W9-AYF-952

National Geographic
Visual History of the World

PHOTOGRAPHIE
NADAR

National Geographic Visual History of the World

NATIONAL GEOGRAPHIC

Washington, D.C.

NATIONAL GEOGRAPHIC

Visual History of the World

Published by the National Geographic Society

John M. Fahey, Jr.	President and Chief Executive Officer
Gilbert M. Grosvenor	Chairman of the Board
Nina D. Hoffman	Executive Vice President; President, Books and Education Publishing Group

Book Division Staff

Kevin J. Mulroy	Senior Vice President and Publisher
Marianne R. Koszorus	Design Director
Kristin Hanneman	Illustrations Director
Rebecca E. Hinds	Managing Editor
Gary Colbert	Production Director

Staff for this book

Jack Bostrom	Text Editor

Copyright © 2005 Peter Delius Verlag GmbH & Co. KG, Berlin

All rights reserved. Reproduction of the whole or any part of the contents without permission is prohibited.

Library of Congress Cataloging-in-Publication data available upon request.

ISBN: 0-7922-3695-5

Printed in China

Staff at Peter Delius Verlag

Publisher: Peter Delius

Authors: Dr. Klaus Berndl, Markus Hattstein, Arthur Knebel, Hermann-Josef Udelhoven

Academic consultants: Prof. Dr. Dominik Bonatz, Dr. des. Christiane Coester, PD Dr. Renate Dürr, Prof Dr. Marie-Luise Favreau-Lilie, Dr. Karl Heinz Golzio, PD Dr. Bernd Hausberger, Prof. Dr. Peter Heine, Prof. Dr. Dr. h.c. Mechthild Leutner, PD Dr. Carola Metzner-Nebelsick, Dr. Heinrich Schlange-Schöningen, Dr. Christoph Studt, Dr. Siegfried Weichlein, PD Dr. Thomas Zitelmann

Staff of the original edition

Editors: Jeannine Anders, Detlef Berghorn, Marit Borcherding, Arthur Knebel, Juliane von Laffert, Christoph Marx; Katja Klinner, Britta Weyer

Picture management: Barbara Schneider, Katharina Franz

Picture research at akg-images: Erich Hartmann, Kai Holland, Anne Meister, Regina Müller, Axel Schmidt, Barbara Weber; Jürgen Raible

Graphic Designers: Dirk Brauns, Florian Brendel, Thorsten Falke, Burga Fillery, Gudrun Hommers

Staff of the English language edition

Translators: David Andersen, Jonathan A. Smale

Editors in chief: Brad Steiner, Rebecca Thomas

Editors: Maria Evans-von Krbek, Ed Naylor; Prof. Michael Alpert, Stephanie Esser, Dr. Stephanie Kramer

All images from akg-images Berlin/London/Paris except for the following from dpa Deutsche Presse Agentur, Hamburg: 11/bottom r., oben 2. v. l., oben r.; 12/1 l., 2 l.; 13/3 l.; 14/1 l., 2 l.; 15/4 l., r.; 224/4; 225/6, 9; 432/1; 456/2, 5; 496/4; 502 box bottom l.; 508/5; 509/6, 7, box l.; 517/25; 528; 530/2; 531/6-9; 532/1; 533/11; 534/box l.; 535/5–7, 10, 11; 537/9, box; 542/box; 543/8, 9; 545/7; 546/5, 7; 547/9–11, 13; 548/1–6; 549/7, 9, 11, box; 551/box; 552/2–5; 553/6–9, box l. and r.; 554/1–4, 6; 555/8–10, 13; 557/box; 559/8, 9, 11; 560/2–5; 561/9–11; 562/1–5; 563/8–10, box; 564/4, box; 565/6, 9, box l.; 566/4–6, box; 567/7–12, box; 568/2–5; 569/6–10, box; 570/1–7; 571/8, 10–12, box; 572/1–3, 5, 6; 573/7–11; 574/1–3, 5; 575/6, 7, 9–12; 576/2; 577/7, 10–13; 578/2, 5, 6, box; 579/7, 9–14; 580/1, 2, 4, 5; 581/7–11, box; 582/1, 2, 4, 5; 583/6–11, box; 584/1–5, box; 585/6–11; 588/1–3, 7; 589/10, 14, box; 590/3–5, box l. and r.; 591/6–11; 592/1–8; 593/9–15; 594/1, 2, 4–6; 595/10, 12, 13, box; 596/1; 597/8, 10–13, box; 598/1, 4, 6; 599/8, 10–13, box; 600/2, 6; 601/8–10, 12, 13; 602/1–4, 6, 7; 603/9, 10, 12–14, box; 604/2–8; 605/9–13; 606/2–4; 607/8–10, 12, 13; 608/2, 4, 5; 609/9–13, box; 610/1–5; 611/11, box l.; 612/1–5; 613/6–11; 614/1–6, box; 615/7, 8, 10, 11; 616/1, 2, 4, 5, box; 618/3; 619/7, 9, 11, 12; 620/1–7; 621/9–13; 622/1, 4, 5, 7, box; 623/8, 10–14; 624/2–6; 625/7–11, box; 626/1, 3; 627/9, 11, box; 628/2, 3, 5–7; 629/8–12, box; 630/3–5, 7, 8; 631/9–13, box; 632/1–8; 633/9, 11, 12, 14, box; 634/1–7; 635/8–14; 639/8, 9, 13; 640/1, 2, 6, box; 641/7, 9–12; 642/1–8; 643/9–14, box; 644/1–6; 645/7–13; 646/1, 2, 4, 5, 7; 647/8, 9, 11; 648/1–5; 649/6–8.

The publishers would like to express their special gratitude to the team at akg-images Berlin/London/Paris who have made their incredible picture archive accessible and thus the extraordinary illustration of this book possible.

Founded in 1888, the National Geographic Society is one of the largest nonprofit scientific and educational organizations in the world. It reaches more than 285 million people worldwide each month through its official journal, NATIONAL GEOGRAPHIC, and its four other magazines; the National Geographic Channel; television documentaries; radio programs; films; books; videos and DVDs; maps; and interactive media. National Geographic has funded more than 8,000 scientific research projects and supports an education program combating geographic illiteracy.

For more information, please call 1-800-NGS LINE (647-5463) or write to the following address:

National Geographic Society
1145 17th Street N.W.
Washington, D.C. 20036-4688 U.S.A.

Log on to nationalgeographic.com; AOL Keyword: NatGeo.

How to Use This Book

The unique design and organization of this extensive volume facilitates its use and enjoyment. Opening the book to any page, the reader can quickly and easily grasp which country and period is being covered.

Section Introductions
summarizes a broad group of subjects, which can span 2-12 pages.

Section Titles
appear on the top of each page.

Page Introductions
summarize the topic covered on the current page.

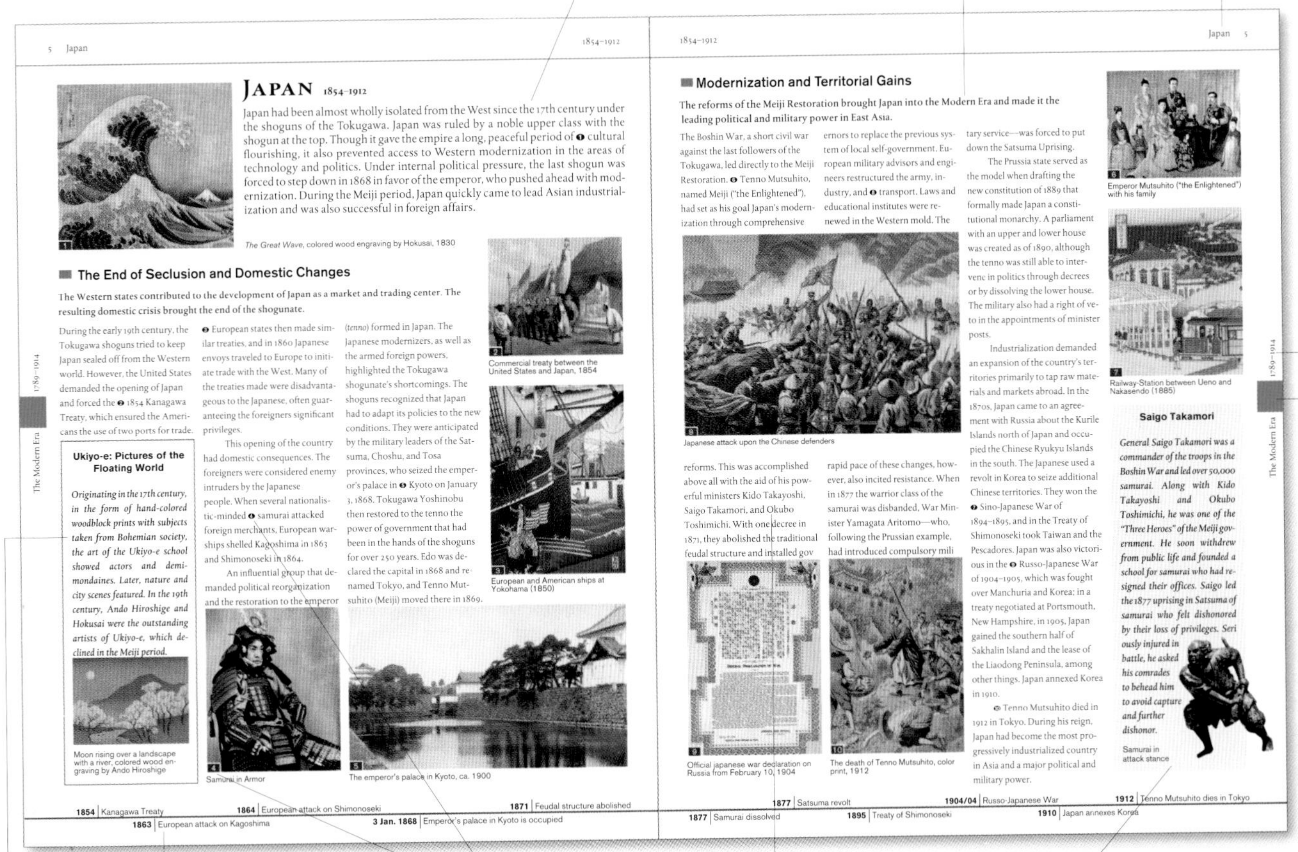

5 Japan 1854–1912

JAPAN 1854–1912

Japan had been almost wholly isolated from the West since the 17th century under the shoguns of the Tokugawa. Japan was ruled by a noble upper class with the shogun at the top. Though it gave the empire a long, peaceful period of ❶ cultural flourishing, it also prevented access to Western modernization in the areas of technology and politics. Under internal political pressure, the last shogun was forced to step down in 1868 in favor of the emperor, who pushed ahead with modernization. During the Meiji period, Japan quickly came to lead Asian industrialization and was also successful in foreign affairs.

1 *The Great Wave*, colored wood engraving by Hokusai, 1830

The End of Seclusion and Domestic Changes

The Western states contributed to the development of Japan as a market and trading center. The resulting domestic crisis brought the end of the shogunate.

During the early 19th century, the Tokugawa shoguns tried to keep Japan sealed off from the Western world. However, the United States demanded the opening of Japan and forced the ❷ 1854 Kanagawa Treaty, which ensured the Americans the use of two ports for trade. ❸ European states then made similar treaties, and in 1860 Japanese envoys traveled to Europe to initiate trade with the West. Many of the treaties made were disadvantageous to the Japanese, often guaranteeing the foreigners significant privileges.

This opening of the country had domestic consequences. The foreigners were considered enemy intruders by the Japanese people. When several nationalistic-minded ❹ samurai attacked foreign merchants, European warships shelled Kagoshima in 1863 and Shimonoseki in 1864.

An influential group that demanded political reorganization and the restoration to the emperor (*tenno*) formed in Japan. The Japanese modernizers, as well as the armed foreign powers, highlighted the Tokugawa shogunate's shortcomings. The shoguns recognized that Japan had to adapt its policies to the new conditions. They were anticipated by the military leaders of the Satsuma, Choshu, and Tosa provinces, who seized the emperor's palace in ❺ Kyoto on January 3, 1868. Tokugawa Yoshinobu then restored to the tenno the power of government that had been in the hands of the shoguns for over 250 years. Edo was declared the capital in 1868 and renamed Tokyo, and Tenno Mutsuhito (Meiji) moved there in 1869.

Ukiyo-e: Pictures of the Floating World

Originating in the 17th century, in the form of hand-colored woodblock prints with subjects taken from Bohemian society, the art of the Ukiyo-e school showed actors and demimondaines. Later, nature and city scenes featured. In the 19th century, Ando Hiroshige and Hokusai were the outstanding artists of Ukiyo-e, which declined in the Meiji period.

Moon rising over a landscape with a river, colored wood engraving by Ando Hiroshige

2 Commercial treaty between the United States and Japan, 1854

3 European and American ships at Yokohama (1850)

4 Samurai in Armor

5 The emperor's palace in Kyoto, ca. 1900

1854 | Kanagawa Treaty
1863 | European attack on Kagoshima
1864 | European attack on Shimonoseki
3 Jan. 1868 | Emperor's palace in Kyoto is occupied
1871 | Feudal structure abolished

1854–1912 Japan 5

Modernization and Territorial Gains

The reforms of the Meiji Restoration brought Japan into the Modern Era and made it the leading political and military power in East Asia.

The Boshin War, a short civil war against the last followers of the Tokugawa, led directly to the Meiji Restoration. ❻ Tenno Mutsuhito, named Meiji ("the Enlightened"), had set as his goal Japan's modernization through comprehensive reforms. This was accomplished above all with the aid of his powerful ministers Kido Takayoshi, Saigo Takamori, and Okubo Toshimichi. With one decree in 1871, they abolished the traditional feudal structure and installed governors to replace the previous system of local self-government. European military advisors and engineers restructured the army, industry, and ❼ transport. Laws and educational institutes were renewed in the Western mold. The rapid pace of these changes, however, also incited resistance. When in 1877 the warrior class of the samurai was disbanded, War Minister Yamagata Aritomo—who, following the Prussian example, had introduced compulsory military service—was forced to put down the Satsuma Uprising.

The Prussia state served as the model when drafting the new constitution of 1889 that formally made Japan a constitutional monarchy. A parliament with an upper and lower house was created as of 1890, although the tenno was still able to intervene in politics through decrees or by dissolving the lower house. The military also had a right of veto in the appointments of minister posts.

Industrialization demanded an expansion of the country's territories primarily to tap raw materials and markets abroad. In the 1870s, Japan came to an agreement with Russia about the Kurile Islands north of Japan and occupied the Chinese Ryukyu Islands in the south. The Japanese used a revolt in Korea to seize additional Chinese territories. They won the ❽ Sino-Japanese War of 1894–1895, and in the Treaty of Shimonoseki took Taiwan and the Pescadores. Japan was also victorious in the ❾ Russo-Japanese War of 1904–1905, which was fought over Manchuria and Korea; in a treaty negotiated at Portsmouth, New Hampshire, in 1905, Japan gained the southern half of Sakhalin Island and the lease of the Liaodong Peninsula, among other things. Japan annexed Korea in 1910.

❿ Tenno Mutsuhito died in 1912 in Tokyo. During his reign, Japan had become the most progressively industrialized country in Asia and a major political and military power.

6 Emperor Mutsuhito ("the Enlightened") with his family

7 Railway-Station between Ueno and Nakasendo (1885)

8 Japanese attack upon the Chinese defenders

9 Official japanese war declaration on Russia from February 10, 1904

10 The death of Tenno Mutsuhito, color print, 1912

Saigo Takamori

General Saigo Takamori was a commander of the troops in the Boshin War and led over 50,000 samurai. Along with Kido Takayoshi and Okubo Toshimichi, he was one of the "Three Heroes" of the Meiji government. He soon withdrew from public life and founded a school for samurai who had resigned their offices. Saigo led the 1877 uprising in Satsuma of samurai who felt dishonored by their loss of privileges. Seriously injured in battle, he asked his comrades to behead him to avoid capture and further dishonor.

Samurai in attack stance

1877 | Samurai dissolved
1877 | Satsuma revolt
1895 | Treaty of Shimonoseki
1904/04 | Russo-Japanese War
1910 | Japan annexes Korea
1912 | Tenno Mutsuhito dies in Tokyo

The Modern Era 1789–1914

Colored Boxes
contain quotations related to the page topic or biographies of important personalities.

Time Lines
give a brief overview of the highlights and events.

Picture Numbers
appear in the text and place images within their historical context.

Colored Tabs
indicate the epoch and chapter of the current topic.

Names of People
mentioned in the text can be found and cross-referenced in the index starting on page 648.

Framed Boxes
enhance the main text with interesting and relevant background information.

The first art by humankind: Cave drawings from the Stone Age **p. 21**

The Sumerians: A high civilization develops in Mesopotamia **p. 34**

The Egyptian pyramids: Grave monuments of the early pharaohs **p. 43**

The "Tower of Babel": Myth-like cross-cultural significance **p. 41**

Imbued with mystery and timeless beauty: the Egyptian queen Nefertiti **p. 45**

The Parthenon temple on the Acropolis: A grand oeuvre of classical Greek architecture representing the power of the Athenian *polis* **p. 87**

The Great Wall of China: Legacy of the first emperors of China **p. 152**

One of the great commanders of Rome: Gaius Julius Caesar **p. 120**

Augustus, the first Roman emperor **p. 122**

Persecution: The prophet Muhammad hides from his enemies **p. 226**

Coronation: Charlemagne, king of the Franks, is crowned emperor **p. 165**

The architecture of the temples embodies the philosophy: Angkor Vat, Khmer temple, in the tropical jungle of Cambodia **p. 246**

Conquest: Spanish soldiers invade the Mexican empire of the Aztecs **p. 335**

Reformation: Luther defends his ideas before Emperor Charles V **p. 256**

The Palace of Versailles: The bedchamber of Louis XIV of France **p. 279**

The Storming of the Bastille: The start of the French Revolution **p. 350**

The French Emperor Napoleon Bonaparte **p. 360**

World War I: Man and animal wear gas masks **p. 440**

Lenin, the head of the Bolshevik October revolution in Russia **p. 480**

World economic crisis: the stock market crash of "Black Thursday" **p. 506**

Advertisement for the international associations of the Nazi SS **p. 510**

Androgynous elegance: Two ladies from the 1920s **p. 506**

Vietnamese children fleeing after a US napalm attack **p. 617**

Denunciation during the Chinese "Culture Revolution" **p. 619**

The people of Berlin celebrate the opening of the Wall **p. 544**

Minutes of terror: A second plane flies into the World Trade Center **p. 643**

Nelson Mandela and Willem de Klerk shake hands, sealing the end of apartheid **p. 633**

The Internet gives up-to-the-minute information about current events but our historical knowledge is based on work done by scholars throughout the centuries.

Moguls past and present: The Australian media mogul Rupert Murdoch, and a depiction of the court of the Indian great moghuls in the 17th century.

WHY HISTORY?

We live in hectic times. Twenty-four-hour news cycles leave us feeling behind the curve or irrelevant. On the ❶ Internet, gossip acquires fact status in a nanosecond. We think sustainable knowledge is only a mouse click away. We Google our history like fast food, ready for quick consumption. The Web has arrived, a virtual volcano spewing in every direction with no barricade to stop the flow of unfiltered words and doctored images. We're stranded, trying to make sense out of the blinding fog of misinformation. Historical truth is a hard commodity to find.

We occasionally need to pause, catch our breath, get a grip on ourselves, straighten our lapels, and realize that world history—like everything else worthwhile—demands high-quality scrutiny. Vetting. That's why in this era of tabloid "truths" I turn to the National Geographic Society, the scientific and educational organization that sponsored Hiram Bingham's rediscovery of Machu Picchu in 1911 and Robert Ballard's successful search for the remains of the *Titanic* in 1985. Many nights I've toiled at the Society's bunker-like headquarters on 17th Street, in Washington, D.C., working on special projects. The building encompasses an entire city block. When you get beyond the supercrocs and dinosaur bones in the museum-like lobby, and enter the private offices and unlocked laboratories, you realize that the Society is, in fact, our cultural-historical-geographic interpreter. Their editors, researchers, scientists, and historians are tireless explorers of truth. And they have no boundaries: Ocean floors, Mars craters, Civil War battlefields and Roman ruins—you name it, National Geographic is exploring and reporting on both the lore and the science; their aim is to educate us about both our world and our galaxy.

Which brings us to this book. Somebody smart once told me that the first rule to garnering knowledge is realizing just how much you don't know. Reading and enjoying the stunning illustrations in this handsome *Visual History of the World* reminded me of that useful piece of folk wisdom. Because we live our lives frontally—day-by-day and hour-by-hour—we seldom have cause to look back. "Everything that belongs to the past seems to have fallen into the sea," novelist Henry Miller wrote perceptively in *Tropic of Cancer*. "I have memories, but the images have lost their vividness, they seem dead and desultory, like time-bitten mummies stuck in a quagmire."

Miller is right. We think of ❷ Rupert Murdoch and Donald Trump as "moguls" but we know nothing about the Indian moghul empire of the 14th century. Some of us pray at Lutheran or Methodist churches on Sunday and call ourselves ❸ "Protestants" without harboring even the vaguest notion of the Peace of Augsburg of 1555. Our collective memory is short-lived. It's hard enough contemplating the hardships of a ❹ World War II era soldier much less evaluating the

The religion of the 340 million Protestants worldwide is based on the Reformation movement initiated in 1517 by the publication of Martin Luther's 95 Theses.

American soldiers in World War II and revolutionaries in Paris on the barricades in 1848: fighting against repression and for the freedom of the citizen.

ancient trials and tribulations of "Peking Man," one of the oldest human archaeological finds ever. He is between 300,000 and 400,000 years old, his body discovered near Beijing in the 1920s. But who knows? Maybe there was a Peking Man 400,000 years before him. We just happened to discover Peking Man. What if we just haven't unearthed his million-year-old predecessors? Sure. He is our descendant, an ancestor from the early dawn of man. But his bones raise more questions than they answer. That is why history is so hard to wrap our hands around. We demand answers but upon procurement they elicit only more questions. It's an exasperating cycle that knocked even the indefatigable Arnold Toynbee and the encyclopedic Durants off their investigatory saddles.

I experienced this answer-and-question cycle while working for National Geographic on a book of visual history called *Mississippi: Making of a Nation*, a work incorporating hundreds of color images and even more historical facts. Along with dreams that fueled the human spirit, the river spawned history: Exploration, empire building, and invention. Each truth we learned in traveling the river—that the Hopewell culture of ancient mound builders lived along the Mississippi's eastern shore and eventually disappeared, for example—caused us to ask more questions, "Why did they disappear?"

Let's face it. The only certainty we have is that nothing is certain forever. Whether we study German princes or Greek gods or Inca rulers or Oceania seafarers, our knowledge of them is bound to be extremely limited. World history, when looked at under a modern microscope, shatters into billions and billions of disparate cultures and peoples and events—each with countless secrets for every fact known about them. Uncertainty reigns supreme in the historical realm and those that tell you they've found definitive answers are wrong. World history is a cyclone that sweeps up every particle or storm cloud that ever existed under its rubric. What isn't world history? No wonder those who really grappled with defining "world history"—like Descartes and Nietzsche—went mad. There is simply too much of it to comprehend so we often ignore the past. Most people can't remember what they thought yesterday let alone what Confucius or Aristotle thought centuries ago. So their solution is reasonable: retreat. Why ponder a vast, insatiable, and indecipherable past?

It's a fair question, "Why study world history?" Too often the rote answer is that it helps us become well-rounded citizens. Nonsense. Most of us do just fine not knowing that Dionysius lived from 430 – 367 B.C. or that *Orrorin tugenensis* "Millennium Man" was found in Kenya in 2000. Why do we need to know that Hephaestian died in 324 B.C. and that Maria Theresa assumed control of Bohemia and Hungary in 1740? How does such factual knowledge enhance our present condition? For my answers I turn to the philosopher William James, who insisted that humans—unlike other creatures—crave, even demand "wild facts without stall or pigeonhole." That is what people want. And in our post-modern era, visual images—like the fine

Mankind continues to probe new boundaries on Earth and in the skies; curiosity and a thirst for knowledge have continuously revised mankind's worldview.

More than just a warehouse for books: The Bibliotheca Alexandrina in Egypt and the Vienna Court Library testify to the culture and spirit of their age.

illustrations in this elegant book—help trigger our buried curiosity. They prove impossible to turn away from, unable to illicit boredom.

Think of Astronaut ❶ Neil Armstrong's most vivid memory as the first to walk on the Moon. When I interviewed him a few years ago about that 1969 Apollo 11 mission, he told me. It was seeing Earth. It was magnificent. From his solar-system perspective, he spoke of seeing Greenland and Antarctica, of watching the sun's rays glint off central Africa's Lake Chad. He saw the world's population as a united entity.

Since it was founded in the late 19th century, the National Geographic Society has championed the dissemination of knowledge of our world, everything from shooting stars to flamingo rookeries to neon motels along forlorn stretches of Route 66. Usually a single National Geographic image tells us more about a particular African civil war or space launch or G-8 summit meeting than reams of journalistic prose. For maximum influence, it's visual imagery that lingers in our consciousness. Images—like those found in this volume—arrest our dormant senses. They stay with us, and become a type of cultural currency. They provoke wonderment. Great imagery offers permanent nourishment. It haunts. Like a Michelangelo statue or a Picasso nude, the perfect photographic image, once seen, endures in one's memory forever.

What is most impressive about this book are the nearly 4,000 illustrations that accompany the text. These visuals help the reader maintain focus. They serve as welcome aids, helping the imagination grapple with historical events. When considering this volume, you may ask: "Why another world history?" This question resonates with me personally. There is nothing more discouraging to an author like myself than to walk through Byzantine ❷ library corridors, eyeing thousands of books neatly lined on overstuffed shelves. Everything is in order but it all feels so sterile and lifeless. And each book seems like a grain of sand on a beach of no return. Too many printed pages to know where to start or what to do. That is why the young often deem history boring. By now the scenario is as familiar as a Norman Rockwell painting: Adolescents go to the library, check out a history book, get bored, and within an hour they are groggy with fatigue, ready to gasp fresh air, or find a good conversation or, better yet, sleep. Most of these yawning library books seem like dead words, a dusty morgue of fanciful erudition and time-honored reason.

This book is not one of those scholarly dry-as-dust tomes. *Visual History of the World* jars the senses—like taking a hard whiff of smelling salts—waking up the comatose mind to the power of the past in a coherent, fun, and inspired way. Its pages are kinetic, sparking in every direction, more alive than just about any other "world history." It's meant to spur on curiosity. It is not an end-all in itself. Whether read from cover-to-cover or dipped into for quick pleasure, the net effect is compelling. Just having this book around the house, sitting on a coffee table or nightstand, makes the owner feel wise. The words and illustrations in this book ring true, and their presentation in "bytes" of information

The inspiring legacy of the pharaohs: The story of Queen Cleopatra, has continued to influence writers, composers and directors

Civilization's development: The futuristic city of Shanghai leads the way into the 21st century, while civilization's roots in ancient cultures continue to fascinate.

allow the reader to have an almost interactive experience. The colors and images dazzle. They cause you to linger, not look to escape. They jump-start the imagination. They make you want to see the ❸ Sphinx and the Great Wall and the Grand Canyon. You start lamenting the fact that you dawdled or doodled your way through high school geography class or college history seminars. Now it's too late.

This last point deserves some elaboration. In our youth, we were all Huck Finns and Tom Sawyers, anxious to escape the repressive shackles of the classroom for the excitements of the Mississippi. Most of us wish that instead of being chained to a nine to five job we could be globetrotters shopping in a Mumbai, India, market or peering out of an open hotel window in the Bernese Alps of Switzerland. History becomes escapism, and the more we know about our past the more places we can escape to. This world history is a sort of magic bus that transports us through time; its sheer vividness makes bygone eras come alive. Centuries enter stage right and left, do a quick jig and then leave, making room for another era to come rumbling into the spotlight. If we can't visit the world's most remote Indonesian islands in the 15th century, or travel ❹ to the present-day Chinese city of Shanghai, at least through these pages we can imagine them.

It's fitting that National Geographic is publishing this world history, for it is an organization with global reach. Although not many in America may know it, the National Geographic Society publishes magazines and books in many languages other than English, including Japanese, Spanish, Hebrew, Greek, French, German, Polish, Indonesian, Korean, Portuguese, Chinese, Czech, Romanian, Russian, Norwegian, Turkish, and Dutch. But their exquisite images don't need translation. They have a universal appeal. A 1985 magazine cover photo, for example, showed an Afghan girl, homeless, her haunting green eyes staring numbly at the photographer's lens. It was heart wrenching. Following Operation Enduring Freedom (the U.S. post-9/11 invasion of Afghanistan) this girl had so touched the heartstrings of the world that a search was conducted to find her. A poor Pashtun woman, living a quasi-nomadic life, she was located in 2002 and the world cheered. The magazine wrote a follow-up account, publishing images of her today. Somehow those pictures of Sharbat Gula—that was her name—spoke to both the horror of war and the resilience of the human spirit throughout history.

Similarly, the National Geographic Society tracks history through the images and illustrations in this hefty book. If I were to inventory this volume in a bookstore it would be shelved under "Usable History." This is a book to own and treasure and use. It is a gift from National Geographic. It invites family participation and household permanency. But don't forget: You're not even close to ultimate knowledge. In fact, your journey has just begun.

Douglas G. Brinkley, New Orleans
June 2005

Prehistory

until ca. 4000 B.C.

When compared to the history of humankind, let alone that of the Earth, the inquiry into the development, roots and relations of humans is very young indeed. Up until the 18th century, the biblical story of human creation—"So God created man in his own image, in the image of God he created him; male and female he created them."—was accepted as an incontestable truth in many parts of the world. Then, however, natural scientists— Charles Darwin the most celebrated among them—appeared. They doubted the special status attributed to humans by the Bible and viewed their development within the context of a theory of evolution. The theory has since been supported and modified by the discovery of skeletal remains, primitive tools, and the remnants of ancient settlements. Their classification, dating, and evaluation using modern technologies has made possible an increasingly accurate perception of human origins.

Reconstruction of a hunting scene from the Old Stone Age, ca. 25,000–30,000 B.C. For the Cro-Magnon man, the mammoth was a desirable prey as use could be made of the meat, hide, and teeth.

The Stone Age: The Beginning of Mankind

1 Evolution from human ape to *Homo sapiens*

From the Beginnings to ca. 4000 B.C.

Even today, no definitive answers to the questions about the origins of mankind have been found. In 1871, Charles Darwin challenged the answers given by the biblical story of creation with his theory of evolution. The evolution theory suggested that man had ❶ descended from anthropoids. Africa, site of the earliest hominoid discoveries, is considered to be "the cradle of mankind." The evolution of today's *Homo sapiens* can be traced by the trail of skeletal remains, tools, and the remnants of settlements—such as cave paintings—that have been left throughout the ages.

It All Began in Africa

With the development of the theory of evolution and the corroborating identification and classification of hominoid finds since the mid-19th century, the hypothesis of an African origin for humans is generally accepted today.

The ❷ story of man's origins and evolution was the subject of fierce controversy throughout the 19th century. There were two schools of thought. According to the creationist doctrine of the monotheistic religions, man had been created by God, after which he did not evolve. In opposition to this stood Charles Darwin's theory of evolution, which stated that life was ❸, ❹, ❺, ❻ continually evolving and emphasized the connection between human origins and the animal kingdom, specifically primates. Darwin's theory proposed a progressive refining of the intellectual, social, and creative abilities of early man. He illustrated this theory with reference to the increasing use of tools and man's lifestyle shift from hunter-gatherer to farmer and animal breeder.

2 Evolution from *Australopithecus anamensis* (blue) to *Homo habilis, Homo rudolfensis, Homo erectus,* and archaic *Homo sapiens* to *Homo neanderthalensis* and *Homo sapiens sapiens.*

Simultaneously the 19th century saw the beginning of a systematic notation and classification of hominoid fossils and stone tools. Of particular concern was the determination of the age of the fossils; however, accurately dating the finds only became reliable with the discovery of the radiocarbon dating method in 1947 by Professor Willard F. Libby of the University of Chicago.

As the oldest hominoids were found in East Africa, a theory proposing Africa as the "cradle of mankind" emerged. This hypothesis was substantiated by the discovery of the "Taung Baby," a 2.2-million-year-old *Australopithecus africanus* in 1924.

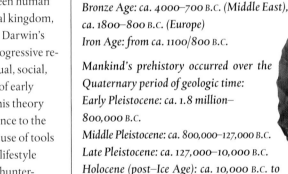

The Divisions of the Prehistoric Periods

Prehistory is divided into the Old Stone Age or Paleolithic period, the New Stone Age or Neolithic period, the Bronze Age, and the Iron Age:

Early or Lower Paleolithic: ca. 2.5 million–250,000 B.C.
Middle Paleolithic: ca. 250,000–30,000 B.C.
Late or Upper Paleolithic: ca. 30,000–10,000 B.C.
Neolithic Period: ca. 10,000/8000–4000/1800 B.C.
Bronze Age: ca. 4000–700 B.C. (Middle East), ca. 1800–800 B.C. (Europe)
Iron Age: from ca. 1100/800 B.C.

Mankind's prehistory occurred over the Quaternary period of geologic time:
Early Pleistocene: ca. 1.8 million–800,000 B.C.
Middle Pleistocene: ca. 800,000–127,000 B.C.
Late Pleistocene: ca. 127,000–10,000 B.C.
Holocene (post–Ice Age): ca. 10,000 B.C. to the present

Paleolithic scraper

3

4

5

6

From left: (3) *Australopithecus anamensis* (ca. 4.2 million B.C.), (4) *Australopithecus afarensis* (ca. 4–3 million B.C.), (5) *Australopithecus africanus* (ca. 2.8–2 million B.C.), and (6) *Homo erectus* (ca. 1.9 million–200,000 B.C.), reconstructions.

ca. 6 0million years ago | *Orrorin tugenensis*
ca. 5.5–4 million years ago | *Ardipithecus ramidus*
ca. 4.2–3.9 million years ago | *Australopithecus*
ca. 4–3 million years ago | *Australopithecus afarensis*

Early Hominoids

According to the most recent discoveries, man's beginnings can be traced back more than six million years. Through a succession of progressive stages, the earliest hominoids developed increasingly greater skills. Slowly man began to leave his African "cradle."

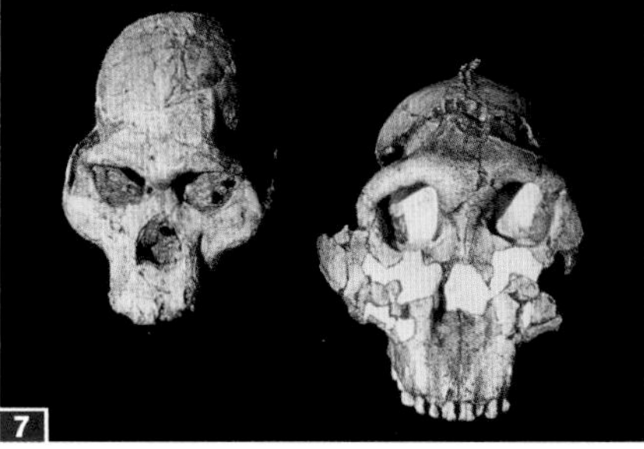

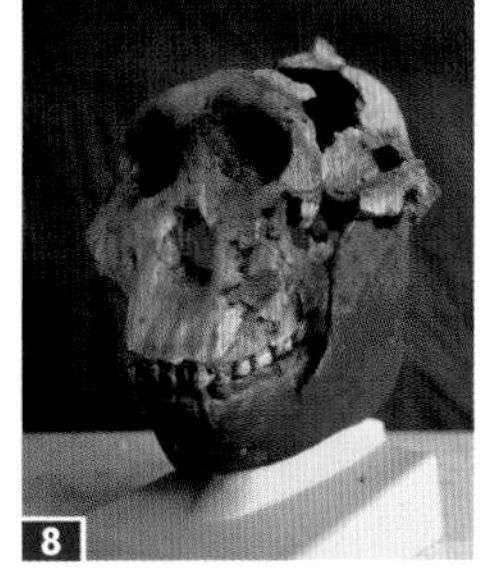

left: Skulls of *Australopithecus africanus* and *Australopithecus boisei*
right: Skull of an Australopithecus with added lower jaw

Following Darwin's theory, paleontologists looked for a "missing link" between man and his nearest relative in the animal world, the chimpanzee. Since then, many hominoid species have been discovered, not all of which are direct ancestors of the modern *Homo sapiens*.

For a long time, the *Ardipithecus ramidus*, which lived 5.5–4 million years ago in present-day Ethiopia, was considered the earliest hominoid. In 2000, however, *Orrorin tugenensis* ("millennium man") was found. It lived about six million years ago in Kenya. The next stage after the Ardipithecus was the 7, 8 Australopithecus, which lived 3.7–1.3million years ago and was already using primitive pebble tools. The *Australopithecus afarensis* became famous through "Lucy," whose skeletal remains were found in 1974.

The next stage of development was the *Homo* genus. *Homo habilis*, which lived 1.5–2.3 million years ago, had a larger brain and ate a broader diet than did previous hominoids. The new diet included meat and animal fats—until then the hominoid diet had been purely vegetarian. *Homo habilis* was the first hominoid to leave the forest and 11 hunt in the savannas. He is credited with the earliest hewn stone tools, which were probably used to break open bones to get at the marrow.

Homo ergaster (*Homo erectus*), which lived approximately 1.8–1 million B.C., settled throughout the African continent and was the first hominoid that resembled modern man in size and proportions. He walked erect only, stored food supplies, and made stone artifacts. About 1.6 million years ago, he made the first completely reworked 9, 10 hand axe that also functioned as a pick. *Homo ergaster* was also the first hominid to travel beyond Africa, gradually populating the nearer parts of Asia and Europe.

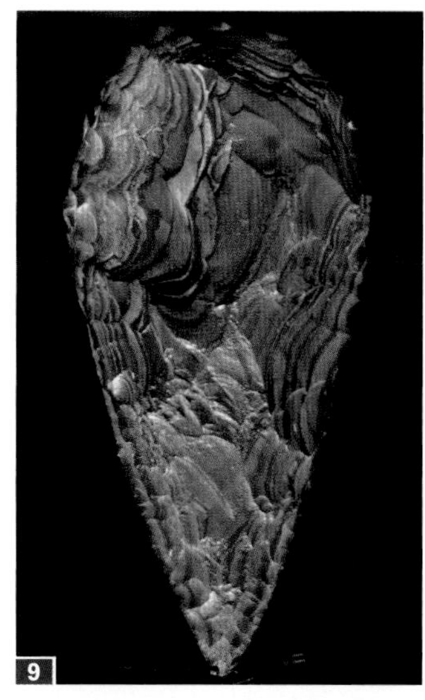

top and above: Flint hand axes, worked tools, Paleolithic period

"Lucy"

No hominoid discovery has elicited such a sensation as the almost complete, 43-inch-high skeleton of a female Australopithecus afarensis found in the Afar region of northeastern Ethiopia in 1974. She was named "Lucy" after a Beatles song that had been playing in the research camp. The press promptly named her the "missing link." She belongs to man's phylogenetic line and possesses all the anatomical prerequisites for walking erect. Her bones and teeth provided valuable information about her lifestyle.

Australopithecines hunting on the plains, Paleolithic period

ca. 2.8–2 million years ago | *Australopithecus africanus*

ca. 2.3–1.5 million years ago | *Homo habilis*

ca. 1.9 million–200,000 years ago | *Homo erectus*

ca. 1.6 million years ago | First flint ax tool

Territorial Expansion

Spreading out of Africa, early man initially settled in Asia and Europe, and then in Australia and the Americas. Due to the climate, it was primarily the robust Ice Age hunters—represented by the Neanderthal and the Cro-Magnon man—who were able to establish themselves in Europe.

It was long believed that early man did not leave his African homeland until ca. 1.4 million years ago. However, in the 1990s, a 1.7–1.8 million-year-old hominoid skull was found in Georgia in western Asia.

The oldest *Homo erectus* fossils have been found in Asia; "Java man," named after the island where the first example was discovered, is today dated to 1.7 million years B.C., while ❷ "Peking man," found in China, is dated to 600,000–200,000 B.C. By that time, *Homo erectus* was probably already using fire and possibly a form of human speech. *Homo erectus* was also the first hominid to live in Europe, which was at that time characterized by extreme ice ages. The European form of *Homo erectus* is named ❸ *Homo heidelbergensis* after a find near Heidelberg in 1907. They are thought to have lived 400,000–800,000 years ago.

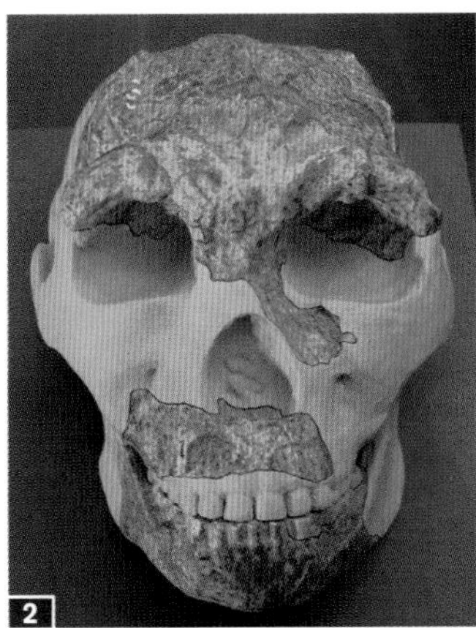

Skull of "Peking man," Middle Pleistocene period

The Late Pleistocene era (127,000–10,000 B.C.) was the age of the Neanderthal. This new hominid, considered to be either a side branch of *Homo sapiens* or a separate subspecies, came about through a series of evolutionary stages and died out about 30,000 years ago. Since the first finding of a Neanderthal skullcap in 1856, this has become the best known example of primitive man.

❶, ❹ Neanderthals were stocky Ice Age hunters with the greatest skull volume of all hominoids known to date. Their wide nose and large nasal cavity were well suited to the cold climate.

Around 40,000 years ago, modern *Homo sapiens*, in the form of the Cro-Magnon man, finally migrated out of Africa to Europe. This direct ancestor of today's man inhabited modern-day Israel as early as 100,000 B.C. ("Proto-Cro-Magnon"). They were taller, more slender and had more stamina than the Neanderthals, but the two coexisted in parallel in Europe for about 10,000 years. Many theories concerning their coexistence and the causes of the Neanderthal's displacement have been suggested. It is generally assumed that there was interaction and a mutual influence between the two hominid genera, but interbreeding of the two is considered highly unlikely.

Homo heidelbergensis hunting

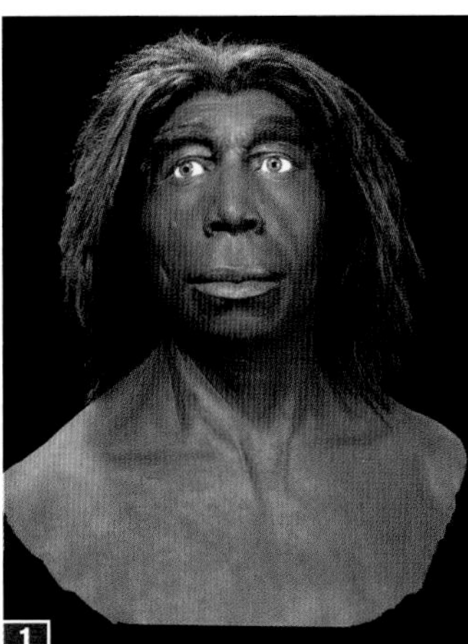

Homo neanderthalensis (ca. 150,000–30,000 B.C.), sculpted reconstruction of a Neanderthal

At least 60,000 years ago, although possibly much earlier, early man settled the Australian subcontinent by way of New Guinea. The first hominids did not reach the Americas, however, until just 11,500 years ago. Ice Age hunters came to the continent via Siberia and Alaska. The oldest finds discovered in America are worked stone arrowheads and spear points. These, known as "Clovis points," are thought to stem from the Clovis culture.

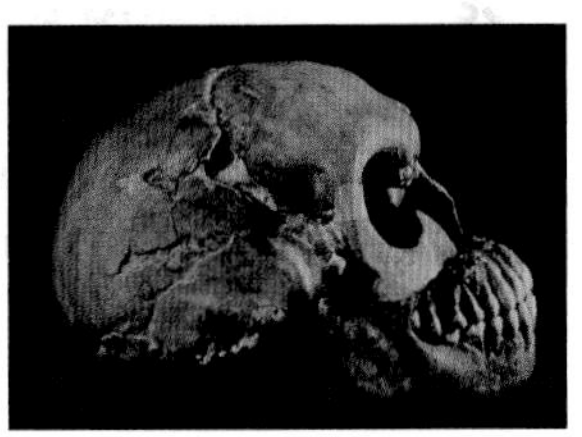

Neanderthal fossils

Following the classification in 1863 of a partial skull found in a cave in the Neander Valley near Düsseldorf in 1856, one of man's early relatives became known as the Neanderthal. Researchers later determined that previously unclassifiable bones discovered in Engis, Belgium, in 1829–1830 and again at Kalpe (Gibraltar) in 1848 belonged to this hominid. The Kalpe skull is much better preserved than the skullcap that was finally identified, and the Neanderthal should perhaps have been named the "Kalpe."

above: Skull found at Kalpe

Neanderthals hunting cave-bears

ca. 1.4 million years ago | Early man leaves Africa

1.7 million years ago | "Java man"

ca. 800,000–400,000 years ago | *Homo heidelbergensis*

ca. 600,000–200,000 years ago | "Peking man"

Campsites and the Use of Tools

The extent of man's development can be gauged by the tools and hunting weapons he used. Another important indicator of this progress is the evidence of dwelling places that housed ever larger groups in increasingly permanent shelter.

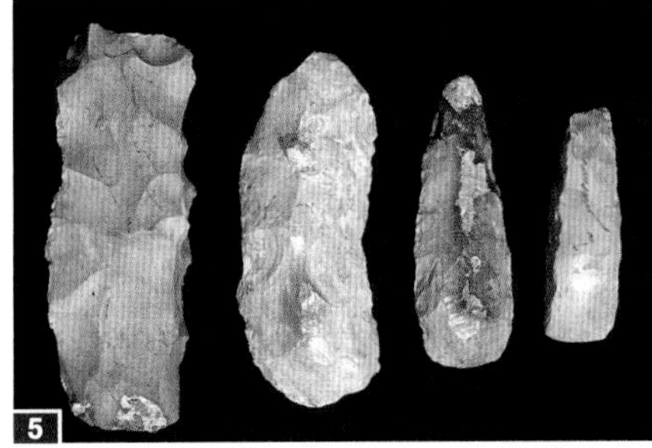

Various stages in the production of the stone ax, worked in the Neolithic period

Alongside skeletal remains, stone artifacts are the best preserved witnesses of the early period of man's existence. The hominids of the Lower Paleolithic made use of materials readily available to them. The first ❻ stone tools were fashioned by striking one stone with another or with a stick to chip flakes off it, shaping the stone into a tool such as a ❺ hand axe. Alternatively, flakes were used to scrape or ❽ chisel the stone into shape. In the Middle Paleolithic, the demands of the hunt necessitated improvements in hand weapons and precisely worked blade points. This resulted in the "thin blade technology"—long, narrow blades of stone or horn used as spear points or harpoons.

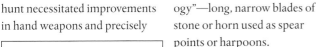

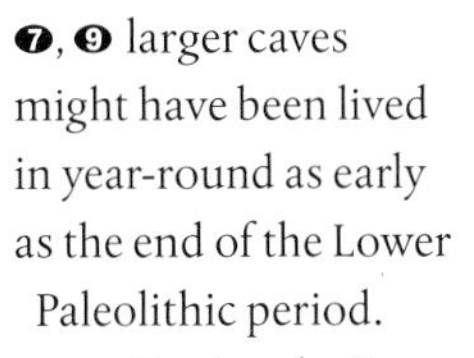

6 Neolithic ax and hammer

Early man used caves for shelter, though possibly not before the discovery of fire in the Lower Paleolithic period, as the caves were often inhabited by cave bears and wild cats. Initially the caves were probably used only in the cold seasons, but some ❼, ❾ larger caves might have been lived in year-round as early as the end of the Lower Paleolithic period.

During the Paleolithic, early people first made their homes in the open—often near rivers or lakes—where they probably built mud huts with leaf roofs. Later dwellings were dug out of the ground. Tent-like constructions made with skins stretched over wooden posts or mammoth tusks began to appear during the Upper Paleolithic period. The dwelling sites of the groups probably changed with the seasons as the groups migrated, but there were also long-term habitation sites such as that uncovered at Willendorf, Austria. The living area was lined with stone slabs and animal skins. Evidence of houses and permanent settlements first appears during the Neolithic period.

7 Cave life in the Paleolithic period

9 Animal herds depicted in cave painting, France; Lower Paleolithic

Mysterious Pierced Staffs

Among the finds associated with Cro-Magnon man are elaborately decorated bone or horn staffs. All of them are pierced. They were first assumed to be cult status symbols and described as "staffs of office." Now it is accepted that they were implements for straightening the stone or bone points set in spear shafts. Cro-Magnons also used spear throwers or atlatls—staffs with a hook on one end; spears were placed against the hook. These increased throwing distance and striking force of the spears.

right: Pierced staffs by Cro-Magnon man

8 Flint daggers

ca. 150,000–30,000 years ago | Neanderthal

ca. 100,000 years ago | Proto-Cro-Magnon in Israel

ca. 60,000 years ago | Settling of Australia

40,000 years ago | Cro-Magnon man in Europe

ca. 11,500 years ago | Settling of the American continent

Fire and the Hunt

The transition from forager to hunter broadened man's diet. In addition, it demanded teamwork; it required an evolution of man's social abilities to enable coordination within an effective hunting group. With the taming of fire, man learned to harness a force of nature. This and associated social changes are considered to be decisive in the development of modern man.

1 Flintstone found at the Messel excavation site, Kalkriese, Germany

The earliest hominoids were probably vegetarians who gathered plants and fruits and unearthed roots and tubers with digging instruments. The expansion of the diet to include meat, which accompanied the move to hunting—although the early ❹ hunters were definitely scavengers as well—was paralleled by a huge development in social intelligence. The hunt required collective effort, skill, strategy, and caution. It required communication within a group and possibly the definition of territories through agreements with other groups. One hunting strategy used by early man was the *battue*, in which the animals were driven into ravines or off cliffs. The essential knowledge of the ❸ prey and its habits also undoubtedly led to the early hunters' first awareness of their superiority over the other animals.

The most important ❷ weapon in the Lower and Middle Paleolithic was the pointed wooden spear or lance, which initially was thrust and later thrown. The bow and arrow did not appear until the Neolithic period. Shortly afterward the dog was domesticated to assist in the hunt.

The preferred prey was the aurochs (or wisent) and red deer in Europe, reindeer and moose in the northern lands, and antelope in Africa. Early man also hunted pachyderms such as the mammoth, forest elephant, and woolly rhinoceros. Cave bears, which played a special role in their cults, were also hunted. These animals became extinct during the transition to the Neolithic period.

The use of fire, verifiable in numerous places as early as the Lower Paleolithic, is seen by many researchers as the truly decisive step in the evolution of modern man. At first, early man probably made use of prairie fire and fire resulting from lighting, until he learned how to create it with ❶ flint stone and control it himself. Thus, he took control of a force of nature for his own protection and as a weapon. He also used it for cooking and roasting his food. Furthermore, it was probably the discovery of fire that made it possible for him to use caves as dwelling places.

Many theories about the division of labor between the sexes during this stage of human evolution have been proposed. Theories have suggested that this may have been the point at which the distinction between the male as hunter, and the female as gatherer and custodian of the fire and children, was first made.

4 Base of hunting group ca. 10,000 B.C., reconstruction sketch after finds

Hunting Techniques

The use of wooden spears for hunting is evidenced by the many animal skeletons that have been found pierced by lances and spears. Near Hannover, Germany, for example, 400,000-year-old horse skeletons were found with three-foot-long lances embedded in their sides. Hunting scenes showing animals shot with spears and arrows are popular subjects of cave paintings. In the wisent hunt in Europe and the bison hunt in prehistoric America, individual animals would be isolated and then hunted. Nets into which animals were driven were also used in the battue for wild horses, red deer, and reindeer.

Mammoth hunt by Cro-Magnon hunting group

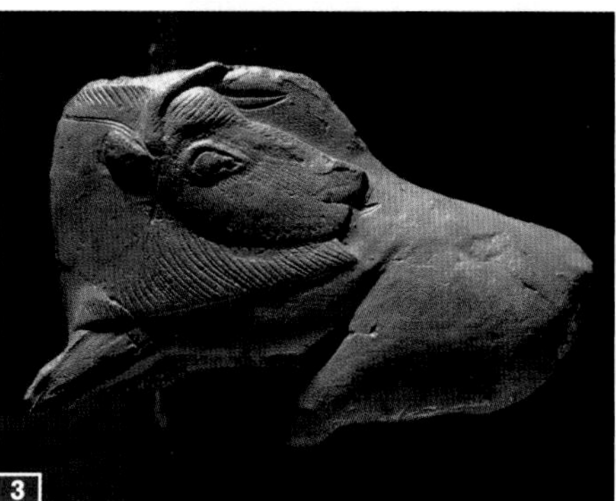

2 **left:** antler spear points 3 **right:** Bison sculpture, bone; both Lower Paleolithic

ca. 2.3–1.5 million years ago | Transition to the hunt

ca. 18–1 million years ago | Development of communication into speech

ca. 2.2 million–130,000 years ago | Wooden spear used as hunting weapon

Language and Burial of the Dead

Mankind's progress also involved the evolution of mental and intellectual abilities. The learning and use of a symbolic language, together with the development of the early death cults, are considered milestones in this respect.

A "psychological revolution" took place hand in hand with the technical and social development of early man. The formation of social groups made it necessary for individuals to express their conscious concerns and feelings as well as to recognize differences. It is assumed that a basic awareness of the self and others and a capacity for simple speech were present from *Homo ergaster* onward.

Language serves as a way of transmitting thoughts, using sounds and words to denote meanings (ideas). Thus, language would have required an ability to conceptualize the ideas communicated through words and symbols. Symbols are characters that—unlike pictographs—do not need to resemble the things they symbolize. These symbols are associated with certain agreed-upon (conventional) meanings, which are then learned by the members of the group.

The use of language therefore implies the parallel development of all these faculties between themselves and others. However, due to the lack of written evidence, only indirect conclusions as to the exact nature and extent of this development are possible.

A higher degree of intellectual abstraction was also a prerequisite for the burial of the dead by early man. With knowledge of the burial rites comes the supposition of an awareness of the mortality of man.

The special burial of human skulls and lower jawbones was practiced as early as the Lower Paleolithic period, particularly by the groups inhabiting present-day China. Middle Paleolithic cave dwellers certainly seem to have performed burial rites. This is evidenced by the ❽ human skeletons found arranged in a way that suggests the dead were buried lying on their backs or squatting, with stone tools as burial objects. The skeletons, and particularly the skulls, were frequently covered with ❺, ❻, ❼ stone slabs. It is unclear whether this was to protect the dead or to protect the living from the spirits of the dead. ❿ Special treatment of the skull has been noted almost everywhere, often with the brain having been removed through holes bored in the rear of the skull.

In Upper Paleolithic times, the bodies of the dead and especially the skulls were generally sprinkled with ocher, a red pigment, and buried in separate stone encasements. Precious ❾ jewelry and finely worked, unused ⓫ stone implements have been found as burial objects inside the skeletons. Teeth with holes bored into them have also been found inside the graves and were probably worn as pendants.

top: Megalith graves, reconstruction drawing
above: Dolmens (megaliths) in Evora, Portugal

Skeleton excavated from middle Paleolithic burial site, Les Eyzies, France

Tumuli (burial mounds) made of stone slabs with stone engravings, France

Burial Rites and Skull Holes

During the Upper Paleolithic, the dead were buried in graves dug especially for this purpose. These were often in the middle of the dwelling area or near a fire site. Presumably the dead were buried there only after the group had moved on.

The circular holes in the back of many skulls are a greater riddle. Probably the brains of the deceased were removed through these holes. However, some skulls have been found in which the cranial bones had partially healed or grown back at the edges, suggesting that the person lived for some time after "trepanation" was performed.

Skeleton of a Neolithic woman buried in a sitting position, found in Backaskog, Sweden

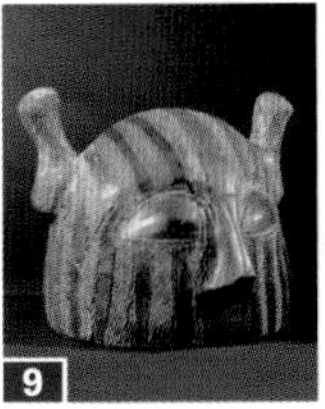

left: Zoomorphic mask; **middle:** human skull with ivory inlay;
right: burial objects from a grave of the Globular Amphora culture, near Berlin

Religion and Cults

A series of prehistoric finds indicates the existence of ritual cults and sacrificial ceremonies. Opinions diverge widely as to whether a form of religion had already developed. It is generally assumed, however, that there was a link between the primitive cults, hunting mysticism, and the preparation of food.

Among the indications of man's psychological evolution, a fundamental one is the emergence of the belief in a transcendental power to whom sacrifices must be made.

Another is the consciousness of a special relationship between man and animal, hunter and prey (animalism), and man and his environment. It is widely accepted that the earliest "religions" or cults were associated with hunting. One of the oldest cult rituals, evidenced since the end of the Lower Paleolithic period, was the ceremonial sacrifice of animals. Examples of this include female reindeer that were submerged in lakes and moors with stones and wooden stakes in their open breast cavities. The buried skeletal remains of animals, especially mammoths, draped with jewelry have also been unearthed.

2 "Venus of Willendorf," statuette, Upper Paleolithic period

3 Female idol, Neolithic period

The cave dwellers of the Middle Paleolithic decorated and reworked the skulls of cave bears and buried them or stood them up behind stone walls. This practice has led to the supposition that a particular cave bear cult existed.

Parallel to the shaman concepts of Siberian hunting tribes, some researchers interpret the decoration and special treatment of animal bones as either a "compensation ritual" for the killing of the animal or an expression of early man's belief that through the burial, the prey would "arise anew." Others theorize that the early humans were sacrificing a portion of the kill to a hunting god or animal totem. Related to this are the representations of half-human creatures, such as the "Sorcerer of ❶, ❹ Trois-Frères," which have been the subject of particularly controversial interpretations.

Cult rituals may also have developed around the dividing up of the kill among the group and the preparation of food around the hearth. Possible evidence of this are the many ❷, ❸ female statuettes with voluptuous forms that have been found around hearths dating back to the Upper Paleolithic. These probably symbolize either fertility or a mother deity.

1 Rock drawing of a human figure, possibly a shamanistic dancer

Another controversial subject is the religious or cult interpretation of the art of early man. The representations of game and hunting themes found in cave paintings may have been intended to invoke success in the hunt or protection against dangerous game.

4 Shaman from the cave at Trois-Frères in French Pyrenees, Paleolithic period

The "Sorcerer of Trois-Frères"

No cave painting has provoked as many different attempts at interpretation as the famous "Sorcerer of Trois-Frères." The name itself is rejected by many researchers. The sorcerer is one of three hybrid creatures discovered on a cave wall in 1916. The painting depicts all three creatures with animal heads and front limbs. The rear part of the body, however, is human. Some researchers, referring to shaman practices in other cultures, see this figure as a "medicine man" dressed in animal skins and an animal mask. They suggest he might be performing a mystical hunting dance as a supplication for the successful outcome of the hunt. Other researchers doubt this theory and see him simply as an imaginative cross between man and animal which testifies to the creativity of early man.

The "Sorcerer of Trois-Frères," cave painting, ca. 14,000 B.C.

ca. 2.3–1.5 million years ago | First animal sacrifices and cult rituals

ca. 3000 B.C. | Development of high religions

ca. 3000 B.C. | First family and clan cave graves

The Art of Early Man

The best known examples of the diverse and impressive artwork of early man are cave paintings. Predominant motifs include game animals and representations of people. Prehistoric art forms—including stone engraving, carvings, and figurines—are diverse in style and allow for a variety of interpretations.

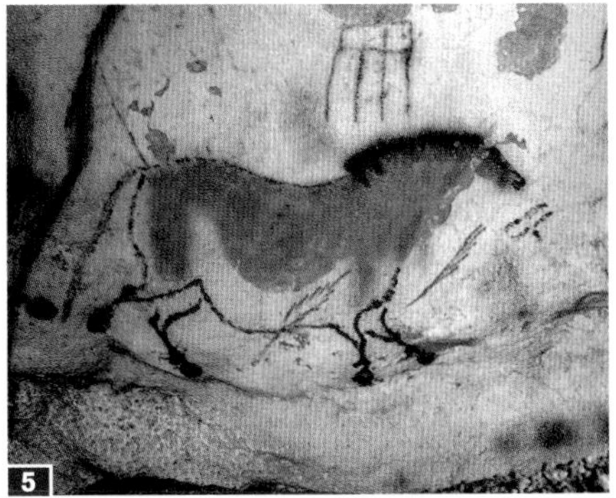

5 Horse, cave painting at Lascaux in France. Lower Paleolithic

❺ Cave paintings and ❾ wall engravings first appeared during the Upper Paleolithic period. The caves of France and northern Spain are particularly rich in art. For a long time, it was believed that motivation for these artworks originated from observation of the cracks and fissures on cave walls, which inspired early man to create first geometric designs and then drawings. However, the painted looping lines have been shown to be no older than the developed picture motifs. Thus from the start the artists must have been aware of the possibility of representing their environment in images.

Generally, it is assumed that the cave paintings did not primarily serve an aesthetic purpose, nor were they the work of one gifted individual but rather represented the world of the group. The dominant theme of the cave paintings is game animals, all depicted in profile and in motion. The rare human figures appear abstract by comparison. The figures are always standing alone and are not uniform in style. Realistic pictographic representations can be seen alongside stark abstractions of human and animal images with overly emphasized details. Another special subject in the caves is the ❽ human handprint.

Even more numerous than the paintings are the cave and rock engravings that occasionally overlap and portray themes similar to the paintings. Engravings are also found on stone, antler horn, and animal bone.

In addition to paintings, sculptured pieces were also produced in the Upper Paleolithic. Many ❻, ❼ small sculptures made of limestone, soapstone, bone, and antler horn—as well as baked-clay figurines—have been found. The smaller ones were probably worn as pendants. The statuettes most often depict ❿ females and are considered to have been fertility symbols. The figures vary from coarse cone shapes to ones with well-detailed facial features.

Painting Techniques in the Upper Paleolithic

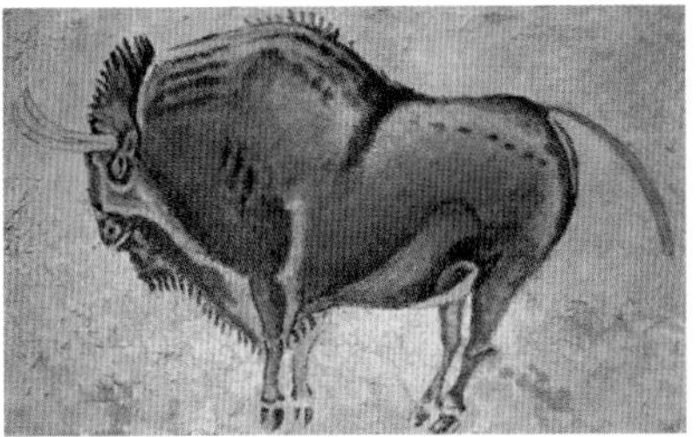

Cave drawing in Altamira, Spain

Upper Paleolithic cave paintings can be found in Western Europe, particularly in France and Spain, the Urals, and Siberia. Cave artists used various iron ochers dissolved in water for coloration. Egg whites, fat, plant juice, and blood created shades from red to yellow and brown (visible in paintings of the wisent of Altamira, Spain, for example) were used in the paintings. Black tones were achieved with animal charcoal or manganese.

Handprints in the caves usually appear in black or red. In some cases, the artist's hand was painted with a liquid color and then pressed against the cave wall (a positive print); in others, the hand was placed on the wall and paint was sprayed around it so that when the hand was removed a negative handprint remained.

9 Fighting ibex, cave wall engraving, Le Roc de Sers in France, Lower Paleolithic

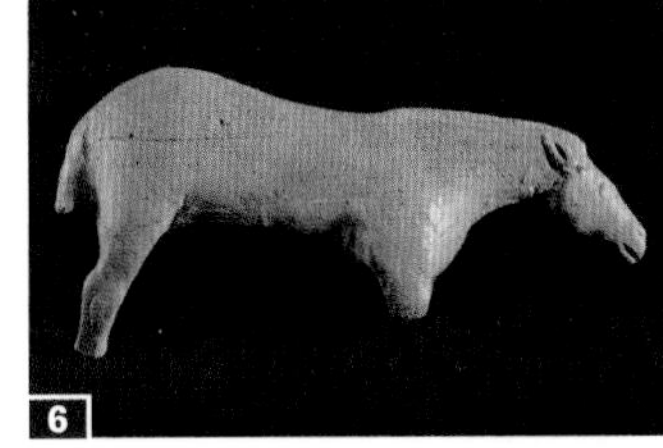

6 Horse, bone carving, Middle Paleolithic

7 Fish, bone carving, Middle Paleolithic

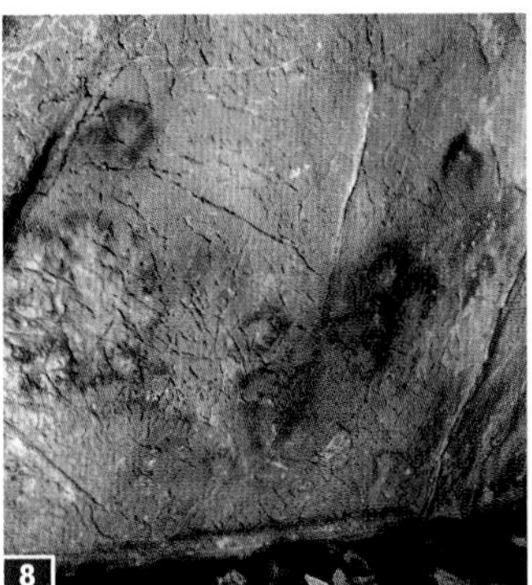

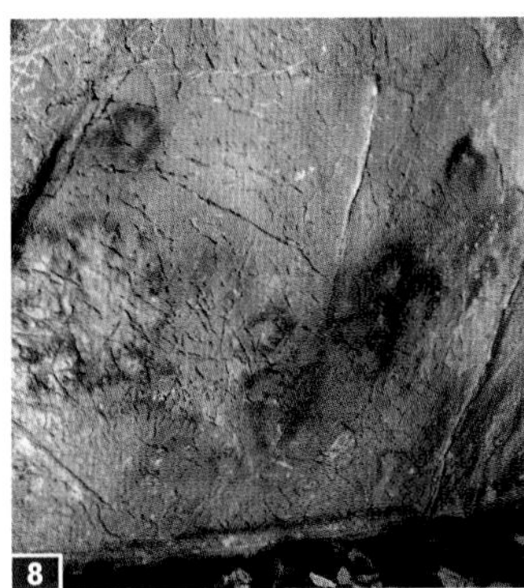

8 Handprint, cave wall

10 Statue, mammoth bone, Paleolithic

between 30,000–10,000 b.c. | "Venus of Willendorf" sculpted

1916 | Discovery of the "Sorcerer of Trois-Frères"

1940 | Discovery of the caves of Lascaux

The "Neolithic Revolution"

During the Neolithic period, a rapid progression of human culture took place—primarily due to the introduction of agriculture and animal domestication. The new sedentary lifestyle demanded new technologies and shaped the beginnings of the modern form of settlement.

The Neolithic period saw a rapid development in many aspects of human culture, characterized by ❺ man's attempts to establish independence from the vagaries of the environment in which he lived. This process was made possible primarily by the broadening of the diet, which was linked to agriculture and the domestication of animals and occurred as a result of sedentary life in ❸, ❹ houses and communities. The hunt continued to play a role in providing nutrition, yet the supply of food was no longer completely dependent on the success of the hunt as there were now alternative food sources.

There was a parallel technological revolution. The introduction of fired ❶, ❷ ceramic vessels, initially used for storing food supplies, defined whole cultural communities, such as the Middle European "Linear Ceramic Culture." Advances also included the use of rotating grindstones and mortars for the processing of plants for food and the construction of houses from clay bricks. Wood was worked at first with chisels and stone axes. Sickle tools were used to cut grasses and grains. After 3000 B.C., metallurgy (initially with copper), using simple pouring techniques, appeared in the Near East.

Agriculture demanded long-term planning as well as knowledge of climatic periods and seasonal cycles. The cultivation of fertile alluvial land began, particularly in Mesopotamia and along the Nile. Goats, sheep, pigs, and later cattle were domesticated for man's use.

New cults also formed around plants and grains. Many Neolithic houses had their own cult niche where offerings such as grain, fruits, and animal remains have been found. The surviving clay, stone, and metal statuettes are thought to be votive offerings, as many have raised arms or open hands in an attitude of supplication. Some represent God.

2 Ceramics stemming from the Funnel Beaker Culture

4 Early Stone Age family in a hut

1 Painted vase and pottery stemming from Neolithic cultures

3 View of Stone Age house interior

Most Neolithic settlements had separate cult edifices. In the Near East, there were early temple complexes. The transition to advanced civilizations began even before 3000 B.C. in these regions with the development of script or hieroglyphics and of religious monarchies.

The "Linear Ceramic Culture"

The oldest culture of the Paleolithic period in Central and Southern Europe is known as the Linear Ceramic Culture. It stretched from eastern France to Hungary in the fifth millenium B.C. The people lived in closed settlements with nave houses and pursued agriculture and animal husbandry.

The culture was named after the ribbon-like decorations typically used on their pottery. These decorations were made up of solid lines and dashes. The Linear Ceramic Culture tribes buried their dead positioned toward the sun, on their side, and with legs drawn up in a sleep-like pose. Some researchers infer from this that they had the concept of an afterlife. Skeletal remains have also been found in a supine position with outstretched arms, reminiscent of certain types of statuettes.

5 Reconstruction of Similaun man "Ötzi" found in the Similaun glacier, Italy

ca. 6700–5700 B.C. | First city-type settlement of Çatal Hüyük

5000–4000 B.C. | Tell-Halaf culture

5000–4000 B.C. | Obed culture in South Babylon und Ur

ca. 5000 B.C. | "Linear Ceramic Culture"

The Tell Cultures

Modern village and city cultures developed from the Tell (Arabic for "hill") settlements of the Near East. These give evidence of a social differentiation between the inhabitants as well as an organized economic life. These communities, identifiable mostly through their characteristic pottery, demonstrate a fluid transition to early advanced civilizations.

The peoples of the earliest known village-like hill communities in the Near East are called Tell Cultures. As a rule, new settlements were built on top of older ones. However, it is possible to date cultural peaks and distinctive fea-

8 Maternal goddess, statue, Anatolia, Neolithic period

tures by excavating deep shafts through the layers. ❽ Çatal Hüyük (p. 50) in Anatolia proved to be a particularly rich site for excavation. Many settlements were enclosed by protective stone walls, which testifies to competition between the sedentary agricultural communities and roaming nomad peoples.

Often the different cultures can be distinguished by their characteristic pottery forms or ceramic decorations: The Syrian ❾, ❿ Tell Halaf Culture, for example, which dominated the Mesopotamian area in the fifth and fourth mille-

6 Stamp, Late Paleolithic period

nium B.C., decorated its ceramics with axes or crosses.

Given the importance of ceramics in determining social and cultural development, a division is made between the "Aceramic Neolithic" (ca. 8000–6500 B.C.) and the "Ceramic Neolithic" after about 6500 B.C.

The Tell Cultures displayed varied building styles—both round and angular—and pottery forms. The discovery of ❻ seals and counting markers indicates an early organization and control of economic life and trade, as well as sophisticated property-ownership relations, which paved the way for more advanced civilizations and societies.

The Obed Culture in southern Babylon and Ur (ca. 5000–4000 B.C.) possessed ❼ houses divided

7 Model of a building with animal skulls on the roof, Neolithic period

into rooms ("middle room houses"), early pottery wheels, seals, stamps, and cult and administrative buildings. It is believed that a cult and administration elite had emerged within the community—a sign of an advanced early civilization. These people dug a system of complex and strategically placed irrigation canals, and signs of a communication network and paths linking the communities have been found. The transition to the metropolitan civilizations of Mesopotamia began with the emergence of urban cultures in the Uruk period around 4000 B.C.

Çatal Hüyük

The large city-like complexes in Anatolia of the early Neolithic period are a treasure trove for archaeologists because of their size and the variety of artifacts found. The clay brick houses possess central rooms that are usually decorated with painted figures, relief figures, and bull heads on the walls. The houses are so close together that the inhabitants had to enter them through a hole in the roof.

Clay platforms are found along the walls under which the skeletal remains of the dead were buried. It is therefore assumed that some of the rooms were used for ancestor-worship. Numerous small sculpted figures indicate the worship of two pairs of deities and sacred animals. The inhabitants used wood and stone vessels but no pottery.

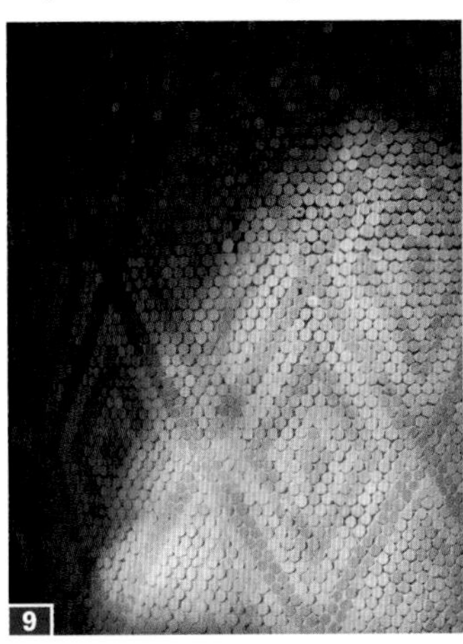

9 Detail from altar, castle of Guzana, Tell Halaf ruins, Syria, from ca. 800 B.C.

10 Hill of ruins of Tell Mardich in Syria: Partial view of the excavation area, showing what was probably a palace during the Bronze Age

since 4000 B.C. | Uruk era: Development of city cultures

4000–2000 B.C. | Harappa culture

since 3000 B.C. | Making of metal tools in the Near East

ca. 3000 B.C. | Development of script in the Near East

First Empires

ca. 7000 B.C.–200 A.D.

The Middle East was the cradle of mankind's first advanced civilizations. In Egypt and the Fertile Crescent, which extends in an arc from the north of the Arabian Peninsula east through Palestine to Mesopotamia, the first state structures emerged in parallel with the further development of animal husbandry, agriculture, trade, and writing. The first great empires, such as those of the Egyptian pharaohs, the Babylonians, the Assyrians, and the Persians, evolved at the beginning of the third millennium B.C., out of small communities usually clustered around a city. Similar development also occurred on the Indian subcontinent and in China, where quite distinct early advanced civilizations took shape as well.

The golden mask of Tutankhamun, a jewel of ancient Egyptian artwork, showing the pharaoh in a ceremonial robe decorated with the heraldic animals, the vulture and cobra, ca. 1340 B.C.

1 Bedouin shepherd with sheep in Jordan

2 Cattle herd at a river in Khuzistan, Iran

3 Camel and rider, ca. 700 B.C.

THE FIRST GREAT CIVILIZATIONS

Long before Greek and Roman antiquity laid the foundations for Western culture, high civilizations were emerging in the Orient, particularly in the fertile "land between the rivers"—Mesopotamia. One of the most important preconditions for the development of such advanced cultures was the development of agriculture and livestock breeding, as both of these demanded increasing investment in organizational structures. The early history of the Ancient Orient was also shaped by the immigration and settlement of ❶ nomad peoples. The relationship between the nomads and the settled peoples was long regarded in terms of certain tribes conquering the lands of others. However, the immigration of small tribes often occurred over the course of centuries and was more of an infiltration. A mutual permeation of culture and religion took place, but so did conflicts over natural resources such as grazing land and water for irrigation.

5 Engraving of carpenter, Babylon, second-third c. B.C.

The transition from small-animal husbandry to ❷ livestock breeding contributed significantly to the settling of nomadic tribes in the Near East. Cattle—which were incorporated into religion as ❹ cult symbols for strength and fertility—were used as draft animals as well as farm and pasture animals. The donkey and particularly the ❸ camel were also domesticated for riding and as pack animals. The camel became the main form of transportation in the caravan trade, while horses were used primarily in warfare.

4 Sumerian bull's head

Wheat and barley were the main crops cultivated. The invention of the field plow, cleverly devised ❻ irrigation systems, and dams and canals to protect against floods all increased efficiency and production within the settlements. The other important task of the growing communities was defense against outside enemies who were competing for resources.

The increasing number and complexity of tasks led to social differentiation between farmers, ❺, ⓫ craftsmen, warriors, and administrators. In addition, there were ❼ priests who performed religious rites and also attempted to determine the favorable times for sowing and harvest through calculations, prophecies, and astrology.

6 Cultivation of grain on artificially irrigated fields

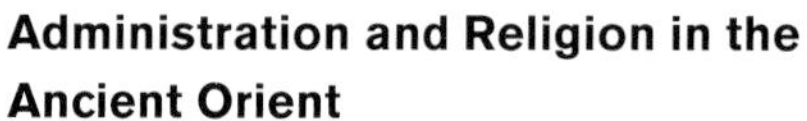

Administration and Religion in the Ancient Orient

Early communities eventually developed into strictly hierarchical class-based societies. The officials, as administrative specialists, held a key position. They controlled the municipal trade and agrarian production. Central ❽ grain silos were usually placed in religious structures, and for this reason it is assumed that the state's property and administration was also concentrated here (that is, a "temple economy"). The ruler, a

7 Statue of a priest

ca. 9000 B.C. | Oldest remains of a town in Jericho
around 3000 B.C. | First Sumerian city-states founded
ca. 2900 B.C. | Unification of Egypt
2500 B.C. | Akkadians take over the Sumerian script
1854–1595 B.C. | Old Babylonian empire

8 Ruins of a grain silo

9 Byblos, ruins of the obelisk temple

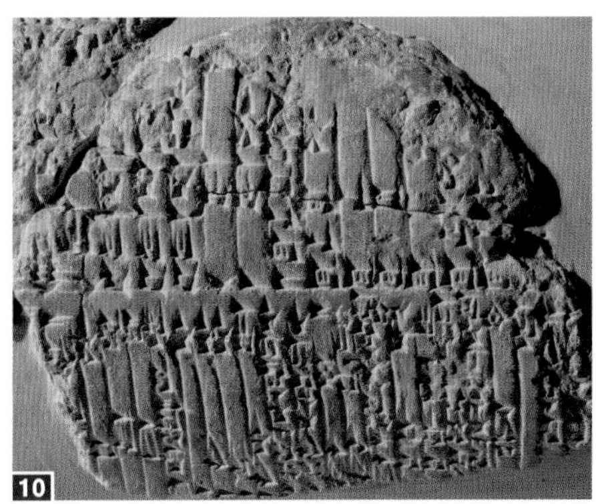
10 Trade record in cuneiform script, ca. second c. B.C.

king or city prince, had a special role. He was the initiator of communal work projects as well as the head of administrative and religious activities. He administered the land in the name of the gods and acted as their earthly representative.

⓬ Religion in Mesopotamia was very complex and, as a result of the steady arrival and settlement of nomadic peoples, new elements were constantly added, and others changed over time, thus testifying to its integrative capacity. Various local heroes, such as Gilgamesh of Uruk (ca. 2700–2600 B.C.), or city tutelary deities, such as Marduk in Babylon, rose to prominence in the pantheon of the gods with the support of the community. For example, Marduk was declared chief god under Hammurapi of Babylon (1792–1750 B.C.). The Achaemenid ruler Cyrus the Great accepted the acclamation of the Marduk priesthood in Babylon and thereby renewed the Babylonian Kingdom. After his victory over Darius III in the battle at Gaugamela, Alexander the Great paid tribute to the city god Marduk in 331 B.C. His rule thereby acquired an element of divine legitimacy. In this way the conqueror made himself the successor of the Babylonian kings.

11 Statuette of a baker, ninth-eighth century B.C.

The Significance and Development of Writing

The change in the cultural development of man that resulted from the invention of writing cannot be overestimated. The earliest known script has been found on small clay tablets that were used in ⓾ commercial transactions. Early Sumerian cuneiform writing developed out of pictographs in which—as in Egyptian ⓭ hieroglyphics—the pictograph resembled the object it was meant to represent. It was a complicated system that was mastered only by specially trained scribes who therefore had a powerful position within the social hierarchy.

Pictographs differed from the earlier symbols and paintings by cavemen because they relied on the systematic coherency of the writing, rather than oral tradition, for the transmission of meaning. The desire to simplify writing led from pictographs to cuneiform script. Characters expressing a sound or a group of sounds replaced the object symbols—and word-phonetic spelling developed. At first a syllabary script emerged in which a character represented a single syllable or combined syllables. Around 2500 B.C., the Akkadians adopted Sumerian syllable writing, which already existed in cuneiform, and expanded it with their own characters. Later, the Elamites, Hurrites, Hittites, Urartians, and other peoples adopted this writing system, and by 1400 B.C. it was in use as the common script for international trade.

12 Sacrificial procession for the goddess Inanna with a bull and other sacrifices, stone vase from Uruk

The most abstract step in the development of writing was the creation of an alphabetic script assigning characters to sounds. With this method, an unlimited number of combinations can be formed with a small number of phonetic characters. The first scripts composed purely of phonetic characters were developed in the Canaanite metropolises of Ugarit (ca. 1400 B.C.) and ❾ Byblos (ca. 1000 B.C.), with alphabets of 30 and 22 letters, respectively. Like all Semitic script, the alphabets of the Canaanites and their successors, the Phoenicians (p. 155)—which became the foundation for Israelite, Syrian, Arabic, and Greek alphabets—had no vowels.

13 Egyptian hieroglyphics in a mural in the tomb of Haremhab, in the Valley of the Kings in Western Thebes, Egypt

The Greek alphabet was the first to include vowel characters, but it otherwise adopted the form and order of the letters from previous alphabets, as well as their use as numeric symbols. The oldest Greek texts are also written, like the old Semitic texts, from right to left.

ca. 1004–926 B.C. | Kingdom of David and Solomon **626–539 B.C.** | Founding of the new Babylonian empire **331 B.C.** | Alexander the Great conquers Babylon

1539–1070 B.C. | New Egyptian Kingdom **883–612 B.C.** | New Assyrian empire **550–330 B.C.** | Persian empire

Nomad woman herding sheep in Ararat, the Caucasus

Migration of Peoples 3000–1200 B.C.

While urban culture was emerging in the Near East, mass ❷ migrations began to take place in Asia. In some cases, these continued for well over a thousand years—lasting longer than the migrations of late antiquity. From 3000 B.C. onward, Semitic peoples from the south and Indo-European peoples from the north migrated into Mesopotamia. At the beginning of the first millennium B.C., the appearance of these seagoing and equestrian peoples triggered great turmoil.

Semitic and Indo-European Peoples

In approximately 3000 B.C., a shift of power took place in the Near East as the result of the immigration of Semitic and Indo-European tribes into the area.

Out of Arabia, Semitic tribes pushed in several waves into the area of the "Fertile Crescent"—that crucial swath of land reaching from Mesopotamia over the coasts of the Eastern Mediterranean and into Egypt. Around 2400 B.C. the Semitic Akkadians subjugated the Sumerian city-states (p. 34) and created an empire. The Canaanites settled in Palestine and founded city-states, as did the Amorites (p. 54) in Syria. The Amorites also established the first dynasty of Babylon and ruled the old Babylonian Empire (p. 40). In the 13th century B.C. the Aramaeans, Semitic ancestors of the Israelites (p. 56), appeared on the scene. They won control from the Assyrians (p. 38) in Syria and Palestine (in the kingdoms of David and Solomon, for example), increasing their influence in Mesopotamia after 1100 B.C. The Aramaic Chaldeans ultimately defeated the Assyrians and founded the Neo-Babylonian Kingdom (625–539 B.C.) (p. 41).

Paralleling this Semitic migration, Iranian Indo-European peoples moved through the ❶ Caucasus into Mesopotamia, beginning with the Gutian invasion in 2150 B.C. that dissolved the Akkadian empire. The Hurrites made up the upper class in the Mitanni kingdom (16th–14th century B.C.; p. 52), which was eventually conquered by the Hittites (p. 50), an Indo-European tribe that settled in Asia Minor around 2000 B.C. The Kassites, who had moved down from Iran, ruled Mesopotamia from about 1530 to 1160 B.C.

The various "peoples" and "tribes" were never clearly defined or distinguishable units. It is assumed that the Hyksos, for example, who invaded Egypt in 1650 B.C., were composed of both Semitic peoples and Indo-European Hurrites. But even the divisions "Semitic" and "Indo-European" are based on the script and languages used by these groups and give little information as to the ethnic composition or indeed precise geographical origins of the tribes they are ascribed to. The Persians and the Medes (p. 60) were not part of this first migration but belong to a later wave of Indo-European migration into the region that occurred in the second century.

The Story of the Biblical Patriarch Abraham

Abraham's story (Genesis 11:10–25:11) mirrors the migration of the Aramaic nomads: In the second half of the second millennium B.C., Abraham led his tribe out of Mesopotamia at God's behest and into Palestine, where they settled despite the resistance of the previous inhabitants. In the traditional Islamic version, he led them to Mecca, where he constructed the Ka'aba and founded the pilgrimage tradition.

above: "Abraham's Exodus," copperplate engraving, 17th century A.D.
left: Abraham's well in Beersheba, Israel

Semitic nomads, Egyptian painting, 19th century B.C.

from 3000 B.C. | Immigration of Semitic and Indo-European tribes
ca. 2400 B.C. | Beginning of the Akkadian empire
from 2150 B.C. | Reign of the Gutians in Akkad
1650 B.C. | Invasion of Egypt by the Hyksos
from 1400 B.C. | Persians settle in Iran

The Sea Peoples and Equestrian Peoples

Around 1200 B.C., the Eastern Mediterranean area experienced great changes. Neither high civilizations, such as the Hittite empire, nor civilizations like the Mycenaeans, Minoans, or Canaanites were a match for the advance of the sea and equestrian peoples.

3 Seaborne procession, Minoan mural, 16th century B.C.

The term "sea peoples," which appears in Egyptian and Hittite sources from around 1300 B.C. onward, refers collectively to diverse foreign tribes. Controversy still exists as to their origins. Speculation has traced them to Illyria (today's Croatia and Slovenia) but also to Asia Minor and the Aegean area.

The ❹ seagoing people at first spread fear among the settled trading tribes, until they—like the Philistines—permanently settled. The Philistines conquered the coastal region of Palestine and Syria and destroyed the Canaanite city-states (p. 54). This facilitated the immigration of the Israelites.

The migratory movements of the Greeks (p. 80), Thracians, Phrygians, and Lydians fit into this pattern of sea peoples' migrations. The Greeks coming out of the Balkans and invading present-day Greece destroyed the cultures of the Mycenaeans and ❸ Minoans. The Hittite empire also went under with the onslaught of the seagoing tribes. The Thracians, Phrygians, and Lydians penetrated Asia Minor from the north; the Greeks and other seafaring peoples fell upon Asia Minor's coasts. The Etruscans also seem to be descended from a seafaring tribe as suggested by the Aeneas saga, which is linked to the founding of Rome.

The most significant equestrian tribes (p. 64) of the period were the Indo-European Cimmerians and ❺ Scythians (p. 65), who advanced out of the Eurasian steppes and into Asia Minor and Iran in the south, as well as modern Germany and Italy to the west. The Cimmerians, who had been expelled by the Scythians, destroyed the Kingdom of Urartu in alliance with the Assyrians. They were then pushed into Asia Minor, where they defeated the Phrygians only to be annihilated by the Lydians. Up until 100 B.C., the Scythians occupied the area of present-day Ukraine, but they were then absorbed by other nomadic and equestrian peoples such as the ❻ Sarmatians.

6 Sarmatian horse soldiers in armor on armored horses, Pillar of Troy, Rome, 113 B.C.

4 Prisoners of the sea peoples who have been tied together by the hair

5 Scythian riders, tapestry, fourth/fifth century B.C.

The Atlantis Legend

Some researchers link the Atlantis legend to the emergence of the seafaring peoples. According to this theory, a great natural disaster set off the migratory movements. Today, archaeologists suspect the epicenter of this disaster was the island of Santorini (Thera) in the Aegean. Here, in the 17th century B.C., a volcanic eruption caused a large part of the island to sink into the sea. Underwater earthquakes and the fallout of ash affected the whole region and might have forced the inhabitants to flee in a long-term migration.

above: Reconstruction of Atlantis following the specifications of Plato

from 1200 B.C. | Great migration of the sea peoples
ca. 1200 B.C. | Collapse of the Hittite empire
from the 9th century B.C. | Immigration of the Medes
714 B.C. | Assyria conquers the Urartu Kingdom
ca. 700 B.C. | Scythians displace the Cimmerians
635–539 B.C. | Neo-Babylonian Kingdom

The Early States of Mesopotamia

ca. 3000–539 B.C.

In contrast to the desert of the Arabian Peninsula to the south and the rugged mountain ranges to the north, Mesopotamia ("land between the rivers"), situated between the Tigris and Euphrates, provided fertile land for cultivation. Early inhabitants, therefore, called their home ❶ Sumer ("cultivated land"). One of the earliest civilization of the Near East developed here. Complex societies flourished and were later organized into city-states like Uruk. Over time, great empires developed who managed to extend their power well beyond the two rivers.

1 The bust of a Sumerian lady of the court at Ur wearing headgear and other jewelry, 300 B.C.

The City-States of Sumer

The advancement of hydraulic engineering led to the formation of the city-states, which were distinguished by functioning administrations.

The first communal settlements grew along the Tigris and Euphrates rivers in response to the development of organized irrigation systems. These settlements merged about 3000 B.C. to form irrigation and flood control provinces. Around 2800–2400 B.C.—the Early Dynastic period—centrally controlled city-states arose and competed with each other for political and economic dominance of the region. The most significant of these were Ur, Uruk, Umma, Lagash, Adab, Nippur, and Kish—whose rulers are known to us through the surviving "kings lists."

Tombs with valuable ❸, ❻ burial objects testify to the high standard of living of the upper social level of the city-states, as well as the ❹ hierarchical nature of these societies, which were dominated by princes, kings, priests, and state officials.

3 A Sumerian helmet made of gold from an Ur king's tomb (third century B.C.)

4 A mosaic from Ur, depicting groups of differing social status within the hierarchy

2 Cylinder seal, second century B.C., and modern molding

In addition to agriculture as the main economic engine, the mass production of pottery is apparent in archaeological finds. Minerals and raw material initially served as payment for the labor. Later, ❷ cylinder seals provided a useful instrument for commercial control and the verification of the delivery of goods. Seals and counter markers served a well-organized food storage system and also property allocation by officials.

Some cities had seaports that later filled with sand as the water level dropped in the Persian Gulf. Through sea and land trade routes, the Sumerian culture expanded into northern Mesopotamia and northern Syria.

Seafaring

In 1977 adventurer Thor Heyerdahl proved that the ancient Sumerians were capable of constructing seaworthy ships by sailing a reed boat replicated from the specifications of an original Sumerian boat.

above: Heyerdahl's reconstruction of a reed boat
right: Sumerian vessel showing a depiction of a reed boat

ca. 3300 B.C. | Sumerians migrate to Mesopotamia

ca. 4000–2000 B.C. | Uruk is the most important Sumerian city-state

ca. 3000 B.C. | Sumerians brew beer

Uruk

One of the most powerful Sumerian city-states was Uruk in southern Mesopotamia.

From its founding around 4000 B.C. until about 2000 B.C. ❼ Uruk was an important trading center. In the center of the city stood many great public buildings that probably served as meeting places and religious buildings. Later these were built upon to create the chief shrine Eanna for the city's goddess ❽ Inanna. The oldest known written tablets, presumably concerned with commerce management, are from this period. At the time there were approximately 20,000 people living in Uruk and a further 15,000-20,000 in the immediate area.

The Construction of the City Wall by Gilgamesh

"[The hero Gilgamesh] built the wall of Uruk-Haven ...
Look at its wall, which gleams like [copper?] ...
Go up on the wall of Uruk and walk around,
examine its foundation, inspect its brickwork thoroughly.
Is not [even the core of] the brick structure made of kiln-fired brick?"

(Gilgamesh epic, first tablet)

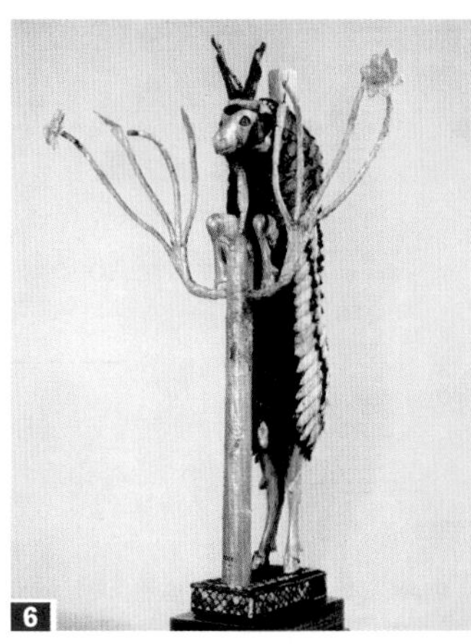

6 "Tree of Life" sculpture, third c. B.C.

Depictions on cylinder seals testify to armed conflicts with neighboring peoples and the punishment of prisoners.

The city was completely reconstructed between 3100 and 2900 B.C. A terrace was raised in the city center, upon which the main temple was built. The terraced temple became the predecessor of later temple towers of the Babylonians, the ziggurats. Writing also evolved, with pictographs transforming into cuneiform.

Uruk is thought to have been the home of the ❺, ❾ legendary ruler Gilgamesh, the hero of the most important ancient Sumerian epic. Gilgamesh is said to have ruled sometime between 2600 and 2700 B.C. and is counted among the kings of the first dynasty of Uruk (ca. 2700–2350 B.C.). Besides numerous heroic deeds, Gilgamesh is credited with the construction of Uruk's six-mile-long (9.7 km) protective city wall.

7 A vase from Uruk decorated with animal depictions, ca. 3000 B.C.

5 Statue of Gilgamesh with a lion, from an Assyrian palace, eighth century B.C.

The epic, handed down in a number of ancient Near Eastern languages and in various versions from the third to the first millennia B.C., in some passages shows parallels to the Old Testament story of Noah and also to the saga of Hercules.

8

9

above: Gilgamesh in battle with two bulls and a lion; modern molding of a cylinder seal from the third century B.C.
left: Facade of a temple of Inanna in Uruk, 15th/14th century B.C.

Lagash and Umma

The history of the Sumerian city-state Lagash in southern Mesopotamia, which competed fiercely with neighboring Umma, is well documented. The rivalry between the city's princes and the priesthood are typical of the political conditions in the Sumerian city-states. Under the reign of Gudea the city enjoyed a period of great prosperity.

King Eannatum of the first dynasty of Lagash (ca. 2494–2342 B.C.) succeeded in temporarily subjugating Umma. The famous ❶, ❺ "Vulture Stele" depicts the vanquished enemy in a net cast by the city god Ningirsu. Internally Eannatum fought the influence of the priest caste, which won the battle by helping the usurper Lugalanda to power. Social tensions lay behind the ascension to the throne of Urukagina, who promptly canceled the debts of the poorer classes and cut back the income of the priests. With the help of these disgruntled clergymen, Lugalzaggesi of Umma then conquered Lagash somewhere around 2250 B.C. He also controlled the cities of Uruk and Adab, and thus declared himself "king of Uruk and of the Land of Sumer." His plans to unite Mesopotamia brought Lugalzaggesi into conflict with the powerful ruler of Akkad, Sargon I, who defeated him before going on to realize the project himself. Lagash experienced its final period of prosperity during the 20 year reign of ❸ Gudea. His rule is associated less with military adventures than with the building of systematic irrigation works and temples of worship.

1 Vultures pick at the bodies of vanquished enemies; detail from the "Vulture Stele," ca. 2454 B.C.

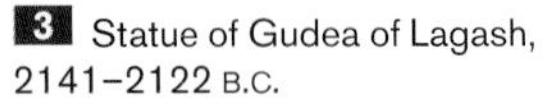

3 Statue of Gudea of Lagash, 2141–2122 B.C.

5 King Eannatum of Lagash leads his army in the battle against the city Umma, fallen enemies lying on the floor; extract from the "Vulture Stele," ca. 2454 B.C.

2 Valley in Luristan, southwest Iran

Proto-Elam and Elam

Concurrently with Sumer, another early high culture emerged in the ❷ southwest of present-day Iran. The Elam kingdom produced the oldest known inter-state treaty.

This little-known culture, identifiable only by a form of script used around 2900 B.C., is referred to as Proto-Elam. Out of it rose the later kingdom of Elam, perhaps as early as 2700 B.C. Around 2300 B.C. the Akkadians occupied the empire until Elam regained its independence in 2240 through an inter-state treaty—the oldest surviving in the world. Several royal dynasties followed, with a supreme monarch—resident in the capital Susa—ruling over several vassal kings. ❹ Women generally played a larger role in Elamitic society than in neighboring Sumer and Akkad. The wife, and often the sister, of the king was a prominent figure. Upon his death, she married his successor. Occasionally successors in the female line predominated.

4 Women spinning, eighth c. B.C.

In the history of Elam, periods of rule by foreign powers alternated with times of Elamite expansion. Around 2004 B.C. the Elamites destroyed Ur. Six hundred years later Elam came under the rule of the old Babylonian Empire. Then in 1155 B.C., the Elamites expelled the Kassites from Babylon, ruling until 1100 when Nebuchadressar I of the second dynasty of Isin pushed the Elamites back out of Babylon and pillaged their capital ❻ Susa. Only in 646 B.C. was Elam finally destroyed by the Assyrians. The area then fell to the Persians and became the central province of the vast empire forged by the powerful Achaemenid dynasty.

2494–2342 B.C. | First dynasty of Lagash
2454–2425 B.C. | King Eannatum
2334–2279 B.C. | Sargon I of Akkad
ca. 2340–2360 B.C. | Lugalzaggesi of Umma
ca. 2300 B.C. | Akkad occupies Elam
2230–2130 B.C. | Rule of the Gutians

6 Reconstructed fortification of Susa, Iran

7 Bronze head of an Akkadian ruler, presumably Sargon of Akkad, 2334–2279 B.C.

The Kingdom of Akkad and the Third Dynasty of Ur

The Kingdom of Akkad (ca. 2334–2154 B.C.) was the first large territorial state in Mesopotamia.

❼ Sargon of Agade founded the Kingdom of Akkad in 2334 B.C. He also founded the new capital city of Akkad, which gave the kingdom its name. Sargon, which comes from the Akkadian title of Sharrukenu ("legitimate king"), conquered Kish. He broke Uruk's domination of Sumer and extended his kingdom to the Mediterranean, Lebanon, and Asia Minor in numerous ❽, ❾ military campaigns, ruling over many city-states and territories. With his royal title of "King of the Four Corners of Earth," Sargon made perhaps the first claim to world dominance. Domestically, he trained administrators—the "sons of the palace"—and was the first monarch to maintain a standing army. The decline of the Akkadian kingdom began around 2250 B.C. The Guti, a mountain people from Iran, then gained dominance over Mesopotamia between 2230 and 2130. Subsequently, the kings Ur-Nammu and Shulgi of the third dynasty of Ur (ca. 2112–2004 B.C.) ruled the most important cities of Sumer and a large part of the Kingdom of Akkad, pronouncing themselves the "Kings of Sumer and Akkad."

The third dynasty of Ur strictly supervised the economy. Huge numbers of laborers and craftsmen were employed in the service of the state in the "grand households," which included the great temples and palaces. The chancelleries produced documentation which bears witness to complex administrative processes. A standardized form was established for the high temples—multi-storied structures with a central flight of steps—called ziggurats. This form was used for the religious edifices erected by and for the kings. The dynasty ended in 2004 B.C. with the destruction of Ur by the invading Elamites. However, the administrative structures survived and were adopted and integrated by the new rulers who established themselves in the dynasty's place.

8 Stele celebrating the victory of an Akkadian king, ca. 2200 B.C.

9 Procession of Akkadian prisoners, ca. 2340–2320 B.C.

Sargon of Akkad

"To Sargon, the king of the land, Enlil gave no enemy from the upper to the lower sea. . . . Sargon, the king of the land, restored Kish, their city he gave them as their abode . . . to Sargon, the king, Enlil allowed no enemy to form. 5400 warriors daily eat their meal before him."

(Text from the Tablet of the Sargon)

2112–2095 B.C. | King Ur-Nammu
2094–2047 B.C. | King Shulgi
1125–1104 B.C. | King Nebuchadressar I of Babylon
2112–2004 B.C. | Third dynasty of Ur
ca. 2004 B.C. | Destruction of Ur
until ca. 1100 B.C. | Hegemony of Elam

The Old Assyrian and Middle Assyrian Kingdoms (ca. 1800–1047 B.C.)

The Assyrian kingdom developed in the north of Mesopotamia at the beginning of the second millennium B.C. Due to their superior methods of warfare, the Assyrians were feared by neighboring peoples.

The city of Ashur was a hub of Mesopotamian trade with Syria, Anatolia, and Iran. Its rulers laid claims to an empire as early as the time of ❷ Shamshi-Adad I and briefly assumed independence (Old Assyrian Kingdom, ca. 1800–1375 B.C.) before coming under the sovereignty of the Hurrites of Mitanni (p. 52).

Assyria became an independent state under the "great kings" of the Middle Assyrian Kingdom (1375–1047 B.C.). In the middle of the 14th century B.C., Ashur-uballit I (1365–1330 B.C.) broke from Mitanni and forged close ties with Egypt and Babylon. Adadnirari I (ca. 1305–1275 B.C.) extended the kingdom at Babylonia's expense and was known by the title "King of All." Assyria's transformation into an expansive military power with a well-trained ❸ army began in the 13th century under rulers Shalmaneser I (1274–1245 B.C.) and Tukulti-Ninurta I (ca. 1294–1208 B.C.). Tukulti-Ninurta I immortalized his deeds in his *Tukulti-Ninurta Epic*, which then became the model for the personal aggrandizement of Assyrian rulers. According to the Assyrian religion, the state god Ashur had destined his people, over whose welfare the ❹ genies watched, for world dominance. The Assyrians subjugated their neighbors in a series of devastating military ❶ campaigns, often conducted with great brutality. The inhabitants of the conquered territories were ❺ deported in the tens of thousands into other parts of the Assyrian Empire, where they were used as forced labor. Revolts of the subjugated regions were considered a crime against the "divine world order" and were crushed with cruel punitive expeditions.

Tiglath-pileser I (ca. 1115–1077 B.C.) extended the empire into northern Syria and Asia Minor. After occupying the Phoenician trading cities, he levied tribute on them. Alongside these military conquests he also promoted scientific research, particularly with regard to zoology, and oversaw the compilation of a great library and encouraged cultural developments. After his death, the expansion of the Middle Assyrian Kingdom came to an end. Pressure from the Aramaean tribes seeking to break into the fertile lands of Mesopotamia, and a revived Babylonian kingdom, ushered in a period of Assyrian decline. The ancient capital of Ashur was later abandoned in favour of Nineveh, a new capital on the banks of the upper River Tigris.

2 Clay tablet bearing the signature of the Assyrian king Shamshi-Adad I, 1813–1781 B.C.

3 Assyrian spear-carrier, eighth c. B.C.

4 Winged genie, ninth century B.C.

1 An Assyrian fighter kills his enemy, ninth century B.C.

The Assyrian Method of Fighting

"Impetuous they are, full of rage, as the storm god transformed, / They plunge into the tangle of battle, naked to the waist, / They test the ribbons; they tear the robes from their bodies, / They tie their hair, the swords they let dance in circles / Jumping about, naked weapons in hand, / The wild warriors, the lords of war, / They stormed ahead, as if lions would seize them."

(from Tukulti-Ninurta Epic)

5 Prisoners of war being carried away into slavery in the Assyrian empire, women and children riding on a wagon drawn by oxen; stone relief, seventh c. B.C.

ca. 1800–1372 B.C. | Old Assyrian Kingdom
1813–1781 B.C. | Shamshi-Adad I
1375–1047 B.C. | Middle Assyrian Kingdom
883–612 B.C. | Neo-Assyrian Empire
883–859 B.C. | Ashurnasirpal II
858–824 B.C. | Shalmanesar III
810–806 B.C. | Regent Queen Sammu-ramat
745–724 B.C. | Tiglath-pileser III

The Neo-Assyrian Empire (883–612 B.C.)

During the period of the Neo-Assyrian Empire (883–612 B.C.), the military power of the Assyrians expanded through Palestine and Israel, and into Egypt.

Assyria experienced a renewed period of expansion under King Ashurnasirpal II (883–859 B.C.). Annual military campaigns were waged in order to break the resistance of neighboring kingdoms, and the conquests were followed by brutal mass executions.

Succeeding Ashurnasirpal, Queen Sammu-ramat, also known as Semiramis, conducted the empire's affairs very successfully. She first acted as regent for her son, Adadnirari III (810–783 B.C.), and then continued to exert a significant influence over the throne even after he came of age. A succession of weak kings, rebellious provincial governors, and the growing power of Urartu threatened the empire. These dangers were averted after Tiglath-pileser III seized power in 745 B.C. and set about refashioning the Kingdom and overseeing renewed military success. He advanced into Gaza in the west, conquered Babylon in the south, and triumphed over the ruler of Urartu (p. 52). In addition to reviving Assyrian military fortunes, Tiglath-pileser proved a capable administrator, strengthening the empire by reordering the provinces and standardizing laws. His economic planning involved the forced relocation of the empire's subjects. His successor, Shalmaneser V, went on to conquer Samaria in 722 B.C. and subjugated Israel, as it had ceased to pay ❻ tribute.

In 721 B.C. a new dynasty was founded by ❼, ❾ Sargon II. His son Sennacherib (704–681 B.C.) destroyed Babylon in 689 and had his capital, ❽ Nineveh, magnificently enlarged by an army of forced laborers. Both Esarhaddon and Ashurbanipal sought to conquer Egypt, but were unable to maintain control due to the great distances involved, as well as domestic intrigues originating with their own relatives. In 646 the Elamites (p. 36) were conclusively defeated and, together with the last small Hittite states (p. 51), absorbed by the new Assyrian Empire during the seventh century B.C.

Ashurbanipal was a great art collector, and in Nineveh he built the largest cuneiform library of antiquity, holding copies of almost all the significant works of the ancient Near East. The empire declined under his successors, until finally—weakened by Scythians' attacks—it fell to the conquests of the Medes and the Babylonians.

6 Emissaries from King Jehu of Israel bring tributes, ninth century B.C.

7 Sargon II (721–705 B.C.) with a high dignitary, perhaps Crown Prince Sennacherib

8

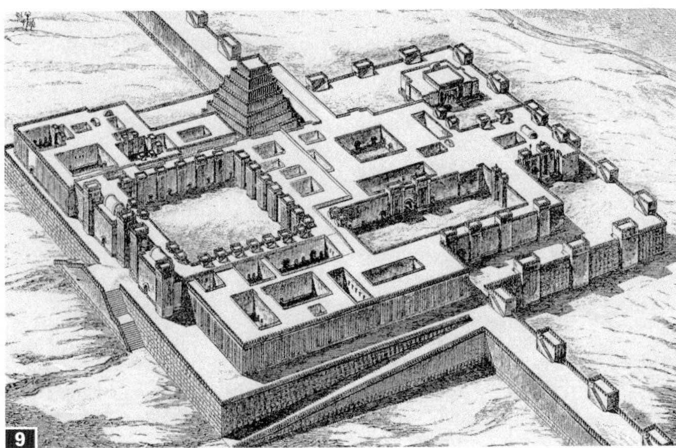
9

top: The king's palace at Nineveh, artist's reconstruction
above: The palace and temple area of Sargon II at Khorsabad (Dur Sharrukin), Iraq, artist's reconstruction

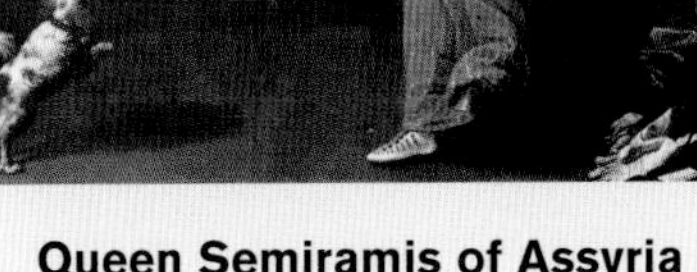

Queen Semiramis of Assyria

Queen Sammu-ramat (Semiramis) of Assyria, who reigned as regent after the death of her husband, is cloaked in legend. She allegedly had innumerable lovers and distinguished herself as a ruler and military commander. She is also credited with the construction of the "Hanging Gardens" of Babylon.

above: *Semiramis Puts Down an Uprising in Babylon*, painting by Matteo Rosselli, 17th century A.D.

721 B.C. | Conquest of Palestine
721–705 B.C. | Sargon II
704–681 B.C. | Sennacherib
689 B.C. | Destruction of Babylon
680–669 B.C. | Asarhaddon
668–627 B.C. | Ashurbanipal
ca. 653 B.C. | Subjugation of Elam
614–612 B.C. | Conquest of Assyria

The Ancient Kingdom of Babylon

The city of Babylon in the heart of Mesopotamia rose to become the new dominant power in the region during the second millennium B.C.

Following the fall of the third dynasty of Ur (p. 37), the old Babylonian Empire was the dominant power in Mesopotamia. The 1st dynasty of Babylon was descended from the Semitic Amorites. Their most famous member was King Hammurapi, who is best known for his ❶ Code of Hammurapi, considered to be the first detailed legal code of antiquity. It presents a collection of cases in 282 provisions for all of the areas of law then recognized. The punishments prescribed for the crimes accorded with the principle of "an eye for an eye, a tooth for a tooth" and went from whipping and maiming to death by impaling, burning, or drowning. Hammurapi, who called himself "the shepherd of the people," described in the foreword of his code how the Babylonian chief deity Marduk had charged him with introducing law and justice to his people.

Soon after Hammurapi's death, the ancient kingdom of Babylon came under pressure from external enemies such as the Hittites (p. 50), who rose to prominence after 1650 B.C. From about 1531 to 1155, the Kassites ruled Babylon; after 1155, it was under the control of the Elamites (p. 36) and the second dynasty of the city of Isin (ca. 1157–1026 B.C.). A prominent representative of this dynasty was Nebuchadressar I, who repulsed the Elamites and Assyrians in successful campaigns.

Eventually Babylon, which had already been weakened by invading Aramaean tribes, came under the rule of the Assyrian Empire.

From the Epilogue of the Code of Hammurapi

I Hammurapi . . . have not withdrawn myself from the men, whom Bel gave to me, the rule over whom Marduk gave to me, I was not negligent, but I made them a peaceful abiding-place. I expounded all great difficulties, I made the light shine upon them. I have not withdrawn myself from the men, whom Bel gave to me, the rule over whom Marduk gave to me, I was not negligent, but I made them a peaceful abiding-place. I expounded all great difficulties, I made the light shine upon them.

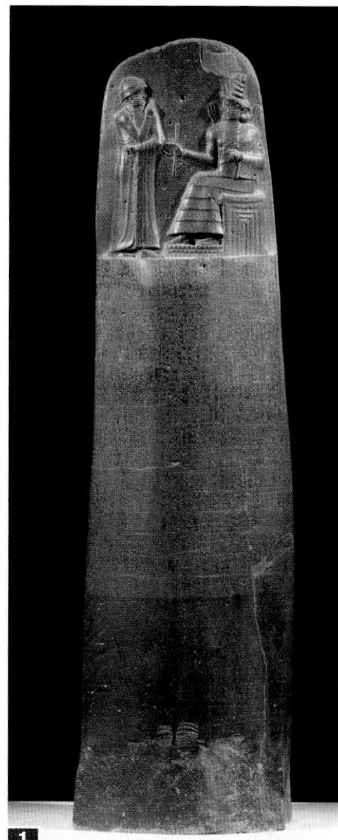

1 Hammurapi's law column, with the king in front of a deity, ca. 1700 B.C.

The Neo-Babylonian Kingdom of the Chaldeans 625–539 B.C.

The greed for power and the luxury of the Neo-Babylonian Kingdom served as the Old Testament model for the depths of iniquity.

The Chaldeans, one of the Semitic tribes of Aramaeans, moved into southern Mesopotamia in about 850 B.C. and rose up against Babylon's Assyrian rulers. Eventually they prevailed. Nabopolassar (625–605 B.C.) founded the Neo-Babylonian Kingdom and defeated the Assyrians in 612 B.C. by capturing and destroying Nineveh on the east bank of the Tigris. Nabopolassar's son Nebuchadressar, known in the Bible as ❷ Nebuchadnezzar II (605–562 B.C.), dedicated himself primarily to ❸ constructing imposing buildings. In the temple district of Babylon, he had a ❺ processional passage and the Ishtar Gate built and decorated with colored relief tiles. The passage led to a massive central ❹ ziggurat, which may have inspired the ❻ "Tower of Babel." His palace's ❾ hanging gardens became one of the Seven Wonders of the Ancient World. Babylon was also a world center for the sciences, above all of

2 Seal with the name and title of Nebuchadressar II, 604–562 B.C.

3 Reconstruction sketch of Babylon under Nebuchadressar II

4 Model of the ziggurat of Babylon built under Nebuchadressar II

ca. 1894–1595 B.C. | Old Babylonian Empire
1792–1750 B.C. | Hammurapi
ca. 1531–1155 B.C. | Kassite period
1125–1104 B.C. | Nebuchadressar I
8th century B.C. | Revolt of the Chaldeans
635–539 B.C. | Neo-Babylonian Kingdom

Festive procession in Babylon; still from the film *The Fall of Babylon*, 1916

Tower Building at Babel by Pieter Bruegel the Elder, 16th century A.D.

Nebuchadnessar Besieges Jerusalem, illumination from a medieval Bible translation, 14th century A.D.

Belshazzar's Fall

In Biblical tradition (Daniel 5), Belshazzar insulted his God, whereupon a hand appeared and wrote "Menetekel" on the wall, which the king interpreted as a warning of the imminent fall of Babylon. The king was murdered that night.

above: *Belshazzar's Feast* by Rembrandt, 17th century A.D.

The Tower of Babel

Nebuchadressar II's tower in Babylon, a five-tiered temple in honor of the chief god Marduk, had a square base of around 300 feet (91 m) per side and was about 295 feet (90 m) high. It was called "Etemenanki" ("House which is the foundation of heaven and earth"). The top was reached by climbing three staircases on the south side. The top levels comprised a two-story temple and were covered in blue tiles. According to Genesis 11: 1-9, it reached to heaven and was a symbol of human pride, which was punished by the Babylonian confusion of tongues.

Slaves transport a stone block, still from the film *Metropolis*, 1927

astronomy, astrology, and the mantic arts.

Militarily, Nebuchadressar II directed his activities against Egypt and then Palestine (p. 57). In 597 B.C. he plundered ❼ Jerusalem for the first time when it refused to make tribute payments, and in 587 he then destroyed the city. Its inhabitants were led into ❽ "Babylonian captivity" and employed as forced labor. Of the Phoenician city-states, only Tyre (p. 55) was able to withstand conquest by Nebuchadressar.

His successors were weakened by family feuds, and eventually the usurper Nabonidus managed to reconsolidate the empire and repulse the invading Medes in 553 B.C. In 550 he installed his son Belshazzar (also known as Nidintabel and Nebuchadressar III) as regent in Babylon and withdrew to the Oasis of Teima. When he returned in 539 it was already too late; the Persians under Cyrus II had annihilated the armies of Belshazzar and entered Babylon.

Reconstruction sketch of the hanging gardens of Babylon, 18th century A.D.

635–605 B.C. | Nabupolassar I

605–562 B.C. | Nebuchadressar II

597 B.C. | Looting of Jerusalem

587 B.C. | Destruction of Judah

572 B.C. | Conquest of Tyro

555–539 B.C. | Nabonidus

550 B.C. | Regent Belshazzar

539 B.C. | Conquest of Babylon

1

ANCIENT EGYPT ca. 2900–332 B.C.

Ancient Egypt's civilization developed on the fertile strip of land created by the Nile in the North African desert. As a result of its relative geographical isolation, Egypt's development differed, in some respects greatly, from that of the rest of the Near East. Although Egypt was subject to outside influences as well, it appears that the principal defining characteristics of its culture remained homogeneous throughout the course of its long history. Its history is characterized by a series of ruling dynasties.

Nilometer used to measure the high-water mark of floods since 2000 B.C.

The Predynastic Period

The upper and lower parts of Egypt were united as early as the predynastic period, creating a single political entity.

Egypt is located in the ❹ Nile Valley, bordered on the East and West by desert. The yearly ❶ flooding which occurs between July and October deposits the fertile silt that is the basis of productive ❸ agriculture on the land bordering the river. The country is divided into Upper Egypt, where the Nile flows through a narrow valley, and Lower Egypt, where the river and its tributaries form a broad delta before flowing into the Mediterranean Sea.

In the early period, ca. 2900 B.C., two warring, independent kingdoms developed in the two areas. According to tradition, it was ❷ Narmer, a Predynastic ruler of Upper Egypt, who conquered the Nile Delta and unified the two kingdoms, establishing the new capital and powerful Memphis on the border of the two. Aha ruled the first dynasty, ca. 2900 B.C.

The separation between Upper and Lower Egypt into autonomous regions occurred repeatedly throughout Egypt's history. Whenever central power began to decline, the individual regions would exert their independence.

2 Votive depicting Narmer, the unifier of the Kingdoms, a prisoner, and the Horus Falcon, ca. 3000 B.C.

The Ruling Dynasties

The chronology of the Egyptian rulers before the arrival of Alexander the Great in 332 B.C. is divided into 31 dynasties.

Early Dynastic Period	(1–2 Dynasty)	2900–2660
Ancient Kingdom	(3–6 Dynasty)	2660–2160
1st Intermediate Period	(7–10 Dynasty)	2160–2040
Middle Kingdom	(11–12 Dynasty)	2040–1785
2nd Intermediate Period	(13–17 Dynasty)	1785–1552
New Kingdom	(18–20 Dynasty)	1552–1070
3rd Intermediate Period	(21–24 Dynasty)	1070–712
Late Dynastic Period	(25–31 Dynasty)	712–332

"Gift of the Nile"

In the fifth century B.C. the Greek historian and traveler Herodotus described Egypt as "a gift of the Nile": "It is certain, however, that now they gather in fruit from the earth with less labor than any other men, for they have no labor in breaking up furrows with a plough, nor in hoeing, nor in any other of those labors which other men have about a crop; but [they wait until] when the river has come up of itself and watered their fields and, after watering, has left."
From the History of Herodotus

3

4

above: Sailing and agriculture
left: View of the Nile showing the bordering agricultural lands

The Ancient Kingdom

In the time of the Ancient Kingdom, the most famous pyramids were built. They testify to the pronounced hierarchical character of the Egyptian society.

Pharaoh Djoser's step pyramid in Saqqara, ca. 2600 B.C.

Ever since the birth of Egyptian culture, the throne was closely linked to religion. At first each pharaoh was considered to be a ❾ representative of the heavenly god Horu. From the fifth dynasty onward, however, the successive pharaohs were revered as the sons of the sun god Re.

The unification of Upper and Lower Egypt was symbolically re-enacted every time there was an accession to the throne, when the pharaoh was crowned with the double crown of both kingdoms. The ruler regularly levied taxes. These depended on the size of the fields and the ❼ amount of livestock each family owned. Furthermore, the population was required to absolve communal duties during the dry and flood periods. These included the digging of canals and dams as well as the construction of the royal tombs. Aside from the pharaoh, the priests, ❽ high officials, and provincial governors owned the majority of property. They were thus able to exert great political influence in the kingdom, particularly as many of these offices became hereditary with the passage of time.

9 Pharaoh Chephren with the Horus Falcon, ca. 2500 B.C.

Sitting scribe, ca. 2500 B.C.

One of the most significant pharaohs of the Old Kingdom was King Djoser of the third dynasty, who commissioned expeditions to the Sinai Peninsula where copper and turquoise were mined. He is also well known for his ❻ Step pyramid at Saqqara. The architect of this structure was Imhotep, who also made a name for himself as a physician, priest, and court official. He was one of history's first universal talents and was later revered as a deity.

The Old Kingdom reached its high point during the fourth dynasty. Pharaoh Snefru led raiding expeditions to ❺ Nubia (present-day Sudan) in the south and to Libya in the west, bringing back spoils such as gold, ivory, and slaves. His son Cheops left behind the ❿ Great Pyramid of Giza, the sole survivor of the Seven Wonders of the Ancient World. Cheops' successors Chephren and Mycerinus also built great burial complexes in Giza. After the reign of Pharaoh Pepy II of the sixth dynasty, who ruled for over 90 years, signs of disintegration began to appear. Power struggles, assassinations at the royal court, and independence struggles led by regional governors led to the demise of the Old Kingdom.

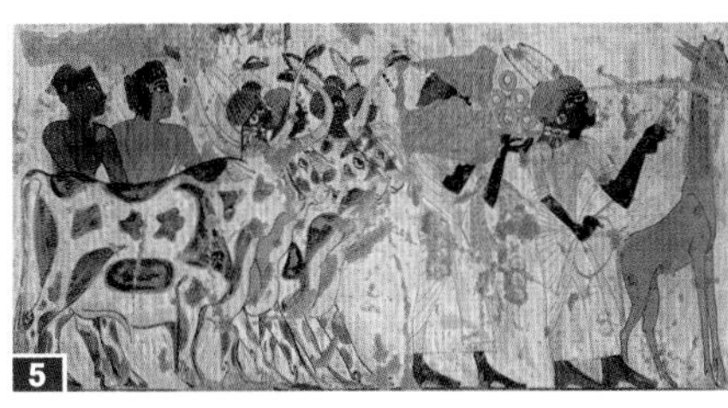

A Nubian family with animals, ca. 1340 B.C.

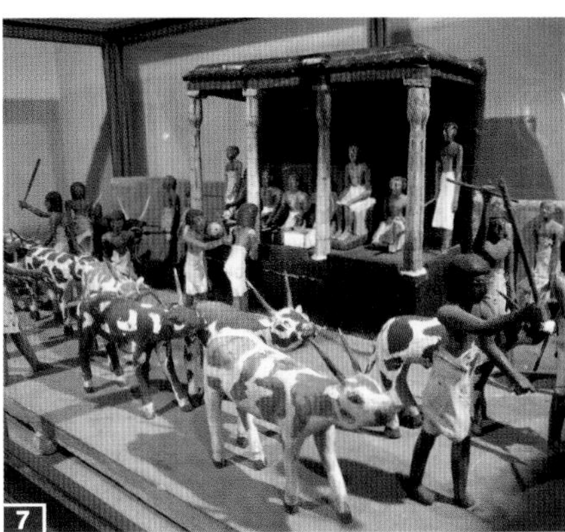

Wood model of a livestock counting, 1990 B.C.

The Pyramids

Pyramids were built from the third through the 17th dynasty, and by the Kushites. The grave mounds of the Predynastic period were the forerunners of the pyramids that developed into the right-angled tombs called mastabas (Arabic: "bench"). The step pyramids of Djoser in Saqqara were constructed by placing several mastabas on top of each other. By the fourth dynasty, pyramids with straight sides were created by filling the steps.

10 The pyramids of Giza, third century B.C.

1 View over the Sacred Lake of the Great Amun-Re Temple at Karnak, East Thebes

First and Second Intermediate Period and the Middle Kingdom 2150–1539 B.C.

The Middle Kingdom era lay between two periods of weakness and division.

During the First Intermediate Period, which followed the fall of the Old Kingdom, Egypt disintegrated once again into many territories, whose rulers fought each other in a civil war. This led to a breakdown in civil administration, trade, and the economy, and the consequent neglect of irrigation and food storage systems meant the population suffered ❸ famines.

The provincial governors of the eleventh dynasty of Thebes in Upper Egypt were finally able to gain supremacy in the power struggle for the reign over Egypt. They conquered Lower Egypt and founded the Middle Kingdom.

The pharaohs of the eleventh and twelfth dynasties disempowered the governors of the provinces and restored a central administration. The shift of the kingdom's capital to ❶ Thebes in Upper Egypt also affected the religious policies of Egypt. The deity Amun, who was particularly worshiped in the new capital, was combined with the sun god Re—whose main temple was in Heliopolis in Lower Egypt, near the old capital of Memphis—to become the official deity of the empire: Amun-Re. A ❷ large temple complex was erected in Thebes to honor and worship him. Thebes was on the site of the present-day villages Luxor and Karnak.

Under Pharaoh Sesostris III (1878–1843 B.C.), far-reaching Egyptian influence—from Nubia across the Sinai to the rich trading cities of Lebanon (p. 54)—was once again restored. Sesostris' son ❹ Amenemhet III (1842–1797 B.C.) diverted a tributary of the Nile to create the Fayoum Oasis. It was here that the last great pyramid was erected for the king. As Theban tradition dictated, later pharaohs were buried in underground tomb complexes in the ❻ Valley of the Kings, west of the capital.

By the dawning of the Second Intermediate Period, following the end of the twelfth dynasty, the country was divided once again into Upper and Lower Egypt. This allowed the ❺ invasion of the Hyksos (in Egyptian, *Hega-khase*: "rulers of foreign lands"), a group of Indo-European tribes (p. 32). They entered Lower Egypt and established their capital Avaris in the Nile Delta. From here they ruled over Lower Egypt as pharaohs, while native dynasties continued to rule Upper Egypt from Thebes.

4 Amenemhet III

2 A pharaoh offering a sacrifice in front of the god Amun-Re of Thebes, ca. 1440 B.C.

3 **left:** Emaciated man with bowl, ca. 2000 B.C.
below: Invasion of Egypt by the Hyksos, woodcarving, 19th century A.D.

5

6 Valley of the Kings, west of Thebes

1842–1797 B.C. | Amenemhet III
ca. 1539–1079 B.C. | New Kingdom
1878–1843 B.C. | Pharaoh Sesostris III
ca. 1650 B.C. | Invasion of the Hyksos

The New Kingdom I ca. 1539–1379 B.C.

Ancient Egypt was at the pinnacle of its political power during the era of the New Kingdom. The pharaohs of the 18th dynasty turned Egypt into the dominant state of the Near East.

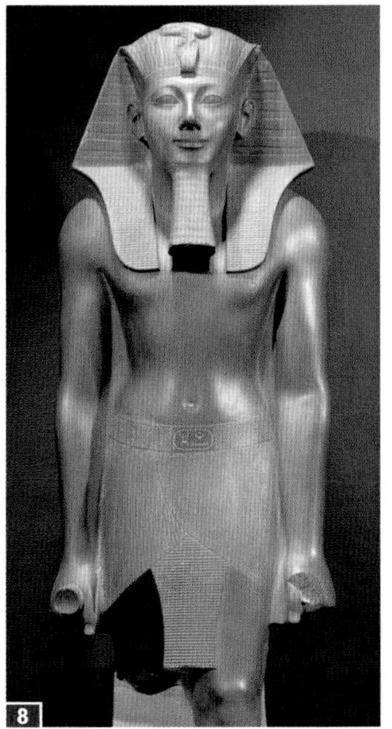

8 Thutmose III, ca. 1460 B.C.

Under Ahmose I, the first pharaoh of the 18th dynasty, the rulers of Thebes were able to expel the Hyksos and extend Egyptian hegemony to the Syrian border. Ahmose's descendent Thutmose I (ca. 1525- ca. 1512 B.C.) conquered the entirety of Nubia and integrated it into the Egyptian Empire.

Thutmose's daughter ❾ Hatshepsut (1503–1482 B.C.) was married to her half-brother Thutmose II. After his death she assumed power, initially as regent for her nephew Thutmose III. She ultimately took the title of pharaoh for herself and ushered in a period of peace and prosperity in Egypt. Great trading expeditions were undertaken, for example, to the land of Punt (present-day Eritrea and Somalia). Like other pharaohs, she had a magnificent ⓫ funerary temple constructed for herself, one of the most significant structures of its kind.

After Hatshepsut's death, ❽ Thutmose III (1504-1450 B.C.) eradicated all memory of his stepmother and aunt. Under him, the New Kingdom was at its most extensive. It reached from the Euphrates in the north into today's Sudan in the south. To counter the growing power of the Hittites, succeeding pharaohs formed alliances with the Mitanni kingdom. This policy of alliances was reinforced through dynastic marriages; ❼ Amenhotep III (1417–1379 B.C.) married not only the Egyptian Tiy but also two Mitannian princesses (p. 52). The reign of Amenhotep III was noted for its ❿ construction and architecture. His long reign was also marked by the gradual decline of the 18th dynasty, which was further accelerated by the religious policies of his son Amenhotep IV (Akhenaton).

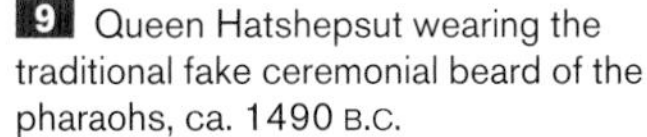

9 Queen Hatshepsut wearing the traditional fake ceremonial beard of the pharaohs, ca. 1490 B.C.

7

above: Giant statue of Amenhotep III and Queen Tiy, ca. 1370 B.C.
below: *Statues of Memnon at Thebes during the Inundation*–remains of the funerary temple of Amenhotep III in West Thebes, painting, 19th c. A.D.

10

Women in Ancient Egypt

Egyptian women enjoyed rights relatively equal to men's. They could independently complete legal transactions and practice most professions. Women also had equal rights with their husbands in marriage. Polygamy was customary only in the royal houses.

Among the wives of the pharaohs, the "great royal consorts" such as Tiy and Nefertiti were able to assert enormous influence. In some cases, women themselves ruled as pharaohs. Sibling marriages were meant to ensure the purity of the divine dynasties. Usually if the pharaoh was the descendent of a concubine—which was true of most of the kings of the 18th dynasty—he would secure his rule through marriage to a half-sister from the main line. In later periods, the "godly wives of Amun" officially stood at the top of Theban theocracy in Upper Egypt.

Bust of Nefertiti, 1355 B.C.

11 Terrace-shaped funerary temple complex of Hatshepsut at Deir el-Bahri in West Thebes, ca. 1470 B.C.

ca. 1525–ca. 1512 B.C. | Thutmose I
1503–1482 B.C. | Hatshepsut
1504–1450 B.C. | Thutmose III
1417–1379 B.C. | Amenhotep III

The New Kingdom II: The Amarna Period 1379–1320 B.C.

Amenhotep IV introduced a form of monotheism and banned older cults. He thereby incurred the wrath of the priests, who feared losing their influence in Egypt.

2 Nefertiti drives though the capital, drawing, 20th century

1 Daughters of Nefertiti and Akhenaton in front of Aten's sun disk, relief, ca. 1355 B.C.

3 Portrait of Akhenaton, ca. 1355 B.C.

The veneration of the sun disk, the Aten, was already common at the pharaoh's court under Amenhotep III. The new pharaoh, Amenhotep IV (1379–1362 B.C.), banned all other cults. He took the name ❸ Akhenaton ("He who is of service to Aten") and founded a new capital city, Akhetnaton ("Horizon of the Aten"), on the plains of Tell el-Amarna in central Egypt. In doing this, he deprived Amun-Re priesthood in Thebes of its power. Under Akhenaton, a new, more ❹ naturalistic art style became popular. In the twelfth year of his reign, however, his zeal for reform let up. ❷ Nefertiti, who until then had appeared as his equal and "great royal wife," disappeared and was replaced by the Mitanni princess Kiya (p. 52). A reason for this could have been the growing threat from the Hittites, which had caused Egypt and Mitanni to ally.

Soon after Akhenaton's death, the old cults were restored. Attempts were made to annihilate memory of the "Heretic King."

Both of the succeeding pharaohs married a ❶ daughter of Akhenaton and Nefertiti to ensure dynastic continuity. The second of them, the young Tutankhaten, changed his name to Tutankhamun in the course of a return to orthodoxy. He was otherwise politically insignificant. The generals had steadily increased their power through continual clashes with the Hittites. Following Tutankhamun's death, military leaders usurped the throne. One of them, Ramses I, established a new dynasty about 1320 B.C.

The Curse of King Tutankhamun

The discovery of the almost undamaged tomb of Tutankhamun in 1922 was the greatest archaeological sensation of the 20th century. But soon many of those involved in the excavation died under mysterious circumstances, and the legend of the "curse of King Tutunkhamun" was born. Today it is believed that the deaths were caused by rare bacteria, fungi, or viruses that were conserved in the burial chamber.

above: Sarcophagus of Tutankhamun

From Akhenaton's Longer Hymn to Aton

"Thy dawning is beautiful in the horizon of heaven,
O living Aton, Beginning of life!
When Thou risest in the eastern horizon of heaven,
Thou fillest every land with Thy beauty;...
For Thou art beautiful, great, glittering...
When Thou settest in the western horizon of heaven,
The world is in darkness like the dead....
Darkness reigns,
The world is in silence.
He that made them has gone to rest in His horizon.
Bright is the earth, when Thou risest in the horizon,
When Thou shinest as Aton by day.
The darkness is banished
When Thou sendest forth Thy rays..."

4 Relief of Tutankhamun and his wife Ankhesenpaaten who ruled for eleven years, here depicted on the back of a king's throne, ca. 1340 B.C.

The New Kingdom III: Ramessid Period 1320–1070 B.C.

The pharaohs of the 19th and 20th dynasties, who almost all bore the name Ramses, were barely able to hold Egypt's great empire together.

5 Mummified body of Ramses II

In the confusion surrounding the throne at the end of the 18th dynasty, Ramses I was able to prevail and founded the 19th dynasty. His two-year reign was spent in heavy fighting.

While Thebes remained the religious center, the capital was moved to the Nile Delta, where the hotly contested front with the Hittites in the north was more easily accessible. The Libyan nomads, who regularly attacked Egypt from the west, were another threat. Ramses I's son, Seti I, fought campaigns in Palestine, Syria and the Sudan, returning home to Egypt with enormous plunder. He continued to build temples, adding in particular many columns to the great edifice at Karnak.

One of the most important ❽ battles against the Hittites (p. 51) and their ally, the Amorite prince of Kadesh in Syria, occurred in 1285 B.C. ❺ Ramses II, grandson of Ramses I, known as "the Great", a vigorous ruler but a cruel and extravagant one whose vast harem gave him 150 offspring, marched against his foes with an enormous army in order to prevent the complete loss of Syria and Palestine, but it was only by good fortune that he did not suffer a crushing defeat. The Battle of Kadesh was a draw and led to a peace treaty signed in 1259 (p. 51). Ramses II's foreign policy problems contrasted with his immense construction activities. The ❾ rock-cut temple of Abu Simbel is the most famous among the many temples that he had built or restored.

Even the most significant pharaoh of the 20th dynasty, ❻ Ramses III (1198–1166 B.C.), who undertook extensive social and administrative reforms, was forced to defend Egypt against fierce attacks. The sea peoples (p. 33), among them the Achaians and the ❼ Philistines, allied with the Libyans and pushed forward into Egypt by land and sea. The pharaoh was unable to prevent either the Philistines from settling in Palestine or the Libyans from settling in Egypt (p. 56). Trade and the tribute payments ceased. The economic problems led to social unrest, which resulted in the first documented strike in history.

Ramses III was eventually murdered, although a memorial to him remained in the form of the huge temples and palaces he had constructed. His successors lost control over the nation. The foreign peoples living in Egypt, descendants of mercenaries or slave laborers, rebelled, while the high priests of Amun in Thebes established a theocracy in Upper Egypt. With the end of the 20th dynasty, Egypt was once again divided up into parts.

The Israelites in Egypt

Among the many foreigners living in Egypt under the Pharoahs were the Israelites, who were ruthlessly exploited as slave labor. At the same time, they were considered a threat:

"A new king came to power in Egypt, and he said unto his people: 'Behold, the people of the children of Israel are too many and too mighty for us... when there befalleth us any war, they also join themselves unto our enemies, and fight against us, and get them up out of the land. Therefore they did set over them taskmasters to afflict them with their burdens. And they built for Pharaoh store-cities, Pithom and Ramses.'"

(Exodus 1:8–11)

8 Ramses II at the Battle of Kadesh, drawing, 19th century

6 Ramses III and one of his sons, wall painting ca. 1370 B.C.

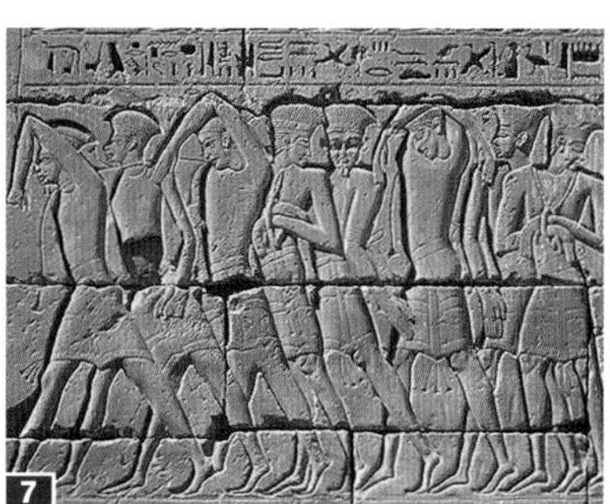
7 Captured Philistines, relief on the funerary temple of Ramses III in Medinet Habu

9 Temple of Ramses II at Abu Simbel

The Third Intermediate Period and the Late Kingdom 1070–332 B.C.

During the Third Intermediate Period, Egypt once again fragmented. The Late Kingdom then saw alternating periods of foreign occupation and independence.

1 Pharaoh Shoshenq I holds Israelite captive, hieroglyphic inscription, ca. 930 B.C.

The pharaohs who followed the 20th dynasty only held sway over the lands of Upper Egypt. The leaders of the Libyan mercenary troops employed by the kings grew in power until one of them, ❶ Shoshenq I (ca. 945–924 B.C.), managed to seize the throne. Through their dynastic connections, the Libyan pharaohs were initially able to exert a certain influence in Upper Egypt, but Lower Egypt eventually disintegrated into a multitude of principalities and kingdoms.

The ❷ high priests of Amun, in Thebes, had already established a form of theocracy in Upper Egypt, which they legitimized through the prophecies of the ❹ "god-wife of Amun." The functions of this high office were usually performed by the princesses of Libya, and later by princesses from the Kushite royal families.

4 The "god-wife of Amun" Karomama, statuette, ca. 870 B.C.

The Kushites began advancing out of Nubia into Egypt in about 740 B.C. They established themselves as pharaohs, first in Thebes and then, under the ❸ 25th dynasty, in Lower Egypt as well. They succeeded in establishing a single Egyptian state in 712.

After 671 B.C., the Assyrians launched repeated invasions of Egypt. They installed Psamtik I, a Libyan prince from the Nile Delta, as governor. In 663, with the help of Greek mercenaries, he declared independence and founded the 26th dynasty. He forced the Kushite god-wife of Amun to name one of his daughters as her successor and thus brought Upper Egypt under his rule by 656. Psamtik I also brought Greek tradesmen to Egypt, who settled primarily in the Nile Delta. Over time, the relationship with the Greeks became ever closer. The pharaohs married Greek women, donated votive offerings to Delphi, and minted coins after the Greek model.

The Persians ❺ conquered Egypt in 525 B.C. and incorporated it into their empire. After many uprisings, Egypt regained its independence only to fall to the Persians a second time in 343. When Alexander the Great conquered the Persian empire in 332 B.C., Egypt also came under his rule and he founded the city of Alexandria. After his death Egypt once again rose to a position of supremacy in the Eastern Mediterranean region under the rule of the Ptolemies.

2 Egyptian priest reading scrolls

3 Taharka, from the 25th dynasty, bows before the falcon god Hemen, statue

Hieroglyphics

Egyptian hieroglyphics were a pictographic script, primarily used on monuments and for religious texts. The Egyptians continued to use simplified forms of hieroglyphics in their daily lives until the time of the early Christians, when they switched to writing the Egyptian language with the Greek alphabet. Over the centuries, the understanding of ancient hieroglyphics was lost. In 1799, a French military officer, who had come to Egypt as part of Napoleon's expedition, discovered the "Rosetta Stone." On this monument from the second century B.C. he found a text chiseled in both hieroglyphics and Greek. With this new evidence, philologists finally deciphered hieroglyphics in 1822.

above: The Rosetta Stone, ca. 196 B.C.

5 Pharaoh Psamtik III defeated and made to submit to his conqueror, Persian King Cambyses, painting, 19th century

Egyptian Religion

The Egyptian religion recognized a multitude of gods. Their relative importance was influenced by social conditions and subject to political changes.

The beginnings of the Egyptian religion can be traced to the fourth millennium B.C. At first, the gods took the form of animals, but later they also assumed human form. Often they were represented as hybrid creatures, for example the falcon-headed god Horus, or the ram-headed god ❼ Amun. Among countless deities, the gods associated with the most important religious centers and the major cities always held a special significance. They were honored across the kingdom, thus asserting a cultural and geographical hierarchy within the framework of the official cult. In the Old Kingdom the sun god Re of Heliopolis, near the capital of Memphis, stood out above all others. With the rise of Thebes during the Middle Kingdom, the city's local god Amun was elevated to the foremost rank of the deities and was then fused with Re to become Amun-Re. Pharaoh Akhenaton attempted unsuccessfully to enforce the worship of Aten, who was not represented in a humanoid form but only by the abstract symbol of a sun disk.

The Egyptians believed that the gods, too, aged and died. ❽ Osiris, represented as a mummy, symbolized death. He was killed and dismembered by his brother, the desert-god Seth, but was resurrected by his sister ❾, ❿ Isis. Osiris was thus also a symbol of ⓫ fertility and lifegiving energy. The first pharaohs were considered to be representatives of Horus, the son of Isis and Osiris.

8 The god Osiris, Egyptian mural, ca. 1306 B.C.

11 Seed bed in the form of Osiris, second century B.C.

12 Group of mourners, mural, ca.1370 B.C.

9 Enthroned Isis breast-feeds a young Horus, seventh c. B.C.

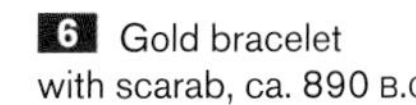

6 Gold bracelet with scarab, ca. 890 B.C.

In the late Old Kingdom references first appear to a tribunal of the dead, where all the dead must account for their actions before Osiris and Re—either to continue to exist as blessed dead or to be damned, the punishment for which was severe and could mean obliteration.

Mummification, burial objects, and tombs such as the pyramids were meant to make the continuation of earthly life possible after death. ⓬ Rituals and incantations were performed for the protection of the dead.

Egyptians used amulets and lucky charms such as ❻ scarabs to ward off danger or to encourage fertility.

The role played by the pharaoh, that of a link between men and gods, decreased with the fall of the New Kingdom and the disintegration of the power. Certain kinds of animals, such as cats and crocodiles, came to be venerated as spiritual mediators. Many of these animals were mummified after death and buried in graveyards or tombs. In the Late Kingdom, Greek influence led to the development of arcane cults, above all those of Isis and Osiris, that would later be popular in the Roman Empire.

7 Statue of the ram-headed god Amun, third century B.C.

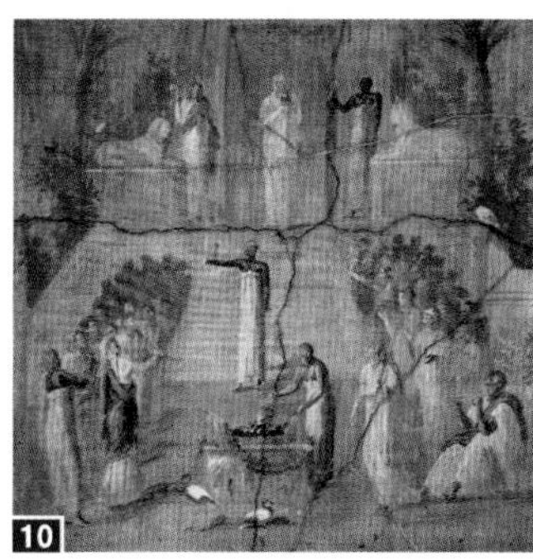

10 Isis cult, Roman mural, first century

From the Book of the Dead:

"I open the channels, in heaven as on Earth. Because I am your loving son Osiris! I have become spirit, sublimated, made holy, and with powerful chants armored...Gods of the immeasurable sky. Godly spirits! All of you, look at me! I have completed my journey and appear before you."

above: Illustration from the *Book of the Dead*, ca. twelfth century B.C.

663 B.C. | Psamtik I founds 26th dynasty
525 B.C. | Persian conquest of Egypt
ca. 404 B.C. | Egyptian revolts
343 B.C. | Persian reconquest
332 B.C. | Egypt under Alexander the Great

THE HITTITES ca. 1570–ca. 650 B.C.

The Hittites were an Indo-European people who migrated out of the steppes north of the Black Sea and into Asia Minor during the second millennium B.C. From there they pushed into Syria and Mesopotamia, where they established an empire that competed with Egypt's New Kingdom for supremacy in the Near East. The empire came to an end under the onslaught of the sea peoples in 1200 B.C.

1 Archer and charioteer, ninth century B.C.

The Old Kingdom ca. 1570–1343 B.C.

The Hittites encountered an old, highly developed civilization in Asia Minor from which they adopted numerous cultural developments and religious concepts.

2 A Hittite couple, ca. 800 B.C.

> **The Hittite Gods**
>
> *The Hittites were called the "people of the thousand gods." Apart from their own, they took up many of the deities and religious concepts of their neighbors. A deity pair associated with the weather and the sun was always at the head of the Hittite pantheon and was worshiped in the official national cult. Above all, vegetation, mountain, and water gods also played a role in daily religious life.*
>
> Hittite gods

One of the oldest cities of the world, Çatal Hüyük (p. 27), existed in Anatolia possibly as early as 7000 B.C. The city on the west coast of Asia Minor, known as ❺ Troy (Ilium) (p. 80) from Homer's *Iliad* and referred to as "Wilusa" by Hittite sources, also belonged to the cultural area of ancient Anatolia. The Hittites first settled, however, in central Anatolia in the land of the Hattis, from whom their name may have derived. There they lived in numerous, independently ruled communities until about 1630 B.C., when King Labarnas II established political unity and moved his capital to the ancient city of Hattusa, after which he took his name Hattusilis I.

Hattusilis expanded the borders of the Old Kingdom that he had founded through ❶ military campaigns in western Asia Minor and northern Syria. His grandson, Mursilis I, conquered the important Syrian trading center, Aleppo, and reached Babylon with his armies around 1600 B.C.

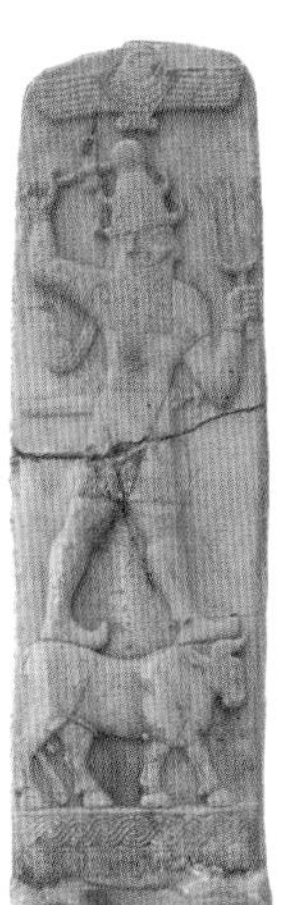

In addition to his role as commander of military forces, the Hittite king also held, together with his queen, religious offices in the state cult as the ❸ weather god and sun goddess respectively. The queen participated in council meetings, had her own chancellery, and also maintained independent diplomatic relations with other princes.

After the death of the king, she retained her offices and titles as his widow. In general, ❹ women, whether they were ❷ married, widowed, or divorced, were well provided for. Hittite law also appears to have been rather progressive in comparison with the other cultures of the Near East, as the death penalty was rarely imposed. The assassination of Mursilis I by his brother-in-law Hantilis around 1590 B.C. led to turmoil around the throne and a revolt of the nobility. Because of the instability in the leadership, the Hittites lost control of Syria to the Hurrite Mitanni kingdom and were forced to focus on Anatolia.

4 **above:** Hittite women, spinning, eighth–seventh century B.C.
left: The Hittite weather god with a bundle of lightning bolts beneath the winged sun disk

5 Artist's reconstruction of ancient Troy

ca. 2000 B.C. | Hittite immigration into Asia Minor
ca. 1570-1590 B.C. | Old Kingdom
ca. 7000 B.C. | Founding of Çatal Hüyük
ca. 1630 B.C. | Political unity under Hattusilis I
ca. 1590 B.C. | Assassination of Mursilis I

The New Kingdom ca. 1335–1200 B.C.

The rise of the Hittites marked the beginning of the New Kingdom. Weakened by fierce battles with Egypt, the empire managed to settle the conflict only to ultimately be destroyed by the sea peoples.

6 The Orontes River in Syria

After a transitional and chaotic phase in which the Hittites contended with enemies such as the Gashga people in their immediate vicinity, Suppiluliumas I (reigned 1380–1346 B.C.), brother of Arnuwanda, established the Hittite empire by defeating the Mitannian kingdom and making vassals of the Amorite princes in Syria about 1335 B.C. (p. 54). He fortified his capital and organized the state, dividing it into provinces ruled by princes. He installed his son Telipinus in Aleppo as priest-king of the weather god, who was worshiped there as well. Suppiluliumas, his son ❼ Mursilis II, (reigned 1345–1315 B.C.), and his grandson Muwattalis (reigned 1315–1290 B.C.) were all drawn into conflicts with Egypt (p. 47), which had been allied with the Mitanni and also claimed hegemony over Syria. In about 1285, Muwattalis and the Egyptian pharaoh Ramses II fought at the ❻ Orontes River in Syria in the ❾ Battle of Kadesh. No clear victor emerged, although Muwattalis was able to maintain his hegemony over Syria. It was only after Hattusilis III signed a treaty with the Egyptians in 1259 B.C. that peace between the two exhausted powers was secured for the remainder of the century. During this period, disputes within the royal family and with the nobility led to political disintegration. Catastrophic crop failures and famine made the import of grain from Egypt necessary and compounded the empire's difficulties. The weakened empire of the Hittites was no longer able to withstand the onslaught of the sea peoples (p. 33), particularly the Greek Achaians.

7 Earthenware plaque with the seal of King Mursilis II in Hittite hieroglyphics and cuneiform script, ca. 1300 B.C.

The line of ❽ Hittite kings ended abruptly with Suppiluliumas II around 1200 B.C. The capital, Hattusa, was completely demolished by unknown attackers. They may have been raiding Gashga peoples, former soldiers, or even the city's own populace. Troy (p. 80), a Hittite vassal state located in present-day Turkey, was also destroyed at this time.

Only in southeastern Anatolia and northern Syria did small, independent Hittite kingdoms survive, lasting into the seventh century B.C. They were finally overrun by the advance of the Neo-Assyrian Empire, while the rest of Anatolia sank into a "Dark Age" until the appearance of the Phrygians and Lydians (p. 53).

8 Statue of a late Hittite king, ninth century B.C.

The Peace Treaty between Hattusilis III and Ramses II

"Look, Reamasesa-mai-amana, the great king, the king of the country of Egypt, is at peace and fraternity with Hattusili, the great king, the king of the country of Hatti. Look, the children of Reamasesa, the great king, the king of the country of Egypt, they will be forever in a state of peace and of fraternity with the children of Hattusili, the great king, the king of the country of Hatti. They will remain in the line of our bond of fraternity and of peace; the country of Egypt and the country of Hatti will be forever in a state of peace and of fraternity as it is with us. ..."

Peace treaty in cuneiform script, 1259 B.C.

9 Three marching soldiers, ninth century B.C.

1335 B.C. | Founding of the Hittite Empire
ca. 1285 B.C. | Battle of Kadesh
1259 B.C. | Peace treaty with Egypt
ca 1200 B.C. | Last Hittite king, Suppiluliumas II
ca. 1200 B.C. | Destruction of Troy

1 Bronze helmet from Urartu, eighth century B.C.

Kingdoms on the Borders of the Fertile Crescent ca. 1500–546 B.C.

Besides the great empires of the Hittites, Assyrians, Babylonians, Persians, and Egyptians, there were many, often short-lived kingdoms in Asia Minor, North Syria, and Mesopotamia. They served as buffer states between the great powers and were frequently occupied by foreign soldiers. They were also sought after as partners in alliances and agreements to secure trade routes passing through their territories. During periods when their more powerful neighboring empires fell into crisis or collapsed, they sometimes won a precarious status of independence and occasionally rose to positions of considerable power and influence in the region.

Mitanni and Urartu

In the north of the Fertile Crescent lay the Mitannian kingdom of the Indo-Iranian Hurrites. After a period of Hittite supremacy, the Kingdom of Urartu supplanted the Kingdom of Mitanni.

Around 1500 B.C., at the time of the fall of the Hittite Old Kingdom, the Hurrites founded the Kingdom of Mitanni, of which they formed only a small ruling

3 Bronze votive tablet from Urartu, showing the weather god Teisheba

elite. At its peak, between 1450 and 1350 B.C., the kingdom stretched from the Mediterranean coast through Syria to East Anatolia, Armenia, and North Mesopotamia, where Assyria was a vassal state of the Hurrites. The first written evidence, using the Akkadian alphabet, dates from the beginning of the third millennium B.C., with inscriptions over the next 2000 years in Akkadian, Sumerian, Hittite, Ugaritic and Hebrew, as well as in Hurrite. At first, Egypt competed with the Hurrites for control of Syria (p. 46), but then the pharaohs of the 18th dynasty formed an alliance with them against the renewed and mounting threat of the Hittites. The alliance was then sealed over many generations through marriage. Eventually, after the Middle Assyrian Kingdom had forcibly liberated itself from Mitannian dominance, the Hurrites were subdued by the Hittites under King Suppluliuna, who elevated the Hittite state to its maximum splendor, in about 1335 B.C.

In Urartu, a region on Lake Van in ❹ East Anatolia, descendents of the Hurrites established various kingdoms after the fall of the Hittite New Kingdom in 1200 B.C. when it was invaded by many tribes. These merged to create a unified state around 860 B.C. The ❷ kings of Urartu expanded their kingdom into the Caucasus, East Anatolia, and northwest Iran. The economy was based primarily on ❶, ❸ ore mining and processing, along with agriculture and trade.

2 Inscription by Sardur III of Urartu, ca. 700 B.C.

Fierce disputes with the Neo-Assyrian Empire over the control of trade routes and ore deposits developed in the eighth century. The Assyrians allied themselves with the Cimmerians (p. 33), an Indo-European nomadic people, and defeated Urartu in 714. The story of Urartu comes to its ultimate end in 640 B.C. with the invasion of the Scythians, who followed the Cimmerians. At the same time, Armenians entered Urartu territory from southwestern Europe. The area remained a bone of contention between the great powers, including the Roman Empire, the Parthians, and the Sassanians.

4 Landscape in East Anatolia

ca. 1500 B.C. | Founding of the Mitanni Kingdom
ca. 1400 B.C. | Alliance between Egypt and Mitanni
ca. 1200 B.C. | Fall of the Hittite New Kingdom
ca. 1100 B.C. | Founding of the Phrygian Kingdom
ca. 860 B.C. | The Urartu kingdoms unite
ca. 750 B.C. | War between Urartu and the Assyrians

Phrygia and Lydia

Following the end of the Hittite empire around 1200 B.C., Anatolia experienced a cultural decline until the Phrygians in the eighth century B.C. In the seventh century the Lydians carved out an extensive area of territory in which they established powerful kingdoms.

The ❼ Phrygians emerged from the Balkans around 1100 B.C. and penetrated into Asia Minor. By the eighth century, there was a thriving Phryrian kingdom in the center of Anatolia that maintained cultural and trade relations with the Greeks in the west and the Urartians and Assyrians in the east. The area's significant deposits of gold inspired the ❿ myth of King Midas, son of Gordius, the legendary founder of the kingdom, and the goddess Cybele. Midas committed suicide at the beginning of the seventh century when the Cimmerians, who were being driven westward by the Scythians, burned the Phrygian capital, Gordium, to the ground.

The ❺ Lydians then gained control of the western part of Asia Minor. They defeated the Cimmerians and attempted to expand their kingdom westward over the Greek colonies on the coast of Anatolia (Ionia), as well as over the entire Anatolian highlands. Their eastern border, by agreement first with the Medes (p. 60) and later with the Persians, was fixed at the Halys River in north-central Anatolia. The last Lydian king, ❻ Croesus—whose ❽ wealth became proverbial—conquered almost all of the Greek coastal cities. He then turned eastward after the Oracle of Delphi prophesied that a great empire would fall if he crossed the Halys. Thus feeling assured of victory, Croesus crossed the river in 546 B.C. and marched against Persia but was defeated by the Persian king Cyrus II—the prophesy came true, but it was his own great kingdom that fell. According to legend, Croesus was ⓫ pardoned shortly before he was to be burned at the stake, and he may later have become an official at the Persian court.

The Phrygians and Lydians lived on, not only in myths but also in the cultural legacy they left to the Greeks and the Romans—the cults of Dionysus and of the "Great Mother" Cybele. They also introduced the practice of ❾ minting coins to Europe.

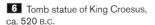

5 Remainder of the Temple of Artemis in the Lydian capital Sardis, steel engraving, 19th century

8 *Solon before Croesus*, Croesus boasts about his treasures before the Athenian lawgiver and traveler Solon, painting by Gerard van Honthorst, 1624

11 Croesus, about to be burned at the stake, is shown mercy by Cyrus, wood engraving, 19th century

6 Tomb statue of King Croesus, ca. 520 B.C.

9 Lydian gold coin from Croesus's reign, sixth century B.C.

7

10

above: Phrygian Bronze Helmet, sixth century B.C.
below: Midas's daughter is turned to gold by his touch, colored lithograph, 19th century

The Legend of Midas

The legend of Midas relates how Dionysus granted the king his wish that everything he touched would turn to gold. However, when even food and drink turned to gold, he was pushed to the verge of starvation. Then the god commanded him to bathe in the Pactolus River to be freed of his gift. It was said that this was the reason the little river in Asia Minor had such a wealth of gold. In another myth, Midas was given the ears of an ass by Apollo because he favored Apollo's rival in a contest he judged. Midas concealed his ears under a Phrygian cap. Erroneously interpreted as the cap of liberty, it later became the symbol of freedom during the French Revolution.

Statue of Paris with a Phrygian cap (fourth century B.C.)

ca. 700 B.C. | Suicide of King Midas
640 B.C. | Invasion of Urartu by the Scythians
546 B.C. | Cyrus II's victory over Croesus
714 B.C. | Urartu defeated by the Assyrians
ca. 700 B.C. | Lydia becomes a trading power
ca. 560–546 B.C. | Reign of Croesus

Syria and Palestine 3000–332 B.C.

❶ Syria and Palestine were of great strategic importance as military, commercial, and cultural crossroads between the early high civilizations of Egypt, Asia Minor, Mesopotamia, and the Aegean Sea. The constant wrestling for control over the area by the bordering powers prevented the formation of a unified state. Only after the upheavals caused by the sea peoples created a power vacuum was it possible for the kingdoms of David and Solomon to emerge, for a short time, as regional powers. At the same time, the Phoenicians built up a trade empire that reached from the coasts of West Anatolia to the edge of the Atlantic.

1 Syrian with lioness and ram, ivory statue, ninth century B.C.

The Canaanites and the Amorites

The Canaanites and the Amorites developed a high civilization that fused together stylistic elements from the whole of the Ancient Orient and demonstrated the bridging role of Syria and Palestine.

The early inhabitants of Palestine are called Canaanites, those of Syria Amorites or East Canaanites. Linguistically both groups belong to the Semites. They never experienced political unity but lived in city-states ruled over by princes or priest-kings. The remains of the Canaanite city of ❷ Jericho date back to around 9000 B.C. and are considered the earliest evidence of urban life. Over the centuries, the rulers of Egypt, the Hittite Empire, Assyria, and Babylon competed against each other for control of Palestine and Syria.

The trading centers situated on the Mediterranean coast held a special position among the city-states. At first, ❸ Byblos was the busiest of them. The city had enjoyed trading relations with Egypt since the third millennium B.C. and was the most important port for exports of Lebanese cedar, as well as ❹ luxury goods that were manufactured there for the Egyptian market. In the middle of the 13th century B.C., Ugarit, situated farther north, replaced Byblos as the preeminent port city. The Mycenaean ❻ merchants had their own quarter in the city, which bears witness to trade relations with the Aegean cultures. By allying alternately with the Hittites and the Egyptians, the ❺ kings of Ugarit were able to maintain their independence until around 1200 B.C., when Ugarit was overrun by the sea peoples and completely destroyed.

Subsequent archaeological excavations of the previous site of the city of Ugarit, present-day Ras Shamra, have uncovered a number of libraries containing ancient manuscripts written in at least four different languages.

2 Foundations of a round tower in Jericho, 7000 B.C.

3 **above:** Ruins of the Temple of Obelisks in Byblos
left: Example of Egyptian gold jewelry from Byblos, 19th century B.C.

4

5 The king of Ugarit hunting, detail on a golden plate, 14th–13th century B.C.

Baal, bronze statue, 14th–13th c.

Baal

Baal, or the female form Baalat, was the name of the chief deity of Canaanite and Amorite cities. They also worshiped other gods, such as the fertility goddess of war, Astarte. In Palestine, the monotheistic cult of Yahweh vied for followers with the older Baal cults and ultimately triumphed over them.

6 Two men agreeing on a contract, limestone relief from the city of Ugarit, 14th century B.C.

ca. 9000 B.C. | Founding of Jericho

ca. 3000 B.C. | Rise of Byblos

ca. 1300 B.C. | Ugarit becomes a trading center

ca. 1200 B.C. | Conquest of Ugarit

ca. 900 B.C. | Rise of Tyre

ca. 850 B.C. | Phoenicians rule over the Mediterranean area

The Phoenician City-States

The Phoenicians are considered the most accomplished seafarers of antiquity. Throughout the Mediterranean and beyond they conducted trade, founded colonies, and spread their culture, which was in the tradition of the Canaanites and Amorites.

Following the devastation caused by the sea peoples, the focus of trade shifted south from Syria towards the territory of present-day Lebanon. The Greeks called this region "Phoenicia" ("purple land") after a precious dye produced there. As in Canaanite and Amorite times, Phoenicia was divided into city-states ruled by ❼ kings and great trading families. With the decline of Mycenaean and Minoan competition, the ⓬ Phoenicians controlled Mediterranean trade as far as the coasts of the Iberian Peninsula and North Africa. They founded numerous ❽ colonies, including Carthage ("new city") around 814 B.C. (p. 106), which was later to become the most important sea power in the Western Mediterranean. The net of Phoenician ⓫ trade relations reached beyond the Mediterranean to the British Isles and the Canary Islands, and it is even possible that Phoenicians circumnavigated Africa about 600 B.C. They kept their knowledge of the ocean beyond the "Pillars of Hercules"—the Strait of Gibraltar—absolutely secret and spread ❿ horror stories about the area to frighten off their competitors.

❾ Sidon and Tyre were the two most important Phoenician city-states, and their rulers were closely tied to the kings of Israel and Judah. In the tenth century B.C., Hiram I of Tyre supported King Solomon in the construction of a fleet for a trading expedition to the Red Sea. Tyre reached its apogee under Ittobaal I, who subjugated rival Sidon in the ninth century B.C. By this time, the Phoenicians were coming under increasing military pressure from the land powers, Assyria and Babylon, who demanded tribute from the cities. Only Tyre, situated on an impregnable island, was able to withstand the enemy forces. Phoenicia lost Sidon but remained independent despite a 13-year siege by Nebuchadressar II of Babylon that ended in 573 B.C. The Persians, on the other hand, accepted the autonomy of the Phoenicians, who made up the majority of the Persian fleet in battles against the Greeks.

It was Alexander the Great who first succeeded in conquering Tyre (p. 96) in 332 B.C., after a seven-month siege during which he built a causeway from the mainland to the island city. The Phoenicians were later ruled by the Diadochoi and the Romans but still managed to keep their cultural and religious identity alive.

7

10 Phoenician silver coin decorated with the image of a merchant ship harried by a sea monster

8

above: Ruins of a Phoenician colony in Sa Caleta on Ibiza, founded ca. 650 B.C.
left: A king with lotus stems, ivory tablet, eighth–seventh century B.C.

9

View over Sidon with Lebanon in the distance, chalk lithograph, 19th century

The Abduction of Europa

According to Greek mythology, Zeus, the father of the gods, assumed the form of a white bull and abducted Europa, the daughter of King Agenor of Phoenicia. By him she conceived Minos, the legendary king of Crete. Much that arrived in Europe from Asia first passed through Minoan Crete, including the Phoenician alphabet.

The Rape of Europa, painting by Rubens, 17th century

11

Phoenician merchants trade, wood engraving, 19th century

12

Phoenician merchant ship at sea, clay relief

ca. 814 B.C. | Founding of Carthage

ca. 600 B.C. | Phoenicians sail around Africa

572 B.C. | Nebuchadressar II besieges Tyre

332 B.C. | Alexander the Great conquers Tyre

The Early Israelites and the Kingdoms of David and Solomon

The Israelites migrated into the region of Palestine in the 13th century B.C. Conflicts in the settlement areas required a military society, which extended beyond individual tribes and became the basis, around 1020 B.C., of national unity.

1 The Israelites conquer the Canaanite city of Jericho

Many of the Canaanite city-states in Palestine were destroyed by the sea peoples around 1200 B.C., after which the ❸ Philistines settled on the coast and established a federation of individual city-states. At the same time, the Semitic Aramaeans moved in, among them the ❶ tribes of Israel. Related folk groups had previously lived in Egypt and are described in the biblical stories of Moses. These Israelite groups had in common the ❼ worship of the god Yahweh. The isolation of this god from the gods of the neighboring peoples and the maintenance of the purity of the Yahweh cult defined their society. Around the year 1020 B.C., the Israelites declared Saul their king and commander for the war against the other Aramaean tribes and the Philistines. They did not, however, grant him any internal authority, for example, to levy a general tax. After ❷ Saul's death, the successful military leader ❹ David, from the tribe of Judah, was chosen as king around 1004 B.C. Unlike Saul, David relied on a private army, which he also used to seize money and estates for himself. He overrode the autonomy of the individual Israelite tribes and established a unified state, with Jerusalem as its capital and political and religious center.

4 David with Goliath's head, bronze statue by Verrocchio, 16th century

3 A Philistine bust, relief, twelfth century B.C.

David subjugated neighboring Aramaean territories until his realm eventually reached from the Euphrates River in the north to the Red Sea in the south. He was succeeded by his son ❺ Solomon, who maintained close diplomatic and trade relations with the Phoenicians, Arabs, and Egyptians. In ❽ Jerusalem, Solomon built a magnificent ❾ temple as the center of the Yahweh cult. There were already signs that the kingdom's power had peaked, however. Some of the Aramaean vassals regained their independence, while tax pressure, unpaid forced labor, and Solomon's tolerance of foreign cultures were stirring up discontent internally among the Israelites. Despite this, Solomon is remembered well by posterity—primarily for his proverbial ❻ wisdom.

7 The Philistines rob the Ark of the Covenant, the holy relic of the Israelites, painting, 19th century

2 Saul commits suicide, book illustration, 15th century

6 Solomon settles an argument of two women claiming to be the mother of a child, book illustration, 13th c.

5 The wedding of Solomon and the Egyptian pharaoh's daughter, painting, 17th century

8 View of the Temple Mount in Jerusalem and the so-called Dome of the Rock, built in Islamic times

1300 B.C. | The Israelites migrate to Palestine
1200 B.C. | Aramaeans' migration
1100 B.C. | The Israelites settle permanently
1020 B.C. | Reign of King Saul
ca. 1000 B.C. | Moses leads the Israelites out of Egypt
1004 B.C. | Kingdom of David

David

After David killed the gigantic Philistine Goliath, Saul had him brought to his court. David was protected from the king's increasing jealousy of his popularity by his love for Saul's son Jonathan. When Jonathan fell in battle against the Philistines, Saul committed suicide and David became king. During his reign, David's own son Absalom rose up in an unsuccessful revolt against him. Later, David fell in love with Bathsheba and deployed her husband's forces in battle in such a way that he would certainly be killed. David's son by Bathsheba, Solomon, succeeded him as king.

David sees the bathing Bathsheba, book illus. ca. 1500

9 Sacrifice scene in the temple of Jerusalem

The Kingdoms of Judah and Israel

The competing claims of Solomon's successors led to a division of the kingdom. But even thereafter, the rulers of Judah and Israel were subject to strong, primarily religious opposition internally, while external pressure from the Assyrians and Babylonians increased.

After his death in 926 B.C., Solomon's kingdom collapsed. His son Rehoboam, who wanted to continue Solomon's centralist policies, was recognized as king by the tribes of Judah and Benjamin, while northern tribes instead chose ❿ Jeroboam I, one of Solomon's old adversaries.

The northern kingdom, Israel, was continually shaken by dynastic change. Under King ⓬ Ahab and his queen Jezebel, a daughter of Ittobaal I of Tyros, social evils and the Baal cult that the queen supported provoked the resistance of the religious leader and prophet ⓭ Elijah. Upon the instructions of another prophet, Elisha, Jehu usurped the throne about 845 B.C. and killed the widowed Jezebel, her son King Joram, and many Baal adherents.

11 King Jehu of Israel and the Assyrian king, sculpture, ninth century B.C.

In Judah, too, where the dynasty of David had retained power, the prophets—Isaiah and Jeremiah in particular—were politically prominent. They criticized not only the religious and social conditions but also the foreign policies of their kings. These policies were greatly influenced by the ⓫ Assyrian dominance of the Near East. Beginning in the ninth century B.C., the Assyrians intervened in the royal succession in Israel and then in Judah, helping enthrone their own candidates, who in return offered tribute payments.

Attempts to win independence with the aid of Egypt led to Israel's destruction in 722 B.C. The Assyrians occupied the land, ravaged Samaria, and displaced the population. After Nebuchadressar II expelled the Assyrians and Egyptians from Palestine, he installed Zedekiah as king in Judah. When Zedekiah rebelled in 587 B.C., Nebuchadressar devastated Jerusalem and annexed Judah. Most of the population was then deported into ⓮ "Babylonian captivity."

13 Prophet Elijah kills a Baal priest, wood carving, 19th century

14 The Israelites are deported to Babylon, painting, 19th century

10 Seal of King Jeroboam I of Israel, tenth century B.C.

12 Ahab and Jezebel arrange the murder of Naboth in order to steal his vineyard, book illustration, 15th century

Criticism of Rulers in the Bible

Criticism of rulers in the Near East as recorded in the Bible is unique in its sharpness. The prophet Jeremiah warned the king of Judah and predicted deportation by the Babylonians: "Say unto the king and to the queen, 'Humble yourselves, sit down: for your principalities shall come down, even the crown of your glory. ... Judah shall be carried away captive all of it, it shall be wholly carried away.'" (Jeremiah 13:18–19)

ca. 1000 B.C.	Foundation of the capital Jerusalem
ca. 971–926 B.C.	Solomon's reign
ca. 950 B.C.	Construction of the Yahweh temple
926 B.C.	Israel is divided
722 B.C.	Israel's occupation by the Assyrians
587 B.C.	Nebuchadressar II destroys Jerusalem

Judaism

Judaism is the oldest of the three great monotheistic religions and provides the historical background to Christianity and Islam. One characteristic of Judaism is an identity which involves membership in both a religion and a people. This complex dualism is embodied by the Jewish state of Israel, founded in 1948, where secularist Zionism and Orthodox Judaism coexist.

Moses sees the Promised Land

The Covenant with God

Jewish tradition teaches that God made a covenant exclusively with the people of Israel. The covenant is a central element of the Jewish religion. God, the creator of the world and of mankind, chose the people of Israel—beginning with the patriarch Abraham—as his people. Being the "chosen people" is at once equally a mark of honor and a burden. Man is directed to follow God's commandments, but, at the same time, is called upon to behave in an ethically responsible way and is accountable for his transgressions. The relationship to God is understood as a dialogue between God and mankind. God often revealed himself to man through prophets who proclaimed his will. Moses stands out among them as the deliverer of the Law—the Torah—which is doctrine, law, and according to Jewish tradition, the complete revelation of God in 613 commandments and prohibitions. It was Moses who transformed the belief in the Jewish tribal god—"God, the Father"—into a belief in a universal god; "Yahweh" was at first only the mightiest among the gods, but then he became the only god.

Moses with the Torah

The Promised Land and the Diaspora

❸ Moses not only brought God's law to the people of Israel but was also called to lead them out of captivity in Egypt to the ❶ "Promised Land." The concept of the Promised Land has played a significant role in Judaism. The patriarchs Abraham, Isaac, and Jacob, with whom the history of Israel begins, were nomads in the land of Canaan. Abraham received the promise that his posterity would be a great people and that God would give them the land of Canaan. The promise was fulfilled after Moses led the people of Israel out of Egypt. After a long trek through the desert, they occupied and settled in Palestine. There followed the founding of the Israelite kingdom and its capital Jerusalem, and the erection of the Jewish shrine, ❹ the Temple. To this day, Jerusalem and the Temple Mount are the most sacred sites of the Jewish faith.

Judaism was also shaped and given its decisive character by the Diaspora communities living as minorities among foreign cultures. This pattern began with the Assyrian conquest of the Kingdom of Israel, which saw the Jews dispersed around the empire. In parallel to this tradition in Palestine, another tradition, the Kingdom of Judah, developed further south in Babylon. It wavered between assimilation and segregation, and had its own liturgy and literature. By the time of Roman rule, this had become the dominant form.

The temple of Solomon, reconstructed model

The Torah and the Talmud: The Literature of Judaism

Judaism is the quintessential book religion, and Christianity and Islam—the other "religions of the book"—also incorporate the Torah. Christianity includes the Jewish Torah as the first five chapters of the Old Testament in its Bible, and through the founder of the religion, Jesus, it has a firm foundation in Judaism. Islam, too, recognizes many of the Jewish prophets and patriarchs. Abraham, or Ibrahim, is considered the arch-patriarch of Islam. The ❺ Torah comprises the absolute core of the Jewish religion. Everyday life is regulated by its laws and prohibitions. Knowledge of the Torah and Torah scholarship enjoy the greatest respect. Since the earliest times, rabbinical commentaries and interpretations have been written down in the ❷ Talmud. There are two different versions of the Talmud, the Palestinian and the Babylonian. The latter was much more influential and has been the subject of countless analyses and interpretations. In Jewish tradition, every word of the Torah has major significance.

The Talmud commentary by Isaac Ben Solomon, manuscript, 16th c.

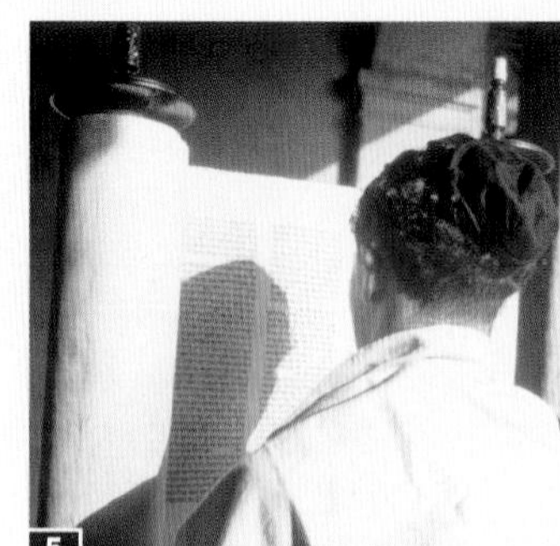

Rabbi reading the Torah

19th–17th century B.C. | Abraham's lifetime according to the Bible

ca. 965 B.C. | King Solomon of Judea

from 9th century B.C. | Scriptures of the Old Testament written

5th century B.C. | Torah becomes canonical authority

Judaism under Arab and Christian Rule

In the Middle Ages, the clash with foreign cultures led to the development of various currents within Judaism. To this day, one differentiates between Oriental, Ashkenazic (Christian Europe), and Sephardic (Moorish Spain and Africa) cultures within Judaism. The influences of Islam

Jews depicted as profiteers, Christian book illustration, ca. 1250

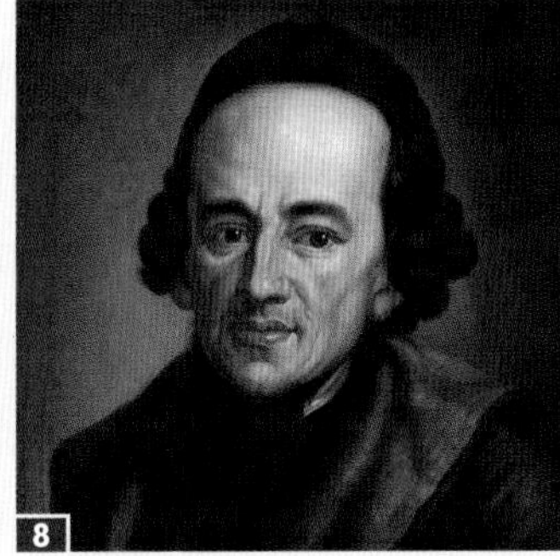

Moses Mendelssohn

and Christianity, as well as the circumstances in which the Jews lived in the various countries, found expression in the religious practice, theology, and self-conceptualization of the Jews.

For centuries the Jewish communities, as members of a fellow religion of the book, enjoyed tolerance under Arab rule, and this made social integration possible. Here, Jewish intellectual life experienced a golden age that radiated as far as France and Italy. The great Jewish philosopher and theologian Maimonides wrote an important commentary to the Talmud in Moorish Cordoba, Spain. The Kabbala, a form of Jewish mysticism, emerged in northern Spain.

In contrast to this, the relationship between the Christian and Jewish communities was strained from the outset. Christianity held the Jews responsible for the death of Jesus, for which they became scapegoats. In addition, the prosperity of individual Jews aroused ❼ envy and resentment, and the Church took advantage of this. In Central and Eastern Europe, the Ashkenazim were driven out of their traditional, hereditary vocations in international trade and money lending, while the skilled trades were denied to them by exclusion from the guilds. They were increasingly driven out of the cities and into the countryside. Horrifying pogroms against the Jews took place as part of the Crusades and reoccurred repeatedly into the late Middle Ages. Out of this experience with all its suffering, the renewal movement of the Chassidim developed. It lived on primarily in Eastern European Judaism. Moreover, in Poland and Russia, where the majority of the West European Jews fled, life in the *shtetl* developed.

In early modern times, the Central and Eastern European Jews

Theodor Herzl

Entrance to Birkenau, the main concentration camp at Auschwitz

continued to be subjected to intense repression. They were, however, allowed to return to the professions of money-lending and merchant trading. Wealthy Jews were important participants in cultural and intellectual life. In the Age of the Enlightenment, efforts toward emancipation and enlightenment, led by ❽ Moses Mendelssohn, were also made in Jewish theology.

The Holocaust and Zionism

European anti-Semitism reached its horrendous climax in the 20th century. The ❻ Holocaust—a product of the murderous ideology of the German Nazi regime—was the attempt to eradicate European Jewry systematically and destroy their culture.

Beginning in 1882 there were repeated waves of Jewish immigrants into Palestine, and that immigration increased dramatically with the rise of Fascism in Europe. Hopes for a Jewish state in Palestine were nurtured by the British Balfour Declaration of 1917. Zionism, a political movement seeking a Jewish homeland, was not a postwar phenomenon. Its roots date back to its 19th century founder, ❿ Theodor Herzl, although the location was at that time subject to debate. Developments during and after World War II, however, accelerated the realization of the Zionist project.

In 1948 the ❾ the State of Israel was founded. Of the roughly 14.4 million Jews in the world today, about 4.7 million reside in Israel. A still larger community is in the United States. Religion plays a significant role in the day-to-day policies of the modern state of Israel. ⓫ Strict religious fractions base their nationalistic claims on their religious convictions. It has proved impossible to reconcile these claims with those of displaced Palestinian Arabs. The conflict continues to this day (p. 596–599).

Foundation of the State of Israel, 1948

Orthodox Jews in Jerusalem, 1962

6th century A.D. | Writing of the Babylonian Talmud finished

from 1882 | Immigration to Palestine

1917 | Balfour Declaration

1948 | State of Israel founded

The Medes and the Persian Empire of the Achaemenids ca. 800–330 B.C.

The Indo-Iranian tribes of ❶ Medes and Persians settled in the western highlands of Iran on the border of Mesopotamia beginning late in the second millennium B.C. The Persians annexed Media in 550 B.C. and founded the last great empire of the Ancient Orient, which survived until it was conquered by Alexander the Great in 330 B.C. The historical assessment of the Persians' rule has often been biased and has judged them to be despotic. This is to overlook the fact that under their rule an immense integrated cultural and economic region was provided with security and stability.

1 Persian and Median soldiers, stone relief from Persepolis, fifth c. B.C.

2 Clay model of two harnessed animals with a driver, art from the Persian culture, ca. 1100 B.C.

5 Cultivated fields, landscape of the former Media, northwest Iran

6 Procession of archers, life-size frieze from Darius I's palace in Susa, ca. 500 B.C.

The Medes and the Rise of the Persian Empire under Cyrus II

Building on the conquests of his Median ancestors, Cyrus II created a world empire.

The only sources of information about the early period of the Medes are Assyrian accounts of conflicts with various mountain tribes. It wasn't until the eighth century B.C. that these tribes were united as a nation under a king. ❸ Media fell under Assyrian and later under Scythian domination. King Cyaxares freed himself from this rule and, together with the Babylonians, destroyed the Neo-Assyrian Empire between 614 and 612 B.C. He and his son Astyages extended their rule all the way to Asia Minor, where they agreed with the Lydians (p. 53) to recognize the Halys River as their common border. The ❺ Median kingdom stretched eastward to Bactria (present-day Afghanistan).

Among the vassals of the Medes were the Persians. Astyages married one of his daughters to the Persian king Cambyses I, the great-grandson of the legendary founder of the Persian ruling house, Achaemenes. Later, however, Cyrus II, the son of Cambyses I, rebelled against Astyages and by 550 had conquered the Median kingdom. From then on, the Medes were equals with the Persians, who adopted many elements of administration, ❼ court ceremony, and ❷ art from their former rulers.

4 The tomb of Cyrus II, located in the royal capital city of Pasargadae

3 Medians paying tribute to the Assyrians

Cyrus II's conquests continued. In 546 B.C. he defeated Croesus of Lydia and subjugated the Greek coastal cities of Asia Minor (Ionia). In 539 he conquered the Neo-Babylonian Kingdom. Babylon—with the ancient Persian capitals of ❻ Susa and Pasargadae and the Median capital Ecbatana—thereafter became one of Cyrus's preferred residences. He allowed the ❽ Jews, living in Babylon since their deportation in 587 B.C., to return to their homeland. Cyrus II's last campaign took him north, where he ❹ died in 530 fighting the Massagetae (p. 64).

7 Persian (left) and Median (right) dignitaries

8 Cyrus II with the Jewish prophet Daniel, painting by Rembrandt, 17th century

614–612 B.C. | Fall of the Neo-Assyrian Empire
ca. 600 B.C. | Foundation of the Median Kingdom
550 B.C. | Achaemenids annex Media
546 B.C. | Cyrus II defeats Croesus of Lydia
ca. 540 B.C. | Cyrus II rules Asia Minor

The Persian Empire under Darius I

Under Darius I (the Great), perhaps the most significant ruler of the Ancient Orient, the Persian Empire of the Achaemenids experienced its golden age.

Cambyses II, the son of Cyrus II, conquered Egypt in 525 B.C. In order to foil an attempted coup, he had his younger brother Smerdis (Bardiya) secretly murdered. In the absence of the king, a Magus named Gaumâta pretended to be Smerdis and claimed the throne. Cambyses II died on the return march from Egypt in 522 B.C., but his cousin Darius stopped the crowning of the "false Smerdis" and restored the rule of the Achaemenids.

With the turmoil around the throne settled, Darius I consolidated his empire from within. He established provinces, which were required to pay taxes. Although the province governors, called satraps, had much latitude, they were controlled by a system of ❾ officials and spies. A well-developed network of roads equipped with a message and postal service and protected by patrols provided improved communications. ❿ Darius also reformed the rule of law and introduced an empire-wide coinage, the daric. In 497 B.C. he completed the construction of a canal between the Nile and the Red Sea that had been begun by the pharaohs. In Persia he laid the cornerstone for the ⓭ palace city of ⓫ Persepolis, which would be developed further by his ⓬ successors. Darius I also promoted ⓮ Zoroastrianism (p. 63) without suppressing the other religions of his multinational empire.

Darius I pushed the boundaries of the Persian Empire to the Indus River in the east and to the Danube in the northwest of Thrace and subjugated Macedonia in northern Greece. He was not always successful in his military undertakings, however, failing in his campaign against the Scythians in 513–512 B.C. From 500 to 494, Darius was forced to suppress the "Ionian Rebellion" of the Greek city-states in Anatolia, and a punitive expedition to Greece ended with his defeat at the Battle of Marathon in 490 (p. 85). Darius I died in 486 while preparing for another war against the Greeks.

9 Persian official in robes, silver statuette, fifth century B.C.

11

above: The ruins of Persepolis
below: Private palace of Darius I in Persepolis

13

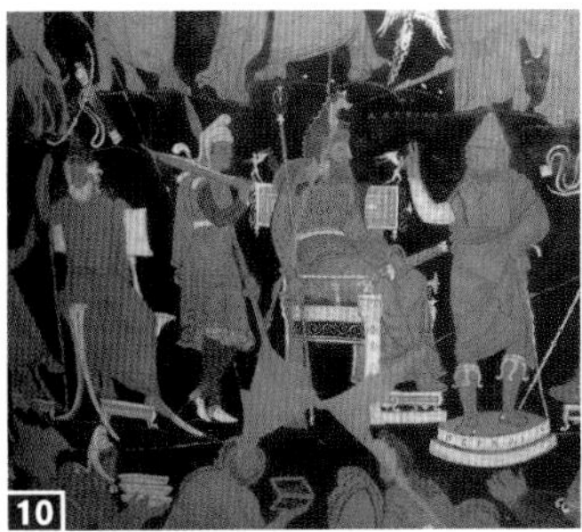

10 Darius I on a throne, painted vase, late fourth century B.C.

12

King Darius Says:

"Ahura Mazda, when he saw this earth in commotion, thereafter bestowed it upon me, made me king; I am king. By the favor of Ahura Mazda I put it down in its place; what I said to them, that they did, as was my desire.

"If now you shall think that 'How many are the countries which King Darius held?' look at the sculptures [of those] who bear the throne, then shall you know, then shall it become known to you: the spear of a Persian man has gone forth; then shall it become known to you: a Persian man has delivered battle far from Persia."

Rock tombs of (from left) Artaxerxes I (or Darius II), Xerxes I (or Artaxerxes I), and Darius I at Naqsh-i-Rustam, near Persepolis

left: Darius I with crown prince Xerxes, stone relief, ca. 485 B.C.
below: Darius I hunting lions, protected by the god Ahura Mazda, round seal print, ca. 500 B.C.

14

539 B.C. | Cyrus II conquers the Neo-Babylonian Kingdom
530 B.C. | Death of Cyrus II
525 B.C. | Conquest of Egypt
520 B.C. | Satraps are established
500–494 B.C. | Ionian Rebellion
490 B.C. | Battle of Marathon
486 B.C. | Death of Darius I

The Persian Empire under the Later Achaemenids

Rebellion in the provinces and intrigue within the royal house weakened the power of the Persians under the successors of Darius I. Warfare against the Greeks remained inconclusive until Alexander the Great conquered the Persian Empire in 330 B.C.

At the beginning of his rule in 486 B.C., ❶ Xerxes I, the son and successor of Darius I, had to crush a rebellion in Egypt. He then attempted to carry out his father's plans for the conquest of Greece (p. 85). Xerxes only succeeded in advancing as far as Athens, and ultimately his fleet was defeated at the Battle of Salamis in 480 B.C., and his army was routed at the Battle of Plataea the following year. By then, Xerxes had already returned to his ❸ capital, where he remained from then on, dedicating himself especially to building activities. He was murdered during a palace revolt in 465.

2 The Athenian Themistocles and Artaxerxes I, steel engraving, 1842

4 Artaxerxes III's tomb, carved into the rock face, near Persepolis

Xerxes' son Artaxerxes I ended the conflict with ❷ Greece by signing the Peace of Callias in 448 B.C. (p. 87). The Persians subsequently shifted their support from one belligerent to another during the Peloponnesian War (p. 90) and in the disputes between Athens, Sparta, and Thebes of the fourth century B.C. In return for this decisive support, the Greek powers fighting Sparta handed over the Ionian cities to the Persians in the "King's Peace" the Peace of Antalkidas (p. 93).

The Persians were expelled from Egypt in 404 B.C., but ❹ Artaxerxes III recaptured it in 343 B.C. He also supported the opponents of Philip II (p. 95) of Macedonia, who had united the Greeks and planned to wage a war against the Persians. Artaxerxes III and his son and heir were both poisoned in palace intrigues. Whereupon Darius III, a member of a minor branch of the Achaemenids, assumed the throne in 336, becoming the last Persian king.

5 Alexander the Great with Darius III's body

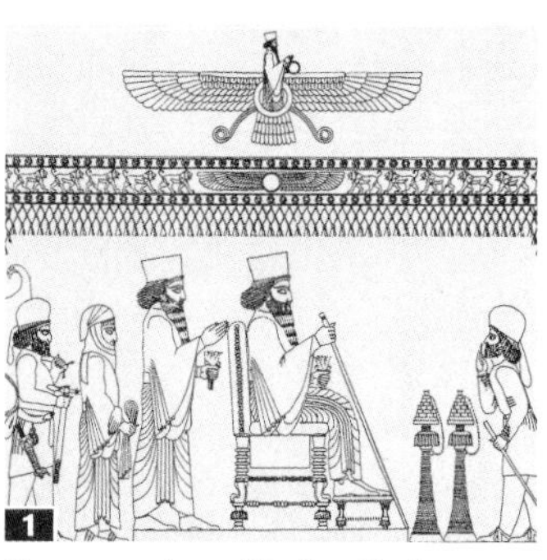
1 Xerxes receives a Median dignitary

In 334 B.C., Alexander the Great of Macedonia opened the campaign (p. 96) against the Persians planned by his father Philip II. Darius III suffered crushing defeats in 333 at ❻ Issus and in 331 at Gaugamela. Following these reverses he fled to the north of Iran, where he was betrayed and ❺ murdered in 330. By 324, Alexander had conquered the whole of the Persian Empire. The Seleucid dynasty that ruled the area after Alexander's death was succeeded by the Arsacids. They presided over a revival of Achaemenid traditions, and this continued under the Sassinian kings who overthrew them in 230 B.C.

6 Darius III at the Battle of Issus

Persia in Greek Historiography

Persian history was retold in Europe in Herodotus's Histories and in the Anabasis by Xenophon. Xenophon was one of thousands of Greek mercenaries who took part in the coup attempt by Cyrus the Younger against his brother, King Artaxerxes II, in 401 B.C. After Cyrus was defeated and killed he led the survivors back to safety.

above: Xenophon

3 The Propylaia of Xerxes I, the "gate to all countries," Persepolis, fifth c. B.C.

ca. 600 B.C. | Zarathustra's era
480 B.C. | Battle of Salamis
479 B.C. | Battle of Plataea
465 B.C. | Death of Xerxes
448 B.C. | Peace of Callias
431–404 B.C. | Peloponnesian War
404 B.C. | Liberation of Egypt
387 B.C. | Peace of Antalkidas

Religion in the Persian Empire

Zoroastrianism flourished under the Achaemenids. The Zoroastrian concept of the afterlife had a significant influence on both Judaism and Christianity.

7 Zarathustra, mural from Syria

The ancient Iranian religion of Zoroastrianism recognized a great number of gods and was probably related to the Vedic religion of ancient India. The rituals of the Magi, a hereditary priestly cast, predominated in the cult. Their name is derived from the Magoi, a Median tribe whose members were renowned for their spiritual practices. The prophet ❼ Zarathustra (or Zoroaster in Greek) appeared around 600 B.C., probably out of the ranks of the ❽ Magi, to proclaim the teachings of the one god ⓫ Ahura Mazda. Zarathustra criticized the Magi for, among other things, their bloody ❾ animal sacrifices and thus earned their enmity. ⓬ King Darius I became a follower of Zarathustra's teachings after thwarting the coup attempt of the Magus usurper Gaumâta. Over time, the Magi adapted to Zoroastrianism and were able to defend their monopoly on religious worship.

According to Zarathustra, Ahura Mazda is the almighty creator of the cosmos and judge at the end of time. He represents the original, right, and good world order and is identified with "the Good Spirit" that opposes "the Evil Spirit." Man is free to decide between these two options but will be judged according to his deeds at the Last Judgment. Along with this dualistic value system, strict purity of ritual is particularly characteristic of Zoroastrianism. Priests were allowed to approach the ❿ eternal flame that burned in the temples in honor of the god only with their mouths covered so they wouldn't desecrate it with their breath. Fire, earth, and water were considered holy elements.

8 Praying man with goat, golden statuette, twelfth century B.C.

During the time of Persian dominance, the Jews came in contact with the concepts of heaven, hell, and a "last judgment," which became an important tenet of Judaism, and later of Christianity and Islam. Manichaeism was formed out of a fusion of Zoroastrianism with Christian and Buddhist teachings and was, for a time, early Christianity's strongest competitor.

Zoroastrianism once again experienced a golden period as the state religion in the Sassanid empire from the third to seventh centuries A.D., only to disappear from Iran almost completely after the Arab invasions that introduced Islam. Many followers of the teachings of Zarathustra emigrated, primarily to India, where they were called "Parsis" after their land of origin, Persia. Today there are around 200,000 Parsis, about half of them in India.

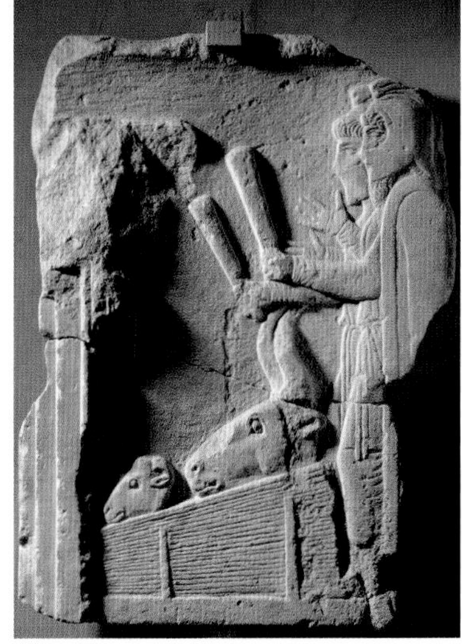

9 Ritual sacrifice of a goat, detail from stone relief, end of the fifth century B.C.

10 Fire altar, Achaemenid temple, known as the Kaaba of Zarathustra, fifth c. B.C.

11 Two sphinxes carry Ahura Mazda, cylindrical seal stamp, ca. 590–330 B.C.

12 Lance bearers in Persian and Median dress under the winged sun of Ahura Mazda, stone relief from Persepolis, fifth century B.C.

343 B.C. | Artaxerxes III recaptures Egypt
336 B.C. | Darius III comes to power
336 B.C. | Death of Philip II
334 B.C. | Alexander the Great opens campaign against the Persians
333 B.C. | Battle of Issus
330–324 B.C. | Alexander conquers Persia
330 B.C. | Death of Darius III

The Nomads of the Eurasian Steppes

Up to the fourth century B.C., Indo-European mounted nomads ranged the wide steppes of the Ukraine, southern Russia, and Kazakhstan until the advancing Huns triggered the "Great Migration of Peoples." But even before this, individual tribes left the region and moved into the Mediterranean area, the highlands of Iran, or India. Some, such as the Hittites, Medes, Persians, or the later Parthians, settled down and established kingdoms. Others stayed on the move and were, like the Cimmerians, eventually annihilated by enemies or withdrew back to their original territory of settlement, as the Scythians did.

1 Tomyris kills King Cyrus II, book illustration, 14th century

3 Sarmatian cavalrymen on armored horses, detail from Trajan's Pillar, Rome, 113 A.D.

The Scythians, Sakians, and Sarmatians

Outsiders have frequently sought to divide nomads of the Eurasian steppes into various peoples and tribes. Greek and Roman authors, in particular, attempted to transcribe the flexible organization of these peoples into categories familiar to them.

2 Fight between a tiger and wolf, Scythian gold plate, sixth c. B.C.

The homeland of the ❷ Scythians is thought to have been in the area of present-day Kazakhstan. Some began to move westward in the first millennium B.C. while the rest—the Sakians—remained. The Scythians drove the Cimmerians, another nomadic people, out of their homeland north of the Black Sea. They ❹ crossed the Caucasus and pushed down into Mesopotamia and Asia Minor.

The Persian kings were constantly at war with the various nomadic peoples on the northern borders of their kingdom. In 530 B.C. ❶ Cyrus II fell in battle against Tomyris, the Queen of the Massagetae, part of the Sarmatian tribe related to the Scythians and Sakians. Darius I's attempt to subjugate the Scythians in 513–512 B.C. also failed. The Persians and other Near East rulers recruited nomads as mercenaries for their armies or made alliances with them. Even in Athens, Scythians were used as police. These peoples and tribes never formed fixed units for a long period of time, but rather joined into confederations under a common figure when an outside threat made it necessary. The Scythian high king Atheas, who died in battle in 339 against Philip II of Macedonia, was one such leader.

Starting in the third century B.C., the Scythians were slowly absorbed by the Sarmatians, and by the first century B.C. only a small group in ❺ Crimea remained. During the "Great Migration of Peoples," most of the Sarmatians merged with the Goths and the Huns. The Sakians arrived in India around 100 B.C., where they established kingdoms that survived for centuries.

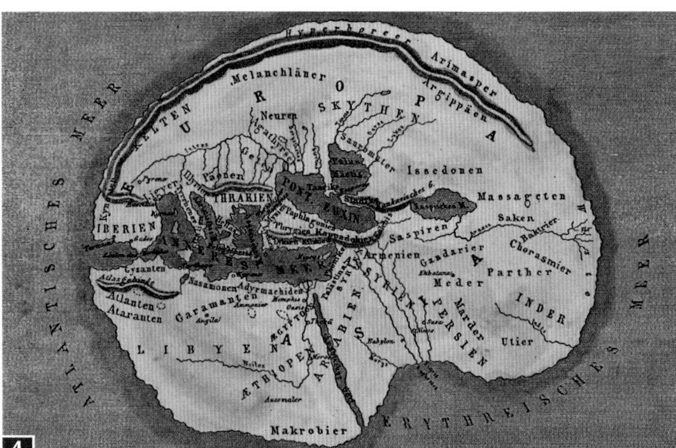

4 The Earth according to Herodotus, showing the Scythians and the Massagetae in the far northeast, wood carving, 19th century

5 Scythians offer milk to the Roman poet Ovid living in exile on the Crimean Peninsula, painting by Delacroix, 19th century

530 B.C. | Death of Cyrus II

ca. 450 B.C. | Herodotus writes about the Scythians

from ca.1000 B.C. | Scythians immigrate into Asia Minor

513–512 B.C. | Persia attacks the Scythians

ca. 350 B.C. | The Scythians and Sarmatians settle

The Scythian Culture and Society

The Scythians left no written records of their own. Greek and Roman sources, along with archaeological finds, provide the only information about their lives.

6 Beard comb with a carved handle showing Scythian soldiers in combat, ca. 500 B.C.

The leaders of the Scythians were princes and were buried in elaborate burial mounds called *kurgans*. The dead were often embalmed and interred in a central burial chamber. Many times, the horses of the deceased were buried with them in adjoining chambers, highlighting the importance of these animals to the Scythians. Weapons and finely worked ❻, ❼ gold objects were common burial gifts; other items included drinking ❾ vessels, jewelry, and armor, and pictures of hunting, battles, or banquet scenes. Domesticated animals seem to have frequently accompanied the dead to their tombs. ❿ Women were also buried with weapons of war, which seems to suggest that not only queens like Tomyris but also common Scythian women may have fought in conflicts. Some historians have cited this as a possible historical basis for the Greek myth of the Asiatic women warriors, the ❽ Amazons.

One of the main facts known about the Scythians was their custom of "blood brotherhood," which was widespread among warriors and formed the basis for lifelong fighting bands. The ❸ mounted warriors were lightly armed and wore coats of chain mail for protection. In the hands of skilled archers, poisoned arrows could do great damage from a distance. For close combat, the short sword, battle-ax, and spiked mace were the preferred weapons. Their battle technique—a short, fast attack followed by immediate retreat—was widely feared and gave them the advantage over unwieldy armies of infantry. The Scythians also practiced trade, agriculture, and herding. Scythian grain, furs, livestock, and slaves were exported through the Greek colonies on the Crimean Peninsula.

7 Gold armband, sixth–fifth century B.C.

8 *The Battle of the Amazons*, painting by Rubens, ca. 1600

The "Wild" Scythians

Come, friends! let's not shout and scream /
like Scythian drunks
but let us study our wine, friends/
and accompany its drinking with beautiful songs.

(Anacreon, Greek lyric poet, sixth century B.C.)

9 **above:** Scythian warriors, gold vessel, fourth century B.C.

10 Women riding on horses in a procession, stone relief, fifth century B.C.

Amazons

Scythian women warriors, who even led armies, perhaps served as a model for the Amazons of Greek mythology. Like the Scythians, the Amazons were supposed to have lived on the shores of the Black Sea. They only temporarily lived together with men. Of their children, they only raised the girls. The girls' left breasts were burned off so that later they would not hinder them shooting the bow and arrow—thus, perhaps, the origin of the name Amazon, from amazós (Greek for "without breast"). Herodotus in the fifth century B.C., however, wrote about a matriarchal society in Asia Minor that also could have served as a model for the Amazons.

above: An Amazon warrior, marble statue, Roman copy of the Greek original, fifth century B.C.

339 B.C. | Atheas is defeated by Philip II
ca. 300 B.C. | Sarmatians join the Great Migration of Peoples
ca. 100 B.C.–100 A.D. | Sakian kingdoms in India
ca. 100 B.C. | Last Scythians remain on the Crimea

The Religions of India, China, and Japan

All present-day world religions originated in Asia. The three major monotheistic religions Judaism, Christianity, and Islam originated in the Near East, and Hinduism and Buddhism, both polytheistic religions, find their roots in India. While ❶ Buddhism has also become popular in the Western world today, religions such as Hinduism in India, Confucianism in China, and Shinto in Japan are closely tied to, and have also significantly influenced, the cultures and social structures of their respective countries and regions.

1 Shakyamuni Buddha with Confucius and Lao-tzu, the three teachers

Hinduism

Hinduism is a religion of India that has diversified into many forms. It resulted from the merging of the Vedic religion, which was introduced by the Aryans, and the religion of the native peoples, but had no known founder. It is difficult to comprehend for members of other religions as it has neither a standardized canon of scripture nor a fixed pantheon of gods, nor an organizational structure that can be compared to that of a church, for instance. Hinduism has no uniform philosophy, and the forms of belief and cult are extremely multifarious. The polytheistic belief in gods such as ❸ Vishnu, Shiva, and Shakti is only one of its manifestations. Coexistent with these are, for example, monotheistic tendencies alongside philosophical speculations that completely reject a personified cosmic guiding force. The one conviction common to all variations is the belief in an all-encompassing world order (*dharma*) that structures human life and its environment, which Buddhism also adopted. Another characteristic is the belief in the eternal cycle of birth, death, and reincarnation, based on the assumption that the conduct and deeds in each life influence the form of existence in the next. Hinduism developed complicated sacrificial rituals, and the priest caste of Brahmans' exact knowledge thereof ensured their considerable influence in Indian society.

4 Hindus doing their ritual washings in the Ganges River in Benares (Varanasi), India

3 Shiva, Brahma, Vishnu, and another deity with the goddess Devi

The caste system is one of the pillars of ❹ Hindu society. It possibly originated from the partition of immigrants from the indigenous population. The individual castes differentiate themselves through specific customs and responsibilities in society. Although social differences between the castes were officially abolished with India's independence in 1947, in effect they continue to exist. Today, Hinduism once again plays a significant role in the national identity of India.

Buddhism

In the sixth century B.C., the "reformer" Siddhartha Gautama (Buddha) rejected the caste system associated with Hinduism and propagated universal compassion and nonviolence toward all living things. He did not see himself as the founder of a religion but rather as an advocate of a self-redeeming doctrine that had strong ethical traits. The underlying belief of Buddha's philosophy was that human existence, fundamentally, meant suffering. His goal was to overcome suffering, which he believed was caused by worldly desires and passions. This goal could be achieved, he believed, by immersion in the true nature of things and the rejection of self and would culminate in *nirvana*. Nirvana, directly translated as "nothing," is the cessation of the reincarnation cycle and the liberation from suffering as a result of this release from existence on Earth.

2 Shakyamuni Buddha, Tibetan statue, eleventh century

As Buddhism spread through Asia, and the monks and laity built their own organizational structures, it absorbed elements of folk religions. The development of the compassionate redemption figure (*bodhisattva*) was one result. Gradually Buddhism

5 Sacrificial ceremony with Buddhist priests and monks in the temple area of Swayambunath in Kathmandu, Nepal

ca. 1000 B.C. | Earliest traces of Hinduism

560 B.C. | Birth of Siddhartha Gautama

6th century B.C. | Buddhism becomes state religion

evolved into a religion with its own temples and cults.

The early rulers of India, from the sixth century B.C. on, installed Buddhism as a form of state religion, so that Hinduism was, at times, completely suppressed on the subcontinent. Buddhism split into several differing schools: Hinayana ("lesser vehicle") Buddhism, with its ❺ austere monks, and the more diverse and liberal Mahayana ("greater vehicle") Buddhism are two of the most significant schools. Contemporary ❷ Tibetan Buddhism headed by the Dalai Lama represents a form of Vajrayana Buddhism.

The Religions of China

The folk religion of China, in which ancestor worship and belief in spirits and nature deities played a large role, is strongly represented to this day. Other important religious currents in China, which have mixed with the folk religion, include Taoism, the teachings of Confucius, and Buddhism.

One characteristic of Chinese thought is the belief in the designed and universal harmony of heaven, Earth, and man. The cosmos is considered a well-ordered organism that is governed by a "Supreme Master," who is not always conceived as a personified unity. People were thought to be linked to and able to communicate with the supernatural world at first through shamans or priests, and later through the emperor. He was the recipient of the "Mandate of Heaven" and was political and religious guarantor for cosmic order on Earth.

6 Lao-Tzu on his way to the mountains, from a Chinese bronze group

Taoism developed in the sixth century B.C. and is attributed to ❻ Lao-Tzu. In his book *Tao Te Ching* ("The Book of the Way and Its Power"), written in the third or fourth century B.C., he described the Tao, or "the Way," as the original source of all existence and power possessed by living things. The T'ai Ch'ai, originally presented as a unity, was split into the opposite forces of ❽ *yin* and *yang*, through whose interplay creative forces resulted. Taoism propagated a withdrawal from the world of human reality and an immersion in nature. It very soon merged with the idea of the deities in the folk religion, stressed magic elements such as the search for the "elixir of life," and developed its own temples.

8 Plate with yin and yang, symbol of the principle of Tao

9 Heaven's king standing on a demon, Tang dynasty

Confucianism

The teachings of China's most successful political philosophy opposed Taoism's retreat from society. The philosophers ❼ Confucius and Mencius (Meng-tzu) developed a doctrine of lifelong learning and personal modesty without withdrawal from the world. The ideal human, according to the philosophy, was the aristocratic "noble" who lived a "humanitarian" life. He would be educated and active as councilor and servant of the state, which needed his service. Confucianism stressed the ritual of ancestor worship and a deep sense of hierarchical family unity. As a result, it quickly became the leading state doctrine of China after 200 B.C. Soon the Confucian attitude and training was compulsory for all civil servants. The doctrine eventually stagnated within a hierarchy, and the state-celebrated Confucius worship took on religious traits, despite Confucius's assertion that he knew nothing of the gods. He did, however, consider religious rites to be of importance, as they strengthened order.

7 Picture of the Chinese philosopher Confucius, ca. 551–479 B.C., stone engraving in Ch'ue-fou

Shinto

The ❿ Shinto religion was tied to the national identity and monarchy of Japan. The story of Japan's origin and the ❾ descent of the emperor Jimmu Tenno from the sun goddess Amaterasu plays a determining role in the religion. Ancestor worship, along with the worship of innumerable deities (*kami*)—primarily clan divinities and spirits of nature—is the most important element of Shinto. The values and behavioral forms transmitted by the Shinto belief system characterize many of the traditions of Japanese society. When Buddhism reached Japan, the two belief systems became closely intertwined, and both continue to coexist to this day.

10 Gate leading to Shimogamo Shinto temple in Kyoto, Japan

ca. 500 B.C. | Confucius

6th century B.C. | Development of Taoism

since ca. 200 B.C. | Confucianism becomes state doctrine

India from the Beginnings to the Invasion of Alexander the Great

From very early times, the culture of the Indian subcontinent was marked by the great number of ethnic and linguistic groups living in the region. This diversity was the result of the many waves of migration which settled the subcontinent. Aryan immigrants put their stamp on the first civilization by introducing into it their gods, caste system, and political order. More complex state structures gradually developed out of the original tribal societies.

1 Citadel of Mohenjo-Daro, Sind Province, Pakistan—after Harappa, the most important excavated city of the Indus culture

2 Harappa royal priest, limestone carving, ca. 2500 B.C.

India's Early Period and the Indus Culture

A great variety of cultural forms took shape early in the history of the subcontinent. The first major culture to assert itself was the Harappa, which arose in the area of present-day Pakistan.

Evidence shows that humans settled India between 40,000 and 30,000 B.C. at the latest. These first inhabitants probably migrated out of Africa by way of the Arabian Peninsula. Several waves of migration followed, resulting in numerous, diverse ethnic groups settling in India. Among the inhabitants, five great language groups developed. The Indo-Aryan (predominantly Hindi) or Indic language, which became the language of religious texts, emerged in northern Sri Lanka and the Maldives. Dravidian, the language of archaic literature, appeared in the south of India and (as Tamil) in parts of Sri Lanka. The other, less widespread language groups were the Austro-Asiatic languages, composed of the Munda tongues; the Sino-Tibetan languages in Kashmir, Nepal, and Bhutan; and the autochthonous remnant languages.

The first inhabitants of the subcontinent were hunter-gatherers, who were superseded by farmers and herdsmen from 7000 B.C. By 6000 B.C. the emergence of a discernible proto-culture began. From this, the ❶, ❽ Indus or ❷, ❸ Harappa culture, which flourished between 2600 and 1900 B.C., evolved on the plains of the river Indus. It is named after the city of Harappa, which was discovered in 1921 A.D. in northeastern Pakistan. The civilization was characterized by advanced agriculture, as evidenced by a highly developed irrigation system and large granaries.

3 Bronze figurine, Harappa culture, ca. 2500 B.C.

4 Indra, Nepalese sculpture, 15th century

The society's administrators used standardized weights, measurements, and ❺, ❼ seals. The Harappa script, which is etched into about 5000 surviving seals and tablets, was in use around 3300 B.C. and has not yet been deciphered. There were large settlements with planned streets, public buildings, and fortified citadels. Archaeological finds indicate sophisticated commercial structures.

In around 1900 B.C., the settlement suddenly fell after being struck by floods and attacked by outsiders. The southern Indus plains were completely given up as a result, but Indus culture lived on in the animal and sacrificial cults of later groups. An example of this is the cult surrounding the ❾ sacred cow.

5 Official seal with animal heads, Indus culture

6 Chariot, bronze model, Harappa culture

from ca. 7000 B.C. | Transition to settled agriculture

40,000–30,000 B.C. | Humans first colonize India

ca. 3300 B.C. | Development of the Indus script

7 Seal decorated with unicorn, Harappa culture

The Arrival of the Indo-Aryans

The invading Indo-Aryan peoples were organized into tribal monarchies. When they arrived, they dominated the culture of India. Nevertheless, there was ultimately an intermixing with the native population.

Among the Indo-Aryans moving into India in the second half of the second millennium B.C. was the Sintasha culture from the eastern Ural mountains. Like the Hurrites of the Mitanni kingdom in northern Iraq and northern Syria, their military superiority was based on their early use of the ❻ chariot. As they pushed into northern India, they introduced the early Aryan gods (Mithra, Varuna, ❹ Indra) to the cultures they encountered.

How the Aryan invasion actually took place is disputed among experts. It was most likely a case of migration rather than conquest. The resettlement probably took place in several waves, coming from the West through Iran.

Along the way, the Indo-Aryans picked up elements of the Oxus culture, which had flourished in southern Tajikistan from around 2400 to 1600 B.C. The greater part of our knowledge about the arrival of the Aryans, and the oldest literary work written in an Indo-European language, comes from the Rig-Veda. Vedism was the earliest Aryan religion of India. In its verses we learn, for example, that the Aryans were cattle breeders. The Aryans did not see themselves as a race—in contrast to later Aryan ideologies of the 19th and 20th centuries—but as members of a particular cultural group who spoke the Vedic (Sanskrit) language. They were soon the dominant class in North India and spoke of other peoples as "enemies" or "slaves." Only after a long period of time did an accommodation with the native population occur.

The Vedas are considered religious texts of purely Aryan origin, although India's early ❿ religions probably arose through a process of fusion of Aryan and native elements. The Rig-Veda refers to the native people as "idol" and "phallus" worshippers and the veneration of the stone Phalli (*lingam*) as fertility symbols can be traced to them. The Rig-Veda also describes the early organization of the Aryans into tribal monarchies, and mentions the Bharata people in Punjab. The Bharata king Sudas is said to have defeated his enemies in the Battle of the Ten Kings by bursting the dams (Rig-Veda 7, 18). Poets played a major role in the Aryan culture as chroniclers of the lives and deeds of the kings.

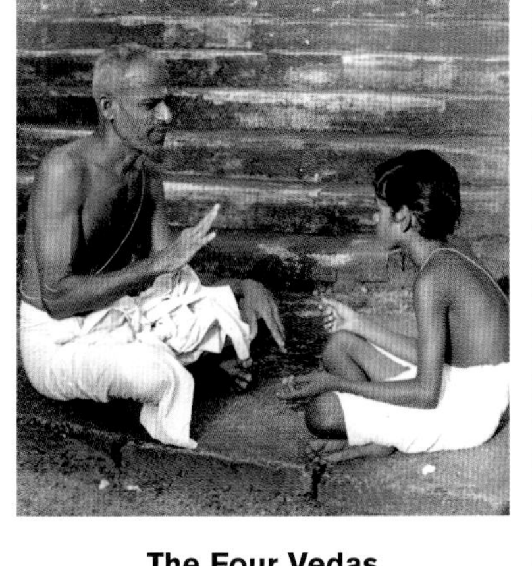

The Four Vedas

The Vedas ("knowledge") constitute India's oldest literature, a collection of religious hymns and verses. They contain the religious, philosophical, and ritual knowledge used by the priests and poets of the Vedic period (between 1500 and 500 B.C.). The canon of the Vedas was compiled around 1000 B.C. The oldest Veda is the Rig-Veda. The Sama Veda, which follows, is made up of melodies and texts to accompany sacrificial rituals. The Yajur Veda contains verses and dietary requirements to go with the sacrifice. The Atharva Veda is primarily composed of magic formulas and poetical-philosophical speculation.

above: Boy receives lessons in the holy Vedas in a Brahman school in Trichur

8 Brick-lined well that supplied the Mohenjo-Daro Citadel, in today's Sind Province, in the southeast of Pakistan

9 Holy zebu bull in India, decorated with richly embroidered cloths

10 Religious scene depicting Indra appealing to the goddess, Indian miniature

The Nations of the Middle Vedic Period

In the Kuru period, India's caste system and complex religious rituals developed. The hierarchical society spread throughout the entire subcontinent.

Around 1000 B.C. India entered the Middle Vedic period. This began in northwest India with the unification of 30 Aryan tribes from the Rig-Veda era to form a great tribal entity: the Kuru-Pancala. The leading tribe, from which the kings were drawn, was the Bharata. Their capital was situated in Hastinapura, present-day Delhi.

During this period, the transition to iron working began and the distinctive "Painted Gray Ware" pottery became prevalent. The Vedic Indians retained a semi-nomadic lifestyle; even the kings did not lead fully sedentary lives. Lower down the social structure, rice farmers were forced off their land to make way for grazing and had their provisions stolen.

An important aspect of the Kuru period was the development of the caste system. There were originally four castes. Two upper classes, the ❺ priests and the nobility, ruled over the two lower castes, which were made up of the farmers, craftsmen, and laborers, and the outcasts (Pariah, or "untouchables").

In religious practice the sacrificial rites, considered to be exchanges of food between the gods and men, became progressively more complex. This practice was thought to preserve the cosmic order. A Brahman was required for the interpretation of the holy texts.

This social system spread to north and east India, including Kashmir and Nepal. Brahman texts speak of a "ritual taking-possession" of the country and the "civilizing" of barbaric tribes by the Brahmans around the year 800 B.C. The tribes of the east were "adopted" into the caste society. The major kingdoms of the northeast, the Kosala and Videha, produced "Black and Red Ware" pottery. The kingdom of Videha, under King Janaka, soon became a model nation of the Vedic order.

2 The birth of Mahavira, Indian miniature, ca. 1400

1 Buddha with disciples

3 Buddha, relief from the Jaulian monastery, ca. third–fifth century

4 Buddha in contemplation

5 *The Priest and the Believer*, Indian miniature, 18th century

ca. 1000 B.C. | Start of the Middle Vedic Period

6th century B.C. | Emergence of Buddhism and Jainism

530 and 519 B.C. | Persian conquest of northwest India

ca. 525 B.C. | Bimbisara adopts Buddhist religion

The Later Vedic Period and the Eastern Nations

In the sixth century B.C., Buddhism and Jainism emerged as religious reform movements. The rise of Buddhism began as the cultural center of gravity shifted toward the eastern Indian states.

The gods Brahma and Krishna, scene from the *Ramayana*

In the Later Vedic period, around 600 B.C., the cultural and political focus of India shifted to the northeast. Concurrently, new groups began moving into the eastern states from Iran and Afghanistan. The kings of Videha and Kosala sent for Brahmans from western India to instruct them in the Vedic laws. Around this time, two reform movements emerged in the east. Both were critical of the caste system and the bloody animal sacrifices that it demanded. The reform movements were the Buddhism of Prince ❶, ❸, ❹ Siddhartha Gautama (Buddha) and the Jainism of ❷ Mahavira.

The Later Vedic period came to an end somewhere around 450 B.C., at least partly due to the Persians' invasion of the Gandhara and Sindh regions of present-day Pakistan in 530 and 519 B.C. New cities and centers of commerce developed. An ambitious class of dealers and merchants prospered, as the luxurious vessels of the "Black Polished Ware" testify. The culture opened itself to the world and flourished. In Gandhara, the alphabet borrowed from further west was modified into a new script: the ❾ Brahmi alphabet from which all present-day Indian alphabets derive. The grand Indian national epic ❻, ❼, ❽, ❿ *Ramayana* was written between 400 and 300 B.C. by the legendary poet Valmiki.

The monkey kingdom, scene from the *Ramayana*

The True Brahman

"The Brahman, truly, was this world in the beginning, the One, the Unending: Unending to the East, unending to the South, unending above and below, unending on all sides. For him there is no . . . location of heaven, not across, nor below, nor above."
From the Upanishads following the Vedas.

Characters of the Brahmi alphabet, second millennium B.C.

While western India had been under Persian influence since the end of the sixth century, the east developed its own structures. In 500 B.C. the kingdom of Maghada, under King Bimbisara, was in a position of dominance. Bimbisara had professed his faith in Buddhism around 525 and sought to promote it, while pursuing a strategy of conquest and marriage. His son Ajatashatru extended the empire to include the tribal federation of the north, and his successor continued this effective strategy. In 364 the usurper, Mahapadma Nanda, toppled them and expanded the empire into central India and Orissa. He and his successors, the Nanda kings, reigned almost up until the invasion of Alexander the Great between 327 and 325 B.C.

The testing of Sita in the fire, illustration of a scene from the *Ramayana*

Rama and Krishna, illustration of a scene from the *Ramayana*

ca. 500 B.C. | Rise of Maghadas

4th–3rd century B.C. | *Ramayana* compiled

ca. 450 B.C. | End of the Later Vedic Period

364–321 B.C. | Period of the Nanda kings

327–325 B.C. | Alexander the Great invades India

Early China up to the Period of the "Warring States" 5000–221 B.C.

Although China was one of the first places of human habitation, its civilization is relatively young compared with other ancient high cultures. In the third millennium B.C., the first communities with a sophisticated civilization began to emerge. From around the 18th century B.C., the ruling Shang and Zhou dynasties centralized power and presided over a period of considerable technical innovation. The empire perceptibly decayed from the eighth century B.C. on and finally ended in a war between its constituent parts.

1 Bronze vessel decorated with human masks and used for ritual meals during the Shang Dynasty era, ca. 1766–1100 B.C.

China's Early Period and the Shang Dynasty

Even the earliest cultures in China produced great technical achievements. These early people and their rulers would later be much celebrated and attain a mythical status in Chinese history.

The ❷ "Peking Man" is among the oldest hominid finds made in China. His remains were found in a cave near Beijing (Peking) and are between 300,000 and 400,000 years old. Subsequently, remains of a 700,000 year-old hominid were discovered near Lantian. Cattle breeders and farmers are known to have settled in villages along the larger rivers in China as early as the Neolithic period. One of the cultures of this period was the Yangshao culture (ca. 5000 B.C.) in northern China, which produced significant pottery. Around 3000 B.C. the group was supplanted by the Lung-shan culture, which was characterized by permanent settlements and technical refinements for predominantly domestic purposes.

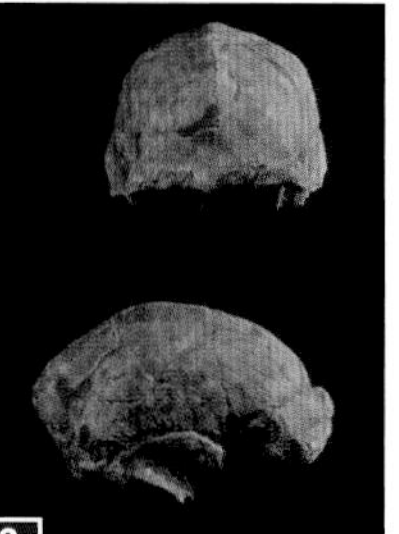

2 Skull of the "Peking Man" (*Homo erectus pekinensis*), discovered in the 1920s

In Chinese tradition, the first state was formed at the end of the third millennium B.C. According to mythology, it was ruled by the sage-kings Yao, Shun, and Yu. They are said to mark the arrival of civilization, particularly through innovations in agriculture and management of water resources, in the region.

Yu is credited with founding the Xia dynasty, which gave way to the ❶, ❺, ❻ Shang dynasty at the start of the Chinese bronze age around 1800 B.C. During the period of the Shang dynasty (ca. 1766–1100 B.C.), the emperor became the political and cultural leader. He was considered the "representative of heaven" and surrounded himself with a great caste of priests. Permanent walled cities were built, some of them at amazing expense, with palaces and temples. The emperor often shifted his ❸, ❹ richly appointed residences. The houses of tempered clay had subterranean storage rooms for food supplies. Among the many technical advances developed in this period were polished ceramics, the farming of silkworms, spoke-wheeled wagons and the plow. The Shang script, pictographic with more than 3000 characters, is a direct predecessor of the modern Chinese writing system.

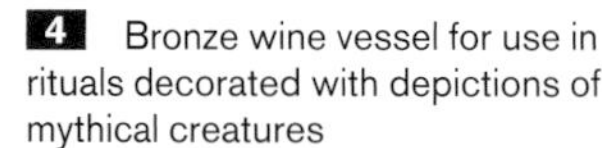

4 Bronze wine vessel for use in rituals decorated with depictions of mythical creatures

3 Bronze vessel used for ritual use with the inscription "Father Chi"

5 Bronze wine vessel in the shape of a pair of owls, Shang dynasty

6 Bronze knife and dagger, Shang dynasty

ca. 5000 B.C. | Yang-shao culture

ca. 3000 B.C. | Lung-shan culture

ca. 2000 B.C. | First state founded

ca. 1800 B.C. | Discovery of bronze

ca. 1766–1100 B.C. | Shang dynasty

The Zhou Dynasty and the "Warring States"

The victory of the Zhou dynasty over the Shang ushered in important changes in China's social structure. The feudal system that developed precipitated a decline in central political authority as regional states asserted their autonomy.

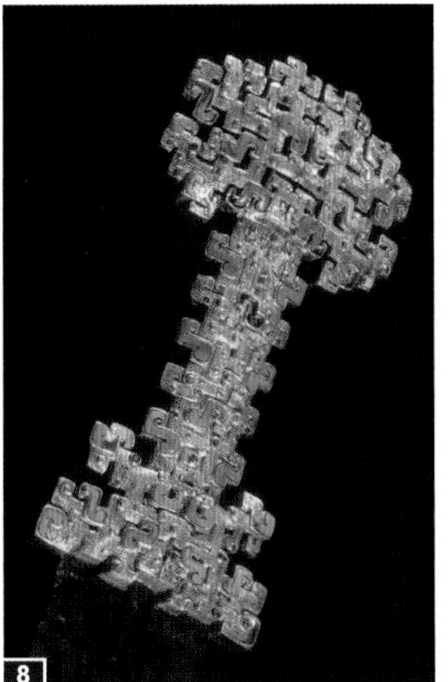

8 Richly decorated dagger handle, made of plaited gold and turquoises, Eastern Zhou dynasty, 771–ca. 256 B.C.

The Zhou, who ruled a small kingdom in the west of China during the Shang dynasty, defeated the Shang around 1050 B.C. and assumed power. They ruled their vast lands through vassals, awarding land to loyal clan chiefs and above all to their family members. Thus historians have traditionally ascribed the emergence of China's characteristic feudal system to the Zhou period. The decentralization of power inherent in this system paved the way for the later formation of more than 1000 "small nations" under the autonomous rule of the local elite. The period also saw traditional social divisions solidify into feudal ones, between the nobility, the military caste and the administrators on the one hand and the serf farmers and craftsmen (the overwhelming majority) on the other. The Zhou are also credited with introducing the concept of a "mandate of heaven," whereby emperors ruled by divine right. The political fortunes of the Zhou dynasty can be divided into two phases. During the first, known as the ❼, ❾ Western Zhou period (ca. 1050–771 B.C.), a strong central government ruled. During the second, known as the ❽, ❿ Eastern Zhou period (771–ca. 256 B.C.), only a puppet ruler, or symbolic figure, remained. He had no real power and was manipulated by rival regional lords. Some sources divide the Zhou dynasty into three phases: the "Early" period (771–722 B.C.); the "Spring and Autumn" period (722–481 B.C.), in which a few larger, autonomous vassal states developed; and the period of the "Warring States" (481–221 B.C.), which takes its name from the *Book of the Warring States* written during the later Han dynasty (p. 153). A period of forced consolidation left seven large states to fight for dominance over China's vast territories. Although marked by violence and war, the period was also notable for its intellectual and technological advances. Perhaps most significant was the transition to a more intensive use of agricultural land, including the introduction of new varieties of crop, in particular rice and wheat. Irrigation techniques and road construction methods were substantially improved, and knowledge of ironworking spread. The period of the "Warring States" was also the golden age of classic Chinese philosophy. It ended with the establishment of the Qin military state.

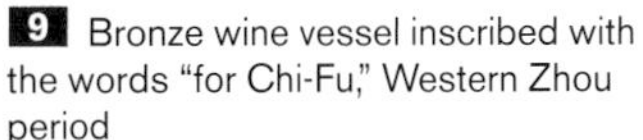

9 Bronze wine vessel inscribed with the words "for Chi-Fu," Western Zhou period

7 Bronze vessel, Western Zhou dynasty, ca. 1050–771 B.C.

10 War drum decorated with dragon handle, from the Eastern Zhou dynasty

The Time of 100 Schools of Thought

In the shadow of the rival lords' conflicts during the period of the Warring States, a number of philosophical schools developed. Almost all of these schools took a position on political questions and endeavored to gain the favor of the rulers. Nine of these schools eventually came to dominate. Among them were the School of Literati (Confucianism); the Taoists; the Mohists, whose moral code shows many parallels with utilitarianist thought; and the Legalists, who advocated strong leadership with strict legal controls. Legalist teachings became state dogma under the Qin dynasty while Mohism died out.

1050–771 B.C. | Western Zhou period

771–ca. 256 B.C. | Eastern Zhou period

481–221 B.C. | Period of the "Warring States"

221 B.C. | Qin dynasty prevails

The Ancient World

ca. 2500 B.C.–900 A.D.

The epics of Homer, the wars of Caesar, and temples and palaces characterize the image of classic antiquity and the cultures of ancient Greece and the Roman Empire. They are the sources from which the Western world draws the foundations of its philosophy, literature, and, not least of all, its state organization. The Greek city-states, above all Athens, were the birthplace of democracy. The regions surrounding the Mediterranean Sea and great parts of Northwest Europe were forged together into the Roman Empire, which survived until the time of the Great Migration of Peoples. Mighty empires also existed beyond the ancient Mediterranean world, however, such as those of the Mauryas in India and the Han in China.

In the famous battle of Issus in 333 B.C., Alexander the Great defeats the Persians under Darius III, detail from a Roman mosaic crafted during the period of the Dominate, found in Pompeii.

1 Greek theater in Syracuse

2 Forum Romanum

3 The Roman theater of Leptis Magna, Libya

The Culture of the Greeks and Romans

The ❶ Greek and ❷, ❸ Roman civilizations of antiquity are regarded today as the origins of Western civilization. The Greek thirst for knowledge and structure and the Roman achievements in political organization have shaped European culture to the present day, and their influence has radiated out to other parts of the world as well.

Greek Literature and Philosophy

There are vastly differing opinions concerning the essential nature of ancient Greek culture. The Greeks are regarded as the true inventors of political and historical thought, but also as the proponents of rationalism and science. Their complex system of myths and gods continues to fascinate, and their sense of art and aesthetics is admired.

5 *Pandora in front of Prometheus and Epimetheus*, from Hesiod's *Theogony*

In addition to their contribution to political evolution, the Greeks influenced Western attitudes and literature with their early epics, particularly ❹ Homer's *Iliad* and *Odyssey* (ninth century B.C.). While ❺ Hesiod, in his *Theogony*, wrote about the fates of the gods, Homer made the human and social aspects of individually fashioned figures the focus of his epic tales. For this reason, the Greeks are considered to be the forerunners of later Western Individualism.

The Greek culture, with its thirst for knowledge, was the first to make the conceptual transition from myths to Logos. The Greeks no longer believed in a world ordained solely by the gods, but sought to understand the world around them by inquiring into the origin of things and the ordering structure of the cosmos. From the ❼ Ionian natural philosophers of the seventh and sixth centuries B.C., the search for the primary building blocks of life and for the governing principles that guide nature dominated Greek thought through the appearance of Socrates, Plato, and ❻ Aristotle. These three great philosophers replaced the capricious gods with natural laws and so stimulated the development of sciences, including mathematics, physics, and engineering.

7 Anaximander, natural philosopher from Milet, with sundial, ca. 610–546 B.C.

4 Homer, Roman marble bust

As a result of intensive observation of nature, biology developed, along with a self-awareness of humans as observers and manipulators of nature. This self-awareness found expression in a desire for political freedom and independence, which for a long time hindered the creation of a united Greek state. It took the wars against Persia and pressure from Macedonia under Philip II and Alexander the Great to bring about a cosmopolitan Hellenism that culturally overarched and politically united the city-states. It was the formation of the Diadoch empires of Alexander and the Diadochi that first made possible the link between Eastern and Western cultural influences that went on to characterize the Mediterranean area.

6 *The school of Aristotle*, fresco by G. A. Spangenberg, 1883–88

The Achievements of Roman Civilization

Roman culture appears more "practical" than that of ancient Greece. Its outstanding contributions to intellectual-historical development lie more in state administration and law—areas in which they shaped sub-

ca. 2500 B.C. | Minoan culture
900 B.C. | Homer's *Iliad* and *Odyssey*
ca. 470 B.C. | Roman Republic founded
ca. 387 B.C. | Plato's academy founded
336–323 B.C. | Alexander the Great's reign
335–334 B.C. | Aristotle's school in Athens founded

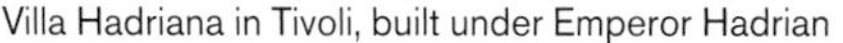
8 Villa Hadriana in Tivoli, built under Emperor Hadrian

9 The Roman aqueduct Pont du Gard, first c. A.D.

10 Arch of Titus, part of the Forum Romanum, 81 A.D.

sequent history—than in philosophy. Collections of laws were written and then continually supplemented—from the biblical Ten Commandments to the comprehensive Justinian Codes. Even the ethical philosophy of ⓬ Cicero or Seneca was written in the service of the Roman Empire and Rome's claim to political and cultural world dominance.

In its early period, ⓮ Rome was a small, free republic with an almost puritanical code of laws. In the course of its ambitious expansion, Rome gradually overwrote its own laws in favor of foreign, particularly Hellenistic, ideas of governance, which it then integrated into its concept of empire; this was particularly the case under the rule of Julius Caesar. The adoption and integration of foreign cults and ideas eventually allowed for the ascendancy of Christianity, a sect of Judaic origin, until it was established as the religion of all territories of the empire. Within its vast realm, Rome projected the image of a disciplined and militarily invincible organizing power.

11 Gladiators, relief, ca. 50 A.D.

Proof of the Roman Empire's impressive engineering capabilities can be seen not only in the many ❿ temples and magnificent buildings in Rome and other important centers but also in the garrisons and settlements constructed throughout the empire, the well-developed road networks, the ❾ aqueducts, the luxurious thermal baths and ❽ villas, and even the capital's ingeniously devised ⓭ sewage system.

13 "Cloaca Maxima" in Rome, sewage pipe leading to the Tiber River

Roman culture demonstrated the intense interaction of the empire's center and its provinces. Rome exported its state and administrative structures and imported finished products, luxury articles, and art—along with ideas and religions. The innumerable military triumphs of the consuls and emperors were celebrated with imposing state celebrations. Under the motto of "bread and circuses," the emperors of Rome, and later also of the Byzantine Empire, entertained the masses with chariot races and bloodthirsty ⓫ gladiatorial combat in great arenas such as the "Circus Maximus" or Colosseum.

The long existence of the Roman Empire is impressive considering the many upheavals, political reorientations, and the constant social unrest that shaped its history. It developed from a republic founded in the sixth century B.C. to a sprawling world empire by the beginning of the Christian era and survived even the fall of the city of Rome itself in 476 A.D. The Roman legacy was carried on not only by the Byzantine Empire, lasting until 1453, but also by Charlemagne at his coronation in 800 as emperor of the Frankish-German Holy Roman Empire. Charlemagne combined the Roman idea of a universal emperor and belief system of Christianity, with its supranational and intercultural ideals, and thereby ushered in the first renaissance of classical thought in the transition from Roman antiquity to the European Middle Ages.

12 Marcus Tullius Cicero, Roman orator, politician, and writer

14 The center of ancient Rome during Emperor Septimus Severus's reign, artist's reconstruction

from 55 B.C. | Cicero writes his major works
from 27 B.C. | Roman Empire
4th c. A.D. | Christianity becomes state religion
476 A.D. | End of the West Roman Empire
527–565 | Justinian I the Great
800 | Charles the Great's coronation as emperor
1453 | Fall of the Byzantine Empire

Crete and Mycenae – The Beginnings of Greek Culture 2500–750 B.C.

Greece was the earliest influential culture of the West. The Minoan and Mycenaean cultures were its first manifestations. The Minoan culture on Crete was characterized by palace cities, extensive trade networks, and sophisticated artwork, while the mainland culture of Mycenae was warlike and its architecture dominated by castles and defensive structures. The myth of the Trojan War, set in the Mycenaean era, clearly illustrates ancient Greece's self-image as a fiercely protective defender of its honor and freedom. The Trojan episode facilitated Greece's assertion of its cultural independence.

1 The Phaistos Disc, burnt clay impressed with Minoan hieroglyphics, 1700–1600 B.C.

Minoan Crete

The ❶ Minoan culture is the oldest precursor of Greek culture. Minoan Crete maintained intensive trade contacts throughout the Mediterranean area. The characteristic cult symbols of the Minoans were the double ax (the sacred *labrys*) and the bull.

3 Sculpture of a goddess, 17th century B.C.

4 Minoan vessel, decorated with the double ax motif

Between 2500 and 1300 B.C., Minoan culture developed on the island of Crete on the southern edge of the Aegean Sea. The oldest high civilization of the area, it has been named after Minos, a mythical ruler of Crete in the city of Knossos. The settlements of the first Minoans—farmers who probably emigrated from Asia Minor—were situated in the east of the island. From here, the Minoans spread throughout Crete.

Crete's favorable geographical position encouraged a flourishing trade with Phoenicia and the states of the ancient Near East. Cultural influences and important raw materials reached Crete from Egypt and Mesopotamia. On Crete, there is evidence of metalworking and the production of faience such as ❷ Kamares ware, which was exported throughout the Mediterranean. The Minoans had a developed commercial and urban life, while they cultivated vines and olive orchards to produce wine and olive oil.

The head of the Minoan pantheon was a great ❸ goddess, so it is often assumed that the original culture was a matriarchy. The Minoan religion, in which the king acted as high priest, had its shrines on mountains or in caves, and practiced human sacrifice to pacify the gods. Nevertheless, there were no monumental statues of deities. The symbols of the great goddess were the ❹ double ax (*labrys*), the ❺ bull, and stylized ❼ bull's horns (*bucrania*). The bull had great significance as a sacrificial animal. The ❻ wall paintings from this period often depict humans leaping over the backs of charging bulls. Indications of a warlike tradition that was characteristic of the later Greeks are less apparent on Crete.

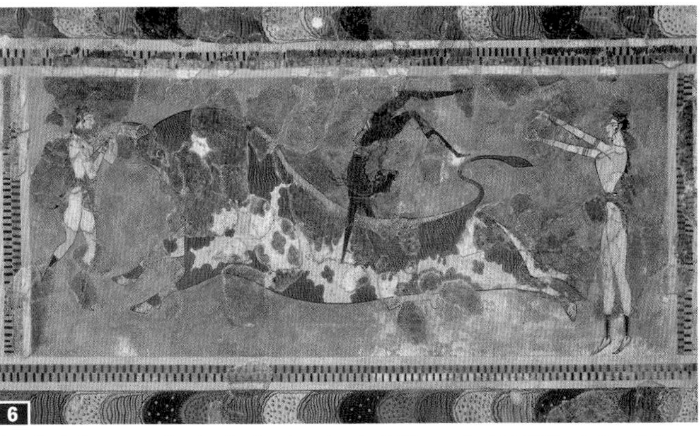

6 Acrobats leap over the back of a charging bull, Minoan fresco, 16th century B.C.

2 Clay vessel, example of Kamares ware, ca. 1800 B.C.

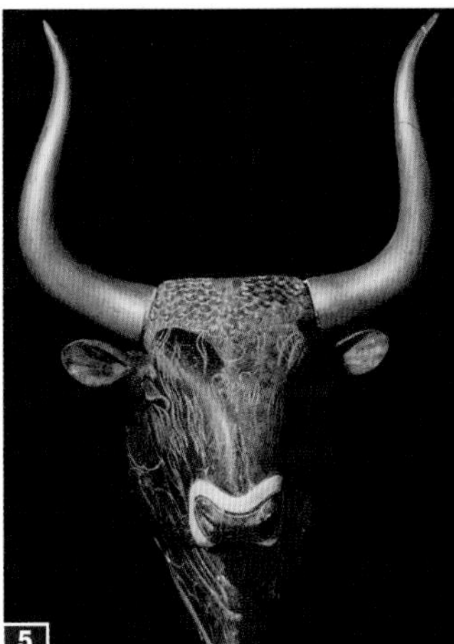

5 Late Minoan vessel for donatives, shaped like a bull's head

7 Set of bull's horns decorate the entrance to the palace of Knossos

2500–1300 B.C. | Formation of the Minoan high culture

from 2000 B.C. | Evidence of Minoan arts, crafts, and trade

ca. 2000–1550 B.C. | First unfortified palaces on Crete

ca. 1750 B.C. | Earthquake destroys the first palace at Knossos

The Palace Cities of Crete

The Minoan palace cities on Crete were political, economic, and cultural centers and were laid out according to a uniform pattern. The most significant of these was the capital palace city of Knossos.

9 Minoan prince carrying lilies and wearing a feather crown, Minoan relief, 16th century B.C.

11 Frescoes in the throne room, Knossos

12 Ceiling frescoes depicting dolphins in queen's Throne Room in the palace of Knossos

The Minoan social order, which centered on the ruler, was reflected in the layout of their cities. The king's palace was always at the center. It served as a political, economic, and cultural focal point. The king probably exercised religious functions, but neither the names nor representations of the rulers have survived. The palaces had a uniform layout. The palace wings contained a great number of rooms in a labyrinth arrangement and were grouped around a rectangular interior courtyard, complete with a modern drainage system providing flushing latrines. Notable colorful ⓫ fresco wall paintings dating back to 2000 B.C. display a wide range of subjects. Art had a primarily decorative function in the early periods, but naturalistic representations of plants, ❾ people, and animals, for example ⓬ dolphins, later came to predominate.

The most important palace on Crete was that of ❽, ❿ Knossos with its two- to four-story palace wings. It was first discovered by archaeologists in 1834 and is situated around four miles from Candia. It was excavated in 1900 by British archaeologist Arthur Evans. Villas and houses were arranged around the palace, while the burial sites were located outside the city. At its height, 80,000 people probably lived in Knossos. There may have been as many as a thousand rooms, all skillfully lit by natural light. An earthquake destroyed the early palace at Knossos about 1750 B.C. It was rebuilt and encompassed more than 200,000 square feet, which suggests that the ruler of Knossos had a position of supremacy on Crete. Subsequent earthquakes on Crete also leveled a portion of these buildings.

Besides Knossos, palace cities existed in Mallia in the north, Zakros to the east, and Phaistos farther south. This last was built on terraces at different levels. There was also the "summer residence" of Hagia Triada. Minoan settlements were found outside Crete on Santorini (Thera), but the island was destroyed by a volcanic eruption around 1628 B.C. About 1450 B.C. Crete, including Knossos, was overrun by the Mycenaeans. The assault of the Dorians around 1230 B.C. led to the destruction of the Mycenaean culture, including the high civilization on Crete. By 1100 B.C., Crete had become part of mainland Greek culture.

8 "Hall of the Double Axes" in the palace of Knossos

10 Palace of Knossos ca. 1520 B.C., model

Minos and the Minotaur

According to legend, King Minos of Crete was the son of Zeus and Europa. He failed to sacrifice a white bull sent from the sea by Poseidon, and for this the sea god took revenge. He made Minos's wife Pasiphae fall in love with the bull, and she bore a half-man, half-bull monster, the Minotaur. The king confined the Minotaur in the Labyrinth constructed by Daedalus. Seven youths and seven maidens were sacrificed to him annually until Theseus finally defeated and killed him. Minos died in Sicily and became a judge of the underworld.

above: Theseus slays the Minotaur, detailed miniature painting on the inside surface of a clay bowl

ca. 1628 B.C. | Volcanic eruption destroys Santorini

ca. 1450 B.C. | Mycenaean occupation of Crete

ca. 1230 B.C. | Dorian occupation of Mycene

from 1100 B.C. | Crete becomes a part of mainland Greek culture

The Mycenaean Culture and Troy

The Mycenaean civilization was characterized by its warrior aristocracy and its fortified cities. The saga of Troy plays an essential part in illustrating the character of these warrior kingdoms.

Mycenaean warriors mount wooden chariots and prepare for battle

Around 1600–1200 B.C., the Achaians migrated from the north into Greece, where they established city-states in the Aegean islands, in Attica, and on the Peloponnesus. Homer uses the term Achaians to refer to all the Greeks. They maintained a ❷ martial social structure, which was mirrored in the arrangement of their palaces, castles, and cities. Most of the castles in which the warrior aristocracy resided were fortified and the cities enclosed by walls. For a long period of time, the most important city was ❹, ❻ Mycenae, after which the whole Aegean culture of this period is named.

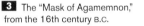

Decorated dagger made of bronze, gold, silver, and niello, 16th century B.C.

The Lion Gate at Mycenae

Little is known of the social organization of the Mycenaean city-state. It was probably a centrally administered palace bureaucracy with close ties between the religious cult and its rulers such as Atreus and his son ❺ Agamemnon. The economy was based primarily on agriculture and ❶ metalworking. There were military conflicts among the various Aegean seats of power, as well as with Minoan Crete and the states of Asia Minor, such as Troy. There is still no clear consensus about the causes behind the fall of the Mycenaean culture. Natural catastrophes or internal social upheaval may have led to the demise of this civilization sometime between 1200 and 1000 B.C.

The destruction of Troy by the Greeks, as immortalized by Homer's *Iliad*, is undoubtedly connected with the migratory movements of aggressive sea peoples such as the Philistines, who drove whole populations from their territories. Nevertheless, the sagas of heroism in the battle for Troy became a model for the whole culture of classical Greece.

German archaeologist Heinrich Schliemann began the ❼ excavation of Troy in 1870 in the mound of ruins at Hissarlik, in modern Turkey. He believed the account in the *Iliad* to be historical reality and therefore dated his finds—treasures of gold and silver from the second stratum of his excavation, which he reached in 1873, including what he believed to be the ❸ "Mask of Agamemnon"—to the time of the Trojan War. However, his oldest finds were distinctly older (ca. 2500–2200 B.C.) than this chronology suggests. In 1874, Schliemann also started excavations of Mycenae, where he found relics of a civilization which linked Greece and Cyprus.

3 The "Mask of Agamemnon," from the 16th century B.C.

The "treasury of Atreus" or the "tomb of Agamemnon," tomb, 14th c. B.C.

Fortified castle in the area of Mycenae, second century B.C.

ca. 1400 B.C. | Enlargement of castle of Mycenae

1600–1200 B.C. | Mycenaean period

ca. 1400 B.C. | Construction of decorated copper graves

Excavation works in Troy, led by Heinrich Schliemann, 1870–1882

From Homer's *Iliad*

"And then, last, Achilles drew his father's spear / from its socket-stand –weighted, heavy, tough. / No other Achaean fighter could heft that shaft, / only Achilles had the skill to wield it well: / Pelian ash it was, a gift to his father Peleus / presented by Chiron once, hewn on Pelion's crest / to be the death of heroes."

The Trojan War

According to Homer's Iliad, the Trojan War began with the abduction of Helena—the wife of Menelaus of Sparta—by Paris, the son of King Priam of Troy. Under the leadership of Agamemnon, king of Mycenae and brother of Menelaus, the Greeks began a ten-year siege of Troy. The climactic episode in Homer's account is the victory of the Greek hero Achilles over the Trojan hero Hector. A ruse by Odysseus (Ulysses in Latin)—the "Trojan horse"—decided the war in favor of the Greeks. The partisanship of the gods and the moral ambiguity of the conflict characterize Homer's work.

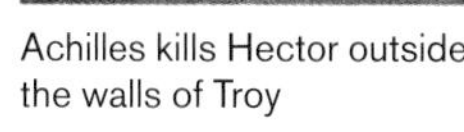
Achilles kills Hector outside the walls of Troy

above: *The Rape of Helena*, oil painting by Guido Reni, 1631
below: The Trojan Horse stands amid the ruins of the fallen city

The Dorian Migrations

The migration of the Indo-European Dorians into Greece led to the gradual settlement of the whole region. Individual clans and communities developed, and these eventually merged together into cities.

The immigration into Greece of Indo-European Dorian tribes out of the Balkan region followed in the wake of the sea peoples around 1000 B.C. In a series of waves, the Dorian Greeks settled first in central Greece and then, about 1150 B.C., also in the Peloponnesus. Dorian tribes settled in the Cyclades, on Crete, and on the coast of Asia Minor as well. They vied with with the Phoenicians for maritime supremacy.

The tribes soon divided into separate subgroups: the Spartans, the Messenians, the Argives, and the Northwestern Greeks, among others. With the development of individual clans and distinct communities came the beginnings of the later city-states and their struggles for independence.

The day-to-day lives of these early Greeks were described by Homer: The house (*oikos*) was the family's living space, and the lot (*kleros*), a clan's or family's portion of land, was the nucleus of its private property. Family members were subordinate to the head of the family. This world was confined within strict boundaries; warfare and cults led to personal ties to aristocracy or warlords. However, with a modicum of politics and administration, several families or communities could ultimately unite and form a city (*polis*), usually located on a fortified elevation.

ca. 1300 B.C. | Construction of castle Tiryns on the Aegean coast

1200–1100 B.C. | Fall of the Mycenaean culture

ca. 1150 B.C. | Destruction of Mycenaean castle

1100–1000 B.C. | Dorian migration

Classical Greece from the Culture of the Polis to the End of Independence 8th–3rd century B.C.

In the wake of the Dorian invasions, city-states with a high degree of political organization developed in the Greek territories. These city-states proliferated around much of the Mediterranean and the Greeks combined their resources in the defense of their territories against the Persians. However, tensions soon developed between the major powers of Athens and Sparta, culminating in the Peloponnesian Wars. The war left Sparta with hegemony over Greece, but eventually its strength also collapsed, sapped by numerous minor wars against other states. After a short period of rule by Thebes, the system of city-states disintegrated as the Greek peninsula was caught up in Macedonian plans for a great empire.

Greek warrior, statuette, mid-seventh century B.C.

top right: Greek youth playing with hoop

The Organization of the Polis

The polis (city-state), where public life was governed and precisely regulated by laws, was based on the political participation of its citizens. The conception of freedom associated with the city-state was central to Greek identity.

The early Greek cities were settlements of between 500 and 1500 ❶ men fit for military service, who lived in the surrounding area. Most of the city-states had a central acropolis ("upper city"). In the eighth century B.C., religious and communal sites and festivals linked the cities. The oracle of ❹, ❺ Apollo at Delphi and the Olympic games of ❸, ❻ Olympia are examples of this tendency.

The Temple of Apollo at Delphi

Relations between citizens, who were the minority of a city's population, were regulated by established laws. The proportion of the population that qualified as citizens, and thus participated actively in public life, varied between city-states. *Polis* was a legal term that described the city and its surrounding area. A council of elders and officials was elected for a fixed period of time by a public assembly of citizens to which they were accountable. The cities demonstrated a large degree of internal cohesion in defending their ideal of self-sufficiency (autarky) against foreign domination. The Greeks considered themselves "politically free"—superior to the "bound barbarians" of the Eastern monarchies.

Greek ❷ society was nonetheless divided into the aristocracy and the non-aristocracy. The aristocracy was distinguished by high levels of property ownership and proficiency in warfare. The non-aristocracy was made up of the rest: free peasants, tradesmen, the landless, and slaves. Slaves became an integral part of Greek society's economic structure at an early stage. They tended to be either former inhabitants of colonized lands, prisoners of war, or indentured servants. Most performed manual labor, but an educated minority held positions as private tutors or secretaries in their master's household. Greek society was patriarchal, though the private ideal was that of a harmonious family life.

Extract from Aristotle's *Politics*

"He who has the power to take part in the deliberative or judicial administration of any state is said by us to be a citizen of that state; and, generally speaking, a state is a body of citizens sufficing for the purposes of life."

above left: The Column of Zeus in the Temple at Olympia, one of the Seven Wonders of the Ancient World
left: The Temple of Apollo, Delphi

Olympia, from left: gymnasium, theater, old wall, Heraion, Kronos Hill, Zeus temple, treasure house, stadium, ceremonial gate

ca. 776 B.C. | First Olympic games
ca. 750 B.C. | Homer writes epics *The Iliad* and *The Odyssey*
ca. 735 B.C. | Foundation of Naxos
8th century B.C. | Building of first centers of worship
750 B.C.–500 B.C. | Wave of Greek settlement in the Mediterranean area
ca. 735 B.C. | Foundation of Syracuse

The Colonization of the Mediterranean Region

An agrarian crisis in Greece led to mass emigration and the colonization of most of the Mediterranean area. Some colonies, particularly those in Sicily, became leading cultural centers.

7 Greek theater in Syracuse, originally constructed in the time of Hieron I, ca. 470 B.C., partially rebuilt in 238 B.C.

The Greeks had long demonstrated an interest in surrounding lands, but it was not until the agrarian crisis of the eighth century B.C. that large-scale colonization began. Increasing indebtedness and servitude among the farmers led to uprisings in many regions and ultimately to migratory pressures.

Between 750 and 500 B.C., a wave of seaborne migration began, from Greece to islands and coastal areas throughout the Mediterranean. In about 735 B.C., colonists founded Naxos at the foot of Mount Etna in Sicily, followed by Syracuse. From 650 B.C., Greeks settled the coasts of Thrace, the Sea of Marmara, and the Black Sea, as well as Asia Minor. Between about 550 and 500 B.C., Ionians occupied Sardinia and Corsica, while Athenians moved into the Tyrrhenian Sea and reached as far as present-day Nice and Barcelona. With a growing population and booming Mediterranean trade, the colonies flourished.

9 Battle of Himera against the Carthaginians, Sicily, 480 B.C.

Most colonies continued to consider themselves part of the Greek cultural world and maintained contact with their parent cities. In the fourth and third centuries B.C., favored by wars on the Greek mainland, ❼, ⓫ Syracuse and ❿ Agrigento on Sicily became the leading ❽ cultural centers of the "West Greeks." At the same time they were forced to defend themselves against the growing threat posed by the ❾ Carthaginians and Etruscans.

The presence of numerous profiteers and exiles contributed to political conditions in the colonies that were frequently unsettled. Military and political leaders often seized power and were known as "tyrants." The tyrants of Sicilian Syracuse—such as Dionysius the Elder, who extended his power into Sicily and southern Italy, or Agathocles, who is remembered for his struggle against the Carthaginians—are a well known group.

10 The *ekklesiasterion*, where citizens' assemblies (*ekklesia*) took place, built in the sixth century B.C. in Agrigento

11 Temple of Apollo and Artemis in Syracuse

8 The Charioteer of Delphi, votive tribute from Polyzalos of Sicily

Dionysius the Elder of Syracuse

Dionysius (ca. 430–367 B.C.) took the rich of Syracuse to court on behalf of the populace, who elected him to a generalship in 405 B.C. He seized power as tyrant the same year, strengthening the army and fortifying Syracuse against the Carthaginians. Dionysius succeeded in conquering Sicily and concluding peace with powerful Carthage in 392. He invited philosophers, including Plato, and poets to his court and became well known as a writer of tragedies.

above: Plato at the court of the tyrant Dionysius in Syracuse

after 550 B.C. | Athenian colonies stretch from Tyrrhenian Sea to Barcelona

405–ca. 367 B.C. | Reign of Dionysius the Elder of Syracuse

after 650 B.C. | Colonization of the Black Sea coast, Thrace, and West Asia Minor

ca. 500 B.C. | Ionian occupation of Sardinia and Corsica

The Omnipresence of War

Due to the regional organization of the city-states, war and conflict increasingly defined the lives of the Greeks. As a result, methods of warfare evolved rapidly.

The self-contained organization of the polis, and the struggle of each for autarky or hegemony, created shifting alliances and led, as is vividly illustrated in Homer's epics, to constant wars, which came to overshadow the lives of the Greeks. There was an underlying sense of Greek cultural homogeneity and unity, but this was not reflected by their political alliances. Thus, the strength of the tightly-bound communities also proved a weakness for the Hellenic world. Greek city-states fought among themselves over land, influence, and privileges. Local conflicts often spread rapidly when neighboring cities intervened. Undeclared minor wars consisting of raids and the theft of goods were commonplace.

4 Hoplite with shield and spear, marble relief, ca. 500–490 B.C.

2 Iron weapons, ca. 820 B.C.

With the increasing size and importance of the cities, warfare with rivals—both on land and at sea—became the main focus of the politicians. Men capable of military service, who usually joined the battles for a couple of months each year, began to enter the service of the warring states as mercenaries, even joining the army of the Persian king.

By the seventh century B.C., individual combat as described by Homer had disappeared in favor of battles between armies. The Greeks adopted the chariot from the East and attacked with ❷ heavily armed and well-armored warriors called ❶, ❹, ❺ "hoplites." They advanced in groups of hundreds—units known as "phalanxes." The art of war increasingly became a profession, with professional strategists and tacticians taking the place of military leaders who had traditionally led the charge. From the sixth century on, the narrow and maneuverable ❸, ❻ trireme ("three-oared") vessel—with 170 oarsmen on three decks and a pointed bow—redefined marine warfare. The ship itself had become a weapon that could ram into other vessels and cause huge damage. Shipbuilding experienced an enormous upswing and brought great prosperity to those cities with shipyards. The procurement of wood, however, cost vast sums of money.

1 Hoplite with shield, helmet, and spear, Greek vase painting

3 Rowers on an Athenian trireme

5 Hoplites putting on armor, Greek vase painting

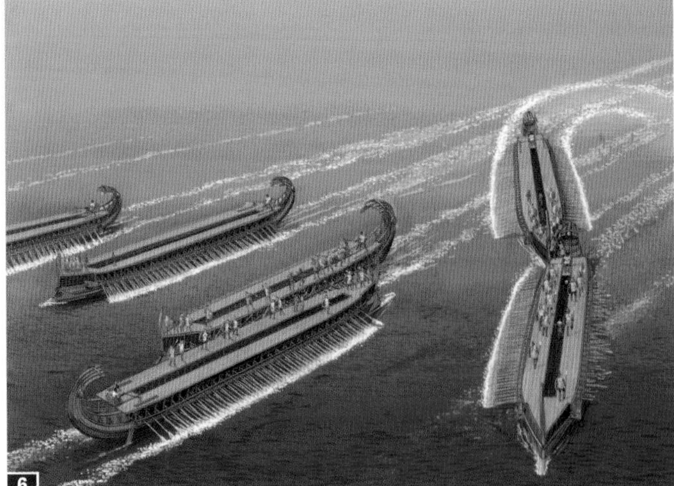
6 Greek triremes carry out maneuvers in the fifth century B.C.

539 B.C.	Cyrus II of Persia conquers Babylon
525 B.C.	Cambyses II of Persia subjugates Egypt
500–494 B.C.	Ionians revolt against the Persians
490 B.C.	Destruction of Eretria
490 B.C.	Battle of Marathon
483–82 B.C.	Fleet construction launched by Themistocles

The Persian Wars

The threat of Persian expansion led to the first military alliance among the Greek city-states. This Greek alliance succeeded in preventing the Persians from entering Europe.

The political changes that took place throughout the Middle East after 550 B.C. finally forced the Greeks to abandon their inward-looking policies. After the Persian kings Croesus and Cambyses II had brought the Middle East—including Egypt and Asia Minor—under their control, Darius I (the Great) sought to extend his realm into Europe. Many of the smaller Greek cities had already sought protection under his rule, and the Greek exiles also counted on him to subjugate the city-states. The Greeks regarded the Persians with a mixture of admiration and contempt; admiration for their ❽ fighting strength and cultural wealth, but contempt for their despotic political system.

8 Persian archer

In 500 B.C., Greek cities in Anatolia, under the leadership of Histiaeus, ruler of Miletus, attempted to revolt against Persian rule. The rebellion failed in 494, but it provided Darius with a reason to move his armies west. In 491, Persian messengers demanded the submission of all Greek cities. When these demands were rejected, the Persian army and fleet were dispatched across the Aegean Sea in 490 to punish Eretria and Athens. The Persians subjugated the Cyclades, destroyed Eretria, and then advanced into the Bay of Marathon. In the face of this threat, Athens and Sparta buried their rivalry and fought together. Under the leadership of the Athenian general Miltiades they defeated the Persians at ❼, ❾ Marathon. A messenger is supposed to have run all the way to Athens with news of the victory, collapsing dead after delivering the message; he was the first ❿ "Marathon runner."

⓫ Xerxes I, whom the Greeks particularly despised, continued the work of his father, Darius, and marched his troops across the Hellespont into Greece in 481 B.C. Responding to the renewed threat, the Athenian statesman Themistocles oversaw the construction of a new war fleet, and once again a Greek alliance was formed, this time led by Sparta. The large Persian army advanced along the Greek coast accompanied by a large fleet. After a dramatic land-battle in the narrow pass of Thermopylae, the Greeks were forced to retreat. The Persians then captured and burned Athens in 480 B.C., marking a low point in the fortunes of the Greeks. Later in the year a Greek victory in a pitched sea battle at ⓬, ⓭ Salamis changed the course of the war. The Greeks chased the demoralized Persian army to Plataea, in Boeotia, where they won a crushing victory in 479 B.C. The Persian threat was thus averted and the episode entered Greek folklore as a glorious triumph.

7 Battle of Marathon, October 9, 490 B.C.

9 Burial-mound of the Athenians who died in the Battle of Marathon in 490 B.C.

10 Messenger brings news of the Greek victory from Marathon to Athens, painting, 1869

11 Xerxes at the Hellespont

12 Ships engage in the Battle of Salamis, September, 480 B.C.

13 Main forces in the Battle of Salamis, the Greek fleet shown in green, the Persian fleet shown in red

From Aeschylus's *The Persians*

"Advance, ye sons of Greece, from thraldom / Save your country, save your wives, your children, / The temples of your gods, the sacred tomb / Where rest your honour'd ancestors."

481 B.C. | Formation of the Greek alliance under Spartan leadership

481 B.C. | Xerxes I of Persia marches into Greece

480 B.C. | Persians burn Athens

late 480 B.C. | Greek naval victory at Salamis

479 B.C. | Greeks rout Persian army

The Rise of Athens

From the beginning Athenian political life was shaped by the legal system. The famous lawmaker Solon was the architect of numerous reforms. After a period under the rule of the tyrants, Cleisthenes broadened citizen participation in government to weaken the aristocracy.

Athens, the city under the protection of the goddess ❷ Athena, whose symbol was the ❸ owl, always held a special position in Greece. It was considered the "cradle of democracy." The highest organ of Athenian government was the *Areopagus* (council). Its members were initially confined to the aristocracy, but later *archons* (rulers)—magistrates who were elected annually for six centuries, came to predominate between 683 and 84 B.C. In 630 B.C. growing social unrest and an attempt to dislodge the council prompted the lawmaker Draco to draw up a harsh code of laws (from which the word "Draconian" derives).

In 594, the Athenians elected ❶, ❹ Solon as archon. He championed the notion of the "rule of law" on all levels and introduced wide-ranging legal reforms. In the sixth century, Athens was suffering from a social crisis brought on by spiralling debt among the poorer classes. Solon sought to remedy this with reforms, establishing legal protection against the arbitrary use of power and abolishing the enslavement of the indebted.

1 The Athenian lawmaker, Solon

Although Solon worked for the balance of the interests of all groups, Peisistratus seized power in Athens as tyrant in 556 B.C. Peisistratus extended Athens's influence beyond the Aegean, laid the foundation for the city's economic rise, further reformed the legal code, and erected grand public structures such as the Temple of Zeus in Athens. His sons Hipparchus (assassinated in 514) and Hippias succeeded him, but when he was deposed and driven out in 510 the old system was restored.

3 Owl of Athena and olive branch on an Athenian coin

In 508–507 B.C. the new archon, Cleisthenes, brought about a complete change in the political structure. He divided Attica into ten geographical sections, called "phyles," which elected their own administrators and provided their own hoplite regiments. Each of these phyles sent 50 representatives to the newly created "Council of the Five Hundred," the highest political assembly, which convened on the Athenian ❺ Agora. In this way Cleisthenes created a system of local administration and severed the ties between the citizens and the aristocracy. Cleisthenes is also credited with instituting ❻ "ostracism," by which supporters of tyranny could be temporarily exiled from the city.

From Solon's *Fragment*

"My heart commands me to instruct the Athenians thus: Where no law is given, much evil will befall the state. Where there is law, the whole is united in beautiful order. Those who do wrong, shackle it by doing so."

(3, 30)

2 The Goddess Athena, bronze statue, ca. 375–340 B.C.

4 Solon defends his laws against criticism from Athenian citizens, painting by Noël Coypel, 1699

5

6

above: Shards of pottery inscribed with the name of Themistocles, an Athenian who was exiled under the ostracism law in 470 B.C.
left: Stele, found on the Agora, celebrating the anti-tyrant law of Eucrates, 337–336 B.C.

683 B.C. | First archons appointed
630 B.C. | Major social unrest
ca. 624 B.C. | Draco's laws enacted
594 B.C. | Solon becomes archon
from 556 B.C. | Tyranny of Peisistratus
527–510 B.C. | Tyranny of Hippias and Hipparchus
514 B.C. | Murder of Hipparchus

7 Pericles

Themistocles

An Athenian army commander, statesman, and archon, Themistocles designed the Piraeus naval harbor in 493–492 B.C. He was never popular with his fellow citizens, despite playing a crucial role in Athens's rise to power, most notably as a commander during the the Battle of Salamis. His enemies and critics managed to have Themistocles ostracized in ca. 470 B.C., and this was followed by the pronouncement of a death sentence. He died or committed suicide abroad sometime after 460 B.C. as a vassal of the Persians.

above: Themistocles

Athens as a Great Power

Athens came to dominate Greece through the Delian League, originally established to fight the Persians. This hegemony inevitably provoked resistance from other city-states, most notably Sparta. Domestically Athenian democracy reached its high point under Pericles.

Athens emerged from the Persian Wars in a position of considerable strength. Under archon ❾ Themistocles, Athens exercised a growing dominance over the Delian League, which had been founded in 477 against the Persians. By extorting financial contributions from the league's members, Athens extended its hegemony over most of Greece. Conflict with the stronger members, above all Sparta, became inevitable. Athens used force to crush revolts in league member cities. Meanwhile, the smoldering war with the Persian Empire finally ended with the Peace of Callias in 448, under which Athens abandoned the attempt to drive the Persians out of the Mediterranean and the Persians agreed to respect the independence of all the Greek cities in Anatolia.

9 Themistocles flees to Artaxerxes

While Athens was pursuing aggressive policies against neighboring states, internally it continued to move towards democracy. Under the leadership of Ephialtes, the Athenians stripped the judicial power from the *Areopagus* in 462–461 B.C. and gave it to the jury courts, thus placing judicial power in the hands of the citizens. Six thousand lay judges were drawn by lots. This was implemented by Ephialtes' protégé, ❼ Pericles, who, beginning in 443, was reelected each year as the strategist who guided Athens's destiny. He established equality before the law and made the city assembly a democratic council before which every citizen had the right to petition. Officials were appointed by drawing lots. The impressive ⓫, ⓬ public buildings and ❽, ❿ theater plays ensured that Pericles' period in office would be considered Athens's golden age.

8 The Dionysios Theater in Athens

10 The Dionysios Theater in Athens today

11 View of the Acropolis in the fifth century B.C., artist's reconstruction

12 The Parthenon or Temple of Athena the Virgin, on the Acropolis, Athens

510 B.C. | Hippias driven from power
508–07 B.C. | Reforms of Cleisthenes
477 B.C. | Delian League founded
462–61 B.C. | *Areopagus* stripped of power
448 B.C. | Peace of Callias
443–429 B.C. | Periclean Age

The Military State of Sparta

Sparta, the most powerful state on the Peloponnesus, was significantly more traditional than other city-states. Its public life was characterized by austerity and martial order, and the state boasted a formidable military force.

1 The landscape of ancient Sparta

Alongside Athens, ❶, ❷ Sparta played a dominant role among the city-states of Greece. Due to the conflict between the two powers, which emerged in the fifth century B.C., comparisons of their political structures and lifestyles have often been drawn that do not do justice to their dissimilar development and background. Sparta's expansion in order to solve its demographic problems began around 720 B.C. when the Spartans occupied Laconia and invaded Messenia. The Messenians rebelled between 660 and 640, which led to the city's subjugation, giving Sparta control over the whole of the Peloponnesus. The conquered peoples became helots, or serfs. Individual tribes of helots were able to gain their freedom through bravery in war, however, and later even acquired the right to Spartan citizenship.

Sparta's social order rested on the upholding of traditional tribal customs such as the petitioning of the gods, communal meals, and the raising of boys from the age of seven by the state rather than the family. The Spartans were famed for their discipline, the austerity of their lives and their obedience to authority. The consequences, however, were that Sparta remained socially and economically backward, for example, not even minting a coinage. By the sixth century B.C. the rule of the aristocracy had been abolished and replaced by a society of equals (*Homoioi*) composed of all able men. They ate their ❸ meals—for example, the notorious Spartan "black soup"—communally. Fifteen men comprised an eating community and undertook the training of their adolescents (*ephebi*). Until the age of 30, the men lived with their military unit and underwent continuous training. This led to the sidelining of marriage and family life and encouraged homosexual relationships. As the men were frequently absent due to war or military training, the women of Sparta led a more liberated life than women in other cities. Aristotle even spoke of an "unbridled regiment of women" in Sparta.

Sparta's political goal was military effectiveness and readiness for battle against outside enemies as well as against possible revolts of the helots. Through physical and weapons ❹, ❻ training, young Spartans were disciplined to fight, kill, and die for the good of Sparta. This archetypal character—readiness for battle and fearlessness in the face of death—is history's image of Sparta.

2 The Agora of Sparta, artist's reconstruction

3 Spartan communal meal

4 Gymnastic exercises of Spartan youths

6 Youths wrestling, marble relief, ca. 500 B.C.

5 Ephebe with pole and sling

Translated from Herodotus' History:

Inscription on Graves of Spartans Killed Defending the Pass of Thermopylae

"Go, stranger, and tell the Spartans that we lie here in obedience to their laws."

ca. 900 B.C.	Foundation of Sparta in the Eurotas Valley
ca. 720 B.C.	Conquest of Laconia and Messenia
ca. 700 B.C.	Lycurgus's constitution
660–640 B.C.	2nd Messenian War
550 B.C.	Foundation of the Peloponnesian alliance
521–490 B.C.	King Cleomenes I

The Political Organization of Sparta

Sparta was ruled by two royal dynasties, though the ephorate occasionally seized the reins of power. The original harmonious relationship with Athens turned into rivalry and confrontation after the Persian Wars.

Sparta's form of government was a monarchy with two lines of kings, the Agiads and the Eurypontids, sharing power between them. The Spartan aristocracy dedicated itself to ❼, ❽, ⓫ warfare and was supported by the taxes of the helot peoples. In the first half of the seventh century B.C., the lawmaker ❿ Lycurgus instituted a political code called the Great *Rhetra* ("agreement" or "law"), which listed Spartan customs and traditions. A council of 28 aristocrats, elected for life, governed with the kings. Beside the council was an assembly (*apella*) of male citizens that approved or vetoed council proposals.

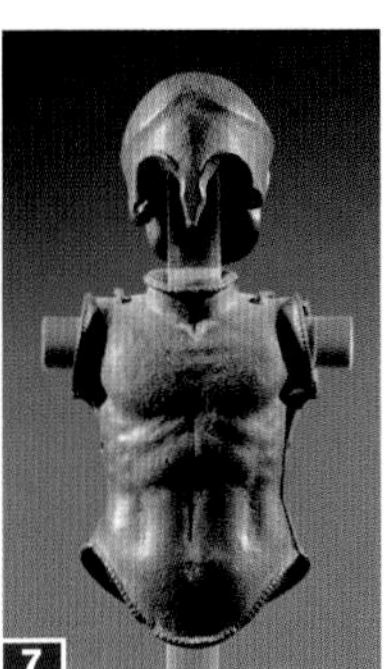

7 Greek helmet and armor

A new institution called the *ephorate* ("overseers") emerged in the fifth century B.C.: this group of five men was at first elected annually by the apella, but soon usurped the leadership of both the council and the apella and eventually displaced the kings from power. It wasn't until 226 B.C. that King Cleomenes III was able to break the power of the ephorate.

11 Spartan hoplite wearing a Corinthian helmet and greaves

Sparta established its domination over the whole of the Peloponnesus, and only few dared to rebel against the powerful state. In contrast to Athens, Sparta was wise enough to demand only men and weapons from other city-states and not to interfere otherwise in their internal affairs.

Sparta's relations with Athens were good at first; the Spartans, under Cleomenes I, helped the Athenians dispose of the tyrant Hippias in 510 B.C. Furthermore, given the Spartans' military capabilities, they carried the burden of the heaviest fighting during the Persian Wars. This is illustrated by the Spartan king ⓬ Leonidas, who in 480 B.C. blocked the advance of the vast Persian army with a tiny force of warriors at the Pass of ❾, ⓭ Thermopylae, buying time for the other Greeks to arm themselves for the Battle of Salamis. The Spartans fought and died to the last man. Afterwards, harmony between the two city-states was replaced by rivalry as Athens sought to expand. The resultant tensions eventually led to the Peloponnesian War.

10 *Lycurgus Demonstrates the Meaning of Education*, painting by Caesar van Everdingen, 1660–61

Cleomenes I of Sparta

Cleomenes I of the Agiad family was king in Sparta from ca. 521 to 490 B.C. He played an important role in deposing the tyrants in Athens. Later, however, he came into conflict with the Athenians. In 494, he dealt Argos, Sparta's traditional enemy, a crushing defeat at Sepeia, and he intervened in several other conflicts. As he wanted to restore a strong monarchy, the ephorates used his absence in war to depose him in 491 and he committed suicide a year later.

8 Duel or ritualized combat between hoplites armed with spears and shields, painting on a Greek vase, ca. 560–550 B.C.

9 Leonidas and his companions before the Battle of Thermopylae, 480 B.C.

12 Leonidas, King of Sparta

13 *Leonidas at Thermopylae*, painting by Jacques-Louis David, 1814

5th century B.C.	Creation of the *ephorate*
480 B.C.	Battle at the Thermopylae Pass
494 B.C.	Spartan victory over Argos
480 B.C.	Alliance made against the Persians
226 B.C.	Reforms of Cleomenes III

The Peloponnesian War

Athens's abandonment of its previous alliance system led to conflict with Sparta. Its ruthless expansionism led to the Peloponnesian War on the periphery of the Greek world.

1 Greek warrior wearing light armor, greaves and helmet with a shield and javelin

In 464 B.C., Sparta suffered a severe earthquake followed shortly afterwards by a helot revolt. An appeal to Athens for help was answered in 462 by Athens's leading statesman and military leader, Cimon, who dispatched ❶ hoplite troops to the aid of Sparta. The democratic forces in Athens used Cimon's absence, and the crushing defeat of his troops suffered at the hands of the helots, to implement a radical change in policy. ❸ Cimon was banished by ostracism, and Athens left the anti-Persian alliance with Sparta in 461. The Delian League was then created, and other states were forced to join and support Athenian expansionist designs. The first inconclusive military conflict with Sparta was settled by a peace treaty in 446–445 B.C., in which both powers agreed not to extend their influence and to allow the neutral Greek states to remain aloof. In the years that followed, however, Athens continued to extend its influence while Sparta sought to maintain the status quo. Thus, the peace became increasingly unviable, and the move to armed conflict was swift.

3 Clay shard inscribed with the name of Cimon, who was banished under the ostracism law

The devastating ❷ Peloponnesian War between the two most powerful city-states began with a flare-up on the fringes of the Greek peninsula between minor powers. However the two giants, Athens and Sparta, were quickly drawn in by their conflicting alliances. ❺ Corinth and Corcyra were quarreling over the possession of their common colony Epidamnos (modern Durrës) on the Adriatic Sea. Corcyra, a neutral power, then sought an alliance with Athens, and Athens—wanting to extend its sphere of influence to include the Adriatic coast—agreed. In 433 B.C. the first clashes occurred at sea, between Athenian and Corinthian ships. In 432, Athens imposed a blockade on Corinth's ally Megara and its Pontian colonies, whereupon Corinth and Megara, both allies of Sparta, pressed for support. After some hesitation, Sparta declared war on Athens in the summer of 432, citing the breach of earlier peace treaties.

2 Two hoplites greet each other before entering battle, Peloponnesian War, marble relief, ca. 420 B.C.

4 Athenians and Corinthians in battle near Potidaea, 431 B.C.

5 Corinthian helmet

464 B.C. | Earthquake disaster in Sparta

462 B.C. | Cimon sends troops to aid Sparta

461 B.C. | Athens cancels alliance with Sparta

446–45 B.C. | Peace treaty between Athens and Sparta

432 B.C. | Sparta declares war on Athens

431–421 B.C. | First phase of the war

The Course of the War

The first phase of the Peloponnesian War was confused, with neither side gaining a decisive advantage. However, once Sparta concluded an alliance with the Persians, Athens was caught on the defensive and ultimately had to capitulate.

The Peloponnesian War (431–404 B.C.) drew most of the surrounding states into one camp or the other. In the first phase (431–421 B.C.), Athens, under Pericles, with its powerful navy, fought defensively on land and offensively at sea. Sparta, under Archidamus II, with its formidable warriors, concentrated on the land war in 431–427 and ravaged Attica in 425. Ultimately the two powers' differing strengths brought the first phase of the war to a stalemate. Pericles' successor, Cleon, continued Athens' imperialistic policies. After gaining an impressive naval victory over Sparta near the island of Sphacteria in 424, he gambled away the chances for a peace agreement by making excessive demands. Negotiations only became possible once Cleon fell in battle at Amphipolis in 422.

6 Foundation of the Heraion of Argos

7 Alcibiades, marble bust

The peace faction in Athens came to power under Nicias and managed to conclude the Peace of Nicias with Sparta in 421 B.C. This restored the territorial boundaries to their pre-war locations. Nonetheless, the main powers' allies continued the conflict. In 420 the pro-war faction, led by ❼ Alcibiades, regained power in Athens and formed an alliance with Sparta's archenemy, the city ❹, ❻ Argos. This did not prevent the latter's defeat by Sparta in 418.

In 415 B.C. a new phase of the war began, as the theater of conflict shifted to ❾ Sicily. However, in 413 the war once again returned to Attica. Athens's situation seemed perilous when Sparta allied itself with the Persians, who supplied large amounts of gold to finance the construction of a Spartan fleet. ❿ Alcibiades was able to defeat the Spartans and the Persians in 411 at Abydus and in 410 at Cyzicus. However, the Athenian naval defeat at Notium in 407 made it evident that the powerful city-state was militarily and financially exhausted.

The destruction of the mighty Athenian fleet by the Spartans at Aegospotami in 405 B.C. proved decisive. The Spartan admiral ❽ Lysander was able to blockade Athens and force the city to capitulate. Athens's dominions were reduced to Attica and Salamis, and it was forced to dismantle its fortifications and relinquish its fleet to the Spartans. The balance of power had shifted; Sparta was now supreme in Greece.

8 Lysander orders the walls of Athens to be torn down

9 The Battle of Syracuse, Sicily, 413 B.C.

10 Alcibiades' victory over the Spartans

The Greek Historian Thucydides

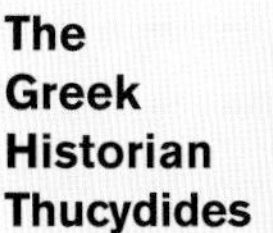

Thucydides, the Athenian historian and onetime general, is the main source of information for scholars about the various phases of the war between Sparta and Athens. Between 431 and 411 B.C., he wrote The History of the Peloponnesian War in eight books, a meticulous account of events. This strategist of Athens was defeated by the Spartans near Amphipolis in 424 and was forced into exile for 20 years. The historian Xenophon took up where Thucydides left off and provided us with the final phase of the war (411–404 B.C.) in his Hellenica.

above: Thucydides, sculpture

421 B.C. | Peace of Nicias
415–413 B.C. | Sicilian expedition
413 B.C. | Alliance between Sparta and Persia
407 B.C. | Athens defeated in Battle of Notium
405 B.C. | Spartan victory at Aegospotami
404 B.C. | Athens surrenders

Intellectual Innovations in the Fifth and Fourth Centuries B.C.

In the two centuries after 500 B.C., significant intellectual developments took place in Greece. This was initiated by the great tragedians and early historians and by the Sophists, whose philosophy was answered by that of Socrates, Plato, and Aristotle.

1 Sophocles

2 Euripides

3 Aristophanes

4 Plato

5 Aristotle

From Herodotus' *History*, Book 1:

"I shall go forward with my history, describing equally the greater and the lesser cities. For the cities which were formerly great have most of them become insignificant; and such as are at present powerful, were weak... I shall therefore discourse equally on both, convinced that human happiness never continues long in one stay."

The fifth and fourth centuries B.C. were a time of ❿ intellectual regeneration in many fields. In the fifth century, the three most important tragedians of antiquity—❾ Aeschylus, ❶ Sophocles, and ❷ Euripides—were all working in Athens. They used myths and historical tales to illustrate subjects such as man's inconstant fate, guilt, and atonement. In the fourth century, similar subjects—but with an emphasis on human weaknesses—were dealt with in comedies, most notably by ❸ Aristophanes.

In parallel to this creative effervescence, the first philosophy of history, or historiography, emerged with Herodotus in the middle of the fifth century. He was followed by Thucydides (p. 91) a few decades later.

6 Logic and Dialectic, typified by Aristotle and Plato, relief by Luca della Robbia, 1437

Herodotus is credited as the "father of history" for his original use of universal historical contexts in writing on the Greco-Persian wars (p. 85). History was no longer seen as merely "a game of the gods" but rather became a combination of forces and people actors; causes and motives were examined and suggested.

In philosophy, the Sophists ("teachers of wisdom") renounced the natural philosophy of the sixth century and set out in a new direction, which led to the end of the old order. As provocative philosophers of enlightenment, they saw thought, critical reasoning, and rhetoric as the basis of all knowledge, behavior, and customs. Man became "the measure of all things." Complementing this, the three great Greek philosophers began the development of ethical thought. ❼ Socrates, who was preoccupied with the moral responsibility of the individual, was put on trial in 399 B.C. and sentenced to drink a cup of poisonous hemlock for "corrupting the youth of Athens." His student ❹, ❻, ⓫ Plato was inspired by the unjust death of his teacher, and took Socrates' teachings, notably his dialogues, as a principle from which he designed an ethics-based, hierarchically structured order of all that exists. In his *Politeia* ("Republic"), Plato contemplated the nature of the ideal state and developed the idea of philosopher-kings. Around 385 B.C. he founded ❽ an academy of philosophy in Athens, where he taught for many years.

Later ❺ Aristotle, whom Plato "converted," took as his starting point individual things and created an all-encompassing system of the sciences. He introduced the thought processes of natural science and the observation of nature into the history of ideas.

7 Socrates

8 *The School of Athens*, fresco by Raffael, 1508–11

458 B.C. | Aeschylus' *The Oresteia* first performed

ca. 445 B.C. | Herodotus' *History*

423 B.C. | Aristophanes' *The Clouds*

ca. 412 B.C. | Euripides' *Iphigeneia in Tauris*

ca. 411 B.C. | Thucydides' *History of the Peloponnesian War*

410 B.C. | Sophocles' *Oedipus the King*

9 Performance of Aeschylus' *Agamemnon* in Athens; the play recounts the return of the King of Argus from the Trojan War, colored wood engraving, ca. 1865

10 Significant artists, poets, and philosophers of the Age of Pericles, print with color added later, ca.1852

11 Plato and his scholars in the academy of philosophy that he established in Athens, steel engraving, ca. 1850

The Political Environment

After the Peloponnesian War, Sparta was forced to defend its supremacy in Greece against the struggle for autonomy by the city-states. It was eventually defeated by Thebes.

The Peloponnesian War (p. 90-91) altered the balance of power. Athens had failed in its imperialist ambitions and was forced to relinquish hegemony to Sparta.

13 Naval engagement during the second Battle of Coroneia in 394 B.C.

However, a general peace on the Greek peninsula proved elusive. The war had left deep scars on almost all of the cities allied with the two main combatants. In virtually every polity, citizens were divided into pro-Athenian advocates of democracy or pro-Spartan advocates of the old oligarchic order. There was social unrest—for example, in Corcyra—and small civil wars.

Following Athens's capitulation in 404 B.C., Sparta's allies—above all Corinth and Thebes—demanded the destruction of the city to break Athenian power once and for all. Sparta, which had already achieved its objectives, opposed this. Meanwhile, the cities formerly under Athenian rule demanded the autonomy that Sparta had promised them during the war—and showed little inclination to exchange Athenian domination for Spartan. However, Sparta removed the democratic governments in these cities and reinstated the old oligarchic parties.

Fresh unrest also broke out on the Peloponnesus. Around 400 B.C., the Persians again occupied the Greek cities in Anatolia. Sparta attempted to force the Persians out with military action in 400–394, but with money and promises of liberation, the Persians persuaded Thebes, Argos, Corinth, Athens, and the central Greek states to side with them against Sparta. Although Sparta had some success against the individual city-states, as in the ⓬, ⓭ second battle of Coroneia (394 B.C.), the alliance backed by Persian gold was too large to overcome. In the ensuing King's Peace of 387–386, Sparta was forced to recognize Persian supremacy in Asia Minor and the autonomy of the other Greek cities. Sparta was visibly weakened—a signal for its former allies to shake off Spartan control once and for all. Thebes took the initiative. Under the command of General ⓮ Epaminondas, who developed a new military strategy with an attack from the left flank, the Theban army defeated the Spartans at Leuctra in Boeotia in 371. Sparta was broken, and within a few decades, Thebes became the leading state in Greece. This lasted until a new power—Macedonia under Philip II—challenged the order.

12 Victory of the Spartans at the second Battle of Coroneia, 394 B.C.

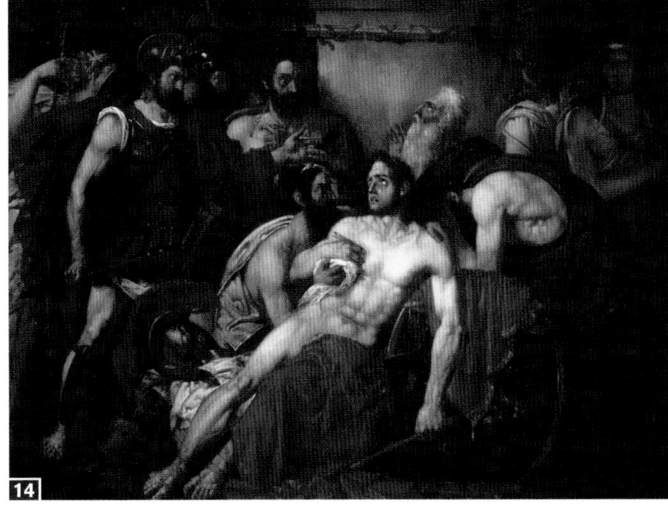
14 *The Death of Epaminondas* after the battle against the Spartans led by Mantineia in 362 B.C., painting by Louis Gallait

387–386 B.C. | King's Peace between Persia and Sparta
371 B.C. | Thebes defeats Sparta at Leuctra
399 B.C. | Death of Socrates
ca. 385 B.C. | Plato founds his Academy in Athens
335–334 B.C. | Aristotle returns from Athens

1 Alexander the Great of Macedonia during the Battle of Issus against the Persians in 333 B.C.

The Rise and Fall of a World Power: From Macedonia to the Diadochoi 7th–1st century B.C.

Initially, the Greeks hardly took note of the Macedonians and regarded them as useful "semi-barbarians" who shielded their civilization from invasions from the north. In the fifth century B.C., however, the Macedonians began to unify as a cohesive nation under a strong monarch and eventually, under Philip II, became the leading power in Greece. From Macedonia, Philip's son ❶ Alexander the Great conquered the known world, although his empire did not survive his death. His successors, the Diadochoi, carried the Hellenistic culture throughout the empire and into the Near and Middle East.

The Rise of Macedonia

Starting in the fifth century B.C., Macedonian rulers were able to develop a relatively cohesive state structure. Macedonia was thus able gradually to build up its influence and become a great power.

2 Philip II of Macedonia, coin

In its early period, Macedonia, in the north of Greece, did not play a strong role in shaping Greek culture. Its populace, predominantly peasants, spoke a distinct dialect and did not regard itself as Greek. Macedonia's early history was characterized by conflicts with the Illyrians and Thracians, its neighbors to the north and south, respectively. By the seventh century B.C., the Argead dynasty ruled in Macedonia. The king was commander of the army, supreme judge, and ritualistic religious leader in one, with his power held in check by an assembly of the army and the warrior aristocracy.

By the fifth century B.C., Macedonia had become a cohesive state. ❹ King Alexander I (the Philhellene) supported the Greeks in the Persian Wars and had, by 480 B.C., extended his kingdom to Mount Olympus and the Pangaion region. He gave his kingdom a more stable structure through military, administrative, and coinage reforms. His successor, Perdiccas II, used clever tactics between the sides of the Peloponnesian War. The rise of Macedonia as a military power began under Archelaus, who made Pella his capital, occupied parts of Thessaly around 400 B.C., and invited famous Greek artists, Euripides foremost among them, to his court.

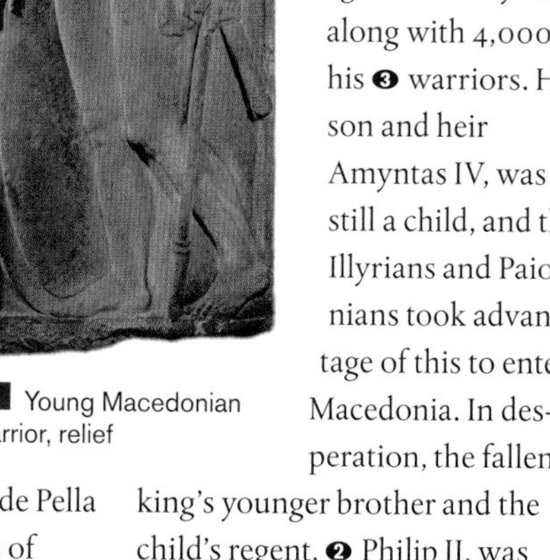

3 Young Macedonian warrior, relief

Macedonia faced catastrophe in 359 B.C. when its king was killed: Perdiccas III, who had won a victory over the Athenians in 360, fell in battle against the Illyrians along with 4,000 of his ❸ warriors. His son and heir Amyntas IV, was still a child, and the Illyrians and Paionians took advantage of this to enter Macedonia. In desperation, the fallen king's younger brother and the child's regent, ❷ Philip II, was raised to the throne and the situation immediately changed.

4 Alexander I of Macedonia has Persians killed by youths disguised as girls, during a feast organized by his father, Philip II

5 Method of attack used by basic unit of the Macedonian phalanx as it was organized under both Alexander the Great and his father Philip II

from 7th century B.C. | Rule of the Argead dynasty
ca. 5th century B.C. | Macedonia becomes a unified state
413–399 B.C. | King Archelaus
359–336 B.C. | Philip II reigns
348–342 B.C. | Occupation of Thessaly, Chalcidice, and Thrace

Macedonia as a Great Power under Philip II

Within a few years, Philip II turned Macedonia into the leading military and political power in Greece. He sought a political and cultural union between the Greeks and the Macedonians under his own leadership.

7 Gold medal with a portrait of Philip II, 336 B.C.

6 The Greek orator Demosthenes rails against Philip of Macedonia

8 Macedonian phalanx

10 The Philippeion, commissioned by Philip II after his victory at Chaeronea in 338 B.C. in honor of his family

11 Mercenaries fighting for Philip II, wood engraving, 1867

❼ Philip II (359–336 B.C) was an outstanding statesman and also a brilliant ❾ military commander. After the death of his brother he governed the country as guardian of his young nephew. Once on the throne, he resolved to capture the various Greek cities. First, he drove the Illyrians and the Paionians out of the country and in the following years conquered a large part of Thrace and the Pangaion. Beginning in 354 B.C. he pushed ever farther into Greece and in 351 conquered the Bosporus. Between 348 and 342 he occupied Thessaly, the Chalcidice, and the entirety of Thrace and incorporated them into his kingdom. Philip built up the Macedonian fleet and reorganized his army. He backed ⓫ mercenaries and professional officers, chose capable generals, and made use of his own military engineers to construct siege devices such as battering rams and catapults. However, the primary reasons for Philip's successes were the weakness and internal strife of the Greek states that had resulted from the Peloponnesian War. The Athenians were particularly anxious about the liberty of the Greek cities. The orator ⓬ Demosthenes warned the Greeks of the "Macedonian barbarian," in his four ❻ Philippics ("speeches against Philip").

Philip's advances led to open war in 340 B.C., during which the Athenians initially gained an upper hand due to their superiority at sea. In the ❿ Battle of Chaeronea in August 338, however, the ❺, ❽ Macedonian phalanx under Philip and his son Alexander won a crushing victory over the "Hellenic League" of Greek cities led by Athens and Thebes. Philip, who called himself the "unifier of Greece," dictated moderate peace terms that allowed the illusion of autonomy, and Athens, Thebes, and most of the other cities joined the Corinthian League and a "Common Peace." Philip then became the undisputed sovereign of the first truly united Greece.

In 337 B.C. Philip called for a war against the Persians to extend his power eastward. In the spring of 336, a great army of Greeks and Macedonians crossed the Hellespont into Anatolia. However, Philip was assassinated in the middle of preparations for war during the wedding feast for his daughter's marriage.

9 Reconstruction of armor from the grave of Philip II in Vergina

12 Demosthenes

The Panhellenic Movement

The term "Hellenes" was taken from Hellen, a mythical patriarch. His sons gave their names to the Aeoleans, Dorians, and Ionians. At first it referred to a tribe in Thessaly, but was later extended to include all Greeks. "Zeus Panhellenios" was declared the universal godhead of all Greeks and was honored in rites on the island of Aegina. Philip II and Alexander used Panhellenism as a political integration strategy and intervened as arbitrators in internal Greek conflicts in its name.

347 B.C. | Demosthenes' Philippics
346 B.C. | Peace of Philocrates between Athens and Macedonia
338 B.C. | Macedonian victory in the Battle of Chaeronea
337 B.C. | Corinthian League
336 B.C. | Murder of Philip II

Alexander the Great and His Campaigns

Alexander rapidly conquered the Near East and Asia as far as India. He was prevented from marching farther by a mutiny of his troops.

❸ Alexander III, son of Philip II, is one of the outstanding personalities of world history. His youthful élan and tactical genius were admired by his contemporaries; his personality and aims continue to present riddles to this day. With his campaigns and his plans for a world empire, he altered Greek identity and Europe's world view, yet ultimately failed as a result of his excesses. Alexander, who was educated by the philosopher ❶ Aristotle, was entrusted by his father with important duties as early as 340 B.C., at age 16, but felt slighted when Philip remarried in 337. Possibly Alexander and his mother Olympias were involved in Philip's murder.

As the new king, Alexander suppressed rebellion in various Greek cities and demonstrated his strength by destroying the city of Thebes in 335 B.C., then took up the aggressive ❺ war against the Persians planned by his father. He crossed over to Asia Minor and defeated the Persian army under Darius III at ❹ Issus in 333, then occupied Syria and Phoenicia in 332. He entered Egypt peacefully in 332–331, had himself crowned ❷ pharaoh, and founded Alexandria. In 331 Alexander crossed the Euphrates and Tigris Rivers into Persia, defeated the Persians once more, and proclaimed himself "king of Asia." The subjugations of Babylon, the imperial capital Susa, and Persepolis were symbolic acts that strengthened his claim as ruler of Persia.

1 Aristotle and his student Alexander

In 327 B.C. Alexander pushed further east, into India, occupying the areas through which he proceeded. He defeated the Indian king ❻ Porus at the Hydaspes River in 326, but as he was preparing to press on to the Ganges, a mutiny of his soldiers forced him to turn back. The army marched along the Indus to the delta, where it split up in 325. Alexander continued back to Iran through the desert of Gedrosia with the major part of his army, while the fleet was sent to explore the sea passage through the Persian Gulf. Alexander's plan to integrate the cultures in his vast empire by making Macedonians and Persians equal in the army and government met with an army mutiny and resistance in Macedonia and the Greek city-states.

3 Alexander the Great

2 Alexander the Great depicted as a pharaoh greeting the god Amun

4 Battle of Issus between the Macedonians under Alexander and the Persians, stone relief, 333 B.C.

5 The aftermath of the conquest of the Persian Empire by Alexander the Great, 334–331 B.C.

6 *Alexander and Porus*, painting by Charles Le Brun, 1673, showing Alexander the Great and the captured Indian king

The Gordian Knot

After Alexander the Great had subjugated Phrygia, he found, in Gordium on the Persian "Royal Road," in the Temple of Jupiter in Gordium, the royal chariot of King Gordius, the yoke of which was knotted up with a rope. According to the oracle, whosoever loosened the knot would rule over Asia. Alexander shouted, "What does it matter how I loose it?" and cut through the legendary Gordian Knot with his sword.

above: Alexander cuts through the Gordian Knot with his sword

335 B.C. | Destruction of Thebes
332 B.C. | Occupation of Syria and Phoenicia
336–323 B.C. | Alexander III (the Great) rule
333 B.C. | Battle at Issus
332–331 B.C. | Occupation of Egypt and founding of Alexandria

Alexander's Goals and Failure

Alexander alienated himself from his troops by demanding he be revered as a deity. His ambitious goal was the cultural unification of East and West in his world empire. Alexander's plans became increasingly unrealistic and his grip on power loosened.

7 Alexander depicted as Amun, coin

Like his father, Alexander went to great lengths to achieve his ambitious goals. He presented himself as liberator of the peoples he conquered and observed their traditions. Along the way, he became increasingly fascinated with Oriental cultures. When he began demanding the Oriental custom of prostration before the king (*proskynesis*) from his subjects, he alienated himself from his old Greek and Macedonian comrades-in-arms, who resisted this "custom of slaves." After the death of his friend Hephaestion in 324 B.C., the king became increasingly isolated and indulged in heavy bouts of drinking. In that same year he declared himself the ❼ son of the Egyptian national deity Amun and forced the Greeks and Macedonians to worship him as a god.

8 Marriage of Alexander the Great to Roxana, Roman mural

Alexander's plans for a cultural fusing of East and West were far reaching. He himself married the Bactrian princess ❽ Roxana in 327 B.C., and he then arranged the ❾ mass marriage of 80 of his close associates and military leaders with Persian noblewomen in 324. These marriages were part of a long-term plan to provide a future elite for his empire that would be personally bound to him and carry the legacy of both cultural areas. Exactly how far his plans extended for a world empire—which also included the founding of a large number of cities—is disputed.

Ultimately, Alexander had to give in to reality and the demands of his army. The situation in Europe and, above all, in Macedonia eventually slipped out of his control. Antipater, Alexander's governor in Europe, was strong enough to resist his command that the Greek cities readmit all their exiles who had served in his army. The last months of his life were overshadowed by megalomaniacal plans, feverish delirium, and contradictory political goals—such as an expedition for the conquest of Arabia. On his deathbed, Alexander took leave of his army and passed his signet ring to Perdiccas, one of his generals, yet he failed to designate a successor to rule Macedonia or any other part of his empire. In June of 323 B.C., Alexander ❿ died in Babylon at the age of 33 from a fever or (as many historians suspect) as a result of being gradually poisoned by one of his many enemies.

Quintus Curtius Rufus, *The History of Alexander*

"To be sure, it is obvious to anyone who makes a fair assessment of the king that his strengths were attributable to his nature and his weaknesses to fortune or his youth."

9 From the throne, Alexander watches the mass wedding at Susa with Stateira, the daughter of Darius, at his side

10 A gravely ill and feverish Alexander takes leave of loyal members of his army from his deathbed

331 B.C. | Alexander proclaimed "king of Asia" after his victory at Gaugamela

327–325 B.C. | March into India

326 B.C. | Victory at the Hydaspes River

324 B.C. | Mass wedding in Susa

The Kingdoms of the Diadochoi

After his death, Alexander's generals divided his empire among themselves. Only those who limited themselves to a distinct territory were able to assert themselves as founders of a dynasty.

1 Roxana, the widow of Alexander the Great, with her son Alexander IV Aigos are received by the Macedonian commander Eumenes

2 Tetradrachmon commissioned by a Macedonian or Seleucid dynasty, ca. 311–280 B.C.

As Alexander had designated no successor, a power struggle erupted immediately after his death in 323 B.C at the early age of 33. He had succeeded in making the concept of monarchy, which had been peripheral to the Greek world, a model for the succeeding Hellenistic kings. The diadem became the symbol of monarchy.

Each of his generals wanted a share of his crumbling empire. Among these *Diadochoi* (successors) there were plenty of strong leaders—in fact, there were simply too many competing against each other. At first, Perdiccas of Orestis, a general who had distinguished himself in the Indian campaign, attempted to use the signet ring he had received from Alexander to legitimize a role as "regent of the empire" until Alexander's young ❶ son, Alexander IV Aigos, came of age. However, those Diadochoi who sought to uphold Alexander's plans for a world empire were defeated, and Perdiccas was murdered in 321 B.C. Only those who chose a specific country in which to build up their power base succeeded. The Diadochoi also carried the cosmopolitan Hellenistic culture, which in many areas fused Greek-Macedonian and Oriental elements, into the empire. Thus Greek culture and philosophy influenced societies in countries far from Greece.

The Diadochoi states were strongly aligned with the personalities of the rulers. Each king legitimized himself as a conqueror and military leader who was able to hold and manage his territory. His power was not limited by a constitution. The successful Diadochoi established ❷ dynasties. These, however, were often characterized by family feuds among the descendants, the *Epigones*.

Many of Alexander's officers established small kingdoms, primarily in Asia Minor. One of these was the Macedonian Philetaerus who, in 283 B.C., founded the kingdom of the Attalids of Pergamon, which has become particularly well known due to its impressive buildings such as the ❹, ❺ "Pergamon altar." ❸ Pergamon became a leading power in Asia Minor, made an alliance with Rome to help bring peace to the region, and brought forth significant cultural achievements. Its library was founded by Attalus I (241-197 B.C), Philetaerus's grandson. Pergamine parchment was pioneered when supplies of Egyptian papyrus for manuscripts were cut off. In 133 B.C. when Attalus III died, Pergamon fell to the Romans.

3 Statue of a dying warrior, found in Pergamon ca. 210 B.C.

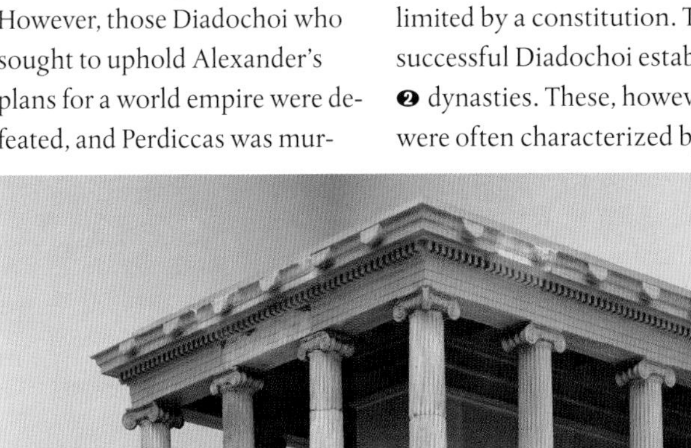

4 Pergamon altar, the lower section of which is a frieze depicting mythological scenes of gods fighting animals and giants, reconstruction of the western section

5 Eastern frieze of the Pergamon altar, showing a battle of gods and Titans

321 B.C. | Murder of Perdiccas

from 312 B.C. | Rule of Seleucus I of Asia Minor

312–64 B.C. | Decline of the Seleucid dynasty in Mesopotamia and Syria

304–30 B.C. | Ptolemaic dynasty in Egypt

The Seleucids and the Ptolemies

The two most important and longest lasting of the Diadochoi kingdoms were those of the Seleucids in Syria and the Ptolemies in Egypt. These kingdoms were ended by Roman conquest.

6 Seleucus I Nicator

❻ Seleucus I Nicator, founder of the Seleucid dynasty, received the province of Babylonia after Alexander's death. Starting in 312 B.C., he extended his rule through Syria and Mesopotamia and eastward into India. In 305 Seleucus took the title of king and solidified his domain through numerous alliances and military expeditions. He brought Greek and Macedonian settlers into his realm and founded many cities. His son Antigonus I Soter (king from 280 B.C.) introduced the Seleucid ruler cult, settled Celts in Galatia, and founded Antioch. The most prominent of his descendents was ❾ Antiochus III the Great (king from 223 B.C.), who subjugated the Armenian, Bactrian, and Parthian kingdoms and, between 202 and 194, occupied Phoenicia, the western and southern coasts of Anatolia, and Thrace. War with Rome in 192–189 resulted when he crossed over to Europe and forced the Greek cities of Asia Minor under his rule. In 189–188 B.C. Antiochus had to withdraw from Asia Minor down to Taurus.

7 Ptolemy I Soter

His successors dissipated their powers in fratricidal wars until the Roman general Pompey dethroned the last Seleucid ruler in 64 B.C. and made a Roman province of what was left of the empire.

9 Antiochus III the Great

As a friend of Alexander, ❼ Ptolemy I Soter, founder of the Ptolemaic dynasty, wrote Alexander's biography and started the state cult around him. He won Egypt in 323 B.C. and took the title of king in 305. In alliance with Seleucus I, he attacked Macedonia several times. Ptolemy solidified his rule in Egypt, generally adopting Egyptian religious concepts and the image of sovereign. He founded the Mouseion, the ❽ Serapeion, and the great ⓬ library of Alexandria. His son Ptolemy II installed the Egyptian national cult around his own dynasty and constructed the ❿ Pharos lighthouse of Alexandria,one of the Seven Wonders of the Ancient World. ⓫ Ptolemy III Euergetes (king from 246 B.C.) advanced to the Euphrates and Asia Minor and defended the empire against the expansionist ambitions of the Seleucids. After him, insignificant and often short-lived kings reigned until Ptolemy XII Neos Dionysos (king 80–51 B.C.), who completely relied on the power of Rome. The story of his daughter Cleopatra VII, the last of the Ptolemaic dynasty, belongs to the Roman era under Julius Caesar (p. 121).

8 Sphinx on the Serapeion in Alexandria

Ptolemy II Philadelphus

Ptolemy II (308–246 B.C., king from 285 B.C.) married his sister Arsinoe II (ca. 316–271 B.C.) according to old Egyptian custom. He extended the kingdom from Egypt into Nubia and the Arabian Peninsula and gained maritime strength in the Mediterranean. The couple, deified as the "Theoi Adelphoi," were generous patrons of the arts and sciences and made Alexandria a cultural center of the world.

above: Ptolemy II Philadelphus and his wife Arsinoe II

10 The Pharos lighthouse in Alexandria, one of the Seven Wonders of antiquity

11 Ptolemy III Euergetes

12 The destruction of the Royal Library of Alexandria by a fire in 47 B.C.

286 B.C. | Foundation of Mouseion and library in Alexandria

283–133 B.C. | Kingdom of the Attalids of Pergamon

223–187 B.C. | Antiochus III (the Great)

192–189 B.C. | Antiochus III fights war against Rome

Macedonia after Alexander's Death

The struggle of the Diadochoi for Macedonia and Greece was played out through family intrigues. Alexander's dynasty fell, and almost all of the Diadochoi joined in the scramble for power in Europe.

1 Olympias, wife of Philip II and mother of Alexander the Great

Upon Alexander's death in 323 B.C., his strongest generals proceeded to divide power. They controlled the richest satrapies. leading the strongest and largest armies, and fought for control of the empire. ❹ Antipater, whom Alexander had appointed viceroy, ruled ❸ Macedonia until his death in 319 B.C . The Macedonians in Alexander's army wanted to hold on to the Argead dynasty and chose Alexander's half-brother Philip III Arrhidaeus as king in 323 B.C. Alexander IV, who was born after the ❷ death of his father, also had dynastic claims. Antipater became regent of the empire in 321, while at the same time ❶ Olympias, Alexander the Great's mother, tried to secure influence as head of the dynasty.

Antipater decided on the loyal general Polyperchon as his successor, but his own son Cassander wanted control and allied himself with Antigonus I, who had established an empire in Asia. Cassander and Antigonus unseated Polyperchon and allied themselves with King Philip III and his wife Eurydice. Polyperchon in turn allied himself with Olympias, and together they had the royal couple killed and from 317 ruled as regents in the name of the child Alexander IV. Thereupon, Cassander started a campaign of revenge against the royal house. He marched out of Athens with the army at his side in 316, had Olympias executed, and drove out Polyperchon. He took the young Alexander IV and his mother Roxana as prisoners and put them to death in 310. With this, Cassander had annihilated Alexander's dynasty. Through shifting alliances with other Diadochoi rulers (Lysimachus, Ptolemy I, and Seleucus I), he was able to gain recognition from all as "viceroy of Europe" by 311 B.C. After engaging in serious clashes with Antigonus beginning in 307, Cassander's position finally became untenable around 300 B.C.

❺ Thessalonica, Cassander's wife, who had tried to decide his succession, was murdered by her son Antipater. In 294 Antipater was finally deposed by Demetrios I Poliorcetes, who gave way to the rule of the Antagonids over Macedonia and Greece.The peace between the successors of Alexander recognized the effective division between Antigonus, who was supreme in Asia; Cassander, who dominated Greece and Macedon; Lysimachus, who ruled Thrace; Ptolemy, who governed Egypt; and Seleucus, who ruled the eastern satrapies. Soon after his death in 297, his dynasty came to an end.

2 Dying Alexander, marble sculpture, second century B.C.

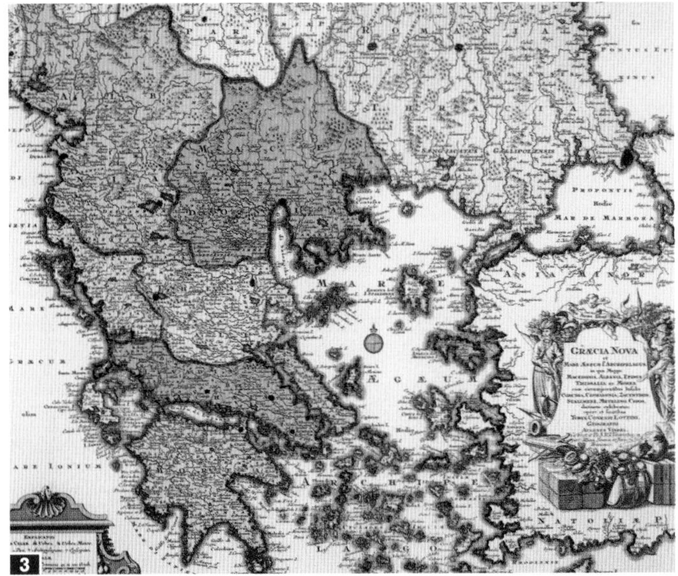

3 Map of ancient Greece showing Macedonia in the north in red, Thracia in yellow, Epirus in green, copper engraving, 18th century

4 King Antipater in battle, copper engraving, 17th century

5 King Antipater I kills his mother Thessalonica

Macedonia under the Antigonids

The descendents of Antigonus I finally succeeded in gaining power in Macedonia and thus over Greece. Their successors waged war against the growing power of Rome.

6 King Philip V forces Theoxena and her husband Poris to commit suicide for fleeing Macedonia

Antigonus I Monophthalmus ("the One-eyed," ca. 382–301 B.C.) and his son Demetrius I Poliorcetes—"the Besieger" —were the last of the Diadochoi to hold onto Alexander's plans for a world empire. From their power base in Asia, they invaded Greece and took Athens claiming to be "liberators." After the expulsion of Cassander, Antigonus assumed the title of king in 306 B.C. and revived the Corinthian League for the liberation of all of Greece. In 301 Antigonus fell at Ipsus against Lysimachus and Seleucus I. Demetrius was able to bring a large part of Greece, Macedonia, and Asia Minor under his control but was captured by Seleucus I in 285 B.C. His son Antigonus II Gonatas (king 283–239 B.C.), however, was able to maintain Antigonid control of Macedonia and most of the Greek cities through alliances until the country was invaded and conquered by the Romans in 168 B.C.

By about 250 B.C. the situation was generally settled, and Macedonia was again the undisputed master of Greece. Demetrius II (king 239–229 B.C.) son of Antigonus I, secured victories over the Celts and the Dardanians and dominated the Aegean Sea, defeating the battle fleets of the Egyptian Ptolemies at Cos in 258 B.C. and at Andros in 245 B.C. Antigonus III Doson (regent, then king 229–221 B.C.) brought Sparta under their sovereignty, and Antigonus united almost all of the Greek peninsula in the "Hellenic League" in 224.

However, conflict began to develop with the rising power of Rome, which sought to hinder Macedonia's consolidation of its strength in Europe.

❻ Philip V of Macedonia (king from 221 B.C.) allied himself with the Carthaginian general Hannibal in 215 B.C. (p. 107) to expand westward against Rome. During the First Macedonian War (215–205 B.C.) Philip was relatively successful, gaining access to the Adriatic Sea, but when a few Greek cities pulled out of the ❽ Second Macedonian War (200–197 B.C.), he was defeated by the Romans. In the following years he became entangled by internal Greek unrest. Philip's son ❼, ❾ Perseus was the last king of Macedonia. After suffering several ❿ defeats by Rome, Perseus was captured in 168 and paraded through the streets of Rome in a victory procession in 167. Macedonia was then divided into four republics and finally made part of the Roman Empire as a new province.

7 King Perseus of Macedonia in profile, contemporary cameo

The Athenian Philosophy

During the period of Antigonid rule over Greece, Athens remained a center of culture and philosophy. In 306 B.C. Epicurus founded his school, whose followers strove for individual happiness and peace. The Stoics, named after their meeting place in the columned hall on the Agora of Athens, first met around 300 B.C. and with their austere rationalism stood in opposition to the hedonism of the Epicureans.

left: The Stoa Poikile ("painted colonnade"), at the Agora in Athens, where philosophy was taught and after which the Stoics were named
above right: The philosopher Epicurus, ca. 270 B.C.

8 The Greeks are set free at the Isthmic Games, 196 B.C., after the Second Macedonian War

9 Perseus marches through the Thessalian canyons to Illyria during the Third Macedonian War

10 Roman legionnaires break the Macedonian phalanx in the Battle of Pydna, 168 B.C.

279–168 B.C. | Rule of Antigonids in Macedonia **215 B.C.** | Alliance between Macedonia and Carthage **171–168 B.C.** | Conflict with Rome

215–205 B.C. | First Macedonian War **200–197 B.C.** | Second Macedonian War **148 B.C.** | Founding of the Roman province of Macedonia

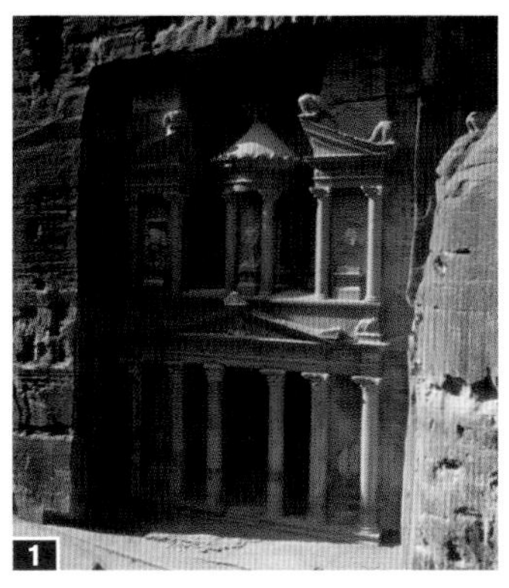

Judea and Arabia before the Romans

ca. 1100 B.C.–136 A.D.

As the Babylonian exile ended in 539 B.C., the returning Jews installed a priestly principality in Palestine, later taken over by the Maccabees. Herod the Great first established a secular kingdom. The ancient Arabian kingdoms benefited from the ❷ Incense Road trade route connecting India and the Persian Gulf with the Mediterranean. These states, and the Nabataea of ❶ Petra, acquired great wealth and made significant cultural developments. While Petra fell to Rome, southern Arabia was occupied by the Sassanids.

1 The "Shelter of the Pharaoh" of Petra, capital of the Nabataea

Palestine from the Persians to the Maccabees

After their return from Babylon, the Jews were able to maintain their cultural and religious autonomy under changing regimes. The Maccabees finally established the first king/high priest monarchy.

When the Persian king Cyrus II conquered Babylon in 539 B.C., he ended the "Babylonian captivity" of Jews captured by Nebuchadressar II in 588 B.C. Most of the Jews returned to the vicinity of Jerusalem, where they erected a shrine to Yahweh. They came into conflict with the Samarians and the Ancient Judeans who had settled there in the meantime. It wasn't until 520–515 B.C. that the Jews were able to reestablish a central Yahweh cult in Jerusalem under a ❸ high priest, who was simultaneously political leader of the Jews.

3 High priest and minor priest

Palestine remained a province of the Persian Empire until 332 B.C., when Alexander the Great incorporated it into his growing empire. After Alexander's death, it ultimately came under the rule of the Egyptian Ptolemies in 301, who allowed the Jews complete religious freedom. Around 200 B.C. a strong Hellenization of the Jewish culture began. In 198, Palestine and Phoenicia came under the domination of the Seleucid Antiochus III of Syria, who confirmed their religious freedom and constitution. His son ❹ Antiochus IV Epiphanes, however, deviated from this policy when he intervened in the conflicts between Jewish priestly families, attempted to introduce the Seleucid cult, and plundered the temple in 168 B.C. A Jewish revolt in Jerusalem was crushed and an altar to Zeus was installed in the temple. The Maccabee family overthrew the high priests in charge and led an uprising of the people.

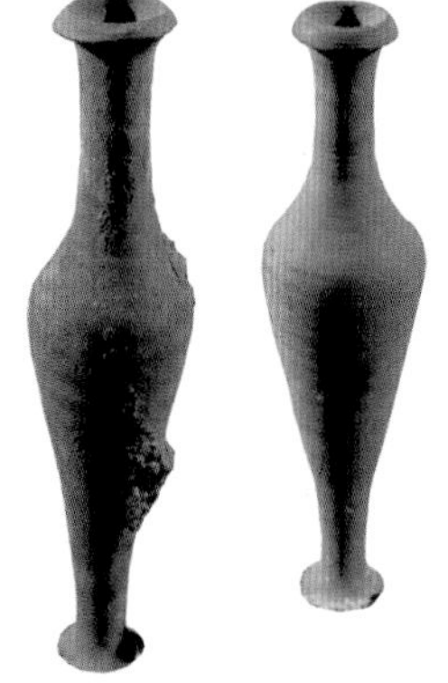

2 Perfume flacon from Jerusalem, first century A.D.

4 Antiochus IV Epiphanes' portrait on a coin

❺ Judas Maccabee ("the Hammer") drove the Seleucids from Jerusalem and restored the Yahweh cult in 164. His successors extended their rule over Judea, made the high priest office hereditary, and Judaized the regions of Samaria, Idumaea, and Galilee.

Power struggles in the first century B.C. allowed the Romans to intervene in Judea, installing Hyrcanus II (76–40 B.C.) but granting him only limited powers. When the Maccabean king ❻ Antigonus Mattathias allied with the Parthians, he was captured and executed in 37 B.C.

5 Judas Maccabee defeats the enemies and purges the temple

6 Antigonus Mattathias calls the Jews to arms

539 B.C. | End of the "Babylonian captivity"
515 B.C. | Completion of the temple in Jerusalem
from ca. 332 B.C. | Palestine under Alexander the Great
from 200 B.C. | Introduction of Hellenism
198 B.C. | Palestine under Antiochus III
168 B.C. | Looting of temple by Antiochus IV

Herod the Great and His Successors

Herod the Great conclusively did away with the rule of the Maccabees and allied himself with Rome. Following rebellions by the Jews, Judea was completely integrated into the Roman Empire.

❼ Herod the Great was from a family that was loyal to the Romans; his father Antipater had been appointed procurator over Judea by Julius Caesar. Herod eliminated the last of the Maccabees and assumed the throne in 37 B.C. Although he married the Maccabean princess Mariamne, his rule was secularly oriented, following the Roman model.

The ruins of Masada, in the background the Dead Sea

Believers during Passover in front of the temple of Jerusalem

Herod suppressed the religious agitators in the land, as well as intrigues in his palace, and was thus able to maintain peace. Under him Judea's economy blossomed, as evidenced not least by his monumental construction projects. He had the ❿ temple erected anew, yet his attempts to culturally unify the Jews ultimately failed. The birth of Jesus Christ falls within his reign, but the ⓫ murder of innocent children of which he was accused is probably a Christian myth.

Upon his death in 4 B.C., Herod's kingdom was divided among his three sons, the Tetrarchs. One of them, Herod Antipas (ruled 4 B.C.–39 A.D.), who received Galilee and Peraea, is known to this day for his marriage to his niece and sister-in-law Herodias and the dance of his stepdaughter, ❾ Salome, performed for the head of John the Baptist. His nephew, Herod Agrippa I, ruled once more over the reunited realm of Herod the Great with great support of Judaism and as a friend of the Romans from 41 to 44.

In 66 A.D., Jewish religious zealots initiated a revolt against Roman rule. The king, Agrippa II, who while of Jewish faith had been raised in Rome, sided with the Romans against the zealots. The revolt led the Roman emperor Titus to seize control of Jerusalem and to order the ⓬ destruction of the temple in 70 A.D. The last stronghold of the Jewish zealots, ❽ Masada, fell in 73 A.D. after the suicide of all the defenders. Judea was made a Roman province with limited autonomy. But even that was permanently lost after the revolt of Bar Kokhba in 132–135, led by the Jewish military commander Simon Bar Kokhba, establishing the independent state of Israel. The Jewish people were then driven out of Judea by the Romans three years later into the Diaspora.

Herod the Great conquers Jerusalem 37 B.C. with the help of the Romans

Salome dancing in front of king Herod Antipas

The Rebellion of Bar Kokhba

Simon Bar Kokhba ("the Son of the Star") led the last revolt of the Jews against the Romans in 132 A.D. The catalyst was the ban on circumcision and the Roman attempt to construct a temple to Jupiter in Jerusalem. Bar Kokhba captured Jerusalem and ruled as "prince of Judea," with messianic traits as defined by ancient Jewish laws. In 135 A.D. he was vanquished by superior Roman strength at Bethar. Thereafter the Jews were forbidden to enter Jerusalem.

above: Silver coins (tetra drachmas), distributed by Bar Kokhba

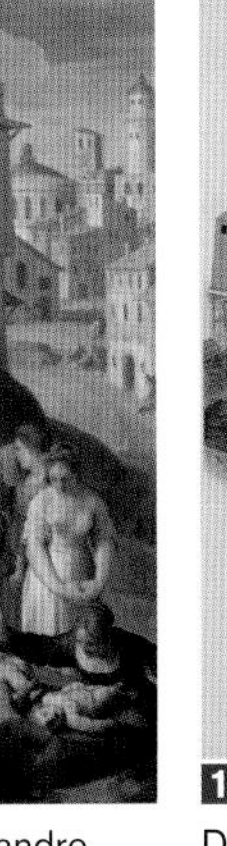
The Bethlehem infanticide, painting by Alessandro Turchi, 1640

Destruction of the temple of Jerusalem by the Romans under Titus, 70 A.D.

167 B.C. | Maccabee Revolt
164 B.C. | Reintroduction of Yahweh cult and reconstruction of the temple
37 B.C. | Herod named king of the Jews
70 A.D. | Conquest of Jerusalem and destruction of the temple by Titus
132–135 A.D. | Revolt of Bar Kokhba

The Kingdoms of South Arabia

Kingdoms in South Arabia grew rich from the ❶ caravan trade of the Incense Road. In the first century A.D. the Himyars of Saba (Sheba) were able to bring the whole region under their control.

1 Caravan on its way to the Red Sea, painting by Alberto Pasini, 1864

The Arabian Peninsula, inhabited since the Paleolithic age, has been home to Semitic tribes since the third millennium B.C. These peoples have generally been referred to as "Arab" and are mentioned in Assyrian sources as early as the ninth century B.C. While the inhospitable central desert was largely crossed only by nomads, a number of city kingdoms developed in the more favorable climes of the south (present-day Yemen and Oman along the coast). Very early on, they built irrigation systems like the ❷ dam of ❸ Marib and profited from the incense trade. They connected the Persian Gulf with India and even China by caravan and shipping trade routes. Incense, myrrh, and spices reached the Mediterranean by way of the militarily guarded caravan stations and cities built on rocky hilltops.

2 Dam of Marib, in present-day Yemen, an irrigation plant, which leads the water out of the wadi to the fields

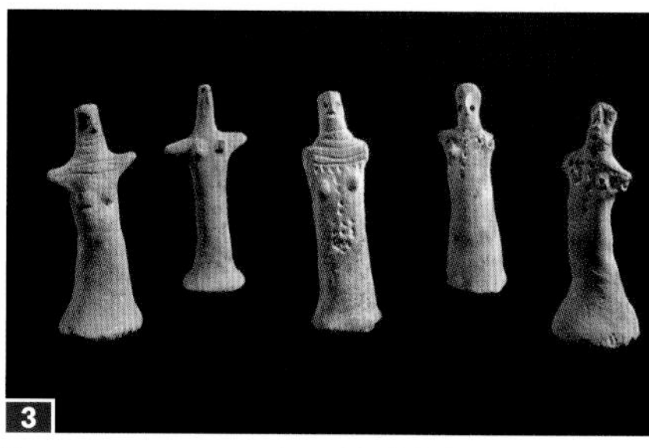

3 Terracotta statuettes from Marib in Yemen

4 Figure with sword and dagger, found in Qataban, first c. A.D.

The South Arabian empire of Saba, or Sheba, initially ruled by priest-princes and then from the fifth century B.C. by kings, developed in the tenth century. Its capital was Marib. The visit of the ❼ queen of Sheba to King Solomon, as reported in the Old Testament, reflects Israel's trade relations with the southern Arabian area. Another state that is mentioned in inscriptions dating back to the tenth and ninth centuries B.C. is ❹, ❺ Qataban, with its capital Timna. This kingdom reached its height in the second century B.C. but was conquered by the ❻ Hadhramauts about 20 A.D. The kingdom of the Hadhramauts, whose capital was Shibam, began its ascendancy at the beginning of the first century A.D., and by 50 A.D. was sovereign over all of southeastern Arabia.

5 Depiction of a goddess carrying an ear sheaf, found in Qataban first century B.C.

At this time, the kingdom of Saba, under the tribe of Himyars, was regaining importance. The Himyars made the rocky fortress Zafar their new capital and conquered the Hadhramauts, bringing all of South Arabia under their rule by around 300 A.D. Following the destruction of Jerusalem in 70 A.D., the Himyarite kingdom experienced a strong influx of Jewish communities and, from the fourth century on, of Christian communities. Originally the Himyarite kingdom had good relations with Christian Abyssinia, but the persecution of Christians by the last Himyarite rulers, who were religiously inclined toward Judaism, resulted in an attack by the Abyssinians in 525. The kingdom was subsequently conquered by the Persian Sassanids in 575.

6 The village Kawkaban in western Hadhramaut

7 The queen of Sheba at Solomon, painting by Veronese, 16th century

10th century B.C. | Development of the Empire of Saba

ca. 10th–9th centuries B.C. | Qataban flourishes

4th century B.C. | Foundation of Petra

164 B.C. | Jewish revolt against the Seleucids

9 B.C.–49 A.D. | Aretas IV

The Nabataea of Petra

The kingdom of the Nabataea also became wealthy through its position on the Incense Road. It had become a leading power in the region by the second century B.C., but ultimately succumbed to the power of Rome.

8 Ed-Deir ("the Convent") of Petra

10 Three containers for incense from the Ancient East, tenth–sixth century B.C.

The Nabataea migrated out of the Arabian Peninsula and into the territory of present-day Jordan in the fourth century B.C. They founded ❽, ❾ Petra (today Wadi Musa) in a rocky basin of soft red sandstone that was accessible only through a narrow ⓭ gorge. Up until the second century B.C. they remained without political ambitions and lived in their secluded valley as herdsmen, caravan guides, and traders, maintaining good relations with Egypt, Persia, and Greece. The Nabataea controlled an important section of the incense route and built warehouses for goods and foodstuffs in the rock faces. Some of these became multistoried dwellings, burial complexes, and shrines in which, at first, ⓫ stone idols and later deified rulers were worshiped. The Nabataea produced finely decorated ❿ pottery, which became a sought-after article in the Orient.

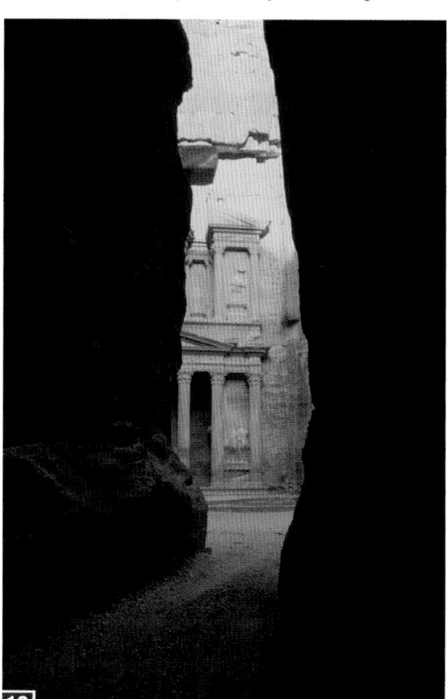
13 The gorge Siq is the main entrance to Petra

Nabataean politics changed in the second century B.C. and the kingdom began to expand. The kings proceeded cautiously in the power struggles between the Seleucids and the Ptolemies, aiding the Jews in their revolt against the Seleucids in 164 B.C.

New times came with Aretas III, who conquered half of Palestine and a large part of Syria from the Seleucids in 84 B.C. The inhabitants of Damascus chose him as king. He went on to besiege Jerusalem in 65 B.C. but was forced to withdraw when threatened with war by the Romans. Still, Aretas III had extended his kingdom from Damascus in the north to Egypt in the west.

11 Anthropomorphic idol with a Nabataean inscription

Aretas IV (9 B.C.–49 A.D.) conducted a victorious campaign in Judea against Herod Antipas, who had divorced his wife, Aretas's daughter, to marry his niece Herodias. Aretas ruled in harmony with the Romans and, with the construction of an aqueduct and the ⓬ amphitheater in Petra, achieved a cultural merging of Nabataean, Hellenistic, and Roman building styles, which is characteristic of the surviving structures that were cut from the living rock. The death of the Nabataean king Rabel II (70–105) provided Rome with the excuse to occupy the kingdom in 105, resulting in Petra's destruction. Emperor Trajan turned it into a Roman province.

Petra Rediscovered

Petra became the capital of the Roman province Palaestina Tertia in 106 and was still the seat of a Christian bishopric into the fourth century. After being overrun by the Arabs in the seventh century, the city decayed and lay completely forgotten in its inaccessible rocky valley until it was identified in 1812 by the Swiss Orientalist Johann Ludwig Burckhardt, following up on reports of indigenous nomads.

9 View of Petra, colored chalk lithograph, 1839

12 The amphitheater in Petra, built in the first century B.C. and extended by the Romans

from 20 A.D. | Hadhramaut kingdom develops
105–107 | Subjugation of Petra by Trajan as Palaestina Tertia
ca. 300 | Himyars conquer the Hadhramauts
525 | Abyssinians invade South Arabia
575 | Conquest by the Sassanids

Carthage: World Power and Rival of Rome 814–44 B.C.

The Phoenician colony of Carthage, traditionally founded in 814 B.C., rose, through trade and shipping, to become the leading power of the Western Mediterranean. Facing conflicts with the Greek colonies on Sicily and later with Rome, Carthage also armed itself militarily. The struggle between Rome and Carthage under ❶ Hannibal was a battle for survival. It culminated in the defeat and destruction of Carthage.

1 Hannibal crossing the Rhone in 218 B.C.

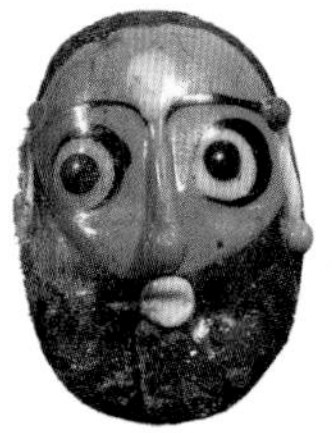

2 Pendants in the form of bearded heads, ca. fourth/third century B.C., found in Carthage

The Rise of Carthage to Military and Economic Power

After Carthage's ascendancy as a trading power, it also became an important military power as a result of its clashes with the West Greeks and Romans in Sicily.

Dido

According to the myth, it was the Phoenician princess Dido who founded Carthage. The Roman poet Virgil tells of her love for the Trojan hero Aeneas. When Aeneas only stops briefly in Carthage on his way from the defeated Troy and then leaves the queen in order to fulfill his destiny and found Rome, she immolates herself on a burning pyre. The story has been a very popular subject among writers, composers, and poets since.

Originally settled by Phoenicians from Tyre, ❹ Carthage was initially very much under Phoenician cultural and religious influence. Its highest god was ❸ Baal Hammon, joined in the fifth century B.C. by the goddess Tanit. The cult was practiced in cave-like ❻ shrines (*tophets*), but whether child sacrifices were made—as was reported—is disputed. Grotesque ❷ clay masks that have been found in the area possibly belonged to a cult of the dead.

3 Statue of Baal Hammon

In the sixth century B.C., the politically independent Carthage began setting up trading colonies in North Africa and on the Mediterranean coasts. Carthage became a great city with, at its zenith, 400,000–700,000 people living in buildings up to six stories tall. The heart of the city was the double harbor (*Cothon*)—a circular inner ❺ military harbor enclosed by an outer harbor for trading vessels—and a city wall 20 miles long was constructed. Carthage was ruled by elected shophets (chief magistrates)—who were both head of state and military leaders—and a senate composed of members of the nobility.

5 Punic defensive military harbor with docks which cannot be observed from the sea, artist's reconstruction

The conflicts with the West Greeks, primarily with the tyrants of Syracuse, began in the fifth century B.C., over bases and trading settlements in Sicily and Sardinia. After several wars and sieges, the Halycus River was set as the boundary line in Sicily in 374 B.C. From the sixth to the third centuries, the Carthaginians maintained trade relations with the Etruscans and the Romans, to whom they were tied by alliance treaties. When the Romans took control of Messina in northeast Sicily in 264 B.C., a conflict ensued. In the First Punic War (264–241 B.C.), the Romans drove the Carthaginians out of Sicily, although a Roman landing in Africa in 256–255 was repelled. In 241, Rome destroyed the Carthaginian fleet. Forced to sue for peace, Carthage withdrew from Sicily and Sardinia in 237.

4 Ruins of Punic Carthage

6 Shrine (*tophet*) of Carthage

814 B.C.	Carthage founded
264–241 B.C.	First Punic War
241 B.C.	Destruction of Carthaginian fleet
218–201 B.C.	Second Punic War
218 B.C.	Hannibal crosses the Alps
216 B.C.	Victory at Cannae
215 B.C.	Alliance with Macedonia

Hannibal and the End of Carthage

In the Second Punic War, Hannibal was able to win several victories against Rome but was then forced onto the defensive. Carthage was totally destroyed in the Third Punic War.

7 Obliteration of Carthage in 146 B.C. in the Third Punic War

8 Hannibal's suicide in Libyssa in Bithynia in 183 B.C.

In 237–236 B.C. the Carthaginian general Hamilcar Barca occupied the south and west of Spain as a power base against Rome. His son-in-law Hasdrubal advanced up to the middle of Spain but concluded a moratorium with Rome in 226. With Hasdrubal's murder in 221, command fell to ❾ Hannibal, the son of Hamilcar Barca, who had ⓬ sworn deadly enmity against Rome as a boy. Hannibal had enormous talent for military and tactical thinking, and he immediately began with the conquest of the area north of the Ebro River in Spain, provoking the Second Punic War (218–201 B.C.). Hannibal famously crossed the Alps with his army and the legendary elephants in 218 and defeated the Romans under Publius Cornelius Scipio, later known as Scipio Africanus, on the Trebia River in 218 and again on Lake Trasimene in 217. By encircling the Romans, he won a major victory at the ⓫ Battle of Cannae in 216. He then tried to force the northern Italian peoples such as the Celts to join him against the Romans, but was only partially successful. However, in 215 he was able to form an alliance with Philip V of Macedonia, another enemy of Rome.

10 Mosaic with scenes of country life on a Roman estate near Carthage

Under the Roman consul and dictator Quintus Fabius, known as "*Cunctator*" ("the delayer"), the Romans consistently avoided direct battle with the Carthaginians and limited themselves to guerrilla attacks. Consequently, Hannibal moved toward Rome in 211 B.C. but was stopped and soon forced out of most of Italy and Spain in 206. In 204, P. Cornelius Scipio landed in North Africa with his Roman legions. Hannibal returned to defend Carthage but was defeated in battle at ⓭ Zama (p. 112) by Scipio in 202. Hunted by the Romans, Hannibal fled through Syria to Bithynia. Threatened with extradition to Rome, he ❽ ended his own life in 183.

9 Portrait bust of Hannibal

Total submission to the power of Rome saved Carthage at first. But the fear of the once powerful city-state, stirred up primarily by Cato the Elder, led to the Third Punic War (149–146 B.C.). Carthage was taken and ❼ obliterated in 146 B.C.—the ground of the city strewn with salt to render it infertile. Resettled under Julius Caesar, in 29 B.C. ❿ Colonia Julia Carthago became the capital of the African province.

Cato's Closing Words

Cato the Elder's closing words of every one of his speeches before the Roman Senate: "Ceterum censeo, Carthaginem esse delendam."

("I declare that Carthage must be destroyed").

above: Cato the Elder

11 Battle of Cannae, 216 B.C.

12 Hamilcar Barka lets his nine-year-old son swear enmity to the Romans, painting by Johann Heinrich Schönfeld, ca.1662

13 Scipio conquers Hannibal in the Battle of Zama, 202 B.C., painting 1521

206 B.C. | Loss of Spain

204 B.C. | Scipio invades North Africa

202 B.C. | Carthage's catastrophe at Zama

183 B.C. | Suicide of Hannibal

146 B.C. | Destruction of Carthage

29 B.C. | Colonia Julia Concordia Carthago

The Etruscans: The League to the Roman Empire 7th century B.C.–1st century B.C.

Between the seventh and first centuries B.C., the ❶ Etruscans thrived as an independent culture in central Italy. Whether they were indigenous to Italy was unclear even in antiquity, as the Etruscans had assimilated the Roman myth about Aeneas and the founding of Rome. The Etruscans believed in predestination and that life was totally controlled by the gods, which is why sacrificial cults and cults of the dead played a special role in their culture. From the fifth century on, their history was closely tied to that of Rome.

1 Terra-cotta model of an Etruscan temple, first half of first century B.C.

The Culture of the League of Twelve Cities

A confederation of twelve Etruscan cities controlled Mediterranean trade at first but were forced onto the defensive by the West Greeks of Sicily.

2 The Etruscan necropolis at Cerveteri

The Etruscans in Italy can be traced back to the seventh century B.C. Today they are no longer regarded as immigrants from the East, although there was a close cultural proximity to the early Greek world as seen in their ❹ script and ❸ vase painting. Evidence of their culture is found primarily in house-like tombs and in the form of ❺ burial objects found in chamber tombs, which were decorated with ❻ frescoes. They built necropolises, for example, at Orvieto and ❷ Cerveteri, with their own road networks. The Etruscans worshiped a number of gods, which were later mixed with the Roman gods. The highest god was Varro, the god of war and vegetation. The prophecies of the ❼ haruspex, who read omens in sacrificial livers and interpreted lightning and bird flights, played a large role in the cult.

The Etruscans were politically organized as a league of twelve city-states, which were ruled by priest-kings. This league was primarily a community based around the shrine to the god Voltumna at Volsinii, but it also pursued common political goals. In the seventh and sixth centuries B.C., the Etruscans pushed out of their core territory, present-day Tuscany, into southern Italy and over the Apennines to the north, and they founded the city of Rome about 650 B.C. by combining existing settlements.

Because of Etruria's wealth of ore, it had many trade contacts, including trade agreements with the Phoenicians, Carthaginians, and Greeks—particularly Sicily, beginning in the fifth century. Over time, the Etruscans increasingly intervened in Sicilian political affairs and came into conflict with the tyrants of Syracuse when the Sicilians extended their sphere of power to the Italian mainland. The destruction of the Etruscan fleet at Cumae in 474 B.C. broke Etruscan political power and made Rome's subsequent rise possible.

6 Etruscan mural in the Tomba dei Leopardi in Tarquinia depicting servants and musicians, first half of the fifth century B.C.

3 Etruscan vase painting, ca. 500 B.C.

4 Sheet of bronze with Etruscan script, end of the third century B.C.

5 Etruscan animal figures, found in the Tomba Bernadini in Palestrina, ca. 640–620 B.C.

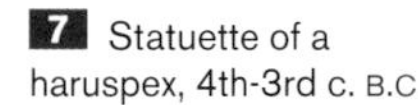

7 Statuette of a haruspex, 4th-3rd c. B.C.

A Life of Luxury

The flourishing trade in mineral resources and other raw materials provided the Etruscan upper class with great prosperity and wealth, as testified to by the luxury articles they left with their dead for the next life. However, the Etruscans also knew how to enjoy this life. Sumptuous celebratory feasts with music and sporting competitions were held. Greek and Roman writers took exception to the loose morals of their neighbors but at the same time admired their cultural achievements.

7th century B.C. | Etruscans settle Italy
from 7th century B.C. | Formation of city-states in Etruria
ca. 650 B.C. | Foundation of Rome
from 6th century B.C. | Expansion into southern Italy
510 B.C. | King Tarquinius flees Rome
ca. 510 B.C. | King Porsenna reconquers Rome

The Etruscans under Roman Rule

As Rome gained power, the Etruscan cities increasingly lost their independence, and the Etruscans became allies—Roman citizens, but without the right to vote. They were later completely integrated into the world empire.

Initially, Rome was part of the Etruscan world and was ruled over by the Etruscan Tarquin dynasty. When they were driven out by the Romans in 510 B.C., the king of the Etruscans, ⑩ Porsenna of Camars (modern-day Chiusi)—who is frequently mentioned in ancient literature—is said to have besieged and taken the city. But his efforts proved in vain. Rome became a republic, and when the people rebelled against the powerful patrician families around 500 B.C., the monarchic form also came to an end in other Etruscan cities.

During the fifth century, the Etruscan cities came under attack by both the ⑪ Celts and an expanding Rome. The clashes between Rome and Tarquinia, the leader of the League of Twelve Cities, spread in 353 B.C. to all the cities of Etruria. The Etruscan city-state of Caere was quickly captured and assimilated by the Romans. Its inhabitants became "allies," Roman citizens with all privileges except the vote. This was the model by which succeeding Etruscan and Italian cities were taken into the Roman Empire; the Etruscan cities of Veii (396), Nepete (386), and Sutrium (383), which had already been conquered, received the same status. Between 310 and 283 the last ❽, ❾, ⑫ Etruscan coalition army suffered crushing defeats against the Romans at the Vadimonian Lake. This sealed their fate as an independent polity.

Economic and cultural decline followed the political fall when the Etruscan cities, now under Roman rule, experienced destruction by attacking Gauls in 225 B.C. and the advance of the Carthaginians under Hannibal in 218–207. The areas around the cities became extensively depopulated as a result of the pillaging and brutal conquest by the invaders, and many Etruscan peasants were forced by poverty into lifelong servitude. The social misery of the Etruscan territories provided a mass base for Roman social reformers like the Gracchi in the second century B.C. and Marius, who built up a voluntary army of poverty-stricken Etruscans, in 87 B.C. The revenge of its enemy Sulla thus hit the region of Etruria particularly hard. Under Emperor Augustus, Etruria was fully incorporated into the Roman Empire and was granted the status of Regio VII, making it a Roman voting district.

8 Statuette of an Etruscan warrior, fourth century B.C.

9 Etruscan chariot from Castro

10 Conquest of Rome by Porsenna 510 B.C.

11 Battle between the Etruscans and the Celts, urn, second century B.C.

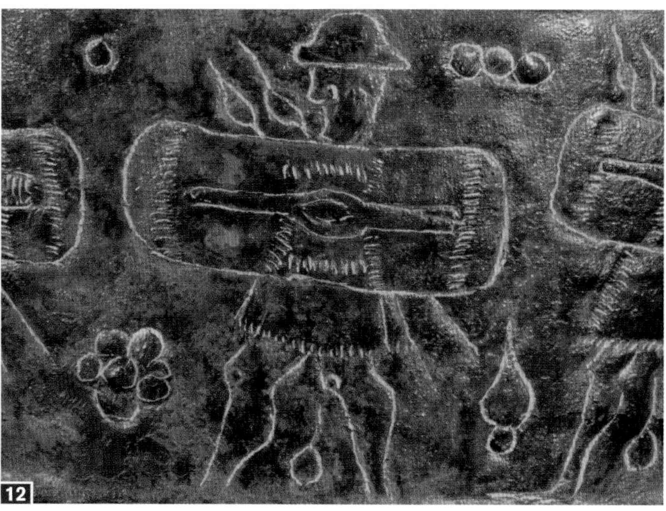
12 Etruscan soldier with rectangular shield

474 B.C.	Etruscan defeat at sea at Cumae / Rise of Rome
from 353 B.C.	Battles between Rome and Etruscan cities
310–283 B.C.	Etruscans defeated by the Romans at Vadimonian Lake
225–207 B.C.	Destruction by the Gauls and Hannibal's advance

Aeneas pays tribute to the Penates, who accompanied him from Troy to Rome

Rome: From the Beginnings to the End of the Republic 753–82 B.C.

Rome's early self-conception was derived primarily from the republican myth of its ❶ founding. Its rise followed the political fall of the Etruscans and their incorporation into the new Republic. Rome first gained control of all of Italy, then spread its hegemony throughout the Mediterranean area and into the Near East. The two pillars of Roman rule were, internally, its republican constitution, and, externally, its expansion. The first crumbled through social unrest, making possible the emergence of military dictators from Marius to Julius Caesar, but the second continued unabated as Rome continued to expand its sphere of influence.

Myth, Founding, and Early Period

The myth of its founding shaped Rome's self-image and its identity as a state. Out of the battle for military power came the disparity in status between the upper (patrician) and the lower (plebeian) classes.

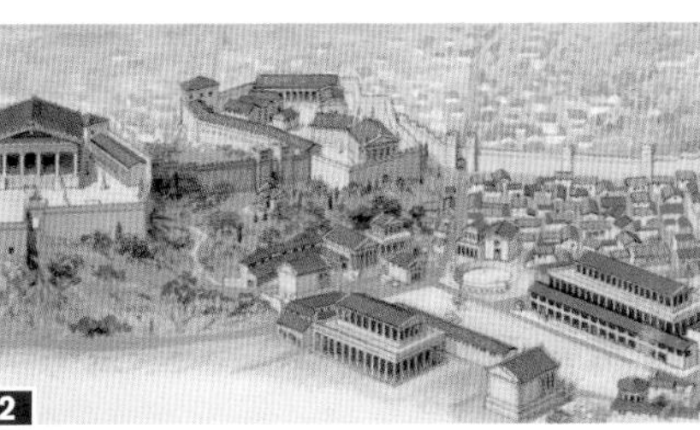
Reconstruction of the Capitol with the temple of Jupiter and Forum Romanum, end of second c. B.C.

Romulus and Remus decide where to build the city of Rome by reading the flight of birds

Reconstruction of the antique Forum Romanum as it looked after its completion, wood engraving, ca. 1880

In no other world empire did the myth of its creation play such a pivotal role in the state as in Rome. The Romans traced their ancestry back to the Trojan hero Aeneas, who—according to Virgil's *Aeneid*—landed in Italy and founded Alba Longa, the mother city of Rome. ❸ Romulus, however, is regarded as the founder—on the traditional date of April 21, 753 B.C.—and first king of Rome.

Altogether, seven kings ruled over Rome, the last of which, Tarquinius Superbus, was toppled in 510 B.C. The cause was, among other things, his son's ❺ rape of Lucretia, the wife of the nobleman Collatinus. It was his nephew, ❻ Junius Brutus, who was said to have initiated the reforms instrumental to the creation of the consulate.

The rape of Lucretia by Tarqinius Superbus's son, *Tarquin and Lucretia*, painting by Tintoretto, 1559

In reality, ❷, ❹, ❼ Rome was founded as an Etruscan colony around 650 B.C., perhaps even as late as 575 B.C. At first it was ruled by Etruscan kings from the Tarquin royal family, but after the defeat of the Etruscans at Cumae in 474 B.C., Rome disposed of their rule. Even during the time of the monarchy, Rome was characterized by the division of its citizens into "horsemen" (knights), from whom the later patrician families descended, and the masses (plebs) who made up the lower military ranks. The supreme commander of the army (*praetor maximus*) made the decisions concerning military leadership posts, all of which were soon filled by patricians. With the adoption of the Greek phalanx form of warfare, the lower ranks became increasingly important; competition for military leadership positions thereafter evolved into a struggle between patricians and plebeians over access to political offices in general and came to characterize Roman history. Early Rome, like the Greek cities, experienced severe social conflicts when, through agrarian crises and overpopulation, farmers and peasants became increasingly impoverished and were forced into bonded servitude.

6 Bust of Junius Brutus

Romulus and Remus

Romulus and Remus were the twin sons of Rhea Silvia and Mars. They were abandoned at the Tiber River and suckled by a she-wolf—which became the symbol of Rome. Romulus later struck his brother dead for jumping over the foundation walls of Rome, as no one was ever supposed to "vault" the impregnable city walls of Rome.

above: *The Capitolian She-Wolf,* Etruscan sculpture, 500 B.C.

ca. 650 B.C.	Founding of Rome by the Etruscans
509 B.C.	Establishment of the Roman Republic
ca. 450 B.C.	The Laws of Twelve Tables
21 Apr 753 B.C.	Founding of Rome according to myth
510 B.C.	Fall of Tarquinius Superbus
from 470 B.C.	Internal power struggles

The Struggle over the Constitution of the Republic

The early laws of Rome and political leadership by two consuls worked towards the realization of the balance between the patrician and the plebeian classes, which was always threatening to tip.

7 Forum Romanum: View of the temple of Saturn, built 498 B.C.

10 Roman soldier, colored lithograph, ca. 1860

The first Roman law code, the Twelve Tables, was drawn up around 450 B.C. under pressure from the plebeians. It remained the basis of Roman law up until the early emperors. It guaranteed, among other things, wide-ranging legal equality of ⓫ patricians and plebeians. The class struggle did not come to an end until 300 B.C., however, when the plebeians were granted access to the higher state offices (magistrate) and positions in the priesthood.

The political system of the new republic was geared toward creating a political balance between the patricians and the plebeians. The ❽ Senate, the supreme advisory body to the magistrate, was forced to accept plebeians. However, as the Senate remained dominated by patricians, the plebeians were granted the influential office of "tribune of the people," which publicly represented the rights of the people and allowed them their own assembly. Rome now had a mixed constitution with monarchic (magistrate), aristocratic (Senate) and democratic (people's assembly) elements.

The seminal event in the struggle for equal rights was the consulship constitution of 367 B.C. It allowed for the ❾ election of two consuls—ideally one patrician and one plebeian—for a one-year term. These two principal magistrates were joined by a *praetor* ("he who goes ahead") as the highest civil court officer and "arbitrator." The two counsuls were each elected for one year during the time of the Roman Republic. They were, in case of war, also joint supreme commanders of the armed forces, as long as no dictator was elected. The two-counsul system remained in force as well during the Roman Empire.

9 Dinar depicting a voter submitting his vote for an election

When internal stability had been reestablished after the ⓬ Gauls sacked the city in 387 B.C., Rome began building up its world empire in the third and second centuries. By subjugating the Etruscans, and with the victory over the central Italian Samnites, Rome gained control over all of Italy and was also able to assert itself in the Mediterranean against the sea powers of Sicily and Carthage. In numerous wars, Rome was able to extend its power from western Europe into Greece and the Near East. The last deadly threat to Rome was the unsuccessful Carthaginian expedition led by Hannibal against Rome between 218–201 B.C.

With its well-equipped and disciplined ❿ army, its system of Roman colonies, and its practice of conferring Roman citizenship or perpetual alliances on defeated and subjugated foes, Rome could concentrate, as Athens had done before it in the fifth and fourth centuries B.C., on the development of internal republican freedom and external expansion.

8 Senators with the son of a senator or philosopher, Fragment of a sarcophagus

11 Romulus divides the population into patricians and plebeians

12 Conquest and plundering of Rome by the Gauls under Brennus, 387 B.C., wood engraving, 19th century

367 B.C. | Constitution creates the consulship
from 3rd century B.C. | Roman expansion in the Mediterranean region
387 B.C. | Looting by the Celtic Gauls
300 B.C. | Plebeians gain access to priesthood and high offices
218–201 B.C. | Hannibal's campaign against Rome

The Crisis in the Republic

The rapid expansion of state power exacerbated the social disparities in Rome. The Senate's brutal suppression of the Gracchi land reform further aggravated the general crisis and led to social unrest which threatened to overwhelm the political structures of the Republic.

2 The death of Tiberius Gracchus, 132 B.C. Steel engraving, 19th century

By the second century B.C., Rome had built a world empire, but culturally it leaned on the traditions of other peoples. In the early period, ❹ Greek cultural influence was significant, while later the Hellenistic culture with its Oriental aspects was more important. Leading patrician families, such as the Fabians, the Julio-Claudians, and the Scipiones, who provided consuls and generals in every generation, enjoyed high esteem and ❺ wealth as a result of military fame and the spoils of war. They ruled the city with their network of clients.

The tributes of subjugated peoples and allies brought enormous amounts of money and precious metals to the city of Rome. Corruption scandals, primarily in the provincial administration, shook the republic. The inequality between the large landowners and the destitute city plebeians threatened to shatter the internal peace of Rome yet again.

3 Coin portrait of Jugurtha, king of Numidia

In 133 B.C., the Roman tribune ❻ Tiberius Gracchus sought to push through a program of land reform entailing a more just redistribution of land, putting himself in open opposition to the Senate. This program was unpopular with many of the patricians, and Tiberius was ❷ killed in 132, along with a majority of his supporters, in the civil war–like battles between the plebeians and Senate troops. His younger brother Gaius Gracchus then took over his reform proposals and planned a plebeian colony in the provinces. He provoked a national crisis when he promised full citizenship for Roman allies. Renewed attempts to revolt were crushed by the Senate and patricians, who forced Gaius to commit suicide.

Ultimately, the Senate and the consuls came out of the conflict weakened, as they had made themselves the advocates of patrician interests against the plebeians.

In this situation, external threats, especially the Jugurthine War (111–105 B.C.) against King ❸ Jugurtha of Numidia and the attacks of the Germanic ❶ Cimbri and Teutoni in northern Italy (113–101 B.C.), highlighted an unexpected explosive force with the state of Rome.

1 Battle between the Cimbri and the Romans under Marius in northern Italy, near Vercelli 101 B.C.

P. Cornelius Scipio Africanus the Elder

Publius Cornelius Scipio Africanus the Elder (ca. 235–183 B.C.), the most significant Roman general before Julius Caesar, participated in the battles against Hannibal. Entrusted with the command of the Roman troops in Spain as proconsul in 210 B.C., he drove the Carthaginians out by 206 and landed in North Africa in 204, where he defeated Hannibal at Zama in 202. Afterward, he fought in Rome's wars against Antiochus III of Syria.

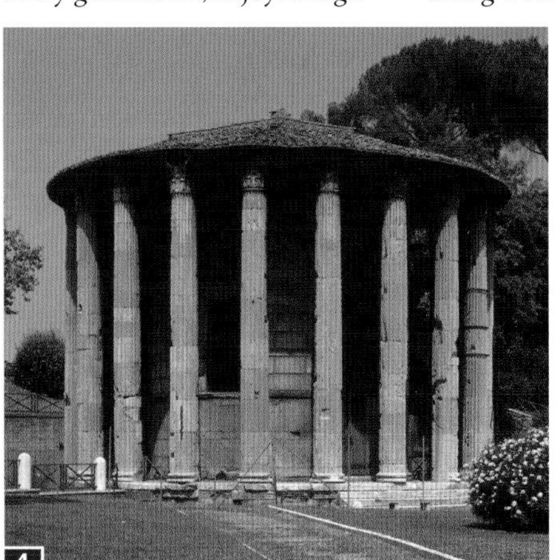

4 The Hercules temple on Forum Roarium in Rome, built in the second century B.C.

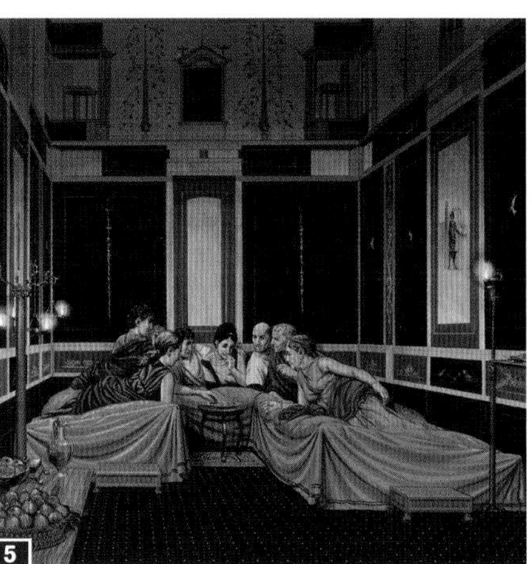

5 Roman banquet feast in the house of a wealthy citizen of Pompeii

6 Gracchus, tribune of the people, wood engraving from 1873, from a play by Adolf von Wilbrandt

133 B.C. | Land reform proposals by Tiberius Gracchus
from 133 B.C. | increased patrician–plebeian tensions
132 B.C. | Death of Tiberius
111–105 B.C. | Jugurthine War
113–101 B.C. | Battle against the Cimbri and Teutons
107 B.C. | Marius appointed consul

The Civil War

The political clashes of the generals Gaius Marius and Lucius Cornelius Sulla resulted in the Roman Civil War that divided the state. After the rule of Marius and Cinna, Sulla established a dictatorship that led to the fall of the republic.

In 107 B.C., the Senate appointed the ambitious general ❾ Gaius Marius to lead Rome in the struggle against external enemies. He completely destroyed and defeated King Jugurtha and the Germanic tribes who threatened Rome from the North. At the same time, he strove for political office, supported by the military power of his troops. He occupied the office of consul several times. Marius took up the cause of the plebeians, formed a volunteer army of semiprofessionals—with a single ensign, the Roman eagle—and opened its ranks to the innumerable destitute plebeians. After military service, these volunteers were given their own land, creating plebeian and soldier colonies in the provinces.

The Senate was split over the issue of land reform when the Italian allies revolted against Rome in 91–89 B.C. and were pacified only when granted full Roman citizenship. During these battles ❽ Lucius Cornelius Sulla particularly distinguished himself as a commander of the troops and the name "Felix"—the fortunate—was added to his name in reference to his luck in war. Sulla was elected consul in 88 B.C., but the Senate relieved him of supreme command in the war against Mithradates VI of Pontus in favor of Marius. Sulla then marched to Rome at the head of his troops, expelled ❼ Marius to Africa, and restored his command. For the first time, a military leader had dared to force his will upon the Senate through military means. The civil war had begun.

❿ Sulla had hardly marched off again to resume the war against Mithradates, when ⓫ Lucius Cornelius Cinna (consul 87–84 B.C.), an ally of Marius's, led his own army against Rome in a bid for power. Cinna occupied the city in 86 and ruled alone as dictator until he was murdered in an uprising of his troops in 84. Sulla returned to Italy the next year, and a majority of the patricians and Senate defected to his side.

In 82 B.C. Sulla entered Rome as dictator and "restorer of the state and the Senate's power." In the following years he ushered in an era of brutal persecution of his opponents. He had the followers of Marius and Cinna hunted down and killed, which led to the bloody extermination of whole families (the "proscriptions"). In 81–80 Sulla rewrote the constitution, strengthening the Senate and limiting the tribunate. Individual state offices and courts were allotted far-reaching new authority and jurisdiction. At the same time he settled 120,000 army veterans in Italy. In 79 B.C., Sulla voluntarily resigned his offices and retired to the country. He died shortly thereafter. Sulla's restoration of the old Roman constitution did not long outlive him—but the example set by him and by General Marius set a precedent for later dictatorships.

8 Lucius Cornelius Sulla, marble bust, ca. 50–40 B.C.

9 General Gaius Marius, marble bust, ca. 90 B.C.

10 Sulla triumphs over Mithradates VI's army in 86 B.C.

7 Marius after his exile by Sulla to Carthage in 87 B.C.

Description of the
Proscriptions:

"Sulla now busied himself with slaughter, and murders without number or limit filled the city. Many, too, were killed to gratify private hatreds, although they had no relations with Sulla, but he gave his consent in order to gratify his adherents."

From Plutarch's Parallel Lives

11 Cinna, depiction from Pierre Corneilles's drama, 1640

88 B.C. | Civil war between Sulla and Marius
89 B.C. | Voting rights granted to Italian allies
86–84 B.C. | Dictatorship of Cornelius Cinna
82 B.C. | Sulla claims dictatorship
81–80 B.C. | Realignment of constitution
79 B.C. | Resignation of Sulla

Biographies
The Emperors of Rome

Caesar (100–44 B.C.)
Was born in a Patrician family; Enlarged the Roman Empire in military campaigns, particularly against the Gauls; by 45, had established personal dictatorship; refused the title of king for political reasons; prepared the change from republic to a monarchical state; had his name, Caesar, adopted as a title by later emperors; was murdered during the Ides of March (March 15) 44 B.C. by a conspiracy of senators in Rome.

Augustus (Gaius Octavius) (63 B.C.–A.D. 14)
As Octavian, was adopted as the son and heir of Julius Caesar in 45 B.C.; claimed his political inheritance after the dictator's death; in 31 B.C., ended a civil war with victory over Mark Antony, a rival for the reins of power; became Augustus, Rome's first emperor, in 27 B.C.; helped Rome achieve a period of prosperity–a cultural golden age celebrated as the "Pax Augustus"; skillfully combined the appearance and rituals of republican government with absolute personal power.

Tiberius (42 B.C.–37 A.D.)
Emperor 14–37 A.D.; adopted by Augustus in 4 A.D., guaranteeing patronage and advancement; led successful military campaigns in Armenia, Rhaetia, Vindelicia, Pannonia, and Dalmatia from 20 B.C. to 9 B.C.; became emperor after a formal vote by the Senate in 14 A.D.; handed over affairs of state to the Praetorian guard prefect Sejanus between 27and 31; spent his last years on the island of Capri.

Nero (37–68)
Emperor 54–68; raised by the philosopher Seneca; reigned at first in close cooperation with the Senate on the Augustan model; had his mother and first wife murdered; ruled increasingly despotically after 62; was suspected of arson after a great fire in Rome in 64; brutally persecuted Christians; committed suicide in 68 after being declared a public enemy by the Senate due to the people's increasing hostility.

Trajan (53–117)
Emperor 98–117; was adopted the son of Emperor Nerva; became the first emperor to come from a province (Spain) in 98 A.D.; significantly extended the Roman Empire through conquests in Asia Minor, the Middle East, and Central Europe; later presided over public building projects and a major extension of the roman road network; opened the age of the adopted emperors.

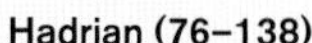

Hadrian (76–138)
Emperor 117–138; supposedly adopted by Trajan in his will; dedicated himself to securing the borders of the empire, particularly through the construction of the defensive walls (known as limes) in Britain and Germany; had the Jewish "Bar Kochba" rebellion crushed in 132; ordered the first Roman codification of laws; dedicated himself to the intellectual refinement of the Roman lifestyle and promoted education for all levels of the empire's population.

Marcus Aurelius (121–180)
Emperor 161–180; was adopted by his uncle Antoninus Pius in 138; became a significant philosopher of the Stoic school; wrote *Meditations*; successfully defended the empire in lengthy wars against the Parthians and Marcomanni; shared power with his adoptive brother Lucius Verus as coemperor; succumbed to the plague in Vindobona (modern Vienna) in 180.

Lucius Septimus Severus (146–211)
Emperor 193–211; born in Leptis Magna in North Africa; established a Roman province in Mesopotamia after defeating the Parthians; increased the power of the army and especially that of the Praetorian Guard; laid the foundations for the soldier-emperors who succeeded him; centralized the imperial administration and instigated wholesale judicial reform.

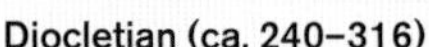

Diocletian (ca. 240–316)
Emperor 284–305; created the tetrarchy (rule of four); decentralized the empire and secured the borders against the Germanic tribes and the Persians; sought a return to traditional Roman values and the original Roman religion; initiated a systematic persecution of the Christians and Manichaeans; carried out military reforms and favored the army, which had proclaimed him emperor in 284; abdicated in 305 according to the tetrarchian order of succession.

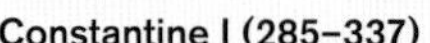

Constantine I (285–337)
Emperor 306–337; initially ruled as a tetrarch; after the Battle at the Milvian Bridge in 312, became the first emperor to adopt Christianity; extended rights of worship to the Christians; became sole ruler in the empire after defeating his last rival in 324; made efforts to bring unity to the Church; renamed Byzantium "Constantinople" in 330, declaring it the "new Rome" in the East; was a generous patron of public building projects; was baptized on his deathbed in 337.

Guiding Principles and Political Organization of the Roman Republic

left: Ruins of the Colosseum in Rome, built 72–82 A.D.

middle: Fight scene on a Trajan column, Rome, built 113 A.D.

right: Cicero before the Senate, fresco, 19th century

Since the earliest times in the history of the Roman Empire, the society and the rights of the citizens formed an integral part of the identity of the state. Even in the period of kings, there were a number of distinguishable political bodies—delegations of nobility, the priesthood, and the people—who advised the king. The monarchy was abolished around 470 B.C. and the Roman Republic was founded.

The guiding principles of the early republic were civic virtues: self-sacrifice for the public good and the equal treatment of all citizens. Early Rome relied on conservative ethics of virtue in issues of state leadership, based on *mos maiorum* (customs of the fathers). Conservative state moralists such as Cato the Elder, Cicero, and Seneca often warned their fellow citizens about turning away from "common decency," which referred less to moral behavior than to the republican principles of respect for all citizens and their interests.

In order to protect the republic from dictatorship, institutions and regulations were established to control the exercise of power. The most significant of these were the annuity (the annual rotation of consuls as head of the state) and the principle of collegiality in the administration of the state—each consul had the right to lodge a veto against the official acts of his colleagues. The supreme decision-making body of the early republic was the Senate. At first, the highest officials of the republic—the magistrates—chose the members of the Senate. The qualities required of officeholders were "dignity," social esteem, experience in service to the republic, and an irreproachable life.

Several factors served to undermine and eventually destroy this balance of power within the state. With the expansion of the empire, it became necessary to leave consuls in office for longer than the stipulated year because they were often far away from the capital carrying out affairs of state or commanding armies. As early as 327–326 B.C. there were departures from the annuity in times of crisis. This practice backfired during the rule of Marius and Sulla, who used claims of a "permanent crisis" to justify staying in the consulate indefinitely.

Another source of abuse was the traditional Roman emergency law of "rule by dictatorship." Whereas the Senate had historically implemented the law for a maximum of six months in times of crises, it was later arbitrarily extended. This was paralleled by the increasing influence of the army on state affairs. Thus the general Sulla named himself dictator for life in 82 B.C., although he gave up his office voluntarily after two years. Julius Caesar, dictator from 45 B.C., strove for the title of king and therefore was assassinated. From 27 B.C. Augustus's principate, which combined his rule as first citizen (*princeps*) with the apparent forms and institutions of the republic, confirmed an irreversible power shift from the Senate to the army.

The Rule of the Generals and Imperial Rome 74 B.C.–192 A.D.

The civil war destroyed the structure of the Roman republic. The seizure of power by the generals Pompey, ❶ Caesar, and Antonius prepared the way for the transition to autocratic imperial rule finally accomplished by Augustus. The era of imperial Rome had begun. After the dynasty of Augustus, other dynasties ruled including that of Julius Caesar and Octavian, with the emperors increasingly coming from the provinces of the empire rather than from the city of Rome itself. Diocletian's tetrarchy restored a strong system of government to the late Roman Empire.

1 Gaius Julius Caesar

Pompey, Caesar, and Crassus

The alliance of the generals Pompey and Caesar with Crassus, the richest man in Rome, ended the Republic. In the ensuing power struggle between Caesar and Pompey, it was Caesar who ultimately triumphed.

After Sulla retired as dictator in 79 B.C., two of his followers tried to seize power. ❸ Gnaeus Pompeius Magnus (Pompey the Great), as a general under Sulla, had liberated Italy's coasts from pirates. Now his political ambition awoke and in 70 B.C. he shared the consulship with Marcus Licinius Crassus, the wealthiest man in Rome. Together they repealed the major part of Sulla's constitution and reestablished the tribunate, which made them very popular in Rome.

3 Gnaeus Pompeius Magnus

After Pompey brought eastern Europe up to Asia Minor under Roman control, everyone expected him to claim the dictatorship, but the opposition of the Senate caused him to delay. Instead, Pompey and Crassus sought an ally from within Marius's powerful party of the people (p. 113). This ally was the general ❼ Gaius Julius Caesar. He was Marius's nephew and was married to Cinna's daughter. In order to get the plebeians on his side, Caesar forced the Senate to pass land reforms and purchase state lands for settlers and war veterans.

5 Caesar crossing the Rubicon River, 49 B.C.

6 Caesar's triumphal procession

As the First Triumvirate, Pompey, Crassus, and Caesar shared power in 60–59 B.C. and effectively repealed the republican constitution. They also divided the provinces among themselves: Pompey took Spain, Crassus took Syria, and Caesar took Illyria and ❷ Gaul.

When Crassus fell against the Parthians in 53 B.C., Pompey (the only consul for 52 B.C.) and Caesar faced each other in a bid for sole power. Both depended on their loyal armies and financial strength. When Pompey's followers attempted to keep Caesar away from Rome so he couldn't campaign for the consulship in 49, Caesar marched out of Gaul with his troops and crossed the ❺ Rubicon River to Rome. Civil war broke out once more, and Pompey was soon forced to flee. Caesar occupied Spain and won the decisive battle at Pharsalus (Thessaly) against Pompey. Pompey fled to Egypt, where he was ❹ assassinated when he arrived on orders of the Egyptian King Ptolemy. Caesar then ❻ entered Rome in 47 B.C. as its undisputed ruler, popular and pardoning most of his rivals.

2 Armor and weapons of Caesar's army in the Gallic War, 58–51 B.C.

4 Murder of Pompey

7 Gaius Julius Caesar

70 B.C. | Consulship of Pompey and Crassus
63 B.C. | Siege of Jerusalem
60–59 B.C. | First Triumvirate of Caesar, Pompey, and Crassus
53 B.C. | Death of Crassus
49 B.C. | Civil war between Caesar and Pompey

The Rule of Caesar to the Victory of Augustus

Caesar's dictatorship was ended by his assassination. In alliance, Antony and Octavian, Caesar's grand-nephew and heir, forcibly assumed power. Octavian eventually became sole ruler.

8 Antony and Cleopatra after the battle at Actium

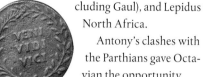

Cleopatra VII

Cleopatra VII, the last Greek ruler of Egypt from 51 B.C. and blessed with legendary beauty, successfully opposed her co-regent and brother Ptolemy XIII with the help of Rome and her lover Julius Caesar. After a stay in Rome, she removed Ptolemy XIII and elevated her son by Caesar to co-regent as Ptolemy XV (Cesarion) in 44 B.C. In 41, she became the lover of Mark Antony, who then moved to Alexandria. Both of them took their lives when Octavian entered Alexandria in 30 B.C., she using the poison of a snake.

above: *Cleopatra VII*, painting by Alexandre Cabanel, 1887

❾ Julius Caesar, supported by his clients and soldiers, solidified his power and defeated the last supporters of Pompey and the Republic in Africa, Spain, and at sea in 46–45 B.C. He then carried out wide-ranging social and legal reforms in the empire. Caesar rejected monarchical titles, but in 44 became dictator for life. However, some senators who still held republican ideals ⓭ stabbed Caesar to death while he was on his way to the Senate on March 15 (the "ides" of March), 44 B.C.

9 Coin from Caesar: "I came, saw and triumphed"

❿ Marcus Antonius (Mark Antony), one of Caesar's generals, called for the banishment of the murderers, who fled from Rome. Then the 19-year-old grand-nephew of Caesar, ⓫ Octavian, made his claim for the inheritance, and signs of a power struggle appeared. As Brutus and Cassius, two of Caesar's assassins, had won the entire east of the empire over to their cause, Octavian and Mark Antony entered into an alliance of convenience. Together with the consul Marcus Aemilius Lepidus, they formed the Second Triumvirate, which lasted from 43 to 33 B.C. In 42 they defeated the republicans at Philippi and then divided the provinces among themselves, Antony receiving the East (and, at first, Gaul), Octavian Italy and the West (eventually including Gaul), and Lepidus North Africa.

11 Bust of Octavian, ca. 40-50 A.D.

Antony's clashes with the Parthians gave Octavian the opportunity to build up his power in Rome. In 33 B.C., he was elected to the consulship, along with one of his followers. In the meantime, Antony had begun an affair with the Ptolemaic queen of Egypt, Cleopatra, to whose charms Caesar had also succumbed. This gave Octavian the excuse to fight Antony, who was married to Octavian's sister. He convinced the Senate that Antony was planning to separate the East from the rest of the Roman Empire. Even Lepidus, who was later compensated with the office of the highest priest (*pontifex maximus*), joined Octavian's side.

Using Caesar's money, Octavian armed an enormous fleet under the command of his friend ⓬ Agrippa, who destroyed the fleets of Antony and Cleopatra in 31 B.C. at ❽ Actium. The next year, Octavian occupied Egypt. With this he unified, for the first time, the empire under one man.

10 Marcus Antonius

12 Marcus Vipsanius Agrippa

13 Murder of Julius Caesar on March 15, 44 A.D., painting, 1815

48 B.C. | Victory of Caesar against Pompey

47 B.C. | Caesar becomes sole ruler

15 Mar 44 B.C. | Murder of Caesar

43–33 B.C. | Second Triumvirate of Octavian, Antony, and Lepidus

30 B.C. | Victory of Octavian over Antony and Cleopatra

The Empire under Augustus and His Family

Emperor Augustus reorganized the political structure of the Roman state. His reforms were successful and the modernized state proved stable under the rule of his successors.

In 27 B.C., the senate bestowed upon the victorious Octavian the title ❶ *augustus* ("the exalted") and the office of *princeps* ("first citizen"). He was ultimately promoted via a number of intermediary offices to the position of *imperator* ("emperor") Caesar Augustus. He was seen as the emperor of peace, a savior who was ultimately venerated as a deity. Augustus carried out a reorganization of the empire's administration, its provinces, and the tax system. He implemented strict moral and marriage laws with the aim of revitalizing the ancient civic virtues of Rome. "*Pax Augusta*"—peace in the empire and an end to all party conflicts—was declared as the highest state goal and integrated into the state religion. Augustus recognized the increasing professionalization of the military and thus set up a standing army of 28 legions. He continued Marius's and Caesar's policy of rewarding veterans with state lands.

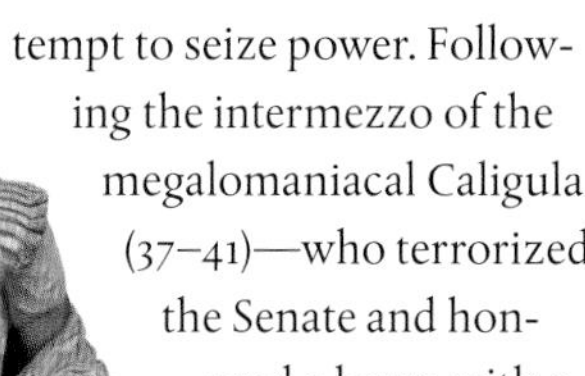

1 Augustus

2 Tiberius

3 Nero

The emperor shrewdly avoided the excessive adulation of his person. He reinforced his position as the focus of centralized power, yet always maintained good relations with the Senate. Rome's economy rapidly recovered from the decline that had resulted from the civil war. The Age of Augustus was not only one of increasing wealth but also of abundance in art and literature.

After Augustus' death in August, 14 A.D., his stepson ❷ Tiberius continued his policies. His attempts at including the Senate in the administration of the government failed, however, and he withdrew, embittered, to Capri in 27. The Praetorian Guard, an elite detail of the emperor's personal bodyguards, which later became a "state within the state," then made its first attempt to seize power. Following the intermezzo of the megalomaniacal Caligula (37–41)—who terrorized the Senate and honored a horse with a consulship—Claudius (41–54), an idiosyncratic but capable regent, became emperor. Under his rule, the transition from republic to a state centered on the emperor was completed, and parts of the British Isles were conquered. His stepson ❸ Nero (54–68) ruled wisely and benignly at first, while still under the influence of his teacher, the philosopher Seneca. But gradually he lost his grip on reality, perhaps due to his inordinate admiration of the Greeks and the cult of his person. The administration of his empire was taken over by minions. ❹ Christians were persecuted and blamed for the devastating fire in Rome in 64. With revolts in the provinces, Nero killed himself in 68, ending the Julio-Claudian dynasty.

The Peace Realm of Augustus

Virgil, The Aeneid, book 1, foretelling the reign of Augustus: "Then dire debate and impious war shall cease, / And the stern age be soften'd into peace: / Then banish'd Faith shall once again return, / And Vestal fires in hallow'd temples burn; / And Remus with Quirinus shall sustain. / The righteous laws, and fraud and force restrain...."

above: Virgil and two muses, mosaic from the house of Virgil in Hadrumetum, Sousse, Tunisia

4 Persecution of Christians after the fire in Rome in 64 A.D.

27 B.C.–14 A.D. | Economic and cultural prosperity
27 B.C. | Beginning of the Imperial Era / Honorary title "Augustus" awarded to Octavian
14–37 A.D. | Tiberius
19 Aug 14 A.D. | Death of Augustus
41–54 A.D. | Claudius
37–41 A.D. | Caligula

The Flavians and the Adopted Emperors

The Flavian dynasty consolidated the Roman Empire. The adopted emperors built on this reinforced empire and ushered in its golden age.

5 Domitian, Marble bust

6 Colosseum in Rome, construction begun under Vespasian, 72 A.D.

7 Trajan gives a speech before soldiers, Trajan column in Rome

8 Marcus Aurelius

In 69 A.D., in the vacuum left by Nero, four emperors claimed Rome. ❾ Vespasian, the governor of Judea and founder of the Flavian dynasty, prevailed. He balanced the treasury deficit through better economic administration and increased taxation—his sewer tax became known by the motto "*Pecunia non olet*" ("Money doesn't stink"). He began the construction of the ❻ Colosseum in Rome, reorganized the army, and tied the provinces closer by extending the right to citizenship. Under his successor ⓫ Titus (79–81), the cities of Pompeii and Herculaneum were destroyed by the ⓬ eruption of Mount Vesuvius. The Flavian era ended with the murder of Titus' brother and successor ❺ Domitian (81–96).

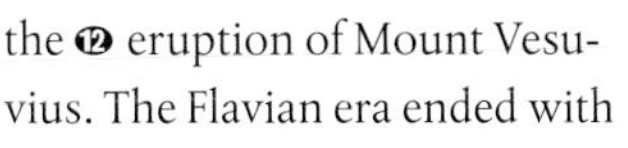

9 Portrait of Vespasian on coin

The ensuing era was that of the "adopted emperors"—each emperor adopted his most capable successor—and is considered the most humane of the Roman Empire. The rule of law was guaranteed and charities and social institutions were founded. ❼ Trajan (98–117), who was proclaimed *optimus princeps* by the Senate, was victorious in wars against the Dacians and Parthians and in North Africa, and the empire was at its most extensive.

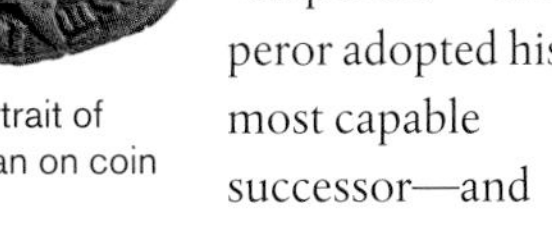

11 Titus

The era of Hadrian (117–138)—a general and admirer of Greek culture—and the peace-loving Antoninus Pius (138–161) is considered to be the golden age of the Roman Empire. Influenced by Stoicism, both aimed for a multiethnic and multicultural empire and developed a defensive foreign policy, which led to securing the borders, for example, in the form of ❿ Hadrian's Wall in Britain. ❽ Marcus Aurelius (161–180), who was sometimes referred to as the "philosopher on the emperor's throne," wanted to dedicate himself to the preservation of peace, yet was forced to wage defensive wars on the empire's borders. These were primarily against the Marcomanni, in northern Italy, and the Quadi in the Danube region, Egypt and Spain. Marcus Aurelius broke with the tradition of adoption and named his son Commodus (180–192) as successor. With Commodus' murder, however, the system of adoption collapsed.

12 Eruption of Mount Vesuvius in 79 A.D.

10 Protective wall between Solawaybusen and the mouth of the Tyne, built under emperor Hadrian, 122 A.D.

The Greek Philosophy of Stoicism

The Greek philosophy of Stoicism became popular in Rome during the 2nd century A.D. The Stoics' ethic was modesty and the conscientious performance of one's duty. Peace of mind—"stoic" calm—justice, rational self-control, and humanity were considered the highest goals. The Stoics' ideal state included the whole world and built on the equality of all men before the law of divine reason. Hadrian, Antoninus Pius, and Marcus Aurelius were all Stoics.

54–68 A.D. | Nero; persecution of Christians
68 A.D. | Nero's suicide
69 A.D. | "Year of the Four Emperors"
98–117 A.D. | Trajan
117–161 | Golden age under Hadrian and Antoninus Pius
161–180 | Philosopher-emperor Marcus Aurelius

The Severan Dynasty

Lucius Septimius Severus consolidated the power of the military within the state and thereby laid the foundations for the reign of the military emperors in the third century A.D. Under the rule of his dynasty, Eastern influences increasingly shaped Rome.

1 Caracalla

Five generals competed for the throne after Commodus's death. The North African ❸ Septimius Severus triumphed in 193. He consolidated the empire, reorganized its finances, and equalized the status of the inhabitants of Italy and the provinces. Septimius Severus transformed the empire into a military monarchy by ignoring the Senate, replacing the Praetorian Guard with his own troops, and appointing loyal military men to increasingly powerful civil offices. He thus led the way for the military emperors that would follow.

His son ❶ Caracalla murdered his co-regent and brother Geta in 212 and encouraged a fusion of Roman and Eastern cults. Supported by the army and the Praetorian Guard, his was a reign of terror. When he failed in his campaign against the Parthians, he was assassinated by the commander of the Praetorians, Macrinus, who himself became emperor in 217–218.

The rule of Caracalla's Syrian cousin ❷ Elagabalus (Heliogabalus, 218–222), a priest of the sun god of Emesa (Elah-Gabal), was a new low point for the Roman emperors. He held extravagant nocturnal celebrations and founded secret cults. His attempt to make the Syrian sun cult the official state cult undermined the identity of the Roman Empire.

2 Elagabalus

His cousin Alexander Severus (222–235) who was born in Palestine tried another course. He strengthened the Senate and, advised by the lawyer Ulpian, governed strictly in accordance with old Roman law. However, it became clear that the emperor could no longer rule against the will of the military and the Praetorian Guard. After the Praetorians ❹ murdered Ulpian in 228, Alexander Severus and his mother, who had great influence over her young son, fell victim to an assassination plot of his officers after his luckless expeditions to Mesopotamia and Egypt and against the Germanic Marcomanni. The army finally achieved total control of the Roman Empire.

The Severan Women

The Severan women consistently played an important role in the reigns of their male relatives. The wife of Septimius Severus, Julia Domna, daughter of the sun-priest Bassianus of Emesa, was highly respected and established a circle of scholars around her. Her sister Julia Maesa was the grandmother of the emperors Elagabalus and Alexander Severus and energetically campaigned for their coronation. Her daughters Julia Soaemias and Julia Mamaea, both mothers of Roman emperors, exercised great influence on the rule of their sons, with whom they were both murdered.

above: Julia Domna, marble bust, ca. 210 A.D.

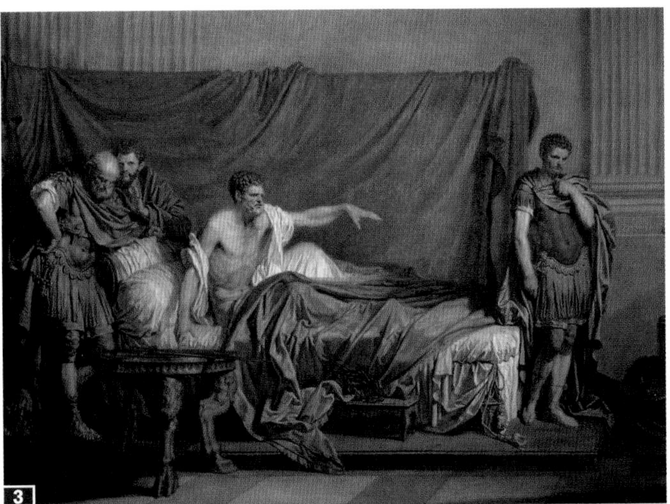

3 Emperor Septimius Severus accuses his son Caracalla of an attempted murder

4 Ulpian's murder before Emperor Severus and his mother, wood engraving, 1876

193 | Septimus Severus founds the Severan dynasty
212–217 | Caracalla rules
218–222 | Cultural decline under Emperor Elagabalus
222–235 | Revitalization under Alexander Severus
235 | Beginning of rule of the military emperors

The Military Emperors 235–284

The period of military emperors (235–284 A.D.), with its unclear succession rules and rapid changes of emperors and usurpers, was extremely unsettled. Only the last of the military emperors were able to achieve stability within the empire.

The 50 years that constituted the rule of the military emperors is also called the "crisis of the third century." It was an extremely turbulent era: 26 emperors and 40 usurpers were crowned—and murdered. Many of the emperors were officers of Illyrian-Pannonian origin; most were at war throughout their reigns. Often, competing emperors appeared and the empire fell apart. Rome was being forced into the defensive; from the beginning of the third century Germanic tribes, primarily the Goths, threatened the empire from the west. By the middle of the century, the Danube region, Asia Minor, and Greece had all been lost. In the Middle East, the newly founded Persian Empire of the Sassanids forced the Romans into retreat there. Emperor Valerian (253–260) was captured by the Persians after a crushing ❺ defeat in 260. In 258 the usurper Postumus separated Gaul from the empire and founded a Gallo-Roman Empire that survived him. The Syrian governor of ⓫ Palmyra, Odaenathus, declared himself independent and forced Rome to recognize him as "governor of all the East." After his death, his widow ❽ Zenobia took the title of empress.

6 Marcus Aurelius Probus

8 Zenobia, Queen of Palmyra, after her arrest by Emperor Aurelian, painting, 1878

10 The Aurelian Wall

It was the last of the soldier-emperors that finally restored stability to the empire. ❾ Claudius II Gothicus (268–270) held off an invasion of the Alemanni in northern Italy and triumphed over the Goths on the Danube. Aurelian (270–75), the most significant military emperor, had the ❿ Aurelian Wall built around Rome and drove the Goths out of upper Italy for good in 270–271. He then marched into the Orient and destroyed the Kingdom of Palmyra (273) and reincorporated Egypt into the Roman Empire. Aurelian reorganized the economy and administration and installed the cult of the Syrian god *Sol Invictus* ("Unconquered Sun") as the unifying cult of the empire; the festival for this god on December 25 was later adopted by the Christians as Christmas. After Aurelian, ❻ Probus (276–282) pacified the recently reclaimed Gaul and pushed the Franks back across the Rhine, which was once again defended as the empire's border. He also settled Germanic tribes as colonists or took them into the ranks of his army. After his ❼ murder, conditions once again became unstable until Diocletian—building on the achievements of Aurelian and Probus—gave the empire a new character.

5 Triumph of Shapir I, king of the Sassanids, over the Roman Emperors Philippus and Valerian in the battle near Edessa in 260

7 Aurelian is murdered near Byzantium in 275

9 Claudius II Gothicus

11 View of Palmyra in Syria

258 | Separate Gallo-Roman empire
260 | Persian captivity of Emperor Valerian
268–270 | Consolidation under Claudius II Gothicus
270–275 | Aurelian
278 | Securing of the Rhine as border of the empire

The Dominate: Diocletian and the System of the Tetrarchy

Diocletian restored the strength of Rome. His dual reign with Maximian and eventually the system of the imperial tetrarchy effectively dealt with an empire that was gradually pulling itself apart.

In November 284, ❶, ❷, ❹ Diocletian, a guard commander of humble origins, seized power and imbued the empire with a new order, thus ending the "crisis of the third century." As war broke out again in Gaul, he made his comrade-in-arms Maximian his co-regent (*caesar*) in 285 and, after he had successfully suppressed the rebellion in Gaul in 286, co-emperor (*augustus*). His rule was initially precarious; he had to simultaneously fight attacks on the Roman borders while stamping out civil unrest within the state.The two emperors divided their duties. Diocletian's main interests lay in an overall reform of the administration and the army. The tax system, the salaries of public officials, and the courts were all completely reorganized, and the provinces were granted greater authority, which contributed to the decentralization of the empire that began to emerge. In the meantime, Maximian rushed from one war to another.

3 "The Tetrarchs," relief at San Marco, Venice, interpreted as Diocletian, Valerius, Maximian and Constantinus

5 Depiction of the Apostle Paul in a mural found in one of the Roman catacombs in which Christians hid

1 Portrait of the Emperor Diocletian, coin

When Britain separated itself from the empire under local usurpers in 286–287 and revolts broke out in the Near East, Diocletian recognized that the empire was no longer capable of being centrally governed and in 293 installed the system of ❸ tetrarchy ("rule of four"). Both regents adopted successors, who were to reign as caesars (junior emperors) and, when the emperors retired, would take their place. Diocletian and Maximian chose, respectively, ❼ Galerius and Constantius I Chlorus as caesars, and the tetrarchs divided their authority regionally. Diocletian, as augustus of the East, ruled from Thrace to the Near East and Egypt, with his capital at Salona (modern Split); Galerius was given the Danube provinces and Greece; Maximian, as augustus of the West, controlled Italy, Spain, and North Africa from his capital in Milan; and Constantius received Gaul and Britain. In conflicts of interest, Diocletian as "senior augustus" had the final word. For 20 years, the system demonstrated an astounding stability, until Diocletian decided that he and Maximian would retire on May 1, 305, and Galerius and Constantius would move up to the position of augusti.

The emperors held to the old Roman deity cult as state ideology and demanded veneration as divine rulers. The Christians' refusal to obey this demand led to their persecution in 299, which intensified between 303 and 305. The Christians were forced to hide in the ❺ catacombs of Rome, and ❻ Diocletian's memory was thereafter reviled in Christian historiography. Nevertheless, he had restored the power of Rome.

2 Diocletian

4 **above left**: Portrait of Diocletian **above:** Jupiter with eagle and small goddess of victory on the reverse side of the same golden coin

6 Reconstruction of Diocletian's palace, which he built around 300 for his retirement in Split near Salona, Dalmatia

286-287 | Britain secedes from the empire

303–305 | Intense persecution of Christians

284–305 | Rule of the two emperors by Diocletian and Maximian

293 | New system of succession ("tetrarchy")

Collapse of the Tetrarchy and the Victory of Constantine and Licinius

The power struggle between the contenders resulted in the collapse of the tetrarchy after 306. With the victory of Constantine the Great and Licinius, the Christians gained their first recognition by the state, and the process by which Christianity became the religion of the Roman Empire began.

8 Portrait of Constantine the Great on a coin

7 Galerius convincing Diocletian to make him caesar

From Galerius's Edict of Toleration of 311:

"Wherefore, for this our indulgence, they ought to pray to their god for our safety, for that of the republic, and for their own, that the republic may continue uninjured on every side, and that they may be able to live securely in their homes."

The tetrarchy was already teetering by 305 because Maximian, in contrast to Diocletian, was reluctant to give up power; furthermore, in addition to his adopted son Constantius, Maximian had a biological son, the ambitious Maxentius, who sought power. While the change of rule ran smoothly in the East and Galerius raised Maximinus Daia to caesar, in the West it came to bitter conflicts. When Constantius, who had stopped the persecution of Christians in his realm, died in 306, his biological son ❽ Constantine, supported by his father's army, seized the imperial throne. Maxentius protested and had himself declared emperor by the Praetorians in Rome. The senior augustus Galerius sent his troops against him but ❾ Maxentius was victorious, and thus a five-year struggle for control of the western Roman Empire began between Constantine and Maxentius.

The situation intensified in 308 when Galerius declared ❾ Licinius augustus of the West. Licinius recognized Constantine as his caesar and convinced Galerius, who had been a persecutor of Christians, to issue an edict of religious tolerance in 311 to bring the Christians to support him—the first official recognition of the Christians by a Roman emperor. Together, Licinius and Constantine were able to prevail against their enemies. In 312 Constantine, who openly favored the Christians, moved with his legions against Rome and defeated Maxentius' troops at the ❿ Milvian Bridge, although his troops were outnumbered by Maxentius's by at least two to one. The next year, Licinius triumphed in the east against Maximinus Daia, also with the aid of Christian soldiers. The victors divided the empire among themselves, Constantine ruling the West and Licinius the East. A new era had begun in the Roman Empire; one which was much more favorable for the Christians.

9 **above:** Maxentius on a coin; **left:** Licinius on a coin

The Victory at the Milvian Bridge in 312

Constantine's politically calculated move to send his troops into battle wearing the Christogram XP—the initials of Christ—was glorified by the early Christian authors Lactanz and Eusebius of Caesarea. Eusebius in his Vita Constantini reported that Constantine, whose troops were significantly outnumbered by those of Maxentius, dreamed before the battle that the sign of the cross appeared in the heavens before him and a voice called, "In hoc signo vincis!" ("In this sign thou shalt triumph").

10 The Battle at the Milvian Bridge, 312 A.D.

306–337 | Constantine I

313 | Victory of Licinius over Maximinus Daia

1 May 305 | Resignation of Diocletian and Maximian

311 | Official recognition of Christianity

313–324 | Joint rule of Constantine (West) and Licinius (East)

From Constantine to the Rise of Byzantium 312–867

In 313 A.D., ❶ Constantine and Licinius issued an edict of tolerance in Milan, putting the Christian religion on equal footing with existing Roman cults. Less than a century later, Christianity would become the state religion of Rome. Constantine was the first to use it as an instrument to strengthen his rule, subjecting the Church to strict political control, a practice followed by his successors. The de facto division of the empire into a Western (Roman) and Eastern (Byzantine) became permanent in 395. While the Roman Empire declined, Byzantium rose as a new power in its own right.

1 Marble bust of Constantine I, the Great

2 The Christian symbol of the fish, early Christian mosaic, fourth c.

Constantine the Great

In 324 Constantine was able to establish sole rule and reorganize the empire. He encouraged Christianity in all areas.

Following the ❺ victory over their opponents in 313, Constantine and Licinius divided the empire between them and issued the Edict of Milan, which guaranteed ❷ Christians the right to practice their religion. Cooperation between the two did not last long, however. From 316 on, military clashes between the adversaries took place. Constantine ultimately triumphed and exiled Licinius.

Constantine increasingly saw himself as the representative of the Christian god and protector of Christianity. He clearly recognized the potential of the new religion and wanted to tie it into the Roman ideology of the state. He reimbursed the Church for confiscated property and financed the construction of ❹, ❻ churches. However, the ❸ "Donation of Constantine" of state-owned land to the church is a myth resulting from a document forged around 850.

Constantine implemented many new laws that were influenced by Christian standards. He repealed punishment such as gladiatorial service, maiming, and limited slavery and passed relatively progressive marriage and family laws. By emphasizing the divine right of kings, he reinforced the role of religious legitimacy in imperial rule. Any offense against a Christian emperor became sacrilege toward God and God's order. The emperor not only intervened in Church politics, but also had the final say concerning matters of faith. Many Christians began to identify with the empire that had previously persecuted them and sought to participate in its affairs. The Church adopted many organizations and state offices into its own structures.

5 Constantine arc, 315 A.D., christened after Constantine's victory over Maxentius at the Milvian Bridge

Excerpt from a Eulogy from the "*Panegyrici Latini*"

"You have, Constantine, indeed some secret with the godly spirit, who, after He has left to the lower gods all concern about us, only you He has dignified by showing himself to you directly. Otherwise, bravest Emperor, give account of how you have triumphed."

3 *The Donation of Constantine*, fresco, 1246

4 The Constantine basilica in Rome, christened by Constantine in 330

6 The Grave Church in Jerusalem, christened in 326

313 | Edict of Tolerance of Milan

314 | Donatist disputes

321 | Sunday introduced as Christian day of rest

324 | Constantine the Great reigns alone

325 | Council of Nicaea called

Constantine's Successors

A fratricidal war destabilized the empire after Constantine's death. Ultimately Constantius II was able to continue his father's policies successfully. The attempt of Julian the Apostate to revert to paganism remained an aberration.

7 Baptism of Constantine the Great by Pope Sylvester I, fresco, 1246

In 330 Constantine renamed the city of Byzantium ⓫ Constantinople as the new capital of the Roman-Christian empire. By 335 he had instituted a system of imperial succession influenced by Diocletian's tetrarchy: His oldest and second sons, Constantine II and Constantius II, were to be augusti, while his youngest son Constans and his nephew Dalmatius would be caesars. However, when Constantine died in 337 in the initial stages of a planned military excursion to Persia, a few days after he had accepted a Christian ❼ baptism, all three of his sons assumed the title of augustus.

A murderous fratricidal war flared up, during which ❿ Constantius II, son of his father's first wife Fausta, had all his relatives by his father's second marriage killed. Out of the struggle for power he emerged triumphant. After he had repulsed the attacking Persians, he actively continued his father's church policies. Because the quarrel over Arianism and other early splinter groups of Christianity threatened to destabilize the empire, Constantius attempted to foster politico-religious unity by particularly emphasizing the overarching position of the Christian emperor. His court ceremonies already bore the features of the ruler's religious zeal that were later characteristic of the Byzantine Empire.

10 Constantius II

Constantius's successor in 361 was his cousin ❽, ❾ Julian, who had held the office of caesar of the West since 355 and had assumed the title of augustus against Constantius in 360. The philosophical and highly educated Julian is one of the tragic figures of late antiquity. Due to his enthusiasm for Greek philosophy and the greatness of ancient Rome, he lost his faith, reverted to paganism and attempted to suppress Christianity and install a neo-Platonic sun cult. He did not persecute the Christians, but his attempt to turn back time led to unrest in the empire. When he fell in battle against the Persians in June 363, his new sun cult broke up and the Christian historians damned him as "the Apostate." His death marked the end of rule by Constantine's dynasty.

Arianism

Arianism, as formulated by the Alexandrian priest Arius, taught that Jesus Christ was divine, but only of like substance to God and there had been a time when he was not of divine substance. The teachings that were finally accepted at the council at Nicaea in 325 were formulated by Athanasius, who stated that Christ "was consubstantial ["of one substance"] and uncreated and co-eternal with the Father." Nonetheless, the "Arian heresy" continued and split Christianity between the 4th and 7th centuries, as some emperors and many of the Germanic peoples were adherents of Arianism.

above: The council at Nicaea 325 in Iznik, fresco, ca. 1600

8 Emperor Julian the Apostate, fresco, ca. 1320/25

9 Julian Apostata, coin portrait

11 Constantine founds Byzantium's new capital under the name Constantinople in 330

337 | Christian baptism of Constantine
363 | Julian dies
330 | Constantinople founded as new imperial capital
361 | Julian the Apostate comes to power

Christianity

Since its beginnings as a Jewish sect, Christianity became established as one of the five main world religions as a result of its interaction with Greco-Roman culture and philosophy. Christianity, particularly in its organized form as a church, has played an important role in world history since its inception, whether as a state religion or as a powerful competitor to secular authority. It wasn't until the separation of church and state in the modern era that the Church lost its direct influence on political events.

1 The Virgin Mary and John witness Christ's crucifixion, mural, ca. 740

2 The Good Shepherd, fresco in Catacomb of Calixtus, Rome, third c.

The Central Message and the Early Church

The Christian image of God is based on that of Judaism; both believe in a benevolent creator and preserver of the world who also demands of man an accounting for his actions. Christianity's central message, however, is the belief in the incarnate son of God, Jesus Christ, who suffered and ❶ died on the cross for the salvation of mankind and was resurrected. His story and message are recorded in the four ❸ Gospels of the New Testament, which is the basis of Christian belief.

3 Handwritten Gospel of John on papyrus, end of the second century

Early Christianity engaged in an intensive spiritual debate with its Jewish and Greco-Roman rivals. Under the influence of the ❺ Apostle Paul, the Church decided upon an active mission to disseminate its message to the heathens and throughout the world. Up until the seventh century, the Church struggled with the definition of its image of God and its role in the world. Often this resulted in wars and persecution. Socio-politically, early Christianity wavered between the commandment of brotherly love, which required active engagement in the world, and the anticipation of the forthcoming Kingdom of God that is "not of this world." The claim of God and Jesus Christ to exclusive divine status kept the Christians, like the Jews, from participating in Roman cults that the Roman Empire mandated in order to maintain the loyalty of all peoples and cultures in the empire.

5 The Apostle Paul, founder of the Church, Serbian mural, ca.1265

4 The Benedictine abbey Monte Cassino, Italy, founded in 529 by St. Benedict of Norcia

Christianity in the Roman Empire

The Christians proselytized in all of the larger cities of the empire, including Rome, so that by the end of the second century A.D. there were already numerous congregations. As they were suspected of disloyalty to the rulers, the Christians often experienced fierce persecution and took refuge in the ❷ catacombs of the cities; when discovered, they most often chose a ❼ martyr's death in keeping with the image of the suffering Jesus and apostles before them. At this time, however, a stable structure emerged that allowed the Church to survive. The "Constantinian Change" occurred with the edicts of tolerance of 311 and 313 and the further policies of Constantine the Great. Christianity became the official religion of the Roman Empire. In the Eastern Roman Empire of Byzantium, the Christian doctrine of salvation was combined with the ancient cult of the ruler, and the emperor became the preordained advocate of the fate of man.

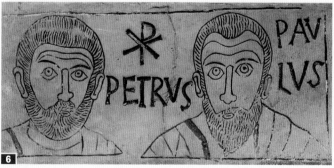

6 The Apostles Peter and Paul, tombstone, after 313

7 Christians condemned to die as martyrs await their death in the arena

ca. 29–31 A.D.	Crucifixion of Christ
until 40	Gospel of Mark is written
64	Persecution of Christians under Emperor Nero
311–13	Constantine the Great's Edict of Tolerance
800	Charlemagne becomes emperor
1054	Eastern Schism
1095	Start of the Crusades

Charlemagne is crowned emperor by Pope Leo III on December 25, 800 in St Peter's Cathedral

The Middle Ages and the Rise of the Papacy

In the early Middle Ages, a surge in the development of European civilization and education was sparked by the work of Christian monastic orders. As a result of endowments, the ❹ monasteries also became powerful landowners. The conversion to Catholicism of the previously Arianist Germanic peoples in the fifth to seventh centuries strengthened the position of the bishop of Rome, the pope. Primarily through his alliance with France, the pope had won independence from Byzantium and built up a papal claim to jurisdictional primacy as the successor of the Apostle ❻ Peter. From the time of the ❽ imperial coronation of Charlemagne by the pope in 800, popes and the Holy Roman Emperors were closely tied. The estrangement from Byzantium led to a schism in 1054 between the papal Western church and the Eastern Orthodox Church, which endures to the present. The ❾ Crusades to the Holy Land initiated by the Western church between 1095 and the 13th century exemplified Christianity's most intolerant and violent side.

With the ⓫ Investiture Controversy in the eleventh and twelfth century, the Church won far-reaching independence from lay interference. Under Pope Innocent III (1198–1216), the papacy reached the zenith of its worldly power—until it went too far. The exile of the popes to Avignon from 1309 to 1377 and the Great Schism of 1378–1417 highlighted that reforms were necessary.

Emperor Henry IV, front, asks Mathilda of Tuscany to mediate in his conflict with Pope Gregory VII in the Investiture Controversy, book illustration

Martin Luther at the Imperial Diet of Worms, 1521

From the Reformation to the Enlightenment

The Reformation in the 16th century was a period of social as well as religious upheaval that can be considered the beginning of the Modern Era. In an attempt to return to the original message of the Gospels and prevent abuses of power by the Church, a number of Protestant churches sprang up. The most important among these were the Lutherans, followers of ❿ Martin Luther; the Reformists, followers of Huldrych Zwingli; and the Calvinists, followers of John Calvin. The first religious wars were ended by the laboriously negotiated Peace of Augsburg in 1555, but the religious disputes broke out violently again in the French Wars of Religion, and above all during the Thirty Years' War.

In the 17th and 18th centuries, Christianity and the churches in Europe found themselves on the defensive as a result of renewed self-awareness resulting from the Enlightenment and the start of the Industrial Revolution. In the 19th century, they allied themselves with the powers of political conservatism. It was only later that they recognized the necessity of reacting to labor issues and socialism. In the "battle for culture" in many countries, the churches lost the supervision of the educational institutions of modern society.

The conquest of Jerusalem by the First crusade under the leadership of Godfrey of Bouillon on the Jul y 15, 1099, book illustration, 14th century

The Churches in the 20th Century and Beyond

In the 20th century, the Eastern Orthodox Church experienced a period of widespread suppression between 1917 and 1991—or an authoritarian binding into the system of "socialism as it was actually practiced." The churches in Western and Central Europe wavered between currying favor with authoritarian regimes and suppression at their hands. After 1945, the Catholic Church reconciled with the Western democracies and opened to the modern age with the ⓬ Second Vatican Council (1962–1965). Protestantism experienced an upswing, particularly in the United States.

Since the late 20th century, the Catholic Church has focused on the "young churches" of Latin America and Africa. In Central Europe the Church is largely limited to a role in community work and providing ethical cues. Whether there will be a return to the Church in post-communist Eastern Europe remains unclear.

Celebration following the end of the Second Vatican Council in Rome, 1965

1378–1417 | Great Schism
1555 | Peace of Augsburg
17th–18th century | Enlightenment
until 1122 | Investiture Controversy
1517 | Beginning of the Reformation
1618–48 | Thirty Years' War
1962–65 | Second Vatican Council

The Roman Empire under Valentinian and Theodosius

The emperors Valentinian I and Theodosius the Great strengthened the Roman Empire for the last time. While Valentinian undertook an internal consolidation, Theodosius made Christianity the state religion.

1 Portrait bust of a youth, believed to be Emperor Gratian or Valentinian II

3 Theodosius I (the Great)

5 The patriarch Ambrosius absolves Emperor Theodosius, painting, 18th century

The rise of Christianity was not greeted favorably everywhere in the empire, and the reaction of Julian the Apostate had met with some approval, above all in the circles of the old Roman elite. However, Christianity as the religion of the empire did not collapse, and the empire was able to withstand the onslaught of the Germanic tribes once more due to the policies of the emperors Valentinian and Theodosius.

In February 364, the officer ❹ Valentinian was declared emperor. At the request of his army, he made his younger brother, Valens, who resided in Constantinople, co-emperor in the East. Valentinian dedicated himself first to the urgently needed strengthening of the empire's borders. In Gaul he pushed the invading Alemanni back across the Rhine and erected border fortifications from the North Sea to Rhaetia. Then he initiated his financial policies, which demanded extreme austerity and economizing and found little favor with the Roman upper class.

His brother in the East had to contend with ❻ Goths and Persians. In 376 he settled the Visigoths in Thrace, but they pushed down to Greece. A military confrontation was unavoidable. His nephew Gratian hurried to his aid with imperial troops, but Valens did not wait and was defeated by the Visigoths in 378 at the Battle of Adrianople. He was killed, and the Goths took Eastern Europe.

Valentinian's successor in the West was his son ❶ Gratian, but general ❸ Theodosius I (the Great) held political leadership, and Gratian selected him as augustus of the East in January 379. Theodosius then concluded a treaty with the Visigoths in 382, granting them territory south of the lower Danube as "federates" of the empire. After Gratian's death, Theodosius dedicated himself to the complete Christianization of the empire, fought against heathen cults and in 392 confirmed the theology of the Nicaean council and Rome as the religion of the empire. Gratian and Theodosius were the first emperors to discard the traditional title of pontifex maximus, which the pope now assumed, and to ❺ subject themselves to the decisions of the Church. Theodosius was religiously and politically visionary and an honest ruler, but his decision to call upon Teutonic army commanders for aid against the usurper ❷ Eugenius left a difficult legacy for his successors.

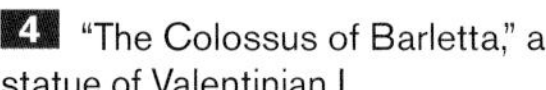

4 "The Colossus of Barletta," a statue of Valentinian I

2 Emperors Eugenius and Theodosius I holding a symbol of victory

6 Peace agreement between the Goths and Emperor Valens, 369

364 | Crowning of Emperor Valentinian I / Brother Valens co-emperor in East
376 | Visigoths settle in Thrace
378 | Battle of Adrianople
379 | Theodosius co-emperor in Constantinople
382 | Peace treaty with Visigoths
383 | Theodosius the Great rules alone

The End of the Western Roman Empire

In 395 the empire was irrevocably divided into the Western and Eastern empires. Until the end of the Western Empire in 476, the emperors were dominated by Teutonic army commanders.

7 Arcadius, son of Theodosius the Great, marble bust, ca. 395

8 Tomb of the Empress Galla Placidia in Ravenna, finished ca. 450

When Theodosius died in January 395, he left the empire divided among his sons. The elder, ❼ Arcadius, received the eastern part with Constantinople; the younger, Honorius, received the western Roman half. The sons and grandsons of Theodosius were for the most part dependent on their Teutonic commanders. Honorius, who shifted the Western capital from Rome to Ravenna in 402, was dominated by his imperial general Flavius Stilicho, a Vandal who from 395 held back the Germanic tribes. The impending invasion of the Visigoth Alaric into Italy evoked an anti-German backlash in Rome and led to Stilicho's execution in 408. Shortly after this, Alaric sacked ❾ Rome in August, 410.

Valentinian III, the last emperor of Theodosian dynasty, was under the influence of his mother ❽ Galla Placidia, who served as

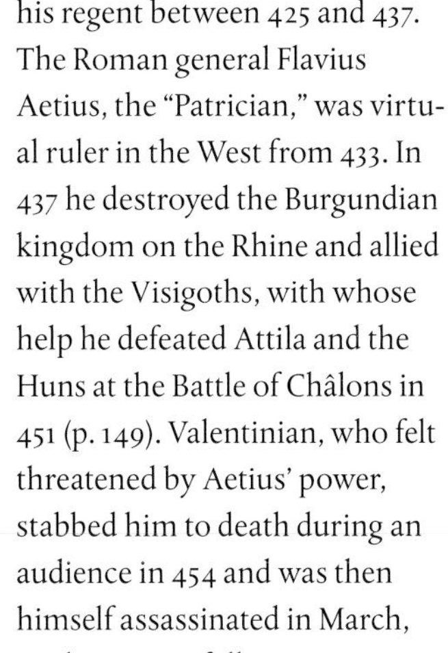

his regent between 425 and 437. The Roman general Flavius Aetius, the "Patrician," was virtual ruler in the West from 433. In 437 he destroyed the Burgundian kingdom on the Rhine and allied with the Visigoths, with whose help he defeated Attila and the Huns at the Battle of Châlons in 451 (p. 149). Valentinian, who felt threatened by Aetius' power, stabbed him to death during an audience in 454 and was then himself assassinated in March, 455 by Aetius' followers.

Thereafter, the decline of the Western Empire took on a rapid pace, particularly as the relationship to the Eastern Empire, which was growing in strength, had been tense since 450. Finally, in 475 Romulus Augustulus ("Little

9 The conquest of Rome by the Visigoths led by Alaric, 410

Augustus") ascended the throne in Ravenna. When Odoacer, a Germanic prince, conquered Ravenna in 476, he ❿ dethroned the last emperor and exiled him. Odoacer became the first barbarian king of Italy, and with that the Latin Western Empire had come to an ignominious end; now the only Roman emperor was the emperor of Byzantium.

Odoacer

Odoacer of the Sciri entered the service of the Western Empire in 470 as a mercenary and, militarily victorious, was declared king by his followers. In 476 he deposed the last Western Roman emperor and gained from the Eastern Empire tacit recognition as ruler of Italy. By strengthening the Senate, he was able to shrewdly balance the Romans and the Germans in Italy. He also reconciled with Catholicism, although he was Arian, and fought off other Germanic tribes. Eventually, the Eastern Empire sent the Ostrogoths under Theodoric against him. At a banquet supposedly designed to celebrate a reconciliation in Ravenna on March 15, 493, he was assassinated by Theodoric.

above: Odoacer's murder in Ravenna on March 15, 493

10 The Germanic army commander Odoacer dethrones Romulus Augustulus in 476, wood engraving, ca. 1880

392 | Christianity becomes state religion
395 | Empire divided in East and West
395–423 | Honorius is West Roman emperor
395–408 | Arcadius is East Roman emperor
451 | Aetius defeats the Huns under Attila
476 | "Romulus Augustulus" dethroned

The Consolidation of the Byzantine Empire

After 450, the emperors of Byzantium were able to strengthen the empire and assert their claim to rule in Europe. As capital of the Eastern Empire, Constantinople assumed the legacy of fallen Rome.

1 The council at Chalcedon, 451 A.D.

Under Theodosius' weak heirs, the Eastern Empire was coming to ruin as a result of enormous tribute payments to the Huns and German princes and was heading for a fate similar to the Western Empire. This changed quite suddenly when a period of capable rule began with Marcian in 450. Marcian refused to pay tribute to the Huns and was able to force them off to the West. Through confederation pacts with the Visigoths and the Gepids, while fending off Arab tribes in Syria and Palestine, he was able to consolidate the empire. In 451 he convoked a ❶ council at Chalcedon in order to condemn Monophysitism, which was dividing the empire.

Church historian Socrates (died ca. 450), describing the

Wealth of Constantinople

"Many come to Constantinople; for the city, although she feeds tremendous masses, has good reserves: By sea she imports from everywhere necessary, but the Black Sea, which is very near, supplies her with an inexhaustible supply of cereal, if she needs this."

Marcian's successor Leo I strengthened Orthodoxy and took up the fight against Aspar, the German general who had been all-powerful in the empire since 424. He created the Isaurian Guard, an elite force made up of Isaurians—a warrior mountain tribe from his homeland—and defeated Aspar in 471, ending the dominance of Germanic generals in the Eastern Empire. His son-in-law Zeno, who was also Isaurian, developed ❸ Constantinople into a new "center of the world" after the fall of Rome. Zeno was more of a diplomat than a warrior and so sent Theodoric, his "son-in-arms," to Italy in 488, where he eventually deposed Odoacer and officially placed Italy under the sovereignty of the Eastern Empire.

2 Emperor Anastasius I, ivory diptych, beginning of the sixth century

3 Constantinople (Istanbul): View over the Bosporus

Now the militarily strengthened empire needed a new internal structure. For the first time, a high administrative official, ❷ Anastasius, assumed the throne in 491. First, he dismissed the Isaurians in favor of the traditional administrative elite and fortified the empire against the Persians and the Bulgarians. Anastasius stood out for his humane legislation and through economical administration was able to accumulate immense state reserves.

❹ Justinian I was able to build on these achievements and, as emperor from 527, led Byzantium to its first golden age. A well-educated Illyrian farmer's son, Justinian had held a leading position in state affairs under his uncle Emperor Justin I (518–527), and in 525 married the actress ❺ Theodora, who proved to be of vital support and virtually coreigned with him.

4 Emperor Justinian with entourage, mosaic, before 547

5 Empress Theodora with entourage, mosaic, ca. 547

450–457	East Roman Emperor Marcian
451	Council of Chalcedon
457–474	Leo I
476–491	Zeno
489	Victory of Theodoric over Odoacer
491–518	Anastasius

The Empire under Justinian and Heraclius

Under Justinian I, Byzantium became the leading power in Europe both politically and culturally. Heraclius reorganized the empire and gave Byzantium a structure that endured to its end.

7 *Mother of God of Vladimir*, icon from Constantinople, 12th–13th century

In foreign affairs, Justinian pursued the establishment of Byzantine dominance in the West, repulsion of the Persians in the East, and above all the elimination of the restless Germanic tribes. The kingdoms of the Vandals in North Africa (533–534) and the Ostrogoths in Italy (551–553) came under Byzantine rule.

In keeping with the idea of ❽, ⓫ imperial divine rule, Justinian elaborated Byzantine court ceremonies in a strongly religious vein ("caesaropapism") and subjugated the patriarchs and popes of Constantinople and Rome. Justinian's most significant work was the civil code of laws begun in 528. The Code of Justinian decisively set the pattern for the whole of European legal history. Under his rule, the empire experienced the first literary and artistic flowering of its own independent culture. He also invested the enormous state budget in buildings of extraordinary magnificence, such as the ❻, ❿ Hagia Sophia in Constantinople, and in the development of the cities.

10 Interior of Hagia Sophia

Justinian's successors were occupied in wars against the Persians, Avars, and Bulgarians and embroiled in religio-political disputes. In 610 the general Heraclius rose to prominence and took the emperor's throne. He went on to mold the character of the Byzantine Empire. At first, however, he found himself on the defensive. In 614 Jerusalem fell to the Persians, and in 626 the Persians and Avars jointly laid siege to Constantinople. However, once the Persians were driven out of Anatolia, things changed. The Byzantines advanced into Persian territory and in 627 reclaimed Jerusalem. Heraclius now restructured the empire, reorganized the Orthodox Church, divided the empire into military districts, and crushed the power of big landowners. Above all, as the official state, administrative, and military language, he replaced Latin with the Greek used by the church and the people. The imperial title of *augustus* was replaced with *basileios*. Heraclius thereby achieved the final stage of development in the Greco-Byzantine character of the empire.

The Heraclian dynasty that ruled until 711, as well as the following rulers, had to contend with ❾ Arab and Bulgarian invasions in the seventh through ninth centuries, which were a mortal threat to the empire. Internally, the empire was shaken from 711 to 843 by violent religious controversy regarding the ❼ veneration of icons. The emperor and patriarchs fell victim to the icon disputes, and several provinces were able to gain their independence by civil war. Despite this, Byzantium's structures and borders remained largely intact.

6 The Hagia Sophia, completed 360; rebuilt under Emperor Justinian 532–537

8 Mary with Jesus between Constantine and Justinian, mosaic, Hagia Sophia

9 The siege of Constantinople by the Arabs in 717, book painting, 13th c.

11 Crucifixion scene with Constantine and Helena under the cross

527–565 | Byzantine golden era under Justinian I
528 | Introduction of Code of Justinian
610–711 | Dynasty of Heraclius
532 | Beginning of construction of the Hagia Sophia in Constantinople
626 | Expulsion of the Avars from Constantinople

Armenia and Asia Minor from the Diadochoi to the Romans 550 B.C.–ca. 200 A.D.

Armenia and the kingdoms of Asia Minor were the point of intersection between the Orient and the Greco-Hellenic—and later Roman—world. Stubbornly protective of their independence, these states were constantly under threat from the great powers, particularly Rome in the first century B.C. Under Mithradates VI, however, Pontus proved to be an opponent the Roman rulers could not easily dismiss.

1 Relief on the Armenian Church of the Holy Cross on the island Ahtamar, with a depiction of George the Dragonslayer

Armenia and Bithynia

Armenia first gained independence from the Seleucid Empire in the second century B.C. It became the first Christian nation around 300 A.D. Bithynia maintained its independence at first, but later came under Roman control.

Armenia was heir to the ancient Kingdom of Urartu. Initially used only by the Scythians and Cimmerians as a passage to other regions, it became a province of the Achaemenid Empire of Persia about 550 B.C. After the conquest by Alexander the Great in 331 B.C., it was awarded to the Seleucids but then occupied by the Parthians. The defeat of Antiochus III of Syria led to a division of the country in 189 B.C.

King Tigranes I was able to unite the region again about 90 B.C. In addition, he enlarged the kingdom in the west, conquering Cappadocia and the remains of the Seleucid kingdom with Phoenicia and Cilicia. In 69 B.C., however, he was defeated by the Romans and lost the conquered territories. Armenia became a contested buffer state between the Romans and Parthians, and later the Sassanids.

Around 300 A.D., Bishop ❸ Gregory the Illuminator converted Armenia to Christianity, creating the first Christian state even before the conversion of Rome. The head of the ❶, ❷ Armenian Church—also known as the Armenian Apostolic or Gregorian Church—is the supreme *catholicos*. The Armenian Church adheres to Monophysitic doctrine and has, up to the present day, maintained its independence from other Christian churches.

The Kingdom of Bithynia in the northwest of Asia Minor was ruled since the end of the fourth century B.C. by a local dynasty able to repel even Alexander the Great and the Diadochoi. In 264 B.C. its most significant ruler, Nicomedes I, founded the capital of Nicomedia, becoming a center of Hellenistic culture. The last Bithynian king, Nicomedes IV (95–75 B.C.), was expelled by Mithradates of Pontus, but returned to the throne in 84 with the help of Sulla. In return, he bequeathed his kingdom to Rome, who took possession in 74 B.C.

2 The Armenian Church of the Holy Cross on the island Ahtamar

3 Gregory the Illuminator, baptizes King Tiridates III, 296 A.D.

Monophysitism

Monophysitism, a religious doctrine founded by Alexandrian theology, states that Jesus Christ, as the son of God, had only one nature (mono physis), the divine. He is seen as the incarnate word of God. In contrast, Catholicism and Orthodoxy teach that Jesus has two natures—divine and human. That "Christ is truly God and truly human" was confirmed by the Council of Chalcedon in 451, whereupon the Monophysite churches—those in Egypt (Coptic), Armenia, and Ethiopia—split away from the Catholic and Orthodox churches.

above: Cyril of Alexandria, icon painting, second half of 16th c.

ca. 550 B.C. | Armenia becomes a Persian province
late 4th century B.C. | Independence of Bithynia
331 B.C. | Armenia passes to the Seleucids
280–250 B.C. | Nicomedes I king of Bithynia
2nd century B.C. | Independence of Armenia
189 B.C. | Division of Armenia

Cappadocia and Pontus

Cappadocia allied itself with Rome, as did early Pontus. However, under Mithradates VI, Pontus became a dangerous enemy of the Roman Empire. After Mithradates was defeated, Rome controlled all of Asia Minor.

4 Mithras shrine in the minor church of San Clemente in Rome

5 Mithras kills the bull, marble sculpture, second c.

6 Mosaic depicting the seven grades of consecration, Ostia Antica, second half of third century A.D.

Cappadocia, in the east of Asia Minor, was originally a Persian province, but gained independence after the death of Alexander the Great. It managed to assert itself against the Diadochoi but eagerly assimilated Hellenistic culture. After 190–189 B.C. Cappadocia was allied with Rome. From 114–113 B.C. it was threatened by Mithradates of Pontus, who styled himself the defender of the kings. About 100 B.C. ❽ Mithradates murdered King Ariarathes VII and installed his own son as Ariarathes IX. After Rome's victory over Mithradates, Cappadocia came under direct Roman control. In 36 B.C., Mark Antony appointed the loyal Archelaus as king, and after Archelaus' death, Tiberius made Cappadocia a Roman province.

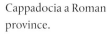

The Kingdom of Pontus on the north coast of Asia Minor was the last significant opponent of Rome. With its capital at Amaseia, the kingdom was politically separated into eparchies, each of which had its own administrative center. Starting in the third century B.C., Pontus brought the Greek cities of Asia Minor under its control. While Pontus had earlier been an ally of Rome, conflict between the two developed under Pontus's son ❼ Mithradates VI Eupator. In 112 B.C., when the Greek cities called for aid against Rome, Mithradates used it as an opportunity to occupy the Bosporus and the Chersonese, as well as to subjugate the Crimea and southern Russia up to Armenia Minor. Attempts to incorporate these territories into his kingdom ultimately led to war with Rome.

7 Mithradates VI Eupator

In the First Mithradatic War (89–84 B.C.), Pontus occupied all of Asia Minor and Greece, but was forced to a settlement after its defeat by Sulla in 84. In 74–73 B.C. Mithradates occupied Bithynia and thereby ignited the Second Mithradatic War. After initial successes, the "Hellenized barbarian" was defeated by Pompey in 63. His successor allied with Rome, which now controlled the whole region of Asia Minor. In 40 B.C., Rome appointed Darius, Mithradates' grandson, king. The kingdom was then dissolved in 64 A.D. and integrated into the Roman Empire as administrative provinces.

It was probably during wars with Mithradates that the ancient Indo-Iranian ❹, ❺, ❻, ❾ cult of Mithras spread through the Roman army. Mithras worship was prominent even in Rome, primarily through its mixing with the state cult Sol Invictus. Numerous Mithras shrines were built. Only with the expansion of Christianity did its influence fade.

8 Mithadates of Pontus stables his son Ariarathes

9 Ritual meal in a Mithras shrine

89–84 B.C.	First Mithradatic War
74 B.C.	Bithynia becomes a Roman province
63 B.C.	Defeat of Mithradates VI by Pompey
64 A.D.	Pontus becomes a Roman province
ca. 300 A.D.	Conversion of Armenia to Christianity

Persia under the Parthians and the Sassanians 250 B.C.–651 A.D.

2 Parthian olive garland, gold, third century B.C.

The Parthian dynasty, and the Sassanians who followed them, were for centuries the most dangerous opponents on Rome's eastern frontiers. The kings considered themselves heirs to the Achaemenid Empire. While the Pathians adopted much from Hellenic tradition, the Sassanians sought to revive Persian traditions such as Zoroastrianism. Rome was also influenced by Persian traditions, the Byzantine Empire inspired by Eastern "divine rule." Exhausted by its struggles with Rome, the Sassanid Empire ultimately succumbed to the Arab Muslim invasions of the seventh century A.D.

left: Statue of a Parthian king, marble, second century B.C.

The Parthian Empire 250 B.C.–224 A.D.

The Parthians emerged as the successors to the Seleucid Empire. They extended their territories westward, which eventually brought them into conflict with the Roman Empire.

Beginning in the fourth century B.C., the Parni, a tribe of nomads, migrated from the southeastern shore of the Caspian Sea into the Iranian highlands. They were known as ❶, ❷, ❹ Parthians after the province of Parthia, which they conquered in 250 B.C. under their first ruler, Arsaces I. He and his successors, the Arsacids, drove the Seleucids out of Iran and under Mithradates I in the second century B.C., out of Mesopotamia. This then became the center of their empire, with its capital, ❻ Ctesiphon, located on the Tigris River. The Parthians adopted the ❸ Hellenistic culture of the Seleucids (p. 99), as well as their administrative structure. The provinces were almost autonomously ruled by independent governors, who were often members of the ruling royal dynasty.

Parthian Temple in the Hellenistic style, Hatra, Iraq

The Parthian Empire reached its greatest extent under Mithradates II "the Great" in the first century B.C., when it stretched from the Euphrates to the Indus. There were clashes with the Roman Empire over the control of Armenia, but neither side was able to gain the upper hand. The Parthians defeated the Roman consul Crassus (p. 120) in the Battle of ❺ Carrhae in 53 B.C. However, during the reign of Augustus the Romans were able to take advantage of the Parthian provincial governors' desire for independence and dynastic disputes over the throne. The Romans thus pursued a policy of divide and rule by supporting different pretenders to the Parthian throne.

Emperor Trajan conquered Mesopotamia in 114 but it was lost again under Hadrian (p. 123). Further Roman campaigns against the Parthians followed at the beginning of the third century. The Parthians were forced to make peace with the Romans in 218, as their empire was starting to collapse from within. Finally, Ardashir, who as a Parthian governor had run Fars (Persis), the ancient Achaemenid home province, ended Arsacid rule in 224 and replaced it with the Sassanid dynasty.

Parthian soldier, color lithograph

Crassus's defeat at Carrhae

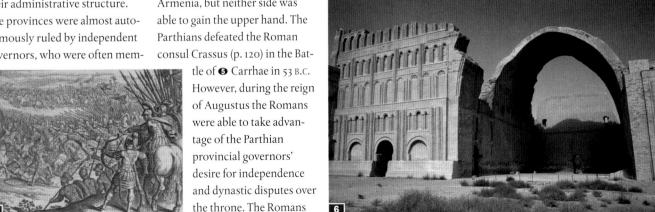

Palace of the King in the Parthian capital, Ctesiphon

2nd century B.C. | Defeat of the Seleucids by Mithradates I
1st century B.C. | Greatest extent of the Parthian Empire
53 B.C. | Triumph over Rome in the Battle of Carrhae
114 A.D. | Conquest of Mesopotamia by Trajan
218 | Peace with Rome

The Empire of the Sassanians 224–651 A.D.

The Sassanians saw themselves as heirs to the Achaemenids and sought to revive their culture. War with the Romans drained the kingdom and it succumbed to the Arab invasions.

The Sassanid ⑩ Ardashir I overthrew the last of the Parthian rulers in 224. To a much greater extent than the Arsacids, the Sassanians identified with the ancient Persian traditions and sought to revive this culture, particularly Zoroastrianism (p. 63). This became the official state religion. The Sassanians attempted to revoke the autonomy of the provinces—which would ultimately result in the downfall of the Parthian Empire—and centralized all authority. The Sassanians continued to pursue the conflict with the Romans and the Byzantine Empire. Shapur I defeated the Romans with ease at Edessa in 260 and even took ⑨ Emperor Valerian (p. 125) prisoner. Under Shapur's successors in the fourth century, Christians were seen as politically suspect and persecuted as potential supporters of Rome. Once the conflict ended, in the fifth century, they were granted freedom to practice their religion.

7 The gold and crystal "Khosru Bowl," decorated with an enthroned Khosrow I

The Sassanid Empire reached the height of its power under ⑦ Khosrow I, who had destroyed the Hephthalite Empire (p. 148) by 560 and conquered southern Arabia by 570. War with the Byzantines culminated in ⑧, ⑫ Khosrow II bringing the Byzantine Empire to the verge of collapse. He occupied Syria and Egypt, before capturing Jerusalem in 614, and stealing holy relics. The Emperor Heraclius (p. 135), however, halted the Persian advance, and won a decisive victory in the Battle of Nineveh in 627. Khosrow II was deposed and ⑪ murdered, while his successor had no choice but to make peace with Heraclius.

8 Khosrow II and the Christian Shirin, illustrated book, 15th century

9 Shapur I takes the Roman Emperor Valerian prisoner, engraving, third century

Persia had been so militarily exhausted by the conflict that it was unable to defend itself effectively against the onslaught of the Arab invaders spreading Islam (p. 226). The last Sassanid, Yazdegerd III, fled eastwards and was murdered in 651. However, the language and refined culture of the Persians fused with the new faith, and marked out the elite.

Manichaeism

In the third century A.D., a Persian thinker, Manichaeus, propagated a dualistic doctrine that integrated elements of Zoroastrianism, Christianity, and Buddhism, and to which he gave his name. He identified God with the kingdom of light that opposed a kingdom of darkness and taught that man must constantly defend himself against the darkness, which threatens him. Mankind is helped in this by redeemers sent by God. Manichaeism strongly influenced both Gnosticism and Christianity. He was persecuted as a heretic and flayed to death in 276 A.D.

above: Manichaeus, third century

10 Ahura Mazda passes the ring of power to the Sassanian Ardashir I, rock relief in Persepolis, third century

11 Khosrow is executed by his own son after his defeat, engraving, 17th century

12 Khosru II and the Christian Shirin, book illustration, 15th century

224 | Sassanid rule begins
260 | Victory of Shapur I over the Romans at Edessa
560 | Khosrow I destroys the Hephthalite Empire
614 | Conquest of Jerusalem by Khosrow II
627 | Sassanids defeated by Heraclius at Nineveh

Celtic bronze helmet, first century B.C.

Celts, Slavs, and Germanic Tribes

6th century B.C.–7th century A.D.

During antiquity, much of Europe was inhabited by the ❶ Celts, Slavs, and ancient Germanic tribes. They were considered uncivilized barbarians by the Mediterranean peoples, although some Greek and Roman writers expressed more favorable opinions. These ancient accounts, medieval epics, and archaeological finds provide what little information there is about these peoples, while elements of their culture and language have survived to this day.

The Migrations of the Celts

The Celts moved out from their original homeland in western France and southern Germany and into western and southeastern Europe. They also settled in northern Italy and the plains of central Anatolia.

The name "Celt" dates from the sixth century B.C. when Greek sources used the term to denote tribes living around the Danube and Rhone rivers. Evidence of the migratory movements of the Celts is found where they ❸ encountered the Etruscans, Romans, and Greeks. In the sixth century they began to settle the plains of the Po River, which had previously been controlled by the Etruscans. In the fourth century B.C., they began to send raiding parties south, even sacking Rome about 390 B.C. In the third century, the Celts pushed through southern Europe and the Balkans into Greece and plundered Delphi. The ❺ Celtic Galli reached Asia Minor as mercenaries of Nicomedes I of Bithynia in 278 B.C. They were defeated in the ❻ "Battle of the Elephants" in 275–274 by Antiochus I of Syria. He then settled them permanently in central Anatolia (Galatia), where they were still living in the first century A.D.

3 A Celt kills his wife and himself after losing a battle, marble statue, third c. B.C.

There is no evidence of a mass Celtic migration into either the Iberian Peninsula or the ❹ British Isles. It is more likely that the indigenous societies adopted aspects of Celtic culture. The bearers of Celtic culture began to spread south from northern Spain in the fifth century B.C. and are referred to as Celtibers. The inhabitants of the British Isles in pre-Roman times were seen as Celts due to their culture and language.

In the early first century B.C., Germanic tribes advancing out of the north drove the Celts of Central Europe out of the valleys north of the Rhine and Danube, until they eventually came under Roman rule. Under Roman influence, an independent ❷ Gallo-Roman culture developed in Celtic Gaul. The Celts on the British Isles, who were never part of the Roman Empire, maintained their independence in ❼ Ireland, Scotland, and Wales. From these regions, tribal groups who spoke Celtic despite having been Romanized migrated into Brittany in the fifth and sixth centuries A.D. The Celtic language and culture has been preserved in these areas up to the present.

The Celtic horned god, Cernunnos, associated with nature and fertility, seated between Apollo and Mercury, stone relief, first century A.D.

The remains of a Celtic ceremonial complex built of stone, consisting of a round room, two galleries, and a tunnel, in Cornwall, southwestern England

Celtic warrior on horseback

6 Celtic warrior trampled by an elephant, terra-cotta statuette, Second century B.C.

Remains of a Celtic fort in Dun Aengus, Ireland, ca. first century B.C.

ca. 390 B.C. | Sacking of Rome by Brennus
ca. 278 B.C. | Looting of Delphi / Campaign against Asia Minor
275–274 B.C. | "Battle of the Elephants"
from 125 B.C. | First Roman conquests of Celtic territory
ca. 1st century B.C. | Celts driven out of Central Eur

The Celts and the Romans

Between 200 B.C. and 100 A.D., the Romans conquered almost all of the Celtic territories.

The first great clash between the Romans and the "Gauls"—as the ❽, ❾ Celts were called—ended in 390 B.C. with the sacking of Rome by the Celtic Senones, under Brennus. The Celts, bribed by the Romans to leave, then withdrew to the north and settled on the Po River plain. The Romans subjugated the region between 225 and 190 B.C.

The conquest of the Celtic regions beyond the Alps began in 125 B.C. and occurred in several stages. The tribes living there frequently quarreled with each other and were incapable of offering collective resistance. Sometimes they even sought help from the Romans against other enemies. Julius Caesar was therefore able to intervene in Celtic affairs when he assisted the Gauls against the Germanic warlord Ariovistus in 58 B.C. By 51 B.C. he had subjugated all of Gaul—present-day France and Belgium—often forming alliances with individual Celtic tribes. The Roman's most stubborn and serious opponent was prince ⓭ Vercingetorix, who in 52 B.C. was proclaimed king by a number of tribes. He was finally captured and became Caesar's prisoner in Alesia. After being paraded through Rome in 46 B.C., Vercingetorix was executed.

8 Gallic warrior with tattoos (left) and Senone chief in full armor, artist's reconstruction

Under Caesar's successors, the boundaries of the empire expanded to the Rhine and Danube so that all of the Celt-occupied areas in central Europe came under Roman control. The Celts on the Iberian Peninsula and in present-day England also succumbed to Roman rule. In 60 A.D., the British Celtic queen Boudicca rebelled against the Romans. After initial success, the rebellion was defeated and Boudicca committed suicide.

9 Tombstone showing the Pannonian Umma in Celtic garb, first c. A.D.

The Romanization of Gaul led to the development of a mixed ⓾ Gallo-Roman culture. The Gauls rapidly adopted Latin, Roman law and administration. They assimilated the civilization and culture of Rome. The Celtic nobility adapted to Roman ways, gained citizenship, and could even be admitted to the Senate, although they continued to prefer life in the country.

Celtic settlements, such as Paris and ⓬ Trier, became flourishing Gallo-Roman cities. Gaul was one of Rome's most important provinces as a result of the revenues generated from the ⓫ export of grains, wine, and finished textile products.

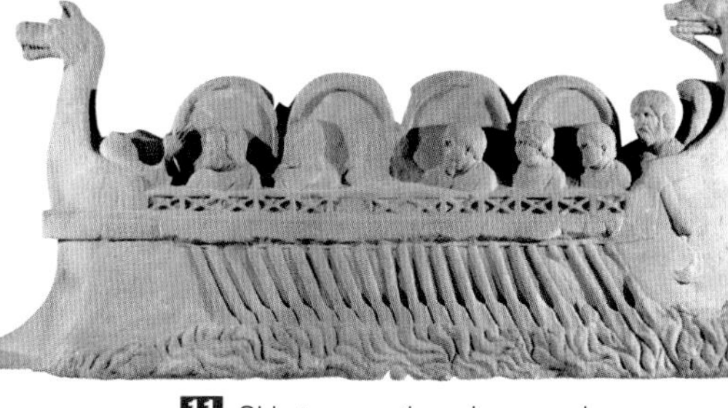

11 Ship transporting wine vessels, detail from a wine merchant's tomb, second–third century A.D.

10 Gallic warriors, stone sculpture, second century B.C.

The Sacking of Rome by Brennus

The Roman writer Livy described the sacking of Rome by Brennus in his History of Rome. According to Livy, Brennus was unable to take the Capitoline Hill because the defenders were alerted to the attack by the cries of geese. Since then, geese have been particularly honored there. Brennus made a deal, accepting 1,000 pounds of gold in exchange for his withdrawal. When the Romans complained that the weights on the scales were too heavy, Brennus threw his sword on top with the words: "Vae victis!" ("Woe to the vanquished!").

Above: Brennus throws his sword onto the scales, steel engraving, 19th century

12 The Porta Nigra, Trier, in Germany, second century A.D.

13 Vercingetorix surrenders to Caesar, wood engraving, 19th century

52 B.C. | Vercingetorix is appointed Celtic king
60 A.D. | Queen Boudicca's rebellion against the Romans
58–51 B.C. | Conquest of Gaul by Caesar
46 B.C. | Execution of Vercingetorix in Rome
5th and 6th centuries | Immigration of Celtic tribes into Brittany

Celtic Culture and Society

The Celtic culture is differentiated from other ancient cultures primarily by its lack of writing. In all other respects, it achieved a very high level in social differentiation, material culture, economy, and trade.

2 Celtic warrior nobility, sandstone statue, fifth century B.C.

5 Celtic burial mound in southern Germany, ninth–fifth century B.C.

7 Celtic woman and her warrior husband, chalk drawing, 19th century

The Celts had no unified national identity, but were instead subdivided into many tribes and clans who alternately formed alliances and fought with one another, according to political necessity. In early times the tribes were led by kings, who were later replaced by assemblies of the nobility. The ❷ princes stood out among the nobles, distinguishing themselves through exceptional wealth and influence. They also led the armies into battle in times of war. They were buried in large ❺ burial chambers with valuable funerary objects. Below the nobility was the broad mass of the ❼ populace, and subordinate to them were the serfs. The rigid system of allegiances and personal loyalties was of great importance. The princes held extensive properties, exacted tolls and taxes, and even minted their own ❸ coins.

3 Celtic gold coin, second century B.C.

Agriculture and animal husbandry formed the basis of the Celtic economy. In addition, ❻ metalworking and ceramic production reached a high level of sophistication under the distinct influence of the Etruscans, Romans, and Greeks. The Celts lived on individual farms or in ❽ villages, with larger settlements growing up around important seats of the nobility. In the second century B.C., ❶ fortified cities were also built.

The ❹ Druids, who formed a priestly caste, enjoyed particular esteem. They performed religious rites and made prophecies, as well as passing legal judgments. ❾ Deities and ancestors were worshiped—occasionally with human sacrifices—in man-made ⓬, ⓭ shrines as well as at springs, rivers, or trees. The Druids imparted their knowledge through an exclusively oral tradition. The history of the Celts was also passed on orally through the poems of the bards, in which—as in the legend of King Arthur—historical events were interwoven with mythical tales.

6 The Gundestrup Cauldron, made of silver, discovered in 1891in a bog in Denmark, 1st c. B.C.

1 Reconstruction of the defensive walls of a Celtic settlement

4 Druidic meeting in a stone circle, still from a film

The Legend of King Arthur

The epic tale of King Arthur reflects the clashes between the Celtic Britons and the Germanic Anglo-Saxons. Some elements reoccur repeatedly in its numerous literary versions. Among these are Arthur's triumph over the Anglo-Saxons, his famous round table, and the unfaithfulness of his wife Guinevere. He has been identified with a number of historical figures, including a Roman named Lucius Castus and the Celtic King Riothamus.

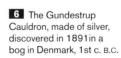

8 Reconstruction of a Celtic village in Ireland

ca. 8th–7th centuries B.C. | First Celtic tribes
2nd century B.C. | First fortified cities
ca. 550 | Slavs besiege Constantinople
from 6th century B.C. | Hierarchic class society
from the 5th century A.D. | Slavic migration to the west and south

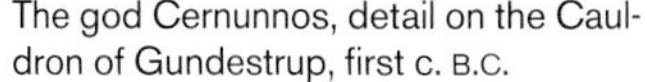

The god Cernunnos, detail on the Cauldron of Gundestrup, first c. B.C.

10 Excavation of a Slavic fortification, in Mecklenburg, northern Germany

Under the Yoke of the Avars

"Each year the Avars came to the Slavs to spend the winter and slept with the wives and daughters of the Slavs: the Slavs tolerated other perfidies as well, and also paid tribute to the Avars. The sons, however, which the Avars had fathered with the women and daughters of the Slav menfolk, would not tolerate this brutal oppression and refused to subject themselves to the Avars."

From the Chronicles of Fredegarius

Above: The Avars humiliate the Slavs, forcing them to draw their carts like packhorses, book illustration, 15th century

The Early Slavs

The advance of the Huns in the late fourth century A.D., and the resulting migratory movements of the Germanic tribes, provided the stimulus for the movement of the Slavs. At first they settled in the regions deserted by the Germans, but then increasingly headed south into the Balkans.

11 Slavic urns, ninth-tenth century

The Slavs probably originated north of the Carpathian Mountains between the Vistula and Dnieper rivers. During the Great Migration of Peoples (p. 146), they spread out and began following the withdrawing Germanic tribes in the fifth century A.D. The Slavs went as far west as the Elbe River and the Baltic Sea and as far east as Kamchatka. In the south, they were at first halted at the Danube, on the border of the Byzantine Empire. However their raiding parties soon led them to Ragusa and up to the gates of Constantinople.

The Slavs eventually crossed the Danube in great numbers and settled the Balkan region. Ancient writers refer to them as Sarmatians and Scythians.

The Slavs of the Danube region were dominated from the sixth to the eighth centuries by the Avars (p. 149), an equestrian tribe. In the ninth century, the Magyars, who originated in the Eurasian steppes, settled in present-day Hungary. The region settled by the Slavs split between western, eastern, and southern Slavic groups, who developed separately from one another.

The basis of the communal life of the early Slavs was the clan, several of which would band together to form a tribe. Ancient descriptions picture them as industrious pastoral peoples. In the sixth century subsistence farming still prevailed and crafts were little developed. Articles such as drinking 11 vessels and tools were produced mainly for domestic needs. Only gradually did clan leaders become a distinct class—and only where the Slavs were not dominated by foreign powers. In the seventh century, the fortified 10 castles were built. Little is known of the religion of the early Slavs except that they worshiped nature deities. Christianity was introduced in the ninth century by Cyril and Methodius, the former giving his name to the Cyrillic alphabet.

12 Cape Arcona on the island of Rügen, a sacred site for pre-Christian Slavs

13 Celtic stone circle in Ireland created ca. 150 B.C.

from the 7th century | First Slavic nobility appears

9th century | Progression of the Magyars / Separation of Slavic regions

from 565 | Invasion of the Avars

ca. 880 | First known writings about King Arthur

The Culture and Society of the Ancient Germans

The ancient Germans were described by Roman writers as an especially warlike people. They successfully defended themselves against Roman conquest and, despite the lack of a unified leadership, came to pose a serious threat to the Roman Empire.

By the first century B.C., the ancient Germans, whose exact origins are unclear, had spread from the northeast down to the plains of the Rhine and the river Danube. German societies were split into various tribes, each dominated by a warrior aristocracy, which based its power on property and personal allegiances. In times of war, kings were also chosen to lead the armies. During the period of the great migrations, the office of king became permanent. The population practiced ❹ agriculture and animal husbandry and was divided into a noble elite, freemen, and slaves. They traded extensively with the Roman Empire. Elected judges officiated at the ❶ community assembly and also heard legal cases. Legal verdicts were aided by oaths and considered the judgment of God. Personal conflicts often resulted in bloody feuds.

3 Two warriors, one with a horned helmet, the other with a wolf mask, perform a war dance for Odin, bronze stamp used for the decoration of helmets, sixth century

2 Illustration of *Twilight of the Gods*, stone relief, tenth century

Despite near continuous ❸ conflict with the Romans, in which Arminius was the greatest threat, from the first century A.D. on, Germans were increasingly recruited into the Roman army as mercenaries, eventually coming to dominate it. The Romans admired the physical size and fighting power of the Germans, as well as their sparse, simple life. The Roman historian Tacitus emphasized the frenzy into which the warriors transported themselves before battle and called it "Teutonic rage."

War and battle also played a large role in German religion and ❷ mythology, which was permeated with the fights of pugnacious gods against giants and demons. The ❺ war god Wodan (Odin), who was most likely also the chief of the Germanic deities, received fallen soldiers in his castle, Valhalla. The gods were worshiped in holy sites or at natural monuments. These rituals apparently included animal, and even ❼ human, sacrifice. The Germanic world of fantasy is known primarily through medieval epics and myths such as the *Edda*, based on early Icelandic poems. The earliest written firsthand accounts—oracles, magic formulas, and curses—were written in runes and date from the second century A.D. Only in Scandinavia were texts of significant length written in runes, most notably on ❻ gravestones.

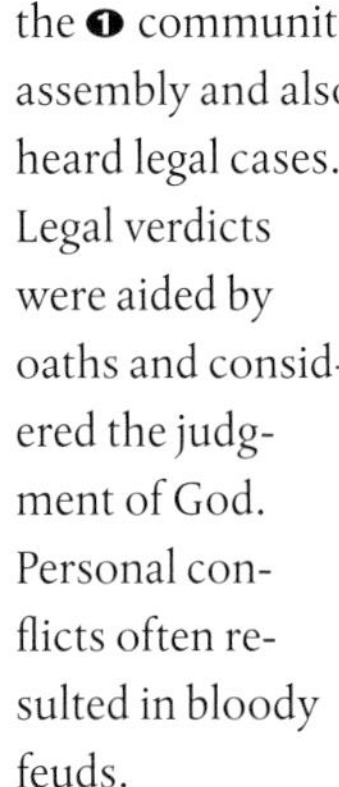

6 Rune engraving showing the arrival of a warrior in Walhall and the story of the blacksmith Wölund, limestone, eighth–ninth century

1 A tribal assembly, known as a "Thing," attended by all freemen

4 Germanic tribal village

5 Germanic gods Odin, Thor, and Frei, tapestry, twelfth century

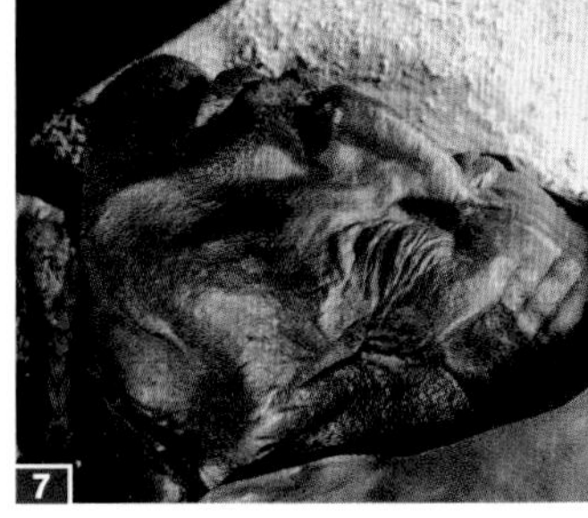

7 Head of a strangled male, human sacrifice, found in a peatbog in Denmark

Tacitus on the Religion of the Germanic peoples

"At a stated time of the year, all the various peoples descended from the same stock, assemble with their deputies in a wood; consecrated by the idolatries of their forefathers, and by their superstitious awe as in times of old. There, by publicly performing a human sacrifice, they commence the horrible solemnity of their barbarous worship."

Above: Giant stones in the Teutoburg Forest, a pagan ritual site

2nd century B.C. | Migration of the Cimbri and Teutons southward

101 B.C. | Marius's victory over the Cimbri and Teutons

58 B.C. | Victory of Caesar over Ariovistus

12 B.C. | Roman occupation up to the Elbe

The Ancient Germans and the Romans

Beginning in the first century B.C., there were constant clashes along the Rhine and Danube rivers between the Germanic tribes and the Roman Empire.

8 Cimbrian women in battle against the Romans, engraving, 19th century

From as early as the first century B.C., there were regular clashes along the Rhine and Danube rivers between the Germanic tribes and the Roman Empire.

9 A legionnaire apprehends a fleeing German woman with her child, plaster mold of a second century A.D. relief

Even before the Great Migration of Peoples (p. 146) that began in the third century A.D., the Romans came into conflict with nomadic Germanic tribes such as the Cimbri and Teutoni, who had moved south during the second century B.C. The defeats inflicted on several Roman armies sent to the aid of threatened Celtic tribes triggered a panic in Rome in 113 B.C., as residents feared another sacking of the city like that of the Celts under Brennus. Under Marius, however, the army turned the tide and ❽, ❾ annihilated the Cimbri and Teutoni around 102–101 B.C. The next great challenge was an invasion of Gaul by the Germanic warlord Ariovistus. Again, the Celts were dependent on Roman aid. Caesar repelled the Germans in 58 B.C. and went on to conquer all of Gaul. From this point on, the Rhine and Danube marked the boundaries of the Roman Empire, but the Germans continued to send small raiding parties into the empire.

From 12 B.C., the Romans sought to eradicate the problem by occupying all the lands up to the Elbe. It was only after the defeat of the Roman governor Varus, in the 9 A.D. ❿ Battle of Teutoburg Forest, that the Romans abandoned these plans of conquest. On the north side of the Rhine and Danube, only the Agri Decumates, in the area between the two rivers, stayed in Roman hands; it was protected by a ⓫ fortified border (a "limes"), reinforced with palisades, trenches, and watchtowers.

Despite the regular incursions, the Romans were able to keep the divided Germanic tribes in check until the second half of the second century, when larger tribes, such as the Alemanni and Franks, began to emerge. It was only with great effort that Marcus Aurelius was able to repel the Marcomanni and Quadi, who had settled between the Elbe and Danube, around 170. The occupation of the Agri Decumates by the Alemanni and the Suebi in 260, along with the settlement of Frankish allies on the empire's territory, foreshadowed the changes that finally led to the fall of the Western Roman Empire.

10 The Battle of Teutoburg Forest, painting, 19th century

Armin of the Cherusci

The Cherusci prince Arminius—later Germanized to "Hermann"—was originally an ally of Rome. He trained in the Roman army, was a citizen of Rome, and fought for the Romans against other Germanic tribes. It was only when the governor Varus tried to introduce the Roman tax and legal systems in Germania that he rebelled and defeated the Roman forces. He was murdered by relatives who feared his growing power around 21 . In the 19th century, with a total disregard for history, he was pronounced the "defender of the Germans."

Above: Collossal statue of Armin (Hermann) of the Cherusci, built in the Teutoburg Forest, 19th c.

11 The Saalburg, a Roman stone fort, on the limes of the Danubian frontier

9 A.D. | Armin's victory in the Battle of Teutoburg Forest
66–180 | Romans war against the Marcomanni and Quadi
2nd century | First runes appear
260 | Alemanni settle in the Agri Decumates

The Great Migration of Peoples 375–568 A.D.

The formation of great tribes on the Rhine and Danube rivers put immense pressure on the Roman Empire in the third century. At first it was possible to hold the ❶ Germans back, and when necessary they were included in the empire, where they were welcomed as soldiers. The appearance of the Huns in 375 changed the situation. They triggered a massive migratory movement that the Roman Empire, which officially divided into Western and Eastern parts in 395, was unable to oppose. The Romans were forced to accept the founding of Germanic kingdoms on imperial territory until finally, in 476, the last Western Roman emperor was deposed by the Germans. Only the Eastern Empire, later Byzantium, survived the upheavals during the mass migrations.

1 Warrior's helmet, seventh century

The Migrations of the Germanic Peoples

The Huns stormed out of the Eurasian steppes in 375, driving some of the Ostrogoths and the Visigoths out of their settled regions north of the Danube and the Black Sea. Other Germanic tribes were also on the move.

3 General Stilicho with his wife and son, ivory carving, ca. 400

Even before the Hun invasion of 375, the Romans were forced to cede territory to the Germanic tribes. The Romans were unable to repel the incursion of the ❷ Franks across the lower Rhine in 350, and were forced to accept a settlement. The Franks were granted the status of allies and pacified with payments of money. Some of their leaders were appointed to posts in the Roman army and, after the fall of the empire, gained independence in Gaul. Some Germanic leaders rose to become imperial generals—even commanders of the Roman army—and, like ❸ Stilicho at the time of the division of the Roman empire in 395, were the power behind weak emperors. The German Odoacer deposed the last Roman emperor in 476.

The ❺ migration of peoples began with the Huns driving the Goths out of their homeland in 375. The Goths, who most likely originated in Scandinavia, settled the area south of the Baltic Sea along the Vistula River during the first and second centuries A.D. and had reached the Black Sea and the Danube by the third century. From there, they raided both Greece and Asia Minor. During the second half of the third century, the Goths divided into the Ostrogoths and the Visigoths.

After the Huns attacked in 375, many Visigoths fled south over the Danube border, and their victory over the ❻ Romans at Adrianople in 378 led to an alliance. After the Roman Empire's division in 395, the Visigoths effectively used the rivalry between East and West Rome to their advantage. The Visigoth king Alaric fought many battles against the Western Roman general Stilicho, invading Italy in 401 and then ❹ plundering Rome in 410. When the Visigoths moved on in 418, the emper-

5 Germanic caravan, wood engraving, 19th century

2 Frankish stone carving, seventh c.

4 The conquest of Rome by the Visigoths under Alaric, wood engraving, 19th century

6 Romans battle the Goths, wood engraving, 19th c.

from the 3rd century	Gothic migration to the Black Sea Region
from 269	Division of the Goths into Visigoths and Ostrogoths
from 350	Invasion of the Franks into the Roman Empire
375	Victory of the Huns over the Ostrogoths / Visigoths cross the Danube border

7 Nicasius, Bishop of Reims, kneels before the Vandals, sculpture, 13th century

or offered them the south of France. There they established a kingdom that later stretched on into Spain.

The majority of the ❾ Ostrogoths initially joined forces with the Huns. After the death of the Hun king Attila, they settled in Eastern Roman territory as allies. The Ostrogoth king, ❽ Theodoric, who was raised in Constantinople, marched into Italy in 488 in the name of the Eastern Roman emperor Zeno, defeated the Western Roman regent Odoacer in 493, and founded his own realm.

8 Theodoric the Great, king of the Ostrogoths, image on a coin, ca. 500

In the meantime, at the turn of the fifth century, another wave of Germanic peoples pushed out of their former settlements in Central and Eastern Europe towards the West. In 406–407 the Vandals and Burgundians crossed the Rhine and moved into Gaul. The ❼ Vandals continued over the Pyrenees, settling in Spain by 409, while the Burgundians established their own kingdom on the Rhine. Under increasing pressure from Visigoth attacks encouraged by the Western Roman emperor, the Vandals under King Gaiseric crossed over to North Africa in 429. There they founded an empire with its capital at Carthage, depriving Rome of lands valuable for growing grain.

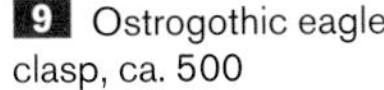

9 Ostrogothic eagle clasp, ca. 500

From the Baltic Sea coast, groups of Angles, Saxons, and Jutes, under the leadership of ❿ Hengist and Horsa, set off in the middle of the fifth century for Britain, which had been abandoned by the Romans around 400. The Germans drove the Celtic Britons into Scotland, Wales, and Cornwall. The Saxons who had remained on the continent were able to fend off the Franks, and Christianization was not widespread until the end of the eighth century.

The last of the important Germanic tribes to join the migration were the Lombards, who until the fifth century had lived between the Elbe and the Danube. Driven out by the equestrian nomadic Avars, under ⓫ King Alboin they left their homeland and occupied a region in northern Italy that came to be named after them—Lombardy—in 568. This is considered the end of the Great Migration.

The widespread migration of peoples led to the fall of the Roman Empire and a westward shift of the areas settled by the Germans and the Slavs who followed. The union of late antiquity and Germanic tradition in the culture of the Visigoths, Franks, Angles, Saxons, and Lombards characterized the culture of Europe in the early Middle Ages.

Ulfilas

During the Great Migration of Peoples, Ulfilas (or Wulfila) was an influential leader of the Germans. In 341 he was ordained "bishop of the Goths" and about 370 he translated the Bible into Gothic. Because he was an adherent of Arius, the Goths and most of the other Germanic tribes came to be called Arians. This led to conflicts with the Romans in the territories conquered by the Germans and hindered an integration of the two groups of peoples. The acceptance of Catholicism by the Franks, and later by the Visigoths and Lombards, eased their acceptance by the native inhabitants and lent their empires greater stability.

above: Ulfilas explains the gospel to the Goths, engraving, 1890

10 Hengist and Horsa land on the British coast, wood engraving, 19th century

11 King Alboin entering Pavia, wood engraving, 19th century

378 | Battle of Adrianople
406–407 | First settlement of the Vandals beyond the Rhine
410 | Looting of Rome by Alaric
429 | Vandals move into North Africa
493 | Theodoric's victory over Odoacer
568 | Lombards occupy land in Italy

Huns in Europe, steel engraving, 19th century

The Nomad Empires of the Eurasian Steppes 3rd century B.C.–7th century A.D.

The Eurasian belt of steppes that stretches eastward from the Black Sea in the west to the Yellow Sea in China has always been inhabited by nomads. Clashes with the Scythians, Sarmatians, or Sakas who lived there played a role in the history of the ancient empires of the Persians, Greeks, and Indians, but these peoples never became organized as a nation. One of the oldest groups was the Xiongnu, who established a great nomad empire at the end of the third century B.C. on the northern borders of China. Their defeat and displacement by the Han dynasty triggered a chain reaction of migratory movements whose western ripples in the fourth century A.D. pushed the ❶ Huns into the Goths and set off the Great Migration of Peoples that altered the make-up of Europe.

Xiongnu, Kushana, and Hephthalites

Even before the rise of the Huns, great nomad empires were formed on the basis of moving confederations of tribes.

Two horse-riders, clay figurines, 2nd–1st c. B.C.

The empires of the ❷ equestrian nomads of the Xiongnu, Huns, and Turkic people, as well as the ❸ Mongolian empire of Genghis Khan in the 13th century, were all based on coalitions of different tribes and peoples. Because the founders of the empires did not define themselves by ethnicity, every group that identified with the interests of the empire—even former enemies—was taken in. Of course, this confederal style easily led to fragmentation of the nomad empires, and most of them were very short lived.

The tribal federation of the Xiongnu, which formed at the end of the third century B.C., presented a serious threat to Han dynasty China, which went to great lengths—from the construction of the Great Wall to offensive military strikes—to rid itself of this opponent. During the course of the second and third centuries, the Chinese succeeded in gradually dividing and driving off the Xiongnu. Parts of the confederation then became dependent on the Chinese and were assimilated; other groups were defeated by the Chinese and driven westward. It seems likely that the Xiongnu, as they withdrew, forced out other peoples and tribes living further west—the Kushana, who then invaded Central Asia and India, for example. Today it is considered doubtful that the Huns who appeared in the fourth century were directly related to the Xiongnu, although it is possible that some remains of the Xiongnu merged into the tribal confederation of the Huns.

In the fifth century, the powerful Sassanians of Persia came into conflict with the nomad empire of the Hephthalites, who were also known as the "white Huns." After the Hephthalites swept south to destroy the remains of the great Gupta empire in northern India, they were themselves annihilated in 567 by the Sassanians under Khosrow I.

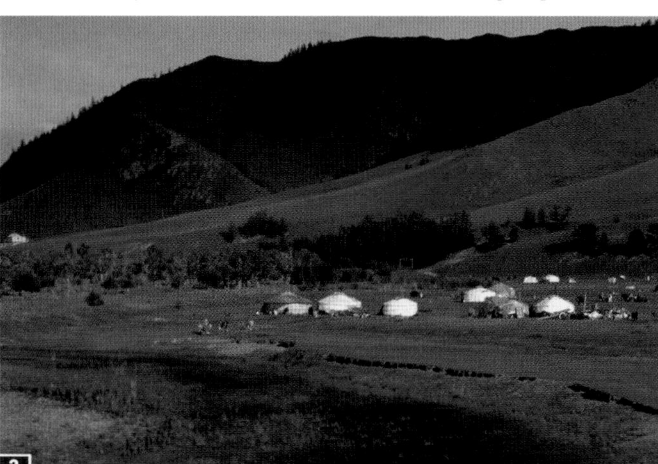
Nomad yurts in the Gobi Desert, present-day Mongolia

The Huns under Attila invade Europe, wood engraving, 19th century

from the 3rd century B.C. | Tribal confederation of the Xiongnu
2nd century B.C.–3rd century A.D. | Expulsion of the Xiongnu from China
375 A.D. | Defeat of the Goths by the Huns
445 | Attila as single ruler over the Huns
451 | Attila's defeat at the Catalaunian Plains

The Huns

The military expeditions of the Huns, particularly under King Attila, the "scourge of God," were so devastating that many in Europe believed that they were experiencing the end of the world.

6 The Huns pour across the steppes north of the Caspian Sea, wood engraving, 19th century

7 Looting of a Gallo-Roman villa by the Huns, wood engraving, 19th century

8 The Battle of the Catalaunian Plains, color print, 20th century

9 *The Meeting between Leo the Great and Attila,* fresco by Raphael, 16th century

The Huns overran the Ostrogoths and the Visigoths in 375, destroying everything in their path. Due to their custom of strapping their children's noses flat from an early age, in order to widen their faces, they were described by early chroniclers as "animal-like creatures"—which only increased the terror they instilled. The Huns were not set on totally exterminating the Germans, though, since they needed them for their army.

East Rome tried to hold off the Huns from its borders with payments of up to 1,500 pounds of gold annually. But despite this, the ❹ Huns under Attila—who had earlier killed his brother and co-regent Bleda in 445—pushed deep into East Roman territory ❻, ❼ devastated the Balkan provinces, and extorted ever greater tribute payments. Attila then turned towards the West, leading his immense, and growing, army of Huns and Germanic tribesmen. Along the way many cities, such as Trier and Metz, were burned to the ground. In June 451, the Franks, Visigoths, and Romans, led by the imperial commander Aetius, brought the Huns' advance to a halt. The resulting ❽ Battle of the Catalaunian Plains, near Chalons-sur-Marne, lasted several days and cost around 90,000 lives.

The Huns and their allies were forced to withdraw toward Eastern Europe, but Attila was still not completely defeated. In 452 he invaded northern Italy and threatened Rome. However, Pope ❾ Leo I managed to persuade the Huns, who were afflicted by starvation and epidemics, to turn back. Attila ❺ died suddenly in 453, just after his wedding celebrations. The Huns split apart in the battles that followed, and were ultimately defeated and dispersed almost as quickly as they had conquered.

Following in the footsteps of the Huns, new equestrian nomads began to move into Europe from the east, among them the ❿ Avars and Magyars. The Avars are credited with introducing the stirrup to Europe, which gave their mounted warriors a major advantage in battle. In Central Asia, the Turkic people took up the legacy of the Huns and from the sixth to seventh century established a great nomad empire that stretched all the way from China to the Caspian Sea.

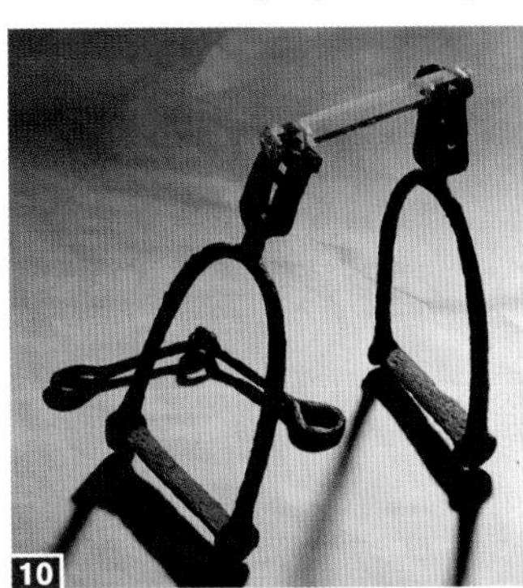
10 A pair of stirrups, an innovation imported into Europe by the equestrian nomads, particularly the Avar nomads

5 Attila dies on his wedding night, wood engraving, 19th century

The Appearance of the Huns

"For by the terror of their features they inspired great fear in those whom perhaps they did not really surpass in war....Their swarthy aspect was fearful, and they had...pinholes rather than eyes.Their audacity is evident in their threatening appearance, and they are beings who are cruel to their children on the very day they are born. For they cut the cheeks of the males with a sword, so that before they receive the nourishment of milk they must learn to endure wounds."

Jordanes, Getica (History of the Goths, ch.XXIII) 551 A.D.

above: Artificially deformed skull of a noblewoman, fifth century A.D.

453 | Death of Attila
6th and 7th centuries | Nomad empires of the Turkic peoples in Asia
452 | End of the Huns' primacy in Southeastern Europe
6th century | Extermination of the "white Huns"

Ancient India 321 B.C.–ca. 500 A.D.

Since the time of Alexander the Great, India had been in touch with Hellenic culture. The rulers of the Maurya Empire in particular maintained contact with the West. The most significant among them was Asoka, who promoted Buddhism. After the fall of the Maurya, local dynasties continually fought against the invading nomads from the Central Asian steppes. Only the Gupta Empire was able to once again unite large parts of India. In the meantime, Hinduism experienced a renaissance and eventually pushed Buddhism out of the subcontinent.

1 The lion capital of the Asoka Column, model for the Indian state crest, third century B.C.

The Mauryan Dynasty ca. 321–185 B.C.

After 321 B.C., the Mauryan Dynasty became the leading power in India. Emperor Asoka made Buddhism the state religion and gave the teaching and missionary efforts decisive impetus.

Alexander the Great marched with his army into the Indus Valley in 327 B.C. and despite great resistance from the hill tribes, he reduced most of their fortresses and defeated King Poros, as well as other local rulers, with his 2,000 war elephants. Alexander's successors in the east, the Seleucids, came into conflict with what had become the dominant power on the Indian subcontinent—the Maurya Empire, which had been founded around 321 by Chandragupta Maurya, in the area of Magadha on the Ganges. Chandragupta defeated Seleucus but eventually reached an agreement with the Seleucids about their common borders. He and his successors maintained close contact with the Greeks, ensuring the continued influence of Hellenic culture in India.

4 Asoka Column, third century B.C.

3 Depiction of the female earth spirit Yakshi, recognized as a symbol of fertility by Hindus, Buddhists, and Jains, sandstone, third century B.C.

Asoka, grandson of Chandragupta, came to the throne between 273 and 265 B.C., and is considered the most significant ruler of the Maurya Empire and of ancient India as a whole. During his reign, the empire included nearly all of the Indian subcontinent and reached present-day Afghanistan. His experiences during a brutal military campaign led to his conversion to ❷, ❸ Buddhism. Accounts and edicts on ❶, ❹ pillars and rock faces testify to Asoka's goals and achievements. While tolerant of other religions, he promoted the spread of Buddhism, even sending missionaries abroad. Around 250 he called a Buddhist council in his capital, Pataliputra, to establish the textual canon of early Buddhism. After his conversion, he refused to wage war. Instead, he sought to extend the social support within his empire. Soon after Asoka's death in ca. 232 B.C., the Mauryan Dynasty began to decline and in 185 B.C. the last Maurya was killed.

2 Buddha, old Indic

From an Edict of Asoka

"All men are my children. What I desire for my own children, and I desire their welfare and happiness both in this world and the next, that I desire for all men.... Your aim should be to act with impartiality."

Fragment of an inscription of an edict by emperor Asoka on a column in a Buddhist column, third century B.C.

ca. 321 B.C.	Foundation of the Maurya empire
ca. 268 B.C.	Asoka ascends to the throne
ca. 250 B.C.	Buddhistic council in Pataliputra
ca. 232 B.C.	King Asoka's death
first century B.C.	Conquest of India by the Sakes
184 B.C.	End of the Murya rule

The Gupta Dynasty ca. 320–550 A.D.

Foreign conquerors and tribes continually pushed out of the northwest into the Indian subcontinent and founded kingdoms, though they tended to be shot-lived. The last great Indian empire of antiquity was that of the Guptas.

5 Ruins of the city Bactra, present-day Balkh, Afghanistan, former capital of Bactria

After the fall of the Mauryan Dynasty in 184 B.C., several forms of states with strong Hellenistic traits established themselves independently in the northwest, stretching from ❺ Bactria (Afghanistan) to the Punjab, whose western part became for some time part of the Parthian empire. They were overrun in the first century A.D. by the nomadic Sakas, who swept down from Central Asia into India and established several kingdoms that survived into the second century under the domination of the Parthians (p. 138) and Kushana (p. 148). The empire of the Kushana in the northwest of India, then disintegrated in the third century under pressure from the intruding Sassanians (p. 139).

At first, orders of Buddhist ❻ monks exercised great power in the numerous Indian states. The princes then promoted the ancient Indian cults and priest castes as a counterweight, which brought about a renaissance of ❽ Hinduism. In this period, the great Indian hero epics ❾ *Mahabharata* and ❼ *Ramayana*, in which the political events of the times are reflected, were written. In the long run, the revitalization of Hinduism pushed Buddhism out of India.

6 Buddhist cave monasteries and temples, second century B.C.–sixth century A.D.

7 Illustration of the *Ramayana*, the life story of Rama, miniature painting, 18th century

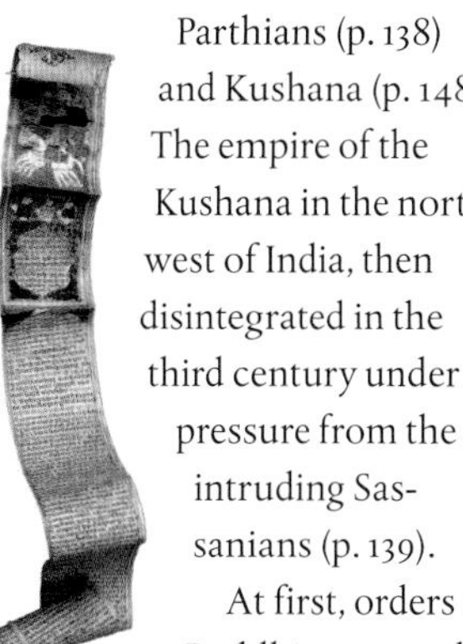

9 The *Bhagavad Gita*, part of the *Mahabharata*, excerpt from a script scroll

10 Shiva as Nataraja, lord of the dance, sandstone from Pratihara, ninth century

In the fourth century Magadha once again became the foundation of a great empire. The local princes of the Gupta Dynasty (320–500 A.D), which reigned during the golden age of Hindu culture, under Chandragupta II and his son Samudragupta, were able to make vassals of the neighboring rulers in quick succession.

Under Chandragupta II, who also stood out as an ⓫ architect, the empire stood at the pinnacle of its power at the beginning of the fifth century, stretching over all of North India. But then it was destroyed by invading Hephthalites (p. 148). The last Guptas in the sixth century reigned only in Magadha, while in the rest of northern India a number of warring powers emerged. Among them only the powerful Hindu dynasty of the ❿ Gurjara-Pratiharas stood out, as they were able for some time to withstand the onslaught of Islamic conquerors, who had been invading India repeatedly since the eighth century.

Several states existed in central and southern India, among which the central Indian Andhra of the first and second centuries is of note. The Tamils were able to maintain their independence and the characteristic features of their southern Indian culture in the great plain of the Carnatic and northern Ceylon even in the times of the Maurya and Gupta empires.

8 The god Vishnu shows sympathy for the animal world, fifth century

11 Vishnu Temple in Deogarh, fifth century

3rd century A.D.	Destruction of Kushana empire by Sassanians
320–500 A.D.	North Indian dynasty of the Guptas
ca. 380–414	Chandragupta II
ca. 500	Hephthalites destroy Guptas empire
750–ca. 1000	Hindu dynasty of Gurjara-Pratiharasharas

China's First Emperors of the Qin and Han Dynasties 221 B.C.– 220 A.D.

In the "Period of the Warring States," China was split into seven individual states that were eventually conquered by the Qin Empire. The "first sovereign emperor" of China, Emperor Qin Shi Huang Di, brought about the political and cultural unification of the country. The succeeding Han dynasty built upon this unification, expanded the area of Chinese rule, and successfully defended itself against the nomadic tribes in the north. In addition, Confucianism became the state ideology during the Han period. Under these first two imperial dynasties, developments that would characterize the history of China for more than 2,000 years were initiated.

1 Armor protection, shown in a third century B.C. clay figure

The Qin Dynasty 221–206 B.C.

China's first emperor created a unified state within a few years and began outwardly fortifying his empire. He ruled the land with an iron fist and in accordance with the state philosophy of Legalism.

3 Qin Shi Huangdi, former Zheng, king of Qin, wood carving, ca. 1640

4 Archaeologists at the excavation of Qin dynasty clay figures

The unification of China into a state in the third century B.C. was accomplished by the western state of Qin, which gave the country its name. Its frontier position opposite Tibet and the territories of the mounted nomads required it to have a powerful army and a tight administration. Its newly conquered territories were not given over to nobles as fiefs but were directly administrated by the ruler, which impeded the development of an aristocratic opposition. From this power base, King ❸ Zheng of Qin was able to conquer the other seven Chinese feudal states by 221 B.C. This ended the "Period of the Warring States" and a unified state with a divine emperor (Shi Huang Di: first august emperor) at its head was created.

The emperor then extended Qin's centralized administrative system over all of China. Disregarding old boundaries, the empire was reapportioned into provinces and districts that were run by imperial administrators. The government was based on the philosophy of the Legalists, who declared that the central laws should supersede all else and instituted the regulation of all areas of life by strict laws and taxes. Within a few years, language, measurements, weights, and coinage had been standardized in the empire. Even the gauge and length of wagons were standardized to accommodate uniform road networks. The people were forced to extend the walls against mounted nomads, which is the first section of the ❺ Great Wall.

2 The grave of Qin Shi Huangdi, with 6,000 life-size men and horses, third century B.C.

After his death in 210 B.C., China's first emperor was laid to rest in an enormous burial monument with thousands of individually crafted ❶, ❷ terra-cotta figures. Its ❹ discovery in 1974 was an archaeological sensation. The Qin dynasty ended shortly thereafter in 206 B.C. with an uprising of the people that brought the Hans to power.

5 The Great Wall of China in the hills near Beijing

221 B.C. | King Zheng becomes the first central sovereign of China

210 B.C. | Burial with terra-cotta figures

ca. 206 B.C. | Beginning of the Han dynasty

from the 2nd century B.C. | Formation of the Silk Road to the West

174 B.C. | Confucianism becomes state cul

The Han Dynasty 206 B.C.–220 A.D.

In the power struggle at the end of the Qin era, a peasant rebel leader, Liu Bang, triumphed and took the emperor's throne in 206 B.C. as Emperor Gaozu.

The most important task of the first Han emperor, Kao Ti (206 B.C.), was defending against the ❻ mounted nomads, above all the Xiongnu. Emperor ❾ Han Wu Ti, the most illustrious of the Han emperors, took the offensive, and his search for allies led the Chinese to their first contact with the West. The Xiongnu were finally defeated and forced westward, displacing Eurasian steppe peoples and ultimately triggering the Great Migration of Peoples (p. 146) in Europe of the fourth and fifth centuries. China conquered eastern Turkistan to the borders of today's Afghanistan, where a trade link to the west—the ❿ Silk Road—developed.

Domestically, Han Wu Ti carried out several reforms that were to have a long-lasting effect. He tried to repair the educational vandalism of Shi-Hwang-ti. He divided the central administration into departmental ministries for the first time. The system of training of ⓬ officials through schooling and examinations was perfected and remained in effect until the 20th century. The basis of this training was a synthesis of Legalism, Confucianism, which stressed the relationship between father and ⓫ son, and the yin–yang nature philosophy. The veneration of Confucius in a state cult began under the Hans. In 174 B.C., Emperor Han Wu Ti made a sacrifice on the philosopher's grave in ❽ Chu Fu, which survives to this day. The Han period was one of the greatest epochs of Chinese prosperity.

7 Generals in their armor, clay figures, Han period

10 A Buddhist shrine on the Silk Road in western China

11 Depiction of model sons, varnish painting on a woven basket, Han period

Han Wu Di's successor increasingly came under the influence of the family of the empress. In 9 A.D., the Hans were even temporarily deposed by the nephew of an empress until in 25 A.D. a distant relative of the Hans, Liu Hsiu, restored the dynasty as Emperor Guang Wu Di. He moved his capital from Xi'an to Luoyang in the east, and his dynasty is therefore called the "Eastern Han" in contrast to the former "Western Han." The empire was stabilized—and even grew—into the first century. However the empress clan began to regain its influence, while palace intrigues were aggravated by the intervention of the eunuchs. The ❼ generals formed a third power factor so that the epoch became known as that of the Three Kingdoms. In 184, the religiously motivated revolt of the Yellow Turbans erupted. The generals involved in crushing the revolt gained a level of autonomy, but then grew in their ambitions and ended up fighting each other in a civil war. In 220, the last Han emperor was forced to abdicate.

From that time until the end of the sixth century, China remained divided into many competing kingdoms.

9 Burial mound of emperor Han Wu Ti first century B.C.

12 Court official, clay, 2nd c. B.C.

6 Horses and riders, terra-cotta figures, second–first century B.C.

8 Statue of Confucius in his commemoration temple in Chu Fu

The Invention of Paper

One of the most important developments of mankind—the invention of paper—was made in China during the Han period. Plant fibers were worked into a mash through soaking in water, boiling, and pulping. The mash was spread into flat forms, and it settled as a thin, cohesive layer. In the 13th century, paper came to Europe by way of Arabia.

Paper manufacture in China, ink drawing, 18th century

141–87 B.C. | Reign of Han emperor Wu Ti
9 A.D. | Revolt of Wang Mang
25 | Beginning of the Eastern Han dynasty
184 | Revolt of the Yellow Turbans
220 | End of the Han dynasty

The First Kingdoms in North and Northeast Africa ca. 1000 B.C.–8th century A.D.

More or less on the periphery of the ancient Mediterranean world, the kingdoms of the ❶ Berbers, Nubians, and Ethiopians developed in north and northeast Africa as early as 1000 B.C. Despite their geographically marginal position, these states and peoples played a significant role in the history of the Egyptians, Carthaginians, and Romans. Intensive trade relations led to a lively cultural exchange. These areas also came into contact with Christianity, where, primarily in Ethiopia, it has maintained a form of its own since ancient times.

1 A fortified Berber village called Ksour, and a citadel, in Tansikht, Morocco

North Africa

While the Phoenicians and the Greeks settled on the coast, the hinterland of North Africa remained in the hands of the Berbers.

North Africa has been inhabited since early times by the Berber peoples, who were partly settled and partly ❹ nomadic. The ❺ Libyans in the east began invading Egypt on a massive scale during the 13th century B.C., but some were also employed by Egypt as mercenaries. Eventually, in the early tenth century, several Egyptian pharaohs were Libyan.

From the ninth century, Phoenician colonies, and in the seventh century ❻ Greek colonies, developed on the North African coasts and would later come under the rule of either Carthage or Egypt. The ❷ Numidians, who were allies of Rome, used the fall of Carthage in the Punic Wars to found a kingdom in present-day Algeria and Tunisia. When battles of succession broke out there in 118 B.C., ❸ King Jugurtha bought the support of Roman senators and so provoked a bribery scandal in Rome. In 112 he resorted to violence and ordered a massacre of his opponents, whereupon Rome felt forced to intervene. The Jugurthine Wars ended in 105 B.C., and the king was executed the following year. But it wasn't until 46 B.C. that Julius Caesar deposed the last of the Numidian kings, who had supported Pompey in the civil war. Another ally of Rome, Mauretania profited from Numidia's fall following this event.

After the ruling dynasty had died out there in 25 B.C., Emperor Augustus installed the Numidian Prince Juba II as king. Mauretania remained independent until 40 A.D. when Caligula had King Ptolemy, a grandson of Antony and Cleopatra, killed.

Under Roman rule, North Africa flourished and became rich through its agriculture and trans-Saharan trade, particularly under Emperor Septimius Severus, who originated from the area and had many of the cities magnificently improved. Christianity also spread early through this area. In Hippo Regius (today's northeastern Algeria), the great church father Augustine acted as bishop and must have seen first-hand the invasion of the Vandals around 430. In the seventh century, Muslim Arabs conquered North Africa and revitalized the region.

2 Roman and Numidian riders going into battle, copper engraving, 18th century

3 King Jugurtha of Numidia, coin, ca. 110 B.C.

4 Farmers herding cattle, rock painting, Sahara, second c. B.C.

5 A Libyan and a Syrian are captured by Pharaoh Ramses II, relief, twelfth century B.C.

6 Temple of Zeus in Cyrene, Libya, sixth century B.C.

8th and 7th centuries B.C. | Peak of the Kushite rule

146 B.C. | Destruction of Carthage

115–105 B.C. | Jugurthine Wars

112 B.C. | Massacre of the Romans in Cista

Northeast Africa

From the beginning, Nubia was under the strong influence of Egypt. The roots of the Kingdom of Aksum in Ethiopia lay, however, in local legend.

8 Colonnade of the Kushite Pharaoh Taharka in the Amun Temple of Karnak, Eastern Thebes, seventh c. B.C.

Early on, the Egyptian pharaohs began to undertake expeditions south into Nubia (present-day Sudan), which was rich in gold. It was ❼ annexed in the 15th century B.C. as the vice-kingdom Kush (or Cush) and colonized. Kush regained its independence in 1070 B.C. and was ruled by native princes, who initially resided in Napata. The Kushites used the internal collapse of Egypt in the eighth and seventh centuries B.C. to extend their ❽ rule over Egypt, where they reigned as the 25th dynasty. The intensive contact resulted in the Nubian culture becoming strongly influenced by the ❾ Egyptian culture. The Kushites built pyramid-shaped temples and burial complexes after the Egyptian model and used the title of pharaoh, demonstrating the extent of this influence. About 530 B.C. the capital was moved from Napata further south to ❿ Meroe, which became an important shipping hub for Nubian precious metals. In the fourth century A.D., Christianity reached Egypt by way of Nubia, but by that time, the kingdom of the Kushites was already in decline. Small Christian kingdoms existed in Nubia, however, into the 1500s.

9 Pharaoh Taharka kneels in front of the falcon god Hemen, seventh c. B.C.

Ethiopians trace their ancestry back to Menelik, the legendary son of the biblical King Solomon and the Queen of Sheba in today's Yemen. Menelik is believed to have brought the Ark of the Covenant to Ethiopia, and it is said to be, until this day, in the town of Aksum.

In the fourth century, King Ezana Meroe, who had inherited the throne when still a child, destroyed the capital of the Kushites and also established Christianity as the state religion. To protect the southern Arabian Christians, Aksum conquered Yemen in the sixth century, marking the kingdom's greatest territorial expansion. The spread of Islam in the surrounding countries beginning in the seventh century, as well as the loss of direct access to the ocean, eventually led to cultural and economic isolation. Aksum's importance diminished after the eighth century, while Ethiopia's political focus shifted to the south, where the protected highlands lie. As a holy city, however, ⓫ Aksum remained the coronation site of the Ethiopian emperors into the 19th century.

7 Nubians pay tribute to Pharaoh Tutankhamen, wall painting, Thebes, ca. 1340 B.C.

The Ethiopian Church

The Ethiopian Church dates back to the missionary work of the Alexandrian brothers Frumentius and Aedesius in the early fourth century. Their opinions conflicted with those of the Catholic Church, particularly on the issue of Christology and on the biblical canon. The head of the church was the Coptic patriarch of Alexandria until 1959, after which the Ethiopian Church installed its own patriarch in Addis Ababa.

Passion scenes in a Coptic church in Ethiopia, mural, 18th century

10 Pyramids of Meroe, lithograph, ca. 1800

11 Church in Aksum, copper engraving, 19th century

40 A.D. | Murder of King Ptolemy of Mauretania

from the 4th century A.D. | Christianity reaches Ethiopia and Egypt

4th century A.D. | Decline of the Kushite empire

from the 7th century | Spread of Islam in Ethiopia

The Middle Ages
5th–15th century

The upheaval that accompanied the migration of European peoples of late antiquity shattered the power of the Roman Empire and consequently the entire political order of Europe. Although Germanic kingdoms replaced Rome, the culture of late antiquity, especially Christianity, continued to have an effect and defined the early Middle Ages. Concurrent to the developments in the Christian West, in Arabia the Prophet Muhammad in the seventh century founded Islam, a new religion with immense political and military effectiveness. Within a very short time, great Islamic empires developed from the Iberian Peninsula and the Maghreb to India and Central Asia, with centers such as Córdoba, Cairo, Baghdad, and Samarkand.

The Cathedral Notre Dame de Reims, built in the 13th–14th century in the Gothic style; the cathedral served for many centuries as the location for the ceremonial coronation of the French king.

1 Tournament, book illustration, 15th century

2 Eltz castle on the Moselle, built 13th century

3 A Lord and his vassal, book illustration, 15th century

The Middle Ages

It was the humanists at the end of the 15th and beginning of the 16th centuries who gave the Middle Ages its name. They saw the Middle Ages merely as a "dark" time between the much-admired antiquity and their own modern times. However, our picture of this period is not shaped solely by this negative evaluation depicting intellectual decay, primitive customs, and lack of personal freedom. There also exist the images of the splendor of life at the royal courts, noble ❶ knights who would throw themselves into adventures for the honor of the king or the love of a lady, of huge ❷ stone castles, and of traveling troubadours and ❺ minstrels. We experience this world through the tales of the High Middle Ages—those of Chrétien de Troyes, Wolfram von Eschenbach, or Gottfried von Strassburg. These, however, as is known today, were idealized constructions of reality rather than its depiction. The literary reports that were passed down nurtured the ardor for the Middle Ages and its transfiguration by the German Romantics of the 19th century, whose sense of identity as a nation was fostered by the image of this supposedly glittering past.

5 A minstrel is given a wreath in return for his services, book illustration, beginning 14th century

Social Order

Society in the Middle Ages was a distinct class structure at whose head stood the nobility and the clergy. Underneath these, the third "estate" comprised the majority of the population, from the poorest beggars to the richest merchants. The discrete hierarchy was justified by the view that each estate had—like the limbs of a body—specific tasks to carry out for one another and the good of the whole. The association into social communities, as represented by the estates, was carried over into other areas of life, where the artisans formed guilds and believers organized into religious fraternities. In this, one sees not only the need for a sense of social security and belonging, but also the desire to find a place in the divine order.

4 Peasants work in the fields around Paris which can be seen in the background, book illustration, ca. 16th c.

Because agriculture was the most significant economic factor in the Middle Ages, the social order was strongly tied to the possession of land: Those who had land at their disposal had power and influence. Feudalism (from the Latin *feudum*, fief), which developed in France in the early Middle Ages, characterized this era in Europe. A fief was lent to a vassal by his lord. After the vassal's death, the land was returned to the lord, although later it often became hereditary in the family of the vassal. If the vassal succeeded in making the fief hereditary in his family, he achieved a degree of independence, and his descendents had the chance to establish their own power base over time.

With investiture, however, a social relationship was also established: The vassal owed the ❸ lord loyalty and service, particularly in the case of war, while the lord on the other hand was obligated to provide loyalty and protection. The king stood at the top of this fiefdom pyramid which encompassed all people from regional princes and high clergy to merchants and down to ❹ the peasants.

Living Conditions

In the Middle Ages, the working and living conditions, particularly of the simple population but also of the lower clergy and nobility, were relatively primitive—in comparison, for example, with those in the concurrently blossoming Islamic culture. Bad nutrition, miserable medical care, and wars and feuds provided insecure living conditions and a very low life expectancy. Mankind was powerless against epidemics such as the plague, or "Black Death," which in the middle of the 14th century took the lives of around 25 million people—a third of the total population—in Europe alone. It appears that movement by the Mongols and

ca. 476 | End of the Roman Empire
568 | End of the Great Migration
800 | Charlemagne is crowned emperor
ca. 1031–1492 | Reconquista
1074–1122 | Investiture controversy
1096 | First crusades

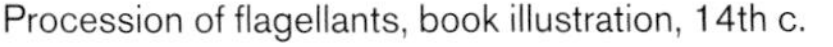
6 Procession of flagellants, book illustration, 14th c.

7 Medieval bathing house, book illustration, ca. 1450

8 Lecture in theology at the Sorbonne, 15th century

merchant caravans brought the plague from Central Asia, where it had presumably already killed as many people, to the Middle East and Europe. Such epidemics made a huge impact on public consciousness, leading to a mood of impending doom and ❻ religious fanaticism, as well as a greed for ❼ life and pleasure.

Culture and Spiritual Life

The Church—and particularly its ❿ monasteries and convents, out of which internal church reforms were initiated—were the carriers and shapers of culture in the Middle Ages. Here, the knowledge of antiquity was preserved through the copying of texts, but also debate over them, and the creation of new religious and philosophical tracts, as well as spiritual compositions for the Mass. The churches and monasteries were responsible not only for the preservation but also for the mediation of education and culture. Monastery and cathedral schools taught the *septem arties liberales* (seven liberal arts): grammar, rhetoric, dialectics, arithmetic, geometry, astronomy, and music. From these schools developed the first ❽ universities in the 12th century, initially as fraternities (*universitas*) of teachers and students. In addition to theology, law and medicine were the most important faculties.

10 Parents bring their child to a convent school to be educated, book illustration, beginning 14th century

It was also theologians who, through the philosophical discipline of scholasticism, set themselves the difficult task of unifying belief and knowledge, of combining theological dogma with scientific discoveries. As a reaction to the rational scholasticism, mystics such as Hildegard of Bingen and Meiseter Eckart sought an individualized internal experience of the divine. Lay movements such as the Beguines attempted, in non-monastic fraternities, to combine a new form of piety (*devotio moderna*) with everyday life. The institutionalized Inquisition (from the Latin for "examination") was one of the innovations of the Church that strongly shaped the negative picture of the "dark Middle Ages." However, it was not only an instrument of repression, although its methods are infamous today; legally it constituted progress, in that it replaced the practice of "God's judgment," as the deciding factor in a trial, with examinations that had to follow certain rules. This opened the way for a modern criminal process trial.

9 Palazzo Comunale in Montepulciano, Tuscany, end of 14th c.

Transition to the Modern Era

The transition to the Modern Era took place in many fields, including philosophy, society, and the economy. With the emergence of the new international financial system and early capitalism after the 13th century, the possession of land became less important and the position of ❾ cities, where capital could be made through other means, primarily through international trade, became more powerful. The ⓫ "middle class" of society gained political influence in relation to the nobility and clergy, as they adapted quicker to these new paths to capital and wealth.

Especially in Flanders and Italy, with their many rich trading cities, the perception of mankind and the environment changed to a more worldly view that saw the here and now as increasingly important, which developed in the late Middle Ages in the wake of humanism and the emerging Renaissance. This was influenced by the rediscovery of texts from antiquity. Ultimately the demand of Catholic dogma for absolute interpretative authority broke up and made way for the scholarship of the Modern Era.

11 *Portrait of Giovanni Arnolfini and his Wife*, painting by Jan van Eyck, 1434

1209 | Franciscan Order founded
1231–32 | Inquisition centralized
1339–1453 | Hundred Years' War
1453 | Ottomans conquer Constaninople
1492 | Columbus reaches the New World
1517 | Beginning of the Reformation

Tomb of Theodoric the Great in Ravenna, built ca. 520

THE GERMANIC EMPIRES 5TH CENTURY–774

The decline of the Roman Empire meant that the Germanic tribes were able to advance into its former territory. Although German peoples had been migrating through Europe since the second century, the large-scale westward advance of the Huns now put pressure on the Germanic tribes inhabiting Eastern Europe. They too moved further west, into Western and Southern Europe, where they founded generally short-lived kingdoms, such as the Ostrogoth empire of ❶ Theodoric the Great.

Vandals, Burgundians, and Anglo-Saxons

In the fifth century, the Vandals, Burgundians, and Anglo-Saxons founded numerous states on the territory of the Western Roman Empire.

Moving from Eastern Europe through Spain, the Vandals arrived in North Africa in 429, and under their king ❷ Gaiseric, founded a kingdom with its capital at Carthage. They conquered the islands of the Western Mediterranean and in 455 ❸ plundered Rome in further campaigns. Later, the state was weakened by struggles over succession in the royal family and religious conflicts, particularly the persecution of Catholics by the Arian Vandals. By 535 the Byzantine general Belisarius had reconquered the Vandal kingdom for the emperor.

The Burgundians left Eastern Europe with the Vandals, but they only traveled as far as the Rhine-Main area, where they possibly made Worms their capital. In 437, this first Burgundian kingdom was destroyed by ❹ Hun mercenaries under the Roman general Flavius Aetius—an event described in the German epic story the "Nibelungenlied." In the following years, Aetius settled the rest of the tribe on Lake Geneva, where the Burgundians built up a second kingdom. In 534, they were defeated by the Merovingians and absorbed into the Frankish empire.

According to legend, the Angles, Saxons, and Jutes—under their leaders, the brothers ❺ Hengist and Horsa—had originally been called by the Britons themselves to help in internal disputes. The Germans settled permanently, however, and pushed the Celtic Britons into Wales and Cornwall. The Germans, who gradually merged to become the Anglo-Saxon people, founded numerous kingdoms, which were only gradually Christianized. One of these was the kingdom of Wessex, which initiated the unification of England in the ninth century.

Gaiseric, king of the Vandals, wood engraving, 1869

The Vandals loot Rome, wood engraving, 19th c.

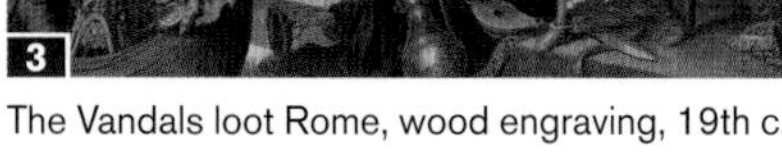

The Burgundians defend themselves against the Huns, painting, 19th century

A king of the Celtic Britons greets Hengist and Horsa

"Nibelungenlied"

The medieval Nibelungenlied preserves the memory of the Great Migration of Peoples. In the second part, it describes the destruction of the Burgundian kingdom by the legendary king of the Huns, Etzel (Attila). The great heroic epic by an unknown author consists of 39 "adventures" and is based on various legendary cycles. It was not until the 18th century that the Nibelungenlied was rediscovered and elevated to the status of a German national epic.

Etzel or Attila, king of the Huns, and the daughter of the Burgundian king, book illustration, 15th c.

5th century | Creation of states by Vandals, Burgundians, and Anglo-Saxons
410 | Sack of Rome by Alaric
437 | Destruction of Burgundians by the Huns
455 | Plundering of Rome by Gaiseric
507 | Death of Alaric II

The Kingdoms of the Visigoths, Ostrogoths, and Lombards

The Visigoths created a kingdom in southern France in the fifth century, but were eventually driven into Spain by the Franks a century later. The kingdom of the Ostrogoths in Italy succumbed to the campaigns of the Byzantines. Eventually it was replaced by the kingdom of the Lombards.

6 Decorative cover of a Langobard bible, ca. 800

After the ⓫ Visigoths under Alaric had plundered Rome in 410, they eventually settled in south western France. Officially still under the sovereignty of the Roman emperor, they founded their own kingdom with Toulouse as its capital. In the second half of the fifth century, King Euric extended Visigoth rule all the way to Spain. His son ❼ Alaric II, however, fell in battle against the Franks in 507 when these breached the treaty made between the two empires a generation earlier. The Visigoths were then forced to withdraw to the Iberian Peninsula, where ⓬ Toledo became their new capital. There the Visigoths, who had previously practiced the Arian religion, converted to Catholicism in 568. This made assimilation into the local population possible. At the same time, the influence of the Church, which had allied itself with the higher ranks of the nobility, weakened the central authority within the kingdom. This facilitated rapid Arab subjugation of the Visigoths by 714-719 (p. 227); Christian rule continued only in the north of the Peninsula (p. 198).

The Ostrogoth king, ❾ Theodoric the Great, was raised as a hostage at the imperial court of Constantinople; his presence guaranteed Ostrogoth compliance with a treaty made between his father and the Byzantine Empire. As an ally of Eastern Rome, he marched to Italy and defeated Odoacer, the local ruler, and built up his own kingdom with ❽ Ravenna as capital. Theodoric unsuccessfully attempted to bind the German states together through dynastic marriages and so create a counterweight to the Eastern Roman Empire; he himself married the sister of the Frankish ruler Clovis I. After his death in 526 the Ostrogoth kingdom was weakened by the strict separation he had established between Arian Goths and Catholic Romans, as well as the resulting conflicts and unclear succession.

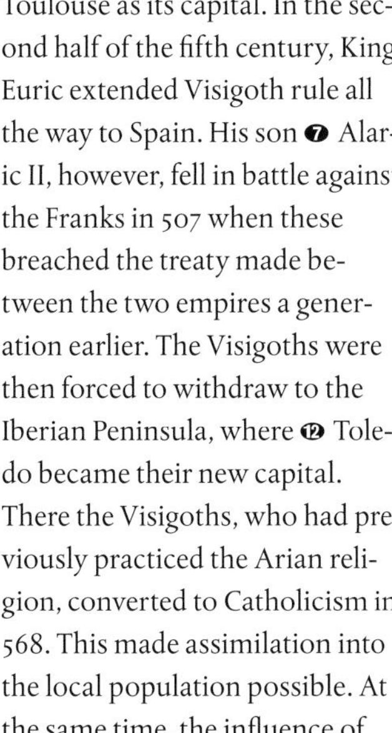

10 A Lombard, lithograph, 19th c.

In 552, the Byzantine general Narses defeated the Ostrogoth king Totila, who had sought to restore the Gothic kingdom in Italy. For a short period Narses controlled Italy. However, the Byzantines were soon driven out by the ❻, ❿ Lombards under King Alboin. The Lombards settled in northern Italy in 568, in the area that came to be known as Lombardy, and later also in southern Italy. Only Ravenna, Rome, the southern tip of Italy, and Sicily remained Byzantine. These territories too were later partially conquered by the Lombards, while in central Italy the papacy gradually developed its own area of control that later became the Papal States. The Lombard kings in fact ruled only northwestern Italy from their capital Pavia, and several ruling dynasties reigned in rapid succession; there were other duchies only nominally subject to the king. Once the Franks under Charlemagne conquered northern Italy in 774 (p. 164), only the Lombard princes in the south remained independent.

7 Alarich II is defeated by Clovis I, lithograph, 19th century

8 Theodoric's palace in Ravenna, mosaic, ca. 500

9 Theodoric the Great welcomes delegates of Germanic tribes, wood engraving, 19th century

11 Visigoth kings, book illustration

12 The Old Town of Toledo with the cathedral on the left and the castle on the right

534 | Victory of the Franks over the Burgundians
552 | Victory of Narses over Totila
714 | Subjugation of the Visigoths by the Arabs
526 | Death of Theodoric the Great
535 | Defeat of the Vandal kingdom by Belisarius
568 | Arian Visigoths convert to Catholicism

The Kingdom of the Franks 486–843

Under Clovis I of the House of the Merovingians, the ❶ Franks gained supremacy in Western Europe. After his death, a dispute that would characterize the social and political history of the Middle Ages—that between a central monarch and local princes—began. The nobility had to be pacified with concessions before they would recognize the king. Frequent divisions of the kingdom under the legitimate heirs so weakened the Merovingians that they were ultimately forced to relinquish their power to the Carolingians, the former mayors of the palace. After a series of successful Carolingians came Charlemagne, the first emperor of the Holy Roman Empire.

1 The Frankish Empire in the age of the Merovingians and Carolingians, copperplate engraving, 17th c.

The Merovingians' Frankish Empire

Beginning with a small region south of the Rhine estuary, the Merovingians created the largest empire of the Germans of the early Middle Ages.

2 The death of Queen Brunhild in 613 following family intrigues, wood engraving, 19th century

4 Victory of Clovis I over Syagrius in the Battle of Soissons, embroidered tapestry, 15th century

The expansion of the Franks ❸ brought them into conflict with Syagrius, the last Roman governor of the region, who was defeated ❹ by the Merovingian Clovis I in 486. Clovis enlarged his domain considerably and, by the time of his death in 511, he ruled an area encompassing present-day France, Belgium, the Rhineland, and southwestern Germany. Clovis was baptized a Christian ❺ by Bishop Remigius of Reims, facilitated the merging of the Franks with the indigenous Gallo-Romans, and also allied the rulers of the Frankish kingdom, and later those of the Holy Roman Empire, with the papacy. In his legal code, the *Lex Salica,* Clovis excluded female accession to the throne. This established the continuity of the Merovingian line and that of their successors—the Carolingians and Capetians—into the 19th century, but also led to major conflicts such as the Hundred Years' War between France and England (p. 179) in the 14th century.

Despite this new regulation of succession, after his death, Clovis's empire was parceled out among his four sons according to the old Frankish custom of drawing lots. Three new kingdoms thus came into being—Austrasia, Neustria, and Burgundy—whose respective rulers attempted to ❷ destroy each other. Chlotar II managed reunification a century later, but at great political cost. In order to gain the support of the nobility, he was forced to agree to the *Edictum Chlotharii* of 614, which stipulated that the royal officials—the counts—were to be chosen from among the property owners of the counties, strengthening the local nobility at the expense of central authority. Furthermore, the three kingdoms were each to have a "mayor of the palace," who would represent the king and hold great authority. The last Merovingian to reign over a unified empire, from 629 to 639, was Dagobert I. ❻ Discord within the dynasty made possible the ascent of the Carolingians.

3 Frankish warrior armed for battle, wood engraving, 19th century

5 The baptism of Clovis I by Bishop Remigius, painting, 19th century

6 King Dagobert I builds the church of Saint-Denis, manuscript, 14th century

486 | Victory of Clovis I over Syagrius
511 | Death of Clovis I
614 | *Edictum Chlotharii*
629–39 | Reign of Dagobert I
687 | Battle of Tertry
714–741 | Reign of Charles Martel

The Rise of the Carolingians

The Carolingian mayors of the palace seized power in the Frankish kingdom

In Dagobert I's Austrasia, the office of mayor of the palace was held by Pépin I, who founded the Carolingian ❾ line. While the Merovingians remained on the throne as puppet rulers, his grandson Pépin II acquired effective power throughout the Frankish kingdom after he defeated the mayor of the palace of Neustria at Tertry in 687.

When Pépin II died in 714, his son, ❼ Charles Martel ("the Hammer"), came to power, though he also never laid claim to the crown. He defeated Germanic tribes such as the Thuringians, bound the Bavarians to the kingdom, and promoted the mission of St. Boniface ❿ in Germany (p. 182). Most famously, he halted the advance of the Arabs into Western Europe, for which he was later celebrated as the "Savior of the West." In 732, Charles defeated an Arab army in battle ❽ at Tours, near Poitiers; seven years later, the Arabs were also driven out of Provence. Charles assembled a heavily armed mounted army—a military innovation that laid the foundation for the European feudal system and chivalry. To pay for their armor, the cavalry were allotted fiefs and had to swear an oath to serve their king when called upon.

In 747 Charles Martel's son, Pépin III, took over the post of mayor of the palace in Austrasia from his brother Carloman, who, after a bloody fight against the Alemanni, retired to a monastery. In 751, Pépin III ended the nominal rule of the Merovingians by exiling the last king to a monastery. He assumed the title of king, the first of the Carolingian dynasty, and three years later he had himself confirmed by Pope Stephen II.

7 Charles Martel slays an Arab, bronze casting, 19th century

Pépin III returned the favor by defending Rome ⓫ against the Lombard princes and offering their captured territories to the pope as the "Donation of Pépin"; These territories later became the basis of the Papal States. Shortly before his death in 768, following the example of the Merovingians, Pépin divided the Frankish kingdom between his sons, Charlemagne and Carloman.

8 The Battle of Tours, near Poitiers, painting, 19th century

9 Pépin and Bega, first of the Carolingian line, painting by Rubens, 17th century

10 Bonifatius baptizes Teutons and then dies a martyr, book painting, 10th century

11 Pépin III and Pope Stephan II defeat the Lombards, copper engraving, 17th c.

The Mayors of the Palace

The mayor of the palace was initially responsible only for the running of the royal household. However, once they began to take on military tasks their political influence increased. The mayors of the palace were not only governors in their respective areas of the kingdom, but under weak kings became the true rulers of these territories. In the end, the Merovingian kings had a merely symbolic function until the Carolingian mayors of the palace finally took the throne for themselves, in name as well as in practice.

King Clovis III, a minor, with the mayor of the palace, Pippin II, wood engraving, 19th century

746 "Canstatte Court Day" bloodbath against the Alemanni

747 Pépin III becomes mayor of the palace in Austrasia

751 Pépin III becomes king

754 Donation of Pépin

768 Death of Pépin III and division of the Frankish empire

Charlemagne's Wars

Charlemagne enlarged the Frankish kingdom by annexing numerous territories.

Pépin III's son, Carloman, died just three years after his father, in 771. His elder brother, ❶ Charlemagne, took Carloman's territories for himself and ignored the custom whereby the lands would be divided between the sons. Carloman's sons then fled to seek refuge in the court of the Lombards, who were at this time threatening the Papal State. When, in 772, ❺ Pope Hadrian I reminded Charlemagne of his duty as protector of Rome, Charlemagne came to his defense in 773–774. The Lombards were comprehensively defeated, and Charlemagne proclaimed himself their new king. Most of northern Italy was thereby incorporated into the Frankish kingdom (p. 190).

1 Charlemagne riding, statue, ca. 870

Since 772 Charlemagne had also been attempting to conquer the Saxons. Initial military successes, attempts at Christianization and even collaboration with the Saxon nobility were not enough to subjugate the free Saxon peasants, who fought against the Franks under ❸ the leadership of Wittekind. After they annihilated a Frankish army in 782, Charlemagne ordered a vengeful massacre. Thousands of captured Saxons were murdered at *Verden an der Aller*. In 785 Wittekind made peace with Charlemagne and was baptized. It still took a long time, however, until all the Saxons submitted to Charlemagne and were baptized as Christians. The Bavarians were particularly reticent and refused to pay taxes to the Church. In the course of his campaign of Christianization, Charlemagne established many new ❷ bishoprics among the Saxons. In Bavaria, which Charles Martel had already conquered, Duke Tassilo III threatened to ally himself with the Avars and secede from the kingdom. He was deposed for this disloyalty at the Diet of Ingelheim in 788.

Charlemagne then began to secure his borders by setting up margravates in which the royal administrators also held military authority. In 796, the Avarian margravate was founded after the Avars in present-day Hungary had been subdued. Further north, treaties with the Bohemians and the Slavic Sorbs regulated the flow of tribute payments, and in 811 Charlemagne made peace with the Danes on the northern border. His only defeats came against the Basques (p. 198) and ❻ the Arabs—the latter triumphing in ❹ the 778 Battle of Roncesvalles, which is described in the medieval "Song of Roland."

5 Pope Hadrian I. greets Charlemagne as he arrives in Rome, illustrated manuscript, 13th century

2 St. Peter's Dome in Minden, seat of the bishopric founded ca. 800 by Charlemagne

3 Wittekind bows before Charlemagne, painting, 19th century

Einhard

Einhard wrote the famous biography of Charlemagne called the Vita Caroli Magni. He entered Charlemagne's palace school around 794 at the age of 25 and was soon employed in diplomatic work. Einhard counseled Charlemagne's son Louis the Pious in his church policies and was the abbot of Seligenstadt monastery until his death in 840.

Einhard writing the life of Charlemagne, manuscript, 14 c.

4 Battle of Roncesvalles, stone relief, twelfth century

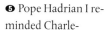

6 Arabs dress as devils to frighten Charlegmagne's army, book illustration, 14th century

771 | Death of Carloman
772 | Crusades against the Saxons
773–774 | War against the Lombards
778 | Battle of Roncesvalles
782 | Saxons under Wittekind defeat the Franks
785 | Peace between the Saxons and Franks
788 | Deposition of Tassilo III

The Empire of Charlemagne

Charlemagne modernized the administration and culture of his empire. Under his successors, however, the Frankish empire fell to ruin. Despite this, the reign of Charlemagne had a major bearing on the course of history in the Middle Ages.

7 Cupola of the Imperial Cathedral in Aachen, built 788–805

By the turn of the ninth century ❽ Charlemagne's empire encompassed major portions of West and South Europe. The papacy wanted to secure the support of the powerful Frankish king for good, and so Pope Leo III crowned Charlemagne ❿ emperor in 800 during the Christmas Mass at St. Peter's Basilica in Rome. The emperor of Byzantium, who considered himself to be the true heir of the Roman Empire, initially refused to accept this.

Only when Charlemagne relinquished territories on the Adriatic, under the Treaty of Aachen in 812, did Byzantium recognize the new empire. Charlemagne ruled his empire from Aachen and wanted to turn the city, his main residence, into a "new Rome." He had an imperial cathedral, with an ❼, ❾ octagonal chapel built. Charlemagne sent *missi dominici*—agents—⓫ to control the counts in whose hands the provinces were placed (p. 162). As long as the laws of the subjugated peoples did not contradict those of Charlemagne, they were allowed to retain them.

When he died in 814, Charlemagne left his whole empire to his youngest son, Louis the Pious. Louis's sons, however—Louis the German, Charles II (the Bald), and Lothair I—later fought for the succession and ended up dividing the empire in the ⓬ Treaty of Verdun of 843. This division roughly established the future frontier between France and Germany. The border territory was named Lotharingia (later Lorraine) after Lothair II. Further divisions and disputes among the successors (p. 180), as well as attacks by the Normans (p. 176) and Magyars (p. 298), saw the empire decline. The Carolingian line died out in the East Frankish empire—today's Germany—with the death of Louis III ("the Child") in 911. In the West Frankish territories—today's France— they ruled until 987.

9 Charlemagne's throne in the Octagonal chapel of Aachen Cathedral, marble, late 8th century

8 Bust of Charlemagne, silver with gold-plating, 14th century

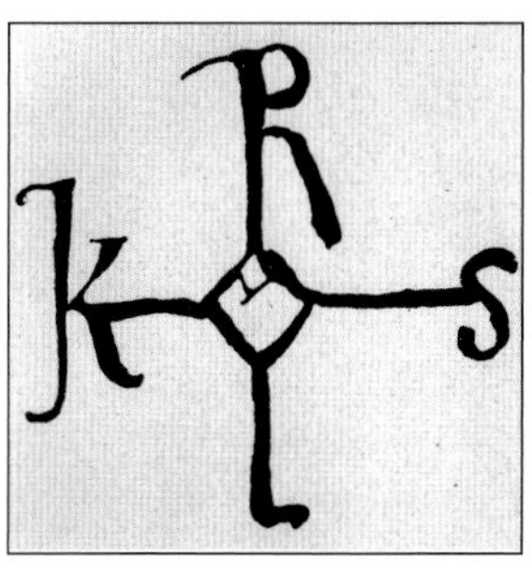

The "Carolingian Renaissance"

The "Carolingian Renaissance" of Charlemagne, who probably could not read or write himself but sought the restoration of the Roman Empire, aimed to fuse Christian, ancient, and Germanic cultures. Under the leadership of the Anglo-Saxon scholar and priest Alcuin, an educational campaign was set in motion and scholars were summoned from all over Europe. The centrally established palace school was emulated throughout the empire in the form of cathedral and monastery schools. In these, monks functioned as the leading disseminators of medieval culture. The Carolingian minuscule' script forms the basis of today's Roman, or Antigua, typefaces.

above: Charlemagne's signature, a monogram written in Carolingian Minuscule script, this became the standard across most of Europe.

10 Pope Leo III crowns Charlemagne, illustrated manuscript, 15th century

11 Charlemagne dispatches messengers to the provinces of his empire, illustrated manuscript, 15th century

12 The signing of the Treaty of Verdun, wood engraving, 19th century

796 | Founding of the Avarian margravate
800 | Charlemagne is crowned Holy Roman emperor
811 | Frankish-Danish peace
812 | Treaty of Aachen
814 | Death of Charlemagne
843 | Treaty of Verdun

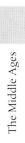

The Holy Roman Empire in the High and Late Middle Ages 911–1519

The German High Middle Ages were marked by three successive ❶ imperial dynasties—the Saxon, the Salian, and the Hohenstaufen—that struggled for unity of the empire and the central authority of the ruler. While the Saxons leaned on the clergy, the Salians and the Hohenstaufens saw the enhanced status of the Church merely as further competition, added to that of the princes, for supremacy in the empire. Attempts to introduce a hereditary monarchy failed. In the Late Middle Ages, the particularism of the princes triumphed over the concept of a centralized state.

The crown of the Holy Roman Empire made of gold, silver and gemstones, tenth–eleventh century

The Beginnings of the Holy Roman Empire under the Saxons

The Holy Roman Empire developed out of the East Frankish empire. The duke of Saxony, Henry I, was chosen as king and consolidated the empire.

The Carolingians, descendants of the Frankish king Charles the Great and his son Louis, had quickly dismantled tribal duchies such as those of the Saxons, the Swabians, the Alemanni, the Thuringians and the Bavarians in the east of their empire. However, they were reintroduced for the administration of the vast realm. Facing threats from the Magyars, Slavs, and Normans, the dukes appointed by the king were granted military authority, and with the decline in royal authority, they became increasingly autonomous. With the end of the East Frankish Carolingians in 911, at a great assembly the German princes chose Duke Conrad of Franconia as king. He was followed in 919 by ❹ Henry I of Saxony, known popularly as "Henry the Fowler." This procedure instituted the concept of a monarchy that was elective rather than hereditary.

Henry immediately signed a ❷ treaty with the West Frankish—that is, French—king, Charles III (the Simple), confirming the independence of the East Frankish or Holy Roman empire. Henry brought the West Frankish Lorraine under his control in 925. In the Battle of Riade in Thuringia in 933, he was able to fend off the ❸ Magyars, who attacked the kingdom in plundering raids.

Henry's successors were remarkable for their energy. After Henry's death in 936, his son Otto I became the first German king to be crowned in Aachen, or Aix-la-Chapelle, thereby establishing a link to the tradition of Charlemagne. As a counterbalance to the nobility, Otto relied heavily on the ❺ Church for support. He increased the Church's possessions as well as the legal authority of its dignitaries. In return, the Church was obligated to provide the ruler with to financial and military support. The celibacy of the clergy prohibited hereditary transmission of offices and fiefs, so after the death of each incumbent, these reverted to the crown. In order for this policy to work, investiture—that is, the filling of ecclesiastical offices—had to be an entitlement of the ruler, not the pope. This led to long-term disputes that resulted in the investiture controversy of the eleventh and twelfth centuries.

Quedlinburg in Saxony-Anhalt, view of the castle, home of the Saxons under Henry I, later a convent founded by St. Matilda and Henry's son Otto

Henry I and Charles the Simple meet before signing the treaty in 921

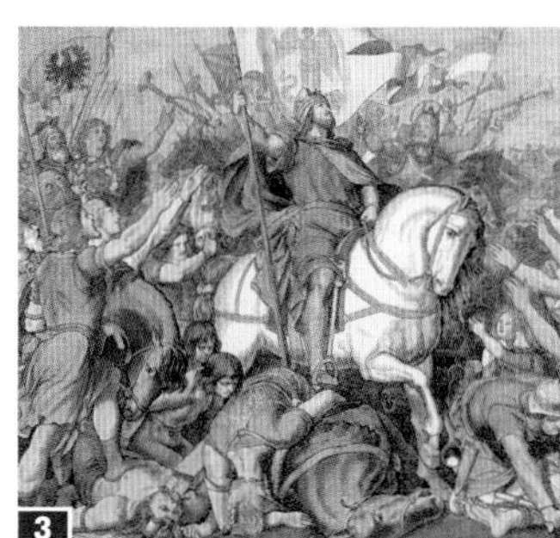

Henry I's victory over the Magyars, wood engraving, 19th century

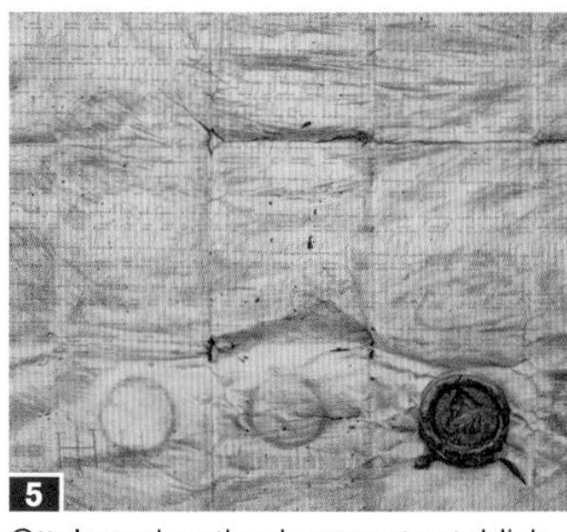

Otto's seal on the document establishing the bishopric of Brandenburg, 948

911 | Election of Conrad I as king
919 | Election of Henry I as king
925 | Incorporation of West Frankish Lorraine
933 | Battle of Riade
936 | Coronation of Otto I in Aachen
950 | Subjugation of Bohemia
955 | Battle of Lechfeld

The Ottonian Renaissance and the End of the Saxons

Otto I (the Great) prevailed in Italy and against the Slavs and was able to maintain his power. His successor, on the other hand, did not have time to consolidate his empire.

In order to control the fractious duchies, Otto I gave Bavaria to his brother Henry and Swabia, which had emerged out of the former Alemannia, to his eldest son Liudolf. Even they repeatedly challenged the authority of the king as did the other dukes.

Otto the Great was more successful in foreign affairs. In 950, he subjugated the Bohemians. He secured the border territories by erecting new marches and bishoprics for converting the Slavs. A plea for help from the widow of the king of Italy, Adelaide of Lombardy (p. 190), took Otto across the Alps for the first time in 951. He married Adelaide and became king of Italy. In further campaigns, Otto was once again able to repulse the Magyars in 955 at ⓫ Lechfeld near Augsburg, defeated the Lombard princes, and prevailed against the Byzantines. In 962, he was crowned Holy Roman emperor by the pope. From this event dates the tradition by which the king crowned at Aachen was entitled to be crowned Holy Roman emperor at Rome. As a means of reconciliation with Byzantium, Otto's son, Otto II, married Theophano, the daughter of the Byzantine emperor.

Otto II reigned for only ten years, from 973 to 983. Within the empire, he had to subdue his cousin Henry II (the Quarrelsome) of Bavaria. Otto's position in Italy was weakened in 982 by a defeat in Calabria at the hands of the Arabs, and the great Slavic uprising of 983 meant the loss of territories beyond the Elbe River.

Following the death of Otto II, Theophano and her mother-in-law Adelaide defended the reign of young ❾ Otto III against Henry the Quarrelsome. Otto later promoted the spread of Eastern missionary work through the founding of archbishoprics in Gniezno in Poland and Gran in Hungary. In Italy, he succeeded in having his cousin Bruno elected as ❼ Pope Gregory V—the first German pope—in 996. Roman ❿ patricians did not like the idea of a ❻ German empire being ruled from Rome, however, and drove Otto out of the city in 1001. The son of Henry the Quarrelsome, from the Bavarian line of Saxons, took the throne as Emperor ❽ Henry II in 1002, but he died without issue, and the dynasty died with him.

8 Henry II's tombstone, sculptures by Tilman Riemenschneider, 1513

7 Pope Gregor y V, copper engraving, 16th century

9 Otto III between two clerical and two secular gentlemen, book illustration, late tenth century

10 Otto III punishes the leader of a rebellion in 998 by gouging out his eyes and chopping off his hands, copper engraving, 17th century

11 Otto I's victory over the Magyars in the Battle of Lechfeld, book illustration, 15th century

6 The four parts of the Empire; Sclavinia (Eastern Europe), Germania (Germany), Gallia (France), and Roma (Italy) pay tribute, book illustration, tenth c.

Theophano

After the death of Otto II, Theophano, the Byzantine princess, took over the regency for the underage Otto III until her own death in 991. During this period, Byzantine culture gained greatly in influence, as she brought many artists with her from her homeland, along with the worship of Saint Nicholas. Her daughters, Adelaide and Sophia, became abbesses in Quedlinburg, Gandersheim, and Essen. These centers of medieval culture in Saxony remained autonomous principalities ruled over by the abbesses until 1803.

Otto II, Theophano, and her son Otto III kneel before Christ, ivory carving in Byzantine style, ca. 983–84

962 | Coronation of Otto I as Holy Roman emperor in Rome
973–983 | Reign of Otto II
982 | Battle of Calabria
983 | Uprising of the Slavs
996 | Election of Gregory V
1001 | Expulsion of Otto III from Rome
1002 | Henry II succeeds Otto III

The Prelude to the Investiture Controversy under the Salians

In their power struggle with the princes, Conrad II and Henry III looked to the cities, the reformed papacy, and the *ministeriales* for support.

In 1024 on the death of Henry II, ❶ Conrad II, a Franconian relative of the Ottonians, was elected king of Germany by the nobles and founded the ❺ Salian dynasty. A hereditary contract concluded under the Ottonians led to the annexation of the kingdom of Burgundy (p. 180) by Germany during his reign in 1033. Though the king now controlled all the passes through the Alps, the cities of Burgundy were becoming more independent. As a counterbalance to the powerful princes, the Lombard cities had been granted privileges by the king (p. 191), but they too had begun to oppose the royal claim to authority. The wealth of the metropolitan bishops and the higher nobility created conflict with the lesser gentry.

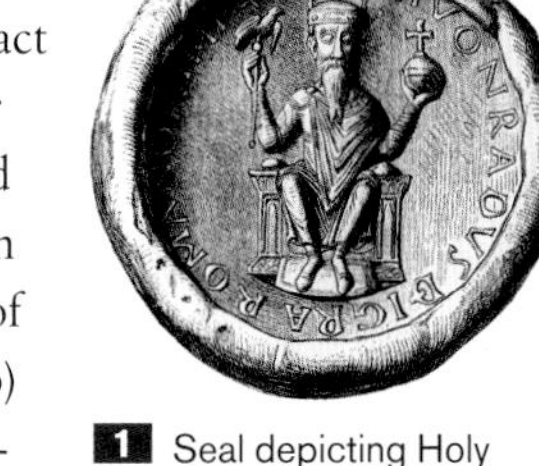

1 Seal depicting Holy Roman Emperor Conrad II

Conrad's son ❷ Henry III, who ascended the throne in 1039, intervened more directly in ecclesiastical affairs. He thought he could control the papacy by standing up for the Cluniac reform movement. He supported the reformers in their fight against marriage of the clergy and simony. Henry succeeded, despite the influence of the opposing Roman aristocracy, in having several ❸ reform-minded popes elected, among them Clement II and Leo IX. Although he was initially successful, his actions created great problems for the Holy Roman Empire in the long run, as the newly acquired self-confidence of the Church made it, in addition to the princes, a powerful opponent of the king—as the reign of his son Henry IV would show.

The German kings came to depend more and more on the *ministeriales,* whose rise to power had begun in the eleventh century. ❹ Ministeriales were originally servants working in the administration and the army who were provided with nonhereditary fiefs. This dependency on their lords made them trustworthy and so they were increasingly entrusted with court offices and the administration of royal property at the state level.

5 Speyer Cathedral, built by Conrad II, where kings of the Salian dynasty are buried

2 Henry III and his wife before the Virgin Mary, book illustration, 1050

3 Henry III designates Pope Clement II in 1046, wood engraving, 19th century

4 Ministers draw up documents, book illustration from the *Codex Manesse*, 14th century

The Cluniac Reform

The Cluniac reform movement was a religious model that initially sought to cleanse the Church of worldly influences. It developed out of the French Benedictine monastery founded in 910 in Cluny and owed its importance to the greatness of its abbots, who were pious and strong-willed. It insisted that the clergy must strictly observe celibacy and prohibited simony—the sale of Church offices—cease. Pope Gregory VII gave the movement a political direction: The new moral superiority was to be reflected in temporal dominance. The popes thereafter claimed supremacy over monarchies and fought the investiture of clergy by the king, particularly in the German empire.

Model of the Benedictine abbey of Cluny, ca. 1900

1024 | Election of Conrad II as king
1033 | Incorporation of Burgundy
1039 | Henry III becomes king
1046 | Election of Pope Clement II
1049–54 | Pontificate of Leo IX
1056 | Henry IV becomes king
1073–85 | Pontificate of Gregory VII / Cluniac reforms

The Investiture Controversy and the End of the Salians

Henry IV struggled with the revitalized papacy for political supremacy, but no compromise was reached between the two powers until his son Henry V took the throne.

When ❻ Henry IV, the son of Henry III, assumed power in 1056, he sought support from the ministeriales, as well as from the increasingly important ❼ cities. In the cities, a self-confident middle class had emerged whose capital provided a counterbalance to the nobility's control over the countryside.

The reform papacy favored by his father had grown to be the chief opponent of Henry IV. ❾ Pope Gregory VII demanded the papacy's complete control over all interests of the Church, particularly over investiture—the right to appoint clergy to their offices. When Henry consequently declared the pope deposed at the Synod of Worms in January 1076, Gregory responded by excommunicating the king, freeing Henry's subjects as well as the princes from their loyalty oath to the king. An assembly of princes held at Tribur demanded Henry's abdication should the excommunication remain in effect. This conflict precipitated the breakup of the feudal system in the Empire and destroyed the sovereignty of the German monarchs. The nobles took advantage of the struggle between emperor and pope to enrich themselves with the wealth abandoned by the bishops.

6 Emperor's seal of Henry IV with the inscription "Heinricus D(ei) Gra(tia) Rex " (Henry, king by the mercy of God)

In 1077 Henry went to see the pope at Canossa, where he regained his right of regency. This put him in a position in 1080 to defeat the rebellion of princes who had elected ❽ Rudolf of Swabia as their king in the meantime. Later, Pope Urban II repeated the ban on lay investiture at the Synod of Clermont in 1095, and even Henry's own children turned against him. Conrad, his oldest, disempowered him in Italy in the 1090s, aided by a rebellion of the Lombard cities. Henry, his second son, whom he had chosen as his successor, pressured by an uprising of the princes, forced his father to abdicate in 1105, becoming Henry V. Henry IV died the following year.

Following revolts, ⓫ Henry V brought about an agreement with the princes at the Diet of the Holy Roman Empire at Würzburg in 1121. The ❿ Concordat of Worms of 1122 finally brought an end to the investiture controversy: The Church would choose who would hold the offices of bishops and abbots, while the king would invest them with their temporal jurisdictions. The imperial Church could therefore not be used as an instrument of power.

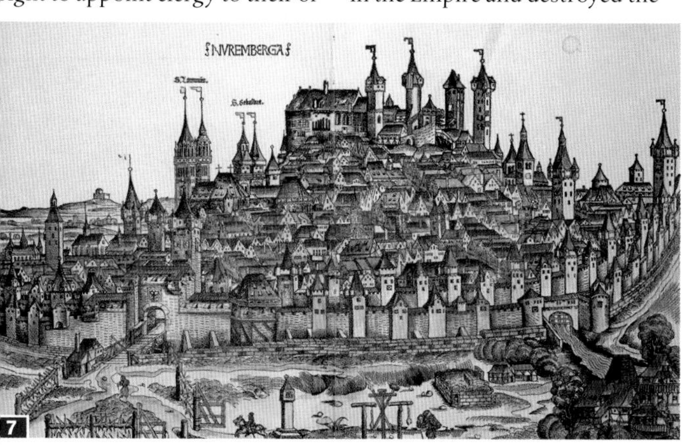

7 View of Nuremberg, city of the Holy Roman Empire, founded in the eleventh century, with the emperor's castle, wood engraving, late 15th century

9 Pope Gregory VII is liberated and dies in exile in 1085; Henry IV with the antipope Clement III, wood engraving, twelfth century

10 Cathedral of Worms, built in the 12th–13th century

The Journey to Canossa

Henry IV went to Canossa in northern Italy to meet Pope Gregory VII and have his excommunication rescinded. The pope is said to have made Henry wait barefoot in the snow and cold of January for three days and nights, as proof of penance. Although a "journey to Canossa" proverbially means to admit defeat, this was actually more of a victory for Henry IV, who regained his freedom to act with the blessing of the Church through the revocation of his excommunication.

above: Henry IV in Canossa in 1077, painting, 19th century

8 Rudolf of Swabia is killed in battle in 1080, wood engraving, 19th century

11 Henry V captures Pope Paschal II, wood engraving, 19th century

1077 | Journey to Canossa
1095 | Synod of Clermont

1076 | Synod of Worms
1080 | Victory of Henry IV over Rudolf of Swabia
1104 | Uprising of the princes
1122 | Concordat of Worms

The Battle between the Welfs and the Hohenstaufens

Neither Conrad III nor Frederick I was able to achieve permanent supremacy over the papacy and the powerful princes of the empire.

1 The battle of Legnano, painting, 19th century

Henry V, the last Salian king, died in 1125, and the Saxon duke Lothair of Supplinburg was chosen as his successor. As emperor, Lothair II allied himself with the Welfs, who reigned over the duchy of Bavaria, to successfully oppose his rival, the Hohenstaufen Duke Conrad of Swabia. Lothair arranged the marriage of his daughter Gertrude to Henry the Proud, the son of the Welf duke. Henry thus inherited both his family's and Lothair's estates, thereby unifying Saxony and Bavaria and making the Welfs the most powerful princes of the empire.

Nevertheless, the princes chose Conrad as the new king to succeed Lothair in 1138. Conrad III deposed Henry and gave his duchy to loyal princes, and the conflict between the Welfs and the Hohenstaufens split the empire throughout the next century. Saxony was given to the Ascanian Albrecht the Bear, and Bavaria went to the Babenberg Henry Jasomirgott. However, Henry the Proud's son ❷ Henry the Lion—who was also the son-in-law of the powerful English king Henry II—regained Saxony only four years later.

To finally bring about a reconciliation, Conrad's nephew and successor Frederick I reinstated the Welfs in Bavaria in 1156, naming Henry Jasomirgott duke of Austria as compensation.

3 Pope Adrian IV (1154–59), copper engraving, 16th century

❻ Frederick I (Barbarossa or "Red-Beard" 1152-1190), son of Frederick II of Hohenstaufen, had to contend with opposition from the (p. 191) Lombard cities in Italy, as well as from the popes, who found support in the Norman kings of Sicily (p. 191). Having reduced Germany to order, he was crowned Holy Roman emperor in 1155. After his ❶ defeat at Legnano in 1176, where foot soldiers for the first time defeated an army of knights, Frederick made peace and temporarily settled the conflicts with the Italian cities, the ❸ papacy, and Sicily.

During the battles in Italy, ❹ Henry the Lion, head of the House of Welf, contrary to his feudal oath, refused to assist the king. In a subsequent trial, Henry was denounced and lost his duchies; the Welfs were allowed to retain only their private estates. Bavaria was given to the House of Wittelsbach, and the greatly reduced Saxony once again went to the Ascanians. Many territories that had been dependencies of Bavaria or Saxony were placed directly under the emperor's authority. Thus the old tribal duchies were dissolved once and for all, and the path was then open for the emergence of smaller territorial states. Henry went to live in exile with his English relatives.

In 1189, Frederick handed over power to his eldest son, Henry, and took over the leadership of the Third Crusade, but after winning two great victories, he ❺ drowned under mysterious circumstances in the river Saleph in Asia Minor in 1190.

2 Tombs of Henry the Lion and his wife Maud of England in Brunswick, chalkstone statues, before 1250

4 Frederic I Barbarossa begs in vain for help from Henry the Lion for the war against the Lombard cities' league, sketch, 19th century

5 Frederick I drowns in 1190 in the Saleph, book illustration, 13th century

6 Frederick I Barbarossa makes Henry II Jasomirgott Duke of Upper Austria and gives back Bavaria to Henry the Lion, painting, 19th century

1125 | Death of Henry V
1138 | Election of King Conrad III
1142 | Henry the Lion reacquires Saxony
1156 | Coronation of Frederick I as Holy Roman emperor
1176 | Battle of Legnano
1189 | Frederick I leads the Third Crusade
1190 | Death of Frederick I, succeeded by Henry VI

The Decline of the Hohenstaufens

The conflict between the Hohenstaufens and the Welfs irrevocably weakened the German monarchy. It continued until the Hohenstaufen line died out.

7 Dankwarderode Castle in Brunswick with dome and lion monument

The Norman kingdom of Sicily became a base for Hohenstaufen rule. ⑩ Henry VI, who followed his father Frederick Barbarossa, as emperor in 1190, married ⑨ Constance, heiress of Sicily. But Henry died before realizing his plans for a hereditary monarchy over Germany and Italy. His underage son Frederick succeeded him only in Sicily, while in the empire the struggle between the Hohenstaufens and the Welfs erupted once again.

In 1198, two rival kings were chosen: the Hohenstaufen Philip of Swabia, a brother of Henry VI, and the Welf Otto IV, a son of Henry the Lion. Pope Innocent III at first supported the Welfs, but when Otto, the sole monarch after the death of Philip in 1208, moved to appropriate Sicily, Innocent changed sides and accepted Frederick II as king of Germany. Otto, though supported by his English relatives, was defeated by Frederick and his ally, the French king Philip II Augustus, in 1214 at the ⑧ Battle of Bouvines, near Lille. When Otto died in 1218, Frederick became the undisputed king, and in 1220 he was crowned Holy Roman emperor.

⑪ Frederick II lived in ⑬ Southern Italy, founded the University of Bologna to train state officials and reigned over Germany primarily through the allocation of royal prerogatives, leaving the sovereign authority and imperial estates to the ecclesiastical and secular princes. This favored the division of the empire and the autonomy of the sovereign princes. In 1226, Frederick tasked the German orders (pp. 222) with the conquest and conversion of Prussia. A reconciliation with the Welfs took place in 1235, when Otto the Child, grandson of Henry the Lion, was named duke of ⑦ Brunswick and Lunenburg. However, the power struggle with the popes continued and resulted in Frederick's excommunication in 1227, which was retracted only after Frederick had undertaken a crusade to the Holy Land in 1228–1229 (p. 221) a vow which he had made at his coronation. In 1239, the pope excommunicated Frederick again, and in 1245 he was even condemned as a heretic by a Church council.

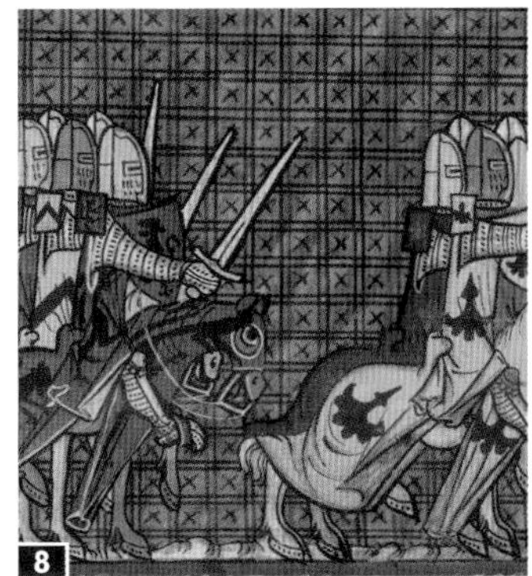
8 The flight of the emperor's army after the Battle of Bouvines, book illustration

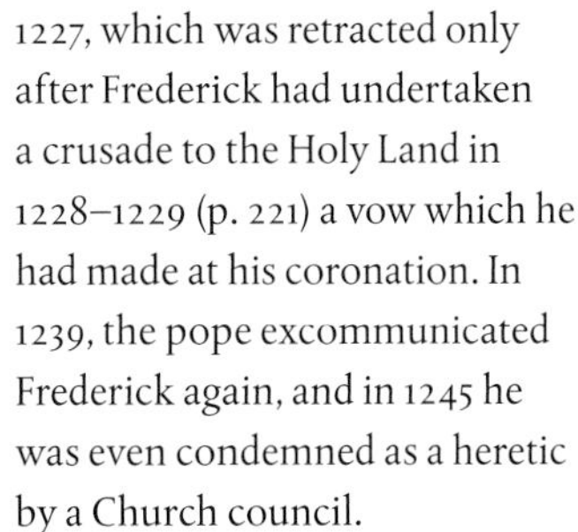
10 Henry VI, wood engraving, 19th century

13 Castel del Monte in Southern Italy, Frederick II's hunting lodge, built ca. 1240–50

When Frederick died in 1250, his son Conrad IV reigned only a short time before his own death in 1254. His son Conradin immediately had to defend Sicily against an invasion by Charles of Anjou, a brother of the French king. Conradin was defeated in 1268 at the Battle of Tagliacozza and was handed over to Charles after having fled the battlefield and was ⑫ executed in Naples. He was the last of the Hohenstaufen dynasty.

9 Crown of Constance, heiress of Sicily, ca. 1200

11 Frederick II, marble sculpture, ca. 1240

12 Execution of Conradin in 1268 in Naples, quill lithograph, 19th century

1214	Battle of Bouvines
1220	Coronation of Frederick II as Holy Roman emperor
1226	Start of the conquest and conversion of Prussia
1227 and 1239	First and second excommunication of Frederick II
1250	Death of Frederick II
1268	Battle of Tagliacozza

The Power Politics of the Houses of Habsburg, Luxembourg, and Wittelsbach

After the breakdown of centralized royal authority, local rulers fell back on their authority over their own lands. This led to conflicts of interests between the empire and the individual dynasties.

Following the end of the Hohenstaufen dynasty, a period known as the Interregnum set in. In 1257, a descendent of Philip of Swabia, the Spanish king Alfonso X of Castile, was elected Holy Roman

4 Rudolf I invests his sons with Austria and Styria in 1282, book illustration, 16th century

emperor. However, he was just as incapable of gaining recognition as his rival, the English claimant, Richard, earl of Cornwall. The absence of both these foreign monarchs made it possible for the local clerical and secular princes to extend their own power.

Gradually, a group of the most important princes, the *Kurfürsten*, emerged and claimed the exclusive right to elect the king.

Following the death of Richard of Cornwall in 1273, the princes elected ❶ Count Rudolf of Habsburg as the new king. Although Rudolf came from a respected and wealthy family, he did not belong to the high nobility. The princes thought they could easily control him, but he energetically set to work eradicating irregularities in the kingdom, for example, by combating the ❷ robber barons. He also established a strong territorial power base for his family. Rudolf I defeated Otakar II of Bohemia (p. 204) in 1278 and ❹ invested his sons as the dukes of Austria and Styria, territories that had been occupied by the Bohemians after the extinction of the Babenbergs.

Following Rudolf's death in 1291 and the brief reign of Adolf of Nassau through 1298, Rudolf's son was elected King Albert I. He ruled only ten years, however, ❸ assassinated in 1308 by his own

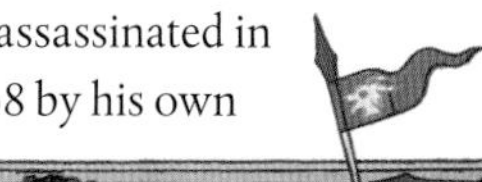

6 Emperor Louis the Bavarian defeats the rival claimant of the throne, Frederick of Austria, book illustration, 14th century

1 Rudolf of Habsburg's tomb in Speyer

nephew, which shattered the Habsburgs' plans for a hereditary monarchy. The elector Baldwin of Trier succeeded in having his brother Henry VII of Luxembourg elected king. Henry's son ❺ John married the heiress of the kingdom of Bohemia, which from then on became the territorial base of Luxembourg power.

❻ Louis IV (the Bavarian), from the House of Wittelsbach, beat a rival Habsburg candidate in the next election, becoming king in 1314. He was ❼ crowned emperor by the people of Rome in 1328, despite having been excommunicated by Pope John XXII in 1324 (p. 193) for having supported an antipope. In 1338, the German electors finally forbade the popes from influencing the election of German kings at the Diet of Rense. Because Louis was too actively enlarging his power base, the princes chose Charles IV—the grandson of Henry VII and son of John of Bohemia from the House of Luxembourg—as rival king and Holy Roman Emperor in 1346. He also gained the crown of Lombardy in 1355. When Louis died in 1347, Charles became the sole ruler.

2 Looting of a village by robber barons, quill lithography, 15th century

3 Murder of Albert I of Habsburg, copper engraving, 17th century

5 Henry VII of Luxembourg invests his son John with Bohemia, after his marriage, wood engraving, 19th century

7 Louis IV the Bavarian is crowned emperor by layman Sciarra Colonna in Rome in 1328, painting, 19th century

1254–73 | Interregnum
1273 | Coronation of Rudolf of Habsburg
1278 | Victory over Otakar II of Bohemia
1291–98 | Reign of Adolf of Nassau
1324 | Excommunication of Louis IV
1328 | Coronation of Louis IV as Holy Roman emperor

The Rise of the Habsburgs

After the end of the Luxembourgs, the Habsburgs were able to establish themselves as the imperial dynasty until the end of the Holy Roman Empire in 1806. Their actual power, however, was based on the family estates, which they enlarged through a judicious marriage diplomacy.

In the ⓮ "Golden Bull" of 1356, Charles IV redefined the election process of the king, specifying three elector archbishops (Mainz, Trier, and Cologne) and four secular ❾ electors (Palatine of the Rhine, Saxony, Brandenburg, and Bohemia). Without the involvement of the pope, the king would be crowned in Aachen and thereby become emperor as well. The seven electors had influence on imperial policies as well as rights within their own territories.

9 The seven electors, book illustration, ca. 1350

Charles had his capital ⓫ Prague magnificently improved and founded the first university on German soil there in 1348.

Charles's son Wenceslas was deposed by the electors because of his lack of interest in the affairs of the empire. Wenceslas's brother ⓭ Sigismund, the German king from 1410, spent his energy in numerous conflicts. Although he was able to end the Great Schism of the papacy (p. 193) through his intervention at the ⓾ Council of Constance in 1414–1418, he was unable to defeat the Ottomans in Hungary (p. 205), an area he had acquired through marriage. The wars against the Hussites in Bohemia (p. 204), where he had succeeded his brother Wenceslas as king in 1419, distracted him from urgent domestic problems in the empire.

8 Albert II of Austria's seal

After the death of Sigismund in 1437, his son-in-law, the Habsburg ❽ Albert II of Austria, inherited Sigismund's lands. But due to Albert's early death in 1439 and that of his son László V (Posthumus) in 1457, the Habsburgs lost both Bohemia and Hungary. Only in the empire and in the Austrian hereditary lands was Albert's cousin Emperor ⓬ Frederick III able, with great difficulty, to hold authority.

Frederick's son Maximilian I, called the "Last Knight," acquired sovereignty over the prosperous Netherlands through his marriage to Mary of Burgundy (p. 181) in 1477, which he was also able to defend successfully against French attacks. In the empire, where he succeeded his father in 1493, his reforms failed in the initial stages, but he was more successful in his marital diplomacy. The marriage of his son Philip the Handsome (p. 296) to the heiress of the Spanish kingdom and the double wedding of his grandchildren Ferdinand and Mary with the heirs of Hungary and Bohemia (p. 302) laid the foundation for the rise of the Habsburgs as a great power that would culminate in the world empire of Charles V, who became emperor in 1519 after the death of his grandfather Maximilian I.

Adage about the marriage diplomacy of the Habsburgs

Bella gerant alii, tu felix Austria nube!—"May others make war, you,lucky Austria, marry!"

Maximilian I with his family: his son Philip the Handsome of Castille and his wife Mary of Burgundy, first row; his grand-sons, the future emperors Ferdinand I and Charles V, as well as Louis II of Hungary and Bohemia, painting, ca. 1515

10 Cardinals leaving the conclave after the election of Martin V at the Council of Constance, book illustration, 15th c.

11 The Charles Bridge in Prague with the Lesser Quarter Bridge Towers, built in the 13th–14th centuries

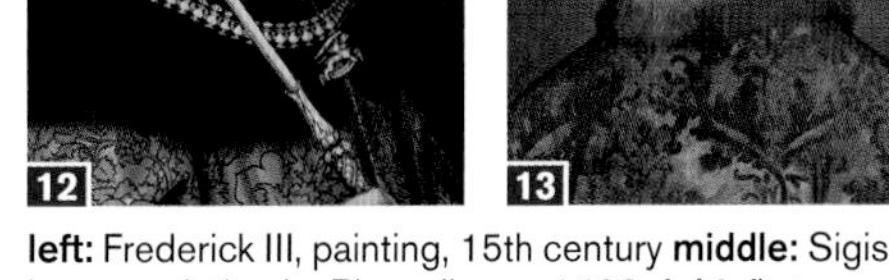

12 13 14 **left:** Frederick III, painting, 15th century **middle:** Sigismund of Luxembourg, painting by Pisanello, ca. 1433 **right:** first page of the "Golden Bull," the empire's constitutional law, enacted by Charles IV in 1356

1346 | Charles IV becomes anti-king
1347 | Charles IV becomes king upon death of Louis IV
1356 | Golden Bull
1410 | Election of King Sigismund
1439-57 | Rule of László V
1493 | Election of Maximilian I
1519 | Charles V takes power

Switzerland 1291–1848

In the 13th and 14th centuries, the ❶ Swiss Confederation developed out of the region's defensive struggles against foreign domination. In the 16th century, it became a center of the Reformation, although large areas remained Catholic. Switzerland gained full sovereignty in the 17th century. Despite great structural and religious differences between the individual cantons, freedom from foreign domination remained a common goal. Nevertheless, it was not until after the interlude of a Helvetic Republic during the Napoleonic era and the great constitutional crisis of the *Sonderbundskrieg* (Special Alliance civil war) in 1847 that a unified federal state was founded.

The Swiss defend themselves against the knights' army of Duke Leopold I of Austria in the Battle of Morgarten, book illustration, ca. 1450

From the Struggle for Independence to Neutrality

The Swiss Confederation developed out of local security alliances against the Habsburgs, Savoyards, and Burgundians.

In the High Middle Ages, today's Switzerland was part of the kingdom of Burgundy and—as part of the duchy of Swabia—of the kingdom of Germany. Many secular and ecclesiastical rulers held power, initially under the control of kings and dukes, but steadily increasing in autonomy. In the 13th century, the decline of the Hohenstaufens, who had reigned over Swabia, accelerated this process. As the ❸ Savoyards in the southwest and the ❹ Habsburgs in the north began to dominate, cities and farm communities that sought to maintain independence allied against them.

The Oath of Rütli for the foundation of the Swiss Confederation, 1291, painting by Henry Fusely, 18th c.

The original cantons of Uri, Schwyz, and Unterwalden united in 1291 in an ❷ "eternal league" (*Ewiger Bund*), which became the nucleus of the Old Swiss Confederation. Once the league had defeated the Habsburgs at Morgarten in 1315, the cities of Bern and Zurich, among others, joined the confederation by 1353. The confederation's Habsburg allies, the Burgundians under Duke Charles the Bold, were defeated in 1476 at Grandson and Morat; Charles himself fell in the Battle of Nancy in 1477 (p. 181). The Swiss intervened independently in the war between France and the Habsburgs in Italy. Though they were able to take Ticino, they adopted neutrality following their defeat by the French at ❺ Marignano in 1515 (p. 294). Clashes still occurred with the Savoyards—who relinquished Vaud and Geneva. Switzerland was also affected by the Thirty Years' War, as was Grisons, which was not then a member of the confederacy. Switzerland's independence was universally recognized at the Peace of Westphalia in 1648 (p. 163).

Chillon Castle on Lake Geneva, rebuilt by the Earls of Savoyen

The Habsburg in Aargau, residence of the Habsburgs since the eleventh c.

William Tell

William Tell is seen as the symbolic figure of Swiss independence. According to legend, he was forced by the Habsburgs' Bailiff Gessler to shoot an apple from his son's head. He later took revenge and in so doing ignited a rebellion against the Habsburgs. Friedrich von Schiller used the tale, which is probably fiction, as the basis for a drama, which in turn inspired Gioahino Rossini's opera of the same name.

Tell shooting the apple from his son's head, colored lithograph, early 20th century

King Francis I of France in the Battle of Marignano, painting by Fragonard, ca. 1836

1291 | Formation of the "Ewiger Bund"
1315 | Battle of Morgarten
1476 | Battles of Grandson and Morat
1477 | Battle of Nancy
1515 | Battle of Marignano
from 1519 | Reformation teachings by Zwingli

Internal Development from the Reformation to the Special Alliance

The present-day Swiss federal state developed during the 19th century out of an alliance of more or less sovereign cantons.

The Swiss Confederation, which used the name of one of the original cantons, Schwyz, as an overall designation, was built up from the 13 old cantons, additional new cantons, and subject and allied territories, all tied to one another through a complex system of agreements and governmental relationships. To the old cantons belong important cities such as Zurich and ❼ Bern. The new cantons were not full members of the confederation; they were tied to the confederation by alliances, but were internally autonomous.

8 Fight in the *Sonderbundskrieg*, wood engraving, 19th century

Among these were the principality of Neuchâtel, the monastery of ❾ St. Gall, the bishopric of Basel, and the city-state of Geneva. There were also separate territories ruled by the old cantons. The

7 View of the city center of Bern in the Middle Ages with the tower of the minster and the cupolas of the *Bundshaus* or federal state building

only common institution of the confederation was the *Tagsatzung* (parliament), in which the emissaries of the cantons consulted.

Religious differences overlapped with structural differences between the cantons during the Reformation. In the 16th century, independent of each other, ❻ Ulrich Zwingli and ❿ John Calvin spread the ideas of the Reformation (p. 264) from Zurich and Geneva, respectively. Violent confrontations took place between Protestants and Catholics during the "Wars of Kappel" in 1529 and 1531, and battles at Villmergen from the 16th through early 18th centuries. As neither side was able to gain an advantage, Switzerland remained divided into Catholic and Protestant cantons.

Switzerland's neutrality was respected until 1798 when Napoleon's troops invaded. Napoleon supported the liberal factions by forming a central state, the Helvetic Republic, although it was exposed from the onset to powerful internal resistance. A compromise between the new centralism and the old federalism was brought about through Napoleon's ⓫ Mediation Act of 1803. The cantons regained their sovereignty after the collapse at the Congress of Vienna in 1815, but disagreements over a common constitution continued. In 1847, the conservative Catholic cantons founded the *Sonderbund* ("Special Alliance") against the liberal Protestant cantons, who held a slight majority in the *Tagsatzung* (federal assembly). A ❽ civil war, the *Sonderbundskrieg*, lasted one month, with fewer than 100 casualties, and ended with the defeat of the Sonderbund. This led to the founding of the Swiss federal state in 1848, centralizing lawmaking, defense, and trade.

6 Ulrich Zwingli, painting, 16th c.

9 Library in the monastery of St. Gall, 18th century

The Swiss Guards

Up until the 19th century, almost every European army employed Swiss mercenaries, as they were considered indomitable and warlike; for the Swiss, the poor mountain regions of their homeland offered few other forms of livelihood. Only the papal Swiss Guard at the Vatican, from 1505, has survived to this day.

Swiss Guard in the Vatican in the uniforms designed by Michelangelo in the 16th century

10 The reformer John Calvin, French painting, 16th century

11 Napoleon Bonaparte receives a Swiss delegation and hands over the Mediation Act, wood engraving, 19th century

from 1536 | Calvin preaches in Geneva
1648 | Peace of Westphalia
1798 | Invasion by Napoleon
1803 | Mediation Act
1847 | Founding of the Special Alliance
1848 | Founding of the Swiss State

France in the High and Late Middle Ages 843–1515

Charles II (the Bald), Charlemagne's grandson, was awarded the western portions of the Frankish Empire—future France—in the Treaty of Verdun in 843. The election of Hugh Capet over the last Carolingians in 987 established the rule of the Capetian dynasty over France, various branches of which ruled into the 19th century. The Capetians gradually built up a centrally governed state despite the resistance of the great princes in their kingdom, particularly in the Hundred Years' War through 1453 against the English kings, who possessed vast estates in France.

1 Reims Cathedral where France's kings were crowned, 13th century

The Rise of the Capetians

Once the threat from the Carolingians had been eliminated, the Capetians consolidated and expanded their rule in France.

3 Coronation of Hugh Capet in Reims in 996, wood engraving, 19th century

The last ❷ Carolingians became enmeshed in struggles with the German Saxons over the possession of Lorraine (p. 180). The Capetians, who as dukes of Paris had gained great prestige in repulsing the Normans, made use of this conflict; members of this family had already been elected in 888 and 922 over Carolingian candidates. When the Carolingian Louis V died without issue in 987, ❸ Hugh Capet took the throne with the help of the Saxons.

The kings at first possessed only a small realm in the Île-de-France around Paris out of which they could finance their reign. Many de facto autonomous dukes and counts ruled the rest of France. Unlike the Holy Roman Empire, where the lack of adult heirs to the throne and consequent dying out of imperial dynasties advanced the development of an elective monarchy, the continuous succession of father to son into the 14th century firmly established a hereditary monarchy in France.

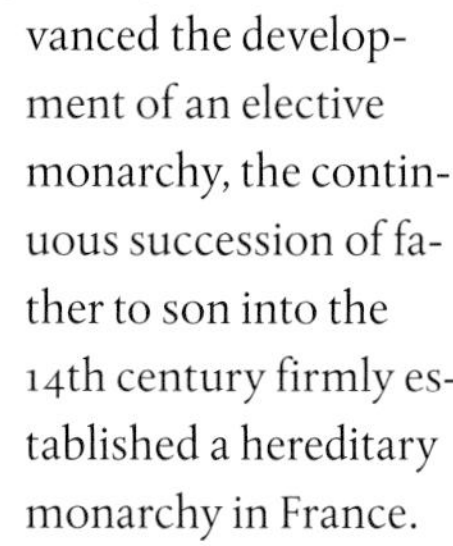
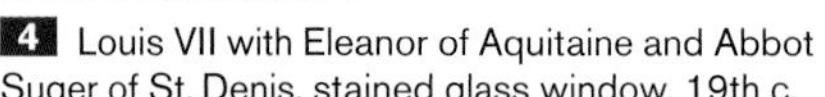
4 Louis VII with Eleanor of Aquitaine and Abbot Suger of St. Denis, stained glass window, 19th c.

The kings sought support for their monarchy particularly from the rising cities and high-ranking clergy. Prominent among these was the ❹ Abbot Suger of ❺ Saint-Denis, who strengthened the kings' central authority, defended against insubordinate vassals, campaigned with ❻ Bernard of Clairvaux for the Second Crusade, and served as Louis VII's regent while the king took part in the Crusade. He also counseled Louis in his divorce from Eleanor of Aquitaine.

2 The Carolingian King Charles II–the Bald,–book illustration, ninth c.

The Normans

A Viking tribe, the Normans not only plundered the coasts of Europe but also in the later half of the ninth century gradually settled the areas they terrorized—for example, Normandy, the region named after them in northern France, which later became the Duchy of Normandy. It was from here that the Normans led by William the Conqueror occupied England in 1066. The English kings, William's descendents, also maintained their territorial interests in France.

Norman ships, *Bayeux Tapestry*, late eleventh century

5 Tombs of the French kings in the Abbey of Saint Denis

6 Bernard of Clairvaux preaches in 1146 on the Second Crusade

843 | Treaty of Verdun

987 | Election of King Hugh Capet

1137 | Marriage of Louis VII and Eleanor of Aquitaine

1152 | Divorce of Louis and Eleanor

The Development of the Estates of the Crown

Philip II Augustus and his successors increased the possessions of the French crown.

The Capetians attempted to enlarge the territories they directly ruled through well-directed marriage diplomacy. In 1137 Louis VII married Eleanor of Aquitaine, the heiress of expansive estates in southwestern France. However, the marriage was not a success and was dissolved in 1152. Eleanor then married Henry II Plantagenet, who was earl of Anjou, duke of Normandy, and from 1154 king of England. Through this union, a dangerous enemy to the French king emerged in his own country. However, the struggle strengthened the French monarchy, which was supported by the popular will and by the Church, at a time when the English king was alleged to have encouraged the murder of the Archbishop of Canterbury, Thomas Beckett.

In order to weaken the English, Philip II, the son of Louis VII from a second marriage, stirred up conflict between Henry and his son Richard the Lion-Hearted, and then between Richard and his brother John Lackland (p. 186). John, as vassal of the French king, later refused to follow summons to the royal court in Paris. A trial in 1204 declared the majority of John's French lands forfeit. John then allied himself with his cousin, the Welf Otto IV, in a war against France, but ❼ Philip was victorious over John and Otto in the Battle of Bouvines in 1214, which earned him the epithet "Augustus." At the same time, a war began against the ❽ Albigenses in southern France, who were supported by nobility, including the powerful ❾ counts of Toulouse and his ❿ vassals. After Philip's death in 1223, his son, and then his grandson (Saint) Louis IX, continued the Albigensian wars. Though they were waged as holy crusades, they also had the goal of gaining the prosperous, culturally and linguistically diverse southern France for the crown.

7 Battle of Philip II Augustus and John Lackland, book illustration, 14th century

8 A heretic is burnt at the stake while Philip II Augustus' looks on, book illustration, 15th century

10 Carcassonne castle, seat of one of the vassals of the counts of Toulouse, built in the twelfth century

9 A Seal belonging to Count Raymond VII of Toulouse, 13th century

The Albigensian Wars

The community of Albigenses, or Cathari, the pure ones—whom the popes considered heretical—formed in the region around the town of Albi in southern France. The Cathars believed in a dualistic division of the world into good and evil, wherein the Roman Catholic Church belonged to the latter. Crusaders from northern France and the Inquisition, established solely for this purpose, eventually exterminated the Cathars over 20 years of brutal persecution.

top: The fortress cathedral Saint-Cecile of Albi, built 13th–15th c.

Eleanor of Aquitaine

The independent Eleanor of Aquitaine was a patron of artists, particularly troubadours. Her lifestyle did not suit her husband King Louis VII of France, who was under the strong influence of his counselor Abbot Suger. She also had a falling out with her unfaithful second husband, Henry Plantagenet, King of England. Eleanor was held under house arrest for years in England because she had supported a conspiracy of her son Richard the Lion-Hearted against his father.

Depiction of Eleanor of Aquitaine on her tomb in Fontevraud Abbey, sculpture, 13th century

1154 | Henry II Plantagenet becomes king of England
1204 | Trial of John Lackland
1214 | Battle of Bouvines
1208-29 | Albigensian wars

France under the Last Capetians

The later Capetians consolidated the power of the monarchy and were able to dominate the papacy.

Louis IX was successful in the war against the ❷ Albigenses and the counts of Toulouse and was able to incorporate southern France into the crown estates. He also kept the upper hand in the ongoing conflicts with the English kings, who, even after the setbacks under John Lackland, held considerable territories in southwestern France. Louis IX was canonized in 1297 for his ❶ crusades (p. 221) to the Holy Land—during the last of which he died in 1270.

Louis's grandson, ❹ Philip IV, was forced to withdraw from Flanders in 1302 following a revolt and the Battle of the Golden

Philip IV the Fair, king of France, steel engraving, 19th century

Ludwig IX. boards for the crusade, book illustration, 15th century

Spurs at Courtrai, in which his army of knights was destroyed by Flemish rebels. Pope Boniface VIII opposed Philip's ❸ taxation of the clergy and in 1302, in the papal bull *Unam Sanctam,* (p. 193) formulated a claim to absolute world supremacy. Philip had the pope kidnapped. Boniface was later able to free himself, but died a short time later.

In 1305, Philip succeeded in having his friend, the archbishop of Bordeaux, elected pope. As Pope Clement V, he designated ❺ Avignon in southern France as the new permanent papal residence (p. 192-193). Philip bought the city, which belonged to the Holy See. The Popes, totally under the will of the kings of France, would live there for nearly 70 years. Philip soon began an assault on the Order of the Knights Templar (p. 221), which had vast holdings in France. All of its leaders were arrested and charged with heresy by 1307. After confessing under torture, the ❻ grand master and other knights were burned at the stake, and the king confiscated the order's assets. At the king's request, the pope in 1312 officially disbanded the order.

After Philip IV's death in 1314, his three sons followed him on the throne in succession, but all died without producing a male heir, bringing the primary Capetian line to an end in 1328. In accordance with the Lex Salica of Clovis I, which allowed succession only through male lineage, Charles IV's cousin Philip VI from the House of Valois became king. However, the English king, Edward III, also laid claim to the French crown as he was the son of Charles IV's sister Isabella. This led to the beginning of the Hundred Years' War.

The papal palace in Avignon, photograph, ca. 1900

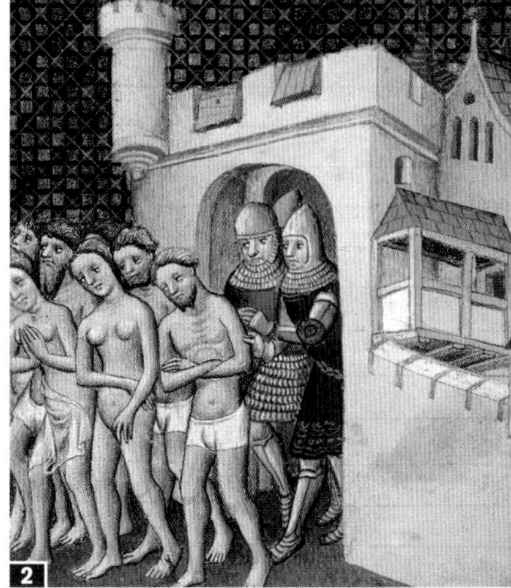
The expulsion of the Cathars from Carcassonne after their capitulation, book illustration, 14th c.

Philip IV and his councillors decide to tax the clergy, book illustration, 14th century

Philip IV watches the execution of Jacques de Molay, last grand master of the order of the Knights Templar, book illustration, early 15th century

1270 | Death of Louis IX
1297 | Canonization of Louis IX
1302 | Battle of the Golden Spurs at Courtrai
1302 | Boniface VIII issues the bull "Unam Sanctam"
1305 | Election of Pope Clement V
1312 | Dissolution of the Knights Templar
1314 | Death of Philip IV
1328 | Death of Charles IV

The Hundred Years' War and the House of Valois through 1515

The war against England brought France to the verge of collapse. After a phase of reconstruction, the Habsburgs became the new opponents.

In 1346, in the Hundred Years' War, the English defeated the French in the ❼ Battle of Crécy. Edward "the Black Prince," son of Edward III, was again victorious

8 *Charles VII of France*, painting by Jean Fouquet, ca. 1444

in 1356 at the Battle of Maupertuis, where he took King John II of France captive. Through the Treaty of Bretigny in 1360, John regained freedom in exchange for a ransom and the secession of land. As he was unable to secure the ransom, he honorably returned to English captivity, where he died in 1364.

Charles V, who had taken over the regency for his captive father, followed him as king. First, he repressed peasant revolts in northeastern France. Then in 1369, he returned to war against England and was able to regain almost all of the English territories.

His son Charles VI acceded to the throne in 1380, but from 1392 was accused of mental insanity and therefore later called Charles the Mad. The struggle for regency among several of Charles's relatives resulted in a civil war. Henry V of England took advantage of this and in 1415 invaded France. After the Battle of Agincourt, Charles was forced to relinquish Normandy to Henry and recognize him as heir to the throne of France in the Treaty of Troyes in 1420. However, both died in 1422.

❽ Charles VII, claimant to the crown as the son of Charles VI, now had the south of France behind him, while Henry VI of England was supported by northern France. In 1428, with the siege of Orléans, the French seemed defeated, yet in the following year, led by ❿ Joan of Arc, the French drove out the English. Burgundy made peace with the French crown in the Treaty of Arras in 1435; Paris was liberated, and by 1453 the English had been expelled from France, with the exception of Calais. The outbreak of the War of the Roses (p. 187) in England deterred further attacks against France.

10 Joan of Arc, sculpture, 19th c.

Charles VII and his successors set to work rebuilding the ❾ country. Louis XI fought Charles the Bold, duke of Burgundy, who strove for autonomy (p. 181). After the latter's death in 1477, Louis lost a major part of the Burgundian realm through the marriage of Charles the Bold's daughter to Maximilian of Austria. This

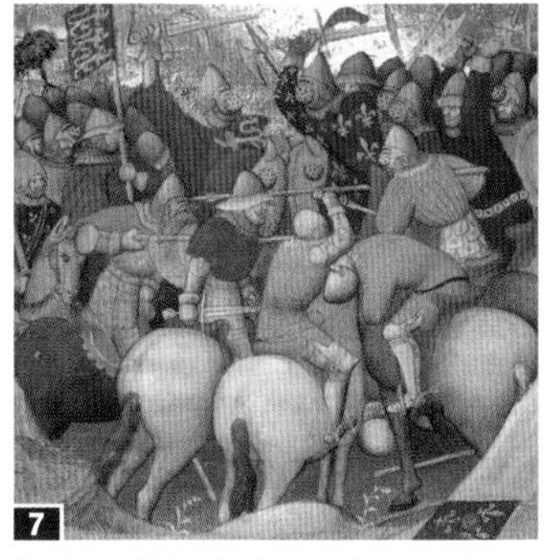

7 Battle of Crécy in the northwest of France, book illustration, 14th century

9 Destitute mercenaries wander the country pillaging and murdering following the Hundred Year War, book illustration, 15th century

strengthened the Habsburgs and they soon became France's new opponents.

The Valois had claims to the kingdom of Naples and the duchy of Milan which ⓫ Louis XII occupied in 1499. He was succeeded in 1515 by his son-in-law, Francis I, under whom conflict with the Habsburgs came to a head.

Joan of Arc, painting by Jean-Auguste-D. Ingres, 1894

Joan of Arc at the stake, wood engraving, 19th century

Joan of Arc

Joan of Arc was born into a family of peasants in 1412 and had religious visions as a child. She felt herself called to be the savior of France. Joan joined the army and was responsible for the victory at Orléans in 1429. Against the will of Charles VII, she continued the war in 1430, in the course of which she fell into the hands of the English. Pro-English clerics in occupied Rouen tried her for heresy and witchcraft. The French king made no attempt to save her, and she was burned at the stake in 1431.

11 Louis XII. during a campaign in Italy, book illustration, early 16th century

1346 | Battle of Crécy
1356 | Battle of Maupertuis
1360 | Treaty of Bretigny
1415 | Battle of Agincourt
21 May 1420 | Treaty of Troyes
1428 | Siege of Orléans
1429 | Relief of Orléans under Joan of Arc
1435 | Treaty of Arras

Map of the divided Carolingian Empire after 870, Burgundy marked in yellow, 17th century

Burgundy and the Netherlands 6th–15th c.

After the ❶ division of the Carolingian empire in the ninth century, France and Germany were unable to resolve the border region lying between them. Lorraine and the kingdoms of Lower and Upper Burgundy emerged from the Middle Kingdom. By the eleventh century these territories had become part of the Holy Roman Empire. In France, a side branch of the French royal family reigned in the duchy of Burgundy. In the 14th and 15th centuries, the dukes succeeded in building a powerful new Middle Kingdom, but it was divided between France and the Habsburgs after the last duke died in battle without a male heir in 1477. Arts in the Netherlands, especially painting and music, flourished under court patronage.

The Forerunners and Rise of the Duchy of Burgundy

During the Middle Ages various kingdoms emerged in the lands of historical Burgundy

In 534, the Franks conquered what, since the time of the Great Migration, had been the kingdom of the Burgundians. In the Treaty of Verdun of 843 (p. 165), the Carolingians divided Burgundy. The northwestern portion—the region of today's Burgundy—went to the West Frankish kingdom, the larger portion to the kingdom of ❷ Lothair I.

Lothair I's "Middle Kingdom" stretched from the North Sea coast to Italy. After his death in 855 it was once again divided among his sons. Louis II received Italy, Lothair II was given Lorraine—which is named after him—and Charles received Burgundy and Provence. Charles died in 863 without issue and his brothers divided his territories among themselves. When Lothair II also died without heirs in 869, Louis II left Lorraine to his uncles Charles the Bald and Louis the German. However after prolonged disputes (p. 166, 176), it fell to the Holy Roman Empire. In 875 Louis II also died without producing a male heir.

Lothair I on the throne, surrounded by guards, book illustration, ninth century

Philip the Bold's wedding with Margaret, Countess and heiress of Flanders in 1369, book illustration

In Lower Burgundy, Count Boso of Vienna, the son-in-law of Louis II, succeeded as king in 879. In Upper Burgundy, a member of the Welf dynasty, Rudolf I, was crowned king in 888. The Welfs supported the Saxons in Italy, who in turn supported the Welfs in the annexation of Lower Burgundy in 933. Rudolf III signed an agreement in 1016 with his nephew, the German king Henry II, that led to the unification of Burgundy—called *Arelat* then after the capital ❸ Arles—with the Holy Roman Empire after Rudolf's death.

The duchy of Burgundy itself evolved from the ninth century out of the West Frankish part of Burgundy. This region was at first ruled by a side branch of the Capetians and in 1364 went to Philip the Bold and the Valois. Through ❹ marriage, Philip acquired Flanders, Brabant, and other territories of the Netherlands, where he first had to suppress the revolts of wealthy cities like ❺ Ghent and Bruges. In this way he created a significant power base for his dynasty.

The Carolingian Church St.Trophime, in Arles, the capital of the medieval kingdom of Burgundy

Medieval merchant houses on the river Lys in Ghent

879 | Government of Lower Burgundy by Boso of Vienne

1407 | Murder of Louis of Orléans

843 | Treaty of Verdun

1016 | Testamentary contract between Henry II and Rudolf III

Burgundy's Golden Age and End of Autonomy

Charles the Bold sought to substantially expand the collection of Burgundian territories, offending France and the Holy Roman Empire. After his death the kingdom rapidly disintegrated.

Like his father, Philip the Bold, John the Fearless interfered in the regency of Charles VI of France. John ordered the ❻ murder of his adversary, Louis of Orléans, in 1407 and in the Hundred Years' War allied himself with Henry V of England against Louis's successor. In 1419, John himself was killed by a supporter of the future Charles VII, heir to the French throne. John's son, ❼ Philip the Good, continued the alliance with the English crown and handed Joan of Arc over to the English troops. But in 1435, he reconciled with Charles VII in the Treaty of Arras, after which Charles released Philip from his obligations as a vassal of the French crown. In the meantime, Philip had acquired further territories in the Netherlands and came to reign over a large complex of lands stretching between Germany and France. In 1464, he called the first ⓫ States-General, a delegation of all the estates over which he ruled. Although the regions always stressed their independence, the first step toward union had been taken.

❽ Charles the Bold, who succeeded his father, Philip, in 1467, wanted to unify his lands in a kingdom that would be independent of France and the Holy Roman Empire. He made a lot of enemies in his efforts to acquire the territories that separated his possessions in the Netherlands from the rest of Burgundy. He provoked Louis XI of France and the Habsburgs by occupying Lorraine, which belonged to the empire. He also put pressure on the free cities in Alsace, which were forced to seek support from the Swiss. Charles suffered a crushing defeat in 1476 at Granson and Morat against an army fielded by the coalition between the Swiss and Lorraine. In 1477, the last duke of Burgundy was killed in the battle at Nancy.

Charles's only daughter ❾ Mary married the Habsburg Maximilian of Austria, who later became emperor. When Mary died in Bruges in 1482, her husband inherited the estates, although he had to ❿ defend them against Louis XI of France. He succeeded in keeping most of the Burgundian territories, although the original West Frankish duchy of Burgundy passed to France.

6 The murder of Louis of Orleans on the orders of John of Burgundy, book illustration, 15th century

10 Battle between the Habsburgs and the French, by Tongern in 1482, wood engraving, 16th century

7 8 9

from left: Philip the Good, painting by Rogier van der Weyden; Charles the Bold, painting from the studio of Rogier van der Weyden, 15th century; Mary of Burgundy, painting by Niclas Reiser, ca. 1500

"The Autumn of the Middle Ages"

Through textile production and international trade, the Netherlands had become the most advanced and wealthy region in Europe. Cities such as Bruges, Ghent, and Antwerp, and particularly the ducal courts in Dijon and Brussels, were centers of art and music. Fashion and court ceremony became the model for Europe. While paintings like those of the court artist Jan van Eyck announced the onset of the Renaissance, the exclusive Order of the Golden Fleece harked back to the age of chivalry.

above: Charles the Bold and the knights of the Order of the Golden Fleece, book illustration, ca. 1475
below: *The Sense of Taste*, tapestry from the southern Netherlands, late 15th century

11 The States-General with the Duke of Burgundy, copper engraving, 18th c.

1419 | Murder of John "the Fearless"
1435 | Treaty of Arras
1467 | Charles the Bold ascends the throne
1476 | Battles at Grandson and Morat
1477 | Battle at Nancy

England in the Middle Ages ca. 450–1485

Between the fifth and seventh centuries, the Anglo-Saxons founded a number of kingdoms on the territory of present-day ❶ England. In the ninth and tenth centuries, they united in defense against the Danish Vikings. Following a period of Danish rule, the French Normans conquered England in 1066. The holdings of the English kings on the Continent provoked France and, together with English claims to the French throne, led to the Hundred Years' War. In the 15th century, the disputes over the royal succession escalated into the War of the Roses. The nobility used the weaknesses of the monarchy to institutionalize their right to a share in decision making through the creation of a parliament.

1 First page of Bede's *Ecclesiastical History of the English People*, ca. 830

Settlement by the Anglo-Saxons and the Founding of Kingdoms

The Anglo-Saxons, and after them the Danish Vikings, conquered wide areas of the British Isles and drove out the native Britons as they settled in their territories. The native British tribes were pushed North and West into Scotland and Wales.

Germanic tribes from the North Sea coast landed in the British Isles around 450. They were initially summoned by the Celtic Britons as mercenaries against the Picts, who were invading from Scotland. However, under their legendary leaders, the brothers ❷ Hengist and Horsa, the Angles, Saxons, and Jutes settled permanently. The native Britons were pushed into the fringe regions of Cornwall and Wales, where Celtic princes were able to maintain their independence until the 13th century.

The occupation and settlement by the Germanic tribes, who merged to become the ❸ Anglo-Saxons, was complete by the seventh century. At that point, there were seven major Anglo-Saxon kingdoms: Mercia, Northumbria, East Anglia, Wessex, Essex, Sussex, and Kent. These were known as the Heptarchy. Northumbria's initial hegemony in the seventh century was overtaken by Mercia in the eighth century. However, it was out of Wessex, in defense against the Vikings, that the eventual unification of England came.

3 Anglo-Saxon helmet, seventh c.

The first raid by Danish Vikings in 793 targeted the ❹ monastery of Lindisfarne off the coast of Northumbria. Further attacks and raids followed until the Danes, from around 866, set about the total conquest of the British islands. From the Thames estuary, they occupied the areas north of the river, the Danelaw. At the same time, Norwegian Vikings conquered the coastal areas and islands of Ireland, Scotland, and England, where they founded kingdoms such as Dublin and the Isle of Man.

2 Hengist and Horsa land on the English coast, steel engraving, 19th century

The Christianization of the Anglo-Saxons

St. Augustine, who was sent by Pope Gregory I to convert the Anglo-Saxons to Christianity, began his mission in Kent in 597. The reigning king, Ethelbert, had married a Christian Frank and, under her influence, converted to Christianity and was baptized. Augustine became the first archbishop of the city of Canterbury, which remains to this day the most important bishopric. Later, Anglo-Saxons themselves became missionaries, such as St. Boniface, who died in 754 and was known as the "Apostle of Germany."

King Ethelbert of Kent is baptized by St. Augustine of Canterbury, copper engraving, 17th century

4 Ruins of the monastery on Lindisfarne or "Holy Island," northeast England

ca. 450 | First landings of Germanic peoples on the British Isles

from 597 | Christianization of the Anglo–Saxons

793 | Viking raid on the Lindisfarne Monastery

from ca. 866 | Conquest of England by the Danes

871 | Alfred the Great crowned in Wessex

The Battle of the Anglo-Saxons against the Danes and Normans

The Danes were unable to conquer the kingdom of Wessex, which became the starting point of England's national unity.

King ❺ Alfred the Great of Wessex came to the throne in 871. At first he made a peace agreement with the Danes, but they did not abide by it. In 878, Alfred defeated the Danes in the ❻ Battle of Edington; in 886, he captured London, and by his death in 899 he had been able to extend his territories even further north. Alfred was also a notable legislator and a translator of historical and philosophical works from the Latin.

His successors continued the fight against the Danes. Alfred's grandson, Athelstan, completed the reconquest in 937 with a victory over the Danes and their Welsh and Scottish allies. Though the Danish kingdom on English soil was eliminated, further attacks ensued from Denmark itself. King Ethelred II tried in vain to buy off the Danes by paying large sums of ❽ "Danegeld" tribute. However, the Danish king Sweyn I Forkbeard forced him into exile with a military campaign of invasions that followed the massacre of England's Danish settlers. Sweyn's son, Canute the Great, eventually defeated Ethelred's son, Edmund II, in 1016 at the Battle of Assandun and was thereafter generally recognized as king of the English. Canute married Emma of Normandy, widow of Ethelred II, and converted to Christianity. After he also became king in Denmark and Norway (p. 201), he ruled over a vast kingdom situated on the coasts of the North Sea that also encompassed northern parts of Germany.

When Canute's son ❼ Hardecanute died in 1042 without an heir, Godwin, earl of Wessex, the leader of the Anglo-Saxon nobility, brought ❾ Edward the Confessor, the son of Ethelred II, out of exile in Normandy and made him the new king. Edward, however, became unpopular because he brought Norman counselors with him into the country and preferred them over the Anglo-Saxon nobility. When his marriage to Godwin's daughter remained childless, he designated his cousin, Duke William II of Normandy, as his successor. But the Anglo-Saxons chose Godwin's son, ❿ Harold II, as king after Edward's death in 1066. Harold was able to repulse an invasion by the Vikings, who wanted to reconstitute Canute's North Sea kingdom, but then was defeated in 1066 at the ⓫ Battle of Hastings by William of Normandy's invading troops. Harold fell in battle, and William the Conqueror had himself crowned king of England.

5 Alfred the Great, painting, 19th century

6 Battle between Anglo-Saxons and Danes, a still from the film *Alfred the Great*, 1969

7 Hardecanute orders the body of his half-brother and usurper, Harold, exhumed, decapitated and thrown into the Thames, copper engraving, 17th c.

8 English coins used to pay the *Danegeld* tribute to the Viking invaders, tenth–eleventh century

9 Edward the Confessor, book illustration, late twelfth century

10 Coronation of Harold II, detail from the *Bayeux Tapestry*, late eleventh century

11 Armed with battle-axes, Anglo-Saxons fight against the Norman cavalry, detail from the *Bayeux Tapestry*, late eleventh century

878 | Battle of Edington
885 | Occupation of London by Alfred
937 | Victory over the Danes
1016 | Canute the Great becomes English king
1066 | Battle of Hastings

Norman Rule in England

William the Conqueror and his successors introduced a well-organized central government to which the nobility and the Church were subordinate.

1 Caen Castle in Normandy, France, one of the largest medieval fortresses in Europe, built by William the Conqueror prior to his invasion of England

2 William the Conqueror lands on the English coast, engraving, 19th century

3 Archbishop Anselm of Canturbury, copper engraving, 18th century

4 Henry I, book illustration, 14th century

Danish Vikings who came to be known as Normans (or Norsemen) (p. 176) settled permanently around the estuary of the Seine in northern France toward the end of the ninth century. In 911, the West Frankish king Charles III was compelled to accept as vassal the Norman leader Rollo, who converted to Christianity and was elevated to count of ❶ Normandy. Through marriage, the counts and later dukes established connections with the French and English royal houses and became a significant power factor. Inheritance claims resulting from this led to the ❷ invasion of England by Duke William, a descendent of Rollo, and his ❺ coronation as King William I (the Conqueror) in 1066 ushering in Norman rule in England.

By 1071, William had conquered all of England. He quickly installed the European feudal system in England. The Salisbury Oath of Allegiance in 1086 swore vassals to loyalty to their sovereign lords. Rebel Anglo-Saxon nobles were dispossessed and their properties divided among the Norman invaders. William filled almost all the higher church, court, and state offices with his ❻ followers. As the Domesday Book of 1086 shows, at that point in time almost all private property was in the possession of the Normans. At the local level, however, the division of the country into shires, with a sheriff as royal officer, was carried over from the time of the Anglo-Saxons.

After William's death in 1087, a quarrel amongst his sons over the succession in England and Normandy developed. His youngest son, ❹ Henry I Beauclerc, emerged the winner. The Synod of Westminster of 1107 that settled the English investiture conflict over the appointing of clergy by laymen took place during his reign. ❸ Archbishop Anselm of Canterbury, a chief advocate of the philosophical movement of early scholasticism, was the King's opponent in the investiture question . In contrast to his son-in-law, the Holy Roman Emperor Henry V (p. 169), however, Henry I asserted his right to the investiture of Church offices, despite opposition.

5 Coronation of William the Conqueror as King of England, in the background towns destroyed during his invasion

6 William the Conqueror feasts with his noble companions, detail from the *Bayeux Tapestry*, late eleventh century

The Domesday Book

In 1086, William the Conqueror ordered a complete survey of all land holdings and income in England. Together with a census of the population, this land register composed the Domesday Book and was the basis for calculating taxes. Nowhere else in Europe was there a similarly comprehensive administration at the time as that of the Normans.

The peasants harvest, supervised by the lord of the manor, book illustration, 14th century

1066 | Coronation of William the Conqueror
by 1071 | Conquest of England complete
1086 | Salisbury Oath of Allegiance
1086–87 | Domesday Book
1087 | Death of William the Conqueror
1107 | Synod of Westminster

The House of Plantagenet

The Plantagenet family attempted to consolidate the English monarchy while further enlarging its possessions in France.

Following the early death of his only son, Henry I forced the nobility to recognize his daughter Matilda as heiress to the throne. In her second marriage, she had wed the Frenchman Geoffrey, count of Anjou, who was named Plantagenet after a gorse-branch helmet decoration he wore in tournaments. When Henry died in 1135, his nephew Stephen, count of Blois, usurped the throne. After a long civil war between the two, Stephen was finally forced to recognize Matilda and Geoffrey's son, Henry Plantagenet, count of Anjou and duke of Normandy, as his successor in 1153. In 1154, after the death of Stephen of Blois, he became King Henry II of England.

In the turmoil, the central royal authority had deteriorated, and the nobility as well as the Church had gained in power. In order to strengthen his position, Henry tried to standardize the legal system. The reforms, however, diminished the power of the church courts; even the clergy was required to submit to the royal secular courts, which led to a ❼ dispute with Thomas Becket, the archbishop of Canterbury.

9 The mythical hero Robin Hood wakes up a sleeping Friar Tuck, wood engraving, 19th century

In 1169, Henry began the conquest of Ireland (p. 188). However, his great success in power politics was his marriage to ⓫ Eleanor of Aquitaine (p. 177), the divorced wife of the French king Louis VII. In uniting Anjou, Normandy, and Aquitaine with the crown of England, the Plantagenets had founded the so-called Angevin kingdom, which challenged the power of the French king in his own country by rivaling his claims to French territories.

8 Richard I, wood etching, 19th century

Henry's successor, his son ❽ Richard I (the Lion-Hearted) (p. 177), who took the throne in 1189, marched off to the Holy Land in the Third Crusade shortly after his coronation.

It was reports of the situation at home that persuaded him to return. However, on his return journey, he was taken ❿ prisoner near Vienna in 1192 by Duke Leopold V of Austria, with whom he had quarreled during the crusade. Leopold V demanded a huge ransom in return for Richard's release. The payments brought England to the edge of bankruptcy. Tax increases and the tyranny of John Lackland, who reigned as regent in the absence of his brother Richard, led to unrest in the population. These were the conditions that gave rise to the legend of ❾ Robin Hood, who stole from the rich to give to the poor.

After his return from captivity in 1194, Richard had to reconquer his lost French possessions, the major part of which had been occupied by Philip II Augustus of France in the meantime. However, he was killed in 1199 in battle against rebelling nobility in Aquitaine.

7 Dispute between Henry II and Thomas Becket, book illustration, 14th century

Thomas Becket

When Henry II decreed in 1164 that the clergy would be held accountable to the secular courts, Thomas Becket, the archbishop of Canterbury, objected. He was murdered in Canterbury Cathedral in 1170 by knights allegedly acting in response to Henry's rhetorical question "Will no one rid me of this troublesome priest?" Deeply distressed, Henry did penance at Becket's grave and repealed his decrees.

Henry II at the grave of Thomas Becket, engraving, 19th century

10 On his return from the crusades, a disguised Richard the Lion-Hearted is recognized and captured near Vienna, book illustration, late twelfth century

11 Tombs of Henry II (foreground) and Eleanor of Aquitaine, in the Church Notre Dame de Fontevraud, in France, painted stone, late twelfth–early 13th century

1135 | Death of Henry I
1154 | Crowning of Henry II
1169 | Beginning of Conquest of Ireland
1170 | Murder of the Archbishop of Canterbury
1189 | Coronation of Richard the Lion-Hearted
1199 | Richard's death

The Struggle with the Nobility and the Development of Parliament

The kings were unable to subjugate the nobles and were forced to grant them a voice in political decision making.

In 1199, Richard's younger brother ❷ John, who as a result of disputes with Philip II Augustus of France had forfeited almost all of England's possessions in France (p. 177), took the throne. King John was also known as John Lackland; as the fourth son he had inherited no land. Following King John's defeat by Philip at Bouvines in 1214, the English nobles rose up and coerced the king into signing the ❶ Magna Carta in 1215, by which the crown was compelled to recognize the rights and liberties of the nobility and Church. The Magna Carta became the foundation of English law.

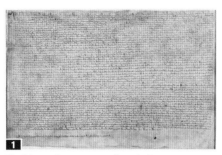

1 The Magna Carta, manuscript, 1215

John's son Henry III, who succeeded his father in 1216, had ambitious plans. He sought to secure the throne of the Holy Roman Empire for his brother, Richard of Cornwall (p. 172), and win the crown of Sicily. Tax demands and the appointment of favorites from southern France to English state ministries led to a revolt of the English nobles, the Barons' War, led by Simon de Montfort in 1258. Although Simon de Montfort was initially one of the favorites promoted by Henry and thus an unlikely leader of the revolt, a feud between the two had developed when de Montfort had married Henry's sister Eleanor without his consent.

Henry was taken captive at the Battle of Lewes in 1264 and forced to agree to summoning a ❹ parliament, which was to include, along with the nobility, gentry from the shires and burgesses from the ❺ towns. Initially the representatives of the nobles, Church, and common people met together; only later did they separate into upper and lower houses. Although Henry's son, Edward I defeated Simon de Montfort in the Battle of Evesham in 1265, he was forced to retain the parliament, as he was dependent upon the cooperation of the nobility and towns to finance his military campaigns. In 1297, he confirmed parliament's right to approve taxes. Despite this, Edward was able to restore the king's authority through a number of reforms. In addition, he succeeded in subjugating the last of the independent Celtic princes of Wales in 1284; the title "Prince of Wales" has been bestowed thereafter upon every English heir to the throne. On the other hand, Edward was only temporarily able to take possession of Scotland (p. 189).

2 King John signing the Magna Carta, steel engraving, 19th century

3 Isabella of France presents her son Edward II of England to her brother Charles IV of France, book illustration, 15th century

His son and successor in 1307, Edward II, was forced to give up his father's conquest of Scotland. He was confronted by a strong opposition of nobles, who opposed the influence of Edward's ❻ favorites, and his excessive financial demands. His own wife ❸ Isabella, a daughter of Philip IV of France, had the king deposed in 1327 with the help of her lover, the exiled baron Roger Mortimer and, it is assumed, had Edward killed.

4 English Parliament with clerical members (left of picture) and secular members, alcove painting, ca. 1400

5 London in the Middle Ages, old London Bridge over the River Thames, wood engraving, ca. 1600

6 Edward II and his favorite, Piers Gaveston, painting, 19th century

1199 | Crowning of King John
1215 | Magna Carta is signed
1216 | Henry III becomes King
1258 | Barons' War
1264 | Battle of Lewes
1284 | Subjugation of the last Celtic princes
1307 | Edward II becomes king

The Hundred Years' War and the War of the Roses

England spent its strength in the Hundred Years' War. The Houses of Lancaster and York, rival claimants, fought over the English crown and the inheritance of the Plantagenets.

When Edward III turned 18 in 1330, he exiled his mother and had her lover executed. As the grandson of Philip IV of France, he had laid ❼ claim to the French throne when the male line of the Capetians died out in 1328, triggering what became the ❾ Hundred Years' War (p. 178-79). The king's eldest son, Edward—known as the Black Prince because of the color of his armor—was especially prominent as an army commander during the initial phase of the war. He died a year before his father in 1376, however, so in 1377 his young son became King ❽ Richard II at the age of ten. Although he successfully put down the Peasant's Revolt in 1381, Richard's reign became increasingly authoritarian and was directed at the claims of the nobility and Parliament, who openly supported a rebellion by Richard's cousin, the duke of Lancaster. Richard was deposed in 1399 and probably murdered. The duke of Lancaster then took the throne as Henry IV.

The war in France flared up again in 1415 during the reign of his son, Henry V (p. 179). But the tide of the war turned against the English after the early death of the king in 1422. By 1453, under Henry VI, England had lost all of its continental possessions, with the exception of the harbor city of Calais. Worse still, the king became mentally ill. Various noble parties contested over the regency. One was led by a cousin of the king, Richard, duke of York, who himself had well-founded claims to the throne as both of his parents were direct descendents of King Edward III. Civil war broke out in 1455. As the House of Lancaster carried a red rose in its coat of arms and the House of York a white rose, the conflict became known as the War of the Roses.

King Richard II worshiping the Madonna, painting, ca. 1395

Richard of York's son, ❿ Edward IV, usurped the throne in 1461 with the help of Richard Neville, earl of Warwick, known as "the Kingmaker." But Neville changed sides and Edward was forced to flee England in 1470. He returned with new troops and defeated Neville and Henry VI's son Edward, both of whom fell in battle. Henry VI was executed in the ⓬ Tower of London in 1471. Edward IV reigned undisputed as king until his death in 1483.

Edward was succeeded by his brother ⓫ Richard III, who had ⓭ Edward's underage sons excluded from the succession. Henry Tudor, a nephew of Henry VI, landed in England as the heir to the House of Lancaster and a descendent of an ancient Welsh royal house. Richard III fell in 1485 in the Battle of Bosworth. The new king, Henry VII, then united the claims of the houses of Lancaster and York by marrying Elisabeth of York, daughter and heiress of Edward IV, and became the first Tudor monarch.

Edward III dressed in the colors of England and France, leopards on a red background, and lilies on a blue background, book illustration, 15th century

English and French knights in battle during the Hundred Years' War, book illustration, 14th century

Edward IV unites the crowns of England, Ireland. and France after his victory over the House of Lancaster, book illustration, 15th century

Richard III, painting, 16th century

The Tower of London, built by William the Conqueror, begun in 1078

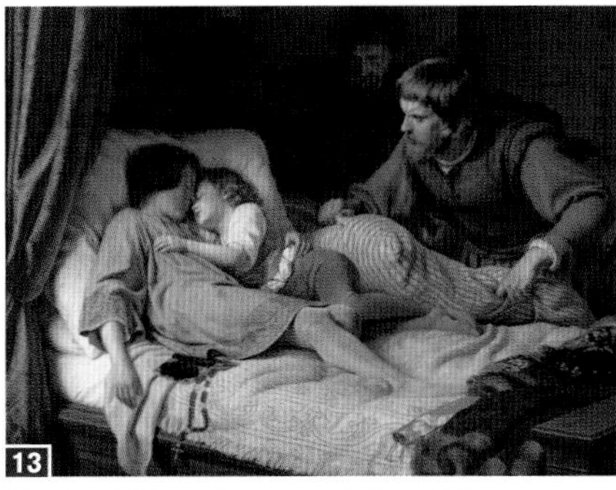

Murder of Edward's sons, painting, 19th century

1327	Edward II deposed
1376	Death of "the Black Prince"
1377	Coronation of Richard III
1455	War of the Roses begins
1461	Throne seized by Edward IV
1471	Execution of Henry V
1485	Battle of Bosworth

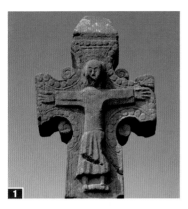

Ireland and Scotland in the Middle Ages ca. 450–1603

In ❶ Ireland and Scotland, neither of which had ever been part of the Roman Empire or conquered by Germans, many Celtic traditions that had disappeared in England were preserved. Both countries, however, were subjected to the English kings' expansionism. The English were able to take advantage of Ireland's internal divisions to subjugate clans and then the entire island, although English control remained weak. Scotland, on the other hand, maintained its independence until the dynastic unification with England.

1 Irish high cross, stone sculpture, twelfth century

Ireland

The rivalry among the clans prevented the development of a unified Irish state and made it possible for the English to extend their rule into Ireland.

The history of Ireland is dominated by the battles of a large number of hostile clans fighting among themselves, each attempting to build up a unified complex of dominions. Four large kingdoms emerged between the fourth and tenth centuries—Connacht, Leinster, ❷ Munster, and Ulster—in addition to numerous other smaller kingdoms. The title of an overall Irish ❸ "high king" remained hotly contested among the clans. In the fifth century, ❺ St. Patrick Christianized the whole of Ireland from the see he established in Armagh. A distinctive Irish type of Christianity, characterized by autonomous ❻ monasteries, developed. The monasteries ushered in a cultural golden age, particularly in literature, while also maintaining the old Celtic epics. Moreover, the monks traveled in active missionary work—for example, Gallus among the Germans on the Continent, and St. Columban of Iona in Scotland in the sixth century.

A plea for help to Henry II of England from a minor Irish king in battle against his rivals brought an ❹ English invasion in 1169. Initially only a portion of the east coast was occupied, and the English kings were satisfied with nominal sovereignty. Not until the time of the Tudors was an attempt made to control the entire island, but then Henry VIII assumed the title of king of Ireland in the year 1541. The deliberate settlement of English people and later also Scots, particularly in Ulster, that began in the 16th century was meant to secure English rule. Religious conflicts developed, however, because the new settlers were Protestants while the Irish remained Catholics. After several rebellions, the revolt of Hugh O'Neill in 1595 became a serious threat to the English crown's rule over Ireland. Despite support from Spain, the Irish were overcome. The Irish supported the pro-Catholic Stuarts in the English civil war and during the Glorious Revolution (p. 285), which they paid for through appalling retaliatory measures and a wide-reaching deprivation of rights by the English up to the 19th century.

2 St. Patrick's Cathedral in Cashel, the former capital of the kingdom of Munster

5 The miracle of St. Patrick, painting by Tiepolo, 18th century

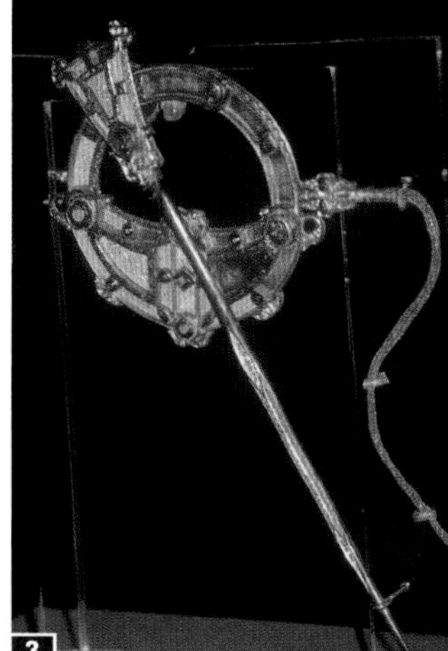

3 Broach from Tara, the seat of the Irish high kings, twelfth century

4 English fleet navigating a stormy Channel on the way to invade Ireland, book painting, ca. 1400

6 The round tower of Clonmacnoise Abbey, built in the twelfth century

5th century | Mission to Ireland of St. Patrick
6th century | Mission to Scotland of St. Columban of Iona
9th century | Merging of the Scots and Pict tribes
1057 | Death of Macbeth
1169 | English invasion of Ireland
1297 | Battle of Stirling

Scotland

The Scottish kings had to establish national unity and independence in the face of the Scottish aristocracy and the claims of the English.

In Roman times Scotland was inhabited by tribes with a ❼ Celtic culture. The Romans called them Picts ("the painted"), because of their tattoos. In the third century, Celtic "Scottis"—after whom Scotland was named—began invading from out of Ireland; they settled and founded a kingdom. In the ninth century, their king, Kenneth MacAlpin, united the Picts and Scots in the Kingdom of Alba.

MacAlpin's descendents died out in 1018. A relative, Duncan I, took the throne, but was murdered by the usurper ❽ Macbeth in 1034. Macbeth then fell in battle against Duncan's son, who became king as Malcolm III of Scotland in 1057.

English influence in Scotland increased during the reign of Malcolm III and afterward. The Roman Catholic Church suppressed the Irish-Scottish form of Christianity. The feudal system in the English form became established in the Southeast and the ❾ Lowlands. The Highlands, however, remained ruled by the clans as in Celtic times.

Ossian on the bank of the Lora invoking the Gods to the strains of a Harp, painting by Gérard,19th c.

Macbeth and the three witches, scene from Shakespeare's Scottish play *Macbeth*, painting, 19th century

Once Malcolm's dynasty was extinguished at the end of the 13th century, the powerful Bruce and Balliol families fought over the succession. Edward I of England saw an opportunity and helped John de Balliol to the throne, in return for which he was to recognize English suzerainty. However, after winning the crown, Balliol refused to submit to English interests, whereupon the English occupied the country. Sir William Wallace and Robert the Bruce organized the resistance against the English occupiers. In extended fighting, Robert, who was crowned king in 1306, was able to defend Scottish independence. The Scots were able to strengthen their position further as England became embroiled in the Hundred Years' War and the War of the Roses.

In 1371, the Stuarts replaced the House of Bruce. Despite the marriage of James IV Stuart to Margaret Tudor, the daughter of Henry VII of England in 1503, clashes with the English continued. Nevertheless, this marriage formed the basis for the claim of James's granddaughter ⓫ Mary Stuart (p.284) to the English throne and led in 1603 to the unification of both kingdoms under Mary's son ❿ James VI of Scotland and I of England.

William Wallace

William Wallace—known as "Braveheart"—led the Scots to victory over a superior English army in the Battle of Stirling in 1297. However, the Scottish nobility refused to support Wallace, who rose out of modest circumstances, and so he was soon defeated by the English in 1298 at Falkirk. Wallace was later betrayed by a Scottish noble, taken captive, and executed in London in 1305.

above: Statue of William Wallace by the walls of Edinburgh Castle

Edinburgh Castle, built from the late seventh century on, in Edinburgh, capital of the Scottish Lowlands

James VI of Scotland and James I of England, painting, 1605

Mary Stuart with her second husband, Lord Darnley, engraving, 1565

1298 Battle of Falkirk
1305 Execution of William Wallace
1541 Henry VIII takes title of Irish king
1306 Coronation of Robert the Bruce
1603 Union of Scotland and England
1595 Uprising of Hugh O'Neill

View over the city center of Siena inTuscany, with the Palazzo Pubblico and the Bell Tower built in the Middle Ages

Italy in the Middle Ages ca. 600–ca. 1500

Northern Italy was closely tied to France and later to the Holy Roman Empire. A Norman kingdom developed in southern Italy, then later went to the German Hohenstaufens and the French and Spanish royal houses. The papacy reached the pinnacle of its secular power in the 12th and 13th centuries. Its influence had decreased again by the Late Middle Ages as it was divided by the Great Schism. Simultaneously a self-confident middle class, whose early capitalist economy expanded over the Continent in the course of the following centuries, emerged in ❶ northern Italy. One northern Italian city-state, Venice, rose to become Europe's most significant economic power.

The Kingdom of Italy After the Carolingians

Several dynasties fought for the monarchy following the end of the Carolingians. Eventually, the Saxon Ottonians added the Italian monarchy to the German royal crown.

❹, ❺ Charlemagne conquered the kingdom of the Lombards (p. 164) in northern Italy in 774. His sons and grandsons ruled over the Italian territories into the ninth century.

After the Carolingians died out, rulers of various families seized the Italian ❷ royal crown; most of these were descended from the female line of the Carolingians, although some were simply usurpers. None of the kings were able to establish a permanent dynasty, however, and thus an unstable period followed in which local nobility and later cities were able to build up their independence.

In 951 the widow of Lothair II, ❻ Adelaide of Lombardy (p. 167), sent a plea to the German king Otto the Great for help against the new king, Berengar II of the House of Ivrea. ❸ Otto defeated Berengar and became king of Italy. He united the kingdom and then integrated it into the Holy Roman Empire. The German kings and emperors never had a power base of their own in Imperial Italy and were instead dependent upon the great nobles, the powerful cities, the Church, and the papacy during their rule. They attempted to play the individual parties off against one other, for example, by granting increased royal prerogatives to win over individual parties, but this ultimately undermined their authority. Thus Italy ultimately disintegrated into numerous independent city states.

Berengar II of Ivrea before Otto I the Great, 1150

The "Iron Crown," the Lombard royal crown with an iron ring within, allegedly made from a nail of Christ's cross, sixth–ninth century

Charlemagne marches into Pavia, capital of Lombardy, wood engraving, 19th c.

Charlemagne holds the Iron Crown, crown of the Lombard kings, drawing, 19th century

Figures of the Empress Adelaide and Emperor Otto I the Great at the dome of Meissen

774 Conquest of the Lombard kingdom
951 Victory of Otto I over Berengar II
1059 Robert Guiscard becomes duke of Puglia and Calabria
1130 Unification of Norman territories
1194 Henry VI becomes king of Sicily
1220 Frederick II is crowned emperor

Southern Italy from the 8th to the 15th centuries

Normans and Hohenstaufens made a model state of the kingdom of Sicily. French and Spanish dynasties fought over the wealthy Hohenstaufen crown.

Lombard principalities had survived in southern Italy. Furthermore, there were still Byzantine bases that had in part fallen into the hands of the Muslim ❽ Arabs who had occupied Sicily and Puglia in the ninth century. Since the eleventh century, Normans in the service of the southern Italian princes as mercenaries had also seized domains for themselves. The popes tried to bring the Normans under their control by legitimizing their rule through official investiture; in 1059 Robert Guiscard was made duke of Puglia and Calabria, and his brother Roger I count of Sicily. ❼, ⓫ Roger II combined the Norman possessions and was granted the title of king by the pope in 1130. Catholic and Orthodox Christians, Jews, and Muslims lived at his ⓭ court in Palermo, a leading European cultural center of the time.

7 Coat for the crowning of Roger II, twelfth century

In 1194, the Hohenstaufen emperor Henry VI, son-in-law of Roger II, gained the crown of Sicily. His son, Emperor ⓬ Frederick II, found Sicily more welcoming than the more northerly parts of the Holy Roman Empire and ruled from his home and power base (p. 171) there. Because of his education, Frederick was known by his contemporaries as "*Stupor Mundi*" ("Wonder of the World"). After Frederick's death in 1250 and that of his son Conrad IV in 1254, Conrad's illegitimate brother Manfred ruled Sicily in the name of Conrad's son, Conradin. In order to eliminate the Hohenstaufens for good, the pope gave the crown of Sicily to ❾ Charles I of Anjou, brother of the French king. Charles defeated Manfred and Conradin, who was ❿ executed in 1268 (p. 171).

Charles's French administrators demanded high taxes from the Sicilians, who rose up in 1282 in the revolt of the "Sicilian Vespers." This enabled Peter III of Aragon, Manfred's son-in-law, to occupy the island. Charles, who died shortly thereafter, retained only his mainland possessions, which became the kingdom of Naples. A number of battles over succession in Naples took place among Charles's descendents. The last monarch of the House of Anjou, Queen Joan II, first designated King Alfonso V of Aragon and Sicily as her heir, then a French cousin, Louis of the House of Valois. After her death in 1435, Alfonso secured the kingdom of Naples for his family. His nephew, Ferdinand the Catholic of Aragon, united Sicily and Naples in 1501. The possessions, along with the Spanish inheritance, went to his grandson, Charles V of the house of Habsburg after Ferdinand's death in 1516.

8 Arabs besiege and conquer Messina in 842–43, book illustration, 13th century

9 Charles I of Anjou travels to Italy by sea (left); his investiture by Pope Clemens IV with the kingdom of Sicily (right), wood painting, 14th century

11 Depiction of Roger II of Sicily crowned by Christ

12 Frederick II receives Arab deputies at his court, painting, 19th century

Salimbene di Adam, from his Cronica, about

Emperor Frederick II

"Frederick . . . was crafty, wily, avaricious, lustful, malicious, wrathful; and yet a gallant man at times, when he would show his kindness or courtesy; full of solace, jocund, delightful, fertile in devices. He knew to read, write, and sing, to make songs and music."

Book illustration to Holy Roman Emperor Frederick II's book on falconry, 13th century

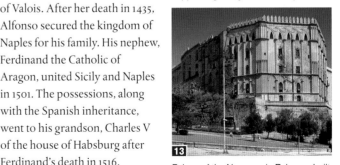

10 Execution of Conradin in Naples, copper engraving, 17th century

13 Palace of the Normans in Palermo, built from the ninth century onward

1254	Manfred becomes regent of Sicily
1268	Execution of Manfred by Charles of Anjou
30 Mar 1282	Sicilian Vespers revolt
1282	Occupation of Sicily by Peter III
1501	Unification of Sicily and Naples

The Papacy in the Middle Ages

The papacy reached the pinnacle of its power in the High Middle Ages, strengthened by the Cluniac and Gregorian reforms. Division in the Church over doctrinal and theological issues as well as secularization led to the gradual decline of the papacy.

The popes—bishops of ❶ Rome and successors to the ❷ Apostle Peter—claimed a position of supremacy within the Catholic Church. Furthermore, once the Roman emperors no longer resided in Rome and the state structure in the Western Empire disintegrated, the popes increasingly assumed secular functions. The extent of their authority is demonstrated, for example, by Leo I, who was able to convince the leader of the Huns, Attila, to halt his march on Rome. (p. 149). The popes based their claims, among other things, on a falsified document known as the ❼ "Donation of Constantine" by which Emperor Constantine the Great supposedly left most of the Western Roman Empire to the papacy. In the East, the patriarch of Constantinople and head of the Byzantine imperial church rejected the primacy of the Roman popes. The final break came in 1054 in the Eastern Schism, when Pope Leo IX and Patriarch Michael Cerularius excommunicated one other.

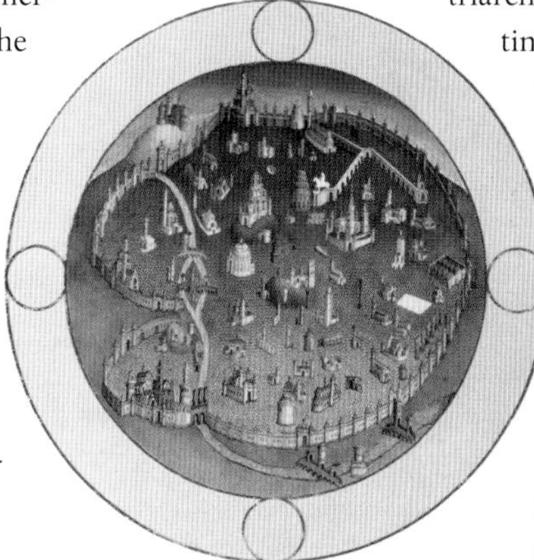

1 Plan of the city of Rome, book illustration, early 15th century

At the turn of the seventh century, ❸ Pope Gregory introduced the central administration of papal lands. From this developed what became known as the Papal States (*Patrimonium Petri*); of the former Papal States, only the Vatican remains under the pope's control today.

In 753 the new Frankish king, Pépin III, extended the Papal States by a bequest of lands known as the "Donation of Pépin." In return for this, he was recognized by Pope Stephen II as the successor to the Merovingians (p. 162). The Franks became the protectors of the Church and defended the popes against Italian princes and Roman patricians. The alliance was cemented in 800 when Pope Leo III ❹ crowned Charlemagne as emperor (p. 165). The Saxon Ottonians (p. 166), who became kings of Italy in 951, continued the traditional close ties between the imperial crown and the papacy. Concurrently, the Cluniac reforms sought a spiritual renewal of the Church and the elimination of abuses such as the marriages of priests, simony and lay investitures.

The Salians, who succeeded the Saxons, helped put a reform-minded pope in office (p. 168). Now politically and spiritually renewed, the papacy turned against the instrumentalization of the Church by secular rulers by taking on the investiture controversy (p. 169). Pope Gregory VII formulated the clergy's position of supremacy over the secular rulers in his "*Dictatus Papae.*" The renewal movement gained further political weight through the Gregorian reforms. The symbolic submission of Emperor Henry IV to Gregory VII in his "journey to Canossa" in 1077 (p. 169) attested to the power of the papacy. The investiture controversy was officially settled in 1122, although the

2 Jesus gives Peter the keys to Rome, as a sign of his supremacy over the other apostles and the Church's right to territory in Rome, painting, 15th century

3 Pope Gregor y I (the Great) studying at his desk in his residence, ivory carving, tenth century

4 Pope Leo III crowns Charlemagne as emperor, copper engraving, 19th c.

5 Pope Martin V is elected at the Council of Constance, book illustration, 15th century

6 Innocent III confirms the rules of the Franciscan order, fresco by Giotto di Bondone, ca. 1300

440–61 | Pontificate of Leo I
600 | Implementation of papal central administration
753 | Donation of Pépin
8th–9th century | Fabrication of the "Donation of Constantine"
ca. 1050 | Beginning of the investiture controversy
1054 | Eastern Schism
1077 | Journey to Canossa

Constantine the Great gives Pope Silvester I the symbols of imperial power, fresco, 13th century

The Pope's palace in Avignon, France, built in the 14th century, papal residence 1309–1377

The Castel Sant'Angelo in Rome on the banks of the Tiber, tomb of Emperor Hadrian, refuge of the popes

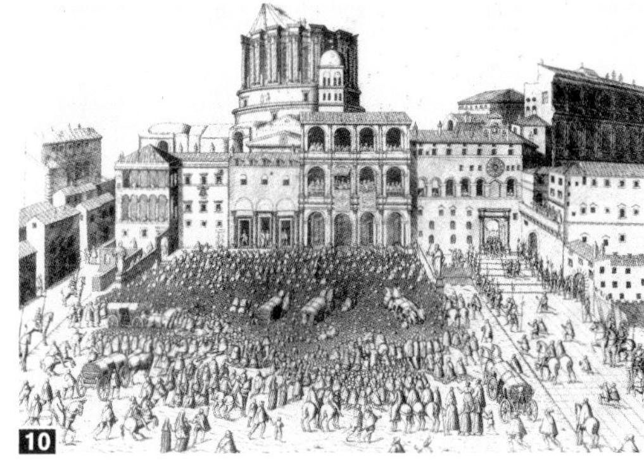
The old St. Peter's Cathedral in Rome, in the background the new cupola, built in Renaissance style

conflict between the pope and secular rulers continued.

Between 1198 and 1216, the papacy under Pope Innocent III was able to take advantage of the power struggle (p. 171) between the Hohenstaufens and the Welfs in the Holy Roman Empire and reach the height of its political power. Innocent called for crusades against the Albigenses (p. 177) in France and the Muslims in the Holy Land and for the ❻ founding of the Franciscan and Dominican orders. In 1231 the latter was entrusted with the Inquisition, which served to combat heresy and monitor the implementation of Church doctrines.

The popes lacked temporal instruments of power such as armies, however, while their ultimate spiritual weapon—the threat of excommunication—had lost much of its impact through its frequent usage. In response to the overreaching claims of absolute world power that Pope ⓭ Boniface VIII formulated in 1302 in the bull *"Unam Sanctam,"*

Crowning of Pope Clement VII, book illustration, 14th century

King Philip IV of France demonstrated the autonomy of the state (p. 178) by forcing the papacy to move to ❽ Avignon in France in 1309. Here it remained until 1377, constantly under the influence of the French kings. Similarly, excommunication by John XXII in 1324 no longer held the power to intimidate the Bavarian emperor Louis IV (p. 172). He continued to support the Franciscans against the papacy in the poverty controversy—the Franciscans saw the poverty of Christ as a model for the Church, a view the papacy did not share.

Because the papal properties in Italy were threatened, Gregory XI returned to ❾ Rome from Avignon in 1377. After Gregory's death, however, conflict erupted between the French and Italian cardinals; both parties wanted to elevate a fellow countryman to the papacy—and both did. In 1378, two popes were elected: Urban VI in Rome and ⓫ Clement VII, who continued to reside in Avignon. The Great Schism (or Western Schism)—after 1409, there were even three competing popes—was finally ended in 1417 at the Council of Constance (p. 173) with the election of ❺ Martin V as the sole pope. During the schism, the spiritual authority of the papacy naturally suffered. Councils such as that of Basel, which met from 1431 to 1449, claimed to supersede the decisions of popes. The popes, however, succeeded in splitting

Pope Pius II, fresco by Bernardino Pinturicchio, early 16th century

the council movement, and in 1459 it was declared heretical by Pius II. Thus a possible instrument of Church reform was also eliminated.

In the 16th century, the inability to make spiritual reforms finally resulted in the rupture of the Catholic Church's authority on spiritual matters by the Reformation (p. 256). The Reformation gained additional impetus from the secularization of the papacy, which was ushered in by ⓬ Pius II and his predecessor Nicholas V, under a series of ❿ Renaissance popes (p. 292).

13 Pope Boniface VIII, gold-plated bronze structure, 1301

1198–1216 | Pontificate of Innocent III
1122 | End of the investiture controversy
1309–77 | Avignon becomes the papal residence
1231 | Centralization of the Inquisition
1409 | Western Schism
1378 | Dual election of Urban VI and Clement VII
1431–49 | Council of Basel
1417 | Council of Constance

Northern Italy under the Salians and Hohenstaufens: Welfs and Ghibellines

Out of the power struggles between the emperor, the pope, the aristocracy, and cities came the feud between the Welfs and Ghibellines.

The new trading routes that the Crusades opened up brought enormous ❸ economic prosperity to the Italian cities in the 12th century. As a counterweight to the popes and the nobility, ❹ emperors had granted the cities increasingly more freedom. The cities, however, now insisted on pursuing their own goals. The investiture controversy had already reduced the emperor's authority. In addition, the conflict between the Welf (or Guelf) and Hohenstaufen houses (p. 170) spread into Italy as both families claimed the rich inheritance of Matilda of Tuscany. When the Hohenstaufen emperor ❻ Frederick I claimed ownership of Italian territories and wanted to enforce his tax demands, the northern Italian cities formed the Lombard League against him. The Lombards defeated the emperor in the Battle of Legnano in 1176 and were thus able to secure their financial and political freedom.

1 The Piazza della Signoria in Florence with the Palazzo Vecchio, the government domicile of the city republic and the Loggia dei Lanzi (right)

3 A clothier at his loom, fresco by Lorenzetti, 14th century

4 Crowning of a German emperor with the Iron Crown of Lombardy, wood engraving, 19th century, after a relief from the late 14th century

6 Frederick I Barbarossa on horseback fights for a Lombard city, painting, 19th century

Mathilda of Tuscany

The countess of Tuscany held a key position due to her wealth and the strategic location of her estates in central Italy. An adherent of Church reform, Matilda mediated between Henry IV and Pope Gregory VII, who met at her family seat in Canossa in 1077. She rewrote her will several times before she died childless in 1115. At one point, she named the Church, and at another point the emperor, as heir to her fortune. Eventually the Welfs, the family of her last husband, also laid claim to the inheritance. The conflict was finally settled in 1213.

Henry IV asks the Countess Mathilde to mediate in his conflict with the pope, book illustration, early twelfth century

Two factions emerged out of this conflict: The Welfs supported the papacy, while the Ghibellines, who got their name from the Hohenstaufen castle of Waiblingen, supported the emperor. The partisanship in the dispute between the Welfs and Hohenstaufens, however, gradually slipped out of focus. "Guelf" and "Ghibelline" evolved into designations for rival factions in many feuds between families or political groups, particularly in the communes, which were split by outright civil wars. For defense they retired to fortified towers, the ❺ "tower houses," which were also meant to demonstrate the families' wealth and power.

The Guelfs in 13th-century ❶ Florence saw themselves principally as good patriots who defended the liberties of the city. They had been exiled from the city but when the emperor died had come back to power. The declaration of the ideal of civic patriotism was meant to keep the hostile Ghibellines out of power. At the end of the 14th century, the Guelfs were mainly the representatives of the ❷ rich upper class in Florence, while the political representatives of the middle class belonged to the Ghibellines.

2 Florentine merchant in his warehouse, wood engraving, late 15th century

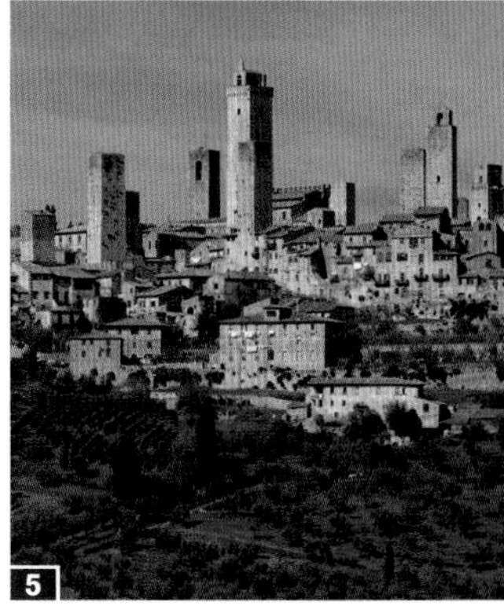
5 The town of San Gimignano in Tuscany, from the Middle Ages, with numerous fortified towers

1096	Beginning of the Crusades
1167	Founding of the Lombard League
1176	Battle of Legnano
12th–13th c.	Fight between the Guelfs and Ghibellines
1312	Coronation of Emperor Henry VII
1395	Giangaleazzo Visconti becomes duke of Milan

Northern Italy in the Late Middle Ages: Signori and Condottieri

New territorial states rose up among the many Italian cities and small dominions. These were characterized by unstable political conditions and conflict with neighboring states.

In the 13th century, after the end of the Hohenstaufen line, there was a power vacuum in northern and central Italy. The popes were then resident in French Avignon, and the papacy would later be split by the Great Schism. In southern Italy, the kings of Naples from the House of Anjou were fighting against the kings of Sicily from Aragon. France was distracted by the Hundred Years' War with England. The German kings and emperors from ever-changing royal houses concentrated primarily on Germany in their power politics (p. 172) and no longer had the resources to be active in Italian politics. The poet Dante expected Emperor ❼ Henry VII of Luxembourg to bring peace and unity to Italy, but the early death of the emperor in 1313 prevented the realization of these plans.

In this chaotic period, northern Italy dissolved into innumerable city-states and dominions. Civil war–like clashes between factions and family feuds between Guelfs and Ghibellines plunged the cities into chaos. Communes were consequently forced to grant near-dictatorial powers to a single strong "city lord," the *signore* (or signori)—when he did not usurp these powers himself. The signori were descended either from old noble families such as the Estes in Ferrara, the Gonzagas in Mantua, or the ❾ Visconti in Milan or, like the Medici in Florence, from the wealthy middle class (p. 294). Some of the signori were able to establish hereditary titles so that city-republics became principalities in the course of time. By ❿ subjugating neighboring signori, they were able to create expansive territorial states. The signori usually engaged mercenary leaders, the ❽ *condottieri*, and their forces for the countless wars against each other.

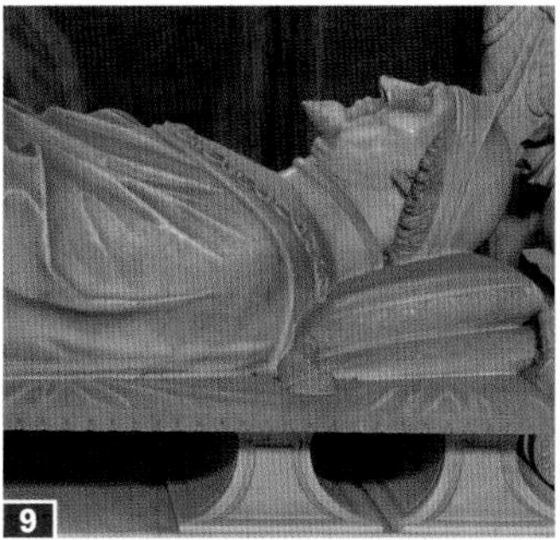
8 Equestrian statue of the Condottiere Gattamelata in Padua, bronze statue by Donatello

7 Henry VII of Luxembourg adjudicates at the trial of the rebellious citizens of Milan, book painting, ca. 1350

The condottieri were eventually also able to establish territories for themselves, as was the case with the Sforzas, for example, who succeeded the Visconti in Milan in 1450.

In the meantime, the Valois in France and the Habsburgs in the Holy Roman Empire consolidated their dominions. The Valois, as relatives of the Visconti and Anjou, laid claim to Milan and Naples (p. 179). The Habsburgs (p. 173) inherited southern Italy along with Spain, and attempted to reestablish the traditional supremacy of the Holy Roman emperor over Italy. Consequently, Italy was caught between the ⓫ fronts of the great powers, and drawn into their conflicts.

9 Grave monument of Giangaleazzo Visconti, first duke of Milan from 1395, marble, 16th century

Italy

"Ah! servile Italy, grief's hostelry! / A ship without a pilot in great tempest! / No Lady thou of Provinces, but brothel!...
And now within thee are not without war / Thy living ones, and one doth gnaw the other / Of those whom one wall and one fosse shut in!"

From Dante's The Divine Comedy (Purgatorio: Canto VI, translation by Henry Wadsworth Longfellow)

Dante Alighieri, painting by Justus van Gent, ca. 1476

10 *The Battle of San Romano* in 1432 between the quarreling city republics of Florence and Siena, painting by Paolo Uccello, ca. 1456

11 1525 battle between emperor Charles V and Francis I of France, near Pavia in Lombardy, 16th-century tapestry

1433	Gianfrancesco Gonzaga becomes margrave of Mantua
1434–64	Cosimo d'Medici the Elder leads the republic of Florence
1450	Rule of the Sforzas in Milan begins
1452–71	Borso d'Este becomes duke of Modena and Ferrara
1525	Battle near Pavia

Genoa and Pisa

Though the sea powers Genoa and Pisa were able to accumulate great wealth, internal instability meant that politically they lost their freedom of action.

The Crusades and the Spanish Reconquista in the Middle Ages ended Muslim rule in the Mediterranean region, and this vacuum was filled by the Italian maritime cities—first and foremost ❶ Genoa, Pisa, and Venice. Initially they profited by using their own fleets to ❹ transport the crusading troops. Then they established trading posts in the Crusader states—in the Byzantine Empire, around the Aegean Sea, and on the Black Sea coasts—and these became significant power bases. The Italians imported coveted goods such as silk, brocade, damask, pepper, incense, porcelain, pearls, and perfume to Europe via Arab middlemen. The Italians also borrowed an efficient accounting system from the Arabs, as well as Arabic numerals. In addition to trade, banking and credit transactions gained in importance.

1 Genoa, wood engraving, late 15th c.

3 The Cathedral of Pisa, built from the eleventh century on, with the Leaning Tower of Pisa, twelfth century

4 Crusaders board ships heading for the Holy Land from a Mediterranean port, book illustration, 15th century

Through naval campaigns against the Arabs during the 11th century, Pisa and Genoa were able to build up supremacy in the Western Mediterranean. The Italian rivals, however, constantly waged war against each other. At first, Pisa dominated, and its great wealth was invested in costly ❸ building programs. In the middle of the 13th century, there was a shift to Genoa's advantage. Emperor Michael VIII Palaeologus granted extensive trade concessions as a reward for Genoa's support in returning him to the imperial Byzantine throne in 1261. In 1284, the Genoese military crushed the Pisan fleet in the naval battle of Meloria.

Domestically, however, Genoa and Pisa were caught up, like most of the Italian communes, in the spreading factional fighting. Ghibelline and Guelf noble families waged war against each other. In addition there were disputes with the *popolo*—literally "the people," but referring to the rising middle class of small merchants and craftsmen, who wanted a share in power. Consequently, popoli and signori from various noble families repeatedly replaced each other as magistrates. By supporting diverse factions, foreign powers were able to gain influence in the city-republics. Pisa was subjugated by ❺ Florence in 1406 and Florence became the new dominant power in Tuscany. Genoa maintained its independence but came under Milanese, ❻ French, and from 1528 Habsburg suzerainty.

2 View into the Basilica of San Marco in Venice with mosaics in the Renaissance style, built in the eleventh century

Lombard and Giro

Many terms used in the financial world—for example, Lombard and giro—are reminders of the fact that the modern economy was first developed in northern Italy. From there, Italian bankers and traders spread early capitalism in Europe. In London, Lombard merchants settled in Lombard Street in London City, which even today is the address of many banks.

Early banking, depiction of a banking house in Genoa, book illustration, late 14th century

5 Victory of the Florentines over Pisa in 1505, fresco, ca. 1570

6 Louis XII of France and his troops attack a Genoese fortress, book illustration, ca. 1510

from 5th c. | First settlements on the lagoon islands
828 | Venetians steal relics of St. Marcus from Alexandria
1202 | Conquest of Zara
1204 | Conquest of Constantinople
1284 | Battle of Meloria

Venice

The Republic of Venice grew rich through control of much of the trade with the East and became a strong power for a time.

The settlements on the lagoon islands of Venice—to which the population had withdrawn during the age of the Great Migrations—were under Byzantine sovereignty and were never part of the Holy Roman Empire. Therefore, Venice was strongly influenced by Byzantine ❷ culture as well. Byzantium appointed the first political leaders, the ❽ doges (from the Latin *dux*, "leader"), in the eighth century, but free election of the doge was established later. The authority of the doges was greatly curtailed in the twelfth and 13th centuries by the Great Council and the Senate, whose members were required to be from leading families of the city whose names had been entered in the "Golden Book" of 1297—by which means the ruling class excluded the broad mass of the population from taking part in the political process. The annually elected Council of Ten and a police state monitored all state institutions, made sure a ❾ political balance was maintained, prevented civil wars, and ensured that Venice was free of the influence of foreign powers that was present in other Italian communes.

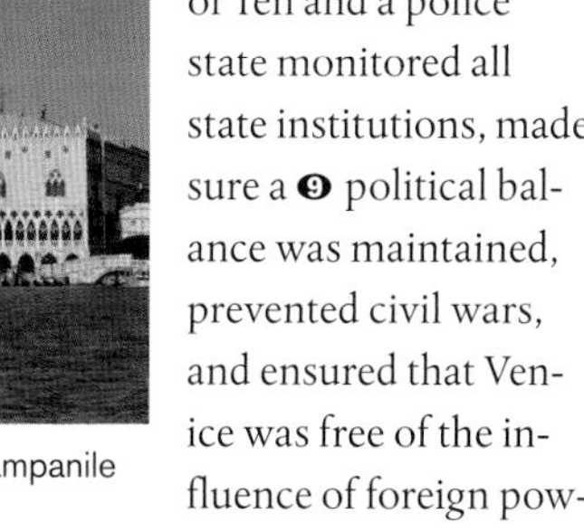

The doge's palace in Venice, left of the Campanile

Venice became extremely rich through its prominent location on the trade routes to the ❼ Eastern Mediterranean via the Adriatic and to Northern Europe via the Alpine passes. The Venetian doge ❿ Enrico Dandolo was able to conquer Constantinople (p. 221) in 1204 with the help of the Fourth Crusade. Venice seized the majority of the spoils and in addition gained vast territories on the Adriatic and Aegean coasts.

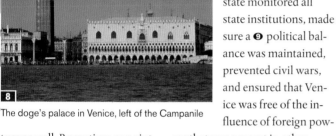

The doge Enrico Dandolo at the storming of Constantinople in 1204, painting by Tintoretto, 1580

Conquest of the town of Zara on the Adriatic by crusaders and Venetians in 1202, painting, 16th century

Venetian deputies at an Oriental court, painting, 15th century

Execution in 1355 of the doge Marino Falier in 1355, who wanted to abolish the republic, and establish a hereditary monarchy, painting, 19th century

When Venice won the power struggle with Genoa for mastery in the Mediterranean in ⓫ the War of Chioggia (1378–1381) it became the greatest and unrivaled trading power in Europe, famous for its naval fleets and skills.

In the 15th century, Venice began expanding its territories on the Italian mainland, the *terra firma*, to guarantee a food supply of the ever-growing city. This resulted in numerous wars over territory, which the Venetians won. A gradual decline began only with the eastward advance of the Ottomans in the 15th century and the shifting of the trade routes from the Mediterranean to the Atlantic in the 16th century.

The Jewish Ghetto

In 1516 the Venetian government resettled the Jewish communities of the city on the island of Ghetto. Despite this, relative tolerance prevailed and many exiled Jews from Spain and Portugal settled in Venice. This ghetto set the precedent for a form of persecution that was forced on the Jews throughout Europe until after World War II.

Synagogue of the Spanish Jews in the ghetto of Venice

Marco Polo

The Venetian Marco Polo set out on a trading journey to China in 1271, where he reportedly became a close friend of Kublai Khan, the Mongol emperor of China. He first returned to Europe in 1295. He had his memoirs recorded, but their authenticity was doubted even by his contemporaries, as his accounts and descriptions were so extravagant and fantastical.

From Marco Polo's travel memoirs: The dog-headed inhabitants of Ceylon trading spices, book painting, ca. 1412

1310 | Introduction of the Council of Ten
1378–81 | War of Chioggia
1453 | Ottoman occupation of the Dardanelles
1489 | Venice conquers Cyprus
1509 | Final subjugation of Pisa by Florence
1528 | Genoa under Habsburg rule

A Muslim and a monk play chess in a tent, book painting, 13th century

Spain and Portugal in the Middle Ages 8th–15th century

Since the eighth century, Christian kingdoms in the north of the Iberian Peninsula had been resisting Arab conquest, and starting in the eleventh century, the kingdoms began the ❶ Reconquista. The Muslim rulers were expelled by 1492. Modern Spain was created through a marriage between the kingdoms of Castile and Aragon at the end of the 15th century. In the 1400s, Portugal became a major sea power.

The Kingdoms of Navarre, Castile, Aragon, and Portugal

From the eleventh century on, the Christian kingdoms in the north of the Iberian Peninsula steadily pushed the Muslims farther south.

Between 711 and 714, Muslim Arabs conquered the Visigoth empire (p. 230). Christian rule in Iberia survived only in the impassable Pyrenees in the north. There, in 718, the Visigoth ❷ Pelayo, leader in the struggle against the Muslims, was chosen to be king of ❸ Asturias—later part of the kingdom of León. At the same time, the Basques made a stand against Charlemagne's conquest attempts—he had set up a short-lived Spanish *marca* (border) in 812. In 824, they chose Inigo Arista as the first king of Navarre. In the ninth century, the county of Barcelona also took shape on the territory of the marca. Around 1016, the Christian kingdoms benefited from ❹, ❻ Muslim civil wars, during the course of which the last Umayyad caliph was deposed in 1031. Numerous minor rulers took his place, but they were too disunited to oppose the *Reconquista* ("reconquest") begun by the Christian kings.

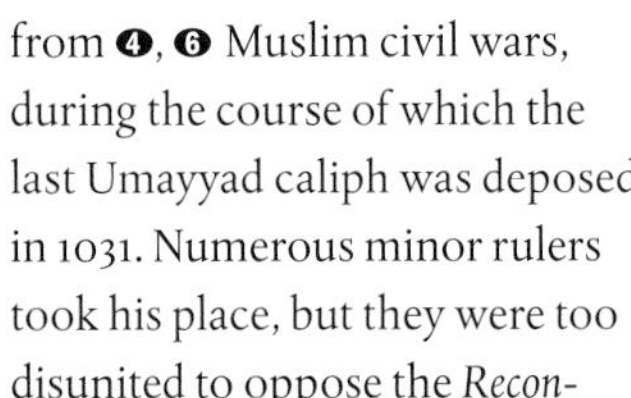

2 Pelayo, bronze

3 Reception hall of the Asturian kings in Oviedo, built ca. 850, later converted into a church

4 Alcázar in Segovia, built 11th/12th c., since 14th c. residence of Castile kings

In the first half of the eleventh century, Sancho III Garcés "The Great" reigned as king over a significant kingdom in northern Spain. After his death in 1035, Sancho's kingdom was divided into three independent kingdoms: Castile, Aragon, and Navarre. In 1038, Ferdinand I "The Great," ruler of Castile, also became king of León through marriage. Aragon and Barcelona were also united through marriage in 1164. The French Count Henry of Burgundy married the granddaughter of Ferdinand of Castile and León and in 1097 received the country of Portugal as her dowry. Henry's son, ❺ Alfonso I, then established his independence from Castile and assumed the title of king in 1139. Thus in the twelfth century there were four kingdoms on the Iberian Peninsula: Navarre, Castile-León, Aragon, and Portugal.

5 Afonso I of Portugal "the Conqueror" takes Lisbon from the Moors in 1147, steel engraving, 19th century

6 Muslim rider in battle, fresco, ca. 1280

711–714 | Arab conquest of the Visigoth Empire
718 | Pelayo becomes king of Asturias
812 | Spanish march founded
824 | Inigo Arista first king of Navarre
1031 | Last Umayyad caliph deposed
1035 | Kingdom divided into Navarre, Aragon, and Castile
1038 | Ferdinand I becomes king of Leon

The Formation of Modern Spain and Portugal

In the course of the Reconquista, the Christian rulers recaptured all the Muslim territories on the Iberian Peninsula.

The Reconquista did not proceed without setbacks. The North African dynasties of the Almoravids and the Almohads, who ruled southern Spain from 1094 and 1147 respectively, were still able to win important victories over the Christian kings in the 12th century. There were isolated incidences of shifting coalitions among the Christians and Muslims, as illustrated by the example of El Cid. Spanish ⑩ knightly orders (p. 222)—such as those of Calatrava, Alcantara, or Avis that kept alive the legacy of the Crusades (p. 218)—played an important role in the Reconquista.

10 Castle of knights of an order in Ponferrada, founded in 1178

The Portuguese kings meanwhile extended their territories along the Atlantic coasts. Lisbon, the future capital, was captured in 1147 and in 1250–51 the Algarve was conquered. ⑫ John I of Avis, crowned in 1385, conquered areas in North Africa in 1415. He and his son, ⑬ Prince Henry the Navigator (p. 298), who fitted out naval expeditions and founded a merchant navy college, initiated Portugal's ascendancy as a sea power.

7 Toledo, the Roman bridge "Puente de Alcantara" and the Alcázar in the background

In 1085 Alfonso VI of Castile had captured the former Visigoth capital of ⑦ Toledo, which then became the Castilian and Spanish capital until the court was moved in 1561 to Madrid. Castile's expansion came to a temporary halt under ⑪ Ferdinand III after he conquered ⑧ Córdoba in 1236. Only the Muslim kingdom of Granada in the extreme south of the peninsula (p. 231) remained.

Concurrently, Aragon was building up its power in the Mediterranean. In 1235 King James I captured the Balearic Islands and in 1238 the port of Valencia from the Moors (Spanish Muslims). His son Peter III occupied Sicily in 1282. Once it had brought Sardinia and Naples (p. 191) under its rule in 1326 and 1442, respectively, Aragon became a dominant power in the Mediterranean.

12 John I of Avis established as Portuguese king in the battle of Aljubarrota in 1385, book painting, 15th c.

13 Henry the Navigator, painting, detail, 15th c.

8 The Cathedral of Córdoba, built into the former Great Mosque known as the Mezquita in the 16th century

El Cid

Rodrigo Díaz de Vivar, known as El Cid (from the Arabic al-sid, "Lord"), fought as army commander for both the Christian and Muslim rulers in the Reconquista. He eventually captured the city of Valencia, which he defended against the Muslims until his death in 1099. El Cid thus came to embody the ideal of chivalry.

The 1469 marriage of ⑭ Ferdinand II of Aragon and Isabella I of Castile, jointly known as the "Catholic monarchs," set the stage for Spain's union and meant that both crowns went to the Habsburgs (p. 296) after Ferdinand's death in 1516. The two rulers completed the Reconquista with the subjugation of Granada in 1492. In Spain and Portugal, the persecution and eventual expulsion of the Muslims and Jews, as well as the so-called Moriscos (converted Moors), were carried out with the aid of the ⑨ Inquisition.

9 Inquisition court under the chairmanship of Dominican friars, painting, end of 15th century

The kingdom of Navarre did not take part in the Reconquista. Several French royal families had succeeded each other since the 13th century. In 1572, Navarre fell to Henry of Bourbon, who also became king of France as Henry IV in 1589, combining both crowns (p. 277). Ferdinand II of Aragon had already seized major parts of southern Navarre in 1512.

11 Ferdinand III "the Holy," book painting, 13th century

14 Ferdinand II and Isabella I, wood engraving, beginning of 16th century

1085 | Alfonso VI conquers Toledo
1139 | Alfonso I becomes king of Castile
1147 | Lisbon captured
1164 | Union of Aragon and Barcelona
1250–51 | Conquest of Algarve
1415 | Parts of North Africa conquered
1516 | Spain united

1 Stave Church, Borgund, Norway, built in the twelfth century

Northern Europe 8th–16th century

From Scandinavia, the Vikings started sailing along the European coasts during the eighth century. Initially they sailed as warriors and pirates, but later also as traders and settlers. In the ninth and tenth centuries, the kingdoms of Norway, Denmark, and Sweden emerged in Scandinavia. ❶ Christianity played a major role in the formation of these states. The kings were constantly opposed by a strong aristocracy. Even the Kalmar Union, which united the three northern kingdoms from the 14th to 16th centuries, could not obscure the structural weaknesses of the kingdoms.

The Vikings and the Kingdom of Norway

Daring seafarers, the Vikings for a time ruled the seas around Europe. Norway experienced a golden age from the 13th century until it came under Danish rule in 1387.

The Scandinavians of the Early Middle Ages were also known as ❷ Vikings, Varangians, or Normans, though they formed no ethnic or political unity. Over

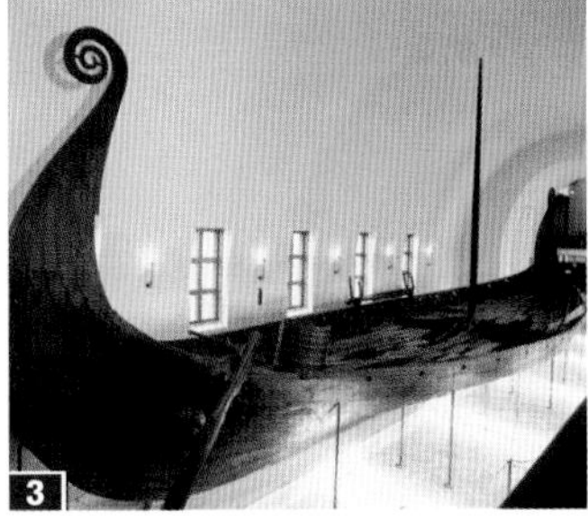
3 The Oseberg ship, found in a large burial mound in Norway, 9th century

time, various groups sailed from their northern homelands due to limited resources and political change, but also out of a thirst for adventure. Viking advances in ❸ shipbuilding technology enabled them to conduct warring and raiding expeditions along the European coasts and even up rivers far into the interior. Trade also played a significant role, as is testified to by the ❺ port cities, such as the North German trading settlement of Haithabu. Eventually, the Scandinavians also appeared as settlers and founders of empires in England, Ireland (p. 182), Normandy (p. 176), and Russia (p. 206). The Vikings also reached Iceland and Greenland and, around the year 1000, led by ❻ Leif Eriksson, the North American coast.

In the homeland of the Vikings, the increasing power of the ❹ kings curbed the former freedom and self-governance of the clans. Opponents of the new kingdoms usually joined the emigrants. ❼ Harold I Fairhair, about 870, was the first to unite the Norwegian monarchies.

4 A king, Norwegian toy figure, twelfth c.

Christianity was introduced, occasionally forcibly. In particular, Olaf I Tryggvason and Olaf II Haraldsson (St. Olaf) used the Church to support the centralization of the state in the eleventh century. As in other European countries, conflicts over the appointing of church offices (p. 169) arose in the twelfth century.

Sverre Sigurdsson was able to strengthen the power of the

2 Tyr, the Norse mythology god of warfare and battle, with a tied wolf of the underworld, bronze relief, sixth c.

monarchy again by 1202. During the reign of his grandson Haakon IV (the Old), Norwegian rule was extended over Greenland in 1261 and Iceland in 1262; for centuries before that, the institution of the Althing, an assembly of all free men in which political and legal affairs were discussed, had governed Iceland. In 1319 the Swedish Folkungs inherited Norway, and in 1380 it was inherited by the Danish queen Margaret I. Norway remained united with Denmark until 1814.

5 Port city of the Vikings, reconstruction drawing, 20th century

6 Leif Eriksson sees North America, painting, 19th century

7 Harold Fairhair and a giant, Iceland

870 | Norwegian monarchies united
940 | Vikings subjugate Haithabu
960 | Baptism of Harold Bluetooth of Denmark
ca. 1000 | Vikings land on Iceland and Greenland
1227 | Battle of Bornhöved
1261 | Norwegian rule of Greenland

Denmark and Sweden

In the Kalmar Union, Denmark attempted to dominate the Baltic Sea region. However, it came up against great opposition, particularly from Sweden.

The development of the Danish kingdom began with Gorm the Old, who about 940 subjugated the Vikings of Haithabu. His son ⑩ Harold II Bluetooth followed him around 950, but was killed by his son Sweyn I Forkbeard in 986. Sweyn and his son ⑫ Canute the Great (p. 183) occupied England and Norway, thus creating a great kingdom along the coasts of the North Sea. Only a few years after Canute's death in 1035, however, England and Norway regained their independence.

Denmark was weakened by struggles over succession in the further course of the eleventh and twelfth centuries. Beginning in 1157, Valdemar I (the Great) was able to conquer territories in northern Germany and along the Baltic coast, but his son Valdemar II was defeated in 1227 at the ⑧ Battle of Bornhöved by the North German princes and the Hanseatic city of Lübeck. Following the Hanseatic War, Valdemar IV Atterdag was forced to recognize the demands of the Hanseatic League in the Treaty of Stralsund of 1370. His daughter Margaret I, widow of King Haakon VI Magnusson of Norway and Sweden, secured the Danish crown for her son Olaf and, after his death in 1387, took over the regency herself. In 1397, she united the three kingdoms as the ⑨ Kalmar Union.

The history of the Swedish monarchy had begun in 980 with Erik VIII Bjornsson. His son Olaf Skotkonung III was baptized in 1008. Nevertheless, the entire period of the High Middle Ages was defined by clashes with non-Christian sections of the population and fighting over the throne by rival dynasties. In 1250, the House of Folkung came to the throne. The founder, Birger Jarl, a regent of the empire, completed the conquest of Finland, which had been the goal of Swedish ⑪ warriors, ⑬ missionaries, and settlers since the twelfth century.

Margaret I of Denmark, the heiress of the last Folkungs, brought Sweden into the Kalmar Union. Sweden, in particular, chafed under the Danish domination of the Kalmar Union. The Swedish nobility rose up against Margaret's successors, particularly against the kings from the House of Oldenburg who reigned after 1448. This ended in 1523 when Gustav I Vasa, king of Sweden, broke away from Denmark.

8 Battle of Bornhöved, book illustration, ca. 1300

9 Kalmar Castle in Southern Sweden, built 12th–16th c.

10 Stone with runes of Harold Bluetooth, ca. 965

11 Mounted warriors on reindeers and soldiers on skis, wood engraving, 16th c.

12 King Canute the Great and his wife donate a cross, book illustration, 1031

13 Bishop Henry of Uppsala, a missionary in Finland, book illustration, ca. 1475

The Hanseatic League

Lübeck and other trading cities joined together between the twelfth and 14th centuries as the Merchants' League of the Hanse. The Hanseatic League maintained common trading posts, secured the routes of their merchant ships—the so-called cogs—against pirate attacks, and intervened in the domestic politics of neighboring countries to gain more favorable concessions. The increasing strength of the Northern European states and the shift of the main trade routes to the Atlantic in the 16th century led to the decline of the Hanse.

Hanseatic League ship

1262 | Norwegian rule of Iceland
1319 | Sweden inherits Norway
1370 | Treaty of Stralsund
1387 | Margaret I of Denmark regent over Norway and Sweden
1397 | Kalmar Union
1523 | Sweden separates from Denmark

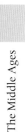

Eastern Europe 10th–15th century

Following the Great Migration of Peoples, the Slavs spread into the areas of Eastern Europe abandoned by the German tribes. Around 900, the Magyars began to settle the central Danube region. In the tenth and eleventh centuries, the historical kingdoms of Poland, ❶ Bohemia, and Hungary emerged. The last to form a unified nation were the Lithuanians in the 14th century. The political development of all these countries was fundamentally characterized by the dominance of the nobility, while the kings continually sought to establish a dynastic rule of their realms.

1 Duke Boleslaw II of Bohemia gives an audience to St. Adalbert, Bishop of Prague, bronze relief, twelfth century

The Development of the Polish State in the Middle Ages

The long-ruling Piast dynasty was unable to establish a strong monarchy. Up until the 13th century, therefore, numerous territories were lost to Germany and other neighboring states.

Under the princely House of Piast, the West Slavic Polanie tribe, which settled between the Oder and the Vistula rivers, became the nucleus of the future Poland. Mieszko I came to power and converted to Christianity in the 960s. Although the Ottonians wanted to prevent too strong a concentration of power in the east, Mieszko I and his son ❻ Boleslaw I Chrobry (the Brave) initially maintained a cordial relationship with the German Saxon Ottonians (p. 167). Only after the end of the Ottonian dynasty did Boleslaw assume the title of king in 1024 and thereby secure Poland's independence.

Boleslaw I's grandson Casimir I Odnowiciel had to contend with pagan revolts and repulse invasions from Bohemia and Kievan Rus. Boleslaw III Krzywousty in 1138 restructured the monarchy such that the eldest member of the dynasty would act as an overlord in the capital ❹ Krakow, while other family members would reign as autonomous princes over the provinces. Instead of the desired stability, however, this resulted in the fragmentation of Poland. The nobility and the Church benefited from the lack of a strong monarchy. After the catastrophic ❺ defeat in 1241 at Legnica (Liegnitz) against the Mongols (p. 237), Poland was saved only by the death of the khan and the subsequent withdrawal of the Mongol army.

In the meantime, the ❷ Germans were steadily encroaching from the west. By the twelfth century, the Slavic tribes between the Elbe and Oder rivers had lost their independence and, with few exceptions, also their cultural identity through the targeted policies of German conquest and ❸ colonization. In the 13th century the indigenous rulers in Pomerania and Silesia promoted the influx of German settlers, and in 1226 the Piast princes of Mazovia sought the help of the German Teutonic Order (p. 222) against the pagan Prussians. The "Germanized" territories leaned politically toward the German king. The Teutonic Knights became an adversary of Poland in the 14th and 15th centuries.

2 Henry I, German king, conquers Brandenburg, colored lithograph, ca.1900

3 The Polish town of Gdansk, which was founded as a German colony in twelfth century near a Slavic castle

4 The king's castle Wawel in Krakow, residence of the dukes and kings of Poland until 1596

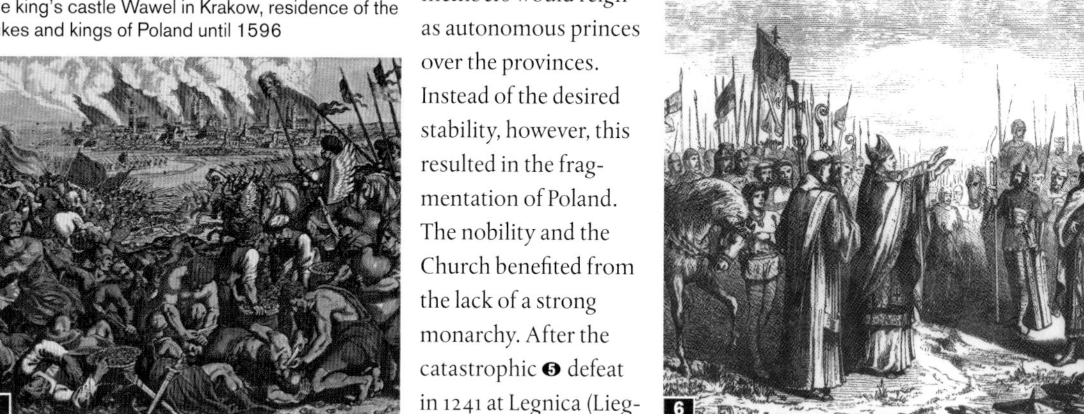
5 Battle of Legnica, copper engraving, 17th century

6 Boleslaw of Poland receives German missionaries, wood engraving, 19th century

966 | Baptism of Mieszko I
1024 | Boleslaw I becomes king
1241 | Battle of Legnica
1320 | Wladyslaw I Lokielek becomes king
1325 | Gediminas takes Kiev

Poland and Lithuania as Major Powers in Eastern Europe

The unified Poland-Lithuania under the Jagiellos became the largest state in Eastern Europe, although the domestic position of its rulers remained weak.

Following a period of Bohemian domination, Poland was reunited by Wladyslaw I Lokielek, who was crowned king in 1320 in Krakow. His son, Casimir III, became king in 1333. He took care of the extensive development of the country and invited ⑩ Jews, who had escaped from pogroms in Western Europe, to settle down in Poland. He reached an agreement with the kings of Bohemia to abandon their claim to the Polish Crown in exchange for Silesia.

As the main line of the Piast dynasty ended with his death in 1370, he bequeathed the throne to his nephew, Louis I of Anjou, king of Hungary, known as the Great, in order to provide a counterweight to the empire. But the Polish nobility used this transition to secure advantages for themselves. Louis was forced to make further concessions in the Pact of Koszyce of 1374 in order to secure the throne for his daughter, Jadwiga. The nobility immediately demonstrated its increased power by forcing Jadwiga to marry ⑨ Jogaila, the grand duke of Lithuania, who was crowned king of Poland in 1386 as Wladyslaw II Jagiello.

Lithuania was at this time still a young, and for the most part pagan, country. The first grand duke of all Lithuania had been Jogaila's grandfather Gediminas, who fought against the Teutonic Order and benefited from the decline of Kievan Rus. In 1325, Gediminas captured Kiev and extended Lithuania's borders far inside today's Russia and Ukraine.

After their union under Jadwiga and Wladyslaw, Poland and Lithuania defeated the Teutonic Knights in the ⑫ Battle of Grunwald (Tannenberg). In the ⑪ Treaty of Torun in 1466, the order was forced to yield large territories to Wladyslaw's son Casimir IV and recognize him as sovereign. The Polish-Lithuanian kingdom now reached from the Baltic Sea to the Black Sea and was the largest territorial state of Europe.

Domestically, the Jagiellon dynasty was locked in contention with the great nobles, known as the magnates. Casimir IV therefore sought support from the lesser nobility, the *szlachta*, who were given tax privileges and admitted to the Polish ⑧ *sejm*, or parliament. There, however, the magnates and the szlachta banded together, holding tight to the principle of the elective monarchy and demanding ever greater liberties from each new ruler. Casimir's successor in 1505 was forced to accept the *nihil novi* ("nothing new") law, according to which nothing was to be decided without the approval of the nobility. Possession of property became a privilege of the nobility, and the ⑦ peasants were forced into serfdom. After 1652, any member of the sejm could alone thwart a decision through the "liberum veto." An aristocratic republic with a monarch evolved. However, the Polish kings of the 18th century were no match for the expansionist drives of the absolute rulers reigning in the neighboring countries of Prussia, Austria, and Russia (p. 302).

8 Quarrels between different factions of the nobility during a session of the Polish parliament

9 Jogaila of Lithuania, crowned Wladyslaw II

11 Treaty of Torun, document with seals

7 Peasant's wedding, engraving, 19th c.

10 Old synagogue in Krakow, built in the 15th century

12 Battle of Grunwald, painting, 20th century

1333 | Casimir III becomes king
1374 | Pact of Koszyce
1386 | Wladyslaw II Jagiello becomes king
1410 | Battle of Grunwald
1466 | Treaty of Torun
1505 | *Nihil novi* law

Bohemia

The Czech Premysl dynasty founded the kingdom of Bohemia. Under subsequent dynasties, there were religious conflicts and disputes with the aristocracy.

In the ninth century, Premyslid princes unified the tribes of West Slavs that had settled in Bohemia. ❷ Prince St. Wenceslas sought ties to the Holy Roman Empire and promoted Christianity. In 929 he was murdered by his brother Boleslav I, who was then forced to accept the suzerainty of the Holy Roman emperor. Bohemia became an autonomous part of the empire, and in 1198 the German emperor bestowed the hereditary title of king on the Premyslids.

King Otakar II of Bohemia occupied Austria in 1251 and also coveted the German crown. When Rudolf I of Habsburg (p. 172) was elected the German king in 1273, Otakar challenged him. Otakar fell in 1278 at the ❸ Battle of the Marchfeld, however, and control of Austria went to the Habsburgs. The Premyslids died out with Otakar's grandson Wenceslas III in 1306.

John of Luxembourg, the son of Emperor Henry VII, then inherited the Bohemian crown by marrying Wenceslas's sister Elizabeth. He was followed in 1347 by his son ❶, ❼ Charles IV (p. 173). The authoritarian regime of Charles's son ❹ Wenceslas IV caused a revolt of the nobility, in which even his relatives took part. The state structure collapsed completely when the conflict with the ❺ Hussites became a civil war. Wenceslas's brother Sigismund was refused recognition as king of Bohemia until shortly before his death in 1437, even though he had been Holy Roman emperor since 1410.

When Sigismund's grandson ❻ László V (Posthumus) died in 1457, George of Podebrady, a local noble who had been regent for the underage László, was elected king. For the first time a king appealed to the moderate Hussites.

In 1471 he was succeeded by Wladyslaw (Ulászló) II, who also inherited Hungary in 1490. The Habsburgs once again gained control of Bohemia and Hungary through the double marriage of his children to the grandchildren of Holy Roman Emperor Maximilian I (p. 302). The position of the Habsburg rulers in Bohemia, however, remained weak. The power of the Bohemian aristocracy was finally broken in the Thirty Years' War when they supported the adversaries of the Habsburgs.

1 Charles IV (left) and his son Wenceslas IV kneel before Mary, painting, 14th c.

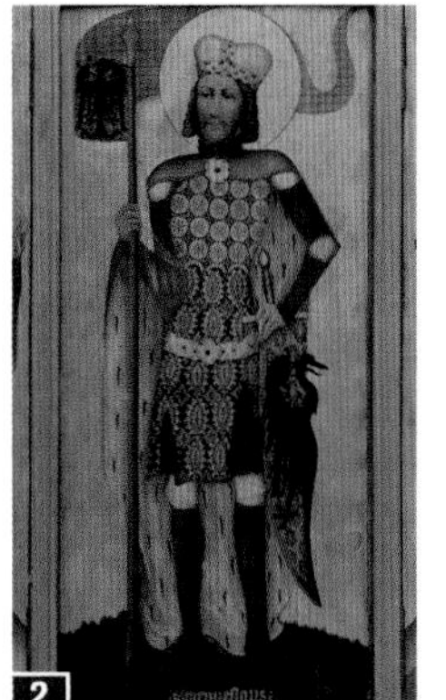
2 St. Wenceslas, altarpiece, 14th century

3 Battle of the Marchfeld, east of Vienna, Austria, painting, 19th century

4 Murder of the clergyman John of Nepomuk, ordered by Wenceslas IV, wooden engraving, 19th century

5 A corral used as a mobile fortress by the Hussites, book illustration, ca. 1450

6 László Posthumus, painting, 15th century

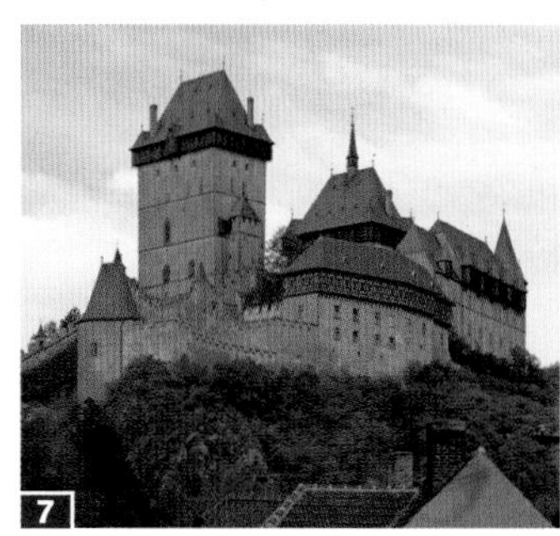
7 Karlstein Castle near Prague, built under Charles IV, 14th century

The Hussites

Jan Hus, a Bohemian reformer, attended the Council of Constance in 1415. He criticized the secularization of the Church and was therefore condemned as a heretic and burned at the stake. His followers in Bohemia rose up against Sigismund of Luxembourg, who had assured Hus safe conduct but was now seen as a betrayer. The Hussites terrorized wide stretches of the empire, and a number of crusades against them failed. Only a division within the Hussites in 1433 made possible a compromise with the more moderate faction and Sigismund's subsequent return to Bohemia.

Jan Hus is burnt at the stake, copper engraving, 17th century

ca. 900 | Magyars advance under Árpád
929 | Wenceslas I murdered
955 | Battle of Lechfeld
1001 | Stephen I becomes the first king of Hungary
1222 | "Golden Bull"
1251 | Otakar II occupies Austria
1278 | Battle of the Marchfeld

Hungary

Hungary became a state under the Árpáds. Even in the face of the Ottoman threat, the self-confident nobility held onto their privileges.

Sigismund escaping over the Danube after the Battle of Nicopolis

Baptism of Stephen I, painting, 19th c.

From the time of the Huns in the fourth and fifth centuries, nomads continually pushed out of the Eurasian steppes into Europe. Around 900, the Magyars, or Hungarians, led by their prince ⓬ Árpád, moved into the power vacuum left by the Avars after their defeat by Charlemagne in 796. The Magyars traveled as far as Rome on their extended plundering raids, and only after their defeat by the German army in 955 at Lechfeld did they settle down in Transdanubia (Pannonia), present-day Hungary.

Prince Geza, a descendent of Árpád, became a Christian and secured a dominant position for his family. His son, ❾ Stephen I (St. Stephen), was crowned the first king of Hungary in 1001. With German help, he built up a government and an ecclesiastical structure. His successors conquered neighboring Croatia and Transylvania, where many Germans settled. In 1222 Andrew II was coerced by the nobles into issuing the "Golden Bull," which recognized the rights of the nobility and Church. The German regions in Transylvania were also granted extensive autonomy. The Árpád dynasty ended with Andrew III in 1301.

Louis II of Hungary and Bohemia, painting, 16th c.

Pressburg, present-day Bratislava, Slovakia, capital of the Hungarian Habsburgs after 1526

Following much turmoil over the throne, a French Anjou came to power in 1307. Louis I (the Great) was enthroned in 1342 and for a time was able to disempower the barons. In 1370, he also succeeded his uncle, Casimir III, as king of Poland. Upon Louis's death, his realm was again split, Poland being bequeathed to his daughter Jadwiga, while his daughter Mary and his son-in-law Sigismund of Luxembourg succeeded him in Hungary. In 1396, Sigismund suffered a crushing defeat against the Ottomans at ❽ Nicopolis on the Danube. In exchange for financial support, the barons were able to demand more and more privileges from the constantly cash-strapped monarch, who became German king in 1410, king of Bohemia in 1419, and emperor in 1433. After the death of Sigismund's son-in-law and heir, Albert of Austria, another struggle for the throne took place. In Hungary, the Hungarian nobleman János Hunyadi (p. 217) prevailed as regent for Albert's son, László Posthumus. After László's death in 1457, the Hungarians elected Hunyadi's own son, ⓭ Matthias Corvinus, as the new king.

During the reign of Matthias, who fostered a brilliant Renaissance court, Hungary reached its greatest territorial size. He occupied wide stretches of Bohemia and Austria during his campaigns against George of Podebrady—who, as a Hussite, had been excommunicated by the pope—and Emperor Frederick III, who claimed László's inheritance. In the end, Matthias reconciled with Frederick and the successor of George Podebrady, Wladyslaw (Ulászló) II, who was elected king at Matthias's death as the latter had no legitimate children. Wladislaw's son ❿ Louis II fell in the Battle of Mohács against the Ottomans, who occupied almost all of Hungary. Only in the ⓫ border region between Hungary and Austria was Louis's brother-in-law, the Habsburg Ferdinand I, accepted as king of Hungary (p. 302).

The Hungarians appropriate land under the leadership of Árpád, painting, 19th century

Matthias Corvinus, marble relief, ca. 1490

1342 Louis I becomes king of Hungary | **1347** Charles IV crowned king of Bohemia | **1415** Murder of Jan Hus | **1437** Sigismund recognized as king of Bohemia | **1457** László V dies | **1490** Wladyslaw II inherits Hungary

RUSSIA 9TH–16TH CENTURY

Under the influence of the Byzantine culture, Slavs and Scandinavian Varangians had been merging in the kingdom of Kiev since the ninth century. The ruling Rurik dynasty involved the country in ❶ struggles for the throne and the division of the dynastic inheritance. The divided principalities found themselves under Mongolian rule from the 13th century. At the same time, Moscow's rise began. Russia was united by Moscow in the 14th and 15th centuries and began its path to becoming a major European power. With the death of the last of the Ruriks, a period of chaos set in, ended only in 1613 by a new dynasty, the Romanovs.

1 Battling Russian principalities of Novgorod and Suzdal, icon, 15th century

Kievan Rus

The Scandinavian Varangians founded the first kingdom on Russian soil.

Scandinavian Vikings, known to Slavs and Byzantines as "Varangians" or "Rus," began moving into the territory of present-day Russia and Ukraine in the eighth century as warriors, traders, and settlers, using large rivers such as the Neva, Don, and Volga as transportation routes. The small defensive nuclei of the steppes became staging posts on a route linking the Baltic to the Volga. Trading links, by way of the Black and Caspian seas, existed as far as the Byzantine Empire and the Abbasid caliphate. In Constantinople, Varangians formed the emperor's personal elite bodyguard.

3 Varangian ship in the port of Novgorod, painting, 1900

According to the Primary Chronicle, the inhabitants of the old Slav trading metropolis of ❸ Novgorod in northern Russia elevated a Varangian named ❷ Rurik to the status of prince in 862 in order to settle their feuds; Varangians also came to power in other towns after being appointed by the Slavs or by taking them by force.

Rurik's successor Oleg the Wise advanced to the south and in 882 occupied Kiev, which became the capital of his realm, known as Kievan Rus. A trade agreement with Byzantium in 911 also opened up the principality to Christianity; Rurik's daughter-in-law Olga was baptized in 957. Her grandson, Vladimir I (the Great), married the sister of the Byzantine emperor and converted to ❺, ❻ Christianity in 988 as part of a pact with Basil II of Constantinople. Kiev became the seat of an Orthodox bishop, who was nominally subject to the patriarch of Constantinople until 1589.

2 Slavic deputies kneel before Rurik, wood engraving, ca. 1890

4 Mosaic in the cupola of St. Sophie's cathedral in Kiev, eleventh century

When Vladimir died in 1015, his sons fought over the throne. Eventually, Yaroslav the Wise prevailed and by 1036 had subdued the whole of Kievan Rus. During Yaroslav's reign, Kiev experienced a golden era in ❹ architecture and culture influenced by Byzantine culture. Yaroslav was the first to codify Russian law—a combination of Byzantine laws and Slavic common law.

The Russian Primary Chronicle

The Primary Chronicle recounts Kievan Rus history up to the twelfth century. It was compiled by an unknown author probably at the end of the eleventh century in Kiev's cave monastery. For a long time, it was known by the name of the monk Nestor, who was thought to have compiled it. However, he only revised it, shortly after 1110.

Manuscript illustration in a medieval Russian chronicle: looting of Kiev by an opposed Russian prince

5 St. Sophie's cathedral in Novgorod, built under Vladimir I in the eleventh c.

6 Baptism of Vladimir I, book illustration, 15th century

862 Rurik named prince | **882** Oleg the Wise occupies Kiev | **911** Beginning of Christianization | **1036** Yaroslav the Wise consolidates Kievan Rus | **1054** Death of Yaroslav

The Rule of the Mongols

The Mongols conquered the internally divided Kievan Rus in the early 13th century and obligated it to make tribute payments.

After the death of Yaroslav in 1054, Kievan Rus was divided among his sons. The eldest member of the Rurik dynasty was supposed to exercise titular sovereignty, yet after every change in ruler there were renewed struggles for the throne and further division of the inheritance. Even significant rulers such as ❽ Vladimir II (known as *Monomakh* or "sole ruler") and Mstislav the Great in the twelfth century were unable to reunite Kievan Rus. To make matters worse, economic decline set in. The profitable Black Sea trade, for example, was lost to the Venetians and Genoese in the 13th century. Only ❼ Novgorod continued to experience growth through trade with the Hanse.

Kievan Rus was politically splintered and shaken by wars and attacks on its borders. Thus the Mongols—known as "Tatars" to the Russians—were easily able to conquer the Russian principalities. The first defeat of the Russians at the Kalka River, northeast of the Crimea, in 1223 was without consequence at first as the Mongols under Genghis Khan (p. 236) considered it only a preparation for further conquests in the future. However, a decade after Genghis Khan's death, his grandson, Batu Khan of the Golden Horde, established the rule of the Mongols in Russia. The Russian princes were forced to pay tribute to the khans, pay taxes, and tolerate political control by Mongol envoys.

8 Crown of Vladimir II (*Monomakh*), ca. 300

In 1240 the Rurik prince Alexander repelled a Swedish invasion at the Neva River, thus acquiring the surname Nevsky. He also ❿ beat back the Teutonic Knights on the frozen Lake Peipus in 1242. In 1263, Alexander Nevsky entrusted the city of Moscow to his son Daniel as an independent principality. Daniel's son, ❾ Ivan I—known as *Kalita* ("moneybags")—bought the favor of the khans and began to subjugate neighboring principalities; in 1328 he assumed the title of grand prince. The head of the Russian Orthodox Church also moved his seat to Moscow.

9 Ivan I Kalita with a silver pot, ca. 1900

Eventually, the Moscow grand princes turned against their Mongol overlords and successfully rebelled against them. Ivan's grandson, Dmitri Donskoi, won the first major victory over the Mongol army in 1380 at ⓬ Kulikovo on the Don, taking advantage of the fact that the Golden Horde had been disintegrating since 1357 and that the plague had hit them especially hard. Competing Turik khanates had emerged from the Crimea to Siberia, and these were later conquered by Russia. The last of these to come under Russian influence was the ⓫ khanate of the Crimean Tatars in the 18th century. At the time it had been under Ottoman suzerainty.

7 View over the city of Novgorod, copper engraving, 17th century

10 Battle between Russians and the Teutonic Order, movie scene

11 Palace of the Crimean Tatar Khans in Bachtshissarai, painting, 19th century

12 Battle of Kulikovo, book illustration, 16th c.

1110 | Nestor revises the Primary Chronicle
1223 | Battle of the Kalka River
1227 | Genghis Khan dies
1240 | Swedes repelled on the Neva
1263 | Moscow made an independent principality
1380 | Battle of Kulikovo

Moscow's Rise

The Muscovite grand princes extended their territories and considered themselves the successors to the Byzantine emperors.

When Constantinople was conquered by the Ottomans in 1453, the grand princes of Moscow deemed themselves to be the legitimate heirs of the Byzantine emperor and defenders of the Orthodox Church. ❶ Moscow was to be the "third Rome." Grand Prince ❻ Ivan III married the niece of the last emperor in 1472 and from 1478 on assumed the title of "Sovereign of All Russia." From Byzantium, he adopted the heraldic double eagle on the Muscovy coat of arms, the court ceremonial, and the autocratic rule that characterized the Russian monarchy until its end in 1917.

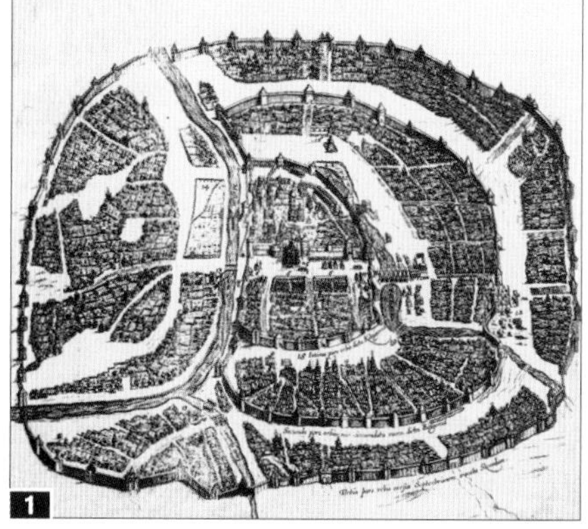

View over the city of Moscow with the Kremlin in the center, copper engraving, ca. 16th century

Ivan had his royal residence in Moscow, the ❸ Kremlin, magnificently improved by Italian architects. In 1478 he annexed the merchant city of Novgorod, which had acquired vast territories in the north of Russia, and in 1480 ended his tribute payments to the Mongolian khans. Ivan and his son Vasily III steadily extended their Russian domain westward at the expense of the Polish-Lithuanian union.

When ❷ Ivan IV (the Terrible) inherited the throne from his father Vasily in 1533, he was just three years old, and a brutal battle for the regency flared up among the noble families, the *boyars*. When he reached adult hood in 1547 Ivan was crowned tsar, the first Russian ruler to use this title formally, and he began to break the power of boyars. With the help of the nobility (who earned their titles through service), the Church, and an elite military unit, the Strelitsi, he reformed the military, the legal system, and the government. To accomplish these ends, he used great ❹ brutality and the *oprichniki*, a bodyguard bound to him by an oath of loyalty. The opposing boyars were persecuted through deportations, expropriations, and liquidations, and their property was divided among the newly titled nobility loyal to the tsar. In 1570, Ivan had Novgorod razed and thousands of citizens murdered because the city had supposedly risen up against his authority. He even killed one of his own ❺ sons in a fit of frenzied rage. Peasants fled the state terror and sought refuge with the Cossacks in the steppe regions north of the Black Sea.

In international affairs, Ivan IV continued the expansionist policies of his predecessors. The khanates of ❼ Kasan and Astrakhan were conquered, which pro-

Ivan IV the Terrible has convicts roasted over an open fire, copper engraving, 17th c.

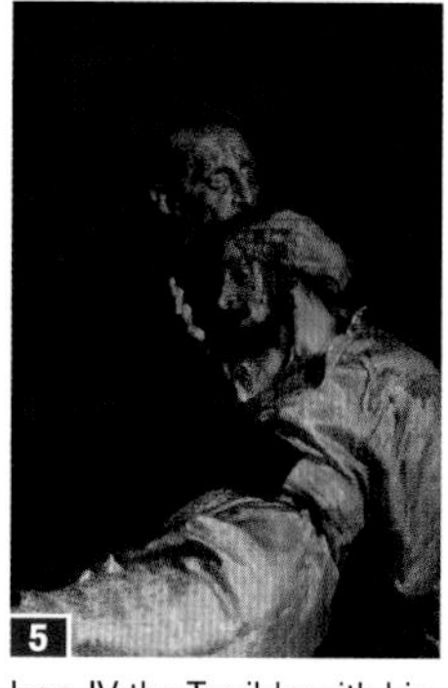

Ivan IV the Terrible with his dead son

Siberia

In 1558 Ivan IV charged the merchant Stroganov family with subjugating Siberia. They hired the Cossack leader Yermak, who in 1584 conquered the capital of the khanate of Sibir. The Cossacks were followed by merchants, fur traders, and settlers. A hundred years later, the Russians had reached the extreme east, where a treaty with China in 1689 established the Amur River as the boundary.

Yermak, the leader of the Cossacks, painting, 18th century

Ivan the Terrible, painting by Victor M. Wasnezow, 1897

The Kremlin with the Cathedral of St. Michael the Archangel

Ivan III, wood engraving, 16th century

1453 | Ottoman conquest of Constantinople
1478 | Conquest of Novgorod
1533 | Ivan IV succeeds to the throne
1547 | Ivan IV crowned czar
1558 | Beginning of expansion into Siberia
1570 | Novgorod destroyed

St. Basil's Cathedral, built by Ivan IV to celebrate his victory over Kasan

voked a retaliatory strike by the Crimean Tatars, who devastated Moscow in 1571. The conquest of Siberia began in the east. In 1584, the northern port of Arkhangelsk was founded on the White Sea to facilitate trade with England.

When Ivan died in 1584, Russia had become significantly larger in territory, but internally was in ruins, the populace in poverty, and the leadership classes split by power struggles that broke out openly after the death of the czar.

The Cossacks

Ever since the 15th century, runaway serfs from Russia and the Ukraine and dispersed Tatars had been settling the steppes between the Black Sea and the Urals. Here they founded communities of free armed peasants and warriors, who chose their leaders by election. The Cossacks (from the Tatar qazaq, "adventurer") had a high reputation as skilled soldiers and were thus often hired as mercenaries by the Poles, Lithuanians, and Russians.

above: Assembly of Cossacks, painting by Ilya Repin, 19th century

The Time of Troubles

After the death of Ivan the Terrible, the *Smuta*—Time of Troubles—began.

❾ Boris Godunov was the regent for his brother-in-law Fyodor I, the feebleminded son of Ivan IV and Anastasia Romanovna. Fyodor's only surviving brother, Dmitri, was murdered in 1591, probably on Godunov's command. When Fyodor died in 1598, ending the main line of the Ruriks, Godunov was elected to the throne. After a severe famine, social unrest and revolts plagued Godunov's reign as he made the serfdom of the peasants even harsher and more stringent.

Following Godunov's death in 1605 and the assassination of his son Fyodor II, Sigismund III Vasa of Poland-Lithuania sought to expand his influence in Russia and supported a pretender who claimed to be Dmitri, the son of Ivan IV. This Dmitri became tsar for a short time before he was assassinated by a boyar, Vasily Shuysky—who was then elected tsar by the boyars in 1606. Further revolts brought another false Dmitri, from Tushino, to prominence. Sigismund then claimed the tsar's throne for his son, the future Wladyslaw IV (p. 302), and had Shuysky deposed in 1610. The Poles ruled in Moscow for two

Michael Romanov ascends the throne, lithograph, 19th century

Whipping in a Russian village, steel engraving, 19th century

years, until the folk hero ⓫ Kuzma Minin put together a Russian army and, with the support of the Cossacks, liberated Moscow in 1612. The following year, the boyars elected a new tsar, ❿ Michael Romanov III, the 16-year-old son of an influential patriarch and—through his great-aunt Anastasia Romanovna—cousin of the last legitimate tsar of the House of Rurik. The Time of Troubles had finally ended, although the disputes over the autocracy of the tsars and the social problems of the starving and impoverished ❽ rural population that had erupted during the Time of Troubles would continue to plague Russia in the ensuing centuries.

Tsar Michael, who ruled until 1633 jointly with his father, the Patriarch Philarete, came to an understanding with Poland-

Boris Godunov, painting by Alexander Yakovlevith Golovin, 1912

Lithuania wherein the Polish territories under Ivan the Terrible's rule were returned.

The imperial dynasty of the Romanovs would rule as Russian tsars for 150 years and five generations from 1613 to 1762.

Prince Dimitrij Poscharsky and Kuzma, painting, 19th century

1571 | Crimean Tatars plunder Moscow
1584 | Port of Arkhangelsk is founded
1584 | Ivan IV dies, Time of Troubles begins
1605 | Death of Boris Godunov
1613 | Michael Romanov chosen as czar
1610–12 | Moscow under Polish occupation

The Byzantine Empire 867–1453

In the ninth through eleventh centuries, the Byzantine Empire once again rose to become a major power, but there were signs of internal discord. Attacks from outside weakened the state, and it did not fully recover from its conquest by the armies of the Fourth Crusade at the beginning of the 13th century. In 1453, Constantinople fell to the Ottomans, an event that sent shock waves through Christian Europe. ❶, ❷ Byzantine scholars who fled to the West brought with them the knowledge of the culture of classical antiquity preserved in the Byzantine Empire, which was central to the Renaissance and the rise of humanism in Italy.

1 John Bessarion, patriarch of Constantinople and scholar, painting, 16th c.

The Byzantine Resurrection under the Macedonian Dynasty

The Macedonian dynasty was able to reestablish the Byzantine Empire's old supremacy in the East.

Byzantine Emperor Basil I (the Macedonian 867–886) rose from modest circumstances. In 867, he ❸ murdered his patron, Emperor Michael III, and assumed the throne. Basil was soon able to ❻ reconquer territories in southern Italy and sought to win over the pope by temporarily relieving the anti-Roman patriarch, Photius I, of his office. Domestically, he had the Imperial Code retailored to allow a more centralized, strongly bureaucratic power for a government in which the emperor was considered the absolute ruler by divine right.

2 Cross of John Bessarion, 14th–15th century

Basil's son, ❼ Leo VI, together with Romanus I Lecapenos, who led the government from 920 to 944, repulsed invasions by the Bulgars, the Russians, and the Arabs. In 922, the emperor sought to reform the system of land ownership, limiting the amount of land that large estate owners could acquire from small proprietors. Leo's son, ❹ Constantine VII Porphyrogenitus, wrote a number of works about the ceremonial customs and administration of the court.

In 963 Constantine's son and successor, Romanus II, was probably poisoned by his wife, Theophano, who then married his successor Nicephorus II Phocas, a successful general who had recaptured parts of Asia Minor and Syria, as well as the islands of Crete and Cyprus.

Theophano then turned to a younger relative of Nicephorus, ❺ John I Tzimisces, and together they plotted the assassination of the new emperor in 969. After this usurpation John married Theophano and quickly embarked on further military campaigns.

4 Constantine VII Porphyrogenitus, gold coin, minted in 945

3 Basil I murders Michael III in his bedchamber, copper engraving, 17th century

5 Aided by Theophano, John I Tzimisces scales the palace walls in order to kill Nicephorus II Phocas, copper engraving, 17th century

6 Basil I in battle against Arab invaders, book illustration, 13th century

Patriarch Photius I

Basil I initially attempted to cultivate a cordial relationship with the Roman papacy and removed Photius I, the patriarch of Constantinople, from office because of his emphasis on the independence of the Byzantine Church from Rome. Pope Nicholas I had also been angered by the success of the Slavic mission of St. Cyril and St. Methodius, initiated by Photius. After the death of his successor in 877, Photius was reinstated, which led to an open breach with Rome.

The "Slavic apostles" Cyril and Methodius, monument in front of the Bulgarian national library

7 Leo VI at Christ's feet, mosaic, ca. 900

867 | Basil I seizes the throne
920–44 | Romanus I Lecapenos leads government
963 | Romanus II murdered
971 | John I conquers eastern Bulgaria
976 | Reign of Basil II begins
1014 | Boris II's victory over the Western Bulgars

The Byzantine Empire and the Crusades

The attacks of the Normans, the Seljuks, and ultimately the crusaders brought the last golden age of the Byzantine Empire to an end.

The new emperor, John I Tzimisces, conquered eastern Bulgaria in 971 and advanced further into Syria and Palestine. He arranged the marriage of Theophano, the daughter of Romanus II, to Otto II, the future Holy Roman emperor (p. 167). John was succeeded in 976 by ⓫ Basil II, another member of the Macedonian dynasty. Basil conquered western Bulgaria after more than a decade of fighting. After the final victory in 1014, he had 14,000 enemy prisoners blinded, which earned him the title of the "Bulgaroctonus" ("Slayer of the Bulgars"). Basil's regency also marked the last great cultural flowering of the Byzantine Empire, which from then on was increasingly forced onto the defensive by the encroachments of its powerful enemies.

The advance of the Muslim Seljuks (p. 232) was particularly threatening. A crushing defeat of the Byzantines at Manzikert in Armenia in 1071 cleared the way for the Seljuks to occupy Asia Minor, where they established the sultanate of Iconium.

8 Alexius I Comnenus, mosaic, 12th c.

At the same time, struggles over the throne grew in intensity. The female members of the court, notably ⓬ Zoe and ❾ Eudocia, played an important role in the dynastic intrigues of the period.

❽ Alexius I Comnenus, who became emperor in 1081, granted Venice, Genoa, and other leading Italian powers broad trading privileges to gain their support against the Normans, who had seized Byzantine possessions in southern Italy. In the long run, however, this undermined the Byzantine economy as the state lost control of its revenues. Despite the break with the Roman Catholic Church in the Great Schism in 1054 (p. 192), Alexius also sought help from the pope in 1095 in his fight against the Seljuks. Although parts of Asia Minor were regained by Byzantium in the wake of the First Crusade in 1096, the new Crusader states in Syria and Palestine soon ceased to recognize the sovereignty of the Byzantine emperor (p. 219).

11 Emperor Basil II stands over the defeated Bulgars, book illustration, early eleventh century

Alexius' grandson, Manuel I, spent much of his reign fighting to regain lost provinces. Meanwhile, in 1175 the Venetians began to support the Normans, and the Byzantine Empire suffered a defeat in 1176 at the hands of the Seljuks at Myriocephalon. In 1185, the Bulgars also made themselves independent of the Byzantine Empire.

Under the influence of Venice, the Fourth Crusade used the ❿ struggle over the throne to sack Constantinople in 1203 and occupy it in 1204. The Byzantine Empire was reduced to a shell of small provinces.

12 Empress Zoe, wife of three Byzantine emperors, golden diadem, eleventh c.

9 Christ crowning Empress Eudocia and her second husband Romanus IV Diogenes, ivory carving, eleventh century

10 Murder of Alexios IV Angelos by Alexius V Dukas Murtzuphlos

Feudalization

From the tenth century, the Byzantine emperors increasingly turned toward granting estates as payment for services rendered. It was also possible for large property owners to be granted immunity from taxes. When the estates and privileges became hereditary, the state also lost its control over the peasants, who had been pressed into serfdom. The authority of the central government in the provinces deteriorated in favor of the newly established domains of a developing nobility.

1054 | Great Schism
1071 | Battle at Manzikert
1096 | Byzantium reconquers parts of Asia Minor
1176 | Battle of Myriocephalon
1185 | Independence of the Bulgars
1204 | Latin conquest of Constantinople

The Latin Empire and Other Successor States

Under the Emperor Michael Palaeologus of Nicaea, the Byzantines reconquered Constantinople.

After the ❸ fall of Constantinople, sacked by the Crusaders on 13 April in 1204, various crusader kingdoms and Byzantine successor states emerged on Byzantine soil. Among these was the empire of ❶ Trebizond founded in the northeast of Asia Minor, where a branch of the Comnenus family reigned until 1461. In Byzantium itself the crusaders chose a Latin, Baldwin Count of Flanders, and crowned him as ❷ Emperor Baldwin I in Santa Sophia. The Patriarch was also a Latin: the Venetian Tomasso Morosini.

Venice also secured numerous strategically located islands and ports, including Crete, most of the Aegean islands, Rhodes, and trading posts in the Pelopponese and Thrace. Crusader leaders built up feudal states after the European model in the kingdom of ❼ Thessaloniki, the duchies of Athens (p. 215) and Naxos, and the principality of Achaea. In theory, suzerainty was held by the Latin emperor of Constantinople, but he was dependent on the support of the feudal lords and Venice, keen to protect its trading privileges, in order to rule.

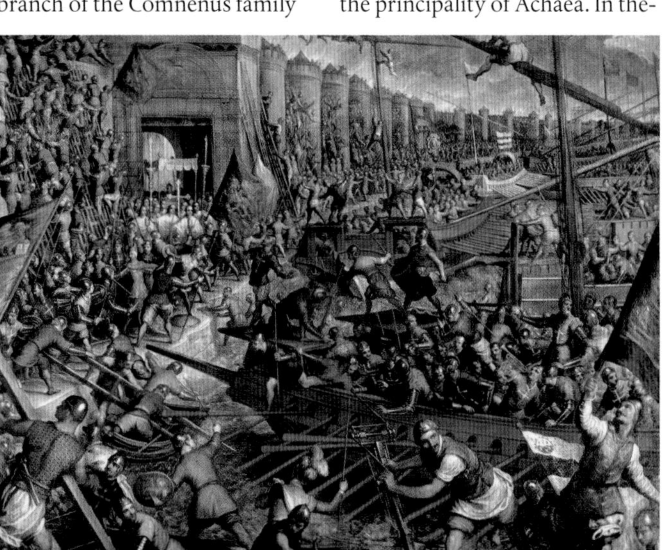

3 The conquest of Constantinople in 1204, painting by Tintoretto, 16th century

Greek Orthodox Christians were placed under Catholic clergy, which provoked violent resistance. They received support from the Bulgarian tsar, Kaloyan Asen, and at the Battle of Adrianople in 1205, Baldwin was seized and killed by the Bulgars. The Latin emperors in Constantinople thereafter followed one another in quick succession.

By the time Baldwin's nephew, ❹ Baldwin II, came to power in 1240, his empire consisted of little more than the city of Constantinople itself. His financial problems were so acute that he even married off his own son in return for a loan from Venice.

In Nicaea, the Byzantine state tradition was preserved by Emperor Theodore I Lascaris after the fall of Constantinople. From there, he and his successors sought to restore the empire. Although John III Ducas Vatatzes failed in the first attempt to retake Constantinople in 1235, he won territory in Thrace and Macedonia in victories over the Bulgars, and in 1246 he was able to reconquer Thessaloniki.

In 1259, Michael VIII Palaeologus usurped the throne from the young John IV Lascaris and founded the ❺, ❻ Palaeologan dynasty. He allied himself with Genoa, Venice's powerful rival in the Mediterranean, and the emerging Muslim power of Asia Minor, and succeeded in recapturing Constantinople in 1261.

The surprise attack was assisted by the absence of the Latin emperor, Baldwin II, who was on a mendicant visit to Western Europe.

Michael Palaeologus thus restored the Byzantine empire, though in a much weakened form. The northern part of the Balkans remained under the control of the Bulgarians and the Serbs, while Thessaly and the Epirus were governed by the Greeks.

5 Manuel II Palaeologus, silver coin, minted ca. 1400

6 "Tekfur Saray," the imperial palace, in Constantinople, built between the twelfth and 13th century

1 Hagia Sophia church in Trebizond, built in 1461 and later annexed by the Ottoman Empire

2 Venetian Doge Enrico Dandolo crowns Baldwin I of Flanders emperor of Byzantium, painting, 16–17th century

4 Venetian merchants meet Emperor Baldwin II, book illustration, ca. 1410

7 The "White Tower" in Thessaloniki, built during the 15th century

1204 | Theodor I Laskaris becomes emperor of Nicaea
1205 | Battle of Adrianople
1240 | Baldwin II becomes Latin emperor
1246 | Reconquest of Thessaloniki
1259 | Michael VIII Palaeologus usurps the throne
1261 | Constantinople recaptured by the Byzantines

The Fall of the Byzantine Empire

After the restoration Byzantium was increasingly undermined by the powerful merchant empires of Venice and Genoa, while the mighty Ottomans finally captured Constantinople in 1453.

Although Michael VIII restored the Byzantine Empire, it was never again able to regain its former strength. The maritime republic of Venice maintained its stranglehold on commerce, while Genoa was rewarded for its help in restoring Michael to the throne with trade privileges and the colony Pera, further undermining Byzantine power. The Latin feudal states held out in Greece, while the Serbs and Bulgars in the north and the successors of the Seljuks to the east all threatened Byzantine borders.

Despite this precarity, Byzantium enjoyed something of a ⓫ cultural resurgence in this period.

9 John VI, surrounded by the clergy at a synod, book illustration, 14th century

10 John VIII Palaeologus, painting by Benozzo Gozzoli, 15th century

Michael's son, Andronicus II Palaeologus, came to power in 1282, but a period of dispute over the throne began in 1321 that brought the state close to complete collapse. After being coerced into recognizing his grandson, Andronicus III, as co-emperor, he was forced to abdicate in 1328. After Andronicus III's death in 1341, ❾ John VI Cantacuzenus, supported by followers of *hesychasm,* usurped the throne in place of Andronicus's son John V. Although John VI was deposed, he regained the throne in 1347 with the help of the Ottomans. In 1354 he was deposed again and sent to a monastery. His son Matthaios, however, ruled until 1382 as despot of Morea, a center of late Byzantine culture (p. 215).

13 The Ottomans conquer Constantinople, 1453, copper engraving, 17th century

The Palaeologans, restored in Constantinople, became increasingly dependent on the Ottomans. The fall of Adrianople in 1362 completed the encirclement of the Byzantine Empire, which soon consisted of just Constantinople and its outlying districts. Calls for aid to the West went unanswered, and the fall of Byzantium was delayed only by the Ottomans' defeat by Tamerlane in 1402 (p. 238).

8 "Greek fire," an incendiary liquid contained in a grenade, used by the Byzantines to set enemy ships ablaze, striking fear into enemy ranks

In 1439 Emperor ❿ John VIII Palaeologus offered to recognize the supremacy of the pope in exchange for military aid against the Ottomans, but the deal failed and provoked violent resistance from the Greek Orthodox population. He was succeeded in 1449 by his brother, Constantine XI, the last Byzantine emperor. When the Ottoman sultan Mehmed II began a siege of Constantinople in 1453, the ❽ encircled populace offered determined resistance with assistance from Venetians and others in the city.

11 Chora monastery in Constantinople (Istanbul), built in the early 14th century, later transformed into a mosque

However, the Ottoman forces, using the heaviest artillery yet seen, were overwhelming. On the night of May 29, 1453, the ⓭ Ottomans broke through the ⓬ walls of the city (p. 309). The last Byzantine emperor died in battle.

Hesychasm

A group of Greek monks from Mount Athos sought to achieve hesychía, ("perfect peace"), and thus a union with God, through the constant repetition of a prayer in time to a breathing pattern. Many followers of this mystic meditation technique were also actively involved in Byzantine politics, as demonstrated by the growing influence of the monks and monasteries. Theologically it was championed by Gregory Palamas, who defended mystic and contemplative prayer against scholasticism.

Monasteries of Meteora in northwestern Thessaly, Greece

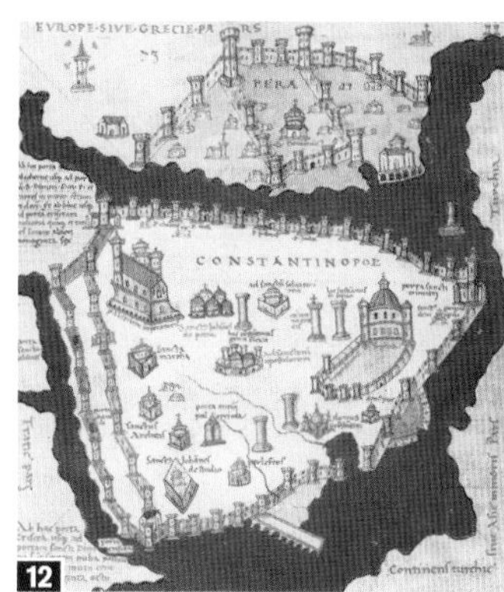

12 Map of Constantinople in the 16th century, with the Genoese trading colony of Pera in green

- **after 1321** | Disputes over the succession
- **1341** | John VI Cantacuzenus usurps the throne
- **1362** | Fall of Adrianople
- **1402** | Ottomans defeated by Tamerlane
- **1449** | Constantine XI becomes emperor of Byzantium
- **May 1453** | Fall of Constantinople

1 Ottoman bridge in Mostar, Herzegovina, built in the 16th century

Southeast Europe 7th–15th century

With the decline of the Eastern Roman Empire in the eighth and ninth centuries, numerous, often short-lived states developed in southeast Europe. Only the Bulgars and Serbs enjoyed periods of supremacy in the Balkans. The region was above all a zone of influence and a military thoroughfare for the neighboring major powers. The last of these was the ❶ Ottoman Empire, which by the 16th century controlled most the region.

The Adriatic Coast

With only a few exceptions, the entire west and northwest of the Balkan Peninsula came under Ottoman or Habsburg control at the end of the Middle Ages.

The Southern Slavic (p. 143) Croats were ruled first by the Byzantine Empire and then by the Franks. In 925 an independent Croatian kingdom emerged, united with Hungary in a personal union from 1102 to 1918, which was ruled by a viceroy called ❸ Ban. After King Demetrius Zvonimir was crowned by the pope in 1076, Croatia aligned itself with the Roman Catholic Church. The ❻ Ottomans' endeavors to conquer Croatia were successfully repelled. By the 15th century, Venice had conquered Dalmatia, the Croatian coastal region, as it came to dominate the Adriatic. The city-republic of ❺ Ragusa, today's Dubrovnik, was able to maintain its independence for centuries, until it was occupied by Napoleon's armies between 1806 and 1808.

3 Miklos Earl Zrinyi, Ban of Croatia, wood engraving, 16th century

Bosnia was initially part of the Byzantine Empire but fell to Hungary in the twelfth century. Viceroy Stephen Kotromanic (Turtko) also conquered the region of Herzegovina. Following additional territorial gains, he named himself king of Serbia and Bosnia in 1377. The kingdom did not survive long after his death, however; the Ottomans occupied Bosnia in 1463 and Herzegovina in 1483.

Of the Slavic territories of the Balkans, only small Montenegro was able to maintain its autonomy against the Ottomans, because the inhabitants had inaccessible mountain fortresses from which they could hold out.

4 Nicholas I Petrovic, prince and (from 1910 on) king of Montenegro, portrait, ca. 1895

2 Prince George Kastrioti, known as Skanderbeg, wood engraving

From 1528, the Orthodox bishops of Cetinje headed a polity that consisted of loosely bound clans, who were at odds with each other. Toward the end of the 17th century, Peter I was able to make the office of bishop hereditary in his family. In 1852, Montenegro became a ❹ secular principality and in 1910 a kingdom that lasted for a mere eight years.

The Albanians, who are not of Slavic descent and are thought by some to be descended from the ancient Illyrians, were also able to resist the Ottomans for a long time. In 1443, ❷ George Kastrioti, also called Skanderbeg, was trained by the Ottomans and fought for them for many years. He later returned to unite the Albanian tribes. In alliance with Naples, Venice, and Hungary, he negotiated a ten-year cease-fire with the Ottomans in 1461. When Skanderbeg broke the agreement after only two years, his allies deserted him, although the Ottomans were not able to conquer the area until his death in 1468.

5 The old town of Ragusa, present-day Dubrovnik

6 The Ottomans besiege Agram (Zagreb), the Croatian capital

925 | Emergence of Croatian kingdom
1076 | King Demetrius Zvonimir crowned by the pope
1102 | Personal union of Croatia and Hungary
1385 | Mircea makes Bucharest his capital
1396 | Mircea accepts Ottoman suzerainty

Greece and Romania

By the 17th century the Ottomans had conquered Greece. They appointed governors from the leading noble families in the Romanian principalities.

After the capture of Constantinople by the armies of the Fourth Crusade in 1204, a large number of independent ⑪ dominions (p. 212) developed in present-day Greece alongside the ⑦ Venetian strongholds. Often these consisted of only a small island or city and were ruled over by Greek, French, or Italian noble families. The most significant territory was the duchy of Athens, where the reigning French dukes were driven out in 1311 by Catalonian pirates, who were themselves ousted in 1388 by the Florentine Acciaioli family. In 1458, the Ottomans took Athens; the Ottoman conquest of the rest of ⑩ Greece was not complete until into the 17th century.

8 Marketplace in the German town of Schässburg in Transylvania, colored lithograph, 20th century

The territory of present-day Romania was the home of the Vlachs, a people descended from the Romanized natives and the Gothic, Slavic, Hun, and Bulgarian invaders. Hungary's expansion in the eleventh century and the increasing number of ⑧ German settlers pushed many of them out of Transylvania into the Carpathian Mountains and beyond, further south and east into Walachia and Moldavia. Out of the Hungarian border provinces, independent states under local princes—the voivods—developed in the 14th century.

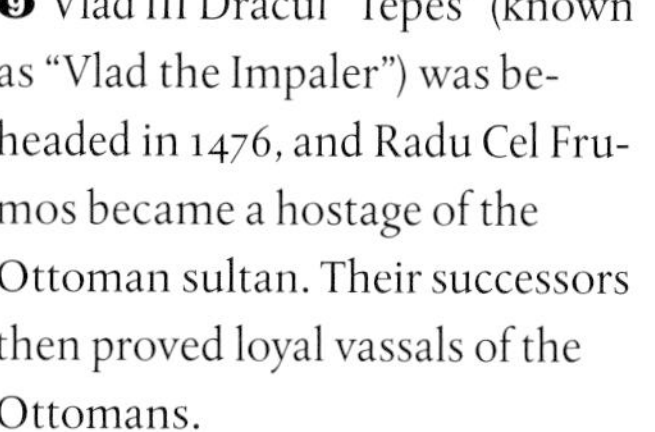

9 Vlad III Dracul, "The Impaler," painting, 16th century

Mircea the Old, the voivod of Walachia, made Bucharest his capital in 1385, and in order to avoid being deposed he accepted Ottoman suzerainty in 1396. His grandsons formed shifting alliances with Hungary and the Ottomans, which allowed them room to maneuver, but this was ultimately an unsustainable policy. The kings met grisly ends: Mircea was buried alive in 1442, ⑨ Vlad III Dracul "Tepes" (known as "Vlad the Impaler") was beheaded in 1476, and Radu Cel Frumos became a hostage of the Ottoman sultan. Their successors then proved loyal vassals of the Ottomans.

11 Ruins of the Byzantine castle in Mistra in the Pelopennesus, 13th–15th c.

⑫ Stephen the Great, voivod of Moldavia from 1457 to 1504, had more success in playing his neighbors off against each other, though in 1513, Moldavia was compelled to recognize Ottoman suzerainty. ⑬ Michael the Brave, voivod of Walachia, together with the Moldavians, was the last to rise up against the Ottomans, but he was murdered in 1601. From the 17th century on, the Ottomans appointed nobles from different families as governors of the Romanian principalities.

7 Venetian fortress near Heraklion on the island of Crete

10 Siege of Rhodes, Greece, by the Ottomans in 1480, book illustration, end of the 15th century

12 Monastery of Voronet, built in 1488 on the orders of Stephen the Great, St. George, its patron saint

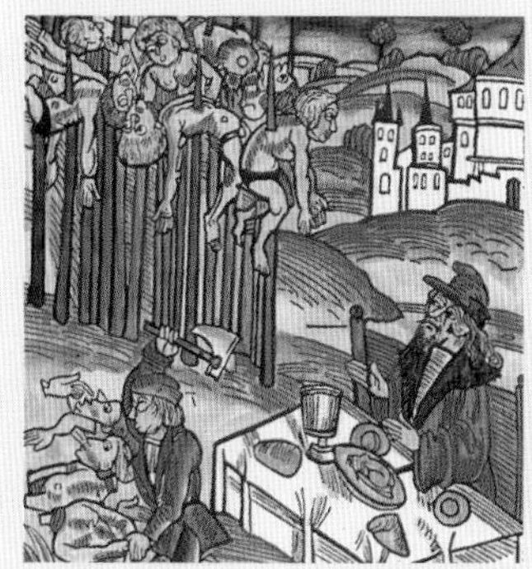

Vlad III Dracul Tepes dining during executions
wood engraving, 1500

Count Dracula

Vlad III and Dracul Tepes were both 15th-century voivods of Walachia. Vlad III was notorious for his preference for executing the condemned by impalement. The Irish author Bram Stoker created the literary figure of Count Dracula at the end of the 19th century by combining these historical figures with popular vampire tales from Transylvania.

13 Michael the Brave is slain by a jealous comrade in arms, copper engraving, 17th century

1458 | Ottomans capture Athens
1463 | Ottoman conquest of Bosnia
1468 | Albania falls to the Ottomans
1476 | Vlad III Dracul executed
1483 | Ottomans conquer Herzegovina

Bulgarian Kingdoms

During the ninth and tenth centuries the Bulgars were the dominant power in the Balkans.

During the fifth century, elements of the Huns (p. 149) withdrew back into the steppes of southern Russia, where they mixed with related Turkic tribes and Slavic ethnic groups to become the Bulgars. Their first major kingdom fell apart around 640 because of the advance of other steppe peoples, dividing the Bulgarian people into the Volga and Danube Bulgars. Thereafter, the Volga Bulgars prospered on the trade route between Kievan Rus and the Islamic lands to the south until their kingdom was destroyed by Mongol invaders in 1236.

Orthodox chapel overlooking Lake Ohrid, in present-day Macedonia, built in the late ninth c.

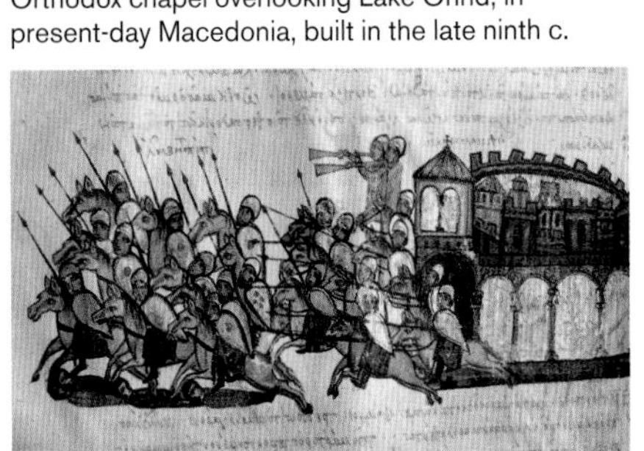

Fights between Bulgars and Byzantines outside Thessaloniki, book illustration, 13th century

The Danube Bulgars established the first Bulgarian kingdom in the Balkans around 681 under their khan, Asparukh, who claimed to be descended from Attila. Boris I introduced ❷ Christianity in 865 to facilitate the unification of the kingdom (p. 210). His younger son, Simeon, whom he had sent to Constantinople to be educated as a monk, usurped the throne in 893. Simeon I ("the Great"), the most significant Bulgarian ruler, waged several ❸ wars against Byzantium but was unable to capture Constantinople. In 925, he assumed the title "Tsar of All the Bulgars." Simeon presided over a cultural golden era in the Bulgarian Empire, promoting the use of the Cyrillic alphabet to enable Slavic translations of the Bible and to facilitate the population's conversion to Christianity.

Soon after Simeon's death in 927, during a time of conflicts with Kievan Rus, the decline of the empire set in. Bulgaria was so weakened in 1014 by its ❺ defeat at the hands of Byzantine emperor Basil II, the "Slayer of Bulgars" (p. 211), that four years later the Byzantines returned to annex all of Bulgaria, managing to hold it for almost two centuries.

The Bulgarian nobles Peter and Ivan Asen used the distraction caused by the attacks of the Seljuks on the Byzantine Empire to proclaim their independence in 1186. They founded the second Bulgarian kingdom, with its capital at ❻ Turnovo. Their brother, ❶ Kaloyan Asen, was recognized as king by Pope Innocent III in 1204. Shortly afterward, however, he turned away from Rome and supported the Greek Orthodox Christians in their struggle against the Latin Empire, defeating Emperor Baldwin I in 1205 at Adrianople. Kaloyan's nephew, Ivan Asen II, expanded the kingdom all the way to the Aegean and Adriatic Seas and in 1235 founded a Bulgarian patriarchate.

Kaloyan Asen in battle, mosaic, 16th c.

Ivan Shishman and his family, book illustration, 14th century

Following the invasion of the Mongols in 1242, the kingdom came under the rule of Mongolian khans. In 1330, Bulgaria was defeated by the Serbs at the Battle of Velbuzhd and was reduced to half of its previous size, thus becoming a relatively insignificant state. Bulgaria's last medieval tsar ❹ Ivan Shishman, participated in the Christian defeat at the Battle of Kosovo in 1389 against the Ottomans, and by 1396 the Bulgarian territories were under the control of the Sultan.

Bulgar prisoners, blinded by Basil II, return from Byzantine captivity, wood engraving, ca. 1900

Fortifications and church of the old town Veliko Turnovo, above the river Yantrain, present-day Bulgaria

ca. 681 | First Bulgarian kingdom founded
893 | Simeon I usurped the throne
1018 | Bulgaria annexed by Byzantium
1167 | Serbian kingdom founded
1235 | Bulgarian patriarchate founded
1242 | Mongol invasion

Serbian Kingdoms

From the twelfth to the end of the 14th century, the Serbs were able to establish a large kingdom in the western Balkan region.

Like the Bulgars, the South Slavic Serbs (p. 143), under Stephen Nemanja in 1167, used the decline of the Byzantine Empire in the twelfth century to establish an independent state. He reorganized the Serbian kingdom and Church. New Serbian bishops were selected and Serbian became the liturgical language. In 1196 he abdicated and retired to a ❼ monastery. His son and successor, ❽ Stephan II Nemanja, initially turned toward the West and was granted the title of king by the pope in 1217. In 1219, as a counterweight to Stefan's pro-Roman policies, his brother ⓬ Sava founded the Serbian Orthodox Church, which later became a key part of Serbian national identity under foreign domination. The monasteries founded by St. Sava became cultural centers. Later in the 13th century, Serbia, which had previously been characterized by clan groupings, developed a feudal state after the Western European model, and the peasants effectively became serfs.

7 Studenica Monastery, the largest in Serbia, founded by Stefan Nemanja after his abdication in 1196

10 Serbian Patriarchate Monastery in Pec, built in the 13th–14th centuries

In 1330 at Velbuzhd, the Serbs won an important victory against the Bulgars, which brought additional territories to the Serbian crown. ⓫ Stephen Dushan, crowned in 1331, continued these expansionist policies and conquered Greece as far as the outskirts of Athens. He had himself crowned "Emperor of the Serbs and Greeks" in 1346 in Skopje and established a Serbian ❿ patriarchate. Domestically, he built up a hierarchical government organized along Byzantine lines and codified the legal system. His son, Stephan Urosh V, crowned in 1355, was unable to hold the empire together and it splintered into a number of principalities in 1371. The North Serbian prince, Lazar Hrebeljanovic, tried in vain to halt the Ottoman advance. The Serbs suffered a massive defeat in the Battle of Kosovo on the "Field of the Blackbirds" in 1389, and Lazar's successors were forced to recognize Ottoman suzerainty.

8 St. Stefan II Nemanja, king of Serbia, portrait surrounded by scenes from his life, Serbian icon painting, 16th c.

12 St. Sava, fresco in the monastery of Decani, Kosovo, 1572

9 János Hunyadi fighting against the Ottomans, wood engraving, 19th c.

11 Stephen Dushan, mosaic, 14th century

In 1456, Belgrade was besieged by Mehmed II. On that occasion ❾ János Hunyadi, the Hungarian regent, succeeded in relieving the city and forced the Ottomans to retreat before he himself died of plague in his army camp. Nonetheless, in 1459 the Ottomans deposed the last of the Serbian princes and integrated the region into their empire.

The Battle of Kosovo, "Field of the Blackbirds"

In June 1389, the armies of the Ottoman Sultan Murad I and the Serbian prince Lazar Hrebeljanovic faced each other at the town of Kosovo Polje, Serbian for "Field of the Blackbirds." With the defeat of the Serbs, the Ottomans became undisputed masters of the Balkans. Mythologized by nationalists in the 19th and 20th centuries, the battle still plays a role in Serbian national sentiment.

Battle at the "Field of the Blackbirds", copper engraving, 18th century

330 | Serb victory over Bulgars at Velbuzhd
1346 | Stephen Dushan becomes "Emperor of the Serbs and Greeks"
28 Jun 1389 | Battle of Kosovo
1396 | Ottoman conquest of Bulgaria
1456 | Seige of Belgrade ended by János Hunyadi
1459 | Serbia annexed by the Ottomans

The Crusades 11th–15th century

The Crusader movement, which began in the eleventh century, was in its causes and effects a multilayered phenomenon. The ❶ Crusades to the Orient led to the expansion of European trade with the Orient. They had a lasting effect on the development of Europe, particularly on its intellectual life. The Crusades in Europe itself, which were directed against the Muslims of the Iberian Peninsula and against heretics and pagans, were also of long-lasting political importance. The consequences of the Crusader idea were fatal for many European Jews, who also fell victim to the crusading armies and the fanaticized population.

1 Christ leads the crusaders, book illustration, 14th century

Background and Causes

Religious, material, and political reasons motivated aristocratic crusaders as well as poorer members of the population to set off for the Holy Land.

The religious life of the Christian West underwent revitalization in the tenth and eleventh centuries. Expressions of this included the reform movements within the Church, such as the Cluniac (p. 168) and Gregorian reforms (p. 192), as well as the emergence of new religious orders such as the Cistercians. This sense of piousness also resulted in an increase in the number of ❷ pilgrimages to sites in Palestine, which had been under Muslim rule since the seventh century.

Into this situation came the ❺ Seljuks (p. 232), whose advance into the Near East in the mid-eleventh century had been noticed in Europe. By 1074 Pope Gregory VII was already planning

3 Knight on horseback, bronze sculpture, 13th century

a Crusade to "liberate" the holy sites and overcome the Great Schism (p. 193). When the Byzantine emperor Alexius I Comnenus turned to Pope Urban II with a request for aid against the Seljuks in 1095 (p. 211)—the same year as the Synod of Clermont—the pope won over the knights and princes of the West for a Crusade in support of the Byzantine emperor. Soon, however, the main aim of the war became to liberate ❹ Jerusalem from Muslim rule.

❸ Crusaders were promised a remission of their sins in the hereafter, which motivated many of the poorer participants. For most of the aristocratic crusaders involved, however, the possibility of material and political gains were also important motivating factors. Many of the younger sons of the aristocracy, who were excluded from hereditary succession in their homeland, saw the Crusades as an opportunity for an activity befitting their station that could lead to military glory, booty, and perhaps even a dominion of their own. At the same time, kings and princes used the Crusades to ideologically legitimize their reigns in their own countries by presenting themselves as truly Christian-minded rulers. Merchants, particularly in the Italian commercial cities, were lured by profits from outfitting and transporting troops, as well as the expansion of their trade interests.

2 The patriarch of Jerusalem shows pilgrims a relic, book illustration, 14th c.

4 The world as a disc with Jerusalem at its center, illustration, ca. 1250

5 Muslims hold a banquet after their victory over the Byzantines, Byzantine book illustration, 13th century

Pope Urban II's Sermon Promoting the Crusade, Clermont, 1095

"They [the Seljuks] have killed and captured many, and have destroyed the churches and devastated the empire. If you permit them to continue thus for awhile with impunity, the faithful of God will be much more widely attacked by them."

Pope Urban II preaches at Clermont

1074 | First Crusade planned
1095 | Synod of Clermont
1096 | First Crusade begins
1097 | Battle of Dorylaeum
1098 | Capture of Antioch
1099 | Conquest of Jerusalem

The First and Second Crusades

The First Crusade resulted in the establishment of crusader states in the Near East. These were soon on the defensive, however. A subsequent Crusade in their defense remained unsuccessful.

The pope's appeal was first answered in 1096 by relatively disordered bands of adventurers and social outsiders led by the monk ❻ Peter of Amiens. After being decimated by the Bulgars, the rest of the People's Crusade was wiped out by the Seljuks in Asia Minor. Around the same time, an army of German crusaders carried out pogroms against the Jews while still in Europe.

7 Muslims are massacred by crusaders in a mosque, wood engraving, 19th c.

The first organized army of crusaders, the "Princes' Crusade," was led by Godfrey of Bouillon, his brother Baldwin of Boulogne, Raymond of Toulouse, and Bohemond of Taranto and was composed of French, Flemish, and southern Italian soldiers. When these crusaders reached Constantinople in 1097, Emperor Alexius I insisted that they swear an oath of allegiance to him, although this oath would not last long (p. 211). Once the Christian army had beaten the Seljuks in 1097 at Dorylaeum, they were able to take Antioch in Syria in 1098. Meanwhile, Baldwin of Boulogne had been accepted as heir by Thoros, the king of Edessa on the other side of the Euphrates. When Thoros was assassinated, Baldwin erected the first of the crusader states there. Bohemond of Taranto then created the first principality in Antioch, and Raymond of Toulouse founded the county of Tripoli. In 1099, they conquered ❾ Jerusalem; Jews and Muslims alike were slaughtered in a ❼ massacre. Godfrey was elected "Protector of the ❽ Holy Sepulchre," refusing to be named king in the city where Christ had died. When he died in 1110, his brother Baldwin succeeded him and assumed the title of king.

By 1144, Edessa had been retaken by the Seljuks, whereupon the Cistercian abbot ❿ Bernhard of Clairvaux called for a second Crusade. Another army set off in 1147 under Louis VII of France and the German king, Conrad III. After a journey involving heavy losses and unsuccessful sieges of Damascus and other cities, the crusaders returned home in 1149.

9 Jerusalem is captured by crusaders, 1099 book illustration, 14th century

10 Bernhard of Clairvaux calls for the Second Crusade, painting, 19th c.

6 Peter of Amiens calls for the Crusade, wood engraving, 19th century

8 The Holy Sepulchre in Jerusalem

Crusader States

The crusaders established several feudal states in Cyprus, Prussia, the Levant, Greece and Israel, along Western European lines. As few colonists from Europe were forthcoming, however, the small group of conquerors, after a wave of persecution and expulsions, adapted to the predominantly higher civilization of the Jews and Muslims and lived, if not with, then alongside them. In addition to warring with the Muslim states, the Christians also often fought among themselves, weakening each other's positions. After two centuries, in 1291, the last crusader state on the mainland fell.

above: Meeting of the Estates in Jerusalem under Godfrey of Bouillon, steel engraving, 19th c.

1110 | Baldwin of Boulogne becomes King of Jerusalem
1144 | Edessa retaken
1147 | Beginning of Second Crusade
1149 | Crusaders return
1291 | Fall of the last crusader state

The Third and Fourth Crusades

Led by Ayyubid Sultan Saladin, the Muslims retook large parts of the Near East, including Jerusalem, although it was then granted to Richard I of England.

The Second Crusade was unsuccessful in the Near East, but it had initiated the Reconquista (p. 199) on the Iberian Peninsula, where the Christians were advancing into the Muslim south.

In the Near East, the Ayyubids (p. 233) had supplanted the Seljuks as the dominant Muslim power. Sultan ❸ Saladin defeated the European crusaders in 1187 at ❷ Mount Hattin and ❶ recaptured Jerusalem, leading Pope Gregory VIII to call for a third Crusade. The rulers of the leading European countries—the Holy Roman emperor, Frederick I (Barbarossa); the heir to the English throne, Richard I (the Lion-Hearted); and King Philip II Augustus of France—answered his call. Frederick won a victory in May 1189 at Iconium in Asia Minor but ❺ drowned in the Saleph River the next year. His son, Frederick VI of Hohenstaufen, led the German contingent to the Holy Land, from which a majority of them sailed home at once; the rest of the Germans, including Frederick VI, died of malaria.

1 Saladin conquers Jerusalem, illumination, ca. 1400

❹ Richard and Philip were able to recapture the important port city of ❻ Acre in 1191. The French king then sailed home to France with his knights following a personal argument between the two monarchs. Alone, Richard was unable to recapture Jerusalem, but he did gain the secession of the coastal regions of Palestine and Syria through negotiations. Saladin also guaranteed Christian pilgrims access to the holy sites.

The Fourth Crusade, initiated by Pope Innocent III in 1202, showed the corruption of the Crusade idea. The crusaders were redirected by the Venetian doge, Enrico Dandolo (p. 197), to ❼ Constantinople, where they deposed the Byzantine emperor and established the Latin Empire that existed from 1204 to 1261 (p. 212).

The Children's Crusade of 1212 was a further low point. Thousands of boys and girls were led by religious fanatics to southern France where they were sold into slavery.

2 Mount Hattin

3 Monument to Saladin in front of the medieval citadel of Damascus, present-day Syria

4 Philip II Augustus of France and Richard the Lion-Hearted of England take the cross, book illustration, 14th century

From Annales Marbacenses, 1238:

The Children's Crusade

"Many of them [boys and girls] were kept back by the inhabitants of the land as farm hands and maidservants. Others were to go to the seaside, where boatmen and sailors would deceive them and ship them off to distant regions of the world."

above: Children's crusade, wood engraving, 19th century

5 Frederick I (Barbarossa) drowns in the Saleph River, wood engraving, ca. 1900

6 After the conquest of Acre, Richard I (the Lion-Hearted) orders the execution of Muslims, wood engraving, 19th c.

7 Conquest of Constantinople, 1204, painting by Eugene Delacroix, 19th century

1187 | Battle of Mount Hattin
1188 | Start of Third Crusade
1189 | Battle of Iconium
1191 | Acre recaptured
1202 | Innocent III calls for the Fourth Crusade
1204–61 | Latin Empire of Constantinople
1212 | Children's Crus

The Last Crusades and the End of the Crusader States

The Mamelukes drove the crusaders out of the Holy Land for good.

Emperor ❾ Frederick II had sworn a crusader's vow and set off in 1228 on the Sixth Crusade. He negotiated the return of Jerusalem, Nazareth, and Bethlehem from the Ayyubid Sultan al-Kamil in 1229. He achieved this through diplomatic negotiations with the Sultan, as a result of which he became popular in the Arab world. Jerusalem was handed over on the condition that Muslims would be allowed to go on pilgrimage to their holy sites.

After the Muslims retook Jerusalem in 1244, King Louis IX of France started out in 1248 on the Seventh Crusade to attack Egypt, the seat of Ayyubid power. Although he occupied Damietta in the Nile Delta in 1249, he suffered a defeat at Mansura and his army was ❿ captured. Louis was freed only after the payment of a ransom. Years later, Louis organized the last great Crusade, the Eighth. The king and many of his knights died of an epidemic outside the walls of Tunis in 1270. Louis was canonized in 1297.

In the meantime, the ⓬ Mamelukes, slaves recruited for the Ayyubids' military, had overthrown their former lords (p. 233). By virtue of their centralist military regime, they were able to overcome the Mongols who invaded Syria in 1260. After that, they concentrated fully on subjugating the crusader states. In 1291, with the capture of ⓭ Acre, the last important bastion of the Christians, the Mamelukes had reconquered Palestine and Syria.

The Christians were forced to withdraw from the Holy Land among them were the orders of Christian knights that had formed during the two centuries of the Crusades. The ⓫ Knights Templar concentrated on the administration of their territories in France, which constituted a threat to the crown, and they were disbanded in 1312 (p. 178). The Teutonic Knights had already sought a new field of activity in the Baltic with the mission of converting non-Christian peoples. Only the Knights Hospitaller continued to fight against the Muslims. In 1309, they moved their headquarters to ⓮ Rhodes, where they held off the Ottomans until 1522. Emperor Charles V allocated ❽ Malta to them, and it was not conquered until 1798 by Napoleon.

8 Knight of St. John of Malta, a Maltese knight, painting by Caravaggio, beginning of 17th century

11 A Knight Templar, wood engraving

9 Emperor Frederick II crowns himself king of Jerusalem, wood engraving, 19th century

10 An imprisoned Louis IX, book illustration, 14th century

12 Mamelukes on horseback, Arabic book illustration, 15th century

13 Fortification in Acre dating from the times of the Crusades

14 Knights of the order of St. John in Rhodes, illustration, 15th century.

Orders of the Knights

The knightly orders founded in the course of the twelfth century combined monkish and chivalrous ideals. Sworn to personal poverty, chastity, and obedience, the members initially dedicated themselves to the protection of pilgrims and caring for the sick. In addition, they increasingly took part in the fighting against the Muslims. The orders quickly developed into significant powers by virtue of their wealthy properties captured in the Holy Land and bequeathed to them in Western Europe.

above: Castle of the Knights of St. John in Syria, built ca. 1142

1228 | Sixth Crusade begins under Frederick II

1229 | Return of Jerusalem, Nazareth, and Bethlehem

1244 | Muslim reconquest of Jerusalem

1248 | Seventh Crusade

1269–70 | Last Crusade

1309 | Knights Hospitaller settle on Rhodes

1312 | Knights Templar disbanded

The Crusades in Europe and the Teutonic Knights

The crusaders also fought against heretics in Europe. Following the forced conversion of the Baltic Prussians, the Teutonic Knights erected a powerful military-monastic state in the Baltic region.

Crusades took place in Europe as well as the Near East. Examples of these include the Reconquista against the Muslims in the Iberian Peninsula and the campaigns against groups considered to be heretical, such as the Albigenses in southern France (p. 177) and the Hussites in Bohemia (p. 204).

Military force was also employed in evangelical missions to non-Christian regions. Pope Eugenius III welcomed not only the Second Crusade to the Holy Land but also the one waged in 1147 against the Wends and Slavs in northern Germany by Henry the Lion, duke of Saxony—although undoubtedly an increase in their territory rather than the missionary work was uppermost in the minds of many of the German princes that took part.

As the Baltic Prussians, or ❷ Pruzzi, who lived on the coast between the Vistula and Neman Rivers offered especially strong resistance to Polish attempts to conquer and convert them, the ❻ Teutonic Knights were summoned to help in 1226. Emperor Frederick II, in the ❸ Golden Bull of Rimini, transferred their future conquests to them as possessions. The actual crusades against the Prussians first began in 1231 under Grand Master Hermann von Salza. In 1237, he merged his order with the Livonian Knights, founded in 1202 in Riga. By 1283 the Teutonic Knights had subjugated and officially Christianized the region, which was named Prussia after the Pruzzi. The whole of the eastern Baltic region except Lithuania then belonged to the Teutonic Knights, who erected their own state there. The head of the order was the grand master, who was elected by the general chapter and who resided in ❹ Marienburg after 1309. Province masters and commanders administered the order's districts. The half-brother commoners were placed beneath the brothers, who were knights and priests. The German patricians of the cities, as well as the Polish and German landed aristocracy, belonged to the upper class. The Prussian peasant farmers were underprivileged in contrast to the great number of new German colonists. Trade with the Hanseatic League brought great wealth.

The last people to convert to Christianity in the region were the Lithuanians, who did so after their union with Poland in 1386. This removed the need for proselytizing, which was the justification for the existence of the order. Furthermore, the order's state found itself in the grip of a powerful enemy, the united Polish-Lithuanian Commonwealth. After a decisive defeat in 1410 at the ❺ Battle of Grunwald and as a result of the two Treaties of Torun of 1411 and 1466, the order was forced to accept territorial losses (p. 203). The last grand master, ❶ Albert of Brandenburg, secularized the remaining territories of the order in 1525 and declared it the Duchy of Prussia, a fief of the Polish king.

1 Albert of Brandenburg, the last grand master of the order of Teutonic Knights, painting, 16th century

3 Golden Bull of Frederick II, 13th c.

2 The Pruzzi kill the missionary Adalbert of Prague, 997, wood engraving, ca. 1900

4 Marienburg Castle in West Prussia, Poland, built ca. 1272

5 Battle of Grunwald, painting, 19th century

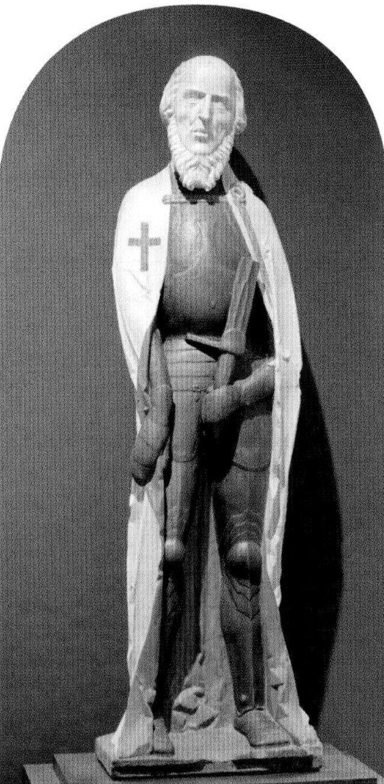
6 Teutonic Knight

1103 | Imperial Peace of Mainz
1147 | Crusade against the Wends
1202 | Order of Livonian Knights founded
1215 | Fourth Lateran Council
1226 | Golden Bull of Rimini
1283 | Teutonic Knights conquer Pruzz

Persecution of the Jews in Europe

Jews were not subjected to a direct campaign during the period of the Crusades but rather to persecution and discrimination.

Anti-Semitism was widespread in medieval Europe. The Jews were maligned as the "murderers of Christ." Accusations of ❽ ritual murder and desecration of the Eucharistic Host stubbornly persisted. A specific law governing the ❼ clothing of Jews was demanded at the fourth Lateran Council in 1215. A ban on ownership of real estate and membership in guilds forced the Jews into the textile trade. As the Christians were forbidden to loan money for interest, another source of income through financial transactions became open to the Jews—which in turn presented a source of new prejudices against Jewish usurers.

7 Man wearing the typical headgear of the Jews, illustration, 14th century

In the religiously inflamed atmosphere linked to the Crusades since the turn of the twelfth century, hate and jealousy repeatedly erupted against Jews in the form of frequent pogroms, during which Jews were tortured and murdered, along with the theft and destruction of Jewish property. A second wave of persecution occurred with the spread of the plague beginning in 1347, when Jews were accused of having poisoned the wells. More than 350 ❾ Jewish communities were destroyed during this period in the German territories alone.

Things were no better for Jews in other regions. In 1290, King Edward I had expelled all Jews from England, and they had been forced to leave ❿ France in 1394 due to alleged ritual murders of Christians. Jews who had lived in relative peace under Muslim rule on the Iberian Peninsula were either expelled or forced to convert during and particularly after the completion of the Reconquista in 1492; in the end, because even the forced converts were not to be trusted, they were completely driven out.

Primarily aimed at maintaining public order, laws were also repeatedly passed to protect the Jews. One example is Emperor Henry IV's Imperial Peace of Mainz from 1103, wherein the Jews were counted among those who were in need of protection—because they did not hold the status of free persons, they were not allowed to carry weapons and could not defend themselves. Rulers placed Jews under their protection in order to secure the high taxes that were extorted from them. They were particularly welcomed as settlers and tradesmen (p. 203) in ⓫ Eastern Europe.

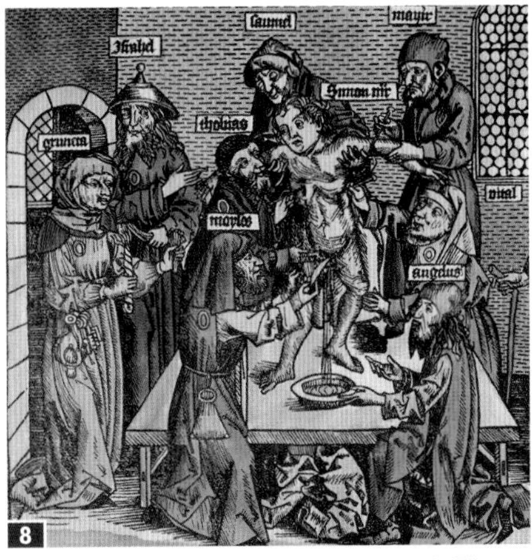

8 Alleged ritual murder of a boy by the Jews in Trient, 1475, wood engraving, 15th century

9 Jewish ritual bath (*mikvah*) in Friedberg, Germany, built ca. 1260

from the chronicle of Salomo bar Simson:

A Crusader Discussing the Persecution of Jews

"See we are on the long journey to the grave [of Christ] and to revenge ourselves on the followers of Islam, although in our midst are the Jews, whose forefathers killed and crucified him. ...Let us take revenge on them and eradicate them among peoples ... or let them take on our beliefs."

The burning of Jews as heretics, wood engraving, 15th century

10 Jews burned at the stake in France, painting, ca. 1410

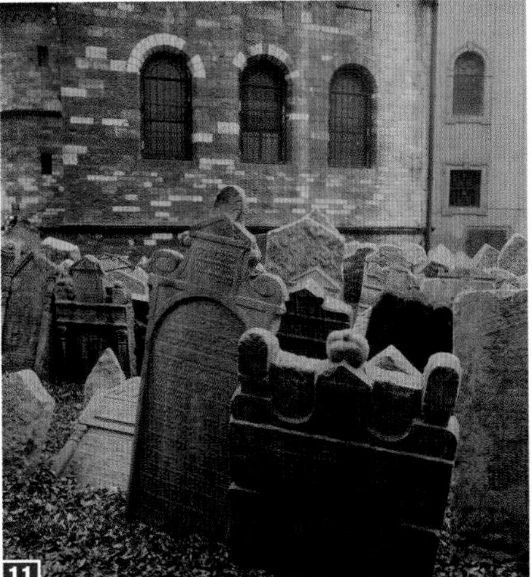

11 Jewish cemetery in Prague, Czech Republic

1290 | All Jews expelled from England
1394 | All Jews expelled from France
1410 | Battle of Grunwald
1411 | First Treaty of Torun
1466 | Second Treaty of Torun
1492 | Expulsion of all Jews from the Iberian Peninsula
1525 | Prussia secularized

Islam

Today, Islam is a subject more prevalent in the media of many Western countries than ever before, although comment is not always well informed. It has been depicted as an actual threat to the West due to the ❹ terrorism of radical Islamists, which reached a climax on September 11, 2001. In the prevailing political climate the distinction between radical and mainstream Islam has sometimes been blurred, and the common elements of Islam, Judaism, and Christianity, as well as the rich intellectual and cultural history of Islamic civilizations, are often overlooked.

Pilgrims in the Great Mosque of Mecca, colored engraving, ca. 1860

The theologization of politics, such as has occurred repeatedly in the history of man all over the world, has always tended toward radicalism and emotionalism and, above all, has often resulted in the suppression of, and intolerance toward, those of other faiths.

During its period of expansion and conquest, Islam, in contrast to Christianity, proved relatively tolerant, because respect toward other religions—particularly the other ❷ biblical religions Judaism and Christianity—is anchored in the Koran. The freedom to practice religion was very much the norm in the great Islamic empires—one need only consider Spain in the Middle Ages or the policies of the Ottoman Empire toward its many Christian subjects. The phrase "better the Turban than the Tiara" refers to the preference of some Orthodox Christians for the Sultan's rule rather than the persecution suffered under Catholics. It is arguably the humiliations suffered during the long years of colonization, and the support of the West for authoritarian regimes in the post-colonial Middle East, that have fed a hostile current of opinion in some Islamic countries vis-à-vis the West.

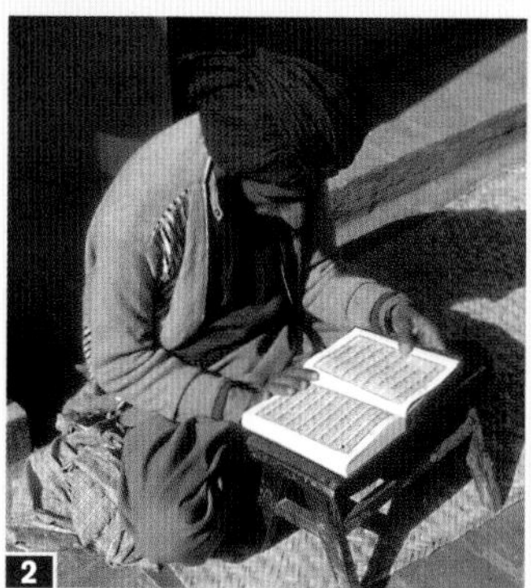

A Muslim reading the Holy Scripture in a mosque in Multan, Pakistan

The Beginnings of Islam

The prophet Muhammad and a small group of his followers, who declared their faith in the one true God, stand at the beginning of the history of Islam. Its development and diffusion were initiated by the Prophet's ❺ emigration, the *Hegira* (Arabic hijrah), from hostile Mecca to more receptive Medina in 622. The move was considered so important by the early Muslims that they used this date as the start of the Islamic calendar. In Medina, Muhammad created the basis for a strong society of believers, with political as well as religious cohesion.

The leader of the Al-Qaeda network, Osama bin Laden (right), speaking at an event

The Religious Teachings of Islam

"There is no god but Allah, and Muhammad is His Prophet." So states the Islamic declaration of faith, the *shahadah*. It contains Islam's two most important principles of faith: monotheism and the belief in the teachings and practices (*Sunnih*) of the Prophet, including the Koran as the instructions of God to mankind that were revealed directly to Muhammad. The Koran proclaims God as the creator of heaven and earth. It demands ❸ obedience to the almighty, omniscient, and merciful God and describes a final judgment in which all mankind must answer to God for their deeds. Heaven awaits the believers, hell the nonbelievers. These aspects are also shared by Judaism and Christianity.

The *Hegira* from Mecca to Medina in 622, copper engraving, 1844

"Ma sha'a Allah"—"It is God's will;" Ottoman-era tile, 19th century

The standards of behavior demanded of Islam's followers are derived from the Koran and the examples of the Prophet. They are set down in Islamic law, known as the *sharia*, which constitutes a comprehensive guide to the righteous life. The most important regulations for the practice of the religion form the Five Pillars of Islam: the repetition of the *shahadah*, the five daily ❼ prayers offered to God, the distribution of alms, fasting during the holy month of Ramadan, and a pilgrimage to ❶ Mecca at least once in a lifetime.

622 | *Hegira* of Muhammad
632 | Death of Muhammad / foundation of "Schiat Ali"
632–661 | Rule of the Four Righteous Caliphs
635 | Beginning of Islamic expansion
661-750 | Caliphate of the Omaijads
680 | Martyrdom of al-Husayn
750–1258 | Caliphate of the Abbasids

Shia and Sunni

The most significant division of Islam was ignited by the issue of who the successor to Muhammad would be. After his death in 632, one group believed that only his son-in-law Ali and Ali's descendents were rightful heirs (*imams*) to the Prophet. This faction is known as Shia and its adherents Shiites—from Shiat Ali ("Party of Ali")—and comprises about 10–15 percent of all Muslims today. Shiites in turn are divided into various groups, according to the number of rightful ❽ imams they recognize: There are the Fiver, Sevener, and Twelver Shiites. Shia also differs from Sunni, the largest group in Islam, in diverging teachings and traditions. The martyrdom of al-Husayn, a grandson of Muhammad, in 680 is very significant to the Shiites.

7 Worshipers perform Friday prayers on the street near to the Bazaar in Istanbul, Turkey

Spread and Expansion of Power

While Islam has been spreading in the world as a result of migration since the end of the 19th century, the expansion of Islam in its early stages took place by military conquest. Within the first 80 years, the caliphs and their army commanders had opened up to Islam an area that reached from the Indus River in the east to Spain in the west. A caliph ruled over the entire great Islamic empire, while his governors ruled in the provinces. From the beginning, the system of rule was autocratic with divine authority invested in the ruler. However they were bound by Islamic law and were often restricted in their authority by influential legal scholars (*Ulema*) and religious clerics.

The first dynasty that reigned over a large Islamic empire was the Umayyads, followed by the Abbasids. Later phases of the expansion were carried out by the Turkic tribes and the Mongols of Central Asia. The last domain that combined major parts of the Islamic world, as well as other faiths, under its rule was the Ottoman Empire, which came to an end in 1923.

The political spread of Islam went with the Islamization of conquered countries, though seldom through forced conversions. Muslims and non-Muslims alike profited from political stability and a good infrastructure.

8 The Golden Mosque Al-Kazimain in Baghdad, a Shiite place of pilgrimage containing the graves of two imams

Pan-Arabism and Pan-Islamism

It was only in the 19th century that, under the influence of imperialism, nationalistic thought emerged in the Islamic world, out of which a secular pan-Arab consciousness developed. At first this new awareness was directed primarily against the Turkish Ottoman Empire and later against the European colonial powers. The Pan-Arab movement, whose most important figure in the 1950s and 1960s was Egyptian president Gamal Abdel Nasser, is based on historical, cultural, and linguistic characteristics, not on religion. It ultimately failed, due to differing ideologies and political goals. The goal of Pan-Islamism, on the other hand, was to foster a religiously motivated cooperation and solidarity. It had also been developing since the 19th century and strove to oppose nationalistic thinking through shared Islamic values.

Islamic States Today

By the end of the 19th century, the influence of Western politics as well as secular nationalism introduced by governments—such as that of Kemal Atatürk in Turkey—had already led to irreversible shifts in Islamic society, including changes in customs, Western clothing, and even the suppression of religion in daily life. A modern implementation of the Islamic principle of unity in religion and politics has succeeded in only a few nations.

One can only speak of "Islamic states" in a few cases. Although the Islamic Republic of Iran was created by a popular revolution of the faithful the civil society is complex. Secular lifestyles in large cities coexist with traditional Islam, although the highest state authority remains the religious committee of the guardian council. The country in which the legal system and public life are probably most determined by the sharia is Saudi Arabia. Most of the nations with Islamic populations have secular—but only in rare instances democratic—governments that profess a separation of religion and state. Islamic ❻ fundamentalism can be judged to be a counter-movement to this secularization of politics as well as to living conditions that often benefit only a privileged minority. A ❾ revival of Islam has been noticeable since the 1960s. Often, however, it is social conflicts and frustration with stifling and corrupt dictatorships that preside over closed economies and high unemployment that encourage the spread of radical and fundamentalist approaches to Islam.

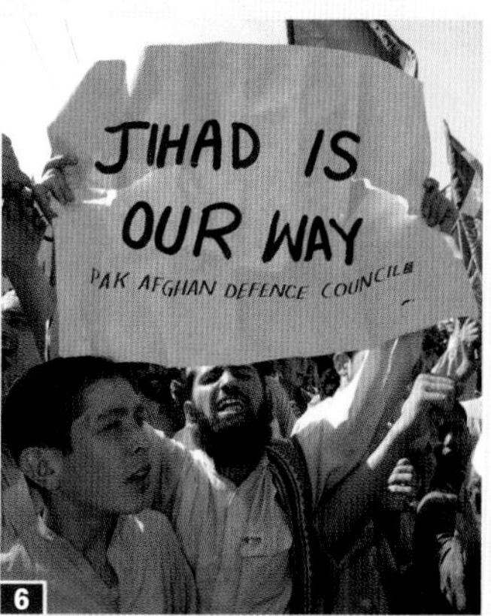

6 Street demonstrators brandishing a poster calling for Jihad ("Holy War")

9 Muslim woman wearing the chador, an outer garment that covers the body, worn by the devout in parts of Iran.

1453 | Ottomans capture Constantinople
1923 | Collapse of Ottoman Empire
1979 | Islamic Revolution in Iran
11th-13th century | Crusades
1492 | End of *Reconquista* in Spain
1956–70 | Gamal Abdel Nasser president of Egypt

The Spread of Islam 622–ca. 1500

Immediately after Muhammad's death, his successors, the caliphs, began to organize a rapidly spreading empire. By the early eighth century, Muslim armies had subjugated an area that stretched from Spain in the west to Pakistan in the east. However, driven by religious schisms resulting from debate concerning the legitimate successors of Muhammad, Islamic rule began splitting into regional autonomous dynasties after 800. Politically, early Islam had been dominated chiefly by Arabs and Persians, but after the tenth century, the Islamized Turkish peoples and, from the twelfth and 13th centuries, the Berber tribes in the west and the Mongols in the east proved to be the principal forces.

1 The Grand Mosque of Mecca with the Kaaba, the main shrine of the Muslims

Muhammad and the "Rightly Guided Caliphs"

Muhammad had already instituted the political organization of Islam, and under his first successors, the "rightly guided caliphs," its first triumphant campaign of expansion was initiated.

The Prophet Muhammad not only formulated the teachings of Islam but also acted as the political leader of a community. Following the Hegira, his migration to Medina in 622, Muhammad organized the ❷ battles and defense of the Muslim community (*umma*), drove out the Jewish tribes, and in 630 conquered ❶ Mecca almost without violence, where he declared the Kaaba to be Islam's main shrine.

Muhammad died on June 8, 632, in ❸ Medina without having designated a successor; therefore four "rightly guided caliphs" were chosen, one after the other, from among his most intimate circle. The first two were the Prophet's fathers-in-law, the last two his sons-in-law. ❹ Abu Bakr, the first Muslim leader after the Prophet's death, held the community together based on the strength of his authority. Under him, parts of Yemen were brought under Islamic rule. It was his successor Umar I ibn al-Khattab, however, who would become the actual creator of the Islamic Empire. In 637 Umar consolidated the internal organization of the empire through military garrisons, land redistribution, pensions, and a poll tax levied on non-Muslims. His generals in 635–637 conquered all of Syria and Palestine, including Damascus and Jerusalem, as well as the Sassanian Persian Empire. They then subjugated Egypt in 639–641 and Iraq in 640–644. His successor, Uthman, dedicated himself primarily to domestic affairs, and in 653 had the ❺ Koran compiled in its present form. In 647, Muslim armies began pushing west out of Tripolitania (present-day Libya) and by 682 all of the North Africa was under Islamic rule.

The fourth caliph, ❻ Ali, was the cousin and son-in-law of the Prophet and is considered by Shiite Muslims to be the true successor (*imam*) of the Prophet. He was a just and brave leader, but politically procrastinating and overly cautious. The first divisions of the Islamic community occurred under his rule, and he eventually lost the struggle against the Umayyads. The rule of these "rightly guided caliphs" is considered in the Sunni tradition to represent the "golden age" of a just and God-pleasing leadership of the Islamic community.

3 Depiction of the main mosque of Medina showing the grave of Muhammad, ceramic tile

2 The battle of Badr in 624: Victory of the Muslims over the people of Mecca, miniature, ca. 1594–95

4 Muhammad and Abu Bakr hide from their persecutors in a cave, Turkish miniature, 17th century

5 Handwritten script from the Koran, probably from the eighth century

6 Muhammad with his daughter Fatima, his cousin and son-in-law Ali ibn Abi Talib and his grand-children al-Hassan and Hussein, miniature, 18th c.

622	Muhammad's migration to Medina
630	Muhammad's arrival in Mecca
8 Jun 632	Muhammad's death
Jun 632	First Caliph Abu Bakr
634	Second Caliph Umar I
635–637	Extensive conquests in Near East
from 637	Improvement of internal organizatio

The Caliphate of the Umayyads

In 661, the Umayyads established a hereditary caliphate and from out of Damascus initiated the rapid spread of Islam to the east and west. In 750, they were deposed by the Abbasids.

The rule of the Umayyad dynasty began in 657, when Caliph Ali lost a battle at Siffin against the rebel Syrian governor Muawiya. After Ali's murder in 661, Muawiya, who already controlled a major part of the Muslim territory by 658, established the caliphate of his family. He made Damascus, where the magnificent ❼ Grand Mosque was built, his capital. ❽ Desert palaces in Syria and Jordan served as recuperative retreats as well as for agricultural purposes. In 674–678 Islamic troops advanced far into Byzantine territory and besieged Constantinople for the first time. Under Yazid I, the family of the Prophet's grandson al-Husayn was killed near Karbala in 680—an event that initiated the Shiite movement. Abd al-Malik began stabilizing the Umayyad Empire's political structures in 685. He wanted to make Jerusalem the new political and cultural focus of his reign, and had the flawless ❾ Dome of the Rock constructed in 691–692.

7 The Grand Mosque of the Umayyads in Damascus, Syria, built in the eighth century

8 Qasr al-Hair ash-Sharki, desert palace in Syria, built starting in 729 under the Caliph Hisham

The second wave of Islamic expansion began under al-Walid I. In 711, Islamic Arabs and Berbers under General Tariq crossed from Africa to Gibraltar and into Spain, destroyed the Visigoth Empire of Toledo, and within a short time conquered the whole Iberian Peninsula as far as Asturias.

Soon they were advancing into southern France, but they were turned back at Tours and Poitiers in 732 by the ⓫ Franks led by Charles Martel. Between 694 and 711, Arab troops also advanced out of southern Persia into present-day Pakistan and conquered Afghanistan, Bukhara, and Samarkand in 704, as well as the Indus Valley to Multan. In 724, Transoxiana and Tashkent also fell to the Islamic forces.

Troops of al-Walid's successors besieged Constantinople again in 717–718 and regularly plundered Byzantine Asia Minor. Caliph Hisham proved himself to be a capable administrative expert by regaining control of the unrest among the Berbers and new Muslims through the just distribution of ❿ monies and the financing of public buildings and municipal water supplies. He also promoted culture, the arts, and education. The bloody elimination of the Umayyad caliphate in 749–750 by the Abbasids, who were related to the Prophet's family, was facilitated by revolts under Hisham's successors and struggles for the throne in the ruling house.

The Tragedy of Karbala

After the abdication of his older brother al-Hassan, al-Husayn, the younger son of Ali, was recognized by the Shiites as the third imam and rightful ruler. In 680, the citizens of al-Kufa persuaded him to rise up against the Umayyads' rule. During a march through the desert, Husayn and 72 family members were surrounded by Caliph Yazid's troops, starved, and annihilated. The tragedy of Karbala on Muharram 10, 680, (October 10 according to the Western calendar) is commemorated by the Shiites in the Ashura festival with plays and flagellant processions.

above: Preperations for the battle of Karbala, Turkish miniature

9 Mosque of Omar, or Dome of the Rock, in Jerusalem, built 688–691

10 Silver coins minted by the Umayyads

11 Battle at Tours and Poitiers in 732

644	Third Caliph Uthman
ca. 653	First official version of Koran
656	Fourth Caliph Ali
657	Rule of the Umayyads
661	Damascus becomes royal residence
680	Murder of Husayn
732	Charles Martel's victory over Tariq
749–50	Umayyads deposed by Abbasids

The Early Abbasids

After removing the Umayyads, the Abbasids took over the caliphate and built up Baghdad as the world center of Islam. However, a rapid decline in power was already evident by the ninth century.

Al-Mansur (ruled 754–775) became the founder of the Abbasid Empire after the Abbasid caliphate had been made secure through the extermination by his brother Abu l-Abbas ("the Bloody One") of all Umayyads, with the exception of Prince Abd al-Rahman (p. 230). He led the Islamic world to a high point In 762, he established a new capital at Baghdad on the boundaries of the Arab and Persian worlds, which became a world center of Islamic culture, science, and art and a prosperous trading city in subsequent centuries. His son al-Mahdi established the dynastic and absolute rule of the caliphs, with Sunni Islam as the state religion. He suppressed internal rebellions but lost Spain, where an independent caliphate had been established at Córdoba in 756.

4 Minaret of the Grand Mosque of Samarra, built in 859

1 Harun ar-Rashid

Al-Mahdi's son was the luxury-loving ❶, ❷ Harun ar-Rashid—known from the "Tales of the Arabian Nights"—during whose reign the empire reached its first high point. The gap between the caliph and the people, however, was growing ever wider. The Barmakid family of viziers, who administered the empire wisely, led the government until 803.

The power struggle among Harun's sons was won in 813 by al-Mamun. He elevated to state doctrine the rationalist teachings of the Mutazilites, who propagated the divine origin of the Koran. He also created an intellectual center with the founding of a comprehensive library in 830, the House of Science in Baghdad. He ordered the writings of the scholars and philosophers of ancient Greece to be translated, thus eventually making them available to the Western world. Al-Mamun began the practice, followed by his successors, of relying on Turkish mercenary troops, converts to Sunni Islam.

In 836 al-Mutasim moved his capital and the Turkish guards from Baghdad, which had been repeatedly shaken by unrest caused by tension between the population and the Turkish troops, to the newly founded ❸, ❹ Samarra. The strict believer al-Mutawakkil limited the influence of philosophers and the Mutazilites during his reign from 847 to 861. Disputes over succession and frequently changing caliphs weakened central power under his successors. The capital was returned to Baghdad in 883, but de facto autonomous local rule developed after 800, and the decline of the empire continued to accelerate. These weaker caliphs, who increasingly came under the control of the Turkish troop commanders, became a power elite under the caliphs in the tenth century.

2 The deputies of Harun ar-Rashids at an audience with Charlemagne

3 Stucco ornaments from Qasr al-Achiq ("the lovers' castle"), built in the late ninth century

Avicenna (Arabic: Ibn Sina)

Centers of Islamic Sciences

In Baghdad and other centers of Islamic sciences, the legacy of Greek antiquity was adopted and further developed, far outstripping progress in the West. It was principally in the areas of mathematics, astronomy, medicine, and optics that supreme achievements were made; philosophy also reached a new high point with the universal scholars al-Kindi and Ibn Sina (Avicenna), both of whom had a significant impact on Renaissance scholarship in Europe. For centuries, the textbooks of Islamic scholars comprised the scientific canon.

762 | Baghdad becomes royal capital
786–809 | Caliph Harun ar-Rashid
830 | Founding of "House of Science"
836 | Samarra becomes new capital
846 | The Aghlabids plunder Rome
932 | Renewal of caliphate under the Buwayhids

The End of the Abbasid Caliphate

The Abbasids' loss of power in the ninth century favored the autonomy of local kingdoms and the Shiite counter-caliphate of the Fatimids. The caliphate ended with the Mongol invasion.

The local kingdoms that developed under the Abbasids mostly proved to be politically strong and made their courts into independent cultural centers. The Aghlabids (800–909), who ruled in eastern Algeria, ❻ Tunisia, and Tripolitania, were able to settle southern Italy and Sicily after 827 and plundered Rome in 846, while the ❼ Tulunids (868–905) and Ikhshidids (935–969) ruled in Egypt, Syria, and Palestine. The Tahirids (821–873) in northeastern Persia (Khorasan) and the Saffarids (861/67–903) in Afghanistan and parts of Transoxiana made themselves independent

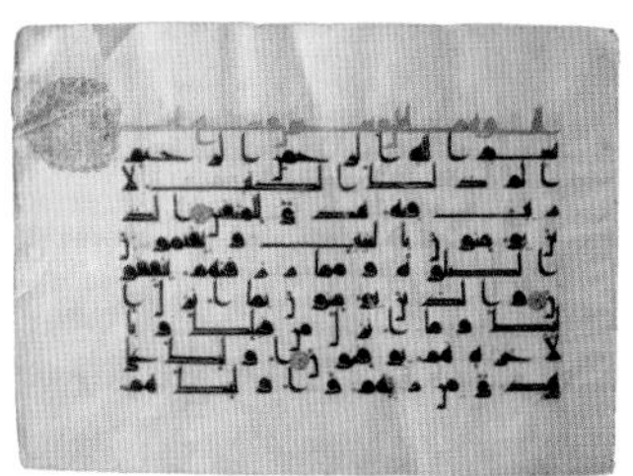
5 Handwriting from the Koran in script of the Kufi from the Grand Mosque in Kairouan, tenth century

and were then supplanted by the Samanids, who resided in Samarkand (p. 234). The Maghreb and Spain withdrew from the control of Baghdad (p. 230).

The Shiite Fatimids became Baghdad's greatest challenge when they advanced out of Tunisia, where they had made ❺, ❽ Kairouan their capital. The Fatimids conquered Egypt in 969, took control of Syria, and erected a Shiite counter-caliphate in the newly founded city of ❾ Cairo. Their founder Ubayd Allah al-Mahdi took advantage of Shiite expectations of salvation to hold his realm together. His successors al-Muizz and al-Aziz made Cairo into a center of science and culture and, with ❿ al-Azhar Mosque, founded a mission center for Shiism (today the leading Sunni school of Islamic theology).

8 The Grand Mosque of Kairouan, Tunisia, first built in 672, enlarged and rebuilt in the eighth century

9 Bab Zuweila, Fatimid city gate in Cairo, eleventh c.

The religious eccentricities of Caliph al-Hakim led to unrest and, in 1017–1021, to the founding of the religious community of the Druze, who worshiped him as a god. In 1036–37 the Fatimid Empire, which was also undergoing an economic decline, lost Syria and Palestine to the Seljuks (p. 232). The Ayyubid sultan Saladin was able to dispose of the Fatimid caliphate (p. 233) in 1171 because of a religious and political schism that had developed in 1094. Out of this schism the sect of Assassins, notorious for their murderous attacks, also emerged.

In the meantime, since 932 the caliphs in Baghdad had become mere puppets of the Shiite military dynasty of the Buwayhid emirs, who reestablished the power of the caliphate and revived Persian culture. The most notable of the Buwayhids, Adud ad-Dawlah, emir of Baghdad from 977 to 983, subordinated the whole of Iraq to his power. Between 1056 and 1062, the last of the Buwayhid line in Baghdad and Kerman was removed by the Seljuks. The caliphs then became pawns of the Seljuks and the Khwarizm-shahs (p. 232, 235). They were able to once again restore their sovereignty to a great extent through an-Nasir and al-Mustansir, who built the Mustansiriya Madrassa in Baghdad. The last caliph, al-Mutasim, refused to submit to the advancing Mongols as demanded and died with thousands of his subjects when they stormed Baghdad in 1258.

6 Ribat, fortress in Sousse, Tunisia, built in the late eighth century

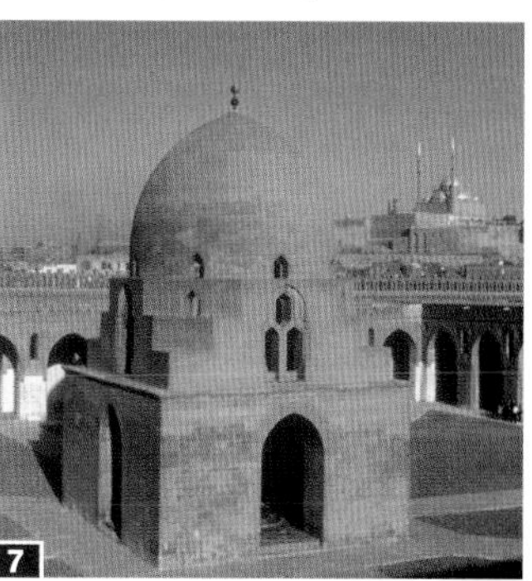
7 The Mosque of Ibn Tulun in Cairo, inner courtyard with fountain, built 876

10 The Al-Azhar Mosque in Cairo, Muslim university since 998, built 970–972

969 | The Fatimids conquer Egypt
1017–21 | Founding of the Druzes
1036–37 | The Seljuks conquer Syria and Palestine
1056–62 | The Buwayhids driven from Baghdad
1171 | End of Fatimid caliphate
1258 | End of Abbasid caliphate

The Emirate/Caliphate of Córdoba

After the Islamic conquest, the Spanish Umayyads guided their empire into a political and cultural golden era. In 929, Abd al-Rahman III assumed the title of caliph.

Since the conquest of the greater part of the Iberian Peninsula (from 711) by Arab and Berber troops, the province of al-Andalus had been ruled by governors of the Umayyad caliphs. Following their removal by the Abbasids, the only surviving Umayyad prince, Abd al-Rahman I, established an autonomous emirate in ❹ Córdoba in 756. Thereafter, al-Andalus experienced an economic heyday due to its excellent state administration, cleverly devised irrigation and cultivation techniques, and extensive trade relations with Africa and the Orient. This was accompanied by an ❸ artistic and intellectual blossoming. Córdoba became an important religious site with its ❶, ❷ great mosque called La Mezquita; the enormous palace-city Medina az-Zahara was constructed just outside the city during Abd al-Rahman III's reign.

Abd al-Rahman I and his son Hisham I consolidated power and several times advanced into southern France. An Orientalization of the cities and refinement of court manners occurred during the reign of Abd al-Rahman II (822–852). The ruler and the nobility emerged as poets and patrons of the arts, and Córdoba was soon able to compete with Baghdad and Samarra as an Islamic center. The central government began to lose its authority under his successors. Local rulers such as the Hafsun family in Bobastro, who controlled large parts of Spain, restricted the power of the emir, as did the Christian kings whose strength was growing and pushed southward from their bases in northern Spain—Asturias, León, and Castile.

Islamic Spain reached its political apogee under Abd al-Rahman III. He not only restored lost power, but after 920 also brought the whole of western Maghreb under his control and gave the empire a well-organized civil and military administration. In 929, he proclaimed himself caliph and thus created a third caliphate alongside those in Baghdad and Cairo. His erudite son, al-Hakam II, had one of the largest libraries of his time built and furthered philosophy, science, and the arts. General al-Mansur assumed the regency for Hisham II, who was underage at the time of his father's death. Al-Mansur restored the military power of the empire in more than 50 campaigns against the Christians and, in 997 conquered Fez, as well as the Christian pilgrimage city of Santiago de Compostela. His son Abd al-Malik held onto power, but the caliphate sank into civil wars and the squabbles of semiautonomous rulers after 1009. The last caliph, Hisham III, died in 1031 and the caliphate splintered into autonomous *taifas* (Islamic city-states) that were later conquered by powers from the north.

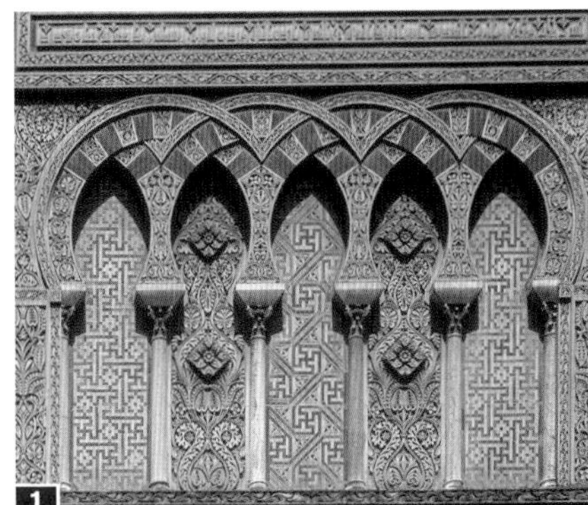

1 View of the east facade of the Grand Mosque, La Mezquita, in Córdoba, Spain, built 785– 990, used as cathedral since 1236

2 Interior of La Mezquita in Córdoba, Spain

3 Ivory box in the style of the Umayyads, from Medina az-Zahra, a palace city near Córdoba

4 View of Córdoba with the bridge over the Guadalquivir and the Grand Mosque with the later cathedral

19 Jun 710 | Battle of Guadalete
720 | Conquest of Narbonne
756 | Founding of emirate of Córdoba
795 | Building of Great Mosque of Córdoba
929 | Caliphate of Abd al-Rahman III
936 | Building of the palace-city Medina az-Zahra
985 | Conquest of Barcelona

Islam in Spain and the Maghreb

The political weakness of the Arabs in Spain led to the rise of the Berber dynasties, which reached from Morocco into Spain. While Islam was being forced to retreat in Spain, the Berbers claimed the Maghreb.

Between 1013 and 1091, al-Andalus broke up into 26 tiny factional states, *taifas*, that were ruled over by Arab or Berber dynasties. In the meantime, the Almoravids, Berber border warriors, rose to power by about 1060, and in 1082 they advanced out of Marrakech into Algiers. Summoned to aid the local kings of Islamic Spain against the Christians of the north, the strictly religious Almoravids, who had started to build up an empire in Morocco, defeated the Christians but then took control of Spain themselves and eliminated the factional kingdoms between 1090 and 1094.

The mosque of Tinmal, Morocco, from the Almohad period, built 1153–54

Beginning in 1124, opposition emerged in ❺ Tinmal, Morocco, in the form of a strict ascetic mass movement, the Almohads, led by the preacher Ibn Tumart. In 1147, their leader Abd al-Mumin did away with Almoravid rule in Marrakech and ❻ Seville and by 1160 had absorbed into his empire almost the whole of Maghreb, including Algeria, Tunisia, and parts of Tripolitania. The Almohads put an end to the religious tolerance previously practiced by Muslim rulers in Spain and restricted free philosophy in favor of orthodox beliefs. After initial military successes in Spain, in 1212 they suffered a crushing defeat by the Christians at Las Navas de Tolosa, and after 1224–1232 they were subjugated by former vassal princes in Spain. Before long, the Christians reclaimed all of Spain except the ❾ Nasrid emirate of Granada, which had been founded in 1232 with the ❼ Alhambra palace as its center of power. This last Moorish stronghold lasted until 1492, when the Catholic kings drove out the last ruler, Muhammad XI, and eliminated Muslim rule in Western Europe.

The Alhambra of Granada, residence of the Nasrids 1231–1492, left, the famous Courtyard of the Lions in the center of the palace grounds

Muhammad XI

Besieged by Christian forces, the Nasrids of Granada had been required to pay tribute to the kings of Castile since 1431. The last sultan, Abu Abdallah Muhammad, also known as Muhammad XI and in Spanish as Boabdil, "the little king," ruled from 1482 to 1492, except when temporarily expelled by his uncle in 1483–1487. He hardly resisted the advance of the Catholic kings and left Granada to them on January 2, 1492. This "farewell of the last Moor" was often artistically represented. He was exiled to Morocco and died in 1527.

right: Boabdil's dagger

The Berber dynasty of the Merinids ended Almohad rule in Morocco in 1269 and stayed in power for 200 years until 1465, building up its residence ❽ Fez with mosques and *madrassas* (Islamic schools) and extending its power over Algeria. The Hafsids, residing in Tunis, were in competition with the Merinids (1229/1236–1574) and ruled the former Almohad lands in Tunisia, eastern Algeria, and Tripolitania. They took the title of caliph after 1258. Under the Hafsids, Tunis became the center of Mediterranean trade in the Magreb.

Torre del Oro, fortification tower in Seville, Spain, built in 1220

The Kairaouine Mosque in Fez, Morocco, founded in the ninth century

The battle of Higueruela on July 1, 1431 between John II of Castile and the Nasrids of Granada, Spain, fresco 16th century

997 | Conquest of Santiagos de Compostela
1031 | End of the caliphate of Córdoba
1082 | Berber conquest of Algiers
1124 | Emergence of Almohads
1212 | Battle of Las Navas de Tolos
1232 | Founding of emirate of Granada
1492 | Expulsion of Boabdil, last sultan

The Seljuk Empire

The Great Seljuks unified their domain under the "Sunni state," which was officially ruled by the caliph. After the disintegration of the Seljuks, only a small branch of the dynasty remained in Anatolia.

Islamized Turkish tribes took over power in the Middle East with the rise of the Great Seljuk sultanate. The Seljuks—named after the legendary tribal founder Seljuk—who at first settled in Transoxiana and followed a religion with shamanic practices, converted to Sunni Islam around 960 under the influence of the Persian Samanids. After their division into several tribal units, they pushed out of Nishapur and, following their victory over the Ghaznavids (p. 234) under the leadership of Tughril Beg, conquered western Iran (1042), advanced to Shiraz (1052), and then took control of Azerbaijan and Khuzestan in 1054. In 1055 Tughril Beg seized Baghdad, freed the caliph from the "protective rule" of the Shiite Buwayhids, and took his place as sultan. His nephew Alp Arslan, who assumed power in 1063, then created the Great Seljuk Empire, along with his exceptional vizier, the statesman and philosopher Nizam al-Mulk. In 1071, he achieved an important victory over the Fatimids, taking Aleppo, over ❶ Byzantium at Manzikert. Following Alp Arslan's murder in 1072, Nizam remained the dominant figure under his son Malik Shah. In 1092, Nizam became the first prominent murder victim of an attack by the Assassins.

As they themselves possessed no religious authority, the Seljuks, now rulers of all the Arab East save the far South of the Arabian Peninsula, acted as ❸ "rulers of the lands of East and West, renewers of Islam" (the title Tughril Beg took in 1062) on behalf of the caliph. They created a great and powerful empire with excellent administration, connected by secure roads, ❺ trade routes, and comfortable ❷ caravansaries from Central Asia across ❻ Persia to Iraq. A network of notable *madrassas*—schools for general education and the teaching of Islam—and the integrated "Sunni state" served to train the future administrative elite efficiently.

3 The mausoleum of Sultan Sandjar, probably the reception hall in the palace of the Great Seljuk in Merv, present-day Turkmenistan, twelfth century

The Great Seljuk Empire disintegrated through struggles over the succession following Malik Shah, and in 1157 it was destroyed by the Khwarizm-shahs (p. 235). However, a Seljuk branch had established its independence in Anatolia in 1078. Its sultan Qilich Arslan II maneuvered between the Crusaders and the Byzantines and created a well-organized and militarily stable state with its capital at ❹ Konya. Ala ad-Din Kay-Qubad I was its most significant sultan, ruling from 1219 to 1237. The westward-moving Mongols increased their pressure after 1242, and the Seljuks suffered a defeat in 1279 against the Ilkhans, the successors of the Mongols in Persia. Masud II, the last sultan of the Anatolian Seljuks, died in 1308.

1 Battles between the Byzantines and the Seljuks in the eleventh century, Byzantine book illustration

2 Former caravansary in Baghdad, built in 1358

4 The Ince Minare Medrese in Konya, Turkey

6 Tiled mosaic in the Mosque of Isfahan, Iran

5 Cobandede Bridge, part of the silk trade route built by the Seljuks, Anatolia, Turkey, 13th century

1042 The Seljuks conquer West Iran | **1055** Tughril Beg captures Baghdad | **1063** Sultanate of Alp Arslan | **1071** Battle of Manzikert | **1092** Murder of Nizam al-Mulk | **1157** Expulsion of Seljuks | **1171** Saladin eliminates the Fatimid

The Ayyubids and the Mamelukes

The time of the Crusades favored the rise of military dynasties in the Middle East. Sultan Saladin became the outstanding general on the side of Islam. He was followed by the Mameluke rulers.

The Seljuks were not able to bring the local dynasties in the Palestine–Syria–northern Iraq area under their control. A Kurdish dynasty established the first political unity in the region under its founder, ❼ Saladin—one of Islam's most important statesmen and conquerors.

Saladin (Salah ad-Din) was initially a military leader for the Fatimids, but he removed them in 1171 and reinstituted Sunnism in their former area of dominion. In quick succession, he seized Tripoli (1172), Damascus (1174), ❽ Aleppo (1183), and Mosul (1185–1186) from the ⓫ Crusaders and local rulers. In 1187 he was able to take Jerusalem (p. 218), which he proclaimed an open city for all religions. A mixture of brilliant tactics,

7 Sultan Saladin

negotiating, and chivalrous generosity characterized Saladin's political dealings, which won him respect even in the West. As the ruler of a reunited Egypt, Syria, and Iraq, Saladin negotiated with the army of the Third Crusade, led by ❿ Richard I (the Lion-Hearted) and persuaded the crusaders to end the weak siege of the city of Jerusalem in 1192.

Saladin's brother al-Adil was able to reunite the empire that fractured upon Saladin's death in 1193, but al-Adil's successors had to use the help of Caucasian military slaves (Mamelukes) against the Crusaders. In 1250–1260, the ❾ Mamelukes removed the last of the Ayyubids and took power for themselves, ruling over Egypt and Syria until 1517 from their capital Cairo. The Mameluke leader Sultan Baybars I, an outstanding military strategist, halted the westward movement of the Mongols in 1260 and restricted the rule of the Crusaders, who were driven out of their last bastions in Tripoli and Acre in 1289–1291 by his successors. The Mamelukes developed Cairo into one of the most important hubs of Asian trade in the Mediterranean and under ⓬ Sultan Barkuk resisted the Mongolian conqueror Tamerlane. They established their religious legitimacy through the Abbasid shadow caliphs, whom they controlled. Mameluke decline began after 1450, and in 1517 they were swept aside by the Ottomans under Selim I (p. 309).

9 The tombs of Mameluke caliphs, in Cairo, laid out 1250–1517

11 Crusaders' castle Montreal, Shobak, in Jordan, built in 1115

8 The Grand Mosque of Aleppo in Syria, destroyed in 1169 and rebuilt under the Ayyubid Nur ad-Din

10 Richard the Lion-Hearted in the Battle of Arsuf against Saladin's troops

The Conquest of Jerusalem

Saladin's victory over the Crusader army at Hattin on July 4, 1187, was a tactical masterpiece that paved the way for the retaking of Jerusalem on October 3. Saladin proved his chivalry when he allowed the inhabitants of Jerusalem to choose the knight Balian of Ibelin as their commander for the defense—although the knight was actually Saladin's prisoner—as he did not want to win a victory over women and children. After taking the city, he spared the Christians and allowed almost all of them to buy their freedom. He also granted freedom to hundreds without any ransom.

above: The 1187 battle of Hattin: The crusaders' defeat against Saladin's army

12 Lamp from Sultan Barkuk's mosque, 14th century

1172	Conquest of Tripoli
1174	Conquest of Damascus
3 Oct 1187	Conquest of Jerusalem
4 Jul 1187	Battle of Hattin
1250-60	Reign of the Mamelukes
Mar 1193	Death of Saladin
1308	Death of Masud I

The Islamic Regional Rulers of the East and Mahmud of Ghazna

Following the Samanids in the East, it was Mahmud of Ghazna and his successors who spread Islam through Central Asia and all the way to India.

The Islamic East went through a development that was generally independent of that of the West. After the Arab armies had advanced as far as Bukhara, Samarkand, and Pakistan after 700, these dominions fell in 821 to the Tahirids (p. 229), whose governors in Samarkand, Ferghana, and Herat were the Iranian ❹ Samanids (from 819). Nasr I used the decline of the Tahirids in 873 to make himself independent as the Abbasid caliph's governor in Transoxiana. He developed Bukhara into his royal residence, and at the end of the tenth century it became a cultural center with Persian characteristics. His brother Ismail conquered Afghanistan and a major part of Persia including ❷ Khorasan by 903. The empire then reached its greatest extent under Nasr II (914–943) stretching from Baghdad, Kerman, and the Persian Gulf to Turkistan and India. His successors lost Khorasan to the Ghaznavids in 994 and Transoxiana to the Qarakhanids in 999. The last Samanid ruler was murdered in 1005 while fleeing.

2 Khorasan ceramic plate, tenth c.

4 The Samanid mausoleum in Bukhara, Uzbekistan, built from the ninth to the tenth century

With this, the Turkish tribes had taken over power in the East. The Ghaznavids, who were originally Turkish mercenaries and generals of the Samanids, installed the dynasty founder Sebüktigin as governor of Ghazna in 977. His son ❶ Mahmud of Ghazna, who assumed power in 998, is one of the great conquerors of Islam. By 999, he had conquered the Samanids in Khorasan and seized major areas of Persia and Punjab with his swift mounted armies. In 1027, he had the caliph in ❺ Baghdad award him the honorary title of "protector of the caliphate" and as a strict Sunni, fought the Shiite Buwayhids. He was driven by religious faith and the quest for wealth. Between 1001 and 1024, Mahmud subjugated the north of India in 17 campaigns and made possible Islam's penetration into India (p. 240). He dealt harshly with the "idolatrous" Hindus and destroyed their temples. Mahmud's son Masud I focused on India and suffered a crushing defeat against the Seljuks in 1040 with the result that the sovereignty of the Ghaznavids became confined to ❸ eastern Afghanistan and northern India. In 1161, the Ghurids of central Afghanistan forced them out of Ghazna and in 1186 out of northern India as well.

1 Victory column of Ghazni, built under Mahmud of Ghazna

3 Kohi-Baba, mountain range in eastern Afghanistan

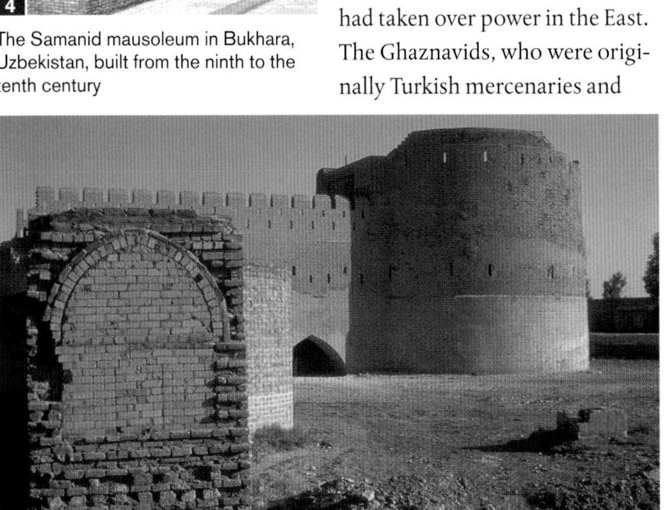

5 Bab El Wastani, one of the city gates of Baghdad, late eleventh century

The Court of Mahmad of Ghazna

The court of Mahmud of Ghazna was a center of Islamic intellectual life. Poets and scientists were generously supported. He also took them with him on his campaigns so that they could conduct their studies there. Among the most notable scientists surrounding Mahmud was the universal scholar al-Biruni, who described the areas of life in his In the Garden of Science, and Firdawsi, who was commissioned by Mahmud to write his Persian book of kings Shah-nameh.

Firdawsi, when he was still an unknown poet meets the court poets of Sultan Mahmud of Ghazna (980), cover picture of the *Shah-nameh* ("king's book") of Firdawsi

Central Asia and the Khwarizm-Shahs

Following the Seljuks and Qarakhanids, the northern Iranian Khwarizm-shahs erected the greatest empire of the old Islamic world. Due to their rapid expansion, they provoked the westward movement of the Mongols.

6 Uighur yurt at the Tian Chi in China

The Qarakhanids were a Turkic people belonging to the ❻ Uighurs who originated in the Asian steppes. They made themselves independent after 840 under a dual khanate in the west and east and converted to Islam in the tenth century. In 992, the Qarakhanids conquered Bukhara and by 999 had appropriated the Transoxianan dominions of the Samanids. They made ❼, ❾ Bukhara their royal residence, and after 1042 Samarkand, too. At first they were able to resist the Ghaznavids and Seljuks, but were finally forced to recognize the sovereignty of these and indeed later became their vassals. Under the rule of the Khwarizm-shahs after 1180, they were removed from the

7 The Kalan Minaret in Bukhara, Uzbekistan, built in the early twelfth century by the Qarakhanids

west khanate in 1210–1211 and from the east khanate in 1212.

The greatest Islamic empire before the western migration of the Mongols emerged under the Khwarizm-shahs (Khorezmi) who settled in Central Asia. Under the rule of the Ghaznavids beginning in 1017, they were conquered by the Seljuks in 1047 and installed as governors in Khwarizm. Konja Urgench remained their capital until 1212, when the last shah moved his government to the capital of Bukhara. In the first half of the twelfth century under Qutb ad-Din Muhammad and Ala ad-Din Atsiz, the Khwarizm-shahs were able to make themselves independent to a great extent and began in 1135 to push the Seljuks in Iran further back. Kiliç Arslan II dislodged the rule of the Great Seljuks over the East in 1157 and assumed their title of protector of the caliph in Baghdad (officially in 1192). Ala ad-Din Tekish conquered Iran with the seizure of Khorasan (1187) and Raj (1192). The Khwarizm-shahs now ruled over a huge empire spanning Turkistan, Iran, and parts of Iraq.

Ala ad-Din Muhammad expanded the empire once again by driving the Ghurids out of Afghanistan in 1206, and in 1210–1212 he overthrew the rival Qarakhanids in Transoxiana. Both territories were absorbed into the empire. Furthermore, he drove the ❽ Qara-Khitai Mongols back to the east. Ala ad-Din was now ruler over an Islamic empire of a size until then unknown. But in overestimating himself, he provoked the invasion of Mongolian army under ❿ Genghis Khan in 1218 by refusing to make amends for the arrest of Mongolian merchants by one of his governors. Ala ad-Din died trying to escape; his son Djalal ad-Din was murdered after an adventurous life as a fugitive in 1231. The empire then fell to the Mongols.

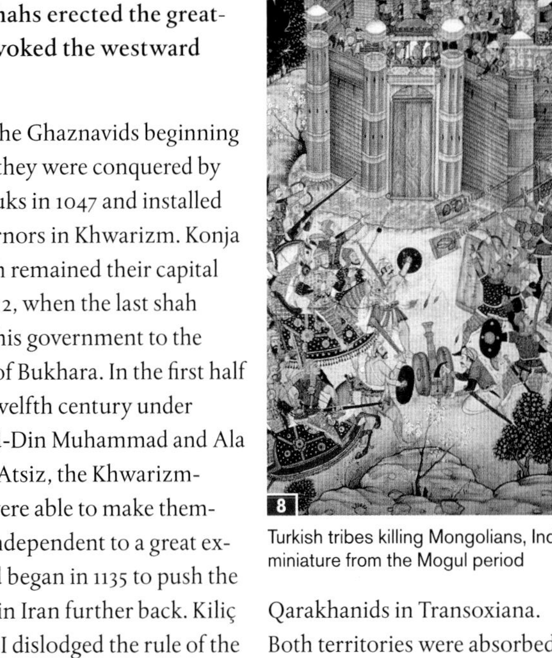

8 Turkish tribes killing Mongolians, Indian miniature from the Mogul period

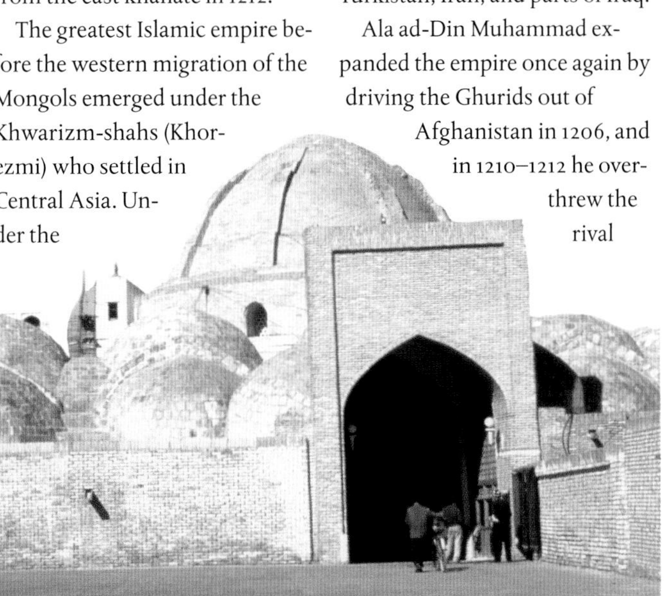

9 Cupola bazaar in Bukhara, with the Kalan minaret left in the background

10 Genghis Khan, wood engraving, 16th c.

1157 | Reign of Khwarizm-Shahs
1187–92 | Conquest of Iran
1206 | Ghurids driven out of Afghanistan
1210–12 | Qarakhanids driven out of Transoxiania
1218 | Invasion of Genghis Khan

The Mongolian Empire and Its Successors 12th–15th century

The conquests of ❶ Genghis Khan and his successors fundamentally changed the structures of Asia and Eastern Europe. The "Mongolian storm" that hit Baghdad in 1258 brought about the end of the old Islamic world. The destructive force of the mounted nomads resulted in the downfall of many cities and kingdoms. The Mongols' religious tolerance enabled them to assimilate into the dominant cultures of the territories they conquered, such as China and Persia. The huge empire founded by Tamerlane in the 14th century saw itself as heir to both the Mongolian and Islamic traditions but rapidly disintegrated after his death.

1 Genghis Khan, founder of the Mongolian empire

The Campaigns of Conquest of Genghis Khan

Genghis Khan united most of the Mongolian tribes and undertook campaigns of conquest in every cardinal direction. With them came dreadful devastation.

Even before the rise of Genghis Khan, Central Asia had been dominated by Turkish and Mongolian ❷ nomadic tribes since the migrations of late antiquity (p. 148). Their strength lay in their ❸ swift and flexible fighting methods, which included attacks by mounted archers in small, mobile units. Between 1133 and 1211, Mongolians of the Qara-Khitai tribal group ruled vast stretches of central Asia, but they were driven back to the east by the Khwarizm -shahs after 1200.

At the end of the 12th century, Temujin, who was descended from the ruling family of a small tribe in the northeast of present-day Mongolia, was able to unite several tribes and assemble a strong army. In 1206, he took the title Genghis Khan ("Universal Ruler") and began his carefully planned campaigns of conquest. First he subjugated southern Siberia in 1207 and in 1211–1216 conquered ❹ northern China. He made an unsuccessful attempt to advance into central China, but the Uigurs submitted to him in 1209. A careless act by the Khwarizm-shahs (p. 235) presented the opportunity for a long-planned campaign in the west. Between 1219 and 1221 Genghis Khan overran Transoxiana and also wide stretches of the Khwarizm territories. In 1220, he founded his capital, Karakorum, in the north of Mongolia. He then captured northern Persia, Armenia, and Georgia and defeated the Russian princes in 1223.

3 Mounted Mongolian warlord, painted ceramic tile

Genghis Khan waged his campaigns with extreme cruelty and presided over widespread plundering and destruction. He did, however, lay the foundation for an empire supported by caravan trade, establishing a huge network of trading posts and communications points; he also kept the Silk Road free of banditry. The Mongolians also demonstrated a pragmatic tolerance of different religions. The subjugated empires were absorbed into a "friendship union" and required to pay tribute, from which considerable Mongolian state rserves were accumulated. Genghis Khan ❺ died in 1227, after which the empire was divided among his ❻ four sons.

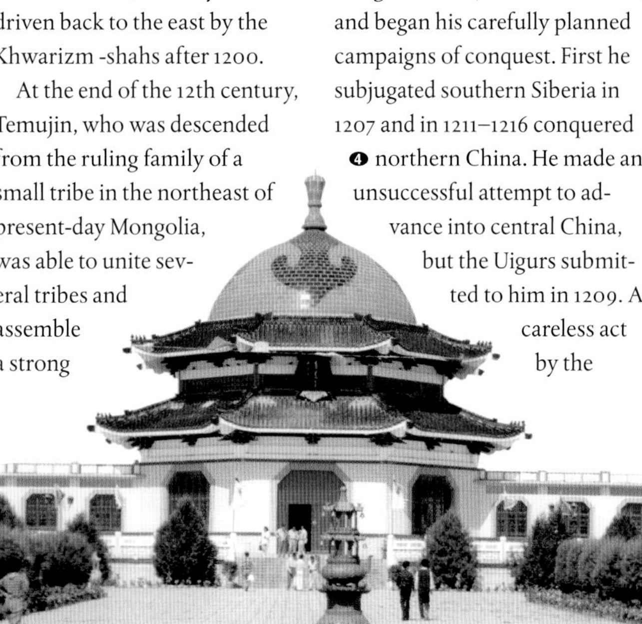

5 Genghis Khan's mausoleum, inner Mongolia

2 Yurts–Mongolian tents–covered with felt, Persian miniature, 14th century

4 Genghis Khan's Mongol army storms a fortress during the invasion of the northern Chinese province of Tangut, miniature painting, ca. 1590

6 Meeting of Genghis Khan's sons, Persian book illustration, 14th c.

1207 | Genghis Khan conquers southern Siberia
1211–16 | Genghis Khan conquers northern China
1220 | Founding of Karakorum
1223 | Genghis defeats the Russian princes
1227 | Death of Genghis Khan

The Spread of Mongolian Rule

The empire may have been divided among the sons of Genghis Khan, but it was the third generation that proved its military power through the conquest of wide stretches of Asia and Eastern Europe.

Genghis Khan's son ❼ Ögödei, who succeeded him as the "great khan," decided in a war council in 1236 to conquer Russia, Poland, and Hungary and from there to move into the rest of Europe. His nephew Batu Khan subjugated most of Western Russia between 1236 and 1242. In 1240, he stormed Kiev and advanced almost to the Baltic Sea. In 1240–1241, his troops devastated Poland and Hungary and annihilated an army of German and Polish knights at ❽ Liegnitz, in Silesia, in early 1241. Europe appeared to lie open to the Mongolians when, in December 1241, Ögödei died and Batu Khan turned his army back east to settle the succession. In 1251, Mangu Khan, another grandson of Genghis Khan, became great khan in Karakorum and began the systematic construction of a great empire. In the meantime, his cousin ❾ Batu and his successors made themselves largely independent and founded the khanates of the Golden and Blue Hordes in Muscovy and Eastern Europe. However, they lost territory in battles against the Russian grand dukes in the 14th century, and in 1502 the states were destroyed. Mangu Khan, whose cultured court was characterized by religious tolerance, respectfully received a papal legation headed by Willem van Ruysbroeck in 1253. He charged his younger brother ❿ Kublai Khan, who in 1260 inherited the title of great khan, with new conquests to the East and South; Kublai Khan then invaded ⓬ China and founded the Yuan dynasty, which survived until 1368. Hülegü Khan conquered Persia and led the Mongolian sacking of Baghdad that ended the caliphate and the old Islamic order in 1258. After disposing of the small principalities in the Middle East, he was finally halted by the Egyptian Mamelukes. Hülegü Khan founded the Il-khan dynasty, which ruled over Iran, Iraq, Syria, East Anatolia, and the Caucasus from the royal palace in Tabriz. The dynasty converted to ⓫ Islam during the reign of Khan Ghazan in 1300.

In 1335, the Mongolian Empire disintegrated into a series of minor principalities. Though it only existed for 150 years, the Mongolian empire affected peoples and states across the known world, from China to Eastern Europe.

7 Great khan Ögödei

10 Great khan Kublai Khan

12 Occupation of fortresses strung along the Yangtse River in 1275 during Kublai Khan's invasion of China, from an Indian miniature, ca. 1590

11 Niche in the Friday mosque in Yazd, Iran, built in 1325–34

8 Battle of Liegnitz, April 9, 1241

9 Batu Khan on his throne, Persian book illustration, 14th century

Baghdad before the Mongolian Attack on February 10, 1258:

"Together with them [two high officials and the army leader of Baghdad], the Baghdad army decided to withdraw, and much of the population hoped in this way to be saved. However, they were divided up between the thousand-, hundred-, and ten-man units of the Mongolian army and were killed. Those who remained in the city dispersed and hid themselves beneath the Earth and underneath the baths."

Rashid ad-Din's Book of The Tribes

The conquest of Baghdad by the Mongols led by Hülegü in 1258, Persian miniature

1240 Ögödei captures Kiev
1241 Death of Ögödei
1241 Battle of Liegnitz
1258 "Mongol Storm" hits Baghdad
from 1260 Conquest of China
1335 Disintegration of Mongolian Empire

The Empire of Tamerlane

After 1370, the conqueror Tamerlane united Islamic and Mongolian traditions in his vast Asian empire. He brought scholars and artists to his capital, Samarkand, making it a center of culture.

In the 14th century, an aggressive expanding empire, combining Mongolian and Islamic characteristics once again emerged in Central Asia. The Jagatai khanate, the descendants of the second son of Genghis Khan, ruled in Central

Conquest of the city of Isfahan by Tamerlane, 1387

Asia, but its dominion had split into various tribal groupings during the 14th century. In the context of this political turmoil, a Turkic prince known as Tamerlane was able emerge as a powerful leader. ❶ Tamerlane seized power in Samarkand in 1366, and in April 1370 united the majority of the khanates of ❺ Transoxiana under his leadership.

In 1370 he occupied the Mongolian vassal Khwarizm, and in 1379 plundered the rebellious Konya Urgench. By 1381 he had conquered most of Afghanistan. He either integrated local rulers into his "union of friendship" or elimi-

After defeating Ottoman armies in Anatolia, Tamerlane takes the Sultan Bayezid I prisoner, holding him in a golden cage, lithograph, 18th c.

nated them. Tamerlane captured ❷ Isfahan in 1387 and seized Shiraz from the Muzaffarids in 1393. By 1391 he had made a fugitive of his most dangerous rival, Tokhtamysh, the khan of the Golden Horde, who had carved out an empire in western Russia and the Caucasus; The conquest yielded enormous treasures that were hauled back to his royal residence in Samarkand. In 1393, Tamerlane occupied Iraq and the of Baghdad, crushing the local warlords ruling there. In 1394, he besieged Damascus, and then plundered it in 1401. In July 1402, Tamerlane annihilated the ❸ Ottomans in Anatolia and took Sultan Bayezid I (p. 308), who had refused the offer of an alliance, prisoner.

The restless general, who ruled his world empire ❹ from his saddle, had already waged a military campaign against India in 1398–1399, in the course of which he occupied Lahore and Delhi and had 100,000 Indian prisoners executed. Tamerlane tended to treat cities and rulers relatively mildly if they surrendered to him, but showed no mercy to those who resisted. The fate of those who rebelled was even worse, as with the cities of Isfahan and Baghdad when they revolted in 1387 and 1401; Tamerlane had 10,000 inhabitants killed and their heads piled up in pyramids outside the city walls.

Tamerlane, artist's reconstruction based on contemporary descriptions

Aside from his conquests Tamerlane, who ruled over one of the largest empires in history, also gathered around him scholars, poets, and court painters. Many of these came from from the occupied territories, carried off to Samarkand where they made the capital the "center of the world" and the "threshold of Paradise," building magnificent mosques and madrassas. Tamerlane was a strict Sunni, but also sought to preserve the pre-Islamic Mongolian nomad traditions. In the autumn of 1404, he set off to the north with an enormous army to conquer China, but died in Utrar on February 19, 1405.

Tamerlane on horseback, atop a mound of skulls

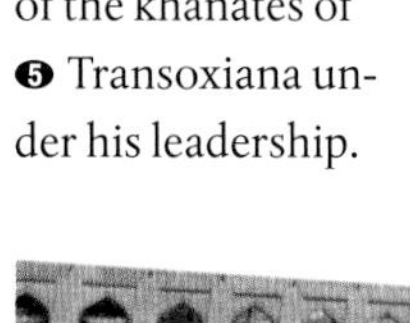
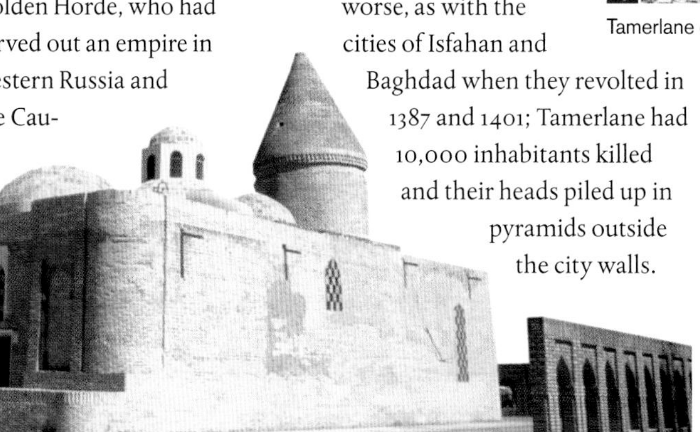

Hiob's well in Bukhara, one of the most important cities in Transoxiana (present-day Uzbekistan) built in the 14th century

1366 | Tamerlane seizes power in Samarkand
1370 | Conquest of Khwarizm
1381 | Afghanistan occupied
1393 | Capture of Baghdad
1394 | Siege of Damascus

The Rule of the Timurids

The empire that Tamerlane founded was divided up among his successors, but these new kingdoms continued to influence Central Asia well into the 16th century.

Tamerlane's heirs, the Timurids, divided the empire among themselves as dictated by Mongolian tradition after Tamerlane's chosen successor—his grandson Pir Muhammad, governor of Kandahar—was murdered in 1407. In the course of time, Tamerlane's youngest son, Shah Rokh, who had reigned in Herat since 1405, established himself as the most important of the heirs and head of the clan. He gained control of Transoxiana and Persia, and most of the rulers of the Uzbeks and the Golden Horde submitted. Iraq, however, was lost to local dynasties. Shah Rokh, a notable patron of the arts and sciences, was one of the more peaceful and cultivated Timurids.

His son, ❼ Ulugh Beg, who had been an autonomous khan in Samarkand since 1409, was one of the most significant scholars of his time. In 1428–1429, he had an observatory with telescopical instruments constructed, from which he made the most exact calculations of the stars possible in the period. The capital, Samarkand, which had been founded by his grandfather Tamerlane, continued to shine under his reign. The rulers were also buried ❽, ❾here in a magnificent necropolis. In 1447, he waged war against his own son Abd al-Latif over the succession to the empire of Shah Rokh. The conflict ended with the murder of Ulugh Beg in 1449 and Abd al-Latif a year later.

Abu Said, a great-grandson of Tamerlane, emerged victorious from the ensuing turmoil to rule over Transoxiana. In 1469, he was taken captive and executed by Turkic tribesmen of the Aq-Qoyunlu, the "White Sheep Turks," who advanced out of Persia. His son, Sultan Ahmad, held on to the Samarkand area, but was constantly under pressure from the Uzbek Shaibanids (p. 317). Ahmad's nephew was Babur, the first great Mogul of India (p. 318). The last Timurid still ruled from Herat over a part of ❿ Afghanistan, but died in 1506 during a campaign against the Shaibanids, after they attacked the city. The last rulers descended from Tamerlane are remembered more for their ❻ patronage of the arts than for their conquests.

6 Timuridian miniature painting from Herat, Afghanistan, ca. 1488

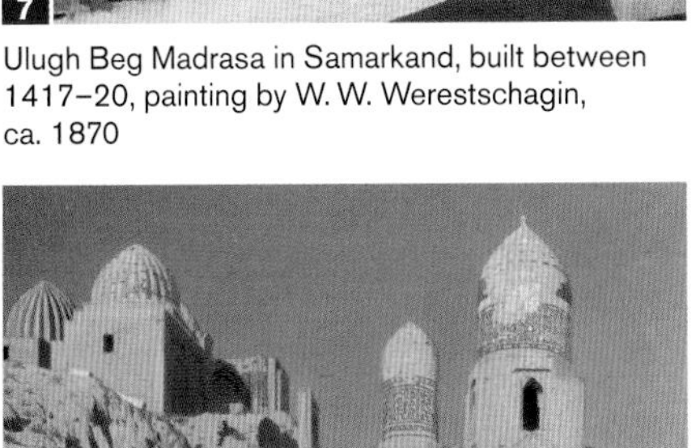

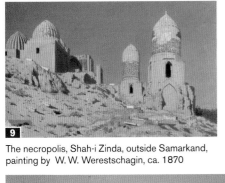

7 Ulugh Beg Madrasa in Samarkand, built between 1417–20, painting by W. W. Werestschagin, ca. 1870

8 Ceramic tombstone from a mausoleum in Shah-i Zinda, Samarkand

9 The necropolis, Shah-i Zinda, outside Samarkand, painting by W. W. Werestschagin, ca. 1870

10 The Blue Mosque in Mazar i-Sharif, Afghanistan, built ca. 1480

The Gur-e Amir Mausoleum

Tamerlane and his successors were buried in the magnificent mausoleum Gur-e Ami, in Samarkand. In 1941, Russian scientists under the direction of anthropologist Mikhail Gerasimov investigated the remains, and Gerasimov reconstructed the facial characteristics of Tamerlane and his sons, Miranshah and Shah Rokh. An examination of Tamerlane's skeleton showed deformities on the right elbow and the right hip; the right kneecap had also grown together with the thigh. He was practically a hemiplegic.

The ruins of the Gur-e Amir mausoleum, painting by W. W. Werestschagin, ca. 1870

1398-99 | Invasion of India
1402 | Victory over the Ottomans
19 Feb 1405 | Death of Tamerlane
1409-49 | Reign of Ulugh Beg
1469 | Abu Said killed by Turkic tribesmen

INDIA 500–1500

The Rajasimhesvara temple in Mahabalipuram, south India, built ca. 690–715 under the Pallava dynasty

For centuries the north of India had experienced periodic Arab invasions and settlement. The arrival of Turkic Muslim invaders from central Asia after 1000 had a more lasting impact, not least through settlement. The Hindu kingdoms of north India were subjugated and by 1206 Delhi and the Ganges valley too. Only the South remained unaffected. Although the destruction of Hindu temples indicates persecution, a pattern of co-existence quickly emerged. Ultimately Indian culture proved adept at assimilating the new influences. The Muslim sultans were successful as military rulers but were displaced by the Moguls after 1500.

The Hindu Empires in India

While northern India fell under the rule of the Muslim sultans, Hindu princes held onto power in most of central and southern India. The Vijayanagar Empire was the last significant Hindu state.

Distinctly Hindu or Dravidian dynasties reigned in central and southern India after 550. One of these was the ❷, ❸ Calukya dynasty that ruled in Bidjapur between 543 and 757 and subjugated a significant part of southern India between 609 and 642. A second ❺ Calukya dynasty ruled between 975 and 1189. They became involved in power struggles with the most important southern Indian dynasty, the ❶, ❻ Pallava of Kanchi, who had spread out in the seventh century into Deccan and the southern tip of India. They were supplanted by the dynasty of the Colas (888–1267), who enlarged their east coast kingdom northward. Under Rajaraja I (the Great), they rose to become the leading power in South India around 1000. They were also a naval power, their fleet sailing in 1001 to Ceylon and in 1014 occupying the Maldives.

The Hindu rulers of central India, including the Pala kings of Bengal (750–1199) or the Kanauj kings (840–1197), were eventually defeated by the advancing Muslim armies. The last great Hindu kingdom, ❼ Vijayanagar (City of Victory), was founded in 1336. Its capital, ❹, ❽ Hampi, was originally built on the site of a temple. It subsequently grew to become the preeminent kingdom in southern India. The flourishing city, with its magnificent temples and palaces, became a center of Indian literature and science. The kings of Vijayanagar regarded the Tungabadhra and Kistna rivers as the southern boundary of Islam and in 1380 compiled a collection of all the Brahman teachings, the *Sarvadarshana Sangraha*. While they successfully held off the invaders for some time, the last ruler, Ramaraja, fell in 1565 at Talikota in battle against the Muslim sultan Ahmadnagar.

Thereafter, only a small Hindu kingdom survived in Madurai. This was in turn annexed in 1684 by the Grand Mogul Aurangzeb.

5 Female dancer, sculpture, late western Calukya dynasty, twelfth c.

3 Vishnu, sculpture from the Calukyan period

2 Shiva, "king of the dance", with 18 arms, sculpture from the western Calukya dynasty, sixth century

4 Vithala Temple in Hampi, capital of the Vijayanagar kings, 16th century

6 Buddha Maitreya, gold-plated bronze sculpture, seventh–ninth century

7 Vijayanagar-style ceiling fresco, in the Virabhadra temple in Lepakshi, 16th c.

8 Narashima, the fourth incarnation of Vishnu, sculpture in Hampi

888–1267 | Cola Dynasty
1001 | Conquests in India led by Mahmud of Ghazna
1206 | Sultanate of Delhi founded

543–757 | First Western Calukya Dynasty
975–1189 | Second Western Calukya Dynasty
1193 | Construction of the Great Mosque in Delhi begins

The Sultans of Delhi

In the wake of the Ghaznavids and Ghurids, military dynasties of Turkish origin increased the spread of Islam in India. They came to an end with the Lodi rulers, who were defeated by the Moguls.

Ever since the first Muslim armies had advanced into Pakistan and India around 700, India had been coveted by Islamic rulers. Mahmud of Ghazna's campaigns of conquest after 1001 (p. 234) put great pressure on the Hindus, whose polytheism the strict Muslims vehemently rejected. The Ghaznavids dominated the north of India at the beginning of the 12th century, but in 1187 they were displaced by the powerful Afghan ❾ Ghurids in Lahore, who had already subjugated Multan in 1175. In 1193 Sultan Muizz ad-Din occupied Delhi and expanded his realm to Gujarat in the south and Bengal in the east. The driving force behind these conquests was the Turkish general Qutb-ud-Din ❿, ⓫ Aybak, who had ended the rule of the Buddhist princes in 1194 with the capture of Bihar, and pushed the Hindus to the south. He felt strong enough in 1206 to depose the Ghurid sultan and founded the "Slave King" sultanate of Delhi. His successor, Iltutmish (ruled 1211–1236) conquered Sind and made Delhi an independent Islamic kingdom.

In 1290, the House of Aybak was overthrown by the Khalji dynasty, which was also Turkish. They fended off the Mongols, conquered all of Deccan (central India), and advanced to Madurai in southern India. The sultanate divided the country into fiefs that were distributed to the Muslim nobility, each of whom was required to provide and maintain troop contingents in case of war. The Khaljis were later followed by the military dynasties of the Tughluqs (1320–1414) and Sayyids (1414–1451), under whom the state administration was Islamized. After 1388, many regions became increasingly independent from the government in Delhi and formed their own sultanates, including Bengal, Deccan, Gujarat, Jaunpur, and Malwa. In 1398–1399, Tamerlane invaded India and temporarily occupied Delhi (p. 236).

After this shattering defeat, effective central authority re-emerged only under the Afghan Lodi dynasty which ruled from 1451 to 1526. Sikandar Lodi again extended the kingdom from the Indus to Bengal in the east. The last Lodi ruler, Ibrahim, fell in battle in 1526 at Panipat against the Mogul leader Babur, who had been summoned by Ibrahim's own emirs to depose him. Babur was then able to take possession of Agra.

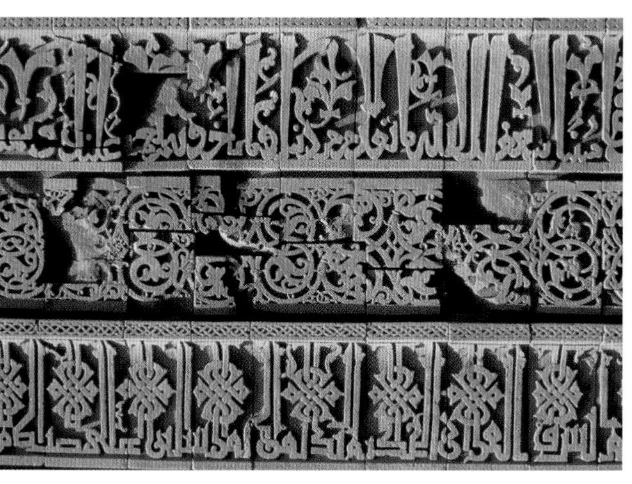

Delhi

After Delhi became the capital of Islamic rule in India in 1193, various "slave kings" erected enormous buildings, often using the remains of destroyed Hindu temples. In the same year Delhi was captured, work began on the construction of the great Quwwat-ul-Islam ("Power of Islam") mosque. In 1236 the magnificent sepulchre of Sultan Iltutmish was integrated into it. Qutb-ud-Din Aybak began construction of the Qutb Minar ("Tower of Victory") in 1192.

above: Detail from the Qutb Minar, near Delhi

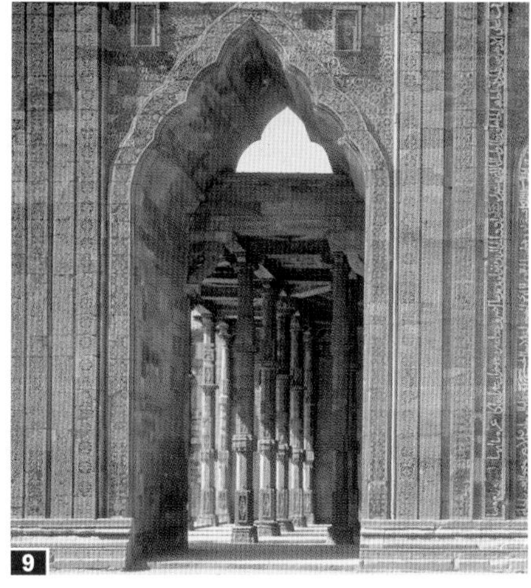

9 Adhaidinkajonpara mosque in Ajmer. The original Jaina school was converted into a mosque after its capture by the Ghurids in 1198

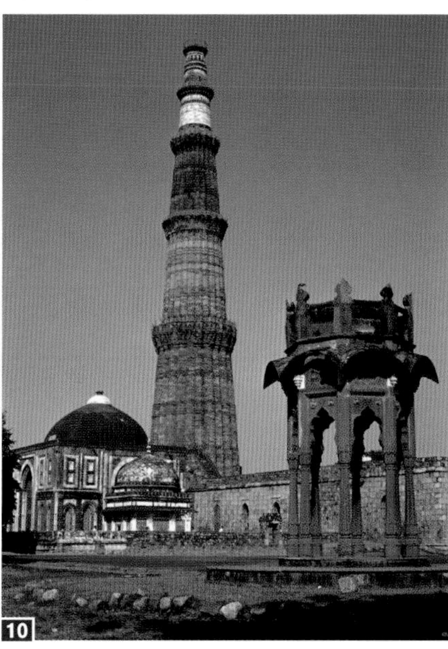

10 The Qutb Minar, "tower of victory," built under Qutb ad-Din Aybak from 1199 on. In front and to the left is the mosque Quwwat al-Islam, the oldest Muslim building in Delhi.

11 Detail from outer wall of the Qutb Minar

1320 | Tughlug Dynasty
1380 | *Sarvadarshana Sangraha* compiled
1414 | Sayyid Dynasty
1290 | Khalji Dynasty
1336 | Founding of Vijayanagar Empire
1398-99 | Occupation of Delhi by Tamerlane
1451 | Lodi Dynasty

China after the Han Dynasty 220–1279

For more than 300 years after the fall of the Han dynasty, China was divided into rival kingdoms. Then the ❶ Tang dynasty ushered in a cultural blossoming in the seventh century. Following half a century of turmoil and division, the Song dynasty began to unify the country once again in 960, although it remained militarily weak. The Songs eventually had to make way for the Chins and withdraw to the south. Here too, however, a cultural golden age began that lasted until the conquest of the Mongols in 1279.

1 Li Yuan, founder of the Tang dynasty, drawing19th century

The Tang Dynasty 618–907

Several centuries of unrest were brought to an end by the Tang dynasty. Chinese culture and territorial expansion both reached high points.

2 Armor-plated and saddled horse from Wei dynasty, fifth-sixth cntury

Following the fall of the Han dynasty in the third century (p. 153), numerous wars took place between three rival kingdoms. Nomads from out of the steppes north of the Great Wall repeatedly attacked, until they were eventually able to bring the north under their control; China then remained divided into north and south until the sixth century. Numerous factions competed for control in the north until the ❷ Wei dynasty was able to bring them under its control in 439. During its brief reign, the Sui dynasty was able to restore the unity of China to a certain extent from 589 to 618, but was defeated in a war against the peoples of southern Manchuria and northern Korea. The uprising led by the later ruler Li Yuan, resulting primarily from domestic policies, prepared the way for the Tang dynasty from 618 to 907.

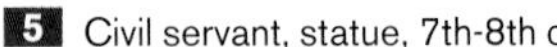

5 Civil servant, statue, 7th-8th c.

3 The view of the citadel near Turfan, built to protect the Silk Road

The Tangs stabilized China from their capital Ch'ang-an (present-day Xi'an) at the eastern end of the ❸ Silk Road. The rulers were not afraid to allow broad tolerance in culture and religion, as the central government was solidly organized with well-trained ❺ civil servants and efficient regulations and laws. Chinese ❻ literature and the arts experienced a golden age. Trade relations by land and sea flourished, and conquests as well as international agreements secured the Tang dynasty's influence all the way into central and southern Asia. In the eighth century, however, China was forced to accept the expansion of the Tibetan Tufan kingdom, which conquered Tang territories.

6 House of the poet Du Fu near Chengdu in the province Sichuan

Domestically, the Tang dynasty failed through its own success. The growth in population brought on by the booming economy destroyed the financial foundation of the state. Emperor ❹ Xuanzong, who tried to make reforms, was weakened by court intrigues that culminated in 755 in a revolt of the governor and general An Lushan. A civil war began, ending eight years later at a cost of millions of lives. The weaknesses of the state led to internal repression. Persecution of the ❼ Buddhists, during which thousands of monasteries and temples were destroyed, began in 845. Regional govenors began to function more independently, until Zhu Wen deposed the emperor, ushering in the Five Dynasties and Ten Kingdoms Period.

4 Emperor Xuanzong flees in 755 from the revolt of An Lushan, painting, 8th c.

7 Bodhisattva Avalokiteshvara, the personification of compassion, marble, 8th c.

since 220 | Division of the empire in Shu, Wei and Wu
589–618 | Unity of China under the Sui dynasty
618–907 | Tang dynasty
755 | Revolt of General An Lushan
from 845 | Persecution of the Buddhists
880 | Revolt under Huang Chao

The Song Dynasty 960–1279

The Song dynasty was able to stabilize the country until China was conquered by the Mongols.

A further revolt in 880 broke the power of the Tang dynasty over China. The country fell apart into minor regimes from 907 to 960, while the Mongolian ⓬ Liao dynasty built up a strong empire in the north between 907 and 1125.

❽ Chao K'uang, the first emperor of the Song dynasty, aceded to the Chinese throne in 960. Over the next 20 years, the Songs captured vast areas of China and ruled the empire from their ❿ capital Kaifeng. Like the Tangs, the Songs organized their power centrally: department ministries controlled corresponding areas of responsibility and the military was placed under civilian officials. In 1004 the Song dynasty, after several uncessful wars, was forced to secure peace with the Liao through tribute payments and the cession of territories they had previously annexed in the north.

8 The first Song emperor, Chao K'uang, drawing, 19th century

11 Three urns with figurative decoration, ceramics, 12th-13th century

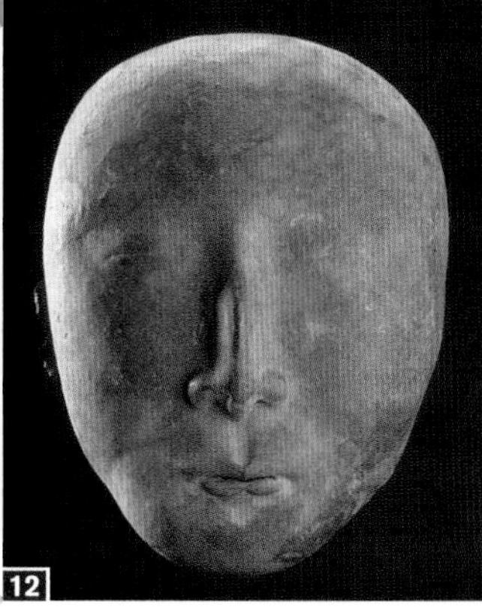

12 Death mask from Liao dynasty times, bronze, tenth-twelfth century

The country prospered culturally and economically in this period until a crisis began around 1050. The population grew faster than the state could assimilate it, and the tax revenues soon could not cover the state's expenditures, particularly for protecting the northern borders. During the reign of Shen Tsung (Chao Hsü) in the eleventh century, comprehensive reforms were carried out, including a land reform in favor of the farmers, who then paid taxes according to their income.

The Songs, together with the Chin dynasty that ruled in Manchuria from 1115 to 1234, defeated the Liao, but they were then forced to the south by the Chins, and in 1126, also lost Kaifeng. This ended the empire of the Northern Song and began the era of the Southern Song, who resided in Hangzhou from 1135. There the Songs once again flourished. Many technological innovations—including book printing with movable type, gunpowder, and ⓫ porcelain—were introduced. Academies trained landscape painters, Neo-Confucianism became the new state philosophy, and the philosopher Chu Hsi created the new Chinese language.

Like many other dynasties, the Songs were forced to give way to the ❾ Mongols coming out of the northern steppes. Genghis Khan had already conquered the Chin empire and its capital Beijing by 1215. In 1279, Kublai Khan also incorporated the Songs into the Mongolian world empire.

9 Mongols storming a Chinese fortress, Indian miniature, 16th century

10 Boat traffic in Kaifeng, painting on silk, ca. 1100

Hangzhou

The Italian traveler Marco Polo visited the capital of the Southern Song dynasty in the 13th century. The 12,000 bridges of the city, which is situated on a lagoon, reminded him of his hometown of Venice. Hangzhou, he said, was "the most beautiful and magnificent city in the world."

View of the lagoon city, French book painting, ca. 1412

907–960 | Period of the decline of the Empire
from 960 | Rise of the Song dynasty under Chao K'uang
1115–1234 | Chin dynasty
1215 | Conquest of the Chin empire by Genghis Khan
1279 | Incorporation of the Song into the Mongolian Empire

Japan ca. 400–1338

Influenced by China, a Japanese empire began developing in the fourth century and experienced its blossoming in the eighth century. During the ensuing period, great ❶ cultural achievements were accompanied by a decline in imperial power. With the emergence of the samurai class between the 8th and 12th centuries, the form of feudalism developed that would remain characteristic for Japan into the 19th century.

1 Pagoda in Nara in the family temple of the Fujiwara, built 710

Development of State and Culture

Following the phase of state building, the Nara Period was a cultural high point.

According to mythology, the state of Japan was founded in 600 B.C. when the god Ninigi descended on Mount Kirishimayana and was the forerunner of Jimmu, the first emperor. In reality, there probably existed only various subkingdoms that were first united into a large empire around 400 A.D. under the ❹ Yamato dynasty, which still reigns to this day. The Yamatos based their claim to rule on their descent from the sun goddess Amaterasu, the highest god in ❻ Shintoism. This combined in the Japanese emperor, the *tenno,* the functions of a high priest and political power.

2 Prince Regent Shotoku-Taishi's marriage to a princess, painting, 14th century

4 Burial gift from a ruler of the Yamato Period, clay sculpture, seventh century

Many cultural achievements were adopted from China, such as script and metallurgy. Buddhist missionaries began arriving on the islands in 552. Empress Suiko and her designated prince regent ❷ Shotoku later promoted Buddhism. In 604, a 17-article constitution was promulgated that contained, among other things, moral maxims and the principle of a hierarchical order of society.

The Taika reforms introduced in 646 followed Chinese precedent and were meant to strengthen centralized imperial power over the aristocracy. The country would be ruled from the capital city Nara through imperial officials. All land was claimed by the emperor, who granted estates to loyal nobility as fiefs.

Japan experienced a cultural high point during the Nara Period, particularly during the reign of Emperor Shomu, who ruled until 756. He modified the Taika reforms in 743, giving the nobility the right to bequeath their properties. Consequently, they were in a position to build up a power base and thus to increasingly weaken central authority over the course of a few generations. The gradual rise of the Fujiwara family, of which Shomu's mother and wife were both members, began during his reign. Shomu also promoted ❸ Buddhism. He had the famous ❺ Todaiji temple with the 48 foot-high *Daibutsu* ("Great Buddha") erected in Nara.

To avoid the growing power of the Buddhist priests and monasteries, Emperor Kammu moved the capital in 784 to Heian-kyo—modern Kyoto—and the Heian Period began.

5 Archway of the Todaiji temple in Nara, built in the eighth century

3 Bodhisattva, from the Nara period, varnished scupture, eighth century

6 Shinto ceremony in Kyoto: Drummer playing the big Taiko drum, which is used to call and entertain the gods

600 B.C.	Mythical founding of Japan
ca. 400 A.D.	End of unification of the partial kingdoms of Japan
ca. 552	Arrival of Buddhist missionaries
604	17-article constitution
646	Taika reforms
710–84	Nara Period

Shoguns, Samurai, and Daimyos

The imperial court lost political power with the development of feudal structures governed over by shoguns and based on military force and samurai warrior groups.

The arts, particularly literature, became highly refined during the Heian Period, from 794 to 1185; the ladies of the court especially were notable authors. While court culture blossomed, the political power of the emperor continued to wane. His functions became limited to ritual religious tasks, while the real power rested with the noble families who had built up their estates into autonomous dominions and then entangled the country in ❾ civil wars. Initially, the ❼ Fujiwara family was the leading dynasty.

During the war to expand the empire into the north in the eighth century, the fighting efficiency of the army of conscripts proved insufficient. The well-trained ❿ samurai (p. 326) mercenaries were much more effective in battle—and also in the civil wars. Certain families specialized in leading these samurai and became a warrior nobility. The system was multi-tiered in which individuals swore allegiance to particular leaders, who in turn were loyal to certain powerful families. Among these dynasties, the Taira and the Minamoto clans increasingly challenged the power of the Fujiwaras.

Villa of the Fujiwara family in Kyoto, built in 1052, later converted into a temple

Burning of the palce in Kyoto during a rebellion in 1159, painting, twelfth-14th century

Helmet and steel face mask of a samurai warrior in the style of the 14th c.

The Tairas displaced the Fujiwaras after a ⓫ civil war in the mid-twelfth century and were in turn defeated in 1185 by the ❽ Minamotos. In 1192, ⓬ Minamoto Yoritomo had the emperor give him the hereditary title of *shogun* ("imperial general") and created the Kamakura shogunate, named after his seat of government. Early in the Kamakura Period, which lasted from 1192 to 1333, however, a shift of power again took place, with the Hojo clan rising to become hereditary regents of the shogunate in 1203, while the shoguns were pushed into the background.

Minamoto no Yoshitsune, the "ideal knight" of the Japanese "middle ages," wood engraving, 19th century

Battle scene during the civil war against the Fujiwaras, painting

The *daimyo* class led the samurai warrior caste during the twelfth century. The Hojos were dependent upon them to drive off the invasion attempts of the Mongol Kublai Khan in 1274 and 1281. They succeeded—purportedly assisted by divine winds, the *kamikaze*—but because it was not a conquest and there were no spoils, the daimyos' loyalty to the central government diminished. Emperor Go-Daigo took advantage of this dissatisfaction in 1333 and overthrew the Kamakura shoguns and their Hojo regents with the help of samurai from the Ashikaga family. This Kemmu Restoration lasted only until 1338, when Ashikaga Takauji (p.326), who himself had hoped to be shogun, took over power in a coup.

From *The Pillow Book* of the Lady of the Court Sei Shonagon

"A groom who is happy to see the father-in-law / A bride, that pleases the mother-in-law A liegeman, who never defames his master ... Men, women, and priests who maintain a lifelong friendship. Many books capture that of which does not know a single one."

Lady of the court, painting, 17th c.

Minamoto Yoritomo, painting,19th c.

784 | Heian-kyo (Kyoto) becomes capital
794–1185 | Heian Period
from 9th century | The Fujiwara clan takes over regency for the tenno
1192 | Naming of first hereditary shogun
1192–1333 | Kamakura period
1333–38 | Kemmu Restoration

1 The coasts of Southeast Asia, Portugesian naval map, 16th century

Southeast Asia 5th–15th century

Once the Burmese Pagan Kingdom and the Khmer Empire of Angkor had divided ❶ Indochina between them, the Thais replaced the Khmer in their position of power and became the main rivals of the Burmese. A number of different kingdoms, both Hindu and Buddhist, followed one another in Indonesia until the Europeans built up their colonial rule in Southeast Asia.

Empires of the Southeast Asian Mainland

While the Khmer were greatly influenced by Indian culture, the proximity to China was evident in Vietnam. New conflicts were ignited by the advance of the Burmese and lastly by that of the Thais.

The area settled by the Khmer stretched from southern Thailand and southern Laos to the Mekong Delta. They were the trading power Chinese sources referred to as "Funan," which flourished from the first or second century A.D. to the sixth or seventh century. In the seventh and eighth century, small Khmer kingdoms emerged that were strongly influenced by Indian culture. Indravarman I was the first to establish a large kingdom; his son, Yashovarman I, founded Angkor ("the city") around 900.

3 Jayavarman VII, sculpture, 12th–13th century

The kingdom of Angkor expanded its power in the tenth century. Its rulers were followers of Shivaism and built monumental temples. The famous temple of ❺ Angkor Wat was built under Suryavarman II. Following an ❻ invasion by the Cham, ❸ Jayavarman VII expanded the Khmer kingdom over large parts of Asia. He was a follower of Mahayana Buddhism and built up the walled capital of Angkor with ❼ numerous Buddhist temples. Raids by the Thai led to the loss of Angkor in 1369 and in 1389. The capital was move south in the 15th century to Longvek, Udong, and Phnom Penh, also for reasons of trade.

The state of Nam Viet (today's North Vietnam) was conquered in 111 B.C. by the Chinese Han dynasty (p. 153). China's powerlessness following the Tang dynasty in 931 made possible the founding of a kingdom called Dai Viet in Tonkin, with its center in the Red River Delta. It was ruled by the Ly dynasty from 1009 to 1225. Chinese influence, as well as the great significance of Confucianism, remained evident. The Ly were followed by the Tran, who ruled from 1225 to 1400 and in 1287 repulsed a Mongol invasion.

2 Pagoda in Pagan, eleventh century

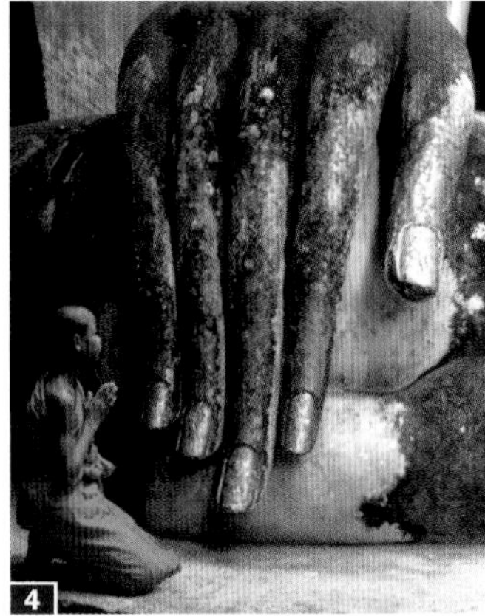

4 Buddhist monk praying in front of the hand of a 48-foot Buddha statue in Sukhothai

The Cham had settled in the southern regions in central and southern Vietnam. There they founded the kingdom of Champa by the fourth or fifth century. In 1177, the Cham conquered Angkor, but in 1181 were beaten back, and from 1192 to 1220 fell under the rule of the Khmer. Champa came under pressure from the Vietnamese and the kingdom was annexed ca. 1471.

The Burmese migrated in the ninth century down into present-day Burma and founded the ❷, ❸ Pagan Kingdom around 849. Until its destruction by the Mongols in 1287, the kingdom shared domination over southern Asia with the Khmer. Two separate state systems emerged after the fall of Pagan, and they were not reunited until the 18th century.

Tribes speaking the Thai language moved into Yunnan in the

5 The Hindu temple complex Angkor Wat or Vishnuloka ("the world of Vishnu"), Cambodia, built in the twelfth century

6 War of the Khmer against the Cham, sandstone relief, ca. 1200

111 B.C. | Conquest of Nam Viet by Han-China — **4th–5th century** | Kingdom of Champa — **7th century** | Kingdom of Nan Zhao — **ca. 849** | Empire of Pagan — **ca. 900** | Foundation of Angkor — **931** | Empire of Dai Viet — **1009–1225** | Ly dynasty in Dai Viet

southwest of China from about the second century B.C. The kingdom of Nan Zhao developed there in the seventh century; the Mongols destroyed it in 1253. The ❹ kingdom of Sukhothai formed in the middle of present-day Thailand in 1238 is considered to be the political and cultural origin of Thailand. The kingdom experienced its high point in the second half of the 13th century under King Ramkhamhaeng, who expanded his dominion to the Gulf of Thailand at the expense of the Khmer and Burmese. Around 1283, he devised the traditional Thai script that is still in use today. His successors dedicated themselves only to religion and science, so that in 1350 the local Thai prince of Ayutthaya (p. 330) was able to take over the kingdom without a struggle.

7 Partial view of the Buddhist temple Angkor Thom, built ca. 1200

8 Temple of Pagan in Burma, present-day Myanmar

The Island Kingdoms of Southeast Asia

Indonesia had always been influenced by Indian culture and religions. Various Buddhist and Hindu kingdoms existed there until Islam began its advance in the 14th century, after being introduced onto the island by Arabian merchants.

Until the 1300s, both Buddhist and Hindu kingdoms existed in the Indonesian archipelago. The most notable Buddhist realm was the maritime kingdom of Srivijaya, which emerged in the seventh century on the southeast coast of Sumatra. From its capital Palembang, Srivijaya spread its area of dominance throughout the South China Sea and adjoining regions. Local rulers began making themselves independent again in the eleventh century. The Shailendra dynasty, which was also Buddhist, left the temple complex of ❾ Borobudur on Java.

The Hindu Majapahit empire, which replaced Srivijaya as the dominant power, was established in 1293 in eastern Java by King Vijaya. It existed until about 1520, experiencing its golden age in the 14th century when King Gajah Mada controlled Indonesia.

Around 1300, Arabian merchants introduced Islam into Indonesia, and it was rapidly accepted almost everywhere. Only the island kingdom of ⓬ Bali remained ⓫ Hindu. In the mid-15th century, the prince of Paramesvara on Sumatra founded the Malacca sultanate, with Palembang as its capital. It was the leading trading hub of the region until it was conquered by the ❿ Portuguese in 1511 (p. 331).

In the 17th century, Java was controlled for the most part by the ⓭ kingdom of Mataram. The Dutch, who had replaced the Portuguese as the most important European trading power, established the trading base of ⓮ Batavia on Java in 1619 and from there brought Indonesia under their control. In 1755, they brought about the division of the once-mighty Mataram into the two principalities of Surakarta and Yogyakarta, thus effectively curtailing its power.

9 Temple of Borobudur on Java, Indonesia, built in the eighth century

10 Portuguese shipwreck, Indian miniature, 16th century

11 Water temple on Bali

12 Pavilon and lotus pond in a palace on Bali, built in the 17th century

13 Nandi bull in a Hindu temple of the kings of Mataram, built in the tenth c.

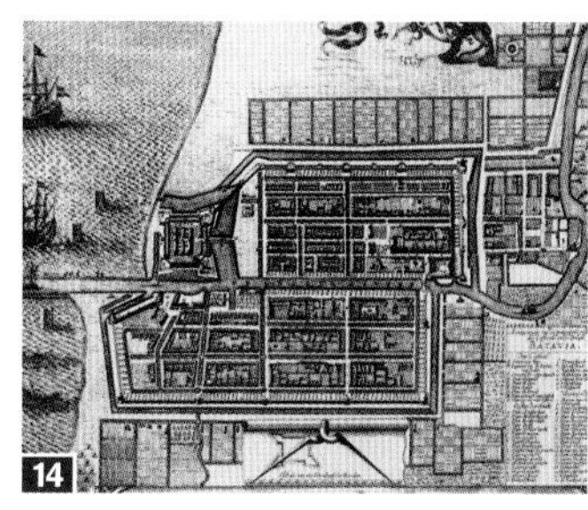
14 Map of Batavia, present-day Jakarta, copper engraving, 17th century

ab 1181 | Expansion of the Khmer Empire under Yayavarman VII
1238 | Empire of Sukhothai
1287 | Destruction of the Empire of Pagan by Mongols
1177 | Conquest of Angkor by the Cham
1225–1400 | Tran dynasty in Vietnam
1253 | Destruction of Nan Zhaos by Mongols

Caravan in the Sahara, film still

Sub-Saharan Africa 5th–15th century

It was not only in the north of Africa that impressive empires developed in the Middle Ages. Especially in western Africa, kingdoms that had become prosperous through ❶ trans-Saharan trade with the African north existed for centuries. Maritime trade also made the cities on the Swahili coasts in the east of the continent rich. Their connections reached into the interior of Africa to the kingdom of Zimbabwe, to which they were drawn by the treasures of its gold mines.

West Africa

From the fifth century, several large kingdoms existed south of the Sahara, controlling the caravan routes there.

Various kingdoms emerged along the caravan routes in West Africa in the Early Middle Ages. The kingdom of Ghana with its capital Koumbi Saleh developed south of Morocco in Mauritania in the fifth century. In the eighth century, Berbers reigned over black subjects until the latter expelled their overlords. The trade in gold and salt led to wealth, but the Arab traders, who had introduced Islam around 1000, were soon followed by conquerors. Ghana was destroyed in the eleventh century by the North African Almoravids. A war ensued, ending in the Islamization of the country.

3 Portugese man with a musket, bronze relief from the Oba of Benin's palace, 16th c.

In 1203, the Soso people conquered Koumbi Saleh and ruled over Ghana for a brief period, but they were subjugated in the mid-13th century by the ❷ Manlinkas, who had founded a kingdom in Mali. The Manlinkas also converted to ❹ Islam. Under their ruler Mansa Musa, a period of great prosperity that spread from the capital of Niani began at the beginning of the 14th century. However, the kingdom disintegrated in the 1400s and was replaced by the Songhai.

The Songhai originated in the Nigerian northwest, and in the eighth century they spread their territory along the Niger River and built up an economically flourishing kingdom around the capital of Gao (p. 332). King Kossoi and his subjects converted to Islam around 1000. The city-state league of Kanem-Bornu that developed northeast of Lake Chad and existed into the 19th century converted to Islam in the eleventh century.

Only in the coastal areas on the Gulf of Guinea was Islam unable to gain a foothold. The Yoruba founded several kingdoms there. Among these, ❻ Ife was the political and cultural center between the eighth and 13th centuries. It was then replaced by the Kingdom of Benin. The kings, called ❺ *obas*, made numerous military expeditions in the 15th century during which captives were taken; beginning in the 16th century, they began to be sold as slaves to the ❸ Europeans.

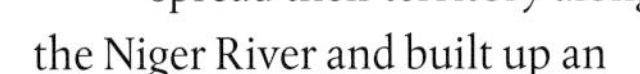

5 An oba of Benin on horseback with two servants, bronze relief, 16th c.

2 Shrine of the legendary patriarch Malinkas, built in the 13th century and renewed every seven years

4 Mosque in Dienné in Mali, ca. 1400

6 Head of a ruler of Ife, brass sculpture, 12th-15th c.

Mansa Musa

Mansa Musa, the ruler of Mali, undertook a pilgrimage to Mecca in 1324 accompanied by a great caravan; he was reportedly accompanied by 60,000 bearers. The amount of gold that Musa spent in Cairo alone ruined the Egyptian currency for decades. Musa had a great mosque constructed in Timbuktu and developed an Islamic school that became a center of Islamic learning.

Caravan of pilgrims on their way to Mecca, painting, 19th century

5th century | Founding of the Ghana Kingdom
8th century | Development of the city-state league of Kanem-Bornu
10th century | Zagwe dynasty
ca. 1000 | Introduction of Islam
11th century | Destruction of Ghana by the Almoravids

South and East Africa

The East African coast was characterized by trade links reaching all the way to China, and Zimbabwe in southern Africa.

Christian Ethiopia shifted its center from Aksum to the highlands so that it could more easily defend against Muslim attacks. There, the Zagwe dynasty took over power in the tenth century. The Zagwe rebuilt Ethiopia from their royal residence at ❼ Lalibela. In 1268, they were supplanted by the Solomonic dynasty, which claimed descent from Menelik, the legendary founder of the nation (p. 155). They were in permanent conflict with their ⓫ Muslim neighbors and rebellious provincial princes. To enforce the state church, which legitimized the rule of the emperor, heretics and Jews were persecuted. In the 15th century, contact was once again established with Europe, primarily with the pope in Rome and Portugal, which actively supported the struggle against the Muslims in the 16th century.

On the East African coast, from the north of Somalia down to Mozambique, a relationship developed between African and Islamic Arab elements, the Swahili culture (from the Arabic *sahil,* "coast"), whose cities were made wealthy and powerful through their ❿ trade on the continent as well as overseas with Arabia, India, and China. ❽ Kilwa in Tanzania held the leading position among the coastal cities in the 14th century.

Their trading partners in the interior were the Bantu tribes, who primarily delivered copper and ivory. The Bantu people had spread out from the interior of the continent to the south and east shortly after the first century A.D., making their linguistic group one of the largest in Africa.

The Bantu-speaking Shona developed a state system in the region of Mozambique and Zimbabwe in the twelfth century. Tens of thousands of people resided within the mighty walls that surrounded the capital ⓬ Great Zimbabwe. Finds of Chinese ceramic from the Ming period attest to its far-reaching trade connections. Zimbabwe's main exports were ores and gold.

The Shona empire was replaced in the 15th century by the Mozambican ❾ Monomotapa, which for a time stretched far to the west. Great bastions were also erected there, but the kingdom had already come under the control of the Portuguese and its decline and ultimate end in the late 1600s could no longer be avoided.

7 Church cut from the rock, dedicated to the Virgin Mary, Lalibela, twelfth century

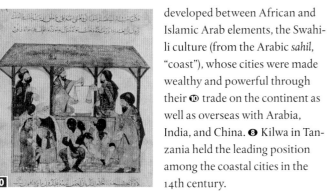

8 Fort in the harbor of Kilwa, Tanzania

9 King of Monomotapa

10 Trade in African slaves, Arabic illumination, 13th century

Bantu

The word ban-tu means "person" and has come to signify a great linguistic family that today is spoken by around 100 million people in southern and central Africa. Half of this number speak the Swahili language. Bantu-speaking peoples migrated from Nigeria and Cameroon through East Africa down to South Africa.

Traditional housing of the Bantu-speaking Zulu in South Africa

11 Battle between Ethiopians and Muslims, painting ca. 1412

12 Ruins of Great Zimbabwe, built from the 13th c. onwards

11th century | Rise of the Mali empire
12th century | Rise of the Shona empire
1268 | Salomonid dynasty
1325 | Pilgrimage of Mausa Musa to Mecca
15th century | Founding of the Monomotapa empire

1 Colossal stone head depicting an Olmec god

The Settlement and Early High Cultures of America ca. 15th century B.C.–15th century A.D.

After the settling of the Americas, various cultures developed in North America, some of which were culturally very sophisticated. Predominantly hierarchically organized empires developed in Central and South America, each of which took over the political and cultural leadership of the region for a certain time. These included the empires of the ❶ Olmec and Toltec as well as the Maya and Aztec in Central America and of the Chimú, Chavín, Moche, Nazca, and finally the Inca in South America.

North America

A large number of diverse American Indian cultures characterized the northern continent.

Nomadic Stone Age hunter-gatherers moved into North America toward the end of the last ice age, roughly 13,000 B.C., across a land bridge that existed at the time between Asia and America. They spread out over the entirety of the Americas in the course of the following millennia.

2 Bison hunt, wood engraving, 19th c.

Around 300 B.C., members of the Hohokam cultures migrated northward from Mexico and settled in villages whose agricultural areas were irrigated by large-scale canal systems. The various American cultures flourished from the beginning of the Christian era until the eighth century. The ❻ cliff-dwelling ❸ Anasazi culture developed around 500 A.D. in the American Southwest. They were settled agriculturalists who dwelled in multistory stone houses and are the predecessors of the ❺ Pueblo Indians, who were then conquered by the Spanish in the 16th century.

3 Clay bowl of the Anasazi culture, 12th-13th c.

The Mississippian culture unfolded about 750 around the city of Cahokia, near modern St. Louis, in which close to 50,000 inhabitants lived. The cultivation of corn served as their basis for life. Presumably the civilization was destroyed by epidemics introduced by Europeans—a fate that many Indian cultures met.

Tribes on the northwest coast existed by fishing, pursued trade with northern Asia, and held potlatches—complex gift-giving rituals which distinguished many of them. They are also known for their wood carvings, particularly their totem poles.

The ❹ tribes of the Great Plains were for the most part nomads, their culture dependent on the ❷ hunting of bison. As they more frequently came into contact with white settlers pushing westward, they were mistakenly thought to be typical of Indian cultures.

4 Totem poles of Indian tribes of the Great Plains of North America

The lifestyles, social organizations, and political institutions of the Native Americans were very diverse. These were partly determined by the living conditions such as climate, terrain, and animal population, but even in similar environments there was a great diversity of social structures: settled and nomadic peoples with or without slaves, hunter and agrarian cultures, patriarchal and matriarchal societies, monarchical and democratic structures. The Wendat (Huron) confederations in the 15th century, and later the five-nation Iroquois League, had a parliament and constituted the first American democracy.

5 Settlement of the Pueblo Indians in New Mexico

6 Cliff dwellings of the Anasanzi culture, ca. 1200

ca. 1500 B.C. | Advanced civilization of the Olmecs

ca. 1000 B.C. | Development of the Chavín culture

ca. 300 B.C. | Northward migration of Hohokam cultures

ca. 0 | Urban culture of Teotihuacán

200 | Development of the Anasazi culture

Central and South America

Sophisticated state-building civilizations developed in Mexico and Peru, some of which covered vast territories.

The nomadic hunter-gatherer communities of Central America became settled agrarian societies about 8000–9000 years ago. The Olmec formed the first advanced civilization; they left behind temple complexes and palaces from about 1200 B.C. The Olmec culture was dominant on the Mexican east coast until about 400 B.C. This culture was long considered to be the oldest in the Americas until 2001 when a city dating back to around 2700 B.C., and testifying to a sophisticated society that built pyramids as old as those of Egypt, was discovered in Caral, Peru.

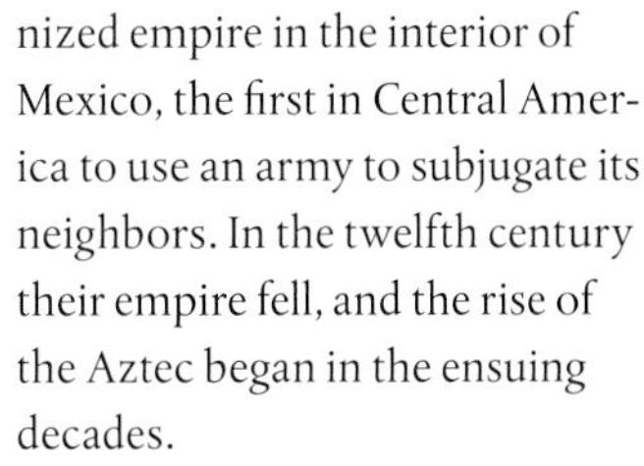

8 Head of a Maya prince, Tuff, ca. 700

Approximately 2000 years ago, a nation developed around the city of Teotihuacán not far from modern-day Mexico City, and it dominated Mexico from 450 to 700. The city at times had more than 100,000 inhabitants and a widespread trading network. It housed ⓫ sun and moon pyramids as well as numerous colorfully painted temples lining a wide thoroughfare.

Between 400 and 1200 A.D., the Toltec formed a militarily organized empire in the interior of Mexico, the first in Central America to use an army to subjugate its neighbors. In the twelfth century their empire fell, and the rise of the Aztec began in the ensuing decades.

The Maya peoples had been laying out settlements on the Yucatan Peninsula since 1200 B.C. Between 300 and 900 A.D., the Classic ⓭ Maya period, numerous ⓬ city-states ruled by ❽ priest-princes formed on the peninsula. For reasons unknown, these were given up in favor of the cities of the Postclassic Period, which were situated further north (p. 334).

11 the 213-foot (65 m) high sun pyramid in Teotihuacán, ca. 0

12 Ruins of the city Tikal, Guatemala

In South America almost 3000 years ago, the Chavín culture emerged in Peru. It lasted into the third century B.C. and was replaced by the Mochica or Moche in the north and in the south by the Nazca. The latter, famous for their rock paintings, survived into the sixth or seventh century. Between 300 and 900, the civilization of the ❾ Tiahuanaco dominated the region around Lake Titicaca, which was possibly developed from the earlier Chavín culture and which influenced the Huari empire that ruled Peru from the seventh to eleventh centuries.

The ❼ Mochica built temples and pyramids that are among the largest in the Americas and created characteristic pottery that occasionally depicted human sacrifice. They gave up their cities at the beginning of the eighth century. The Chimú, who had an intricate irrigation system, succeeded them about 200 years later on the Peruvian coast. Their empire and its capital Chan Chan, which had around 50,000 inhabitants, was conquered by the Inca in 1470.

13 Mayan vessel showing a palace scene, decorated clay

The ❿ Amazon region was first settled by humans in the third millennium B.C. The people occupying the southern tip of South America nearly 10,000 years ago were almost completely eradicated by colonization and epidemics.

7 Mochica culture vessel in the shape of a head, clay, first c. B.C.-sixth c. A.D.

9 Gateway of the Sun from the Tiahuanaco culture, Bolivia, model

10 Indians from the Amazon region wearing traditional garments

ca. 750 | Development of the Mississippian culture
1470 | Conquest of the Moche empire by the Incas
300–900 A.D. | Old Maya empire
from the 12th century | Rise of the Aztecs
16th century | Conquest of the Pueblo Indians by the Spaniards

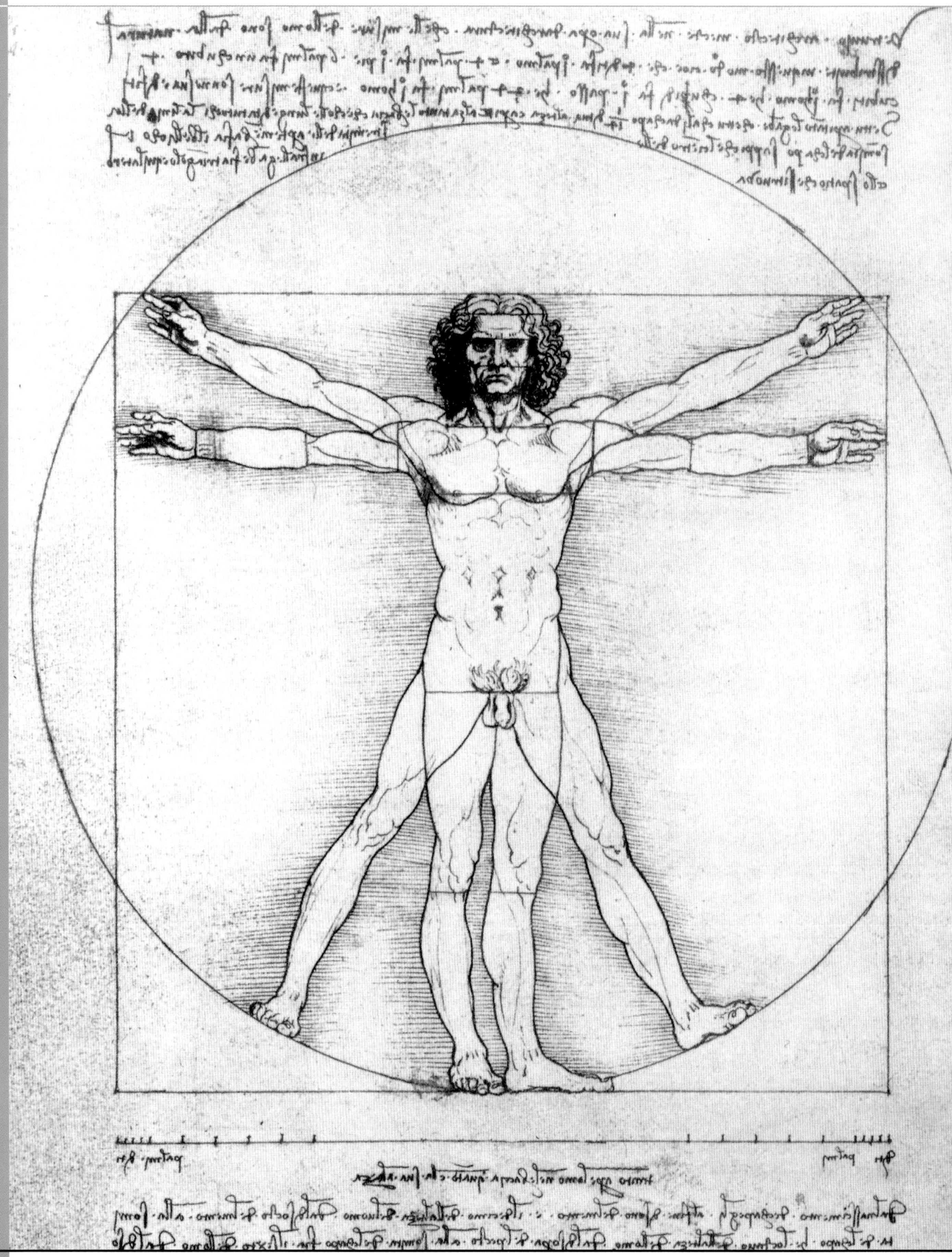

The Early Modern Period

16th–18th century

The smooth transition from the Middle Ages to the Modern Age is conventionally fixed on such events as the Reformation and the discovery of the "New World," which brought about the emergence of a new image of man and his world. Humanism, which spread out of Italy, also made an essential contribution to this with its promotion of a critical awareness of Christianity and the Church. The Reformation eventually broke the all-embracing power of the Church. After the Thirty Years' War, the concept of a universal empire was also nullified. The era of the nation-state began, bringing with it the desire to build up political and economic power far beyond Europe. The Americas, Africa, and Asia provided regions of expansion for the Europeans.

Proportions of the Human Figure by Leonardo da Vinci (drawing, ca. 1490) is a prime example of the new approach of Renaissance artists and scientists to the anatomy of the human body.

Breaking out of the worldview of the Middle Ages

Humanist scholars including Luther and Erasmus

Map with Columbus, Vespucci, Magellan, and Pizarro

The Early Modern Period

The beginnings of the Early Modern Period can be seen around 1500 in the reshaping and expansion of the ❶ worldview of the Middle Ages that was taking place. Despite symbolic dates such as the discovery of the New World by Christopher Columbus in 1492 and the beginning of the Reformation in 1517, this transformation did not take place abruptly but took the form of cumulative changes throughout the era.

Humanism and the Renaissance

As early as the 14th century, Italian authors such as ❺ Dante, Petrarch, and Boccaccio built on the ideals and erudition of the scholars of antiquity. In contrast to the universal world view that was prevalent during the Middle Ages, the Humanists (Latin: *humanitas*, "humanity") placed humankind at the center of their conceptualization of the world. The ideas of the *Renaissance* (French, "rebirth") emerged from a interaction with the teachings and philosophies of antiquity. This led to a new independence of the sciences and a disentanglement of philosophy from Christian dogma and to a flourishing of the arts. Cosmopolitan scholars such as Erasmus of Rotterdam tried to unify humanism and Christian piety, while from the court of the Medici in Florence and the papal court of Rome, Renaissance art and its innovations spread throughout Europe.

Dante, Petrarch, and Boccaccio, painting by Giorgio Vasari, 16th century

Reformation, Counter-Reformation, and Nation-States

Even before ❷ Martin Luther initiated the Reformation, criticism of the increasingly worldly Church had been growing. Jan Hus (p. 204) of Bohemia, for example, was a significant reformer who, however, failed due to resistance from the aristocracy. In contrast Luther, during the peasant wars, for example, explicitly put himself on the side of the princes, who in turn supported the Reformation because they hoped for an increase in power through the development of national churches. The Catholic world responded to the Reformation with an internal renewal of the Church. A significant agent of this renewal was the ❹ Jesuit order, which saw its duty in missionary work and also in combatting heretical movements. The Jesuit order also took over the development of the Catholic educational system. The Counter-Revolution was based on the redefinition of the Catholic faith and Church in the Council of Trent. The Council of Trent laid down the principles of Catholic faith in the same way that the "Augsburg Confession" definitively set down the tenets of the Protestant faith.

Ignatius of Loyola, founder of the Jesuit order, 17th century

Inventions and Discoveries

The rapid spread of the Reformation was facilitated by the invention of the ❻ printing press around 1445 by Johannes Gutenberg, as communication of new ideas was much facilitated and speeded up by this new medium which made possible the mass production of texts that could be carried far from where they were written. Discoveries in the field of natural sciences, such as that of the heliocentric universe by Copernicus in 1507, revolutionized the world view of the time. A thirst for new discoveries and the search for new trading routes led to great ❸ sea voyages: The search for sea routes to India led the Portuguese to sail around Africa at the end of the 15th century; Christopher Columbus landed in America in 1492; Magellan sailed around the world for the first time from 1520 to 1521. In the wake of beginning world trade and colonialism, European states established hegemony in many parts of the world. As a result of this they damaged and destroyed

Johannes Gutenberg at his printing press, etching, 18th century

1445 | Invention of printing press
1507 | Theory of the heliocentric universe
1530 | "Augsburg Confession"
15th century | Beginning of the Era of Absolutism
1492 | Landing of Columbus in America
1517 | Beginning of Reformation

7

Chinese Pavilion in Sanssouci, Potsdam, Germany
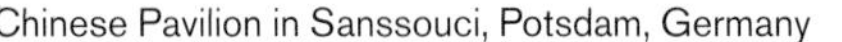

8

Newton discovers gravity by observing a falling apple

9

A middle-class cultural Salon in Paris, 18th century

many cultures and forced millions of people into slavery. The discovery of new societies, however, also resulted in a fascination for the ❼ "exotic," particularly the cultures of Persia, China, and that of the Ottoman Empire. In the 17th and 18th century, elements of each of these were imported to Europe. In the Ottoman Empire, in Persia, and in India under the Great Moguls, and in China under the Manchu dynasty— states that were at the height of their power and prosperity between the 16th and 18th century—serious conflict with the Europeans did not take place and their excursions were given only marginal attention.

Absolutism and Enlightenment

In the Early Modern Era, absolutism—the concentration of undivided power in the hands of the Princes—prevailed as the form of government in many countries. It was based on theories formulated by political philosophers such as Niccoló Macchiavelli (p. 295), Jean Bodin, and Thomas Hobbes from the 16th and 17th century onwards. In these tracts, concepts such as that of the *raison d'état* ("reason of state") and the absolute sovereignty of the ruler were developed. The primary instruments of power of the absolutist princes were the standing army and an administrative bureaucracy that was solely responsible to the ruler.

11

René Descartes, painting, ca.1640

A particular form of absolutism emerged in conjunction with the Enlightenment of the 18th century that attempted to apply humanism, as well as the philosophical and scientific discoveries of the 17th century, throughout society. Since the 17th century scholars such as ⓫ René Descartes, John Locke, Baruch de Spinoza, and Gottfried Wilhelm Leibniz had found methods to free deduction from religious dogma. Scientists such as Galileo Galilei and ❽ Issac Newton shaped a new worldview based on knowledge gained through scientific discovery. The great Enlightenment philosophers of the 18th century such as Montesquieu and Voltaire championed freedom of the spirit, of religion, and the decoupling of knowledge from religious doctrine. They also demanded a review of the methods of government on the basis of reason and an image of mankind that presumed the equality and community of all mankind. The philosophers Jean-Jacques Rousseau and ❿ Immanuel Kant, however, attacked absolutism through their critiques of the politics and institutions of the state, and above all of the church.

Enlightened Absolutist princes took advantage of the already present structures of church and state to achieve their goals: the good of the state and the welfare of their subjects. The centralization of the state was in this way pushed forwards, while the influence of the church, particularly in the school and education systems, was decreased. However, even the reform-minded monarchs such as King Frederick the Great of Prussia or Emperor Joseph II were not prepared to give their subjects, particularly the upward striving bourgeoisie, a political voice. The division of powers, for example, demanded by the Enlightenment philosophers was never implemented.

10

Immanuel Kant, painting, 18th century

The Rise of the Bourgeoisie

Humanism and the Reformation particularly influenced the thinking of the European middle classes, which had become wealthy through early capitalism. This new wealth brought with it respect and a new and influential position in society. In order to maintain a counterweight to the power of the princes and the church, the absolutist princes leaned on the middle classes: with access to a university education, increasing numbers were able to hold state offices. In the state economies, trade and business, which lay in the hands of the middle classes, was promoted. Also in ❾ cultural life the middle classes took on increasing significance. Despite this, the bourgeoisie, as the middle classes became known, were prevented from taking part in political decision-making processes. The conflicts that arose out of this contradiction culminated in the French Revolution of 1789, which, together with the American Declaration of Independence, marked the beginning of the "Age of the Bourgeoisie" and the rise to power of the middle classes.

1534 | Foundation of the Jesuit order
1545-63 | Council of Trent
17th–18th century | Age of Enlightenment
1776 | American Declaration of Independence
1789 | French Revolution

The German Empire: The Reformation and Its Consequences 1517–1609

With the support of powerful protestant German princes, the Reformation initiated by Martin Luther was carried through rapidly in large parts of the empire. Following the first religious wars, the Peace of Augsburg created a balance of power between Catholics and Protestants, but the peace was unstable, as it made no concessions to the Calvinists. Thus conflicts as a result of confessional differences took place even after the Peace of Augsburg. Through a series of stages, the conflict progressively intensified through to the eve of the Thirty Years' War.

1 The German Emperor Charles V, painting by Jakob Seisenegger, 1532

Reformation and the Peasants' War

Martin Luther's Reformation of the church was radical, as it was associated with socially revolutionary demands.

3 Martin Luther, painting, 1528

After the death of Maximilian I, his grandson ❶ Charles V was elected Holy Roman Emperor in 1519—his election was ensured by the payment of enormous bribes to the electors. The Habsburgs raised the money by going into debt with the merchant house of ❷ Fugger, whose trading network covered the whole of the known world. Meanwhile, the Reformation had begun.

Initially the Reformation was a reform movement within the Church that had been incited by the Church's practice of selling indulgences. In 1517 in Wittenberg, ❸ Martin Luther made public his 95 theses to reform the church. He broke with the church in 1520 when the pope threatened him with excommunication, and in 1521 Luther defended his theses at the ❻ Diet of Worms. The movement developed momentum through the backing of powerful German princes. Elector ❼ Frederick of Saxony sheltered Luther in Wartburg Castle, where he worked on a translation of the Bible into German.

The Reformation soon became linked to the social upheaval of the time. In 1522–1523 there was an uprising of imperial knights under ❹ Ulrich von Hutten and Franz von Sickingen, who saw themselves as representatives of humanism and the Reformation, in opposition to the Catholic German princes. Peasants rebelled against the aristocratic landowners in 1524–1525, plundering manors and monasteries in Franconia and Swabia. Luther sided with the princes against the peasants, while the radical reformer ❺ Thomas Münzer led the peasants in Thuringia. In 1525 the peasant army was defeated at Frankenhausen by the princes, and Münzer was executed. In 1533–1534 the radical Anabaptists seized control of Münster.

2 Anton Fugger burns the first debenture bonds of Charles V, in 1535

4 Humanist, writer, and imperial knight Ulrich von Hutten

Thomas Müntzer, "Manifesto of the Mansfeldian Youths" from 1524:

"Go to it, go to it, while the fire is hot. Let not your sword become cold, do not let it become lame! Forge, clink clank, on the anvil of Nimrod, throw their tower to the ground! It is not possible, as long as they live that human fear should become empty. One can tell you nothing of God, while they govern over you. Go to it, go to it, while it is day. God precedes you, follow, follow!"

5 Thomas Münzer, engraving, 1608

6 Martin Luther before Emperor Charles V at the Diet of Worms on April 17–18, 1521, painting by Anton von Werner, 1900

7 Frederick III, (the Wise) Elector of Saxony

31 Oct 1517 | Luther publishes his theses

Dec 1520 | Luther burns the Papal Bull excommunicating him

5 Jan 1521 | Luther excommunicated

3 May 1521 | Luther's stay in Wartburg castle

8 May 1521 | Edict of Worms

1524 | Beginning of the Peasants' Wa

The Organization of the Protestants and the Religious Peace of Augsburg in 1555

After 1530, a large portion of the empire became Protestant. The emperor won the religious wars against the Schmalkaldic League, but the Protestants, who were supported by France, the rivals of the Habsburgs, won the balance of power in the Peace of Augsburg of 1555.

8 The later German king and Emperor Ferdinand I, painting, 1521

9 Count Philip the Magnanimous of Hesse, painting, ca. 1534

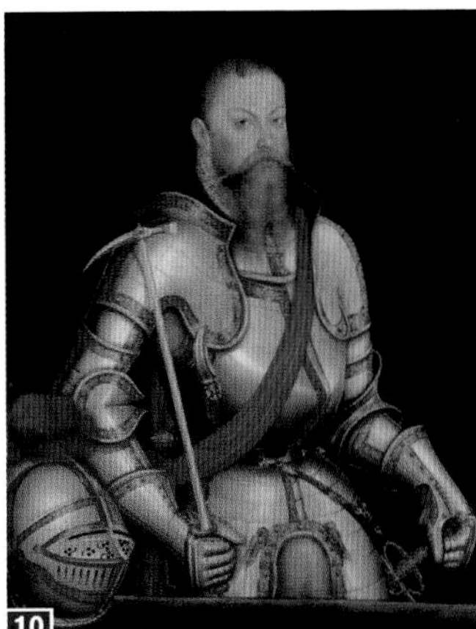

10 The elector Duke Maurice of Saxony, painting by Lucas Cranach, 1548

Holy Roman Emperor Charles V ruled a vast empire on which "the sun never set"—it spanned Spain, the New World, Austria, northern Italy, and the Netherlands. He completely understood the necessity of Church reforms, yet his claim to a universal empire also required that all his subjects be of a unified religion. He therefore saw the Reformation as a politically destabilizing factor and fought energetically against it. As he was often absent from the empire, he had his brother ❽ Ferdinand I crowned Roman king of the Germans in 1531. Ferdinand was then responsible for negotiation between the Protestant and Catholic imperial princes and maintaining peace.

The elector of Saxony and Count ❾ Philip the Magnanimous of Hesse placed themselves at the head of the Reformation movement and supported Luther in developing evangelical state churches. The new state churches did not answer to a higher church authority, which meant a huge increase in their power and influence. In 1530, the Protestant princes formulated their "Augsburg Confession" and presented it before the Diet, and in 1531 they organized as the Schmalkaldic League. When Brandenburg declared itself on the side of the Reformation in 1539, the whole of the southwest, east, and north of the empire—with the exception of Brunswick-Wolfenbüttel—was Protestant. The German princes secularized Catholic dioceses and installed their younger sons in them as hereditary rulers, hereby forcing the emperor's hand, by challenging his rule in numerous territories of the empire.

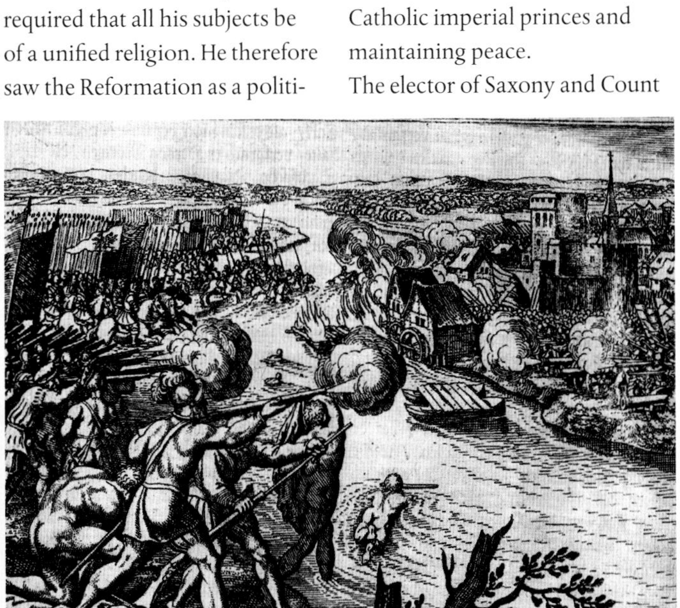

11 Emperor Charles V triumphs over the Saxon army in the Battle at Muehlberg during the Schmalkaldic War of 1546–1547, copper engraving, 17th century

In the wars of the protestant ⓫ Schmalkaldic League, Charles V defeated the Protestants under the leadership of Saxony and Hesse, captured Count Philip, and transferred the Saxon electoral lands and titles to Duke ❿ Maurice of Saxony, who had fought on his side. However, Maurice then changed sides and marched to Austria as leader of the regrouped princes' opposition in 1551–1552, forcing the emperor to flee. In 1552 Maurice extracted from King Ferdinand the Peace of Passau, which guaranteed the Protestants freedom of religion. This treaty prepared the way for the Peace of Augsburg between the emperor and the Protestants, which was signed on September 25, 1555. It stipulated that each prince could determine the religion of his territories and that of his subjects ("*Cuius regio, eius religio*"). Maurice of Saxony was also able to acquire vast lands and power for his family.

Henry the Younger of Brunswick-Wolfenbüttel

Henry the Younger (1489-1568), who strongly opposed the Reformation, was an absolutist ruler of Brunswick-Wolfenbüttel since 1514, remained a strict Catholic and loyal to the emperor while the other Welfs became Protestant. He fought against the Protestant cities of Brunswick and Lübeck. An intensive literary polemic was created around "Hank of Wolfenbüttel"; Martin Luther wrote "Against Hanswurst" about him in 1541. His ousting in 1542 eventually provoked the religious wars of the Schmalkaldic League. When Henry died in 1568, his son Julius converted to Protestantism.

May 1525	Battle of Frankenhausen
1530	Augsburg Confession
1531	Founding of Schmalkaldic League
1533–34	Anabaptist rule in Munster
1546–47	Schmalkaldic War
1555	Peace of Augsburg

Biographies
The Reformers

Martin Luther (1483–1546)
Joined Augustinian order in 1506; ordained as priest in 150;, taught Bible studies in Wittenberg from 1512; published the *95 Theses* demanding reform of the Church in 1517; placed the suffering and death of Christ and the doctrine of the redemption of mankind through grace at the center of his theology; translated the Bible into German and wrote the German Mass; married the former nun Katharina von Bora in 1525; protected by German princes.

Thomas Müntzer (ca. 1490–1525)
Studied and first encountered Luther in Wittenberg; began preaching in Zwickau in 1520; moved to Allstedt in 1523; broke with Luther in 1524 due to differences over his populist socially revolutionary ideas; played a large role in radicalizing the Thuringian peasants as preacher and agitator, later becoming their leader; was captured by Catholic forces in the Battle of Frankenhausen in 1525, tortured, and then beheaded.

Huldrych Zwingli (1484–1531)
Pastor in Glarus from 1506 to 1516; ordained as priest in Zurich in 1518; spearheaded the Reformation there from 1524; saw the presence of Christ not actually but symbolically in the sacrament, which caused a split with the Lutherans; founded the Reformed Church; as a Swiss Protestant army chaplain, killed in 1531 at the Battle of Kappel against the Catholics.

Johannes Calvin (1509–1564)
Studied law in Paris; preacher and church organizer in Geneva from 1536; was banished in 1538 when he attempted to introduce theocratic rule; returned in 1541 and succeeded in establishing his own strict Reformation Church; took Zwingli's position on the issue of the sacrament and promoted the concept of a dualistic predestination of mankind, either to blessedness or damnation; promoted an austerity and a pessimistic view of human nature that shaped the idea of a "Protestant work ethic."

Philipp Melanchthon (originally Schwarzert) (1497–1560)
Was professor of Greek in 1518 in Wittenberg and one of the first supporters of Luther; wrote numerous theological works on the Reformation; composed the Augsburg Confession and oversaw the reordering of the regional churches; became the spiritual leader of the Lutherans after Luther's death and sought conciliatory talks with Catholics and Calvinists; attempted to integrate humanist ideas into the Reformation.

Johannes Oecolampadius (originally Husschin) (1482–1531)
Tutored the princes of the Electoral Palatinate from 1506; colleague of the humanist Erasmus of Rotterdam from 1515; became parish priest, preacher, and professor in Basel in 1522 and introduced the Reformation there between 1528–29; was the most significant reform theologian of Switzerland; took a leading role in numerous theological disputes and worked alongside Zwingli as leader of the Swiss Reformation.

Johannes Bugenhagen (1485–1558)
Ordained as a priest in 1509; later taught Bible studies in a seminary; moved to Wittenberg in 1521 to became a parish priest, a professor of theology, and Luther's confessor; was leading church organizer of the Reformation; founded most of the Reformed Churches in northern Germany, Denmark, and Norway.

Martin Bucer (1491–1551)
Joined Dominican Order in 1506; joined the Reformation in 1518; worked as a pastor and reformer in Strasbourg, a center of the early Reformation; endorsed Zwingli's and Calvin's view on the issue of the sacrament; aligned himself with the Baptists on some theological questions; was expelled from Strasbourg by command of the Holy Roman Emperor in 1549; took refuge in England at the invitation of the archbishop of Canterbury.

Desiderius Erasmus (ca. 1466–1536)
Born the illegitimate son of a priest in Rotterdam; was himself ordained as a priest in 1492; worked as an influential theologist, philologist and publicist; criticized the worldliness of the Church and the cult of relics; as a humanist, argued for the respect of each person's freewill, and criticized Luther's excessive determinism; attempted to avoid aligning himself with either of the two sides in the schism but was attacked by both as a result.

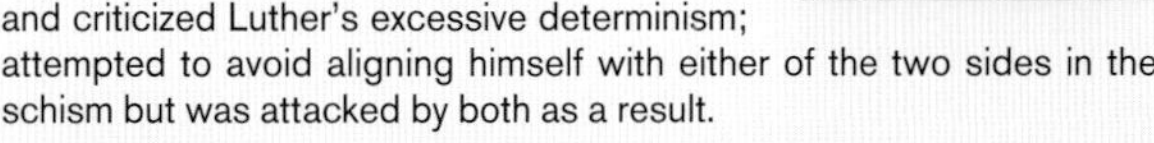

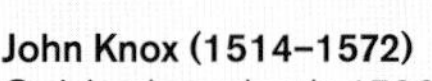

John Knox (1514–1572)
Ordained as priest in 1536; became supporter of the Reformation in 1546; worked as reform preacher from 1549 in the English-Scottish border region; fled from the Catholic restoration in England in 1554; took refuge in Geneva where Calvin was based; returned to Edinburgh in 1559 as a priest and preacher; successfully worked to establish Calvanism in Scotland; wrote his *Confessio Scotia* (Scottish Confession) for the Calvinist church there in 1560.

The Origin and Course of the Reformation

The Reformation was ignited by the Church's sale of "indulgences," which promised liberation from punishment for temporal sins in the afterlife. The Church enriched itself by selling this spiritual forgiveness, a practice that reached a high point in the 16th century when the papacy used the profits from this to finance the rebuilding of St. Peter's in Rome. This caused the Augustinian monk Martin Luther—who countered the concept of purchased salvation with the doctrine of redemption through the grace of God—to criticize the basic teachings of the Church in 1517, which eventually resulted in the establishment of Protestant communities and churches throughout Europe.

left: St. Bartholomew's Day Massacre in1572 in Paris, painting, 16th century

middle: Group of reformers, among others Martin Luther, Desiderius Erasmus and Philipp Melanchthon, copy of a painting by Lucas Cranach the Younger

right: "Le Paradis", Protestant church in Lyon, France, painting, 17th century

Radiating from Germany, Reformation movements sprung up all over Europe in the 16th century. In many cases, these differed fundamentally from the teachings of Luther. The Lutheran Church spread primarily in Scandinavia and the Baltic States, as well as in the German Empire, while the teachings of John Calvin spread out of Switzerland into France, the Netherlands, England, Scotland, Poland, Hungary, and elsewhere. The basis of the Calvinist theology was the doctrine of predestination—God's preselection of each individual as either saved or damned. The Calvinists believed that the nature of this selection, though immutable, was detectable by the circumstances of one's life, wealth, and fortune. This doctrine had a significant influence on the development of Western Europe and North America.

In England, the Reformation took on a unique form through the creation of the Anglican Church. Its legal structure was acquired in 1534 through the designation of Henry VIII as the supreme head of the Church of England, through the Act of Supremacy.

The Huguenots in France formulated their creed in 1558 at their first national synod in Paris. The French Reformation found its followers particularly among the nobility, which was always in contention with the strict Catholic monarchy. Following the slaughter of Huguenots in the Saint Bartholomew's Day Massacre in 1572, a religious civil war broke out. Continuing persecution later resulted in the emigration of around 200,000 Huguenots in 1685.

Smaller spiritual movements also emerged, such as that of the Anabaptists, who espoused adult baptism as a conscious "baptism of faith," and communal property.

The Division of the Empire and Calvinism

Despite being left out of the Peace of Augsburg, Calvinism was later able to gain a foothold in the empire while the emperor endeavored to reach religious compromises.

The German Emperor Charles V, archduke of Austria, and also Charles I of Spain, painting by Titian, 1548

The French-Swiss reformer John Calvin, painting in the style of the Flemish school, ca. 1530

The German Emperor Ferdinand I, archduke of Austria, king of Bohemia and Hungary, painting, ca. 1550

Fatigued and sick with gout, ❶ Charles V gave up the throne in 1556, splitting his enormous empire between his brother Ferdinand (the Austrian line) and his son Philip (the Spanish line). ❸ Ferdinand, who in 1526 had inherited the crown of Bohemia and Hungary, received Austria and the title of emperor in 1558. The religious and political peace in the empire remained volatile. Ferdinand had been able to include a clause in the Peace of Augsburg stipulating that a prince was required to relinquish his power if he converted to Protestantism, but the Protestants were always able to work around this requirement. Furthermore, the Catholic majority of the seven electoral votes was minimal after Brandenburg, the Palatinate, and Saxony had become Protestant.

The Emperor Maximilian II, painting by Anthonis Mor, ca. 1560

Meanwhile, the Reformation movement was also divided by doctrinal differences. In 1525 ❹ Huldrych Zwingli, a former Roman Catholic priest, had brought the Reformation to Zurich, but his version differed from the Lutheran, above all over the issue of Communion. Of even greater consequence was ❷ John Calvin's 1541 brand of Reformation in Geneva, which introduced a severe church discipline and established a form of theocracy in the city. Calvinism spread rapidly to France, the Netherlands, and the west of the empire. In 1560s the Palatinate electorate under Frederick III the Pious converted to Calvinism, and western German earldoms such as Nassau followed. Because the Calvinists had not been included in the Peace of Augsburg, the Palatinate leaned heavily toward France under Frederick III and even more so under his son John Casimir, bringing the emperor into great difficulties.

Charles V and Ferdinand I had repeatedly urged the pope to make the reforms to the Catholic Church that were finally made by the Council of Trent, which met intermittently between 1545 and 1563 and which redefined Catholic doctrine. Ferdinand remained a Catholic but was ready to make concessions, for example, over the issue of the marriage of priests, which he was prepared to allow in view of the many priests cohabiting. His son ❺ Maximilian II, emperor from 1564, was indifferent to religion, if anything leaning slightly toward Protestantism. The political lines were vague: Saxony under ❻ Elector August (elector since 1553) fought for the rights of the Protestants, but remained staunchly on the side of the emperor; on the other hand, the Catholic dukes of Bavaria were ready to weaken the Habsburgs to their own advantage. Protestantism was at the height of its power in the empire under Maximilian, when most of the important imperial cities had become Protestant.

Huldrych Zwingli, former Catholic priest and German-Swiss reformer, painting by Hans Asper, 1549

Elector August of Saxony, painting by Zacharias Wehme, 1586

1540 | Jesuit order founded
1545–63 | Council of Trent
1556 | Abdication of Charles V
1563 | Beginning of Counter-Reformation in Bavaria
1564 | Maximilian II elected emperor
1576 | Rudolf II elected emperor

The Counter-Reformation and Intensifying Religious Differences within the Empire

Spreading from southern Germany, the Catholic Counter-Reformation gained ground. The confessional differences sharpened, culminating in the outbreak of the Thirty Years' War.

7 John Sigismund von Brandenburg in a dispute with Wolfgang Wilhelm von Neuburg over the Jülich-Clevian succession, color print, 19th century

8 The German Jesuit Petrus Canisius preaches before Pope Gregory XIII and Emperor Rudolf II, painting, 1635

The beginning of the Catholic Counter-Reformation can be tied to the founding of the order of Jesuits by Ignatius of Loyola in 1540. The Bavarian dukes, among others, joined this order in 1564. The driving power behind it was the cardinal of Augsburg, Otto Truchsess of Waldburg, who unified Catholic forces. In 1563 he handed over the University of Dillingen, which he had founded in 1554, to the ❽ Jesuits, who were taking control of universities and establishing Catholic seminaries in all of the empire's territories. Also, in Austria where the Protestants had won significant freedoms, Archduke Ferdinand—later Emperor Ferdinand II—increased his efforts for a return to Catholicism from 1594.

Under the Emperor Rudolf II, whose reign began in 1576, the religious differences increased, especially after 1600 when the increasingly mentally ill emperor retired from public view. The occasion that sparked the war came during the crisis of Cologne in 1582–83, when Archbishop Gebhard Truchsess of Waldburg—a nephew of Cardinal Otto—attempted to transform Cologne into a hereditary Protestant principality with the aid of Protestant German princes and Dutch Calvinists. As this would have meant the loss of the majority in the Electoral College, Catholic forces, with the help of Spain, drove the archbishop out of Cologne and installed the young line of Bavarian Wittelsbachs, which ruled until 1777.

Since 1606 the fraternal feud in the House of Habsburg had been weakening the central power. ❿ Archduke Matthias won control over Hungary (1608) and Bohemia (1611) from Rudolf, who was by then almost incapable of governing. The emperor allied himself with the Protestant estates of Bohemia and granted them religious freedom in 1609. All signs pointed to a storm in the empire when in 1607 ⓫ Duke Maximilian I of Bavaria occupied the Protestant city of Donauworth, where a Catholic procession had been attacked, and reestablished Catholic rule. As a result, the Protestant Union was formed in 1608 and, in response, the Catholic League in 1609. The ❾ battle lines of the Thirty Years' War had been drawn and the ❼ Jülich-Clevian dispute gave a foretaste of what was to come.

The Dispute over Succession in Jülich-Cleves

By 1609, the religious wars were already imminent when the last Catholic duke of Jülich and Cleves died and a dispute over the succession flared up. The princes of Brandenburg and Neuburg, both Protestant, each laid claim to the duchy. They agreed upon a division of the territory in 1614 only after the Brandenburgs had secured Dutch help by converting to Calvinism, and the Neuburgs had received aid from the Wittelsbachs and the Spaniards once they had converted to Catholicism.

9 A protestant flyer with a polemical depiction of the "real church of Christ" (Protestants) confronting the "antichrist" (Catholics) copper engraving, 1606

10 The German emperor Matthias, painting, ca. 1580

11 Maximilian I, Duke and since 1623 first Elector of Bavaria, painting, ca. 1620

1582–83 | Crisis of Cologne
1607 | Occupation of Donauworth by Maximilian I of Bavaria
1608 | Protestant Union founded
1609 | Catholic League founded
1609–14 | Jülich-Clevian dispute of succession

The Thirty Years' War 1618–1648

In the Thirty Years' War, the growing tensions between the Holy Roman Emperor and the Catholic powers on the one hand, and the Protestant regions and estates on the other, erupted into violence. The conflict began in Bohemia but soon spread throughout the empire and drew in almost all the European powers. Spain supported its Catholic relations, Denmark and Sweden supported the Protestants, and France was mainly interested in weakening the Habsburgs. In the Holy Roman Empire, and especially in Bohemia, whole districts were devastated by passing armies which would terrorize the local population and requisition their property.

The Battle of White Mountain in Bohemia, painting by Pieter Snayers, 17th century

The Palatine-Bohemian Phase 1618–1623

In Bohemia the country princes disposed of the Habsburg Ferdinand II and chose Elector Count Palatine as king. However, he was soon expelled by the Catholic League.

During his lifetime, the childless Emperor Matthias, who succeeded his brother Rudolf in 1612, assigned the crown of Bohemia (1617) and Hungary (1618) to his cousin, ❹ Ferdinand II. The Bohemian country princes, who were mainly Protestant, feared that the Jesuit-educated Ferdinand would suspend the Letter of Majesty of 1609. This had stipulated that all subjects should enjoy freedom of conscience in religious matters. Insisting on their right to freely elect their king, the princes deposed him and voted in the leader of the Protestant Union, ❺ Elector Frederick V of the Palatinate, as his replacement in 1618. The election caused bitter enmity between the religious parties of the Bohemian aristocracy. On May 23, 1618, Protestants threw the Catholic imperial governors, Slawata and Martinez, and a secretary out the window of the ❸ Prague Castle (the ❷ "Prague defenestration") and thus threw down a challenge to the Habsburgs. The violent conflict had begun.

Ferdinand II

Prague Castle

Ferdinand sent his cousin, Duke Maximilian of Bavaria and head of the Catholic League, to Bohemia with troops under the command of the Bavarian ❻ General Tilly. On November 8, 1620, the league's forces ❶ defeated those of the Protestant princes at the Battle of White Mountain, near Prague. Frederick V, mocked as the "winter king" for his short-lived reign, was forced to flee to Holland. A tribunal then convened in Bohemia, and 21 leaders of the rebellion were executed, while a large amount of Protestant property was confiscated. The crown of Bohemia became the property of the Habsburgs until 1918.

In 1622 troops of the Catholic League and of Spain occupied the Palatinate, and in 1623 they made Maximilian elector palatine, whereupon power relations in the Electoral College shifted significantly in favor of the Catholics. The Protestants in the empire felt challenged and threatened.

The "Prague defenestration", 1618

Elector Frederick V of the Palatinate

Bavarian General Tilly

From
Mother Courage and Her Children
by Bertolt Brecht

I won't let you spoil the war for me. / It is said it kills off the weak, but they're done for in peace, too. / It's just that war feeds its own better, / and if it gets the best of you / then you're simply not there for the victory. / War is nothing more than business, / but with bullets instead of cheese.

Helene Weigel as "Mother Courage"

1618 | Emperor Matthias designates Ferdinand his successor
23 May 1618 | The Prague Defenestration
1622 | Catholic League troops occupy the Palatinate
1623 | Palatinate electorate given to Duke Maximilian

The Danish War 1625–29

Denmark allied itself with the Protestants of Lower Saxony and fought against a northward attack by the imperial troops under Wallenstein.

Albrecht von Wallenstein, painting by Anthony van Dyck, 17th century

In his battle against Frederick V, Tilly advanced well into Westphalia. The Protestants of northern Germany feared Catholic domination and prepared their ❽, ❿ troops under Ernst of Mansfeld and Christian of Brunswick-Wolfenbüttel. The war thus began to spread beyond Bohemia. Christian IV of Denmark led the Protestant forces, together with Duke von Holstein, the most senior Protestant prince in the region of Lower Saxony.

On the Catholic side, the rise of ❼, ⓬ Albrecht von Wallenstein commenced. The Bohemian aristocrat had converted to Catholicism, acquired an immense fortune through the purchase of confiscated Protestant goods, and offered his services to the emperor. An excellent strategist, he quickly made a name for himself as a military commander. Wallenstein marched his army to northern Germany and there defeated Ernst of Mansfeld at ⓭ Dessauer Bridge on April 25, 1626. Shortly afterwards, Tilly also defeated Christian IV at the Battle of Lutter am Barenberg on August 27, 1626.

In 1626 Wallenstein, now commander in chief of the imperial army and duke of Friedland, and Tilly went on to conquer Holstein, Schleswig, and Jutland, expelling the dukes of Mecklenburg and appropriating their lands. The Danish king was forced to agree to the Peace of Lübeck in 1629. Ferdinand II now stood at the height of his powers, and on March 6, 1629, he decreed his Edict of Restitution, which demanded that the Protestants ⓫ return all the secularized Church lands and called on the Catholic imperial estates to actively re-Catholicize. However, Wallenstein's draconian demands alarmed many; at the Diet of Regensburg in 1630, his enemies and rivals, notably ❾ Maximilian of Bavaria, conspired to secure his dismissal from the post of commander in chief of the imperial armies.

Castle Güstrow, Wallenstein's residence in Mecklenburg, north Germany

Wallenstein's palace in Prague, built in 1621

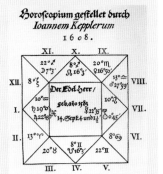

Band of soldiers attacking local peasants, wood engraving, 17th c.

Maximilian I of Bavaria, painting, 17th century

Albrecht Eusebius von Wallenstein (1583–1634)

Wallenstein was convinced of the power of the stars over his fate. He had the famous astronomer John Kepler draw up his horoscope.

Horoscopium gestellet durch Ioannem Kepplerum 1608.

Horoscope made for Wallenstein by the astrologer John Kepler, showing the position of the planets on the day of his birth

Band of soldiers robbing and killing their victims, wood engraving, 17th c.

Wallenstein's victory in the Battle at the Dessauer Bridge, 1626

1625–29 Danish phase of the war
25 Apr 1626 Battle at the Dessau Bridge
27 Aug 1626 Tilly's victory at Lutter am Barenberg
6 Mar 1629 Edict of Restitution
1629 Peace of Lübeck
1630 Wallenstein's dismissal

The Swedish War 1630–1635

The plight of the German Protestants caused the Swedish king to act. After a triumphant march through Germany, King Gustav fell in battle against Wallenstein.

Sweden was alarmed by the advance of imperial power in northern Germany and the Baltic region where, by the Peace of Lübeck of 1629, Christian IV of Denmark had agreed not to intervene in German affairs. Fearing for his hegemony in the North, the Swedish Lutheran ❶ King Gustav II Adolph championed the cause of the German Protestants. In 1630, encouraged and financially supported by Cardinal Richelieu of France who also wished to reduce imperial influence, Gustav moved south and began his march through Germany. The Swedish army was a formidable and well-disciplined fighting unit. The imperial forces under Tilly were not strong enough and suffered a defeat against the ❸ allied Swedish and Saxon forces at ❷ Breitenfeld on September 17, 1631.

King Gustav II Adolph of Sweden

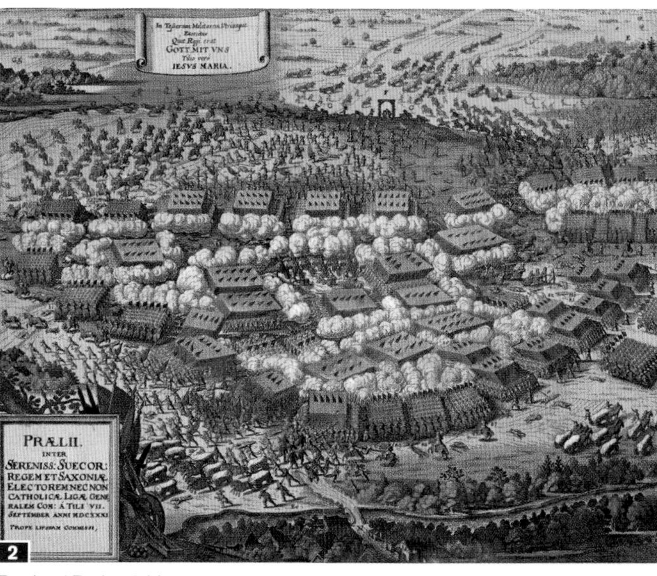

Battle of Breitenfeld, 1631

Commemoration of the Protestant alliance between Gustav II Adolph of Sweden, the Elector John George I of Saxony, and George William of Brandenburg, 1631

Duke Bernhard von Weimar

From Mainz, Gustav pushed southward in spring 1632 to occupy Augsburg, and in May of 1632 moved into the Munich residence of the Elector Maximilian, who had fled to Nuremberg. The city of Munich offered heavy bribes to prevent the Swedish and Saxon armies from looting, but many churches and monasteries in southern Germany were devastated by Swedish soldiers.

At this point the emperor had no choice but to reappoint Wallenstein as commander of the troops. Wallenstein cut off Swedish support in southern Germany and forced Gustav to confront him in Saxony. At the ❺ Battle of Lützen on November 16, 1632, Gustav was killed, but the Protestants still triumphed. However, the Swedish chancellor, Axel Oxenstierna, could not keep the Protestant alliance together, particularly as Wallenstein and the Saxon commander, Hans Georg von Arnim, were secretly negotiating peace. The strange behavior of Wallenstein, who probably wanted to join the Protestant troops under ❻ Bernhard von Weimar at this stage, convinced Emperor Ferdinand of his commander's betrayal, and he gave his consent for ❹ Wallenstein's murder in Eger by a group of his officers.

Murder of Wallenstein by his officers in Eger, February 25, 1634

Gustav II Adolph prays for victory before the Battle of Lützen, 1632

Battle of Nördlingen, 1634

The subsequent defeat of Weimar and the Swedes at ❼ Nördlingen led to the Peace of Prague between the emperor and most of the Protestant princes of the empire on May 30, 1635. Ferdinand abandoned the implementation of his Restitution Edict, and all sides agreed to expel foreign powers and mercenaries from the empire. A general war weariness saw all sides embrace the peace.

1630 | Gustav II Adolph arrives in Pomerania
17 Sep 1631 | Battle of Breitenfeld
16 Nov 1632 | Battle of Lützen / Death of Gustav II Adolph
25 Feb 1634 | Wallenstein murdered
Sep 1634 | Battle of Nördling

From the Franco-Swedish Phase to the Peace of Westphalia

1635–1648

France engineered the continuation of the war. The last phase was particularly devastating for the civilian population until the Peace of Westphalia ended the conflict in 1648.

The end of war in Germany was not in the interests of France, since it was clearly placing a major strain on the rival Habsburgs. Cardinal Richelieu (p. 278) of France continued to support the Protestant commanders with large sums of money and urged them to pursue the war. With this assistance, Swedish general Johan Banér defeated the imperial forces at ❽ Wittstock in 1636, and again at Chemnitz in 1639. Duke Bernhard of Saxe-Weimar also triumphed over imperial troops at Rheinfelden in 1638. In 1645, the Swedes marched as far as Vienna, while French troops were forced back in Bavaria.

8 General Banér in the Battle of Wittstock, 1636, wood engraving, 19th c.

After three decades of war the empire was devastated. Whole regions in northern Germany, the Palatinate, and Brandenburg were depopulated and desolate and would remain so for decades; in some parts of the empire, as much as half of the population had ❿ died. Prosperous cities had been reduced to small towns or even large villages.The people, particularly the ⓫ peasants, had suffered appalling hardships: torture, famine, and disease. Bands of desperate people wandered through Germany begging and stealing whatever they could.

From 1644 to 1648, representatives of all powers took part in peace negotiations at ⓬ Münster and Osnabrück, which after long and hard bargaining led to the ❾ Peace of Westphalia. Bavaria retained the title of elector palatine, and an eighth electorate was created for the reinstated son of the "winter king." Switzerland and the Netherlands officially resigned from the Imperial Alliance, and the power of the emperor was restricted to Hungary and Bohemia, his hereditary lands. The princes of the empire gained significantly in power and created their own alliance of sovereign states, of which the emperor was only the nominal head. The actual victors were France and Sweden, who gained territory and underlined their status as great European powers. The Netherlands, too, profited from the weakening of the empire. The Peace of Westphalia established the principle that states could not interfere in each others affairs on grounds of religious differences.

10 Mass public hanging, etching, 1632

11 Peasants flee from the advancing armies, ca. 1645

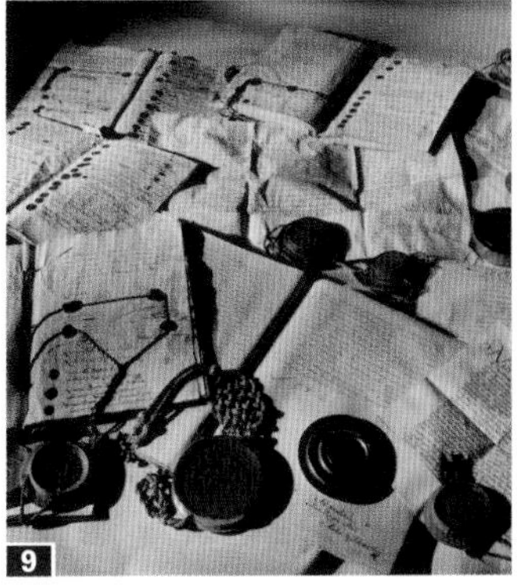

9 Documents marked with the seals of the combatants establishing the Peace of Westphalia in 1648

Song of Praise for the Peace by Paul Gerhard

Praise God! A noble word of
Peace and joy rings out,
Which will from now on still
The spears and swords and their murdering.
Take courage and take once more to your string,
Playing O Germany and sing songs,
In a high full choir,
Lift your spirits to your God and say,
Lord, Your mercy and goodness
Still remains eternal.

Peace of Münster is announced to a crowd in the town square

12 Peace negotiations in Münster, 1648

1635 French phase of war begins
30 May 1635 Peace of Prague
1636 Battle of Wittstock
from 1636 Franco-Swedish Alliance
1639 Battle of Chemnitz
Oct 1648 Peace of Westphalia signed

The Castle of Nymphenburg in Munich

The Holy Roman Empire under Enlightened Absolutism 1648–1806

The Peace of Westphalia brought the German states complete independence and some, most notably Prussia, would become European powers. Absolutist monarchies came to predominate as a form of rule. The Enlightenment and the belief in reform and progress are reflected in the "enlightened absolutism" of Prussia and Austria. Influenced by the French Revolution and under pressure from Napoleon's military victories, the Holy Roman Empire was finally dissolved in 1806.

The Absolutism of the German Princes

With the 18th century came new wars that taxed the empire. Of all the German princes, the electors of Saxony and Bavaria were the most significant.

By 1700, the empire had largely recovered from the damage done by the Thirty Years' War, but new wars—the Eight-Year War (1689–1697), the War of the Spanish Succession (1701–1714; p. 280), and the Great Northern War (1700–1721; p. 305)—brought fresh strife.

The German princes of the Baroque period sought to rule like kings. ❶ Prestigious buildings, after the French model, turned the greatest courts into cultural centers and drove the less wealthy into debt and ruin. The most magnificent German court was maintained by Elector Frederick Augustus II of Saxony, who in 1697 also took the throne of Poland. Known as ❷ "Augustus the Strong," he commissioned a number of ❻ architectural projects and was infamous for his numerous love affairs. He made a disastrous attempt to annex territories from Sweden during the Great Northern War, and was temporarily driven out of Poland.

left: Augustus the Strong **middle:** Maximilian II Emanuel, Elector of Bavaria **right:** Klemens August, Elector of Cologne

The Battle of Hochstadt, August 13, 1704

❸ Maximilian II Emanuel of Bavaria was governor of the Spanish Netherlands. In 1683 he was among those who fought the Turks (p. 310) outside Vienna and later fought on France's side in the War of Spanish Succession. After the French defeat at ❺ Hochstadt he was forced out of Bavaria—occupied by the Austrians—and not allowed to return until 1714. Maximilian's son Charles Albert (elector from 1726) occupied Bohemia in 1740 before being elected Holy Roman emperor, as Charles VII, in Frankfurt in 1742. His brother ❹ Klemens August, "the sun prince," was elector of Cologne from 1723. In 1714 George Louis, of the House of Hanover, became King George I of Great Britain and Ireland, and his descendants ruled until 1901.

The "Zwinger," a baroque castle in Dresden, painting by Canaletto

The Persecution of the "Witches"

The last "witch-trial" in Germany took place in 1775 at the abbey of Kempten. Her story is similar to that of many other victims: The maid Maria Anna Schwegelin had lost her employment, after a suitor had broken their marriage engagement. The woman was put away into a workhouse, where she had to bear the continuous ill-treatment of an attendant. After several arguments the attendant accused her of being in league with the devil, and branded her a "witch."

A witch prays to a demon, wood engraving, 16th century

1683 | Ottomans lay siege to Vienna
1689–97 | The Eight-Year War
1700–1721 | The Great Northern War
1701 | War of the Spanish Succession begins

The End of the Empire

Napoleon abolished many of the smaller priestly principalities. Austria's defeats saw the larger German princes assert their independence from the Holy Roman Empire after 1801.

The priestly principalities of the empire were also under absolutist rule. The ruler was often a Prince-Bishop, who held both spiritual and temporal authority over his realm. Both Catholic and Protestant bishops usually originated from ruling royal houses or great noble families and often held several dioceses in their hands. The southwestern German Catholic area was shaped by the 8 Schönborn family. After 1719, the imperial chancellor and elector of Mainz since 1694, Lothar Franz, gave the most important bishoprics to his four nephews; Johann Philipp Franz in Würzburg, Friedrich Karl in Bamberg and Würzburg, Cardinal Damian Hugo in Speyer and Konstanz, and Franz Georg as elector of Trier. They built up the residences of 10 Würzburg and Bamberg as well as the palaces of 9 Bruchsal and 11 Pommersfelden and ruled in a manner that has come to be known as enlightened absolutism.

7 Karl Theodor, Baron of Dalberg

While the princes of the Rhine were swept aside by the French Revolutionary armies after 1792, other German princes successfully allied with Napoleon to weaken Austrian influence. After the 1801 Treaty of Luneville (p. 360) between France and Austria, which headed the Holy Roman Empire, Mainz elector and imperial chancellor 7 Karl Theodor Baron of Dalberg succeeded in bringing about the Diet's Recess on February 25, 1803. The west side of the Rhine was annexed by France and many of the smaller principalities were abolished, but the major German princes received compensation and their dominions were extended at the expense of city-states and through the requisitioning of Church land. After further defeats Austria's Francis II laid aside the crown of the Holy Roman Empire and declared it dissolved.

The Napoleonic wars had a lasting impact on the political map of Germany, consolidating what had been a patchwork of small states into fewer but larger and more powerful states (p. 364–365).

10 The bishop's residence in Würzburg; frescos painted by Giovanni Battista Tiepolo

8 Frederick Charles Schönborn

9 The Castle of Bruchsal, begun in 1722

11 Hall of Mirrors in the Castle of Weissenstein, Pommersfelden, built between 1711 and 1718

1704	Battle of Hochstadt
1742	Charles VII elected emperor
1801	Treaty of Luneville
25 Feb 1803	Diet's Recess
6 Aug 1806	End of the Holy Roman Empire

The Rise of Austria from Leopold I to Charles VI

Under Leopold I and his sons, Austria increased its power in Europe. Under the command of the talented general, Prince Eugène of Savoy, Austrian forces succeeded in halting, and then reversing, the advance of the Ottoman Turks. Meanwhile the Emperors managed to keep France in check.

While Ferdinand III (emperor from 1637) presided over major disruption in the empire resulting from the Thirty Years' War, Austria's political and economic ascendance began under his son ❷ Leopold I, who became emperor in 1658. First, Leopold had to defeat the powerful Turkish army (p. 310) that had advanced out of the Balkans and in 1683 reached the gates of Vienna. An imperial army, under Charles V of Lorraine and the Polish king John III Sobieski, saved the city. They pushed back the Turkish army after a narrow victory at the ❶ Battle of Kahlenberg. Thereafter Leopold promoted himself as "vanquisher of the Turks." In 1696 work began on the building of his imperial residence, the ❸ Schonbrunn Palace.

Despite the victory at Vienna, Leopold was still forced to fight a war on two fronts. While he confronted France's claims to hegemony in the west and in the north of Italy, he continued to fight the Turks, who were allied with France, in the east. His brilliant general, ❹ Prince Eugène of Savoy, proved himself by comprehensively defeating the Turkish army at Senta, on the River Tisza, in 1697. In the Peace of Karlowitz (1699), dictated by the emperor, Austria took all of Hungary, Transylvania, and Croatia from the Ottomans. When war broke out again in 1717, Eugène captured Belgrade. The subsequent Peace of Passarowitz (1718) gave Serbia to Austria and definitively ended the westward advance of the Ottoman Empire.

1 The Battle of Kahlenberg on September 12, 1683, detail from the tapestry

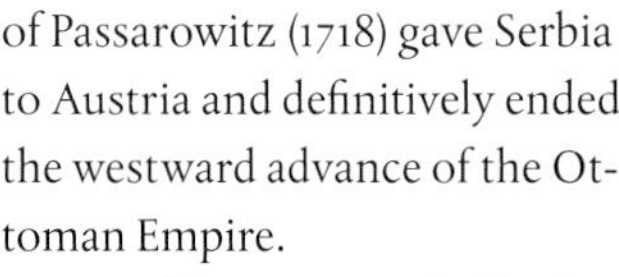

Leopold was succeeded by his oldest son, Joseph, in 1705. As ❻ Joseph I, he reorganized the government administration and forcibly repressed revolts in the kingdom of Hungary (p. 303), whose Magyar nobility tended to jealously guard their autonomy and ancient privileges . After his death in 1711 the imperial crown fell to his brother, ❺ Charles VI, who had until then held the throne in Spain (p. 300).

Under Charles VI Austria grew in economic and military power. As he had no male heirs, his major concern after 1713 was convincing the German princes to recognize his ❼ "Pragmatic Sanction," which changed the rules of succession to secure the crown for his daughter, Maria Theresa. The emperor made concessions to achieve this, but Prussia and Bavaria soon found reasons to disregard the agreement.

2 Leopold I in theater costume, painting

3 Interior of Schonbrunn Palace

4 Prince Eugène of Savoy

5 Charles VI (and Charles III of Hungary)

6 Joseph I

7 The "Pragmatic Sanction," 1713

1683 | Battle of Kahlenberg
1696 | Construction of Schonbrunn Palace begins
1697 | Battle of Senta on the River Thisza
1699 | Peace of Karlowitz
1713 | "Pragmatic Sanction"
1718 | Peace of Passarowitz

Austria under Maria Theresa and Joseph II

Maria Theresa defended the Habsburg Empire against Prussia and introduced reforms. These were accelerated by her son, Joseph II, in the spirit of enlightened absolutism.

8 rancis Stephen of Lorraine, Holy Roman Emperor Francis I

9 oseph II with his brother and successor, Leopold II, family portrait

In 1740 ⑩ Maria Theresa inherited the thrones of Bohemia and Hungary. She immediately had to defend her birthright against king Frederick II of Prussia, who annexed Silesia, and Charles Albert of Bavaria, who occupied Bohemia (p. 270). In the ⑪ War of Austrian Succession (1740–48), she succeeded in driving the Bavarians out of Bohemia, but Silesia remained Prussian. However, in 1745, Frederick II recognized the election of Maria Theresa's husband, ⑧ Francis Stephen of Lorraine, as Holy Roman emperor Francis I. The royal pair, together with their 16 children, founded the royal house of Habsburg-Lorraine.

Maria Theresa sought to bring greater uniformity and centralization to Austria through cautious reforms. Notably she reorganized the legal system, and improved education provision through a general school reform in 1774. With her chancellor of state, Prince Kaunitz, and in alliance with France (p. 281) and Russia, she attempted to win Silesia back (p. 275) from Prussia in the Seven Years' War (1756–1763). However, the war was not a success and the Treaty of Hubertusburg left the country financially ruined.

After Francis's death, his eldest son, ⑨ Joseph II, became co-regent of Austria but did not attain real power until 1780. Strongly influenced by the ideas of the Enlightenment, he pushed through the enactment of many liberal reforms, such as the abolishment of torture and serfdom, complete freedom of the press, the emancipation of the Jews, and a reduction in the pomp of the court. In his Edict of Toleration (1781), Joseph granted complete freedom of religion, and later established new schools and orphanages. However his ambitious reform plans relied too much on central authority in a multi-ethnic state where special privileges for regions and groups were the rule. Thus Joseph's hasty attempts to impose enlightened ideas through despotic means swiftly ran into opposition and the results fell well short of his radical ambitions. His brother and successor Leopold II was more cautious but attempted to maintain the overall direction of the reforms. However, his son, Francis II, was forced to give up the imperial crown of the Holy Roman Empire in 1806 (p. 364).

10 Maria Theresa of Austria, portrait, 1750

Joseph II, portrait, 1785

Extract from Joseph II's *Edict of Toleration*, December 21, 1781

"As we are convinced that every coercion that violates the conscience of humans is highly damaging; that in contrast extraordinary advantage for religion and the state come from true tolerance as prescribed by Christian love, so we have decided to implement these in all our hereditary lands."

11 Prussia defeats the army of Austria and Saxony at Hohenfriedberg

739 | Treaty of Belgrade
1740 | Maria Theresa comes to the throne
1745 | Francis I Stephan of Lorraine elected emperor
1756–1763 | Seven Years' War
1780 | Joseph II becomes sole regent
21 Dec 1781 | Joseph II's *Edict of Toleration*

The Rise of Prussia

After the Hohenzollern family had established themselves in Brandenburg, the Great Elector Frederick William made the region one of the leading forces in the empire. His son Frederick I secured the royal status of Prussia's rulers.

1 Joachim II from the House of Hohenzollern, elector of Brandenburg from 1535 to 1571, copper engraving, 1570

In 1411 King Sigismund made the Margraves of Nuremberg from the House of Hohenzollern governors of the province of Brandenburg. Four years later he granted them the title of elector. The first rulers quickly established their authority in the cities. ❶ Joachim II joined the Reformation movement in 1539 but, like his successor, stood by the emperor. The rise of Brandenburg began with ❷ John Sigismund, who converted to Calvinism in 1613. In 1614 he acquired Cleves, Mark, and Ravensberg on the Rhine during the dispute over the Jülich-Cleves succession (p. 259).

In 1618 he inherited ducal Prussia, which had been founded in 1525 on the lands once held by the Teutonic Order (p. 222).

Brandenburg was ravaged by the Thirty Years' War, as troops of both sides marched through to battle. When ❸ Frederick William, the Great Elector, came to power in 1640, he resolutely set about reconstruction. After centralizing the tax system he acquired further territories (East Pomerania, Minden, and Halberstadt) through playing the emperor and France against one another. In 1675 he defeated the Swedish army at Fehrbellin and drove them out of Germany by seizing Swedish Pomerania and Rügen. His Potsdam Edict of Tolerance (1685) was a landmark, and paved the way for receiving the Huguenots (p. 279) who were driven out of France. The absolutist ruler left his successors a centralized state with a strong standing army, which was well on the way to becoming a major European power.

3 Frederick William, "Great Elector" of Brandenburg, portrait painting, 1649

His son ❹ Frederick III, together with his wife, the Welf princess Sophie Charlotte, turned the country into a glittering baroque state. They promoted the arts, built palaces (such as Berlin's Charlottenburg), and founded universities. In return for providing military aid to the emperor in the War of Spanish Succession, he was granted the royal status he had desired. On January 18, 1701, in Königsberg he had himself ❺ crowned Frederick I, marking the arrival of a powerful new dynasty in Europe.

2 John Sigismund, elector of Brandenburg

4 Frederick III, elector of Brandenburg, later Frederick I, king of Prussia

5 Coronation of Frederick I on the January 18, 1701 in Königsberg, painting, 19th c.

Allegory of the reception of Protestants from Salzburg as they arrive in Frederick William I's Prussia

The Huguenots

When the Great Elector invited the Huguenots to settle in the cities and barren stretches of land in Brandenburg-Prussia, more than 20,000 accepted his invitation. By 1700 they made up about a third of the population of Berlin. Among them were craftsmen, who brought new skills with them from France, as well as prosperous merchants, who developed the city's connections to international trade, providing a major boost to the Prussian economy.

18 Apr 1525 | Teutonic Order's lands become Ducal Prussia
1618 | John Sigismund inherits Prussia
1640 | Frederick William becomes Great Elector
1660 | Prussia gains sovereignty
1675 | Battle of Fehrbellin
1685 | Edict of Tolerance of Potsda

Prussia under the Soldier King and Frederick the Great

Through the creation of an effective centralized administration and a powerful army, the Soldier King, Frederick William I, and his son, the enlightened despot Frederick the Great, turned Prussia into one of the greatest powers in Europe.

6 Frederick William I inspecting the results of his education reforms in a Prussian school, painting

In 1713 Frederick William I, the "Soldier King," came to power. He was determined to cement his father's legacy with further reform to increase his dynasty's power and prestige. A straight-laced and thrifty Puritan, he sought to introduce a martial discipline into the bureaucracy and other aspects of the Prussian state. His was the largest standing army in Europe, accounting for three-quarters of the state's expenses. The mercantilist economy was forced to serve the needs of this military force. More progressively, he introduced ❻ compulsory primary education in 1717 and prohibited the physical punishment of serfs. Frederick William was pragmatic in foreign affairs, maintaining the alliance with Hanoverian England despite personal antipathy toward its rulers and occupying former Swedish West Pomerania without resistance in 1720. In 1732 he allowed the Salzburg Protestants, who had been expelled from Austria, to settle in the region, which boosted Prussia's economy. Prussia's "greatest domestic king" determined the character of the Prussian state until well into the 19th century.

His son ❼ Frederick II (the Great), despite severe conflicts with his unyielding father during his youth, retained Frederick William's system of government—contrary to expectations—yet was simultaneously a passionate adherent of the Enlightenment and French aesthetics. As the ❾ "philosopher of Sanssouci" and a ❽ talented flutist, he surrounded himself with eminent free-thinkers and artists, including ❿ Voltaire. He also used the army to expand Prussian territory, wresting Silesia from Austria in the War of Austrian Succession (1740–48). During the ⓫ Seven Years' War (1756–1763), Prussia was brought to the verge of destruction by the alliance of Austria, France, Russia, and Saxony, and was saved only by the death of the Russian empress in 1762 (p. 307). In 1772 Prussia participated, along with Russia and Austria, in the first partition of Poland (p. 303). Domestically, Frederick bound the aristocracy into the leadership of the state and army and improved the educational system. The cost of his wars was borne by his subjects, but he made Prussia a dominant power and established the "Prussian myth."

10 King Frederick II dining in Sanssouci, with guests including Voltaire and Friedrich von Stille, painting by Adolph von Menzel, 1850

Frederick the Great, 1743

"I hope posterity will know to differentiate in me the philosopher from the prince, the gentleman from the politician. I must admit: it is hard for he who is pulled into great European politics to maintain his honest and pure character."

7 Frederick II, known as "the Great"

8 Frederick the Great gives a flute concert, painting by Adolph von Menzel, 1850/52

9 The Palace of Sanssouci in Potsdam

11 Frederick the Great in the Battle of Zorndorf on the August 25, 1758 during the Seven Years' War

1698 | Construction of Berlin Palace
18 Jan 1701 | Frederick I crowned first king of Prussia
1713 | Frederick William I comes to power
1717 | Education reforms
1740–48 | Silesia conquered
1772 | Prussia participates in the first partition of Poland

France: From the Wars of Religion to the Eve of the Revolution 1562–1789

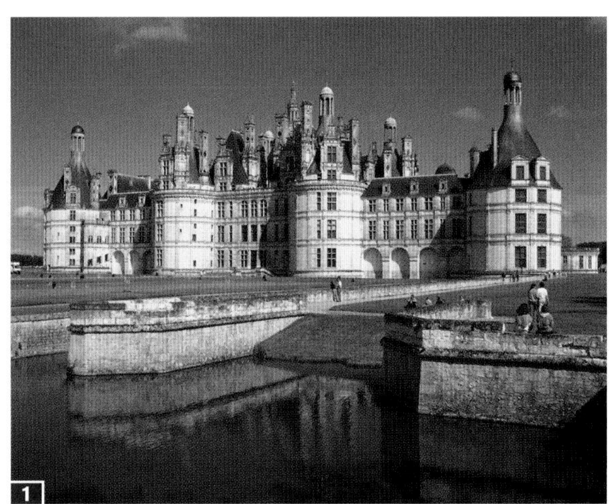

The last kings of the House of Valois were bested by the Habsburgs in the struggle for supremacy in Italy. Domestically, they had to contend with religious schism and a powerful and fractious nobility. The kings of the House of Bourbon presided over conflict between Catholics and Protestants. After compromises failed, a policy of repression saw the forced expulsion of the Protestant Huguenots. A series of capable kings and ministers built up an absolutist monarchy and made France a great European power. French became the universal language of European diplomacy and aristocratic society while Paris became the center of European culture. Under weaker successors, costly wars drained the royal coffers, and political and economic crises paved the way for social upheaval and revolution.

1 The Castle of Chambord, built by Francis I

The Struggle Against the Habsburgs

Francis I and his successors tried to weaken the power of the Habsburgs. The spread of Calvinism led to the first conflicts. At the same time, Renaissance ideas and culture became predominant in France.

In 1515 ❶, ❷ Francis I, a member of a side branch of the House of Valois, ascended to the throne of France. During his reign, the French court developed into a center of the European Renaissance, attracting important artists such as ❺ Leonardo da Vinci and Andrea del Sarto. Francis also spent money building up a considerable collection of Italian paintings including works by Titian and Raphael.

In foreign affairs, the king, like his predecessors, continued to compete with the Habsburgs for dominance in central Europe and Italy. Having lost out to Charles V for the emperor's crown in 1519, Francis was then defeated by him in the Italian Wars. Despite these reverses, Francis managed to cause his adversary considerable difficulty by allying himself with the Ottoman Empire and forcing the emperor into a war on two fronts. In the end, neither side managed to prevail.

Francis I was succeeded in 1547 by his son ❸ Henry II, who was married to Catherine de Médicis. She was the niece of Pope Clement VII, an ally against the Habsburgs (p. 292). Henry was under the political influence of his mistress, Diane de Poitiers, and on her advice, he took repressive measures against the ❹ French Protestants—even though he supported the Protestant princes of Germany with money and weapons—in their rebellion against the Habsburgs. Henry only accepted Habsburg dominance in Italy after a costly war that ended with the signing of the Treaty of Cateau-Cambrésis in 1559.

In the same year, the king was accidentally wounded in a joust and died from his injuries. His eldest son Francis II died one year after acceding to the throne. Charles IX and Henry III proved to be weak kings. The latter struggled to cope with the intrigues of his mother, Catherine, and the Duke of Guise, and with the religious turbulence that soon engulfed France.

3 Double grave monument of Henry II and Catherine de Médicis in the Abbey of St. Denis near Paris

4 The Protestant church "Le Paradis" in Lyon, painting, 17th century

2 Portrait of Francis I, bronze medallion by Benvenuto Cellini, 16th century

5 Francis I at the death bed of Leonardo da Vinci, painting by Jean-Auguste-D. Ingres, 19th century

1515 | Reign of Francis I begins
1519 | Charles V elected Holy Roman Emperor
1547 | Henry II ascends the throne
1559 | Treaty of Cateau-Cambrésis
1562 | Edict of St. Germain
1562 | Ambush of the Huguenots in Vassy

The Guise brothers, leaders of the Catholic faction; from left: Duke Charles of Mayenne, Duke Henry I of Guise, and Cardinal Louis of Lorraine, portrait from the 16th century

The French Wars of Religion and the Edict of Nantes

Bloody religious wars engulfed France during the reign of the last Valois king, Henry III. His successor, Henry IV of the House of Bourbon, was the first to be able to restore calm to the country with the Edict of Nantes.

Originating in the Swiss Cantons (p. 175), Calvinism gradually spread to France and steadily gained followers from the middle of the 16th century on. They were called Huguenots, a French derivative from the German word *Eidgenossen* ("Swiss confederate"). A substantial proportion of the nobility became Huguenots—particularly the Bourbons, who not only had large holdings in France but also ruled as sovereign kings in neighboring Navarre (p. 199). Being relatives of the Valois, they also had hereditary claims to the French throne. The mighty Catholic ❻ dukes of Guise were hostile to them.

Catherine de Médicis tried to play the factions off against one another to preserve the authority of the crown. To bind the Bourbons to her, she married off her daughter, Margaret, to Henry of Navarre in 1572. At the same time she planned to do away with the leader of the Huguenots, ❿ Gaspard de Coligny. When the assassination attempt failed, Catherine and the House of Guise, fearing revenge, initiated a massacre of thousands of Huguenots who had remained in Paris after the wedding on the ❾ night of St. Bartholomew's. Henry of Navarre fled to his kingdom, and his marriage to Margaret was later annulled.

A civil war broke out in France between the religious factions, including the nobility and the royal family. The "Holy League" of Catholics, founded in 1576 under the leadership of the dukes of Guise, allied with the Habsburgs, while the Huguenots were supported by England. In 1574, Catherine's third son, Henry III, then reigning as the king of Poland, ascended to the French throne (p. 302). He had no children and when the last of his brothers died in 1584, Henry of Navarre became the successor. Five years later, a monk murdered ❽ Henry III, and the Bourbon Huguenot Henry of Navarre succeeded him as ❼, ⓫ Henry IV. In order to be recognized as king, he converted to Catholicism in 1593, famously saying, "Paris is worth a Mass." In 1598 he signed the Edict of Nantes that granted rights to France's Protestant minority. He was murdered in 1610.

Henry IV on horseback and wearing a suit of armor, statue, Paris

Excerpt from the Edict of Nantes, issued by Henry IV:

"We forbid all our subjects, of some state and quality that they are, to renew the memory, to attack, to feel, to scold, or to provoke each other by reproach of what took place, for some cause and excuse whether it is, to compete for it, to dispute, quarrel or offend itself or take offence actually or at word, but contain itself and live peacefully together as brothers, friends and fellow countrymen..."

Henry IV signs the Edict of Nantes, wood engraving, 19th century

Dominican monk murders Henry III, copper engraving, 17th century

The St. Bartholomew's Day Massacre, 23–24 August,1572

Gaspard de Coligny, portrait, 16th c.

Coronation of Henry IV in Chartres,1594

23–24 Aug 1572 | Saint Bartholomew's Day Massacre
1576 | Founding of the "Holy League"
1589 | Assassination of Henry III
1593 | Henry IV converts to Catholicism
1598 | Edict of Nantes

The Rise of France under Henry IV and Cardinal Richelieu

Under the leadership of the cunning strategist Cardinal Richelieu, France was able to weaken the power of the Habsburgs in the Thirty Years' War and to centralize the French state.

1 Ravaillac, the murderer of Henry IV, is quartered, colored copper engraving, early 17th century

After the turmoil of the Wars of Religion, Henry IV and his minister Sully set about reconstructing France. But in 1610 the king was murdered by the Catholic fanatic ❶ Ravaillac. ❹ Maria de Medici, the mother of Henry's son who was still a minor, ran the affairs of state for him. In 1616, she brought the future Cardinal Richelieu into the court. He won the confidences of the reserved ❸ Louis XIII and rose to become the leading minister in 1624. Such was his power that, following a conspiracy, he even forced the queen mother to flee the country.

Internationally, the gifted and unscrupulous power broker Richelieu sought to make France the leading power in Europe, while domestically he worked to strengthen the monarchy. He began by abolishing some of the special privileges of the nobility and oversaw a military campaign to crush the power of the French-protestant Huguenots. Provincial revolts against tax rises were also brutally suppressed. At the same time, he was a generous patron of the ❺ arts and founded the *Académie française.*

In foreign affairs, he seized the chance offered by the Thirty Years' War to weaken France's major rival, the Habsburgs. With cool calculation, he supported the Protestant princes against the Catholic emperor with both money and weapons. He also persuaded Gustav II Adolf of Sweden to fight the Habsburgs. Richelieu died in 1642, followed a year later by the king he had served, Louis XIII. France profited from the cardinal's aggressive policies in the Peace of Westphalia signed in 1648 (p. 269). The country gained territories in Alsace and the Pyrenees at the expense of the Habsburg Empire.

After his death, another Cardinal, the Italian ❷ Mazarin, became first minister of the French government. He initially ruled with Anna of Austria, Louis XIII's widow, who acted as regent for her son, Louis XIV.

2 Cardinal Mazarin, copy of a painting by Champaigne, 17th century

3 Queen Anna of Austria, King Louis XIII, and Cardinal Richelieu, still from the film *The Three Musketeers*

The Three Musketeers

Today, Richelieu is less known for his political achievements and services to the arts and culture – he was elected principal of the Sorbonne in 1622 – than for the role he plays in Alexandre Dumas' novel The Three Musketeers. In it the young guardsman d'Artagnan fights together with the three inseparable musketeers Athos, Porthos, and Aramis against the sinister Richelieu. With the help of the mysterious Lady de Winter, the jealous cardinal is determined to uncover a love affair between Queen Anna of Austria and the English prime minister, Buckingham.

above: Duel between the king's musketeers and Cardinal Richelieu's guard, watercolor sketch

4 Triumph of the regent Maria de Medici, painting by Rubens, 1623

5 The chapel of the Sorbonne, sponsored by Richelieu

1610 | Murder of Henry IV by Ravaillac
1624 | Richelieu becomes de facto ruler of France
1631 | Treaty of Barwalde
1635 | *Académie française* founded
1642 | Richelieu's death

The reign of the the "Sun King" Louis XIV

Cardinal Mazarin continued Richelieu's policies and established the foundations of the absolutism of Louis XIV. During his reign France became the leading European power, both culturally and politically. The opulent royal court at Versailles became a model for rulers throughout the continent.

Inciting a crowd against Mazarin, the Louvre of Paris in the background, etching, 17th century

Though the Peace of Westphalia in 1648 marked a major success for Mazarin, his domestic power base was weak. In a series of armed uprisings known as the *Fronde*, dissident French nobles ❻ revolted against the authority of the king and his ministers between 1648 and 1653. It proved to be the last revolt of the French nobility, and henceforth they would be subordinate to the power of the ruling monarch and his royal court.

Upon the death of the cardinal in 1661, ❼ Louis XIV took personal charge of the affairs of state. The ❾ Palace of Versailles, the new royal residence located outside the capital Paris, became a symbol of the king's alleged claim "*L'état c'est moi*" ("I am the state"). Woods and ❿ landscaped parks ran up to the palace, with the Hall of Mirrors and the ❽ Royal Bedchamber as its center. The vast court of almost 20,000 people was the physical embodiment of Louis XIV's claim to rule by "divine right." His palace and his court were imitated by princes throughout Europe.

As in Versailles, everything in the state was supposed to be concentrated on the monarch known as the "Sun King." He did not tolerate overweening ministers like Richelieu or Mazarin. Several ministers together saw to the details of government for him. The finance minister, Jean-Baptiste Colbert, was also in charge of building up the fleet and an active colonial policy focussed on North America and India. Under his supervision the royal coffers swelled. His rival, the Minister of War, François Michel Louvois, built up one of the mightiest armies in Europe and pressured the king into an expansionist foreign policy. Despite fighting a series of wars both in Europe and the New World, France made few territorial gains.

King Louis XIV of France, painting by Rigaud, 1701

The French Protestants suffered as Louis XIV sought to establish the supremacy of the French Catholic Church with himself at its head. He revoked the Edict of Nantes in 1685 and expelled the Huguenots from France. The flight of the Huguenots was a major loss to the French economy because the Protestants had played a significant role as merchants and skilled manufacturers. These refugees successfully established themselves in neighboring Protestant countries, building thriving communities in both Amsterdam and London.

Voltaire, the Political Philosopher on King Louis XIV:

"He had failings and afflictions and he made mistakes - but would those who judge him have equaled him, if they had been in his place? One will not be able to speak his name without awe."

above: Louis XIV, marble bust by Bernini, 1665
right: A young Louis XIV as the "Rising Sun," sketch for a ballet costume

The lavishly decorated royal bedchamber in the Palace of Versailles, near Paris

The Palace of Versailles, originally a hunting lodge but by 1682 Louis XIV's main residence

View from the Palace of Versailles, across the formal gardens, down towards the Grand Canal

1643 Cardinal Mazarin takes over affairs of state
1648 Peace of Westphalia
1648–1653 Civil wars of the Fronde
1661 Reign of Louis XIV begins
1685 Revocation of the Edict of Nantes

The Wars of Louis XIV

In his attempts to enlarge France's borders, Louis XIV drew other European states into a series of conflicts. The War of the Grand Alliance and the War of the Spanish Succession were inconclusive but nonetheless showed that France could not maintain its hegemony on the continent.

Louis XIV, with the help of his generals Condé, ❶ Turenne, ❷ Vauban, and Vendôme, waged numerous wars of aggression. Although territories were gained in the campaigns against Spain and the Netherlands—Spain, for example, was forced to relinquish Burgundy and parts of its Dutch territories in the Peace of Nijmegen in 1679—French expansionism led to a permanent alliance among the Habsburgs and most of the German princes, England, and the Netherlands.

Louis used the death of the Palatinate elector as an opportunity to make hereditary claims in the name of his sister-in-law, Elizabeth Charlotte, duchess of Orléans. In 1688 he occupied the Palatinate and other parts of the Holy Roman Empire, and in the process his armies pillaged a number of cities, including ❹ Heidelberg. This aggression ensured the unity of the Grand Alliance against France. A drawn-out war followed, in which the French navy was destroyed by a combined Anglo-Dutch fleet, but France held its own on land. The 1697 Treaty of Ryswick did little other than restore the pre-war status quo.

Plan of the city of Freiburg showing the defenses established by Vauban, ink sketch, 1685

The ❺ War of Spanish Succession began in 1701 after the line of the Spanish Habsburgs (p. 297) died out, and the throne was claimed by both the Austrian Habsburgs and the French Bourbons. Louis wished to place his grandson, Philippe Duke of Anjou, on the Spanish throne, while the Habsburgs backed a non-Bourbon candidate. Despite the defeat of the French armies in the war that followed, Philippe was confirmed king of Spain in 1713 at the Peace of Utrecht. However, he was removed from the French line to prevent a union of France and Spain. The Austrian Habsburgs also gained most of the former Spanish territories (p. 300) in the Low Countries and Italy.

Despite Louis XIV's attempts to expand his dominion through war and diplomacy, a policy that placed a ❸ heavy burden on the French population, French supremacy was replaced by a new balance of power in Europe, with the Habsburgs and English kings able to counterbalance France.

1 Henri de La Tour d'Auvergne, Count of Turenne, painting by Le Brun, 17th c.

Collecting the taxes: "The nobleman is the spider, the peasant the fly", satirical cartoon, 17th c.

The Castle of Heidelberg, seized by the French army during the War of the Grand Alliance

Victory of the Austrians and British, led by Prince Eugène and the Duke of Marlborough, over the French army at Malplaquet, 1709

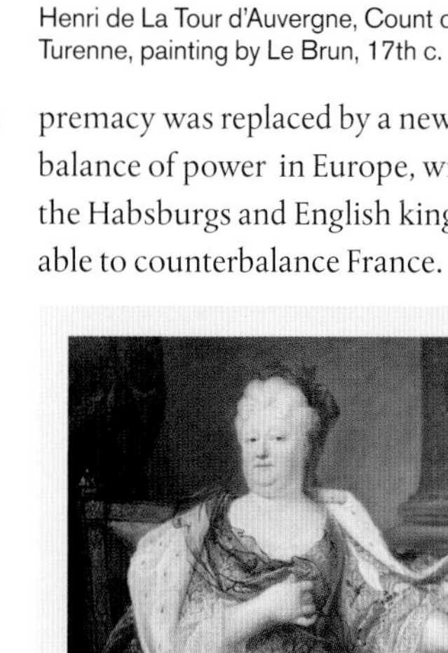

Liselotte of the Palatinate

Princess Elizabeth Charlotte, "Madame," was married to Philippe I, duke of Orléans and brother of Louis XIV, in 1671. The completely unpretentious duchess was known as "Madame." She had a difficult position at the French court alongside "Monsieur," her husband, who did not bother to conceal his numerous homosexual affairs. She vented her anger in innumerable often caustic letters to her German relatives: "Being a Madame is a wretched trade."

above: Elizabeth Charlotte of the Palatinate, Duchess of Orléans, portrait, ca. 1715

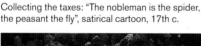

1667 | War of Devolution in the Spanish Netherlands
1679 | Peace of Nijmegen
1688 | War of the Grand Alliance begins
1697 | Treaty of Ryswick
1701 | War of the Spanish Succession begins
1713 | Peace of Utrecht

France under Louis XV and Louis XVI

Louis XIV's heirs possessed neither his political ambition nor his abilities, but they were confronted by endemic financial crises. At the same time the institution of absolutist monarchy came under increasing attack from radical writers inspired by the ideas of the Enlightenment.

Louis XIV outlived both his son and his grandson and was followed to the throne in 1715 by his five-year-old great-grandson ❻, ❽ Louis XV.

Even after coming of age, Louis XV left the running of the government to the acting regent Cardinal Fleury. The cardinal cleaned up the state finances and tried as far as possible to keep France out of international conflicts. Louis's marriage to Maria Leszczynska—daughter of the Polish king Stanislaw I, who had been deposed and wanted to regain his throne—was the only entanglement. Instead of his throne, Stanislaw received the duchy of Lorraine in 1737, which reverted to France after his death in 1766.

7 Voltaire, sculpture by Houdon, 1778

After the death of Fleury in 1743, Louis increasingly came under the influence of his mistresses. Perhaps the most significant of them was the ⓭ Marquise de Pompadour. She originated from the bourgeoisie and maintained an influence over French policies—even after her sexual relationship with the king ended—for almost 20 years, until her death in 1764. She was influential in France's alliance with Austria against Prussia and England in the ❿ Seven Years' War (1756–1763), which ended in defeat and humiliation for France. The huge expense of fighting against England in the New World, where France lost her last colonial possessions, took a massive toll on the royal finances.

The court was maintained in luxury at enormous expense, while the living standards of the ⓫ common people, on whom most tax burden fell, remained low. At the end of Louis' reign, France was virtually bankrupt. At the same time, the ideas of the Enlightenment were gaining currency. ❼ Voltaire, Montesquieu, and Rousseau developed their ideas of a just and enlightened society and attacked the despotism of absolutist monarchy. Many minor writers popularized these ideas in satirical poems and pamphlets that stirred up resentment towards the king's lifestyle.

Louis XV's successor in 1774 was his grandson Louis XVI, who had been married since 1770 to ⓬ Marie Antoinette, a daughter of Maria Theresa. She was widely attacked in the radical press, which dubbed her "the Austrian bitch." As the financial situation worsened, Louis looked to reform but failed to win the cooperation of the nobility, who sought to protect their ❾ privileges. In an attempt to break the deadlock, the king summoned the States General in 1788, an assembly of the clergy, nobility, and commoners that had not met since 1614. Radical populist figures, backed by the hungry crowds of Paris, quickly came to dominate the assembly, firing the opening salvos of the French Revolution.

9 A peasant carries the nobility and clergy on his back, cartoon satirizing the social order, 18th century

11 *Old Peasant Couple Eating*, painting by Georges de la Tour, ca.1620

6 Louis XV's crown

8 Louis XV, painting by Maurice-Quentin de La Tour, 18th century

10 French Québec in ruins after bombardment by the British fleet in 1759 during the Seven Years' War

12 Queen Marie Antoinette, portrait by Élisabeth-Louise Vigée-Lebrun, 1783

13 Madame de Pompadour, portrait by François Boucher, 1756-58

1715 | Death of Louis XIV
1715–1743 | Cardinal Fleury is regent for Louis XV
1756-63 | Seven Years' War
1774 | Louis XVI comes to power
1788 | Summoning of the States General

Flagship of the British Royal Navy

The Rise of England 1485–ca. 1800

The history of modern England began with the reign of the Tudors in 1485. They turned England once more into a player in European politics. The Stuarts, who reigned from 1603, united England and Scotland into an empire that has been named Great Britain since 1707, but did not succeed in establishing absolutism after the French model. Parliament was able to impose a constitutional monarchy during the civil war between 1642 and 1649 and finally in the "Glorious Revolution" of 1688–89. Furthermore, in the Act of Settlement parliament ensured that any future monarch of England would be Protestant. In 1714, the elector of Hanover inherited the British throne. In the 18th century, Great Britain finally became a world power through its ❶ sea trade and colonial policies.

England under Henry VII and Henry VIII

The first two Tudor rulers ruthlessly expanded the power of the monarchy. England was severed from the ecclesiastical sovereignty of the pope, and opposition in the country was suppressed.

In 1485, ❷ Henry Tudor, the Lancastrian heir, defeated Richard III from the rival House of York at Bosworth Field and seized the throne as Henry VII. He ended the War of the Roses (p. 187) by marrying Elizabeth of York, Richard III's niece. With strict economizing and high taxes, he brought the state finances into order. He also centralized jurisdiction in the royal supreme court.

The ascent to the throne of his son ❸ Henry VIII in 1509 was greeted at first with enthusiasm. Initially, his politics were determined by Cardinal ❺ Thomas Wolsey, who developed royal centralism and abroad followed a seesaw policy between the Habsburgs and France. In 1528, Henry decided to divorce his wife, Catherine of Aragon, the aunt of Charles V, partly because of the lack of a male heir but also because of his love for Anne Boleyn, a lady of the court. Under pressure from the Habsburgs, the pope wouldn't allow the divorce, and the process took years.

During this period, Henry's reign degenerated into tyranny. Cardinal Wolsey was dismissed in 1529 and charged with high treason. Thomas More, Wolsey's successor as lord chancellor, was executed. With the aid of the new, unscrupulous lord chancellor Thomas Cromwell, the king severed the English church from the papacy in 1534, creating an Anglican state church with the king as its head. Catholic ❻ church properties were confiscated or given to nobility, and monasteries were disbanded. After his first divorce, Henry VIII married five more times; two of his ❹ wives were executed. No English king had ever possessed so much personal power, which Henry used to dispose of opposing nobility and adversaries of his church policies.

Henry VIII, painting by Hans Holbein the younger, 1540

Henry VII's coat of arms with the white rose and the red rose, the symbols of houses of Lancaster and York

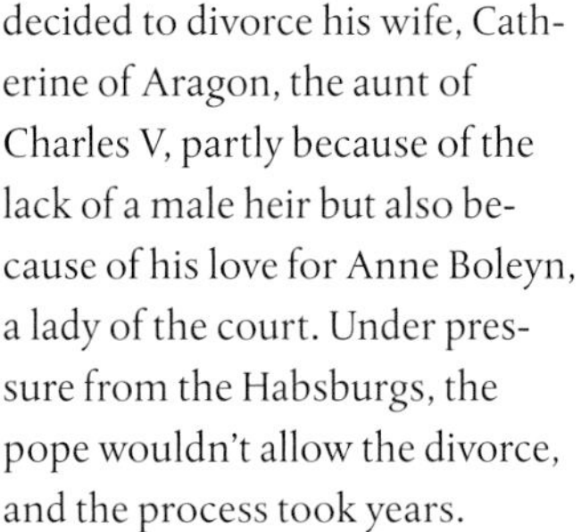

left: Henry VIII and his wives; Anne of Cleves, Kathryn Howard, Anna Boleyn, Catherine of Aragon, Catherine Parr, Jane Seymour, lithograph, 19th century
near right: Hampton Court Palace near London, residence of Cardinal Wolsey, later confiscated by Henry VIII during the church reforms
far right: Byland Abbey in Yorkshire, former Cistercian abbey, abolished by Henry VIII

1485 | Reign of Henry VII begins
1509 | Cardinal Wolsey rules under Henry VIII
1516 | Thomas More's *Utopia*
1529 | Wolsey dismissed
1534 | Anglican Church splits from Roman Church
1535 | Thomas More murdered
1547 | Edward VI crowned

The Reign of the Tudors to Elizabeth I

Anglicanism strengthened its position during the reigns of Henry VIII's children, with but one interruption for a short phase of Catholic revanchism. Elizabeth I's naval policies simultaneously made England a great European power.

Henry VIII was followed in 1547 by his young son Edward VI, whose regency was contested by the dukes of Somerset and Northumberland. During his reign, the Anglican archbishop of Canterbury, Thomas Cranmer, formulated the creed and in 1553 the 42 articles of faith of the Anglicans as well as the renowned Book of Common Prayer. Edward was followed to the throne in 1553 by his elder sister ❼ Mary, the Catholic daughter of Henry's first wife Catherine of Aragon. In 1554, she restored papal jurisdiction in England and married her cousin Philip II of Spain. Her brutal persecution of Protestants—among them Archbishop Cranmer, who was burned at the stake in 1556—earned her the nickname "Bloody Mary."

In 1558, Mary's Protestant half-sister ❾ Elizabeth I, the daughter of Anne Boleyn, came to power. Though declared illegitimate, she had been magnificently educated in the "new learning" of the Renaissance. At first she acted cautiously in religious affairs, but then in 1564, with the "Thirty-Nine Articles" she finally secured the position of the Anglican state church. After the elimination of Mary Stuart's claims to the throne (p. 284), Elizabeth supported the Protestant Netherlands in their struggle for liberation, which led to war with Spain. The English fleet annihilated the numerically far superior Spanish ⓫ Armada in 1588, which dramatically marked the end of Spanish supremacy at sea and the rise of English sea power. Afterward, Elizabeth had Spanish ships captured in an unofficial war by privateers like ❽ Francis Drake. It was increasingly clear that England was becoming a leading European power.

8 Sir Francis Drake, miniature, 16th c.

Domestically, the unmarried queen understood how to deftly play her ❿ favorites and aides against each other and assert the monarchy's authority. The Elizabethan Age produced a tremendous upswing in trade, as well as significant cultural achievements, of which the works of ⓬ William Shakespeare are a shining example. In 1584, Elizabeth gave Sir Walter Raleigh permission to set up the first English colony in North America. It was named Virginia after the "virgin queen." In 1600, the East India Company—an important factor in trade and colonial policies—was chartered.

10 Elizabeth I surrounded by her household, painting, ca. 1580

7 The Catholic Queen Mary Tudor, painting, 16th century

9 Elizabeth I with the Armada in the background, painting, 1588

11 Confrontation of the English Navy (left) with the Spanish Armada (right), copper engraving, 18th century

Thomas More

Thomas More, who in 1516 wrote about an ideal state in the novel Utopia, became lord chancellor of England in 1529 after long experience as a member of Parliament. As he rejected the divorce of the king and the Reformation, he stepped down, but he was still accused by Henry VIII of high treason for refusing to recognize the Act of Supremacy that designated the king as head of the church and beheaded in July 1535. In 1935, the Catholic Church canonized him as a martyr.

Arrest and execution of Thomas More, painting, 16th century

12 London Globe Theatre reconstructed to look as it did in Shakespeare's time

1554 | Re-Catholicizing of England under Mary I
1554–1558 | Persecution of Protestants
1558 | Elizabeth I becomes queen
1564 | Elizabeth I's "Thirty-Nine Articles"
1584 | First English colony in North America
1600 | Founding of the East India Company

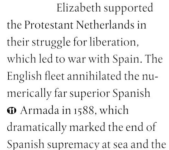

The Reign of the Stuarts

The personal union of the crowns of England and Scotland was brought about by James I, the son of Mary Stuart, in 1603. He and his son Charles I failed with their idea of an absolute monarchy, and Charles was executed.

When the House of Tudor died out with Elizabeth I in 1603, King James VI of the Scottish ❺ Stuarts succeeded in England as James I. James's mother, ❶ Mary Stuart, known as Mary Queen of Scots, a granddaughter of Henry VII (p. 189) and a Scottish queen since birth, had raised a claim to the English throne in 1558. The Catholic queen saw in Elizabeth only the illegitimate child of Henry VIII and not a rightful claimant to the throne. During her reign in Scotland, a Calvinistic Reformation took place under ❸ John Knox that combined with civil wars and acts of violence even in the immediate surroundings of the queen. In 1578 Mary was deposed by a rebellion of Protestant nobles and imprisoned. She managed to escape to England, but was held captive there as well. When her intimate friends and England's Catholics tried to set her free, Queen Elizabeth had her charged with high treason and, in 1587, ❻ executed.

Mary Stuart, painting, 16th century

James I and VI, painting, 17th century

❹ James I tried to bring about a reconciliation between the faiths. He wanted to establish royal absolutism in England after the union of the two kingdoms, but failed due to the resistance of Parliament. The dispute over royal rights continued, but James adopted the Anglican state church model, which disappointed the Catholics. He insisted on the principle of the Divine Right of Kings to rule.

James's second son ❷ Charles I, who took over the throne from his father in 1625, also tended toward absolutism and approached Spain against the will of Parliament. Up until 1640, he reacted to the resistance of the members of Parliament by repeatedly dissolving Parliament or not calling it into session, which inflamed the temper of the country. His unfortunate ecclesiastical policies led to revolts in Scotland and his permanent financial crisis forced him to summon the so-called Long Parliament, which ousted the king's favorites and leading ministers, and stayed in session until 1653. The parliamentary majority led by John Pym allied itself with the Scots, and in 1642 a civil war broke out, with the king and the royalist minority opposing the parliamentary majority, whose troops were commanded by Oliver Cromwell. After several defeats, in 1644–45 the king fled to Scotland but was handed over to the English Parliament in 1646. In 1647 he escaped and war broke out again, but in 1648 Charles I was recaptured and, after a trial before the Lower House, ❼ executed for high treason in London in 1649.

The Stuart king Charles II from three perspectives, painting by Paul van Dyck, ca. 1635

John Knox, copper engraving

Holyrood Palace, the residence of the Scottish kings, construction begun in1528, 19th century photograph

The execution of Mary Stuart, on February 8, 1587 in Fotheringhay

Execution of Charles I in front of the Banqueting House in London, copper engraving, 17th century

1587 | Beheading of Mary Stuart **1625** | Charles I becomes king **1642** | Civil war beaks out **1646** | Charles I is handed over to the Parliamentarians

1603-25 | Reign of James I **1640** | Calling of the "Long Parliament" **1644–45** | Flight of Charles I **30 Jan 1649** | Beheading of Charles

The "Glorious Revolution"

Oliver Cromwell abolished the monarch and ruled as lord protector over England, but in 1660 the Stuarts were restored to the throne. The Catholic James II was removed from power in the "Glorious Revolution" of 1688–89.

❽ Oliver Cromwell, leader of the English Puritans, abolished the monarchy in 1649 and proclaimed England a Protestant "free state," in the first stage of the English civil war. There was an immediate uprising by the Scots and Irish in 1649–1650, which Cromwell bloodily suppressed. Although he aspired to a republic, Cromwell dissolved Parliament in 1653 and, when it did not settle its internal strife, made himself "lord protector" with ⓭ dictatorial powers, refusing the title of king. In foreign affairs, Cromwell strengthened England's supremacy at sea through well-directed colonial and trade policies and prevailed over the Netherlands in their trade rivalry. After his death in 1658, his son Richard could not hold onto power and abdicated, clearing the way for the restoration of the Stuarts.

In 1660 ❾ Charles II, the son of Charles I, returned from exile. Though the new monarch punished the republicans, he worked for a political reconciliation of all parties. The Habeas Corpus Act, an important milestone in civil rights—under which no person may be held in custody without judicial review and being duly charged with an offense—was passed by Parliament in 1679.

8 Parliament in session, back of the state seal created by Oliver Cromwell in 1651

During Charles II's reign, the ❿ "Great Fire of London" broke out in 1666. It destroyed large parts of the city and made extensive reconstruction of the city necessary.

When Charles's Catholic brother, ⓬ James II, ascended to the throne in 1685, some of the nobles arose in protest but were subdued. Overturning a ban instituted by Charles II, James gave government posts to Catholics, and he proclaimed religious freedom for Catholics and those diverging from the state church in 1686–87. The birth of his son in 1688 fed fears of a permanent Catholic and absolutist monarchy in England. Parliament, the army, and the middle class then offered the crown to the Protestant regent of the Netherlands, ⓫ William of Orange. In the "Glorious Revolution" of 1688–89, William landed in England and expelled James to France in December 1688. William III and his wife Mary II, James II's Protestant daughter from his first marriage, then ascended the throne as joint sovereigns after they had acquiesced to the "Declaration of Right" presented to them by Parliament and later incorporated into an Act of Parliament known as the Bill of Rights. The Bill of Rights established the rights of Parliament in relationship to the crown and a constitutional monarchy controlled by Parliament.

11 William of Orange, the future king William III, sails to England, painting, 1689

13 Puritans under orders from Oliver Cromwell search and arrest noblemen, painting, 19th century

12 James II's cruelties to the Protestants in Ireland, copper engraving, 17th century

9 Charles II, painting, 17th century

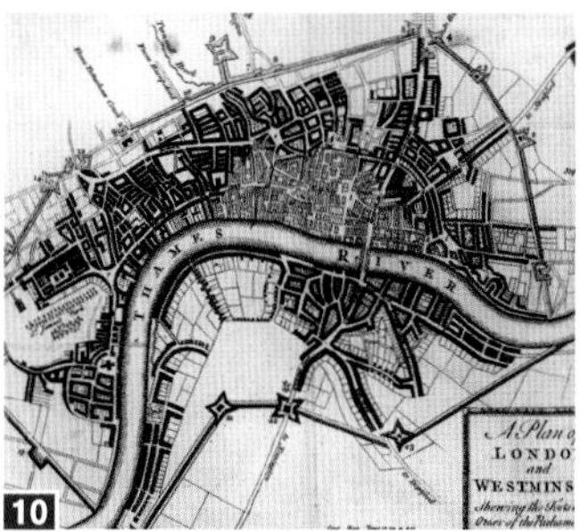

10 Map of London after the fire of 1666, copper engraving, 18th century

The Gunpowder Plot

Catholic nobility loyal to James I swore to blow up Parliament when it opened in 1605. They hid a great quantity of gunpowder in the cellar of Parliament, but the conspiracy was betrayed and the plotters caught and executed. The failure of the Gunpowder Plot is still celebrated in Great Britain on November 5 as Guy Fawkes Day.

Execution of the participants in the Gunpowder Plot, copper engraving, 17th century

1649–50 | Scots and Irish revolt

1679 | Passing of "Habeas Corpus Act"

1688–89 | "Glorious Revolution"

1649 | Oliver Cromwell proclaims England a Commonwealth

1686–87 | Religious freedom for Catholics

1689 | "Bill of Rights"

The Reign of the House of Hanover

England fought against France's supremacy in Europe and developed its colonial territories. In 1714, Parliament established the succession of the Protestant Welfs (or Guelfs).

As regent of both countries, ❶ William III ended the conflict between England and the Netherlands. He defeated the Irish, who had supported James II, in the Battle of Boyne in 1690, and the Scots at the massacre of Glencoe. The king's engagement on the Continent, where he was fighting in alliance with the Habsburgs against Louis XIV's claims, was unpopular in England because he used English troops to defend his Dutch interests.

When the king died in 1702 at the start of the War of Spanish Succession, his sister-in-law ❷ Anne (1665–1714), the last of the Protestant Stuarts, followed him on the throne. During her reign, in 1707, England and Scotland were unified into Great Britain, with a single Parliament. However, Anne was a weak monarch who was under the controlling influence of the ❹ Duke and Duchess of Marlborough.

1 William III depicted during the Battle of Boyne, painting, 18th century

In 1704, the English occupied Gibraltar and Menorca. After the victories of Marlborough and Prince Eugène of Savoy over the French in the ❺ battles of Hochstadt and Blenheim in 1704, Oudenaarde in 1708, and Malplaquet in 1709, Great Britain was the primary benefactor at the Peace of Utrecht in 1713 which put an end to the War of the Spanish Succession. It was allowed to keep its conquests and received part of the French colonies in North America.

2 Memorial for Queen Anne Stuart in front of St. Paul's Cathedral, London

3 George I, colored copper engraving, ca. 1730

In the Act of Settlement (1701), Parliament had excluded Catholics and anyone married to a Catholic from the succession to the throne as well as establishing that parliament determines who succeeds to the throne.

Thus the electoral widow Sophie of Hanover, a grandchild of James I, was the next Protestant heir apparent. After Anne's death, Sophie's son, Elector George Louis of Hanover, ascended the throne as ❸ George I. Great Britain and Hanover were ruled in personal union until 1837. The reign of the House of Hanover continued until Queen Victoria's death in 1901.

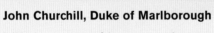

John Churchill, Duke of Marlborough

John Churchill had a very successful career as a military commander in the army under James II. He later shifted his allegiance to William of Orange, though he still maintained contact with James, which brought him under suspicion of treason. His wife, Sarah Jennings, was a close friend of Anne Stuart, who after ascending to the throne made Churchill commander-in-chief of the English troops in the War of Spanish Succession and in 1702 elevated him to duke of Marlborough. He was victorious over the French and was regarded as the savior of the motherland. In gratitude, Anne gave him land and money and had Blenheim Palace built for the duke and his wife. Sir Winston Churchill, a descendent of the first duke, was born there in 1874.

above: Blenheim Palace, Oxfordshire, built by John Vanbrugh and Nicholas Hawksmoore

4 John Churchill, first duke of Marlborough, painting, 1705

5 Battle of Hochstadt, copper engraving, 18th century

1690 | Battle of Boyne
1701 | "Act of Settlement"
1704 | Occupation of Gibraltar and Menorca
1707 | Union of England and Scotland forms Great Britain
1714 | George I becomes king

The Hanoverian Kings and the Growing Power of the Prime Minister

Parliament continued to gain power under the kings of the House of Hanover. Great Britain was able to expand its colonial territories at France's expense, but was forced to accept the American colonies' independence.

❼ Robert Walpole (1676–1745) was the first "modern" British prime minister in that he established collegiate Cabinet responsibility. He served the Hanoverian kings as Secretary for War, Chancellor of the Exchequer, and then Chief Minister. Completely trusted by King ❻ George I and then after 1727 by his son ❿ George II, as well as by a majority of the Whigs in Parliament, he determined Great Britain's policies between 1721 and 1742. He tried to ensure peace in foreign affairs, and when Great Britain became involved in the War of Austrian Succession, he resigned in 1742.

7 Sir Robert Walpole, Earl of Oxford, copper engraving

The Catholic pretender to the throne, Charles Edward Stuart—a grandson of James II and commonly known as Bonnie Prince Charlie—used a British defeat by the French as an excuse to land in Scotland. After initial successes, he and his Scottish supporters from the highland clans were crushed at ⓫ Culloden in 1746.

The balance of European powers remained a foreign policy aim. Upon the urging of ❽ William Pitt the Elder, Great Britain intervened in the Seven Years' War and, under the Treaty of Paris in 1763, was able to take the French colonies in North America and India. George II was followed by his grandson, ❾ George III, in 1760. To become independent of the Whigs and gain more weight in the government, he turned to the Tories. His policies led to the war of independence of the American colonies (p. 342). The focus of political decision making now clearly rested in Parliament. The king's mental illness also weakened the position of the crown. From 1811 until the death of George III in 1820, his son, the future George IV, reigned as regent. The most important prime minister under George III, ⓬ William Pitt the Younger, reduced state debt and brought the East India Company under government control. In 1793, war with France (p. 360) began.

Whigs and Tories

An election party of the Whigs, copper engraving by Hogarth, 1755

Two factions confronted each other in the British Parliament: the Whigs and the Tories. They were the only political parties in Britain until the mid 19th century. Both terms were originally derisive nicknames: "tory" came from an Irish word for outlaws, "whigs" were Scottish Presbyterian rebels. The Whigs stood for political and economic liberalism, a strong Parliament, and religious tolerance, the conservative Tories defended the rights of the Anglican Church and crown.

6 The Composer Handel and King George I at the Thames enjoying a performance of Handel's "Water Music", steel engraving, 19th century

8 William Pitt the Elder, Earl of Chatham, mezzotint, 18th century

9 George III, painting, 18th century

10 London at the time of George II, royal barque on the Thames and St. Paul's cathedral in the background, painting by Canaletto, 18th century

11 Charles Edward Stuart, called "The Young Pretender" or Bonnie Prince Charlie, in the battle of Culloden, steel engraving, 19th century

12 Caricature of William Pitt the Younger at a Parliament debate entitled "The Back-Less Pitt," etching, 1792

1721–42 | Robert Walpole leads the government
1763 | Treaty of Paris
1775–83 | American War of Independence
1784 | Government takes control of East India Company
1793 | Declaration of war on France

The Netherlands: From the Struggle for Independence to the French Occupation 1477–1795

The independence that the Habsburgs fought for after the Reformation led to the Netherlands' fight for liberation from the rule of the Catholic kings of Spain. It culminated in 1581 in the independence of the Protestant northern provinces under William I of Orange. The fight between the Calvinist-dominated north and the Habsburg-loyal, Catholic south was drawn out until 1621. The United Provinces of the Netherlands, under the regency of the House of Orange, experienced its golden age as a naval, trading, and ❶ cultural power in the 17th century but was eventually displaced by Great Britain.

1 *The Nightwatch*, a depiction of the Amsterdam citizens' brigade, painting by Rembrandt, 1642

The Beginnings of the Struggle for Liberation

The prosperous and self-confident Netherlands, under the influence of the Reformation and Calvinism, became involved in progressively more serious conflicts with their sovereign rulers, the Catholic Habsburgs.

In 1477, the Netherlands, which belonged to the dukes of Burgundy, was transferred to the Habsburgs through the marriage of Mary of Burgundy to the future Holy Roman emperor Maximilian I of Austria. Maximilian combined most of the provinces into the "Burgundian Circle" in 1512. The privileges of the circle were greatly enhanced by his grandson Charles V, who ruled the Netherlands from 1506.

Calvinism gained a foothold in the Netherlands from 1540 on. An uprising occurred in Geneva, Charles's birthplace, in 1542, and radical Calvinists organized ❹ organized the destruction of Catholic churches. The monarch Mary of Hungary, Charles's sister, pursued a policy of compromise, but when Charles ❺ abdicated in 1555 and the Netherlands fell to his son Philip II of Spain, Philip rejected any conciliation with the Protestants. He made his half-sister ❻ Margaret of Parma regent in 1559, and she reintroduced her aunt's policy of compromise, but by then the almost completely Calvinist nobility of the Netherlands demanded the withdrawal of the Inquisition and the Spanish as well as religious freedom.

3 Caricature depicting Duke of Alba and his violent regime in the Netherlands; the dead bodies of Egmont and Hoorn lie at his feet, copper engraving, 16th century

After fruitless negotiations, Philip II decided on harsh measures and in 1567 sent the ❸ Duke of Alba into the Netherlands leading Spanish troops, whereupon the regent stepped down. Alba restored monarchial rule by force, capturing the leaders of the opposition, the counts Egmont and Hoorn, in September and had them beheaded in June 1568 in Brussels. Now the whole of the Netherlands was in open rebellion; the war of independence had begun. The Protestants, who were mockingly called *Geusen* ("beggars") by the Spanish, adopted the name for themselves and involved the Spanish in a guerrilla war. The Spanish answered with brutal ❷ retaliatory measures.

2 Mass executions in the Netherlands, copper engraving, 16th century

4 Looting and destruction of a Catholic church by the Calvinists, copper engraving, 16th century

5 Charles V assigns rule over the Netherlands to his son, Philip II, painting, 19th century

6 William of Orange protests at an audience with Margaret of Parma, painting, 19th century

1477 | The Netherlands falls to the Habsburgs
1512 | Founding of the "Burgundian Circle"
1542 | Calvinist uprising in Geneva
1555 | Philip II of Spain governs the Netherlands
1559 | Margaret of Parma becomes regent of the Netherlands

The Dutch War of Independence

The struggle for Dutch independence from Spain intensified under the repressive rule of the Duke of Alba. It culminated in independence in 1581. The leaders of the freedom fighters were William I of Orange and his family.

7 William of Orange, painting, 16th century

In 1556 Calvinist riots provoked Philip II of Spain to increasingly repress religious dissidents in the Netherlands. In 1568 ❼, ❾ William I of Orange, of the House of Nassau-Dillenburg and originally a confidant of Charles V, took over the leadership of the Dutch Protestants. The Dutch republic owed its existence to William's devotion to the cause of independence from Spain.

William and his brothers John VI, the reigning duke of Nassau-Dillenburg, and Louis were leading exponents of a combative Calvinism in the empire. Louis traveled throughout Bohemia and Hungary to forge alliances with radical Protestants. Since 1567, about 60,000 of the empire's persecuted Calvinists had poured into the Netherlands and had fortified the resolve for freedom there. In 1572, William pushed into the Netherlands with Protestant troops and seized several cities from the Spanish. In the face of these successes, Philip II recalled the Duke of Alba as governor-general in 1573.

9 Equestrian statue of William of Orange

Following negotiations over a cease-fire, the final phase of the revolt began in 1576. William enacted laws for the northern provinces, but a union with the southern provinces failed due to ❽ Geusen unwillingness to compromise in matters of religion. In 1579, the seven northern provinces of Holland, Friesland, Gelderland, Zeeland, Overijssel, Utrecht, and Groningen—the United Provinces—formed the Utrecht Union, with William as its *stadhouder* or governor, and officially broke with Spain in 1581 to form the Republic of the United Netherlands. In 1579, the southern provinces had joined together in the Union of Arras and recognized the Spanish governor-general, ⓫ Alexander Farnese, duke of Parma; they later formed the ⓬ Spanish Netherlands, which was ruled by the Habsburgs. The war, however, continued because Farnese wavered between peace negotiations and waging war. Philip II put a price on ❿ William's head in 1580, and he was shot by a Catholic fanatic in Delft in 1584.

8 Catholic Geusen loot a farm in the southern provinces, painting, ca. 1600

10 William of Orange's tomb in the "Nieuwe Kerk" (New Church) in Delft, painting, ca. 1651

Declaration of Independence of the United Provinces to Philip II, 1581 Dutch Act of Abjuration

"A prince is constituted by God to be ruler of a people, to defend them from oppression and violence as the shepherd his sheep; and whereas God did not create the people slaves to their prince . . . but rather the prince for the sake of the subjects . . . to govern them . . . and support them as a father his children. . . . And when he does not behave thus, but . . . exacting from them slavish compliance, then he is no longer a prince, but a tyrant."

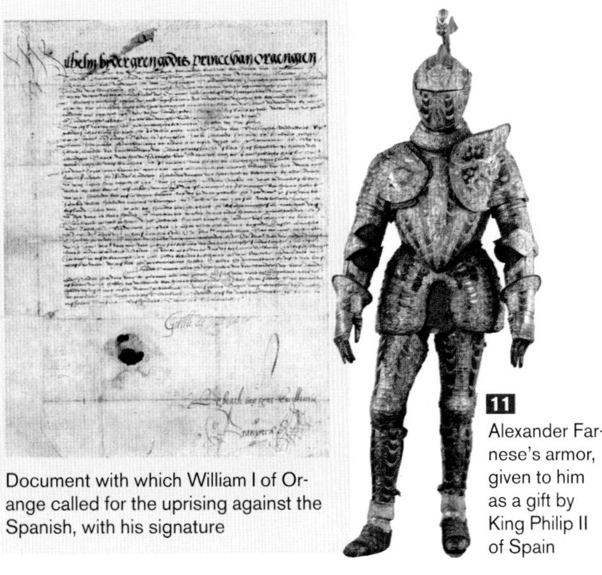
Document with which William I of Orange called for the uprising against the Spanish, with his signature

11 Alexander Farnese's armor, given to him as a gift by King Philip II of Spain

12 Grande Place in Brussels, capital of the Spanish Netherlands

1568 | Executions of opposition leaders Egmont and Hoorn
1579 | Declaration of independence by "Utrecht Union"
1584 | Murder of William of Orange

1567 | Magaret is deposed by Philip II
1568 | War of independence begins
1579 | Formation of the "Spanish Netherlands"

The Independent Netherlands to the Middle of the 17th Century

The war of the United Provinces against the southern Netherlands ended in 1609. A power struggle then developed between the *stadhouder* (governor) from the house of Nassau-Orange and the powerful merchants over who would rule the United Provinces.

1 Isabella Clara Eugenia of Spain, painting by Rubens, ca. 1613/15

2 The fleet of the Dutch East India Company, painting, 1675

After declaring independence, the United Provinces had to continue to fight against an invasion of Spanish forces under the command of Alessandro Farnese; internally it took action against the Catholics. In 1584 the Stadhouder William of Orange was murdered by a Catholic fanatic. In 1585, Antwerp was taken by Farnese, and the United Provinces accepted an offer of aid from Elizabeth I of England, who sent 8000 English soldiers under the command of the Earl of Leicester to their aid. The war dragged on with varying intensity until Maurice of Nassau, son of William of Orange, after two years of campaigning finally succeeded in expelling Spanish forces from the Protestant Netherlands in 1607. Finally, in 1609, the governor-general of the Spanish Netherlands, Archduke Albrecht of Austria and his wife ❶ Isabella Clara Eugenia, a daughter of Philip II, concluded a truce. In 1621, Philip III of Spain finally recognized the independence of the United Provinces.

The northern Netherlands recovered rapidly from the wars and, due to the powerful ❹ middle class in its cities, soon rose to become perhaps the wealthiest nation of Europe in the 17th century. For a time it was the leading ❷ naval and colonial power, with territories reaching from North America (New Amsterdam, later New York) and the Caribbean to Indonesia and Japan. It also dominated culturally, particularly in the field of painting. Political relations within the United Provinces were difficult, however, as they decided in 1590 against having a single head of state.

In 1585, the eldest son of William I of Orange, ❸ Maurice, replaced him as stadhouder of the provinces. Holland, financially the strongest of the United Provinces, was dominated by a rich ❺ merchant and legal elite, whose leader, Johan van Oldenbarnevelt, was the second political head alongside Maurice beginning in 1586. Although Maurice wanted to continue fighting, van Oldenbarnevelt accepted the truce with the Spanish Netherlands in 1609 in the interests of continuing trade. A power struggle developed, and Maurice ousted van Oldenbarnevelt and had him executed in 1619. The conflict was symptomatic of the unsettled power struggle between the Orange governors and the municipal representatives, which would dominate Dutch history until 1786. Maurice's half-brother, ❻ Frederick Henry, succeeded him as stadhouder in 1625, conquered fortresses in the south from the Spanish during the Thirty Years' War, and turned his court in The Hague into a center for arts and culture.

3 The "Mauritshuis" in The Hague, home of Maurice of Orange

4 Wedding portrait of a Haarlem merchant, painting by Frans Hals, c. 1622

5 Representatives of the cloth merchants' guild, painting by Rembrandt, 1662

6 Frederick Henry depicted as messenger of peace and independence, painting by Jordaens, 1652

1609	Ceasefire
1621	Recognition of independence
1652–54	First Anglo-Dutch naval war
1665–67	Second Anglo-Dutch naval war
1667	Navigation Act
1667–68	France attacks
1668	Alliance with England against France
1672	Murder of de Witt

The Netherlands up to the French Occupation

In 1672, the House of Orange was finally able to prevail with William III. His heirs were driven out in 1795 by French revolutionary troops, and later controlled by Napoleon.

Frederick Henry's son, William II, attempted to occupy ❼ Amsterdam in 1650 and make himself king but died before he could. The ruling grand pensionary of Holland, Johan de Witt, who represented the liberal bourgeoisie of the cities hostile to the centralizing monarchy, was forced into two naval wars with England over the Navigation Acts. These effectively broke Dutch naval supremacy. In 1667–1668, France seized parts of the Spanish Netherlands, whereupon de Witt made an alliance with England in 1668 and forced Louis XIV to withdraw. But then England changed sides, joining France in an attack on the United Provinces, particularly Holland, by land and by sea. Consequently, de Witt was literally torn to pieces in a rebellion in August 1672 and William III of Orange, the son of William II, was installed as supreme commander and stadhouder. He ended the war with England in 1674 and with France in 1678. In 1689 he was ❽ granted the English throne as James II's son-in-law. The prosperity of the country was maintained by the Dutch East India Company, founded in 1602, and ❾ colonial territories in Africa (Cape Colony), the Americas (Guyana, Netherlands Antilles), and Asia (Indonesia).

7 The mayor's house on the "Damplatz" in Amsterdam, painting, ca. 1668

After William III died in 1702, there was no unified leadership until 1747 when William IV Friso, a member of the House of Orange, became stadhouder of the United Netherlands. From 1780 to 1784, his son and successor William V waged war against Great Britain over colonies, which weakened the Netherlands as a colonial power; to prevail against the French, he supported the ❿ "Patriots" in 1785 and 1787, who had ousted him from office as *stadhouder* in some provinces.

The Spanish Netherlands went to the Habsburgs in 1713 in the Peace of Utrecht, which ended the War of Spanish Succession, and were thereafter called the ⓫ Austrian Netherlands. Occupied by French revolutionary troops in 1792, the southern provinces were incorporated into France in 1794. The following year, the French also occupied the United Provinces, drove out William V, and proclaimed it the Batavian Republic. In 1806, Napoleon Bonaparte made this French satellite state into a kingdom and handed it over to his brother Louis.

8 William III of Orange, king of England, painting, c. 1700

9 Whipping of a black slave in Dutch Guyana, copper engraving, 18th century

10 Caricature of the suppression of the uprising against William V of Orange, etching, 1787

11 Laeken Castle near Brussels, built for the governor of the Austrian Netherlands, Maria Christina of Austria, between 1782 and 1784

Intellectual Freedom in the United Provinces

During the 17th century the United Provinces were a stronghold of intellectual freedom in Europe. Hugo Grotius, the famous scholar of international law, was the pensionary (chief magistrate) of Rotterdam from 1613 to 1618. The founder of modern Rationalism, René Descartes, found refuge in the Netherlands in 1628–1648. The Jewish philosopher Baruch de Spinoza also lived in The Hague.

HVGONIS GROTII
DE
IVRE BELLI
AC PACIS
LIBRI TRES.
In quibus ius Naturæ & Gentium: item iuris publici præcipua explicantur.

MOENO-FRANCOFVRTI,
Typis & sumptibus Wechelianorum, Danielis & Davidis Aubriorum & Clementis Schleichii.
ANNO M.DC.XXVI.

Grotius' *De iure belli ac pacis* ("on the law of war and peace"), 1626

1672	William III of Orange becomes *stadhouder*
1689	William becomes heir to English throne
1713	Peace of Utrecht
1792	France occupies the Netherlands
1795	Proclamation of the "Batavian Republic"
1806	Louis Bonaparte becomes king

1 View of Pont Sant' Angelo and St. Peter's Basilica, Rome

The Italy of Popes and Princes

ca. 1450–ca. 1800

Between the 15th and the 18th centuries, Italy was contested by the rulers of France, Spain, and the Holy Roman Empire. It disintegrated into interdependent political structures that quarreled with each other and maneuvered between the great powers. The popes and the northern Italian princes were united by ruthless power and family politics in their battle against municipal freedoms and fashioned their courts into shining centers of the ❼ arts and literature.

2 Enea Silvio Piccolomini, the future Pope Pius II, being crowned as poet laureate by Emperor Frederick III, fresco by Pinturicchio, ca.1502

The Renaissance Papacy

The popes of the Renaissance were politically unscrupulous and had a love of splendor and worldly pleasures. They made their families exceedingly rich and were also patrons of the arts.

In the Papal States, the "Renaissance papacy" began in the middle of the 15th century. While its first representatives in the mid- to late 1400s, notably Nicholas V and ❷ Pius II (formerly the celebrated poet Enea Silvio Piccolomini), were significant and respected humanists, moral decay set in with the pontificate of Sixtus IV in 1471. The popes sold Church offices and favored their families. ❶ Rome became a city of frivolous celebrations, rather than of religious piety. Popes and cardinals, who were mostly members of leading noble families and related to one another, enriched themselves with church properties and monies. However, the court of the Renaissance popes was also a center of culture and the arts where significant artists such as Raphael and ❼ Michelangelo were commissioned by the ecclesiastical princes to create artworks.

The integrity of the papacy reached a low point with the self-aggrandizing Alexander VI between 1492 and 1503. His successor, Julius II, personally fought at the head of his troops in defense of the Papal States and against the rivalling Italian cities, while the popes from the Medici family, ❹ Leo X and Clement VII, were patrons of the arts. Clement VII allied himself with France (p. 276) against the Holy Roman emperor and consequently provoked the plundering of Rome by imperial mercenaries in the ❸ *sacco di Roma* in 1527. ❻ Paul III (Alessandro Farnese) and Julius III were transitional popes who, although they continued to live like Renaissance princes, were coaxed by Emperor Charles V into making reforms. ❺ The Council of Trent, which was convened in 1545 and lasted until 1563, eventually introduced a far-reaching program of internal ecclesiastical reorganization after years of debate.

3 Charles' mercenary army ridicule the pope during the *sacco di Roma*, copper engraving

4 Pope Leo X, copy after the painting by his protégé Raphael

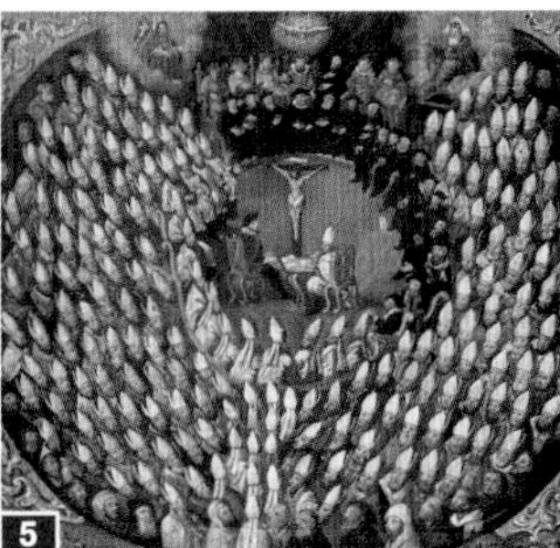

5 Congregation of the Council of Trent, painting, 18th century

6 Paul III's Palazzo Farnese in Rome, built 1534–89

7 The creation of Adam, from ceiling fresco of the Sistine Chapel painted by Michelangelo, 1511

1447 | Founding of the Vatican library
1506 | Start of the reconstruction of St Peter's in Rome
1527 | *Sacco di Roma*
1536 | Start of the reform papacy
1542 | Reintroduction of the Inquisition

Cesare Borgia

"On the evening of the 31st of October 1501, [Alexander's son] Cesare Borgia hosted in his rooms in the Vatican a party with 50 honorable prostitutes, referred to as courtesans, who after the meal danced with the servants and others present, first in their clothes and then naked. After the meal the candelabras with the burning candles were stood on the floor and chestnuts spread around them, which the naked prostitutes collected on their hands and knees and crawling between the candelabras, watched by the Pope, Cesare, and his sister Lucrezia [Borgia]."
by Johannes Burcardus, Alexander VI's master of ceremonies

above: Cesare Borgia, painting, ca. 1520

10 Pope Benedict XIV, painting, 18th c.

The Papacy during the Counter-Reformation

A moral renewal of the papacy occurred under the influence of the Counter-Reformation, but it also brought about a curbing of intellectual and scientific freedoms, and the papacy ignored the Enlightenment for a long time.

After the reform plans of popes such as Hadrian VI, Pius III, and Marcellus II failed because their pontificates were too short, Paul IV in 1555 and Pius V in 1566 were able to establish an uncompromising papacy of the Counter-Reformation. The moral renewal

9 Tomb of Pope Alexander VII in San Pietro di Vaticano, designed by Bernini, 1676–78

under these popes, however, was accompanied by the Inquisition's reign of terror. Among the Italian clergy active at this time was the later canonized Carlo Borromeo, who as cardinal-archbishop of Milan after 1560 worked toward comprehensive Church reform.

Popes who held fast to the concept of the Counter-Reformation included Gregory XIII, who introduced the modern Gregorian calendar in 1582, and Sixtus V, who rid the Papal States of its bands of robbers and developed papal centralism through a complete reorganization of Church administration that remained in force into the 20th century. In the 17th century under Paul V and Urban VIII, Rome once again became a world center of ❾ art and culture, but it was also under them that the dispute with ⓫ Galileo Galilei about the Copernican conception of the world took place. Gregory XV founded the Congregation for Propagating the Faith (*Propaganda Fide*) in 1622, which was responsible in the following centuries for coordinating the spread of Catholic missionary work all over the world. Innocent XI stood out among the successors of Urban VIII, bringing about a grand coalition of European powers against the Ottomans' 1683 siege of Vienna.

The papacy closed its mind to the enlightening currents of the 18th century through censorship and the banning of books. The liberal and enlightened ❿ Benedict XIV, who was described by Montesquieu as the pope of the scholars, demanded internal ecclesiastical enlightenment, but his successors rescinded his reforms—provoking the opposition of enlightened absolutism,

8 Pope Pius VI and the Emperor Joseph II, copper engraving, 18th c.

which had by that time established itself in the Catholic countries. Austria, Spain, and Portugal forced the reactionary Clement XIV to dissolve the powerful order of the Jesuits in 1773. His successor, ❽ Pius VI, was a victim of these developments; in 1782 he traveled to Vienna in a fruitless attempt to persuade Emperor Joseph II to tone down measures against the Church (p. 273). In 1797 Pius lost the papal enclave at Avignon in southern France, and in 1798 he was captured by French troops who had occupied Italy on Napoleon's orders and was deported, along with a major part of the Church's treasures, to France.

11 Galileo defends himself before the inquisition court, painting, 17th century

1545–63 | Council of Trent
1582 | Gregorian calendar reform
1622 | *Propaganda Fide*
1633 | Galileo's trial
1773 | Jesuits disbanded
1798 | Capture of Pius VI

The Nobility and the Papal States in Northern and Central Italy

The numerous Italian princes' palaces became, despite their comparatively minor political importance, significant centers of the Renaissance and the baroque. They were matched in their displays of splendor by the confident noble families in the city-republics.

2 Lorenzo de Medici, painting by Vasari, 16th century

While the Kingdom of Naples and Sicily was ruled over by Spain or by Spanish collateral family branches into the 18th century, local ruling dynasties of varying origins (p. 195) reigned in the north and center of the Italian peninsula. The Milanese Sforza family, descended from a mercenary soldier (*condottiere*), was ousted in 1515 when Francis I of France occupied Lombardy after his victory at Marignano. Following success over the French at ❶ Pavia in 1525, the Habsburg emperor Charles V then seized Milan as an imperial fief.

The history of the Medici family in ❸ Florence was eventful. They rose to become the unofficial rulers of the city and particularly distinguished themselves as patrons of the arts. Cosimo the Elder summoned the sculptor Donatello to his court in the 15th century. Michelangelo and Botticelli worked for his grandson ❷ Lorenzo the Magnificent in Florence. After Lorenzo's death, however, the family was driven out by the monk ❹ Savonarola, who established a form of theocratic republic in 1494. The Medici returned in 1513. After the murder of Alessandro de' Medici—who, as son-in-law of Charles V gained the title of duke of Florence for his family in 1532—Cosimo I, a distant cousin, took over the dukedom in 1537 and became a leading power in northern Italy. Cosimo established himself as absolute ruler, founded the famous collection of paintings in the Pitti Palace, and conquered Siena, which he absorbed into Tuscany in 1555. In 1569 he was elevated to grand duke of Tuscany. When the Medici line died out in 1737, the grand duchy was given to Francis Stephen (later Emperor Francis I) in exchange for Lorraine (p. 281). His son Peter Leopold, the later Emperor Leopold II, transformed Tuscany into a model state of enlightened absolutism and a center of independent sciences through extensive social reforms.

The ancient royal house of Este was granted the imperial fiefs of Modena and Reggio by the emperor in 1452 and in 1471 was awarded ❺ Ferrara as a dukedom by the pope. Ercole I laid out Ferrara as a modern city with wide, straight streets. His son Alfonso I was married to the pope's daughter Lucrezia Borgia. When the direct line died out with Alfonso II in 1597, the pope took back Ferrara as a papal fief in 1598, but Este relatives still ruled in Modena until the French occupation in 1796.

The main branch of the Gonzaga family reigned in Mantua. Margrave Giovanni Francesco III was married to ❻ Isabella d'Este, who made Mantua into an important cultural center. Their son Federigo II gained the title of duke in 1530. The extinction of the direct line in 1627 led to the War of Mantuan Succession (1628–1631). The emperor seized Mantua as an imperial fief in 1708.

Pope ❼ Paul III of the House of Farnese made his illegitimate son Pier Luigi the duke of Parma and Piacenza in 1545. However, the duke was murdered and the land

1 The Battle of Pavia, wood engraving, ca. 1530

3 The Cathedral of Florence with the bell tower by Giotto di Bondone and the dome by Brunelleschi

4 Savonarola's execution in Florence, painting, ca. 1500

5 Castello Estense in Ferrara

1452 Este rule in Modena and Reggio | **ca. 1500** Medici rule in Florence | **1515** French occupation of Lombardy | **1525** Charles V seizes Milan as an imperial fief | **1528** End of French rule in Genoa | **1545** Farnese rule in Parma and Piacenza

6 Isabella d' Este, Duchesse of Mantua, painting by Rubens, ca. 1605/08

7 Pope Paul III and his nephews, painting by Titian, 1546

was then occupied by imperial troops. His son Ottavio was able to regain the estates in 1538 through his marriage to Margaret, the illegitimate daughter of Emperor Charles V. Their son Alexander became governor of the Netherlands in 1578. The Farnese line died out in 1731, and Parma was initially seized by the emperor as an imperial fief, but eventually in 1748 through marriage came into the hands of the Spanish Bourbons (p. 300), who also ruled Naples and Sicily.

8 Andrea Doria depicted as sea god Neptune, by Bronzino, ca. 1530

Another papal family, the della Rovere, gained possession of Urbino. Here, the governor and condottiere Federigo da Montefeltro received the ducal title in 1474 and founded a dynasty, into which the nephew of Pope Julius II and great-nephew of Pope Sixtus IV, Francesco Maria della Rovere, married in 1508. Urbino was independent until 1631 when it reverted to the Papal States.

❽ Andrea Doria, who fought against the Ottomans as an admiral for Emperor Charles V, put an end to the French rule of Genoa in 1528 and reintroduced the old constitution of the aristocratic republic with the election of a doge as head of state every two years. In compensation for having lost the Mediterranean trade to the Venetians and the Turks, the Genoese rose to become the most important bankers of the Spanish crown. In contrast to ❿ Venice, Genoa was able to maintain a leading position in commerce. The Venetian republic had lost almost all of its territories in the Eastern Mediterranean to the Ottomans by the 18th century. The shifting of world trade to the Atlantic led to the gradual decline of the city. In 1797, the French occupied both Venice and Genoa, abolished the rule of the doges, and made both cities satellite states of the French Republic.

The most significant dynasty in Northern Italy was the house of Savoy. From ❾ Turin it ruled the Duchy of Savoy and Piedmont . It alternatively allied with the French and the Habsburgs in order to maintain its independence and expand its territories. After the Spanish wars of succession it gained the island of Sardinia and ⓫ its crown.

As in the other Italian states, branches of the Bourbons or respectively the Habsburgs ruled, it was able to lead the Italian independence movement in the 19th century as it was the only authentically "Italian" royal dynasty.

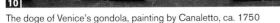

10 The doge of Venice's gondola, painting by Canaletto, ca. 1750

Niccolò Machiavelli

A diplomat and member of the government of the republic of Florence, Niccolò Machiavelli—in his work, Il Principe (The Prince), in 1513—developed the principle of pragmatic politics as a fundamental law for modern European states: "The end justifies the means."

above: Niccolò Machiavelli, painting, 16th century

9 The Basilica of Supergra containing the House of Savoy mausoleum, Turin

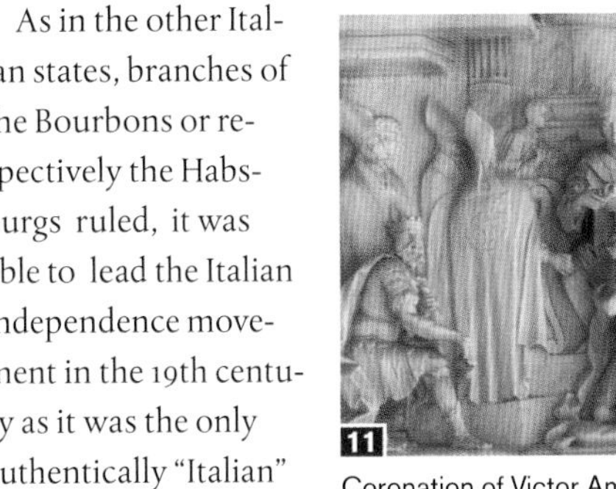
11 Coronation of Victor Amadeus II, Duke of Savoy, marble relief, 1713

1555 Conquest of Sienna | **1578** Alexander Farnese governor of the Netherlands | **1598** Ferrara becomes papal fief | **1628–31** War of Mantuan Succession | **1737** Medici government ends | **1796** French occupation of Modena | **1797** French occupation of Genoa and Venice

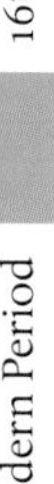

Spain and Portugal 1500–1800

Voyages of discovery and merchant shipping made Portugal and Spain the leading sea powers of Europe during the fifteenth and sixteenth century. Under ❷ Philip II, Spain also became the major force behind the Counter-Reformation. A rapid economic and political decline took place in Portugal after 1580 and in Spain after 1600, accelerated by the often weak and conservative governments. This decline lasted until around 1750, when reforms associated with enlightened absolutism elsewhere were carried out in ❶ both countries. In the wake of the French Revolution, both countries fell under Napoleon's control.

1 Map of the Iberian peninsula, 1577

right: Philip II of Spain 2

Spain from the Catholic Kings to Philip II

The union of the kingdoms of Castile and Aragon paved the way for the final defeat and expulsion of the Arab Muslim and the rise of the Spanish kingdom. Under Charles V and Philip II, Spain became the leading Catholic power in Europe.

4 Isabella I, portrait, ca. 1500

5 Ferdinand II, portrait, ca. 1500

Spain was unified by the marriage of the "Catholic monarchs" ❺ Ferdinand of Aragon and ❹ Isabella of Castile in 1469. In 1492, they ❸ drove out the last of the Iberian Muslim rulers from Granada and then completed the *Reconquista* through the expulsion or forced baptism of Jews and Moors. In the same year, ❼ Christopher Columbus landed in America and claimed it for Spain. The royal heir to the Spanish throne, Joanna the Mad, married the Habsburg Philip the Handsome, the son of Emperor Maximilian I, in 1496. When Isabella died in 1505, Joanna was already mentally ill and was unable to govern in Castile. After Philip's death in 1506, Ferdinand of Aragon established his rule over all of Spain.

3 The handing over of the key to Granada by the last of the Muslim rulers after the city's surrender, stone carving, ca. 1500

Only after Ferdinand's death in 1516 was his grandson Charles I, who became the Holy Roman Emperor Charles V in 1519, able to take up his inheritance. The Spanish cities rebelled against his Dutch advisors in 1520. Spanish conquest in the New World brought vast quantities of gold into the country but did not lead to any long-term improvements in the state finances. During his frequent absences, Charles left the regency to his wife Isabella of Portugal or his son Philip II.

6 The Escorial Palace, residence and place of burial for the Spanish kings since 1563, built by Juan Bautista de Toledo and Juan de Herrera

When Charles I abdicated in 1556, Spain along with its overseas possessions, the Netherlands, and Italy, were inherited by his son, Philip II. He became the leading figure of the Catholic Counter-Reformation in Europe. The extremely duty-conscious and hard working monarch took personal charge of the administration of the kingdom from his ❻ Escorial Palace in Madrid. He was determined to combat the spread of Protestantism in Europe by any means. This led to the secession of the Netherlands, where Calvinism was strong, after a protracted war that began in 1568 (p. 288).

7 Columbus returns with gifts from the New World, painting by Delacroix, 1839

1469	Spanish Union
1480	First Inquisition court in Seville
1492	Columbus reaches America
1506	Death of Philip the Handsome
1516	Charles I becomes king of Spain
1520	Revolt in Spanish cities
1556	Philip II becomes King of Spain

High Point and Decline of Spanish Power

Spain's dominant position in Europe and the New World, attained under Philip II, declined under his successors. Under the last Spanish Habsburg the country was practically bankrupt, and its political influence greatly diminished.

Philip III on horseback, portrait by Velasquez, ca. 1634

From a position of strength, Philip II projected Spanish power across Europe. He supported the Austrian Habsburgs against the Protestants, ended the war with France in 1559, and married Elizabeth of Valois, the daughter of Catherine de Médicis, in his third marriage. In the context of the Counter-Reformation he financed the Catholic League (p. 277) in the French Wars of Religion, but was unable to prevent Henry of Navarre from becoming king of France in 1589. In 1571 a Spanish-papal fleet under Juan de Austria won a major ❾ naval victory over the Ottomans at Lepanto. However, Spanish naval supremacy was broken in 1588 when a large invasion fleet, the Spanish Armada, was defeated off the British coast in 1588 (p. 283).

The windmills of La Mancha, setting for the famous 17th century novel *Don Quixote* by Miguel de Cervantes, who also fought in the Battle of Lepanto

In 1598 Philip II was succeeded by his son, ❽ Philip III, who fell under the influence of royal favorites. He further stretched the state finances by underwriting the Catholic powers in the Thirty Years' War. In the same period, Spanish art and ⓫ literature was in full bloom at his ❿ courts. ⓬ Philip IV was forced to declare the state bankrupt in 1627 and accept the loss of territory in the Treaty of the Pyrenees in 1659 after heavy defeats by the French. The repeated intermarrying of Austrian and Spanish Habsburgs began to show clear signs of degeneration. ⓭ Philip's son Charles II, the last of the Spanish Habsburgs, was both impotent and mentally ill. Even before his death, the dispute over his succession flared up at the royal court. When he died in November 1700, the War of the Spanish Succession began.

Philip IV, portrait by Velasquez

Charles II, portrait by Velasquez

Celebration of the victory over the Ottomans at the Battle of Lepanto, including Pius V, Philip II, Doge Alvise Mocenigo of Venice, and Don Juan de Austria, painting by El Greco, ca. 1577

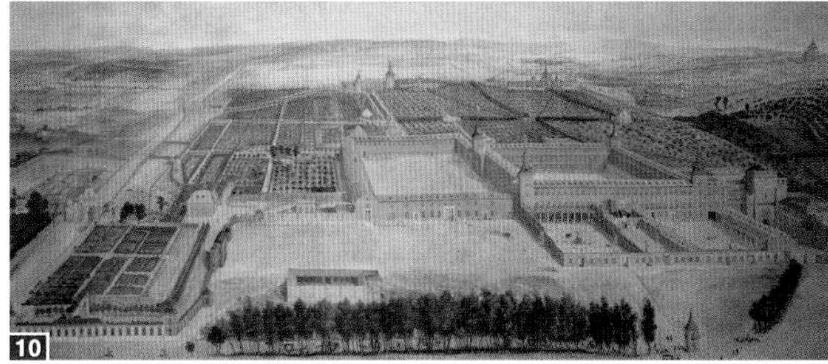

Palace Buen Retiro and gardens in Madrid, painting, 17th century

Philip II, on the Defeat of the Spanish Armada Sent to Invade England:

"We must praise God for all that He does. And I thank Him for the mercy shown. In the storms which the Armada had to sail through, they could have suffered a worse fate, [and] that their misfortune was not greater is thanks to the pious and ceaseless prayers sent to heaven for their successful return(...)" *Extract from a letter to the Spanish bishops, 1588*

above: English naval victory over the Spanish Armada, engraving, 17th c.

1571 | Battle of Lepanto
1588 | Defeat of the Spanish Armada
1589 | Henry of Navarre becomes king of France
1627 | State bankruptcy
1659 | Treaty of the Pyrenees
1700 | War of the Spanish Succession

Portugal at Its Zenith as a Naval Power

Voyages of discovery, merchant shipping, and a well-run fleet made Portugal the leading sea power at the end of the 15th century. When the reign of the House of Aviz came to an end to be replaced by the Spanish Habsburgs, the country lost its dominant position.

Since the time of Henry the Navigator in the first half of the 15th century, Portuguese explorers had dedicated themselves to finding a sea route around Africa to India and establishing bases on the African coast. John II (ruled 1481–1495) launched a major fleet-building program, had ❼ sea charts drawn up, and outfitted explorers and soldiers. In 1487–1488 Bartolomeu Dias sailed to the Cape of Good Hope. Ten years later, ❷ King Manuel I the Fortunate sponsored the expedition of ❶ Vasco da Gama, which sailed around Africa and reached the coast of ❸ India in May 1498. Pedro Alvars Cabral claimed part of today's Brazil for Portugal in 1500, thus securing Portugal's position in South America—confirmed by the papal "division" of the New World between Spain and Portugal in the Treaty of Tordesillas signed in 1494.

King Manuel I the Fortunate with St. Hieronymus in Belem in the Hieronymus monastery, donated by the king, sculpture, 16th c.

Manuel centralized the government as an absolute ruler and expelled the Moors and Jews—refugees from Spain—to North Africa in 1496. During his reign, and that of his son John III, Portugal reached its zenith as a maritime power. The Portuguese constructed forts and trading stations along the African and Indian coasts and controlled the spice trade to Europe. Working with certain African tribal chiefs, they transported a great number of slaves for the European markets. Portuguese ❻ caravels ruled the world's seas. Francisco de Almeida, the first Portuguese viceroy in East India in 1505, and ❹ Alfonso de Albuquerque, secured Portuguese dominance in the Indian Ocean and took trading cities such as Goa and Malacca. Their successors conquered the Moluccas (Spice Islands) and Ceylon.

4 Afonso de Albuquerque

Vasco da Gama before an Indian sovereign, wood engraving, 19th century

Baroque church dating from the time of the Portuguese in Goa

Sebastian, King of Portugal painting, 1571

John's grandson, ❺ Sebastian, succeeded him in 1557 and dreamed of a revival of the Crusades. He invaded North Africa with a large army in 1578 but was defeated by the sultan of Morocco at Ksar el-Kebir. As his body was never found, the Portuguese believed for a long time that he would return victorious, a rumor which several adventurers used to their advantage. His great-uncle, Cardinal Henry, who had already reigned as regent for the young Sebastian, succeeded him as king and had to pay an enormous ransom for the survivors in North Africa. The royal line of Aviz came to an end with the death of Henry in 1580.

Portuguese sailing boat, book illustration, 16th century

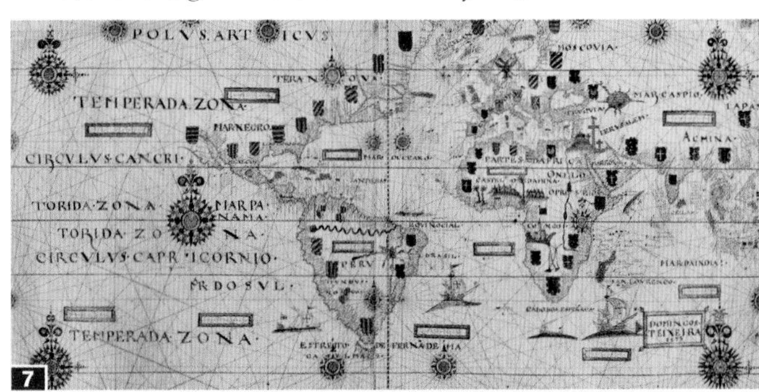

Portuguese map of the world, 1573

1487 | Navigation of the Cape of Good Hope
1494 | Treaty of Tordesillas
1498 | Sea route to India discovered
from 1505 | Portuguese viceroy in East India
1578 | Battle of Ksar el-Kebir
1578 | Attack on North Africa

Portugal up to the Occupation by Napoleon

Neither under the Spanish nor under the House of Bragança did Portugal regain its former importance. Following reforms under Pombal, the country was occupied by Napoleon in 1807.

Philip II, King of Spain and Portugal, bronze sculpture, ca. 1570

A typical country estate of the nobility, in Villa Real in the north of Portugal, built in the 18th century

Heretics being burnt at the stake by Jesuits, copper engraving, 1723

Since time immemorial, Portugal's rulers had made marriage alliances with the Spanish ruling houses. ❾ Philip II of Spain, an uncle of King Sebastian, rejected claims by related dynasties in 1580 and occupied Portugal, which he absorbed into his empire. Portugal was further undermined through the weaknesses of the Spanish Habsburgs after 1598. The Dutch replaced their hegemony in the Indian Ocean and seized the Moluccas in 1663 and Ceylon in 1668.

A Portuguese ❽ revolt against Spain, supported by England, brought John IV (of the Bragança dynasty, a side branch of the old royal house) to the throne in 1640. In 1654, he drove the Dutch out of the coast of Brazil and permanently secured it as a possession of Portugal. During the reign of John's successor, Portugal sought support from Great Britain against Spain. The country's economy suffered as a result of mass emigration to Brazil by those seeking to escape the rigidly hierarchical society, in which most of the land ❿ was in the hands of the nobility. Change came in 1750, when Joseph I, an adherent of enlightened absolutism, came to the throne. His chief minister, the Marquês de Pombal, used an earthquake that struck ⓬ Lisbon in 1755 as an excuse to institute radical changes. He had the city rebuilt, improved its infrastructure, and worked to revive the economy. Between 1761 and 1763, he banned slavery in Portugal. He expelled the Jesuits, who had led ⓫ the Inquisition, from the country in 1759–1760 and, Portugal contributed to the order's dissolution in 1773 through pressure on the pope. Pombal cemented a form of enlightened absolutism, reformed the universities, and brought Portugal into line with the more progressive of Europe's regimes.

Joseph's death in 1777 meant the fall of Pombal, because successive rulers again came under the influence of the Church. Since Portugal remained aligned with Great Britain, Napoleon occupied the country in 1807 and expelled the regent John VI, who set up a secondary royal court in Brazil.

Uprising in Lisbon against the Spanish king, etching, 18th century

The Lisbon Earthquake

On November 1, 1755, a massive earthquake and subsequent tidal wave destroyed the city of Lisbon and took the lives of about 60,000 people. The event became a much-discussed subject in Enlightenment Europe. The optimism of the proponents of the Enlightenment was greatly shaken, and Voltaire wrote a mocking poem in 1756 which he entitled "Poem on the Lisbon Disaster; or, An Examination of the Axiom 'All Is Well.'"

above: The Lisbon earthquake, sketch, 18th c.

Ships entering the port of Lisbon with the central Praça do Comércio in the background, painting, ca. 1800

- **1580** Philip II occupies Portugal
- **Dec 1640** Portuguese revolt
- **1654** Portuguese establish colony in Brazil
- **1 Nov 1755** Lisbon earthquake
- **1759–60** Jesuits expelled
- **1761–63** Slavery abolished
- **1807** Napoleon invades Portugal

Spain under the First Bourbons

As the Habsburg dynasty died out, the new Bourbon line temporarily brought Spain under the influence of France. Under mentally ill monarchs Spain lost territories and influence.

In 1700 Charles II, the last Habsburg, who had no heir, bequeathed the Spanish throne to his great-nephew ❷ Duke Philip of Anjou, the grandson of Louis XIV of France. The Austrian Habsburgs countered this with their own claims to the throne. They were supported by the British, who feared French hegemony. In the War of Spanish Succession, the two sides fought for their claims. However, when the Habsburg pretender Charles III succeeded his brother Joseph I as Holy Roman emperor, his erstwhile allies began to fear an increase in Habsburg power. In the end, the inheritance was divided: The grandson of Louis XIV was recognized as King Philip V of Spain in 1713–1714 by the treaties of Utrecht and Rastatt but was forced to renounce his and his descendents' claims to the French throne. The Habsburgs also received the Spanish possessions in the Netherlands and Italy, while Great Britain gained Minorca and Gibraltar. The psychologically unstable ❶ Philip V (ruled 1700-1746) was heavily influenced by his second wife ❹ Isabella Farnese, princess of Parma and Piacenza, who wished to secure crowns for her own sons. Through military and diplomatic pressure following the War of Polish Succession in 1734–1735, the Habsburgs were forced to relinquish Naples and Sicily. After the War of Austrian Succession in 1748, they lost Parma and Piacenza as well. Philip's attacks of depression soon escalated into phases of mental breakdown and paranoia, and he spent much of the time in retreat at his ❸ residences outside Madrid. Meanwhile, the aristocracy, who under the last Habsburgs had already made themselves largely independent on their country estates, blocked all social reform to alleviate the situation of the majority of the population who suffered from poverty and illiteracy.

1 Philip V, portrait by Rigaud, 18th c.

3 The gardens of La Granja de San Ildefonso, Philip V's summer residence

In Philip's son Ferdinand VI, who succeeded him in 1746, the hereditary depression intensified into chronic mental illness. As he was incapable of governing, Chief Minister Marquis de la Ensenada ruled in his place. While in office he reformed the Spanish finances, making Spain independent of France, and began to introduce a range of Enlightenment-inspired political reforms in the country.

4 Philip V and Isabella Farnese and family, painting by Van Loo, 1743

2 King Louis XIV proclaims the Duke of Anjou to be king of Spain, color lithograph

Farinelli

The Italian castrato singer, Farinelli, performed at the Spanish court from 1737. Born Carlo Broschi in 1705 in Italy, he first performed publicly in 1721 and was soon a celebrated star around the opera houses of Europe. Under Philip V and Ferdinand VI, he initially sang for a small circle of the illustrious—it is said that he was the only one who could please the depressive Philip—but then rose to become the "maître de plaisir" and an esteemed political advisor in the Spanish court.

Carlo Broschi, known as Farinelli, painting, 18th century

1700 | War of the Spanish Succession
1704 | British seize Gibraltar
1713 | Peace of Utrecht
1714 | Treaty of Rastatt
1734–35 | War of the Polish Succession
1748 | War of the Austrian Succession

Spain during the Reigns of Charles III and Charles IV

Charles III enacted reforms in the spirit of enlightened absolutism. Under his son Charles IV, the chief minister, Godoy, presided over a political reconciliation with the French Republic.

A reversal of conditions in Spain took place when Ferdinand VI was succeeded by his half-brother ❺ Charles III in 1759. As king of Naples and Sicily since 1735, Charles had already initiated social and economic reforms in southern Italy with the aid of his chief minister Tanucci. The single-minded and industrious king now brought enlightened absolutism to Spain. He began an extensive settlement program to recultivate the rural regions that had been barren for centuries, ordering modern techniques and new strains of plants for the peasants. Along with a number of ❻ palaces and hunting lodges, he built orphanages and workhouses for vagrants. He improved roads, established banks and carefully controlled colonial revenues. Charles III even took on the Catholic Church. He ended the Church's monopoly over education and abolished the ❾ courts of Inquisition. In foreign affairs, Charles formed an alliance with France in 1761 and participated in the Seven Years' War against Great Britain, which was allied with Prussia against France. In 1767, he expelled the Jesuits from Spain, confiscated much church property, and distributed it to the ❼ peasants.

Royal palace of Madrid, designed by Juvara, construction begun under Philip V and completed under Charles III, photograph, ca. 1890

A Village Bullfight, traditional pastime of the peasants, painting by Goya, ca. 1819

Charles III was succeeded in 1788 by his son ❽ Charles IV, who left much of the affairs of government to his energetic wife, Maria Luisa of Parma, and her protégé, ❿ Manuel de Godoy, who as chief minister from 1792 continued the policies of Charles III. Initially Godoy had been an opponent of revolutionary France, but in 1796 he entered into the alliance of San Ildefonso with the French Republic, which obliged Spain to take part in the war against Great Britain. In 1805, the British fleet under Admiral Nelson destroyed the French and Spanish fleets at Trafalgar. As a result Spanish trade routes were decimated.

In 1807, Godoy even attempted to negotiate with Napoleon over the division of French-occupied territories in the hope of gaining southern Portugal as part of the Spanish kingdom. In 1808, however, Godoy was ousted from Aranjuez in a popular uprising. To prevent Spain from defecting to the growing enemy camp, Napoleon forced Charles III and his son Ferdinand to renounce the throne and installed his own brother, Joseph, as king.

5 Charles III on horseback, 18th c.

Charles III, on the Clergy:

"The Bishops have nothing to give away; everything they own belongs to the poor; therefore they should sell it and distribute it as alms."

above: The Cathedral of Santiago de Compostela, built in the 18th century

8 Charles IV and Maria Luisa with their children, family portrait by Francisco Goya, 1800

9 Public humiliation of man condemned by the Inquisition, painting, 19th c.

10 Manuel de Godoy during a military campaign against Portugal, painting by Francisco Goya, 1801

1759	Charles III comes to power
1761	Alliance with France
1767	Jesuits expelled
1796	Alliance with San Ildefonso
1805	Battle of Trafalgar
1808	Joseph Bonaparte becomes king of Spain

Eastern Europe and Scandinavia 1500–1800

Poland experienced a turbulent period due to its elective and weak monarchy that struggled to maintain its authority in the face of an aristocracy that strove for independence. It was then divided up between the Great Powers in the partitions of Poland. In Hungary and Transylvania the Ottomans and Habsburgs fought for power. Protestant ❷ kings in Denmark and Sweden attempted to strengthen central authority and expand their sphere of influence. Sweden rose to become a European power under Gustav II Adolph after 1648, but Russia was able to break Sweden's dominance in the north after the death of Charles XII.

1 The Wawel Cathedral in Kraków used for the coronation ceremonies of Polish kings and built in the Italian Renaissance style

2 The Danish "Crown of the Absolute Monarchs," made in 1670-71

Poland and Hungary in the 16th and 17th Centuries

The aristocracy's right of election and the disputes with its neighbors weakened the Polish kingdom. Hungary came under the rule of the Ottomans and the Habsburgs.

The position of the Polish kings was traditionally weak because it was an ❸ elective monarchy. The nobility held the peasants in servitude and expanded its privileges at every election in the Sejm or Diet. Sigismund I of the Jagiellon dynasty, king from 1506, was a promoter of the ❶ Renaissance and humanism. He ended the disputes with the Habsburgs in 1515 and with the Teutonic Order over East Prussia in 1525. His son Sigismund II Augustus unified the Lithuanian provinces with Poland in the ❺ Union of Lublin in 1569.

After the end of the Jagiellon line, the aristocracy forced through religious freedom and the right of resistance with the election of Henry of Valois in 1572, later Henry III king of France (p. 277). In 1587 ❻ Sigismund III brought the Catholic line of the House of Vasa to power. His son Wladyslaw IV pushed far into Russian territory, but Wladyslaw's brother ❹ John II Casimir later had to contend with the revolts of the Cossack leader Bogdan Chmelnizkij, who was supported by Russia and the Polish peasants, founded his own state in the Ukraine, and placed himself under the czar in 1654. When Ukraine was lost to Russia, the king abdicated.

A branch of the house of Jagiellon had ruled in Bohemia and Hungary since the 15th century. A pact was made with the Habsburgs for the ❼ double wedding of the children of King Wladyslaw II, Louis and Anna, with the grandchildren of Holy Roman emperor Maximilian I, Ferdinand and Mary, in 1515. When the young King Louis II fell in the Battle of Mohacs against the Turks in 1526, his brother-in-law, Ferdinand I claimed Bohemia and Hungary. But Ferdinand was only able to hold Bohemia; the Ottomans, who supported their own kings, occupied most of Hungary for a century and a half.

4 John II Casimir, 18th c.

3 Polish general assembly for the election of a king in a field near Warsaw, copper engraving, 17th century

5 Unification of Poland and Lithuania in the Lublin, wood engraving

6 Portrait of Sigismund III Vasa, king of Poland and briefly king of Sweden, ca. 1600

7 Double wedding between the Habsburg and the Jagiellon dynasty in 1515

since 1386 | Jagiello rule in Bohemia and Hungary
1515 | Poland gains Prussia as fief
1525 | Secularization of Prussia
1526 | Battle of Mohacs
1541 | Turkish Hungary becomes Ottoman province
1569 | Lublin Union

Hungary and Poland to the 18th Century

The power struggle between the Ottomans and the Habsburgs also raged in Hungary and neighboring Transylvania. At first, Poland fought against Sweden in the Great Northern War but then came under the influence of Russia and finally ceased to exist as a state due to the Three Partitions.

The battle for Hungary and Transylvania sapped the strength of the Habsburgs in the East. The Ottomans had supported local nobility against the Habsburgs over the centuries, beginning with John Zápolya, who was *woiwode* (governor) of Transylvania from 1511 and king of eastern Hungary from 1526. The Protestant Bethlen Gábor, for example, prince of Transylvania in 1613 and king of Hungary in 1620, pushed into Bohemia and Austria. The Habsburgs were first able to extend their rule over all of Hungary only after the victory of Prince Eugène of Savoy in 1697. For the last time, in 1704, ❽ Ferenc II Rákóczi, prince of Transylvania and Hungary, once again led a revolt against the Habsburgs but in 1711 was forced to relinquish all his titles. Nevertheless, Hungary, which persisted in striving for independence, remained a hotbed of conflict until the end of the Habsburg monarchy.

❾ John III Sobieski, who was elected king of Poland in 1674, helped defend Vienna against the Turks. His attempt to establish a hereditary monarchy failed, however, due to the resistance of the nobility. Instead, the Saxon elector ⓫ Frederick Augustus I (the Strong) was elected as King Augustus II in 1697 (p. 270). He was driven out of Poland in the Great Northern War (p. 305) in 1701 by Charles XII of Sweden but was able to regain the crown after Charles's defeat at Poltava in 1709.

John III Sobieski with captured Ottomans, etching, 18th century

Upon Augustus's death in 1733, the Polish nobility chose the Polish noble ❿ Stanislaw I Leszczynski, the father-in-law of Louis XV of France, who had once already been installed as king between 1704 and 1709 by Charles XII. However, Russia and Austria, fearful of losing their influence, forced the election of Augustus III, the son of Augustus the Strong, in 1733–1734. The consequent War of Polish Succession ended with a Europe-wide exchange of lands. Stanislaw Leszczynski received Lorraine (p. 281) as compensation and Francis Stephen of Lorraine got Tuscany (p. 294). Augustus III continued to reign in Saxony and Poland. After his death, Empress Catherine II of Russia put her former lover ⓬ Stanislaw II Poniatowski on the throne in 1764. The king tried to make reforms, but Russia obstructed them. In opposition, the National Polish "Confederation of Bar" rebelled, while in support, the Ottomans started a war with Russia. After her victory, the empress undertook the ⓭ First Partition of Poland in 1772, in which Russia, Austria, and Prussia annexed large tracts of land for themselves. In two further partitions in 1793 and 1795, Poland was completely divided up. King Stanislaw II abdicated and the old Polish Empire ceased to exist.

Ferenc II Rákóczi, portrait, ca. 1700

Stanislaw I Leszczynski, steel engraving, 18th century

Charles XII of Sweden encounters his opponent in war, Frederick I Augustus (the Strong) of Saxony and Poland, wood engraving, ca. 1860

Stanislaw II August Poniatowski, copper engraving, 19th century

Artistic representation of the first partition of Poland, with Catherine II of Russia, Stanislaw II of Poland, Joseph II of Austria and Frederick II of Prussia, copper engraving, 18th century

Freedom of religion in Poland
1701 | Great Northern War
1709 | Battle of Poltava
1733–34 | War of the Polish Succession
1795 | Completion of the partition of Poland

Denmark and Sweden to the 17th Century

The kings in Denmark and Sweden carried out the Reformation, attempted to prevail against the nobility, and became involved in the Thirty Years' War. Sweden was one of main benefactors of the war's peace treaty in 1648.

1 Christian IV, ca. 1640

Traditionally in Denmark and Sweden, the nobility tried to maintain their independence, while the kings sought increased central authority and supported their countries' sea power. ❷ Christian II, king of Denmark and Norway from 1513, brutally established his dominance over Sweden with the "Bloodbath of Stockholm"—the mass execution of his opponents in 1520.

3 Queen Christina of Sweden on horseback, ca. 1652–54

Just three years later, however, he was driven out by the Swedish noble Gustav Erickson, who was elected the new king. As ❹ Gustav I Vasa, he established the modern nation-state of Sweden and introduced the Reformation in 1527.

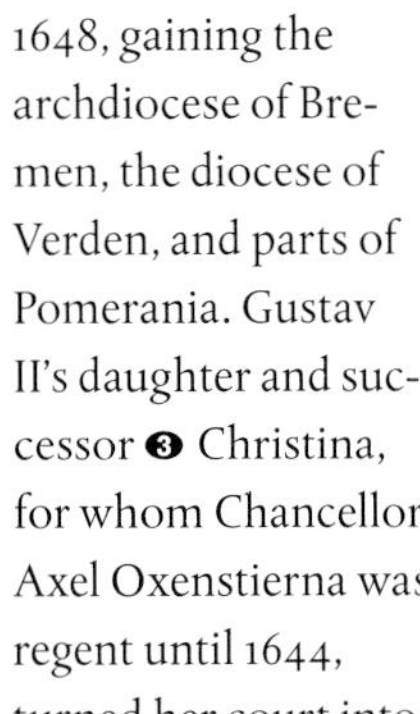

2 Christian II, painting by Lucas Cranach the Elder, ca. 1523

His successors built upon this foundation in wars of shifting alliances against Denmark, Poland, and the Hanseatic city of Lübeck, which controlled the Baltic Sea trade. King Gustav II Adolph was thus able to gain territories in the Baltic from Russia in 1617 and from Poland in 1629, making Sweden the leading power in the north. In 1630, he intervened in the Thirty Years' War (p. 268) as leader of the Protestant powers. Sweden also acquired land from Denmark in 1645 and was among the winners of the Peace of Westphalia in 1648, gaining the archdiocese of Bremen, the diocese of Verden, and parts of Pomerania. Gustav II's daughter and successor ❸ Christina, for whom Chancellor Axel Oxenstierna was regent until 1644, turned her court into a center of scholars but then abdicated in 1654, converted to Catholicism in 1655, and died in ❻ Rome in 1689. The kings of the House of Palatinate-Zweibrucken, who inherited Sweden from the Vasas in 1654, continued to develop Sweden's power and influence.

In Denmark the strengthening of the monarch's authority was served by the introduction of the Reformation in Denmark and Norway in 1536, because it placed the church under the control of the head of state. ❶ Christian IV centralized government and in 1625 entered the Thirty Years' War (p. 267). In 1645, he was forced to recognize Sweden's hegemony in the Baltic region in the Peace of Brömsebro. His son, ❺ Frederick III, broke the power of the nobility in an alliance with the clergy and middle class in 1660, introduced the hereditary monarchy, and established absolutism by the Royal Law of 1665.

1616 Poem by Gustav II Adolph:

Some day virtue will reward you, / When you have become Dust, / With high glory eternal / As you were promised.

Gustav II Adolph, 17th century

4 Gustav I Vasa, 19th-century painting

5 Frederick III, ca. 1648

6 Festivities for the reception of Christina of Sweden in Rome

1520 | Bloodbath of Stockholm

1523 | Gustav I Vasa elected king

1527 | Introduction of the Reformation in Sweden

1536 | Introduction of the Reformation in Denmark

1645 | Treaty of Brömsebro

1654 | Sweden invades Poland

Northern Europe in the 18th Century

Charles XII once again made Sweden the predominant power in northeast Europe, but with his death, all that was gained was lost again. Enlightened absolutism could only be hesitantly implemented in Denmark and Sweden.

❼ Charles X Gustav of the house Palatinate-Zweibrucken, who inherited the Swedish throne from his cousin Christina of Vasa in 1654, extended Swedish possessions in wars against Poland and Denmark—which was forced to relinquish all of southern Sweden, including Skåne and Halland, by the Treaty of Roskilde in 1658. Although his son ❽ Charles XI lost Pomerania to Brandenburg (p. 274), he did finally break the power of the Swedish aristocracy by seizing the crown estates and establishing absolutist rule. Denmark, Russia, and Poland allied against his son Charles XII, who succeeded him in 1699, to regain lost territories from Sweden, but the king invaded Denmark and forced it to accept peace, and then in 1700, leading his troops, destroyed the Russian army at ⓫ Narva. In 1702 Charles XII expelled Augustus the Strong of Saxony and Poland out of Livonia, then in 1702 out of Poland as well, and in 1706 he invaded Saxony. In 1709, however, he suffered a crushing defeat against Czar Peter the Great on the plains of Poltava and was forced to flee to Turkey; he finally fell in Norway in November 1718. The Great Northern War, begun in 1700, was finally concluded at the Treaty of Nystad in 1721. Sweden was forced to turn over its possessions in the Baltic and southwest Finland to Russia.

8 Statue of Charles XI in Karlskrona, 19th century

Domestically, marriages and the inheritance of succeeding reigns by the German houses of Hessen-Kassel and Holstein-Gottorp weakened royal power in Sweden.

⓬ Gustav III Vasa restored the absolute power of the king in 1772 through a coup d'état and abolished aristocratic privileges in 1789. His was a splendid court, and he founded the Swedish Academy in 1786, but he was murdered in March 1792 by a conspiracy of nobles during a masked ball. His son Gustav IV Adolph waged unsuccessful wars against Napoleon and was deposed by his officers in 1809.

Denmark's inflexible absolutism prevented necessary reforms. Two chief ministers, Johann Hartwig Graf Bernstorff and his nephew Andreas Peter Graf Bernstorff, tried to govern in the spirit of enlightened absolutism. In 1771–1772, the physician of the mentally ill King ❿ Christian VII and lover of the Queen Caroline Mathilde, ❾ John Frederick of Struensee, intervened in politics with radical reforms, including the abolition of torture and censorship, but he was overthrown early in 1772 and executed.

10 Christian VII, copper engraving

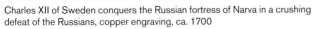

11 Charles XII of Sweden conquers the Russian fortress of Narva in a crushing defeat of the Russians, copper engraving, ca. 1700

7 Charles X Gustav, painting, ca. 1652

9 Struensee is led away to his execution, quill lithography, 19th century

12 Murder of Gustav III in the Stockholm opera house, wood engraving, 19th c.

1658	Treaty of Roskilde
1665	Royal Law in Denmark
1700	Battle of Narva
1721	Treaty of Nystad
1772	Gustav III Vasa's coup
1809	Deposing of Gustav IV Adolf

Russia's Rise as a Great Power 1613–1801

The rule of the Romanov dynasty which began with the election of Michael Romanov in 1613 stabilized the turbulent political conditions in Russia following the "Time of Troubles." Supported by an absolute authority, Czar Peter the Great could push through an authoritative and broad ❶ modernization of the Empire in all fields. His successors continued this modernization and, particularly under Catherine the Great, carried out aggressive Russian expansion policies, particularly against Poland and the Ottoman Empire. Catherine ruled as one of the most powerful "Enlightened monarchs" of the eighteenth century.

1 Caricature referring to the modernizing reforms of Peter the Great: A "reactionary's" beard is cut off, wood engraving, ca. 1700

Russia under the First Romanovs

The ruling Romanov dynasty reintroduced the autocracy of the czars and began to reconquer the lands lost to Poland and Sweden under previous rulers.

The election of ❷ Michael Romanov as Russian czar in 1613, ended the "Time of Troubles" (*Smuta*) (p. 209). His father Fyodor, the Orthodox patriarch of Moscow, stood behind his election. Another relative, the patriarch Philaret, governed Russia jointly with the czar until 1633.

Czar Michael I made peace with Sweden and Poland in 1617–1618, whereby Novgorod was brought back into the empire. The Church reforms led to the Great Schism. Michael's son ❸ Alexis curtailed the rights of the aristocracy and the Church further. The serfdom of the peasants was definitively laid down in law at this time. As a result of the support of the Cossack leader Bogdan Chmelnizkij (p. 302), Russia won back parts of Ukraine with the old Russian capital of Kiev in 1654–1667, leading to conflicts with the Ottomans and the khans of the Crimea in the Ukrainian south.

3 Alexis I and his second wife, medal produced to commemorate the occasion of their son Peter's birth in 1672

2 The Election of Michael Romanov to Czar, watercolor painting, 19th century

After Alexis' death in 1676, his children from two marriages fought for succession. His son Fyodor III became czar but died six years later. Fyodor's sister Sophia then served as regent for her mentally deficient brother Ivan V and underage half-brother ❺ Peter I; in 1686 she allied with Poland and joined the Holy League against the Ottomans. When Peter reached maturity, Sophia tried to retain power and get rid of Peter. However, he preempted her and took power in a coup in 1689, exiling ❹ Sophia to the Novodevichy convent. That year, Peter, who was sole ruler after the death of Ivan, brutally put down the ❻ *streltzi* uprising by a military unit of Sophia's supporters.

4 Sophia in exile in the convent, painting by Ilja Repin, 1879

5 Peter I the Great, painting by Jean Marc Nattier, 1717

6 After his return from Western Europe, Peter I has participants in the *streltzi* uprising executed

1613	Czar Michael I Romanov
since 1696	Reform phase under Peter the Great
16th May 1703	Founding of St. Petersburg
1714	Introduction of a line of succession
1721	Dissolution of the Patriarchy
1725	Catherine I crowned

From Peter the Great to Catherine the Great

Peter the Great's reforms made Russia a modern European great power. His successors, particularly Catherine the Great, carried out the expansion of the empire.

Fascinated by Western European culture, ⑩ Peter I (the Great) undertook a journey to Prussia, England, and Holland in 1697–98, where he was trained as an ordnance soldier and ⑧ shipbuilding engineer. He completed his expansion of the army and fleet and then, in the Great Northern War, conquered Swedish territory in the southwest of Finland and in the Baltic region, giving Russia access to the Baltic Sea (p. 305). Here, on the estuary of the Neva River, he founded his new capital, ⑨ St. Petersburg, which was designed after the European example. Internally Peter initiated comprehensive modernization. He broke the power of the Church by disbanding the patriarchy and appointing a holy synod along the Lutheran model. The economy and social order were reformed by the establishment of early manufacturing organizations, expansion of the infrastructure, recruitment of foreign workers, founding of education institutions, and regulation of the aristocracy and administration.

8 Peter I learns shipbuilding in the Netherlands, wood engraving, 19th c.

10 Peter I founding St. Petersburg, painting, 19th century

11 Elizabeth, daughter of Peter I, painting, ca. 1744–51

9 Peter and Paul Fortress in St. Petersburg, with the Cathedral where the Romanovs are interred

As he had had his own son killed, Peter's widow Catherine I succeeded him in 1725. In 1741 his youngest daughter ⑪ Elizabeth came to the throne. She joined in alliance with Maria Theresa of Austria against Prussia in the Seven Years' War in 1756, and their forces had brought Prussia to the brink of total collapse when Elizabeth died in 1762. This alone saved Frederick the Great, as Elizabeth's successor Peter III was an admirer of the Prussian king and ended the war immediately. In order to control Peter, Frederick had negotiated his marriage to Sophie von Anhalt-Zerbst, the daughter of a Prussian general, in 1745. Peter's reign was brief, however, as his wife, aided by a military putsch, disposed of him and took the throne as ⑦ Catherine II within the year.

Influenced by Enlightenment ideas, Catherine II (the Great) communicated with many of the most significant thinkers of Europe, yet also gave away thousands of serfs as presents to her numerous lovers and favorites.

Catherine adopted strongly imperialist policies and conclusively turned Russia into a great power. In the Russo-Turkish War, Russia destroyed the Turkish Fleet in 1770 and conquered the northern Caucasus, ensuring Russian access to the Black Sea. Crimea, which had less than a decade earlier become independent, was annexed. In the three partitions of Poland in 1772, 1793, and 1795 (p. 303), Russia pushed its boundaries gradually west.

Catherine's son, ⑫ Paul I, took part in the Second Coalition in the Revolutionary Wars against France. In 1801, his plans for the conquest of India led to his murder by military officers.

12 Paul I, painting, late 18th century

7 Catherine the Great, painting, 18th c.

Prince Potemkin

Prince Potemkin was a favorite and political advisor of Catherine the Great. He was a capable administrator and initiated ambitious constructions of city and settlement projects in the south of Russia. Those jealous of him defamed him by suggesting that he set up false facades—"Potemkin villages"—faked civic improvement with which to impress the Czar during her tour of the country.

above: Prince Potemkin

1755 | Founding of the University of Moscow
1756 | End of the Seven Years' War
1762 | Catherine the Great crowned
1768–74 | First Russo-Turkish war
1801 | Murder of Paul I

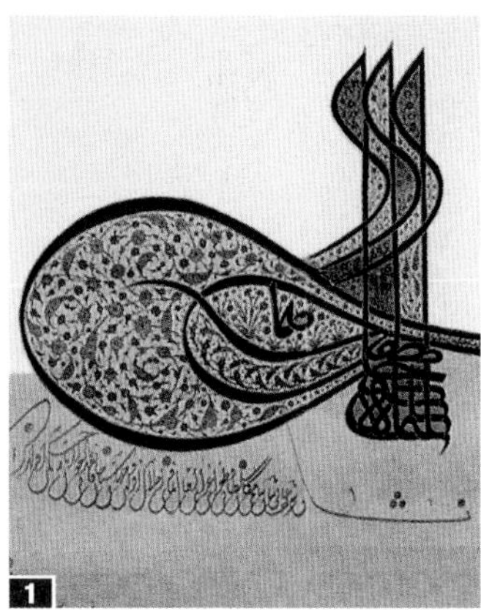

The Ottoman Empire, the Great Power of the East ca. 1300–1792

The Turkmen tribal group of the Ottomans, based in northwestern Anatolia, pushed steadily westward. After the capture of Constantinople in 1453, Sultan Selim I made the Ottoman Empire a major power by 1516-1517 with the conquest of the Near East and large parts of Africa. Under his successors, particularly ❶ Suleiman the Magnificent, the Turkish presence became a determining factor in European politics. After several successful advances against the Habsburg Empire, the Ottomans were forced onto the defensive by the Austrians and Russians after 1697. Internal political reforms were slow.

1 Sultan Suleiman the Magnficent's "tughra," the official seal or signature of a sultan

The Rise of the Ottomans

The early Ottoman sultans consolidated their power in Anatolia and began the conquest of the Balkans. In 1453, Mehmed II took Constantinople and ended the Byzantine Empire.

2 Osman I with his army commanders, colored lithograph

❷ Osman I, the dynasty founder from whom the name "Ottoman" is derived, led an independent tribal group in northwestern Anatolia around 1300. The tribe's warriors had dedicated themselves to a *jihad* against Byzantium. Osman's son Orhan took the title of sultan, made Bursa his capital, and conquered East Anatolia. In 1354, he gained control of Gallipoli, a foothold in the Crimea, which he then used as a base to begin his conquest of the Balkans. Murad I conquered Bulgaria in 1385-86 and triumphed over the Serbs in 1389 in the Battle of Kosovo, at the Field of the Blackbirds.

5 Interior of the Hagia Sophia, finished in the sixth century, mosque since 1453

During the 14th century, the Ottoman tribal federation became a solid state structure. The sultans armed their military well and created an elite corps made up of Islamized Balkan Christians—the much-feared ❸ Janissaries. Bayezid I permanently subjugated Bulgaria in 1393, but suffered a crushing defeat near Ankara in 1402 against the Central Asian conqueror Tamerlane. A reorganization of the state interrupted further expansion until Mehmed I brought Asia Minor and a large part of the Balkans under his control again.

The siege of Constantinople began in 1422 under Murad II, who had subjugated all of Anatolia. In 1439 Murad annexed Serbia—which he crushed in 1448 in the second Battle of Kosovo—into his empire, and repelled the last Christian Crusade in 1444 at Varna. ❹ Mehmed II was able to conquer Constantinople on May 29, 1453, bringing an end to the Byzantine Empire. He had many churches converted into mosques, including the ❺ Hagia Sophia, and built the Topkapi Palace, where the sultans would reside from then on.

4 Sultan Mehmed II

3 Janissary soldier

Critobulus of Imbros, History of Mehmed the Conqueror, 15th century, on

The Conquest of Constantinople:

"... but when Sultan Mehmed saw that the Palisade and the rest of the part of the walls (of Constantinople) had been pulled down and was naked of men and without defenders... he immediately called in a loud voice, 'We have the city, my friends, we have her already. With a small effort and the city is conquered. Do not get weak, but go with courage to the work and prove yourselves brave men and I will be with you.'"

The Ottoman army base outside Constantinople

ca. 1280–1324 | Reign of Osman I
1354 | Conquest of Gallipoli
1389 | Battle of the Field of the Blackbirds
1393–96 | Conquest of Bulgaria
1396 | Battle of Nicopolis
1402 | Battle of Ankara
1451–81 | Reign of Mehmed I

The Zenith of the Ottoman Empire

Mehmed II's successor, Selim I, was responsible for making the Ottoman Empire a world power. During the reign of Suleiman the Magnificent, the empire was at its political and cultural peak.

Sultan Bayezid II

The architect Sinan

Mehmed II considered himself the next world conqueror. While he avoided internal unrest by granting Christians and Jews cultural freedom through payment of a poll tax, his forces overran Serbia, Bosnia, and Albania and occupied the last Christian territories in the Peloponnesus in 1458-1462. He annexed Serbia in 1459 (p. 217). The Ottomans soon controlled the Eastern Mediterranean and the Black Sea through the conquest of Trebizond (p. 212) in Asia Minor and the subjugation of the khans of the Crimea in 1475, and then obligated to tribute payments. In 1480 Mehmed landed in southern Italy and was preparing to advance on Rome, the "heart of Christianity," when he died in the spring of 1481.

A time of military inactivity under the pious sultan ❻ Bayezid II ended in April 1512 with a coup d'état by his son, Selim I (the Grim). At his accession to the throne, Selim proclaimed that he was going to be lord of all civilization and successor to Alexander the Great. He was the creator of the Ottoman world empire. In 1514 he defeated the Safavid rulers of Persia at ❾ Chaldiran (p. 314), occupied Azerbaijan and East Anatolia, and subjugated Kurdistan, which gave him control of the trade routes to Persia. The sultan used the Egyptian Mamelukes' call for aid against the Portuguese to occupy Syria in 1516 and seize Egypt in 1517. With that, Selim had doubled the area of the Ottoman Empire. He deposed the last caliph in Cairo, assuming the title himself, and took over the protectorate of the Islamic holy sites of Mecca and Medina. In order to secure the power of the sultan domestically from rivals and to avoid struggles of succession, he introduced the practice of a sultan murdering all of his brothers upon assuming the throne.

Selim's son ❼ Suleiman I (the Magnificent) led the Ottoman Empire to cultural grandeur. He dedicated himself to the modernization of the government, especially the legal and tax systems. He had magnificent ❿ mosques constructed by his brilliant master builder ❽ Sinan. Suleiman's armies pushed west. In 1521, they took Belgrade, which became their main base in the Balkans in the ensuing period, and they crushed the Hungarians in 1526 at Mohács.

In 1529, the Ottomans approached ⓫ Vienna for the first time and besieged the city, but this was unsuccessful and they were forced to withdraw. The 16th century was marked by the Ottomans' eventful battles against the Habsburgs and Spanish in the Balkans, their control of North Africa, and their domination of the Mediterranean.

7 Sultan Suleiman the Magnificent

The Suleiman Mosque in Istanbul, 16th century

Battle against the Persians on the plain of Chaldiran on the August 23, 1514

The Ottomans besiege Vienna under Suleiman II from September 8 to October 15, 1529

1453	Conquest of Constantinople
1514	Battle of Chaldiran
1516	Conquest of Syria
1517	Conquest of Egypt
1520–66	Reign of Suleiman II
1521	Taking of Belgrade
1526	Battle of Mohács
1529	First Siege of Vienna

The Time of the Grand Viziers

Suleiman I's successors were generally weak rulers whose grand viziers ruled in their stead. Nevertheless, in 1683 the Ottomans once again stood at the gates of Vienna.

2 The naval battle of Lepanto on the 7 Oct 1571

In the middle of the 16th century, Selim II and Murad III ushered in the period of the rule of insignificant sultans with no interest in state affairs. They abandoned themselves to immense luxury and became wrapped up in household intrigues, and the reign of the grand viziers began. Thanks to Grand Vizier Mehmed Sokollu, the empire remained politically stable even after its defeat at the hands of an allied Christian fleet in the naval Battle of ❷ Lepanto in 1571. The Turks opened diplomatic and trade relations with England in 1580 and with the Netherlands in 1603. Caucasia, with ❶ Tbilisi and Tabriz, came under Ottoman control in the 1579-1590 war against Persia, but after 1603 they were lost again to Shah Abbas the Great.

4 The Grand Vizier Kara Mustafa

Revolts in Anatolia and Kurdistan provided signs of the internal disintegration of the empire. The Janissaries had become a powerful state within a state. But in 1622 when they murdered Sultan Osman II, who had attempted to curb their power, his brother Murad IV broke the Janissaries' dominion with barbaric ritual punishment. He was able to subdue the revolts of the Kurds and Druze in Syria, and in 1638 managed to ❸ retake Baghdad from the Safavids. During this period, many Albanians and Bosnians and a portion of the Bulgarians in the Balkans converted to Islam.

From the middle of the 17th century, the governance of the empire was in the hands of the Albanian Koprulu family of grand viziers, who proclaimed a war on corruption and strengthened the central authority. They were also able to snatch Crete from the Venetians in 1669 and Podolia from the Poles in 1672.

The ambitious ❹ Kara Mustafa became grand vizier in 1676 and marched his troops through Hungary. In 1683, he besieged Vienna, but the combined armies and their Polish allies defeated the Turks at the ❺ Kahlenberg heights and drove them back; Charles V of Lorraine and Louis William of Baden-Baden then pushed the Ottomans out of ❻ Hungary. In 1687, the Venetians occupied parts of the Peloponnesus, including Athens. A return to rule of the Koprulu grand viziers did not end Turkish losses in the Balkans.

5 The Battle of Kahlenberg Heights, Sept. 12, 1683

6 Austrian imperial troops attack an Ottoman army base

1 Triumphant parade of the Ottoman army outside the walls of Tbilisi in Georgia after the Persians had abandoned the city in Aug 1578, book illustration

3 The taking of Baghdad by the Ottomans

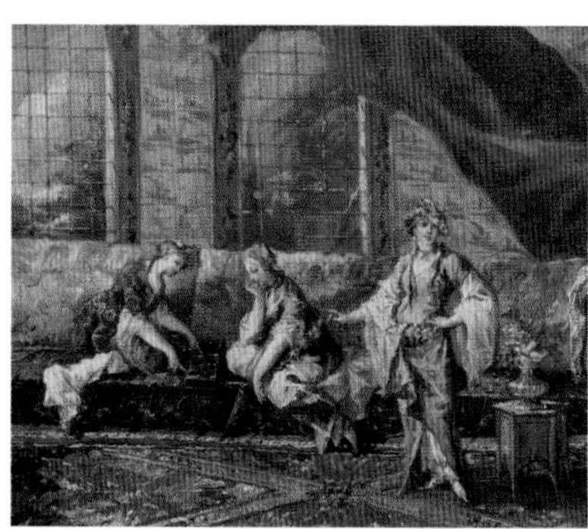

The Harem

The wives of the sultan, his concubines, and the countless servant girls who served them lived in the harem, closed off from the outside world and guarded over by eunuchs. At the head of the harem was the powerful mother of the sultan, with whom the women who had borne the sultan sons vied for power. The sultans' sons were also raised here in this "gilded cage." It was no wonder that many of them were blind to reality or even psychologically disturbed when they finally came to power.

above: Members of the sultan's harem play a game, painting, Francesco Guardi, 18th c.

1565–79 Grand Vizier Mehmed Sokollu | **1571** Battle of Lepanto | **1579–90** War against Persia | **1656–76** Grand Viziers Mehmed and Fasil Ahmed Koprulu | **1669** Conquest of Crete | **1676–83** Grand Vizier Kara Mustafa | **1683** Siege of Vienna

The Empire between Decline and Reform

The Ottoman Empire was forced onto the defensive in the Balkans through the victories of Prince Eugène of Savoy and pressure from Russia. Necessary internal reforms were late in coming and strongly opposed.

8 Sultan Ahmed III in one of the courts of the Topkapi Palace, painting, 18th c.

Defeated by the Austrian general Eugène of Savoy in 1697 at Zenta, the Ottoman empire lost Hungary, Transylvania, and Slavonia to Austria, Podolia to Poland, and the Peloponnesus and parts of Dalmatia to Venice under provisions of the Treaty of Carlowitz; in 1700 Azov went to Russia. When Sultan ❽ Ahmed III granted asylum to Charles XII of Sweden in 1709, he provoked a war with Russia in 1710-1711, which the Ottomans won. In 1717, however, ❼, ❾ Belgrade was lost to the Austrian Empire, which by the Treaty of Passarowitz in 1718 also took the Banat, northern Serbia, and Little Walachia.

These military failures led to the overthrow of Ahmed III in 1730 and a renewed reign of the Janissary corps, which retook northern Serbia and Little Walachia in 1736-1739. While a military pact was made with Austria, Russia with its expansionist ambitions had become the major enemy of the Ottoman Empire by 1741. An alliance between the Ottomans and Prussia in 1761 ushered in cordial relations that continued up to World War I. The Russians advanced into Moldavia and Transcaucasia during the First Russo-Turkish War (1768-1774) and in 1770 destroyed the Turkish fleet. In 1774-1783, the Ottomans lost ❿ Crimea to Russia and Bukovina to Austria. Catherine the Great of Russia then usurped the protectorate over the Christian princes Georgia in 1784. The Turks once again went to war in 1787-1792 against Russia and Austria. Russia made further territorial gains and replaced the Ottoman Empire as the dominant power in the Black Sea region.

7 The Ottomans hand over Belgrade to the Austrians in 1717, painting

The Tulip Era

The short period between 1718 and 1730 during the reign of Sultan Ahmed III is referred to as the Tulip Era. Following the Treaty of Passarowitz, Ottoman interest in the European baroque culture grew, as did Western interest in the Orient. During the Tulip era in Turkey there was an a cultural blossoming of the arts. The tulip, an extremely popular and—as tulip bulbs could be sold for their weight in gold—valuable export from Turkey, became a symbol for the era.

Example of the famous ceramic tiles produced in Iznik, Turkey, with tulip, carnation, and rosette motif

9 The Battle for Belgrade, center Prince Eugene of Savoy, August 18, 1717

10 The Russian deputy sovereign visits the Grand Vizier in 1775 for negotiations

1689–91 Grand Vizier Fasil Mustafa Koprulu | **1697** Battle of Zenta | **1699** Peace of Karlowitz | **1718** Peace of Passarowitz | **1768–74** First Russo-Turkish War | **1770** Destruction of Ottoman fleet | **1787–92** Second Russo-Turkish War

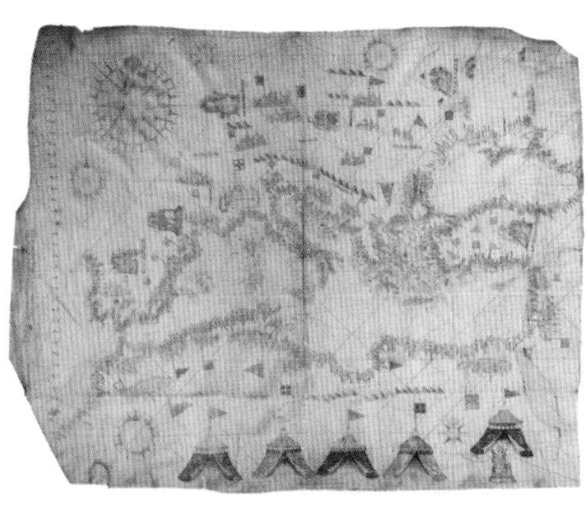

North Africa 16th–18th century

Algeria, Tunisia, and Libya were fiercely contested during the 16th century. The Ottomans eventually prevailed, yet the local elite was able to win increasing political and cultural freedom and became effectively independent by the 17th century. Morocco had particular difficulties defending itself against Portuguese conquest attempts. Under local dynasties, the land grew in prosperity and stability, but, like the whole of the Maghreb, it drew Europe's colonial interest around 1800.

1 Naval map of the Mediterranean and the Black Sea, 1551

2 The Corsair Khayr ad-Din Barbarossa

Algeria and Tunisia in the 16th–18th centuries

The eastern area of the Maghreb was at first fought over by Spain and the Ottomans. The Ottomans were able to uphold their rule for a long time, but the regions won a large degree of autonomy despite their formal suzerainty.

3 Liberated Christians in Tunis express their gratitude to Emperor Charles V

While Syria-Palestine and Egypt had been firmly under the control of the Ottomans since 1517, the coasts of Algeria, Libya, and Tunisia were actively fought over in the 16th century. In the ❶ Mediterranean, the Spanish and the Ottomans competed for both military and commercial supremacy. The Barbary pirates, or corsairs, were a constant source of uncertainty as they often changed allegiance and plundered coastal towns. The most successful of them during this period were the two brothers ❷ Khayr ad-Din. Attacks on Spanish galleons by Khayr ad-Din (Barbarossa) provoked Emperor Charles V into occupying ❸, ❻ Tunis in 1535 and besieging ❺ Algiers, the most important centers on the North African coast.

In the long run, it was the Ottomans who—at least nominally—won supremacy over the eastern Maghreb: Cyrenaica in 1521, Tripolitania (Libya) in 1551, Algeria in 1556, and Tunisia in 1574. From 1587 until 1671, Algeria was administered by a Turkish governor (*pasha*) until the local Janissaries took over rule as *deys* who were only officially dependent on the sultan; this system lasted until the French occupation of 1830. The Ottoman pasha was also deposed in Tunisia in 1591 in favor of a largely autonomous dey. In 1640 Hammuda ibn Murad seized power and founded the dynasty of the Muradid beys that stayed in power until 1702; they were followed in 1705 by Husain ibn Ali, whose dynasty of ❹ Husainid beys ruled until the declaration of the republic in 1957. In Tripolitania, the Qaramanli dynasty ruled from 1711 until 1832 as autonomous beys. Their ships' troops were feared as pirates. Even before 1800, this region was being eyed by France as potential colonial territory.

5 View of the important coastal city of Algiers from the sea

4 Muhammad III, Bey of Tunis (1859–82)

6 Market place in Tunis, painting, 19th century

The Siege of Malta

After the Turks captured the headquarters of the Order of St. John of Jerusalem on Rhodes in 1522, Emperor Charles V gave the Order the island of Malta in 1530 as a fiefdom. From here they continued to defy the Muslim world. A Turkish-corsair fleet tried to conquer Malta in 1565, but the Knights of St. John, supported by the Spanish, held the island, despite a four-month siege. The hero of the defensive battle was the order's grand master, Jean Parisot de La Valette.

above: Turkish forces besiege Malta, May 1565

1472 | Wattasid rule in Morocco begins
1515 | Portuguese besiege Marrakech
1517 | Ottomans occupy Syria-Palestine and Egypt
1521 | Ottoman conquest of Cyrenaica
1524 | Start of Sa'did Dynasty rule in Morocco
1556 | Ottomans conquer Algeria

Morocco under the Wattasids and the Early 'Alawites

The Wattasids and the later dynasties of the Sa'did and 'Alawites defended Morocco's independence. Morocco experienced stability and prosperity under Mawlay Ismail and his successors as a result of its strategic position for trade.

The capital Marrakech, which lies in an oasis where date palms grow

⑩ Morocco did not come under the rule of the Ottomans, but was forced to defend its independence against Portugal. The Wattasids, who had ruled Morocco since 1472, lost Melilla to the Spanish in 1497 and then Agadir and large expanses of their coastal regions in 1504 to the Portuguese, who then besieged ⑦ Marrakech in 1515. In 1524 the Sa'did dynasty rebelled in southern Morocco, and in 1554 they deposed the last of the Wattasid rulers. Muhammad al-Mahdi, the founder of the Sa'did dynasty, assumed the title of sultan, made an alliance with the Ottomans, and declared himself a descendent of the Prophet Muhammad (*sharif*), and even a caliph of Islam. His descendant, ⑧ Ahmad al-Mansur, crushingly defeated the invading Portuguese under King Sebastian in 1578 at Ksar el-Kebir, and through tight administration led the country to considerable prosperity. Through the policy of *makhzan*, a system of awarding land, he was able to make the elite of the country beholden to him. His sons divided the land in two ruling lines that governed Fez (until 1626) and Marrakech (until 1659).

The Sa'did sharifs were followed in 1666 by the 'Alawite dynasty of sharifs, who still rule Morocco today. Mawlay ar-Rashid, the first ruler, established himself in Fez and, in alliance with the Ottomans, conquered Marrakech in 1669 and finally all of Morocco. His son, ⑨ Mawlay Ismail, succeeded him in 1672 and was the most important ruling public figure of Maghreb in the 18th century. Politically shrewd, ostentatious, and violent, he broke the resistance of the local sheiks and religious brotherhoods, created a personal elite corps of 150,000 black slaves, and built the magnificent "imperial city" of Meknes. He maintained trading relations with many European powers.

Everything Mawlay Ismail had gained was at stake in the fratricidal war of his seven sons. However, his grandson, Mawlay Mohammed, was able to restore stability through the reorganization of the administration system, and finances and by fostering the economy through the granting of trade licenses, primarily to France and the United States. His son Mawlay Suleiman continued these policies by easing tariffs for the European powers. After 1810, he changed his originally liberal policy concerning religion and persecuted religious brotherhoods and banned local customs, which led to general unrest. Around 1800 Morocco's prosperity caught the interest of France and Spain.

Detail from the Sadier tombs at Marrakech, built under Sultan Ahmad al-Mansur

The stables in Mawlay Ismail's Meknes

Moroccan landscape, small settlement with the Atlas Mountain range that stretches across northern Morocco in the background

May–Sep 1565 | Siege of Malta
1574 | Ottomans occupy Tunisia
1578 | Battle of Ksar el-Kebir
1640 | Muradid Bey rule in Tunisia begins
from 1666 | 'Alawite dynasty rule in Morocco
1705 | Husainid Bey Dynasty rule in Tunisia
1711 | Qaramanli Dynasty rule in Libya

Persia under the Safavids and Qajars ca. 1450–1921

The rule of the Shiite Safavids introduced a period of independent religious and cultural development in ❶ Persia after 1500. In particular Shah Abbas the Great, through his military and economic policies, made the country a major power in the Near East. For this reason, it was constantly in competition with the Ottoman Empire. Following the Safavids, Nadir Shah erected a short-lived empire that fell apart again under his successor. The Qajars, who came to power in 1796, were the first dynasty able to restore Persia's unity. At the same time, the Central Asian Uzbek empire was flowering under the Shaybanids.

1 Map of Persia, 1681

The Beginnings of the Safavids and the First Safavid Shahs

Shah Ismail established Safavid rule in Persia in 1501. He laid the groundwork for the Shi'ite identity of the country, which was used as a foundation by his successors.

In the power vacuum left by the local dynasties, the heirs of the Timurid Empire established the Sufi Order of the Safavids, which converted to Twelver Shiism in the 15th century. The hereditary sheikhs of the order also fostered a military basis among their followers and were able to extend their power. The founder of the dynasty, and the first shah was Ismail I (ruled 1499-1524), ruler of the town of Ardevil, who descended from the Sassanid dynasty. A Shi'ite, he conquered all of Iran and Iraq and drove the Uzbeks east by 1507. In 1514, at Chaldiran, he suffered defeat against the Ottomans under Sultan Selim I (p. 309).

Shah Ismail focused on domestic development. He concentrated religious and secular authority and made Twelver Shiism the state religion, dramatically influencing Iran's development as a nation-state. Ismail's rule, based on his own charisma, showed itself to be unsturdy under his son Tahmasp I, who succeeded him in 1524. The new shah, who was himself artistically talented, promoted painting and calligraphy. During his reign, magnificent editions of the Persian national epic, ❷, ❸ *Shah Namah*, and the "Khamsa" by Nizami were created. During the course of his entire reign, Tahmasp was forced to wage war against the Uzbeks over Khorasan in the east and with the Ottoman Turks over Azerbaijan in the west. In 1548 he moved his capital from Tabriz to Qazvin. In 1554 he occupied Georgia, where he increased military recruitment of Caucasians, and in 1555 exchanged Iraq for Azerbaijan in a peace settlement with the Ottomans. The reigns of Tahmasp's sons, Ismail II (ruled 1576–77) and Mohammad Khudabanda (ruled 1578–1587), almost led to the collapse of the state structure. Mohammed's son Abbas, who was declared shah in Herat in 1581, entered Qazvin in 1587 and forced his father to abdicate. In 1592 he moved the capital again from Qazvin to Isfahan.

2 From the *Shah Namah* or "Book of Kings" by Firdausi, 1567

3 From the *Shah Namah* or "Book of Kings" by Firdausi: Ardashir's fight against Arduwan, book illustration, 16th century

The Safavids

The Safavids came out of a Sufi order of Shi'a Islam. It was founded about 1300 by Sheikh Safi od-Din (1252–1334) in Ardabil in present-day Azerbaijan. Because of his socially revolutionary orientation and active proselytizing in neighboring countries, he soon became very popular. He supported himself militarily with his own troops, who were named Kizilbash ("redheaded ones") after their red turbans. The order founded the Safavid Dynasty in 1501.

Dance of the Dervishs, book miniature from the "Khamsa" by Dschami, early 16th century

1501 | Rule of the Safavid Shahs in Persia
1507 | Conquest of Iran and Iraq by Ismail I
1514 | Battle of Chaldiran
1554 | Occupation of Georgia
1581 | Shah Abbas I the Great
1590 | Ottomans gain Azerbaijan and Kurdista

The Safavid Empire under Abbas the Great

Shah Abbas the Great led the Safavid Empire to its political, and economic zenith. The first of his successors were able to govern using the structures he had created. Encouragement of immigration and trade enriched his country. He rebuilt the capital, Ispahan.

Shah Abbas I (the Great; 1571-1629) was the most eminent of the Safavid rulers. He energetically oversaw the reorganization of the state. In 1590, he made peace with the Ottomans, at first conceding Georgia, Armenia, Azerbaijan and Kurdistan to them territories which he would later recover. He created a standing army of Christian Caucasians, Armenians, and Circassians under British officers that he organized after the model of the Turkish Janissaries. In 1598 Abbas retook Khorasan from the Uzbeks, and he then annexed Bahrain in 1601, captured Azerbaijan, Armenia, and Georgia between 1603 and 1608, and in 1623–24 retook Kurdistan as well as Iraq from the Ottomans, making Persia the supreme power of the Near East.

Persian Carpets

The renown of Persian carpets, which persists to this day, was established during the reign of Abbas the Great. Carpets were already being manufactured in Persia, but only then did the export to Europe begin. Here they served, not as floor coverings as in the East where people prayed sitting, but as luxury coverings for tables and beds. The designs changed in this period from representations of figures to arabesques, blossoms, and leaves. The material—silk—was provided by the Armenians settled in nearby Isfahan, who monopolized the silk trade.

top: Carpet with trees, birds and a deer; in the center a pond with ducks, 16th century

5 Wall hanging from the Lutfallah-Mosque, Isfahan, early 17th century

Abbas's greatest accomplishments were in the area of domestic politics. He settled Caucasian craftsmen in Iran and invited Christian and Jewish traders and merchants into the country, which brought the people prosperity and the state coffers enormous wealth. ❹ Isfahan, his new capital, was ❺ magnificently rebuilt. Under Abbas, the leasing and tax systems were simplified, and he maintained close ❻, ❼ trade relations with the Moguls in India. Abbas seized the trading center of Hormuz from the Portuguese in 1622, from which he controlled the trade of the Persian Gulf. At this point, Europeans also discovered Safavid Persia; trade delegations, artists, and adventurers came into the country in swarms, some of them personally received by the ❽ shah. When Abbas the Great died in 1629, Persia stood at its political and economic peak, a modern empire with diplomatic contacts throughout the world.

7 Caravan on the Shahrestan Bridge in Isfahan

It was during the reign of Abbas's grandson Safi I, who killed his family during a fit of paranoia, that Iraq was lost to the Ottoman Turks in 1638. It was thanks to Grand Vizier Mirza Taqi that Armenia wasn't lost as well. Safi's son Abbas II was the last of the strong Safavid leaders, securing the streets and trade routes, and maintaining intensive economic exchange with European colonies. In his fight against corruption and the arbitrary use of power, he reformed the legal system.

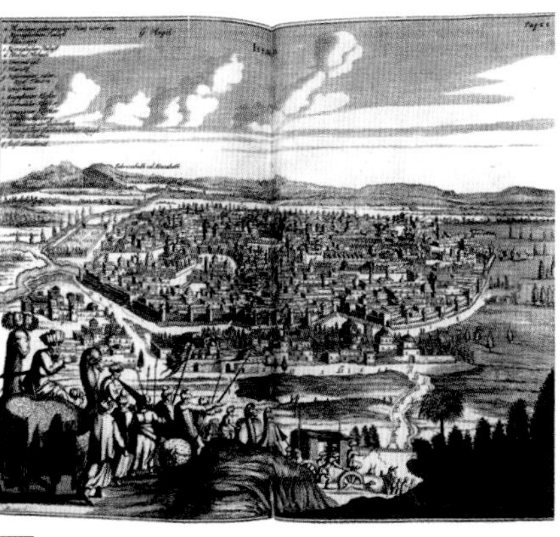

4 Isfahan, copper engraving, 1681

6 *The Caravan of the Persian Shah*, painting by Alberto Pasini, 1867

8 Reception by a Persian Prince, miniature, end of the 16th century

1598 | Conquest of Khorasan

1601 | Annexation of Bahrain

1603–08 | Conquest of Azerbaijan, Armenia, and Georgia

1623–24 | Conquest of Kurdistan and Iraq

1629 | Death of Abbas I the Great

1638 | Ottoman conquest of Iraq

From the Last of the Safavids to the Qajars

During the reigns of the last Safavid rulers, the empire experienced its decline and fall. Only the conqueror Nadir Shah was able, in 1736, to once again create a great empire. After a short reign by the Zand, the Qajars came to power.

1 Afghan

2 Qajar

The "Peacock Throne"

When Nadir Shah defeated the Indian grand mogul, he took the Moguls' treasures for himself, bringing them back to Persia. In addition to the Peacock Throne and the famous Koh-i-noor diamond, which is today part of the British Crown Jewels in the Tower of London, they became a symbol of the shahs.

top: The Grand Moghul Shajahan on the Peacock Throne, Persian miniature

Following the reign of Abbas II (ruled 1642-1667), signs of a Safavid decline could be seen. He sought French aid against Constantinople, in return for commercial preferences. His son Safi II left the running of the government largely to palace eunuchs. In 1668 he assumed the throne for a second time under the name of Shah Suleiman, while his hostile neighbors pushed into Iranian territory unimpeded. Safi's son Sultan Husein (ruled 1694-1722) submitted himself completely to the rule of Shiite clerics. When he began forced conversions of the Afghan Sunnis, who had been subjugated in 1648, he provoked a revolt of the Afghans. In 1709 they murdered the Persian officials and soldiers and declared Afghanistan independent. In 1719 the Afghans marched into Persia under their leader Mir Mahmud and conquered the country. Sultan Husein was executed in 1726.

Although Mahmud declared himself shah in 1722, two shadow rulers of the House of Safavid continued to claim control until 1736. During the reign of the last Safavid, Abbas III, General Nadir of the Afshar, a Turkmen tribe, rose to power. Nadir drove the ❶ Afghans out of Isfahan in 1726 and by 1730 out of all of Persia, seized Azerbaijan and the Caucasus from the Ottomans, and then ascended the throne in 1736 as Nadir Shah. He moved his capital from Ispahan to Mashhad, on the route to India reoccupied Afghanistan in 1738, pushed into India taking Peshawar and, reaching Delhi in 1739. Afterward, he turned to Central Asia and conquered Chiva and Bukhara. In June 1747, Nadir Shah was murdered by his own emirs.

The Afshar dynasty didn't outlive Nadir Shah for long. His grandson lost the empire in 1749, Afghanistan, Azerbaijan, and a large part of Persia proclaimed themselves independent. The Kurdish military leader Karim Khan Zand (ruled 1750-1779) established the Zand dynasty in central and southern Iran, with its capital at Shiraz. After his death in 1779, his sons fought each other until being replaced in 1794 by the ❷ Qajars.

The Qajars were Turkmen nomads from the northwest of Iran and followers of the Safavids. Their leader, Agha Muhammad Khan, made Tehran his capital in 1786, deposed the last Zand ruler in 1794, and then took the title of shah of Persia in 1796. The Qajar dynasty that he founded ruled until 1925. When he was murdered in June 1797, the dynasty was so well established that his nephew Fath Ali Shah (ruled 1797-1834) was able to assume power without opposition. Under his rule, Iran began a close ❸ association with the great powers of Europe, primarily the British who were concerned about the expansionism of Russia.

3 Asker-Khan, the Persian legate in France, painting by Joseph Franque

1648 Subjugation of Afghanistan | **1709** Afghan revolt and declaration of independence | **1719** Afghan conquest of Persia | **1730** Afghans driven out of Persia | **1736** Nadir Shah comes to power | **1736-1738** Nadir Shah's conquests in Central Asia | **1739** Persia expands to Delhi

Central Asia

Under the Uzbek successor dynasties following the Timurids, Central Asia—especially the capitals Bukhara and Samarkand—remained a cultural center of eastern Islam. During the 18th century, however, they fell under Persian and later Russian suzerainty.

4 Chanaka Nadir Diwan-Begi, an inn for pilgrims in Buchara, build in 1620

The cultural blossoming under the Timurids continued under their successors, the Uzbek tribal confederation. Beginning in 1500, the ❻ Uzbek leader Muhammad Shaybani Khan seized the territories of the Timurids, occupying Herat in 1507 and establishing the rule of the Shaybanids, a dynasty with Mongolian roots. He fell in 1510 at Merv against the Safavids attempting to conquer Khorasan, but his rule over Bukhara and the capital Samarkand was established. Ubaydallah and his successors further built up both cities with numerous mosques, ❽ madrassas, and inns for ❹ pilgrims. The former tribal warriors soon assumed the courtly culture of the cities and supported the ❼ Naqshbandi order, so that the region became a center for Islamic mysticism. Since 1540 one line had ruled in Bukhara, and Abdallah II, the last of the Shaybanids, was able to reunify the empire out of Bukhara in 1583 and successfully expanded his domination to the west, east, and north.

5 Alim Khan, the last Emir of Buchara

In 1599, Baqi Muhammad, leader of another Uzbek tribal confederation, the Djanids (or Astrakhanids), took control over Central Asia. They made Bukhara their capital and once more developed it splendidly, reigning there until 1785. In the 18th century, various conquerors cast an eye on Bukhara. Nadir Shah of Persia occupied large parts of the empire after 1737, including Balkh, Chiva, and Bukhara. Chiva remained under Persian and Turkmen domination until 1770. Czarist Russia, which was expanding eastward, sought to influence the politics of the khanate, until finally bringing the area under its control in the 19th century.

8 The madrassa Mir-i Arab in Buchara, built 1535-1536

9 The conquest of Samarkand by the Emir of Buchara, 1868. painting

6 Uzbek commander Muhammad Shaybani Khan, painting, 1873

7 Members of an Islamic Order in Tashkent, painting

After Kokand and other regions had detached themselves from the central regime beginning in 1732, a rapid loss of power and a civil war among the Djanids occurred in 1747. The rulers fell under the regency of the related Mangits from around 1753 until Amir-i-Masum Shah, who acted as regent in Bukhara beginning in 1770, assumed the title of "prince of the believers" and established the khanate of the Mangits in 1785. He was able to assert himself in the Bukhara region in the early 19th century, but following ❾ internal unrest, the area fell under Russian rule between 1868 and 1873. The last ❺, ❿ Mangit khan was deposed in 1921.

10 Setareje Mahe Chase, the summer residence of the last reigning Emir of Buchara, Said Alim Khan

1747 | Nadir Shah murdered
1749 | Independence of Azerbaijan and Afghanistan
1779 | Qajar Dynasty in Iran
1796 | Agha Muhammad Khan becomes Shah of Persia
1868–73 | Russian supremacy in Central Asia

A Mogul ruler in the region of Agra, Indian miniature, ca. 1650

Mogul India and the European Trading Companies 1526–ca. 1800

The Indian Mogul Empire had existed since 1526, blossoming under Akbar's rule beginning in 1556. The splendor and luxury for which the Moguls are famed developed under his successors. After the death of Aurangzeb, the last important ❶ Mogul ruler, the empire declined both politically and culturally, while the European trading companies that had established themselves on the coasts of India since 1500 increasingly influenced political affairs. The Portuguese, initially the most powerful European state in India, were later pushed aside by the Dutch and British. Eventually, the British politically and economically dominated the subcontinent.

The First Moguls to Akbar the Great

Babur, founder of the Mogul Empire, established his authority over wide areas of India, which were, however, lost again under Humayun. It was not until Akbar the Great that the empire was finally consolidated.

By 1526 ❸ Babur had conquered the north and middle of India, founding the Mogul Empire, which in the 16th and 17th centuries would reach almost unbelievable standards of splendor together with immeasurable wealth. The name of Babur's dynasty, the Moguls (Mongols), reflects his Central Asian heritage: He was directly related to Tamerlane on his father's side and Genghis Khan on his mother's. In 1497 Babur became the ruler of Samarkand. He went on to conquer Kabul in 1504 and then pushed steadily southward into India from Afghanistan through the Khyber Pass, taking Lahore in 1524. After his victory over the last Lodi ruler at Panipat in 1526, Babur controlled the majority of India and made Agra his capital.

Just how unstable his empire was became evident under his son, Humayun, who was driven out of India and into Persia by the brilliant commander Shir Shah Khan, who took Agra, Delhi and Lahore, in 1540. Shir Shah established his own dynasty, consolidating and giving firm institutions to the Mogul empire, but his kingdom collapsed after his murder in 1545 and had disappeared by 1555. Humayun returned from Persian exile but had a fatal accident shortly afterward.

His son ❷ Akbar the Great ascended the throne at the age of 13 in 1556. He shaped the Mogul Empire and guided the Indian-Islamic culture to a new golden age. A capable general as well as politician, he extended the empire in all directions and controlled the area from Kabul and Kashmir in the west to Bengal in the east. Northern Deccan to the south, including the Rajput states of Rajasthan and Gujarat, were also parts of his empire. Akbar erected the royal city of ❹, ❺ Fatehpur Sikri as his new capital. He created a new class of nobility loyal to him from the military aristocracy of various tribes, implemented a modern government, and supported the economy. At the same time, he intensified trade with the European trading companies. Akbar allowed free expression and discussion of all religions—even Christianity and Judaism—at his court and organized colloquia and debates.

Babur, the founder of the Mogul dynasty in India, miniature, 17th century

The private audience hall of the emperor in Fatehpur Sikri

Akbar crosses the Ganges, Indian miniature, ca. 1600

The residence Fatehpur Sikri, illustration from the *Akbar-name*, ca. 1590

1504 | Babur seized Kabul
1526 | Founding of the Mogul Empire
1540 | Moguls driven out of India
ca. 1542 | Shir Shah Khan founds his own kingdom
1545 | Shir Shah Khan murdered
1555 | Shir Shah's dynasty dissolves

The Empire at the Height of Its Splendor

Akbar's successors Jahangir and Shah Jahan were politically weak but are notable as great patrons of the arts and architecture. Their love of extravagance brought the state into difficulties.

6 The mausoleum of Akbar in Sikandra

A tolerant and far-sighted ruler, Akbar attempted to resolve the smoldering differences between Muslims and Hindus in his empire by establishing a new religion with strong characteristics of a ruler cult. *Din-i-Ilahi* ("Divine Faith") was a mixture of Islam, Hinduism, and other religions, but it failed due to the massive resistance of the Islamic court orthodoxy. Akbar's grand buildings — court studios in which magnificently illustrated books, ❽ carpets, and jewelry were created—served both political and symbolic functions.

❻ Akbar left his successors an internally stable empire, but before long the first signs of political weakness emerged. Akbar's son ⓫ Jahangir, who succeeded him in 1605, was addicted to opium, neglected affairs of state, and came under the influence of rival court cliques. The grandeur of the arts and ❿ immense court administration that developed under his reign fascinated foreign envoys. Great Britain in particular had been trying to establish diplomatic and economic relations since 1609 and was granted numerous trade privileges. Jahangir's reign was weakened by rebellions in his own family and in Deccan beginning in 1620. During the reign of his son ❼, ❾ Shah Jahan, the splendor and luxury of the court reached its zenith. He collected tens of thousands of jewels, exported the products of the Indian painting schools to the world, and commissioned the construction of the ⓬ Taj Mahal near Agra.

Shah Jahan was not only an enthusiastic builder but also a distrustful personality who took ruthless measures against his adversaries, suspected as well as real. As a strict Muslim, he attacked the Portuguese colony in India and left Christian captives who refused conversion to Islam to die in prison. The "grand mogul" retreated to his harem palaces, isolated from the outside world, and left the government of his empire increasingly to his ministers and eunuchs. The maintenance of the court began to cost more than taxes brought in. In June 1658 Shah Jahan was deposed by his sons.

above: Shah Jahan
right: Shah Jahan's favorite wife Mumtaz-i-Mahal

8 Indian carpet from Madras

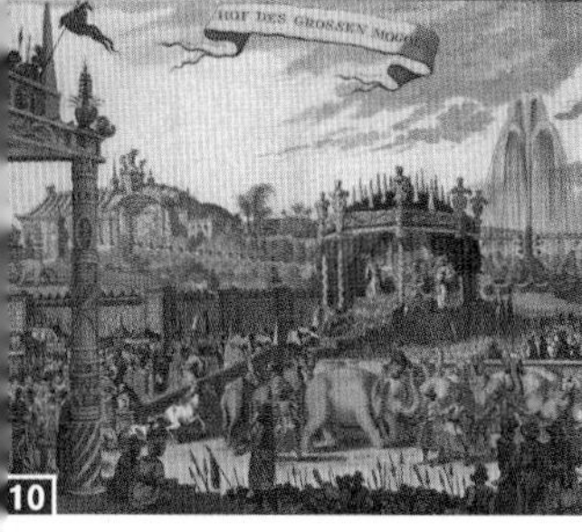
10 Court of the great Mogul, engraving by Jan Caspar Philips, 18th century

11 Jahangir with a picture of the Virgin Mary

Taj Mahal

Between 1632 and 1648, Shah Jahan had the Taj Mahal constructed out of white marble by 20,000 workers as a mausoleum for his favorite wife Mumtaz-i-Mahal ("Pearl of the palace"), who died in childbirth in 1631. A planned parallel mausoleum for Shah Jahan himself, to be built out of black marble, was never constructed. The Taj Mahal, whose interior is equally magnificently constructed and in which Shah Jahan was also laid to rest, is often called the "Eighth Wonder of the World."

above: The Taj Mahal in Agra. The central building with its 22 cupolas and minarets (ca. 131 ft high), made of marble and red sandstone that must be continually renovated due to its porosity.

12 Ornaments with blossom motifs in the Taj Mahal

1556 Akbar the Great takes power
1605 Rule of Jahangir
1609 Diplomatic relations established with Great Britain
1631 Attack on the Portuguese Indian colonies
1658 Shah Jahan deposed

Aurangzeb and the Decline of the Moguls in India

During Aurangzeb's reign, the empire gained political strength once more, but his religious conservatism and intolerance undermined the stability of society. His successors became mere decadent shadow rulers.

1 The great Mogul Aurangzeb

3 The conquest of Kandahar by Aurangzeb

The conflict that had been building among the four sons of Shah Jahan and Mumtaz-i-Mahal since 1644 flared up immediately after their father was deposed. At first it seemed that the eldest, Prince ❷ Dara Shukoh, a supporter of the arts and of dialogue between religions, would prevail. However, the third son ❶ Aurangzeb, allied with Islamic orthodoxy against his brother and ascended the Mogul throne in June 1658 under the name of Alamgir ("world conqueror"). In 1659 he defeated Dara Shukoh and had him executed. Aurangzeb was a strictly orthodox Muslim, popular for his application of Sharia law. A talented military commander, he doubled the empire's territory, and the Mogul Empire reached its greatest expanse when he seized Deccan, ❸ Kandahar, and Kabul. In 1687, he conquered the Kingdom of Golkonda, the most significant state on the Indian subcontinent.

2 Dara Shukoh with his army

Domestically, Aurangzeb brutally suppressed all "unorthodox" movements with the help of secret police. His ruthless drive for the conversion of the Hindus and Sikhs—including the execution of the Sikh guru Tegh Bahadur in 1675—sowed the seeds for the political decline of the Mogul Empire. Aurangzeb had Hindu temples systematically razed to the ground and erected ❹, ❺ mosques in their place. In 1679 he reintroduced the poll tax for non-Muslims, which had been abolished under Akbar. When Aurangzeb, the last powerful Mogul, died in March 1707, many parts of the empire were in open revolt.

Aurangzeb's son, Bahadur Shah I, was able to make favorable contracts again with the princes of Bengal and the English trading companies, reform the tax system, and repeal the harsh religious policies of his father. However, after his death in 1712, the Mogul dynasty sank into chaos and violent family feuds. In the year 1719 alone, four Moguls successively ascended the throne. In 1739 Nadir Shah of Persia invaded India and plundered the treasures of the palaces (p. 316). The succeeding Moguls ruled only nominally and never left their palaces, where the British eventually found them vegetating under indescribable conditions. After a crushed rebellion which he led in 1857–58, the last "Mogul," Bahadur Shah II, was deposed by the British, who then took control of the country.

British Ambassador Sir William Norris, 1701, Describing his Encounter with Emperor Aurangzeb

"He was completely white, the clothing, the turban, and the beard and was carried by a crowd of humans in open gentleness. But he himself saw no one, as his eyes were directed towards a book in his hands, which he read during the entire way, not letting himself be distracted by any other object."

6 The Portuguese seafarer Vasco da Gama, who discovered the sea route to India, Portuguese book illustration, 1683

4 Mosque of Gyanvapi, built by Aurangzeb, in Benares on the Ganges, watercolor by R. Smith, 1833

5 The mosque of Gyanvapi with neighboring ghats in Benares, steel engraving, ca. 1850

1497–98 | Sea route to India discovered
1531–58 | British conquest of Indian west coast
1612 | Naval battle of Suali
1658 | Aurangzeb comes to power
1675 | Tegh Bahadur's execution
1679 | Reintroduction of poll tax for non-Muslims

From European Trading Companies to British Domination

The Portuguese controlled European trade with India in the 16th century, but after 1600 they were pushed aside by the Dutch, British, and French. The British eventually gained political control throughout the region as well.

7 The St. Alex Church in Calangute, Goa, built in 1515

During the rise and fall of the Mogul Empire, the ⓬ European trading companies were establishing themselves on the Indian coasts. Following ❻ Vasco da Gama's discovery of a sea route to India in 1497–1498 (p. 298), the Portuguese—having defeated the combined fleets of Egypt and Gujarat at Diu in 1509—reached

8 A frigate of the kind used by the East India Company off of the Indian Coast, from two perspectives, painting by Thomas Whitcombe

❼ Goa in 1510. From there they proceeded to conquer the west coast of India in 1531–1558 and establish a ❿ trade monopoly of goods from India and Indonesia in Europe.

In the 17th century, the Dutch and English entered into competition with the Portuguese, after Queen Elizabeth granted the British ❽ East India Company a monopoly over British trade with India in 1600. The British, who had already established a trading post in Agra in 1608, defeated the Portuguese in a naval engagement near Surat in 1612 and went on to set up outposts on both the east and west coasts of India. In 1658, Chennai (Madras) became the headquarters of the ⓫ East India Company, which had been diplomatically represented at the court of the Moguls since 1603. In 1668, the British also took Mumbai (Bombay) from the Portuguese. Meanwhile, the Dutch East India Company was able to establish itself in Surat in 1618 and Bengal in 1627 and drove the Portuguese out of Ceylon in 1638. That led to the bitter and bloody ⓭ struggle between the British and the Dutch, which the British eventually won.

9 Warren Hastings

In 1664, the French under Finance Minister Jean-Baptiste Colbert also entered the competition for Indian trade. The French *Compagnie des Indes Orientales* seized bases on the west and east coasts in 1668 and won, in 1739, the southern portion of the Kingdom of Hyderabad. Joseph François Dupleix, governor-general of the company from 1742 to 1754, was able to spread French influence across all of the southern Indian principalities. There were several clashes between the French and British in southern India between 1746 and 1763, which the British eventually won under the leadership of Robert Clive. In 1765 Lord Clive became governor of East India, and the East India Company was given Bengal, Bihar, and Orissa (Kalinga), making British dominance of the subcontinent a fact.

❾ Warren Hastings, the first governor-general of Bengal from 1772 to 1785, put a complete end to French influence there and paved the way for British political domination of India. In 1784, the East India Company was placed under the control of the British government, which instituted British universities in India and anglicized Indian society to a far-reaching extent. After the last Mogul had been deposed, India was governed by a British viceroy, or *Raj*, from 1858 until Indian independence in 1947.

10 European merchant ships, presumably Portuguese, at the Indian coast, Indian miniature, late 16th century

11 Two British officers of the East India Company are entertained with music and dance

12 Europeans smoking a water pipe, Indian miniature, ca. 1760

13 British warships at an island in Dutch East India, painting by Dominic Serres the Elder

687 | Conquest of Golkonda
1690 | Calcutta founded
1707 | Aurangzeb dies
1739 | Persian invasion
1746–63 | Anglo-French war over southern India
1784 | East India Company under British government
1858 | East India Company dissolved

China under the Ming and Manchu Emperors 1368–ca. 1800

The native Ming dynasty established itself in China in 1368, but the central power of the ❶ emperor was already in decline by the 15th century. The country was under constant pressure from Mongolian tribes and also had to defend itself against the advance of the Europeans. Economic prosperity led to an enormous increase in the population. The country expanded into Central Asia under the Manchu emperors, but was showing internal stagnation in its bureaucratic and intellectual traditionalism.

1 The Forbidden City, residence of the emperor since the Ming era

The Beginnings of the Ming Dynasty

In 1368, the Mings drove the Mongolians out of China, but they were constantly forced to defend their rule against internal and external enemies. However, the court eunuchs eventually came to exercise real power.

❷ Zhu Yuanzhang, a former Buddhist monk, drove the Mongolian Yuan dynasty out of China from the south and founded the Ming dynasty as Emperor Hung-Wu. A cruel despot, ❸,❹ officials and ministers were limited to counseling functions, and the administration of the 13 provinces was carried out directly by the ruler—in this case a ruler who penalized the slightest infraction with cruel punishment. As the peasants had supported his rise to power, the emperor instituted a redistribution of land, made taxes more equitable, and established a work colony for the destitute. Defense against the Mongols and Japanese invasions on the coasts remained a pressing military problem during the whole of the Ming period. As early as 1387, China began building fortifications on the east and southeastern coasts and continued construction of the ❺ Great Wall.

Emperor Chengzu, who ascended the throne in 1402, built a fleet of ships and intensified overseas trade. The eunuchs were now increasingly replacing the officials in the internal administration until they became, under Chengzu's successor, the actual instrument of rule. The leading eunuch Zheng undertook sea voyages to Africa and developed a market for African products in China; an endeavor which he did not persue. After Chengzu, there followed a series of weak or very young emperors, who were effectively controlled by court cliques and the eunuchs, while Mongolian leaders were able to advance several times as far as Nanjing and Beijing. By 1550 all of the court offices and control of the bureaucracy were in the hands of the cliques and court favorites. Through the reinforcement of the teachings of Confucius in the academies and civil service schools, the internal structure of the state was able to remain relatively stable despite occasional rebellions in the rural provinces.

3 A civil servant (right) and a military servant (left) from the Ming era

2 Zhu Yuanzhang, Emperor Taizu

4 Portrait of an educated dignitary from the Ming era

5 The Great Wall

Wang Yangming

The greatest Ming philosopher, Wang Yangming (1472–1529), worked to counter the intellectual torpor in China. He combined Neo-Confucianism with Chinese Buddhism and reinforced the intellectual fusion of both systems. Furthermore, he developed the idea of "intuitive" as opposed to rational knowledge of what is good and bad, with which many political decisions were justified.

1368 Ming Dynasty founded
1402 Emperor Chengzu
1421 Extension of the Great Wall
1516 First Portuguese base in Canton
1563 Elimination of Japanese pirates

The End of the Mings and Beginning of Christian Influence

The power of the Mings decreased during the 16th century until the Manchus deposed them in 1644. At the same time Europeans, the Jesuits in particular, were able to gain a foothold in China.

As the Ming emperors had to station large armies on the coasts and the northern and southern borders of the empire to defend against external enemies, colonies were established in the borderlands, leading to the settlement of previously uninhabited regions. Due to the Mongolian threat, the capital was also moved from Nanjing to Beijing.

The economy of the Ming period was based primarily on expanded trade and agriculture; experiencing an upswing in the 1600s with the cultivation of new, economically useful plants such as potatoes, ❻ tobacco, corn, and peanuts. As a result of the general prosperity, the population surged. A merchant and banking class emerged in the rapidly growing cities, making its way into the state administration, while the emperors remained weak through an extravagant lifestyle and the power of the eunuchs.

8 Vase with a dragon motif, beginning of 15th century

During the reign of Emperor Wan Li, the country was shaken by innumerable revolts. In addition, a Japanese attempt to occupy the Chinese vassal state of Korea in 1592 was answered with a costly defensive battle in 1593–98. Between 1594 and 1604, China also unsuccessfully attempted to decrease the influence of the East India Company through wars in Annam, Burma, and Siam.

6 Ivory tobacco tin

After the Portuguese had established a trading colony in ⓫ Canton in 1516—particularly for the ❼ tea trade—and Macao as a trading base in 1567, Christians began missionary work in China. The Jesuit ❿ Matteo Ricci lived in Beijing from 1601 and as a scholar had access to the highest court circles. In 1613, the emperor entrusted the Jesuits with reforming the calendar, and ❾ Johann Adam Schall von Bell, who worked on it, soon became director of the ⓬ imperial observatory, was conferred the rank of first-class mandarin, and functioned as the regent of the young emperor from 1651. The Jesuits assumed Chinese clothing and manner and considered Confucianism to be compatible with Christianity.

During the reign of the last Ming emperor, despite the political weaknesses of the empire, China experienced a blossoming of literature, science, the arts, and above all, ❽ porcelain production. The political weakness was exploited from the end of the 16th century on by Jurchen tribes in Manchuria, who, under the leadership of Nurhachi, rose up against the Chinese administrators and allied themselves with the Mongolians. By 1621 they had conquered Manchuria and under their leader Abahai marched toward Beijing. In 1636, the Manchus (Jurchen) proclaimed themselves an imperial dynasty under the name of Da Qing ("Great Purity"). When the last Ming emperor, Chongzhen, committed suicide in 1644, the Manchus entered Beijing.

7 A tea manufactory in China: Tea is pressed, packed, and sold to European merchants, 18th century

9 Johann Adam Schall von Bell

10 The Italian Jesuit Matteo Ricci

11 European trade branches in Canton

12 The royal observatory in Beijing

1567	Portuguese trading colony in Macao
from 1581	Jesuit mission in China
1592	Japanese attack Korea
1593–98	War against Japan
1636	Qing Dynasty founded
1644	Manchu capture Beijing

The Reign of the Manchus

The foreign Manchu rulers soon assumed Chinese customs, promoted science and the arts, and expanded Chinese influence into Central Asia. This last imperial dynasty lasted over 250 years.

The ❶ Manchus, or Qings ruled over the last Chinese imperial dynasty (1644–1911). To consolidate power they had to first crush the revolts of rival tribes and do away with the remaining Mings in the south. They secured their influence in politics and the administration and then demanded the adoption of their customs, including the wearing of pigtails and traditional Manchu dress. Thousands of the ❷ native Chinese officials committed suicide, but the majority of the Chinese population soon accustomed themselves to the political and cultural dominance of foreigners.

The long reigns of the three Manchu emperors between 1661 and 1796 were political, economic, and cultural high points. The emperors promoted the publication of encyclopedias and literary works, and the educated officials and upper class occupied themselves with literature and painting. Christianity was initially tolerated if the representatives were open-minded scholars.

❹ Emperor K'ang-hsi brought about an extensive reconciliation of the various peoples of the empire, moved against official corruption, and integrated Taiwan into the empire after expelling the Dutch in 1662. By 1681, he was able to establish the central government's authority over all parts of the land. K'ang-hsi entered into a treaty with Russia in 1689—the first Chinese treaty with a European power—ending Russian encroachment in the Amur River region. In 1696, he drove off the Jungars, who had been advancing into East Turkistan and Outer Mongolia since 1678. When the Jungars occupied Tibet in 1717–1718, K'ang-hsi began an ❸ intensified Chinese engagement in Central Asia. Tibet was taken back in 1720 by the Chinese and integrated into the empire as a protectorate with authority administered by resident commissioners or *ambans.*

Although relative economic prosperity continued, the population explosion created a food crisis. The population of China rose (according to a popular census) from 60 million in 1578 to more than 100 million in 1662, 143 million in 1741, 275 million in 1796, and 374 million by 1814. Agricultural land-use, however, was not able to keep pace with territorial expansion and population growth. Farming methods also remained underdeveloped.

1 Emperor Schi-tsu, the founder of the Manchu (Qing) Dynasty

2 Infantrymen escorting two dignitaries by horse

3 The Panchen Lama lodged in this temple near Beijing when he visited the Qing court in 1780.

4 Emperor K'ang-hsi's second journey to the south, rolled picture by Wang Hui, silk painting, ca.1700

1662 Annexation of Taiwan
1681 Rule established over entire empire
1689 Treaty with Russia
1696 Jungars repulsed
1705 Ban on Christianity
1717–18 Junggars occupy Tibet

China under Yung-cheng and Hung-li

The preferential treatment of Christians ended abruptly under Yung-cheng. Hung-li then led the empire to international splendor and high esteem once again, but internally the seeds of intellectual inflexibility and corruption were being sown.

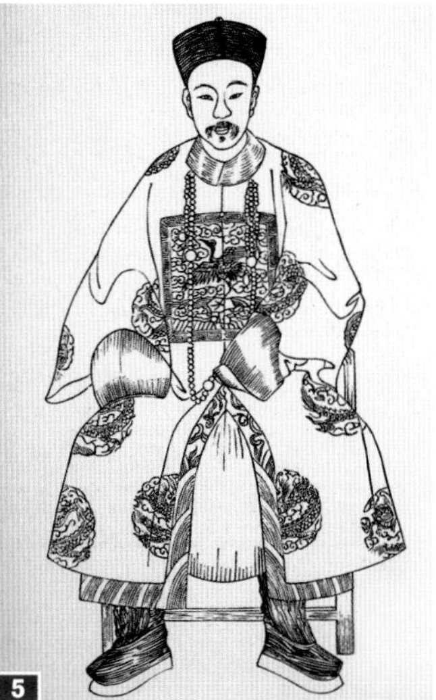
5 Emperor Yung-cheng

K'ang-hsi's son ❺ Yung-cheng instituted a complete change in politics and culture in China. He institutionalized imperial power in 1729 by replacing the ponderous "inner cabinet" with a modern state council as advisory body. He also prevented the influence of imperial relatives, excluded eunuchs from higher offices, and installed an information service and a secret police. He increased the wages of the civil servants to discourage second incomes and integrated the finance and tax systems. The open influence of Christians in China also ended during the reign of Yung-cheng. In 1705, the pope had declared Confucianism and Christianity to be incompatible, and Catholic missionaries had begun preaching against ❽ Confucius. The emperor thereupon banned Christianity, expelled the missionaries, and persecuted native Christians.

China reached the greatest extent of its expansion during the long reign of ❻ Hung-li (1735–1796). It was simultaneously forced to wage colonial wars for many years, bringing Uighurs, Kazakhs, Kirghiz, and Mongols under Chinese rule. Beijing was magnificently built up with ❼ residences and ❾ temples, yet the empire was showing signs of intellectual ossification: the Chinese civil service exams were filled with more questions about orthodox Neo-Confucianism than practical knowledge, necessary political and economic reforms did not occur, and the state administration became extremely conservative. The arbitrary use of power by officials provoked revolts of the populace, and mafia-like secret societies frequently controlled whole regions. The government was forced to undertake a campaign against the strongest of them, the White Lotus society, between 1793 and 1803. The British sent ❿ diplomatic missions to the imperial court in 1793 and 1816 to gain trade concessions, but the court firmly held to its policy of isolationism and turned the British away. Despite this, from 1816 on, the British East India Company increasingly brought opium into the country and the smoking of opium became widespread among the Chinese.

6 Emperor Hung-li

7 A palace for the summer in Beijing, built under emperor Qianlong 1711–96, Chinese silk painting

8 Worshippers at a statue of Confucius

9 The sky temple in Beijing

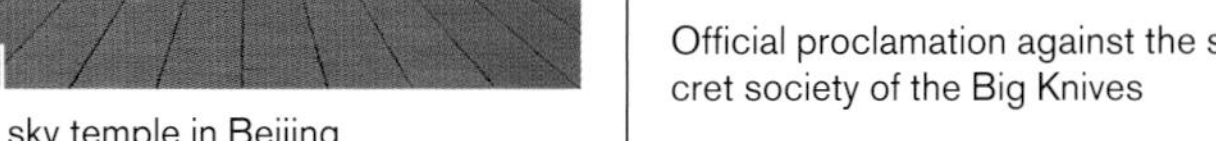
Official proclamation against the secret society of the Big Knives

Secret Societies

Secret societies and secret sects run throughout China's history. Mostly they originated out of local cult societies, founded by charasimatic leaders. They attracted charismatic members with religious and socially utopian promises of salvation, and trained fanatic fighters. The bloody Taiping Rebellion, which cost 20 million Chinese lives in 1850–1864, and the Boxer Rebellion of 1900 against Western influence have their roots in these secret societies.

10 Lord Macartney's diplomatic mission to facilitate the trade with China, caricature from 1792/93

1720 | Tibet retaken
1729 | "Inner cabinet" abolished
1793–1803 | "White Lotus" revolt
1850–64 | Taiping Rebellion
1900 | Boxer Rebellion

Japan from the Muromachi Period to the Tokugawa Shogunate 1338–1868

During the Muromachi period of the Ashikaga shogunate, which began in 1338, political power in Japan was transferred to the military aristocracy and regional warlords. Their rivalry favored the rise of local centers, European trade, and Christianity. Starting in 1560, the three great "unifiers" of the country centralized political and military power. The Tokugawa shogunate of the Edo period pursued a policy of isolationism that brought inner stability but also persecution of Christians, and sealed off the country from European influences into the 19th century.

1 Theater performance, detail from a colored tapestry, Muromachi Period

The Muromachi Period (1338–1573)

The shogunate of the Ashikaga brought the military aristocracy to power in Japan permanently. As the central power became weaker and weaker, the rise of the local military warlords began.

In the Muromachi period, governmental power went from the imperial government to the military aristocracy—the *samurai*, or *bushi*. The ❸, ❹ *bushi* were swordfighters who despised court life and lived in the provinces on their estates. They gave their personal allegiance to a local prince and had their own personal followers. The samurai code of ethics required them to fight for honor and family and, when necessary, to commit ritual suicide (*hara-kiri*). Their heroic deeds were immortalized in the cultic plays of the ❶, ❷ Noh theater.

The Muromachi period began with a power struggle. In 1334 Emperor Go-Daigo (p. 245), based in Kyoto, tried to reestablish the power of the emperor that had been lost to the shoguns in 1185—whereupon the military leader, Ashikaga Takauji, installed a new imperial line loyal to him. In 1338 Ashikaga conquered the shogunate for himself and his family. The shogun became the sole ruler, with the emperor as a mere figurehead. Military leaders in the provinces, the *shugo*, gradually established civil administration and tax sovereignty for themselves. In 1379, under the third shogun Yoshimitsu, the center of power was moved from ❺ Kyoto back to Kamakura. The sixth shogun, Yoshinori (1428-1441), was the last to intervene strongly in the political fate of the country; his successors dedicating themselves primarily to the arts. The Onin War of 1467-1477 erupted over the succession of the shogunate and devastated many provinces.

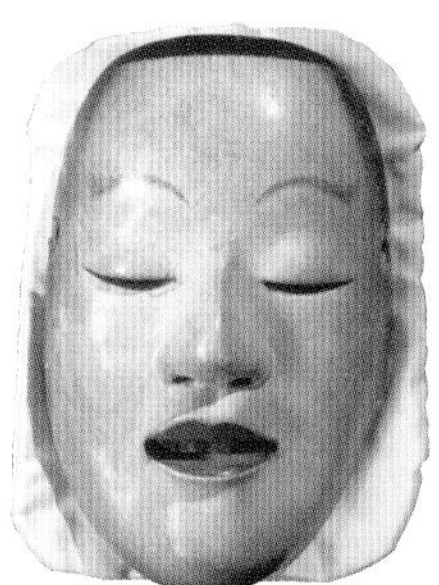

2 Noh theater mask, ca. 1500

The power of the shugo brought the country considerable economic growth and great cultural achievements, with many provincial courts able to compete with the major courtly centers. The development of fleets by the princes of coastal provinces led to vigorous trade with China but also attacks on China's coasts.

3 An actor playing a Samurai, colored wood engraving, early 19th century

4 Japanese Samurai sword with an ivory sheath, 18th century

5 The Kinkakuji Temple, or "Golden Pavilion" in Kyoto, built in 1397

The Samurai

The Japanese knights, the samurai, lived according to the code of bushido, which fused three traditions. From Zen Buddhism came the ideal of inner peace and fearless composure, and from Shintoism, the honoring of the family and ancestors as well as unconditional loyalty to the prince. Finally, Confucianism imposed on the bushi the requirement of service for the good of society and country, and the protection of the weak. Samurai were also expected to be literate and take interest in the arts.

Armament of a samurai, 16th–17th century

The Reign of the Daimyo

The rule of rival local princes, the *daimyo*, favored the rise of Christianity in Japan. From 1560, the three great unifiers of the country formed a new, strong centralized power.

The political weaknesses of the last Ashikaga shoguns after the Onin War led to the effective takeover of power by provincial princes, who were known as *sengoku-daimyo*, or feudal lords. The most powerful daimyo—there were between 200 and 300 in Japan—were able to raise armies of more than 10,000 men and replaced the individual combat of the ❻ samurai with the besieging of cities and the storming of strongholds by organized infantry troops. They pursued their own, shifting alliance policies. The rivalry among the daimyos also favored the spread of European influence and ❼ Christianity in Japan.

In 1543 ❾, ❿, ⓫ Portuguese merchants from Macao landed in Japan for the first time, south of Kyushu. Because the daimyo of Kyushu—and soon other daimyos as well—hoped to gain power through European trade, they granted the merchants favorable concessions. In 1571, the port of Nagasaki became the Portuguese base in Japan, and in 1579 municipal authority was even transferred to them. There were always Christian missionaries in the retinue of merchants. The cofounder of the Jesuit order, ❽ the Spaniard Francis Xavier, had already landed in Kyushu in 1549 and was honorably received by the local daimyo. The work of Gaspar Vilela in Kyoto made it a center of Christian missionary work in 1560. By 1582 there were already 200 churches and 150,000 Christians in Japan.

A new period of political strength began in 1560 under the three great unifiers—the shoguns Oda Nobunaga, Toyotomi Hideyoshi, and Tokugawa Ieyasu. They, too, were at first local daimyo, but were able to consolidate their power and influence through clever alliance and war policies. They recognized the need for a consolidation of the central authority and worked for policies that resulted in the expansion of trade and the importation of Western firearms.

Nobunaga began to eliminate his daimyo foes in 1560, seized Kyoto in 1568, broke the resistance of the Buddhist monasteries, and in 1573 ended the reign of the Ashikaga shoguns, whose authority, by this time, existed only in name. His rule also saw the development of the tea ceremony and kabuki theater.

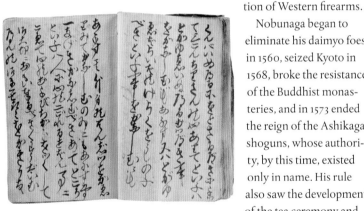

7 Book of Catholic faith in Japanese handwriting, 17th century

6 Japanese helmet, decorated with a war fan, 16th century

8 The missionary Francis Xavier

9 Portuguese trading ship in the port of Nagasaki, detail from a Japanese folding screen, 17th century

10 A Jesuit and a Portuguese merchant in Japan, detail from a Japanese folding screen, 17th century

11 Portuguese merchants, detail from a Japanese folding screen, 17th century

1543 | Portuguese merchants land in Kyushu
1549 | Jesuit mission under Francisco Xavier
1560 | New political strength of Oda Nobunaga begins
1568 | Conquest of Kyoto
1573 | Last Ashikaga shogun

The Reign of the Unifiers

The political reorganization by Oda Nobunaga, Toyotomi Hideyoshi, and Tokugawa Ieyasu fundamentally changed the structure of Japan. Ieyasu was the first to be able to institute a dynasty of his family.

1 Osaka Castle, built 1583–1587 by Toyotomi Hideyoshi

Nobunaga established his power over the land by making vassals of the local daimyo or by fighting against them with his massive armies and siege techniques. At the Battle of Nagashino in 1575, his troops were the first to use firearms on a large scale. By 1582 Nobunaga had brought the greater part of Japan under his control. He then decreed a standardization of weights and measurements, taxes, and commerce laws, did away with the power of the local guilds, and supported the merchants.

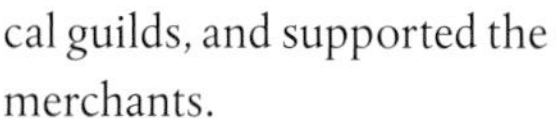

2 Box depicting the preparation of tea, lacquer-work

After Nobunaga's death in 1582, his general ❸ Toyotomi Hideyoshi was able to gain control, occupying Kyoto in 1584 and allying himself with the powerful Tokugawa Ieyasu. In 1585, Hideyoshi eliminated the last of the daimyo with brutal force, while trying to win over the traditional elite for a constructive policy of peace, rewarding even former rivals with estates once they had proved their loyalty. He brought the daimyo together in a union and made himself the supreme feudal lord. In order to control them, he often held their families as "hostages of honor" at his court. From 1583 on, Hideyoshi built ❶ Osaka Castle as his capital and in 1591 he appointed himself regent for the emperor. He occupied Korea in 1592, but was forced to withdraw from the continent two years later.

In domestic policies, Hideyoshi undertook sweeping reforms. He had the whole country surveyed in order to reorganize the villages and family seats. He then put the villages together into production units and calculated the tax rate according to the whole village. This measure was accompanied by a separation of ❷ farmers from the warrior class, ❺ tradesmen, and merchants that would prove decisive in the future. The farmers were forced to give up their weapons, while the bushi were kept out of the villages and were allocated to their princes in personal allegiance. In 1590, after a last victory over the Hojo (p.245), Hideyoshi was the undisputed master of Japan, but his attempt to establish a shogunate for his family failed.

3 Audience hall of Hideyoshi in Kyoto, partial view of the interior, 16th century

When Hideyoshi died in 1598, his powerful ally ❹ Ieyasu, after a decisive victory in the Battle of Sekigahara, assumed power and was able to establish the Tokugawa shogunate in 1603 that his family would hold until 1867. Ieyasu built upon the achievements of his predecessor and laid the foundation for a rather conservative, isolationist form of politics, which, however, contributed to lasting peace and internal stability. He also centralized all of Japan's economic and trade policies, preventing local daimyo from trading with Europe.

4 The Japanese national coat of arms, the chrysanthemum, at the Higashi-Honganji Temple, founded in 1602 by Ieyasu

5 Merchants at the market and bathing people at the Shijo Gawa River in Kyoto, detail from a colored folding screen, ca. 1550

1575 Battle of Nagashino | **1584** Kyoto occupied | **1585** Country is re-surveyed | **1586** Osaka castle built | **1590** Victory over the Hojo | **1592** Occupation of Korea | **1603–1867** Tokugawa Shogunate | **1614–15** Osaka taken

The Tokugawa Shogunate 1603–1867/68

After forcefully bringing peace to the country, the Tokugawa shoguns suppressed Christianity and resolved to seal the country off from European influences. This continued until the 19th century.

Taking over for Hideyoshi, Ieyasu first had to contend with a renewed rebellion of the daimyo families. He defeated his greatest rival, Ishida, and his "western alliance" in 1600. By the time he finally gained full control in 1603, 87 daimyo families had been eradicated. The centers of Tokugawa power were ❽ Kyoto and especially Edo (present-day Tokyo). In 1605 Ieyasu officially transferred the shogunate to his son Hidetada, who played only a background role until Ieyasu's death in 1616. In the meantime, Ieyasu wiped out the last of the rebelling daimyos while ❾ seizing Osaka in 1614-15.

The third Tokugawa shogun, Iemitsu, completed the development of Ieyasu's system of rule and finally brought peace to the empire through strict military controls. Iemitsu, who enacted strict nationalistic marriage and dress regulations, forced the daimyo to recognize him as the sole lawgiver and in 1635 put all religious institutions under the supervision of the shoguns. The system of personal loyalty and allegiance was anchored at all levels. In 1639, the policy of "locking up the country," which isolated Japan from the outside world for 200 years, was proclaimed. As early as 1622, ❼ Christians had begun to be persecuted, and they were now perceived as foreigners. Religious and cultural policies gained extreme nationalistic characteristics after the ❻ foreigners had been expelled and the native Christians executed.

After Iemitsu, the Tokugawas increasingly refrained from active politics and left the government to the military leaders. The eighth shogun, Yoshimune, whose reign began in 1716, was able to reestablish the power of the shogunate through governmental and economic reforms. He encouraged new land reclamation and the cultivation of crops such as sweet potatoes and mulberry trees for the breeding of silkworms. He also standardized the legal system and cancelled the debts held by farmers. Yoshimune also loosened the ban on the import of European publications in order to become acquainted with new administrative and agricultural breeding methods. His policies were actively resumed by the eleventh shogun, Ienari, from 1787. Japan experienced a new upswing, but the policy of isolationism remained in place until the country was forcibly ❿ opened by the United States in 1853–54.

Revolt of the Christians

The religio-political measures of the first Tokugawa shogun provoked the revolt of the Christians of Shimabara in 1637–38. The shogun brutally crushed the uprising, and initiated the extermination of Christianity in Japan. Even when restrictions on the import of Western writings were moderated in 1720, no publications with Christian content were allowed to enter the country.

Depiction of the Virgin Mary in a plaster form. Persecutors of Christians recognized Catholics by their refusal to desecrate the form by stepping on it.

6 A native boy shows a great bird to a European, colored woodcarving, 18th century

7 Martyridom of the Jesuits in Japan, painting, 1622

8 Nijo-jo Castle in Kyoto, residence of the Tokugawa Dynasty in the imperial city, built 1603-1626

9 The conquest of Osaka 1615, detail from a folding screen, 17th century

10 Delivery of a letter from US president Fillmore to the Japanese emperor by a delegation on 14 June 1853, lithography, 19th century

1622–23	Christians persecuted
1637–39	Christians of Schimabara revolt
1639	"Policy of locking up the country"
from 1720	European books allowed
1853–54	The opening of Japan
1868	Last Shogun abdicated

Southeast Asia 1500–1800

Burma and Siam were particularly significant kingdoms between the 16th and 18th centuries. The Portuguese and other Europeans established relations with trade agreements, particularly in Siam. While the French asserted themselves in Annam in the 18th century, the Portuguese were able to control the Malay Archipelago at first—and with it a monopoly on the spice trade—only to gradually lose it to the Dutch in the 17th century. Many South Asian kingdoms experienced a renaissance through trade with the Europeans.

1 Burmese rowing boat

Burma and Siam

The kingdom of Burma was able to temporarily extend its influence to Siam. The Portuguese, and later other European powers, made advantageous trade agreements with Siam (Ayutthaya).

After the fall of the Kingdom of Pagan in 1287, the Shan tribes established a kingdom in Upper Burma. The Mon, who founded principalities in the ninth and tenth centuries before the arrival of the ❶, ❷ Burmans, ruled in the south. In 1531, the Toungoo dynasty from Lower Burma unified the country. King Tabinshwehti subjugated the Mon and, with the aid of Portuguese firearms, conquered central Burma, establishing its capital at Pegu in 1559 and Ava in 1635. By 1559, his successor gained the principalities of the north and the Shan states. The empire was at its zenith and magnificent buildings were erected. In the 17th century, British and Dutch trading companies began establishing bases in the empire. After attacks by the Chinese and Siamese, the Toungoo dynasty fell in 1752.

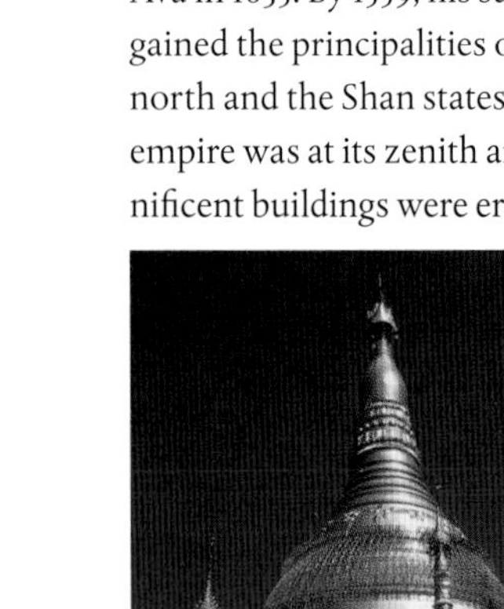

5 The Shwe Dagon Pagoda in Rangun, Burma, altered in 1768–73

The Burmese chief Alaungpaya unified ❺ Burma (present-day Myanmar) in 1753. His son Hsinbyushin, bringing many scholars to his court, rebuilt Ava as his capital in 1765 and between 1764 and 1767 pushed far into Siam. Burma occupied a large part of Siam by 1785, until the British, attacking from India, brought Siam under its control after the first Anglo-Burmese War (1824–26).

3 Head of a Buddha, Siamese sculpture in the Ayutthaya style

The Ayutthaya Kingdom in Siam (present-day Thailand), which had existed since the 14th century and stretched over the Malay Peninsula to Malacca, destroyed the Khmer Empire in 1431. King Ramathibodi II in 1516 allowed the Portuguese to set up trading posts. His successor fended off the Burmans, and in 1549 besieged Ayutthaya. The kings had been using European weapons against the Burmese since the 16th century, in exchange for which the Europeans were granted favorable trade agreements with Siam—a trading center for products from China and Japan. Religious tolerance in Siam also allowed for the influence of European culture.

France sent Jesuit missionaries to ❸ Buddhist Siam in 1662 and the French East Indian Trading Company came to Ayutthaya in 1680. However, ❹ French political intervention proved excessive and in 1688 King Phetracha had them expelled. Two years later, the Dutch forced the king to grant them a monopoly on the trade in animal skins by blockading the Menam River. After 1700, this trade brought considerable prosperity to Siam. Thai literature and art reached a high point during the reign of King Boromokot.

Starting in 1770, the general Phraya Taksin reconstituted the Kingdom of Siam, and made vassal states of ❻ Laos and Cambodia; at his death, the kingdom was as powerful as ever. In 1782, General Phraya Chakri ascended to the throne as Rama I and founded the Chakri dynasty, which still reigns in Thailand today.

2 Elegant man and woman from Annan, colored wood engraving

4 The French ambassador arrives at the palace of the Siamese king

6 That Luang, Buddhist temple near Vientiane, Laos, 1566, reconstructed 1930

1431 | Ayutthaya destroy Khmer Empire
1516 | Portuguese trading posts in Southeast Asia
1521 | European discovery of the Philippines
1531 | Toungoo Dynasty in Burma
1544 | Conquest of Central Burma
1549 | Ayutthaya conquered by Burma
1662 | Jesuits in Siam

Indochina and Indonesia

The French gained influence in Indochina, while the Portuguese and Dutch waged war over the foreign trading posts in the Indonesian Archipelago.

In 1428, Annam in Indochina, under Emperor Le Loi (Le Thai-to), the founder of the Le dynasty, broke away from China. Through efficient administration, Annam under Le Thanh-tong in 1471 occupied the remainder of the Champa Empire. Central power declined during the 16th century, and the country was ruled up to the 17th century by two great families, the Trinh and the Nguyen, who for a long time fended off landing attempts by the Europeans. France negotiated the first foreign basing rights in the region, with ❼ Nguyen Anh in Indochina in 1787, who declared himself Emperor Gia Long in Vietnam in 1802.

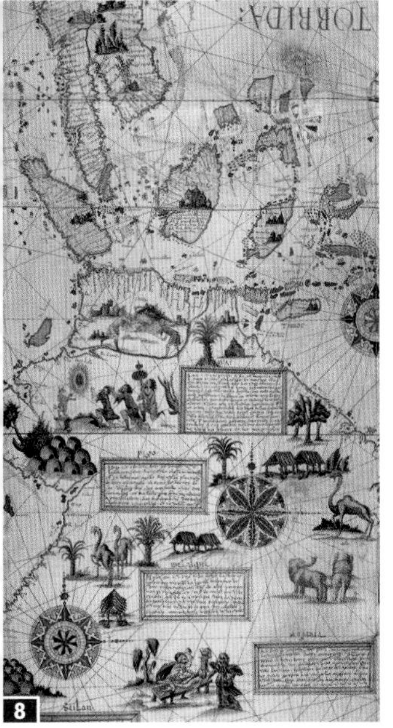

8 Map of the Malay Archipelago, detail from a map of the world by Pierre Desceliers, 1550

Muslim merchants and the Portuguese fought over influence in Indonesia and the ❽ Malay Archipelago. In 1511, the Portuguese conquered ❾ Malacca and made it their main base; from there, they set up trading posts in ❿ Java, Ambon, Banda, Ternate, and elsewhere and monopolized the spice trade. During the 16th century, a major part of formerly Buddhist Indonesian territory converted to Islam.

The chartering of the Dutch East India Company in 1602 led to bitter fighting. The Dutch established themselves in Jakarta in 1610 and then in 1619 set up Batavia as their administrative center. They seized Malacca from the Portuguese in 1641, Sulawesi (Celebes) in 1666, and finally Ambon and Ternate in 1683 and so controlled the region, but were forced to allow British trade in their regions in 1784. The Dutch East India Company declared bankruptcy in 1798 and was dissolved by the Dutch government, which took over administration of the company's territories.

7 Nguyen Anh at the age of eight during his visit to Versailles, 1787

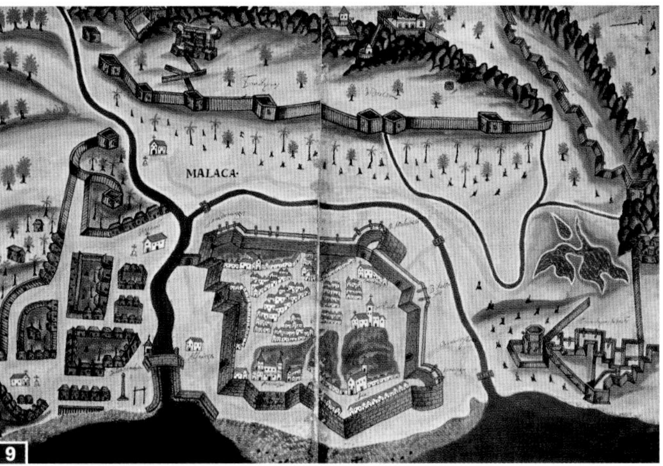

9 Harbor and capital of Malacca founded by the Srivijayan prince Parameswara, map of the city as a Portuguese trade base

10 Dutch trading center at the coast of Bantam, Java

The Philippines

By the end of the 15th century, Islam had spread from Borneo and Sulawesi to the Philippines. Magellan reached the island group in 1521 on his voyage around the world and clashed with the inhabitants. The islands were claimed by Spain and named after King Philip II in 1543. The structures of the local tribal governments were considered "primitive" and the northern islands were soon Christianized and economically developed by Catholic padres following the South American model, while the southern islands remain Islamic to this day.

Magellan fighting against the natives on the Phillippine island of Cebu

1680	French East Indian Trading Company in Siam
1688	French expelled from Siam
1752	Fall of the Toungoo Dynasty
1753	Founding of the new Burmese empire
1770	Paya Tak reconstitutes Siam
1782	Chakri Dynasty founded in Siam
1785	Occupation of parts of Siam

Africa 1500–1800

The diversity of African social development can be accounted for only to a certain extent. From the 16th to the 19th century, Africa became a focus of European trading interests. The coastal regions primarily drew the interest of the Portuguese and other European powers, who organized a complex slave and commodities trade with the African kings and chiefs, playing rival tribes against each other. In the North African kingdoms, there were constant struggles between Islam and Christianity in the upper classes, while the common people held fast to their traditional religions. Ethiopia had a special position in North Africa.

1 Map of the Indian Ocean showing East Africa, 16th century

East Africa, the Kongo Kingdom, and the Songhai Empire

While the Portuguese controlled trade on the African east coast, a Christian kingdom was established in the Kongo Kingdom. The Muslim Songhai Empire resisted Christianization.

The arrival of the Portuguese on the African continent in 1498, a year after Vasco da Gama had discovered India, changed the dynamics of Africa, especially on the ❶ east coast. Portuguese commercial enterprise would know no limits. The Portuguese used the rivalry between the coastal ❻ chiefs and city-states to destroy the trade there, eliminate Muslim traders, and gradually bring the entire coast under their control. In the meantime, the kingdoms of central Africa were able to survive, while Zanzibar became a new center for Arab traders under the rule of Oman.

In the the ❺ Kongo Kingdom, King Nzinga Nkuwu asked the Portuguese king to send missionaries to his Kingdom in 1482 and converted to Christianity in 1491 as John I. He and his son Afonso I (Nzinga Mbemba I) constructed Christian churches and monasteries. The Kongo Kingdom experienced considerable prosperity as a result of the influx of Christian merchants and artisans, but the Kingdom's Christian upper class also participated in the ❹ slave trade of the poorer subjects. The Christian Kongo Kingdom declined in the 17th century and in 1668 the capital São Salvador do Kongo was devastated and plundered during attacks by neighboring non-Christian tribes.

5 The king of Kongo receives a delegation, copper engraving, 1686

3 Bronze head of an Oba, a king of Benin

The most important Yoruba state, the Kingdom of ❸ Benin, traded with the ❷ Portuguese from 1486 and allowed them a trading post in the country. British expeditions to Benin beginning in 1530 led to regular clashes with the Portuguese, but the kingdom profited from the slave trade. The ban on slavery in 1691 led to the disintegration of the Kingdom of Benin.

Portugal also opened diplomatic relations and trade in 1484 with the Mali Empire, which went under in the 16th century with the expansion of the Muslim Songhai Empire. Songhai had already risen to become a prosperous kingdom in the 11th century through intensive trade contacts with the Arab world. Sonni Ali the Great turned the empire into the leading power in the Sudan by 1464 through expansion and in 1476 conquered Djenné.

6 Monomotapa of the Bantu Empire, copper engraving, 17th c.

2 Portuguese with helmet and trident, sculpture from Benin, 17th c.

4 Handcuffs of slave traders in sub-Saharan Africa

❼ Muhammad Ture founded the Askia dynasty in the Songhai Empire in 1493, which became a leading power in Upper Africa with a standing army, but was defeated by Morocco in 1590–1591.

7 The Tomb of Muhammed Ture of the Asaki dynasty in Gao, Mali

1476 | Conquest of Djenné

from 1482 | Christianizing of the Kongo

1493 | Askia Dynasty in Upper Africa

1527 | Somali Empire attacks Ethiopia

1543 | Ethiopian victory under Negus Claudius

Bornu, the West Coasts, and Ethiopia

Bornu became a strong Islamic empire, while the African west coast fell under the trade control of European powers. Ethiopia was largely able to maintain its own independent form of Christianity.

9 Castle at the Gold Coast, present-day Ghana, copper engraving, ca. 1750

The rising Bornu Empire under Ali Dunamani, who had reigned since 1472, replaced the declining Kanem Empire on Lake Chad. Ali expanded his empire in all directions with his armored cavalry and carried on trade with North and West Africa. Idris II continued this expansion and trade, which reached their height during the reign of Idris Alooma in 1580–1617. Northern Cameroon, northern Nigeria, and even the Yoruba nations were then under the influence of Bornu, but its supremacy declined in the 17th century. Islam had been advancing since the 1500s in the Hausa and Fulbe states, which had been largely able to retain their independence.

Competition developed among the European great powers for West African trade products, and the British and French eventually triumphed. In the 18th century, the British controlled the trade in the Gambia, Sierra Leone, and the Gold Coast (present-day Ghana), while the French dominated Senegal, French Guinea, and the Ivory Coast. ❾ Ghana, Togo, Nigeria, the Kongo, and Angola were centers of the ebony trade.

10 Banquet, where wine is served in round clay jugs, Ethiopian book illustration, 17th century

The Christian emperors in ❽ Ethiopia had been fighting the advance of Islam in Africa since the 14th century. Although they were determined to maintain political and ❿ cultural independ-

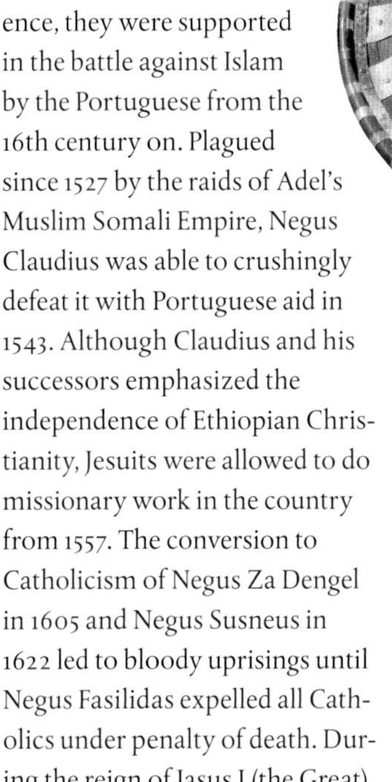

ence, they were supported in the battle against Islam by the Portuguese from the 16th century on. Plagued since 1527 by the raids of Adel's Muslim Somali Empire, Negus Claudius was able to crushingly defeat it with Portuguese aid in 1543. Although Claudius and his successors emphasized the independence of Ethiopian Christianity, Jesuits were allowed to do missionary work in the country from 1557. The conversion to Catholicism of Negus Za Dengel in 1605 and Negus Susneus in 1622 led to bloody uprisings until Negus Fasilidas expelled all Catholics under penalty of death. During the reign of Jasus I (the Great),

8 Leather buckle from Ethiopia

Ethiopia once again attained a political and cultural zenith at the turn of the 18th century but then sank into anarchy due to palace intrigues and the invasions of hostile neighboring tribes, finally crumbling into small local kingdoms. This condition persisted until Theodor II's reign in 1855. Theodore, a native of Amhara, married the daughter of the previous ruler.

The Ancient American Empires and the Conquest by Spain and Portugal

As in Southeast Asia, the Portuguese were forced out of Africa after 1600 by the Dutch. In 1637 the Dutch West India Company drove the Portuguese out of Elmina on the Gold Coast, took over the slave trade there, and made its own contracts with the Fanti chiefs of the Coast. In 1641, the Dutch occupied Luanda Island in Angola; they finally succeeded in expelling the Portuguese from Angola by force of arms in 1648. A largely peaceful reconciliation in trade eventually developed between the Portuguese and the Dutch.

Dirck Wilre, General Director of the West India Company on the south coast of Africa, painting by Peter de Wit, ca. 1669

1557 Jesuit mission in Ethiopia
1590–91 Moroccan victory over the Songhai
1637 Dutch oust Portuguese from Elmina
1641 Dutch occupy Luanda Island
1648 Dutch driven out of Angola by Portugal

The Ancient American Empires and the Conquest by Spain and Portugal ca. 1500–1800

The regionally splintered late ❶ Mayan cultures, as well as the Aztec and Inca peoples, built up—even as late as the 15th century—large and effectively administered empires in Central and South America. Their rapid collapse in the face of the Spanish conquest in the 16th century may be connected to the conquistadors' ability to exploit the enormous concentration of religious power in the hands of the native rulers. Under Spanish and Portuguese rule, it was primarily the missionaries who converted the Indians, though some of these clergymen also fought for the Indians' rights. Africans were also brought as slaves to the New World and exploited. Under the direction of the Jesuits, semi-autonomous Indian reservations were set up.

1 Maya incense holder in the form of the rain god Chac, painted clay

The Late Maya Empire

The late Maya culture was divided into a number of separate states. These were weakened by political strife in the 15th century and were conquered by the Spanish in the 16th century.

The Old Maya Empire and its temple cities were established by 300 A.D. In the fifth and sixth centuries, the Maya culture spread widely. An efficient agricultural system permitted a substantial increase in the population. In 987, the New Empire of the Maya emerged in the Yucatan under the leadership of the Toltec, who had emigrated from Campeche and mixed with the ancient Maya. Other city-states joined the new entity. By 1204, the Cocom of Mayapán, who may have originated in Mexico, had assumed leadership of the empire. Some Maya tribes, led by Xiu of ❷ Uxmál, rebelled against their harsh rule in 1441. Political unification eluded the Yucatan, as 18 tiny city-states fought among themselves. Epidemics and natural catastrophes also served to weaken the states prior to the arrival of the Spanish.

4 Mayan temple in Yucatan, built ca. twelfth century

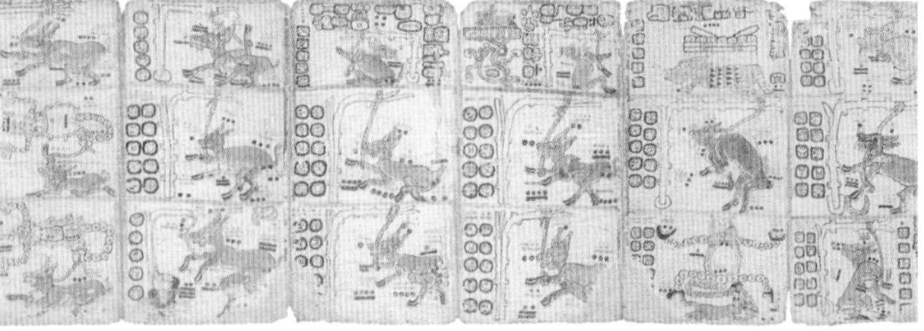

5 Maya fortune-telling calendar, known as the Tro-Cortes codex, which was probably made in Yucatán using the hieroglyphic script, 14th century

In the highlands of present-day Guatemala were the Toltec-influenced states of the ❸ Quiché, the Cachiquel, and the Tzutuhil, with their capitals at Utatlán, Iximché and Atitlán, respectively. Toltec tribes also settled areas of present-day Nicaragua, northwest Honduras, and El Salvador.

Despite its political decline, ❹ Maya culture was highly developed in the pre-Columbian period. The Maya used a ❺ hieroglyphic script, a numerical system, and a calendar that was more precise than the Gregorian calendar used in 16th century Europe. The people lived in large cities with stone houses and surfaced roads. Surpluses in the cultivation of maize supported artistic activities and skilled trades. The society was hierarchically structured, with the nobility and priests forming the ruling caste. Slaves were acquired through taking prisoners in war or debt servitude. The Maya traded over long distances, but metals and wagons were unknown to them.

2 Farmers in Uxmál

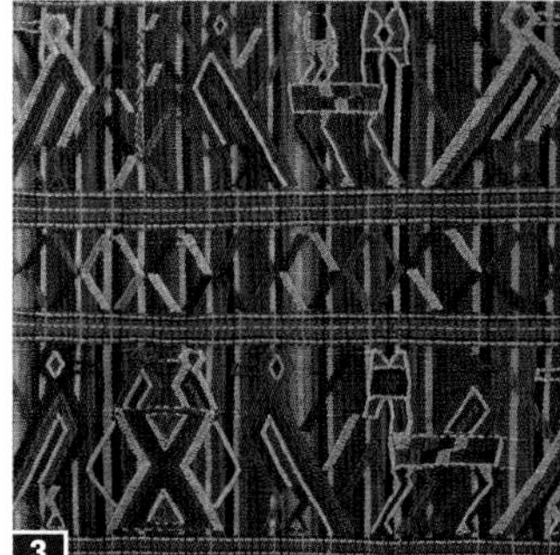

3 Traditional Quiché cloth decorated with animal motifs

Favored by this political fragmentation, the Spanish were able to conquer the highlands of ❻ Guatemala by 1525 and Yucatan by 1541, but the Guatemalan lowlands eluded Spanish control until 1697.

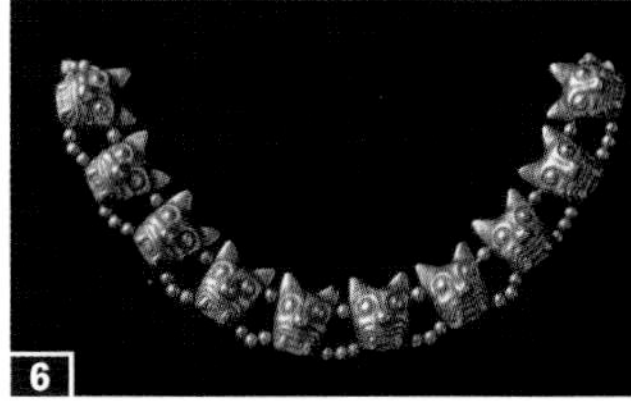

6 Necklace with jaguar-shaped beads, Guatemala, ca. 1200–1500

987 | New Maya Empire founded
1100 | Aztecs migrate into Mexico
1204 | Rule of the Cocom of Mayapán begins
1375 | Aztec capital Tenochtitlán founded
1441 | Maya tribes under Xiu revolt

The Aztec Empire

In alliance with other cities, the Aztec ruled a mighty empire from their capital, Tenochtitlán, but in the 16th century they were rapidly subjugated by the Spanish conquerors.

The Aztec first migrated into Mexico around 1100. At first they were vassals of the Tepanec but steadily gained in strength. In 1375 the Aztec founded their capital, ⓫ Tenochtitlán, and then in 1428 they rebelled against the domination of the Tepanec, whose empire they destroyed in 1430 in alliance with the city-states of Tetzoco and Tlatelolco. The Aztec rulers Moctezuma I, Axayacatl, and Ahuitzotl expanded the ❼ empire to the northeast in the second half of the 15th century, and peoples as far south as Guatemala paid tribute to them. They declared themselves the heirs of the Toltec and identified their ❾ war god Huitzilopochtli with the sun god, thus ❽ religiously legitimizing their policy of conquest. The Aztec Empire maintained alliances with its partner city-states, and all three profited from the enormous tributes and slaves that the subjugated peoples were forced to provide. At the time of the Spanish conquest, the empire was composed of 38 city-provinces.

7 Aztec warriors, Indian drawing taken from the *Historia de las cosas de Nueva*

10 Moctezuma II

In 1502, ❿ Moctezuma II Xocoyotzin, who would lead the empire to its zenith and then its rapid demise, came to the throne. He subdued the Mixtec in the highlands of Oaxaca and annexed the allies of Tetzoco in 1516. Moctezuma built up Tenochtitlán into the largest and most magnificent city in the Americas, with a population of about 300,000 people. The society was strictly hierarchical, and religiously charged court customs allowed the ruler to stand far above his people. The nobility was hereditary, but warriors with outstanding service could also aspire to enter the noble caste.

In 1519 Moctezuma cordially welcomed the ⓬ Spanish under Hernán Cortés, because a prophecy had announced the return of the god Quetzalcoátl. Cortés, however, treacherously took the ruler captive and used him to subdue the people. The Spanish put down a rebellion against the ⓭ destruction of Inca religious sites in 1520, and in the course of this Moctezuma was killed by a thrown stone. The Spanish went on to occupy the whole Aztec Empire by 1521.

8 Headdress of an Aztec priest, early 16th century

9 The Aztec god of war, Huitzilopochtli, lithograph

Human Sacrifices

The war and sun god of the Aztec, Huitzilopochtli—meaning "blue hummingbird of the south"—was regularly offered bloody human sacrifices on the temple platform's stone sun altar. The victims were usually anacesthetized with intoxicating beverages before the chief priest sliced the hearts out of their living bodies. According to contemporary reports, in the final years of the Aztec Empire about 20,000 people were sacrificed annually, and human remains have subsequently been found that seem to confirm this.

above: Human sacrifices on the sun altar in Tenochtitlán

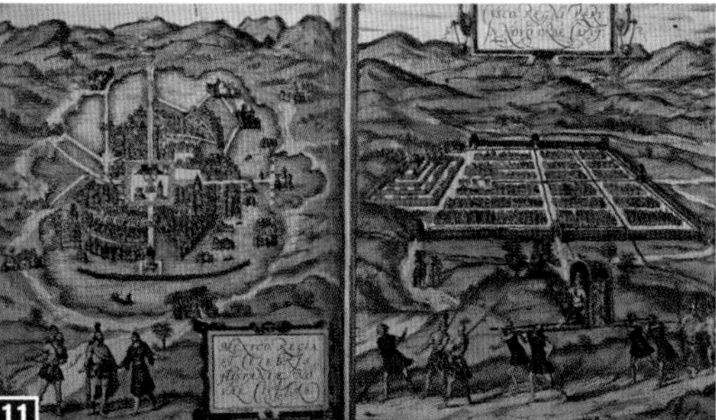

11 The Aztec capital city Tenochtitlán (left) and the Incan capital city Cuzco (right)

12 Hernán Cortés leading his soldiers to the Aztec leader Moctezuma

13 Hernán Cortés destroys the religious sites of the Aztecs, 1520

1519 | Hernán Cortés arrives in Tenochtitlán

1520 | Death of Moctezuma

1521 | Spanish occupy Aztec Empire

1525 | Spanish conquer highlands of Guatemala

1541 | Spanish conquer Yucatán

The Rise of the Inca Empire

From their capital Cuzco, in present-day Peru, the Inca built the greatest empire in South America in the 15th century and ran a centralized government that organized almost all areas of life.

Following the collapse of the Tiahuanaco culture in the central Andes (part of present-day Peru and Bolivia) around 1100, local coastal cultures arose and formed numerous small states. The Inca, who inhabited the Cuzco Valley, gradually gained dominance under the ruler Manco Capac, who according to Inca tradition had migrated from Lake Titicaca around 1200. "Inca" appears to have originally been the name of the ruling family, then of the ruler, and finally the name of the whole people. The ninth Inca ruler, Pachacutec Yupanqui, who came to power around 1438, embarked on a series of military conquests that provided the foundations for the government of the Inca Empire. The capital

1 Headdress made of plaited lama hair decorated with feathers, 15th–16th c.

Cuzco grew rapidly, and other cities such as ❷ Machu Picchu were founded with ❹ monumental cult edifices. Pachacutec's son, ❸ Topa Yupanqui, conquered the Bolivian highlands and pushed into present-day northwest Argentina, subduing the coastal areas of the Chimú Empire and expanding Inca territory southwards. He sent raft expeditions out into the Pacific Ocean, which probably got as far as the Galapagos Islands. At the beginning of the 16th century, under Huayna Capac, the empire was further enlarged to include much of present-day Colombia and reached its political and ❶ cultural zenith. The "Empire of Four Parts" was the mightiest realm in ancient America, ruling the surrounding peoples.

4 Carved rock sundial for cult ceremonies, Machu Picchu, Peru

The Inca state had a tightly centralized administration and a carefully planned economic structure. At its head was the ❻ ruler, the Sapay Inca ("highest Inca"), revered as the son of the ❺ sun. In the empire's strict hierarchy, the Inca people constituted the nobility, while the subjugated peoples were used as laborers. All subjects were combined into administrative units and were required to accomplish specific labor and military services for the good of the state. Everything was recorded by means of knotted strings called ❼ *quipu*. An excellent network of paths through the mountains permitted the rapid transport of troops, news, and some produce between cities. Like the Maya, the Inca did not have knowledge of metallurgy or the wheel. A common language of the empire, Quechua, was used to simplify administration. For every 10,000 inhabitants of the Inca Empire, there were 1330 state officials, selected according to their abilities and trained for specific responsibilities and positions.

2 The ruins of Machu Picchu, Peru

3 Topa Yupanqui on his throne with his wife at his side, artist's reconstruction from written descriptions, 1870

5 Inca sacrifice to the sun god, colored copper engraving, 17th century

6 Inca ruler, wood engraving, 16th c.

7 Inca *quipu*, 1430–1532

1438 | Inca military expansion begins
1527 | Death of Huayna Capac
1527 | Conflict over the royal succession
1533–39 | Spanish conquest of the Inca Empire
1533 | Murder of Atahualpa

The Structure of the Inca Empire and the Spanish Conquest

Agrarian collectivism was overseen by the Inca Empire's administration, but the passivity of the masses and a fratricidal war facilitated the civilization's rapid conquest by the Spanish.

In Inca society the land belonged to the village community, which allocated certain areas of arable land to individual families, according to their size. Each family could live from the yield, but the community was also required to pay taxes for the support of the ruler, the priests, and communal buildings. Individuals also had to cultivate the community's fields to support the elderly, the ill, and those otherwise unfit for work. Woods and pastures were common land for the use of every member of the community, but the home and farm were family property. Harvest surpluses were delivered to central silos where they were stored for times of famine. Agricultural productivity was raised through ❽ terracing and irrigation systems and the use of fertilizer, primarily guano. The breeding of animals, notably the llama, and fishing along the coast, also played a significant part in the Inca economy. The manner in which the absolute authority of the ruler and his state rested on divine ritual and went unquestioned may have made the structure more fragile, assisting the Spanish conquest.

In 1527, Huayna Capac died without designating a successor. Both his eldest son Huáscar, in Cuzco, and his favorite son Atahualpa, in Quito, laid claim to the throne. resulting in a fraticidal war that seriously weakened the empire. The Spanish under Francisco Pizarro used this division to their advantage to conquer the Inca Empire. At first they sided with ❾ Atahualpa, who was victorious when Huáscar was captured and murdered by his troops in 1532. But then Pizarro had Atahualpa ❿ imprisoned in 1533 and strangled, leaving the state without a Sapay Inca and thus paralyzed. The Inca Empire was largely conquered by 1539.

9 Atahualpa, son of Huayna Capac

Resistance to the Spanish continued after 1535 in the border provinces of Vilcabamba under the leadership of a member of the former ruling family, Manco Capac II, whom the Spanish themselves had installed in 1533. He was murdered in 1544, but the Vilcabamba region was still able to resist the Spanish until 1572. A last revolt of the Inca, which attempted to restore the old religion, failed in 1565. Despite repression and conversion, ⓫ Inca culture survived and influenced the European colonists who came and settled in the former empire.

8 Irrigation of the Inca terraced fields, wood engraving, ca. 1560

The Revolt against the Spanish in 1780–81

Attempts by Spanish government officials (corregidores) to force the indigenous peoples to adopt 18th-century Spanish lifestyles resulted in a revolt in Peru in 1780–1781 which was led by a descendent of a noble Inca family, Tupac Amaru. The revolt was violently crushed, but the corregidores concerned were replaced by new officials who then allowed the indigenous people greater independence.

10 Atahualpa is seized by Pizarro's soldiers, 1532

11 Drinking vessel in a mixed Incan-Spanish style, ca. 1650

1535 | Inca revolt in Vilcabamba led by Manco Capac II

1544 | Manco Capac II murdered

1572 | End of revolt in Vilcabamba

1780–81 | Tupac Amaru leads failed revolt

Spanish and Portuguese Domination of the Americas

The Spanish and the Portuguese colonized the "New World" after 1500. Black slaves were brought from Africa to work on the plantations and farms of the colonizers.

1 Columbus lands in the Americas, 1498

4 Cortés conquers Mexico, colored lithograph

Soon after their arrival in the Americas, the Spanish and Portuguese began to lay claim to the land. In 1498 ❶ Christopher Columbus reached the mainland for the first time (in present-day Venezuela) and the following year, Amerigo Vespucci landed on the coast of Colombia. The Europeans proceeded to explore and conquer much of the continent: the area of Mexico by ❸, ❹ Hernán Cortés in 1519–1521, Peru by ❷ Francisco Pizarro in 1531–1534, Chile in 1535, Paraguay in 1536, and Bolivia in 1538. In 1535, the Spanish king, Charles V, appointed ❺ Antonio de Mendoza viceroy of "New Spain," which encompassed present-day Mexico and most of Central America. In 1543 the viceroyalty of Peru was formed, comprising all of Spanish South America and Panama. The conquests were retrospectively given the legal title of "missionary work," although this concept long remained controversial among theologians.

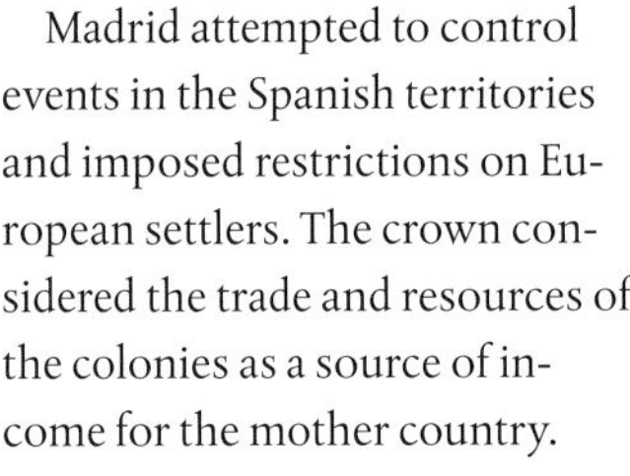

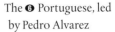

2 Francisco Pizarro, copper engraving, 1673

The ❻ Portuguese, led by Pedro Alvarez Cabral, arrived in Brazil in 1500 and established trading posts there. The Portuguese crown first claimed the country as its property in 1534. From 1549 Brazil was administered by a royal governor-general.

Madrid attempted to control events in the Spanish territories and imposed restrictions on European settlers. The crown considered the trade and resources of the colonies as a source of income for the mother country. ❼ Monastic missionaries converted the Indians to Christianity—sometimes forcibly—but also protected them from the ❽ arbitrary actions of the conquerors. In 1542 they were able to enforce a legal ban on Indian slavery, and in the same year the Dominican father, Bartolomé de Las Casas, the "apostle of the Indians," drew up his *Leyes Nuevas* ("new laws"). These established the equality of the Indians and their liberation from forced labor. However the Church was silent on black slavery, and ❾ Africans were soon transported to work on the plantations of South America and the Caribbean islands. By the time slavery was abolished in 1850, between four million and ten million Africans had been transported to Brazil alone.

Initially whole tribes of Indians were eradicated by infections carried by the Europeans, but over time the South American-born Europeans (*creoles*), Indians (*mestizos*), and black Africans (*mulattos*) born in the New World mixed. The Europeans, however, continued to form the ruling class.

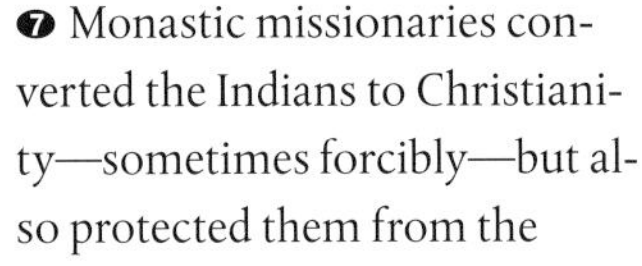

6 Battle between the Indians and Portuguese, ca. 1550, colored copper engraving

7 A Franciscan monk preaches to the Indians

8 Spanish oppression of the native Indians, colored copper engraving, 1596

3 Hernán Cortés, painting, 16th century

5 Antonio de Mendoza, painting, 1786

9 African slaves at a market in Brazil, ca. 1768

1498 | Columbus lands on the Venezuelan coast

1499 | Vespucci lands on the Colombian coast

1519 | Cortés arrives in Mexico

1529 | Francisco Pizarro becomes governor of Peru

1535 | Francisco Pizarro founds the city of Lima

The Indian Reservations

Under the direction of the Jesuits, autonomous Indian reservations were established during the 17th century. In the 18th century, the Creoles became increasingly politically conscious and sought independence from the motherland.

Under Las Casas, bishop of Chiapas from 1544, the ⑩ Dominicans and later the Jesuits began the ⑪ conversion of the Indians. They started in the jungles of Guatemala and founded mission reservations in which the tribal chiefs remained in office with the recognition of the king of Spain. Similar reservations were later set up in Mexico. Protective regulations for the Indians, such as payment for services rendered and prescribed work and rest periods, were often not respected by the local authorities. In 1601 a royal decree gave the rules the force of law—yet they were still routinely disregarded.

In 1604, the Jesuits succeeded in having the province of Paraguay transferred to their control, and in 1609 founded a *reducción* (reservation) for the Guarani as a semi-autonomous Indian settlement. The Indians lived in supervised settlements and cultivated communal lands for two or three days of the week, the yield of which was used to pay Spanish taxes and church construction. The remaining days of the week the Indians worked their own land for their family. All children received an education a part of which was training in a skilled trade. The Jesuits kept their own ⑫ militia to guard against the raids of slave traders from neighboring Brazil. Similar reservations were set up in Ecuador, northern Bolivia, and northwest Mexico, but they deteriorated after the expulsion of the Jesuits from Paraguay between 1759–1767.

The enlightened government of Charles III of Spain carried out reforms in the second half of the 18th century. These included measures to improve the legal status of Indians and the legal equality of the Creoles and immigrant Spaniards in the appointment to offices. However ownership of the best land and access to office remained the preserve of the Creole elite. This class slowly became acquainted with the concepts of the Enlightenment and the French Revolution. Spanish America saw the Napoleonic occupation and the de facto deposition of the royal house in Spain in 1808 as an opportunity to assume home rule. The hour of the struggle for liberation under Simon Bolívar had come.

10 Dominican monks baptize Indians, ca.1600

11 A Christian sermon in a pictorial script which was developed by the Jesuit missionaries to assist them in converting the Indians of Paraguay, extract written on parchment, 17th century

The Pizarro Brothers

The Pizarro brothers are prime examples of the conquistador spirit. Francisco had himself declared governor of Peru in 1529 and founded Lima in 1535. In 1537–1538, trapped with his brothers in Cuzco, he had a disagreement with the Spanish general, Diego de Almagro, who had hurried to save him. Francisco had Almagro executed in 1538 but was then himself murdered by Almagro's son in 1541. Francisco's brother Gonzalo rebelled against the Spanish viceroy in 1546; he was imprisoned and executed. Their youngest brother, Hernando, went to Spain in 1539 to explain Almagro's execution and was imprisoned until 1560.

The arrest of Gonzalo Pizarro

12 Indians obstruct a Spanish officer from entering their reservation, wood inlay, 17th century

1604 | Jesuits take control of Paraguay
1609 | *Reduccione* (reservations) founded
1710–17 | French colonize Louisiana
1718 | New Orleans founded
1759–67 | Jesuits expelled from Paraguay

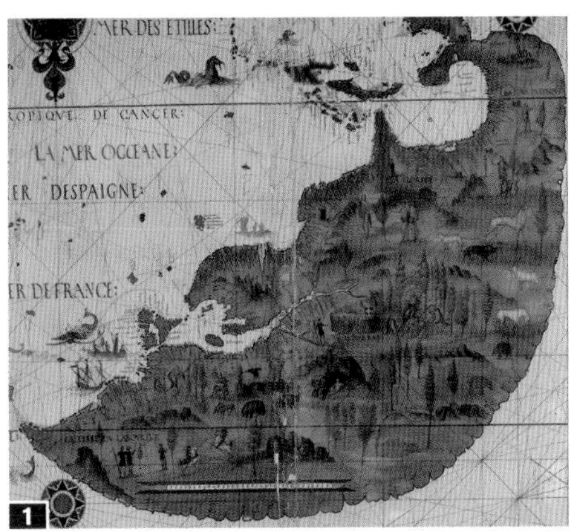

Map of North and Central America, colored lithograph, 19th century

North America to the Founding of Canada and the US 1497–1789

A race began between the British and the French for the colonization of ❶ North America. It ended with the British claiming the area of the later eastern United States and the French pushing north. Canada was eventually divided between the British and the French. In the northeast of the present-day United States, emigrating Puritans and private proprietors and companies founded the New England colonies. In the 17th and 18th centuries, they won cultural independence and political confidence and resisted taxation by the British motherland. The conflict escalated into a war lasting from 1775 to 1783, defined by the United States' Declaration of Independence in 1776, and resulting ultimately in a new constitution for a federal United States of America.

The Fight for the Coasts and the First Colonization of North America

On the coasts of America, Great Britain and Spain fought battles for naval supremacy. During the 16th century, the British and the French began the exploration of North America.

While Spain and Portugal were conquering Central and ❺ South America, it was primarily the British and French who established themselves on the coasts of North America. In 1497, just five years after Columbus's first voyage, John Cabot, in the service of the English king, reached the North American coast in Labrador. French exploration began with Jacques Cartier, who sailed through the Gulf of St. Lawrence and up the St. Lawrence River in 1534–1541. The buccaneer Walter Raleigh landed at Cape Hatteras in North Carolina in 1584, claimed the entire Atlantic coast between the 35th and 45th parallels for England, and named the area ❸ Virginia in honor of the "virgin queen" Elizabeth I; in 1607 it officially became a British colony (and in 1624 a Crown colony). Henry Hudson investigated the East Coast of North America for Great Britain in 1609, while the French missionary Jacques Marquette and fur trader Louis Jolliet discovered the Mississippi River Valley from Wisconsin to Arkansas. Louisiana became the center of French colonization in the Mississippi area in 1716–1717, and in 1718 the French founded the city of New Orleans.

Sir Henry Morgan, privateer and vice-governor of Jamaica, copper engraving

Naval battle of the British fleet against the French fleet near Domenica in the Caribbean, 1782

In the conflict between the sea powers of England and Spain, English privateers seized many transports of Spanish gold and goods returning to Europe from the Spanish colonies. The ❹ Caribbean islands, the Antilles, and parts of the Central American coasts remained contested areas from which freebooters, independently or under the mandate of the European sea powers, seized ships and set up their own, occasionally highly organized "buccaneer states." The most famous privateer was ❷ Henry Morgan, occupied and ransacked trading vessels around Spanish Panama with his British-supported "filibusters," and in 1674 he was knighted before returning to become the British representative governor of Jamaica in the following year.

First British settlement in Virginia, 1584, copper engraving, 1590

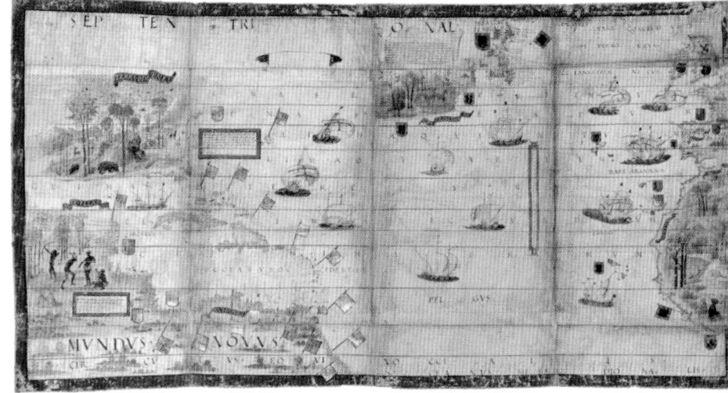

Naval map of the South Atlantic with the continents South America and Africa, drawing, ca. 1519

1497 | John Cabot lands in Labrador

1607 | Virginia becomes British colony

1608 | Founding of Quebec

1620 | Founding of Plymouth

1623 | Founding of New Hampshire

1626 | Founding of Sale

The Establishment of the New England Colonies 17th to 18th century

The earlier British colonies were established and settled either by Puritans driven out of England or by private entrepreneurs. They were soon increasingly prosperous both economically and culturally and developed their own social and political structures.

6 Battle between feuding Indian tribes

At the beginning of the 17th century, North America seemed like the promised land to many groups of English Puritans, who were oppressed by the state church and government in Britain. Their desire to live by the principles of a puritanical Christianity shaped the identity of America and later the United States. In 1620 the ❾ Pilgrim fathers, 102 Puritans who wanted to break with the Church of England because they felt it had not fully carried out the reforms started in the Reformation, sailed to the New World in the ⓬ Mayflower. They landed in ❽ New England. As they had the official right to colonize the area, they signed a charter they had drafted themselves, the "Mayflower Compact," in which they vowed to form an autonomous community and subsequently founded the colony of Plymouth. Other, related colonies followed: New Hampshire (1623), Massachusetts Bay (1630), Connecticut (1634), and Rhode Island (1636). After 1630 the whole of Massachusetts was settled by the "Great Migration" of the Puritans. The founding fathers at first tried to live peacefully with the native ❼ Indians, and this was initially successful while the colonies were still small. With time, however, the settlers constantly expanded their territories and began repeatedly interfering in the ❻ feuds between the Indian tribes.

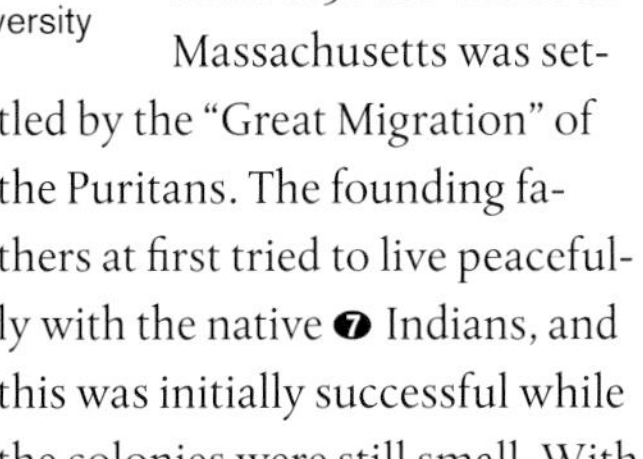

11 Engraving at the main entrance of Harvard University

7 Indian village in present-day North Carolina

The British government assigned the development of the land both to corporate enterprises and individuals with "free letters," or charters for colonization. Thus the colonies of Maryland (1634) and Carolina (1663), divided into North and South in 1729, arose. The first black slaves were brought to North America in 1619.

The Dutch were also active in colonization on a smaller scale; they settled in present-day ⓾ New York, founding the colony of New Netherlands and its capital New Amsterdam in 1624. However, the British took the area from the Dutch in 1664; Charles III assigned it to his brother James, duke of York, after whom it was renamed "New York." The duke sold the area of present-day New Jersey to a private individual. A part of this land was acquired in 1674 by William Penn, the leader of the Quakers, who in addition bought Pennsylvania—named after him—in 1681 and Delaware in 1682. In 1733 the last private colony, named Georgia after King George of England, was founded.

After beginnings full of privations, the New England states blossomed by the end of the 17th century, due to the colonists' pioneering spirit and Protestant work ethic. The first American universities were founded, including ⓫ Harvard (1636), Yale (1701), and Princeton (1746).

8 *Landscape in New England*, painting by Frederick Edwin Church, 1851

9 The pilgrims arrive in America

10 View over the city of New York, copper engraving, 1776

12 The Mayflower's voyage

William Penn

William Penn

As a Quaker, William Penn was persecuted in England where he was expelled from Christ Church, an Oxford college, for his beliefs. Yet as the son of Admiral Sir William Penn he also had some influence at court. Penn was able to persuade the government to assign him territories in the New World, where he founded colonies of peaceful Quaker communities. His drafted the first plan to unify all North American colonies (1696) and to found a "league of nations" for Europe (1693).

from 1630 | "Great Migration"
1630 | Founding of Massachusetts
1634 | Maryland colony
1634 | Founding of Connecticut
1636 | Founding of Rhode Island
1663 | Carolina colony, divided in 1729

Canada and Resistance to the Crown by the New England Colonies

In the fight for colonial territory, French explorers pushed ever further north into Canada. The New England states united after 1765 in resistance against British paternalism.

The French concentrated in the north of the North American continent. In 1603 the French officer ❶ Samuel de Champlain, who initially set off to Canada as part of a fur trading expedition, began the exploration and settling of Canada. He founded Quebec in 1608. The area around the Gulf of ❸ St. Lawrence was referred to as "New France." The defeat of France in the Spanish War of Succession led in 1713 to the Peace of Utrecht, which transferred Newfoundland, Acadia, and areas of the Hudson Bay to Great Britain.

1 Samuel de Champlain

3 The French seafarer Jacques Cartier travels down the St. Lawrence River, 1534–1542

The attempt of the British to expand their control westward into Ohio led in 1754–1763 to a colonial ❹, ❺ war between France and Great Britain. In the Peace of Paris in 1763, which ended the Seven Years' War, France had to concede the rest of Canada, which later saw an influx of British loyal to the king. The legacy of this maneuvering is seen in the bilingual nature of Canada to this day. The Quebec Act (1774) recognized the validity of both British and French law in the recently acquired area, and the Canada Bill (1791) later split the territory into the predominantly English Upper Canada (later Ontario) and the French Lower Canada (Quebec).

In the 1754–1763 war for the American colonies, known as the French and Indian War, the ❷ New England colonies remained loyal to the British. However, economic power had strengthened their confidence, and the link to the motherland had grown weaker with each new generation of American-born colonists. To pay the debt that had accrued fighting France in North America, King George III attempted—against the advice of leading statesmen—to raise finances through an increase of taxes in the 13 American colonies. The colonies, however, demanded representation by their own delegates in the British parliament in exchange, which London was not prepared to grant. In other areas, too, the colonies saw their freedom being restricted. The high import taxes on all goods from the British motherland were particularly offensive and led to widespread boycotts. As an expression of protest, a group of colonists from Boston, Massachusetts. staged the ❻ "Boston Tea Party" in 1773; dressed as Indians, they stormed British ships coming into Boston Harbor and threw their cargo of tea overboard. In response, the crown suspended the constitution of the Massachusetts colony. Armed conflict was not far off.

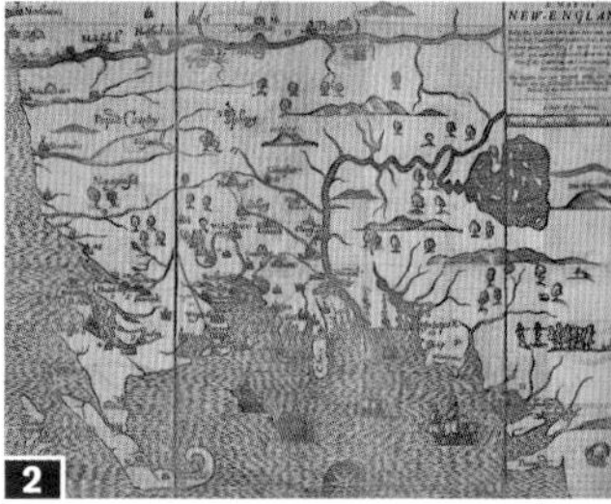
2 Map of New England, wood engraving, 1677

4 The death of General Wolfe in the battle against the French at Quebec on the September 13, 1759

5 Conquest of the French fortress Louisbourg by the British, 1758

6 "Boston Tea Party" on the December 16, 1773, colored lithograph, 1846

1713 | Peace of Utrecht
1754–63 | The French and Indian War
13 Sep 1759 | Battle of Quebec
1763 | Peace of Paris
1773 | "Boston Tea Party"
1774 | Quebec Act

The War against the British and American Independence

Friction between London and the colonies led to the American War of Independence in 1775 and a formal declaration of independence in 1776. The Americans won the war in 1783 with French aid.

In September–October 1774, at the Continental Congress in Philadelphia, the delegates of the 13 British-American colonies decided not to accept any taxation without direct representation in Parliament and demanded the reinstatement of the Massachusetts constitution. London responded by sending troops to restore order in the colonies. After the first hostilities, a second congress of colonists decided in May 1775 to establish a combined army, under the supreme command of ❼, ❾ George Washington, later supported by the French ⓫ Marquis de Lafayette and the Prussian Baron von Steuben, who contributed to the professional organization of the army.

In the meantime, independence was implemented politically: on July 4, 1776, the ⓭ 13 colonies (Massachusetts, New Hampshire, Rhode Island, Connecticut, New York, New Jersey, Pennsylvania, Delaware, Maryland, Virginia, North Carolina, South Carolina, and Georgia) adopted the ❽ Declaration of Independence in Philadelphia as an agreement between the people and government, emphasizing the freedom and equality of all humans. After this, the new states ratified republican constitutions.

The badly armed and discordant, yet enthusiastic American troops achieved a major victory in October 1777, forcing the British troops to capitulate at Saratoga. With this, the American ambassador in Paris, ❿ Benjamin Franklin, was able to negotiate an alliance with France in February 1778. With the help of French naval units, Washington eventually cornered the previously victorious British southern army and in October 1781 forced it to ⓬ surrender. The French brokered the Treaty of Paris, which ended the Revolutionary War with advantageous conditions for the colonists on August 3, 1783. London was forced to recognize the independence of the United States, and the entire territory east of the Mississippi River, south of the Great Lakes, and north of Florida fell to the newly founded nation.

Under the Articles of Confederation, ratified in 1781, the states joined together in a loose league, in which the individual states had great autonomy. This was replaced in 1788 by a constitution that strengthened the federal government, and George Washington was elected the first president of the United States in 1789.

7 Washington crosses the Delaware before the Battle of Trenton, 1776

9 George Washington

10 Benjamin Franklin

11 Washington receives Lafayette

12 The surrender at Yorktown on the October 19,1781

8 Declaration of Independence of the United States of America, July 4, 1776

Virginia Declaration of Rights

Section 1

That all men are by nature equally free and independent and have certain inherent rights, of which, when they enter into a state of society, they cannot, by any compact, deprive or divest their posterity; namely, the enjoyment of life and liberty, with the means of acquiring and possessing property, and pursuing and obtaining happiness and safety.

13 Signing of the Declaration of Independence by the 13 colonies of America, 1776

4 Jul 1776 | Declaration of Independence
1777 | British surrender at Saratoga
1777–81 | Articles of Confederation
1789 | George Washington elected first president
1791 | Canada Bill
1812–14 | War for Canada

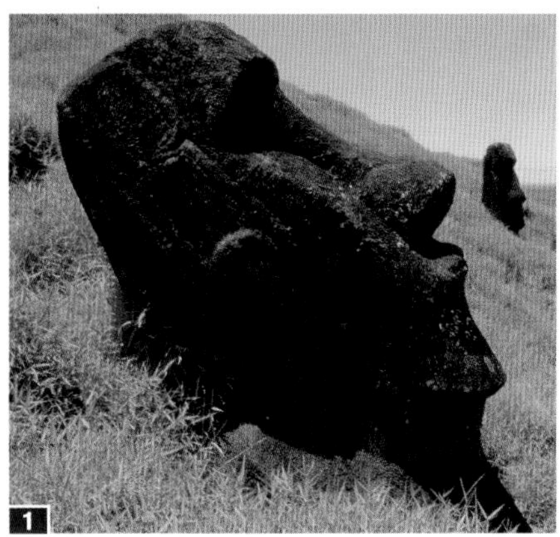

Oceania and Australia to the Arrival of the Europeans 16th–18th century

The native inhabitants of Australia, New Zealand, and the ❶ islands of Oceania were able to develop their ancient culture over a long period of time. In the 16th and 17th centuries, the seafaring European nations arrived on the islands and mainland of Australia, but comprehensive European exploration did not occur until the 18th century. The explorers saw the inhabitants of the South Sea Islands as "noble savages" because of their harmonious lifestyle and lack of private property. After the loss of the American colonies, the British used Australia as a penal colony.

1 Moai, monolithic stone statues on Easter Island

Oceania

The diverse cultures of the Pacific islands formed predominantly local communities scattered across large areas. They were encountered by the European nations in the 16th century and gradually colonized.

Various cultures developed on the islands of New Guinea, Melanesia, Micronesia, and Polynesia. They had in common ❷ village settlements, the use of ❸ stone tools, agriculture, the breeding of animals, and fishing. Most of the societies were based on hierarchy and were led by a king or chief and a priest caste.

Settlement took place over a prolonged period of time in various waves of migration, notably the Austronesian migration that began around 750 B.C., and the Malayo-Polynesian migration that began around 500 B.C. By 700 A.D. Raiatea, one of the Society Islands, was the center of the Polynesian world. Between 900–1000 the ❻ Polynesians reached and settled Easter Island, Hawaii, and New Zealand, establishing the Maori culture.

3 Ceremonial Axehead of the Maori chiefs

At the beginning of the 16th century, Spanish and Portuguese seafarers arrived in Oceania, initiating two centuries of European exploration. Magellan passed several Pacific islands during his 1519–1521 circumnavigation. In 1526 the Portuguese Jorge de Menezes claimed the island of New Guinea, while in 1524–1564 Spanish voyagers charted the majority of the islands of Micronesia. The Dutchman Abel Tasman, who came to New Zealand in 1642, was the first to make a more exact survey of the Melanesian region. In 1722, his countryman Jacob Roggeveen named Easter Island after the date of its sighting. On his three voyages between 1764 and 1780, James Cook, commissioned by the British Royal Society, traveled to ❺ Tahiti and circumnavigated New Zealand for the first time. In 1772–1775 he arrived in New Caledonia and mapped the ❹ New Hebrides, the Marquesas, and Tonga.

2 Matavae, a village on the island of Tahiti

James Cook

On three voyages to the South Pacific, Captain James Cook, one of the last great seafaring discoverers, explored Oceania, Australia, and New Zealand. In 1773, he became the first navigator to cross the Antarctic Circle, searching for the mysterious Terra Australis ("southern land"). On his third voyage, he looked in vain for a northern passage from the Pacific to the Atlantic. In February 1779, he was killed in Hawaii by a group of islanders.

above: James Cook

4 James Cook in the New Hebrides in 1774, painting by William Hodges

5 *Woman holding a fruit*, Tahiti-inspired painting by Paul Gauguin, 1893

6 Polynesian woman from the Tonga islands, 1895

ca. 24,350 B.C. | Evidence of first settlements
1526 A.D. | Jorge de Menezes reaches New Guinea
1605 | Willem Jansz sights Australia
1642–44 | Abel Tasman's voyage of exploration
1642 | Tasman gives his name to the island of Tasmania
1643 | Tasman reaches New Zealand

Australia up to British Colonization

The Australian native inhabitants, the Aborigines, constitute an independent cultural society. Europeans first arrived in Australia in the 17th century, but colonization by the British only began in the second half of the 18th century.

The Australian ❽ native inhabitants lived as hunter-gatherers and killed wild animals with throwing spears or wooden clubs. They fashioned vessels and tools out of wood, bone, and shells. Their extensive ❿ religio-cultic concepts often revolved around the relationship between the living and totem animals and their ancestors, and are often presented in colorful rock paintings. The oldest settlement finds in Australia have been dated as early as 24,350 B.C. The earliest immigrants probably came through Southeast Asia and Melanesia.

9 Group of English convicts deported from England to the penal colony, working the land, steel engraving, 1835

Lack of written evidence and the heavily mythological form of the oral histories make a more exact dating extremely difficult. The Aborigines still represent an independent cultural society in Australia today.

The arrival of Europeans in Australia began in 1605 with the Dutch captain Willem Jansz. The ❼ barren, arid land and the often hostile behavior of the Aborigines offered the Dutch little incentive to colonize, though they anchored off the north coast several times. Commissioned by the governor of the Dutch Indies, Anthony van Diemen, ⓬ Abel Tasman undertook a voyage of exploration around Australia in 1642–44. He charted the island named after him, Tasmania, in 1642, and the South Island of New Zealand and the Tongan and Fijian islands in 1643. Australia was then called "New Holland," although the Dutch did not pursue their colonial interest.

8 Portrait of an Aborigine woman

⓫ William Dampier, a British sea captain, reached the northwestern coast of Australia by way of the Marianas and the Moluccas in 1699 and was the first to describe the native inhabitants and their culture. In April 1770, Captain Cook, after crossing the Pacific Ocean, landed on the southeast coast of Australia in Botany Bay, south of modern Sydney, and claimed the land for the British crown, naming it "New South Wales." His companion, the naturalist Joseph Banks, provided the crown with a description of the land, which raised great interest back in Britain, even more so after the loss of the American colonies (p. 343). London decided to use Australia as a penal colony for ❾ British prisoners, who were to cultivate the land under strict supervision. In January 1788, the first prisoner ship, carrying 730 convicts, anchored north of Botany Bay. There, the New South Wales penal colony was established; Sydney was founded nearby for the colonial officials. Convicted prisoners continued to be deported to Australia until 1868. The last of the prison colonies, located on the island of Tasmania, was closed in 1877.

7 The Australian interior or "outback"

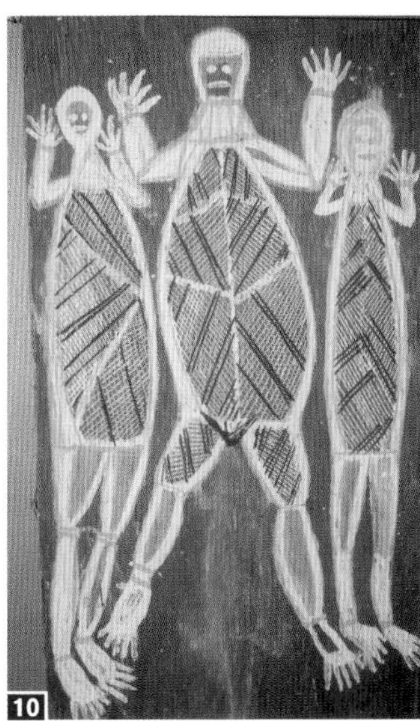

10 Three ghost figures, an Aboriginal painting on tree bark

11 The English discoverer and privateer, William Dampier

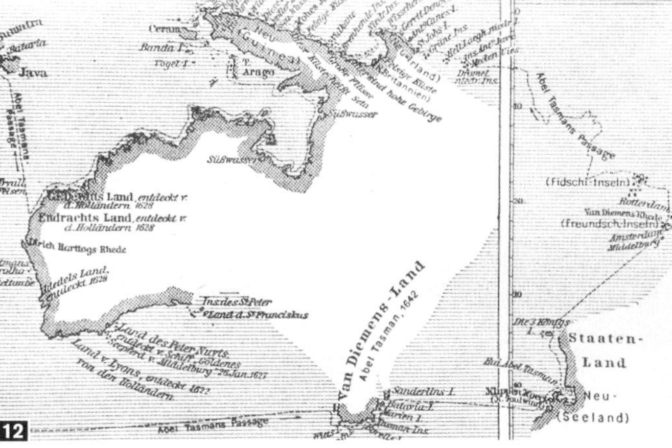

12 Route traveled by the Dutch explorer Abel Tasman, who in the 17th century searched the Pacific Ocean for new trade routes for the Netherlands

1699 | William Dampier reaches Australia
1722 | Discovery of Easter Island
1768–71 | First circumnavigation of New Zealand
1770 | James Cook lands in Botany Bay
1788 | First British convicts arrive in Australia
1877 | Closure of last penal colony on Tasmania

The Modern Era

1789–1914

In Europe, the revolutionary transformation of the ruling systems and state structures began with a bang: In 1789 the French Revolution broke out in Paris, and its motto "Liberté, Egalité, Fraternité"—Liberty, Equality, Brotherhood—took on an irrepressible force. A fundamental reorganization of society followed the French Revolution. The ideas behind the revolution were manifest in Napoleon's *Code Civil,* which he imposed on many European nations. The 19th century also experienced a transformation of society from another source: The Industrial Revolution established within society a poorer working class that stood in opposition to the merchant and trading middle class. The nascent United States was shaken by an embittered civil war. The economic growth that set in following that war was accompanied by the development of imperialist endeavors and its rise to the status of a Great Power.

Liberty Leading the People, allegory of the 1830 July revolution that deposed the French monarchy, with Marianne as the personification of liberty, contemporary painting by Eugène Delacroix.

1 First edition of the Napoleonic code, March 21, 1804

2 George Stephenson's "Rocket" steam engine

3 Everyday poverty in a laborer's cottage

The Civic Age

Criticism of authority and tradition on all levels grew with the rationalist and emancipatory ideas of the Enlightenment. The French Revolution of 1789 broke up the old order of the three estates and, with its motto of ❹ "Freedom, Equality, Brotherhood," laid the foundations for a new pan-European social order based on the principles of personal freedom and equality before the law. In the course of the 19th century, the middle class, often champions of liberalism, increasingly came to dominate public life.

4 Red "cap of liberty" and the motto: "Unity, indivisibility of the Republic, liberty, equality, brotherhood or death," French revolutionary poster, 1792

Path to the Political Emancipation of the Citizen

Napoleon ended the French Revolution with his coronation as ❻ emperor of France in 1804 and, through military conquest, set about reordering continental Europe according to his own vision. Although he was ultimately defeated at the Battle of Waterloo in 1815, and the other powers attempted to restore the pre-revolutionary conditions in the 1815 Congress of Vienna, Napoleonic rule left deep traces across Europe. The ideas spread by the revolution and the Napoleonic reforms that followed made a return to the old structures of rule impossible. With Napoleon's ❶ civil code, the areas of Europe he conquered experienced a civic law that shaped the demands of later nationalist and liberal movements for constitutional protection of citizens' rights.

6 Emperor Napoleon, portrait by Jean-Auguste-Dominique Ingres

The tensions between the old ruling powers and bourgeois movements demanding a political voice eventually culminated in the European revolutions of 1848. The threat of civil disorder was initially successful in forcing through constitutional reform, but the movements lacked unity, and much was clawed back once order was restored. The 1848 revolutions nonetheless marked the entry of the middle class into the ranks of those seeking to preserve social order. The middle classes tried to imitate the ❺ lifestyle of the aristocracy. Bourgeois society and the workers would never again find themselves on the same side of the barricades.

5 Ball held at the Court of Vienna

Changes in Society and the Economy

At the beginning of the 19th century, industrialization, which had already begun in Great Britain in the 18th century, gathered pace in many parts of the European continent with inventions such as the ❷ steam engine. The implementation of new technologies created a rapid transformation of working and living conditions, often initially for the worse. With the emergence of a growing pool of undifferentiated "wage labor," a new stratum—the working class—was formed. The industrial workers lived in workers' quarters in the expanding cities marked by squalid conditions. As economic conditions in the countryside continued to deteriorate, rural workers lost their livelihood and moved into the cities to seek work. Many people also emigrated, particularly to America. They fled from ❸ poverty and the increasingly authoritarian backlash that followed the 1848 revolutions.

The emerging industrial labor force was often politicized and organized.

1789 | Outbreak of the French Revolution
1804 | Napoleon's coronation as emperor of France
1823 | Monroe Doctrine
1830 | First railway in the world opened in England
1848 | European revolutions

7 Karl Marx

8 Steel mill, painting by Adolph Menzel

9 Battle of Verdun, 1916

The demands of the workers were often related to wages and hours, but in many places they also joined movements with demands including universal male suffrage and the relief of poverty. More systematic political ideologies, notably anarchism and socialism as expounded in the popular *Communist Manifesto* by ❼ Karl Marx and Friedrich Engels, vied for influence among the urban working class. By contrast, although many radical leaders had bourgeois origins, the middle class as a whole became increasingly conservative, identifying its interests with the preservation of property rights.

The expanding economies of the ❽ Industrial Revolution demanded access to new sources of raw materials and markets outside Europe. At the same time, the flood of labor to the cities and the lack of regulation contributed to appalling urban working and living conditions.

Nation-States and Imperialism

In addition to the Industrial Revolution, increasing nationalism—in the form of imperialism—became a major source of great power engagements outside Europe, especially in the later decades of the century. This made a decisive contribution to the outbreak of World War I. In the second half of the 19th century, nations increasingly linked their emerging identities with competition for world power. As well as bringing power and prestige to a nation, colonies were a source of valuable raw materials, markets for industrial goods and, in some cases, strategically vital naval bases. Influence in the world meant economic power. Furthermore, imperialism was underpinned by the presumptions of 19th century social science, which lent intellectual cover to imperialist ventures. At its simplest imperialism was perceived, or at least presented, in paternalistic terms. The self-image of British imperialism, for example, was that of the world's greatest empire nurturing the development of subject peoples around the globe until such time as they would be ready to govern themselves—although of course only Britain would be able to determine when this might be.

Once Tunisia had been occupied by France, and Egypt by Great Britain, at the beginning of the 1880s, the contest between the European powers for territories began. The United States, which made its own colonial acquisitions in the Pacific, accelerated US hegemony in Central and South America with the 1823 Monroe Doctrine. The Great Powers also included the new Italian state and the German empire. The overlapping of interests, particularly in what became known as the "scramble for Africa," led to open conflict. At the Berlin Congo conference of 1884, an agreement was reached as to the spheres of interest of the Great Powers in Africa, considerably reducing the costs of imperialism to the point where a carving-up became viable.

10 German cartoon: "German imperialism soars," the British lion prevents the German imperial eagle from flying

However the European powers also followed an alliance policy that anticipated the fault lines and fronts of World War I. The first military conflict of the Great Powers after the Vienna Congress was the Crimean War of 1853–1856. Great Britain and France fought on the side of the Ottoman Empire against Russia in the Black Sea region. This strained relations between Austria and Russia, as the weak Austro-Hungarian Empire sought to remain neutral despite its alliance with Moscow. The expansionist drives of the Great Powers inevitably created conflicts. Great Britain and France had overlapping claims in Asia and Africa that threatened to turn into a major war. However, neither side could afford such a course, and the *Entente Cordiale* (French: "friendly understanding") of 1904 secured an alliance between Great Britain and France. ❿ Imperial Germany then sought to catch up with Britain and France by acquiring its own colonial empire, and this competition led to an ⓫ arms race. By the beginning of the ❾ First World War in 1914 the major powers were thus entangled in a complex web of alliances and a growing competition for colonial empire.

11 Cartoon on the naval arms race: "In the kitchen of the fleet chef"

1853–56 | Crimean War
1882 | Britain takes control of Egypt
Jul 1914 | Outbreak of World War I
1848 | *Communist Manifesto* published
1871 | German *Reich* founded
1884 | Berlin Congo conference

The French Revolution 1789–1799

The French Revolution had far-reaching consequences not only for France but for all of Europe as it challenged the fundamental institutions that shaped the political structure of Europe. It was an attempt to establish in common laws the equality of all persons regardless of their origin. The Revolution led by the bourgeoisie had as its goals the abolition of aristocratic rule, a constitution, and intellectual freedom. It stressed social mobility without class barriers ("Let ability win through!") and strove for a moral society, the nation, in which the common good took precedence over self-interests: "Liberty, Equality, Brotherhood!" Radicalism, however, along with outside pressure, transformed at times the rule of virtue into a despotism of its own kind.

1 The storming of the Bastille on July 14, 1789

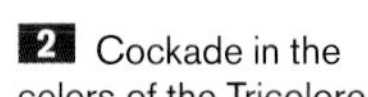

2 Cockade in the colors of the Tricolore

Beginning of the Revolution

The internal crisis of the monarchy brought about the convening of the Estates General in 1789. At the same time, the destitute masses revolted in Paris.

In May 1789, King Louis XVI summoned together representatives of the three estates, aristocracy, clergy, and bourgeoisie, to bring France's catastrophic financial situation under control. The third estate, the bourgeoisie, composed 98 percent of the population and carried the tax burden but in fact had few rights. On June 20, 1789, to counter the attempt of the king and the aristocracy to dissolve the National Assembly, the members took the ❹ "Tennis Court Oath" not to disband and announced their opposition. The king, however, installed an ultra conservative government, after which the people of Paris revolted and on July 14, 1789, stormed and destroyed the ❶ Bastille– a prison and symbol of the power of the state. The Revolution had started.

3 National Guard planting a liberty tree, gouache, ca. 1790

Two days later the National Assembly forced the king to accept the revolutionary Tricolore in the ❷ national colors blue-white-red as symbol of the "alliance of king and people." A revolutionary fervor spread throughout the country. On August 8, 1789, the rights of man were declared and everywhere ❸ "liberty trees" were planted in celebration.

Freedom of the press made possible a flood of new newspapers and pamphlets. Diverse opinions and parties developed. The National Assembly carried out judicial and constitutional reforms and abolished the feudal system in France. The new system of census voting provoked a major confrontation because it allowed only the wealthiest taxpayers to take part in the political process. The poor and peasants, who had been involved in the events since the beginning, fought for universal suffrage.

At first, the monarchy was retained as the form of government. Most of the members of the Assembly, above all ❺ the powerfully eloquent leader of the early revolutionary phase, Honoré Gabriel Riqueti Comte de Mirabeau, supported a constitutional monarchy based on the English model.

5 Mirabeau during the session of the Estates General on June 23, 1789

4 The National Assembly takes the Tennis Court Oath in Versailles on June 20, 1789

Declaration of Man and of the Citizen, 1789

"Men are born and remain free and equal in rights. Social distinctions can only be founded on communal utility." (Article 1)

above: Declaration of Man and of the Citizen, 1789

20 Jun 1789 | "Tennis Court Oath" **26 Aug 1789** | Declaration of Man and of the Citizen **14 Jul 1790** | Celebration of the constitutional consecrat

14 Jul 1789 | Begin of the revolution with storming of the Bastille **5 Oct 1789** | Bread March by the women of Paris

Phase of Radicalization

Between 1791 and 1792 the Revolution became more radical when it faced massive resistance to its ideas in France and abroad. Some French provinces were in open revolt and the revolutionary masses in Paris became even more active.

6 Battle between the French Revolutionary Army and the Coalition Army in Valmy on September 20, 1792

The Sans-culottes

The sans-culottes ("without kneebreeches") saw themselves as true revolutionaries. They rejected the wigs and kneebreeches of the aristocracy and were recruited from the ranks of wage-earners and urban proletariats who fought early on and in the foremost ranks. The journal that served as their voice was the "Père Duchesne" of the social revolutionary J.-R. Hébert.

Armed Sans-culotte in uniform

The radicalization of the Revolution was triggered by the undiplomatic behavior of the king, as well as outside pressure. ❼ Even after Louis XVI swore upon the constitution at the celebration of the inauguration of the constitution at Champ de Mars, he attempted unsuccessfully to block it. He fled from Paris in June 1791 with his family, but his flight was stopped near Varennes and the king was taken prisoner.

The radical parties of the Revolution demanded the abolition of the monarchy and the declaration of a French republic. In 1791, the majority of the nobility fled from France and as emigrants worked against the Revolution from abroad, seeking support from powerful parties throughout Europe. Internationally, fear of the revolutionary forces taking power in France grew. In February 1792 the emperor of Austria and the king of Prussia formed a pact against the Revolution.

The "Girondists" now became the leading party. They were political moderates but supported the war that began in April 1792. The initial battles ended devastatingly for the Revolutionary Army. Only after the Austro-Prussian commanding general threatened Paris with conquest and destruction in July 1792 did a patriotic zeal seize the entire country. The *sans-culottes* controlled the events; ❽ ten thousand French citizens armed themselves and marched off to war. ❻ 50,000 revolutionary soldiers defeated the allied troops near Valmy on September 20, 1792 and in November 1792 the Revolutionary Army marched into Belgium and Germany.

The revolutionary momentum was now directed against the king, who had been held in Temple since August 1792. After the discovery of his clandestine correspondence, he was sentenced to death as a "treasonable conspirator, rebel, and public enemy," and ❾ guillotined publicly in Paris on January 21, 1793.

7 Louis XVI and Marie Antoinette swear upon the constitution

8 Arming of the people at the Hôtel des Invalides

9 Execution of Louis XVI on the Place de la Concorde in Paris

1789–1914 The Modern Era

20–21 Jun 1791 | Escape of the royal family to Varennes
20 Apr 1792 | Declaration of war on Austria
10 Aug 1792 | Storming of the Tuileries Palace by sans-culottes
20 Sep 1792 | Battle of Valmy
21 Jan 1793 | Execution of Louis XVI

The Jacobins verses the Girondists

The issue of a war against the German Empire sparked a struggle for power between the pro-war Girondists and the anti-war Jacobins.

Jean-Paul Marat gives a speech

Since the middle of 1792, a struggle for control over the direction of the Revolution had been playing out between the moderate Girondists and the radical clubs of the Cordeliers and ❷ Jacobins — named after their meeting place in a monastery in the rue St. Jacob. The leaders of the Girondists were Jean-Pierre Brissot and the minister of the interior, Jean-Marie Roland. They argued for the war and the export of the Revolution to the rest of Europe. They particularly attempted to check the mob rule of the streets of Paris after the storming of the Tuileries Palace in August 1792. On the radical side stood tribunes of the people. Among these was the leftist social revolutionary Jacques René Hébert, mouthpiece of the sans-culotte movement, and also, notably, the friend of the people," ❶ Jean-Paul Marat, a radical speaker who described himself as "the eye of the masses." These radicals created a fermenting, turbulent and violent climate within the city, which was particularly apparent when the slaughter of the enemies of the Revolution in September 1792 ("September Massacres"), was tolerated by Justice Minister Danton. In March 1793, the radicals succeeded in establishing the dreaded Revolutionary Tribunal. In summary trials, they proceeded with extreme severity against actual and supposed enemies of the Revolution. Concurrently, the war on the borders continued.

The arrest of Hébert, who was then freed by the people, and the charge against Marat by the Girondists, precipitated a conflict in which the Girondists were defeated by the Jacobins in June 1793. Shortly thereafter, the representatives of the Département Gironde were executed or forced to commit suicide. The reign of the Jacobins began and Marat, as the leader of the people, joined them. However, the "friend of the people" was violently stabbed to death in his bath on July 13, 1793, by the Girondist Charlotte Corday d' Armont. The cult surrounding Marat, now the "Martyr of Liberty," became a weapon against all anti-revolutionaries. The revolts against the Jacobin reign, which first broke out in Vendée and in Lyon, led to bloody civil war in some provinces and ruthless verdicts from the victorious Jacobins throughout the whole country.

Jean-Paul Marat:

"500 or 600 chopped-off heads would have secured peace, liberty and happiness for you. A misunderstood humanitarianism made your arms lame and hindered you from administering the blows. It will cost the lives of millions of your brothers."

above: Portrait of Jean-Paul Marat

Club of Jacobins, January, 1792

Women in the Revolution

Women from all levels of society saw the Revolution as an opportunity for political participation. Manon Roland de la Platière, a member of the bourgeoisie and the wife of the Girondist minister of the interior, hosted a salon for supporters of the revolution in Paris. From the start, for example during the storming of the Bastille, women were to be found in the front ranks of the revolutionary masses. They were ridiculed by their opponents as "soldiers in skirts" but played a significant role in the French Revolution, particularly in the sans-culotte movement.

above: Armed revolutionary
right: Manon Roland de la Platière

1792–93 | Power struggle of Girondists and Jacobins
Mar 1793 | Revolutionary Tribunal established
2 Jun 1793 | Girondists defeated
13 Jul 1793 | Murder of Marat
1793–94 | Power struggle between Danton and Robespierre
5 Apr 1794 | Danton executed

Prussia's Rise and Austria's Decline

The Seven Weeks' War of 1866 ended Austrian influence in German politics. Thereafter the North German confederation was dominated by Prussia.

Wilhelm I, son of Frederick William III, succeeded his brother Frederick William IV as king of Prussia in 1861. He was a ruler of absolutist and autocratic ideas. When he became embroiled in a ❺ constitutional conflict in 1862, he entrusted the office of Prussian minister-president and foreign minister to Otto von Bismarck. His first action was to defy the Prussian Chamber of Deputies and push through a set of military reforms, setting the tone for his period in office. Bismarck snubbed the Habsburgs by boycotting the 1863 Frankfurt Diet of Princes, which was convened to discuss Austria's reform proposals for the German Confederation. He then turned to Russia to secure its neutrality in any future conflict with Austria. Despite these tensions, Austria and Prussia together defeated Denmark in 1864 in a ❻ war over Schleswig and Holstein.

5 Cartoon of Bismarck's contempt for the constitution

In 1866 Bismarck reignited the dispute over supremacy by occupying Holstein. Austria secured a resolution of the Diet of the German Confederation to mobilize the neutral Confederation troops, whereupon Prussia declared war on Austria. Prussia and its 18 allied North German states defeated Austria and its 13 German Confederate state allies on July 3, 1866, at ❼ Königgrätz. The resulting Treaty of Prague, signed on August 23, dissolved the German Confederation. Prussia dominated the North German Confederation that was founded shortly afterwards and was soon joined by the South German states.

However, Bismarck had yet to achieve formal German unity under Prussian leadership. The ❽ Franco-Prussian War, which ended in France's defeat at the Battle of Sedan on September 1, 1870, provided the opportunity. On January 18, 1871, in the Hall of Mirrors at the Palace of Versailles, ❾ Wilhelm I declared himself emperor of a new unified Germany. Although Prussia had secured Germany a leading role in Europe, its arrival alarmed the other major powers. France, which lost Alsace-Lorraine after its defeat, was particularly alarmed and hostile.

6 Storming of the Danish trenches during the war over Schleswig and Holstein, 1864

7 Bismarck and General Moltke near Königgrätz

8 Prussian and French troops skirmish during the Battle of Wörth, 1870

9 King Wilhelm I of Prussia is declared German emperor in the Hall of Mirrors in the Palace of Versailles, following Prussia's crushing victory over France, 1871

Otto von Bismarck

Otto von Bismarck:

"Germany does not look to Prussia's liberalism, but to her power. ... Not by speeches and majorities will the great questions of the day be decided—that was the mistake of 1848 and 1849—but by blood and iron."

From a speech delivered to the Prussian Chamber of Deputies, September 30, 1862

from 1862 | Bismarck minister-president in Prussia
1863 | Frankfurt Diet of Princes
1864 | War with Denmark over Schleswig and Holstein
23 Aug 1866 | Treaty of Prague
1 Sep 1870 | Battle of Sedan
18 Jan 1871 | William I proclaimed German Emperor

Imperial Germany 1871–1914

After the founding of the Reich, Bismarck pursued an alliance policy meant to create a European balance of power while largely isolating France. Domestically he fought the power of the Catholic Church in the *Kulturkampf* ("cultural struggle"). He also sought to control the spread of socialism through the carrot-and-stick method of enacting social reforms while banning socialist organizations and literature. After Bismarck's dismissal in 1890, the German Reich found itself hemmed in on two fronts by an allignment between Russia and France as allies—exactly the situation he had always sought to avoid. The Belle Époque, in both domestic and foreign politics, was an era in which potentially explosive tensions emerged.

1 Berlin Congress June 13–July 13, 1878: Bismarck and the Russian deputy Earl Shuvalov

European Alliance Policies

The Three Emperors' League, the Triple Alliance, and the Reinsurance Treaty temporarily protected the German Empire within the network of European great powers.

The German Reich that came into existence through the constitution of April 16, 1871, comprised 22 individual states and three free cities. The constitutional monarchy was now governed by an imperial chancellor, who was appointed by the kaiser (emperor) and, as was the case with ❸ Bismarck, served as Prussian prime minister and foreign minister.

Alliances forged under Bismarck temporarily protected the German Empire within the network of European powers. In 1873 Bismarck formed the Three Emperors' League with Austria and Russia. By the time of the ❶ Berlin Congress in 1878, however, the alliance was already tottering, and Germany abandoned it in favor of a ❺ pact with Austria; this became the ❷ Triple Alliance when Italy joined in 1882.

3 Otto von Bismarck

The ❹ Balkans remained an area of contention, where the competing interests of Austria and Russia created friction. To avoid escalation, Germany entered into the Reinsurance Treaty with Russia in 1887, which bound both to neutrality. When Great Britain allied itself to Italy and Austria—and thus indirectly with Germany—through the Mediterranean Entente in 1887, all European major powers except France were now tied with Germany through alliances. However, the Reinsurance Treaty was not renewed after Bismarck's forced dismissal in 1890. Russia instead concluded a military pact with France in 1892, thus placing Germany between the pincers of two major allied powers.

2 Caricature depicting the Triple Alliance of Imperial Germany, Austria and Italy, showing Bismarck as lion tamer

Wilhelm II, after Bismarck's Dismissal

"The post of duty officer on the ship of state has fallen to me. The course stays the old one. Full steam ahead."

The captain leaves the ship; caricature about the dismissal of Bismarck by Wilhelm II

4 Russian-Turkish war, 1877–78

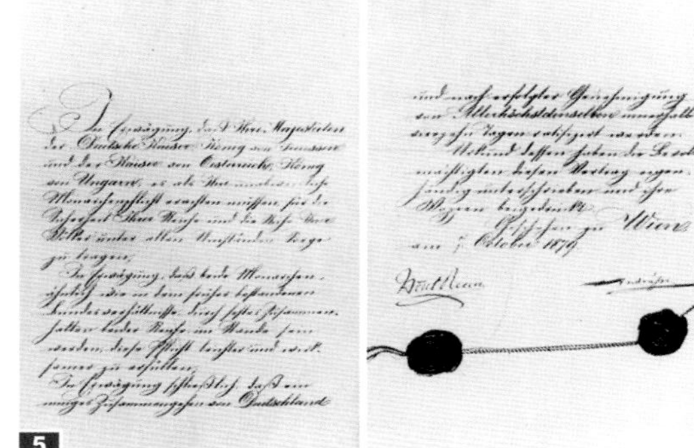

5 German-Austrian pact, signed on October 17, 1879

18 Apr 1871 | Constitution of the German Reich
1873 | Viennese stock-market crash
1873 | Three Emperors' League
1878 | Anti-socialist law
1878 | Berlin Congress
1879 | Dual Alliance
1881 | Three Emperors' League renewed

Domestic Political Failures

Bismarck was as unsuccessful in his battle against the Catholic Church as he was in his struggle against the labor movement.

Bismarck's free trade policy, aided by the high reparations payments of the French, led to an economic upswing in the founding years of the German Reich marked by building activity and stock speculation, although that slackened after the ❽ Viennese stock market crash of 1873. Bismarck then introduced protective tariffs in 1879 that split the ⓫ National Liberal party, which had stood by him until then.

The National Liberals represented the hopes particularly of the upper middle class for industrial progress and of Protestant, middle-class intellectuals for a stemming of the Catholic influence that was represented in the *Reichstag* (Parliament) by the ❿ Center party; for this reason, they supported Bismarck in the ❻ *Kulturkampf*, or struggle, against the political influence of Catholicism. Laws were enacted in the early 1870s disallowing the Catholic clergy from making political statements in office, putting their training under state control, banning the promulgation of the Jesuits, transferring the supervision of schools to the state, and making possible the closing of monasteries. Some of the priests who refused to recognize the laws were prosecuted. The measures, however, remained ineffective and Bismarck was forced to repeal most of them in the 1880s.

Kaiser Wilhelm II

Bismarck combated the spread of socialism among the workers with a two-pronged strategy. The antisocialist law of 1878 was meant to "counter the efforts of social democracy, which is a danger to the public": labor movement organizations and pamphleteering were banned. This too proved unsuccessful, however. By the time the law was repealed in 1890, the Social Democratic Party had been formed and its share of voters had tripled. The gradual introduction of ❾ social security from 1883 to 1889 addressed some of the workers' concerns but was meant to preempt more far-reaching political demands.

On June 15, 1888, ❼ Wilhelm II became kaiser after the death of his father Friedrich III who had ruled for only 99 days following the death of his own father Wilhelm I in the same year. Bismarck was as little in agreement with Wilhelm's desire to conciliate workers with more social reforms as he was with the other ideas of the new kaiser. Consequently, Wilhelm dismissed the "Iron Chancellor" on March 20, 1890.

Kulturkampf 1871–89, Caricature about Bismarck and Pope Leo XIII

Viennese stock market crash on May 9, 1873

"Year of the Three Emperors"

1888 is called the "Year of the Three Emperors" in Germany. When Kaiser Wilhelm I died on March 9 at age 91, his son Frederick III was already seriously ill with cancer of the larynx and unable to speak. He was only able to breathe through a silver tube that had been inserted into his windpipe. The people had set hope in him because of his liberal political convictions, but he died that summer. His son, Wilhelm II, succeeded him.

above: Memorial coin for the "Year of the Three Emperors"

Caricature about the social laws: The unemployed demand work instead of social welfare

The leader of the Center party: Windthorst, von Mallinckrodt and Reichensperger

Rudolph von Benningsen, leader of the National Liberal party, wood engraving by A. Neumann, ca. 1880

1882 | Triple Alliance
1883–89 | Socialist Laws
1887 | Mediterranean Entente
1887 | Reinsurance Treaty
15 Jun 1888 | William II proclaimed Kaiser
20 Mar 1890 | Bismarck dismissed

The German Reich from 1890 to 1914: The "New Course"

With the dismissal of Imperial Chancellor Bismarck in 1890, two years after he had ascended to the throne, ❶ Wilhelm II rang in a new era. However, the Wilhelminian society persisted in its outdated traditions.

Wilhelm II did not continue Bismarck's hard-line strategy. His "New Course" promised to end internal political stagnation. The Catholics, who had been alienated in the Kulturkampf, were given compromises; the anti-socialist law was not renewed; and the new labor law that, for example, banned child labor, showed the protective side of the monarchy. But the kaiser's social interest evaporated when the workers, even after these "gifts," could not be wooed away from the Social Democratic party.

In Count ❸ Leo von Caprivi, Wilhelm now had a less domineering imperial chancellor at his side who would not hinder him in his "personal reign." Caprivi did not remain in office for long, however. His pragmatic and conciliatory domestic politics went too far for the conservatives, and his trade policies, while making Germany a leading economic world power in the 1890s, earned him the enmity of big property owners. Caprivi was forced to resign as Prussian minister-president in 1892 and as imperial chancellor in 1894 because he had planned, as had Bismarck before him, to topple the Reichstag.

2 The Social Democrat August Bebel holding a speech in the Reichstag

Central to the nature of Wilhelminian Era was the inner contradiction between economic modernization and the traditionalism of the elite. The ❹ aristocracy, which had set the tone socially, attempted to hold onto its leading role. This, however, had long been lost to the upper middle class, which controlled both industry and the financial market. A consequential modernization was not allowed to take place, particularly in Prussia, the most influential part of the Reich. There, the composition of the state parliament was determined up until 1918 by the three-class franchise so that it increasingly contrasted with the more progressive ❷ Reichstag. The Zabern Affair in 1913 proved what was true for the whole of the Wilhelminian Era: a parliament against an authoritarian government responsible only to the kaiser could accomplish nothing.

1 Kaiser Wilhelm II

3 Count Leo von Caprivi

4 A ball during the Wilhelminian period, painting by Adolf von Menzel, 1878

The Zabern Affair

The Zabern Affair of 1913 made the impotence of the Reichstag clear. After German soldiers arrested protesters in Saverne (German: Zabern), Alsace, without legal grounds, Imperial Chancellor Theobald von Bethmann Hollweg, albeit reluctantly, supported the Prussian minister of war, Erich von Falkenhayn, in a cover-up together with the kaiser that denied abuse of power on the parts of the soldiers. The Reichstag passed, for the first time, a vote of no confidence in the government on December 4, 1913, and demanded the chancellor's resignation. However, there was no constitutional basis for this move, and it proved unsuccessful.

above: Theobald v. Bethmann-Hollweg, left
left: Erich von Falkenhayn

Diplomacy without a Touch of Tact

Wilhelm II proved to have little skill in foreign policy. Germany became increasingly isolated in Europe through imprudent diplomacy.

Wilhelm II began the foreign affairs segment of his New Course by abandoning Bismarck's policy of the European balance of power. Germany would now aim for an imperialistic world policy. His new chancellor, Caprivi, refused Russia a renewal of the Reinsurance Treaty of 1890. France saw its chance and allied itself with Russia in 1894, which made a two-front war against Germany possible.

5 Cartoon depicting the first Morocco crisis, 1905/06

In spite of the theory of the inevitability of Anglo-German rivalry, Wilhelm sought close contact with Great Britain, recognizing the British protectorate over Zanzibar in exchange for Heligoland, but then antagonized the British in 1896 with his ❽ Kruger telegram—a message congratulating the president of the South African republic of Transvaal, Paul Kruger, on a victory of the Boers over the British. Furthermore, Wilhelm wanted to build up a ❾ German fleet with the help of Admiral von Tirpitz and consequently started an arms race with Great Britain in the mid-1890s that brought Germany to the limit of its financial resources. When Germany approached the Ottoman Empire in 1898 and started constructing the ❻ Berlin-to-Baghdad railroad in the Near East, the British considered it an intrusion into their sphere of influence and so allied first with France in 1904 and then also with Russia in 1907, thus creating the Triple Entente, which left Germany isolated except for Austria-Hungary.

In colonial affairs, the German Empire wanted its "place in the sun," as Foreign Minister von Bülow expressed it in 1897. Germany became politically involved in Africa, China (p. 417), and the Pacific. Rebellions, such as those of the ❼ Herreros and Hottentots (Khoikhoi) in German Southwest Africa, were brutally suppressed. The conflict with France in ❺ the Morocco Crises of 1905 and 1911 soon left Germany alone in Europe, without an alliance partner other than the Austrian-Hungarian Empire, and militarily encircled. Germany decided to expand her military and naval might despite British efforts at a rapprochement. When the Austrian heir to the throne was shot in Sarajevo in 1914, World War I was unavoidable.

The "Hun Speech"

In his infamous "Hun Speech" of July 27, 1900, Kaiser Wilhelm II sent off the troops leaving for China to put down the anti-foreigner Boxer Rebellion with the words: "Pardon will not be given. Prisoners will not be taken. Whoever falls into your hands is forfeit. Once, a thousand years ago, the Huns under their King Attila made a name for themselves... May you in this way make the name German remembered in China for a thousand years so that no Chinaman will ever again dare to even squint at a German!"

above: Kaiser Wilhelm II bids an expeditionary corps in Bremerhaven farewell as they leave to put down the Boxer rebellion, June, 27 1900

6 Berlin-to-Baghdad railway, built 1903–1940

7

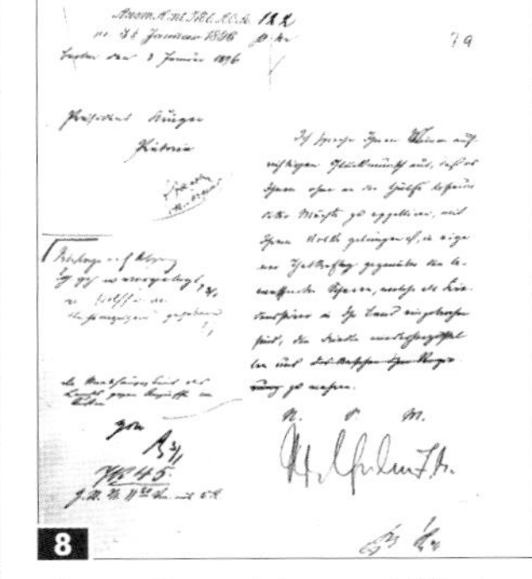
8

above: Kruger telegram; Wilhelm congratulates the president of the Boers, Paul Kruger, on his victory over the British
left: Herrero uprising in German South West Africa, 1904/05

9 "S.M.S Kaiserin Augusta," second-class protected cruiser

1898	Beginning of the navy development program
1903	Construction of the Berlin-Baghdad railroad
1905	First Morocco crisis
1911	Second Morocco crisis
1912–13	Balkan Wars
1913	The Zabern affair
28 Jun 1914	Franz Ferdinand murdered

Karl Lueger, the anti-Semitic mayor of Vienna, at a ball

AUSTRIA-HUNGARY 1867–1914

Austria, politically weakened both domestically and abroad, was forced to relinquish its leading role in Germany after its defeat by Prussia in 1866. Conservative forces sought to retain the old Habsburg glory, but the progressive industrialization had its consequences. Growing nationalism within the individual ethnic groups in the multiethnic state, especially that of the Hungarians and Slavs, consistently wrested new concessions out of Vienna, and in the process fostered Austrian xenophobia and ❶ anti-Semitism. In the midst of this powder keg—which would explode into World War I in 1914—one of the most important cultural currents of the 19th and 20th centuries developed in the form of Viennese modernism.

The Institution of the Dual Monarchy

Austria and Hungary formed a personal union in 1867. In the period of liberalization that followed, nationalist and anti-Semitic currents also became apparent.

The Hungarian parliament, which had existed briefly during the 1848 revolution (p. 372), was reinstituted in 1867, and a Hungarian Ministry was created. The Austrian imperial chancellor, ❷ Count von Beust, was forced to make concessions to the Hungarian representatives, Ferenc Deak and ❹ Count Gyula Andrassy. The union between Austria and Hungary was now merely pragmatic; they were united only by a common monarch—the Austrian emperor, who was also crowned ❺ king of Hungary—a combined army, and the ministries of foreign affairs, war, and finance.

Friedrich Ferdinand Count von Beust, wood engraving

On December 21, 1867, ❸ Kaiser Francis Joseph I proclaimed the December Constitution which remained in power until 1918 and regulated the representation in the parliaments of the two countries. These bodies, together with the monarch, now made the policies of the country. In 1868 Prince Karl Auersperg became Head of the Government. He introduced liberal figures into his Cabinet. A ten-year liberalization began, during which progressive laws were implemented. In 1868 the influence of the Catholic Church on education and family policies ended. In the succeeding year, general compulsory military service and free compulsory education were implemented.

Count Gyula Andrassy, ca.1865

Count von Taaffe, as prime minister of Austria, dealt strongly with the Christian conservatives and laid the cornerstone for the Austrian social state. However, in order to obtain majorities, he had to seek support primarily from the Slavic members of the imperial council and make allowances, particularly those of the Czechs. Czech became the official language in Bohemia in 1880 and, in 1882, the language of instruction at the University of Prague. Through his "pro-Slavic" multinational policies, Taaffe nurtured the antipathy of nationalist and anti-Semitic conservatives, such as the mayor of Vienna, Karl Lueger.

Kaiser Francis Joseph I, painting, 1895

Coronation of Francis Joseph I as king of Hungary in Budapest, June 8, 1867, wood engraving, 1889

1866 | German War
1867 | Personal union of Hungary and Austria
21 Dec 1867 | December Constitution
1875–90 | Magyarization in Hungary
1879 | Dual Alliance

The Alliance Policies of the Danube Monarchy

The multinational policies of the multiethnic state failed. Meanwhile, the Danube monarchy sought to ally itself with Germany against Russia.

The imperial and royal monarchy of Austria-Hungary did not succeed in integrating the many ethnic groups under its rule. This phenomenon, paradoxically, led to a certain stability, given that no significant union was possible between so many competing nationalities. Meanwhile the civil servants remained loyal to their Habsburg paymasters.

Germans and Hungarians were favored with regard to voting rights and participation in the political process. As a result, the dual monarchy controlled its minorities with police force. The Hungarian government's Magyarization of the southern Slavic efforts at liberation from the 1870s contributed to the tension in the Balkans, which helped to precipitate World War I. These efforts led in 1914 to the assassination of the heir to the Austro-Hungarian throne the Archduke Francis Ferdinand—nephew of the Emperor and hated by Serbs because of his strong opposition to separatist movements—by a Serbian nationalist.

In foreign affairs the Danube monarchy was forming alliances. In 1872 it formed the Three Emperors' League with Germany and Russia. In the context of the steady decline of Ottoman power in that region and given Austrian suspicions of Russian expansionism—and support of Slavic nationalists—in the Balkans, it entered the ❻ Dual Alliance with Bismarck's Germany. In addition, Austro-Hungary guaranteed to come to Germany's aid if the latter were faced by a combined Russian and French attack. In 1882, the alliance was expanded into the Triple Alliance with the addition of Italy. Increasingly, the other European powers felt threatened by this concentration of power. Consequently, in 1907, Great Britain, Russia, and France formed the Triple Entente. This divided Europe into the two military blocs between which a world war would break out seven years later.

Signing of the Dual Alliance on 17 Oct 1879: Kaiser William I and Kaiser Francis Joseph with Bismarck and Andrassy, their ministers of foreign affairs

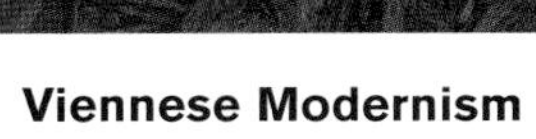

Members of the "Viennese Secession" **right:** Egon Schiele, self-portrait, 1912

Exhibition hall used by the "Vienna Secession" movement, built in 1897-98 by Joseph M. Olbrich

Viennese Modernism

During the two decades around the turn of the 20th century, "Young Vienna," a literary current of Jugendstil (Viennese Art Nouveau), formed around Arthur Schnitzler and Hugo von Hofmannsthal, whose play, "Everyman," captured Vienna's zeitgeist of morbid superficiality and profound decadence. Other period authors still famous today are Karl Kraus, Robert Musil, and Hermann Broch. In painting, which distanced itself from the Belle Époque's passion for grandeur, Egon Schiele and particularly Gustav Klimt, a founding member of the "Viennese Secession" movement, made names for themselves. The Late Romantic Gustav Mahler and the twelve-tone serialists Arnold Schoenberg and Alban Berg stood out as composers, Adolf Loos and Otto Wagner as architects. Schnitzler's friend Sigmund Freud developed psychoanalysis, which strongly influenced Viennese Modernism.

Gustav Mahler, painting, ca. 1905

Sigmund Freud, father of psychoanalysis, 1909

1880 | Czech official language Bohemia
1882 | Founding of Czech University of Prague
1882 | Triple Alliance
from 1883 | Czech majority in provincial parliament
1907 | Triple Entente

France 1814–1914

After Napoleon I, France returned to the circle of European great powers. The Bourbons tried to restore their prerevolutionary monarchy, but political suppression and social injustice led to several ❶ revolts which increasingly gained momentum and strength. The Second Republic, which resulted from the revolution of 1848, was once again transformed into an empire through a coup d'état by President Louis-Napoleon. With time, however, the social desire for liberal policies grew again, and the conservatives found themselves under increasing pressure. The empire ended with its defeat by Germany in 1870–1871, and the Third Republic finally vanquished "Bonapartism" in the struggle between republican and conservative ideas.

Liberty Leading the People, allegory of the July Revolution depicting liberty as Marianne, icon of the French Republic, painting by Eugène Delacroix, 1830

The Reign of the Bourbons and the Revolution of 1830

France became a constitutional monarchy under the Bourbons, whose restoration policies resulted in the July Revolution of 1830.

On June 4, 1814—almost exactly a year before Napoleon's final defeat at the Battle of Waterloo and exile on Elba—France received the *Charte constitutionelle,* a new charter for a constitutional monarchy. It included some democratic elements such as the *Code Civil* and a two-chamber parliamentary system with a Chamber of Notables chosen by the king and an elected Chamber of Deputies. The Bourbon ❷ Louis XVIII headed a restoration regime that favored the aristocracy and property-owning bourgeoisie. This policy was continued after the intermezzo of Napoleon's Hundred Days (p. 367) in 1815. In 1818 the Congress of Aachen, a follow-up conference to the Congress of Vienna, resolved to recognize France once again as a European major power. Louis's brother Charles was a leading member of the ultraroyalists, who gained great influence in domestic politics

after 1820. They succeeded in pushing through restrictions on the right to vote, reestablished press censorship, and restored to the Church its properties. When Louis died in 1824, ❸ Charles X ascended the throne and continued his reactionary policies by, for example, compensating the aristocracy that had emigrated during the French Revolution. The liberal middle-class opposition under the leadership of ❻ Adolphe Thiers won a majority in the lower chamber in 1830, whereupon Charles dissolved it. The next day, the ❹ July Revolution began, which resulted in the ❺ abdication of Charles X and his emigration to England. King Louis-Philippe took the throne.

King Louis XVIII

Charles X, King of France

July Revolution: Street fighting in the Rue de Rohan on July 29, 1830

King Charles X emigrates to Great Britain following his abdication in 1830

Adolphe Thiers, president of the Third Republic from 1871–73, ca. 1860

4 Jun 1814 | *Charte constitutionelle*
1818 | Congress of Aachen
from 1824 | Monarchy of Charles X
1830 | July Revolution
1830 | Charles X abdicates
1830–48 | "Citizen King" Louis

The Revolution of 1848 and Louis-Napoleon's Coup d'État

Social problems during the reign of Louis-Philippe culminated in the February Revolution of 1848 and a new constitution which introduced a conservative presidential system that was soon replaced by a second empire.

The workers and the middle class, who had until then been underrepresented due to the census suffrage (voting only by owners of substantial property), wanted a republic. But the upper-middle-class deputies who dominated the second chamber decided to continue with the constitutional monarchy under the ❽ "Citizen King," Louis-Philippe of Orléans. In the following years, France experienced rapid industrialization, which resulted in grave social problems. Thinkers and social philosophers such as Pierre-Joseph Proudhon and ❾ Charles Fourier, who were critical of society, expressed the demands of the lower classes for improvement in their living conditions.

The criticism of the conditions first erupted in weavers' rebellions in Lyon in 1831 and 1834. Crop failures and economic crises, as well as an unbroken desire for real democracy rather than a government which was seen as ever more corrupt than the last, eventually led in 1848 to the ⓬ February Revolution. The provisional government proclaimed the Second Republic, and Louis-Philippe and Prime Minister François Guizot took their leave. After the suppression of a workers' ❼ revolt in June of the same year 3by the newly elected moderate government, France enacted a constitution in November 1848. In December Louis-Napoleon, a nephew of Napoleon I, was elected president by the people.

Louis-Napoleon sought support from the lower middle class, rather than from the parliamentary majority, with the aim of restoring Bonapartism. When his government's four-year term reached its end in 1851, he dissolved the parliament and had his most important opponents ❿ arrested. In January 1852, a referendum decided on a new constitution that provided for a term of office of ten years. A few months later, Louis-Napoleon declared the end of the Second Republic, and on December 2, 1852, he ⓫ ascended the throne as Emperor Napoleon III.

7 Barricade battle during the workers' revolt in June 1848

8 The "Citizen King" Louis-Philippe swears upon the charter of Aug 7, 1830

9 Charles Fourier

10 *Coup d'état* by Louis-Napoleon on February 2, 1851, and the imprisonment of representatives of the opposition

11 From left to right: Napoleon III, his son Louis-Napoleon, Napoleon I Bonaparte, and his son Napoleon

"Enrichissez-vous!"

In response to the demand of the people to abolish census suffrage, François Guizot, the moderate liberal prime minister for Citizen King Louis Philippe, is said to have answered: "There will be no reform. Get rich, and then you can vote."

Pierre-Joseph Proudhon (1809-1865), a printer and later journalist, formulated his famous statement "Property is theft" in an 1840 pamphlet entitled What Is Property? As an anarchist, Proudhon rejected every form of state and dreamed of a society in which people lived and worked of their own accord, with no self-interest but rather in the interest of all. Proudhon was a member of the Constituent Assembly after 1848 and was arrested as an opponent of Louis-Napoleon in 1849. Following his release in 1852, he lived in exile in Belgium, but was able to return to France, where he hoped to be able to further the cause of social reform, after being pardoned in 1862.

Proudhon and his children, 1863, painting by Gustave Courbet

12 February Revolution of 1848: The Tricolor remains the national flag of the second Republic

1831	Weavers' Revolt in Lyon
1848	February Revolution
1848	June Revolt in Paris
Nov 1848	New constitution accepted
Dec 1848	Louis-Napoleon becomes president
2 Dec 1852	Monarchy of Napoleon III

The Second Empire

Napoleon III's reign began in an authoritarian vein which he had to abandon in favor of liberal developments.

In Napoleon III's empire, the parliament was of little significance; the Church and the army had greater influence in the running of the state. The lower middle class accepted the authoritarian state out of fear of socialist violence. The lower class was pacified by the creation of jobs in the wake of "Haussmannization"—the renovation and modernization of Paris. Baron Georges-Eugène Haussmann, prefect of the Seine *département* which included Paris, redesigned the city and laid out wide, corridor-like ❶ boulevards and parks such as the Bois de Boulogne. The 1889 ❹, ❺ public exhibitions held in

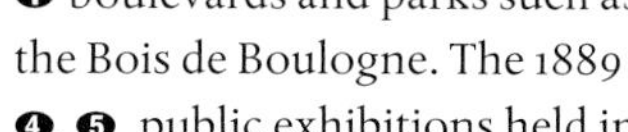

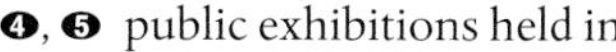

4 Eiffel Tower in Paris, inaugurated on the occasion of the 1889 world exhibition

2 Abdelkader

Paris demonstrated France's industrial progress.

France fought in the Crimean War from 1853 to 1856 against Russia on the side of the Ottoman Empire. Its participation in the Franco-Sardinian War against Austria in 1859—which France won primarily through its victory in the ❻ Battle of Solferino on June 24, 1859—was also profitable due to the capture of Nice and Savoy. After France annexed Algeria in 1834 and finally conquered it in 1847 in the struggle against ❷ Abdelkader, it was agriculturally exploited by the *Colons*, European settlers who were mostly French. France was also able to prevail in Indochina (p. 420), Syria, and Senegal. It was a different matter in Mexico, whose French-installed emperor was overthrown (p. 434) in 1867. The plan to absorb regions of Luxembourg and Belgium also failed.

Domestically, the liberal opposition was victorious in 1869. Napoleon III was forced to compromise with the democrats and relinquish a large part of his authoritarian regime in the *Empire libéral*. The Franco-Prussian War of 1870–1871, provoked by Prussia, resulted in the ❸ Battle of Sedan on September 1, 1870, and the downfall of the Second Empire. The emperor was taken prisoner, and, in the course of the negotiations, France had to cede Alsace and Lorraine to Germany.

3 The French defeat at Sedan, September 1, 1870

1 *Boulevard des Italiens* in Paris

Charles Baudelaire

The poet Charles-Pierre Baudelaire (1821–1867) was arguably the most important French lyricist of the Modern Era. He became famous through his major work, a collection of poems entitled Les Fleurs du Mal ("The Flowers of Evil") which was published in 1857 and triggered a scandal in bourgeois French society. After a trial for offending the public morals, he had to withdraw six of his poems. The most important themes of his "aesthetic of the ugly" were, in contrast to Romantic literature, death and eroticism. He particularly influenced English writers such as Edgar Allan Poe. He lived in Belgium for a number of years, but died of syphilis in Paris, the city of his birth, on August 31, 1867.

above: Charles Baudelaire, self-portrait from 1860

5 The Aquarium in the 1867 world exhibition in Paris

6 Emperor Napoleon III during the Battle of Solferino

1834 | Annexation of Algeria
1847 | Conquest of Algeria
1853–56 | Crimean War
1859 | Franco-Sardinian War
26 Jun 1859 | Battle of Solferino
1869 | *Empire libéral*
1870–71 | Franco-Prussian War

The Third Republic

The Second Empire was followed by the Third Republic, which was confronted by domestic political scandals. Internationally, France was able to reintegrate itself step-by-step into the community of European states.

Shortly after the capitulation of the French army under the Comte de ❼ Mac-Mahon at Sedan in the Franco-Prussian War, the Third Republic was proclaimed in Paris. In 1871, the National Assembly chose Adolphe Thiers as head of the new government.

The communists and socialists, who had joined together to run the ❾, ❿ Commune of Paris, set up a form of socialist republic that was crushed by Mac-Mahon's troops in the "Bloody Week" in May. Mac-Mahon was elected president or "placeholder for the monarchy" by the conservative majority, but he stepped down in 1879 because of the growing strength of the republicans.

The moderate republican majority under State President Jules Grévy existed until 1887 but then began to crumble due to crises and scandals. The economic crisis of 1882 had worsened the mood of the people and provided a boost for the conservatives. ❽ Georges Boulanger sought revenge against Germany following the loss of Alsace-Lorraine in the Treaty of Versailles in 1871 and united conservatives, radicals, and monarchists in an authoritarian-nationalistic movement called "Party of the Dissatisfied" that seriously threatened the Republic. The republicans' victory in the 1889 election prevented a dictatorship of the Boulangers. The Republic was shaken in the 1890s by the Panama scandal and the Dreyfus Affair, which caused political polarization. The majority coalition of republicans and left-wing radicals that existed from 1898, together with the socialists Aristide Briand and Prime Minister Georges Clemenceau, instituted the separation of church and state as well as enacting social welfare measures in 1905.

In foreign affairs, France pursued an alliance policy to preserve its colonial interests and protect itself against a possible war with Germany. In 1902, it received Italy's assurance of neutrality in case of a German attack. The alliance between France and Russia in 1894 was expanded to include Great Britain and became the Triple Entente in 1907. The anti-German mood of the French citizens, exacerbated by the Morocco Crisis, was personified from 1913 by the President ⓫ Raymond Poincaré, who aimed to regain territories lost to Prussia.

7 Marshall Comte Maurice Mac-Mahon, second president of the Third Republic

8 Georges Boulanger, leader of the opposition nationalists' party

9 The commune of Paris builds barricades at the Place de la Concorde

10 The ruins of the town hall that was set on fire by communards in Paris on May 24, 1871

The Dreyfus Affair

Captain Alfred Dreyfus, a Jew, was wrongly accused of spying for the Germans and thus arrested and tried for treason. A military court sentenced him in 1890 to life imprisonment on Devil's Island and expelled him from the army. The Dreyfus Affair split the nation. While, for example, Émile Zola obtained a reopening of the trial with his open letter "J'accuse," anti-Semites, nationalists, and antiparliamentarianists gathered together in the opposition camp. In 1898, the principal piece of evidence, a document, was shown to be a forgery, and Dreyfus was cleared in 1906. The affair was a struggle between restorative and republican ideas, and the Republic emerged from it strengthened as liberal ideals triumphed.

Cover page of the *Le Petit Journal* of January 13, 1895: Degradation of Alfred Dreyfus

Le Petit Journal

Le nouveau Président de la République
M. RAYMOND POINCARÉ

11 President Raymond Poincaré on the cover of *Le Petit Journal* of January 26, 1913, shortly after coming to power

Mar–May 1871 | Commune of Paris revolt
1890–1906 | Dreyfus Affair
1905 | Separation of church and state

1871 | Adolphe Thiers becomes head of government
1875 | Proclamation of the Third Republic
1892–93 | Panama scandal
1907 | Triple Entente

Great Britain 1830–1914

England's economic development was almost half a century ahead of the Continent's due to its early industrialization, but the working conditions were devastating and led to impoverishment of the workers. This made worker protection laws necessary, along with the gradual extension of suffrage to ever-widening sections of the population, to alleviate the social tensions. Under ❶ Queen Victoria, whose reign began in 1837, the economy flourished at first, but social problems remained and the worker movement demanded further reforms. The British colonial empire was gradually restructured in the 19th century to become the Commonwealth of Nations.

Queen Victoria I of Great Britain and Ireland and Empress of India, portrait commemorating 50 years on the throne in 1887

Political Reforms of the Constitutional Monarchy

The 1830s and 1840s saw a series of successful reforms in Great Britain.

After the death of ❸ George IV (p. 287), William IV, a king eager for reform, took the throne. Suffrage was modernized in the Reform Act of June 1832, and at the same time an increase in Parliament's power was passed; because the ❷ population in the cities had rapidly grown due to migration from the countryside, the division of the seats in Parliament no longer corresponded to the number of voters, and therefore the voting districts were reallocated in favor of the cities. The Municipal Corporations Act of 1835 also provided for the election of city councils. The protest against the liberal suffrage reform of 1832 was the hour of birth of the Conservative and Unionist party of Great Britain, which endeavored to gain the increased number of voters. But the British Conservative party split in 1846 when Prime Minister Sir Robert Peel moved toward free trade.

Poor quarter in London ,ca. 1850

Cartoon about the reform laws concerning the emancipation of Catholics: "The Mountain in Labour –or much ado about nothing"

Reforms were also necessary in the relationship between the confessions. Compared to the members of the Anglican Church, Catholics were greatly restricted in their civil rights. It was not until April 1829 that—through the influence of, among others, ❺ Prime Minister Arthur Wellesley, the duke of Wellington—the ❹ Roman Catholic Relief Act was passed. Known as the "Catholic Emancipation," this law ended official discrimination against Catholics and allowed them to become members of Parliament.

George IV, King of Great Britain when he was still Prince of Wales, painting by Thomas Gainsborough, 1781

Prime Minister Arthur Wellesley, Duke of Wellington, painting by Francisco Goya, 1814

The Chartists

Though the suffrage reform of 1832 meant a strengthening of the middle class, the number of voters was still very small—about four percent of the population. Consequently, in 1837 a London workers association presented the House of Commons with a "People's Charter." The Chartists demanded universal male suffrage, with elections to represent the actual proportions of the population, secret ballots, and the payment of MPs so that poorer members could afford to stand for Parliament. Parliament rejected this, despite petitions with up to three million signatures and a general strike. The leaders of the Chartists were arrested during unrest in Wales in 1839.

Friedrich Engels speaks at an assembly of the chartists in 1843

1802 | Factory Act passed
1815 | Corn Laws
16 Aug 1819 | "Massacre of Peterloo"
1819 | Ban on children working in cotton mills
1824 | Introduction of right to strike
Apr 1829 | Roman Catholic Relief Act passed

The Social Reforms of "Manchester Capitalism"

Over time, various innovations and a series of laws implementing social reform improved the living conditions of the lower class in Britain.

6 Women work in a cork factory

On August 16, 1819, a demonstration of workers was suppressed in the "Peterloo Massacre" when the cavalry charged at a crowd that had gathered in the streets of Manchester. It was soon clear to conservatives that reforms were needed to maintain domestic peace. The first of the Factory Acts had already been passed in 1802, making night work for children punishable and limiting the workday for apprentices to twelve hours. The ⑩ employment of children under nine in mills was forbidden in 1819. In 1824 workers were granted the ⑦ right to strike and form coalitions.

As there was no state control, however, these laws were easy to circumvent. The first effective factory law was passed in 1833. It limited the number of hours a day ⑥ women and children could work; children under age 13 were allowed to work no more than nine hours a day. A supervisory department controlled the implementation of the law. Some of the improvements in working and living conditions are attributable to ⑪ Anthony Ashley Cooper, the seventh earl of Shaftesbury. He encouraged "social housing" and provided schools for the children of the poor. He also introduced a number of social laws, including the 1842 ban on women and children working in mines and, in 1847, the regulation of the ten-hour workday for women and youths ⑨ working in factories.

To maintain a high price for British grain, Parliament in 1815 passed a tariff against imports, known as the Corn Laws, but the resulting high price of bread elicited insurrections among the populace. George IV reacted by restricting civil rights, particularly the right to assemble and freedom of the press. Only after heavy pressure was applied by the Manchester School—a group of textile manufacturers led by ⑧ Richard Cobden who, because of their interest in free trade, had allied with the workers—were the Corn Laws repealed in 1846. The Anti–Corn Law League founded by Cobden and John Bright in 1838 demanded general public education and suffrage reform.

Robert Owen

In 1799, at the age of 28, Robert Owen became co-owner of a cotton mill in New Lanark, Scotland. The early socialist did not allow child labor, limited the workday to ten and a half hours, and so became a supporter of early labor protection laws. His workers lived in a housing estate built for them, their children attended school, and they could buy food inexpensively at shops he subsidized. Despite these additional costs, his factories were economically successful. The Cooperative Movement, founded in 1844 in Rochdale, England, took up his ideas, which are still accepted today.

School in New Lanark, founded by Robert Owen

7 Impoverished worker with his family during the dockworkers strike of 1889 in London

8 Richard Cobden

9 Pump station at a canal in Birmingham, with Watt's easy working pumping machine

10 Child labor in an English coal mine following the industrial revolution, painting, 19th century

11 Anthony Ashley Cooper, seventh Earl of Shaftesbury, painting, ca. 1870

1832 | Reform Bill
1835 | Municipal Corporations Act
1837 | "People's Charter"
1838 | Founding of the Anti-Corn-Law League
1844 | Cooperative Movement launched
1846 | Conservative Party splits

Economic Growth and the Welfare State in the Victorian Age

The economic boom in the first years of Victoria's reign slowed, and social issues once again became a focus of politics.

1 Crystal Palace in London Hyde Park, built for the World Exposition in 1851

2 Queue of people waiting outside a shelter for the poor and homeless

Following a turbulent reform era, Great Britain experienced calmer decades. The Great Exhibition in 1851, featuring the famous ❶ Crystal Palace, was a symbol of the flourishing economy. Because the reform of the 1830s had established parliamentary structures, the Europe-wide revolutions of 1848 left Britain unaffected.

The boom was followed by a crisis, which exacerbated the social problems. The unions, which had organized in 1868 as the Trade Union Congress, saw an increase in membership. The strike by London dockworkers in 1889 was a sign of the unions' growing self-confidence. Many ❷ destitute workers ❸ emigrated to America or Australia.

3 Emigrants climb aboard an overcrowded ship

The Irish Fight for Independence

An enormous increase in population in Ireland, along with the potato blight of 1845, resulted in a terrible famine that lasted until 1849. Prime Minister Lord John Russell largely denied state aid to alleviate the crises and instead sent soldiers to counter outbreaks of unrest. More than a million Irish died of hunger and epidemics, and about twice as many emigrated. The nationalists demanded political independence for Ireland, and secret societies such as the Fenians murdered British government representatives. It wasn't until 1921 that Ireland—with the exception of the North—became independent.

above: Starving rural population outside a poorhouse during the great famine in Ireland that lasted from 1845–1849

The Labour Representation Committee, founded in 1900 and renamed the Labour party in 1906, gained influence. Liberals David Lloyd George and ❹ Winston Churchill fought for the welfare of the people. Within a few years, pensions, unemployment insurance, and national health insurance had been introduced and a minimum wage agreed upon for certain groups.

William Gladstone's amendment to the reform bill of 1867 had secured suffrage for urban workers, and in 1884 farm hands were also given the vote. The House of Lords' power to veto legislation was curtailed in 1911. ❺ Suffragettes campaigned for women's right to vote.

4 Winston Churchill in the Camberwell Labour Exchange, an employment agency, ca. 1910

Queen Victoria I

Queen Victoria of England and Empress of India took the throne on June 20, 1837, and shaped a whole era of Great Britain's history during her 64-year reign. The Victorian Age was characterized by economic prosperity and the British Empire's position of leadership in the world. The Victorians also stood for a conservative lifestyle and prudery. Queen Victoria's husband, Prince Albert of Saxe-Coburg-Gotha, introduced conservative opinions to the originally more liberally inclined queen. She is the longest ruling monarch in British history.

above: Queen Victoria I celebrating her Golden Jubilee

5 Cover page of the magazine *The Suffragette* edited by Christabel Pankhurst, May 23, 1913

20 Jun 1837 | Coronation of Victoria I
1839 | Durham Report
1842 | Opium War
1845–49 | Famine in Ireland
1851 | World Exhibition in London
1858 | Sepoy Rebellion
1868 | Trade Union Congress

Colonial Policies and the Path to World War I

Great Britain expanded its vast colonial empire, but increasingly came into conflict with the German Empire, which wanted its own "place in the sun."

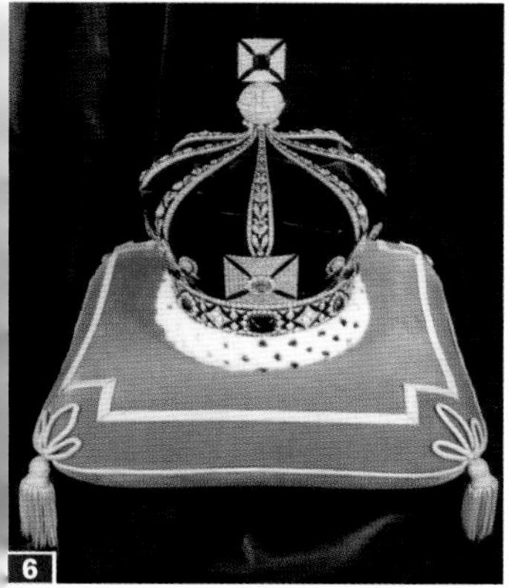

6 Crown of the Indian emperor, made for the crowning of George V as emperor of India, 1911

The long reign of Queen Victoria (1837-1902) was marked by imperial claims that continued the steady expansion of the colonial empire. When the East India Company was dissolved in 1858 in the wake of the Sepoy Rebellion (p. 414), the ❻ British crown took over the government of India, which was put under the rule of a British viceroy, and Victoria assumed the title of "Empress of India" in 1876. The colonies at ⓫ Hong Kong—which England had secured on a 99-year lease through the Treaty of Nanjing that ended the 1842 Opium War—and Singapore ensured Asian expansion possibilities into China and the Pacific, but also brought Great Britain into conflict with Russia.

10 Soldiers of the Indian auxiliary troops and British soldiers in the First World War

In the "scramble for Africa," Great Britain got into disputes with France and Germany over the last colonizable regions of the world. Egypt was occupied by Britain in 1882 primarily because of the Suez Canal (p. 410). In the 1890s, Britain almost came to war with France over control of Sudan, later ruled as an Anglo-Egyptian condominium in "the ❼ Fashoda Incident." Both powers then allied themselves against the ❾ German Empire in 1904 in the Entente Cordiale, which Russia also joined in 1907.

8 Advancing Indian auxiliary troops of the British army during the fights south west of Ypres in May 1915, design for a lamp shade

Early on, the colonies with large populations of European immigrants demanded self-rule. The transformation of the empire into the Commonwealth of Nations of the 20th century began with the Durham Report of 1839, which introduced the union and self-government of the ⓬ Canadian provinces. The colonies thus remained in the trusteeship of the motherland until they were released into political independence. The settlement territories joined together into large federations and adopted constitutions after the British model. Canada, Australia, New Zealand, and parts of southern Africa were defined as "dominions"—governmental regions within the British Empire that were technically autonomous—at the colonial conference of 1887. With their ❽, ❿ entrance into World War I on the side of the motherland, the standing of the colonies and dominions changed, and they were recognized as autonomous nations of an imperial commonwealth in 1917.

A number of additions to the British Commonwealth were made after the end of the First World War, when some former German and Ottoman colonies became British protectorates and mandates.

7 The Egyptian flag is flown in Fashoda, Sudan, after the retreat of the French forces in 1898

9 Caricature "The future on the water– he dares to venture onto the seas in search of power"

11 Harbor of Hong Kong, 1847

12 St. Lawrence River, Quebec, Canada, painting, ca. 1850

1882 | Egypt becomes a British protectorate
1887 | Colonial conference
1889 | London dockworkers strike
1898 | Fashoda crisis
1900 | Founding of the Labour Party
1904 | "Entente cordiale" signed
1921 | Ireland gains independence

1 William II, King of the Netherlands

The Benelux Countries 1815–1914

Austria was forced to cede its territories in the southern Netherlands (p. 291) to France under the terms of the 1797 Treaty of Campo Formio. At the Congress of Vienna this area was joined with the united Netherlands, which were supposed to act as a buffer zone to France. However confessional, political, and cultural differences led to the separation of Belgium in 1830. At this point in time the industrialization process in the Netherlands and in Belgium began. The Belgian economy benefitted from colonial territories in Africa. The Dutch kings also ruled over Luxembourg as Grand Dukes. Differences in the laws of succession led to Luxembourg's separation from the Netherlands in 1890.

The Netherlands and Luxembourg

Democratic structures were gradually implemented in the Netherlands, which was ruled by the Orange-Nassau dynasty. Luxembourg became independent in the 1890s.

The Congress of Vienna in 1815 created the United Kingdom of the Netherlands, including present-day Belgium, the former Austrian Netherlands. During the course of the Revolution of 1845, King ❶ William II, son of the conservative William I, was forced to agree to a constitutional monarchy. After his death the following year, his son ❻ William III took the throne. During his reign, the parliament was able to significantly expand its authority. In the 1880s, the Netherlands experienced an economic boom that also promoted the development of the ❷, ❹ workers movement, out of which the Social Democratic Workers party emerged in 1894.

3 Napoleon III, French Emperor, painting by F.X. Winterhalter, 1857

Luxembourg had been granted the status of a grand duchy at the Congress of Vienna but was governed over until 1867 by the Netherlands. It was thus able to profit from the Netherlands' new liberal constitution in 1848. In 1898 ❺ Queen Wilhelmina ascended the throne. Luxembourg law did not allow for a female monarch, however, and the country was therefore released from its union with the Netherlands.

When ❸ Napoleon III purchased the country in 1867, this created a crisis, as Prussia did not approve. The London Conference of May 11, 1867, ended the Luxembourg crisis by assuring its independence and neutrality. This agreement was disregarded by the Germans at the beginning of World War I when they occupied the country.

2 *Worker at the loom*, one of many paintings by Vincent van Gogh of weavers working at machines, 1884

4 Congress of the socialist Second Internationale in Amsterdam, August 14-20, 1904

5 Festivities celebrating Wilhelmina's majority on August 31, 1890

William I of the Netherlands

William I, steel engraving, 19th c.

William I of Orange-Nassau, the dynasty that governed the Netherlands, fought against the French revolutionary army between 1793 and 1795 and later lived in exile in England. He was crowned king of the Netherlands and grand duke of Luxembourg on March 16, 1815. His insensitive policies toward the Belgians resulted in that country declaring its independence in 1830. In the Netherlands, he refused any restrictions of his authority by the parliament and therefore had to abdicate in favor of his son, William II.

6 William III, King of the Netherlands and Grand Duke of Luxembourg, ca. 1865

1797 | Treaty of Campo Formio

16 Mar 1815 | William I crowned king of the Netherlands

25 Aug 1830 | Revolt in Brussels

26 Sep 1830 | "September Revolution" in Belgium

4 Oct 1830 | Belgium declares independence

Belgium's Political and Economic Progress

Belgium had a liberal state system as early as 1830, was the most industrialized country in Europe after Great Britain, and also endeavored to gain colonies in Africa.

In 1815, the Congress of Vienna merged the Catholic region of the Austrian Netherlands with the Republic of United Netherlands situated north of it, which was reigned over by the Protestant House of Orange-Nassau. Dutch became the official language, which wounded the national pride of the French-speaking population. This and other discriminatory policies, as well as political and economic restrictions, led to a rebellion in Brussels on August 25, 1830, in the wake of the Parisian July Revolution. Dutch soldiers were then chased out of Brussels during the September Revolution ❽ on September 26, and on October 4, 1830, the provisional Belgian government proclaimed the country's independence. Belgium adopted a liberal constitution on February 7, 1831, and installed a constitutional monarchy. The anglophile Leopold I of Saxe-Coburg-Saalfeld was crowned ❾ king on June 4, 1831. In 1839, Luxembourg ceded the western Walloon region to the newly independent Belgium. The Netherlands, however, did not recognize Belgium's independence until the London Protocol of April 19, 1839, but then the country's borders were fixed and its neutrality guaranteed by the Great Powers.

8 Revolution of the Belgians against the Dutch rule under William I in 1830, wood engraving, 1864

❼ Belgium led the Continent economically in the first half of the 19th century. Domestically, the conflict between Catholic and liberal thought over the educational policies of 1879 were resolved with a liberal school law. Differences between the French-speaking Walloons in the south and the Flemish speakers in the north were not only linguistic and cultural but also represented a difference in wealth as industrialization had been more advanced in the south.

7 The "castle in the-air," world exhibition in Antwerp, Belgium, 1894

Universal male suffrage was first implemented in 1893 as a result of a ❿ general strike initiated by the Social Democrats.

Belgian Colonial Politics

King Leopold II sponsored the exploration of central Africa by, among others, Sir Henry Morton Stanley. The result of his expedition was the founding of the Congo Free State (later Zaire). The king was its personal sovereign with a neutral status at the Berlin Congo conference of 1885. When the inhuman methods he used to exploit the country and the unrest that resulted from them became known, he was forced to cede Congo to Belgian governmental control in 1908. His successor, Albert I, who was crowned the following year, restructured the organization of the colony.

above: The ivory stock of Congo documents the exploitation of Africa's natural resources, wood engraving, 1890
top: Sir Henry Morton Stanley and some of his African companions, wood engraving, 1890

9 Coronation ceremony of King Leopold I on 4 June 1831 at the Palace Royale in Brussels, painting from 1856

10 The military puts down the strike by the miners of Mons, 1893

7 Feb 1831 | Liberal constitution in Belgium

11 May 1867 | London Conference

1885 | Berlin Congo conference

1890 | Luxembourg gains independence

1890 | Wilhelmina becomes Queen of the Netherlands

1 Garibaldi monument, Rome, built in 1895

Italy from the Congress of Vienna to the Eve of World War I 1815–1914

After the reestablishment of the Italian kingdoms and states at the Congress of Vienna, restorative and conservative policies could not prevent the emergence of a national unification movement and the creation of the Kingdom of Italy. However, political unification did not lead to a social or economic unification. The poor agricultural south had little in common with the industrialized north, and the latter dominated the politics of the new state. The government of Prime Minister Crispi, who wanted to give Italy more weight internationally, was replaced by the era of Giolitti, under whom social reforms were made and the economy blossomed.

The Call for Freedom and the Violent Unification Movement

The restoration of the prewar kingdoms and states in Italy stood in opposition to the national unification movement.

During the Congress of Vienna, Italy was largely restored to its pre-Napoleonic condition: Naples and Sicily were reunified as the ❸ Kingdom of the Two Sicilies, the Kingdom of Sardinia was reunited with Piedmont and Savoy, and Lombardy and the Veneto became part of the Austrian Empire. In addition to the regional realignment, the *Code Civil* and the political reforms from the Napoleonic era were also revised. The absolutist policies of the Italian kingdoms caused outrage, particularly among the liberal middle classes, who demanded political representation and the national independence of Italy.

The activities of secret societies such as the ❺ Carbonari and Giovane Italia were an expression of the national unification movement known as the *Risorgimento* ("resurgence"). King Charles Albert of Sardinia-Piedmont was unsuccessful in his attempt to conquer the Italian regions of Austria in 1848–1849 and had to abdicate in favor of his son ❹ Victor Emmanuel II. In 1849, Pope Pius IX was briefly expelled from the Papal States, and a ❻ republican commune was declared in Rome by Giuseppe Mazzini and ❶, ❷ Giuseppe Garibaldi. They were hopelessly outgunned when Louis-Napoleon's French troops intervened to restore the pope, and the commune fell in July.

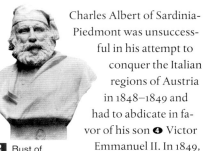

2 Bust of Giuseppe Garibaldi, ca. 1870

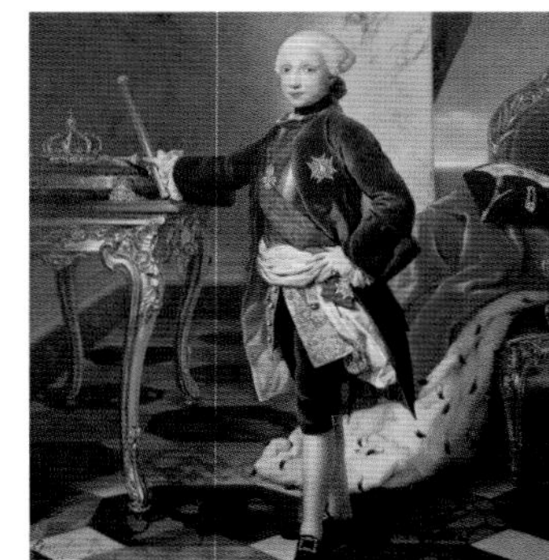
3 Ferdinand IV, King of the Two Sicilies, painting by A. R. Mengs, 1760

4 Victor Emmanuel II, King of Italy

Giuseppe Mazzini

Giuseppe Mazzini

Giuseppe Mazzini (1805–1872), who initially belonged to the Carbonari, founded the Giovane Italia ("Young Italy") secret society while in exile in 1831. He was sentenced to death in absentia for encouraging the Sardinian-Piedmontese army to mutiny. All rebellions that he instigated failed: in Piedmont in 1833, in Bologna in 1843, in Calabria in 1844, and in Rimini in 1845. Further uprisings in Mantua and Milan were equally unsuccessful. Mazzini, whose aim was the unity of Italy as a democratic republic, refused the crown after Italy unified as a monarchy. He died in Pisa in 1872.

5 Secret meeting of the Carbonari, wood engraving, 19th century

6 Crowd in front of the church of St. Maria Maggiore as the Roman republic is proclaimed, February 9, 1849, wood engraving, 19th century

Feb 1849 | Proclamation of the Roman republic
24 Jun 1859 | Battle of Solferino
May 1860 | "Expedition of the Thousand" under Garibaldi
1870 | Rome occupied by Italian troops
1871 | Rome becomes official capital of Italy
1878 | "Italia Irredenta" founded

The Path to Unity and International Dreams

Cavour and Garibaldi successfully fought for the unity of Italy. Internal reforms were accompanied by the attempt to turn Italy into a major European power.

After the Revolution of 1848, Sardinia-Piedmont retained its parliamentary constitution. The count of Cavour, ⑩ Camillo Benso, who became prime minister of the kingdom in 1852, decided on reforms and sought an alliance partner for the unification of Italy. With French assistance, Cavour triumphed over Austria in the ⑨ Battle of Solferino on June 24, 1859, which brought him Lombardy. In 1860, Emilia-Romagna, Tuscany, Modena, and Parma-Piacenza all voted to join Sardinia-Piedmont. In May 1860, Garibaldi's ⑧ "Expedition of the Thousand" conquered the Kingdom of the Two Sicilies. When the Marches and Umbria acceded, almost all of Italy was united in a single state.

7 King Umberto I and crown prince Victor Emmanuel of Italy, the future King Victor Emmanuel II

10 Camillo Benso di Cavour, ca. 1855

The Kingdom of Italy was proclaimed, with ⑪ Victor Emmanuel II as king, and the first parliamentary elections were held in 1861. Italy acquired the Veneto in a war against Austria in 1866 but decided to forego Trentino and Istria. After the occupation of the Papal States in 1870, the pope ruled over only the Vatican and Rome, which finally joined Italy as its capital in 1871. The liberals, under Prime Minister Agostino Depretis, provided for social improvements and expanded the electorate, though only to seven percent of the population. Founded in 1892, the Partito Socialista Italiano became the main socialist party in Italy.

11 Monument to Victor Emmanuel II in Rome, built between 1885 and1911

During the reign of ⑦ King Umberto I after 1878, the organization "Italia Irredenta," dedicated to the incorporation of "unsaved Italian areas," was founded. Trentino and Istria stood at the center of these efforts and shaped the alliance policies of the new state until World War I. As Prime Minister, Francesco Crispi strove for a stronger and more credible Italy and also sought to acquire new colonies with the support of its two partners, Austria-Hungary and the German Empire, in the 1882 Triple Alliance. Its humiliating defeat in a war against Abyssinia in 1896, however, dashed Italian hopes of acquiring an East African empire.

After Umberto was assassinated in 1900, Victor Emmanuel III came to the throne. The left-wing prime minister Giovanni Giolitti pushed through numerous reforms in the years that followed: The right to strike and social security were introduced, and electoral suffrage was extended to almost all adult males. Internationally, Giolitti ensured continuity. In 1911, Italian forces occupied the city of Tripoli, and in a war against the Ottoman Empire, Italy seized control of the Dodecanese and the rest of Libya. At the outset of World War I Italy remained neutral but on 26 April 1915, Italy signed the "secret treaty of London" with the Entente powers. The treaty offered Italy Trieste, the South Tirol, and Dalmatia in exchange for entering the war. Italy duly declared war on Austria-Hungary on May 23, 1915, and on Germany on August 28, 1916.

8 Garibaldi's "Expedition of the Thousand" lands at Quarto, near Genoa, May 6, 1860

9 The Bersaglieri, an elite corps of the Piedmontese army, guarding Austrian prisoners captured during the 1859 war, in which Piedmont and France defeated the Austrian Empire in Northern Italy

Pope Pius IX

Pope Pius IX, from a noble Italian family, proclaimed the infallibility of the pope in 1870 and is said to have left the Papal States with the words, "I might be infallible, but in any case I am bankrupt."

above: Pius IX, pope 1846–78

1892 | Founding of the first Italian socialist party
1896 | War against Abyssinia
1900 | Assassination of Umberto I
1911 | Italian forces occupy Tripoli
1911-12 | War against the Ottoman Empire
24 Jun 1915 | Treaty of London

Portugal and Spain 1814–1914

Economically and politically, ❶ the Iberian Peninsula fell behind the rest of Western Europe and suffered a loss of both wealth and prestige as a result of the South American colonies' independence. Portugal was unable to industrialize during the whole of the 19th century, and democratization was achieved only after the turn of the century. In Spain, too, modernization progressed only haltingly after the restoration of the Bourbons; the power of Catholicism, the army, and the absolutist nobility was still too strong. Following the more settled 1870s and 1880s, political colonial conflicts resulted in destabilization that once more put the brakes on liberal reform.

The river Duoro, which flows from the high mountains near Soria across the Iberian Peninsula, near its mouth into the Atlantic ocean at Porto

Portugal: The Liberal Struggle and State Bankruptcy

The struggle between conservative and liberal political forces in Portugal hampered the country's modernization and made land reform impossible. In 1911 Portugal became a republic.

The Portuguese ❷ King John VI returned to Portugal from his Brazilian exile (p. 299) in 1821, a year after Portugal had been transformed by a liberal revolution into a constitutional monarchy. His son, as Emperor Pedro I of Brazil, proclaimed the colony independent to save it for the crown. In Portugal, the queen and her son Miguel attempted a coup against John VI in 1824, which was thwarted with the aid of the English.

When John VI died in 1826, Pedro—still in Brazil—took the Portuguese throne as King Pedro IV and strengthened the rights of the king through a new constitution. He then granted a constitutional charter and abdicated in favor of his daughter, Maria da Gloria, but the Holy Alliance forced him to make his brother Miguel regent in 1827. The regent then had himself proclaimed King Miguel I in 1828 and reintroduced absolutism. Again the English came to Portugal's aid, and Pedro was able to restore his daughter to the throne in 1834 as Queen ❹ Maria II. In the ensuing years, the liberal Septembrists and the conservative Cartists struggled against each other; in 1836 a revolution restored the 1832 Constitution and a people's rebellion in 1846–1847 was suppressed. The governments of kings Pedro V and ❻ Louis I were marked by internal political turmoil in which foreign powers sometimes intervened. By 1892 the country was also bankrupt.

Under Louis's successor, the weak ❺ Charles I, Prime Mnister João Franco abolished the *Cortes*—the parliament—in 1907 and set up a dictatorship. In the next year, Charles and his eldest son Louis Philip were both assassinated. Thereupon the 19-year-old Manuel II ascended the throne. Despite coalition governments, amnesties and liberal legislation, the inexperienced king of Portugal was driven into ❸ exile in Great Britain following a republican coup d'état. On August 31, 1911, a new democratic constitution was proclaimed. In 1916, Portugal entered World War I against Germany. The Portuguese forces suffered heavy losses, but as a victor Portugal obtained some minor colonial territories from the dismantled German Empire in the final peace settlement.

Manuel II flees Portugal in 1911

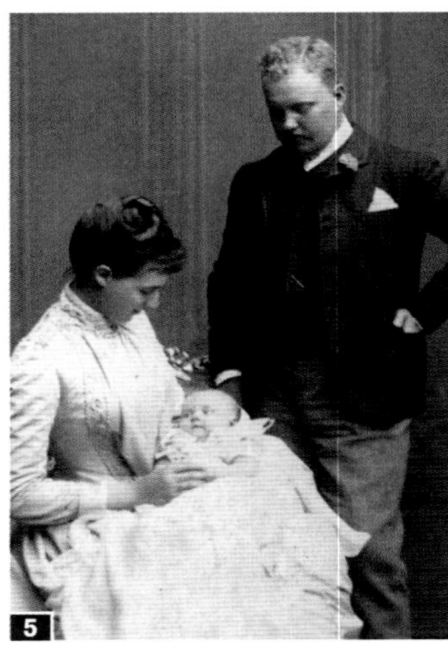

Charles I, king of Portugal, with his wife, Amelie, and their firstborn child, Louis Philip, 1888

John VI, king of Portugal

Maria II da Glória, queen of Portugal

Louis I, king of Portugal

1822 | Independence of Brazil
1828 | Independence of Uruguay
1834 | Maria II da Glória becomes queen
1846/47 | People's rebellion
1847–74 | Carlist Wars
1876 | New constitution in Spain
1892 | Bankruptcy of Portugal

Spain: Family Feuds and Sluggish Modernization

Carlist wars and rebellions obstructed Spain's progress in the 19th century. The flourishing period that began just after 1876 was already over by the turn of the century.

❼, ❾ King Ferdinand VII of Spain, even more than most other European monarchs after the end of the Napoleonic wars (p. 361), pursued a restoration policy of extreme reaction. After he returned from France in 1814, he restored the Inquisition and then repealed the 1812 constitution that had given the word "liberal" to the world. A popular revolution in 1820 was crushed with French help, and Ferdinand's absolute authority was restored. In 1831 he designated his newborn daughter ⓬ Isabella as the new queen rather than his brother Don Carlos. This triggered the turmoil of the Carlist wars that lasted more than 40 years, at the end of which Isabella's son ⓭ Alfonso XII took the throne after the very brief First Republic.

9 Ferdinand VII, king of Spain

12 Isabella II, queen of Spain

13 Alfonso XII, king of Spain

Alfonso XII did away with absolutism in the constitution of 1876, which prohibited both the king and the army from interfering in politics. The next two decades were marked by stability and growing prosperity.

❽ Carlist revolts were suppressed, as was ⓫ the Cuban revolt of 1878, although it flared up again in 1895. The United States then ❿ intervened in Cuba, sparking the Spanish-American War of 1898, in the course of which Spain lost Cuba, Puerto Rico, the Philippines, and Guam to the United States.

7 Silver coin worth eight *real*, depicting King Ferdinand VII and the royal Spanish coat of arms, minted in 1822

10 Spanish cartoon questioning the motives behind US support for the 1895 anti-Spanish revolt on Cuba: "I've had my eye on that morsel for a long time, guess I'll have to take it in!"

The Spanish defeat produced domestic instability. Anarchist and socialist factions gained in strength, and regionalist movements sought autonomy. The conservative head of government from 1907, Antonio Maura, demonstrated little understanding for the liberals, and in 1909 he attempted to use workers from Barcelona in the conflict over Spain's control of Morocco. A revolt resulted, and Maura was replaced by the more liberal José Canalejas y Méndez; however, his promising reforms were cut short when he was murdered in 1912. Spain remained neutral during World War I, which allowed it to profit from record exports.

8 Zumala-Carregui, commander of the forces of the royal pretender Don Carlos, conquers Bilbao in June 1835, during the Carlist Wars

11 Cubans burn down the sugar refinery at Los Ingenios, near Trinidad de Cuba, during the 1878 revolt

The Carlist Wars

The Carlist wars stemmed from the disputed succession of Ferdinand VII, who had designated his daughter Isabella II as heir to the throne. The Carlists, who wished to bring Ferdinand's brother Charles to the throne, waged war against the followers of Isabella's mother, María Cristina. The Carlists, whose strength was in rural northern Spain, fought against the more urbanized south. In 1839, the Carlists were defeated, but Isabella's coronation in 1843 triggered a second Carlist war. Isabella remained in power until the "glorious" revolution of 1868. In 1870 Amadeo, the son of the Italian king, came to the throne, but was forced to step down in 1873. After the First Republic, a military coup in 1874 placed Isabella's son, Alfonso XII, on the throne and brought an end to the Carlist wars in 1876.

Revolt against Queen Isabella II, Madrid, 1868

1895 Cuban revolt
1898 Spanish-American War
1906–08 Dictatorship of João Franco
1908 Charles I assassinated
1910 Proclamation of the republic
31 Aug 1911 Passing of the democratic constitution

Scandinavia ca. 1800–1917

The Scandinavian countries of Denmark, Norway, and ❶ Sweden gradually developed into modern democracies over the course of the 19th century. At the turn of the 20th century, they began developing into the social welfare state models that have typified Scandinavia ever since. At the same time, Denmark suffered territorial losses and economic problems, while Finland remained largely dependent on Russia, even after its political independence. Sweden experienced economic growth, but its union with Norway was not of long duration as Norway strove successfully for national autonomy.

Moon rising over Valdres, painting by Eugene, Prince of Sweden, 1890

Descent of Denmark and Finland into Dependency

Denmark lost Norway to Sweden, following which it also experienced a severe economic crisis. Finland was able to win independence from Russia in 1917.

In 1801 and 1807, ❸ the British Royal Navy destroyed the Danish fortifications and fleet in ❷ Copenhagen, which was resisting the British blockade of Western Europe. Denmark was then forced to ally with Napoleon, but as a result lost control of Heligoland and Norway to Sweden in the Treaty of Kiel in 1814. This loss of many markets led to inflation, great poverty and eventually the bankruptcy of the state in an economic crisis that lasted until 1828. The country became a constitutional monarchy with universal suffrage and universal education in 1849. A year earlier, Denmark had fought with Germany over ❻ Schleswig and Holstein, and in ❺ 1864 a second German-Danish war erupted, in which Denmark lost both duchies along with Lauenburg. After that, it maintained neutrality, even during World War I. A parliamentary constitution and the socialist legislation under Minister-President Jacob Estrup in the 1890s won Denmark a reputation as a "model social state."

Bombardment and occupation of Copenhagen by British Navy in 1807

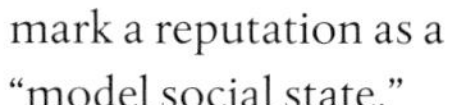

Russia's plan to annex all of Finland was implemented following the Treaty of Tilsit in 1807. Finnish nationalist efforts following Napoleon's defeat were unsuccessful under the restoration policies of the Russian tsar ❹ Nicholas I Liberal reforms by Alexander II—including equality for the Finnish language, reinstatement of the Finnish state parliament in 1869, and the creation of a conscript army in 1878—were repealed by Alexander III. In 1899, Finland lost its autonomous status through the February manifesto of Nicholas II, although it was reinstated for a time after the revolution of 1905 in Russia. On December 31, 1917, Vladimir Lenin confirmed Finland's independence.

above: Nyhavn in Copenhagen, part of the original harbor
left: Bust of the Russion tsar Nicholas I, marble, Christian Daniel Rauch

Søren Aabye Kierkegaard

Denmark produced one of the greatest philosophers of the 19th century during its period of crisis. Søren Aabye Kierkegaard was born in 1813 in Copenhagen. After finishing his studies, he published—over a period of only ten years beginning in 1843—the philosophical papers that set the foundation for existentialism as one of the most significant philosophical movements of the 19th and 20th centuries. Kierkegaard died in Copenhagen in 1855.

above: Søren Kierkegaard

Storming of the trenches of Düppel near Sonderburg, Denmark, by Prussian troops on 18 Apr 1864

Danes flee Flensburg ahead of Prussian troops, 1848

1814 | Treaty of Kiel
1815 | Norway granted own administration
1821 | *Storting* abolished
1848–50 | 1st German-Danish war
1864 | 2nd German-Danish war

Sweden's Modernization and the Union with Norway

Sweden became a modern democracy in the 19th century. It united with Norway, which then chose independence at the turn of the century.

A coup in 1809 forced the ❽ abdication of the Swedish king Gustav IV Adolph in favor of his uncle Charles XIII, who in turn was forced to cede significant Finnish territories and the Åland Islands to Russia. In 1814, Sweden gained Norway from Denmark, but also yielded its Pomeranian region, the last of its German territories.

8 An officers' coup forces the abdication of the Swedish king Gustav IV Adolph 13 March 1809

Charles adopted the French marshal ❿ Jean-Baptiste Bernadotte as the heir to his throne in order to gain support from France. Under the name Charles XIV John, Bernadotte became the king of Sweden and Norway in 1818, both of which flourished both economically and ⓫ culturally. His son ❼ Oscar I (1844-1859) supported liberal reforms and the pan-Scandinavian movement, which had the goal of uniting the Scandinavian nations. Oscar's son, Charles XV, continued these reforms and turned Sweden into a modern constitutional state. His brother ❾ Oscar II continued to improve social legislation. During the reign of ⓬ Gustav V, Sweden established universal suffrage and wise measures of social welfare.

The Swedish-Norwegian Union of 1815 had granted Norway its own administration, legislation, and army but all under the Swedish king. The Norwegian parliament abolished the *Storting*, or higher nobility, in 1821. The European revolutions of 1848 resulted in an increased national enthusiasm and consequently a desire for autonomy. Universal suffrage was introduced in 1898, and in 1905 the Norwegians voted to sever their ties with Sweden. In November 1905 ⓭ Prince Charles of Denmark was crowned Haakon VII, king of Norway. Norway carried out exemplary social legislation and remained neutral in World War I, as did all the other Scandinavian nations.

Considerable numbers of emigrants left Sweden and Norway in the second half of the 19th century—about 1.5 million people from Sweden and another 100,000 from Norway—particularly to North America.

Swedish socialism was aided by the growth of industry, though it was successful mostly in the rural parts of the country which were attracted by theories of cooperation and social security.

10 Bernadotte as Charles XIV John, king of Sweden and Norway

7 Oscar I, king of Sweden and Norway, champion of a united Scandinavia

9 Oscar II, last king of Sweden and Norway before separation of the thrones

The Two Norwegian Languages

Under the banner of patriotic nationalism, the Norwegians wanted their "own" national language. Until this point, a Norwegian dialect of Danish, Riksmål ("national language"), had been the official written language in government and literature. The philologist Ivar Aasen then created Landsmål ("country language"), based on old rural Norwegian dialects, mid-century. Today, both languages—now named Bokmål ("book language") and Nynorsk ("new Norwegian")—are equally supported by the government and are both taught in schools.

11 The Norwegian composer Edvard Grieg, painting by Lenbach

12 Gustav V, king of Sweden, with his wife Victoria von Baden

13 Haakon VII, King of Norway and formerly Prince Charles of Denmark

1898 | Universal suffrage in Norway
1899 | February Manifesto
1905 | Norway cuts ties to Sweden
1909 | Universal suffrage in Sweden
31 Dec 1917 | Finland gains independence

Czars' residence: Winter Palace, St.Petersburg

Russia from the Treaty of Tilsit to the Abdication of the Last Czar 1807–1917

Russia remained isolated from many of the political and economic developments that transformed Western Europe in the 19th century. Domestically autocratic and with an economy long based on a semi-feudal agricultural system, Russia faced a growing gulf between the vast majority of the population and the high nobility. Although Russia conquered large territories, its failures in foreign affairs weakened ❶ czarism. Tentative reform initiatives were always followed by periods of extreme reaction which forced moderate liberals toward radicalism. With the onset of industrialization urban workers joined radical intellectuals in the Revolution.

Expansionism, Poland, and the Decembrist Rebellion

Russia was able to expand its vast territory and Poland fought unsuccessfully to regain its independence. Young liberal army officers sought to bring about reform in a failed revolt.

The pact with Napoleon in the Treaty of Tilsit in 1807 gave the Russian Czar ❷ Alexander I the opportunity to expand his own empire. Russia gained the Åland Islands and Finland from Sweden in 1809 and Bessarabia after the Russo-Turkish War of 1806–1812. In 1813 it seized Dagestan in a war with Persia; Czar Paul I had already occupied neighboring Georgia in 1801. After Napoleon had been defeated in his Russian campaign and definitively eliminated at the Battle of Waterloo, the 1815 Congress of Vienna also awarded Russia the major part of the Grand Duchy of Warsaw.

Soldiers and citizens prepare for the defense of the Polish capital, Warsaw, against Russian attack in 1830

The Polish Prometheus as personification of the rebels, in the talons of the eagle, heraldic symbol of czarist Russia

Poland was not prepared to accept the foreign rule of the Russians. Although it initially remained an independent kingdom, resistance—particularly the ❸ November 1830 insurrection—was suppressed, and Poland lost its autonomy. A further Polish uprising in 1863 was ❹ crushed, and Russia completely dissolved the kingdom five years later.

Domestically, Alexander I initially introduced some liberal reforms, such as the reorganization of the government and education system. The Holy Alliance that Russia formed with Austria at the Congress of Vienna in 1815 for the purpose of preserving the monarchical order in Europe led to the czar's post-1820 restoration policy. In effect Russia became a bulwark against political radicalism in Europe, intervening to support regimes threatened by popular unrest. Within the Russian Empire, Alexander increased censorship and police powers.

Czar Alexander I Pavlovitch, portrait by François Gérard, 1814

Decembrists

Many Russian intellectuals were influenced by Western reform ideas and opposed an autocratic Russia. Some formed secret societies. Shortly after the death of Alexander I, a group of young liberal officers who wished to establish a constitutional monarchy organized a revolt in December 1825 in St. Petersburg. Though their demands were moderate Nicholas was deeply alarmed by the events. The extreme reaction and harshness of his reign is often linked to the effect of this revolt on the young czar. Six hundred of the Decembrists were subsequently condemned, five executed, and more than 100 exiled.

Execution of Decembrists on board the Russian warship *Grand Duke Vladimir*

Medallion with the leaders of the Decembrist revolt: Pestel, Ruilejev, Bestuchev, Muravjev, Kachovski

1806–12 Russo-Turkish War | **1807** Treaty of Tilsit | **1813** War with Persia | **1825** Decembrists's uprising | **14 Sep 1829** Treaty of Adrianople | **1830** Revolt in Poland

Territorial Gains and the Crimean War

Nicholas I intensified repressive policies and led his country to war in the Crimea.

❻ Nicholas I, brother and successor to Alexander I, increased repression through a clampdown on liberal universities and the arrest of dissidents. Following the European revolutions of 1848, he tightened these measures further and sent Russian troops into Austria to fight the Hungarian revolt there. Furthermore, he planned to Russianize the non-Russians in his empire in language and religion to make them loyal subjects.

Externally he continued an expansionist course. In 1828, Persia was forced to cede territories in Armenia. The sixth Russo-Turkish War secured sovereignty for Russia in the Caucasus and a "protectorate" over ❼ Walachia and Moldavia in the Treaty of Adrianople on September 14, 1829. Nicholas I occupied these territories militarily in 1853 with the aim of taking control of the Dardanelles, thereby fulfilling a long held ambition to gain naval access to the Mediterranean. This alarmed other major powers and drove his country into the calamitous Crimean War.

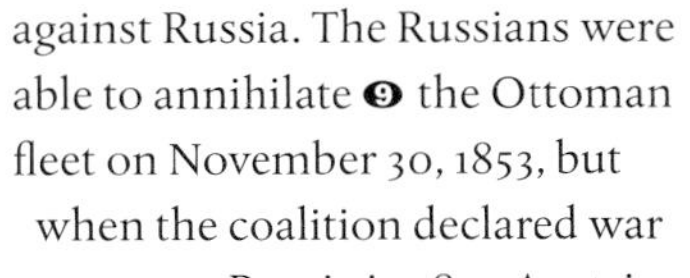

6 Czar Nicholas I Pavlovitch

The Ottoman Empire allied itself with France, Great Britain, and the Kingdom of Sardinia against Russia. The Russians were able to annihilate ❾ the Ottoman fleet on November 30, 1853, but when the coalition declared war on Russia in 1854 Austria failed to enter the war on the side of its longtime ally, Russia. The Habsburgs's neutrality ended up alienating both sides. In September, the Allies then launched an attack in the Crimea against the main port of the Russian Black Sea fleet, ❺ Sevastopol. After an 11-month siege of the city, the Russians surrendered on September 9, 1855. Under the terms of the subsequent ❽ Treaty of Paris of March 30, 1856, Russia lost Armenia and southern Bessarabia, as well as its protectorate over the Danubian principalities. The Black Sea was declared a neutral demilitarized zone, which represented a major setback to Russian ambitions in the region.

5 The capture of Fort Malakoff in Sevastopol by the French General Mac-Mahon, September 8, 1855

7 Villagers in Walachia

8 Paris Congress from January to March 1856

9 Destruction of a part of the Ottoman fleet by the Russians in the port of Sinope, November 10, 1853

The Crimean War

The significance of the Crimean War lay less in the conflict over a particular region. Rather, it was a turning point in the 19th century that sealed the end of the European balance of power that had been in place since the Congress of Vienna. For the first time in four decades the Great Powers engaged in a major war and the Holy Alliance of Austria and Russia was torn apart. The modest success of the British and French forces also helped to preserve the weak Ottoman empire from Russian expansionism. Russia's role in continental affairs, developed under czars Alexander I and Nicholas I, was significantly weakened by the Crimean War.

1853–56 | Crimean War
Sep 1854 | Siege of Sevastopol begins
9 Sep 1855 | Fall of Sevastopol
30 Mar 1856 | Treaty of Paris
1863 | Polish revolt

Russia under Alexander II

Czar Alexander II expanded the empire to the Pacific Ocean. Cautious reforms did not satisfy the reform movement, and the czar was assassinated by radical militants in 1881.

1 Construction of a bridge over the river Jenisseij, part of the Trans-Siberian railroad, built between1891 and 1904

2 Office of Czar Alexander II in the Winter Palace in St. Petersburg

3 Alexander II, Czar of Russia and Grand Duke of Finland, in military uniform

❷, ❸ Alexander II, who succeeded his father in 1855, ended the Crimean War. Following this fiasco in the south, Russia turned to focus its expansionist plans on the east. In 1856, Russia annexed portions of Sakhalin Island and in 1858 seized all the territory up to the Pacific coast, where ❻ Vladivostok was founded in 1860. The czar sold Alaska to the United States in 1867.

In 1891 the ❶ construction of the Trans-Siberian Railroad began, connecting the empire's far-flung provinces. Russia seized further territories in the southeast during the 1860s and 1870s so that the borders of the empire extended almost as far as India.

Alexander II complied with the desires for reform in Russia by abolishing serfdom in 1861, followed three years later by the introduction of *zemstvos*—elected institutions of local government—and compulsory military service. But these measures did not satisfy the opposition and secret societies remained active. The self-styled ❹ Narodniki ("Friends of the People") group was active primarily in rural areas.

4 Vera Ivanova Sassulitch, member of the Narodniki in Michajlovka, near the city of Smolensk

A rebellion by Serbs and Montenegrins against Turkish rule in 1876 presented Russia with another opportunity to realize its ambitions in the Dardanelles. Russia took the side of the rebels, igniting the Eighth Russo-Turkish War in January 1877, which further ❺ weakened the Ottoman Empire. In the Treaty of San Stefano, on March 3, 1878, Russia gained large areas of Ottoman dominions and consequently gained hegemony over the Black Sea region. The Great Powers substantially revised this settlement at the Berlin Congress (p. 380)—under the Treaty of Berlin of July 13, 1878, which cut back Russia's influence—but they did not resolve the "Eastern Question" of the disintegrating Ottoman Empire or prevent the looming crisis in the Balkans.

5 Capitulation of Turkish fortress Plevna, in present-day Bulgaria, December 10, 1877: The wounded Osman Pasha is presented to Czar Alexander II

6 The port of Vladivostok on the Pacific coast, founded in 1860

Peter Kropotkin

In 1862, at the age of 20, Peter Alekseyevich Kropotkin joined the army. During his period of service he worked as a geographer in Siberia. In the 1870s he traveled to Western Europe for the Russian Geographical Society where he became acquainted with revolutionary social theories, and became a convinced anarchist. After returning to St. Petersburg in 1874, he was arrested for agitating against the czar but was able to escape to Western Europe two years later. He was put under house arrest for four years in France in the 1880s and then lived in exile in England until 1917. There he wrote a number of papers, notably his famous blueprint of an anarchist utopia, Mutual Aid (1902). Disillusioned with the statism of Lenin's Bolshevism after his return to Russia, he gradually removed himself from political life.

above: Prince Peter Alexseyevich Kropotkin

1860 Founding of Vladivostok
1861 Serfdom abolished
1864 Introduction of compulsory military service
1867 Alaska sold to USA
1876 Serbs and Montenegrins revolt
1877 Eighth Russo-Turkish War
3 Mar 1878 Treaty of San Stefano
13 Jul 1878 Treaty of Berlin

The Russo-Japanese War and the First Revolution

The war against Japan was lost, which indirectly triggered the revolution of 1905, but the czar was once more able to regain control.

7 Assassination of Czar Alexander II by radical militants, March 13, 1881, in St. Petersburg

8 Czar Nicholas II Alexandrovich

11 Pogrom against the Jews in Russia in the second half of the 19th century

12 Cossack infantry in the Russo-Japanese War, 1904-1905

❼ Alexander II was assassinated with a bomb in 1881 by members of the terrorist group Narodnaya Volya ("People's Will"). His son and successor, ❾ Alexander III, repealed many of his liberal reforms. The authority of the zemstvos was truncated, censorship was increased, and the political police force was strengthened. Nationalist policies were also pursued in earnest: ⓫ discrimination against the Jews increased, and the Russianization of ethnic minorities was pushed further. All of these measures provided a boost to the anti-czarist resistance. Although Russia was still far from industrialized—economic measures were implemented in the 1880s in order to increase factory production—socialist ideas were slowly spreading among the workers. The organizations that formed were often led by exiles.

In international affairs, Russia allied with France against the Central Powers in 1890, thus establishing the constellation of the warring factions in World War I. The last czar, ❽ Nicholas II, who was crowned in 1894, continued to pursue an expansionist policy in the east. This brought Russia into conflict with the emerging power of Japan, which was also seeking to establish an empire on the Asian continent. A quarrel developed over Manchuria and the ⓬ Russo-Japanese War began with a Japanese attack on the Russian harbor of Port Arthur. Despite its numerical superiority

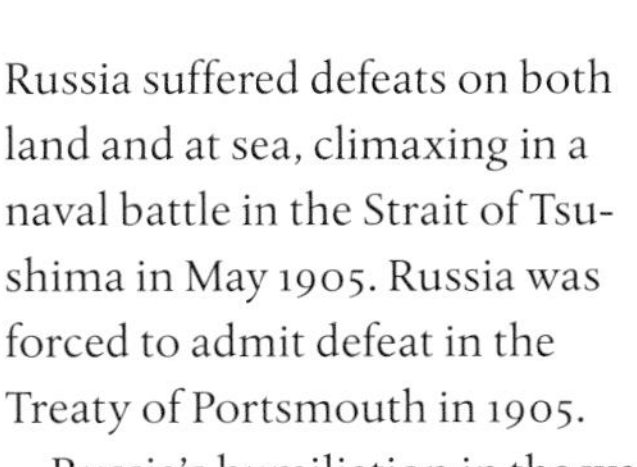

Russia suffered defeats on both land and at sea, climaxing in a naval battle in the Strait of Tsushima in May 1905. Russia was forced to admit defeat in the Treaty of Portsmouth in 1905.

Russia's humiliation in the war revealed the weaknesses of the czarist government, and this inspired a ❿ revolution in 1905. The result was a new census suffrage law that provided a conservative majority in the third Duma, the legislative assembly, which convened until 1912 but accomplished nothing. The need for change was highlighted in World War I. The October Revolution (in November by the western calendar) of 1917 resulted in the abdication of the last czar. Shortly afterwards, Nicholas II and his family were murdered in 1918.

9 Czar Alexander III Alexandrovich, who repealed his father's reforms, portrait by Ivan Nikolajewitsch Kramskoj

10 Lenin with revolutionaries during the revolt in December 1905

The "Bloody Sunday"

A meeting of the zemstvos in St. Petersburg demanded democratic changes from the czar. A rally on January 22, 1905 was attended by almost 200,000 people. Hundreds were killed when soldiers opened fire on the orders of the czar's uncle. This "Bloody Sunday" provoked outrage nationwide. Despite Nicholas II's October manifesto, uprisings occurred everywhere. The government ended the revolution at the beginning of 1906 with the aid of the military. The Duma that had been promised was dissolved following its protests against the new antidemocratic "fundamental law of the empire" of May 6, 1905.

above left: "Bloody Sunday" in St. Petersburg, January 22, 1905
above right: Caricature of Nicholas II, 1905

from 1891 | Construction of the Trans-Siberian Railroad
1904–1905 | Russo-Japanese War
1905 | First Russian Revolution
22 Jan 1905 | "Bloody Sunday"
May 1905 | Battle of Tsushima
7 Nov 1917 | Second Russian Revolution

THE BALKANS 1821–1914

Until the middle of the 19th century, the Balkans were almost completely in the hands of the Ottoman Empire, but it was in a process of decline, and by the outbreak of World War I in Europe its control had shriveled to a narrow strip of land. The Greeks were the first to rebel ❶ against the Turks in their war of independence in the 1820s. They were followed by other nationalities, who were supported by Russia, which saw itself as the patron of the Slavic nationalist movement. But the Balkan countries also fought among themselves over territory, which created an explosive political situation that was partly responsible for the start of World War I.

1 Colonel Favier leads the Greeks in the battle against the Turks, decorative wallpaper, 1827/28

Liberty in Greece

Greece's successful war of independence made it the first country on the Balkan Peninsula to free itself from Ottoman rule.

Patriotic nationalism in Greece increased at the end of the 18th century and led the Greeks to liberate themselves from Ottoman control (p. 408). Though the rebellion of ❷ Alexander Ypsilantis, the leader of the Hetairia Philikon secret society, failed in 1821, the Peloponnesus region also rose up, led by ❻ Bishop Germanos of Patras. Europe supported the Greeks: money and, above all, volunteer fighters such as ❸ Lord Byron, came to Greece to join the ❺ fight for independence. Many of these were romantics, motivated by the idea of liberating a country descended from Ancient Greece .

2 Ypsilantis

3 Lord Byron

The long struggle was accompanied on both sides by ❼ massacres of the civilian population. The Peloponnesus was almost completely retaken by the Turks, but the sultan, Mahmud II, had to ask the Egyptian viceroy, Muhammad Ali, for help. The Egyptians reconquered the southern Peloponnesus in 1826. Russia, Great Britain, and France then sent a fleet to Greece that annihilated the Turkish fleet at Navarino in 1827. Russia was also victorious in the Russo-Turkish war in 1829, and Greece—which at first consisted mainly of the Peloponnesus—was granted the status of an independent kingdom at the London Conference on February 3, 1830.

4 George I, King of Greece

The first king of the Hellenes was Otto of Bavaria, who was crowned in 1832. With little success, he struggled with internal uprisings that led to his abdication in 1862. His successor in 1863 was Prince William George of Denmark as ❹ George I, who ruled for 50 years before he was assassinated in 1913 in Salonika. Over time, the Greeks were able to significantly expand their territory through wars against the disintegrating Ottoman Empire and in the Balkan Wars of 1912–13.

6 Bishop Germanos of Patras blesses the flag of an independent Greece, painting by Theodoros Vryzakis

7 *The Massacre of Chios*, retaliatory strike of the Ottomans in April 1822, painting by Delacroix, 1824

5 Hellas with her "children" Kapodistrias, Ypsilatni, Lord Byron and the bishop Germanos and others, painting by Theodoros Vryzakis

Count Ioánnis Antónios Kapodistrias

Count Ioánnis Antónios Kapodistrias was foreign mi nister of Russia and a negotiator for Tsar Alexander I at the Congress of Vienna in 1815. He quit the Russian service when a dispute developed between him and the tsar over the fate of Greece. Kapodistrias then participated in the Greek war of independence and was elected president of an independent Greece in 1827. He was assassinated on October 9, 1831, in Nauplia.

above: Ioánnis Antónios Kapodistrias

1821 Revolt led by Ypsilanti
1827 Battle of Navarino
1829 Russo-Turkish War
1832 Otto of Bavaria king of Greece
1885 Serbia wages a war against Bulgaria
1908 Annexation Crisis

The Balkan Powder Keg

The Balkan nations were able to liberate themselves and gain independence from the Ottoman Empire but fought among themselves over land.

Bulgaria, Romania—created in 1861 out of the unification of Walachia and Moldavia—Montenegro, and Serbia became autonomous under the Treaty of San Stefano following the Russo-Turkish War of 1877–78. Bulgaria became a principality obligated to pay tribute to the sultan. Serbia had dreams of a greater Serbian Empire, however, and in 1885 ❾ King Milan I Obrenovic waged a war against Bulgaria over Macedonia; Austria-Hungary made sure that Serbia gained only a small western region. Prince Alexander I of Bulgaria lost his throne in a coup to ❿ Ferdinand I of the House of Saxe-Coburg-Gotha, who made himself tsar of Bulgaria in 1908 and proclaimed the country independent.
Bosnia and Herzegovina were occupied in the same year by Austria-Hungary, creating an ⓫ annexation crisis that almost led to war with Serbia, which saw its dreams of a great Serbian Empire as destroyed.

Serbia, Montenegro, Greece, and Bulgaria formed the Balkan League and declared war on the Ottoman Empire in October 1912 and in short order captured almost all of its European territories and reduced it to its present territories. The Treaty of London on May 30, 1913, left the Turks with only a small piece of territory in Europe, but did not resolve the problem of control over Macedonia, contested between Bulgaria and Serbia. Consequently, Serbia and Greece began the ❽ Second Balkan War against Bulgaria on June 29, 1913. By July, Romania, the Ottoman Empire, and Montenegro had joined in against Bulgaria. The Treaty of Bucharest of August 10, 1913, stated that Bulgaria was to cede territory to Romania; Macedonia was absorbed for the most part by Serbia and Romania; and Albania became independent.

Unfortunately, that still did not eliminate the tension in the Balkans. Serbia had become significantly stronger, which the multinational state of Austria-Hungary, with its strong and vocal slavic population, regarded with distrust. When the heir to the Austro-Hungarian throne, Archduke Franz Ferdinand, was ⓬ shot on June 28, 1914, in Sarajevo by Gavrilo Princip, a Serbian nationalist, it led to the July Crisis during which Serbia was unable to fulfil an Austo-Hungarian ultimatum and Vienna declared war on Serbia. This escalated when the other European nations intervened and it ultimately led to World War I.

8 The inhabitants of Melknik burn their city before they flee

9 King Milan I Obrenovic

10 Ferdinand I

11 Analogy of the Annexation Crisis: The peal bell can not ring because each nation pulls it in a different direction

12 Assasination of the Austro-Hungarian heir to the throne, Franz Ferdinand, by Gavrilo Princip

The Congress of Berlin

From June 13 to July 13, 1878, the Great Powers—Austria-Hungary, Great Britain, France, Italy, Russia, and the German and Ottoman empires—sat down together in an attempt to defuse the Balkan situation. The other powers were particularly interested in halting Russia's advance on the Black Sea in the direction of the Dardanelles, which would put it in a position of dominance. Among other things, the north of Bulgaria was declared independent and Eastern Rumelia in the south was made an autonomous province.

The Congress of Berlin, painting by Anton von Werner, 1881

Mar 1912 | Balkan League founded
Oct 1912 | First Balkan War
30 May 1913 | Treaty of London
29 Jun 1913 | Start of Second Balkan War
10 Aug 1913 | Treaty of Bucharest
1914 | July Crisis

The Ottoman Empire ca. 1800–1914

The ❶ Ottoman Empire, which at its height stretched from the Mediterranean to Persia, experienced political and economic decline during the 19th century. From the late 1700s, the Ottoman government had instituted reforms from above, but these were not supported by the old elite and, later, did not go far enough to please the increasingly strong and liberal reform-minded younger generation. The period of reforms was accompanied by a great loss of territory that was the start of the breakup of the great empire.

The palace Dolmabahçe Sarayi near Istanbul, capital of the Ottoman Empire, completed in 1843

Territorial Losses and Internal Reforms

The Ottoman Empire suffered territorial losses at the end of the 19th century primarily in the Balkans. Domestically, the sultan prepared reforms.

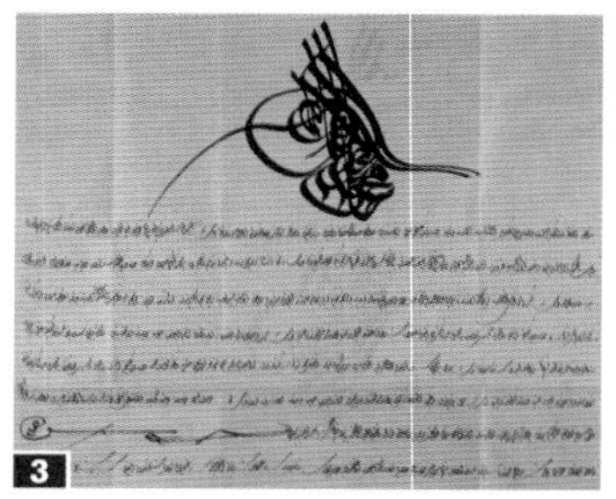

Decree signed by Sultan Mahmud II

The French Revolution and the Wars of Liberation against Napoleon also awoke thoughts of freedom and nationalistic feelings in the European territories dominated by the Turks. ❷ Greece revolted and finally gained its independence in 1829, while the rest of the Balkans was in rebellion during the whole of the 19th century. The European great powers, above all Russia, increasingly intervened, and they supported the independence of Bulgaria, Romania, Serbia, and Montenegro at the Congress of Berlin in 1878.

Memorial to Count von Moltke, military instructor for the restructuring of the army of Mahmud II, Istanbul

In North Africa, Egypt, too, sought independence from the Ottoman Empire. Despite initial support of the Turks by an alliance of Austria, Prussia, and Great Britain, the Egyptians succeeded in 1841. The Maghreb states increasingly came under the influence of Europe. In 1830, France occupied and then colonized Algeria, and in 1881 it made Tunisia a French protectorate.

Domestically, the Ottoman sultans had to contend with a weakening of their central power. The first so-called reform sultan was Selim III, who ascended the throne in 1789 and reorganized the state, its financial administration, and the army according to Western European models. He was not able to withstand the resistance of the traditional elite, however—particularly the military Janissaries, who finally murdered him. His plans were later carried out by ❸ Mahmud II, who destroyed the Janissaries after a ❹ revolt in 1826 and replaced them with a conscription army controlled by the central government. He also fostered the sciences by establishing state schools in which he advocated a general secularization. The Tanzimat reform era, a new phase of reforms, was instituted under Sultan Abdülmecid I. Along with a new ❺ restructuring of the army, the administration was reorganized in line with the French model and the legal standardization of all of the empire's subjects was carried out. New roads, ❻ railroads, and a telegraph system were constructed. For this purpose, foreign loans were drawn, but the government was unable to pay the interest on them after 1875. This, together with corruption and the enormous luxury in which the sultans lived—Abdülmecid had just had a huge new ❼ palace built on the shores of the Bosporus—finally led to the financial ruin of the Ottoman Empire.

Suppression of the Janissary revolt of 1826

Railway viaduct at the narrow pass of Ushak

Attacking Janissaries engage Greek fighters during the Greek war of independence from the Ottomans, painting by Eugéne Delacroix, 1827

Stairwell in the Dolmabahçe Sarayi palace

1826 | Janissaries eliminated
1829 | Greece gains independence
1830 | France occupies Algeria
1841 | Egypt gains independence
1875 | State bankruptcy
1877 | Parliament created

End of the Reforms and Rise of the Young Turks

The Young Turks wanted the political and economic modernization of their country, but failed with their policies.

After the death of ❽ Sultan Abdülmecid I, his brother Abdülaziz ascended the throne in 1861, but he was forced to abdicate in 1876 and was replaced by Abdülhamid II. He put a constitution in force, guaranteed freedom of religion and the press, and installed a ⓫ parliament in 1877—which he then dissolved again when the empire had to defend itself against the pressure of the Europeans. Russia declared war on the Ottoman Empire. By the Treaty of San Stefano of 1878, Turkey surrendered Bessarabia. The Congress of Berlin (1878) marked a further loss of Ottoman territory.

9 Enver Pasha

Abdülhamid's reign soon became a dictatorial and centralized one. The ❿ mass murder of 200,000 Armenians in 1896 occurred during his reign. Although the sultan was able to improve the economic situation, his autocratic regime stirred up resistance from liberals, who organized in the Young Turk movement. A revolt took place in 1909 with the support of General ❾ Enver Pasha.

The Young Turks assumed power, restored the constitution and parliament, and ruled for ten years under the nominal regency of ⓬ Mehmed V. They attempted to modernize the country by curtailing the influence of religion in schools and the legal system while seeking to kick-start industrialization. But even this couldn't save the "sick man of Europe."

The two ⓭ Balkan Wars of 1912–1913 further weakened the declining empire and left it only a small piece of land—Eastern Thrace—in Europe. The Turkish government tried to remain neutral during World War I, but was pulled in on the side of the Central Powers by a promise of German support and funding and the need for allies against Russia.

8 Sultan Abdülmecid

10 Massacre of the Armenians in the Turkish part of Armenia, 1896

11 The first Turkish parliament meets in the year 1877

12 Prince Reshad is proclaimed Sultan Mehmed V

13 The Turks flee from the conquered areas of the Balkan states

The Young Turks

This movement had been formed by Midhat Pasha in 1868, with the aim of reforming Turkish institutions. Around the 1880s, many officers, officials, and intellectuals, mostly young, who were not in agreement with the autocratic running of the Turkish state and sought a revitalization of the country, began uniting. The Young Turks advocated a strategy of liberalization, with the goal of establishing a constitutional monarchy, but were still forced at first to act from abroad. Various groups joined together and were able to depose Sultan Abdülhamid II and install Mehmed V on the throne. The Young Turks were not able to put the Ottoman Empire back on its feet, however, and were forced to hand over the government in October 1918.

Sailors loyal to the Sultan shoot their Young Turk commander, who wanted them to attack the sultan's palace

Egypt 1798–1914

Since being conquered by Sultan Selim I in 1517, Egypt had been administered by governors from the Mameluke dynasty. This regency ended with the success of Napoleon's campaign. After the expulsion of the French, the Ottoman officer ❶ Muhammad Ali Pasha ruled Egypt autonomously and with his policies laid the foundation for the modern Egyptian state. To accomplish this, the country borrowed heavily, which strained the treasury but was profitable for European powers—especially Great Britain, which occupied Egypt at the end of the 19th century.

1 Muhammad Ali, governor of Egypt

Egypt under Muhammad Ali

Muhammad Ali extended Egypt's borders and began modernization.

Napoleon landed at Alexandria in 1798 and began the conquest of Egypt, which was accompanied by ❸ the research and plundering of Egypt's archaeological treasures. The French defeated the ❷ Mamelukes near the ❹ pyramids, presenting a challenge to Great Britain, which had its own interests in North Africa and the Ottoman Empire. When the Ottomans expelled the French in 1803, Egypt became autonomous, although it formally still belonged to the Ottoman Empire.

❺ Muhammad Ali Pasha, an Albanian who had fought against Napoleon as a Turkish officer, became the Ottoman governor of Egypt in 1805. He used the weaknesses of the Mameluke upper class to strengthen his power and destroyed them in 1811. In the following years, he invested in developing industry and agriculture. To gain control of the trade routes, he extended the country's borders to the east and south. Muhammad Ali's son Ibrahim Pasha defeated the Wahhabis living in the Arabian Peninsula in battle in 1819 and conducted further campaigns in 1820–1822 in the Sudan and in 1833 in Syria.

Only a few years earlier, the Egyptian fleet had helped Sultan Mahmud II against the Greeks. Now the Egyptians attacked the Ottoman Empire. The advance of the Egyptians was halted only by the intervention of Prussia, Austria, Great Britain, and Russia—who had an interest in saving Constantinople from being conquered. Ibrahim Pasha's fleet was defeated in the ❻ naval Battle of Navarino in 1827. The Egyptians still had control of Syria but lost it when they attacked the Ottoman Empire for a second time in 1839. Egypt then became a viceroyalty and Muhammad Ali was awarded hereditary rule over Egypt.

The Suez Canal

A route between the Mediterranean and the Red Sea has existed sporadically since antiquity. Spurred by the investigations of Napoleon's scientists, Egypt granted the Frenchman Ferdinand de Lesseps permission to build a canal in 1854. The construction took ten years. After the opening of the canal in 1869, a majority of the stock of the company owning the concession came into French possession, while the rest was Egyptian. The Suez Canal was of particular interest to the British because it shortened the sea journey to India. Consequently they bought the bankrupt Egyptians' share of stocks in 1875 and then militarily occupied the canal in 1882.

above: Viscount Ferdinand de Lesseps

5 Muhammad Ali, accompanied by his son Ibrahim Pasha

2 Mameluke warrior

3 Scientists measure the Sphinx in Giza as part of the Egyptian expedition

4 Napoleon defeats the Mamelukes in the battle at the pyramids

6 Naval battle at Navarino on October 20, 1827

1798 | Napoleon lands in Egypt
1798 | Battle near Pyramids
1803 | French withdrawal from Egypt
1811 | End of Mameluke aristocracy
1827 | Naval Battle of Navarino
1839 | Loss of Syria

The Internal Development of the State and Growing Influence of the European Powers

The building of the Suez Canal and the development of its infrastructure led Egypt to financial ruin while it fought against the revolt in Sudan. Great Britain occupied the Suez Canal and later controlled the entire country.

The ships of the sovereigns cross the Suez Canal for the first time on November 17, 1869

Muhammad Ali died in 1849 and his successors continued with the modernization of the country but came increasingly under the influence of European powers. Muhammad Ali's fourth son ❽ Said Pasha incurred huge debts abroad, which increased again as a result of the development projects of his successor ❾ Ismail Pasha. The building of factories, the development of roads and the postal system, and particularly the construction of the ❼ Suez Canal—commissioned by Said Pasha in 1854—overburdened the state treasury. The growing debt forced the Egyptians to accept French and British ministers in their cabinet in exchange for finances. Ismail Pasha, who had once so victoriously fought in the south of the land and extended Egyptian hegemony to the borders of Ethiopia, was deposed and replaced by his son Tawfiq Pasha, who restructured the country's public finances.

Ismail Pasha

Meanwhile, Great Britain was working on securing ❿ control over the Suez Canal. After the British acquired the Egyptian allocation of stock in 1875, a rebellion of Egyptian officers under War Minister Arabi Pasha broke out against Tawfiq very conveniently in 1881. In 1882 the Christians of Alexandria were massacred, which led to British intervention. The British crushed the rebellion and then in 1882 took full control of the country with a powerful garrison. Egypt had became an Anglo-Egyptian condominium to which Sudan was added between 1895 and 1899. The dynasty of Muhammad Ali remained on the throne with Abbas II Hilmi Pasha, but the ⓫ British governor-general ruled the land. Abbas, who supported Egyptian efforts to regain self-government, was replaced by his uncle Hussein Kamil in 1914. In order to prevent Egypt from supporting the Central Powers in World War I, as the Ottoman Empire had done, it was declared a British protectorate.

Cartoon of the relationship between Abbas II Hilmi and the occupying British power

Said Pasha

The occupation of the Suez Canal by British troops

The Mahdi Rebellion

Grave monument of Muhammad al-Mahdi in the Great Mosque of Omdurman, Sudan

After Muhammad Ali, the Egyptians continued the conquest of Sudan in 1874, which from 1877 was placed under the administration of British governors. In 1881 a rebellion led by Muhammad Ahmad broke out against the occupation. As the self-proclaimed Mahdi, "the (divinely) guided one"—the messianic deliverer expected by Muslims—he supported a war against Egypt, conquering Kordofan in 1883 and, two years later, Khartoum after his victory over the English. He was then recognized as ruler of East Sudan, though he died the same year in Omdurman. The Mahdi State existed only until the invasion of the Egyptians and British, who defeated the Mahdists in 1898 at Omdurman. From 1899, Sudan was also an Anglo-Egyptian condominium.

1854 | Commission to build Suez Canal
1881 | Putsch by Arabi Pasha
1881 | Mahdi revolt
1882 | British occupy Canal Zone
1914 | Egypt becomes British protectorate

Persia and Afghanistan ca. 1800–1914

Competition between Great Britain and ❶ Russia over control of the "Asian hub" heavily influenced the history of Afghanistan and Persia in the 19th century. Russian plans for expansion in southern Asia presented a threat to India, the "crown jewel" of the British Empire. The European powers were threatening Persia and Afghanistan externally and striving for influence internally, destabilizing regimes in both countries. The discovery of oil in Persia in 1908 raised the stakes, but Afghanistan managed to secure a degree of autonomy as a buffer state between the Russian Empire and British India.

Reception in the Russian embassy in Teheran in the 1830s

Persia: Dependency on the British and Russians

Two great powers, Great Britain and Russia, vied for control of Persia, and this was reflected in the increasing influence of these two on Persia's internal politics.

Fath Ali, the shah of Persia, suffered numerous defeats at the hands of the Russians during his reign. In the treaties of Golstan in 1813 and Turkmanchay in 1828, the Persians lost all their possessions in the Caucasus. In the 1870s and 1880s, the Russians again put further pressure on the country, occupying the Persian territories east of the Caspian Sea and south of the Aral Sea, and in 1884 the area around Merv.

The internal strains grew as well. ❷ Shah Nasir ad-Din, who had traveled throughout Europe, pursued a cautious reform policy during his 1848–1896 reign, which introduced a measure of European liberal thought into his country. Great Britain had a particularly strong interest in and influence over the Persian economy. As a result, the shah was forced to contend with powerful pro-British merchants who opposed the autocratic system and demanded a hand in decision making, while any concessions to reform were met with accusations of Europeanization from the influential Shiite clerics.

Since the 1840s, the shah had been fighting the Bab movement, which later gave rise to the ❸ Baha'i faith. He used harsh measures against this Islamic offshoot group and almost completely eradicated its followers after an attempted assassination in 1852.

Internal tension grew with every concession the shah made to the British, who, for example, demanded permission to build a railroad and industrialize the country. The granting of the tobacco trade monopoly to Britain provoked widespread protest. In October 1906, the shah was forced to summon a national assembly and establish a constitution, turning Persia into a constitutional monarchy. Shah Muhammad Ali, who came to power the following year, attempted to reverse these changes, but ❹ unrest and rebellions forced him to abdicate. When Russia and Britain signed the Anglo-Russian Entente of 1907 in St. Petersburg, they divided Persia into respective zones of influence which they proceeded to occupy in 1909.

Oilfields in Persia

Oil field in Baku

Oil reserves were first discovered in Persia in 1908, and within a year the first processing refinery had been built. The Anglo-Persian Oil Company developed oilfields in the southwestern province of Khuzestan on the Persian Gulf, which today is thought to have more than 10 percent of the world's known oil reserves. The British government secured a controlling interest in the company and occupied the region on the pretext of securing its commercial interests, which had previously been designated as "neutral territory" in an agreement with Russia. However, the British attempt to gain complete control of the country and the oil in the following decades failed, partly due to the hostility of the Persian population to foreign occupation.

Shah Nasir ad-Din

Abdu'l-Baha, son of the founder of the religion of the Baha'i, preaching the Baha'i faith in Constantinople

Rebel fighters during the unrest that led to Muhammad Ali's abdication in 1907

1813 | Treaty of Golstan
1826 | Conquest of Kabul
1828 | Treaty of Turkmanchay
1838–42 | First Anglo-Afghan War
1852 | Assassination attempt on Shah Nasir ad-Din
1855 | Treaty of Peshawar

Afghanistan: Precarious Independence

The Russians and British effectively neutralized each other in their struggle for strategic hegemony in Central Asia, thus permitting Afghanistan a precarious independence.

Ahmad Shah Durrani, who ascended to the throne in 1747, founded what is today known as Afghanistan. He expanded it in all directions, particularly into northern India. However, the empire had collapsed completely by 1818 due to internal divisions. In 1826, Dost Muhammad Khan captured Kabul and established a new emirate, which soon presented a threat to the interests of the British and Russians.

After Dost Muhammad opened ❺ negotiations with the Russians, the British took the initiative and marched in. During the First Anglo-Afghan War of 1838–1842, the British seized Kandahar and Ghazni. Shah Shuja, a grandson of Ahmad Shah Durrani, was installed as a sovereign acceptable to the British. A counterattack by Akbar Khan, son of Dost Muhammad, proved successful, and the British troops were forced to withdraw. Dost Muhammad once again took over his emirate, and the conflict ended peacefully with the Treaty of Peshawar in 1855.

When ❻ Shir Ali Khan decided to resume dialogue with Russia in 1878 and refused to accept British representation in Kabul, the British army once again invaded Afghanistan. This time, there was no reaction from the Afghans to the conquest of ❾ Kabul during the ❽ Second Anglo-Afghan War of 1878–1879. In the ❿ Treaty of Gandamak that ended the war, Yaqub Khan permanently conceded the ❼ Khyber Pass and other territories to Great Britain; the British made guarantees of protection from foreign aggression but retained the right to import British products and control Afghan foreign affairs. In 1893, the Durand Treaty fixed the frontiers of Afghanistan with British India, which forms the present Afghan-Pakistan border.

In 1907 Afghanistan became independent indirectly, when Russia and Great Britain reached an agreement to abandon territorial claims there. Afghanistan effectively became a buffer state between the two major powers, and despite the Anglo-Russian alliance, Kabul remained neutral during the First World War. Britain, however, retained its influence in the country, and especially Afghan foreign policy, until 1919, when the heir to the throne was assassinated due to resentment of the pro-British stance of the monarchy.

5 An Afghan diplomatic envoy with his entourage, Russia, 1830s

6 Shir Ali Khan gives instructions to his men during the Second Anglo-Afghan War of 1878–1879

Sayyid Jamal ad-Din al-Afghani

Sayyid Jamal ad-Din, who was born near Kabul in 1838, was an Islamic reformer and political activist. He preached that original Islam was the way to unite the Muslims and resist European colonization of Islamic territories. He studied at the madrassa (theological school) in Kabul and then lived in India, Arabia, Turkey, and Egypt and also traveled to Europe, Russia, and the United States. The British deported ad-Din from Egypt in 1879. He then drew public support in Persia by denouncing the dependence of Islamic rulers on Europe and advocating reform. He was again deported, this time to the Ottoman Empire, where he was arrested in 1896 after Shah Nasir ad-Din was shot by a militant suspected to be a follower.

7 Summit of Mount Hindukush

8 Fortress occupied by British troops on the frontier with the Russian empire

9 Conquest of Kabul by British forces in 1879

10 Signing of the Treaty of Gandamak, May,1879

1878-79 | Second Anglo-Afghan War
1893 | Durand Agreement
1906 | National Assembly called
1907 | Treaty of St. Petersburg
1909 | First oil refinery
1909 | Persia occupied by Russia and England

The goddess Durga fights the demon Mahishasura

India ca. 1800–1914

The imperial rule of extensive areas of India by the British required a large administration and the co-option of local elites. Ironically the forced unification of the vast fragmented subcontinent served to raise awareness of common history, ❺ culture, and ❶ religion. This led in the course of the 19th century to concrete demands, first for participation in government, and eventually for self-determination. The Indian National Congress was the organ of the Liberal Nationalists, which began the struggle for independence in the 20th century.

The city of Delhi ca. 1850

Expansion of British-ruled Territories in India and the outbreak of the Sepoy Rebellion

The East India Company pushed further into the country. The introduction of a Western-style administration and education system led to the emergence of an Indian intellectual class that soon began to demand democratic rights.

India was a patchwork of 500 separately governed territories which the British appropriated piece by piece during the wars against the Maratha Confederation in 1775–1782, 1803–1805, and 1817–1818. The conquered territories were either administered directly by the British or left under the rule of ❹ Indian vassal princes. Only the Sikhs and the Gurkhas were truly independent of British rule.

The development of the administration system and infrastructure was given priority—the construction of an enormous ❸ railroad network, which opened in 1853, to open up the interior of the country, better roads, and a reliable postal system. A unified, national legal system and a single currency were also introduced.

At the beginning of the 19th century the need for qualified Indian workers led to the introduction of Western educational institutions where Indians qualified as officials, lawyers, and teachers. In 1857 universities opened in Madras, Bombay, and Calcutta, and a wealthy few came to Britain to study. A small class of Indians with Western education thus emerged, and some came to express anger over the conquests and annexations of the British. Political organizations were soon composing petitions that demanded democratic rights and access to things. These critical voices were all but ignored by the British at first, but this changed with the Sepoy Rebellion of 1857 in ❷ Delhi which, though limited to northern and central India, affected the whole of the country. The mutiny was provoked by the use of cartridge grease which, containing both pork and beef, defiled both Hindus and Muslims.

Platform of an Indian railway station on the network that opened in 1853

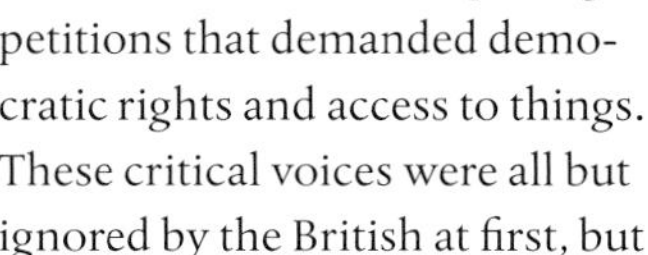

Indian astrolabe

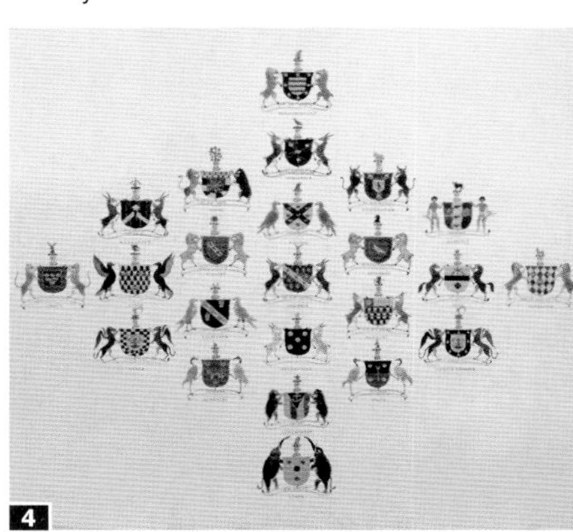

Emblem of the Indian Rajas

The Uprising of the Sepoys

The Sepoys were Indian soldiers primarily from the Punjab region, which had been annexed in 1849. In 1857 the Sepoy Rebellion (or Indian Mutiny) erupted. Resentment of the gulf between the British officer class and the common soldiers was one of the main causes, as was the fear of Christian missionary efforts sparked by insensitivities to religious practices. The Sepoys liberated imprisoned soldiers in Meerut, near Delhi, killing British citizens in the process. This mutiny ignited the rebellion of the recently disempowered upper class in Oudh, and princes, lords of manors, and peasants fought side by side. Delhi was seized and the last Mogul, Bahadur Shah II, was proclaimed emperor of India. Delhi and the encircled British seat in Lucknow were retaken by the British in 1857.

Execution of Indian soldiers following the mutiny's suppression

1849 British annex the Punjab
1857 Sepoy Rebellion
1858 East India Company dissolved
1858 British rule in India
1877 Victoria becomes "Empress of India"

The Awakening of the Indian Nation

The Indian educated class organized itself into political movements and demanded a voice in the running of British India.

Following the Sepoy Rebellion of 1857, the last Mogul, Bahadur Shah II, was banished, and the British crown took direct control of India. The East India Company was dissolved in 1858 and

Hindi begging the British for food, ca. 1873

❻ Queen Victoria assumed the title of "Empress of India" in 1876; from this time until Indian independence, the British monarch was simultaneously the ❾ Emperor of India. The governor-general, formerly the head of the East India Company, was then appointed viceroy. In addition to India, his domain included the present-day states of Sri Lanka, Pakistan, Bangladesh, and Myanmar.

In the second half of the century, the British continued the development of the administration and infrastructure. Revenues

Indian military units revolt against the British occupying forces

gained from property taxes, the opium monopoly, and a salt tax were sent to London, while the Indian people suffered under the ruthless exploitation of their country. Millions lost their lives in ❼ famines.

The new generation of Indian intellectuals increasingly absorbed ideas of democracy and nationalism; the latter began to develop strongly in the 1870s. On the one hand there was the desire for recognition by the West; on the other there was ❿ cultural and religious pride. These contradictory desires shaped the nationalists' debates into the 20th century. The government of the liberal viceroy Lord Ripon gave the nationalists further impetus. In 1885 the Indian National Congresswas founded, which would lead first to negotiations with the British and later an independent India. In 1906, Indian Muslims formed their own party, the Muslim League, which better represented them as a minority.

When the British wanted to divide the Bengal region to form a province with a Muslim majority, there were attacks against the British, boycotts, and a ❽ revolt. The British were forced to abandon the division. Because the rebellious Bengals had become a danger for the viceroy, the seat of government was moved from Calcutta to Delhi in 1911.

George V, king of Great Britain and Ireland, is crowned Emperor of India during a lavish ceremony held in Delhi, in 1911

Sitar player, miniature from Dhubela, Rajasthan, ca. 1800

Victoria, Queen of Great Britain and Ireland, Empress of India

Sir Rabindranath Tagore

In 1913, Rabindranath Tagore became the first Asian to win the Nobel Prize for literature. This increased the Indian sense of nationalism, as the Indian culture was now in some respects recognized by the West as an equal. Tagore did what he could for the farmers in the villages of Bengal. Among other things, he established a cooperative grain silo and had roads and hospitals built. He criticized the English school system and the neglect of the mother tongue that it caused. He founded a school after the ancient Indian model called Ashram in Shantiniketan, West Bengal, where a university still operates today.

above: Rabindranath Tagore

1885 | Founding of the Indian National Congress

1905 | Revolt in Bengal

1906 | Muslim League founded

1911 | Delhi becomes seat of government

1913 | Rabindranath Tagore awarded Nobel Prize for literature

China to the Last of the Emperors

ca. 1840–1912

The high point of the Manchu Dynasty (1644–1912) had passed. China was increasingly losing political and economic power to the British, who had prevailed in two Opium Wars. The British, Russians, and French were claiming more and more Chinese territory for themselves. Internally, the Manchus had to contend with secret societies and religious movements, as well as the widespread opium use within the country. Weakened in this way, the Manchu state broke apart after hesitant reforms and was replaced in 1912 by a republic.

1 Chinese poster against increasing European influence in the country

The Opium Trade and European Treaty Ports

The Opium Wars forced ❶ European economic and cultural influence upon China.

Ever since the British had begun importing opium from India into China, China's trade balance had significantly worsened. The import of opium into China was banned under Chinese law, as the country was able to manufacture enough for medicinal purposes domestically. The use of opium was banned in 1810. When the imperial Chinese government in Canton confiscated large amounts of opium, it led to the ❷ First Opium War in 1840, because the British refused to relinquish the drug trade. An expeditionary force with warships militarily enforced the continuation of the trade. The weakened Chinese were forced to agree to the first "unequal treaty," which was signed in Nanjing on August 29, 1842. It stipulated the payment of war reparations by the Chinese, the cession of Hong Kong to the British, and the opening up of five further ports to British trade. But the new conditions still did not go far enough for the British because they did not coincide with their concept of free trade.

4 Hung Hsiu

The Europeans also won the Second Opium War, or Lorcha War (1856–1860). In the ❸ Treaty of Tientsin in 1858, they secured ten more "treaty ports." When the Chinese resisted and mishandled British prisoners, 20,000 British and French soldiers destroyed the ❺ emperor's summer palace. The Treaty of Beijing in 1860 legalized the opium trade. In addition, cheaper European products flooded into China after the import duty was lowered, destroying the Chinese economy and its chances of modernization.

Internally, the *Taiping* (Great Peace) movement—a synthesis of traditional religious and Christian views demanding an egalitarian social system—became a serious opponent of the Manchus. Its followers revolted against the imperial government under the leadership of ❹ Hung Hsiu in 1851 in the Taiping Rebellion and erected their own state, which encompassed a large portion of southern and southeastern China with Nanjing as its capital. The rebellion was ended in 1864 by the Manchus with British and French aid and cost the lives of 20 million people. After that, Muslim uprisings shook the province of Yunnan between 1864 and 1878. In Sinkiang, on the western rim of the Chinese Empire, Yakub Beg established a Muslim Turkish empire from 1865 to 1877 as khan of Kashgar.

2 The English force the Chinese to buy British opium from India

3 Treaty of Tientsin between England and China, June 26, 1858

5 The emperor's summer palace in Beijing

1840 | First Opium War
29 Aug 1842 | Treaty of Nanjing
1851 | Taiping Rebellion
1856–60 | Second Opium War
1858 | Treaty of Tientsin
1860 | Treaty of Beijing
1864–1878 | Muslim revolts in Yunnan

The End of the Empire

China's influence in Asia diminished. The Boxer Rebellion demonstrated the weaknesses of the Manchu government, and it was soon replaced by a republic.

After China had already lost its northern territories to Russia in 1860, it lost Vietnam to France in the Sino-French war of 1884–1885 and Burma to Great Britain in 1886. The intervention of Japan and China in a revolt in Korea in 1894 then triggered the ❼ Sino-Japanese War. Despite China's superiority in troops, the war—especially after the lost naval battle in the estuary of the Yalu River—ended with defeat and a large loss of territory. Influence in Korea, which then became independent, had to be given up.

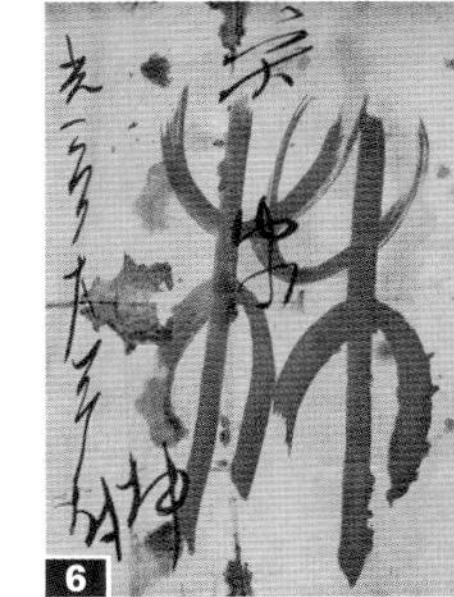
Amulette of the Boxer

Toward the end of the 19th century, the voices that demanded ever more reform, after the Japanese model (p. 418), finally reached Emperor Te Tsung. He was willing to transform China into a constitutional monarchy with further modernizations. But a coup d'état by the powerful dowager empress Tz'u-hsi and her conservative followers put an early end to the reforms phase. In 1899 she recognized the ❻ secret society of the Boxers, which then gained ground. The Boxers denounced the exploitation of the country by the Europeans and strove for a restoration of China's former greatness. To this end, they ❽ attacked foreign installations and murdered Europeans. The ❿ Boxer Rebellion of 1900, which was ❾ crushed by the Japanese, Europeans, and Americans, led to even greater restrictions on China's sovereign rights.

Only after the Russians and Japanese had divided Manchuria into spheres of influence in 1904–1905 was the Chinese court ready for reforms. A constitution and the formation of a parliament were planned, but only hesitantly enacted. In 1911 there was a military revolt in Wuchang that spread through the empire and finally forced the last emperor, P'u-i, to abdicate. P'u-i had ascended the throne as an infant in 1908, after having been designated the successor to the throne by dowager empress Tz'u-hsi as she lay dying. The republic that was proclaimed at the end of the year by the revolutionaries around ⓫ Sun Yat-sen was governed by General Yuan Shikai from 1912. Under an agreement signed with the new Chinese leadership, P'u-i retained his imperial title. It also stipulated that he was to be treated with the same official protocol as a foreign leader.

Battle during the Sino-Japanese War 1894–1895

Group of armed Boxers

European troops defeat the Boxers and carry out punitive expeditions

Boxer Rebellion in Beijing

Sun Yat-Sen

The Boxer Rebellion

The murder of the German ambassador, Baron von Ketteler, on June 20, 1900

The Boxer Rebellion was triggered by the murder of the German ambassador, Baron von Ketteler, in Beijing in June 1900, and the siege of the foreign embassy quarter by the secret society of the Boxers. It was finally crushed by an international expeditionary force including Japanese, European, and American troops which occupied Beijing on August 14, 1900, and made several bloody punitive expeditions under a German general, Field Marshal Count von Waldersee, against the insurgents. The Boxer protocol of September 1901 ended the conflict and committed China to, among other things, large reparations payments and the toleration of foreign military bases.

1865 Muslim Turkish Empire in Sinkiang
1884–85 Sino-French War
1894 Sino-Japanese War
14 Aug 1900 Boxer Rebellion
Sep 1901 Boxer protocol
1911 Military revolt in Wuchang
1912 Proclamation of the republic

Japan 1854–1912

Japan had been almost wholly isolated from the West since the 17th century under the shoguns of the Tokugawa. Japan was ruled by a noble upper class with the shogun at the top. Though it gave the empire a long, peaceful period of ❶ cultural flourishing, it also prevented access to Western modernization in the areas of technology and politics. Under internal political pressure, the last shogun was forced to step down in 1868 in favor of the emperor, who pushed ahead with modernization. During the Meiji period, Japan quickly came to lead Asian industrialization and was also successful in foreign affairs.

The Great Wave, colored wood engraving by Hokusai, 1830

The End of Seclusion and Domestic Changes

The Western states contributed to the development of Japan as a market and trading center. The resulting domestic crisis brought the end of the shogunate.

During the early 19th century, the Tokugawa shoguns tried to keep Japan sealed off from the Western world. However, the United States demanded the opening of Japan and forced the ❷ 1854 Kanagawa Treaty, which ensured the Americans the use of two ports for trade. ❸ European states then made similar treaties, and in 1860 Japanese envoys traveled to Europe to initiate trade with the West. Many of the treaties made were disadvantageous to the Japanese, often guaranteeing the foreigners significant privileges.

This opening of the country had domestic consequences. The foreigners were considered enemy intruders by the Japanese people. When several nationalistic-minded ❹ samurai attacked foreign merchants, European warships shelled Kagoshima in 1863 and Shimonoseki in 1864.

An influential group that demanded political reorganization and the restoration to the emperor (*tenno*) formed in Japan. The Japanese modernizers, as well as the armed foreign powers, highlighted the Tokugawa shogunate's shortcomings. The shoguns recognized that Japan had to adapt its policies to the new conditions. They were anticipated by the military leaders of the Satsuma, Choshu, and Tosa provinces, who seized the emperor's palace in ❺ Kyoto on January 3, 1868. Tokugawa Yoshinobu then restored to the tenno the power of government that had been in the hands of the shoguns for over 250 years. Edo was declared the capital in 1868 and renamed Tokyo, and Tenno Mutsuhito (Meiji) moved there in 1869.

Ukiyo-e: Pictures of the Floating World

Originating in the 17th century, in the form of hand-colored woodblock prints with subjects taken from Bohemian society, the art of the Ukiyo-e school showed actors and demimondaines. Later, nature and city scenes featured. In the 19th century, Ando Hiroshige and Hokusai were the outstanding artists of Ukiyo-e, which declined in the Meiji period.

Moon rising over a landscape with a river, colored wood engraving by Ando Hiroshige

Commercial treaty between the United States and Japan, March 31, 1854

European and American ships at Yokohama

Samurai in armor

The emperor's palace in Kyoto, ca. 1900

1854 | Kanagawa Treaty
1863 | European attack on Kagoshima
1864 | European attack on Shimonoseki
3 Jan 1868 | Emperor's palace in Kyoto occupied
1871 | Feudal structure abolished

Modernization and Territorial Gains

The reforms of the Meiji Restoration brought Japan into the Modern Era and made it the leading political and military power in East Asia.

The Boshin War, a short civil war against the last followers of the Tokugawa, led directly to the Meiji Restoration. ❻ Tenno Mutsuhito, named Meiji ("the Enlightened"), had set as his goal Japan's modernization through comprehensive reforms. This was accomplished above all with the aid of his powerful ministers Kido Takayoshi, Saigo Takamori, and Okubo Toshimichi. With one decree in 1871, they abolished the traditional feudal structure and installed governors to replace the previous system of local self-government. European military advisors and engineers restructured the army, industry, and ❽ transport. Laws and educational institutes were renewed in the Western mold. The rapid pace of these changes, however, also incited resistance. When in 1877 the warrior class of the samurai was disbanded, War Minister Yamagata Aritomo—who, following the Prussian example, had introduced compulsory military service—was forced to put down the Satsuma Uprising.

Japanese attack upon the Chinese defenders

The Prussia state served as the model when drafting the new constitution of 1889 that formally made Japan a constitutional monarchy. A parliament with an upper and lower house was created as of 1890, although the tenno was still able to intervene in politics through decrees or by dissolving the lower house. The military also had a right of veto in the appointments of minister posts.

Industrialization demanded an expansion of the country's territories primarily to tap raw materials and markets abroad. In the 1870s, Japan came to an agreement with Russia about the Kurile Islands north of Japan and occupied the Chinese Ryukyu Islands in the south. The Japanese used a revolt in Korea to seize additional Chinese territories. They won the ❼ Sino-Japanese War of 1894–1895, and in the Treaty of Shimonoseki took Taiwan and the Pescadores. Japan was also victorious in the ❾ Russo-Japanese War of 1904–1905, which was fought over Manchuria and Korea; in a treaty negotiated at Portsmouth, New Hampshire, in 1905, Japan gained the southern half of Sakhalin Island and the lease of the Liaodong Peninsula, among other things. Japan annexed Korea in 1910.

❿ Tenno Mutsuhito died in 1912 in Tokyo. During his reign, Japan had become the most progressively industrialized country in Asia and a major political and military power.

Official declaration of war by Japan on Russia from February 10, 1904

The death of Tenno Mutsuhito, color print, 1912

Emperor Mutsuhito ("the Enlightened") with his family

Railway station between Ueno and Nakasendo

Saigo Takamori

General Saigo Takamori was a commander of the troops in the Boshin War and led over 50,000 samurai. Along with Kido Takayoshi and Okubo Toshimichi, he was one of the "Three Heroes" of the Meiji government. He soon withdrew from public life and founded a school for samurai who had resigned their offices. Saigo led the 1877 uprising in Satsuma of samurai who felt dishonored by their loss of privileges. Seriously injured in battle, he asked his comrades to behead him to avoid capture and further dishonor.

Samurai in attack stance

1789–1914 The Modern Era

1877 | Samurai dissolved
1877 | Satsuma revolt
1895 | Treaty of Shimonoseki
1904–05 | Russo-Japanese War
1910 | Japan annexes Korea
1912 | Tenno Mutsuhito dies in Tokyo

Southeast Asia until 1914

Apart from Siam—present-day ❶ Thailand—nearly all of Southeast Asia came under the colonial rule of European powers during the 19th and early 20th centuries. In addition to the British, who had been expanding their Indian empire eastward by annexing ever more colonial territory to it, Holland—with control of Indonesia—and France were the most significant colonial powers in Southeast Asia. Trapped between British-occupied Burma and French-ruled Indochina, Siam was able to escape colonization only through the wise politics of kings Mongkut and Chulalongkorn. These kings opened up the country to Western notions of modernization and industrialization.

1 Guard figure at the Wat Phra Kaeo (Temple of the Emerald Buddha) in Bangkok, 19th century

The French and British Conquest of Southeast Asia

Indochina and Burma fell victim to the expansionist ambitions of France and Great Britain.

In 1802 the French ended the local power struggles in Vietnam by helping Nguyen Anh defeat the ruling Tay Son dynasty. Nguyen centralized administration, following the Chinese model, and significantly expanded his dominion. He claimed the title of Emperor from 1806 on and made efforts to win landowners over to his side against the rebelling peasants, but his successor Minh Mang was no longer able to prevent the uprisings. The ❸ persecution of Christian missionaries under Minh offered the French and the Spanish the opportunity to attack Vietnam. The Spanish withdrew, but the French commander stayed on, governing with the help of his officers, and thus established the beginning of the French empire in the Far East. By 1867 they had conquered Cochin China, the southern part of Vietnam; Annam and ❷ Tonkin, the middle and northern parts of Vietnam, became ❹ protectorates in 1883–1884.

In the first half of the 19th century, Cambodia was besieged by Siam and Vietnam. In 1845, the two powers finally agreed on joint administration of the old Khmer Empire. On the request of the Khmer king Norodom, the French—primarily interested in rice and rubber—established a ❺ protectorate. They supported the monarchy and acted as its advisors. A national administrative elite was trained and the infrastructure of the country was modernized. The ❻ "Union of Indochina," combining Vietnam and Cambodia, was the largest French colonial possession apart from its African territories.

Meanwhile, Burma—now known as Myanmar—came into Britain's range of vision. When the Burmese occupied large parts of Siam, the East India Company used the opportunity for an expansion of its sphere of influence. In the First Anglo-Burmese War in 1824, which began with the conquest of the capital Rangoon, the British made only small territorial gains. In the Second Anglo-Burmese War, Great Britain was able to annex the south with its fertile rice plains and as a result of this became the most important Asian exporter of rice. After the Third Anglo-Burmese War in 1885, all of Burma was a British colonial territory.

2 French-Chinese war over the province of Tonkin, the Battle of Nam Dinh, 1883, contemporary lithograph

3 Execution of the French missionary Pierre Borie, 1838

4 Establishing the French protectorate over Annam, 1883

5 Cambodia as French protectorate, painting, 1885

6 Captives of the French in Indochina

1802 | Deposition of Tay Son dynasty
1806 | Emperor Nguyen Anh
1824 | First Anglo-Burmese war
1855 | Bowring Treaty
1863 | France "protective rule" in Cambodia

Modernization and Independence in Siam

Kings Mongkut and Chulalongkorn opened Siam up to Western influences, and in this way the country was able to avoid colonization.

8 Chakri Maha Prasat (Grand Palace) in Bangkok, built under Rama V

The ruling dynasty of Siam, the ❽ Chakri, was confronted with the expansion designs of the British. Therefore, in 1826, Siam entered into a trade agreement that increased the position of power of the British—whose merchants had been present since the early 17th century—but prevented total colonization. This strategy remained that of future Siamese kings: making concessions to Western modernization ideas to the point where they could use their advantages and simultaneously defend against the occupation of their country.

With Vietnam coming under French rule, Siam was threatened by both the French in the east and the British in Burma. Having little choice, the Siamese king Mongkut (Rama IV) made the Bowring Treaty with Britain in 1855, which granted concessions such as a British consulate in Bangkok and gave the British advantages along the lines of the "unequal treaties" of the Europeans with China. Mongkut, a former monk who had unearthed the records of King Rama Kamheng of the 13th century that are important for Thailand's identity, had intensively investigated the European world of ideas. After his accession to power in 1851, he gave up the previous policy of isolation. Advised by Europeans, he improved the infrastructure of the country with new streets and canals, modernized agriculture, and created a military after the European example.

Mongkut's son ❼ Chulalongkorn (Rama V) continued his father's direction during his long ❾ reign from 1868 to 1910. The administration was reformed and organized along more strictly centralized lines, and a modern justice system, based on the ideas of a European constitutional state and respect for human rights, was implemented. Chulalongkorn did away with slavery. Hospitals were constructed, the postal system built up, road works continued, and the construction of a railway network begun. Franco-British negotiations concerning the frontiers of their colonies with Siam took place in 1895.

In the course of the creation of French Indochina, ❿ Siam lost Laos and regions in Cambodia and Siam itself. But the Siamese heartland was preserved from colonization and kept its independence.

7 Chulalongkorn (Rama V), King of Siam, with his family, photography, ca.1905

Chulalongkorn

Rama V, better known as Chulalongkorn, was crowned king of Siam in 1868. He shared the opinion of his father, King Mongkut, that his country had to modernize following European models. As the first Siamese king since Rama Kamheng to leave his country, Chulalongkorn traveled to India, Burma, Java, and Singapore in 1871 and visited Europe in 1907. He was able to fend off many attempted coups, but as a result was only able to carry out cautious reforms. The "Beloved Great King," as the Thai people called him, died on October 23, 1910; October 23 is now honored as a Thai national holiday.

Funeral procession for the Siamese king Chulalongkorn

9 Visit of Chulalongkorn (Rama V), King of Siam, to Otto von Bismarck in Friedrichsruh, 1898

LE CONFLIT AVEC LE SIAM

10 French gunboats make the claim to Laos in Siam, contemporary newspaper

1867 | French conquest of Cochin China

1868–1910 | Rule Chulalongkorn (Rama V) in Thailand

1885 | Burma becomes a British colony

1885 | Loss of the eastern Mekong-Area

1907 | Loss of Battambang and Siam Reap

African State Building and Colonization 1814–1914

At the turn of the 19th century, Africa was hardly colonized at all, apart from the coasts. The European outposts became unprofitable after the ❶ slave trade was banned at the Congress of Vienna in 1814–1815; African states on the west coast and the East African sultanate of Zanzibar, however, lived off the slave trade until well into the 19th century. The states formed in Africa were often kept under the "protective rule" of European countries. However, many independent African states were able to assert themselves until the Europeans pushed into the interior and divided Africa among themselves at the Berlin Conference of 1884–1885.

1 British soldiers deliver the message to the African people that the slave trade has been abolished, colored etching, 19th century

State Building in the 19th Century

In both West and East Africa, which were shaped by the slave trade of the preceding centuries, states were founded that outlasted the colonial period.

During the Vienna Congress of 1814–1815, the European colonial outlawed the ❹ slave trade, though not the ownership of slaves, which had been a source of great wealth for West African states such as Ashanti, Dahomey, and regions of present-day Ghana, as well as the East African sultanate of ❺ Zanzibar. In the course of the 19th century, numerous African states were newly reestablished or expanded. In 1822, freed slaves from the United States founded the settlement of ❸ Liberia, which became an independent republic in 1847. An Arabic trading empire in the eastern Congo region was founded by Mohammed bin Hamad (Tippu Tib) in 1870 for purely economic reasons.

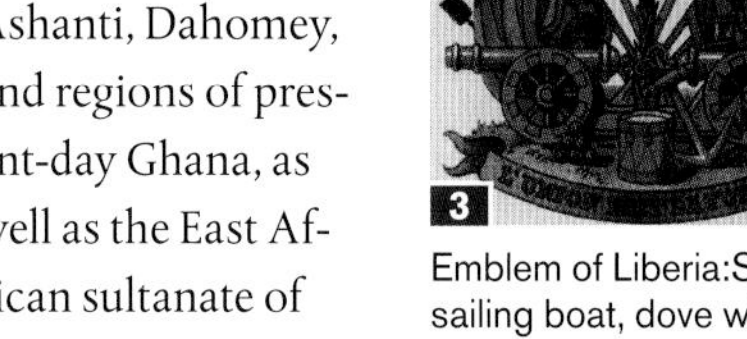

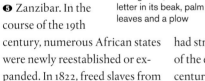

3 Emblem of Liberia:Sun, sailing boat, dove with a letter in its beak, palm leaves and a plow

In Abyssinia (Ethiopia), Ras Kassa reunited the empire in 1853 after the governors of the provinces had strongly curtailed the power of the emperor (p. 333) in the 18th century. He ruled as Emperor Tewodros II until 1868 and was replaced by John IV, who was helped by the British. During his reign, John successfully repelled attacks by Egyptian military units. His successor ❷ Menelik II allied with Italy, which exercised its influence over Abyssinia. When the Abyssinian empire terminated this alliance, the Italians declared war. In the Battle of Aduwa, ❻ Menelik's troops triumphed, and in the peace of Addis Ababa in 1896, the independence of the country was secured.

In West Africa at the beginning of the 19th century, Usman dan Fodio called for a jihad or holy war against the Muslims of the Hausa city-states in present-day northern Nigeria. With his forces' victory, dan Fodio began to set up a great Islamic empire. A few years later, his son Mohammad Bello created a caliphate that was divided up into emirates. With conquests as far as the land of the Yoruba and victory over Adamawa (present-day northern Cameroon), he ruled from Sokoto over the Fulani Empire. Even as a British protectorate, the emirs did not lose their power, and the empire outlasted the colonial era.

2 Menelik II, Emperor of Abyssinia

4 Slave hunters attack a village to capture villagers, wood engraving, 1884

5 American and British trading ships in the harbor of Zanzibar

6 Menelik II in the battle of Aduwa

1814–15 | Slave trade banished at the Vienna Congress
1822 | Foundation of Liberia
1828 | Murder of Zulu king Shaka
1837 | "Great Trek" of the Boers
1839 | Founding of the Republic of Natal
1847 | Independence of Liberia

South Africa between the Boers and the British

In South Africa, the warrior state of the Zulus emerged and soon came into conflict with the Boers. Great Britain, despite great resistance, conquered the Boer Republic.

In South Africa, ❼ Shaka founded the state of the ⓫ Zulu, which he ruled as king until his murder in 1828. He practically became master of South Africa from the Cape Colony to the Zambesi river. He supported his power within the empire on a strict organization and administration of the nation. His military reforms, the introduction of a new battle order, and the deployment of a new throwing spear for close combat provided the success of the Zulus in their campaigns. Through the conquest of large territories, the Zulus put the Bantu people, particularly the Herero and the Matabele, to flight. Shaka's half-brother and successor continued his policies, yet soon came into conflict with the Boers, the descendents of Dutch settlers in the Cape Colony. In 1806 the Boers had come under British rule. Due to internal tensions, particularly resulting from the banning of the slave trade, which, following the teachings of the Dutch Reformed Church, the Boers believed was biblically ordained, around 5000 Boers set off from the Cape Colony in 1837 on a "Great Trek" into the interior of the country, where they came upon the Zulus. The Zulus killed Piet Retief, the leader of the Boers, but in the ensuing battle in 1838 under Andries Pretorius, the Boers killed more than 3000 Zulus. After the victory, the Boers founded the Republic of Natal in 1839, but this too was annexed by the British in 1843.

9 Cecil Rhodes

In the 1850s Britain recognized the independence of the South African Republic (Transvaal) and the Orange Free State—Boer republics founded shortly after Natal. However, when diamonds were found in the border regions between the Cape Colony and the Boer areas and gold was found near Johannesburg, the British once again increased the pressure on the Boers. After the annexation of Transvaal in 1877, the Boers rose up and defeated the British. In the following years, ❾ Cecil Rhodes, prime minister of the Cape Colony from 1890, encircled the Boer republics with the conquest of Rhodesia and Bechuanaland. With the deployment of troops, the British provoked the president of Transvaal, ❽ Paul Kruger, to declare war in 1899. In the Boer War, the British lost initial battles against generals ⓬ Smuts, Botha, and Hertzog in Natal and the Cape Colony. However, in 1900 British troops captured the capital of the Orange Free State, Bloemfontein; Johannesburg fell in May and Pretoria, the capital of Transvaal, in June.

8 Caricature of "Ohm" Kruger and King Edward VII of England: "Mr. Kruger's new ashtray"

Kruger fled to Europe, but the Boers began a guerrilla war. For two years they resisted the British attacks, until Lord Kitchener defeated them. He allowed the destruction of Boer farms and the internment of women and children in ❿ concentration camps. In 1902 Transvaal and the Orange Free State were declared British colonies with administrative autonomy. The Boer states were integrated in the Union of South Africa in 1910 and became dominions of the British Empire.

7 Monument for the Zulu king, King Shaka, erected at the site of his murder in Stanger, Kwadukuza, his former place of residence

10 British concentration camp where the Boer were interned from May 1900

12 Jan Christiaan Smuts, later Prime Minister of South Africa, 1910

11 Zulu women dancing at a wedding, 1970

1853 | Refounding of the empire of Abyssinia
1877 | Annexation of Transvaal by the British
1896 | Peace of Addis Ababa
from 1899 | Boer War
1902 | Peace of Vereeniging
1910 | Union of South Africa founded

Africa: The Apportionment of the Continent by the Europeans

With Henry Morton Stanley's expedition, the push into inner Africa began. In order to avoid war, the colonial powers agreed among themselves on the division of the continent at the Berlin Conference.

In the wake of discussions originating from the new philosophies that emerged from the Enlightenment, the ❸ slave trade caused widespread human rights protests, and a general ban on slave trading was incorporated into the documents of the Congress of Vienna in 1815. The British Navy played a significant part in suppressing the slave trade. The African bases of European trading companies thus lost their main source of income and much of their economic value, which was subsequently diminished further as a result of the opening up of the Suez Canal in 1869, significantly shortening the sea trade routes to India. ❷ Henry Morton Stanley's ❶ exploration of the Congo region gave the Europeans the opportunity to force their way into the interior of the continent. In 1878, Stanley joined the Belgian ❹ king Leopold II and helped him to establish his rule over the "Free State of Congo," which he established under his personal control. Not long after, the leading world powers divided up the continent definitively at the ❺ Berlin Conference of 1884–1885.

In the 1880s, the economic value of the colonies began to increase again as the raw material needs of the expanding Industrial Revolution once again made them economically profitable; some of the colonies even brought the European colonial powers enormous wealth. In addition, through the belief in their own civilizing superiority, the European nations wanted to carry their ideals out into the world, with little regard for the existing culture of the colonized lands.

Berlin Conference of 1884-85

At the Berlin Conference of 1884-85, the colonial powers sought to agree on and define their interests in Africa. Following their signing of the general act in February 1885, the result for Africa was disastrous. The agreement allowed whichever European country that explored an African territory and claimed possession of it to keep the land as long as it informed the other signatory powers of this. As this gave the territorial rights to whoever was there first, a final stage of the "scramble for Africa" began. Similar rules held for the settlement of the coasts: The borders of coastal colonies could be pushed as far into the interior as desired, until they reached the territory of another power. Borders were drawn arbitrarily and ignored African cultural boundaries. The legacy of this agreement has been numerous wars between African states and peoples up to the present time.

above: The Berlin Conference, November 15, 1884–February 26,1885

1 Stanley's expedition transports a boat through the jungle

2 Henry M. Stanley and his officers, wood engraving, ca.1890

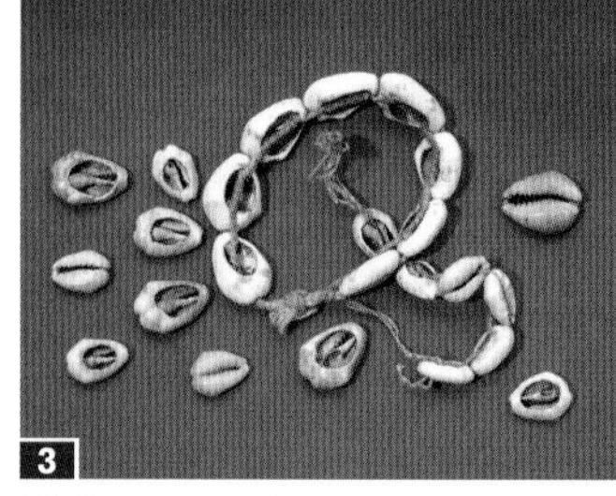

3 Shell money made of cowry, used as method of payment in the slave trade in Africa

4 Leopold II, the Belgian king

5 Bismarck carves up the African cake, caricature, 1885

1869 | Suez Canal opened

from 1878 | Belgians establish "Free State of Congo"

1881 | France annexes Tunisia

1884-85 | Berlin Conference

The Great Colonial Powers

France's and Great Britain's zones for expansion overlapped south of Egypt and the Fashoda Crisis almost led to war.

Under ❼ Prime Minister Benjamin Disraeli, the British had aggressively worked to set up a world empire (p. 393) since the 1870s. The intention was to acquire as much land, and thereby economic power, as possible. Raw materials, labor, markets, and—last but not least—soldiers from the colonies made Great Britain a world power.

Queen Victoria and Prime Minister Benjamin Disraeli

A decade later, at the height of the power of the Third Republic, the French pushed toward the same goal. In the same way as the British conquered ❻ Egypt in 1882, France capitalized on Tunisia's poor economic situation and violently established ❽ "protective rule" in 1881. France, from its coastal bases in Senegal, the Ivory Coast, Dahomey, and the Congo, established a colonial network that stretched over West Africa and was connected to the northern French colonies of Tunisia and Morocco by the Sahara.

The French conquests soon led to conflict with Great Britain, which planned the so-called Cape-to-Cairo Road, a contiguous chain of colonies from the Cape of Good Hope to the Mediterranean Sea together with an accompanying railway. The ❾ Fashoda Crisis of 1898 nearly caused a war between France and Britain, which was avoided only by the restraint of the middle-ranking officers who were in command of the military forces which faced each other.

While those two colonial powers had divided the majority of Africa between them, Germany and Italy also endeavored to acquire regions in Africa. The Germans had engaged themselves—first as private trading colonies, then subordinated to the German empire in 1891—in Togo and Cameroon as well as in German East Africa (Tanganyika) and German Southwest Africa (Namibia), where in 1904 and 1905–1907 they put down with ❿ great brutality uprisings of the Herero and the Maji-Maji. Italy's dream of an East African colonial empire burst when the Italians, after the obliterating defeat in the Battle of Aduwa, were expelled by the Abyssinians in 1896 (p. 422). Until 1936, when Italy took control of most of Abyssinia, Italian possessions were limited to Eritrea and Italian Somaliland.

Disraeli at the Suez canal, the shortest route to India: "Oh, why does this passage to my home not belong to me?", caricature, lithograph

Uprising by the native population of Tunisia following France's occupation of the country, colored lithograph, ca.1910

The Fashoda Crisis of 1898

After Lord Kitchener had destroyed the Sudanese "Empire of the Mahdi," he marched south, where he met French troops under Jean-Baptiste Marchand in Fashoda and forced them to retreat. Great Britain saw the Sudan as a part of British Egypt, but the French saw it as a free area that could be occupied. French foreign minister Théophile Delcassé proffered a compromise. In 1899 it was decided that the British would have sovereignty over the Upper Nile region, while France would control the area of Darfur to Lake Chad—the so-called Equatorial Africa.

above: The French major Jean-Baptiste Marchand meets the envoy of the British, General Kitchener, in Fashoda, drawing, 1898

The conflict between the colonial powers England and France: France is depicted as Little Red Riding Hood, England as the wolf, caricature, 1898

Skulls of Hereros who were executed or died in action are packed and sent to the Pathological Institute in Berlin, photograph, 1905

1891 | Togo and Cameroon colonized by the Germans
1896 | Battle of Aduwa
1898 | Fashoda Crisis
1904 | Herero uprising
1905–07 | Uprising of the Maji-Maji

The United States: Beginnings and Rise to World Power 1789–1917

The ❶ United States, spiritually still strongly rooted in the European tradition, strove to develop its own identity. A foreign policy of isolationism, manifested in the Monroe Doctrine, was implemented. During the 19th century, the territory of the United States increased through the purchase and annexation of land. After 1828 the differences between the Southern and Northern states became increasingly apparent, particularly over the issue of slave ownership. The Civil War from 1861 to 1865 traumatized the young country. Nevertheless, the Union was preserved with the North's victory. After the Civil War, the country's economic and technological ascent began. The entry of the United States into World War I in 1917 signaled the abandonment of isolationism.

1 The Statue of Liberty in New York, unveiled on October 28, 1886

Founding Years

In the early years, there was intense debate over the sociopolitical orientation of the young republic. The unfortunate involvement of the United States in European disputes led to the isolationist policy of the Monroe Doctrine, which was formulated in 1823.

After the 13 original states ratified the US constitution in 1787, two years after it had been drafted in Philadelphia, George Washington was elected the first president, with John Adams as vice president, serving a term from 1789 until 1797. The political options open to the young nation were explored during the first years. Two positions developed: a course toward a strong national government that would promote industry and commerce, advocated by Alexander Hamilton and others and later adopted by the Federalist party; or an agriculturally oriented America with strong individual states, an idea endorsed by the Democratic party headed by Thomas Jefferson. In 1794 farmers were forced to accept a federal excise tax on whisky.

3 Farmers and settlers trek to Black Hills

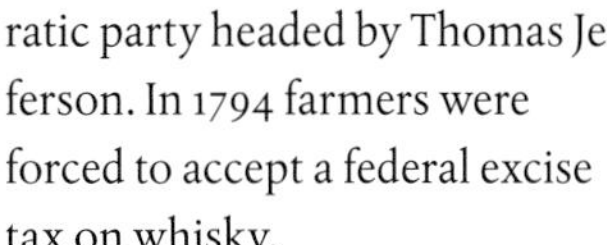

While Washington had promoted a policy of noninterference, the question of whether to ally with France or England arose during the presidency of John Adams (1797–1801). The question was whether to tolerate the Royal Navy stopping and searching United States ships and pressing American seamen into the Navy. In 1803, ❷ Thomas Jefferson (1801–1809) bought the vast stretch of land between the Mississippi River and the Rocky Mountains—the Louisiana Purchase—from France, doubling the territory of the United States. In foreign affairs, the United States became embroiled in the war between Napoleon and Great Britain, leading to war against the British under President Madison. The experience led to James Monroe's (1817–1825) declaration of the Monroe Doctrine on December 2, 1823, stating that the United States would neither interfere in European conflicts nor tolerate colonization attempts by European powers in the Americas.

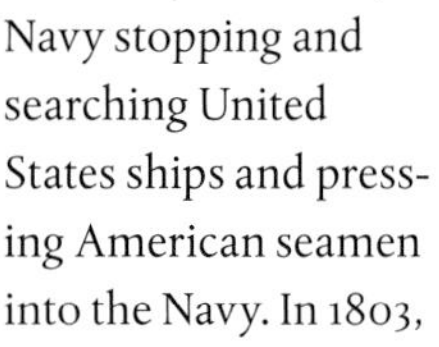

2 Thomas Jefferson

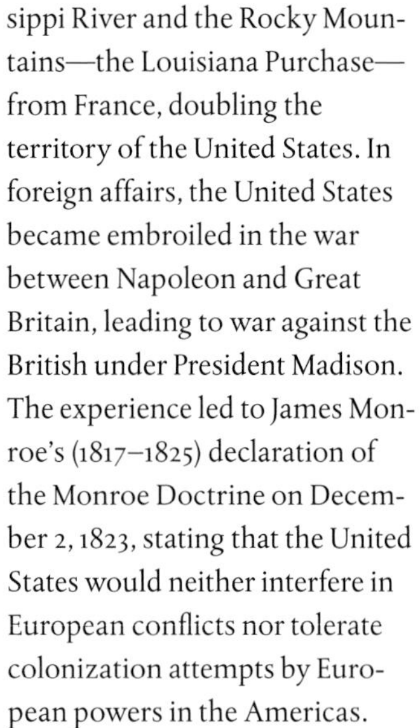

With the economic upswing after the War of 1812 came the development of the Midwestern territories by ❸ farmers searching for new land. This precipitated continuing conflicts with the Indian tribes which had been driven north or settled in reservations.

The Supreme Court

The young United States endeavored to follow the separation of powers advocated by the French philosopher Montesquieu. John Marshall, who served as Chief Justice of the Supreme Court from 1801 to 1835, repeatedly restricted the presumption of authority of presidents Jefferson and Madison. In the case of Marbury v. Madison in 1803, he succeeded in establishing the right of the Supreme Court to review the constitutionality of federal laws and, when necessary, to nullify them.

George Washington, 1793

"'Tis our true policy to steer clear of permanent alliances with any portion of the foreign world."

above: George Washington

4 An Indian reservation, photo, 1906

1787 Ratification of the Constitution | **4 Feb 1789** George Washington becomes 1st president | **1797** John Adams becomes 2nd president | **1801** Thomas Jefferson becomes 3rd president | **1803** "Louisiana Purchase" | **18 Jun 1812** US declares war on England | **2 Dec 1823** "Monroe Doctrine"

Political Reorientation and Expansion

Under President Jackson, popular democracy and party dominance began to shape the political system of the United States. President Polk annexed areas in the West, further expanding the territories of the nation, pushing its borders ever further towards the Pacific.

6 Sioux and General William T. Sherman signing the Treaty of Fort Laramie, 1868, which granted the Sioux an unclaimed territory

The economic crises of the 1820s, after which many farmers found themselves in debt to the banks, was followed by a political U-turn. ❼ Andrew Jackson (1829–1837) was the first president who was not from the Eastern elite. He pursued a "policy of the common man." In 1832–1836, he destroyed the Second Bank of the United States and developed an aid program for farmers and settlers. His style of "Jacksonian democracy" marked US politics until 1860. It involved the domination of the middle class over the economic elite, the development of the party system, and political dominance of the west and south over the northeast.

7 Andrew Jackson

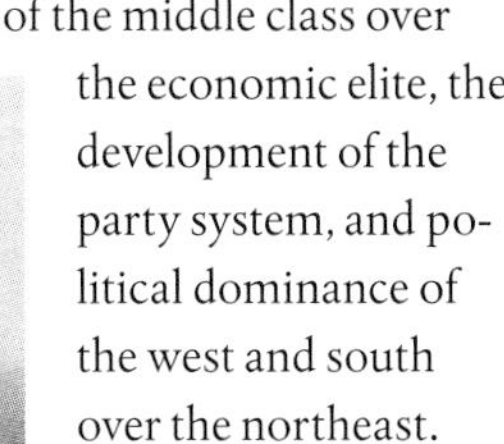

8 James K. Polk

Protective tariff laws that had been passed in 1828, over the vehement objection of the Southern states and their spokesman John Calhoun, led to the Nullification Crisis, a controversy over the right of states to negate federal laws. Jackson threatened the South with military intervention and in this way saved the Union.

9 Gold-diggers search for gold in a river, ca. 1890

Starting in 1830 Jackson implemented a ruthless Indian policy. ❺ Indian tribes were forced west to ❻ unclaimed territories or were settled in ❹ reservations that were constantly encroached upon by the relentless expansion.

Texas declared its independence from Mexico in 1836. Mexico then sent military forces to reestablish its authority. After a series of defeats, including the massacre of American settlers by Mexican troops at the Alamo in San Antonio in March 1836, the Texans finally crushed the Mexican army at San Jacinto.

A period of US weakness ended with the presidency of ❽ James K. Polk (1845–1849). Polk proclaimed that it was the "manifest destiny" of US citizens to inhabit the whole continent, and he pushed the admittance of Texas as a state through Congress in March 1845. With this, he knowingly provoked a ❿ war with Mexico, which began in June 1846. The US troops were victorious. In February 1848, Mexico was forced to sue for peace, and California and New Mexico were annexed. Furthermore, the government had signed the Oregon Treaty with Great Britain, securing the territory between the Rocky Mountains and the Pacific for the United States. The US-Canadian border was set at the 49th parallel.

By 1848, the territory of the United States had doubled once more and gold mines were discovered in California. The ❾ Gold Rush began. In the Western towns, it was the "law of the gun" that reigned.

5 Geronimo, the last Apache chief

The Nullification Crisis

In November 1832, the state of South Carolina under John Calhoun's leadership threatened secession from the Union—a threat later made good in 1860. President Jackson spoke of treason and made preparations for military intervention, but escalation was averted. The conflict, which smoldered until the Civil War, began at a presidential dinner in April 1830. Jackson proposed a toast: "Our federal Union—it must and shall be preserved," whereupon Calhoun countered: "Our Union—next to our liberties, most dear."

10 Capture of the capital of Mexico by US troops under General W. Scott, September 14, 1847

1829 | Andrew Jackson becomes president
1830 | "Indian Removal Act"
1836 | Independence of Texas
1845 | James K. Polk becomes president
Mar 1845 | Texas admitted
Jun 1846 | War against Mexico
5 Jun 1848 | Oregon Treaty

The Start of the Civil War

In protest over the election of antislavery candidate Abraham Lincoln as president of the United States in 1860, eleven Southern states seceded from the Union. In consequence a bloody civil war began in 1861.

1 Slaves on a cotton farm in the southern states, wood engraving, 1885

The unresolved issue of ❶ slave ownership created a deep chasm between the overwhelmingly middle-class, commerce-oriented Northern states and the patriarchal, agrarian South. Slavery had already been abolished in all states north of Maryland by the end of the 18th century, but the South, with its extensive plantation economy, could not survive without the slave labor that constituted the work force.

The dispute heated up again following the war against Mexico in 1848 when newly acquired territories—California, New Mexico, and Texas—were to be incorporated into the Union as states. The North wanted to ban slavery in all of them; the South wanted it to be the prerogative of the individual states to decide. Internal disagreement over the slavery issue weakened the leading Democratic party, while diverse antislavery factions gathered in the new Republican party. In 1860, for the first time, a Republican candidate, Abraham Lincoln, won the presidential election (1861–1865). Thereupon, South Carolina seceded, declaring its independence from the Union in protest. Another ten states (Mississippi, Florida, Alabama, Georgia, Louisiana, Texas, Virginia, Arkansas, Tennessee, and North Carolina) joined in seceding, and in February 1861 they formed the Confederate States of America with its own constitution and president, ❸ Jefferson Davis.

On 12 April 1861, troops from South Carolina fired upon the Union troops stationed in ❹ Fort Sumter in Charleston, and the ❷ American Civil War began. After initial Confederate successes, the momentum changed in favor of the Union in 1863.

2 Defeat of the Union troops in the battle of Bull Run, July 21, 1861

4 Attack at Fort Sumter in Charleston, 1861

3 Jefferson Davis

The Republican Party

The Republican party was formed in 1854 by the unification of antislavery factions from the Democratic and Whig parties. Its foremost goal initially was to engineer the repeal of the Kansas-Nebraska Act of 1854, which allowed the western territories to implement slavery. The Republicans were represented and supported chiefly in the northern and western states.

Abraham Lincoln

Abraham Lincoln, Gettysburg Address, November 19, 1863

"It is rather for us to be here dedicated to the great task remaining before us—that from these honored dead we take increased devotion to that cause for which they gave the last full measure of devotion—that we here highly resolve that these dead shall not have died in vain—that this nation, under God, shall have a new birth of freedom—and that government of the people, by the people, for the people, shall not perish from the earth."

6 Nov 1860 | Abraham Lincoln elected president
24 Dec 1860 | South Carolina secedes
18 Feb 1861 | Jefferson Davis President of "Confederate States of America"
12 Apr 1861 | American Civil War begins
1–3 Jul 1863 | Battle at Gettysburg
9 Apr 1865 | End of Civil War

The Union's Victory and Reconstruction

From the victory of the Union in 1865 until 1877, American politics were dominated by disputes over the reconstruction of the ruined South in the wake of the Civil War. The construction of the transcontinental railroad brought with it economic growth .

5 Celebratory procession following the abolition of slavery, 1865

At the beginning of 1864, Lincoln appointed General ❼ Ulysses S. Grant as supreme commander of the Union forces. Grant forced the Confederacy's leading general, ❽ Robert E. Lee, to surrender on April 9, 1865, at Appomattox, Virginia, in effect ending the war. Five days later, Lincoln was shot and killed by a fanatic Southerner in Washington, DC. On December 18, 1865, slaves were ❺ liberated through the 13th amendment to the constitution.

Like Lincoln, his successor, Andrew Johnson (1865–1869), advocated a Reconstruction policy of reconciliation with the South, which was so devastated that its agricultural production would not reach even half its 1860 level until 1870. The majority of the radical Republicans in Congress, however, insisted on a thorough dismantling of governmental and social structures, and they installed military administrations to control the Southern states.

The Freedman's Bureau, which was set up in 1867 for the protection of the freed slaves, was overwhelmed by the more than three million liberated slaves—almost half of the Southern states' total population. Social attitudes in the South were slow to change, especially in relation to civil rights for former slaves. A racist movement that encompassed numerous secret societies, the largest being the ❻ Ku Klux Klan, terrorized the freed slaves. Fundamental reform of Southern society stalled in its initial stages under Grant, who was less successful as president (1869–1877) than he had been as a general. His second term in office was overshadowed by corruption scandals.

Following the withdrawal of Union troops from the South in 1870 and the official end of Reconstruction, the old systems of white supremacy soon crept back again onto the plantations, if not as open slavery. At the end of the 19th century, strict racial segregation was introduced, affecting schools, public transportation, and restaurants.

After the Civil War, the North experienced a strong economic upswing, particularly through the construction of the ❾ transcontinental railroad. By 1893, five rail lines had been completed, opening up the thinly-settled West.

7 Ulysses Grant, commander of Union forces

8 Robert Lee, commander of Confederate forces

6 Procession of the Ku Klux Klan

9 Atlantic Pacific Railway, 1868

Indian Uprisings

Sitting Bull

The opening of the West by settlers, gold miners, and the railroad was carried out at the expense of the Native Americans. Their land was ruthlessly expropriated, they were resettled in reservations, and tribes that defended their territory were dealt with harshly, even annihilated. Among the largest conflicts was the Battle of the Little Bighorn in 1876, where the Sioux led by Chief Sitting Bull overwhelmed an attacking expedition led by George Armstrong Custer. When a new uprising threatened in 1890, an attempt was made to arrest Sitting Bull, during which he was killed. Two weeks later, on December 29, 1890, the US Cavalry massacred 200 Sioux at Wounded Knee in South Dakota.

The Battle of Little Bighorn

1865 | Lincoln assassinated

18 Dec 1865 | Final liberation of the slaves

24 Dec 1865 | Foundation of Ku Klux Klan

May 1869 | Transcontinental railroad finished

29 Dec 1890 | Massacre at Wounded Knee Creek

Economic Rise

The rapid growth of US cities between 1877 and 1897, swelled by immigrant labor and industrial workers, was accompanied by social and economic problems.

"Haymarket Riots," Chicago, 1886

State Street, Chicago, 1903

The rise of the United States as a world power began with its rapid economic progress. Following the construction of railroads, the discovery of ❹ oil led to further economic expansion and wealth as well as capital for further economic investment. John D. Rockefeller founded the Standard Oil Company in 1870, creating the first "trust" in the United States; by 1911, it controlled about 90 percent of the oil business. In 1873, Andrew Carnegie began building up the steel industry.

The rapid growth of the ❷ cities and the steady rise in the number of predominantly destitute ❸ immigrants from Europe and Asia led to the development of ethnic neighborhoods in the big cities and a huge rise in number of industrial workers. There were no binding regulations covering labor conditions. Wildcat strikes and acts of violence were the order of the day, and unions were organized only locally.

The ❶ "Haymarket Riots" in May 1886 demonstrated the urgent need for social solutions. Two days after police shot six strikers during a mass demonstration, twelve people, including several police, were killed in a bomb attack. Four "anarchists" were hanged as a result, although there was no proof of their guilt. The Haymarket affair directly inspired the celebration of May 1st as International Workers' Day.

While the unions were consolidating their organization, the economic middle class demanded that politics finally be brought into line with the expansive economic development of the country. An explosive issue was protective tariffs, which favored the sale of American over foreign goods within the United States, but also hurt those sectors that were dependent on imported commodities. President Grover Cleveland (1885–1889 and 1893–1897), an opponent of prohibitively high tariffs, was unable to prevent his successors from placing record tariffs on dutiable goods in 1890 (the "McKinley Tariff") and 1897 (the "Dingley Tariff"). By 1909, protective tariffs were set at 57 percent.

In 1893, a collapse of the foreign markets and risky speculation by the trusts resulted in a serious economic crisis in the United States.

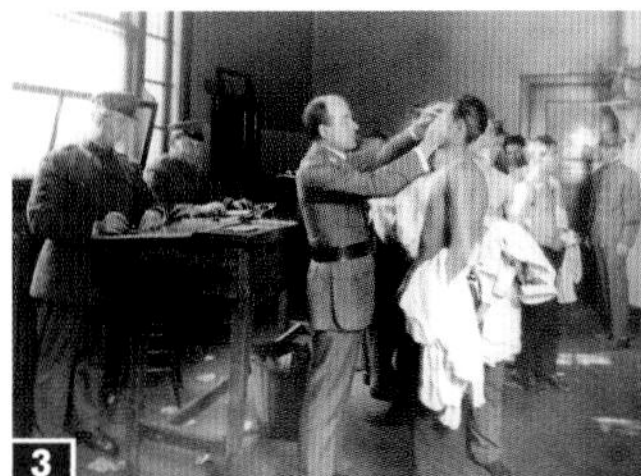
Medical examination of immigrants, Ellis Island, New York, 1900

The Trusts

A trust (short for "trusteeship") is an amalgamation of formerly independent companies into a single joint-stock company with the goal of controlling the market, that is, creating a monopoly in a specific industrial sector. In contrast to a cartel, a trust is a tightly organized unit of administration and capital. Since trusts were first created, the US government has been trying to abolish them to ensure free competition, though often with only moderate success. Important US antitrust laws include the Sherman Act (1890), the Elkins Act (1903), and the Federal Trade Commission and Clayton Act (1914).

"Standard Oil" share

J. D. Rockefeller, 1936

Oil field in California, 1925

1870	Foundation of "Standard Oil Company"	1–4 May 1886	"Haymarket-Riots"	25 Apr 1898	Declaration of war on Spain
since 1873	Development of the steel industry	1890–97	Setting of the protective tariffs at over 50%	6 Sep 1901	McKinley assassinated

The Policy of Imperialism

In 1897–1898, McKinley and Roosevelt intensified US imperialistic expansion into Latin America and the Caribbean regions. President Wilson concentrated on domestic and internal policies after 1913, but the political situation in the world forced him to enter the World War I on the side of the Allies in 1917.

Republican William McKinley was the first "modern" president of the United States (1897–1901). He strengthened the personal authority of the president, raised protective tariffs, introduced the gold standard for the dollar, and built up the confidence of commerce, industry, and the labor unions in the government. In 1898, McKinley intervened in Cuba's fight for liberation from Spain. The interest of the government directed itself toward the new markets and sources of raw materials of Latin American and the Pacific region all the way to the Far East. Cuba became a republic in the Treaty of Paris, and the Philippines, Guam, and Puerto Rico were ceded by Spain to American possession, which led in 1899 to the formation of a critical anti-imperialism league in Democratic circles.

Following McKinley's assassination in September 1901, his successor Theodore Roosevelt (1901–1909) stepped up the expansion policy. Domestically, he brought about more effective control of the trusts and actively settled labor disputes. Reelected in 1904, he intervened in several Central American countries and mediated the Russo-Japanese War of 1904–1905, for which in 1906 he became the first American awarded the Nobel Peace Prize. After installing a US-dependent government in Panama in 1903, Roosevelt acquired control of the Canal Zone for the United States and had the ❺ Panama Canal built (dedicated 1914), connecting the Atlantic and Pacific oceans. In 1913, ❻ Woodrow Wilson brought the Democrats to power again (1913–1921). Wilson curbed the expansion policy and concentrated more intensely on domestic issues. His "New Freedom" program aimed at social reform. Wilson followed a liberal cultural policy and promised to respect the rights of other nations.

Wilson responded to the outbreak of World War I with a declaration of neutrality. His course was controversial, but his promise of noninterference secured him reelection in 1916. However, he was pushed into action particularly by Republicans, especially since unrestricted submarine warfare was affecting US shipping. With the approval of Congress, Wilson declared ❼ war on Germany on April 6, 1917.

5 Opening journey on the Panama Canal 1914

President McKinley on the Monroe Doctrine

"Isolation is no longer possible or desirable. The period of exclusiveness is past. The expansion of our trade and commerce is the...problem. Commercial wars are unprofitable. A policy of good-will and friendly trade relations will prevent reprisals."

above: William McKinley

6 President Woodrow Wilson

The Roosevelt Corollary

On December 6, 1904, President Theodore Roosevelt amended the Monroe Doctrine with his own "Roosevelt Corollary." He proclaimed an American right to intervene in the Western Hemisphere (Latin America and the Pacific region) and justified the entitlement of the United States to exercise international police powers in Latin America. The role of the United States as a "world policeman"—which remains controversial to this day—began with him.

Theodore Roosevelt

7 American soldiers set sail for Europe, 1917

14 Sep 1901 | Theodore Roosevelt becomes prasident
6 Dec 1904 | Proclamation of the "Roosevelt Corollary"
1913 | Woodrow Wilson becomes president
15 Aug 1914 | Panama Canal opens
1916 | Reelection of Wilson
6 Apr 1917 | US declares war on Germany

Latin America 1810–1914

When Napoleon occupied the Iberian Peninsula, the Spanish and Portuguese colonies in Latin America saw the defeat of the European metropoles as an opportunity for self-determination. In the next two decades, most of the South American states were able to gain independence under the leadership of the native Creoles—the descendents of Spanish colonists. Brazil was the only country to free itself from its motherland without military battles, however. Civil wars and internal political struggles shaped events in most of the states of Latin America for a long time after independence. The political organization of the states alternated between ❶ monarchies, dictatorships, and republics.

1 Emperor's palace in Petropolis near Rio de Janeiro, Brazil, built in 1845

The South American Wars of Independence

Simón Bolívar fought for the independence of Venezuela and Colombia, while José de San Martín liberated Chile. Together the two commanded forces that expelled the Spaniards from Peru and the rest of the continent.

❷, Simón Bolívar (1783-1830), one of the leaders of the Wars of Independence, was born into an aristocratic family of Spanish descent in Caracas, Venezuela. After his mother's death when he was nine years old, he spent several years in Spain, where he formed a poor impression of the Court of Charles IV. After two years in revolutionary France, he returned to ❸ Venezuela but was again in Paris for the coronation of Napoleon Bonaparte as Emperor. Together with ❹ Francisco de Miranda, the "Father of South American Independence," he helped free Venezuela from Spain in 1811–1812, although Spain was later able to reestablish its rule. From New Granada (which included present-day Colombia), he resumed his battle, and Venezuela was again freed in 1817. In 1819 Bolívar announced the unification of Venezuela with New Granada to create Gran Colombia, of which he became the first president. Panama joined Gran Colombia in 1821 and Ecuador was added in 1822.

2 Simón Bolívar

To the south, local elites in Río de La Plata province had used the weakness of the central government in Napoleonic Spain to dislodge the viceroy in 1810. In 1816 a congress in Tucamán proclaimed the independence of the United Provinces of Rio de La Plata (present-day Argentina, Uruguay, Paraguay, and Bolivia). Once the local Spanish forces had been expelled from the northwest of the region in a series of pitched battles, an Argentine army under ❺ José de San Martín set off to free Chile and Peru. Along with the Chilean revolutionary Bernardo O'Higgins, San Martín crossed the Andes mountains. The rebel army beat the Spanish in 1817 at Chacabuco, and he was able to proclaim the independence of Chile in 1818. When San Martín marched on to Peru and reached ❻ Lima, the Spanish had already abandoned the town and Peru declared itself independent in 1821. San Martín became president and joined the army of Simón Bolívar, who had marched down to Peru from the north. The battles at Junín and Ayacucho in Peru in 1824 marked the end of metropolitan Spain's dominion over South America.

4 Francisco de Miranda

3 The "Libertador" Simón Bolívar entering Caracas, Venezuela, in 1813

5 Unveiling of the memorial for José de San Martín, 1909

The city of Lima, ca. 1850

1816 | United Provinces of Rio de La Plata
1817 | Battle of Chacabuco
1817 | Independence of Venezuela
1818 | Independence of Chile
1819 | Gran Colombia established
1821 | Independence of Peru
1824 | Battles at Junín and Ayacucho
1828 | Santa Cruz takes power

Development after Independence

Once independence had been achieved, many of the new South American states experienced political turbulence and military dictatorships.

When Peru and Venezuela seceded from Gran Colombia in 1830, ❽ Bolívar resigned and the country broke up into New Granada—after 1861, Colombia—Bolivia, and Ecuador. During a civil war in Bolivia in 1828, the Peruvian general Andrés Santa Cruz took power and forced the unification of Bolivia with Peru in 1836. However, before long Argentina and Chile dissolved this confederation and deposed Santa Cruz.

8 Simón Bolívar

In the following decades General Ramón Castilla was able to bring stability to Peru. The country experienced an economic revival, and the raw materials guano and niter brought wealth. In Bolivia, however, internal stability continued to prove elusive. Bloody civil wars shook the country. Similar struggles took place in many of the other newly independent Southern American countries: At the center of these conflicts lay disagreements over the political structure of the state.

In Argentina, the policies of General Juan Manuel de Rosas, who sought national unity through authoritarian means, brought stability to the country for a long time. In 1852, ❼ General Justo Urquiza toppled the dictatorship and, once the federal constitution came into effect, became president of the Republic of Argentina. The province of ⓫ Buenos Aires, which had been forced to accept the constitution during the civil war, rose up under General Bartolomé Mitre in 1861 and established his presidency. The 1879–1880 "conquest of the desert," led by Julio Argentino Roca against the Indians, brought the country huge areas of agricultural land in the ❾ pampas. With Chile he agreed on the division of Tierra del Fuego. The United States acted as adjudicator for a dispute in which Argentina seized regions of Brazil in 1895, and in 1902, through the mediation of Great Britain—which had conquered the Falkland Islands in 1833—it gained ❿ Patagonia from Chile.

Chile only managed to expel the last Spanish troops in 1826. The restorative constitution of General Joaquín Prieto was opposed by the liberals until 1859, but to no avail. Prieto's and the succeeding governments worked toward a stable internal political situation, which helped to bring about an economic and cultural resurgence. The mining of copper, silver, and niter, the opening-up of markets for agricultural products, the development of ship and rail transport networks, and the improvement of education, were the cornerstones of this boom. In 1891, acting president José Manuel Fernández was toppled, and the ensuing civil war ended with the storming of the capital, Santiago, at the cost of more than 10,000 lives.

7 General José de Urquiza is killed on April 11, 1870, in San José

9 Ostrich hunting on horseback in the Argentinian pampas

Nitrate War 1879–1883

In 1879, a Chilean nitrate company in Antofagasta, then part of Bolivia, objected to a tax increase. Chile then occupied the port and conquered the provinces of Tacna and Arica in Peru, an ally of Bolivia. Bolivia gave up the fight, and Chile occupied Lima, Peru, in 1881. Under the Treaty of Ancón, signed on October 20, 1883, Peru lost Tacna, Arica, and Tarapacá to Chile. With the loss from Antofagasta and the province of Atacama, the Bolivian state no longer had access to the sea.

above: Nitrate is quarried in Chile

10 Ushuaia, world's southernmost city, founded in 1868 on the Beagle channel, Tierra del Fuego Island, Argentina.

11 Buenos Aires, capital of an independent Argentina and its largest port city, in the 1840s

1830 | Decline of Gran Colombia
1831 | Government of Prietos in Chile
1852 | Fall of de Rosas' dictatorship in Argentina
1879–80 | "Conquest of the Desert"
1881 | Chilenian occupation of Lima
1879–1883 | Nitrate War
20 Oct 1883 | Peace of Ancón

Mexico in the 19th Century

Mexico won its fight for independence. Under alternating monarchies and republics, the gradual liberalization and development of the economy took place.

Antonio López de Santa Anna

Porfirio Diaz, Mexican president

General Agustín de Itúrbide signs the Mexican declaration of independence

In New Spain (Mexico), the demand for independence and self-determination grew as it did in the rest of Spanish America. In 1810 a village priest, Miguel Hidalgo y Costilla, called upon the people to fight the Spaniards. The declaration of independence was proclaimed in 1813 and a republican constitution decreed. The country did not officially become independent, however, until the military leader of the Creoles, ❸ Agustín de Itúrbide, allied with the leader of the rebellion, Vicente Guerrero, and proclaimed a monarchy in 1821. The Creole upper class and the higher clergy had joined with Guerrero to prevent the acceptance of a liberal Spanish constitution. Itúrbide reigned for a short period as Emperor Agustín I of Mexico, until he was toppled by ❶ Antonio López de Santa Anna in 1823.

A republican and federal constitution was adopted in 1824, and Guadalupe Victoria was elected president. The young republic was divided by conflicts between the proponents of a centralized state and those of a federalist system. Victoria was ousted by Santa Anna in 1833, who long maintained influence over politics in the country. The United States of Central America, which included most of the present Central American countries, seceded from the republic of Mexico in 1838–1839.

After a war against the US, Mexico was forced to cede its territory north of the Rio Grande in 1848. The US also intervened in its internal politics, supporting the liberal Benito Juárez against conservatives. As president, Juárez had plans to develop the country and sought to default on interest payments to foreign lenders. Upon hearing this, the countries concerned—Great Britain, Spain, and France—invaded Mexico City in 1863 and appointed the Austrian archduke Maximilian as emperor. However, Juárez reconquered the country and had ❹ Maxmilian shot in 1867 under martial law.

Through a coup d'ètat, the liberal General ❷ Porfirio Diaz came to power in 1876 and furthered internal peace and economic development. Under his government, the resentment of the landless peasants exploded in the ❺ Mexican Revolution of 1910 under the leadership of Emiliano Zapata, Francisco Villa, and Venustiano Carranza. Following the revolution's success, Carranza became president of Mexico and adopted a liberal constitution in 1917.

Execution of the Emperor Maximilian, painting by Édouard Manet, 1868–69

Supporters of the revolutionary Emiliano Zapata marching during the Mexican Revolution

The Mexican Revolution

After the reelection of Diaz, a revolution led by politicians broke out in 1910. Before long, however, this developed into an uprising of the peasants (campesinos) who had lost property due to Diaz's policies. In the south they fought under Zapata for the recovery of their lands; in the north under Villa, they fought for the independence of small agricultural undertakings. After a number of conflicts among the leaders, Carranza defeated the others and installed himself as president. In office he enacted agrarian reforms.

Zapata, portrait in a leaflet distributed in the Mexican revolution

1810 | Struggle for independence in Mexico begins
1821 | Official independence of Mexico
1825–27 | War between Brazil and Argentina
1825 | Independence of Brazil
1828 | Peace of Montevideo
1840–48 | War between the US and Mexico

Brazil in the 19th Century

Brazil was the only country of Latin America to gain its independence peacefully, separating from Portugal in 1822.

At the beginning of the 19th century, Brazil was the place of refuge for the Portuguese king John VI, under British naval escort, after he had been expelled by Napoleon. He made ❻ Rio de Janeiro the capital of the Portuguese kingdom. Rio was opened to international trade. Ministries and many other organs of government were established. Rio saw the construction of hospitals, theaters, libraries, naval and military academies, and a school of medicine. After the Congress of Vienna, John returned to Europe in 1821 to rule in Lisbon, while his son ❼ Pedro remained behind as regent. However, Pedro resisted the plans of Portugal's parliament to turn Brazil into a colony once again and put himself at the head of the Brazilian independence movement. This was influenced by autonomist movements and liberal ideas from all over the Continent. On September 7, 1822, he declared independence on the banks of the River Iparanga in Sao Paulo and in the same year was ❿ crowned Pedro I, emperor of Brazil. He was a constitutional monarch. After a campaign against Portuguese forces, in which a British admiral, Lord Cochrane, commanded the newly-formed Brazilian fleet, the Portuguese were forced to evacuate Bahia and in 1825 Portugal recognized Brazil's independence.

7 Pedro I, Emperor of Brazil

After a war with Argentina between 1825 and 1827, Brazil lost the province north of Río de La Plata—later Uruguay—in the Peace of Montevideo in 1828. This external failure, as well as conflicts with the parliament and the leading social classes, forced Pedro I to abdicate in 1831.

Under the liberal government of ❽ Pedro II after 1840, the country stabilized. The economy developed well, with a high rate of European immigration and the growth of ❾ coffee farming, particularly in the south of Brazil. The biggest internal problem was ⓫ slavery. When an influential group of opponents demanded its abolition, Pedro II outlawed it in 1888, but without compensating the slave owners. He thereby drove this powerful group into the republican camp. After an uprising by the garrison of Rio de Janeiro in 1889, under General Manuel Deodora da Fonseca in 1889, Brazil became a republic. Fonseca ensured he was the first president.

In 1891, an assembly decided on a new constitution for the United States of Brazil. Fonseca was deposed the same year by Floriano Peixotos, and a series of dictators followed. Up until the First World War, the territory of Brazil expanded due to treaties made with neighboring states. During the course of the war, industrialization began as new markets opened and the country's infrastructure was strengthened.

6 Copacabana district in Rio de Janeiro, ca. 1915

8 Pedro II, Emperor of Brazil, ca. 1870

9 Coffee farming in Brazil

10 Acclamation of Pedro I in Rio de Janeiro,1822

11 A slave being whipped in Brazil

2 Feb 1848 | Treaty of Guadalupe Hidalgo
1864 | Maximilian crowned emperor
1867 | Maximilian executed
1876 | Coup d'ètat by Porfirio Díaz
1888 | Slavery abolished in Brazil
1889 | Brazil becomes a republic
1910 | Mexican Revolution

The World Wars and Interwar Period

1914–1945

The first half of the 20th century saw the world entangled in two global wars, conducted with an unprecedented brutality. The First World War developed from a purely European affair into a conflict involving the colonies and the United States. It altered Europe's political landscape and shifted the power balance worldwide. In World War II, the nations of Europe, Asia, the Americas, and Africa were drawn into the conflict through the aggressive policies of an ambitious Nazi Germany. The war was conducted with the most up-to-date weapons technology and cost the lives of more than 55 million people. The Holocaust, the systematic annihilation of the European Jews, represented an unparalleled moral catastrophe for modern civilization.

The re-integration of war veterans was problematic to the societies of all nations who had participated in the World Wars; maimed war veterans often ended up begging on the streets.

1 The end of the European monarchs, caricature, 1918

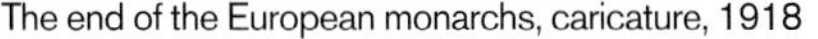

2 British geographers change the map of Europe

3 Parade in the Red Square, Moscow, 1927

The Age of World Wars

Rampant nationalism and an international arms race made European politics potentially explosive at the beginning of the 20th century. It took only the assassination of the Austro-Hungarian heir apparent in July 1914 to ignite a world war that tore apart the ❶ old state structures. Totalitarian political forces emerged, strengthened by the social and economic crises of the postwar period. In 1939, German Nazism plunged the world into the most devastating war in history. At the war's end in 1945, Europe lay in ruins.

Consequences of World War I: Reorganization of States

The First World War, waged with all the resources then available, shifted worldwide power relationships and redrew the ❷ map of Europe. Even the militarily victorious nations Great Britain and France were economically weakened by the war. The United States profited most from the war, replacing Great Britain as the dominant world power, and it sought to bring peace to Europe based on the principle of the right to national self-determination. The postwar order created in Paris by the victorious powers was contradictory, however. It became the source of new conflicts and thereby set the stage for the next war. The military losers bristled at being assigned sole responsibility for the war and saw the reparations that they had been saddled with as greatly unjust. Germany in particular, which was forced to cede its colonies and large parts of its empire, sought revisions in the treaty from the start. The breakup of the multicultural empires of Austria-Hungary and the Ottomans created unstable nation-states in Eastern and Central Europe with strong ethnic minorities. In the ❺ Near East, the victorious powers broke their promise to grant national independence. The former territories of the Ottoman Empire were divided into British, French, and international mandates. Great Britain's inconsistent posture toward Jewish immigration into Palestine set the groundwork for the Arab-Israeli conflict that would erupt after 1945.

5 Jews demonstrate for the right of free immigration to Palestine, New York, 1920s

Totalitarianism: Communism and Fascism

World War I mobilized and politicized whole nations for the first time. It shook up the established social order in many countries and led to revolts and revolutions. Centuries-old monarchies collapsed in Russia, Germany, Austria, and Hungary. Parliamentary democracies were established, with mixed success, in many places. The most momentous development proved to be the ❸ Bolsheviks' victory in Russia in 1917. The founding of the Soviet Union in 1922 influenced the internal development of the whole of Europe. The Soviet goal of a communist world revolution stirred up fears of left-wing communist uprisings by broad sections of the populace in the unstable European democracies of the ❹ postwar period. In response, new right-wing fascist factions gained strength everywhere. Although these varied greatly from country to country, they all had a militarily nationalist, radical antidemocratic and anticommunist position in common. These movements gained the upper hand in Germany and Italy against the backdrop of the worldwide economic depression. In Spain a fascist regime was establsihed only after a bloody civil war . Authoritarian systems also established themselves in South America, and a nationalist military leadership in Japan sought to establish a colonial empire in Asia. In China, the most populous nation of the world, nationalist and communist factions fought for control. Among the leading powers, only France, the United States and Great Britain retained their liberal democratic systems despite economic crises.

4 Paying out unemployment money, 1930

28 Jul 1914 | Start of World War I

1915 | Einstein's *General Theory of Relativity* published

1917 | Balfour Declaration

1919 | Treaty of Versailles

1922 | Founding of the Soviet Union

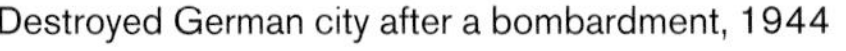
Destroyed German city after a bombardment, 1944

Alexander Fleming, the discoverer of penicillin, 1940

Assembly of cars on a production line, US, ca. 1940

Terror and Total War

An aggressive fascist movement gained power in Germany in the form of Hitler's National Socialist party. The German Reich started ❻ World War II in 1939 with the goal of reorganizing Europe according to Nazi racial theory. An extermination campaign was begun against entire ethnic groups in Eastern Europe, which culminated in the mass murder of millions of European Jews. The United States, Great Britain, and the Soviet Union formed an alliance that finally put an end to the Nazis' rule of terror and occupied Germany in 1945. Germany's ally Japan surrendered only after the first atomic bombs had been dropped. World War II, which was waged with highly developed technology and an enormous numbers of soldiers, cost the lives of more than 55 million people. The carpet bombing by the air forces claimed appalling numbers of victims and destroyed complete cities. As a result of the war, the Soviet Union and the United States rose to become the two world superpowers. After 1945, the differences between them, however, led to the ideological division of both Europe and the entire world.

The Dawning of Modern Mass Culture

The development of science and technology in the industrialized nations between the wars fundamentally altered daily life. In 1915, physicist ❾ Albert Einstein published his *General Theory of Relativity* and revolutionized the concept of time and space. In 1929, bacteriologist Sir Alexander Fleming discovered the medical use of ❼ penicillin. Thanks to the ❽ assembly line, the car became the means of transport for the masses. Life in the cities became more hectic and dynamic, as new and more efficient technology led to an increase in the pace of everyday life. Communication over further distances and within a shorter amount of time was made possible, and increasing numbers of people began to move further away from their place of origin in the search of work and happiness, aided by the new mobility given them by the car. New technology also revolutionized the entertainment industry: Radio and ❿ film sprung up as the dominant entertainment media. A consumer and leisure-oriented culture that set new fashions developed. Daily newspapers, made possible through cost-efficient technology that facilitated the mass production of the printed word, courted the favor of a growing number of readers. Neon advertising and oversize billboards established a new aspect of consumer-orientated commercialization on the streets. The entertainment industry with its ⓫ nightclubs and dance halls came to define a lifestyle associated with the mystique of the "Roaring Twenties."

The dancer Josephine Baker, star of the interwar period, ca. 1930

Albert Einstein, ca. 1930

Access to consumer goods and the spread of lifestyles through the media began to blur the lines between the middle class and the working class. The roles of the sexes began to change. The feminist movement achieved political emancipation; women's rights to vote and run for office were introduced in most of the industrial nations after 1918. Women also increasingly ⓬ entered paid employment, although they often remained blocked from positions of responsibility for a long time to come. These changes took place primarily in the industrialized United States and Europe. Much of the rest of the world took little part in this revolution, sometimes even countering the modern Western lifestyle with more traditional cultural beliefs and practices.

Myrna Loy and William Powell, film stars of the thirties

Geography students survey land, United States, 1920

1929 | Discovery of penicillin
1 Sep 1939 | Start of World War II
from 1929 | World economic crisis
30 Jan 1933 | Hitler comes to power in Germany
8 Aug 1945 | First atomic bomb dropped

The First World War 1914–1918

World War I is considered the "first calamity of the 20th century." Stemming from the imperialist policies of the European powers and the entwined alliances that resulted, the "Great War" claimed a total of around 10 million dead and 13 million wounded. The mobilization of whole nations and the previously unknown ❶ brutality of trench warfare triggered social upheavals, whose political and social consequences shaped the twentieth century.

Soldiers and mule wearing gas masks, 1916

The Outbreak of World War I

The immediate cause of the war was the assassination of the heir to the Austrian throne in June 1914. The "July Crisis" soon escalated as the alliance system saw the European powers mobilize one after another for war.

Following the ❸ assassination of Archduke Franz Ferdinand and his wife Sophie by Serbian nationalist Gavrilo Princip on June 28, 1914, in Sarajevo, Austria-Hungary wished to effect a quick retaliatory strike to restore its political influence over Serbia. As Russia supported Serbia and the German Reich supported Austria through their respective alliances, an escalating crisis threatened the peace of Europe.

The Great Powers stood behind their alliance commitments in the following month of frenzied diplomatic activity, known as the July Crisis. Austria's Emperor Franz Josef I delivered a highly provocative ❺ ultimatum to Serbia, after making sure of Germany's support; he was reassured by Kaiser Wilhelm II of his unconditional support—the so-called "blank check" conveyed on July 5–6, 1914. British attempts to mediate failed, and so Austria-Hungary declared war on Serbia on July 28, 1914.

Assassination of Franz Ferdinand in Sarajevo, June 28, 1914

Czar Nicholas II's Russia reacted with a ❷ general mobilization on July 30 that continued even after a German ultimatum demanded it end. The German Reich then declared war on Russia on August 1. Because France, an ally of Russia and a potential party to the war, was itself mobilizing troops, Germany felt threatened from both sides and two days later declared war on France as well. The extent to which German military planners engineered the war is still disputed by historians, but in the circumstances the best chance for a German victory in a two-front war lay in taking advantage of Russia's slow mobilization process by rapidly defeating France. The long prepared Schlieffen plan involved a rapid attack on France via Belgium. This inevitably drew Great Britain into the war since German troops thereby ❹ violated Belgium's neutrality. The British had long felt challenged by the aggressive ❻ navy-building policies of the German Kaiser, and British policy was not to allow a hostile power to gain control of the Flemish coast. Through the automatic inclusion of the British dominions Canada, Australia, New Zealand, and South Africa in the war, the conflict quickly became a global war. In Europe, as British foreign minister Edward Grey put it, "the lights went out."

Kaiser Wilhelm II talks to members of the navy, 1915

The Austrian envoy hands over the ultimatum to the Serbian government, July 1914

Czar Nicholas II meets Russian soldiers before they enter battle, August 1914

German troops march into Antwerp, August 1914

The Opponents in World War I:

The "Central Powers"
Austria-Hungary, Bulgaria, Germany, Turkey

The "Entente Powers"
Belgium, France, Italy (1915), Japan, Russia, Serbia, the United Kingdom and US (1917).

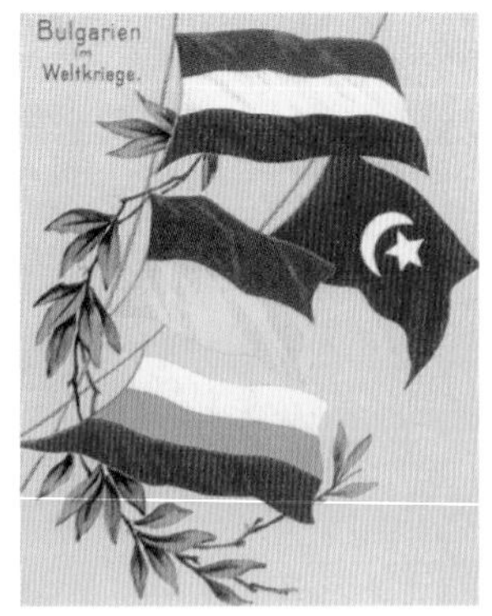

The flags of the Central Powers

28 Jun 1914 | Assassination in Sarajevo
Jul 1914 | July Crisis
28 Jul 1914 | Austria-Hungary declares war on Serbia
30 Jul 1914 | General mobilization in Russia
1 Aug 1914 | Germany declares war on Russia
3 Aug 1914 | Germany declares war on France

The Course of the War 1914–1916

The German westward advance was halted just 25 miles from Paris, and the Western Front then stagnated into trench warfare. The Central Powers gained territory in the east and southeast of Europe, but without decisively weakening the Entente powers.

Both the Germans and the French went to war on a wave of ❾ popular enthusiasm in August 1914. The first battles were actually fought on Belgian territory, however, because the French generals knew of the German plan to march into France through Belgium and met the advance. The swift march to Paris that had been hoped for by the Germans was stopped just short of Paris by a counteroffensive of the Entente powers. The Germans were forced to retreat by the "Miracle of the Marne." The Western Front then stagnated over a length of nearly 500 miles, and the years of ❼ trench warfare's deadly attrition began (p. 442).

From the start, both sides employed poison gas as a weapon of mass destruction. Following France's use of non-lethal tear gas in 1914, the Germans employed deadly chlorine gas for the first time in 1915 near Ypres in Flanders. Although expressly forbidden in the rules for land wars laid down by the 1907 Hague Conference, ❿ gas warfare was waged on all fronts.

On the Eastern Front, the Russian army marched into East Prussia in the middle of August 1914, but was defeated in the battles of Tannenberg and the Masurian Lakes and by February 1915 had retreated. The German army, led by Supreme Commander Paul von Hindenburg, then seized Russian Poland, Kurzeme, and Lithuania, after which the offensive became stuck in East Galicia. Attacks from both sides followed without significant gains, until the Russian Revolution of 1917 (p. 480) decisively changed the situation on the Eastern Front.

The Balkan region, where the conflict had begun with Austria-Hungary's declaration of war, became a second arena of conflict. ❽ Serbia was defeated by Central Powers troops in October 1915 to secure the land routes to the Ottoman Empire. The Entente allies Romania and Montenegro were also occupied at the end of 1916. Entente troops were forced back, taking a stand in Saloniki, and in 1917 forced Greece, which had been neutral up until then, into the war. But no major breakthroughs occurred on the boundaries of the Southeastern Front.

7 French soldiers biding their time in the trenches, 1915

Schoolhouse in Soldau, Serbia, destroyed during the Winter Battle of Masuria, 1915–16

9 German volunteers on a train to France, August 1914

10 Soldiers blinded by poison gas, 1918

Fritz Haber

The German chemist and Nobel prizewinner Fritz Haber gained dubious fame through his role in the arms race to produce chemical weapons. After the outbreak of war, he put his research institute at the disposal of the German military, and he personally supervised the first gas attacks on the front. He was also the scientist who developed the gas Zyklon B, which the Nazis later used to exterminate the Jews in their death camps. Haber himself had to flee Germany after 1933 because of his Jewish ancestry.

Fritz Haber

4 Aug 1914	German troops march into Belgium
4 Aug 1914	Great Britain declares war
26–30 Aug 1914	Battle of Tannenberg
6–15 Sep 1914	Battle of the Masurian Lakes
1915	Battle of Amselfeld
1916	Capture of Bucharest
1917	Russian Revolution

The War of Attrition on the Western Front

On the Western Front, the two sides ground each other down in the *Materialschlacht* ("battle of materials"). The entry of the US into the war tipped the balance in favor of the Entente Powers.

At the beginning of 1916, the German military leadership was determined to break the ❺ stalemate on the Western Front by any means. Without any real prospects of territorial gains, the aim of the subsequent war of attrition was to bleed the enemy into defeat. The months-long battle for ❷ Verdun became a fight for each foot of ground and resulted in 700,000 dead and wounded on each side. During the unsuccessful British-French counterattack on the ❸ Somme, 57,000 British soldiers died within the first hours; in total, more than a million died on both sides. Both of the battles demonstrated the pointless ❻ mass death of technological war and the serious effects on the psyche and morale of the soldiers. It had become impossible to launch a successful attack on deeply dug-in defensive positions without huge losses. Germany and France weakened each other with no prospect of a victory by either side. Due to these failings, the military leadership on both the French and German sides changed; Robert Nivelle took over from Joseph Joffre in France, and in Germany Erich von Falkenhayn was replaced by Hindenburg, who ultimately ended the attack on Verdun.

At sea, the superiority of the Entente powers—thanks primarily to the British war fleet—had been overwhelming from the beginning. Consequently, ignoring international law, Germany used its ❹ submarines to destroy merchant ships of both warring and neutral nations beginning in 1915. After the sinking of the ❶ *Lusitania*, a passenger steamer used to transport munitions on which 100 Americans also lost their lives, the United States broke its neutrality with vehement protests, causing Germany to terminate its unrestricted submarine warfare. However, after the Battle of Jutland at the end of May 1916, which caused heavy losses for the British, the German Reich decided to resume its unrestricted submarine warfare on February 1, 1917. The United States then declared war on Germany, and later on Austria-Hungary as well. With the ❼ entry of the United States into the war on the side of the Entente powers, the course of the war finally turned against the Central Powers. From then on, the Central Powers were at a hopeless material disadvantage.

1 The sinking of the torpedoed *Lusitania*, carrying American civilians, 1915

2 French propaganda poster with the exhortation to hold the fortress of Verdun, 1916

3 French artillery with British guns on the Somme, 1917

4 German navy poster: "Submarines out!," 1914

5 Improvised graves on the Western Front, 1916

6 English military cemetery on the Somme, drawing by Louis Étienne Dauphin, 1916

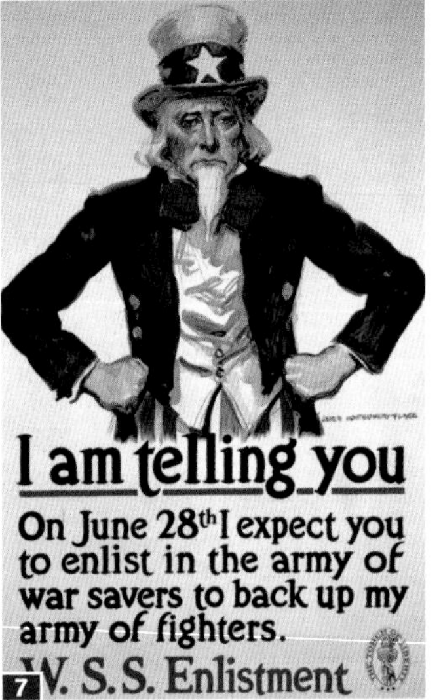

I am telling you
On June 28th I expect you to enlist in the army of war savers to back up my army of fighters.
W. S. S. Enlistment

7 US poster for the recruitment of volunteers, 1917

Psychology

World War I provided an endless stream of test subjects for the fledgling science of psychology. Many soldiers on the Western Front suffered from severe traumatic and hysterical disorders. In the face of bloody slaughters and confinement in the trenches, the soldiers turned into neurotic palsy victims and psychosomatic paralytics. Their example disproved the widely prevailing belief of the time that hysteria was nothing more than a "woman's illness."

8 Dec 1914 | Naval battle of the Falkland Islands

22 Feb 1915 | Beginning of unrestricted submarine warfare

7 May 1915 | Sinking of the *Lusitania*

21 Feb–21 Jul 1916 | Battle of Verdun

31 May–1 Jun 1916 | Naval battle of Skagerrak

24 Jun–26 Nov 1916 | Battle of the Somme

Secondary Theaters of War and the First Resistance Movements

The colonial possessions of the European powers meant that the theaters of war were spread throughout the world. Due to the enormous material and human sacrifice, the first mutinies occurred in 1917 on all sides.

The European colonial powers fought each other on the high seas worldwide. German cruisers fought under the flag of their Turkish allies in the Black Sea against Russia; they also destroyed a British cruiser squadron at Coronel, Chile. The British destroyed German warships at the Falkland Islands off the coast of Argentina. Japan joined the naval war of the Entente Powers as the first independent overseas ally in 1914 because Germany had been unwilling to relinquish its Chinese territorial holding of ❾ Kiaochow.

The Entente Powers fought in Africa for the German colonial possessions. Togo, Cameroon, and German Southwest Africa were conquered in the first years of the war. The Germans were able to hold onto German East Africa until the end of the war in 1918, but only with the help of the ⓫ Askari and other native soldiers.

In the Near East, the ❽ Ottoman Empire joined the Central Powers early on, but despite much support, it was unable to wage a multi-front war. Though successful against the British and Australians in the Gallipoli Peninsula in 1915, the Turks collapsed in Sinai and Palestine. The defeat of the Central Powers in 1918 resulted in the complete dismantling of the empire. Like Austria-Hungary, it was reduced to its core country, Turkey (p. 486).

In order to keep the worldwide machinery of war running, the domestic economies in the warring nations were adjusted to the needs of the ❿, ⓬ war industry. As the war went on hunger and malnutrition fostered resistance to the war—especially in Germany which was losing the war and suffering under a blockade. Discontent also spread to the front. In August 1917, German sailors refused orders because of the bad supply situation. The first civilian revolts took place in January 1918 when workers in German cities went on strike for a swift peace settlement, but the German military leaders continued fighting. Some resistance was seen in other countries as well. Mutinies of French soldiers on the Western Front occurred after battles involving heavy losses, and a group of Russian soldiers deserted after a failed offensive against the German army in May 1917, avowing friendship and brotherhood with the enemy.

8 Soldiers of the Ottoman army, part of the Axis alliance, 1916

11 Askari troops in German East Africa, 1915

12 Women working in the French war industry, 1915

9 German war postcard referring to the fight for Kiaochow, 1914

10 US poster with an appeal for the conservation of food supplies for the soldiers fighting in Europe, 1918

Aerial Warfare

For the first time, war was also waged in the air. The Germans employed the rather sluggish Zeppelin airship, while the British performed reconnaissance with small, maneuverable airplanes. Grenades were thrown by hand, and pilots fought dogfights over the front lines.

British plane hit by the German Luftwaffe, artist's impression

1 Feb 1917 | Unrestricted submarine warfare continues
6 Apr 1917 | US declares war on Germany
7 Dec 1917 | US declares war on Austria-Hungary
28 Oct 1918 | Mutiny of German deep sea fleet

The Collapse of the Central Powers and the Armistice 1918

Although the Entente had the advantage in every area after the United States entered the war, the Central Powers were unshakably set on a military victory.

After his electoral victory in 1916 ❶ US president Woodrow Wilson sympathized with the Allies and provided financial support to them. Under the slogan "Peace without victory" he supported the idea of a balancing peace, whereas France and Great Britain aimed for the complete defeat of the German Reich. On April 6th, 1917, the United States declared war on Germany because the latter insisted on maintaining its policy of unrestricted sinking of neutral merchant shipping by submarines, which could not rescue survivors. By June 1917, the first US troops had landed in France. On January 8, 1918, Wilson gave a speech proposing 14 points, which formed the basis of the later peace treaties, though significantly modified.

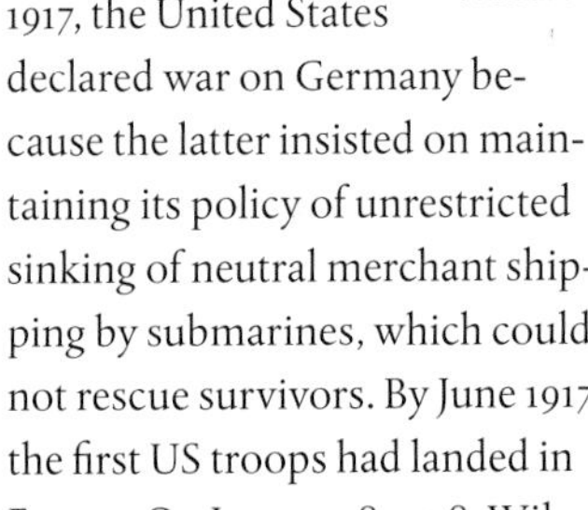
US President Thomas Woodrow Wilson

The most important provisions were the evacuation of all territories seized by the Central Powers, the ❷ return of Alsace-Lorraine to France, international disarmament, the right of all peoples to national self-determination, and the general joining together of all nations for the mutual guarantee of political independence and territorial integrity.

The German Reich, however, continued to pursue the goal of a "victorious peace," particularly given that there had been a permanent cease-fire on the Eastern Front since December 1917 after the revolutionary developments in Russia (p. 480). This had allowed substantial numbers of German troops to be switched to the Western Front. In the Treaty of ❸ Brest-Litovsk on March 3, 1918, the Central Powers coerced the Soviets to relinquish Poland and Kurzeme. Ukraine, and later the newly founded Baltic states, would also become formally independent but remained under German control. Portions of Georgia and Armenia fell to the Ottoman Empire.

The Germans' hopes for a military victory in the West after the end of the conflict in the East quickly proved to be illusory. After the Entente Powers' successful counter-offensive in the summer of 1918, German troops were pushed back all the way to the borders of the Reich. When, at the end of October, Germany's main allies, Austria and the Ottoman Empire, collapsed and made peace on their own, the German Reich was finally defeated. To avoid a bitter peace, the German government accepted the "14 Points" as the conditions for peace negotiations.

Signing of the Armistice of Compiègne, November 11, 1918

Marshal Pétain rides triumphant through a conquered Metz, 1918

Peace of Brest-Litovsk: Trotsky (right) and other Russian deputies on their way to the negotiation, 1918

The events in Germany came thick and fast. German sailors' refusal to put to sea for a naval battle on October 28, 1918, was the prelude to the ❺ November Revolution that ended in the overthrow of the monarchy (p. 448). On November 9, the kaiser ❻ abdicated and a German republic was proclaimed in Berlin. Two days later, Matthias Erzberger, as representative of the German Reich, signed the ❹ Armistice of Compiègne. The war was ❼ over.

German mutineers, November 1918

Wilhelm II leaves Berlin on November 9 for exile

Soldiers heading home

12 Dec 1916 | Germany's first offer of peace
22 Jan 1917 | Wilson propagates "peace without victory"
8 Jan 1918 | Proclamation of the "14 Points"
3 Mar 1918 | Treaty of Brest-Litowsk
3–4 Oct 1918 | Germany's peace offer to Wilson
23 Oct 1918 | Acceptance of "14 point" peace plan

The Peace Settlements

After a power struggle among themselves, the victorious powers agreed upon harsh peace terms for Germany in the Treaty of Versailles. The Germans were forced to take sole responsibility for the war and pay heavy reparations to the countries they invaded.

The victorious Allied powers met in January 1919 in Paris to discuss a new postwar order. The negotiations of the more than 100 delegates lasted into June. The peace discussions were dominated by the U.S. president ⓭ Woodrow Wilson, British prime minister ❽ David Lloyd George, French prime minister ❾ Georges Clemenceau, and to a lesser extent Italian prime minister Vittorio Emanuele Orlando. Neither defeated Germany nor Bolshevik Russia were invited.

8 David Lloyd George

The goals of the victorious powers were widely divergent. Wilson wanted to secure a permanent peace and create a corresponding organization with the formation of a League of Nations. Great Britain wanted to spare Germany—mostly out of fear that the defeated Central Power might embrace Bolshevism. France, on the other hand, wanted to fundamentally weaken its powerful neighbor. In the final Treaty of ❿ Versailles, a compromise prevailed, with harsh terms but no dismantling of Germany, and the US desire to establish a League of Nations. The German National Assembly at Weimar voted to accept the terms by 237 against 138. Germany ⓬ signed the peace terms on June 28, 1919, though with no real alternative.

9 Georges Clemenceau

Germany lost about 13 percent of its pre-war territory. Alsace-Lorraine was returned to France and Germany lost territory to Poland, Czechoslovakia, and Lithuania.The left bank of the Rhine was to be ⓫ demilitarized and occupied by the Allies; the German army was to be reduced to 100,000 men without a General Staff. The reparations had not yet been fixed in the treaty, but it was clear that the amount would be large; the German Reich ended up paying 53 billion marks in gold by 1932. The "War Guilt clause" that held Germany fully responsible for the war was particularly resented.

Separate peace treaties were signed with the other Central Powers. At St. Germain on September 10, 1919, the Austro-Hungarian Empire was dismantled. Austria (forbidden from uniting with Germany) and Hungary became two small states and had to recognize the independence of Czechoslovakia and Poland, as well as the loss of all other imperial territories. In the peace treaty of Sèvres of August 10, 1920, the Ottoman Empire was carved up in accordance with a prior agreement between the Allies: The Bosporus, the Dardanelles, and the city of Constantinople were placed under French and British control.

Graf Ulrich von Brockdorff-Rantzau, foreign minister of the Weimar Republic, in the peace negotiations at Versailles:

"We know the force of the hate that confronts us here. It is asked of us that we confess ourselves to be solely responsible for the war. Such an admission coming from my mouth would be a lie."

Graf Ulrich von Brockdorff-Rantzau

10 Conference room in Versailles, 1919

11 Decommissioning a German tank, 1920

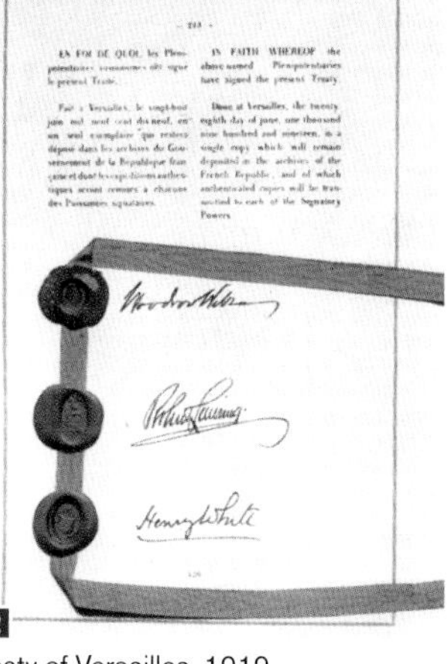
12 Treaty of Versailles, 1919

13 US President Wilson in Paris, 1918

Nov 1918	November Revolution
9 Nov 1918	Proclamation of the Republic
11 Nov 1918	Armistice of Compiègne
18 Jan 1919	Paris Peace Conference
28 Jun 1919	Signing of Treaty of Versailles
10 Sep 1919	Treaty of St.-Germain

Ideologies of the 20th Century

After the social and moral upheavals of World War I, the proponents of two opposing totalitarian political models for the restructuring of society came to power. With National Socialism, inhuman fascism triumphed over the democratic movement that had established the unstable and weak Weimar Republic in Germany. The other ideology that came to influence world politics was ❶ Communism. Both models saw themselves as a radical counterpoint to the "Western" model of a liberal democracy.

1 Communists Marx, Engels, Lenin, Stalin and Mao, Chinese poster

Democracy: Self-Determination of the Citizens

Abraham Lincoln described democratic rule, which is based on the principle of sovereignty of the people and the equality of all, as a "government of the people, by the people, for the people." The ❻ United States under President ❹ Woodrow Wilson justified its entry into World War I ideologically, stating that its aim was "to make the world safe for democracy."

After the war, demands for greater self-determination by groups sharing a cultural or national heritage led to electoral reforms in almost all countries of Europe. Initially the predominant form of democracy was that which

2 Polling station in Spain, 1936

relied on nonviolent party competition, guaranteed individual rights and minority rights, and let each citizen participate in elections according to the ❷ rule of the majority. In the face of the social crises of the postwar societies, however, many democratic governments were crushed between the radical right and radical left-wing parties. Of the major powers, only the traditional democracies of Great Britain and the United States proved immune to totalitarian promises of utopias for world happiness.

4 Woodrow Wilson

After World War II, liberal democracies reasserted themselves in Western Europe. Since the collapse of the Soviet Empire in 1989–1991, almost all of Eastern Europe and many other parts of the world have committed to democratic principles, although many struggle to establish a true democratic form of rule.

6 Stamp with the New York Statue of Liberty

Communism: Deliverance Claims and Paternal Dictatorship

With their 1848 *Communist Manifesto*, Karl Marx and Friedrich Engels conceptualized a new historic-philosophical theory that was used as the ideological foundation of the revolutionary workers' movements of the 20th century. The manifesto instructed the workers that their historical duty was to free all of mankind from repression and injustice ("Proletarians of the world, unite") inherent in society as it was in the early 20th century.

5 Call for the class struggle, 1919

Marx and Engels interpreted history as a series of ❺ class struggles between rulers and the ruled. Only with the historically necessary victory of the proletariat over the bourgeoisie would the free self-development of every human be possible. The middle-class capitalist society had to be overcome and the means of production converted to common property—only this would free humankind from all pressures.

3 Soviet propaganda poster, 1945

In the name of communism, the October Revolution led by Vladimir Lenin in 1918 triumphed in Russia, but the ❸ Union of Socialist Soviet Republics remained the only socialist country until 1945. There, a socialist "dictatorship of the proletariat" through a revolutionary party cadre was supposed to create the conditions for a future true communist "classless society." With their self-conception as the historical vanguard of a communist world revolution, the Soviet Communists under Lenin legitimized their absolute claim to leadership of all other Communist parties. Under Josef Stalin, the Soviet Union became a totalitarian dictatorship

1848 | *Communist Manifesto*
1918 | Wilson's "14 Points"
1918 | October Revolution in Russia
1920 | Mussolini comes to power in Italy
1922 | Founding of the Soviet Union
1933 | Hitler comes to power in Germany

and systematically eliminated its political opponents.

Only after the central role of the Soviet Union in World War II in the victory and the spread of Communism throughout the world did certain states seek their own, national form of communism. During the Cold War after 1945, a particular movement referred to as "Eurocommunism" emerged in many countries of the West. It evolved into socialism, represented throughout Europe by socialist parties within the democratic system. With the upheaval in Eastern Europe in 1989 and the collapse of the Soviet Union in 1991, Communism lost its power base. As the only major Communist power remaining, China ostensibly bases its authority on the state teachings of Marx and Engels.

7 Victory Parade of the fascist Falange in Spain, 1939

Fascism: Violence and the Cult of the Leader

The right-wing Italian nationalists around ❾ Benito Mussolini called themselves fascists, after the old Roman power symbol, the *fasces*—rods bundled around an ax. When he came to power in Italy in 1920, Mussolini set up a new type of dictatorship that was the forerunner and example—though never a totally emulated model—for fascist movements throughout the world.

11 Adolf Hitler, NS painting, 1935

In some European states, diverse authoritarian groupings

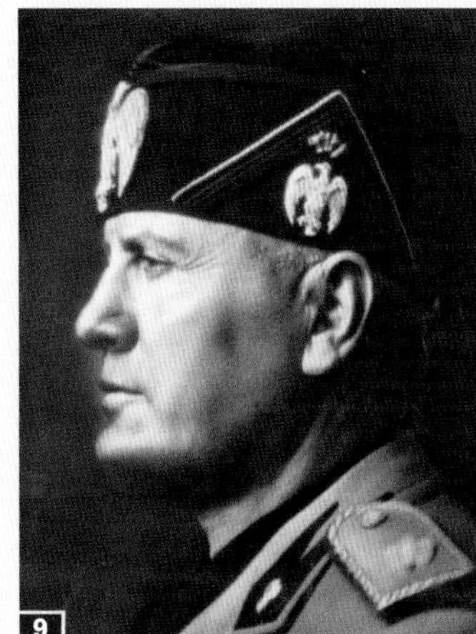
9 Benito Mussolini, 1935

with fascist traits won control over the state apparatus. After the ❼ civil war in Spain in 1939, General Francisco Franco set up a dictatorship. In Portugal, António de Oliveira Salazar created the "Estado Novo" ("New State"), while in Austria a particular form of Austro-fascism developed. In South America there were also authoritarian regimes with fascist characteristics. Notable similarities among these fascist movements included hierarchical organizational structures, the cult around a socially integrative leader figure, suggestive symbolism, and total mass mobilization that left hardly any rights to the individual. The state controlled all areas of life with its political police force.

Ideologically, the fascist state increasingly followed an "anti" ideology: antidemocratic and antiliberal, anticommunist and anticapitalist, antimodern, yet extremely nationalistic and prone to use violence as the decisive measure of politics. Racism, however, was not a central element of fascism. After World War II, fascism lost practically all significance.

National Socialism: Anti-Semitism and Ideology

German National Socialism or Nazism, with its leader (*Führer*) ⓫ Adolf Hitler, was in its state structure a particular variety of fascism. However, due to the central significance of anti-Semitism, race ideology, and the doctrine of ❽ *Lebensraum* ("living space"), in its political ideology, it had an unprecedentedly all-encompassing worldview. Nazism defined history as the battle between peoples for the expansion of each nation's *Lebensraum*. Ultimately the "racially most valuable" people, the Aryans, would rule as the master humans over the inferior peoples. Nazi propaganda defamed particularly the Poles, Russians, and Slavs as "subhuman." Hitler promoted the war in the East as the battle for *Lebensraum*.

The main enemy, in the National Socialist worldview, was ❿ "world Jewry," which did not want to recognize these "natural laws." The Jews were said to control international movements of all kinds—of democracy, pacifism, communism, and capitalism—and had destroyed the national "purity" of nations, according to Nazi philosophy.

8 "Blut und Boden"–The *Lebensraum* myth: Sword over the swastika, 1933

The central aim of the Nazis was therefore the persecution of Jews. Directly after coming to power in Germany, the Nazis began to force citizens of Jewish belief out of all areas by legal, economic, and criminal means, discriminating against them, disenfranchising them, and locking them up.

During World War II, the Nazi regime organized a factory model of mass murder of the European Jews. In the extermination camps, hundreds of thousands of Jews were systematically killed. In total, the number of Jewish victims was around six million. Further victims of Nazi terror included minorities such as the Sinti and

10 Anti-semitic NS Propaganda, 1942

Roma, homosexuals, and political opponents such as communists and socialists. After the victory of the Allies over Nazi Germany, the ideology of National Socialism was internationally outcast.

1939 | Franco dictatorship in Spain
27 Jan 1945 | Liberation of the concentration camp Auschwitz
1945 | Fall of the Nazi regime
1946 | Communist People's Republic of China
1989–90 | Democratic revolutions in Eastern Europe
1991 | Collapse of the Soviet Union

The Unpopular Democracy: The German Reich 1918–1933

Funeral of the victims of the November Revolution, Berlin, Jan 1918

Parliamentary democracy prevailed in Germany in the ❶ revolution of 1918. However, it was never completely accepted by a broad section of the population, and its existence was threatened from the start by radical political forces. The feeling of national humiliation, economic problems, and the internal weaknesses of the democracy made possible the rise of National Socialism under Adolf Hitler, who was named chancellor of the republic in 1933.

The First Years of the German Republic

Hyperinflation and attempted coups from groups from across the political spectrum kept the republic from finding peace and stability in its early years.

The German monarchy collapsed in the wake of social unrest in November 1918. Social Democrat ❷ Friedrich Ebert took over responsibility for the government in the transitional period. The moderate left emerged triumphant in debates at worker and soldier councils over the question of the form of government. A national assembly in Weimar drafted a democratic constitution on January 19, 1919, and established a parliamentary republic with Ebert as president. Fearing Karl Liebknecht would proclaim a socialist republic, another Social Democrat, ❸ Philipp Scheidemann, proclaimed the German Republic on November 11.

Philipp Scheidemann talks to the people, reconstructed picture, 1918

The radical left felt betrayed by the government due to the lack of social measures. The military suppressed ❹ revolts and voluntary military groups, known as *Freikorps* ("Free Corps"), made up of soldiers returning from the war, terrorized the country. Officers of the Freikorps murdered Liebknecht and Rosa Luxemburg, the leaders of the German Communist party.

The right wing considered the government, which had signed the "dishonorable treaty of Versailles" (p. 445) to be agents of the French state—"fulfillment politicians". The signatory of the armistice, Matthias Erzberger, was murdered by right-wing extremists. The ❻ monarchist Kapp Putsch in 1920 and Hitler's 1923 Beer Hall Putsch, were crushed. The finances of the German Reich were catastrophic; the war had consumed vast sums and the victorious powers demanded reparations. To avoid bankruptcy, more money was printed and ❺ inflation skyrocketed. In October 1923, a US dollar cost 40 billion reichsmarks.

Friedrich Ebert, ca. 1918

Government troops during the general strike in Berlin, March 3–12, 1919

Banknote of the German Reichsbank, November 15, 1923

Distribution of flyers during the Kapp Putsch, March 1920, in Berlin

The Hitler Beer Hall Putsch 1923

Adolf Hitler, who was previously unknown, attempted to establish a right-wing dictatorship in Germany with a "March on the Feldherrnhalle" (Bavarian War Ministry) in Munich on November 9, 1923. While in prison following the suppression of the putsch attempt, he wrote his ideological work Mein Kampf. Hitler was released early for good behavior in 1924 and promised to seek power by legal means.

After the failed coup of the NSDAP: the accused; in the middle the main initiators Kriebel, Ludendorff and Hitler, Munich, February 1924

9 Nov 1918 | Transitional government under Ebert
15 Jan 1919 | Liebknecht and Luxemburg murdered
19 Jan 1919 | Weimar constitution passed
13–17 Mar 1920 | Kapp Putsch
1922 | Inflation begins
Fall 1923 | "Cabinet of the Great Coalition"

The Fall of the Weimar Republic

After a short interim of stabilization, Hitler's National Socialists received a boost from the world economic depression. With the aid of the German National party, Hitler took over power in Germany in 1933.

The republic seemed to settle down to transient stability after 1924. The economy recovered with a new currency and the regulation of reparations payments under the Dawes Plan. Culturally, Berlin was a world leader. Foreign Minister Stresemann pursued a path of reconciliation with Germany's neighbors, recognizing the western border with France in the ❼ Locarno Treaty of 1925. Germany signed a friendship and neutrality treaty with the Soviet Union and was accepted into the League of Nations.

The election of the committed monarchist Paul von Hindenburg as president in 1925, however, symbolized the republic's disfavor among a wide section of the population. The world economic depression in 1929 strengthened the enemies of the state and initiated the disintegration of democracy. After the collapse of Hermann Müller's Social Democratic government in 1930, President Hindenburg named Heinrich Brüning chancellor by emergency decree, responsible solely to the president and not to the parliament. Brüning's economic policies increased ❽ mass unemployment; by the beginning of 1933 there were almost six million people out of work.

Growing poverty, fear of losing social status, and the lack of prospects drove many, particularly the middle class and youths, into the hands of Adolf Hitler's radical ❾ National Socialist German Workers' party (NSDAP)—the Nazi party—and presented it with an enormous increase in votes in the 1930 Reichstag election. The anti-Semitic and nationalistic smear campaign against the system and the "November criminals" popularized the ⓫ "dagger thrust legend," according to which the German politicians of the revolution of 1918 had stabbed the undefeated German army in the back by signing a peace treaty with the Allies. When in 1932 the National Socialists became the strongest party after the elections, the Center Party attempted to profit from the Nazis' mass popularity by joining them in a coalition supporting the "Enabling Act."

9 Election poster of the NSDAP, 1932

On January 30, 1933, President ❿ Hindenburg named Hitler chancellor of the National Socialist–DNVP coalition. "In two months we will have pushed Hitler into a corner so that he squeaks," promised Vice Chancellor Franz von Papen, who was allied with the DNVP—a statement that would quickly prove to be a fatal miscalculation.

7 **From left**: Gustav Stresemann, Austen Chamberlain, Aristide Briand, the Locarno Treaty, 1925.

8 Unemployed workers read job listings, Berlin, 1932

The "Golden Twenties"

Berlin was an open-minded metropolis with a thriving art and cultural scene throughout the Weimar Republic period. Be it the silent films of Fritz Lang, the new Expressionism in painting and poetry, the political theater of Bertolt Brecht, or the glamour of the entertainment industry, personified by Marlene Dietrich, for example—cultural life in the German capital was vibrant and drew intellectuals from all over the world. The victory of National Socialists in Germany abruptly put an end to this creative epoch.

top: Actress Brigitte Helm, 1929
above: Playwright Bertolt Brecht, 1930

10 Hindenburg and Hitler drive through Berlin, 1933

11 The "Stab in the Back" propaganda picture, 1924

8–9 Nov 1923 | Beer Hall Putsch
16 Aug 1924 | Dawes Plan
1925 | Locarno Treaty
Apr 1925 | Hindenburg elected president
30 Mar 1930 | Brüning named chancellor
Jul 1932 | NSDAP becomes strongest party
30 Jan 1933 | Hitler named chancellor

1 Imperial eagle and swastika, symbols of National Socialist ideology

Under the Swastika: Nazi Germany

1933–1939

With Hitler's takeover of power, a twelve-year totalitarian regime began in Germany. In 1939 it brought war and racist terror to the world. The "Führer"-led dictatorship attempted to reform state and society to conform to ❶ National Socialist ideology. Despite the Nazis' brutal suppression of the opposition and single-minded removal of the Jewish population from national life, the world underestimated the nature of the regime and its contempt for human life, and thus World War II erupted.

Setting Up the Dictatorial "Führer State"

Within a very short time, Hitler controlled the state institutions in Germany and the Nazi party and dissolved the democratic structures of the Weimar Republic.

The restructuring of the German state from a democracy to a dictatorship took place between January 30, 1933, and August 2, 1934. When it was over, all power was united in the person of ❷ Adolf Hitler. Without formally repealing the Weimar constitution, the Nazi ideology (p. 445) was able to dominate state and society as apparently legal prerequisites were created to invalidate the democratic constitution.

After the ❹ burning of the Reichstag building in Berlin on February 27, 1933, the Nazi party's private army—the storm troopers or SA—began the first acts of persecution against Social Democrats and Communists.

Moreover, Hitler used the opportunity to suspend basic political rights by emergency decree. This made the persecution of political rivals legal and removed it from state intervention or control.

In the last semi-free election on March 5, 1933, the Nazis failed to gain an absolute majority despite massive intimidation of the public. In the first session of parliament, all the legislators—except the Social Democrats and Communists, who had already been arrested—approved an ❻ "Enabling Act" that transferred full legislative power to Hitler's party government.

The Nazi government did away with German federalism and instituted one-party rule. By 1934, the state parliaments had all been dissolved and replaced by regime-conforming "Reich governors." After the Social Democratic party was banned in July 1933, all of the other opposition political parties disbanded in quick succession or, as was the case with the allied DVNP, were forced to retire. The Nazi party proclaimed itself the state party.

A short while later, Hitler purged his party of internal opposition. Even the SA, which was demanding to take over the country's military power, was seen as a threat. Under the pretense of preventing a putsch, the leadership of the ❸ SA was murdered with the support of the German army on July 30, 1934. This arbitrary action was afterwards legitimized as "national self-defense."

When the president of Germany, Hindenburg, died on August 2, 1934, Hitler claimed the office of head of state and proclaimed himself "Führer and chancellor" of the German Reich. The ❺ German army was compelled to swear a personal oath to Hitler. Germany had irrefutably become a Führer state.

2 Adolf Hitler, 1937

3 French caricature commenting on Hitler's liquidation of the SA, 1934

4 Burning of the Reichstag building, February 27–28, 1933

5 The German army marches through Berlin, 1934

6 Hitler during his government statement on the "Law to Remedy the Needs of People and Country," known as the "Enabling Act," March 23, 1933

27 Feb 1933 | Burning of the Reichstag building

5 Mar 1933 | NSDAP fails to gain absolute majority

10 Mar 1933 | Public book burning

23 Mar 1933 | "Enabling Act"

Jul 1933 | Ban of Social Democratic party

Control over Society

Propaganda, ideological persuasion, and violence were the methods with which the Nazis controlled and manipulated the German population.

An anarchistic juxtaposition of state and party systems, rather than the hierarchically organized power bloc as suggested by propaganda, characterized the Nazi state. Hitler remained the only point of reference of rivaling power groups. Alongside the terror, successes in foreign affairs (p. 453) and well-directed social measures strengthened the Führer's status among the German people. Thanks to ⑩ governmental job creation, unemployment sank by half within two years. By 1939, the massive armament programs intended to make the economy capable of war had even caused a labor shortage.

To pacify the coercively organized economic laborers in the "German Workers' Front," the workers received somewhat extravagant wages, protection against job loss, and paid vacations. The ⑪ Nazi party organization *Kraft durch Freude*—Strength through Joy—organized events and inexpensive trips. Thus the regime kept an eye on the "national comrades" even during their time off. The European day of the labor movement, May 1, became a public holiday known as the "Day of National Labor."

Special attention was given to the indoctrination of youth. All youth groups were absorbed by the ⑦ Hitler Youth and the ⑫ League of German Girls. Beginning in 1936, all ten- to 18-year-olds had to become members. The Reich Chamber of Culture, under the aegis of ⑧ Propaganda Minister Joseph Goebbels, supervised cultural life. Literature that did not conform to the party line was destroyed in public book burnings.

National Socialism's quest for totality was amplified by a network of state surveillance agencies. After the elimination of the SA, Heinrich Himmler's elite *Schutzstaffel* ("defense squadrons")—known as the ⑨ SS—became the most important instrument for fighting political opponents in 1934. All police and secret service departments were placed under its control. The SS took over the administration of the concentration camps. In 1939, about 25,000 "undesirable" persons were serving sentences in five of these camps.

7 Members of the Hitler Youth and the League of German Girls sing, 1937

8 Propaganda Minister Joseph Goebbels, 1931

9 Himmler (left) and Hitler inspect a defense squadron, 1935

10 Unemployed people are put to work building the motorway, 1933

Public Book Burning in 1933

The Nazi student association initiated the public book burnings that took place in the German university cities on March 10, 1933. Following a diatribe from Goebbels against "un-German" literature in Berlin, the works of Walter Benjamin, Erich Kästner, Thomas Mann, Sigmund Freud, and Carl von Ossietzky, among others, were set ablaze. Hundreds of writers emigrated, among them Bertolt Brecht and Stefan Zweig. While in prison, Ossietzky was awarded the Nobel Peace Prize in 1935; after three years in a concentration camp he died in 1938.

Book burnings in Berlin, March 10, 1933

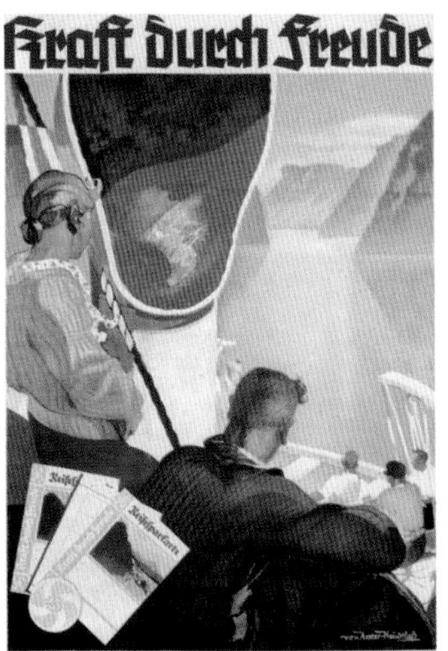

11 Poster promoting a *Kraft durch Freude* holiday: "You too can travel now," 1938

12 Poster promoting the building of youth hostels, 1933

2 Aug 1934 | Hindenburg dies
from 1936 | Compulsory membership in Hitler Youth / League of German Girls
30 Jul 1934 | SA leaders murdered
1935 | Nobel Peace Prize for Carl von Ossietzky
from 1936 | Extensive arms programs

The Persecution of European Jewry

Through a gradual progression of steps up to 1939, German Jews lost their rights, were dispossessed, and were forced to emigrate.

1 SA men hang up posters appealing to Germans to boycott Jewish businesses, April 1, 1933

After the takeover by the Nazis, there were uncontrolled outbreaks of violence in many places against the Jewish population by gangs of SA thugs incited by the anti-Semitic newspaper *Der Stürmer*. In response to protests from business and the old elite, the Nazi leadership tried to steer the persecution of the Jews onto a more regulated track through centrally directed actions and sham legislation.

In April 1933 Propaganda Minister Goebbels organized a ❶ nationwide boycott of Jewish businesses. The "Law to Restore Career Civil Service" of April 7, 1933, launched a flood of discriminatory decrees that forced Jewish people out of their professions and by 1939 had completely isolated them socially. Along with government service, the Jews were banned from cultural professions and forbidden to work as ❷ physicians or lawyers.

Eventually every contact with the "Aryan" population was forbidden. The ❹ race laws of 1935 deprived Jews of all political rights. Every citizen of the Reich had to prove his or her "German-bloodedness." A Jew was defined as anyone who was "descended

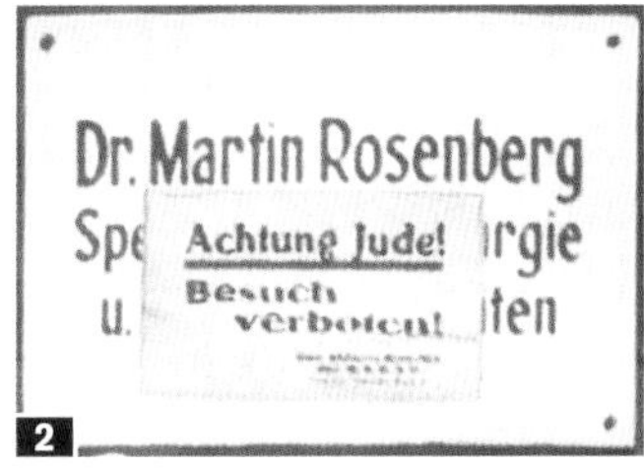

2 Sign of a Jewish physician with a cautionary notice pasted over it: "Warning: a Jew!", 1933

3 Arrested Jewish men in Baden-Baden, November 9, 1938

from, according to race, three full-blooded Jewish grandparents." The whole absurdity of the Nazi race ideology (p. 445) is shown by the criterion for being a "full-blooded Jew" as membership in the Jewish religion.

The Nazi leadership used an attempt to assassinate a German diplomat as a pretext to stage a full-scale ❺ pogrom against the Jews in November 1938. All across Germany on the night of November 9–10, 1938, synagogues were set afire and ❻ Jewish businesses destroyed. Almost 100 persons were murdered and about 30,000 were carried off to ❸ concentration camps. An "atonement payment" of a billion reichmarks ($400 million) was imposed on the German Jews. All Jewish capital assets were confiscated; real estate, stocks, and jewelry were sold under duress. The liquidation of all Jewish businesses and enterprises followed. The economy was thus forcibly Aryanized.

The Nazi leadership next moved on to a program of forced emigration and established a Head Office for Jewish Emigration in 1939. However, financial straits and the restrictive immigration regulations of foreign nations made leaving the country difficult. Emigration was finally banned in 1941 after the new strategy of exterminating the Jews was adopted. The organized mass murder of Jews—along with Sinti and Roma (gypsies), homosexuals, and other minorities (p. 520)—began in Poland.

5 *Reichskristallnacht* 1938: a burning synagogue in Bielefeld

6 The day after: passersby in front of a vandalized Jewish shop

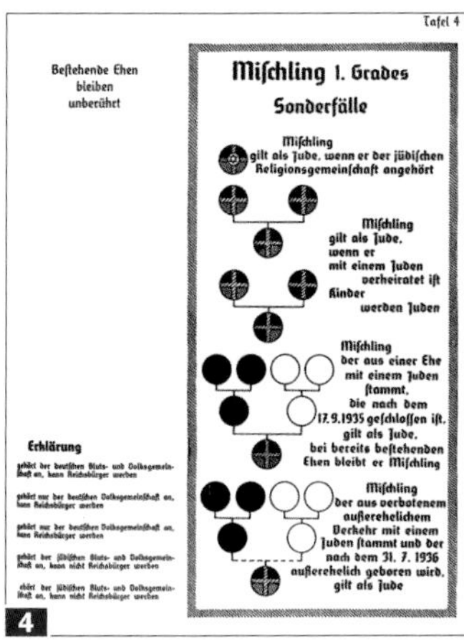

4 Chart purporting to show genetic relationships between the races, 1940

Emigration

A total of almost a million people, the vast majority of them Jewish, were forced or went voluntarily into exile from Germany after 1933. However, the formation of a united, powerful opposition was unsuccessful. The writer Thomas Mann put a face to "the other Germany" with his critical speeches from the United States. Many exiles joined the armies of their host countries during World War II.

Thomas Mann (left) with his family in American exile, 1940

1933 | Germany leaves the League of Nations
Apr 1933 | Nationwide boycott of Jewish businesses
1935 | "Race Laws"
1935 | Saarland joins the German Reich
1935 | Reintroduction of the Wehrmacht
1936 | Olympic Games in Germany

Nazi Foreign Policies through 1939

The Nazi leaders were tactically clever in disguising their plans of conquest as a peaceful policy to revise the Treaty of Versailles.

Hitler had planned a great war since the beginning of his rise to power. In a secret speech to German officers in February 1933 he openly spoke of the goal of "conquering new living space in the East and its ruthless Germanization." In order to restore Germany's position of power necessary to accomplish this, the Nazi leadership successfully ❽ revised the restrictions imposed by the Treaty of Versailles (p. 447). To pacify their war-weary European neighbors, they veiled their goals in an official policy of rapprochement.

Despite ❼ leaving the League of Nations in 1933, Hitler avowed the German desire for peace and stood by Western cultural heritage. The Reich Concordat with the Vatican, which was meant to secure the rights of the Catholic Church in Germany, nonaggression pacts with other states, and the hosting of the 1936 ❿ Olympic Games seemed to confirm this. When Saarland clearly voted to join the German Reich in a plebiscite in 1935, the Western allied powers acknowledged the Germans' right to self-determination and accepted the subsequent violation of the Versailles Treaty. Hitler reintroduced military conscription in 1935, announced rearmament, and signed a naval fleet agreement with Great Britain (p. 464). A year later, he occupied the ⓫ demilitarized Rhineland region. Involvement in the Spanish Civil War (p. 473), the ❾ "Berlin–Rome Axis" (p. 471), and the Anti-Comintern Pact with Japan (p. 498) were coalitions with a clear anti-Soviet orientation that presaged later war alliances.

While the Western Powers had accepted the invasion of Austria in 1938 (p. 455) and its unification with Germany and had even legalized the annexation of the Sudetenland through the Munich Agreement (p. 465), they gave up their policy of appeasement after the breakup of Czechoslovakia (p. 479) in March 1939 and threatened war if Germany attempted further territorial expansion. Poland was invaded by Germany under a pretense on September 1, 1939, and the Second World War had begun (p. 510).

8 Propaganda poster promoting the annexation of Austria: "Bit by bit, Adolf Hitler tore up the Treaty of Versailles!", 1938

7 The empty seats of the German delegation after it left the League of Nations, 1933

9 Stamp showing Hitler and Mussolini, entitled "Two nations, one battle," 1938

10 Official English-language poster of the 1936 Olympic Games

The 1936 Olympic Games in Berlin

Germany deceived the world during the Olympic Games of 1936 with a demonstration of cosmopolitan culture. Jazz was allowed to be played in the bars and the persecution of political opponents and Jews was put on hold. The perfectly staged Olympic propaganda film by Leni Riefenstahl also impressed the world and was generally positively received.

Entartete MUSIK
EINE ABRECHNUNG VON STAATSRAT DR.H.S.ZIEGLER

above: Under the Third Reich jazz was labeled "degenerate" and prohibited, poster, 1938
right: Still from Leni Riefenstahl's Olympics "Festival of the Nations," 1936

11 The reconstituted German Wehrmacht marches into the demilitarized Rhineland on March 7, 1936

1936 | "Berlin-Rome Axis" founded
1938 | Germany invades Austria
1 Sep 1939 | Germany invades Poland
9/10 Nov 1938 | *Reichskristallnacht*
1939 | Creation of the "Head Office for Jewish Emigration"
1941 | Ban on Jewish emigration

Austria: From Habsburg Empire to German "Ostmark" 1918–1945

The multinational state of Austria-Hungary crumbled after the end of World War I, losing three-quarters of its previous territory. The existence of the newly founded Republic of Austria, a small country, was threatened from the beginning by economic problems and political radicalism. The establishment of a partially fascist regime in 1933 could not prevent the Nazi German Reich from absorbing ❶ Austria shortly afterward.

1 The German Armed Forces cross the Austrian border, 1938

The Fall of the Habsburg Monarchy

After the disintegration of the Habsburg Empire in 1918, the German-speaking heartland reconstituted itself as the "Republic of Austria," but the Allies prohibited the merging of this truncated state with the German Reich.

World War I, which developed out of Austria's retaliatory strike against ❺ Serbia for the murder of Archduke Franz Ferdinand in 1914 (p. 440), brought the downfall of the Habsburg dual monarchy. ❻Militarily Austria-Hungary had taken on too much and was dependent on the German troops. When the Austrian fronts collapsed in the spring and summer of 1918 (p. 444), the disintegration of the empire was inevitable. Supply blockages led to civil revolt, mutinies took place in the army and navy, and the various nationalities in the empire fought for their independence.

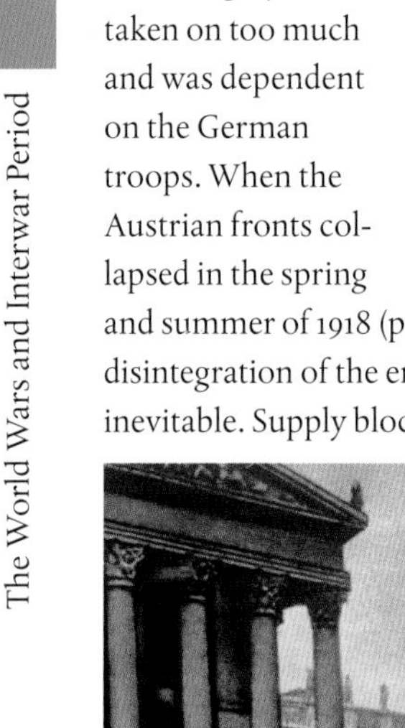
3 Dr. Karl Renner

As early as 1917 the Poles, Czechs, and Slavs had formed governments in exile, and in October 1918 Hungary declared itself independent of Austria. The last Habsburg emperor ❷ Charles I refused to participate in the new government. He was deposed in 1918. In 1919, the Austrian national assembly officially repealed the Habsburg right to rule and confiscated their fortune.

On November 12, 1918, the ❹ "German-Austria" Republic was proclaimed; its chancellor was the Social Democrat ❸ Karl Renner. The state also declared itself part of the German republic, but the Allies prohibited this annexation of Austria to Germany in the Treaty of St. Germain in 1919 (p. 445). The treaty also forced Austria to cede further territories: South Tirol was given to Italy and the German Sudeten territories to Czechoslovakia. From the beginning, the much smaller Austrian state had to struggle with severe economic problems. In 1922, the League of Nations granted the republic a large credit to revitalize the state finances—under the condition that it would irrevocably refrain from a union with the German Reich. The republic slowly began to be consolidated with the introduction of the schilling as currency in 1924.

2 Emperor Charles I

4 Proclamation of the republic of Austria

5 Anti-Serbian violence in Sarajevo, after the assassination on June 28, 1914

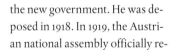

6 Battle against Italy, postcard

1917 | Governments in exile of Poles, Czechs, and Slavs
Oct 1918 | Hungary's independence from Austria
Nov 1918 | Charles I renounces the throne
12 Nov 1918 | Proclamation of "German-Austria" Republic
1919 | Treaty of St. Germain

Austria's Anschluss with the German Reich

Internal political radicalization led to the establishment of an authoritarian government in Austria in 1933. The Austro-Fascists, however, were only able to delay Austria's eventual assimilation into the Nazi German Reich.

The ideological polarization between the national political parties of the Austrian republic, the Christian Socialists, and the Social Democrats, intensified after 1927. At the same time, clashes between fascist and socialist factions shook the nation. As the government had shown itself incapable of dealing with the continuing economic crisis and social unrest, Chancellor ❼ Engelbert Dollfuss, in a couplike move, suspended parliament in 1933 and by emergency decree established a dictatorship—"Austro-Fascism"—modeled on that of Fascist Italy. He gave the Home Guard police authority, founded the nonpartisan ❽ Fatherland Front while banning all other political parties, reintroduced the death penalty, and set up detention camps to incarcerate regime opponents. A putsch by the Social Democrats in February 1934 was brutally crushed.

Chancellor Engelbert Dollfuss

Dollfuss was killed during a coup attempt by Austrian National Socialists in July 1934. His successor, ❾ Kurt von Schuschnigg, dedicated himself particularly to the struggle to maintain Austria's independence now that the *Anschluss* (union) with Germany, desired by some Austrians since the late 1920s, had become a threat with Hitler's accession to power in 1933. It was clear that if this were to occur, Austria would have to subordinate itself to the German Nazi party. Schuschnigg put his hopes in close relations with Italy, which had proclaimed itself a guarantor of Austrian sovereignty and had also dispatched troops to the Brenner Pass on the Austrian border during an attempted Nazi takeover in 1934. Schuschnigg, however, was pressured by Hitler in 1936 to accept the "July Agreement" that obligated Austria to adopt a "more German" foreign policy and to release all Nazis held in custody. Two years later, he was forced to appoint a leading Austrian Nazi, ❿ Arthur Seyss-Inquart, as minister of the interior.

Detainees liberated from Mauthausen, 1945

Schuschnigg's last attempt to prevent assimilation by the German Reich was to call for a ⓬ plebiscite on Austrian independence. The vote was set for March 13, 1938, but on March 12, ⓭ German troops marched into Austria, and two days later Hitler delivered a speech on the Heldenplatz in Vienna in front of cheering masses. The Anschluss was approved by an overwhelming majority in the plebiscite. Even the socialist leader Karl Renner publicly voted for it, and churches were festooned with swastika banners. Austria was then renamed German "Ostmark." In April, the first concentration camp was erected in ⓫ Mauthausen.

Federal Chancellor Dollfuss approves a parade by the Fatherland Front

Kurt von Schuschnigg (left) pays Mussolini (middle) a visit, 1934

Arthur Seyss-Inquart with Adolf Hitler, 1938

Poster with Schuschnigg's appeal to vote for the independence of Austria, in March 1938

Parade of the German Armed Forces in Vienna on March 15, 1938 after their invasion of Vienna on March 12

1924 | Introduction of the Schilling
1933 | Parliament dismissed
Feb 1934 | February putsch by the Social Democrats
Jul 1934 | Putsch by National Socialists
1936 | July Agreement
1938 | Seyss-Inquart becomes minister of the interior

Switzerland: Island of Stability 1914–1945

Switzerland, a parliamentary federal republic since 1848, remained ❶ neutral during both world wars despite its position in the center of the European continent. Neither the economic problems of World War I nor its encirclement by the Axis powers in World War II was able to fundamentally endanger the democratic tradition of Switzerland. However, in order to avoid occupation by Hitler's Germany, Switzerland followed a controversial policy of compromise with the Nazis, despite official neutrality, as a result of which it was viewed with skepticism by the Allied powers.

Swiss soldiers protect the border, 1939

Strict Neutrality in the First World War

Switzerland's perpetual neutrality, as guaranteed at the Congress of Vienna in 1815, remained intact during World War I. Despite economic and social difficulties, the traditional democracy remained stable.

Even in the 19th century, Switzerland played an exceptional role in Europe. As an independent nation since the late Middle Ages, except for a short time after 1798 when it had been under French control, and without expansionist aspirations, it had long been a venue for international negotiations. The Congress of Vienna (p. 367) had granted the Swiss, in the interest of all of Europe, permanent neutrality, and World War I did not alter this. The small nation did not interfere with the Great Powers' war aims and had no raw materials essential to war. During the war, the Swiss army was provisionally mobilized but never saw action. However, the populace suffered due to a war-related economic crisis, causing the introduction of a war tax. As imports were difficult, attempts were made to strengthen the Swiss economy. The cultivation of grain was promoted, and the ❷ Swiss railway became the first to use electric instead of coal-burning, steam-driven engines.

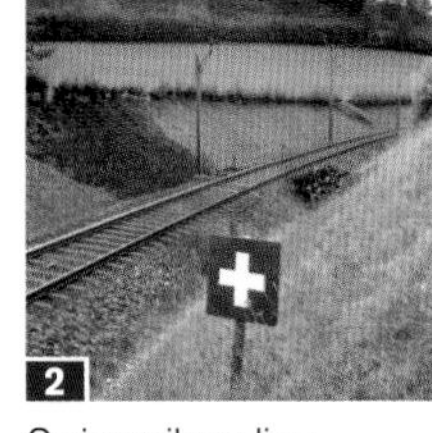

Swiss railway line

The growing poverty of the people brought about a leftist-oriented revolt in 1916. However, the great general strike of 1918 was less an attempt at revolution than a call for social change; the strike was ended by military force, but state social reforms worked to relieve the tension. The liberal democratic tradition of the ❸ federal republic, which had existed since 1848, withstood the postwar turmoil unaffected. The Treaty of Versailles (p. 445) unconditionally reaffirmed the neutrality of the Swiss, and ❺ Geneva was chosen as the headquarters for the ❹ League of Nations initiated by U.S. President Woodrow Wilson; Switzerland joined in 1920.

Later, the threat of the Axis powers to Switzerland's strict neutrality in World War II would present a greater challenge than that of World War I.

The Swiss Houses of Parliament in Bern

Liechtenstein

The tiny principality of Liechtenstein, situated between Austria and Switzerland, has been sovereign since 1806. Following the economic crisis in the wake of World War I, Liechtenstein leaned economically and politically on Switzerland. Like its neighbor, it too remained neutral during the Nazi period. To this day, the princes of Liechtenstein have more rights than any of the other European monarchs.

top: Liechtenstein coat of arms
above: Vaduz Castle, Liechtenstein

Meeting of the League of Nations in Geneva, 1934

The League of Nations complex in Geneva

1806 | Liechtenstein gains sovereignty
1815 | Swiss neutrality guaranteed
1863 | Red Cross founded
1882 | St. Gotthard Pass railroad built
10 Aug 1914 | Swiss army mobilized
1918 | "General strike"

The Nazi Threat

In the 1930s, liberal and neutral Switzerland became the first retreat for German refugees. At the height of World War II, the Swiss were able to maintain their independence only through accommodation of Nazi Germany, although this was limited.

Although economic problems had been increasing in Switzerland since 1927, the influence of emerging front movements that had close ties to the Nazis in the 1930s remained marginal and was unable to shake the parliamentary federal republic. Once the Nazis took power in Germany, many refugees sought refuge in neighboring Switzerland, though often only as an intermediary station. "The boat is full" was a slogan often used to limit immigration; by the end of World War II, more than 20,000 Jews had been turned back at the border.

The latent external threat surrounding the Swiss caused them to move closer together and united them domestically. Switzerland was released in 1938 from its obligations to take part in League of Nations sanctions. The Swiss National Exhibition in 1939, actually an agricultural and industrial show, turned into a demonstration of independence, freedom, and willingness to ❽ defend these ideals. The military mobilization ❼ during World War II was primarily symbolic. Switzerland remained ❾ unoccupied and provided humanitarian services. However, Federal Council member Marcel Pilet-Golaz implemented a highly controversial policy of compromise with the Axis powers—in principle the enemy—that was financially advantageous for the Swiss. The ❿ Saint Gotthard Pass railroad tunnel between Italy and Germany was at the disposal of military transports, and restrictions were placed on the freedom of the press in 1939. The economy profited from the increased export and delivery of weapons to the German Reich.

After 1945, lucrative gold and foreign currency transactions also gave a negative edge to Swiss neutrality. ❻, ⓫ Gold that the Germans had plundered—especially Jewish property confiscated by the Nazis—was deposited in Swiss banks. The voluntary economic collaboration resulted in a short-term international isolation of Switzerland after the war.

6 Gold ingot of the German Reichsbank , 1941

10 Advertising poster for the Saint Gotthard Pass railroad, 1924

The International Committee of the Red Cross (ICRC)

The International Committee of the Red Cross (ICRC), a neutral medical and aid organization for the casualties of war, was a Swiss idea, proposed by Swiss businessman Jean-Henri Dunant and founded in 1863. It was the beginning of the growth of a worldwide movement that developed over the course of the 20th century into an aid organization that transcends cultures and nations. The Red Cross was active on all fronts in both world wars and allowed the wounded to recover as patients in neutral Switzerland and provided them with free medical attention. The ICRC was awarded the Nobel Peace Prize in 1917 and in 1944.

Japanese Red Cross first aid attendants in France, 1914

top: US poster, 1914, recruiting for the Red Cross

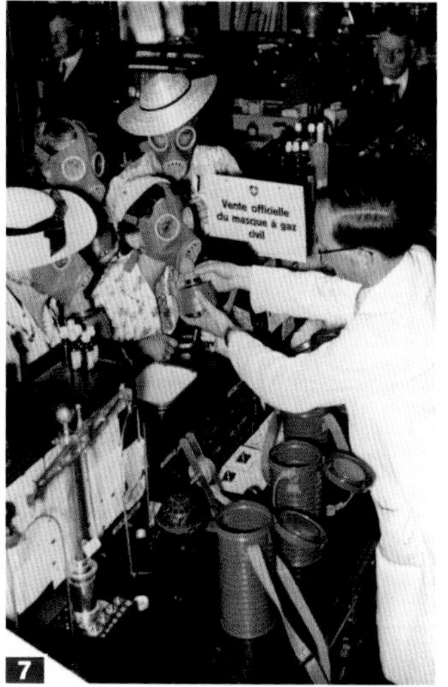
7 Gas masks are fitted and sold in a pharmacy, 1938

8 Protecting the Swiss border, 1939

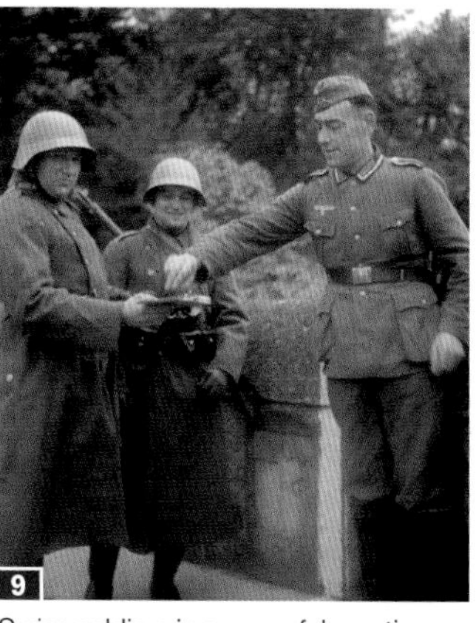
9 Swiss soldiers in a peaceful meeting with German soldiers at the Swiss border, 1939

11 Gold ingots in a bank safe, 1941

Nov 1920 | 1st conference of League of Nations in Geneva
1931 | Economic depression
1938 | League of Nations confirms absolute neutrality
8 Sep 1939 | Press censorship
1939 | Swiss National Exhibition
1949 | Switzerland joins UNESCO

France: Insecurity and Occupation

1918–1945

Despite ❶ victory in World War I, France still felt threatened by its German neighbor. Politically unstable at home and weakened by the war, France initially saw its security as guaranteed only through the pursuit of a "harsh course" against its "traditional enemy." However, in the face of Hitler's aggressive power politics in the 1930s, France seemed almost paralyzed. After the Blitzkrieg in 1940, the German army occupied the north of France and the French Vichy regime collaborated with the Germans.

1 Victory celebrations in Paris, 1919

Turbulence in Domestic Affairs between the Wars

Despite numerous changes of government and economic tension, the antidemocratic movements in the Third Republic were unable to seize power.

In the period between the wars, France had to struggle domestically against the economic, financial, and social consequences of the Great War. The war had cost the lives of about ten percent of the adult male population, in addition to the 4,270,000 wounded. However, in comparison to Great Britain (p. 462) and Russia (p. 480), France remained relatively stable economically and remained a leading continental power with increased territories. During the 1920s French industrial production grew significantly with state support.

Eventually the effects of the worldwide economic depression reached France, albeit later than in the fully industrialized nations as its ❸ agrarian sector was still very large. The number of unemployed began to rise in 1931, which shook the stability of the Third Republic. The administrations came and went as if through a revolving door—a total of 41 times by 1940. The few senior ministers who remained in office, such as Raymond Poincaré and ❷ Édouard Daladier, provided the only elements of continuity in the leadership.

3 French farmer with horse-drawn plow in the 1940s

In 1924, the right-wing Bloc National governed with a majority; a leftist socialist reform cartel then took power for two years. Meanwhile, disagreements between the moderate parties strengthened both left- and right-wing radicalism. The Communists consistently won about ten percent of the votes in the ❺ elections, but never really posed a threat to established policies. Right-wing antidemocratic radical groups such as the Action Française and Croix du Feu (Cross of Fire), an organization of World War I veterans, gained influence in the 1930s; the latter attempted a ❹ coup in February 1934 but it quickly fizzled out.

2 Édouard Daladier making a radio address to the French people, 1938

In 1936, Socialist prime minister ❻ Léon Blum organized and led the leftist Popular Front—a coalition of the Socialists, Radical Socialists, and Communists—in order to avert the rise of a fascist regime like that in Italy. Among other popular reforms, he introduced the 40-hour working week and entitlement to paid holidays.

4 Coup attempt in Paris, February 1934

5 Election posters

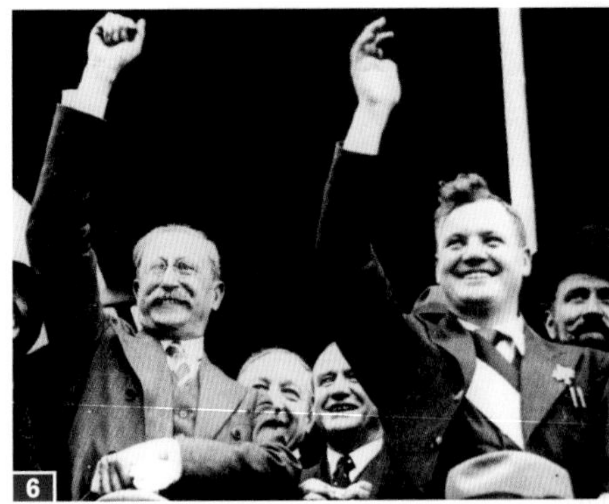

6 Leon Blum (left) with the leader of the Communists

1923 | French occupy Ruhr area

1925 | French withdrawal from Ruhr area

16 Oct 1925 | Locarno Pact

1932–40 | Albert Lebrun presidency

Jun– Dec 1932 | Herriot's radical majority cabinet

1934 | Attempted putsch by radical right

Between Retribution and Appeasement: France's Foreign Policy up to 1939

The fear of renewed German aggression fundamentally determined French foreign policy between the wars.

In the peace negotiations of 1919, France believed its national security could be fulfilled only through the maximum territorial and economic weakening of Germany. In the Versailles Treaty, (p. 445) France was awarded Alsace-Lorraine, German colonies such as Cameroon, the occupation and economic exploitation of the ❼ Saarland, and a large share of reparations. In addition to the agreed reduction of the German army to 100,000 men and the abolition of the General Staff, France demanded the complete demilitarization of the Rhineland to serve as a buffer zone.

Due to the growing differences among the other Allies and the lack of a military security guarantee from the United States, which had retreated into extreme isolationism, France pursued an intransigent reparations policy at the beginning of the 1920s—despite the German Reich's inability to meet the immense demands. French president ❾ Poincaré ordered the occupation of the ❿ Ruhr, Germany's industrial center, on January 23, 1923, to enforce the payment of reparations, over the objections of the United States and Great Britain. The new leftist government of 1924 introduced a conciliatory policy of rapprochement toward Germany, however, and because of the population's ❽ passive resistance the Ruhr was evacuated in 1925. Germany guaranteed the inviolability of her Western borders with France and Belgium in the Locarno Pact of 1925.

8 German poster calling for passive resistance under the slogan: "No! You won't make me do this!" 1923

France attempted to counter Nazi Germany's aggressive power politics that began in 1933 (p. 450) with a system of international alliances, including the 1935 mutual assistance pact with the Soviet Union and the Anglo-French military alliance. Under the influence of Great Britain, and because of divisions within the Popular Front government, France pursued a policy of appeasement toward Germany in 1938. Prime Minister Daladier and Foreign Minister Bonnet tolerated the annexation of Austria and signed the ⓫ Munich Agreement (p. 465). The French policy of appeasement, reflecting the desire of both leaders and people to avoid another war, continued until the invasion of Poland.

9 Raymond Poincaré

10 French soldier guarding a confiscated coal wagon, 1923

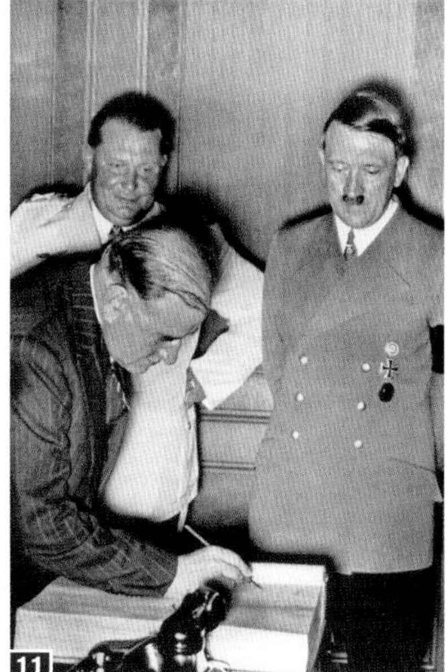

11 Munich Agreement; Daladier signs Hitler's guestbook, 1938

7 Foreign soldiers guard the elections of the referendum in the Saarland concerning a return to the German administration

The Maginot Line

To protect themselves against a new German invasion, the French erected the Maginot Line between 1926 and 1936, a huge barrier of fortifications on the northeastern border with Germany. It was named after the French minister of war and consisted of artillery and infantry emplacements, communications and bunker complexes that cost about three billion francs and was considered impregnable. When war arrived, Nazi Germany simply avoided the fortifications by invading via neutral Belgium, and France surrendered within six weeks.

top: Draft of the subterranean bunker complex of the Maginot Line
above: French bunker on the Maginot Line destroyed by a German attack, 1940

1935	Franco-Soviet mutual assistance pact
1936–37	Popular Front cabinet led by Leon Blum
Sep 1938	Munich Agreement
Nov 1938	General Strike
Aug 1939	Anglo-French military alliance
2–3 Sep 1939	Germany declares war on France

The Vichy Government, 1940–1944

After Germany's occupation of half of France in May 1940, a German-friendly government based in the town of Vichy was set up to administer the unoccupied regions.

France declared war on Germany after Hitler's invasion of Poland on September 3, 1939, but still refrained from active military engagement, relying on the elaborate fortifications of the Maginot Line. Then in May 1940, German troops suddenly ❷ marched through Belgium into France. The French were stunned by the rapid advance, known as blitzkrieg ("lightning war"), and resistance broke down after only six weeks (p. 510); ❶ Marshal Henri-Philippe Pétain asked for a cease-fire on June 16, 1940. In order to humiliate France, the resultant ❹ treaty was signed in a railway carriage in the woods of Compiègne—the same place where the French had forced the armistice on the Germans in 1918 to end World War I. The Third Republic had fallen apart.

Marshal Henri-Philippe Pétain

While German troops occupied the north and west of France, including Paris, an État Français was established in Vichy, in France's unoccupied south. This authoritarian government saw itself as a partner of the German Nazi regime but was recognized by the United States and the Soviet Union, among others. The 84-year-old Pétain became head of state with considerable power at his disposal; his deputy was ❸ Pierre Laval, whom Pétain had arrested at the end of 1940 because he had argued for entry into the war on the side of the Germans. Despite extensive compromises, the Vichy regime continued to come under increasing German pressure. In April 1942, Laval was installed as prime minister and took over the leadership of the state.

In the wake of the Allied landings in North Africa, the German army occupied the remainder of France, turning the Vichy regime into a fascist police state. From the summer of 1942 onward, the French police played a substantial role in the ❺ deportation of French Jews to death camps. The Allied invasions at Normandy on June 6, 1944 and on the Mediterranean coasts (p. 523) led to the collapse of the Vichy regime and the liberation of Paris.

Victory parade of German troops through Paris, 1940

Vichy leaders Henri-Philippe Pétain and Pierre Laval (right), 1942

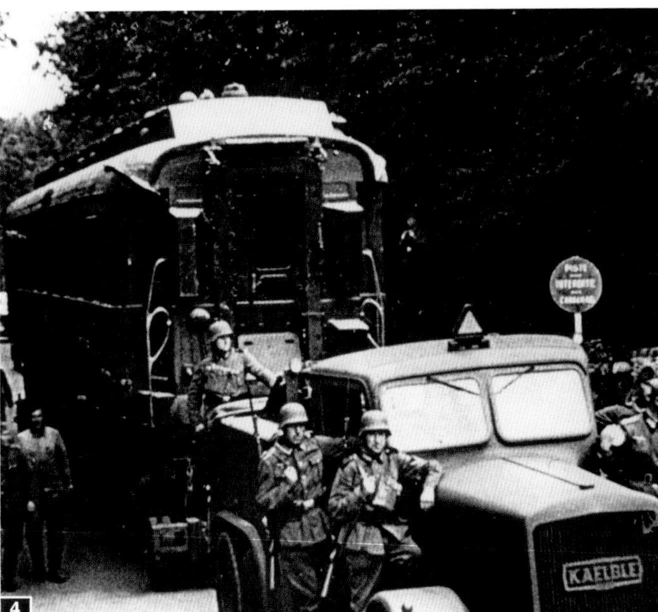

Armistice of Compiègne: The historic train carriage, where the German surrender in the First World War was signed, is used for the French surrender, 1940

Arrested Jews are loaded onto a truck by the German SS and the French police, ca. 1942

May 1940	Germans invade France
5–24 Jun 1940	Battle for France
16 Jun 1940	Armistice signed in Compiègne
10 Jul 1940	Formation of Vichy government led by Pétain
24 Oct 1940	Pétain refuses to enter war

The Resistance and the Rise of Charles de Gaulle

The French leader in exile, General Charles de Gaulle, united small resistance groups into a powerful political force in 1943. This formed a provisional French government directly after the Allied liberation in 1944.

After the occupation of Paris by the German army, French fighters—the Résistance—organized in small groups and waged war through ❼ acts of sabotage and strikes against the occupiers and the Vichy collaborators; they also aided the politically or racially persecuted to flee. The Germans dealt harshly with the insurgents: A total of about 30,000 Resistance fighters were executed, and 75,000 died in concentration camps. In 1944, German SS troops wiped out the village of ❻ Oradour-sur-Glane as a retaliatory measure for partisan attacks.

In exile in London, ⓫ General Charles de Gaulle had in 1940 already formed the ❽ Free French movement, which saw itself as the legitimate representative of France, and built a government in exile—receiving a death sentence in absentia for high treason from the Vichy government. In May 1943 de Gaulle united the different factions of the resistance, such as Combat and Franc-Tireur, into a National Council of the Resistance. At the same time, the exile government moved to Algiers and recruited North African freedom fighters for the insurgency.

The Resistance supported the advance of the Allied troops after their landing in Normandy in June 1944. They organized a revolt in Paris on August 18, 1944, shortly before the Allies arrived in the capital. A week later, de Gaulle entered Paris. The National Council of the ❿ Resistance was then recognized by the Allies as the provisional government. De Gaulle was able to unite the somewhat conservative members of the government in exile with the left-wing, and frequently communist, resistance movement.

Pierre Laval was executed in October 1945; Marshal Pétain was sentenced to death but was later pardoned and exiled to the island of Yeu. Acts of mob violence, including lynchings, against citizens suspected of collaboration were frequent, particularly against ❾ women thought to have "fraternized" with Germans.

7 French saboteur attaches dynamite to the railway tracks, 1944

8 Meeting of the Free French movement in Algiers, 1943

6 The village Oradour-sur-Glane after an attack by the German SS, 1944

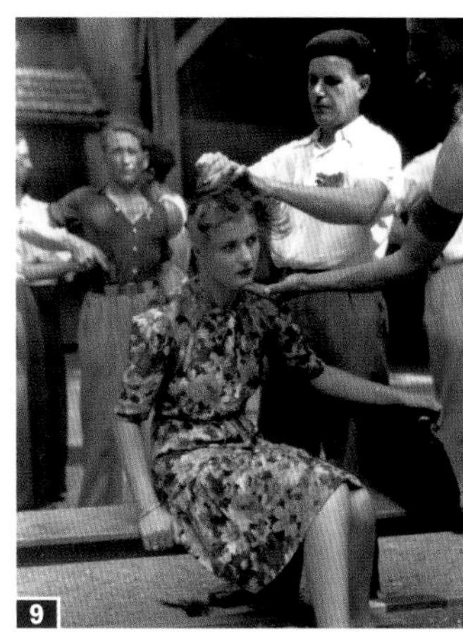
9 A woman suspected of collaboration has her head shaved in public, 1944

Charles de Gaulle Broadcasting from London, June 18, 1940

"I invite the officers and the French soldiers who are located in British territory or who would come there... to put themselves in contact with me. Whatever happens, the flame of the French resistance must not be extinguished and will not be extinguished. Tomorrow, as today, I will speak on Radio London."

above: Charles de Gaulle inspects French army in exile

10 A rebellion in Paris by French resistance fighters, 1944

11 Charles de Gaulle

Apr 1942 | Laval becomes president

6 Jun 1944 | Allies land in Normandy

18 Aug 1944 | Resistance organizes revolt in Paris

25 Aug 1944 | de Gaulle enters Paris

Britain between the World Wars

1919–1939

The British Empire attained its greatest territorial extent after World War I but lost power due to the internal weakening of the kingdom. The ❶ economic and political problems at no time threatened the democratic traditions of Great Britain but did force it into a defensive peace policy to preserve its interests at any cost. Until 1939, it was indecisive and uncertain in the face of the German Nazi regime's aggressive policies.

1 London transport workers on strike, 1936

Economic Weakness in the Wake of the Great War

After emerging victorious from World War I, structural problems and massive debt plunged Great Britain into an economic crisis that lasted into the middle of the 1930s.

Superficially, the end of World War I brought the United Kingdom only success. The German Reich was bankrupt and its fleet was at Britain's mercy. Furthermore, Great Britain had gained the majority of the German colonial possessions and parts of the Ottoman Empire under a ❹ mandate from the League of Nations. But these territorial gains had been paid for by 900,000 dead and two million wounded Britons, as well as a serious weakening of the economy. The cost of the conflict had increased the national debt tenfold by 1918, and Great Britain was now indebted to the United States and had lost its position as the world's primary financial power.

3 Winston Churchill, 1915

Fiscal dependency, outdated technology in essential industrial sectors such as steel and coal, and the weak buying power on the Continent resulted in a long-lasting economic depression. The situation became even more critical when Chancellor of the Exchequer ❸ Winston Churchill restored the pound to the gold standard in 1925, which led to an enormous increase in the price of British exported goods. Unemployment increased rapidly among the workers. Beginning in 1919 prolonged ❷ strikes demanding social improvement—influenced by the Russian Revolution (p. 480)—repeatedly stopped work in essential industries, greatly damaging the economy. The climax was a miners' revolt in 1926 that was supported by a ❺, ❻ general strike of the labor unions. In the end, the workers' struggle ended in a bitter defeat for the consolidated labor unions. The government then passed the Trade Disputes and Trade Union Act of 1927. This legislation outlawed sympathetic strikes and mass picketing, severely curtailing the ability of organized labor from different sectors to collaborate.

2 Striking textile workers in front of the union office in Lancashire, 1929

4 British military police in the British mandate territory of Palestine, 1938

Anti-German Sentiment

Anti-German sentiment in Great Britain during World War I became so strong that in 1917 the royal family decided to change its German surname, Saxe-Coburg-Gotha. The descendents of Queen Victoria's line have used the family name "Windsor," after the royal residence of Windsor Castle, ever since.

above: Windsor Castle

5 Counter-demonstration by aristocratic British women against the general strike, May 1926

6 Traffic jam in central London as public transport workers join the general strike, May 1926

1919–22 Wave of strikes by the miners

1920 Unemployment insurance introduced

1922 "Transport and General Workers' Union"

1924 Formation of 1st Labour cabinet

Feb 1924 Recognition of USSR

Oct 1924 Conservative election victory

A Bulwark of Democratic Stability

The traditional parties, together with the rising Labour party, attempted to come to grips with the social and economic problems Britain faced. Radical forces in the parliamentary monarchy that were opposed to the system found no support.

The United Kingdom's fundamental parliamentary-democratic constitutional order remained stable between the wars despite the ongoing economic and social crisis. Revolutionary parties of the masses, unlike those on the Continent, stood no chance. The National Fascist party, founded in the 1930s by Sir Oswald Mosley, remained of as little consequence as the Communists.

In 1918, parliamentary law became fully democratized. All males over 21 and all women over 30 were entitled to vote. In 1928, women were given voting rights equal to those of men.

Domestically, the Labour party gained strength during the war. Labour grew at the expense of the Liberals to become the strongest opposition party and broke the traditional Liberal–Conservative two-party system. In 1924 the first Labour politicians came to power with the support of the

8 Stanley Baldwin

Liberals. However, when the Labour prime minister ❼ Ramsay MacDonald recognized the Soviet Union, he was voted out after only eleven months in office, and the Conservative ❽ Stanley Baldwin took over affairs of state. Nevertheless, in 1929 Labour won again and MacDonald formed his second cabinet.

Two years later, when unemployment support was cut back at the height of the economic depression, the Labour government collapsed. Under pressure from ❿ King George V, MacDonald then agreed to head a coalition national government, with a cabinet made up only of Conservatives and Liberals, until 1935. The unity government tried in vain to solve the economic problems with retrenchment and tax increases, but not until government stabilization measures and rearmament began in 1937 was there a noticeable drop in unemployment. In 1940, the Labour party joined an all-party wartime government under ❾ Winston Churchill.

7 Labour Party conference in London, 1929; McDonald (center) became a pariah for the Left

9 Winston Churchill, 1939

Edward VIII

Following the death of his father, George V, Edward VIII reigned for less than a year before Prime Minister Baldwin forced him to abdicate in 1936, because he insisted on marrying the twice-divorced American Wallis Simpson even after the explicit disapproval of the cabinet. Edward was downgraded to "Duke of Windsor" and thereafter led a luxurious playboy lifestyle with his wife, mostly in France.

above: Edward, Duke of Windsor, with his wife, 1937

10 The Royal family, 1929; King George V in the center

- **1925** Pound stabilized
- **1926** Miners and labor unions strike
- **1927** Trade union law
- **1929–31** MacDonald's second cabinet
- **1934** Beginning of rearmament
- **1940** Coalition cabinet led by Churchill

British Foreign Policy between the Wars

The United Kingdom sought to secure the British position of world power by a policy of preserving international peace. Strong nationalist movements in the colonies led to the crumbling of the British Empire.

The conviction that ❷ Great Britain should seek peace at all costs to maintain the empire's worldwide sphere of influence, formed the core of British foreign policy after 1919. The consequent avoidance of conflict, preference for diplomatic negotiation, and striving to protect imperial trade were the key principles of the British "peace and trade" foreign policy up until 1939.

Houses of Parliament, London, ca. 1900

In the League of Nations, Great Britain demanded that the organization take on the regulation of armament production and became the driving force in international disarmament efforts after WWI. Great Britain, Belgium, China, France, Italy, Japan, the Netherlands, Portugal, and the United States resolved to reduce the size of Pacific fleets at the ❹ Washington Conference of 1920–1921; in the process, Great Britain agreed to allow the United States equal strength in its battle fleet and so relinquished its traditional naval superiority. In Europe Britain supported the peace efforts of the former belligerents:

Locarno Treaty, 1925; from left: Gustav Stresemann, Austin Chamberlain (half-brother of Neville), and Aristide Briand

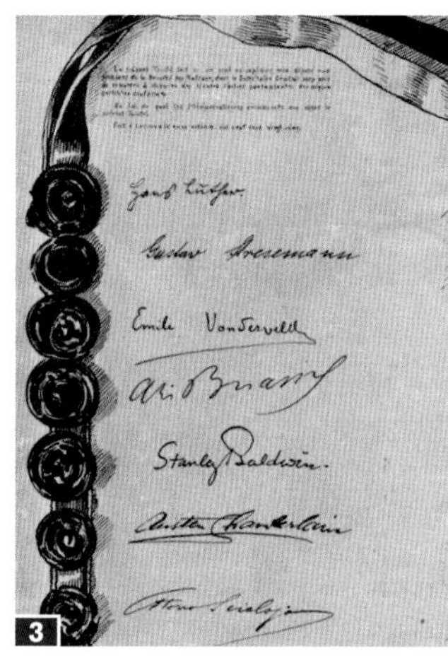

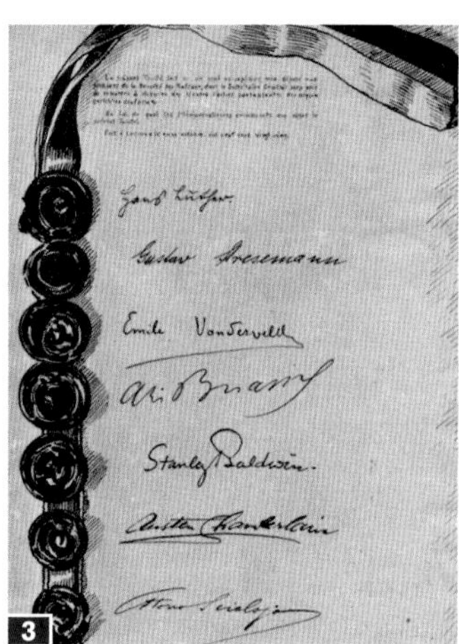

Locarno Treaty, signatures

In 1925, Great Britain, France, Belgium, Italy, and Germany signed the ❶, ❸ Locarno Treaty, which included a declaration of intent to resolve all conflicts without resort to the force of arms.

The British Empire found itself confronted by nationalist movements in many of its colonies. Centuries-old Irish efforts to gain independence culminated in the division of the island in 1921; southern Ireland became independent (p. 466). Britain, whose complete name since 1801 had been the United Kingdom of Great Britain and Ireland, modified its name in 1927 to the United Kingdom of Great Britain and Northern Ireland. In other parts of the world, the empire also had to relinquish territory. It gave up its protectorate of Egypt in 1923 (p. 502), and in 1932 consented to Iraq's independence (p. 488). Great Britain and the now autonomous dominions of the British Empire founded the ❺ Commonwealth of Nations (p. 500) in 1926.

To a great extent, Britain remained calm in the face of Japan's imperialistic strivings in East Asia (p. 496) and those of Italy in the Mediterranean. Increasingly, the focus in East Asia was on Hong Kong and Singapore. However, the powerful movements for independence in India were still suppressed by force (p. 492).

British Prime Minister Neville Chamberlain

"Ever since I assumed my present office my main purpose has been to work for the pacification of Europe, for the removal of those suspicions and those animosities which have so long poisoned the air... The question of Czechoslovakia is the latest and perhaps the most dangerous."

Arthur Neville Chamberlain, 1938

Washington Conference, 1920–21

Empire Conference establishing the Commonwealth, 1926

1920 | Government of Ireland Act
1920–21 | Washington Conference
1921 | Division of Ireland
1923 | End of the British protectorate in Egypt
1926 | Commonwealth of Nations founded
1932 | Independence of Iraq

Appeasement of Nazi Germany

In an attempt to avoid another war in Europe, Great Britain at first tolerated the aggressive revisionist politics of the Nazi regime. Only after the invasion of Poland in 1939 showed that diplomacy was futile did the British government declare war on the German Reich.

Great Britain had already warned its partners against isolating the German Reich during the peace negotiations in 1919 and later criticized France's huge reparation demands. In the 1920s it put its weight behind the economic and political rehabilitation of Germany, expecting therewith the pacification of Central Europe and an increased market for British goods. Hitler's rise to power did little to change this policy, even if Great Britain did gradually begin to ❾ rearm.

7 The German envoy Ribbentrop outside the German consulate in London, June 4, 1935

British leaders believed that war should be avoided through negotiation and accepted Germany's more moderate revisionist demands. In the ❼ Anglo-German Naval Agreement of 1935, Hitler was granted a fleet equal to 35 percent of the capacity of the British Navy and parity in the submarine fleet. The deployment of German troops into the demilitarized Rhineland in 1936 and the union with Austria in 1938 (p. 454) were tolerated, although both were clear violations of the Treaty of Versailles. The British prime minister, Neville Chamberlain, even ❻ accepted the annexation of the German-speaking territories of Czechoslovakia under the Munich Agreement in 1938, and appeared to have saved the peace at the last minute.

6 Chamberlain (left) visiting Hitler (middle) to discuss the Sudeten Crisis, 1938

When Hitler again violated the treaty and marched into Prague in March 1939, Chamberlain recognized the failure of his appeasement policy and began to make the initial ❽ preparations for war. Universal conscription was introduced, and Poland and Romania were assured of military support in case of a German invasion. Following Hitler's invasion of Poland, Great Britain met its obligations and declared war on Germany. Chamberlain, widely discredited by appeasement's failure, announced his resignation in 1940 and was succeeded by ❿ Winston Churchill.

Munich Agreement

In the Munich Agreement, Great Britain and France granted the Nazi regime control over the German-speaking Sudeten territories after Hitler had declared these his "last territorial demands." Although Britain and France had signed defensive alliances with Czechoslovakia, neither felt prepared for war, and the idea of another European conflict aroused dismay among the populations of both countries. Some were also sympathetic to German grievances over the territorial losses imposed after World War I. Czechoslovakia, whose territory was at stake, was excluded from the negotiations, and the agreement that emerged was dubbed the "Munich dictate" by angry Czechs.

Chamberlain talking to the Italian dictator Mussolini at the Munich Conferences, 1938

8 Prime minister Chamberlain (front row, middle) and his war cabinet (Churchill, second row, middle), February 1939

9 Production of grenade launchers for the British Navy, 1940

10 Winston Churchill signs autographs, 1940

Jun 1935 | Anglo-German Naval Agreement
1936 | Death of George V
Sep 1938 | Munich Agreement
1937–40 | Government of Neville Chamberlain
Apr 1939 | Reintroduction of universal conscription

Ireland: Division and Independence 1914–1949

In ❶ Ireland in 1921, the nationalist movement won a partial victory in its struggle for independence against Great Britain; in exchange, however, it had to agree to the division of the country. After years of civil war in Ireland over the question of unity, the island was officially divided in the 1940s. While Northern Ireland remained part of the United Kingdom, the majority of Ireland became an officially independent republic in 1949.

Street in an Irish village, ca. 1930

From the War for Independence to the Anglo-Irish Treaty

Ireland won the status of an autonomous dominion in 1922 after a bloody war of independence, while the northern province of Ireland remained a British possession.

The smoldering conflict between the Irish and the British (p. 392) reignited in 1914 when the British government passed a Home Rule Bill that guaranteed Ireland partial autonomy, including the Protestant parts of the North which were opposed to the bill. The decision to suspend the bill as war broke out was met with nationalist outrage. The militant Irish Volunteers occupied public buildings in Dublin on April 24, 1916, and proclaimed an Irish Republic in the ❸ Easter Rising. The British military brutally suppressed this revolt; hundreds of people were killed, and the leaders were arrested and executed or condemned to long ❺ prison sentences. Further ❹ radicalization on both sides followed, initiating a new phase of violence.

Under Eamon de Valera, an illegal revolutionary parliament was formed; most of its members were from the Sinn Féin ("We ourselves") political party. A year later the military unit called the Irish Republican Army (IRA) was founded to attack British authority. In 1921 the British government and Sinn Féin agreed to a cease-fire and signed the Anglo-Irish Treaty, which gave Ireland the official status of a "free state." Excluded from this were six counties of the mainly Protestant province of ❷ Ulster, which had voted to remain part of the United Kingdom. In 1922, the Irish Free State gained the status of a dominion. The acceptance of this partial sovereignty was approved by the Irish parliament, the Dail, by a narrow majority of 64 against 57 votes. On December 6, 1922, the new Irish constitution came into effect.

Town hall in Londonderry in the province of Ulster, Northern Ireland

"Bloody Sunday" of 1920

"Bloody Sunday"—November 21, 1920—was representative of the brutal cycle of violence in Ireland: Following the execution of 14 British officers on the orders of Michael Collins, a leading Irish nationalist, a unit of British soldiers opened fired into an Irish crowd during a Gaelic football match in Dublin, killing many civilian spectators.

Victims of street fighting in Dublin, 1920

The city center of Dublin after the suppression of the Easter Rising, 1916

Remains of a train derailed by a terrorist attack planned by the IRA, 1916

Prison where the Easter Rising leaders were held

1914 | Home Rule Bill repealed
24 Apr 1916 | Sinn Féin movement Easter Rising
1918 | de Valera's revolutionary parliament
1919 | IRA founded
21 Nov 1920 | "Bloody Sunday"
1921 | Cease-fire

From Civil War to Independence

The division of Ireland led to bloody altercations within the Irish independence movement over the question of unity. The southern republic of Ireland gained full sovereignty in 1949 and left the Commonwealth.

The Anglo-Irish Treaty divided not only the country, but also the Sinn Féin independence movement. Supporters and opponents of the treaty now fought among themselves. The radicals under de Valera, the later Fianna Fáil party, accepted the exclusion of ❼ Northern Ireland, but strove for a reunification. The Fine Gael, under Prime Minister Thomas Cosgrave, sought equality with Great Britain. The IRA was divided as well, with one part joining the official Irish army while ❾ radical "irregulars" fought

6 US soldiers at base in Northern Ireland during WW II, 1942

against the government of the Irish Free State in 1922–1923. Over time, the radicals lost support, and de Valera ordered the end of hostilities. Isolated ❽ acts of terror took place into the 1930s, after which the IRA was banned. A new constitution introduced universal adult male and female suffrage as well as proportional representation. Ireland became a member of the League of Nations. The constitution established Gaelic (also called Erse) as the official national language. In March 1932 de Valera was elected prime minister and refused the oath of allegiance to the English king. His Fianna Fáil party has stayed in power almost continuously since then, but the desired reunification of the country did not occur and the division became cemented.

After a constitutional change in 1937, southern Ireland called itself Eire. It stayed out of World War II, while ❿ Northern Ireland ❻ participated as part of the United Kingdom. On April 1, 1949, Eire left the Commonwealth, and on April 18, officially proclaimed itself the Republic of Ireland.

8 Extinguishing fires after an IRA bomb attack in London, 1939

10 Monastery of Clonmacnoise, province of Leinster

7 Parade for the opening of the parliament in Belfast, Northern Ireland, 1925

9 Irish volunteers with cannons and armored cars acquired for their fight against the British army, 1921

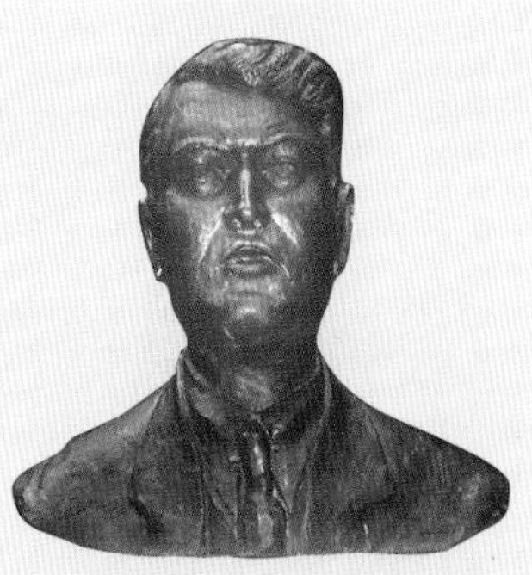

Michael Collins and Eamon de Valera

Michael Collins and Eamon de Valera were leaders of Sinn Féin and also symbolically represent its division. Shaped by the Easter Rising of 1916, both were members of the underground government, de Valera as chairman of Sinn Féin and Collins as the founder of the IRA. After the peace agreement with Great Britain, their paths diverged: Collins accepted the secession of Northern Ireland and joined the official Irish army. De Valera fought first violently and then peacefully for unity. While Collins was shot in an ambush in 1922, de Valera stayed at the top of Irish politics until 1973.

above: Eamon de Valera, 1932
top: Monument to Michael Collins in Dublin

6 Dec 1921 | Anglo-Irish Treaty signed
1922 | Proclamation of the Irish Free State
6 Dec 1922 | Irish constitution accepted
1932 | De Valera refuses oath to Crown
1937 | Southern Ireland renamed "Eire"
18 Apr 1949 | Eire leaves Commonwealth

Belgium and the Netherlands: Objects of German Power Politics

1914–1945

While Belgium became the military invasion route for the German armies during both world wars, the Netherlands survived the Great War unscathed. In World War II, however, it could not hold off the ❶ attack of the Germans and became an occupied territory of the Nazi Reich.

German forces invade the Netherlands, 1940

Belgium: Victim of Two World Wars

As a strategically important country between Germany and France, Belgium unwillingly became a combat zone in both world wars.

Before attacking France in 1914, Germany demanded free passage through Belgium in an ultimatum (p. 440). ❸ King Albert I, who wanted his country to remain neutral, refused, and on August 4, German troops proceeded to occupy the country. The country's neutrality was guaranteed by the Great Powers, which brought Great Britain into the war. The Belgian army mobilized when the country's neutrality was violated, but Liege, Namur, and Brussels soon fell. Almost the entire country was occupied and the strong resistance of the Belgians was answered with brutal retaliations by the German soldiers, notably in ❷ Louvain. The government was forced into exile. Western Belgium, where the French and German troops met, became a battlefield; many cities were ❻ destroyed and parts of Flanders ❹ utterly devastated.

King Albert I of Belgium, ca. 1910

At the end of WW I, Belgium annexed the German-speaking region of Eupen-et-Malmédy. A military accord was made with France, and a defensive alliance against Germany was signed with Great Britain. In 1925, Belgium joined the ❺ Locarno Treaty, which was meant to secure Belgium's borders. All this was to no avail, however, when Germany again invaded France through Belgium in May 1940. A few weeks later, the Belgian army under King Leopold III, who was taken prisoner, capitulated. The Belgian government escaped to London where it remained in exile for the remainder of the war. Leopold was suspected of collaboration and was forced to resign.

The burnt-out library of Louvain, 1914

Battlefield at Passchendaele, 1917

The Locarno Conference, 1925

Ypres after German bombardment, 1915

Atrocity Propaganda

Lurid propaganda was used by all sides in World War I. During the Belgian campaign, the British started a rumor that German soldiers hacked off the hands of children so that they would no longer be able to use a weapon. Although not a single example of this was found, the propaganda lived on. The rumors probably arose from the German view that civilians must not resist an occupying power. Thus hostages were taken and franctireurs were shot.

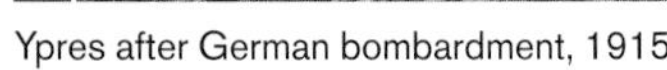

French propaganda postcard, 1914

2 Aug 1914 | Germany issues ultimatum to Belgium

4 Aug 1914 | Germans occupy Belgium

1917 | Universal right to vote in the Netherlands

1918 | Netherlands grants Wilhelm II asylum

1920 | Belgian-French Defense Alliance

1922 | Belgian-British Military Alliance

The Netherlands between Independence and National Socialism

Despite economic problems, the Netherlands was able to assert its neutrality until 1940 and remained politically stable. After the country was occupied by German troops, the new rulers implemented Nazi policies in the Netherlands, including the deportation of Dutch Jews to death camps.

The Netherlands survived World War I without internal upheaval, and coped well economically despite sheltering almost a million refugees who flooded out of Belgium in 1914. However, the blockade imposed principally by the Royal Navy had a restrictive effect on Dutch maritime traffic with countries which Britain and France feared could supply Germany. A severe shortage of coal led to the near-paralysis of Dutch industry. With the introduction of universal suffrage in 1917, the constitutional monarchy was democratized further, though a socialist revolution instigated by Pieter Jelles Troelstra was unsuccessful. The outbreak of the world economic crisis in 1929 (p. 506) caused a rapid increase in unemployment in the kingdom, however.

Externally the Netherlands committed itself to strict neutrality, but it was naturally interested in maintaining good relations with its German neighbor. For this reason, the government granted asylum to Wilhelm II in 1918.

8 Anti-Semitic caricature from the Netherlands, 1939

10 Official sign during the German occupation of Holland reads: "No admittance for Jews!", 1941

The Bombardment of Rotterdam

Like Guernica, Coventry, and Dresden, the Dutch city of Rotterdam stands as a symbol of the terror of modern air warfare against civilian populations. During the German Luftwaffe air raid on May 14, 1940, large parts of the city were completely destroyed, around 78,000 people were made homeless, and 900 people were killed.

above: The city center of Rotterdam, flattened except for the church of St. Laurentius, 1940

The 1933 victory of the National Socialists in Germany divided the Netherlands. Dutch supporters of Hitler, who organized themselves under ❼ Anton Adriaan Mussert, remained a minority, but after the first immigration wave of Jewish refugees, fears of ❽ Judaization became widespread, particularly in Protestant circles. The government followed news of German aggression with anxiety and ordered a general mobilization in 1939.

The army of the Netherlands was no match for the German attack in May 1940. After the bombardment of Rotterdam, the government capitulated and fled to London along with the royal family. The Nazi Reich's commissioner, Arthur Seyss-Inquart, began to align the Dutch state with the economic and social policies of the Nazi regime. Dutch citizens had to do forced labor, the concentration camps Westerbork and Vught were set up, and the ❿ systematic extermination of Jews began. While some volunteer ❾ Dutch SS divisions formed and others collaborated, a resistance movement that fought the regime with raids and acts of sabotage also established itself.

In September 1944, the Allies reached the Netherlands, and ⓫ liberated it on May 5, 1945. The Dutch East Indian colony (p. 526), occupied by the Japanese in 1942, was returned after the war.

7 Meeting of the Dutch National Socialist movement led by Anton Adriaan Mussert (middle), 1941

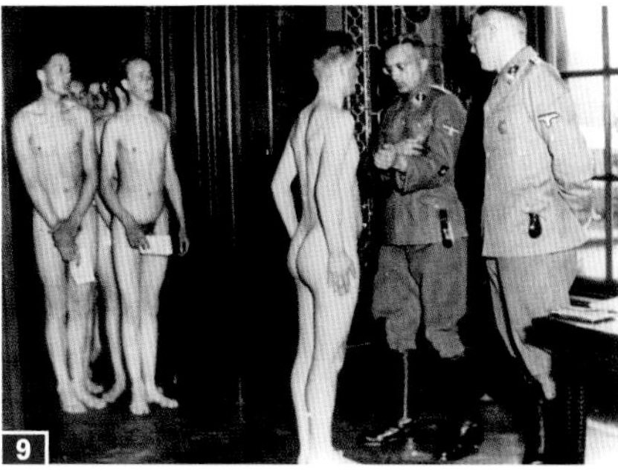

9 Physical examination of volunteers for the Dutch SS divisions, 1940

11 US forces liberate the Netherlands, 1945

1939	Mobilization
10 May 1940	German invasion of the Netherlands
14 May 1940	Bombardment of Rotterdam
14 May 1940	Capitulation of the Netherlands
Jun 1940	Belgian government in exile in London
5 May 1945	Liberation of the Netherlands

Italy under Fascism 1919–1945

The economic crisis and the dashed expectations of acquiring a colonial empire after World War I radicalized Italy's political right and led in 1922 to the establishment of Europe's ❶ first fascist dictatorship under the leadership of Benito Mussolini. He cleverly exploited Italian aspirations to "Great Power" status. After moving closer both ideologically and politically to the German Nazi regime, "Il Duce" led Italy into World War II against the Allies on Germany's side.

1 Meeting of the Fascist chamber in 1939

2 Benito Mussolini, 1940

The Rise of Mussolini

Mussolini's Fascist movement emerged victorious in 1922 out of the domestic turmoil that followed World War I. The ambitious Mussolini turned the state into a personal dictatorship, while retaining a nominal monarchy.

By extending the possibility of territorial gains and financial advantages, Great Britain, France, and Russia convinced the formerly neutral Italy into World War I (p. 397) in 1915. Emerging on the victorious side at the end of the war despite a marginal military contribution, Italy nevertheless resented how it had been sidelined during the peace negotiations. With half a million dead and an economic depression, internal divisions brought the country to the brink of civil war.

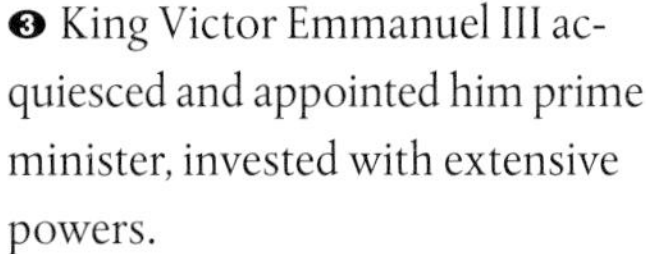

3 King Victor Emmanuel III

The nationalist right, under the slogan of "Mutilated Victory" and led by ❷ Benito Mussolini, turned into a violent and thuggish mass movement. In Rome and elsewhere, the ❺ Fascisti fought fierce street battles against socialist and communist groups, while the moderate parties were incapable of controlling the situation. When Mussolini marched on Rome in October 1922 and demanded the power of state, ❸ King Victor Emmanuel III acquiesced and appointed him prime minister, invested with extensive powers.

With the king's approval, Mussolini used the internal crisis that resulted from the murder of Socialist leader Giacomo Matteotti in 1925 to resolutely build up a "leader dictatorship." All opposition parties were outlawed, the parliament was dissolved, individual civil rights were repealed, and Mussolini's personal power was institutionalized. The Church and the king retained their rights within the framework of the regime. In 1929, Mussolini and Pope Pius XII concluded the ❹ Lateran Treaty, which granted the Vatican autonomous status.

Mussolini initially maintained his distance from Hitler and the German Nazi regime, even promising to protect Austria from a forced union with Germany. In 1935, he formed the Stresa Front with France and Great Britain to prevent further violations of the Versailles Treaty by Germany. However, dreams of empire soon saw him change his policies and alignments.

5 March of the Fascist youth organization "Balilla" in Italy, 1939

4 Signing of the Lateran Treaty in 1929; Mussolini (right) and Cardinal Gasparri, (seated)

The 1922 "March on Rome"

The Fascist demonstrations of October 27–31, 1922, became known as the "March on Rome" and served as a model for Hitler's followers. Fascist groups advanced to within a few miles of Rome following Mussolini's declaration in Naples that he would use force if necessary in order to take over the government. The large protest marches, attended by around 30,000, that converged in Rome on October 30 in fact took place without Mussolini—he had already been made prime minister the day before.

The March on Rome, 1922

26 Apr 1915	Secret London treaty
26 Aug 1915	Italy declares war on Germany
1919	Fascisti gather around Mussolini
Oct 1922	"March on Rome"
Nov 1922	Mussolini gains unlimited authority
1929	Lateran Treaty

Alliance with the Nazi Regime

During the 1930s, Italy and the German Reich increasingly leaned toward each other. Mussolini hoped to realize Italy's imperialist dreams of a new Mediterranean empire by fighting alongside Hitler in World War II. However, abject military failures soon left him dependent on Hitler.

Mussolini's campaign against ❻ Ethiopia (Abyssinia prior to WWI) in 1936 (p. 505) was the beginning of his cooperation with Hitler's Nazi regime and of the so-called ❼ Berlin–Rome "Axis." Germany was the only nation that supported the unprovoked Italian attack on a nation that had long been independent. Following a full-scale invasion that involved the use of tanks, bombers, and chemical weapons against the non-mechanized Ethiopian army, Victor Emmanuel III was proclaimed "emperor of Ethiopia."

The Italian-German relationship strengthened in the ensuing years. Italy resigned from the League of Nations in 1937 and did not protest when Hitler annexed Austria into the German Reich in 1938 (p. 455). Together, Italy and Germany supported the coup led by General Francisco Franco (p. 473) in the Spanish Civil War. Italian Fascism also moved closer to National Socialism ideologically. Whereas the racial supremacy doctrine had not initially been part of the Italian fascist agenda, in 1938 most of the Jews in Italy lost their civil rights and were excluded from public offices. In May 1939, the two ❽ dictators concluded the "Pact of Steel," a friendship and alliance agreement that defined the conditions for a common European war.

While Italy still reacted hesitantly to Germany's invasion of Poland in 1939 (p. 510), the rapid German victory against France erased all doubts and Italy declared war on the Allied powers on June 10, 1940. Mussolini's goal was to conquer the ❾ Mediterranean region, including Greece and North Africa, and found a new "Roman" Empire. The Tripartite Pact of September 27, 1940, committed Italy, Germany, and Japan to wage war against any nation siding with the Allies. Military failures (p. 523) soon ensured ❿ Italy's complete dependence upon Germany's political and military leadership and fanned the flames of internal crisis that ultimately culminated in Mussolini's downfall. Following airstrikes and the Allies' invasion of Sicily, the king forced Mussolini to resign on July 25, 1943, and had him arrested. When General Eisenhower announced a cease-fire with Italy a little while later, German troops occupied Rome. Mussolini was freed by German paratroopers and under the protection of German troops founded the fascist "Italian Social Republic" in Salò, northern Italy. On July 9, 1944, Rome was taken by the Allies, and following the surrender of German armed forces in Italy, Mussolini's puppet government was dissolved. Communist partisans ⓫ executed the former dictator on April 28, 1945, as he was fleeing to Swizerland.

6 Italians enter Gondar in Ethiopia, 1935

8 Hitler on a state visit to Italy in 1938

7 Italian Fascist symbols being erected in preparation for Mussolini's visit to Berlin in 1937

9 Italian torpedo boat in the Mediterranean Sea, 1942

10 German Stukas flying across the Mediterranean region to help the Italians, 1941

11 The bodies of Mussolini and his girlfriend Clara Pettaci, who were publicly hanged by partisans in 1945

1936 | Ethiopia conquered
May 1939 | "Pact of Steel"
10 Jun 1940 | Italy declares war on the Allies
27 Sep 1940 | Tripartite Pact
25th Jul 1943 | Mussolini taken prisoner
9th Jul 1944 | Allies take Rome
28th Apr 1945 | Mussolini murdered

1 Spanish civil war, the front at Malaga, 1936

Spain and Portugal 1914–1945

In Portugal and Spain, strong right-wing authoritarian movements gained influence in the 1930s. While a dictatorial system was quickly established in Portugal, a bloody and devastating ❶ civil war with international involvement raged in Spain between leftist and rightist forces from 1936 to 1939. The victorious General Franco erected a brutal and long-lasting military dictatorship in Spain.

2 Military parade in 1928 on the anniversary of the May 28 1926 coup

Portugal: The Salazar Regime

In the 1930s, Premier Salazar used the political turmoil of the postwar period to build up a dictatorial system, which remained largely uninvolved in world politics.

❸ Portugal supported the Entente in World War I, even sending a poorly-prepared division which was destroyed on the Western Front, but domestically chaotic conditions had reigned since the founding of the republic in 1910 (p. 398). The government changed hands 44 times before the republic finally collapsed in ❷ May 1926 following a military coup. The new head of government, General António de Fragoso Carmona, named ❹ António de Oliveira Salazar as his finance minister in 1928. Salazar succeeded in the rapid economic consolidation of the state.

Salazar founded the fascist União Nacional in 1930, which under his leadership shaped politics in Portugal well beyond World War II. In 1932 he became prime minister and in 1933 institutionalized the "New State" (Estado Novo) through a new constitution and a dictatorial government on a corporative basis, which economically bound employers and employees in a ❻, ❼ state-controlled, hierarchical political system and society.

In international affairs, Salazar supported the insurgents under General Francisco Franco during the Spanish Civil War of 1936–1939, and after Franco's victory, the two countries signed a nonaggression pact. Salazar at first pursued a neutral course in World War II but in 1943 joined the Allies and allowed the stationing of air force and naval units on the Portuguese ❺ Azores Islands.

3 Traditional fishing on the Atlantic coast of Portugal, photography 1930s

4 António de Oliveira Salazar, ca. 1950

5 Portuguese backup troops embark and are sent to the Azores, 1941

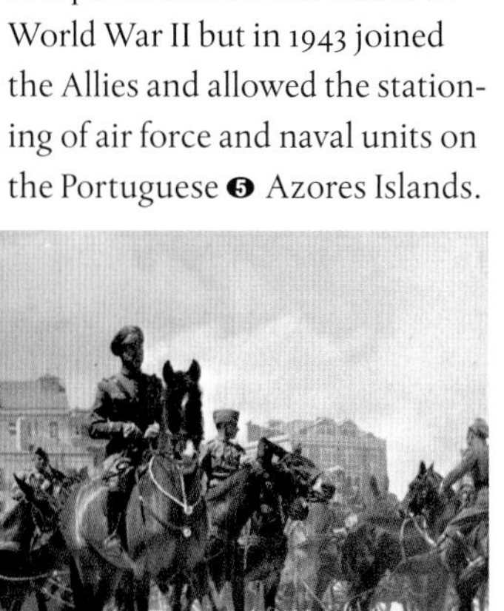

6 Mounted members of the state-controlled paramilitary organization "Légion Portuguesa," 1936

7 Parade of the state-controlled youth organization "Mocidade," 1936

1923 Military coup led by de Rivera | **1926** Republic of Portugal dissolved | **1928** Carmona becomes head of government | **1930** "União Nacional" founded | **1931** 2nd Republic in Spain founded | **1932** Salazar becomes premier

Spain: Civil War and the Franco Dictatorship

Domestic tensions in Spain erupted in the Spanish Civil War in 1936. This led to a fascist dictatorship under Francisco Franco in 1939.

Spain was shaken by political unrest for more than 20 years following World War I. Corruption, separatist aspirations—for example, in Catalonia—and the long struggle to pacify the protectorate in the northern part of Morocco against Abdel Krim, leader of the independence movement, weakened the parliamentary monarchy and led to a military coup by General Miguel Primo de Rivera in 1923. He installed a personal dictatorship that was tolerated by King Alfonso XIII. Despite the successful conclusion of the Moroccan war, however, he had to step down in 1930 due to unresolved social problems and the overstretching of the economy in the boom years of the twenties. In the San Sebástian pact of 1930, republican political parties, as well as ⓫ intellectuals such as José Ortega y Gasset, resolved to overthrow the monarchy. In 1931, they were successful and the king was forced to leave the country. The Second Republic was founded, but quickly came under fire from radical political forces on both the left and right. Violent ❿ uprisings and revolts for social reform by the unionized workers occurred in 1933, as did a strengthening of the fascist movement. In 1933, the antidemocratic ❾ Falange party was formed; it later became a decisive instrument of Franco's dictatorial government. General strikes and political murders further widened the gulf between the conservative-nationalist forces and the republicans and radical socialists. General Franco's right-wing revolt against the leftist Peoples' Front government in 1936 ignited a three-year ⓬ civil war that aroused international attention and was waged with foreign military support on both sides. The republic broke up in January 1939 following the capture of Barce-lona by ❽ Franco's troops.

Franco built a dictatorial regime in devastated Spain, outlawed the formation of political parties, and suppressed all opposition. More than 350,000 opponents were executed and hundreds of thousands incarcerated.

Franco's regime remained largely neutral in World War II, despite joining the Anti-Comintern Pact. Combat units dispatched to fight Bolshevism on the Eastern Front were sent back in 1944. As the defeat of the Axis powers loomed, Franco approached the Allies and curbed the persecution of Communists.

International Brigade

Many left-wing idealists, including artists from throughout the world, fought in the International Brigade against Franco's troops. André Gide, George Orwell, Egon Erwin Kisch, and Ernest Hemingway, among others, came from France, Great Britain, Germany, and the United States as fighters or reporters for the republic.

above: Volunteers of the International Brigade, 1936

10 Insurgents burn churches and monasteries, 1931

8 Francisco Franco, 1935

9 Young Spaniards learn to march in the manner of the Falangists, 1935

Guernica

The total destruction of the small Basque city of Guernica by the German Luftwaffe on April 26, 1937, during the Spanish civil war, offered a foretaste of the bombing raids of World War II. The attacks were directed exclusively at the civilian population in order to break the morale of the Republican troops. Picasso's famous oil painting "Guernica" was meant to condemn this terrible act of destruction to the world.

Destroyed Guernica, 1936

11 Students call for the Republic, 1931

12 Spanish refugees on the border to France, 1939

1933 | Constitution of the "New State"
1933 | "Falange Espanol" founded
July 1936 | Military revolt led by Franco
Sep 1939 | Franco becomes head of government
1939 | Spanish-Portuguese Alliance
Jan 1939 | Republic dissolved

Scandinavia and the Baltic 1917–1944

Following World War I, all of the Scandinavian countries moved toward the development of democratic welfare states. In international affairs, only Sweden was able to maintain the Scandinavian tradition of neutrality throughout World War II, while Denmark and Norway were occupied by German troops, and Finland fought hard to preserve its recently won independence. The newly created independent ❶ Baltic states found themselves squeezed between the aggression of Germany and Russia.

Freedom memorial in Riga, Latvia, built in 1935

The Baltic Republics' Brief Independence

With German aid, the Baltic states became independent following World War I. From 1939 on, they were invaded and occupied first by Hitler and then Stalin. After World War II they were annexed and became republics of the Soviet Union.

In the Treaty of Brest-Litovsk of 1918 (p. 444) between Germany and Russia, the Bolsheviks had been forced to guarantee the independence of their Baltic provinces in northeastern Europe. Through long struggles, Estonia, ❷ Latvia, and Lithuania established themselves as liberal constitutional states by 1920. Germany sought to play the role of guarantor of their sovereignty against attacks from Poland and the Soviet Union. In 1920, the former German port of Memel was taken over by Lithuania; in 1924, it gained autonomy until it was once more assimilated into Hitler's fascist Reich in 1939. Under the ❸ Nazi-Soviet Pact of 1939, the Baltic states were at the mercy of Hitler and Stalin. In the accord's secret protocol, the Nazi regime recognized the whole Baltic region and Finland as a ❻ Russian sphere of influence. Hitler had shortly beforehand signed a nonaggression pact with Latvia. In 1940, the Red Army marched into the Baltic States. Stalin forced Lithuania, Latvia, and Estonia to accept Soviet naval bases and garrisons; Russia had long sought access to warm-water ports and control of the Baltic Sea. The German army retook the territory during its invasion of Russia and carried out a systematic elimination of the Jewish population. Germans were ❹ resettled further west. In the hope that Germany would support the independence of the small republics after the war, many ❼ anti-communists and anti-Semites from the Baltic area, especially Lithuania, volunteered for the Waffen SS. As the Soviets began to push westward, Estonia, Latvia, and Lithuania again fell to the ❺ Red Army in 1944. After the war, they were incorporated into the Soviet Union and did not regain their independence until the fall of the USSR.

Soviet Socialist propaganda after the annexation of Latvia

Ministers of State sign the nonaggression pact: (seated from left to right) Munsters of Latvia, Ribbentrop of Germany, Selter of Estonia, 1939

Arrival of the Red Army in Vilnius, Lithuania, July 1944

Volunteers from the Baltic SS divisions being inspected by a Nazi official, 1944

Parliament of the republic of Latvia in the capital Riga, ca. 1930

Arrival of Baltic Germans in Stettin as part of the resettlement, Oct 1939

Volunteer Corps

Long after the official end of World War I, German volunteer corps continued to fight against the Red Army in the Baltic states. They were officially supported by the Western governments which sought to crush the nascent Bolshevik Revolution in Russia. After many bitterly fought battles, the volunteer corps were defeated and returned to Germany in mid-December 1919.

Volunteer corps soldiers return from the Baltics to Berlin, 1919

6 Dec 1917 | Finland declares independence
1918 | Baltic states gain independence
1932 | USSR nonaggression pact with Finland
23 Aug 1939 | Nazi-Soviet Pact
Oct 1939 | German nonaggression pact with Latvia
30 Nov 1939 | Red Army marches into Finland

Scandinavia and Finland through World War II

While the Scandinavian countries were all able to remain neutral during the First World War, only Sweden avoided being pulled into the hostilities by German aggression during the Second World War.

Sweden, Denmark, and Norway did not join the conflict during World War I, although the Entente occasionally boycotted Sweden because of its lively trade with the German Reich, and Norway sent out its merchant fleet against the Central Powers. Still, the nonaligned status of the Scandinavian countries was never challenged by either side and, after the war, there were no social upheavals. The Scandinavian monarchies became parliamentary democracies in the interwar period and steadily developed as welfare states. The Social Democrat majority reduced the effects of the economic depression (p. 507) on the population through increased state services.

Finland was a special case in the Scandinavian world due to its proximity to ❿ Russia. As a former dominion of the czar's empire, Finland took advantage of the turmoil of the Russian Revolution (p. 480) to declare its independence on December 6, 1917. Despite a nonaggression treaty signed in 1932, the relationship with the Soviet Union remained tense, and in accordance with the Nazi-Soviet Pact that assured German acquiescence, the Red Army invaded Finland on November 30, 1939, in order to prevent future German threats to the Soviet Union moving through Scandinavia. However, only after Soviet bombing of Finnish cities and fighting which inflicted grave losses on the Russians was the ⓬ "Winter War" decided in the Soviet Union's favor, and it was able to retain only about 10 percent of ❽ Finland as the Western powers threatened to intervene. Following Hitler's invasion of the Soviet Union in 1941, Finland allied with Nazi Germany against the Soviet Union.

Norwegian fascist leader Vidkun Quisling (right) and Heinrich Himmler, 1942

Sweden emerged from World War II unscathed. Through making concessions to Nazi Germany, such as permission to allow German troops through Swedish territory, it was left in peace and granted refugees asylum in the country until the end of the war. At the end of 1943, though, Sweden began to lean more decidedly toward the Allies.

⓫ Denmark and ⓭ Norway were occupied by German troops on April 9, 1940. Resistance developed in Norway from the beginning. About 40,000 Norwegians were deported into concentration camps, and a Norwegian fascist leader ❾ Vidkun Quisling was appointed prime minister by the occupying forces in 1942.

When the Germans began deporting Jews from Denmark in 1943, the situation became critical. Martial law was imposed following strikes and acts of sabotage. Danish fishermen carried 7900 Jews to safety over the straits to Sweden. Denmark was liberated by British troops, who did not have to fire a shot, in May 1945. The German occupying forces in Norway also surrendered without offering any resistance.

Finnish soldiers on skis, 1939

Swedish volunteers fighting for the Finnish against Russia, 1940

Finnish soldiers fleeing from the Red Army are brought home under the protection of German soldiers, 1918

German armored convoy in Denmark, 1940

German soldiers in Norway, 1940

1939–40 | Soviet-Finnish Winter War
9 Apr 1940 | German occupation of Denmark and Norway
1940 | Norwegian exile government in London
1942 | V. Quisling made prime minister
1944 | Red Army annexes the Baltic Republics

Poland 1914–1939

After 123 years of foreign rule, Poland was restored as a ❶ sovereign state after World War I, but the existence of the nation was constantly threatened from without because of border disputes. Internal political strife and unresolved problems with minorities also affected the country. Germany and the Soviet Union carved up Poland between them in 1939.

Celebration of Polish independence, painting, 1918

The Polish State until 1921

Poland proclaimed itself an independent state in 1918. The wrangling over the final positions of the borders, however, dragged on until 1921.

Since 1795, the Polish territories had been divided between Prussia, Austria, and Russia. The outbreak of World War I revitalized the Poles' hopes for the restoration of their sovereignty. Polish ❸ legionnaires supported the Central Powers, which proclaimed the restitution of the Polish hereditary monarchy in 1916. The looming defeat of the Central Powers and the assurances of the Entente Powers regarding Poland's sovereignty initiated a change of mood in favor of the victorious powers.

After the overthrow of the czar, the provisional Russian government recognized the Polish right to self-determination in March 1917 (p. 480), and in 1918 in the Brest-Litovsk Treaty relinquished its Polish territories. Following the capitulation of the Central Powers, Jozef Pilsudski proclaimed Poland independent on November 11, 1918, and named himself the provisional head of state of the republic. He built the state of an independent Poland.

The Treaty of Versailles in 1919 granted the new nation the province of Poznan as well as broad sections of West Prussia to create the "Polish Corridor," a narrow strip of territory along the Vistula River with access to the Baltic Sea. Pilsudski, however, sought the restoration of the borders of 1772 (p. 304), which would include the Russian-dominated Byelorussia, Ukraine, and Lithuania. The Lithuanian Vilnius territory was brought under Polish sovereignty through military action. A Polish advance on ❷ Kiev in March 1920 then triggered the Polish-Soviet War. The Soviet counteroffensive failed with the Polish victory in the Battle of Warsaw (the "Miracle on the Vistula"). The subsequent Treaty of ❹ Riga on March 18, 1921, moved the Polish–Russian border about 150 miles to the east.

The League of Nations divided the ❺ disputed Polish-German Upper Silesian territories in 1921. Poland received the coal-rich ❻ eastern Upper Silesia; the other territories went to Germany. The city of Danzig was declared a free city, a further sore point in the Polish–German relationship.

2 Conquest of Kiev by the Red Army, 1920

3 Polish soldiers, 1915

4 Polish delegation at the Riga Conference, 1921

5 Polish workers take up arms during the dispute over Upper Silesia, 1921

6 *"God, let my native soil stay German!"* Propaganda poster during the Upper Silesia dispute, 1921

1916	Kingdom of Poland proclaimed
11 Nov 1918	Poland regains independence
Apr–Oct 1920	Polish-Soviet War
1921	Military alliance with France
18 Mar 1921	Treaty of Riga
1926	Coup led by Pilsudski

Brief Sovereignty

Even the domestic transition from a democracy to an authoritarian state could not prevent Poland's powerful neighbors Germany and the Soviet Union invading Poland and dividing the country between them in 1939.

After the boundaries were agreed upon, Poland re-formed as a democratic constitutional state in 1921. The internal consolidation of the newly formed nation was made difficult from the outset by its underdeveloped economy and the nationalist protectionism that was prevalent in inter-war Central Eastern Europe. The fierce rivalry among the political parties meant the rapidly changing governments failed to coordinate the diverse administrative and economic systems created during the partition and to integrate the minorities. Less than 70 percent of the population living within Poland's new borders was Polish, and the minorities were granted only a restricted franchise and influence in parliament. There were numerous Ukrainian uprisings in East Galicia.

7 Funeral of Jozef Pilsudskis, 1935

The founder of modern Poland, ❽ Pilsudski, proclaimed himself to be the savior of the nation and carried out a military coup in 1926. While formally retaining the democratic constitution, he set up a dictatorial regime that suppressed the opposition. The regime was based on his personal prestige and deteriorated after his ❼ death in 1935. A succession of military leaders determined the course of the state thereafter.

9 Hitler revokes his nonaggression pact with Poland, 1939

Due to border disputes, Poland was continually threatened by its powerful neighbors, Germany and the USSR. It signed an alliance with France in 1921, but this had little effect. Nonaggression treaties negotiated with the Soviet Union in 1932 and with Germany in 1934 quickly proved to be nothing more than a ❾ temporary cease-fire. In a secret protocol of the Nazi–Soviet nonaggression pact of August 23, 1939, also known as the Ribbentrop-Molotov Pact after the foreign ministers of the two countries who negotiated the secret clause, the two powers agreed to partition Poland. The German "Blitzkrieg" poured across the Polish ❿ western border on September 1, 1939; Soviet troops invaded the eastern part two weeks later. The simultaneous attack ensured that the ill-equipped Polish army's brave resistance was short-lived, and on September 27, the Germans occupied Warsaw.

8 Polish leader Jozef Pilsudski at a military parade, 1926

10 German soldiers tear down a barrier on the frontier with Poland, 1939

"Free City" of Danzig/Gdansk

Hitler used the status of Danzig (Gdansk in Polish) as a free city under international law as a pretext to unexpectedly start a war against Poland in 1939. The internationally mandated city had, since its establishment in the Treaty of Versailles, been a source of contention to German nationalists. Danzig had a German majority and it was an economically important port city.

Nazi victory parade through the streets of Danzig/Gdansk, Poland, 1939

1914–1945 The World Wars and Interwar Period

1932	Non-aggression pact with USSR signed
26 Jan 1934	Nonaggression pact with Germany signed
1935	Pilsudski dies
23 Aug 1939	Anglo-Polish alliance
1 Sep 1939	Germany invades Poland
27 Sep 1939	Occupation of Warsaw

Hungary and Czechoslovakia 1914–1945

Out of the remnants of the dual monarchy of Austria-Hungary, the new states of ❶ Hungary and Czechoslovakia emerged in 1918. However, both became caught in the web of the expanding German Reich in the 1930s as a result of their geographical proximity to Germany. Under German pressure, Czechoslovakia was divided up in 1938 and dissolved as a nation before a part of it was annexed by the German Reich. Hungary's radical right-wing regime was sympathetic toward the Nazis and fought on the side of the Axis powers in World War II, following which the government crumbled with the end of World War II.

1 Elizabeth-Bridge in Budapest, Hungary, built 1897–1903

Hungary: From Republic to Right Wing Regime

Following the first postwar revolutionary years, an authoritarian regime established itself in the drastically reduced state of Hungary. It was sympathetic toward Germany during World War II.

Following the collapse of the Habsburg dual monarchy in 1918 (p. 444), Count Mihály Károlyi used the middle class–democratic "Aster Revolution" in Hungary to take over the government, proclaiming a republic on November 16. From the beginning, it was burdened by party conflicts and territorial losses. Hungary was compelled to vacate areas in the south and east of the country as a result of the Treaty of Versailles in 1919. The Czechs occupied Slovakia, the Romanians Transylvania, and the Serbs southern Hungary. The treaty also forced the reduction of the Hungarian army and obliged the nation to pay reparations. Károlyi resigned in protest, and the Communists, led by ❷ Béla Kun, proclaimed a Soviet republic in March 1919.

3 Participants in the peace conference of Trianon

4 Hitler and Horthy, 1941

Opposing pressure from the right and waging a war against Czechoslovakia and Romania over lost territory brought down the leftist regime. At the end of the war, the ❸ Treaty of Trianon in 1920—by which Hungary lost two-thirds of its territory—ushered in the peace. Revisionist demands from then on determined Hungary's politics and encouraged nationalist movements.

In 1920 Hungary once again became a monarchy. The parliament chose ❹ Miklós Horthy as regent of the empire and established a right wing regime. The central domestic problem was a financial crisis that was only temporarily relieved by a loan from the League of Nations in 1923. The economic depression of the 1930s brought a further shift to the right. The national socialistic ❺ "Arrow Cross" gained popularity, and internally and in foreign affairs the government sought to move closer to Hitler's Germany. Anti-Semitic laws restricted the rights of the Jews in public life.

Germany's and Italy's "Vienna Arbitrations" (1938 and 1940) satisfied some of Hungary's territorial demands: Part of Slovakia and the areas occupied by Romania were returned to Hungary. In alliance with Germany, Hungary marched into Yugoslavia in 1941 and participated in Hitler's Russian military campaign. When in 1944 Hungary sought a cease-fire, German troops occupied the country, but quickly lost it again to the advancing ❻ Red Army. By April 4, 1945, the Soviets had conquered Hungary completely.

2 Communist leader Béla Kun holds a speech before the public, 1919

5 Tragedy following the pogroms of the national socialistic "Arrow Cross," 1944

Monarchy

With the proclamation of March 23, 1920, Hungary became a monarchy without a monarch. The Hungarian people rejected the claims to the throne of the former Austrian emperor and Hungarian king, Charles IV. When Charles attempted to seize the crown on his own authority, he was arrested in October 1921 and sent into exile on Madeira.

The former emperor Charles in exile with his family, 1921

6 Russian soldier on the lookout, 1945

1918 | Treaty of Pittsburgh
16 Nov 1918 | Republic of Hungary proclaimed
1 Aug 1919 | Béla Kun flees
1920 | M. Horthy chosen as regent of the empire
1918 | Czech and Slovak government in exile
Mar 1919 | Soviet republic proclaimed
4 Jun 1920 | Treaty of Trianon

The Republic of Czechoslovakia 1918–1938

The Czechoslovakian republic, founded in 1918, was broken up in 1938 and added to the German Reich as the "Protectorate of Bohemia and Moravia."

During World War I, Czech and Slovak emigrants sympathetic to the Allies and escaping military service in the Austrian forces formed governments in exile in the United States; in the Pittsburgh Treaty of 1918, they resolved to unite the two nations in one state after the war. In 1920, the National Assembly chose the Czech ❽ Tomás Masaryk, who had formed Czech regiments in the Allied service, as president of the new parliamentary democratic republic. He remained in power, together with the long-standing foreign minister Edvard Benes, until 1935 but failed to form a common national identity among the assorted ethnicities of the different states. The population of the new multinational state was only about 60 percent Czechs and Slovaks; alongside Hungarians, Ukrainians, and Poles, the Sudeten Germans were the largest minority with almost 25 percent. Encouraged by the Nazis' takeover of power in Germany, the Sudeten Germans increasingly aspired to autonomy.

Konrad Henlein, nationalist gymnastics teacher

Together with ❼ Konrad Henlein's Sudeten German Homeland Front (from 1935, the Sudeten German party), Hitler precipitated the Sudeten Crisis in 1938. Neither the 1920–1921 alliance with France and Poland nor the ❾ "Little Entente" with Yugoslavia and Romania were able to withstand the territorial claims of the Nazi regime. In the Munich Agreement between the Great Powers (p. 465), Czechoslovakia had to relinquish the ❿, ⓫ Sudetenland to Germany. The breakup of the state could no longer be prevented. Poland and Hungary were granted territories in the border regions. The day after Slovakia proclaimed its independence under German protection on March 14, 1939, German troops marched into the remains of Czechoslovakia and placed it under the rule of the German Reich as the Protectorate of Bohemia and Moravia. Czechoslovakia was dissolved. There was hardly any rebellion against the German occupation. The first ⓬ revolt did not take place until May 1945 in Prague.

Benes, now president, worked on rebuilding a Czechoslovakian state from his exile in London. The government in exile concluded an agreement in 1943 on the occupation of the territory by the Red Army. On September 10, 1945, Czechoslovakia reconstituted itself under the protection of the Soviets.

Wehrmacht soldiers take down the border sign to the Sudetenland, 1938

State President Tomás Masaryk, 1926

Meeting of the "Little Entente," founded in 1920, Kamil Krofta (right), foreign minister of Czechoslovakia

Slovakia

Following Slovakia's declaration of independence, a fascist satellite state of the German Reich was created there. It participated in the German invasion of Poland in 1939, joined the Tripartite Pact in 1940, and from 1941 was involved in the extermination policies against the Jews. Following its occupation by the Red Army in April 1945, Slovakian president Jozef Tiso and three ministers were hanged.

Father Jozef Tiso is congratulated following his election

Sudetenland 1938: Evacuation of Czech citizens

Corpses following the Prague revolt, 1945

1938 | "Sudeten Crisis"
29 Sep 1938 | Munich Agreement
2 Nov 1938 | First arbitration decision of Vienna
15 Mar 1939 | Protectorate of Bohemia and Moravia
10 Sep 1945 | Czechoslovakia reconstituted
4 Apr 1945 | Red Army conquers Hungary

The Soviet Union 1917–1939

The Russian czar was deposed in 1917, even before the end of World War I. The radical left-wing Bolsheviks emerged victorious out of the dispute between the democratic transitional government and the revolutionary Soviet Council of Soldiers' and Workers' Deputies. They came to power in the October Revolution in 1917 under the leadership of ❶ Lenin, ended the war, suppressed counterrevolutionary uprisings in a civil war, and constituted the first Communist-ruled state in the world: the Union of Soviet Socialist Republics (USSR). After Lenin's death in 1924, the Soviet Union became an increasingly centralized personal dictatorship under Stalin in the 1930s. Stalin oversaw a massive industrialization program and forcibly collectivized agriculture, while millions fell victim to the regime's repression.

Lenin at the unveiling of the Marx-Engels memorial on the Place of the Revolution in Moscow, 1918

The End of the Czar's Empire

The deposing of Nicholas II in 1917 resulted in a tension-filled coalition between the liberal government and the Soviet Council of Soldiers' and Workers' Deputies.

The large numbers of war dead, supply shortages, and corruption during the course of ❷ World War I led to growing dissatisfaction with the czarist autocracy among the Russian people. The ❹ calls for an end to the war became louder not only in the civilian population but also in the military. Avowals of friendship and brotherhood with the enemy even took place among the soldiers (p. 442).

The situation escalated in March 1917 when military units in St. Petersburg refused ❺ Czar Nicholas II's order to deal severely with striking workers. The military allied itself with the strikers and forced the czar to abdicate on March 15, 1917, in the February Revolution. Nicholas and his family were ❼ executed on July 17, 1918 by the Council of Ekaterinburg, where they were confined due to alarm at the rapid approach of White Russian forces which wanted to release the czar.

Lenin leading the people in the Russian Revolution, painting by Alexandre Gerassimov, 1930

Demonstration, 1917

A provisional government under Prince Lvov was set up. It proclaimed the right of political freedom and was supported by moderate Social Democrats, the Mensheviks. Parallel to this, in many cities workers and soldiers organized into ❸ Soviet councils that demanded more social changes and saw themselves as a counter to the power of the provisional government.

In April 1917 the Communist revolutionary leader of the Bolsheviks, Vladimir Ilich Ulyanov, known as ❻ Lenin, returned to St. Petersburg from his exile in Switzerland. In his "April Theses," he demanded an immediate peace settlement and the redistribution of land to the peasants. He also demanded an end to the coalition of the provisional government and exclusive power to the Soviets. The Bolsheviks' attempted coup in July 1917 failed, however.

The Russian Calendar

Until 1918, the Russian calendar was based on the old Julian calendar, from which the name "February Revolution" derives. According to the Gregorian calendar customary in the Western world, it was March 15. Similarly, the "October Revolution" took place on November 7 according to Western dating.

Russian prisoners of war in East Prussia, 1915

Meeting of the Petrograd Soviet council, March 1917

Czar Nicholas II

Palace in Ekaterinburg, where the czar and his family were executed on July 17, 1918

15 Mar 1917	February Revolution
April 1917	Lenin returns from exile
Jul 1917	Bolsheviks attempt coup
7 Nov 1917	October Revolution
Mar 1918	Government moved to Kremlin in Moscow
17 Jul 1918	Czar Nicholas II murdered

The Bolshevik Victory

A civil war broke out after the October Revolution as western governments armed the counterrevolutionary "White Army." By 1922 the Red Army had emerged victorious.

As the liberal provisional government under the new prime minister, ❽ Aleksandr Kerensky, continued the war and did not give in to the demands for social improvement, the conflict between the Soviets and the government became increasingly critical in the second half of 1917. Lenin and the Bolsheviks once again planned an armed uprising against the government after September 1917.

The ❾ October Revolution finally erupted on November 7, 1917. ⓫ Leon Trotsky led the Bolshevik Red Guard in occupying the most important points in St. Petersburg and ⓬ stormed the Winter Palace, the seat of the provisional government. Kerensky's government was arrested, and Lenin formed the Council of People's Commissars, the first Soviet government.

The Bolsheviks ended the war against the Central Powers with the Treaty of Brest-Litovsk (p. 444) on March 3, 1918. The harsh terms dictated by Germany were accepted by Lenin, as Russia was in turmoil. Large property owners and industry owners were expropriated without compensation, banks were nationalized, opposition parties were banned, and the democratic parliament was abolished. The newly founded security agency, the Cheka, was meant to secure the exclusive authority of the Bolsheviks. The first phase of the revolutionary reformation of Russia ended with the move of the Soviet government to the ⓭ Kremlin in Moscow in March 1918.

But the government was still by no means secure. A counterrevolutionary alliance of monarchists, Mensheviks, and nonsocialist powers had formed a ❿ "White Army" in 1918 that fought the Bolsheviks' ⓮ "Red Army" in a bloody, almost three-year-long civil war. Despite support of the Whites from Russia's World War I allies, the tightly led Red Army finally prevailed at the beginning of 1922. With Georgia, Ukraine, Armenia, and Azerbaijan, the Reds conquered even states that had declared their independence after the Treaty of Brest-Litovsk. The Polish-Russian war of 1920–1921 (p. 476) and the terrible famine in Russia in the winter of 1921–1922 no longer posed serious threats to Bolshevik power. By 1922, the new socialist state had almost reached the same extent as the former Russian empire.

In the same year, the Russian Soviet Federated Socialist Republic united with the Soviet republics of Ukraine and Belarus to form the Union of Soviet Socialist Republics (USSR). The Soviet Union was the world's first Communist country and was hailed by socialists around the world.

9 Cartoon: *The Proletarian's Hammer Strikes Back*, 1917

8 Aleksandr Kerensky (on car) at a parade, 1917

10 General Yudenich of the White Army forces with his staff, 1919

11 Leon Trotsky, 1917

12 Storming of the Winter Palace, 1917

13 Lenin's mausoleum (right), Red Square, Moscow

14 Red Army cavalry, 1919

1918 | Founding of the White Army

3 Mar 1918 | Treaty of Brest-Litovsk

1920–21 | Polish-Russian War

1921-22 | Red Army prevails

1922 | Founding of the USSR

Stalin's Rise from 1924 to 1929

After Lenin's death, Stalin took over the leadership of the party and by 1929 was undisputed leader of the country. In foreign affairs, the Soviet Union was primarily concerned with consolidation.

After Lenin fell ill in 1922, internal power struggles over succession within the party determined the domestic development of the country. Stalin used his power as general secretary of the Communist party to place his followers, particularly Kamenev and Zinoviev, in important government and party posts and give his office a key position in the party structure. Although Lenin in his "political will" had recommended the replacement of Stalin—whose ambitious nature he suspected—as general secretary, Stalin was able to overcome his rivals after Lenin's ❷ death on January 21, 1924. However, civil war and international intervention to crush the revolution created permanent fears.

By 1929 Stalin had been able to eliminate his competitors in the party and government leadership through shifting coalitions. In 1927, he forced his most powerful rival, Leon Trotsky, out of the party and in 1929 had him expelled from the country; Trotsky

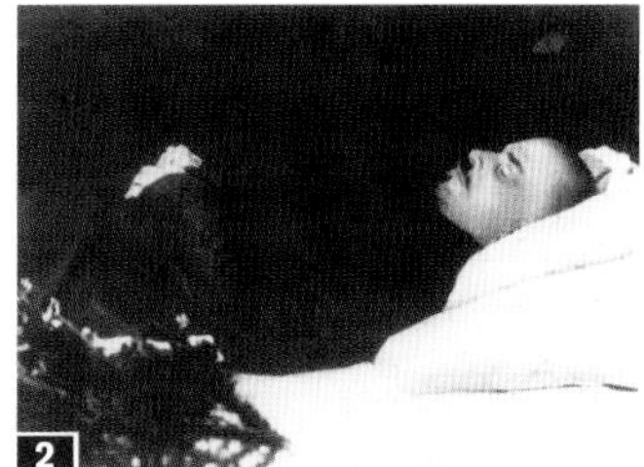

Lenin lying in state, 1924

was murdered by the Soviet secret service in his ❸ Mexican exile in 1940. Whereas Trotsky had maintained that the Soviet Union could be secured if ❶ Communist revolution were continued in the highly industrialized nations of Europe, Stalin primarily concentrated on the ruthless establishment of a socialist social order in his own country from 1928 on. With the increased industrialization and ❹ forced collectivization of the economy, Stalin's dictatorship became a bloody system of suppression in the 1930s.

The Communist state had been recognized by most of the European nations by 1924. The priority of the Soviet Union's foreign relations under Stalin was to secure its own system of rule. The USSR joined the League of Nations in 1934 and signed diverse nonaggression pacts and treaties of mutual assistance. After Nazi Germany's rearmament in the 1930s, (p. 453) the Western powers' concessions in the Munich Agreement (p. 465) reinforced Stalin's reservations with respect to the capitalist nations, especially after their betrayal of democracy in the Spanish Civil War. Stalin therefore decided for the ideologically paradoxical ❺, ❼ alliance with Germany. This allowed the Soviet Union to participate in the ❻ division of Poland and was intended to avert major military conflict. Hitler broke the treaty on June 22, 1941, when German forces began to invade (p. 512).

Collective farm, 1931

German-Soviet meeting at the demarcation line in occupied Poland, 1939

Foreign Minister Molotov and Hitler in Berlin, 1940

French cartoon satirizing the Nazi-Soviet Pact, 1939

"Workers of the World Unite!", Soviet poster, 1932

Trotsky's arrival in Mexico, 1937

Joseph Stalin, the "Man of Steel"

Stalin's real name was Iosif Vissarionovich Dzhugashvili. He was the son of a shoemaker and was set to become a priest, but because he had organized demonstrations and strikes, he was excluded from the Orthodox seminary in 1899. Only after Lenin's arrival in St. Petersburg did Stalin, a member of the Russian Social Democratic party, join the radical Bolsheviks. Lenin regarded his organizational talent highly, and only later recognized his immense hunger for power.

above: Soviet propaganda poster, Lenin and Stalin, 1944

21 Jan 1924 | Lenin's death

1927 | Leon Trotsky expelled from the Party

1928 | Stalin forces farm collectivization

1932 | "Social Realism" movement

1934 | USSR joins the League of Nations

Stalin's Reign of Terror in the 1930s

Stalin's personal dictatorship of state and party reached its bloody pinnacle with his large-scale political purges in the 1930s.

After the 1920s, Stalin's dictatorship was linked to a growing personality ⓬ cult and the development of the state as a tight, centrally controlled administrative machine. Stalin's policies were declared socialist dogma, and in 1936 the hegemony of the Communist party at all levels of society and state was officially established. The state secret police kept the population under surveillance and eliminated any opposition with ⓫ shootings, forced labor, and deportations to Siberia.

Without regard for human life, forced farm collectivization was introduced in 1928; the farms were to be combined into great production cooperatives. The farmers who owned medium and large tracts were defamed as "enemies of the people" and "exploiters"; their land was expropriated, and they were sent off to ❽ work camps in Siberia. A temporary, massive collapse of agriculture was the result; in the Ukraine four million people ❾ starved to death.

9 Dead children, winter of 1921-1922

Between 1935 and 1939, Stalin eliminated all potential or imagined opponents in the "Great Purges." The ⓭ persecution took place at all levels of party, state, economic, and cultural groups. Millions of people were sent to penal or work camps, accused of being "vermin," spies, or saboteurs. Opposition to official views was labeled "deviationist" and the holders were often accused of acting on behalf of foreign powers. Between 1937 and 1938, Stalin had the majority of the military leadership elite eliminated; 35,000 officers were arrested, and about 30,000 were executed. Non-Russian peoples also were victims of Stalin's persecution. The ⓾ Volga German Republic was dissolved in 1941 and its inhabitants put into camps. Prominent party members were accused of being "counterrevolutionaries" in three great public show trials and sentenced to death. Of the members of the party's Central Committee elected in 1934, two-thirds did not survive the years 1937 and 1938.

By the end of the wave of terror in 1939, practically the entire revolutionary elite of 1917 had been extinguished and replaced in all areas of the party structure by "apparatchiks" whose loyalty to Stalin was assured.

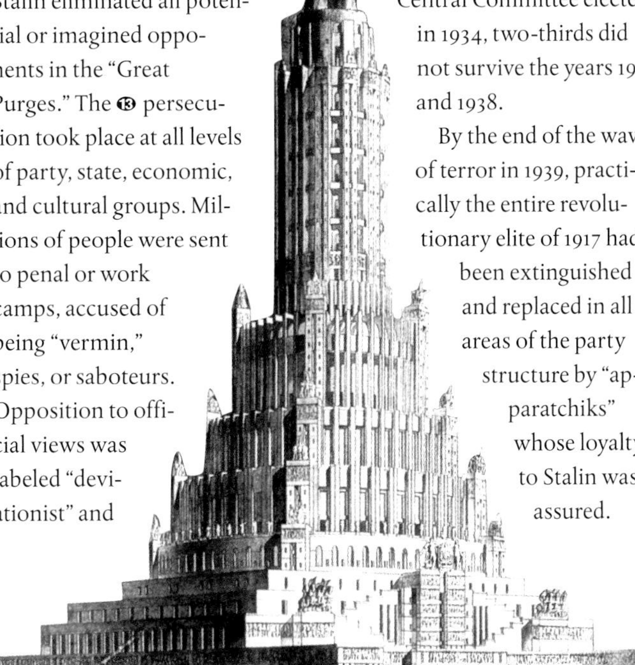

12 Model of the Soviet Palace of Culture including a memorial to Lenin, almost 1600 feet (500m) tall, designed by Boris M. Iofan 1933

Social Realism

In 1932 "social realism" was enforced in all cultural fields. Literature and the visual arts were supposed to educate the Soviet citizens in the spirit of socialism. The central motif was the "working hero," representing socialist progress. Sculptures and murals of working men and women adorned buildings across the Soviet Union.

above: Poster, 1942

8 Forced laborers in a quarry, 1930

10 Meeting of a community of Volga German farmers to organize collectivization, 1931

11 Mass graves from the Stalin era near Kursk, only discovered in 1987

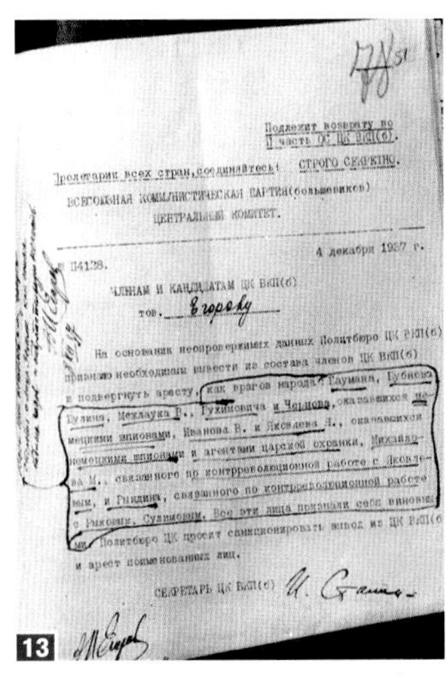

Подлежит возврату во II часть ОС ЦК ВКП(б).

Пролетарии всех стран, соединяйтесь! СТРОГО СЕКРЕТНО.

ВСЕСОЮЗНАЯ КОММУНИСТИЧЕСКАЯ ПАРТИЯ(большевиков)

ЦЕНТРАЛЬНЫЙ КОМИТЕТ.

4 декабря 1937 г.

№ П4128.

ЧЛЕНАМ И КАНДИДАТАМ ЦК ВКП(б)

тов. Егорову

На основании неопровержимых данных Политбюро ЦК ВКП(б) признало необходимым вывести из состава членов ЦК ВКП(б) и подвергнуть аресту, как врагов народа, Баумана, Бубнова, Булина, Межлаука В., Рухимовича и Чернова, оказавшихся немецкими шпионами, Иванова В. и Яковлева Я., оказавшихся немецкими шпионами и агентами царской охранки, Михайлова М., связанного по контрреволюционной работе с Яковлевым, и Рындина, связанного по контрреволюционной работе с Рыковым, Сулимовым. Все эти лица признали себя виновными. Политбюро ЦК просит санкционировать вывод из ЦК ВКП(б) и арест поименованных лиц.

СЕКРЕТАРЬ ЦК ВКП(б) И. Сталин

13 1937 order for a mass arrest of senior party figures signed by Stalin

1935–39	Stalin's "Great Purges"
1936	Stalin consolidates his leadership position
1939	Nazi-Soviet Pact
1940	Trotsky assassinated in Mexico
1941	Republic of Volga Germans dissolved
22 Jun 1941	German invasion of the Soviet Union

Southeast Europe between the Wars

1914–1945

In the wake of the Ottoman Empire's decline, independent kingdoms were founded in almost all of the states of southeastern Europe at the start of the 20th century. In the powder keg of the Balkans, Croatia, Serbia, and Slovenia united after 1918 to form the new state of Yugoslavia. German troops occupied Yugoslavia in World War II. The ❶ advance of the Red Army after 1944 then brought all of the Balkan states under the influence of communism. Greece alone was able to maintain its independence from communism after the war.

1 Red Army occupies Bulgaria; Communists build a new government, Sept. 1944

2 Constantine I, King of the Hellenes

Greece

Greece was shaken by domestic crises following World War I and a lost war against Turkey. When the Germans occupied the country in 1941, the Greeks successfully resisted.

At the outbreak of World War I, Greece's ❷ King Constantine I was determined to protect the neutrality of his country, while Prime Minister ❸ Eleutherios Venizelos favored entering the war on the side of the Entente. Against the will of the king and the Greek people, he asked the British and French to set up a base in Thessaloniki. Constantine abdicated in 1917 in favor of his son Alexander, whom the ❺ Entente forced to declare war on the Central Powers through a coastal blockade. As a reward for this, Greece was granted a sizable amount of territory after the end of the war in 1918. The conflict with Turkey over Izmir led to a two-year war that ended in defeat for the Greeks. More than a million Greek inhabitants were driven out of Turkey, and Turks in Greece emigrated back.

3 Eleutherios Venizelos

The republic was proclaimed in 1924. However, after several dictatorships, domestic stability was restored when Prime Minister Venizelos took office in 1928. The world economic crisis (p. 506) hit Greece hard, and in 1932 Venizelos was not reelected. Radical right- and left-wing groups were able to build up their strength during the depression. In 1935, the Royalists repealed the constitution and declared a monarchy under ❻ King George II. The king was unable to bring about domestic peace, though, and so ❼ Gen. Ioannes Metaxas seized power in a coup in 1936 and established a military dictatorship based on fascist ideology. Through an attempted invasion by the Italians in 1940, which the Greeks were able to repulse, Greece was dragged into World War II. German troops occupied the country in 1941. The Communists organized a partisan resistance movement against the occupiers and brought a large part of the country under their control. The ❹ German troops withdrew in October 1944. When the conservative republican government in exile was installed in Athens under the protection of the British, the Communists incited a revolt that, after clashes with British troops, was ended in a cease-fire. Despite an agreement, the government, with British assistance, was in control only in the cities.

4 German tank in Athens, 1944

5 French and British troops in Thessaloniki, 1915

6 King George II oversees a maneuver, 1940

7 General Ioannes Metaxas (second from the right)

1916 | Rival government in Thessaloniki
1917 | Constantine I abdicates
1918 | Proclamation of the "Kingdom of the Serbs, Croats, and Slovenes"
1924 | Proclamation of the Republic of Greece
1928 | Venizelos takes power
1935 | Monarchy under George II proclaimed

The Balkan States

With the founding of Yugoslavia at the end of World War I, a new state came into being in the Balkans. Along with Bulgaria and Albania, it was caught in the sphere of influence of the Axis powers in World War II.

Caricature of Bulgaria's entry into the war, which was "pushed" by the Central Powers, 1915

The Yugoslavian prince regent Paul with his wife on a state visit to Berlin, 1941

Following the disintegration of the great empires in the First World War (p. 440), Montenegro, Bosnia-Herzegovina, and Croatia united with the Kingdom of Serbia. On December 1, 1918, King Peter I proclaimed the "Kingdom of the Serbs, Croats, and Slovenes," which was renamed Yugoslavia in 1929. The state was unstable, however, due to social and economic problems, particularly the opposition of the Croats to the almost exclusive Serbian leadership. During the 1930s, it increasingly came under ❾ German influence, and in 1940 Yugoslavia was partitioned by Hitler's troops and divided among the Axis powers. The Communists under Tito took the leadership of the partisan fighters against the occupiers and in 1944 agreed with the royal government in exile concerning a provisional government (p. 580).

Bulgaria suffered great losses following World War I. Having already suffered territorial losses in the Second Balkan War (p. 407), Bulgaria, as an ❽ ally of the Central Powers, was put under a heavy burden of reparations by the Treaty of Neuilly. It lost Western Thrace to Greece, thus depriving it of access to the Aegean.

Czar Boris III of Bulgaria together with his family, 1940

To protect itself from the territorial claims of its neighboring countries, Bulgaria under ❿ Czar Boris III moved closer to the Axis powers in 1939, and in 1941 it became a signatory of the ⓫ Tripartite Pact. Following the invasion by the Red Army in 1944, the Communists took over government in Sofia. Bulgaria then signed a treaty with the Soviet Union and declared war on Germany.

In 1912–1913, Albania gained its sovereignty after the Balkan wars (p. 407), but during World War I, the country was contested by the hostile Great Powers. Albania was the only Balkan state whose territory remained unchanged after the war; the claims of Greece, Yugoslavia, and Italy were disallowed at the Paris Peace Conference (p. 445). Italy, which had occupied the north of the country during World War I, recognized Albania's independence in 1921. ⓬ Ahmed Bey Zogu, who governed the Albanian republic as president from 1925 and then from 1928 as King Zog I, unsuccessfully sought to rid the country of Italian influence. In April 1939, Mussolini occupied the country, and ⓭ King Victor Emmanuel III of Italy was installed as king of the Albanians. Italy used the country as a base in World War II. Resistance formed against the occupying power, although the Albanian Communists and nationalists also fought against one another after 1943. The Communists prevailed in 1944, and Enver Hoxha took over the leadership of the country.

Yugoslavia becomes a signatory of the Tripartite Pact, 1941

Ahmed Zogu, president of Albania from 1925 and king from 1928, photo, 1930

Reception of the Albanian delegation in the Roman Quirinal palace on the occssion of the proclamation of King Victor Emmanuel III as king of Albania, 1939

1936 | Ioannes Metaxas attempts military putsch
Apr 1939 | Italian troops occupy Albania
1940 | Italian invasion of Greece
1941 | Bulgaria joins the Tripartite Pact
1941 | Greece occupied by German troops
1944 | Tito government in Yugoslavia

The Decline and Fall of the Ottoman Empire 1914–1945

Between 1878 and 1918, the Ottoman Empire lost over three-quarters of its territory. The remaining parts were occupied by the Allies after World War I. The downfall of the Empire gave ❶ Mustafa Kemal (later "Atatürk") and his followers the opportunity to carry out reforms. After a four-year struggle for independence, the Turkish Republic was declared and an era of political and social upheaval ensued.

Mustafa Kemal Atatürk, "Father of the Turks"

The End of the Ottoman Empire

The Ottoman Empire disintegrated during World War I. The occupation by victorious foreign troops was followed by a succession of wars for independence.

When World War I erupted, the already weakened Ottoman Empire at first sought to remain neutral. However, upon the instigation of the Young Turk minister of war, ❷ Enver Pasha, Turkey ❹ entered the war in November 1914 on the side of the Central Powers. Three of Turkey's five armies were placed under the command of the German general Liman von Sanders. The Turkish navy attacked British and French shipping in the Black Sea.The consequences of the war were fatal to the empire. With British support, Arabia was able to free itself from Ottoman control; part of Palestine was promised to the Jews in the Balfour Declaration as a national homeland; and after the defeat of the Central Powers, the Entente occupied most of what was left of the empire. In the Treaty of Sèvres in 1920, the Turkish state lost its sovereignty.

Resistance to the occupying regime was organized under the leadership of Mustafa Kemal. The struggle for independence began in 1919 when Kemal and the ex-naval officer Rauf Bey convoked a nationalist congress at Erzerum on July 23. The Congress created the Nationalist Party, which established its headquarters at Ankara, overthrowing the feeble regime in Istanbul on October 5, 1919, and achieving overwhelming victory at the subsequent elections. Its first success came with the recognition of the eastern borders by the young Soviet Union. France was also forced to renounce its territorial claims in 1921. The ❺ war against Greece, which sought to annex Constantinople and large parts of Anatolia, ended with the expulsion of not only the Greek army but also a large portion of the long-established ethnic Greek civilian population.

Turkish soldiers who fought with the Central Powers

Mustafa Kemal with his unit during the Greek-Turkish war, 1921

The town square in Izmir

Enver Pasha

The fight for independence ended with the destruction of ❸ Izmir. The occupying powers concluded the Peace of Mudanya with the government on October 11, 1922. International recognition of the Turkish state followed a year later with the Treaty of Lausanne.

The massacre of the Armenians, color print from the French newspaper *Le Petit Journal*, 1916

The Genocide of the Armenians

After the turn of the 20th century, attacks against the Christian Armenian minority occurred frequently in Turkey. In 1915, under the pretext of treason—the Armenians supposedly having collaborated with Russia—Turks began a campaign that cost the lives of an estimated 1.5 million Armenians. Most died on "death marches" into the desert. To this day, Turkey denies that a genocide took place, but the United Nations and the European Union recognize a genocide.

from 1915 | Forced relocation and massacre of Armenians
from 1919 | Struggle for independence under Mustafa Kemal
1920 | Treaty of Sèvres
1922 | Sultanate abolished
1923 | The republic is proclaimed

The Founding of the Turkish Republic

Following the successful conclusion of the struggle for independence, Mustafa Kemal proclaimed the Republic of Turkey in 1923. A phase of intensive modernization began.

❽ Mehmed VI, the last Turkish sultan, had hardly any influence over political events, as the reform movement under Kemal had already won the upper hand in internal political affairs. In the course of the struggle for independence, Kemal formed an opposition government to the sultan's court. He abolished the sultanate in 1922, before he was even elected as the first president, and later also eliminated the caliphate and other religious courts. Kemal proclaimed the republic on October 29, 1923 and moved the capital to Ankara.

The following 15 years of Kemal's governance saw radical political and social change for Turkey. The "clothing reform" of 1925 banned the ❿, ⓫ veil for women and the fez for men. In the same year, the Gregorian calendar and the metric system were adopted, followed later by the ❻ Latin alphabet. Legal systems were absorbed piecemeal from various European nations: Swiss civil law, German commercial law, and Italian criminal law were taken over and implemented. The enforcement of monogamous marriages and social equality between men and women were introduced, though they succeeded only partially; in 1930, women were given voting rights and, four years later, the right to stand for office.

Kemal, who was honored with the epithet "Atatürk" (Father of the Turks), died in 1938. His successor as president was his comrade-in-arms ❾ Ismet Inönü, who sought to continue Turkey's modernization.

Internationally Turkey strove to maintain its sovereignty. During World War II, Turkey remained neutral. In 1934 it signed the ❼ Balkan Entente with Greece, Romania, and Yugoslavia. Turkey also became a charter member of the United Nations. When the Soviet Union once again attempted to exercise control over the region of the Bosporus and Dardanelles straits, Turkey sought closer ties with the United States. This was fundamental to US containment policy, which focused on checking the spread of Communism in Europe. In 1952, Turkey was admitted to NATO after it fought alongside the US in the Korean War.

"Kemalism"

The political and social ideology named after Kemal Atatürk is based upon the "Six Pillars" which was formulated in 1931 by his party. The six pillars are: nationalism, laicism, republicanism, statism, modernism, and populism. Its goal is the building of a modern, Western-oriented nation in which economic and social development is state-directed. Although the state religion was abolished and the clerics strictly excluded from state affairs, Islam still plays a major role in the national concept of a Turkish identity. In 1925 religious opposition parties were banned.

top: Memorial of the 1928 Republic of Istanbul; Kemal Atatürk with his comrade-in-arms

6 Atatürk champions the Latin alphabet on a visit to the provinces, 1929

7 Turkish envoy, second from left, signs the Balkan Entente, September 4, 1934

8 The last sultan, Mehmed VI, at his enthronement 1918

9 From left: Ismet Inönü, Kemal Atatürk, and a young female pilot, 1937

10 Veiled Turkish woman, in traditional Turkish dress, 1917

11 Young Turk after the "clothing reform," ca. 1935

1923 Caliphate abolished | **1930** Introduction of women's right to vote | **1938** Atatürk dies

1923 Treaty of Sèvres revised | **1925** Soviet-Turkish nonaggression pact | **1930** Pact of friendship with Greece

The Reorganization of Arabia 1918–1945

With the end of ❶ World War I and the disintegration of the Ottoman Empire, the Arab world faced a new beginning and a period of political restructuring. The desires for national independence and self-rule of the countries that had previously been Ottoman provinces, collided with British and French "Great Power" colonial interests in the oil-rich region and led to constant tension. In Palestine, Arab and Israeli territorial claims, which could not be resolved by the British Mandate, overlapped. The foundation for the present-day conflict in the Middle East was laid (p. 596-599).

1 Capture of Jerusalem by the British under General Allenby, December 1917

Postwar Political Reorganization in Syria, Lebanon, and Palestine

Great Britain and France divided the territories of the defeated Ottoman Empire between them following World War I. In Palestine, Great Britain failed to successfully mediate between Arab and Jewish interests and solve the territorial conflict.

2 Rebellion against British rule in Palestine: "Holy War" against the British supremacy is declared, 1915

In order to weaken its World War I opponent, the Ottoman Empire, the British government supported the nationalist dreams of the Ottoman provinces of Syria, Lebanon, and Iraq, promising them ❹ independence if they fought on the side of the Entente. The British officer and archaeologist Captain T. E. Lawrence, later known as "Lawrence of Arabia," successfully organized an ❸ uprising of the Arabs against the Turks, which significantly contributed to the downfall of the Ottoman Empire. At the 1920 Conference of San Remo, however, the Entente powers disregarded their promise of Arabian independence and focused instead on consolidating their influence. France was given a League of Nations mandate to rule over Syria and Lebanon, while Great Britain took control, also as the mandatory power, over ❷ Palestine and Iraq. When Syria declared itself an independent "United Kingdom" in the same year, the French military intervened and banished King Faisal. In other colonial areas as well, resistance to the Europeans took on strength. In Iraq the British had to defend against numerous insurrections, and in Palestine the British occupation was unable to satisfy the demands of the League of Nations for a balancing of Arab and Jewish interests.

3 Castle in the desert, near Qasr al-Azraq, Jordan, in which Lawrence of Arabia had his battle headquarters

4 Arabs celebrate the fall of the Ottoman Empire and the liberation of Mecca, June 1916

Lawrence of Arabia

Thomas Edward Lawrence, known as "Lawrence of Arabia"

The archaeologist Thomas Edward Lawrence from North Wales became legendary as Lawrence of Arabia through his leadership in the battle for Arabian independence. From 1916 to 1918, he worked toward inciting an Arab rebellion against the Ottomans. After the war, he saw the imperialist reorganization of the region as a betrayal of his Arabian friends; he refused all awards and lived reclusively until his death in 1935.

Oil Production in the Near East

The major powers' demand for oil had increased steadily since the beginning of industrialization. In 1920, the oil-rich provinces of Baghdad, Mosul and Basra were combined under British mandate to form present-day Iraq. The British shared the rights to the oil deposits with France, the US, and the Netherlands. The payment the Iraqi government received in exchange for oil was a small fraction of the profits.

Oil production in Iraq, 1937

1881 | First Jewish immigration to Palestine
1917 | British conquest of Palestine and the Balfour Declaration
1918 | End of the Ottoman Empire
1919 | Weizmann-Faisal-Agreement
1920 | Conference of San Remo

Palestine: A Religio-Political Conflict Is Born

After 1917, Arabic and Jewish national movements collided over the issue of the religio-historically sensitive region of the territory of Palestine.

5 Street scene in Jericho, ca. 1900

6 Transjordanian emirs

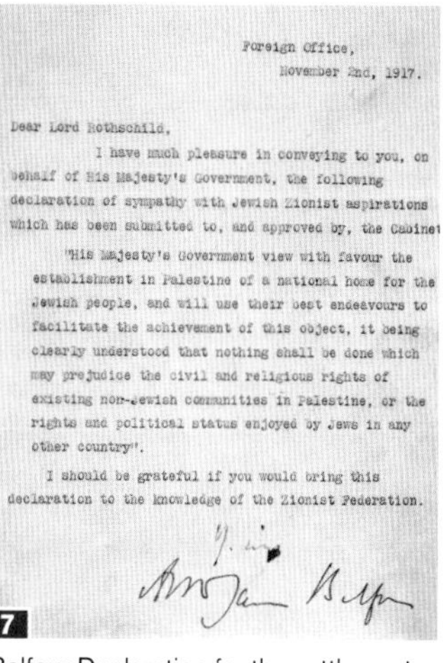

Foreign Office,
November 2nd, 1917.

Dear Lord Rothschild,

I have much pleasure in conveying to you, on behalf of His Majesty's Government, the following declaration of sympathy with Jewish Zionist aspirations which has been submitted to, and approved by, the Cabinet.

"His Majesty's Government view with favour the establishment in Palestine of a national home for the Jewish people, and will use their best endeavours to facilitate the achievement of this object, it being clearly understood that nothing shall be done which may prejudice the civil and religious rights of existing non-Jewish communities in Palestine, or the rights and political status enjoyed by Jews in any other country".

I should be grateful if you would bring this declaration to the knowledge of the Zionist Federation.

Yours,
Arthur James Balfour

7 Balfour Declaration for the settlement of Jewish immigrants in Palestine, 1917

Even by the end of the 19th century, the Arab nationalist movement had provided for a revitalization of Islam and had increasingly begun to defend itself against the secularization promoted by Ottoman rule. At the same time, Jewish nationalism—Zionism—also increased, seeking to unite Jewish people throughout the world in the "Land of the Fathers," in Ottoman-controlled ❺ Palestine. As the Zionist cause was thus anti-Turkish, and as many of the young men of the exiguous Jewish population of Palestine enrolled in British forces and provided military intelligence, Great Britain promised the Jews a "national homeland in Palestine" in the ❼ Balfour Declaration of 1917. Conflicting expectations were thereby created in the Arab and Jewish nationalist movements, both of which expected their own to be fulfilled when the Ottoman Empire collapsed and Great Britain conquered Palestine.

Negotiations between the Zionists and Arab nationalists led to the Weizmann-Faisal Agreement in 1919, in which the Arabs accepted the ❽ immigration of the Jews as long as Arab independence in Palestine was secure. These initial declarations on both sides were forgotten, however, when territorial conflicts began.

Arab ❾ resistance against the Zionist settlement of Palestine became increasingly strident. In response, the British government restricted Palestine to the area west of the Jordan River and created the semi-independent ❻ Emirate of Transjordan in the east. During World War II, Transjordan fought with the British including the 1941 invasion of pro-German Iraq.

9 Anti-Zionist demonstration by Arabs in the region controlled by the British mandate, March 1920

The conflict between Jews and Arabs increased when Nazi persecution increased Jewish immigration to the region during the 1930s (p. 452). The Arab Palestine Uprising in 1936–1939 demanded an independent state and an end to Jewish immigration. In response, Jews demanded the right to unlimited immigration and demanded the creation of a Jewish state in Palestine at a 1942 New York conference.

8 View of the camp of Jewish immigrants in Palestine, 1920

Jewish Immigration to Palestine

The first wave of Jewish immigration to Palestine occurred in 1881 after the pogroms against the Jews in Russia. The increasing anti-Semitism throughout Europe around the turn of the century strengthened the Zionist movements, which demanded the creation of a Jewish "homeland secured by public law" in Palestine. In 1896 Theodor Herzl published the programmatic book The Jewish State, in which he laid out the conditions of national Jewish self-rule, and a year later he called the first Zionist congress. Despite Arab protests, the Jewish proportion of the Palestine population increased from less than 10 percent at the turn of the century to 30 percent at the end of World War II.

Arrival in the port of Tel Aviv, 1936

Theodor Herzl

1920 | Founding of Iraq under British mandate

1920–21 | Creation of the Emirate of Transjordan

1932 | Independence of Iraq

1936–39 | Arab Palestine uprising

1946 | Independence of Jordan

Iran and Afghanistan: Battle for Independence ca. 1900–1945

Afghanistan and ❶ Persia (Iran after 1935) had to defend themselves against the imperialist interests of the Great Powers in the first half of the 20th century, and both were more or less successful in their struggles for independence from Great Britain. Domestically, those in power strove for modernization based on the Turkish model; this was more fully realized in Persia than in Afghanistan. During the World Wars, the Entente powers and then the Allies used Iran against its will as a military base for their troops.

1 Mountainous region in Loristan, Iran

Persia/Iran: Modernization in the Shadow of the Great Powers

In 1905 Persia was divided between British and Russian spheres of influence, with a neutral zone in between. Then, during World War I, it was occupied by Russia, Great Britain, and Turkey.

After the Bolsheviks came to power (p. 481) in 1917, Russia withdrew from Persia and recognized its sovereignty. In response, Britain occupied the country in 1919, but it was unable to force a protectorate treaty upon Persia and ultimately also withdrew. For fear of Soviet expansion, the British demanded that a stable Persian government be set up.

❷ Colonel Reza Khan, the minister of war, took power through a coup in 1921 and consolidated Persian central authority. In 1925, he had the parliament depose the last of the Qajars and elect him shah. As Reza Shah Pahlavi, he began in an authoritarian manner to westernize the country culturally, intellectually, and industrially, following the example of Atatürk (p. 486). For example, he had the Trans-Iranian Railway built and introduced European legal systems through the passage of civil and criminal codes. From 1929, men were required to wear Western-style clothing, women gave up the ❸ veil, hospitals and new roads were built, and in 1935 the first modern university opened in Tehran. Nevertheless there was little progress in the country because the system existed to serve the shah. Through land reform, the shah forced the ❺ nomads to settle in specially constructed villages. Revolts against his policies were brutally ❹ crushed and opposing tribal leaders were killed.

6 Mohammad Reza Pahlavi, 1937

3 Women wearing the chador, 1930

5 Nomadic boy with lamb, 1937

Internationally, Persia strove to maintain its autonomy. In 1933, it forced a new agreement upon the Anglo-Persian Oil Company under conditions more favorable to Persia and in 1935 changed the official name of the state to Iran. Nevertheless, the attempt to remain neutral during World War II again failed, as British and Soviet troops in 1941, and later also Americans, occupied the country to keep the great oil reserves out of German hands. The presence of a large number of German agents in Persia was a cause of anxiety for Britain. The shah, who sympathized with the Axis powers, was compelled to abdicate and was sent into exile. His son ❻ Mohammad Reza Pahlavi became his successor to the throne and cooperated with the Allies. Roosevelt, Stalin, and Churchill reassured Iran of its postwar independence at the ❼ Tehran Conference in 1943 and held out the prospect of economic aid. Accordingly, the United States and Great Britain left the country in 1945, the Soviets one year later.

2 Reza Shah Pahlavi, 1925

4 Persian prisoners, ca. 1928

7 Stalin, Roosevelt, and Churchill at the Tehran Conference

30 Dec 1906	Persia's constitution on Belgian model
1919	3rd Anglo-Afghan War
8 Aug 1919	Treaty of Rawalpindi
8 Aug 1919	Independence of Afghanistan
1925	Reza Shah Pahlavi enthroned
1926	Soviet-Afghan non-aggression pac

Afghanistan: Liberation from British Influence

Afghanistan was finally able to achieve its independence from Great Britain in 1919. Only limited state reforms after the Turkish model could be achieved over the opposition of conservative forces.

❽ Afghanistan was able to maintain its neutrality in World War I under Amir Habibullah. At first it did not defend itself when British India occupied parts of southeastern Afghanistan beyond the Durand line (p. 413). In 1919, however, ⓫ Amanullah—the son and successor of Habibullah, who had been murdered the same year—started the Third Anglo-Afghan War by crossing the frontier into India in May 1919 and was able to make initial gains against the British. In the Treaty of Rawalpindi on August 8, 1919, Great Britain finally released ❾ Afghanistan into independence, recognizing the Durand line as the border.

Young Afghan Movement

The Young Afghan movement developed against the backdrop of British domination at the beginning of the 20th century. Influenced by pan-Islamic enlighteners of the 19th century and the ideas of the Turkish politician Atatürk, they wanted to renew the nation.

9 Street scene in Afghanistan

11 Amanullah watches a German Army exercise in Berlin, ca. 1925

Amanullah Shah identified with secularly oriented young Afghans and introduced a sweeping modernization program following the model of laicized Turkey. He sent young men abroad to study and planned a wide, if unrealistic, program of public works. However, his plans to give women equal rights, secularize the legal system, and institutionalize the protection of religious minorities crumbled against the resistance of the conservative forces in the country that held tight to their ❿ tribal traditions and religious supremacy. In 1929, internal revolts led to Amanullah's abdication.

Following nine months of bloody rule by Habibullah II, Mohammad Nadir Khan seized Kabul in October and, as Nadir Shah, took power. Taking into account conservative political sentiment, he proceeded cautiously to continue his predecessor's reform policies. He fell back on the Sharia—Islamic law—as a legal foundation and made ⓭ Sunni Islam the state religion.

Under his successor Zahir Shah, Afghanistan was also able to maintain its neutrality throughout World War II. A non-aggression pact had already been signed with the Soviet Union in 1926. The Allies accepted Afghanistan's neutral position, although they insisted that ⓬ Zahir Shah expel the diplomatic representatives of the Axis powers from the country.

8 Rock face with Buddhist cave monasteries and "Little Buddha," Afghanistan

10 Afghan dignitaries, ca. 1910

12 Mohammad Zahir Shah, 1937

13 The Blue Mosque in Kabul, Afghanistan

INDIA'S PATH TO INDEPENDENCE UNTIL 1947

❶ Mohandas Gandhi (also known as Mahatma) was the most significant figure of India's struggle for independence from Great Britain. His program of passive resistance and noncooperation was supported by the public and became a powerful protest movement that forced the British to make more concessions, until India was at last granted independence from the British Empire in 1947. The Muslim minority in India also was given Pakistan as a separate state in the same year.

1 Mohandas Kamarchand Gandhi, known as Mahatma Gandhi

Gandhi's Nonviolent Struggle

The British massacre in Amritsar in 1919 gave new impetus to the Indian independence movement. Gandhi's campaign of civil disobedience then developed into a powerful political force.

Despite military loyalty to the British in ❸ World War I, the Indian independence movement's hopes for political equality were not fulfilled at the end of the war. Although high-level political reports proposed more representative government, particularly at a local level, together with the admission of natives to all levels of the public service, additional emergency laws further restricted the Indians' right to partake in decisions, which only strengthened the nationalist Indian National Congress party led by Gandhi and ❷ Jawaharlal Nehru.

3 Indian troops in World War I

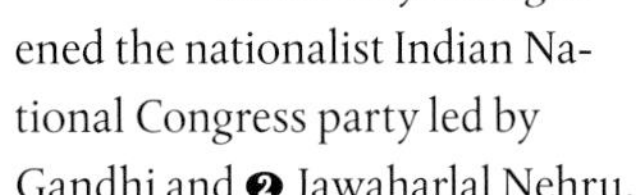

After the British bloodily suppressed a protest meeting in 1919 in Amritsar, Gandhi carried out his first campaign of "civil disobedience" and "noncooperation." It rapidly grew into a powerful mass movement and made Gandhi the undisputed leader of the dominant Congress party. He called for a boycott of the British organs of state and championed the revitalization of the basic Indian ❹ crafts industry.

4 Gandhi at the spinning wheel

The success of the campaign was reinforced when the Muslim League, led by ❺ Muhammad Ali Jinnah, also joined it. The British participation in the destruction of the Ottoman Empire (p. 486) had increased their aversion for the occupiers. Gandhi broke off the campaign in 1922 when excited ❻ demonstrators violated the ban on violence. Gandhi was sentenced to six years in prison but was released in 1924. It was not until 1930 that he became politically active again.

6 Political unrest in Calcutta

2 Jawaharlal Nehru

5 Gandhi with Muslim leader Muhammad Ali Jinnah

Noncooperation and Passive Resistance

Noncooperation and passive resistance were methods that Gandhi had used in his successful battle for the rights of the Indian minority in South Africa. He also followed this path in India, because he believed that British rule was made possible only through the cooperation of the Indian people and that this method could thus force political change. He believed that the Indians should defend themselves by "holding fast to the truth," ("satyagraha") an ancient Indian idea. If one refers to a truth, one has to prove it and alone carry the burden of proof. One should do no harm to anyone, except, at most, oneself. For that reason, Gandhi equated "holding fast to the truth" with nonviolence.

1919 | British massacre in Amritsar
1920 | Constitutional reform
1920–22 | First "Satyagraha" campaign
1924 | Gandhi released
1928 | Nehru's report
1930 | Second "Satyagraha" campaign
1930–32 | "Round Table"-conferences

Independence and Division

The British reluctantly gave in to the pressure of the Congress party and granted independence to India and the separate Muslim state of Pakistan following World War II.

The refusal of the British to grant India its demands for sovereignty in 1930 triggered a second mass movement. To protest against the British monopoly of the salt industry, Gandhi led several thousand people in a demonstration march to the salt fields on the coast. Numerous nonviolent protests followed throughout the country. A constitutional conference in London in 1931 brought only partial success: The salt monopoly was lifted by the ❼ Gandhi-Irwin Pact, but the demand for national self-determination was again rejected.

The Government of India Act passed by the British Parliament in 1935 allowed the Indians to build autonomous governments at the provincial level but left the central government under the British unchanged. The act had to satisfy a huge range of opinion and at the same time see to the protection of Indian minorities. In 1936, the Congress party emerged as the winner of the elections in the provinces; however, in protest against the British governor's emergency laws, they only partly took over their ministerial offices. When the viceroy, Lord Linlithgow, proclaimed India's entrance into World War II in 1939 without guaranteeing later independence, the ❽ Congress party refused its support and called for renewed ❾ civil disobedience. ❿ Gandhi answered a halfhearted British concession in 1942 with the demand to "quit India." Thereupon the complete leadership of the Congress party was arrested. The course of the war and the mounting inner tension in India, however, increased the pressure on Great Britain to find a cooperative solution.

The Muslim League had distanced itself from the Hindu-based Congress party at the end of the 1930s. Muhammad Ali Jinnah, who held the view that Hindus and Muslims were two distinct nations, increasingly demanded the creation of a separate state in the north of the subcontinent after 1940. In order to avoid a bloody civil war between Hindus and Muslims, the British decided after World War II to partition the country in two. In 1947, ⓫ Pakistan (the Muslim areas) and India (the Hindu areas) were granted independence as dominions. Gandhi, who unwaveringly spoke for peace between Muslims and Hindus, was assassinated in 1948 by a fanatical Hindu.

8 Indian National Congress party

10 Prison cell crowded with arrested supporters of the independence movements

11 Mass exodus of Hindus and Sikhs from Pakistan, 1947

7 Gandhi on the way to sign the Gandhi-Irwin Pact, 1931

9 Women demonstrate for Indian independence from Great Britain

The "Salt March"

The "Salt March" to the ocean caused a great international sensation. Mahatma Gandhi and his followers took only a few lumps of salt from the ocean, but thus symbolically violated the British salt monopoly. Sixty thousand participants were arrested, Gandhi among them. This number of prisoners far exceeded the capacity of British jails.

Demonstrations against the British monopoly on the salt trade in India

12 Sep 1931 | Gandhi-Irwin Pact
1935 | Government of India Act
1939 | Congress government resigns
1940 | "Pakistan Resolution" of the Muslim League
1942 | "Quit India" resolution
1947 | Indian Independence Act
30 Jan 1948 | Gandhi murdered

China between Empire and Communism 1911–1949

For more than a century, between 1811 and 1949, China was characterized by the ❶ fight against Japanese expansionist aspirations, the struggle for national unity, and bloody domestic ideological disputes. The internal power struggle between the Republicans and the Communists was briefly set aside in the face of Japanese imperialism. Following World War II, with Soviet aid, Communism prevailed and restructured the country politically and economically.

Guards with machine guns along the Great Wall of China

Civil War and Japanese Aggression

The end of the Empire saw political chaos and territorial breakup in the Republic of China. Japan exploited the turmoil, launching a military invasion as it sought to build an empire in Asia.

At the end of 1911, Republican revolutionaries led by Sun Yat-sen and Gen. ❷ Yuan Shikai forced the last emperor of the Qing dynasty, P'u-i, to abdicate. A republic was proclaimed in 1912. Yuan's attempt to found a new dynasty failed in 1915 due to resistance in the provinces. The government disintegrated with his death in 1916, and until 1928 China experienced continuous civil war. Warlords ruled, particularly in the north of the country. Japan sought to capitalize on the chaos for its own purposes. Its "21 demands" of 1915 sought the colonization of the whole country.

China entered World War I in 1917 hoping to gain allies in its defense against Japanese imperialism. When by 1919 these expectations proved illusory, Chinese nationalism increased. Sun Yat-sen began militarizing the Republican National Party (Kuomintang) in 1923 with the aim of unifying the country. After Sun's death in 1925, Chiang Kai-shek took over the leadership of the party. With the capture of Beijing in 1928, he succeeded in subduing the warlords in the north and became president of the republic. By 1937 Chiang had essentially restored China's unity, but his government ground itself down in domestic conflicts with the Communists.

Japan had already occupied ❸ Manchuria on the Chinese mainland in 1931 and proclaimed the state of Manchoukuo. When Beijing was attacked in 1937, Chiang had no choice but to form a ❹ united front with the Communists in order to defend the country. The Japanese army, however, continued to advance further into the country. Following the violent ❺ subjugation of Nanjing, known in China as "the rape of Nanjing," the government was forced to withdraw to the west.

When the United States declared war on Japan in 1942, China received American material and military support. Following the Japanese surrender to the Allies, the Japanese left Nanjing, and the puppet state of Manchoukuo disintegrated.

P'u-i, the Last Emperor

P'u-i, the last Chinese emperor, had just turned five when he was forced to abdicate in 1912. In 1924, he placed himself under the protection of the Japanese, who proclaimed him emperor of their puppet state, Manchoukuo, in 1934. At the end of World War II, P'u-i fell into Soviet captivity and was detained in custody for "reeducation" until 1959.

The Chinese imperial couple P'u-i and Wan Jung, ca. 1934

Yuan Shikai gives the order to cut off the emperor's traditional plait, 1912

Chinese soldiers in the battle against the occupying Japanese forces in Manchuria, 1932

Communist meeting to discuss the "united front," 1937

Japanese troops invade and lay waste to Nanjing, 1937

1912 National People's Party (KMT) founded | **12 Feb, 1912** Last emperor abdicates | **15 Feb, 1912** General Yuan Shikai's presidency | **1915** Japan's "21 Demands" | **1916–28** Civil War | **1917** China enters WW I | **1919** Start of "Fourth of May Movement" | **1921** CCP founded

The Rise of Communism under Mao Zedong

The influence of the Communist Party under Mao Zedong grew steadily through the 1920s and 1930s. Despite being brutally persecuted by the government, the Communists were able to prevail over the Republicans after World War II.

With China's entry into World War I and the Bolshevik victory in Russia, Western revolutionary thought penetrated China and found expression in the "Fourth of May Movement." The Chinese Communist Party (CCP) emerged in 1921 from the movement's Marxist study groups. With Soviet help, the groups became an important power in the country.

In the wake of national unification efforts, the Communists at first united with the Republican party in 1922. The influence of the Communists steadily increased, however, culminating in a rift between the parties in 1927. ❻ Chiang Kai-shek's forces then persecuted the Communists. During the worst attack, in Shanghai on April 12, 1927, thousands of Communists and union members were ❼ massacred. The CCP then withdrew its ❽ People's Liberation Army into the countryside and built up a local government. After carrying out an agrarian revolution, it set up a Soviet-style republic in Yiangxi province in southeastern China.

To evade the pressure from the "extermination campaigns" of the Republican government, the CCP was forced to move with its troops to the north of the country. Under their new undisputed leader, ⓫ Mao Zedong (p. 618), the Communists managed to escape in 1934-1935 on the "Long March" through western China to Yan'an, which they built up to be their central base.

The CCP steadily expanded its control during the ❾, ❿ war with Japan. When the Soviet Union occupied Manchuria in 1945, the CCP seized power there. By 1949 Communists controlled the whole of the Chinese mainland with Soviet support. Mao proclaimed the People's Republic of China on October 1, 1949.

The Fourth of May Movement

Named after the date of a Beijing student demonstration against the pro-Japanese government, the Fourth of May Movement became a nationwide political emancipation movement of intellectuals, students, and workers in 1919. Its demands, along with national independence, included the rejection of traditional Confucianism, more civil rights, and social reform within the state.

Student demonstration, 1919

6 Chiang Kai-Shek, Koumintang politician, with his wife, 1927

The "Long March"

The Communists' Long March to the north of China took place in 1934–1935 over a distance of some 6000 miles. Many soldiers gave up along the way; others died of illness, of exhaustion, or in battle. In the end, only about 8000 of the original 90,000 reached Yan'an. The CCP later used the Long March as a symbol of the socialist struggle in China.

Mao Zedong

7 Execution of a Chinese communist student, 1927

8 Communist fighters on the "Long March," 1935

9 Shanghai shortly after a Japanese air-raid bombing, 1937

10 Japanese infantrymen with Chinese prisoners during WW II

11 Mao Zedong speaking at a Communist conference, 1933

1923	Militariziation of the Republican National Party
12 Apr 1927	Communists executed and persecuted
1928	Beijing taken and China united
1931	Japan occupies Manchuria
1934-35	"Long March"
1937–45	Sino-Japanese War
1 Oct 1949	Proclamation of the PRC

1 US bomber attacks Japanese destroyer, ca. 1943

Imperial Japan and Southeast Asia

1914–1945

Aggressive expansionist policies and increasingly fascistic nationalism characterized the politics of the Japanese empire from 1914 to 1945. Beginning in 1931, Japan waged a brutal war of conquest against China that lasted almost 15 years. Japan overextended itself with its surprise attack on the ❶ United States in 1941, and despite its military strength, supremacy over the whole of east Asia was clearly unsustainable. The country's inevitable defeat was hastened when the US destroyed two Japanese cities with atomic bombs. Most of the southeast Asian nations won their independence after the war, though some had to fight prolonged conflicts with the Western colonial powers.

Development of Japanese Imperialism up to 1931

Japan expanded its sphere of influence when it gained control of the former German colonies in the Pacific after World War I. Nationalist ideas and the imperial cult increasingly gained influence in the economically flourishing country as it sought to expand into Asia.

Japan further developed its position of supremacy (p. 418) in East Asia after the death of Emperor ❹ Meiji in 1912 and the ascension to the throne of his son Yoshihito. At the outbreak of war in 1914, the Japanese foreign minister stated that while Japan had no desire to become embroiled in war, she would stay loyal to her alliance with Great Britain and protect its interests. When Germany refused to relinquish its lease hold and naval base at ❸ Tsingtao in the Chinese province of Shantung,

3 Government building in Tsingtao, capital of Kiaochow, 1913

Japan joined World War I on the side of the Entente. Japanese forces occupied all German colonies in the Pacific: the Marshall, Marianas, Palau, and Caroline Islands. After the war, the League of Nations transferred these islands and Tsingtao to Japan to administer as mandated territories. Although Tsingtao was given back to China in 1922 under the Shantung Treaty, the islands' territorial status quo was confirmed in other international treaties. In the ❷ "Four Power Treaty," France, Great Britain, Japan, and the United States agreed to respect one another's Pacific possessions and to help in case of an attack by an outside power. In the "Nine Power Treaty" of 1922, Japan guaranteed China national sovereignty.

2 "Four Power Treaty," November 1921

Economically, after a short postwar weakness, a period of strong growth began in Japan. Even the ❻, ❼ devastating earthquakes around Tokyo and Yokohama in 1923 only slightly affected this trend. The global economic depression after 1929, however, brought this to an end, particularly affecting ❺ silk farmers.

The country became formally democratized after the war. The electorate was broadened tenfold to 14 million, and universal suffrage was introduced in 1925. Politically more important, though, was an ultranationalistic group of military officers that over the course of the 1920s gained increasing influence with the government and emperor through extraparliamentary committees such as the "Secret State Council" and the "Military Senate." They pushed for conquests to secure new resources.

4 Emperor Meiji in military uniform, portrait, late 19th century

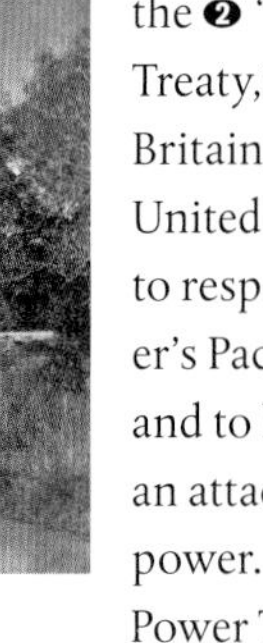

5 Japanese silk painting, ca. 1850

6 Damage wrought by earthquakes, 1923

7 Victims of the earthquake, 1923

Japan's War of Conquest in China 1931–1945

The decade-long Japanese conquest of China began with the occupation of Manchuria in 1931. Domestically, the right-wing military hierarchy tightened its grip on power in the empire, silencing more moderate civilian voices.

❾ Emperor Hirohito took the throne in 1928, but from 1932 on, the army emerged as the sole power factor in the country. Japan rejected the Washington accords of 1922, which had sought to avoid a naval arms race. Chauvinistic and antidemocratic military groups determined Japanese politics behind the scenes in the 1930s, leading to the official collapse of the entire parliamentary system. In 1940, the old political parties were compelled to dissolve, and a sort of conglomerate party emerged in their place: the Imperial Rule Assistance Association (*Taisei Yokusankai*). A new government under Prime Minister Prince Fumimaro Konoe nationalized the economy and put restrictions on important civil rights.

8 Marco Polo Bridge near Beijing

9 Emperor Hirohito, 1930

At the instigation of the military, Japanese troops invaded ❿ Manchuria in 1931 and managed to occupy the entire region in a few months. They created the puppet state of Manchoukuo headed by the former Chinese emperor P'u-i, who was named ⓫ emperor of Manchoukuo in 1934. Japan continued its expansion and colonization of China, also seizing Yehol province. China, militarily inferior and divided (p. 494), could do little to resist the occupiers. In 1935, Shanghai was captured in a brutal campaign.

Japan gradually pulled away from international agreements. When the League of Nations refused to recognize Manchoukuo in 1933, Japan announced its resignation from the organization. In 1936, it terminated the naval fleet agreement, and soon after, Japan declared its withdrawal from the London disarmament conference and signed the ⓬ "Anti-Comintern Pact" with Nazi Germany.

The ⓭ Sino-Japanese War began in July 1937 with a clash between Chinese and Japanese soldiers on the ❽ Marco Polo Bridge near Beijing and lasted until September 1945. Within a short time, Japan had annexed the north of China and almost the entire coast. Further advances into the interior were halted in 1938 only by the rugged mountains of central China. The devastating war claimed enormous losses among the Chinese population; estimates range as high as 20 million dead—the majority of them civilians. With its defeat at the end of World War II, Japan was forced to withdraw from China completely.

Poem by Ushiyama Kinichi

In honor of the German–Japanese alliance:

"The alliance has been created, blood brothers equal,
The countries of both united strive to ascending power,
Brilliant the culture, the justice commanding awe,
German soul, how you equal the Japanese."

Japanese and Nazi banners on the occasion of the visit of the Japanese foreign minister to Berlin, 1941

10 Japanese soldiers in occupied Manchuria, 1945

11 Emperor P'u-i on a state visit to Japan with Emperor Hirohito, Tokyo, 1935

12 Signing of the Anti-Comintern Pact, November 25, 1936

13 Japanese infantry in winter uniform, in front of armored train, ca. 1937

1935 | Conquest of Shanghai
1936 | Termination of naval agreement
1936 | Japan withdraws from London disarmament conference
1936 | Anti-Comintern Pact signed
Jul 1937 | Incident on the Marco Polo Bridge

The Struggle for East Asia in World War II

Japan fought the Allies for hegemony over the entire East Asian region in the War in the Pacific of 1941–1945. The dropping of the atomic bombs on Hiroshima and Nagasaki forced Japan into unconditional surrender.

Japanese surprise attack on Pearl Harbor, December 7, 1941

The outbreak of war in Europe in 1939 did not alter Japan's imperialist aims: the project of "reordering east Asia." Its goal was to unite the entire region—from India to Manchuria to Australia—as the "Greater East Asia Co-Prosperity Sphere" under the political and economic hegemony of Japan, using the "divine emperor" Hirohito to legitimize this claim to dominance ideologically.

As a safeguard against interference, Japan signed the Tripartite Pact with Germany and Italy on September 27, 1940, although it did not commit itself to aid in case of war. Japan also signed a neutrality pact with the Soviet Union on April 14, 1941. An attempt at rapprochement with the United States, which had canceled its trade agreement with Japan in 1939, failed. When Japanese troops marched into Saigon in July 1941, US president Roosevelt imposed an oil embargo on Japan. As a result, Prime Minister Konoe resigned, and his extremely nationalist successor, General Hideki Tojo, decided to attack the Americans.

On December 7, 1941, the Japanese bombed the US Pacific Fleet base at ❶ Pearl Harbor, Hawaii. The resulting entry of the United States into the hostilities turned the European war into a world war.

In the ❷, ❸ War in the Pacific, Japan was able to conquer all of east Asia by 1942. In rapid succession, Japan occupied the Philippines, Hong Kong, Singapore, and Burma. It advanced to India's borders and was on the brink of conquering Australia. The situation finally began to change with the British invasion of Burma in 1943. Then, after American landings in the Mariana Islands and the crushing defeat in the aircraft carrier battle at ❹ Saipan, the war cabinet under Tojo stepped down.

When the Americans captured the islands of Iwo Jima and Okinawa and cut off fuel supplies, Japan's defeat became inevitable, as the desperate deployment of ❺ kamikaze pilots showed. Despite this Japan refused to surrender on the terms that the Allies demanded. On August 6 and 9, 1945, the US dropped atomic bombs on the Japanese cities of Hiroshima and Nagasaki, a demonstration that forced Hirohito to announce Japan's ❻ unconditional surrender.

Atomic Attacks on Hiroshima and Nagasaki

The United States ended World War II with the dropping of atomic bombs on Hiroshima and Nagasaki and ushered in the nuclear age. The devastating destructive force of the new weapon shocked the world. Between them the two bombs are thought to have caused more than 200,000 civilian deaths, perhaps half instantly and half in the fallout. The morality of the attacks are still disputed. Strategically, it saved the lives of US soldiers and served as a demonstration of American power, improving the US position in negotiations over the postwar world order.

Atomic explosion over Nagasaki, April 9, 1945

Japanese destroyer opens fire on British cruiser, 1943

US war plane takes off from an aircraft carrier, 1944

US troops march across the island of Saipan, 1944

Japanese kamikaze pilots praying before their final flight, 1945

Japanese soldiers taken prisoner in Guam, 1945

1939 | US terminates trade agreement
27 Sep 1940 | Tripartite Pact
1941 | Ho Chi Minh founds Viet Minh
14 Apr 1941 | Soviet-Japanese neutrality pact
7 Dec 1941 | Attack on Pearl Harbor
8 Dec 1941 | US and Great Britain declare war on Japan

East Asia's Path to Independence

The states of east Asia emerged from Japanese rule and decades of colonial domination following the end of World War II.

At the beginning of the 20th century, nearly all of east Asia was ruled by the western colonial powers: Indochina belonged to France; the Philippines to the United States; India, ❼ Malaya, and the northern part of Borneo to Great Britain; and today's Indonesia to the Netherlands. On the mainland, only ❽ Siam (present-day Thailand) was officially independent, but even it was subject to French and Japanese influence. Korea had been a Japanese protectorate since 1905.

7 Japanese inspect a captured British plane, Malaya, 1941

Internally, resistance groups such as the communists, which appeared for the first time in Indonesia in 1914 and in other East Asian countries toward the end of the 1920s, posed little threat to the colonial rulers. Only in Burma in 1937 did domestic dissent achieve a significant goal, when an uprising of nationalist students triggered the country's breaking away from the British Indian empire, and Burma was granted partial autonomy.

Japan's plans for a Greater East Asia Co-Prosperity Sphere implied driving the Europeans out of the region, which all east Asian resistance groups welcomed in principle. But it also promoted a split in the anticolonial resistance. Left-wing groups did not want to be ruled by a Japanese divine emperor and formed anti-Japanese communist people's armies, for example, in the Philippines and Malaya. In contrast, nationalists hoped that a pro-Japanese position would help them gain national sovereignty more quickly. A ❾ volunteer army in Burma supported the Japanese, and there was a similar body in India. The reaction in present-day Vietnam was different. When Japan occupied the eastern part of the country in 1941, the nationalists and communists joined together against the Japanese under the leadership of Ho Chi Minh in the League for the Independence of Vietnam, the ❿ Viet Minh.

Following Japan's surrender in 1945, the colonial powers gradually withdrew from the region. Vietnam, Korea, the Philippines, Indonesia, Cambodia, Laos, and Burma proclaimed themselves sovereign states by the end of the 1940s. Malaya gained independence only in 1957. The humiliating loss of British Singapore and Hong Kong greatly reduced the power and prestige of the colonialist powers in southeast Asia.

8 Bangkok, capital of Siam, ca. 1930

9 Japanese soldiers in Burma, 1944

10 Ho Chi Minh (foreground) with Viet Minh forces, 1950

Ho Chi Minh

Ho Chi Minh ("He who enlightens") was the charismatic leader of the Vietnamese liberation movement and in 1945 became the first president of the Democratic Republic of Vietnam. In the 1960s he was the figurehead of the Vietnamese struggle against the military intervention of the United States (p. 617). Ho was born in 1890 in Annam, went to France in 1917, and was a founding member of the Communist Party there. After his deportation to Moscow in 1923, he became the Comintern functionary in Southeast Asia. An advisor to the Chinese Kuomintang troops in the Soviet Union in 1938, he returned to his homeland only after the Japanese invasion in 1941.

Ho Chi Minh, ca. 1960

2 Jan 1942	Manila occupied
3–7 Jun 1942	Battle of Midway
Jun 1944	Naval battle at Saipan
6 and 9 Aug 1945	US air force drops atom bombs on Hiroshima and Nagasaki
2 Sep 1945	Democratic Republic of Vietnam constituted

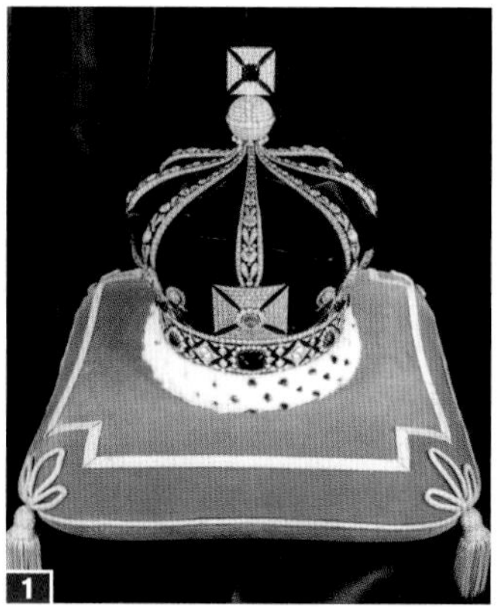

Crown of George V, Emperor of India, 1910

The British Commonwealth: Emancipation of the British Colonies 1914–1945

Step by step, in the wake of strengthened and ever more vocal national movements, the colonies of the British global empire were granted independence. At first they became self-governing dominions of the British Empire, following which the colonies became completely autonomous in 1931 under the Statute of Westminster. A community of equal and sovereign states under the protection of the British crown, the ❶ British Commonwealth took the place of the British Empire.

Dominion: The Preliminary Stage to Independence

Great Britain granted numerous colonies domestic self-rule as "dominions" at the beginning of the 20th century, yet it was not until 1931 that they officially gained complete independence.

London Conference, 1926

King George V

In 1867, Canada became the first British crown colony to be granted independence. It was followed in the early 20th century by Australia, New Zealand, Newfoundland, the South African Union—composed of Cape Province, Natal, Transvaal, and the Orange Free State—and, in 1922, Ireland (p. 466). As dominions, they became sovereign nations with self-rule according to international law. But the bond with Great Britain, particularly in issues of world and security policies, stayed intact, and the ❸ British monarch remained the formal head of state. When Britain declared war on Germany in 1914, the ❺ dominions were automatically also at war. After the war, however, they defended themselves against having British will imposed. In 1919, they individually signed the Treaty of Versailles and joined the League of Nations.

At the ❷ London Conference of 1926, the "Balfour Formula" promised the dominion's independence, which came into effect in 1931 with the Statute of Westminster. As "autonomous communities within the British Empire, equal in status," they were free of British influence in legislation, domestic and foreign policies but "united by a common allegiance to the Crown, and freely associated as members of the British Commonwealth of Nations" (❹ Balfour). All of the sovereign colonies voluntarily joined the Commonwealth, from which they could withdraw. Australia joined in 1942 and New Zealand in 1947. Newfoundland was a special case. It was once again directly governed by Great Britain from the 1930s and became a part of Canada in 1949.

Canadian soldiers on the western front, 1916

Arthur James Balfour, British foreign secretary

The Dominion of South Africa

The Dominion of South Africa began setting the foundations for the future apartheid state in 1910. The British and the white "Afrikaners," descendents of Dutch colonists, were united in the suppression of the black Africans. For non-whites, ownership of land was allowed only within reservations, forms of employment were greatly restricted, and migration to urban areas and sexual relations with whites were prohibited. In 1912, black Africans founded the African National Congress as a common protest organization against injustice.

right: Durban, in the South African province of Natal, ca. 1910
left: Mausoleum of John Langalibalele Dube, ANC founder, Inanda, Natal

1867 | Canada made dominion
1912 | African National Congress (ANC) founded
1919 | Dominions join League of Nations
1922 | Ireland made dominion
1926 | Formulation of "Balfour Formula"

The Disintegration of the British Empire

At the end of World War I, the British Empire was larger than ever before. But financial burden and powerful independence movements in the colonies brought the empire to a gradual collapse after World War II.

The British Empire expanded one last time after the First World War. Great Britain took over the League of Nations mandates of Palestine, Iraq, and the former German colony of ❻ Tanganyika. It also gained influence over New Guinea and Namibia because the former was governed by the British dominions of Australia, the latter by South Africa.

In terms of actual control, however, British power was becoming ever weaker in the regions it controlled. The motherland was suffering under a difficult economic crisis (p. 462) and thus reduced funds and the size of its administration and military in the colonies. In addition, after ❽ World War I the African and Asian peoples demanded, if not complete ❿ independence, at least more self-determination and an end to denigration at the hands of white Britons. In contrast to the dominions that had been granted independence and could decide whether or not they wanted to become members of the newly founded British Commonwealth, the remaining colonies were compelled to do so. Britain's situation worsened further after ❼ World War II. Financial problems and increasingly powerful movements aiming for ❾ independence in the colonies accelerated the breakup of the empire. In 1947, India, the most important of the British colonies, shook off British rule (p. 492). Burma and ⓫ Ceylon followed in 1948. The phase of decolonization could not be halted.

7 Australian soldiers in the service of the British crown, Burma, 1944

6 Young Bantu women, 1936

8 Indian soldiers, 1914

10 Gandhi when he was an activist in South Africa, 1913

Crown Colonies

The British world empire possessed Crown colonies on every continent except Antarctica after 1918. In Asia, these included India, Burma, Malaya, North Borneo, British New Guinea, and Sarawak. In Africa (p. 502)—apart from the special status of Egypt—there were the Gold Coast (Ghana), Sudan, St. Helena, Nigeria, British Somaliland (Somalia), Sierra Leone, Aden, British East Africa (Tanzania, Uganda, and Kenya), and Gambia. In the Americas, British Guyana, British Honduras, and the islands of Barbados, Jamaica, Bermuda, and the Bahamas were all British possessions.

Luxury hotel in Aden, ca. 1890

9 Independence negotiations between the British viceroy Lord Mountbatten and the leader of the Indian Muslim League, Mohammed Ali Jinnah (right), 1947

11 Tea harvesting in Ceylon

1931 | British colonies become members of Commonwealth

1948 | Burma and Ceylon gain independence

1931 | Statute of Westminster

1947 | India's independence

1948 | Palestinian mandate relinquished

1 Frenchman with natives from Cameroon, ca.1917

Africa under Colonial Rule through 1939

With the exceptions of Ethiopia and Liberia, Africa was completely divided up among the European colonial powers by the end of the 19th century. In World War I, German colonial masters were replaced by British, ❶ French, or Belgian rulers. The same thing happened to the Italian colonies in World War II. The South African Union had been granted the status of a dominion since 1910, and Egypt gained limited sovereignty in 1922. Only after World War II did liberation movements start to organize in the rest of Africa.

Africa in the First World War

Germany lost its African colonies with its defeat in World War I. They were placed under mandates by the League of Nations in 1920 although still administered as colonies.

The African war zones during World War I were Egypt (p. 504) and particularly the German colonies. The British, French, and Belgians and their colonial troops were able rapidly to conquer Togo, Cameroon, and ❺ Southwest Africa. Only in German East Africa (present-day Tanzania) was the ❷ Askari colonial force under General von Lettow-Vorbeck able to defend the colony through the end of the war; the army there ceased hostilities only after receiving explicit instructions to do so from Berlin in November 1918.

3 Colonial troops in the service of France

The colonial powers in World War I relied on troops from the native peoples. Segregated from the white soldiers and paid much less, almost half a million Africans fought on the side of the ❸ French, for example; Senegalese and Moroccan tirailleurs were also deployed in ❹ Europe. The desire for independence increased after the end of the war. In the eyes of the returning soldiers, the colonists had morally discredited themselves in the "war of the white tribes." The reinforcement of the peoples' right to self-determination through the Treaty of Versailles initiated the trend toward decolonization.

2 Askari colonial forces fighting on the side of Germany in World War I

New forms of colonial rule represented a first step toward formal emancipation of the colonies. In 1920 the former German colonies were placed under the mandate of the League of Nations. This theoretically imposed limits on the powers of the colonial administrators, as they now had to answer to a larger and officially organized international public. In practice, however, little changed for the African people; they remained at the mercy of European power interests.

4 African soldiers of the French Army fighting at the western front near Verdun during World War II

5 Farmers in southwest Africa

Liberia

How notions of colonists' superiority—which stemmed from the racism of European and American colonists—became embedded in African politics can be seen in the case of Liberia. It was founded as an American colony for the settlement of free slaves and had been a republic since 1847. According to the constitution, only American immigrants had civil rights—the native population was treated as slaves. The settlers' feeling of superiority was similar to that of the white settlers in other colonies. It was not until the 1940s, under President William V. S. Tubman, that native Africans were granted the vote.

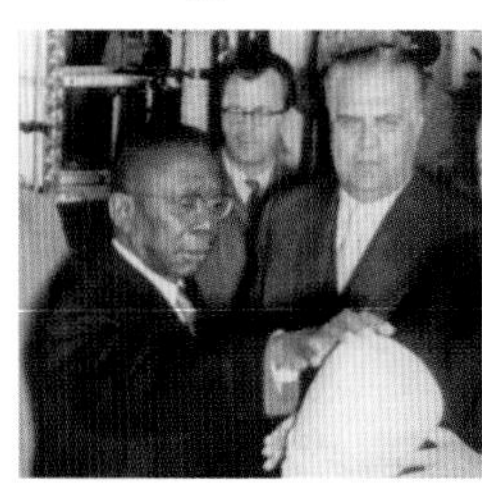

President William Tubman

1934 | South Africa's independence

1939 | South Africa severs relations with Germany

1929 | World economic depression

1936 | Formation of "Native Council" in South Africa

African Economic Development

The world economic depression of 1929 abruptly ended Africa's economic upswing. World War II later placed more instruments of power in the hands of the colonies.

World War I had proven to the warring colonial powers the extent of Africa's economic potential and its importance in supplying both raw materials and manpower for the war effort. The same powers then began the systematic economic development and exploitation of the continent by developing its ❼ infrastructure following the war. A ❻ railroad network spanning all of Africa, corresponding almost to that of the present day, had been built by the end of the 1920s.

The global economic depression of the 1930s interrupted the modernization push that had meant relative prosperity for the inhabitants. European import goods were suddenly unaffordable, and about half of the African wage earners lost their jobs. The Africans stood helpless in the face of these developments, while the white colonial authorities attempted to stabilize profits through tax increases, among other things. Many Africans tried to earn their living in urban ❽ industrial areas, thus beginning the expansion of the cities; in the countryside, there was a return to older forms of exchange such as bartering.

The outbreak of World War II in 1939 improved material conditions and brought a noticeable economic improvement. As the white population for the most part had to return to their homelands for military service and the need for raw materials increased, many new jobs were created. This strengthened the influence of the indigenous population. Europe's dependency on a functioning colonial economy presented the Africans with the opportunity to obtain pay increases and better working conditions. In 1940 Great Britain passed the Colonial Welfare Act, with the goal of preventing further strikes in the areas they controlled. In 1951, it became the first colonial power after the war to grant an African state—❾ Libya—sovereignty, thereby launching a wave of more or less violent decolonization.

6 Oldest steam engine of the Zambesi Sawmill Railway, built 1925

8 Worker in a copper factory in the Belgian Congo

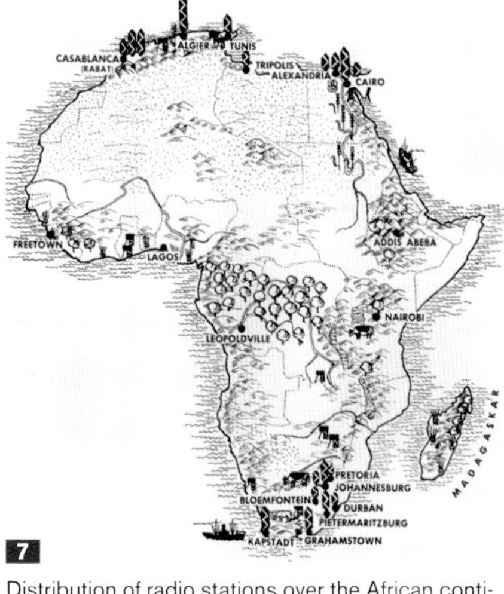

7 Distribution of radio stations over the African continent, 1936

The Pan-African Movement

The importance of the pan-African movement grew after World War II. Active participation in the war and the experience of being economically indispensable reinforced the self-confidence of the Africans in relation to the colonial powers, as they realized the reliance of their colonial masters on their countries and resources. Serious efforts toward autonomy were still absent, however; past Western influences were still too strong for a return to the traditional order, yet too weak for the formation of national states along the European model.

Traditional and modern methods for crossing the desert, 1911

Independence movement in Senegal, 1947

9 Modern housing estate for Italian colonists in Tripoli, Libya, 1935

1940 | Colonial Welfare Act
1944 | Universal suffrage in Liberia
1946 | "French Union" founded
1956 | "Union of African Workers" founded

Ethiopia and Egypt: Between Subjugation and Independence

UNTIL 1945

Ethiopia and ❶ Egypt hold a special position in Africa's colonial history. Egypt had been occupied by the British since 1882 and was formally tied to the Ottoman Empire until 1916. However, it was never fully subjugated and was able to bring about the withdrawal of the British army in 1936. Ethiopia (known as Abyssinia before the First World War) was conquered in a brutal campaign by Mussolini's army but was restored to independence in 1941.

1 US transport plane delivering supplies to the Allied troops in Egypt, 1943

Egypt: Between Sovereignty and British Custodianship

Egypt was an important field of operations for the British military in both world wars. Even as a sovereign state, it was bound to Britain in World War II through alliance commitments, though some nationalists looked to the Axis powers for help in ending British influence.

In 1882, British troops occupied Egypt and took control of the country, albeit without terminating its official status as part of the Ottoman Empire. Widespread reforms were carried out under the leadership of Sir Evelyn Baring. At the outbreak of World War I, however, Great Britain officially declared Egypt a protectorate, imposing martial law and cutting the last ties to the Ottomans.

3 Memorial to Saghlul Pasha, founder of the Wafd party, Alexandria

British troops halted an Ottoman-German offensive against the Suez Canal in 1914 and then used Egypt as a base for attacks on Syria and Palestine.

In 1919, Great Britain prohibited the participation of the Egyptian nationalist ❸ Wafd party in the Versailles conferences, resulting in fierce strikes and unrest that were answered with arrests and hangings. In response, the British granted the country independence in 1922, while still maintaining its military presence and remaining in charge of foreign affairs in order to protect their own interests. When ❷ King Fuad I died in 1936, Great Britain reaffirmed Egypt's sovereignty in an alliance treaty and withdrew its troops, except from the Suez Canal zone. It insisted, however, on the right of intervention in case of war, and so Egypt was once again occupied during World War II and used as a military base in fighting the Italo-German alliance. The ❻ British army defeated German forces in 1942 at El Alamein (p. 511) and forced a withdrawal to Libya. Egypt's ❹ King Farouk I was forced to replace his pro-Axis government with a pro-British one. It was not until 1945 that Egypt officially declared war on Germany. With the exception of their forces securing the ❺ Suez canal, the British once again withdrew from the country in 1946 but still retained explicit control of Sudan.

2 King Fuad I

5 The Suez Canal, a key waterway for international trade, 1940

4 King Farouk I at his wedding, 1938

6 Tank division of the Anglo-Egyptian Army, mobilized to counter the Italian threat in Ethiopia, 1940

1882 | British occupation of Egypt
1894 | Italian invasion of Abyssinia
Oct 1896 | Treaty of Addis Ababa
1922 | Egypt gains independence
1930 | Haile Selassie I enthroned
1930 | Ethiopia joins League of Nations
Oct 1935 | Italy invades Ethiopia

Ethiopia under Haile Selassie I

Due to its modern state structure, Ethiopia was long able to maintain its independence. Italy occupied the country only between 1936 and 1941.

Italian infantry during the invasion of Ethiopia, 1935

Haile Selassie wearing the imperial robes, 1930

The Treaty of Addis Ababa in October 1896, following the uprising under Emperor Menelik of Shoa, ensured the independence of Ethiopia—then still known as Abyssinia—for 40 years, while Eritrea remained under Italian control (p. 422). Ethiopia held fast to its course of modernization even after the death of Menelik II in 1913. His grandson Lij Yasu was deposed by public proclamation and succeeded by Menelik's daughter. Ras Tafari Makonnen became king in 1928 and two years later was enthroned as emperor under the name ❽ Haile Selassie I. He enshrined suffrage and civil rights in a new constitution and brought his country into the League of Nations in 1930. No international intervention took place, however, when Italy seized control of ❼, ❿ Ethiopia under the Fascist leadership of Benito Mussolini (p. 470). In October 1934, Italy manufactured a frontier incident and used it as a justification for war after Ethiopia refused impossible conditions. From October 1935 until May 1936, Italy fought a campaign with modern aircraft, tanks and chemical weapons against Ethiopian cavalry, which provoked an international scandal.

On May 5, 1936, Italian troops captured the capital Addis Ababa. The emperor was forced into exile in London, and Ethiopia was combined with Eritrea and Italian Somaliland to form the colony of Italian East Africa. The people bitterly resisted the invaders in a ❾ guerrilla war and in 1940 supported the British offensive against the Italians in Africa. Haile Selassie returned from exile and retook the throne, ruling up until 1974.

Ethiopians fight guerrilla war, 1941

Ethiopian tribal chief, captured by Italian soldiers, 1936

The Rastafarians

The Rastafarians are members of a religion created after the crowning of Haile Selassie (Ras Tafari). They believe him to be the one true god. Particularly popular in the Caribbean region, the Rastafarian movement considers its members to be the descendents of the Ethiopian kings from the line of Solomon and the Queen of Sheba. It combines social demands with the aspiration to return to Africa. Its members are supposed to pursue natural lifetyles, and they wear their hair in dreadlocks. The Rastafarians are best known for reggae music, which developed in the 1940s and gained global popularity.

King Solomon receives the Queen of Sheba

1936 | British army withdraws from Egypt

5 May 1936 | Italians occupy Addis Ababa

Dec 1940 | British reoccupy Egypt

1941 | Ethiopia liberated

Oct 1942 | Battle of El-Alamein

Feb 1945 | Egypt declares war on Germany

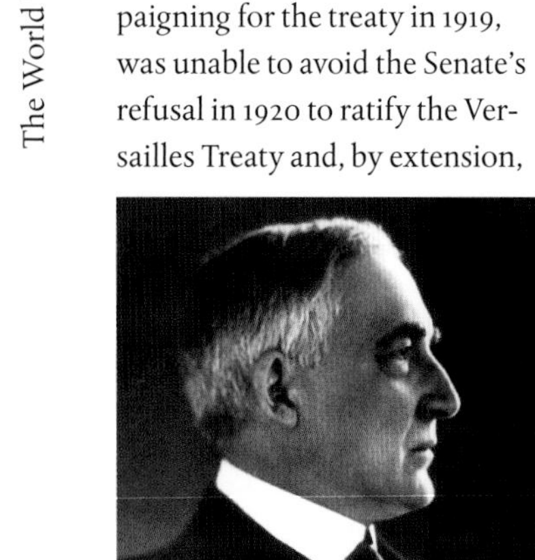

Euphoria and Depression: The US between the Wars 1917–1945

Following the end of World War I, the United States returned to its traditional isolationism. This period saw the beginning of an economic ❶ boom, but blind faith in progress led to euphoric overconfidence in the financial markets. When the speculation bubble burst in the stock market crash of 1929, the entire world economy collapsed. The interventionist New Deal policies of Franklin Delano Roosevelt's government alleviated many of the effects of the Great Depression. In 1939, the officially neutral United States began de facto support of England in the war against the Axis powers, and in 1941, it officially entered the war.

1 Building the Empire State Building, built 1930–1932

Isolationism and Prosperity

The United States withdrew from Europe after the First World War. Technical progress and spectacular growth rates in the "Roaring Twenties" made the increase in general prosperity seem as if it would never end.

After a long period of hesitation (p. 431), the United States under President Woodrow Wilson entered World War I (p. 442) in 1917 with the goal of bringing long-term peace to Europe. After the victory over the Central Powers, Wilson succeeded in having the formation of a League of Nations, intended to help secure future world peace (p. 445), included in the Treaty of Versailles. The US Senate, however, was concerned about potential restrictions on American foreign policy. Wilson, who suffered a stroke while campaigning for the treaty in 1919, was unable to avoid the Senate's refusal in 1920 to ratify the Versailles Treaty and, by extension, the United States' entry into the League of Nations. His successor, ❺ Warren G. Harding, concluded separate peace agreements with the former war enemies in 1921. Until well into the 1930s, the principle of nonintervention in European conflicts remained the determinant of US foreign policy.

Domestically, rapid industrial modernization produced a prospering economy and increasing affluence within the population. Construction and the automobile industry particularly boomed. Efficient production methods, reductions in prices, and rising incomes for the first time allowed the development of a consumer society, with new forms of mass entertainment such as radio, movies, and sports. Glittering parties, ❷ limousines, and the newly rich "self-made men" shaped the glamorous image of the ❻ Roaring Twenties.

In contrast, social ❸ conservatism and xenophobia molded the intellectual climate, particularly in rural America. The most visible expression was Prohibition. The racist ❹ Ku Klux Klan gained in popularity, particularly in the South.

2 The luxury lifestyle: a couple standing in front of their limousine, ca. 1935

3 Arrest of women wearing too-revealing bathing suits, New Jersey, 1920

4 Members of the Ku Klux Klan at a meeting, 1940

5 Warren Gamaliel Harding, 1923

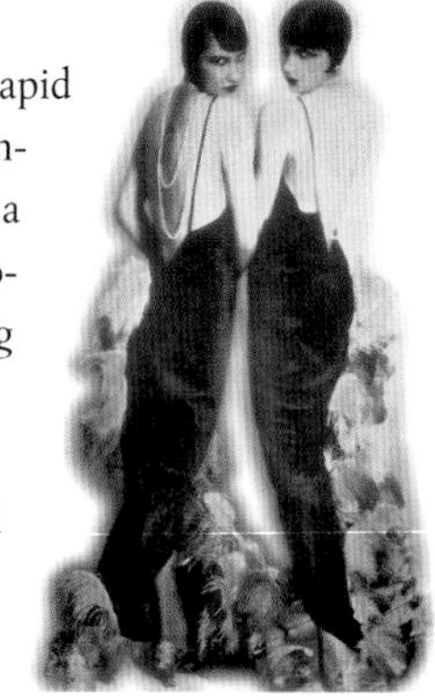

6 Two ladies wearing 1920s Charleston dresses

Prohibition

In 1920, Prohibition—a ban on the consumption and sale of alcohol—became a federal law. Thereupon, however, smuggling and the trade in privately distilled ("bootleg") liquor immediately began to flourish, and alcohol continued to be dispensed in illegal bars known as "speakeasies." In 1933, the law was repealed.

Hiding alcohol during prohibition: a candlestick is used to conceal an alcohol bottle, ca. 1926

1917 | US enters World War I
1920 | Refusal to sign Treaty of Versailles
1920 | Prohibition law comes into effect
1929 | New York stock market crash
from 1930 | Mass unemployment
1932 | Roosevelt's "New Deal" policy
1933 | Prohibition law repealed

The World Economic Crisis and Entrance into the War

The American stock market crash in 1929 sparked a worldwide economic crisis that surpassed all previous recessions. The United States entered World War II under the leadership of President Roosevelt.

7 An unemployed man with a banner demanding work rather than charity, Detroit 1932

8 Investors observe the share prices at the stock market, 1929

The flourishing economy of the 1920s led to excessive investment and stock buying. When in October 1929 the overextension became clear, ❽ prices on the New York Stock Exchange plummeted. The crash in prices led to the bankruptcy of a third of all American banks. Mortgages were foreclosed and farmers ruined. Lack of capital and companies going out of business resulted in the collapse of industrial production and the domestic market. The gross national product, private incomes, and foreign trade shrank to half their previous size by 1933. The result was record ❼ unemployment. By 1933, almost 15 million Americans had lost their jobs.

The crisis rapidly spread to the European nations due to the global nature of the economic network. Europe, which had become the United States' largest debtor after World War I, had financed its postwar upswing with American credit. This was no longer available after 1929, causing bankruptcies throughout Europe as well, and high unemployment followed, particularly in industrialized countries such as Germany. Interrelated drops in prices and production eventually led to a worldwide recession that reached its low point in 1932.

While the crisis strengthened antidemocratic forces, particularly in Germany (p. 449), US President ❿ Franklin Roosevelt began to build up a welfare state after his election in 1932. His "New Deal" policies fought unemployment through government employment programs and antipoverty efforts and set up the first stages of a social safety-net system with the ⓫ Social Security Act. But the crisis was reversed primarily by the national armaments program of 1938.

Although the United States had established its neutrality in 1935, in the face of German power politics (p. 453) Roosevelt began to speak in 1937 of a future fight for survival between democracy and dictatorship. The defense budget was increased in 1938 and a military draft was introduced in 1940. Once war broke out in Europe in 1939, the United States officially reaffirmed its neutrality but. from 1940 on. supported especially Great Britain with arms deliveries for the war being waged against the Axis powers.

After the Japanese attack on the US fleet at ❾ Pearl Harbor (p. 498) in December 1941, the United States entered the war, taking over the leadership of the alliance against the Axis (p. 423). Its immense resources of manpower and materials proved decisive for the Allied victory in 1945. Roosevelt, who against political tradition was elected president for third and fourth terms, died on April 12, 1945, before the end of the war.

9 After the aerial attack by the Japanese: wrecked ships in the port of Pearl Harbor, December 7, 1941

10 President Roosevelt in the Oval Office at the White House, Washington, 1936

11 Postmen in New York submit requests for social security, 1935

1935 | US commits to neutrality
1938 | Armament program stepped up
1940 | Reintroduction of the military draft
since 1940 | Pursuance of the Land-Lease system
Dec 1941 | US enters World War II
12 Apr 1945 | Roosevelt dies

Latin America 1914–1945

Due to a booming export economy after World War I, ❶ Latin America experienced a period of relative domestic stability. However, social tension resulting from the world economic depression in the 1930s brought authoritarian regimes backed by the military to power almost everywhere. These regimes gained popularity due to their social reforms. In international affairs, almost all the Latin American states proclaimed solidarity with the United States and declared war on Germany and Japan during World War II.

"Christ the Redeemer" statue in Rio de Janeiro, built in 1931

Pan-Americanism and Economic Strength

In the 1920s, the economic strength and domestic stability of the Latin American countries led to greater equality with the booming United States.

After the civil wars and coup attempts of the initial phase of independence (p. 423), the Latin American countries achieved internal consolidation after the 1880s. Politically, from the start of World War I, European influence in Latin America began to weaken, while US supremacy gradually increased. The Pan-American Union, an organization of all American states, was founded in 1889 for the promotion of mutual solidarity, but it soon developed into an instrument through which the United States could influence the economies and politics of the nations to the south.

Domestic tension—such as the general strike in Buenos Aires in 1919, uprisings in Brazil in 1924, and the brief intermezzo of a military dictatorship in Chile in 1924–1925—remained the exception during the general peace of the interwar period.

US President Franklin D. Roosevelt, 1936

The opening of the hemisphere to the world market played an essential role in this stabilization. The thriving ❷ export of raw materials created high growth rates through the end of the 1920s, and the ❹, ❺ building industry flourished as well. As everywhere else, though, the world economic crisis would abruptly end the economic growth and cause political turmoil.

The economic successes of the 1920s enabled the Latin American states to gain more equality in the Pan-American Union. At a conference in Santiago, Chile, the Latin American countries were able to achieve the election of the chairman of the Pan-American Union's administrative council; until then, the US secretary of state had held this office. ❸ President Roosevelt adopted the "Good Neighbor" policy in 1930, which aimed to combine US claims to hemispheric leadership with mutual respect and solidarity on both sides. In 1933, the United States signed a resolution that banned intervention in the domestic affairs of other American nations. American troops were withdrawn from the Dominican Republic, Haiti and Nicaragua.

Copacabana in Rio de Janeiro, 1935

Selecting coffee beans, Brazil

Faced with the outbreak of war in Europe in 1939, a common defense against foreign threats took priority at the Pan-American Union conference in 1940 in Havana. When the United States declared war on Japan and Germany on December 11, 1941, the Central and South American nations entered the war one after another.

Salvador de Bahia, Brazil: elevator connecting upper and lower city, built in 1930, photo, 2004

1889–1890 | Founding of the Pan-American Union
1919 | General strike in Buenos Aires
1924 | Rebellion in Brazil
1924–25 | Military dictatorship in Chile
24 Oct 1930 | Putsch by General Vargas in Brazil

Latin America's Crisis during the Depression

In Latin America, social unrest resulting from the world economic depression brought military-supported dictatorships to power during the 1930s. In Brazil, Getúlio Vargas established a personal dictatorship that combined subjugation with social charity.

The global economic crisis (p. 506) hit the ❽ export-dependent economies of Latin America especially hard and led to an economic breakdown. As a result, political uprisings took place everywhere. Dictatorships, mostly of military origin, came to power promising to create jobs and fight ❻, ❾ poverty.

Many Latin American states attempted to reduce their dependency on foreign trade and investments through government-controlled economic policies. Consumer goods were to be produced domestically and the corresponding industries set up. Brazil exemplified this model. ❼ Getúlio Vargas, a failed candidate at the 1929 elections, led a revolt in 1930 in the wake of the world economic depression. He instituted wide administrative reforms. After defeating the 1932 insurrection in Sao Paulo, his status was legitimized by an election in 1934, and he then governed from 1937 with dictatorial authority, alternately supported by the communists and the fascists. Attempts to overthrow him from both sides were suppressed. Following Portugal's example (p. 472), Vargas established an authoritarian state he called the "New State" (*Estado Novo*), in which the individual person or minority factions were subordinate to the national whole. Social conflicts were to be regulated not by a "class struggle" but by cooperation between institutions and organizations. Despite the authoritarianism, the reforms made Vargas popular, particularly among the poor. Trade unions were allowed, and pension and health insurance schemes were set up. The state also guaranteed a minimum wage.

7 General Getúlio Donelles Vargas

Although at the outset of the Second World War Vargas declared himself favorably disposed towards the Axis, after the United States declared war, in 1942, Brazil entered the war on the side of the anti-Hitler coalition, and in 1944 it sent troops to Europe—the only Latin American country to do so. An expeditionary corps of more than 25,000 men fought on the Italian front until the end of the war. Nevertheless, after the defeat of Hitler by the democracies, Vargas's position as dictator became unsustainable. Vargas was ousted by the military in 1945, yet, as a result of his enduring popularity, he was elected president once again in a free election in 1950. However, political scandal led him to commit suicide in 1954.

6 Slum area in Buenos Aires, Argentina

8 A boy harvesting coconuts, 1935

9 A boy offering a captured sloth for sale, 1935

Argentina

Several generals and conservative politicians including Uriburu and Justo, backed by the armed forces, came to power in Argentina in the 1930s, but they were unable to solve the economic problems or control the growing domestic radicalism. The country doggedly avoided entering the war in favor of the Allies and even occasionally indirectly supported the Axis powers. The Army, however, was very much in favor of Germany, and it rebelled in 1943: Colonel Juan Domingo Perón, vice president and war minister since 1943 and later president (1946-1955, 1973-1974) granted German secret agents asylum in Argentina.

President Perón with his wife Evita in Buenos Aires, 1952

Entry papers of Josef Mengele, a doctor in the concentration camp of Auschwitz, who settled in Argentina in 1945 under a false name

1940 | Pan-American conference in Havana

1944 | Brazil deploys troops to Europe

from 1937 | Vargas' government with dictatorial authority

1942 | Brazil joins anti-Hitler coalition

THE SECOND WORLD WAR 1939–1945

With its attack on Poland in September 1939, the German Nazi regime under Hitler (p. 450) initiated the most devastating military conflict in world history to date. Before the unconditional surrender of Germany and Japan in 1945, World War II claimed the lives of some 62 million people. The heavily ❶ ideological aspect of the war led to incomprehensible crimes against humanity. World War II fundamentally altered the international political situation. The victorious United States and the Soviet Union became the leading world powers.

Allied forces propaganda poster, 1943

Blitzkrieg: German Victories up to 1940

A heavily armed Germany controlled almost the entire European mainland in 1940. It failed to conquer only Great Britain.

Germany's invasion of Poland on September 1, 1939, ignited the Second World War. France and Great Britain declared war on Germany, although they did not actively intervene in the Eastern European conflict. Poland's army, which in part still operated with cavalry units, was ❹ no match for the Wehrmacht and Luftwaffe. Poland capitulated after the bombing of Warsaw on October 6. In accordance with the secret agreement with Germany (p. 476), ❺ Soviet troops invaded Poland from the east on September 17 and immediately integrated the eastern parts of the country into the Soviet Union. Germany annexed areas in northern and southern Poland and from the remainder formed the ❷ "General Government of Poland," which would become an area in which Nazi racial fanaticism (p. 520) would play out.

4 Polish war prisoners, September 1940

2 Stamp of the General Government, 1941

German and Russian soldiers allied in Poland, 1939

In order to cut Germany off from raw material sources in Scandinavia at the beginning of the war, the British ❻ Royal Navy blockaded the German merchant marine traffic in the Baltic Sea. A German–British "race to Scandinavia" began in April 1940. Germany occupied Denmark without resistance. Norway was conquered by June, despite heavy British and Norwegian resistance and serious losses on the part of the German navy. Sweden was forced into cooperation with Germany (p. 475).

British submarine returning from Norwegian waters, 1940

Starting on May 10, 1940, German troops rapidly invaded the Netherlands, Belgium, and Luxembourg. Even France could not put up sufficient resistance to the German blitzkrieg tactics; it surrendered on June 22. Three-fifths of France was occupied by Germany; in the southern part of the country, the ❸ pro-German Vichy government (p. 460) was created.

In order to free up resources for his *Lebensraum* ("living space") policies (p. 446) against the Soviet Union (p. 512), Hitler hoped for a peace settlement with Great Britain. When Britain refused to surrender, German ❼ air attacks (p. 524) began in August 1940 to prepare the island for invasion. After heavy losses against the Royal Air Force, they were terminated in October.

Youth organization established under Pétain, similar to the Hitler Youth, 1941

"Blitzkrieg"

The swift, initial successes of the German army are known as the blitzkrieg ("lightning war"). Sudden, unexpected, coordinated assaults by the combined German armed forces did not give the enemy time to organize a stable defense and thus won them many victories.

German fighters approaching England, 1940

1 Sep 1939	German invasion of Poland
17 Sep 1939	Soviet attack on Poland
starting 27 Sep 1939	Bombardment of Warsaw
6 Oct 1939	Capitulation of Poland
9 Apr 1940	Occupation of Denmark
9 Apr–10 Jun 1940	Occupation of Norway

The Balkan Campaign and the War in North Africa (1941–43)

The failed attempts at conquest by its alliance partner Italy forced Germany into costly campaigns in the Balkans and Africa.

Hungarian artillery, 1941

Training German *Luftwaffe* troops in Romania, 1940

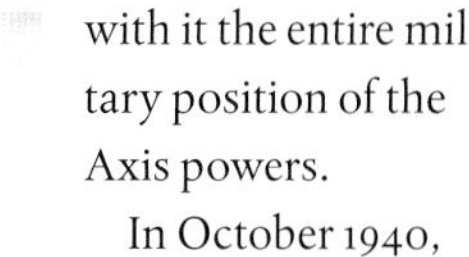

Romanian refinery goes up in flames following British bombardment, 1943

Landing of German paratroopers on the Greek island Crete, 1940

Germany, Italy, and Japan joined together in the Tripartite Pact on September 27, 1940, to form the Axis. However, Japan (p. 498) and Italy pursued their war aims in "parallel wars." ❾ Romania and ❽ Hungary joined the Axis powers in 1940 and Bulgaria in 1941.

Italy under Mussolini (p. 470) aspired to domination of the complete Mediterranean region, which Mussolini resolved Italy should control rather than Great Britain, as well as conquests in Africa, but it failed in its offensives. This repeatedly obliged its alliance partner Germany to supply military support. Deployment on these additional fronts weakened the ❿ German army and with it the entire military position of the Axis powers.

In October 1940, Italy attacked Greece, which was supported by Great Britain, from its province Albania, but British troops forced the Italians back into Albania. In order to restore the reputation of the Axis powers, secure access to Romanian oil wells, and shield the planned German attack on the Soviet Union from a threat from the flank, Hitler decided in April 1941 on a ⓫ Balkan campaign, resulting in the rapid surrender of the armed forces of Yugoslavia and Greece. Yugoslavia was crushed (p. 485), and British troops withdrew from Greek territories.

Another failed Italian offensive against British-dominated Egypt in 1940 (p. 504), which resulted in the annihilation of the Italian units in Libya, forced Germany to intervene militarily in North Africa. The highly efficient German Africa Corps under General Erwin Rommel forced the British out of Libya and back to the Egyptian border between February and April 1941. In January 1942, German tanks began to move into the ⓬ Egyptian desert in an advance which, had it been successful, would have brought the Germans to the oil fields of Iraq, but they were halted at the Battle of El Alamein. By February 1943, a ⓭ British counteroffensive had pushed the Germans back all the way to Tunisia. The fighting in Africa ended on May 13, 1943, with the capitulation of the German-Italian armies.

Erwin Rommel, 1942

Erwin Rommel

Erwin Rommel, the "Desert Fox," was respected even by his foes for his strategic military skills. After he had ordered the retreat out of El Alamein against Hitler's orders, he was transferred to the French front. Although he was not actively involved in the putsch attempt against Hitler, he sympathized with the military resistance movement and, as a long-time confidant of Hitler, urged him to initiate peace negotiations in 1944. Following the failed assassination attempt of July 20, 1944 (p. 525), he was branded a traitor and forced to commit suicide.

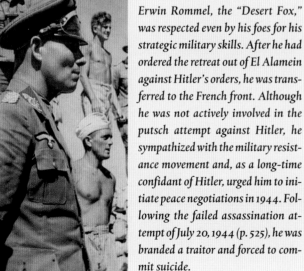

Motorcycle soldiers during the war in the North African desert, 1942

General Bernard Law Montgomery, commander-in-chief of the British troops in North Africa, 1942

10 May 1940 | Beginning of the Western Campaign
22 Jun 1940 | Capitulation of France
from Aug 1940 | Air "Battle of Britian"
2 Sep 1940 | Tripartite Pact
May 13, 1943 | Capitulation of the Axis powers in Africa
Apr 1941 | Beginning of the Balkan Campaign

Operation Barbarossa: The German invasion of the Soviet Union

The German attack on the Soviet Union was initially devastating and forced the Russians to withdraw all the way to Moscow in the winter of 1941. Despite appalling casualties suffered in the Battle of Stalingrad in 1942–1943, the Red Army managed to break out and surround the German besieging forces. This victory marked a crucial turning point in the war against Nazi Germany.

Hitler had planned his ❷ ideological "main war" against the Soviet Union since the summer of 1940. In violation of the German-Soviet nonaggression pact (p. 482), Operation Barbarossa began on June 22, 1941. A vast army of more than three million soldiers, 3500 tanks, and 2000 aircraft invaded the Soviet Union.

1 Workers in the Soviet armaments industry, 1941

As Stalin had not been expecting a German attack at that point in time and the ❶ arming and reorganization of his army was not yet complete, it seemed that the German intention of crushing the Soviet military within a few weeks was realistic. By encircling the Soviet armed forces, the Germans were able to obliterate a significant proportion of them, and by October they had reached as far as Moscow.

4 Soviet propaganda poster: "For our home! For Stalin!", 1944

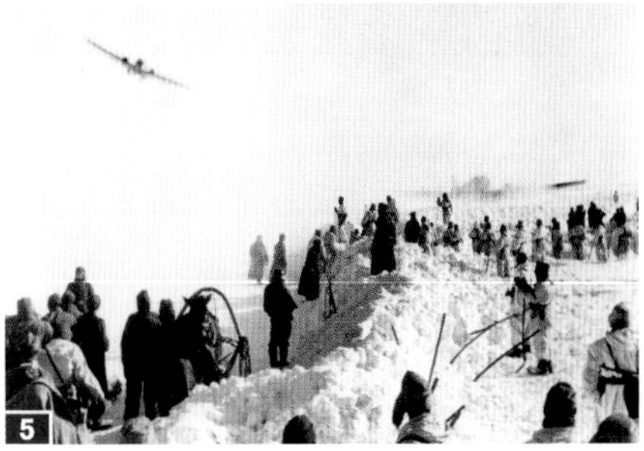

With all his energy, Stalin in the meantime had organized his defenses. A considerable part of the armament industry was moved east, and areas abandoned to the invaders were first stripped of all resources. ❹ Appeals to patriotism—the war became known as "the Great Fatherland War"—and revulsion at the savagery of the occupation forces toward civilians rallied the Russian people. The sheer size and boundless resources of the country inevitably worked in their favor. Thanks to the neutrality pact signed with Japan in 1941 (p. 498), Stalin was able to redeploy troops from the Far East to the Moscow front. Meanwhile, German operations were slowed by extreme weather conditions and the vast distances; the advance on Moscow became bogged down in mud. The Germans were not prepared for the onset of the Russian ❺ winter with –40°F (–40°C) temperatures. Despite a collection drive for winter clothes among the German population, many soldiers froze to death. The German army retreated for the first time. The defeat outside Moscow shattered German plans for a quick victory. Supply difficulties and the long-term materiel superiority of the Soviets undermined German hopes for outright victory.

The real turning point was the Battle of Stalingrad in the winter of 1942–1943. After besieging the strategically important city in the summer of 1942, the 250,000 German soldiers were surrounded by Soviet troops. The entire army ultimately surrendered, following fighting that inflicted ❻ great losses on both sides and on the city's civilian population.

2 Nazi propaganda in Russian against "Jewish Bolshevism," 1942

Treatment of German ❼ prisoners matched that suffered by Soviets during the invasion. After the last German offensive at ❸ Kursk, the Red Army gradually regained lost territory and in January 1945 finally crossed over the eastern border into Germany.

3 Partisans place dynamite at a railway near Kursk, 1943

5 German soldiers supplied by air at Stalingrad, 1942

6 Fallen German soldiers near Stalingrad, 1943

7 German prisoners of war near Stalingrad, 1943

Wars of Ideology and Extermination

During the campaign of conquest against the Soviet Union, the Nazi leadership put its genocidal program into action.

Ukranians murdered by the Soviet secret service, accused of collaborating with the Germans, 1942

In accordance with their ideology (p. 446), the Nazi leaders planned the war against the Soviet Union not simply as a military operation but rather as a "war of two ideologies"—a "battle of extermination" against what they called the "Jewish-Bolshevik" system. The Polish campaign had already been presented as a struggle of the German "master race" against Slavic ❾ "subhumans" and as a struggle for *Lebensraum* ("living space") in the East. Tragically, the invaders were initially greeted as liberators in many of the Soviet republics, such as ❽ Ukraine (p. 481), which were suffering under Stalin's regime. In a number of countries, notably Lithuania, anti-Semitism was very strong, and the local population eagerly joined in the massacres of Jews. Nevertheless, from 1941 the German occupiers brought their own terror and destruction to the Soviet Union.

According to Hitler's personal instructions—the "Commissar's order" of June 6, 1941—all captured political leaders of the Red Army were to be shot immediately. This was primarily carried out by Heinrich Himmler's SS troops (p. 451) who followed in the wake of the army, but the army was also involved in Nazi extermination policies. "Ruthless measures" were also to be taken against Soviet prisoners of war. More than 3.3 million of them died from starvation, torture, execution, or slave labor.

Soviet propaganda poster urges Russians to take revenge on Nazi Germany, 1943

In June 1941, four SS task forces followed the German army east and immediately began mass executions to eradicate "racial inferiors" systematically, particularly ⓫ Jews, who were rounded up, shot in fields and forests, and buried in mass graves which they themselves had to dig. The organized mass murder of the European Jews had already started in Poland (p. 520).

The "General Plan East" of 1942 resulted in the decimation of the Slavic peoples through the deportation and forced labor of about 30 million and the step-by step "Germanization" of Eastern Europe. The conquered regions of Byelorussia and Ukraine were placed under the Reich's Ministry for Occupied Eastern Territories. As a result of the triumphs of the Red Army, the realization of this plan became impossible.

The violence and inhumanity of the German occupiers radicalized the resistance on the Soviet side. Propaganda chief Ilya Ehrenburg called for violent ❿ revenge. Many German prisoners of war died under wretched conditions. Soviet resistance groups also waged a ⓬ partisan war against the German occupiers. This in turn was crushed with violence as villages were razed and children were shot.

When the Red Army reached German soil in 1945, the Soviet soldiers treated the German population with the same brutality (p. 526). The Soviet Union lost a total of 28 million people in World War II, of whom more than half were civilians, far more than any other country.

"The Subhuman," cover page of a Nazi propaganda magazine, 1942

Ilya Ehrenburg

The Russian writer and journalist, born in Kiev, wrote in the journal Soviet News on March 8, 1945: "The only historic mission, as far as I can see it, is modestly and honorably to diminish the German population."

above: Ilya Grigoryevich Ehrenburg, 1935

Execution of Jews by German troops, near Sniatyn, Poland 1941

Byelorussian partisan with his daughters, 1944

1914–1945 The World Wars and Interwar Period

16 Sep–18 Nov 1942	Conquest of a large part of Stalingrad by German troops
after 19 Nov 1942	Russian counteroffensive
22 Nov 1942	Encircling of German troops in Stalingrad
31 Jan–2 Feb 1943	Capitulation of Germany in Stalingrad

Biographies
The Commanders in Chief

Adolf Hitler (1889–1945)
Lived as an unemployed artist in Vienna; went to Munich in 1913 and enlisted in the German army in 1914; in 1919, joined the radical German Workers' Party, which was renamed the National Socialist German Workers' Party by the time he assumed the leadership in 1921; made a political breakthrough to the national level in the 1930 elections; as chancellor from 1933, established a totalitarian state and in 1939 unleashed the Second World War; became supreme commander of the German army in 1941; initiated a plan to systematically exterminate Europe's Jewish population following the invasion of the Soviet Union in 1941; escaped an assassination attempt with only minor injuries in 1944; committed suicide in Berlin on April 30, 1945.

Joseph Stalin (1878–1953)
Joined the Central Committee of the Bolshevik party in 1912; as general secretary of the Communist party from 1922, systematically built up his power base in the Soviet Union; established dictatorial rule with a personality cult after Lenin's death and disposed of his rivals in the party in the "Great Purge" of 1936–1938; occupied eastern Poland in 1939, and in 1940 provoked the Russo–Finnish War (the Winter War); after Hitler's invasion of the USSR in 1941, proclaimed the "Great Fatherland War" and took over supreme military command until 1945; repulsed the German attack and advanced into Central and Southern Europe, where he imposed Soviet-style Communist rule; came into sharp conflict with the US-led Western world; died in March 1953.

Winston Churchill (1874–1965)
Worked as a war correspondent during the Boer War before entering politics; after World War I, became secretary of war and later chancellor of the exchequer in a Conservative administration; gave early warnings about Hitler; became prime minister of an all-party coalition government in 1940 and a symbol of British resistance; forged a strong coalition with Roosevelt and Stalin; had early suspicions of Soviet designs on Eastern Europe; coined the phrase "The Iron Curtain" in 1946; was reelected prime minister 1951–1955.

Franklin D. Roosevelt (1882–1945)
Elected President of the United States in 1933; established American recognition of the Soviet Union in 1933 and sought to end US neutrality at the beginning of the war in 1939; supported Hitler's opponents from 1940 with the "Lend-Lease" scheme; entered the war after the Japanese surprise attack on Pearl Harbor as one of the "Big Three" alongside the USSR and Britain; later widely criticized for acquiescing to Stalin's postwar plans for Central and Eastern Europe; died shortly before the end of the war to be succeeded by Harry S. Truman.

Charles de Gaulle (1890–1970)
Commanded a tank brigade against the Germans at the outset of World War II before entering the government; made a radio appeal from London after the French defeat calling on mainland France and its colonies to resist the Nazi occupation; united various resistance factions and built up separate political and military structures; placed himself at the head of a provisional government-in-exile in 1944 and participated in the Allied liberation of France in 1944; served as president 1944–1946; successfully fought to establish France's place among the victorious powers after 1945; as president, founded the Fifth Republic in 1958.

Benito Mussolini (1883–1945)
Founded the "Fasci di Combattimento" after being expelled from the Socialist party in 1919; overthrew the government in Rome in 1922 and placed himself at the head of a fascist dictatorship; invaded Ethiopia in 1935 and annexed it to Italy; entered World War II in 1940 as Hitler's ally; following humiliating military defeats, was arrested by the king in 1943; after rescue by German commandos, set up the Republic of Salò in Nazi-occupied northern Italy; was captured and shot by Italian partisans while attempting to flee toSwitzerland on April 28, 1945.

Hirohito (1901–1989)
Became the 124th emperor of Japan in 1926; his role in the country's expansionist policies after 1937 is disputed–accused by some of influencing the offensive plans of the military-dominated government and agreeing to the attack on the US military base at Pearl Harbor; urged an end to hostilities after the United States dropped atomic bombs on Hiroshima and Nagasaki; announced Japan's surrender on August 15, 1945, over the radio, breaking the traditional imperial silence for the first time; renounced claims to divinity during the American occupation after the war.

Tito (1892–1980)
Joined the Communist party of Yugoslavia in 1920 and its Central Committee in 1934; organized a strong partisan army following the Nazi occupation of Yugoslavia in 1941; promised the restoration of an independent Yugoslavia in which all nationalities would have equal rights; with Red Army assistance, succeeded in liberating Yugoslavia and dominating competing resistance groups in 1945; as Marshal Tito, became leader of the provisional government in 1943; from 1953 until his death, was president of the Socialist Federal Republic of Yugoslavia.

World War II: An Overview

left: Allied troops land in Normandy, June 6, 1944

middle: Hitler declares war on Poland in the Reichstag on Sep 1, 1939

right: View over the destroyed city of Hiroshima after the atomic bombing

The political order established at the end of World War I favored the victorious powers and reinforced "revisionism" in Germany, an attitude exploited by the National Socialists. Italy and Germany formed the core of the Axis powers in 1936 and Japan joined them in 1940. The Soviet Union and the United States entered the war in 1941 and, together with Great Britain, formed the core of the Allied coalition that opposed the Axis.

Nazi ideology prescribed the need for Aryan "living space"—*lebensraum*—in the east and planned to reorganize the continent according to fascist "racial hierarchies." To this end, Germany invaded Poland on September 1, 1939, quickly defeating the Polish forces.

With the German army's rapid surprise attacks, dubbed the "Blitzkrieg," Hitler secured supremacy on the European mainland. In quick succession, Denmark, Norway, Belgium, Luxembourg, and the Netherlands were overrun. France capitulated in May 1940. The German attack on Great Britain failed. German troops marched into Greece in 1941 and, together with their Italian allies, into Yugoslavia. They supported Italy's campaign against Libya in Africa, but were temporarily halted there by the British.

The attack against the Soviet Union began in 1941. German troops initially made rapid advances, but were halted in December 1941 just outside Moscow. Following behind the advancing units, SS troops routinely murdered political opponents and "racially inferior" people, while others were systematically deported from German-occupied territory to concentration camps.

After the Japanese attack on the US naval base at Pearl Harbor, Hawaii, on December 7, 1941, the United States officially entered the war. By this time, the military superiority of the Allies became apparent. The Axis front in Africa collapsed in May 1943, and in September Allied troops toppled Mussolini in Italy. The Allies landed on the Normandy coast of France on June 6, 1944. They met fierce resistance but marched into Paris on August 25. By the end of 1944, the Red Army had pushed the Germans back as far as Warsaw and Budapest.

Despite the hopelessness of their situation, the Nazi leaders would not consider surrender, so the Allies advanced into German territory from all sides at the beginning of 1945, occupied the country, and forced the surrender of the German Reich on May 8, 1945.

Hostilities continued in the Pacific. The Japanese army had occupied much of Southeast Asia by 1942 until halted by an Allied counteroffensive in 1943 and slowly pushed back. To force a quick surrender, the US government decided to drop two atomic bombs on Japanese cities: Hiroshima on August 6 and Nagasaki on August 8, 1945. The Japanese signed an unconditional surrender on September 2, 1945. World War II, which cost more than 55 million lives, had finlly ended.

The Murder of the European Jewry

After unleashing the war, the Nazi leadership radicalized the persecution of Jews and introduced systematic mass murder in the occupied East.

1 Yellow Star of David from the Nazi period, 1941

The racist policies (p. 452) of the Nazis were spread all over Europe with the German military victories throughout the war until 1941. The isolated position of the Jews was intensified. By 1941, Jews in all of the German-controlled territories were forced to wear the ❶ yellow Star of David. The organized concentration and deportation of European Jews in Polish ghettos began in the summer of 1940. Many Jews were used as ❷ slave labor following the principle of "extermination through labor." Under the direction of SS leader ❹ Himmler, the number of concentration camps in the occupied territories increased to 22 by 1944, with 165 labor camps annexed to them.

In the summer of 1941, Hitler decided to have all Jews within the areas over which he had control murdered. Under the chairmanship of ❸ Reinhard Heydrich, high-ranking bureaucrats at the Wannsee Conference in Berlin in January 1942 defined the groups of persons to be killed and planned the cooperation of the departments most effective in the implementation of the murder operations.

The mass executions by the SS following the invasion of the Soviet Union (p. 512) marked the beginning of the organized genocide to which almost the entire Jewish population of the Baltic states, Byelorussia, and Ukraine fell victim. Extermination camps, in which Jews were murdered primarily with poison gas, were erected in Poland from autumn 1941: Treblinka, Belzéc, Majdanek, Sobibor, and Chelmno. Millions of Jews were transported in cattle cars from all parts of Europe to these camps. The largest "death factory" was ❻, ❼ Auschwitz-Birkenau. At least a million persons died in its ❺ gas chambers alone. From arrival at Birkenau to completed cremation generally took no more than 90 minutes. When the Red Army was closing in at the end of 1944, the gassing was stopped and the camps disbanded, yet innumerable people still died on the death marches to the West in the spring of 1945.

A total of about six million European Jews fell victim to Nazi racist fanaticism. At least 500,000 other "undesirables," primarily Sinti and Roma ("Gypsies"), were also ❽ murdered.

2 Jewish slave labor in the Warsaw ghetto, ca. 1942

3 Reinhard Heydrich, 1940

4 SS leader Heinrich Himmler

5 Gas chamber in Auschwitz

6 Selection process at the ramp in Birkenau, 1944

7 Identification photos of a Hungarian boy in the concentration camp Auschwitz, 1942

The Concentration Camp Theresienstadt

Theresienstadt, 35 miles outside Prague, served as a stopover on the way to the extermination camps. In Nazi propaganda films, the world was shown peaceful life in a camp designed with the needs of the people in mind. Even the foreign representatives of the Red Cross who visited Theresienstadt were fooled.

Theresienstadt, today the Terezín Memorial

8 Corpses of prisoners in the concentration camp

1940 | Founding of the "Viking Division"

31 Jul 1941 | Hitler initiates the "Final Solution of the Jewish Question"

Summer 1941 | Building of the concentration camp Auschwitz

Sep 1941 | Jews forced to wear the Star of David

Pillage and Persecution: The German Occupation Policy

Alongside the reordering in the East modeled on the Nazi ideology, economic exploitation characterized the German occupation policy in all the captured lands. More than a few locals cooperated with the Nazi occupiers.

In Poland, Denmark, Belgium, France, Yugoslavia, Greece, parts of the Soviet Union, and later Italy, Hungary, and Slovakia—in the whole area under German control or influence—the Nazi occupation policy was designed for, in addition to the extermination of the Jews, the exploitation of the countries for German war aims. Local ❾ industries and agriculture were made subordinate to the requirements of the German war economy. In order to meet the need for armament materials in the course of the war, Nazi leaders also increased the use of ❿ foreign workers in the homeland. At first, only prisoners of war were forcibly transported to Germany and coerced to work, but later it was ⓭ civilians, too. German industry employed a total of around 12 million forced laborers during the war.

10 Foreign worker from Eastern Europe, wearing the sign *Ost* ("East"), 1943

Whereas in the Eastern countries the subjugation of the Slavic peoples (p. 512) took priority, German administrators actively tried to enlist the ⓫ support of the local populations in the occupied countries of Western and Northern Europe. In these areas, the people mostly maintained a passive wait-and-see attitude; only a few put up any resistance, and there were some who were even willing to cooperate with the Germans.

9 German soldiers at the fish market in Copenhagen, 1940

The mass deportation of Jews from all over Europe to the extermination camps would not have been possible without collaborators. In addition, a total of 21 ⓬ foreign volunteer units provided support to the German army in its campaigns of conquest. The first were the Norwegians, Danes, Finns, Dutch, and Belgians who formed the "Viking Division" in 1940. The Germans received a particularly great influx of support at the beginning of the attack on the Soviet Union. A captured Russian lieutenant general, ⓮ Andrei Wlassow, built up an anti-Communist army of prisoners of war and Russian volunteers in 1942. When Germany's defeat became foreseeable, military support sank. Nevertheless, at the beginning of 1945, the volunteer units still comprised around a million non-Germans.

11 Poster promoting the international unit of the Waffen SS in France, 1941

12 Mohammedan volunteers as mountain soldiers of the Waffen SS, 1944

13 Poster for the recruitment of Dutch people for work in the agricultural sector in the East, 1942

14 General Andrei Wlassow inspecting his troops, 1944

20 Jan 1942 | Wannsee Conference
1942 | Creation of a Russian voluntary formation under Wlassow
30 Apr 1942 | Mobilization of concentration camp inmates for the military economy
from 1943 | Increasing deportation of civilians for forced labour

The War Conferences of the Allies

Following the German attack on the Soviet Union, the United States, Great Britain, and the Soviet Union formed a common alliance against Germany. At several conferences, the "Big Three" decided upon the essential outline of a postwar European order.

The German attack on the Soviet Union (p. 512) in the summer of 1941 pushed the contrasting ideological and political power interests of the three great powers—the United States, Great Britain, and the Soviet Union—into the background in favor of an anti-Hitler coalition. In October they signed a mutual armament agreement. The United States had already obligated itself in March 1941 to support all enemies of Germany through the Lend-Lease Act. In January 1942, the United States and Britain created a ❶ joint military staff for strategic coordination of the war.Throughout the war convoys endured harsh weather conditions and extreme danger to transport valuable cargoes and supplies to Russian Murmansk.

Conference at Casablanca, 1943: Roosevelt and the French general Henri Giraud (right)

Conference at Tehran, 1943: Stalin, Roosevelt, Churchill (from left to right)

Atlantic Charter, 1941: Churchill talking to Roosevelt (left)

Despite the Japanese attack on Pearl Harbor (p. 498), U.S. President Franklin Roosevelt and British Prime Minister Winston Churchill agreed that victory over Germany should be the first priority. In the ❷ Atlantic Charter of August 14, 1941, they announced "the end of Nazi tyranny" to the suppressed countries of Europe, proclaimed the right of free self-determination of nations, and declared the rejection of political and economic imperialism as the principles of the future postwar order. Tensions developed within the anti-Hitler coalition in 1942 because Stalin was worried that the territories in Poland and the Baltic region he had gained under the Nazi-Soviet pact (p. 476) would not be recognized and was aggravated by the continual postponement of a "second front" in the West that would relieve pressure on the Red Army. Stalin even explored the possibilities of peace talks with Hitler. However, he aligned himself with the demand by the United States and Britain for Germany's unconditional surrender at the conference at ❹ Casablanca on January 24, 1943. In ❺ Tehran, at the first conference of the "Big Three" in late 1943, Roosevelt and Churchill took the successes of the Red Army into account (p. 512) and agreed to the "shifting west" in favor of the Soviet Union.

Shortly before Germany's final military defeat (p. 526), the ❻ partition of Germany into four occupation zones with a common control council and with the participation of France was decided at ❸ Yalta in February 1945.

Churchill (left) and Dwight D. Eisenhower, commander in chief of the Allied Forces from 1944, March 1945

Roosevelt and Churchill agreed to give Stalin a free hand in politically reorganizing Eastern and Southern Europe in exchange for his aid in the war against Japan (p. 498) after Germany's capitulation. This paved the way for the foundation of the Communist "satellite states" of the Soviet empire (p. 576-579) after 1945.

Conference at Yalta, 1945

Map showing the German occupation areas, 1945

March 1941 | Lend-Lease Act

14 Aug 1941 | Atlantic Charter

11 Dec 1941 | Germany and Italy declare war on the US

1941 | Unification of the three great powers in an anti-Hitler coalition

7 Dec 1941 | Japanese attack on Pearl Harbor

The Advance of the Allies

The German army was forced to retreat on all fronts by the Allied advance from 1943. The successful Allied invasion of the French mainland in June 1944 finally brought the decisive turning point in favor of the Allies.

8 Aftermath of the attack on Pearl Harbor by the Japanese, 1941

As in World War I, the entry into the war of the materially superior United States and its huge manpower in the form of the ❼ US armament industry ensured the downfall of the Axis powers. The European conflict had become a worldwide war following the ❽ Japanese attack on the American naval base at Pearl Harbor (p. 498) and the subsequent declarations of war on the United States by Germany and Italy on December 11, 1941. The overwhelming strength of the Allies pressing against the German occupation troops from the west and south from 1943 onwards put them on the defensive and forced them to retreat back to the borders of Germany.

Following the German-Italian surrender in North Africa (p. 511), the Allies invaded ⓫ Italy in July 1943. The Fascist government fell apart when Mussolini was overthrown on July 25, 1943 (p. 471). Italy's new government surrendered and then joined the Allies in the war against Germany. Beginning in 1943, the German allies Romania and Bulgaria had been forced successivelyby the Allies to accept a cease-fire, and German troops had had to evacuate Greece and parts of Yugoslavia. Soviet troops stood outside East Prussia in August 1943.

11 US troops in Naples, 1945

12 Landing of the Allied force in Normandy, June 6, 1944

The second front in the West that Stalin had demanded was established with the landing in Normandy of an enormous ⓬ Allied force on June 6, 1944. In an immense military operation, 326,000 soldiers with more than 50,000 vehicles went ashore on the French Atlantic Coast within five days, suffering ❾ heavy losses in the process, as 10,000 aircraft secured the airspace above. On August 25, 1944, ❿ Paris was retaken with the support of French troops—who were evacuated to Great Britain before the German occupation in 1940—and the French resistance movement (p. 461). In the East (p. 512), the Red Army had advanced to the German border.

Nevertheless, the Germans continued to offer determined resistance despite the hopelessness of the situation. The Nazi leadership mobilized the population to "total war" (p. 525). Only the bloody conquest of all of Germany could end the war (p. 526).

9 Omaha Beach, cemetery for American soldiers in Normandy

7 Poster promoting the recruitment of American women for industry, 1943

10 German soldiers surrender in Paris, August 25, 1944

D-Day

The Allied invasion in France was the largest military operation of the war and went down in history as "D-Day." The term does not stand for "Decision Day" or "Disembarkation Day," as is often assumed, but rather is the military convention for denoting the first day of a military operation. The capitalized D, being the first letter of "day," is used to emphasize this. The actual name of the operation was "Operation Overlord."

Eisenhower talking to soldiers of the Allied forces, June 1944

14–24 Jan 1943	Conference at Casablanca
Jul 1943	Landing of the allies in Italy
25 Jul 1943	Fall of Mussolini
6 Jun 1944	Landing of the allies in Normandy ("D-Day")
25 Aug 1944	Allied reconquest of Paris
4–11 Feb 1945	Yalta conference

Air Warfare

The battle in the air, waged with the cutting-edge technology of the day, caused heavy losses on both sides. The Allied bombing raids on Germany in the final stages of the war were primarily intended to demoralize the population.

1 US bombers attack Frankfurt, January 29, 1944

2 Nuremberg, 1945

3 London after a bomb attack, 1940

4 Dresden, 1945

5 After a bomb attack in Dresden bodies are burnt because of the danger of an epidemic, February 1945

Aerial warfare had played a decisive role since the beginning of the war. Successfully tested in the Spanish Civil War (p. 473), the German pinpoint bombing of military targets effectively contributed to the conquest of Poland in 1939 and Norway in 1940 (p. 510). In May 1940, the Germans for the first time destroyed an entire city, Rotterdam. The air war was radicalized by deliberate "carpet bombing," that is, the systematic saturation bombing of an inhabited area. Both sides gradually accepted the mass murder of civilians and employed it as an instrument of warfare. The German bombing raids on ❸ London and Coventry during the air war over England in 1940–1941 (p. 510) aimed not only to destroy armaments factories but also to undermine the morale of the civilian population.

By 1943 the Allies, superior both in material and manpower, were forcing the Germans completely onto the defensive in the air war. Well-directed air attacks on German positions on the front lines cleared the way for Allied advances on the ground (p. 523). From 1942, ❶ American and British bombing raids had been reaching cities in the north and west, particularly the industrial regions on the Rhine and in the Ruhr Valley, with increasing frequency. In order to break the resistance of the German civilian population, complete ❷ cities were also purposefully destroyed. In both daylight and nighttime offensives, Allied bombing raids had by 1945 reduced to rubble major areas of Cologne, Lübeck, ❻ Berlin, ❹ Dresden, and Hamburg, among others, and had forced the German population to live in overcrowded ❼ air shelters or to flee to the eastern regions of the Reich. Almost two million tons of bombs were dropped; nearly every fifth family was homeless. At war's end, 51 million cubic meters of debris lay in Berlin; in Hamburg, it was close to 36 million, in Dresden 25 million, and in Cologne 24 million. Altogether, ❺ around 600,000 Germans lost their lives in the Allied bombing attacks.

6 Anhalter Station in Berlin after its destruction, 1945

7 Homeless families seek shelter in a bunker, 1944

The War at Sea

The Allies had the upper hand in the naval war after 1943. Up until then, the Germans had been able to disrupt the Allies' merchant marine traffic effectively in the Atlantic with their submarines, but in March 1943 the supreme commander of the German navy, Karl Dönitz, broke off warfare in the Atlantic due to the high losses suffered.

Karl Dönitz plans a submarine attack, 1943

May 1940 | Destruction of Rotterdam

1940–41 | Battle of Britain

30–31 May 1942 | Bombing of Cologne

18 Feb 1943 | Proclamation of "total war"

20 Jul 1944 | Attack of Colonel Count von Stauffenberg on Hitler

Total War and Resistance in Germany

The Nazis began to mobilize the entire population after 1943 despite the hopeless military situation. An attempted putsch on July 20, 1944, failed.

The closer they came to military defeat (p. 523), the more the Nazi leaders fanatically tried to mobilize the last reserves at home and on the front lines, attempting to force an exhausted and starving population into action in defense of their hometowns. After the defeat at Stalingrad, Propaganda Minister Joseph Goebbels proclaimed the start of "total war." (p. 512). All males between 16 and 65, as well as females between 17 and 45, could be called up in defense of the Reich in order to achieve the "final victory." After August 1943, Hitler Youth members were shipped out of "defense fitness camps" (p. 451) directly to the front. Large segments of the population were conscripted to work in the armaments industry, and forced laborers were more intensely recruited. ❾ "See-it-through" slogans, promulgated either by propaganda posters or over the ❽ *Volksempfänger*—mass-produced radios for the general populace—were meant to inspire the "home front willing to sacrifice" to maximum performance. Martial criminal law was made stricter; deserters were shot or hanged on the spot by a drumhead court-martial to intimidate the people.

8 The *Volksempfänger*, a very cheap radio; no foreign programs could be received, 1938

The terror against civilians became more radical once the ❿ German resistance had entered the public consciousness for the first time with a failed assassination attempt on Hitler on July 20, 1944. Germans taking a stand of resistance in the ⓬ church and ⓫ political opposition had been struggling since 1933, unsuccessfully, in a police state (p. 450) against a regime that was still supported by a considerable portion of the population. The risks were high and many paid with their lives.

9 "See-it-through" slogans, 1945: "Frankfurt will be held!"

10 Court-martial where suspected resisters were condemned, 1944

11 Helmuth James Count von Moltke, founder of the resistance group *Kreisauer Kreis* before the court-martial, executed in 1945

12 Dietrich Bonhoeffer, member of the political opposition, executed 1945

From Joseph Goebbels's Sportpalast Speech, February 18, 1943

"The English maintain that the German people are resisting the government's total war measures. They do not want total war, but capitulation! I ask you: Do you want total war? If necessary, do you want a war more total and radical than anything that we can even imagine today?"

Goebbels makes his speech in the Sportpalast, February 1943

The Assassination Attempt of 1944

The bomb attack aimed at Hitler carried out by Colonel Count von Stauffenberg on July 20, 1944, in the Führer's headquarters in Poland had been planned since 1943 by a group of conspirators from all sections of the resistance. It was supposed to launch an immediate overthrow; after the death of Hitler, party and governmental offices were to be occupied and a new government put in place that would end the war. When Hitler survived the attack with only slight injuries, the coup attempt quickly collapsed. About 200 members of the resistance were executed and a further 7000 incarcerated.

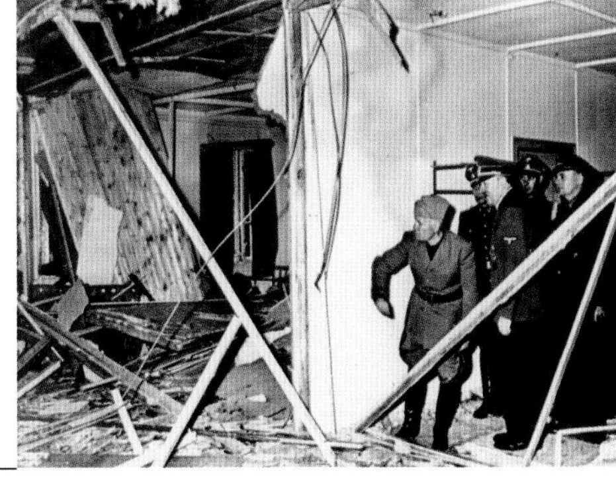

above: Colonel Count von Stauffenberg, 1934
right: Hitler shows his destroyed headquarters to Mussolini

25 Sep 1944	Conscription of able men between 16 and 65
13–14 Feb 1945	Destruction of Dresden
5 Mar 1945	Decrease of all food rations
19 Mar 1945	Hitler gives "Nero Order"
12 Apr 1945	Hitler's order for defense of cities

The Military Collapse of Germany

Germany surrendered unconditionally on May 8, 1945, only after the Allied forces had conquered the entire country. Hitler avoided capture by committing suicide.

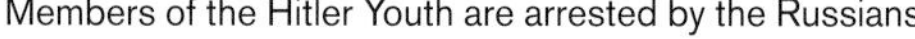
1 Members of the Hitler Youth are arrested by the Russians

2 Soviet flag flying over the German Reichstag, April 30, 1945

3 Soviet soldiers in the ruins of the Reich Chancellery in Berlin, May 1945

The last German offensive in the Ardennes in southern France failed in December 1944. American, British, and French troops pushed from the west onto German soil at the beginning of 1945 and, despite desperate resistance, conquered the contested cities one after another. On April 25, American and Soviet soldiers shook hands at Torgau on the Elbe.The Red Army crossed the German eastern frontier on January 1945 and launched its attack on Berlin. In the course of this assault, brutal acts of revenge for German atrocities committed on the Russian front were carried out on the German civilian population, particularly on women. Despite overwhelming Soviet superiority, the Germans continued to offer heavy resistance. Hitler now had ❶ children, the aged, and the sick armed and sent to the front. Berlin fell on May 2 after a brutal 13-day battle for every street and building; on April 30 the ❷ Soviet flag flew over the Berlin Reichstag. Hitler and ❺ Goebbels had committed suicide in an underground bunker of the ❸ German chancellery: Hitler on April 30, Goebbels the day after. As many as 200,000 Red Army soldiers and around 50,000 Germans lost their lives in the ❹ battle for Berlin alone.

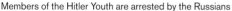

4 Rubble at the Brandenburg Gate in the capital of Berlin, 1945

The German army signed the ❼ unconditional surrender of Germany first on May 7 at Allied Headquarters in Reims, and a day later at Soviet Headquarters in Berlin-Karlshorst; it came into effect the next day. All of Germany was occupied, and the entire armed forces became ❻ prisoners of war. World War II in Europe had ended. Japan, however, surrendered only after the first atomic bombs had been dropped in early August (p. 498).

6 German prisoners of war are transported to the Soviet Union, May 1945

The "Nero Order"

In mid March 1945, Hitler issued the so-called Nero Order, instructing Armaments Minister Albert Speer to destroy Germany completely. With no regard for the civilian population, any installation in Germany that could be used by the enemy in any way—industrial complexes, supply and transport systems—was to be destroyed as the army retreated. The order was generally ignored.

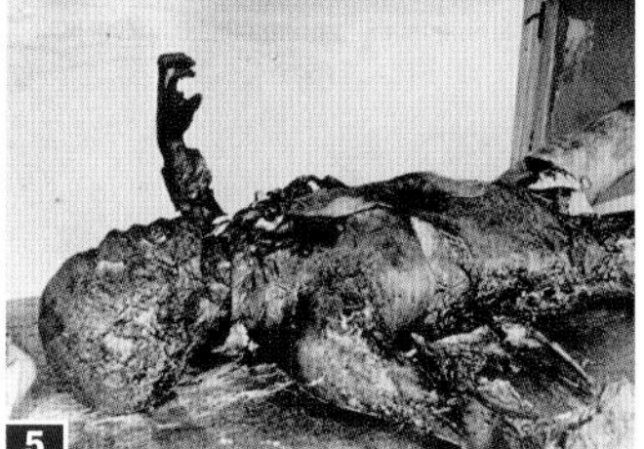
5 Joseph Goebbels's body in Hitler's underground bunker, 1945

7 Field Marshal Keitel signs the unconditional surrender on May 8, 1945

Dec 1944 | Failure of the Ardennes Offensive

Jan 1945 | Beginning of the attack on Berlin

30 Apr 1945 | Berlin taken by the Red Army / Hitler's suicide

8 May 1945 | Unconditional surrender of Germany

Germany in 1945

The Allied victors laid out the political and economic framework for the reorganization of Germany at the Potsdam Conference. Reconstruction from the ruins began.

In accordance with the agreements of the Allied war conferences (p. 522), the victorious powers divided German territory into American, British, Soviet, and French ❾ occupation zones. Concurrently, Berlin and Vienna (p. 546) were subdivided into four city sectors. At the conference in ❽ Potsdam in July 1945, new US President Harry S. Truman, Stalin, and Churchill—who was later replaced by the new prime minister Clement Attlee—emphasized their common responsibility for Germany. An ❿ Allied Control Council was to exercise the supreme power of governance. The German economy would be placed under Allied control. The victors agreed upon demilitarization, denazification, and decentralization as the political principles for rebuilding Germany. The principles were later divergently implemented according to the individual ideology in the occupation zones (p. 538).

8 Potsdam Conference in July 1945. Seated from left to right: Attlee, Truman, and Stalin

10 Seat of the Allied Control Council in Berlin-Schöneberg, 1954

11 Boy cycling through the rubble, Berlin, 1945

Beginning in November 1945, the leading representatives of the Nazi regime were ⓬ put on trial in Nuremberg for war crimes, crimes against humanity, and crimes against the peace (aggression). Most of the representatives were hanged. The examination of every individual German as to his or her involvement in the Nazi system was only halfheartedly pursued with the beginning of the East–West conflict (p. 532).

As planned in the Allied war conferences (p. 522), the north of East Prussia was permanently annexed to the Soviet Union and the remaining German territories east of the Oder-Neisse line were made part of Poland. The resettlement of the German population of Eastern Europe was approved. More than 16 million Germans were ⓮ driven out, often brutally; more than two million died while fleeing.

Meanwhile, in the ⓯ ruins of Germany, reconstruction began. Unlike during the period after 1918, the victors supplied fuel and food to the starving. ⓰ Women primarily accomplished the heavy labor of clearing the cities of ⓫ rubble. The first steps toward democracy were taken under Allied control with the reestablishment of the Social Democratic and other political parties in June 1945. ⓭ Culturally there was also a rebirth; newspapers boomed, and the theaters and concert halls were once again overfilled.

9 Guards on the border between the American and the Soviet occupation zones in Berlin

12 One of the main defendants tried in Nuremberg: Hermann Göring, 1945

13 Poster for a café with dancing, among the ruins of Hannover, 1946

14 Refugees arrive in Berlin, 1945

15 Munich in ruins, 1945

16 Women clear the rubble in Berlin, 1945

Jun 1945 | Founding of new political parties

Jul 1945 | Potsdam Conference

2 Sep 1945 | Capitulation of Japan

after November 1945 | Nuremberg Trials

The Contemporary World

1945 to the present

After World War II, a new world order came into being in which two superpowers, the United States and the Soviet Union, played the leading roles. Their ideological differences led to the arms race of the Cold War and fears of a global nuclear conflict. The rest of the world was also drawn into the bipolar bloc system, and very few nations were able to remain truly nonaligned. The East–West conflict came to an end in 1990 with the collapse of the Soviet Union and the consequent downfall of the Eastern Bloc. Since that time, the world has been driven by the globalization of worldwide economic and political systems. The world has, however, remained divided: The rich nations of Europe, North America, and East Asia stand in contrast to the developing nations of the Third World.

The first moon landing made science-fiction dreams reality in the year 1969. Space technology has made considerable progress as the search for new possibilities of using space continues.

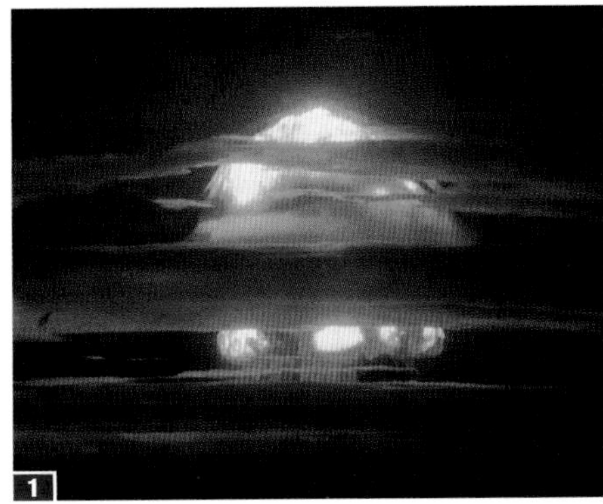
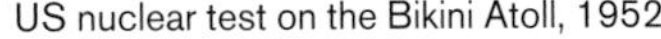

1 US nuclear test on the Bikini Atoll, 1952

2 Disarmament negotiations in Moscow, 1991

3 The Love Parade music festival, Berlin,1997

Contemporary History since 1945

The outcome of World War II in 1945 was devastating: Approximately 55 million deaths worldwide, some 20 million refugees, and wide swaths of Europe and Asia destroyed. The mass murder of the European Jews by the Nazi regime and its collaborators meant an upheaval in modern civilization to an extent previously unknown. Many efforts of international politics in the immediate postwar period were aimed at preventing future catastrophes of this kind.

Between the East–West Conflict and Globalization

The world political situation between 1945 and 1989 was definitively shaped by the East–West conflict. The new leading powers—the United States and the Soviet Union—each attempted to leave their stamp on the postwar order. Due to their opposing views of government and economics, a fault line quickly became visible, and soon the world powers stood opposite one another in a "Cold War." An increasing number of nations became involved in the face-off and aligned themselves with one of the two power blocs. The competition expressed itself in an accelerating arms race that meant a growing danger of global ❶ nuclear annihilation. To avoid being subsumed by the bloc system, many former colonies, the majority of which gained independence after World War II, became part of the Nonaligned Movement.

4 West German border guards at the Berlin Wall, 1978

The end of the Cold War came with the opening of the western Hungarian border and the fall of the ❹ Berlin Wall in 1989 and was ❷ cemented in 1991 with the dissolution of the Soviet Union. Though the world did find peace, the number of wars and conflicts between individual states—often ethnically or religiously motivated—has increased and nuclear, biological, and chemical weapons have come into even more hands.

In the meantime, world politics is now strongly defined by the process of globalization. Europe, East Asia, and North America are the centers of this development, but through the integration of the whole world into an overarching economic and communication network, political and economic decisions often have cross-border effects. Since 1945, as in no other time period before, mankind has made progress in almost all areas of knowledge. However, the fruits of this progress are unequally distributed. It is mainly the Western industrialized nations that have benefited from the wealth globalization has brought. The world political conflict lines no longer run between East and West but between North and South, between rich and poor. Another new source of conflict is international terrorism. Combating it and its causes effectively is a major challenge of the 21st century.

Lifestyle and Values

In the affluent countries of the world, lifestyle and general values concepts have changed enormously in the last 50 years. As the length of education has increased, ❸ youth, which was previously only a short preliminary stage before adulthood, has lengthened to become a stage of life in itself. Tied to wealth and beauty, youth has become an ideal that shapes economics, advertising, and everyday life. Since the 1960s, a new leisure culture has emerged; vacations and travel have become important elements of modern life and a booming industrial sector. Since the 1970s, automation in almost all fields has meant that much of the heavy physical labor of working life has been taken away. This has opened up new jobs, particularly for women. These new jobs are often found in the service sector, which has a high standing everywhere.

A development that has taken place very recently in the Western world is a turn away from traditional Christianity combined

5 Yin and yang: Taoist symbol showing the balance between opposites

1945 Potsdam Conference | **1948** Soviet blockade of West Berlin | **1962** Cuba-Crisis | **1968** Student movement in industrial nations | **1969** First human on the moon | **1973** First oil crisis | **1985** Gorbachev comes to power

6 Demonstration against "un-Islamic" clothing, Iran, 2004

7 Buddhist monks surf the Internet, 2005

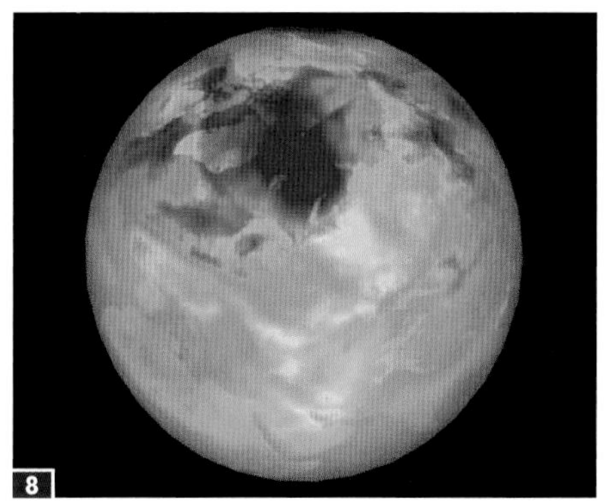
8 Ozone hole (dark blue) over the Antarctic, 2000

with an intensified search for the meaning of life. The orientation toward esoteric or ❺ East Asian lifestyles has increased, yet the search for happiness has been subordinated to constantly changing fashions. On the other hand, at the turn of the millennium, religious fundamentalism, particularly in Islam and Christianity, has strengthened in ❻ opposition, sometimes violently expressed, to the new Western lifestyle characterized by unchecked worldliness and secularism that has spread throughout the world as a standard.

The Mass Market of Culture and Knowledge

Cultural trends today circulate ever faster and wider and are increasingly subordinated to the laws of the marketplace. While, for example, music in the 1940s was limited to recreational and free-time entertainment, since the 1970s it has accompanied people wherever they go. Thus popular music has gained significance in comparison to classical music. Pop music exceeds itself in the rapid development and displacement of separate fashions and styles to satisfy the demand for easily consumed entertainment.

10 *Streifenbild IV* by Sigmar Polke, 1968

"High culture" has become more diverse and complex. New styles and trends, such as ❿ abstract painting, have established themselves worldwide. By the 1970s at the latest, talk of phases and movements was almost impossible, and one can now talk at most of schools. Distinctions between different art forms are no longer as clear-cut as they once were.

The developmental acceleration since 1945 also characterizes science. Never before have there been so many scientists, never before has research advanced so rapidly, and never before was there such a strong differentiation between research areas. English has asserted itself as the universal language of science. Newspapers present research findings quicker than books can, but the fastest and simplest form of knowledge communication today is the ❼ Internet, to which an increasing number of people have access.

Successes and Dangers of Progress

The scientific and technological successes of the last 60 years have been astounding. Cars, airplanes, radio, television, mainframe and personal computers, and the Internet have made the world smaller. In 1969 the first humans stood on the ❾ moon, and after 1987, the space station Mir made prolonged life in space possible. Medicine has made such progress that fear of epidemics such as cholera and polio no longer defines life, although new epidemics such as AIDS continue to emerge. At the turn of the millennium, telecommunication became mobile. Almost all the knowledge of mankind is available and can be accessed anytime, anywhere.

9 First moon landing by the United States, July 20, 1969

Even at the pinnacle of the belief in progress, however, the downside to the "always more, always further" motto became obvious. With the 1970s oil crisis, an end to the oil supply became conceivable, and the consequences this could have worldwide became foreseeable. Global damage to the environment and the advanced destruction of the ❽ Earth's atmosphere have emerged as the downside of industrial progress. Even the supposedly clean nuclear energy has, after the nuclear reactor catastrophe of ⓫ Chernobyl, left damage that will continue to have an effect for centuries. In a globalized world, the protection of the environment can, like the struggle against poverty and the containment of violence, perhaps only be achieved through agreements on a global scale, between states. These are the challenges with which the world is faced in the 21st century.

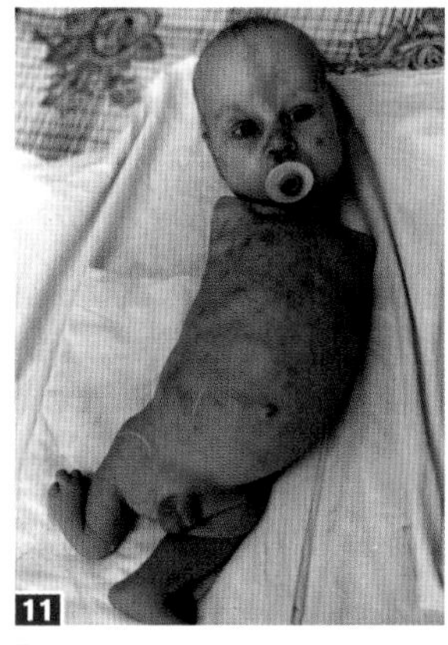
11 Baby malformed by the effects of the Chernobyl disaster, 1986

1986 | Nuclear accident in Chernobyl
1987 | AIDS becomes a public concern
9 Nov 1989 | Fall of the Berlin Wall
1991 | Dissolution of the Soviet Union
11 Sep 2001 | Terror attack in New York, Virginia, and Pennsylvania

Trends in World Politics since 1945

After the dissolution of the anti-Hitler coalition in 1945, the Cold War between the superpower nations—the United States and the Soviet Union—defined international relations until 1989. Conflicts between the ideological and military systems of the superpowers split the world into hostile blocs of countries and hindered the functioning of the United Nations as an instrument of global peace. The collapse of the Soviet empire in 1989 ended the ❶ Cold War, but fundamentalist terror and the uncontrolled proliferation of weapons of mass destruction created new problems and fields of conflict.

View of a painted wall on the Eastern side of the former Berlin Wall, 1990

The Cold War

After 1945, the European continent and virtually the entire world divided into the spheres of influence of the new superpowers, the United States and the Soviet Union.

Millions of refugees, deportees, ❷ prisoners of war, and concentration camp prisoners, referred to collectively as "displaced persons," presented postwar society with an integration problem.

Churchill, Roosevelt, and Stalin had already defined their claims in Europe in 1944 (p. 522). Following the war's end, the victors installed their political systems in the territories they controlled.

Vietnam War: A civilian shows the body of his child to soldiers from the South

The division of Germany into four occupation zones prepared the way for the national partition into the Federal Republic of Germany (FRG) and the ❸ German Democratic Republic (GDR) in 1949 (p. 539). Parliamentarian democracy in the West opposed the dictatorial "peoples' democracies" in the East. In 1946 Churchill coined the term "Iron Curtain" to describe the unyielding separation between the Eastern and the Western Blocs. Europe was also economically divided. Reconstruction in the West was supported by the ❺ Marshall Plan; its counterpart in the eastern Bloc was the Soviet sponsored Council for Mutual Economic Assistance (Comecon).

The division into two hostile blocs affected the whole world. With the victory of the Communist party in China, the most populous country in the world became a member of the socialist camp. The first "proxy war" between the East and the West broke out in ❻ Korea in 1950 (p. 622), followed by later wars in ❹ Vietnam (p. 617) and Afghanistan (p. 608). The Cuban Missile Crisis in 1962 almost resulted in nuclear war. During the period of détente in the 1970s, several control agreements were meant to curb armament on both sides. The Conference on Security and Cooperation in Europe (CSCE) attempted to introduce a process of détente beginning in 1974 by addressing economic and human rights issues.

The Cuban Missile Crisis

The stationing of Soviet nuclear missiles in Cuba led to the Cuban Missile Crisis, a confrontation between the United States and the Soviet Union in October 1962. President Kennedy demanded the removal of the weapons. When First Secretary Khrushchev refused, the US imposed a naval blockade, in the direction of which Soviet ships carrying missile components continued, having already set sail from Russia. At the last minute Khrushchev ordered the fleet to turn around and the missiles to be dismantled.

Khrushchev and the Cuban President Fidel Castro in New York, September 24, 1960

Posters with photos of missing German soldiers in the camp for those returning home, Friedland, 1955

Marx, Engels, Lenin: poster for a march in East Berlin, 1988

Train cars are delivered to the German State Railway as part of the Marshall Plan, November 1948

During the Korean War, US Marines keep a watch on North Korean prisoners, 1950

1944 | Declerationof the "United Nations" in Washington

4–11 Feb 1945 | Yalta Conference

1945 | Founding of the International Bank for Reconstruction and Development

24 Oct 1945 | Founding of the UN

The United Nations

The world community created the United Nations after World War II as an instrument to secure global peace. To this day, however, it remains dependent on the interests of the superpowers.

The United Nations organization emerged directly out of the military alliance against Germany. Initially, only countries that had declared war on the Third Reich by March 1, 1945, were eligible for membership, which allowed the admission of a large number of South American and Middle Eastern nations which had declared war on the Axis powers at the last moment. East and West Germany were not allowed to join until 1973. The aims of the ❼ United Nations since its founding on October 24, 1945, have been to secure world peace and to promote international cooperation. The UN's major organs are the General Assembly; the ❽ Security Council, with permanent and changing members; the Secretariat; and the International Court of Justice.

8 Meeting of the UN Security Council in New York to discuss the uprising in Hungary, November 1956

10 Stonehenge, England, given world cultural heritage status by UNESCO in 1986

11 British peacekeeping troops from the United Nations in former Yugoslavia, 1995

The East–West conflict, however, impeded the creation of a global system of peace. Unanimous decisions in the Security Council were repeatedly thwarted by use of the veto by one superpower or the other. The policy of détente at last led to joint treaties between the world powers, for example over the nonproliferation of nuclear weapons.

The nature of United Nations was altered by the decolonization process after World War II (p. 626). The number of members tripled, and the issues to be dealt with included the question of how to integrate the new members into the UN and the global order. Many former colonies joined, reducing the dominance of the industrial countries. The superpowers therefore tried to enlist the support of the nonaligned states. The UN guidelines were adjusted to new political requirements. Besides the protection of children (UNICEF), ❿, ⓬ world cultural heritage (UNESCO), and ❾ health (WHO), since the 1970s it has also been the United Nations' goal to reduce disparities between the North and South and to halt the overexploitation of natural resources.

The instruments for securing peace have changed since the 1960s. Initially, the organization was limited to diplomatic means, but now it can also deploy armed ⓫ UN peacekeeping troops, which are recognizable by their blue helmets. Despite some successes, the conflicts of interests of the member states that supply these troops have repeatedly hampered the ability of the United Nations to serve as "world police"—even after the end of the Cold War. Whether the United Nations can be made capable of meeting the new demands of the 21st century has been a subject of intense discussion within the world community.

12 UNESCO helping illiterate people in Mexico, 1980

7 United Nations Building, New York, lit up for the 50th anniversary of the founding of the UN, 1995

9 Blood test results are examined as part of the campaign by the World Health Organization against glandular fever, Angola, 1959

after 1945 | Beginning decolonialization
1946 | Dissolving of the League of Nations
Sep 1949 | Founding of the People's Republic of China
1950–53 | Korean War
Oct 1962 | The Cuban Missile Crisis

Decolonization and the Dissolution of the Blocs

A period of decolonization began during the 1950s. Some of the states that emerged fell into neither the Western nor Eastern camps. Soviet reform policies starting in 1985 induced the implosion of the Eastern Bloc and ended the Cold War.

With India's release from British guardianship (p. 493) in 1947, after a long political struggle and the partition of the subcontinent into two mutually suspicious nations, India and Pakistan, a period of global decolonization began. In 1949, Southeast Asian countries such as Indonesia became independent, and in the 1950s and 1960s almost all of the colonies in ❸ Africa gained autonomy (p. 626-629). The number of sovereign states rose from around 50 in 1900 to 180 in 1990.

The process of decolonization took place either violently, as was the case in Algeria, or through agreement, as in the case of India. Some of the colonial rulers—in both blocs—were replaced by dictatorial regimes. Dictatorship and the resultant corruption have been characteristic of many African independent countries. To avoid becoming pawns of the major powers, Third World countries in 1955 formed the Nonaligned Movement.

The end of the rigid bloc confrontation began in 1985, when ❷ Mikhail Gorbachev assumed office as the general secretary of the Communist Party of the Soviet Union. Increased armament, inefficient state structures, and rigid dogmatism had brought the USSR to an economic and social crisis during the preceding Brezhnev era (p. 588). Gorbachev began a radical reform policy, with the bywords *glasnost* ("openness") and *perestroika* ("economic and political reform"). The claim to Soviet supremacy over the Eastern Bloc states was relinquished. Whereas the Soviet Union had sent ❹ tanks in response to the 1968 Czech uprising demanding reform, the suppressed societies in the satellite states now used their new freedom of movement for revolutionary change. ❶ Demonstrations, strikes, and mass exoduses in 1989 brought the communist regimes to the point of collapse. With the disappearance of the Eastern Bloc, the Cold War ended after nearly four decades almost without violence.

1 GDR citizens demonstrate for free elections, Leipzig, 1989

2 Standing in front of a statue of Lenin, Gorbachev addresses the Congress of People's Deputies, 1989

3 Nigeria: Celebrations on the occasion of the fifth anniversary of independence, 1965

4 Soviet tanks in Prague, 1968

The Nonaligned Movement

In April 1955, 29 countries, primarily from Asia and Africa, prepared the way for the nonaligned states movement. Nations such as China, India, Indonesia, and Yugoslavia condemned the confrontation of the blocs. The term "Third World" was coined there to differentiate the movement's members from countries aligned with the superpowers.

5 Nonaligned states conference in Bandung, Indonesia, April 1955

"Life punishes those who come too late!"

This famous statement by Mikhail Gorbachev was never actually made in public. When Gorbachev was met by East German general secretary Erich Honecker at the Berlin airport on October 5, 1989, Gorbachev said on East German state television: "I believe danger only awaits those who don't react to life."

Soviet General Secretary Mikhail Gorbachev greets Erich Honecker, 1987

The New World Order

The West's peaceful victory in the Cold War brought freedom and democracy to Eastern Europe. Wider access to weapons of mass destruction and the growth of international terrorism, however, presented the world with new challenges.

The ❽ fall of the Berlin Wall on November 9, 1989, symbolized the victory of the freedom-seeking movements in Eastern European nations and the rapid collapse of the Soviet empire. In effect, it initiated German reunification along Western lines. East Germany became a part of the Federal Republic of Germany and a year later a member of NATO.

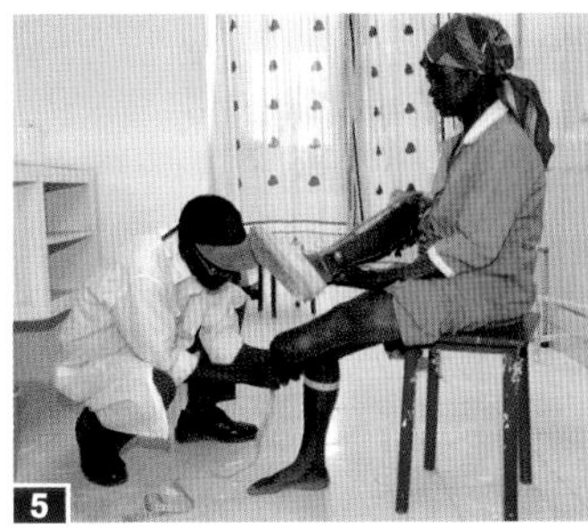

5 Angolan woman maimed by a land mine is fitted with an artificial limb in a local hospital, 2003

7 Debris in New York after the World Trade Center attacks, September 11, 2001

The Warsaw Pact, the Soviet bloc's defense alliance, fell apart, and its Eastern European member states joined the Western alliance after the United States made security reassurances to the Soviet Union and its successor Russia. At the turn of the millennium, a group of Eastern and Central European states, including Poland and the Baltic States, joined the ❻ European Union (p. 536). The Commonwealth of Independent States (CIS) replaced the collapsed Soviet Union.

9 Civil war in former Yugoslavia in 1992: a sign in Sarajevo tells people to beware of snipers

10 Child soldier of the Union of Congolese Patriots

The collapse of communism brought democracy and Western civil rights to all of Europe. The decline and fall of the heavily armed Soviet Union, however, bore new dangers. The few that have prospered have become the new international super-rich, while the removal of basic social services previously provided by the state has left the poor, the sick, and the old in a much worse condition. As central control waned, weapons of mass destruction and nuclear know-how came into the hands of smaller and often unstable states, increasing the potential for a nuclear war. In addition, conventional weapons such as rifles and ❺ land mines were sold without controls and in enormous amounts on the black market. They were used in many brutal ❿ civil wars, for example, in the former ❾ Yugoslavia at the beginning of the 1990s (p. 581) and in Somalia in 1995.

A new threat for the world community was created by the use of ⓫ terror as a political means by non-state interest groups working through globally organized networks. After the ❼ terrorist attacks on New York and Washington, DC on September 11, 2001, by fundamentalist Islamists the United States and its allies called for a political, economical, and military "war on terror." The sociopolitical consequences of this for democracy remain unforeseeable.

6 The European Union Parliament meets in Brussels, 2005

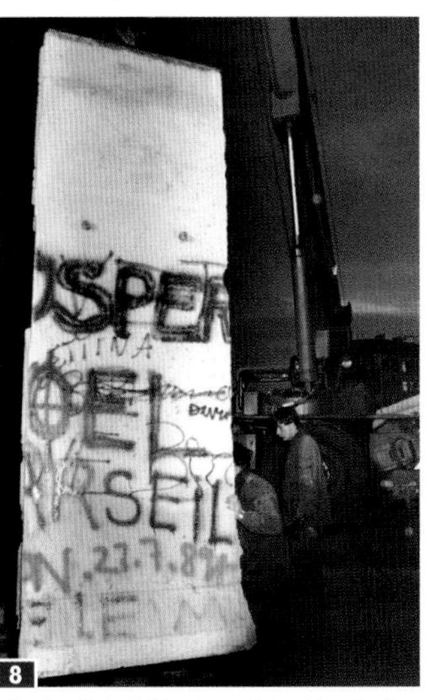

8 The Berlin Wall is demolished by Berlin citizens, 1989

11 Reconstruction of a British bank in Istanbul, Turkey, after having been destroyed by a bomb attack, 2003

9 Nov 1989 | Fall of the Berlin Wall

1 Jul 1991 | Dissolution of the Warsaw Pact

8 Nov 1991 | Founding of the CIS

11 Sep 2001 | Terror attacks in New York and Virginia

The Path to European Unity

Immediately after the war, Europe had to be rebuilt. In the western half of the continent, the United States ❶ fostered the establishment of market economies, while in the east the Soviet Union saw to the installation of centrally planned economies. The political structures also developed in divergent ways, and two political and economic blocs became established. Until the end of the confrontation between these two blocs, European interest in integration was confined to the West. After 1989, the expansion of the union eastward made it possible to overcome the division of the continent.

1 German poster promoting the Marshall Plan, 1948

Between Division and Rapprochement in Europe

The different economic policies of the Allies divided Europe into two opposing camps and resulted in cohesion within the blocs.

George Marshall, the US secretary of state, announced a reconstruction program for Europe on June 5, 1947. The ❷ "Marshall Plan" was formally offered to all European states, but the Soviet Union refused to participate and prevented the acceptance of the plan within its sphere of influence. The distribution of Marshall Plan aid in Western Europe was taken over by the OEEC, a supranational board that was succeeded by the Organization for Economic Cooperation and Development (OECD) in 1961. In Eastern Europe, the Council for Mutual Economic Assistance (Comecon) oversaw the development of centrally planned economies.

3 "What's behind it?" Booklet about the Schuman Plan: Robert Schuman (left) and Konrad Adenauer, 1951

Plans for European unity in Western Europe emerged as soon as World War II was over. These were implemented initially on an economic and military level. French foreign minister ❸ Robert Schuman, for example, encouraged the joint management of coal and steel production, which was intended to benefit economic development and also to contribute to the prevention of war in Europe. France, Germany, the Benelux states, and Italy became members of the Monetary Union in 1951. The ❺ Treaties of Rome followed in 1957, containing a protocol to found a European Economic Community (EEC) with the aim of establishing a Common Market and a unifying economic policy. Further elements were the founding of the European Atomic Energy Community (Euratom) for peaceful nuclear energy research and development.

4 NATO conference in Paris, 1959

5 Signing of the Treaties of Rome on March 25,1957, in Rome

The Western European countries moved closer together militarily as well. In 1948 France, Great Britain, and the Benelux states signed the Brussels Defense Community treaty. This was superceded by the North Atlantic Treaty, signed in 1949 by ten states of Western Europe as well as the United States and Canada, which led to the foundation the military and defense alliance of the ❹ NATO (the North Atlantic Treaty Organization). In response, the military ❻ Warsaw Pact was founded in Eastern Europe, and the division of the continent had become fact.

2 Marshall Plan aid for France: tractors from the United States arrive in Le Havre; ca. 1948

6 The GDR becomes a member of the Warsaw Pact in 1956

5 Jun 1947 | Signing of the Marshall plan
1948 | Brussels defense treaty
1949 | NATO Treaty
1955 | Founding of the Warsaw Pact
1957 | Treaties of Rome

From the European Community to the European Union

In 1965 the European Community was founded. Later restructured as the European Union, in the course of its existence it has taken up numerous new members and expanded geographically. Simultaneously its economic and political challenges have grown.

The development of Europe as a political union was initially slow. France refused political involvement in a supranational framework. Instead it intensified cooperation with Germany: On January 22, 1963, French president Charles de Gaulle and German chancellor Konrad Adenauer signed the ❼ Élysée Treaty, which called for mutual consultation on all important decisions concerning foreign policy and in cultural areas. However, the process of European economic integration could not be forestalled. In 1965 the European Coal and Steel Community, the European Economic Community (EEC), and Euratom formed the European Community (EC). A European Council was founded, in which individual governments were represented, along with a joint ⓫ commission that guards the interests of the EC on an international basis. Further governmental organs include the ❿ European Parliament, which is elected directly by the people of the member states, and the European Court of Justice.

7 The treaty concerning the cooperation between Germany and France is signed in Paris at the Elysée Palace on January 22, 1963, by Konrad Adenauer and Charles de Gaulle

A further milestone on the path to a united Europe was the Maastricht Treaty, signed on February 7, 1992. It forms the basis for a joint European foreign and security policy, closer cooperation in the areas of justice and home affairs, and the creation of an economic and currency union. The European Community became the European Union (EU) on November 1, 1993. In 1999 the ❽ euro replaced the local currencies of twelve EU countries. From that point on, the ⓬ European Central Bank became responsible for EU monetary policy.

8 The euro: the currency of the European Union

Several additional European states strove to take part in the strengthening European Union. Whereas before the disintegration of the Eastern Bloc in 1989 only Western European states had joined, since then many countries in Eastern and Central Europe have applied for membership; ten of them were accepted into the union in 2004.

EU laws now noticeably affect the work of national governments, which has led to criticism of the lack of transparency in the decision-making structures and the paternalism of the ❾ Brussels bureaucracy. Each country has different future goals; whether the EU should be oriented more along political or economic lines is debated. The 2001 Treaty of Nice has left open both options.

Members of the EC / European Union
with their dates of accession:

1958: Belgium, France, Italy, Luxembourg, the Netherlands, West Germany
1973: Denmark, Ireland, the United Kingdom,
1981: Greece
1986: Portugal, Spain
1995: Austria, Finland, Sweden
2004: Cyprus, Czech Republic, Estonia, Hungary, Latvia, Lithuania, Malta, Poland, Slovakia, Slovenia

Poland becomes a member of the EU on May 1, 2004; a Polish and a German border official open the border crossing

9 Farmers demonstrating against the agrarian reform of the EU "Agenda 2000" in Schwerin, Germany, 1999

10 House of the European Council and the European Parliament in Strasbourg, France

11 View of the European commission building in Brussels, Belgium

12 The European Central Bank building in Frankfurt

22 Jan 1963 | German-French Treaty
1965 | Combination of the ECSC, the EEC, and Euratom to the EC
7 Feb 1992 | Treaty of Maastricht
1999 | Introduction of the euro
2001 | Treaty of Nice

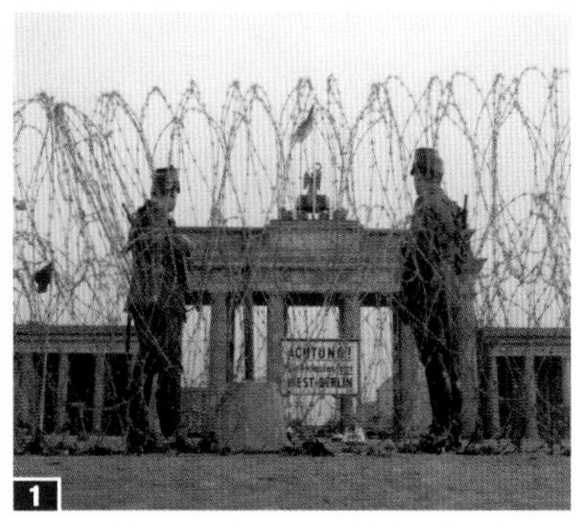

GERMANY SINCE 1945

Even after the defeat of the Nazi regime, Germany was seen as the "key to Europe." Due to its economic potential and strategic position, it became hotly contested between West and East. This brought with it the ❶ partition of the country. The symbolic focus of the Cold War (p. 532) was the city of Berlin, a city partially controlled by Western forces in the middle of the Soviet occupation zone. In 1989 the fall of the Berlin Wall at the Brandenburg Gate became the symbol of the demise of the Communist state system.

Brandenburg Gate in Berlin is blocked off with barbed wire on August 14-15, 1961

The "Zero Hour"

With the surrender of the German armed forces, fascist rule came to an end. The aftermath of the Nazi destruction policies, as well as hunger and displacement, shaped the first postwar years.

The political reconstitution of Germany lay in the hands of the ❺ Allies. They had already agreed on the division of the country and its capital into four zones of occupation, the creation of an Allied Control Council, and the demilitarization and denazification of the country. Austria was reestablished as a separate republic, though it was granted sovereignty only after ten years under Allied administration. Saarland came under French control, and the land east of the Oder and Neisse rivers was transferred to Poland, which fell under Soviet control. In the Sudetenland region annexed to Czechoslovakia, the German population that had not yet fled was ❷ displaced.

Trial against prisoners of war in Nuremberg; in the first row from the left: Göring, Hess, Ribbentrop, Keitel

Important components of the demilitarization of Germany included the dissolution of the army and the Prussian state. Denazification culminated in the ❸ Nuremberg trials of Nazis concerning the crimes committed under Hitler.

Criticism of the dissimilar practices of the Allies quickly began. In the Soviet zone, denazification was linked with political reform. After 1946, every German in the Western zones had to complete a ❹ form for political inspection. Numerous perpetrators were able, through attestations of discharge or so-called "Persil certificates" (named after a German laundry detergent), to "wash themselves clean."

The democratic reconstitution of West Germany began on a regional level. The federal states were created, and in the fall of 1946 the first elections took place. In the East, the Soviet occupation army had called for the formation of political parties in June 1945 but heavily supported the German Communist Party, which was led by Soviet immigrants of the "Ulbricht Group."

Refugees from the East on their way to Berlin, 1945

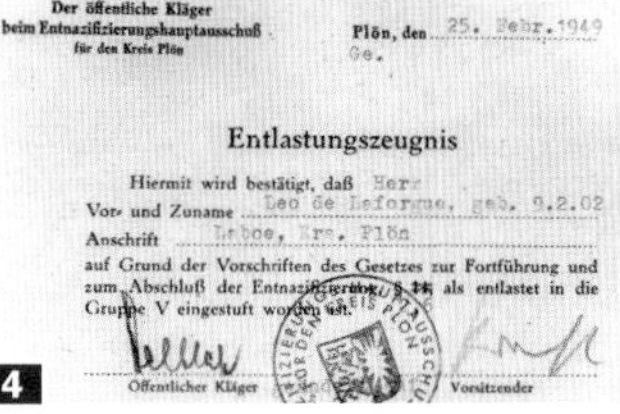

Der öffentliche Kläger
beim Entnazifizierungshauptausschuß
für den Kreis Plön

Plön, den 25. Febr. 1949
Ge.

Entlastungszeugnis

Hiermit wird bestätigt, daß Herr
Vor- und Zuname Leo de Leforme, geb. 9.2.02
Anschrift Laboe, Krs. Plön
auf Grund der Vorschriften des Gesetzes zur Fortführung und zum Abschluß der Entnazifizierung § 14 als entlastet in die Gruppe V eingestuft worden ist.

Öffentlicher Kläger — Vorsitzender

Attestation of discharge, 1949

The Allied Control Council

The four commanders in chief of the Allied forces took over the government responsibility for "Germany as a whole" with the Berlin Declaration of June 5, 1945. The Control Council had no executive power and so was reliant on the cooperation of the respective military governors in each region. The diverse interests of the Allies prevented agreement on almost every issue related to demilitarization and denazification. In March of 1948, the Soviet representatives withdrew from the Control Council, and it never convened again.

Onlookers outside a Control Council meeting

Americans and Russians shake hands on a destroyed bridge near Torgau, April 25, 1945

6 Jun 1945 | Berlin Declaration of the Allied Control Council
1945–46 | Energy crisis and food shortage
Apr 1946 | Founding of the SED
1 Jan 1947 | Unification of the American and British occupation zones
3 Mar 1948 | Dissolution of the Allied Control council

The Founding of the Federal Republic of Germany and the GDR

In Germany, cooperation between the centrally planned economy of the Soviet occupation zone and the market economy of the other zones did not take place even in the most extreme situations.

During the harsh (6) winter of 1945–1946, energy and food supplies in Germany were exhausted. The immediate hardship was eased somewhat by the (8) CARE (Cooperation for American Remittances to Europe) packages that were sent to individuals in Germany beginning in August 1946. After the failure of the Soviets to provide sufficient food supplies, the Western allies blocked the payment of German reparations to the Soviet Union. The July 1946 suggestion from the United States for the economic unification of the occupied zones was refused by the Soviet Union, as it suspected economic imperialism was behind the suggestion. As early as 1945, land reforms and expropriations had paved the way for a centrally planned economy in the Soviet zone. In April 1946, the Social Democratic party and the Communist party in the Soviet zone merged as the Socialist Unity party; other political parties were then forcibly integrated into this single party.

The Americans and British unified their occupied zones on January 1, 1947. A currency reform was implemented in the combined zone as part of the newly created (9) Marshall Plan (p. 536) to help a destroyed Europe recover; the new (10) German mark was introduced on June 21, 1948. When the Western powers introduced the German mark in their sectors of Berlin, the Soviets responded with a blockade of the city. For eleven months, Berlin was supplied by an (7) air bridge: some 277,000 flights brought 2.3 million tons of goods into the city before the Soviets lifted their blockade in May 1949.

10 Temporary money, 1948

Thus, currency reforms were followed by the founding of two German states. In July 1948 the Western allies asked the prime minister of the federal states to call for an election of a constituent National Assembly. The ministers instead worked out a Basic Constitutional Law. Signed on May 8, 1948, by the Parliamentary Council, which was made up of the federal state parliaments, it was approved by the Western allies and proclaimed on May 23, 1949. In the Soviet zone, a People's Chamber that was dominated by the Socialist Unity party signed a draft constitution in May 1949, which it claimed applied to all of Germany; on October 7, 1949, the (11) German Democratic Republic was officially founded. With the establishment of the competing states, the division of Germany for the next 40 years was sealed—even as both sides claimed to speak for Germany.

6 Women warm their hands after clearing up the rubble, 1945–1946

7 Arrival of a "raisin bomber" bringing food to Berlin, 1948

8 Distribution of CARE packages, 1946

Ernst Reuter

Born in 1889, Ernst Reuter was a Social Democrat from 1912 and briefly a member of the German Communist party. After his 1933 internment in a concentration camp, he went to Turkey as an adviser in 1935. In 1947 he was elected mayor of Berlin but was prevented from taking office until 1948. As mayor from 1950 until his death in 1953, he led the resistance against the Berlin Blockade in 1948–1949: "Peoples of the world, look to this city."

Rally in front of the Reichstag: Ernst Reuter asks for help against the Berlin Blockade, September 9, 1948

9 Houses are built for refugees to replace emergency accomodations

11 Founding of the German Democratic Republic (GDR) on Oct 7, 1949; Wilhelm Pieck at the microphone

21 Jun 1948 | Introduction of the German Mark
24 Jun 1948 | Beginning of the Berlin Blockade
May 1948 | Signing of the Basic Law
May 1949 | End of the Blockade
Oct 1949 | East Berlin becomes the capital of the GDR
7 Oct 1949 | Signing of the proposed constitution

East Germany: The Ulbricht Era 1948–1971

The Stalinist government of East Germany had to struggle against popular resistance to it among the people. Consolidation was only possible through coercion.

❶ Walter Ulbricht (1893-1973), a founder of the German Communist Party, was the first secretary of the Socialist Unity party of Germany from July 1953, the same year the German Democratic Republic was accepted into the Council for Mutual Economic Assistance, the Soviet counterpart to the Marshall Plan (p. 536). The Socialist Unity party had presented the first five-year plan in 1951.

In 1952 the Western allies rejected Stalin's suggestion for a neutral Germany, so the aim of Soviets became the integration of East Germany into the Eastern Bloc. The establishment of an army posed economic difficulties for the young republic, which were to be solved by overtime and the reduction of wages. Resistance in the party and society was broken through "cleansings" and repression. When the party increased the work requirements for industrial factories in May 1953, uprisings took place in Berlin and almost all other large cities on ❷ June 16 and 17—the first people's rebellion in an Eastern Bloc country. ❹ Soviet tanks suppressed the uprising, and in its wake, the state government bolstered the secret police of the Ministry of State Security—a force referred to as the "Stasi"—headed by ❻ Erich Mielke.

Walter Ulbricht

Uprising in East Berlin; a burning police station, June 17, 1953,

Sign at the border between East and West Germany, 1988

Uprising in East Berlin; Soviet tanks at Potsdamer Platz, June 17, 1953

Under massive pressure, the ❺ nationalization of agriculture into production cooperatives and of businesses into people-owned enterprises was carried out. The level of production, however, did not improve, which fanned opposition to the government among many parts of the population.

The short political "thaw" after 1956 did not alter the inadequate situation. The most visible form of resistance was citizens "voting with their feet"—leaving the country. It was determined that ❸ sealing of the borders was necessary to save East Germany from economic collapse, and on August 13, 1961, construction of the Berlin Wall was started. Many citizens lost their lives trying to cross the wall.

In the following years, the import of food from the Soviet Union to East Germany provided some relief. The political system opened itself slowly and economic reforms led to briefly to a mood of new beginnings.

"Voting with the Feet"

In the first year of the German Democratic Republic, 130,000 of its citizens fled to the West; in the year of the 1953 uprising, it was 330,000. In total, some 2.5 million people—a seventh of the population, of which 60 percent were employed—had left East Germany by the time the wall was built.

GDR border officials arrest a citizen who was trying to flee through the sewage system, 1962

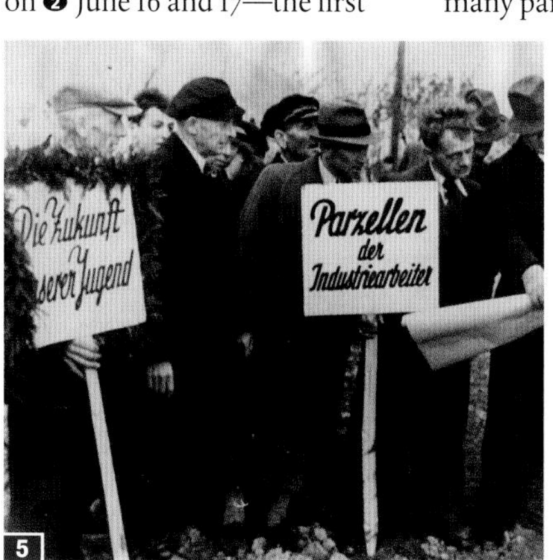

A former manor is divided into lots and given to industrial workers, 1945

Erich Mielke, minister of state security in the GDR from 1957-1989, in 1980

1951 | First five-year plan

Jul 1953 | Walter Ulbricht becomes general secretary of the SED

1953 | Death of Stalin

16–17 Jun 1953 | East Berlin uprising

1954 | Recognition of GDR sovereignty by the USSR

East Germany: The Honecker Era 1971–1989

The supply situation improved, yet due to its high debts, East Germany was dependent on the West. The refusal to reform led to the demise of the state.

Honecker portrait on display, 1986

East German general secretary ⓫ Erich Honecker, who took office in 1976 after the death of Walter Ulbrich, proclaimed "real existing socialism"—meaning that one should no longer hold off for a coming communist paradise but should attempt to improve contemporary living conditions. In fact, the national income of the country rose steadily until it reached its highest level in 1975, giving East Germany the highest ⓬ standard of living in the Eastern bloc. ❿ Housing reform was implemented; while West Germans spent 20 percent of their income on rent, an East German spent only five percent. Medical care was free, and family support led to an increase in the birth rate.

In 1974, East and West Germany were welcomed into the United Nations together, and the equal participation of both states in the Conference for Security and Cooperation in Europe (CSCE) (p. 532) was a successful step on the way to international recognition. In September 1987, when Honecker was received in Bonn by West German chancellor Helmut Kohl with all the honors of a state leader, de facto recognition had been acknowledged.

The country could not finance the desired increase in social spending, however. Due to inadequate modernization, productivity stagnated. The finance gaps were bridged by credits from the West. In 1983 Bavarian prime minister Franz Josef Strauss provided a billion-mark loan, which gave the East Germans some breathing space. Wages once again rose, yet there was less and less to buy. The average citizen had to wait ten years for a car, and the only choice was the locally manufactured and poor quality Trabant, known as the ❾ Trabbi. Television sets were present in 90 percent of the households, however, and most of them could receive broadcasts from the West. In response to the growing discontent, the state government increased ❼ propaganda and the development of the Stasi.

The expatriation of the politically critical singer Wolf Biermann in 1976 pushed the East German cultural elite into the opposition. Under the protection of the church, the environmentalist and ❽ peace movements gathered. In 1984, 32,000 citizens applied for permission to leave the country; by 1988, this figure had risen to 110,000. Honecker's refusal to implement the reforms recommended by Mikhail Gorbachev proved disastrous and within a few months would bring the East German regime crashing down in ruins.

Members of the peace movement demonstrate in Dresden, 1987

A "Trabbi," ca. 1970

View from within the ruins of the newly constructed buildings for the social housing program in Berlin, ca. 1955

Erich Honecker, front, at the eighth party meeting of the SED, June 15, 1971: In front of the committee, from left to right: Stoph, Brezhnev, Ebert, Sindermann

Commercial Coordination

Since the 1960s the Stasi officer Alexander Schalck-Golodkovski had built up a shadow economy empire to supply foreign currency for the servicing of foreign government debt. Rubbish was imported, and expropriated antiques, weapons, and the blood of East German citizens were exported. Political hostages who were bought free by the Western powers were also a source of income.

Uniforms of the GDR youth organizations Young Pioneers and Free German Youth Organization (FDJ), 1972

13 Aug 1961 | Building of the Berlin Wall
1962 | Dissolution of the Soviet command in East Berlin
1974 | Entry of the GDR in the UN
1976 | Erich Honecker becomes General Secretary
1983 | Taking-on of the "billion-mark loan"

West Germany: From Adenauer to Brandt 1949–1974

Konrad Adenauer tied the Federal Republic into the Western alliance. Willy Brandt's primary foreign policy achievement was the easing of tensions with countries from the Eastern Bloc.

While the Socialist Unity Party ruled as the single party in East Germany, the Federal Republic built up a multiparty system, dominated by the Christian Democratic Union and the Social Democratic Party. On August 14, 1949, the first election for the Bundestag took place. ❶ Konrad Adenauer of the Christian Democrats was elected federal chancellor with a one-seat majority.

Konrad Adenauer

Prof. Dr. Walter Hallstein

Adenauer's policies were aimed at tying the country into the Western alliance system. He pushed through West Germany's entry into the ❺ European Coal and Steel Community, Euratom, and the European Economic Community (p. 536). In 1951, the Treaty of Paris paved the way for the Federal Republic to become a sovereign state and join NATO in 1955. Adenauer sought reconciliation with France, which led to the Élysée Treaty in 1963. It called for close cooperation in foreign, defense, and education policies. In 1952 Adenauer signed the Luxembourg agreements with Israeli Foreign Minister Sharett, which became the basis of reparations (*Wiedergutmachung*) legislation. Adenauer insisted that the Federal Republic represented all German citizens. This attitude was mirrored in the ❷ Hallstein doctrine of 1955: Bonn broke off diplomatic relations with any state—except for the USSR—that recognized East Germany.

Demonstration against the war in Vietnam, Berlin, February 18, 1968

Television: an example of the new prosperity, 1952

Adenauer's successor was the former minister of economics, Ludwig Erhard, who went down in history as the father of the ❹ economic "miracle." When Erhard's government coalition broke in 1966, he resigned. A coalition of the Christian Democrats and the Social Democrats took over government. The next chancellor, Kurt Georg Kiesinger, was heavily criticized for his earlier Nazi party membership.

In the face of a lack of opposition in the Bundestag, an ❸ extraparliamentary opposition formed as a protest against solidified structures, the Vietnam War (p. 617), and the Emergency Acts of 1968. This movement molded the societal climate into the 1970s.

In 1969 a social-liberal coalition of the Social Democrats and the Free Democratic Party took power under Willy Brandt, promising to modernize the country. Brandt's principal foreign policy achievement was the policy of détente with the East, culminating in the completion of the Eastern Treaties (1970–1973). His recognition of the Oder–Neisse line as the border between Poland and East Germany was opposed by the Christian Democrats.

Compensation

Adenauer sought reconciliation with the young state of Israel. In the reparations treaty signed with Israel on September 10, 1952, West Germany pledged to pay three billion marks in material value to Israel. The agreement was approved on March 18, 1953, only after the third reading; numerous delegates refused their consent, on the basis that the Federal Democratic Republic was a state unrelated to the Third Reich. The votes of Social Democrats secured the acceptance of the draft.

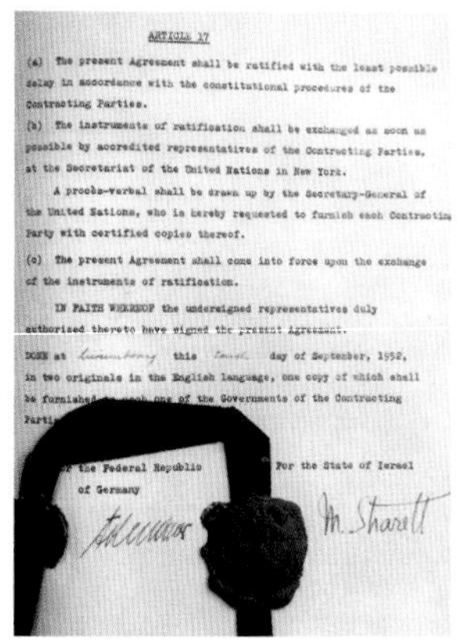

ARTICLE 17

(a) The present Agreement shall be ratified with the least possible delay in accordance with the constitutional procedures of the Contracting Parties.

(b) The instruments of ratification shall be exchanged as soon as possible by accredited representatives of the Contracting Parties, at the Secretariat of the United Nations in New York.

A procès-verbal shall be drawn up by the Secretary-General of the United Nations, who is hereby requested to furnish each Contracting Party with certified copies thereof.

(c) The present Agreement shall come into force upon the exchange of the instruments of ratification.

IN FAITH WHEREOF the undersigned representatives duly authorized thereto have signed the present Agreement.

DONE at [illegible] this [illegible] day of September, 1952, in two originals in the English language, one copy of which shall be furnished [illegible] of the Governments of the Contracting Parti[illegible]

[illegible] the Federal Republic of Germany — Adenauer

For the State of Israel — M. Sharett

German–Israeli treaty, 1952

Talks prior to forming the European Coal and Steel Community; including Robert Schuman and German Chancellor Adenauer, 1951

14 Aug 1949 | First Bundestag election

Sep 1949 | Konrad Adenauer becomes Federal Chancellor

18 Mar 1953 | Reparations treaty with Israel

1955 | Soveignty of the GDR; Entry into NATO

1955 | Hallstein doctrine

1963 | Signing of the Élysée Treaty

West Germany: From Schmidt to Kohl 1974–1989

In the mid-1970s West Germany suffered an economic crisis, but the European integration process and the opening to the East continued.

When it emerged that one of Chancellor Brandt's personal assistants, ⓾ Günter Guillaume, was an East German agent, Brandt resigned in 1974. His successor in office was Helmut Schmidt. During Schmidt's time in government, the first harsh economic crisis hit the Federal Republic.

Helmut Schmidt, left, on his visit to East Germany; Erich Honecker, right,1981

Economic summit on July 16, 1978 in Bonn; from left to right: Carter, the Japanese Prime Minister Fukuda, Schmidt, and the French Giscard d'Estaing

After the general elections: Helmut Kohl is sworn in as chancellor, 1982

The domestic climate was shaped by the terrorist acts of the Red Army Faction and the countermeasures of the state. In foreign policy, Schmidt set out on the course of compromise: He visited ❼ East Germany and took part in meetings of the Organization for Security and Cooperation in Europe (OSCE). Closer European unity was achieved together with French president Valéry Giscard d'Estaing; in 1975, the two government leaders initiated the ❾ economic and political cooperation of the then G-6 states (today the G-8).

Around 1980, politics once again became dominated by world political tensions. Schmidt advocated the stationing of intermediate-range nuclear missiles in Europe, which was opposed by the burgeoning ❽ peace movement and parts of his own party. This, and worries about the environment, became the impetus for the founding of the ❻ "Greens" movement, which was soon able to enter parliament as the fourth political party.

In 1982 the social-liberal era ended when the Free Democratic Party withdrew from the government coalition and instead formed an alliance with the Christian Democrats. ⓫ Helmut Kohl became the new chancellor and Hans-Dietrich Genscher the new foreign minister. Kohl's government was able to stabilize state finances, lower tax burdens for businesses and private households, and curb inflation. It was unable to manage the unemployment situation and many necessary reforms were not made. Among the people, disenchantment with politics took hold and electoral participation dropped.

Pins with the symbol of the peace movement

Chancellor Willy Brandt (left), together with his personal assistant Günter Guillaume

Externally, Kohl's government continued the policies of its predecessors: Contacts to the East were built up and European unity was promoted in partnership with the French.

Election poster of the "Greens": "We have only borrowed the Earth from our children," 1983

The Red Army Faction

In the 1970s the left-wing terrorism of the Red Army Faction shaped the political climate in West Germany. The group's methods included attacks, kidnappings, murders, and blackmail, which they used to destabilize the state. More than 45 people fell victim to their attacks, including the president of the German Employers' Association, Hanns-Martin Schleyer. Most of the terrorists were arrested. The Red Army Faction stopped fighting in 1992 and dissolved in 1998.

Red Army Faction on a "wanted" poster put up by the Federal Criminal Police Office, 1972

since 1968 | Creation of the APO
1969 | Willy Brandt becomes chancellor
1970–73 | Conclusion of the Eastern Treaties
1970 | Kidnapping of Schleyer by the RAF
1980 | Founding of the "Greens" party
1982 | Helmut Kohl becomes chancellor

German Reunification 1989–1990

The rapid collapse of the East German government accelerated the unification process. The Kohl–Genscher Government won the support of the four Allies for the reunification of Germany.

After the opening of Hungary's western border in the furtherance of *perestroika* (p. 589) on September 11, 1989, tens of thousands of East German citizens left their country for the West. Others fled through the West German embassies in Warsaw and Prague. That month, peaceful protests began against the East German government's unwillingness to reform, and the number of participants in the ❷ "Monday demonstrations" increased steadily. On October 23, 300,000 people

2 One of the demonstrations that were held every Monday, Leipzig, Oct. 1989;

marched through central Leipzig under the slogan "We are the people." On ❹ November 4, 1989, a million citizens gathered at Alexanderplatz in Berlin to demand freedom of opinion, freedom to travel, and free elections. The Socialist Unity Party finally opened the ❺ border to the Federal Republic on November 9, 1989, but by then the aim had gone beyond simply reforming the German Democratic Republic. Instead, demands for unification of the two German states became louder.

Willy Brandt on German Reunification, November 1990

"Now what belongs together will grow together".

Willy Brandt during a rally of the Social Democrat Party in Leipzig, February 25, 1990

The first ❻ free elections to the *Volkskammer* in East Germany took place on March 18, 1990, and the Socialist Unity Party's successor—the Party of Democratic Socialism—won only 16 percent of the votes. The conservative Alliance for Germany, under Minister-President Lothar de Maizière, took power and began negotiating a reunification treaty with the West German government.

The rapidly worsening economic situation in East Germany and the continuing wave of departures led to the ratification of an ❶ economic, currency, and social union between the two states. It came into effect on July 1, 1990, as an important first step to reunification. The actual merger of East and West into a single Germany could only be achieved with the acquiescence of the victorious powers of World War II, however, and so the ❸ "Two Plus Four Agreement" was negotiated among both German governments and the foreign ministers of the Allied forces, giving back full sovereignty to a unified Germany 45 years after the end of the war. The reunification was sealed on October 3, 1990.

3 Meeting prior to the "Two Plus Four Agreement," Genscher (third from left) and Meckel (second from right)

1 The unification treaty between the FRG and the GDR is signed, 1990

The Accession

On July 22, 1990, within the territory of East Germany, the East German states of Brandenburg, Mecklenburg–Western Pomerania, Saxony-Anhalt and the Free States of Saxony, and Thuringia were refounded. These five new states joined the Federal Republic on October 3, 1990, and the German Democratic Republic ceased to exist. A day later the Bundestag had its first session in Berlin. Five former East German politicians were sworn in as new state ministers.

4 Demonstrators in front of the Palace of the Republic in East Berlin, November 4, 1989

5 Berlin, after the border at the Glienicke Bridge was opened, November 10, 1989

6 Election posters for the Volkskammer in East Germany on March, 18 1990

11 Sep 1989 | Opening of the Hungarian border

9 Nov 1989 | Opening of the East-West German border

18 Mar 1990 | First elections to the Volkskammer

23 Oct 1989 | March of 300,000 people through central Leipzig

Germany in the Present

The unified Germany had to fight economic and domestic difficulties even as it actively participated in the project of European integration.

The protest movement in East Germany gave birth to numerous opposition parties and organizations which were so large that the state's repressive apparatus could not contain them. In 1990, East German civil rights groups joined together with the West German Greens to form "Alliance 90–The Greens." The representatives of these civil rights movements played a decisive role in the ⓫ dissolution of the GDR's Ministry for State Security and the public release of secret service documents.

The first German Bundestag elections brought a clear victory for the governing coalition under Chancellor Helmut Kohl, showing broad public support for the unification process. Still, the implementation of the unification proved to be an immense economic and political challenge. The ❽ ailing industries in the East almost entirely collapsed, in the context of the competitive West German industrial structures and the ensuing loss of jobs and social welfare cuts led to mass protests in many eastern German towns.

7 German UN peacekeeping soldiers

1990 Treaty on the Final Settlement with Respect to Germany,

Article 1.1

The united Germany shall comprise the territory of the Federal Republic of Germany, the German Democratic Republic, and the whole of Berlin. Its external borders shall be the borders of the Federal Republic of Germany and the German Democratic Republic and shall be definitive from the date on which the present Treaty comes into force. The confirmation of the definitive nature of the borders of the united Germany is an essential element of the peaceful order in Europe.

8 The Wildau Company, starting in 1951 an East German state-owned mechanical engineering company, in 1994

9 The new Federal Chancellery in Berlin, built between 1997 and 2001

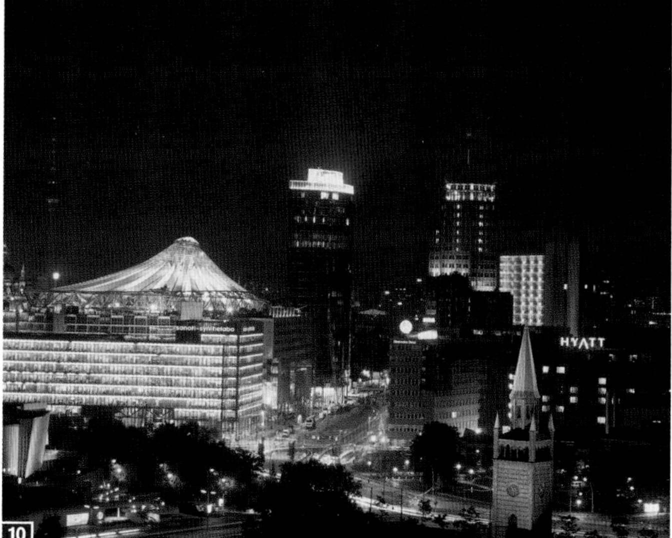

10 The modern architecture of Potsdamer Platz, all built since 1989 on the site of the former no-man's-land around the Berlin Wall, 2000

About a year after unification, numerous attacks by right-wing radicals on foreigners and asylum seekers shook the country. The excesses were watched with worry both inside and outside the country, particularly given Germany's historical record of fascism and xenophobia. At the end of 1992, however, 100,000 people staged a demonstration against racism and intolerance.

Today Germany is the most populous nation in Europe and is still ❿ economically strong. After the successful reunification, it has actively campaigned for the unification of Europe: the currency union and enlargement of the European Union to the east (p. 537) have been shaped by German initiatives. During the time of the Cold War, Germany had foregone worldwide involvement, but since the collapse of the Eastern bloc, the country has taken on increasing global responsibilities. An important expression of this was the participation of German soldiers in the ❼ UN peacekeeping operation in Kosovo in 1999, agreed by the Red-Green coalition under ❾ Gerhard Schröder, who won the Bundestag elections in 1998.

11 The former GDR Ministry of State Security in Berlin-Lichtenberg

1 Jun 1990	Economic, currency, and social union
3 Oct 1990	Reunification
1990	Formation of the Alliance 90–The Greens
2 Dec 1990	First German Bundestag elections
1998	Gerhard Schröder becomes chancellor

1 British soldiers before Schönbrunn Castle in Vienna, April 1945

AUSTRIA SINCE 1945

Austria's independence was restored after the end of ❶ World War II. In 1955 it achieved total sovereignty through the Austrian State Treaty with the Allies, on the condition of its perpetual neutrality. This later helped Austria to maintain relations with both Western countries and the nations of the Eastern bloc. Since the end of the Cold War and Austria's entry into the European Union, the neutrality policy has again become a topic of discussion. Domestically, the republic was characterized over the decades by the major political parties that formed a coalition government for a stable balance of interests.

Independence and Neutrality

Following the end of the war, Austria once again became independent and obligated itself to strict neutrality. The Republic became the seat of many international organizations.

With the approval of a broad section of the populace, Austria annexed itself to the German Reich in 1938 (p. 455). The restoration of an independent Austria after the war was envisioned in 1943 by the Allies, who agreed to divide the country following the same model used in Germany; Austria and its ❻ capital Vienna was divided into four ❸ occupation zones and a common control council was set up. The Social Democratic Party, the Communist Party, and the mainstream Austrian People's Party were able in 1945 to settle on a declaration of independence and a provisional government headed by the Social Democrat Party leader, Karl Renner. A modified form of the constitution of 1929 came back into force, and all the National Socialist laws added during the period of annexation were annulled. The first election on November 25, 1945, resulted in a majority for the People's party, which formed a coalition government with the Social Democrats and Communists.

2 The Allies withdraw after the signing of the state treaty, 1955

5 OPEC headquarters in Vienna

After prolonged negotiations between the Austrian government and the Allies, a ❹ state treaty was concluded in 1955 and was signed on May 15 in Vienna, restoring the ❷ sovereignty of the nation. A condition insisted upon by the Allies was the assurance of "everlasting" neutrality, which was established in the Federal Constitutional Law on the Neutrality of Austria on October 26. This day has been celebrated as a national holiday since 1965.

In 1960, Austria, like all neutral European states, joined the European Free Trade Association. Austria developed close economic ties especially with its neighboring Eastern bloc states. Austria has been a member of the United Nations since 1955, and Vienna became one of the four official ❼ UN sites in 1979. Furthermore, thanks to its neutral status, Austria has become home to numerous significant international organizations, among them the International Atomic Energy Agency (IAEA), the Organization for Security and Cooperation in Europe (OSCE), and the ❺ Organization of Petroleum Exporting Countries (OPEC).

3 The Allies shake hands; (from left) American, British, French, and Soviet military police show their support and cooperation in Vienna

4 The signatories of the state treaty on the balcony of the Belvedere Castle, May 15, 1955

6 Destroyed houses on the banks of the Danube, Vienna, 1945

7 UN complex in Vienna

1938 | Austria annexes itself to the German Reich

1943 | Allies agree on Austria's independence

25 Nov 1945 | First elections

15 May 1955 | Austria's sovereignty

26 Oct 1955 | Constitutional Law on the Neutrality of Austria

Economic Development and the Neutrality Crisis

Austria became a service industry nation with a strong tourism sector. Since the 1990s, alongside the major parties, the right-wing populist Liberal Party has been gaining popularity.

The Marshall Plan (p. 536) provided Austria with the economic means with which to develop a new economy in the first postwar years. Heavy industry and banks were nationalized in 1946. Also facilitating recovery was the "social partnership," a close cooperation of the major economic interests with the government, which is still in practice today. The intervention by the Soviets in their occupation zone in Lower Austria led to an industrial flight to the traditionally purely agrarian west, which permanently altered the economic and social structure of the country. Since the 1970s, the service sector has surpassed all others. To this day, Austria owes its supranational importance primarily to ❽, ❾, ❿ tourism—particularly in the Alpine regions—and Vienna's status as center for headquarters and congresses.

9 Skiers in the Karwendel range, 2003

The People's Party and the Social Democrat Party have been forming predominantly coalition governments since 1947, although occasionally the People's Party has governed alone. For a long time, only the Liberal Party stood in opposition to the major parties. Founded in 1949, the Liberal Party emerged out of the electoral alliance of independents, a sort of catch-all for less incriminated ex-National Socialists. Beginning in the 1990s, the party rapidly gained popularity under its right-wing populist chairman, Jörg Haider. In the National Council elections of October 3, 1999, it became the second strongest party after the People's Party and with them formed the government in place since 2000. The Greens have established themselves since 1986 as a second opposition party.

12 Bruno Kreisky, 1973

13 The Austrian Chancellor and chairman of the SPÖ, Franz Vranitzky, 1992

Austria has used its neutrality as an active peace policy since Chancellor ⓬ Bruno Kreisky's term of office (1970–1983). Among other things, the country has provided military contingents for the peacekeeping activities of the United Nations (p. 533) in the Golan Heights and Cyprus, as well as in Bosnia-Herzegovina and Kosovo. In addition, Austria participates in the NATO Partnership for Peace program.

Austria's neutral status, however, has been an issue of discussion domestically since the 1980s, when membership in the European Community was proposed in order to be a part of the European Common Market (p. 537). In 1989, the government of ⓭ Franz Vranitzky made a formal application, resulting in EU ⓫ membership in 1995 and the Euro monetary system in 1999. Austria, however, has never officially given up its neutrality.

8 View over Salzburg; the Fortress Hohensalzburg in Salzburg, (front right) Kollegien Church, 2002

10 "Fiaker," an Austrian coach, Salzburg

11 Celebrations on the Heldenplatz in Vienna following Austria's assumption of the European Union presidency in1998

The Waldheim Affair

Kurt Waldheim, ca. 1985

The election of Kurt Waldheim as Austrian federal president in June 1986 provoked controversy at home and abroad because he had been an officer in the Nazi German army. Waldheim had been UN general secretary from 1972 to 1981 and entered the elections as a People's Party candidate. He commented on his past in the following way: "I did nothing different in the war than hundreds of thousands of other Austrians, namely, fulfilled my duty as a soldier." Although it could not be proven that he was guilty of any war crimes, Waldheim remained internationally isolated.

1955 | Austria joins UN
1960 | Austria joins EFTA
1970–83 | Federal Chancellor Bruno Kreisky
June 1986 | Waldheim Affair
1989 | Government of Franz Vranitzky makes formal application to EU
1995 | Austria joins the EU

SWITZERLAND SINCE 1945

The traditionally stable Swiss governmental system rests on consensus, direct democracy, and federalism. Switzerland is one of the wealthiest countries in the world as a result of its finance industry. The service sector has also come to play a significant economic role. Relations with the European Union are close, but Switzerland continues to ❶ reject membership, as it does not want to compromise its traditional policy of neutrality.

1 "No" ballot papers from the referendum on EU membership, December 6, 1992

Economic Boom and Criticism after World War II

Switzerland experienced a rapid rise in its economy after World War II. The conduct of the banks cooperating with the Nazis during the war became the subject of sharp criticism.

As a neutral state, Switzerland dissolved its extremist left- and right-wing political parties and was not an active participant in World War II (p. 457) although it was obliged to have commercial relations with the Axis Powers. Its production facilities remained to a great extent undamaged. This facilitated the country's swift ❷,❹ economic resurgence after the war. Switzerland has achieved one of the highest per capita incomes in the world, with low unemployment and a low budget deficit. The service sector has grown to play an increasingly large role; its main business sectors are banking and insurance as well as ❺,❻ tourism. Switzerland preserved its strict neutrality, remaining outside the United Nations (until 2002) and the North Atlantic Treaty Organization, although it did decide to join the European Organization for Cooperation and Development.

3 Headquarters of the Swiss UBS bank in Zurich, 2001

As a ❸ financial center, Switzerland—which owes its leading position to the combination of strict banking confidentiality, the neutrality of the country, and the security of its "Swiss numbered accounts"—came under criticism after the end of the war. The Nazis had moved a major part of the valuables they had stolen during their time in power to Switzerland, and Swiss banks profited greatly from their crimes. In 1946, the remaining German assets were transferred to the Allies for reparations. Treaties with Poland and Hungary in 1949 resulted in the return of assets to the heirs of victims there. In 1962, a law was passed to force the banks to provide information on and pay out the remaining fortunes of those persecuted by the Nazi regime. In 1995 Switzerland was once again accused of having profited from the smuggling of stolen goods. In response, the Swiss government set up an international commission of experts to investigate, but foreign pressure increased to the point that a payment was agreed upon before the investigation was completed. Despite this process, the conduct of the banks had damaged Switzerland's reputation to some extent. Switzerland's refugee policies during the war also came under fire. Around 25,000 Jewish refugees were turned back at the Swiss border. In 1996, the president of the confederation, Ruth Dreyfuss, made a formal Swiss apology for this.

2 An economically profitable Swiss tradition: chocolate by Lindt and Sprüngli

4 Handmade Swiss watches have long been a desired quality item: modern Swatch watches, 2003

5 The Matterhorn mountain in the Swiss Alps

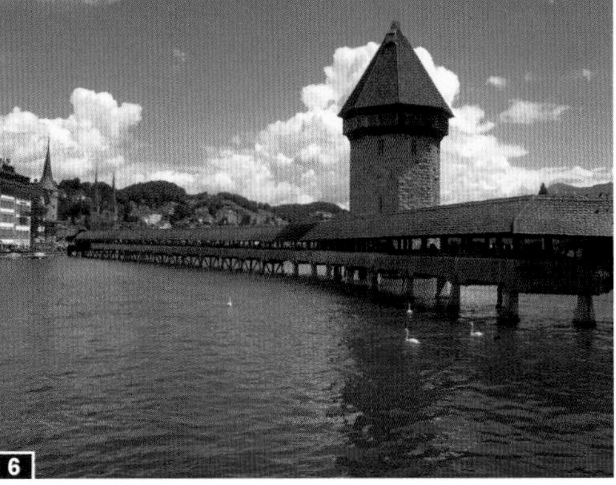

6 The Kapel bridge over the Reuss River, Lucerne, 2000

1848 | Signing of first constitution
1946 | German assets transferred to the Allies
1949 | Reparation treaties with Hungary and Poland
1953 | Introduction of the "Magic Formula"
1962 | Repayment law

The Political System and Neutrality

Switzerland remains a parliamentary federal state with 26 cantons committed to neutrality. Political decisions are made by consensus.

The federal constitution Switzerland adopted in 1848 remained in force through 1999, with only one revision in 1874; a new constitution came into force in 2000. Since 1959–1960, Switzerland has been a concordance or "consensus democracy," in which as many parties, associations, and social groups as possible are included in the political process and decisions are made by consensus. This principle is the basis of the ⓫ Federal Council. According to the so-called "magic formula," it is composed of representatives of four parties, who jointly seek political solutions. This system of government is very stable due to the lack of any opposition. The national government, however, only holds the authority mandated to it by 22 cantons, themselves in turn dependent on the "grassroots" democracy of the 3000 municipalities, and decisions on the federal and canton levels can be contradictory. Women were granted suffrage on the federal level in 1971, for example, but the women in ❼ Appenzell have been able to vote in their canton only since 1990.

The Swiss people have a long tradition of sometimes voting directly on important issues in open-air assemblies, especially in some mountain cantons where in the spring the citizens vote by a show of hands. This is particularly true with respect to changes to the constitution. Consequently, the Swiss decided by referendum against joining the European currency system in 1992, against joining the European Union in 2001, and in favor of membership in the ❿ United Nations in 2002. Although Switzerland was a founding member of the European Free Trade Association (p. 551) in 1960, which does not conflict with the political principle of their neutrality, most Swiss citizens felt that EU membership would mean political ❾ integration into the community of European nations. Switzerland is already closely linked economically with the European Union through bilateral contracts, such as the agreement on ❽ Alpine transit for heavy traffic, but the abandonment of traditional neutrality is rejected by most of the citizens.

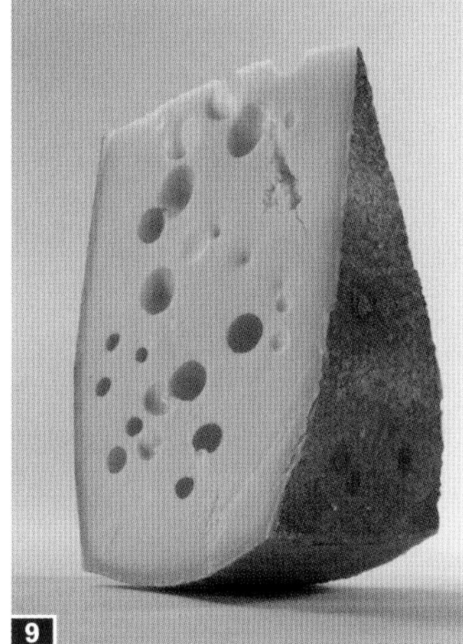

9 Swiss raw milk cheese does not conform to EU regulations

7 The electors of the community of Hundswill, Appenzell, return after meeting to vote on the issue of suffrage for women, 1989

8 Bridge of the North-South railway of the Gotthard Pass that runs through the Swiss Alps

10 Posters in favor of (right) and against (left) Swiss membership in the United Nations, during the second referendum in Switzerland on the United Nations membership February 2002

11 Federal Council meeting room

The Magic Formula

The "magic formula," introduced in 1953, describes the longtime composition of the Swiss Federal Council: two members each from the Liberal, Christian Democratic, and Social Democratic Parties and one from the Swiss People's Party. This splits the cabinet seats between the main four parties. The magic formula was altered in 2003 when, after successes at the polls, the People's Party claimed a second seat in the council and the Christian Democrats were forced to give up a seat.

above: The seven members of the Swiss government, 1999

1971 | Women's right to vote introduced

1990 | Women's suffrage established in Appenzell

2000 | New constitution passed

2001 | Referendum against joining EU

2002 | Joins UN

Great Britain: From Commonwealth to European Union since 1945

Despite the loss of its former position as a superpower, the ❶ United Kingdom was influential in the global reorganization after 1945. As a close ally of the United States, politically the country stood opposed to the Soviet Union in the division of Europe and the world. Great Britain was one of the founding members of the United Nations and is a permanent member of its Security Council. The process of decolonization contributed to fundamental changes in the country and its foreign policies. Since 1973, Great Britain has been a critical but active member of the European Community.

London, Trafalgar Square, ca. 1950

The Transformation of a Global Power

Great Britain's foreign policies after 1945 were determined by the confrontation of the Cold War and decolonization.

Winston Churchill, the British prime minister until July 1945, played a decisive role in the conferences of the Allied powers during the war (p. 532) and took a hard line toward his erstwhile partner Joseph Stalin. In the ❷ postwar Potsdam Conference, the Allies reached relatively consensual agreements on the division of zones of occupation, but the conflicting policies of the Cold War began soon afterward. The British had little room to maneuver in the shadow of the new superpowers, the United States and the USSR. The debt caused by the war tied the country to the United States, to which it already had a sense of connection through their historically and culturally determined "special relationship." As founding member of the ❸ United Nations and a former Ally, Great Britain was granted a permanent seat on the UN Security Council (p. 533).

Signing of the UN charter, 1946

In 1945, British possessions still spanned a quarter of the Earth. However, by 1947, ❺ India, the centerpiece of the empire, had been granted independence (p. 493), and almost all of the British colonies cut ties with their former motherland within the next 20 years. They stayed united as the British Commonwealth of Nations (p. 500), later renamed the Commonwealth of Nations. To this day the British monarch is the head of the Commonwealth, although this position holds no political authority.

Just how limited London's international influence had become was demonstrated particularly in the ❹ Suez Crisis of 1956. Together with France, Britain occupied the Suez Canal after it was nationalized by Egyptian president Nasser (p. 600). The operation failed because of the opposition of the Soviets and the Americans. Politics were no longer possible without both superpowers.

Elizabeth II

Born in 1926, Princess Elizabeth married Philip Mountbatten, who was given the title the Duke of Edinburgh, in 1947. She succeeded her father, George VI, to the throne in 1952. Queen Elizabeth II has been the head of state of the monarchy of Great Britain for half a century and thus also the head of the 53 member states composing the Commonwealth of Nations. She embodies continuity in a time when Britain has fundamentally altered.

Elizabeth II, queen of the United Kingdom and Ireland, head of the Commonwealth, ca. 1953

Potsdam Conference, July 17–August 2, 1945; Churchill, Truman, and Stalin in front of Cecilienhof Palace

Warships on the Suez Canal, November 1956

Lord Mountbatten, General Governor of India, with his wife during a celebration in the seat of the governor, New Delhi, 1948

1945 | Labor government under Clement Attlee
17 Jul–2 Aug 1945 | Potsdam Conference
1946 | Bank of England nationalized
1947 | India's independence
4 Sep 1949 | NATO founded
1949 | Iron and steel industries nationalized

Postwar Economic Development

Extensive social and economic reforms were carried out in Britain after the war in order to alleviate the postwar problems. Economic and political involvement and cooperation with the Continent increased.

After ❻ World War II, in the United Kingdom, a national consensus calling for better living conditions emerged, which allowed a fundamental political and social restructuring of the state. In 1945, the newly elected Labour government of Prime Minister ❼ Clement Attlee instituted an extensive program of state welfare reform, featuring the introduction of a free national health service and unemployment insurance. The ❽ Bank of England was nationalized in 1946, followed by telecommunications, civil aviation, major sections of the energy and transport sectors, and in 1949 the iron and steel industries. The pendulum swung back in 1951 when Churchill returned to office for a second term, and he and his Conservative successors steered again toward economic liberalism. This meant a temporary break from further development of the welfare state and ushered in the beginning of reprivatization.

7 Clement Attlee, photograph, ca. 1935

Due to its very close economic links to the nations of the Commonwealth (p. 500) and its international interests that transcended Europe, Great Britain initially remained outside the newly founded European Community. Nevertheless, to intensify its economic contacts and trade with the Continent, Great Britain cofounded the European Free Trade Association in 1960. However, this contract group could not compete with the economic success of the larger European body, and in 1973 Britain chose to join the European Community after a first attempt in 1963 was vetoed by the French President de Gaulle. Military and political ties to the Continent and the United States were guaranteed through its ❾ NATO membership.

6 Damage in London after an air raid; the cupola of St. Paul's Cathedral in the background, photograph, 1941

The European Free Trade Association

The European Free Trade Association (EFTA) was founded in Stockholm on January 4, 1960, with the aim of promoting growth and prosperity in the member countries and trade relations and economic cooperation in Western Europe and the world. Its founding members were Austria, Denmark, Great Britain, Norway, Portugal, Sweden, and Switzerland, later joined by Finland, Iceland, and Liechtenstein. Because Austria, Denmark, Finland, Great Britain, Portugal, and Sweden have since joined the European Union, so EFTA now has only four member states. With the exception of Switzerland, these EFTA states formed the European Economic Area in 1994 to participate in the Single Market with the EU member states.

above: Conference of the EFTA Council of Ministers in Bern, October 11, 1960

8 Bank of England, built from 1788 to 1833, photograph, 2000

9 The British foreign secretary Anthony Eden (middle) at a NATO Conference in Paris, 1952

1951 Churchill reelected
1952 Elizabeth II crowned
1952 NATO Conference in Paris
1956 Suez Crisis
1973 Britain joins EU
4 Jan 1960 EFTA founded

1945 to the present
The Contemporary World

British Domestic Politics from the 1960s to the Present

Relative economic prosperity reigned in Great Britain through the 1960s. Thereafter, the country was gripped by a long-lasting economic crisis.

Britain, the birthplace of industrialization, had already lost its industrial and technical lead to European and American competition as far back as 1900, but as London was then the flourishing ❶ hub of world trade, the British did not tailor their economic policies to this development. When the pound continually weakened during the 1960s, however, the roots of the economic crisis were laid bare: The British economy threatened to collapse as a result of outdated production facilities, loss of production through numerous strikes, and the overstretching of the budget through steadily rising social expenditures. Conservative and Labour governments replaced each other, neither able to control the financial crisis.

Beginning in 1979, the newly elected Conservative prime minister, Margaret Thatcher, followed strict liberal economic policies. These included the state's withdrawal from the economy, extensive privatization, and tax relief, but also a ❸ reduction in workers's rights and state social benefits. As a result, inflation slowed and investment rates increased, but large numbers of companies also went bankrupt. The number of unemployed reached a record three million in August 1982, and the disparity in incomes widened even more. With decreasing popularity in the electorate, the Conservative Party rebelled at the beginning of the 1990s, when a further recession was begun and Thatcher wanted to introduce a ❹ poll tax despite nationwide resistance. The party elected ❷ John Major her successor as prime minister in 1990, but the privatization of railways, postal services, and coal mining that he implemented was no more popular. In 1992 the value of the ❺ pound fell dramatically again, forcing Britain to pull out of the European Monetary System, which controls monetary stability in Europe.

John Major, British prime minister, 1992

The parliamentary elections of 1997 brought a landslide victory for the Labour party under the leadership of Tony Blair. The new prime minister, leading a party he referred to as "New Labour," attempted to find a "third way"—one that would equally consider free enterprise and social demands—in which to lead the country. Tony Blair was reelected in 2001 with a clear majority. In May 2005, he became the first prime minister in history to win a third term.

Royal Exchange in London, 2000

Miners on strike in Nottinghamshire, 1984

Demonstrators against the poll tax, 1991

Hustle and bustle at the stock exchange in London

Margaret Thatcher

The chemist and barrister Margaret Thatcher was a Conservative member of Parliament in the House of Commons from 1959 to 1992. She became leader of the opposition in 1975, then prime minister from 1979 to 1990; since 1992, she has sat in the House of Lords as Baroness Thatcher of Kesteven. As a result of her inflexible determination, she was dubbed the "Iron Lady." The term "Thatcherism" was coined for the reduction of state economic and social involvement and giving the "powers of free enterprise" free reign in the battle against inflation.

Margaret Thatcher, 1983

from 1949 | Pound devalued
1960 | Great Britain applies to join EEC
1973 | Great Britain joins EEC
from May 1979 | Margaret Thatcher elected Prime Minister
1982 | War over the Falkland Islands
1982 | Record unemployment

British Foreign Policy from the 1960s to the Present

Skepticism of the European Community in Great Britain remained even after the country joined it. The relationship to the United States has characterized foreign policies.

As early as 1960 and shortly after the founding of the European Free Trade Association (p. 551), Great Britain applied for membership in the European Economic Community. The application was denied twice due to the veto of France, but in 1973 Great Britain became a member. By that point, though, the growth spurt that the EEC members had experienced as a result of the introduction of the free market had already slackened. Instead, the explosion in the price of oil in 1973 and the resulting economic crisis put the brakes on economic development. Consequently, EEC membership hardly had a noticeable positive effect in Britain. In 1984, Prime Minister Thatcher was able to gain a considerable reduction in Britain's membership contributions to the community.

Great Britain's relationship to the European Community remained inconsistent also in the ensuing period. The criticism reached a high point when the European Union imposed a ban on British beef imports in 1996 in the face of massive outbreaks of the cattle disease BSE on the island. Anxiety about being dictated to by the EU leadership in Brussels is generally behind the British skepticism of the Union. Nevertheless, the establishment of closer ties to the Continent continues. An illustration and important contribution to this is the ❾ railway tunnel under the English Channel, which connects Great Britain and France and was completed in 1994. The British government pulled out of financing the project, but an international consortium guaranteed the completion of the project.

Alongside European involvement, the historical relationship with the United States characterizes British foreign policy. American satellite information helped the British win victory over Argentina in the ❽ war over the Falkland Islands, a British crown colony, in 1982. As its most significant ❼ ally, Great Britain has assisted the United States in its ❻ military actions against Iraq.

7 British Prime Minister Tony Blair (left) and US President George W. Bush, 2004

6 British aircraft carrier on its way to the Gulf region, January 2003

8 War over the British crown colony Falkland Islands: British paratroopers search Argentinian prisoners of war for weapons, 1982

9 Irish construction workers celebrate the breakthrough of the first tube of the railway tunnel under the English Channel, 1990

BSE

Bovine spongiform encephalopathy (BSE), commonly called "mad cow disease," is a disorder that causes changes in the brain. The processing of infected sheep carcasses into animal feed enabled the transmission of the disease to cattle and eventually even to humans. The disease first appeared in Great Britain in 1986. The European Union's 1996 import ban on British beef led to a severe crisis in livestock farming. So far, only control on the production of feed meal or respectively the banning of the use of sheep carcasses in feed production in 2000 has proven effective in the fight against BSE.

Early diagnosis of BSE is still problematic

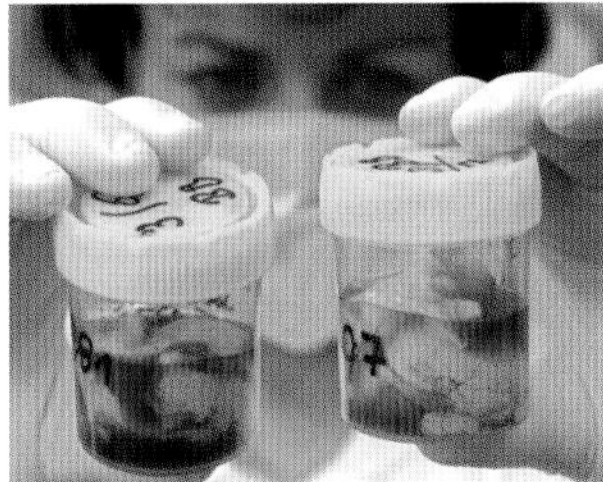

The brain of a cow is examined in a laboratory with safety precautions

1990 | Prime Minister John Major elected
1992 | Pound devalued again
1994 | Euro Tunnel opened
1996 | BSE crisis
1997 | Tony Blair wins elections

IRELAND SINCE 1945

The Republic of Ireland (*Eire*) left the British Commonwealth in 1949. Despite this, economic relations with the United Kingdom remained close, due to historical ties and geographic proximity. Ireland, more than Britain, benefited from joining the European Union in 1973. The country rose to become a prosperous EU nation. This independent flourishing growth facilitated the achievement of an agreement in the ❶ Northern Ireland conflict.

1 Scene from the civil war in Belfast, mother with child passes while a British soldier holds a machine gun, 1996

Economic Development

The Irish economy has been growing steadily since the 1960s. It was also given a boost by Ireland's EU membership, as a result of which capital was invested in the national economy.

Ireland remained neutral during World War II. Nonetheless, the country suffered under the postwar recession, which was alleviated by monies allocated through the Marshall Plan (p. 536). In the 1950s, Ireland again went through an economic depression. The balance of payments was negative, inflation high, and the number of emigrants grew steadily. Some improvement was seen at the end of the decade. The ruling Fianna Fáil party (p. 467), under Seán F. Lemass, who served as prime minister from 1959 to 1966, used the ensuing economic boom to push through liberal economic policies.

Great Britain was and remains Ireland's most important trading partner. In rapid succession, the two island nations concluded numerous trade agreements, and the tense ❷ relationship between them relaxed through the granting of mutual advantages in the economic exchange. Irish economic policies, however, also aimed to conquer other markets, specifically the ❹, ❺ tourism industry. The economic situation improved, if not without interruptions; inflation rates and the ❻ number of unemployed repeatedly shot up. ❸ Membership in the European Community in 1973 had long-term positive effects on the Irish economy; financial aid allocated by the community was invested, with an eye on the future, in the transport and education systems. The industry also boomed as Ireland became a popular holiday destination. As the economy grew, unemployment was reduced and the population soared from 2.9 million in 1970 to 3.6 million in 1998.

3 Heads of state and government of the European Community in front of the state department of the Irish capital in Dublin, 1990

2 Anglo–Irish Ulster agreement is signed; British Prime Minister Thatcher (right) and her Irish counterpart Fitzgerald, November 15, 1985

4 House on the senic Ring of Kerry with a 99-mile coastline, one of the finest in Europe

5 Pub in Dublin, 2002

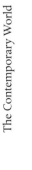

6 Old man begs in the streets of Dublin, 2003

Modern Irish Literature

Samuel Beckett, ca. 1960

Irish literature experienced a phase of renewal and flowering in the 20th century, in English as well as Gaelic. After independence, there was a decline in the heroic mood and a spread in the tone of disenchantment. P. O'Leary and P. H. Pearse wrote short stories in Gaelic. Internationally renowned novelists included Liam O'Flaherty, Flann O'Brien, and Brendan Behan, who wrote in both Gaelic and English. James Joyce gained world fame with his novel Ulysses, as did his friend, the dramatist and poet Samuel Beckett, who won the Nobel Prize for Literature in 1969. His drama of the absurd, Waiting for Godot, was one of the seminal pieces of modern theater. Ireland produced yet another important dramatist in Sean O'Casey.

1921 | Division of Ireland
1949 | Ireland leaves Commonwealth
1955 | Ireland joins UN
1959–66 | Prime Minister Seán F. Lemass
1967 | Northern Ireland Civil Rights Association founded

The Northern Ireland Conflict

After seceding from the Commonwealth, the young republic became a member of several international organizations. Its domestic politics were overshadowed by the Northern Ireland conflict.

The separation from the British Commonwealth and the proclamation of the Republic of Ireland in 1949 dissolved the last constitutional ties to the United Kingdom. Citizens of Ireland nevertheless continued to enjoy free entry to England and voting rights there. New links were soon created within international organizations; Ireland joined the United Nations in 1955. However, the country that was divided in 1921 (p. 466) was shaken in the 1950s by renewed eruptions of the conflict over Northern Ireland. The banned Irish Republican Army (IRA) made its presence felt once more with attacks on posts on the ❽, ⓬ border with the British province of Northern Ireland. The ❾ Irish government tried to master these attacks through common action with authorities in the north, which resulted in a government crisis in the Irish republic.

7 Exterior of a house in a Catholic district of Derry, painted in memory of a schoolgirl who was killed by a rubber bullet fired by a British soldier

10 Prime Minister Tony Blair (center) with the Protestant Ulster Unionist (UUP) David Trimble and the Catholic Social Democrat (SDLP) John Hume in Belfast, 1998

In 1967, the Northern Ireland Civil Rights Association was founded in Northern Ireland as a civil rights movement intended to fight for equality for the Catholics in the north. However, the protests that were peaceful at first were answered with violence. A bloody civil war—the "Troubles"—developed in Northern Ireland in the late 1960s in which close to 4000 people had died by the end of the 1990s. Two antagonists faced each other in the North: the ⓫ Protestant unionists, who wanted to retain the union with Great Britain, and the Catholic ❼ nationalists or republicans, who sought to merge with Ireland. A climax of the confrontations was reached on January 30, 1972, ⓭ Bloody Sunday, when 13 Catholics were shot by the British military. The British government dissolved the Northern Irish parliament in March, to which the IRA responded with numerous bombings. Negotiations between Dublin, Belfast, and London failed.

A breakthrough was achieved with the ❿ Good Friday Agreement, concluded on April 10, 1998, and signed by the governments of the United Kingdom and Ireland and the political party leaders of Northern Ireland. Ireland agreed to abstain from its constitutional goal of reunification, cooperation between all the governments was resolved, and the paramilitary units, in particular the IRA, agreed to a decommissioning of weapons. Britain promised a significant troop reduction and police reform, as well as allowing the greater participation by the Catholic Sinn Féin party in the government of Northern Ireland. Separate referendums in both countries helped achieve the success of the agreement, and life in Northern Ireland gradually began to become less marred by violence.

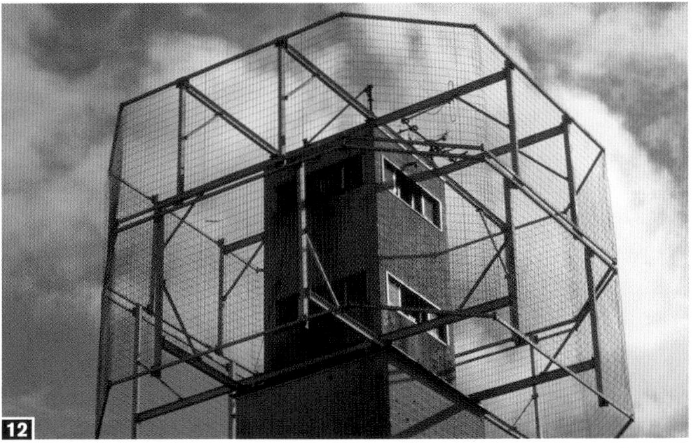

12 British army watchtower, barred as a protection against stone throwers in Derry

8 Road in a Catholic and Protestant area closed off by a steel gate, Belfast, 2004

9 Stormont Castle in Belfast, seat of the parliament and cabinet of Northern Ireland, 2004

11 Painted exterior of a house with a Protestant UFF (Ulster Freedom Fighters) slogan, Belfast

13 Bloody Sunday 1972: A member of a British paratrooper unit beats a demonstrator

30 Jan 1972 | Bloody Sunday

10 Apr 1998 | Good Friday Agreement

1969 | Samuel Beckett awarded Nobel Prize for literature

1973 | Ireland joins EC

France since 1945

France had suffered greatly through World War II. General ❶ de Gaulle's provisional government took action against the collaborators and tackled reconstruction. The Fourth Republic did not last long, however. A revolt in the colony of Algiers led to a crisis in the government and finally to the founding of the Fifth Republic. As president, de Gaulle followed a policy of independence from the power blocs of the Cold War. His successors returned to a stronger engagement within Europe.

Beginning of the German-French friendship: President de Gaulle (right) meets the German chancellor Adenauer

From the Fourth to the Fifth Republic 1946–58

In the first postwar decades, France became an industrialized nation. The unstable Fourth Republic collapsed in 1958 and was replaced by a presidential system.

By the end of the war, France was in many regions a ❸ destroyed country. Though Paris was largely intact, other cities, especially ports such as Le Havre and Brest, lay in ruins. After the "cleansing" of society of perhaps thirty or forty thousand actual and supposed collaborators, the ❷ provisional government under Charles de Gaulle (p. 461) began reconstruction. Banks, insurance companies, and large enterprises such as Renault and Air France were nationalized, and welfare reforms were carried out. The state used economic planning to steer development beyond the reconstruction phase, transforming France from a predominantly ❺ agrarian country to an ❻ industrial nation in the second half of the century.

Allied advance towards a damaged city in Normandy, 1944

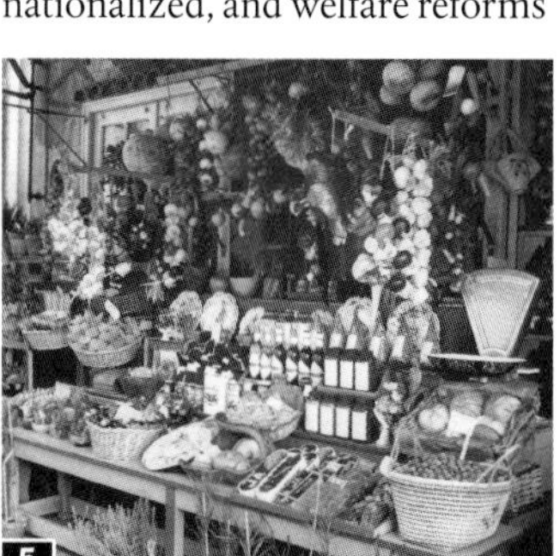

Shop selling regional products, ca. 1960

Citroën DS, the flagship model of the French carmaker, 1960

After de Gaulle resigned, the constitution of the Fourth Republic was adopted on October 13, 1946. The National Assembly gained authority; the president and the government were subordinated to it. Women's suffrage and proportional representation were adopted from the provisional republic, but the latter led to a political division. The government changed almost every six months, which inhibited the functioning of the executive.

The Fourth Republic eventually broke down in 1958 over the issue of the ❹ Algerian War of Independence (p. 595). In order to prevent a military dictatorship and civil war, the National Assembly decided to recall ❼ de Gaulle to power. His government worked out the details of the constitution of the Fifth Republic. It was presented to the public in a referendum and was passed with an overwhelming 79 percent in favor. The Fifth Republic remains in force to this day.

The Fifth French Republic

According to the constitution of the Fifth Republic, adopted in 1958, France is a presidential democracy. The head of state and the head of government both share the running of the country. The president, who is elected directly by the people, however, has had special powers since 1962. He chooses the head of government and the cabinet, is commander in chief of the armed forces, has the right of veto over laws passed by parliament, and has the power to dissolve the National Assembly.

Opening meeting of the National Assembly which decided on the constitution in a liberated Paris, 1944

State crisis after an army putsch in Algiers: demonstration, Paris, May 1958

Charles de Gaulle (right) with President René Coty, 1958

13 Oct 1946 | Constitution of the Fourth Republic

1946–54 | War of liberation in French Indochina

1954 | War of independence begins in Algeria

1956 | Morocco granted independence

1957 | Tunisia granted independence

From Colonial Power to Development Aid

Decolonization was a crisis-ridden process for France, particularly in the case of Algeria, but later new forms of cooperation with former colonies were found.

8 The Viet Minh on top of a shot-down French B26, 1954

A ❽ war of liberation took place in the colony of French Indochina (p. 420) in 1946–1954, involving heavy losses on both sides, after which France declared its withdrawal from the region. The protectorates of Morocco and Tunisia were given independence (p. 594) in 1956 and 1957, respectively, but the colony of Algiers, home to about a million European settlers, was retained as part of France. A law entitled Algerian Muslims to be elected as deputies to the National Assembly in Paris and set up an Algerian legislative assembly with equal representation of French and natives, though the latter outnumbered the former by six to one. The Arab population demanded their freedom and waged a bitter war of ❾ independence (p. 595) after a revolt in 1954. The French military stationed in Algiers acted on its own, taking advantage of the weakness of the Paris government, which was ready to recognize the right of the Algerians to self-determination. Radical French Algerians founded a terror group, the *Organization Armée Secrête* (OAS). Because Egypt was supporting the Algerian freedom movement, France, together with Great Britain, occupied the Suez Canal, but they were forced to withdraw by the United States, the Soviet Union, and the ⓫ United Nations. Against the embittered resistance of several generals, ❿ de Gaulle initiated political negotiations with the Algerian government in exile. The Treaty of Evian of April 8, 1962, brought Algeria independence from France.

The plebiscite to introduce the constitution of the Fifth Republic in 1958 was held not only in the motherland but also in the overseas territories. A rallying point for the colonies was the provision in the constitution for the founding of a "Communauté française"; acceptance of the constitution meant admission into this community. Only Guinea rejected membership. With the amendments to the constitution in 1960, former colonies that had already gained independence could also join, and most of the former French African territories did so.

France sought thereafter to develop equal partnerships with its former colonies. French development aid focused to a great extent on these countries, and cooperation in foreign, security, cultural, and economic policies was regulated by treaties.

9 The Algerian War of Independence 1954–1962: French propaganda postcard with laughing French soldier and Algerian children

10 Charles de Gaulle during his visit to Algiers, June 1958

France's Overseas Possessions

Iles de Saintes, Guadeloupe

The four overseas départements of French Guyana, Guadeloupe, Martinique, and La Réunion are legally almost completely equal in status to the French départements or counties. The French overseas territories of French Polynesia, New Caledonia, and Wallis and Futuna in addition have their own executive and an advisory parliament. French laws are valid there only if expressly so designated, although Paris can intervene in the governing of the land by decree.

11 Suez conflict 1956–1957: A United Nations peacekeeping force watches the retreat of the warring troops

Economic and Domestic Policies of the Fifth Republic since 1958

The constitution of the Fifth Republic concentrated power in the office of president.

After the end of the colonial wars, de Gaulle was able to improve the state finances. ❷ Economic growth soon picked up as trade barriers across Europe fell. However, as French society changed along with the economy, the paternalism and conservatism of de Gaulle and of public life in general seemed to many to be increasingly outdated. In 1968, this frustration among the younger generation erupted into protests after a dispute between students and university authorities. It broadened when unionized workers joined the radical students and intellectuals in challenging the government. ❻ Demonstrations, factory sit-ins, and ❹ street fighting took place, culminating in a general strike. Although de Gaulle survived the immediate state crisis, he was weakened and resigned in 1969.

3 François Mitterrand, 1991

4 Students in street fights with the police, Paris, 1968

His successor, ❶ Georges Pompidou (1969–1974), introduced reforms, but the energy crisis of 1973 proved a set back. The government of ❺ Valéry Giscard d'Estaing (1974–1981) was particularly successful in foreign affairs; together with German chancellor Helmut Schmidt, he instituted an annual summit meeting of the heads of state of the leading industrialized nations, then known as the Group of Six or G-6, which was meant to fight the economic crisis. In France, however, unemployment continued to rise.

A left-wing government came to power with the election of ❸ François Mitterrand (1981–1995) as president and the victory of his Socialist party in the parliamentary elections of 1981. Mitterrand sought more state planning and a redistribution of income, but the budget deficit and a double-digit rise in prices forced him to change course by 1983. His room to maneuver was further reduced by the establishment of the European Common Market in 1984.

2 Baker's shop in France, ca. 1960

Mitterrand lost his absolute majority in parliament in 1986, and the Gaullist ❼ Jacques Chirac became prime minister, marking the beginning of the phase of "cohabitation." This occurred again after the 1997 elections, when President Chirac had to share his power with Lionel Jospin, the socialist prime minister. A major upset also occurred in the 2002 presidential elections when the far-right leader Jean Marie Le Pen came in second with almost 20 percent of the vote.

1 Inauguration ceremony of the French President Georges Pompidou (front) in Paris, June 20,1969

5 French President Valéry Giscard d'Estaing (left) meeting the German chancellor Helmut Schmidt in Bonn, capital of West Germany (FRG), 1975

6 Student demonstrations, Paris, 1968

Cohabitation

In France's semipresidential system of government, both the president and the prime minister have important powers. "Cohabitation" is the name given to the situation in which the two offices are held by different parties. The two leaders must continue to conduct affairs of state despite their political rivalry. In 1984, Mitterrand made a tacit agreement with Chirac over the division of responsibilities: the president took the lead in foreign policy while the prime minister concentrated on domestic policy.

7 President Jaques Chirac, 2003

24 Jan 1960 | Revolt breaks out in Algeria
21-22 Apr 1961 | French army coup in Algeria
1963 | Franco-German Treaty
May 1968 | Unrest and general strike
28 Apr 1969 | Resignation of de Gaulle

France in Europe

De Gaulle's policy of a "Europe of Nation States" stressed the autonomy of France. The "grande nation" has nonetheless been central to the European integration project since the 1950s.

France and Germany have long been considered the ❽ engines of the European Union. Both nations have played key roles in shaping the evolution of postwar Europe. France's role has undergone significant changes over the last 50 years. After the bitter experience of defeat on the part of the German Reich during World War II, its first concern was to establish safeguards against its neighbor, in cooperation with Great Britain and the Benelux countries. The first European treaties—agreements on atomic energy and the joint management of coal and steel (p. 536)—were signed with the intention of making a future war between the two nations impossible.

9 The new Airbus A380 jumbo jet, a collaborative industrial venture of France, Germany, the UK, and Spain, 2004

As France's colonial empire dissolved, the country's leaders increasingly looked to ❾ Europe. However, France was still concerned with further securing and building up its own independent position of power within and outside the community. The ❿ Franco-German treaty of 1963 (p. 542) tied the onetime adversaries tightly together. London's application to join the European Community was twice vetoed by de Gaulle because he feared that Great Britain's entry would endanger France's leading role in Europe. France's withdrawal from the military part of NATO also served primarily to demonstrate France's independence.

After de Gaulle's resignation, France's European policies changed. Under Pompidou, France finally agreed to Britain's EC membership; under Giscard d'Estaing and Mitterrand, France reengaged with the process of integration. As president of the European Commission, Frenchman Jacques Delors was also a key architect in the launch of the European single market in the 1980s. The historic 2004 enlargement, which saw eight former communist countries join the EU, was the culmination of a ⓫ long political process supported by France. However in recent years there have been signs that the French people have become increasingly anxious about the direction of the European project. The French electorate's rejection of the new EU constitution in a referendum on May 29, 2005 seemed to confirm the trend.

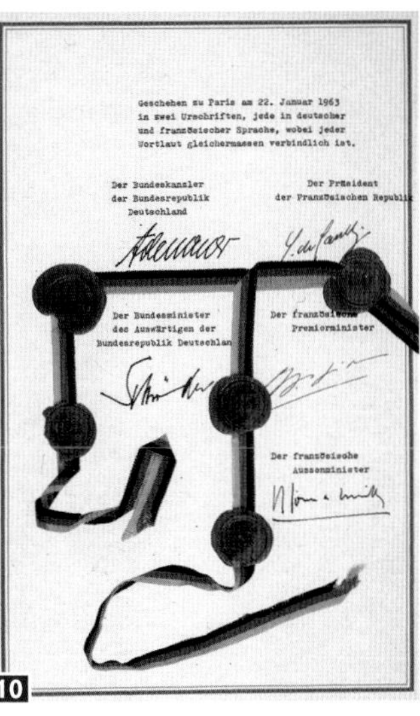

Geschehen zu Paris am 22. Januar 1963
in zwei Urschriften, jede in deutscher
und französischer Sprache, wobei jeder
Wortlaut gleichermassen verbindlich ist.

Der Bundeskanzler
der Bundesrepublik
Deutschland

Der Präsident
der Französischen Republik

Der Bundesminister
des Auswärtigen der
Bundesrepublik Deutschland

Der französische
Premierminister

Der französische
Aussenminister

10 The Franco-German treaty, signed by Charles de Gaulle and Chancellor Konrad Adenauer, in Paris, 1963

8 70th German-French conference; in the center Jaques Chirac, directly to his left the German Chancellor Helmut Kohl; Weimar, Germany, 1997

11 Heads of states and governments after finalizing plans for the admission of new members to the European Union, Amsterdam summit, 1997

François Mitterrand

François Mitterrand joined the French resistance in World War II and in 1944 became a minister in de Gaulle's provisional government. He was a member of parliament and a minister in the Fourth Republic. In the Fifth Republic, he united the splintered left in the Parti Socialiste, of which he served as chairman until 1980. In 1981 Mitterrand became France's first Socialist president and served until 1995. After initial setbacks in economic policy he withdrew to a more statesmanlike role. Mitterrand smoothed the way to German reunification and gave impetus to the European integration project.

President Mitterand throws flowers into the River Seine, where right-wing extremists murdered a Moroccan, Paris, 1995

1969–74 Pompidou presidency
1974–81 Giscard d'Estaing presidency
1981 Mitterrand elected president
1986 Chirac becomes prime minister
1 May 2004 Enlargement of the EU to 25 members

Belgium, the Netherlands, and Luxembourg since 1945

After the end of World War II, Belgium, the Netherlands, and ❶ Luxembourg decided to cooperate economically, culturally, and politically under the collective name Benelux. They integrated themselves into the emerging Western security structures, giving up their traditional neutrality by joining NATO. The Benelux states were also founding members of the European Economic Community in 1957. Within this framework, all three countries rapidly recovered from the war and became prosperous and stable liberal democracies. The course of development of each state differed in some important respects, however.

1 Street decoration marks the marriage of the Luxembourgian grand duke, 1953

The Benelux Idea

During the war, Belgium, the Netherlands, and Luxembourg were all occupied by the Nazis. Out of this common experience the Benelux Union was created. All three countries became respected bastions of liberal democracy and provided many leaders for international organizations.

Belgium, the Netherlands, and Luxembourg were among the first victims of the Nazi war of conquest (p. 468-469). These traumas left a particularly strong mark on Luxembourg, where in the postwar period French language and culture were privileged over German. In order to be able to demonstrate more strength in the future, the governments in exile of the three nations decided upon a customs and economic union in September 1944, introducing the collective name "Benelux"; the customs union came into force on January 1, 1948. In 1949 the three countries agreed on a "pre-union," which was meant to coordinate their economic structures and dismantle trade restrictions. In 1958, a full economic union was established in the Treaty of Benelux Economic Union. Internal borders were abolished in 1970. From then on, the three countries spoke with one voice, gaining added weight through their common actions, and this became a model for the process of European unification.

3 NATO Secretary General Willy Claes, 1995

With a total population of 27 million at the beginning of the 21st century, the Benelux states are jointly the fourth-largest economic player in the world. Even if the Benelux Union in recent times has been eclipsed by the steadily expanding ❺ European Union, the continuing close cooperation ensures the three countries power to achieve their aims that is many times greater than other, solitary EU member states.

Another political change took place in the postwar era. By taking part in the Marshall Plan (p. 536), the Benelux states firmly aligned with the US the Cold War period, ending their traditional neutrality. They joined the United Nations as founding members in 1945, and in 1948 they signed the Brussels Treaty with Britian and France, seeking to establish collective defense arrangements. They also became founding members of ❷, ❻ NATO in 1949. Of the ten NATO secretaries-general, four have come from the Benelux countries: Paul-Henri Spaak and ❸ Willy Claes from Belgium, and Dirk Stikker and ❹ Joseph Luns from the Netherlands.

2 Flags of the member states in front of the NATO headquarters in Brussels

4 NATO Secretary General Joseph Luns, 1976

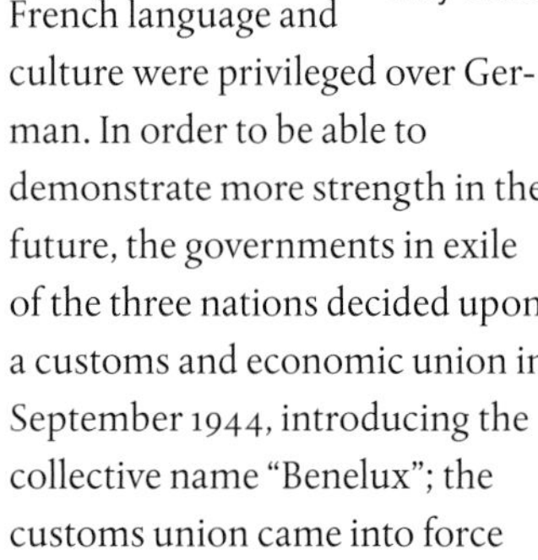

5 The seat of the Council of Europe in Brussels, 2003

6 Meeting of the NATO Security Council in Mons, Belgium, 1949

1945 | Benelux states join the United Nations
1 Jan 1948 | Benelux customs union
1948 | Brussels Treaty concerning defense
1949 | Benelux entry into NATO
1951 | Baudouin I accedes to the throne

Belgium from Centralized to Federal State

After the war, the center of ❼ Belgium's economy shifted to the Flemish part of the country. The conflict between the Flemish and the Walloons led to the establishment of a federal state.

Belgian heavy industry, which had emerged almost unscathed by World War II, provided the country with a strong economic base in the late 1940s. Once the importance of industry diminished, however, Belgium fell into an economic crisis. This was offset by the positive effects of the Benelux Union and membership in the European Economic Community that was founded in 1957 (p. 536). Whereas the Francophone Walloon part of the country had dominated the economy in the preceding decades, new investment flowed primarily into the Flemish areas, especially the ❿ port of Antwerp. The Flemish region now took over the lead role, which stirred up conflict between the two ethnic groups and repeatedly led to domestic crises. Several constitutional reforms were made, and Belgium became a federally organized parliamentary democracy in 1993, composed of the regions of ❽ Flanders, Wallonia, and the capital region of ❾ Brussels. The economy and administration have been decentralized, and the regions were granted cultural autonomy.

8 Flemish coat of arms

10 Heavy cranes load ships on the docks of the Belgian port of Antwerp

The early postwar years were overshadowed by a dispute concerning King Leopold III, who stood accused of treason and collaboration with the Nazis. Leopold returned to the Belgian throne in 1950, but unrest forced him to abdicate in favor of his son Baudouin I in 1951. Baudouin was able to hold the country together through strict impartiality in the ethnic conflict. He was followed on the throne by his brother, Albert II, but Albert did not come into a trouble-free inheritance. A bribery scandal in which many ministers were involved led to the resignation of the government in 1994, and new elections brought a breakthrough for the right-wing parties.

Belgium was shaken between 1990 and 2000 by numerous corruption scandals and the botched investigation of child molester and murderer Marc Dutroux. In October of 1996, 325,000 citizens gathered for the ⓫ "White March" in Brussels—a silent demonstration against political intrigue, moral decay, and the laxity of the justice system in the trial of the pedophile serial killer and his associates.

7 The "Atomium", the main attraction at the 1958 world exhibition in Brussels

9 Town hall in the gothic quarter of the Belgian capital of Brussels

Baudouin I

Baudouin I, King of the Belgians from 1951

Baudouin (Boudewijn in Flemish), born in 1930, returned to Belgium in 1950 with his father Leopold III, who had been taken prisoner by the Nazis and transported to Germany. Baudouin succeeded to the throne in 1951. In 1960 he declared the Belgian Congo's independence. King Baudouin died in 1993 after a popular 42-year reign. The Belgian royal house serves as a unifying and stabilizing factor in a federal state threatened by cultural divisions.

11 Mass demonstrations in the wake of a pedophile scandal, 1996

1958 | Treaty of Benelux Economic Union

1960 | Independence of Belgian Congo

1970 | Abolition of internal borders

1993 | Death of Baudouin I

Oct 1996 | White March in Brussels

Luxembourg

Luxembourg's development has been determined by its relationship to its neighbors. The steel industry and financial sector are equally dependent on cooperation with the bordering nations.

As early as the 1920s, ❶ Luxembourg, an independent grand-duchy, bordered to the west and north by Belgium, was able to establish a customs, trade, and currency union through its economic association with Belgium. The iron and steel industries were of particular international significance because of the rich ore deposits in Lorraine. Furthermore, Luxembourg was of high strategic importance for armies attempting to move through Belgium into France. After the end of World War II, the Grand Duchy of Luxembourg began by joining the Benelux customs union and then became a champion of the ❷ European Coal and Steel Community (ECSC) and was thus involved in the process of European unification. Appropriately, the ECSC high authority chose Luxembourg as its seat in 1952; the treaty had a fixed term of 50 years, and the high authority was abolished in 2002. Other important European offices are also located in Luxembourg, including the ❺ European Court of Justice and the European Investment Bank.

Signing of the ECSC treaty, 18 April 1951

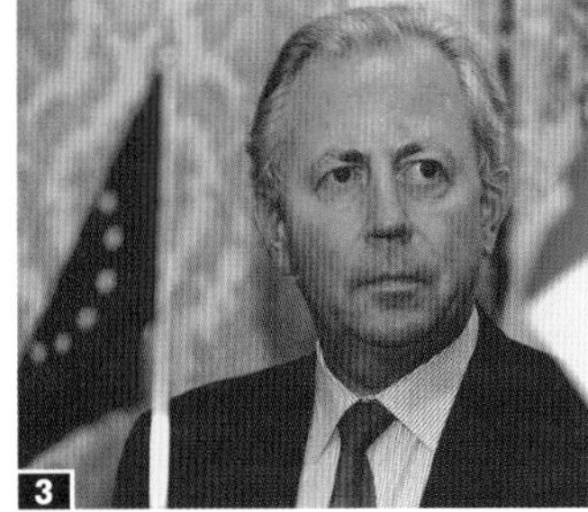

Jaques Santer, president of the EU commission, 1996

Luxembourg gave up its neutrality in 1949 and joined NATO. Its foreign policies are almost exclusively determined by EU policies. The long terms of office of Luxembourg politicians especially qualify them for the European stage. Among them are ❸ Jacques Santer, president of the European Commission from 1995 to 1999, and the current prime minister of Luxembourg, Jean-Claude Juncker, who has made a name for himself as a negotiator within the European Union. Being a small nation, Luxembourg is very intent on not being left out of European committees. Since 2003, the Benelux states have been demanding a commission that is smaller and therefore more capable of acting, whose seats would be equally allocated according to a rotation system.

Luxembourg is one of the most important ❹ finance centers of the world. Financial management is of vital significance to the country. EU efforts to create an interest tax and the abolishment of bankers' confidentiality are therefore seen as an economic threat. A related EU law was prevented by Luxembourg's veto in 1989.

The old town of Luxemburg along the River Alzette, in the Grund Valley

Building of the DG Bank Luxembourg on the Kirchberg in Luxemburg, 1997

The original seat of the European Court of Justice in the Kirchberg area where many European institutions are clustered, Luxembourg

Charlemagne Prize to the People of Luxembourg

The people of Luxembourg were awarded the Charlemagne Prize by the city of Aachen in 1986. Since 1950, this award has been presented annually for services to European unity. The Luxembourgers were deemed worthy of the prize because, as founding members of the European Union, they were among the first committed Europeans, and Luxembourg politicians have made essential contributions to the unity of Europe. The medallion was given to Grand Duke Jean representing the citizens of Luxembourg.

Former Grand Duke Jean with his wife, 1953

1945 | Independence of the Dutch East Indies

1949 | Luxembourg joins NATO

1952-2002 | Seat of the European Coal and Steel Community in Luxembourg

1958 | Construction of the Europort begun

The Netherlands

After World War II, the Dutch economy was dominated by industry and services. The social structures also changed.

The Netherlands conducted massive "cleansings" and criminal prosecutions of collaborators (p. 469) after 1945. It was estimated that close to two per cent of the Dutch population had collaborated with the German occupiers. Over 90,000 people were arrested and the Dutch Nazi, Anton Mussert, was condemned to death. Unlike neighboring Belgium, the Netherlands had suffered great ❻ destruction in the war, but with assistance from the Marshall Plan, it achieved a rapid recovery. The Netherlands could no longer continue as an agricultural and colonial power. The Dutch East Indies (modern Indonesia) had been occupied by Japan and in 1945 proclaimed its independence, which was recognized by the Netherlands after difficult negotiations and fighting in 1949. In 1963 the territory of Western New Guinea was handed over to Indonesia, and in 1975 Surinam gained independence.

The process of decolonization contributed to the Netherlands' transformation to an ❾ industry- and service-oriented nation after the war. The Dutch iron processing, electrical appliance, and ❿ petrochemical industries are among the most successful economic sectors worldwide. The Dutch social structure also changed in the mid-1970s. Up until then, individual social groups had lived side by side as "pillars," culturally inclusive communities with their own social facilities who hardly ever came in contact with one other. There were Catholic, Protestant, Social Democrat, and Liberal pillars. As religions lost their significance, these firmly set worlds gradually dissolved. The student unrest of the 1960s also provided for a more porous social structure.

7 Juliana of the Netherlands

After 1945, a coalition government of Catholics and the social democratic Labor party was established; it lasted until 1958 when Labor withdrew. Thereafter, the Netherlands was governed by a shifting coalition of centrist parties; Labor has sat on the government benches only occasionally since then.

8 The dutch Queen Beatrix, 2004

The monarchy suffered a crisis in the 1970s. The husband of ❼ Queen Juliana, Prince Bernhard, was involved in a bribery scandal and in 1976 resigned from his military offices. ❽ Princess Beatrix, the heir to the crown, had married a German diplomat in 1966, triggering heated domestic political debates. Nevertheless, after her mother's abdication in 1980, Beatrix was able to once again win over the people to the idea of monarchy.

6 Ruins of the Dutch city of Rotterdam following the bombardment, 1940

The Europort

Between 1958 and 1981 an outer harbor for Rotterdam was constructed on a branch of the Rhine for large ships. The Europort is one of the most modern and, when measured by goods turnover, largest port complexes in the world. Grouped around it are the oil and chemical industries and warehouses for automobiles, grain, and iron ore.

above: Deap-sea container ships in the Europort

9 The Erasmus Bridge that spans the River Maas, Rotterdam

10 Oil tank of the Shell refinery in Rotterdam

1963 | Independence of West New Guinea

1975 | Independence of Surinam

1980 | Beatrix becomes Queen of the Netherlands

1986 | People of Luxembourg receive the Charlemagne Prize

Italy since 1945

Although Italy suffered considerable ❷ destruction during World War II, the former ally of the German Reich (p. 471) was rapidly reconstructed with the help of American financial aid. The ❶ Italian economic miracle of the 1950s, saw a boom in its film industry, tourism, and industrial production. The Italian political system is "stably unstable." A serious problem in the country was, and continues to be, organized crime and corruption, which in individual cases reaches all the way into state institutions and the economy. The economic policy system collapsed in the 1990s, though this did not result in structural changes.

1 "Fiat 1400, the progressive car," advertisement for Italy's leading car manufacturer, 1951

Italy's Political System since 1945

Italy founded a constitutional republic after World War II. The Christian Democratic party was a member of the subsequent governments in shifting ruling coalitions.

3 Guests in Harry's Bar in Venice, ca. 1950

4 Aldo Moro, ca. 1971

As the result of a plebiscite on June 2, 1946, Italy became a republic with a parliamentary democratic constitution. ❺ King Umberto II, who had taken over from Victor Emmanuel on May 9th, 1945, in the hope of preserving the monarchy which had been gravely compromised by its tolerance of Mussolini's unconstitutional regime, left the country. The Republican majority was two million from the 23,400,000 votes cast. The centrist Christian Democratic party became the leading force in politics. It governed from 1947 to 1953 with an absolute majority in a Chamber of 556 seats and thereafter in changing coalitions where it regularly had more than a third of the votes. The Socialist party lost its number two position in the parliamentary landscape in the 1950s to the Communists, while the Neo-Fascists established themselves on the extreme right. Between 1945 and 1989, there were 48 changes of government. The causes for this were peculiarities in the Italian constitution as well as the attempt to keep the Communists permanently out of government coalitions.

In the second half of the 1970s, Christian Democratic president ❹ Aldo Moro was in favor of coming to grips with the economic crisis by means of a "historical compromise," that is, with the support of the Communists, but he was kidnapped and murdered in March 1978 by the leftist terrorist group the Red Brigade.

Government crises continued to shake Italy into the early 1990s. Diverse coalition governments were formed with three or four parties. There was practically no effective opposition left. The parties permeated Italian ❸ social and political life almost completely, creating a client or patronage system that was maintained through corruption.

2 The damaged monastery of Montecassino, 1944

5 King Umberto II at his wedding to Maria Jose, Rome

The Italian Constitution

Italy's constitution was a compromise, drafted in the postwar era by an amalgamation of anti-Fascist parties and came into force in 1948. Characteristic of it is the great opportunity given to the citizens for taking part in legislation as well as the composition of the two-chamber parliament. A vote of no confidence in the government from one chamber alone can bring it down. The president has little formal influence and no authority to set guidelines. In a coalition, this arrangement considerably weakens the executive powers of the government.

House of Representatives, Italian parliament, Rome, 1999

1929 | The Vatican becomes a sovereign state

1946 | Departure of Umberto II, the last king

2 Jun 1946 | Parliamentary-democratic constitution

1947 | End of the coalition with the Communists

1949 | Founding member of NATO

Economic Development and Integration into the European Union

The Marshall Plan and European integration assisted Italy's economic development and stabilized economic policy.

7 Signing of the Treaty of Rome in 1957; on the right, the Italian President Antonio Segni

8 Alscide de Gasperi, ca. 1950

The ❾ Partito Comunista Italiano (PCI) was one of the strongest Communist parties in postwar Western Europe. The US-funded Marshall Plan (p. 536) was designed to restrict its influence and prevent it from gaining further support among the poverty-stricken post-war population. In 1947, President ❽ Alcide de Gasperi, a Christian Democrat, terminated the coalition with the Communists, who from then on remained excluded from government. The reconstruction of the ❿ economy and the implementation of social and agrarian reforms began with the help of the money that flowed into the country at the time. Despite the remarkable economic recovery, however, the number of emigrants continued to remain high.

9 The founder, general secretary and leading theorist of the Commmunist Party of Italy (CPI), Antonio Gramsci, ca. 1920

Italy was among the founding members of NATO in 1949, the European Coal and Steel Community in 1951, and the European Economic Community, which was established by the ❼ Treaty of Rome in 1957. The Common Market had a very positive effect on the Italian economy. Northern Italy's industries in particular were able to link up with the rest of Western Europe, which remains a vital market today. The process of European integration also proved to be beneficial in other areas. In order to join the European Monetary System, it was necessary to reduce debt and lower the inflation rate, thus stabilizing the economy. Both chambers of parliament gave their approval for the implementation of the necessary measures. In 1999, Italy, along with ten other nations, entered the last stage of European economic and currency union and introduced the euro as the new common currency. The economically supportive and politically stabilizing effects of the European process of unification are directly noticeable in pro-Europe Italy, which has joined the ❻ Group of Seven, the organization of the leading industrialized states, which is now the Group of Eight (G-8). This integration gives Italy the opportunity to help shape supraregional economic issues and political processes, despite its comparative economic weakness.

6 G7 Conference concerning the employment policy, 1996

10 Production line packaging cheese, Monza, 1950

The Vatican

The Vatican City, which is located in the middle of the Italian capital Rome and is the seat of the Roman Catholic Church, is a UNESCO World Heritage site. Although Italy sees itself as a laicized state, the significance of the Curia in an almost exclusively Catholic country is not only of a religious nature. The Vatican is also an economic factor and was able to exert political influence through the Christian Democratic party.

St. Peter's Square with St. Peter's Basilica, the center of the Vatican City, Rome

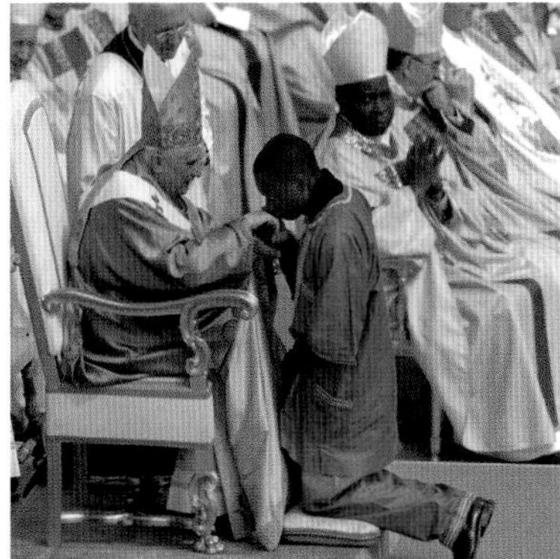
Inauguration of Pope Benedict XVI on St. Peter's Square in Rome, April 24 2005

1951 Founding of the European Coal and Steel Community
1955 Italy becomes a member of the United Nations
1957 Founding member of the EEC
1978 Murder of Aldo Moro
1999 Introduction of the euro

The Peculiarities of the Italian Economy

Since the late 1960s, the signs of an economic crisis in Italy had been multiplying, as industrial production stagnated. Organized crime played a role in this development.

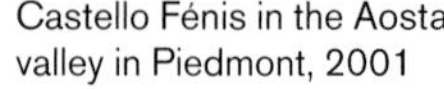
Castello Fénis in the Aosta valley in Piedmont, 2001

Turin in Piedmont with the cupola its architectural symbol, the Mole Antonelliana, 2001

Despite the successes of the postwar period, the Italian ❶ economy showed distinct symptoms of a crisis from the late 1960s on. Inflation was high and the lira was weak. The national debt in 1997 reached a high point of 120 percent of the gross national product, of which 42 percent was earned by state enterprises. This high percentage of state enterprises contributed to the origin of the crisis: Companies that came into difficulties could seek state support or sell company shares to the state. Once they regained economic health, these shares could be repurchased. In this way, unproductive sectors came under the responsibility of the government and restoring these companies to profitability was done at public expense.

Italy suffers a strong north–south disparity. The Northern Italian regions of Lombardy, ❷, ❸ Piedmont, and Veneto, along with Latium in the central region, are industrialized to a high degree and have well-developed service sectors. ❹ Northern Italy is among the wealthiest regions of Europe. The south of the country, the "Mezzogiorno," is primarily ❻ agrarian. Its population density is irregular, with heavy concentrations side by side with deserted areas. Structural aid from the state and the European Union has been unable to alleviate the economic weakness of this region. This seemingly insurmountable division of the country impairs social and political stability. Separatism is an oft-expressed political demand in the north; in the south, large sections of the population migrate north—or leave the country—because of high unemployment. Furthermore, Southern Italy remains a region plagued by ❺ organized crime, or the Mafia. The struggle against this is becoming increasingly difficult as much of the Mafia's capital has flowed into the legal economy and it has many and diverse international ties at its disposal.

The Mafia

Originally a secret society of major Sicilian landowners and their field guards, the Mafia today is a synonym for organized crime that has long since extended far beyond Sicily throughout Europe and into the United States. The main sources of income are drug trafficking, arms smuggling, prostitution, human trafficking, and the extortion of protection money. In addition, the Mafia engages in subsidy fraud and corruption in the allocation of public commissions in the building trade, for example, through blackmail of influential figures. Their code of conduct is characterized by the obligation of secrecy (omertà) and revenge (vendetta). The secret cooperation of state officials and the mafiosi has, over the course of time, made the Mafia a political player in Southern Italy.

A special unit of the police in the fight against the Mafia, on a mission, Naples, 2004

Fiat factory in Turin, ca. 1965

The fashion capital Milan: Models pose in a shop window, 2002

The Napolitan Mafia boss "Lucky" Luciano at home, 1958

Picking of world-renowned Italian olives in the agrarian south, Sicily, 2004

1980 | Bomb attack on Bologna station
1990 | Strong devaluation of the lira
1992 | Corruption scandals lead to state crises
1992 | Scalfaro becomes president

The Italian "Revolution" of the 1990s

The Italian political system collapsed at the beginning of the 1990s. It was not reformed despite an unprecedented wave of trials against corrupt industrialists, public officials, and politicians.

Bettino Craxi, president 1983–1987

Di Pietro, former investigator of corruption

Massimo D'Alema, leader of the PDS party

The structural problems of ⓫ Italy's political system escalated in the 1990s. After the breakdown of the Eastern Bloc in 1989 the exclusion of the Communist party (p. 565) from government was no longer justifiable when it had widespread support. The intertwining of political parties with the economy and state also came under increasing criticism. Though the collapse of the lira at the beginning of the 1990s promoted Northern Italian exports, it wiped out huge amounts of savings. The call for separatism in the northern regions became louder; the Lega Nord party demanded the division of the country in order to detach itself from the backward South.

A few committed public prosecutors took action against organized crime, and the Mafia defended itself with ⓬ terror attacks. The Mafia's connection to the judiciary and politicians came into the open. Even previously respectable politicians such as Christian Democrat Giulio Andreotti and Socialist ❼ Bettino Craxi were charged. After the corruption of the parties in the allocation of public commissions became public, first the Christian Democrats, followed by almost every other party, disbanded. Whole government departments were brought to a standstill through the arrest of public officials. By 1994, 6,059 persons had been investigated, half of whom went to jail. This operation, called "Mani pulite" (Clean hands), was conducted by the Milan public prosecutor, ❽ Antonio di Pietro. Even new parties such as Lega Nord and Silvio Berlusconi's Forza Italia had to explain themselves to the Italian courts.

New Christian Democratic parties emerged from the former Democrazia Cristiana party. The terms Socialist, Republican, Social Democrat, and Liberal became meaningless. The Communist party reestablished itself as the ❾ *Partito Democratico della Sinistra* (Democratic Party of the Left). ❿ Forza Italia and Lega Nord gained in popularity, as did the successor of the Neo-Fascists, the Allianza Nazionale.

After the elections of 1994, more than 70 percent of the members of parliament were new. Despite this, neither chamber could agree upon a reform committee. The proposal to introduce the majority electoral system to concentrate political power was rejected in a referendum in 2000 after minor parties and the Forza Italia spoke against it. Therefore reforms to the political system did not take place.

The Italian tricolor in Rome

Mafia-assassination of Judge Borsellino in Palermo, Sicily, in which five died and 17 were injured, 19 June 1992

Silvio Berlusconi campaigning, 2004

Silvio Berlusconi

Since he was first elected prime minister, as chairman of the right-wing Forza Italia party, which he founded in 1994, media tycoon and current president of Italy Silvio Berlusconi has been the dominant figure in Italian politics. The powerful politician has had to defend himself several times in front of a court and is strongly criticized for his heavy influence on the media both domestically and internationally.

above: The Italian media tycoon and prime minister Silvio Berlusconi, 2000

1994 | Berlusconi becomes prime minister

1994 | Founding of the Forza Italia

1996 | Prodi becomes prime minister

2000 | Rejection of the majority voting system

2001 | Reelection of Berlusconi as prime minister

Spain: From Military Dictatorship to Constitutional Monarchy since 1945

Gen. Francisco Franco was Europe's last fascist dictator. After the end of World War II, the country was politically and economically isolated, and the situation improved only with the opening up of Spain to the world economy in the mid-1950s. Spain became industrialized and developed a tourism industry that attracted visitors from across Western Europe, but still remained a dictatorship until ❶ Franco's death in 1975. His successor, King Juan Carlos I, oversaw a smooth transition to democracy. This opened the way to membership in the European Economic Community and a rapid rise in living standards.

General Franco with his successor Juan Carlos, 1970

Franco's Dictatorship 1945–1975

Fascist Spain was gradually able to free itself from its isolation after the war, but only limited political reforms were achieved.

❷ Francisco Franco, the dictator who had emerged victorious out of the Spanish Civil War (p. 473), restored the Spanish monarchy in 1947 and named himself president (*Presidente del gobierno*). Don Juan Carlos de Borbón refused to accept the crown from him, however, leaving Spain a kingdom without a king. A monarchical opposition sprang up, which Franco suppressed as brutally as he had the liberals. There existed strict censorship of the press, and the Catholic Church dominated the educational system.

Gen. Francisco Franco y Bahamonde

Prime Minister Luis Carrero Blanco

Politics of the Cold War facilitated the ending of Spain's international isolation in 1953 through an agreement granting the United States use of military bases. In the same year, a concordat was signed with the Vatican, and in 1955 Spain became a member of the United Nations.

During the 1960s, alongside economic reforms and cosmetic changes to the constitution, limited political reforms were made. Workers, supported by elements of the Church, were granted the option to form independent unions and to strike. ❹ Opposition movements in the Basque region and Catalonia vehemently demanded independence.

The aging dictator's regime lost its stability. He named Prince Juan Carlos heir apparent to the throne in 1969 and two years later made him his deputy. Franco also made ❸ Luis Carrero Blanco prime minister, though he himself remained head of state. In December 1973, Carrero Blanco was murdered by the Basque separatist movement ETA (p. 571), and political repression was once again increased. Franquists and reformers were irreconcilable under Prime Minister Carlos Arias Navarro after 1974, but the old dictator Franco ❺ died on November 20, 1975.

The six suspects put on trial for membership in an illegal Basque nationalist group

Tomb of Franco in the "Valley of the Fallen Soldiers" (*Valle de los Caidos*), a memorial to those who died during the civil war

Franco's Regime

General Franco supported his regime with a state party—the fascist nationalistic Movimiento Nacional—but also relied on the military and the Church. Their support increased the dictator's credibility significantly. But the Falange—the nucleus of the Movimiento Nacional—lost political power as soon as Spain held free elections in 1977.

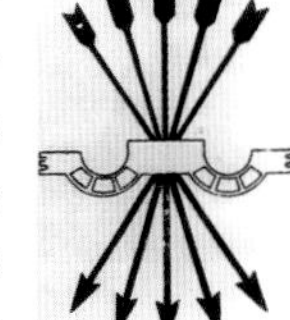

above: Insignia of the fascist Falange group

1928 | Founding of the Opus Dei movement
1947 | Reintroduction of the monarchy under Franco
1953 | American-Spanish agreement over military bases
1955 | Spain joins the United Nations

Economic Development until 1975

Spain's transition from a backward agrarian economy country to an industrialized nation and tourist destination began slowly in the 1960s. The distribution of wealth remained unequal.

As Spain was excluded from the distribution of the Marshall Plan monies (p. 536), the autarkic economic program of the state party, the Falange, continued in force after 1945. The focus of reconstruction after 1939 and the civil war was heavy industry, though not until 1950 did industry reach the production level of 1929. Spain was still an agrarian land—although it was unable to feed its population sufficiently in the 1940s and 1950s. Four-fifths of the population belonged to the impoverished ❻ lower class.

The crisis-ridden situation improved, after the 1953 military base agreement with the United States brought with it US economic aid. Radical economic reform was introduced with the announcement of a stabilization plan, which was a prerequisite for Spain's acceptance into the International Monetary Fund (IMF) in 1958. The economic opening of the country stimulated industry; by the end of the 1960s, 33 percent of the workforce was employed in that sector.

Under the influence of the new power elite—members of the right-wing conservative Opus Dei, among others—trade tariffs were liberalized and money was borrowed from foreign creditors. The decade of the 1960s was a time of privatization and acceptance of foreign investment. Economic plans and guidelines were introduced. The first four-year plan of 1964 focused on transport and energy; the second, through 1971, promoted public education and agriculture. In 1970, Spain signed a free trade agreement with the European Economic Community (p. 536) and became one of the largest ❼ industrial nations in Europe. Growth rates exceeded five percent by 1974. Tourism played a significant role, and Spain became Europe's number-one ❿ vacation destination. A generation of working-class Britons enjoyed their first foreign holidays on package tours to the south coast of Spain. Money sent home by Spanish "guest workers" from wealthier countries such as Germany and France also served to boost the country's living standards and provided the regime with vital foreign currency.

However, the benefits of this economic growth were not evenly distributed. Tourism was largely limited to the Mediterranean coast, and revenues went to a wealthy few or corrupt officials. Much of the country's interior was also bypassed by industry as new ventures were concentrated around Madrid, ❾ Barcelona, and the northern Basque region, resulting in large-scale ❽ migration from rural areas to the cities.

7 Factory in Sant Adria del Besos

9 Tourists sitting in a street café in Barcelona, 2002

6 Slums in a suburb of Madrid, ca. 1950

8 An abandoned farm in Extremadura

10 Cala Bassa beach in the Spanish Mediterranean island Ibiza, 2000

Opus Dei

Opus Dei ("Work of God") is an influential right-wing conservative lay movement within the Catholic Church. It was founded by a Spanish priest, Josemaría Escrivá de Balaguer y Albas, in 1928 with the goal of establishing Catholic principles in private and professional life. Opus Dei has come under heavy criticism for its cooperation with Franco and its sect-like recruiting methods, as well as its heavy-handed treatment of opponents within the Church.

Josemaría Escrivá de Balaguer y Albas, canonized in 2002

1958 | Stabilization plan
1964 | First four-year plan
1969 | Nomination of Juan Carlos as the heir to the throne
1970 | Free trade agreement signed with the EEC
20 Nov 1975 | Death of Franco

The Development of the Constitutional Monarchy since 1975

King Juan Carlos I helped shape the transformation of the Franco dictatorship into a democracy. This system change took place largely peacefully.

Juan Carlos I ascended to the Spanish throne ❶ on November 22, 1975. Together with the premier he appointed in 1976, ❸ Adolfo Suárez, the king introduced the structure of a democratic system. Suárez's middle-of-the-road Democratic Center Union won a victory in the election of the constituent National Assembly in 1977. A new constitution, approved by the people with a large majority in 1978, made Spain a constitutional monarchy. This and the dissolution of the former state party, the *Movimiento Nacional* (p. 568), in 1977 brought an end to the fascist system shortly after Franco's death.

However, this change did not take place completely without resistance. On February 23, 1981, ❹ Lieutenant Colonel Antonio Tejero stormed parliament with members of the paramilitary *Guardia Civil* and took members of parliament hostage. The military took a wait-and-see stance, even approving in part. It was the king's staunch public declaration of his belief in democracy that thwarted the attempted coup.

The elections in 1982 brought a change in government. The winning party was the leftist Spanish Socialist Workers' party. Prime Minister ❺ Felipe González Márquez was confronted with a dissatisfied military and a rise in unemployment. At the same time, Spain was moving closer to Europe and the West. In 1982 Spain became a member of NATO and on January 1, 1986, joined the ❷ European Community. After losing the election in 1996, González relinquished the government to the conservative Popular Party. Spain's recurring problems awaited the new premier, ❻ José María Aznar: The concentration of industry in a few centers, a weak middle class close to ❼ the poverty line, and a high unemployment rate.

Spain has made the jump from an agrarian country to an industrial nation within one generation. Its political processes also harmonize well with those of the rest of Europe, despite its history as a dictatorship.

1 On November 22, 1975, two days after Franco's death, Juan Carlos takes his oath on the Bible and the constitution, becoming king of Spain

2 The Spanish national flag is raised in front of the headquarters of the EC in Brussels on December 25, 1985

3 Adolfo Suárez is sworn in as prime minister with the Spanish king

4 The rebel Antonio Tejero holding a raised gun in the Spanish parliament

5 Felipe González Márquez

6 The Spanish prime minister, José María Aznar (left), congratulates his successor José Luis Rodriguez Zapatero, who was elected in 2004

7 Beggar in front of a bank in Madrid, 2002

Juan Carlos I

Juan Carlos, born in 1938, attended several military academies and the University of Madrid. In 1969, he agreed to be Franco's successor, taking over on November 22, 1975. With the aid of a reform program he had introduced and owing to his personal authority, he was able to transform the Spanish dictatorship into a democracy without great political upheaval. Juan Carlos's greatest hour came during the attempted coup in 1981. With his appearance as the supreme commander of the military on television and with a speech unambiguously in favor of the new form of government, he was able to isolate the leaders, bring the military over to his side, and secure the new democratic system.

1953 | ETA founded

1975 | Basque, Catalan, and Galician declared state languages

1977 | "Falange" dissolves

1978 | New constitution passed

The Regions of Spain

The Spanish regions gained more rights through democratization. At present, Spain is transitioning into a federal state.

In a concession to the desire for cultural identity in the Basque Region, Catalonia, and Galicia, King Juan Carlos granted the Basque, Catalan, and Galician languages the status of official state languages in the respective regions in 1975. However, this was not sufficient for those striving for autonomy. In September 1977, ❿ Catalonia demanded self-governing rights that the region had already been granted once in 1931. Demonstrations in other regions followed. New parties were formed that raised the demand for autonomy.

A national solution was found in the constitution of 1978. Under Article Two, Spain was divided into 17 autonomous regions. The whole national parliament, the *Cortes*, from then on faced a Senate made up of regional chambers. The authority of the regions, as differentiated from the functions of the central state, is laid out in the text of the constitution.

The regions have the right to self-government in, for example, public works, environmental protection, and economic development; the national government regulates ❽ defense and foreign policy, among other things. The particulars of power vary from region to region, but Catalonia, ⓫ Galicia, and the ❾ Basque Region have had a high degree of autonomy from the outset.

Not all sections of the populace reacted favorably to this development. Even the process of democratization was threatened at first through acts of violence and terrorist attacks. The armed forces rejected the efforts toward decentralization, and many attacks by the extreme right took place. The right wing repeatedly called for the military to take over the government. On the other hand, the Basque separatist terror organization ETA continued to fight for complete sovereignty of the Basque Region by means of ⓬ assassinations and kidnappings.

Since 2002 there have been increased discussions in Spain over a new form of the power relationship between the regions and the central state. In addition, because the Senate has demonstrated itself to be rather weak until now, more independence continues to be demanded by the different Spanish regions.

9 The Guggenheim Museum in the Basque city Bilbao

10 Catalonian flags in Barcelona

8 Spanish crown prince Felipe visits soldiers on a Spanish air force base, 2002

11 Wind turbines on the Galician coast, 1998

12 An ETA car bomb attack in Santander, 2003

ETA

ETA ("Euskadi Ta Askatasuna"—Basque Country and Liberty) is an underground movement that developed as a students' group in 1953 from the Basque National Party (PNV) and reconstituted itself as ETA when the PNV seemed too moderate to them. Their goal is the formation of a Basque state out of the Basque regions in Spain and France. Their terrorist attacks increased after Franco's death. ETA has been blamed for about 800 deaths since 1968. Thousands demonstrated against ETA terror in 2000. The government refuses to negotiate with ETA as long as it refuses to lay down its arms.

Car bomb explodes, Madrid, 2000

23 Feb 1981 | Tejero's coup attempt
1982 | Felipe González becomes head of government
1982 | Spain joins NATO
1 Jan 1986 | Spain becomes member of EC
1996 | José María Aznar becomes prime minister

The Tejo Bridge in Lisbon, built under the Salazar regime in 1966

Portugal since 1945

The Estado Novo, the "new state" of the dictator ❶ Salazar, was an authoritarian, clerical, fascist system. The dictatorship was ended in 1974 by the peaceful "Carnation Revolution." The Portuguese colonies then gained their independence. After the first presidential elections in 1976, Portugal moved in the direction of a parliamentary democracy. In 1986, Portugal was accepted into the European Community, which improved the economic situation of the country.

The Estado Novo

The regime of Salazar followed a strict economic policy. In foreign affairs, it was oriented toward the Western camp during the Cold War and fought a brutal colonial war in Africa.

Following a coup d'état by the army in 1926, ❻ Antonio de Oliveira Salazar came to power in 1932 (p. 472). Under his dictatorial regime, Portugal maintained through most of World War II, but toward the end of the war, the dictator allowed the Allies to establish military bases on the Azores Islands. This alignment in foreign policy was maintained, and in 1949 Portugal was among the founding members of NATO. Entrance into the United Nations did not take place until 1955, and membership in the Organization for Economic Cooperation and Development came in 1961.

Domestically, the corporative governmental system based on privilege continued after 1945. Despite a few relaxations, censorship, the secret police, and the one-party system continued to keep the population suppressed. Although Salazar was able to reduce the state debt with his rigid economic policy, he did little to promote industry, and the agriculture sector remained in crisis. Only a few foreign investors were allowed into the country. Consequently, many ❹ Portuguese had to search for work abroad.

Catholic Baroque Church in Goa, India, built by the Portuguese in the 17th century

A unit of the rebel liberation army in the colony of Portuguese Guinea in West Africa, 1968

In 1951, Salazar declared the Portuguese colonies to be overseas provinces to prevent their independence. Despite that, in 1961 the Indian army occupied ❸ Portuguese possessions on the subcontinent, and in Angola, Mozambique, and Guinea ❺ demands for independence grew louder. A bitter and brutally waged colonial war followed, burdening the Portuguese national budget to such an extent that Salazar was forced to open Portugal to foreign investors.

Portuguese guest-workers in France build themselves provisional accommodations, 1963

In September 1968 Salazar suffered a stroke and stepped down from office. His successor, ❷ Marcelo Caetano, eased censorship laws and attempted a mild liberalization in the political sphere, but the reforms were halfhearted. In 1974 it became increasingly clear that the colonial war in Africa could not be won militarily, while there was no political solution in sight. The sense of crisis was exacerbated by the effects on Portugal's weak economy of the world economic depression that had begun in 1973. In this context the armed forces overthrew the government in a bloodless coup, with considerable support from the Portuguese people. The peaceful popular uprising was called the "Carnation Revolution" and signaled the end of both the dictatorship and Portugal's colonial empire.

Marcelo Caetano, 1973

Portuguese dictator António de Oliveira Salazar at his desk

1932 | Salazar comes to power
1949 | Portugal becomes a founding member of NATO
1955 | Portugal joins the United Nations
1961 | Portugal becomes a member of the OECD
1961 | Colonial war begins

The Carnation Revolution and Its Consequences

After the peaceful overthrow of the dictatorship, Socialist leaders launched a nationalization program, but it was reversed by subsequent governments.

The ❾ military coup of April 25, 1974, was carried out by a group of officers who called themselves the Movement of Armed Forces (MFA). The resulting two-year-long ⓫ Carnation Revolution, a period of liberalization and democratization, received its name from the flowers soldiers put in the muzzles of their rifles. In 1974, the MFA junta installed the conservative General Antonio de Spínola as president, but he resigned after only four months because he disliked the leftist direction of the revolution. In March 1975, he attempted an unsuccessful right-wing countercoup.

Socialist MFA officers then founded a revolutionary council and called an election for the constituent assembly that set Portugal on the road to socialism. Censorship was lifted and the ❼ secret police disbanded. The government nationalized the banks, transport, heavy industry, and the media. All of the colonies were given their ❽ independence by 1975, but this brought almost a million settlers back to the motherland, which greatly burdened the country's economy.

The moderate General Antonio Ramalho Eanes outpolled a radical left candidate in the first presidential elections after the adoption of a new constitution in April 1976. The chairman of the Socialist party, Mario Soares, formed a minority government that survived only two years. In 1979 a non-socialist party won the election for the first time after the Carnation Revolution. The governing party agreed with the Socialist opposition on the amendment of the constitution, which came into effect in 1982 and revoked some socialist elements dating from the days of the Carnation Revolution. The revolutionary council was abolished, and most of the nationalized industries were reprivatized. Following a process of reform and preparation, Portugal officially joined the ❿ European Community on January 1, 1986. Although Portugal today remains one of the poorer EU member states it achieved ⓬ impressive rates of economic growth during the 1990s, and living standards rose significantly. Since 2004, the conservative Portuguese politician Jose Manuel Durão Barroso has held the post of president of the European Commission.

8 In the Portuguese colony of Guinea (present-day Guinea-Bissau), independence fighters declare their victory, 1973

9 A group of jubilant soldiers after the coup against the dictatorship, April 25, 1974

11 An angry crowd blocks the path of a tank carrying fleeing members of the government, April 26, 1974

7 During their arrest, three secret policemen from the Salazar regime are protected from an angry Portuguese crowd, Lisbon, 1974

10 Mario Soares (front) signs the treaty of Portuguese accession to the EC

12 The 1998 World Exhibition held in Lisbon

Fado

Fado, which means "fate" in Portuguese, probably dates back to the time when Portugal was a major seafaring power with distant colonies. African slaves in Brazil are said to have developed fado as a dance, and it was only later that it was sung in Portugal. Maybe it was sailors who sang these melodies because they were full of desire for their home. In the nineteenth century, singing fado was still considered indecent and heard only in shady harbor areas. It was only later that fado became socially acceptable, and famous "factistas" made it well-known internationally.

1973 | World economic crisis
1974 | Regency of Antonio de Spínola
1 Jan 1986 | Portugal enters the European Community
1968 | Resignation of Salazar
1974 | Military coup by the MFA and "Carnation Revolution"
1975 | All colonies granted independence

Oresund bridge between Denmark and Sweden, which also connects Sweden to the European mainland

Northern Europe since 1945

The ❶ Scandinavian states became increasingly integrated into the world economy after 1945. Sweden and Finland remained politically neutral and strongly promoted understanding and peace in the world. To facilitate cooperation, the Scandinavians founded the Nordic Council. They were involved to varying degrees in the process of European unification. The Nordic countries, with their state welfare structures, are among the most prosperous nations of the world.

The European North after 1945: The Commonalities

The plan for a Scandinavian defense alliance failed after 1945, but Northern Europe came together on a cultural and political level.

Of all the Scandinavian states, only Sweden did not suffer from the consequences of World War II. After the experience of occupation and deportation on a massive scale (p. 475), the Northern European nations planned their own Scandinavian defense alliance to protect their coasts and hinterlands from attack. Though this failed in 1949, cooperation on other levels was intensified.

Sweden, Denmark, and Norway studied a possible customs union and founded the Nordic Council in 1952; ❺ Iceland joined the council in the same year and ❹ Finland joined in 1955. The Nordic Council is a common advisory body to which representatives are sent by the national parliaments. Its goal is working to promote cooperation among the Scandinavian states and the standardization of legislation in economic, social, and cultural areas. In 1971, the Nordic Council of Ministers was added to complement the committee. Although both are only advisory bodies, they have done much to promote the close collaboration of the countries. The strong social democracies in all the states played an essential part in bringing the political culture and living conditions into line. Due to this political stability, communism has played hardly any role in political life, except in Finland. There was a strong belief in the social market economy and the entire North set about building up welfare states, which are funded by high taxes.

❸ Liberalism in the Scandinavian countries led to a greater tolerance toward ❷ alternative lifestyles. Economic slumps brought on by world economic crises, among other things, have always been brought under control by the government. Concern for maintaining their regional achievements and autonomy has determined the relationship of the Northern European states to the European Union, to which they are tied either by treaties.

Pippi Longstocking, the title figure of numerous books by the Swedish author Astrid Lindgren, embodies the ideals of freedom and an anti-authoritarian education; movie still

Hippy commune in the Danish capital Copenhagen, 1972

The senate house, built in 1822, in the Finnish capital Helsinki

The Icelandic capital Reykjavik, with around 115,000 inhabitants

Greenland

The world's largest island belongs to the smallest Scandinavian nation, Denmark. The United States built military bases on the western coast of Greenland in 1945, for which a defense treaty was signed with Denmark in 1951. The island gained self-rule in 1979 but remains a Danish territory. Together with Denmark, Greenland joined the European Community in 1973, but then left it following a plebiscite in 1985.

A fishing village in Greenland, 1990

1945 | American military bases built in Greenland

1951 | Danish-American defense alliance signed

1952 | Nordic Council founded

1960 | Denmark and Norway join EFTA

The European North after 1945: The Differences

Differences among the Nordic states exist in their military ties, their economic bases, and their relationship to the European Union.

Unlike Norway, in 1945 Denmark did not suffer widespread destruction as a result of the war. Both nations were able to benefit from the Marshall Plan program (p. 536), Norway receiving as much as $35 million, and both were among the founding members of NATO in 1949. A plan for a collective military pact between all the Scandinavian nations had to be abandoned. Iceland and Greenland signed defense agreements with the United States within the framework of NATO. Sweden and Finland, on the other hand, decided on neutrality.

❼ Norway and Denmark's close trading partnership with Great Britain induced them to join the European Free Trade Association (EFTA) in 1960 (p. 551), but their paths diverged when it came to membership of the European Community. While Denmark became an EC member state in 1973 after approval in a referendum, the Norwegian population rejected membership first in 1972 and again in 1994. Norway is nevertheless tied to the European Union, which is its main partner in the European Economic Area (EEA). Its ❿ extensive oil deposits have made it one of the richest nations on Earth.

A British frigate collides with an Icelandic patrol boat thought to have destroyed its nets, 1976

The Soviet first secretary Leonid Brezhnev at the CSCE summit in Helsinki, 1973

Iceland has not joined the European Union in order to protect its fishing industry. With membership, its fishing grounds would be opened up to European competition, which would have serious consequences for the local economy. The extension of its waters triggered a fishing dispute in 1973 known as the ❻ "Cod War," in which Iceland and Britain came close to an armed conflict. Iceland has been a member of EFTA since 1969 and the EEA since 1993.

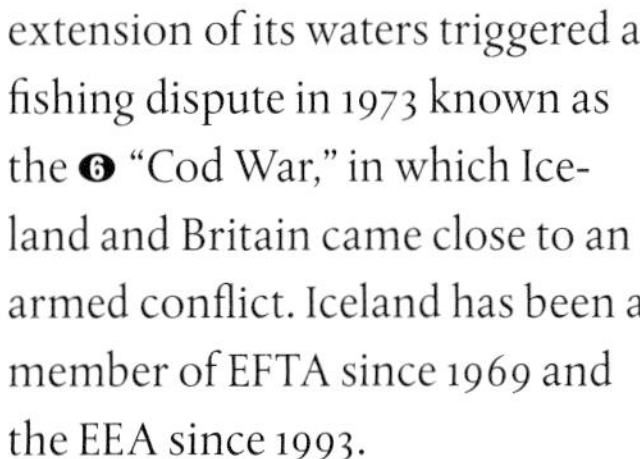

⓫ Sweden and Finland have been EU members since 1995, but there exists much skepticism in both countries regarding the community. As small nations, in terms of population if not geographical size, they are afraid of not having their concerns heard. While Finland nonetheless introduced the euro through the European Economic and Currency Union in 1999, the Swedish population declared itself against the introduction of the common currency in September 2003. Denmark has also maintained its national currency.

Finland and Sweden have both played important roles in overcoming supraregional conflicts. The first ❽ Conference for Security and Cooperation in Europe met in Finland in July 1973. The resolutions made there bolstered demands for civil rights around Eastern Europe, among other things. Sweden's ⓬ Dag Hammarskjöld was twice general secretary of the United Nations in the 1950s, and he was posthumously awarded the Nobel Peace Prize in 1961 for his numerous efforts in the cause of peace. Sweden produced yet another committed foreign diplomat in ❾ Olof Palme. Twice prime minister, Palme was involved particularly in disarmament initiatives and worked as a UN negotiator. His murder on February 28, 1986, was a great shock both nationally and internationally.

King Harald V of Norway and Queen Margarete II of Denmark in the Norwegian capital Oslo, 1997

Funeral procession for Olof Palme, 1986

A drilling rig in the North Sea oil fields that lie off the Norwegian coast, 2003

The Swedish royal couple, Carl Gustav XVI and Silvia, with their children, 2004

Dag Hammarskjöld with the Israeli Prime Minister Golda Meir, 1956

1973 | Greenland and Denmark join EC

1973 | First CSCE in Finland

28 Feb 1986 | Olof Palme murdered

1995 | Sweden and Finland join EU

Eastern and Central Europe since 1945

After the end of World War II, the states of Eastern and Central Europe came under the communist control of regimes loyal to the Soviet Union. After the formation of popular front governments, power was taken over by the Communist party, whose rule was secured and protected by the Red Army. The economies of these so-called vassal states were geared to the requirements of the Soviet Union as were their political decisions. When the USSR was forced to carry out reforms in its own country and the regime could no longer find support within its sphere of influence, the regimes collapsed.

1 Destruction of the Stalin memorial in Budapest during the public uprising in Hungary, 1956

Hungary, 1945 to the Present

The Hungarian revolt of 1956 was brutally suppressed. Hungary was the first Eastern bloc country to open its borders to the West in 1989.

Nazi Germany's ally Hungary, which had declared war on the Soviet Union, was occupied by the Red Army toward the end of World War II (p. 478). Budapest fell after a seven-week siege. Despite the relatively low proportion of pro-Communist votes in the elections of 1945 and 1947, the People's Republic of Hungary was proclaimed on February 1, 1946. Supported by the Soviet military, the Hungarian Communist party took over the administration, forced the parties into line, and united with the Social Democrats to form the Hungarian Workers' party. ❹ Mátyás Rákosi took the post of general secretary and followed a strict Stalinist course of "cleansings" and show trials, including those of Protestant and Catholic leaders.

After Stalin's death in 1953, the new prime minister, ❸ Imre Nagy, attempted to relax the authoritarian system. He ended the forced collectivization of agriculture, eased the speed of industrialization, and put a stop to state terror. His program was thwarted, however, by the Stalinist resistance led by Rákosi. The population then ❶ revolted on October 23, 1956, out of discontent with the Communist party and the running of the government. Nagy formed a coalition government and announced Hungary's resignation from the Warsaw Pact. He paid for his commitment with his life in 1958 when he was executed.

Following the suppression of the revolt by the ❺ Soviet military, the new party leader ❻ János Kádár took control of the government in 1956. He eliminated internal party opposition and leaned heavily on the support of the Soviets. Individual economic initiatives were allowed at the beginning of the 1960s. This "Goulash Communism" brought about a certain economic rebound.

Following Kádár's resignation as party chief in 1988, reforms could no longer be halted. The opening of the Hungarian-Austrian ❷ border in September 1989 punched a hole in the Iron Curtain that had divided East and West and increased the pressure for reform in the entire Eastern bloc. After the first free elections in Hungary, the Democratic Forum took over the reins of government in 1990. Soviet troops left the country in 1991, and Hungary joined NATO in 1999. In 2004, the country was taken into the European Union along with nine other states.

2 Dismantling the border fence between Austria and Hungary, May 2, 1989

3 Prime Minister Imre Nagy, 1954

4 Mátyás Rákosi, 1952

5 Soviet tanks in Budapest, 1956

6 János Kádár, 1956

1 Feb 1946 | People's Republic of Hungary proclaimed
1947 | Presidency of Gomulka in Poland
1953 | Death of Stalin
23 Oct 1956 | Hungarian people's revolt
1958 | Execution of Imre Nagy
Dec 1970 | Warsaw Treaty
1980 | Solidarity founded

Poland, 1945 to the Present

Poland's population repeatedly forced reforms and government change. The country was the first Eastern bloc nation to succeed in changing its political system.

Poland was forced to make especially great sacrifices in World War II: six million Poles died—including 90 percent of the Jewish population—and 38 percent of the national wealth was lost. After the war, in which the Polish government in exile continued the struggle from London, the Allies decided to place Germany's eastern territories under Polish administration, while at the same time Poland was forced to relinquish its eastern territories to the USSR. As Russian troops advanced into Poland, the Communist Party formed the Committee of National Liberation in Lublin. From 1944 onwards, this body held power in those areas not directly incorporated into Russia. The result was a massive resettlement that greatly changed the makeup of the population.

8 The Palace of Culture in Warsaw, Poland in the socialist style of the Stalinist era, modeled on the "Seven Sisters" in Moscow, built 1952–1955

10 Pope John Paul II is welcomed by the public in Warsaw, 1979

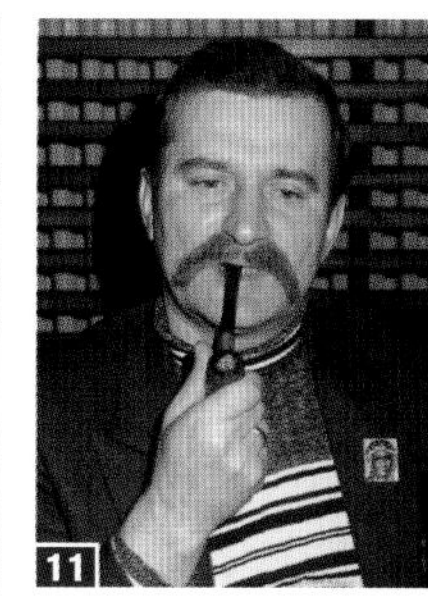
11 Lech Walesa, leader of Solidarity, 1981

After the first elections in 1947, the government led by ❾ Wladyslaw Gomulka tried to pursue a path to ❽ socialism in accordance with Poland's political and social distinctions, but the system was compelled to conform to the Soviet Union's guidelines in December 1948. The Polish Catholic Church was persecuted. After Stalin's death in 1953, unrest forced repeated attempts at reform and changes in leadership. Gomulka returned to power from 1956 to 1970.

In December 1970, Poland and the West German government under Chancellor Willy Brandt signed the Warsaw Treaty. This milestone in the history of reconciliation between Germany and Poland involved a nonaggression treaty and the recognition of the Oder–Neisse line as Poland's western border.

In 1978, Karol Józef Wojtyla, the Catholic cardinal of Krakow, was elected pope. His return to ❿ Poland as John Paul II in 1979 became a triumphal procession. It demonstrated the identification of the Polish nation with Catholicism, and accelerated the loss of power of the state party.

Poland's economic situation became increasingly critical in 1980. The rise in meat prices triggered a nationwide wave of strikes in July. The most significant demand of the interplant strike committee was to permit the existence of free, party-independent unions, and the government finally acquiesced. In October 1980, the independent trade union "Solidarity," under the leadership of ⓫ Lech Walesa, was officially registered. It soon represented 90 percent of the organized workers. In the summer of 1981, the Soviet Union threatened the Polish government with an invasion if it could not control the situation.
In response, Prime Minister ⓬ General Wojciech Jaruzelski declared martial law on December 13, 1981, which lasted until July 1983. Solidarity was banned and its leading members interned. The Church could not be neutralized, nor could the union be intimidated over the long term.

In 1988, the government was compelled to hold ⓭ round table talks with the opposition to negotiate reforms. One of these was permission for private enterprises and opposition groups. The first free elections in 1989 brought a victory for Solidarity. Poland thus became a parliamentary democracy, joining ❼ NATO in 1999 and the European Union in 2004.

7 The Polish president Alexander Kwasniewski (right) and US president George W. Bush at the NATO summit, June 27, 2004

9 Wladyslaw Gomulka (right) talking with Leonid Brezhnev and Walter Ulbricht (left), ca. 1968

12 Prime Minister General Wojciech Jaruzelski, 1984

13 Representatives of government and opposition at the round table in Warsaw, 1989

13 Dec 1981	Declaration of Martial law in Poland
1989	First free elections in Poland
Sep 1989	Opening of the Hungarian-Austrian border
1990	First free elections in Hungary
1999	Hungary and Poland join NATO
2004	Hungary and Poland join the EU

Czechoslovakia and the Czech and Slovak Republics SINCE 1945

The "Prague Spring" reform experiment of Czechoslovakia's government was forcibly crushed. The "Velvet Revolution" of 1989–1990 led to the country's division three years later.

In 1945, Czechoslovakia, which had been dismantled by the Nazi regime (p. 479), was restored to its previous borders with the exception of the region of Carpathian Ruthenia (Carpatho-Ukraine). The expulsion of the ❷ German and Hungarian minorities at the end of the war proved a long term economic loss.

Germans who were expelled from Czechoslovakia have retained their traditions and in some cases their claims to land, 2004

During a communist-organized rally, posters of Klement Gottwald and Joseph Stalin are carried through the streets, Prague, 1948

Václav Havel, 2004

Vladimir Meciar, 2004

In 1947, the Soviet Union forced Czechoslovakia to reject the assistance offered by the Marshall Plan (p. 536). In the meantime, the Communists under Klement Gottwald seized the key positions in the state. President Edvard Benes resigned in protest, and the non-Communist ministers stepped down in June 1948. ❹ Gottwald became the new president and formed a Communist government. In 1949, Czechoslovakia joined the Council for Mutual Economic Assistance (Comecon). In 1952, the country was shaken by show trials and the subsequent executions of prominent Communists.

❸ Alexander Dubcek was elected the new state and party head in 1968. He wanted to liberalize the system and implement "socialism with a human face." The Soviet Union was unable to stop the reforms through diplomatic political means, so on August 21, 1968, ❶ troops from the Warsaw Pact marched into the capital of the country and crushed the "Prague Spring." Under the new party leader, Gustáv Husák, Czechoslovakia became one of the Communist states most loyal to the Soviet Union party line. Nonetheless, in 1976–1977 a new opposition group, Charter 77, developed in the wake of the final resolution of the Conference for Security and Cooperation in Europe (CSCE) in Helsinki in 1975.

After the end of the Cold War, the effects of the process of change were evident in the entire Eastern bloc, including Czechoslovakia. The Communist Party's dictatorship was ended by the peaceful "Velvet Revolution" in 1989–1990. Dramatist and civil rights champion ❺ Václav Havel was elected president in 1990, and Dubcek was elected chairman of the Federal Assembly. The socialist state was on its way to becoming a federal state, but Slovakia, under its emergent leader ❻ Vladimir Meciar, sought independence. Since no agreement could be reached, the country was divided into two sovereign states on January 1, 1993. In 2004, the Czech Republic and Slovakia were accepted as EU members.

The tanks of the intervention troops are surrounded and blocked by the population during the "Prague Spring," 1968

Charter 77

The name of the most famous opposition movement in the Eastern bloc referred to the demand for civil rights in the final resolution of the CSCE. The charter quickly gained more than 800 signatories, including the writers Václav Havel and Pavel Kohout. They highlighted human rights violations in regular publications. The leading members became national political figures in the years of upheaval following 1989.

Václav Havel (left) in a discussion with other dissidents in his apartment in Prague, 1985

Alexander Dubcek, 1968

1948 | Edvard Benes resigns
1949 | Czechoslovakia joins Comecon
1965 | Ceausescu takes office
1968 | Alexander Dubcek's government
21 Aug 1968 | Prague Spring crushed

Bulgaria, Romania, and Albania, 1945 to the Present

The authoritarian Communist state systems of these three Balkan states collapsed in 1989. Despite their transition to democracy, these countries remain among the poorest in Europe.

After the end of World War II, the Communist Party in Bulgaria, led by its general secretary ❽ Georgi Dimitrov, began building up a Soviet-style "people's democracy." The opposition was violently eliminated. ⓫ Todor Zhivkov was first secretary of the Communist Party from 1954 to 1989. Between 1962 and 1971, he held the office of prime minister, and in 1971–1989 he was chairman of the council of state. Attempts to "Bulgarianize" the large Turkish minority after 1984 caused a mass exodus. The political upheaval of 1989 destabilized the government. An economic crisis in 1996–1997 led to major unrest. The parliamentary elections of 2001 were won by the party of the former king, ❾ Simeon II, who had promised an improvement in living standards.

In 1944, Communist partisans led by ❼ Enver Hoxha took power in Albania. As head of the party, he ruled autocratically and brutally eliminated any opposition. At first he turned toward Yugoslavia (p. 580), then China from 1961 to 1977, and finally he completely isolated the country internationally. His successor, Ramiz Alia, cautiously began to open up the country to the outside world in 1985. The process of reform accelerated after 1989, and the first multiparty elections were held in 1991. After 1995, governments came and went in rapid succession. In 1997, hundreds of thousands lost what little money they had in a stock investment scam. In the subsequent disturbances, barracks were stormed and large numbers of weapons were stolen. Since 1989 people have been ⓮ emigrating on a large scale. Today poverty and corruption rates are high, while the relationship to the Albanian majority in Kosovo remains contentious.

Simeon Sakskoburggotski, former king

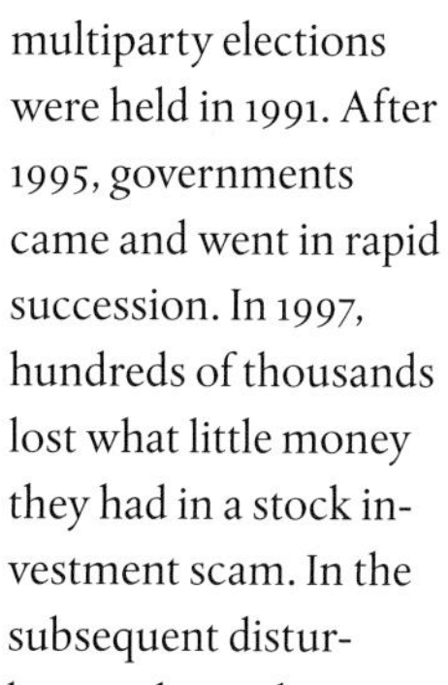

Dictator Nicolae Ceausescu, 1984

Romania lost Moldavia to Ukraine after 1945 but gained Transylvania and with it a German and Hungarian minority. The Stalinist Communist Party head, Georghe Gheorghiu-Dej, made the country a part of the Eastern bloc, but after 1960, he sought greater independence from Moscow. His successor as state and party head after 1965, ❿ Nicolae Ceausescu, continued this policy and received ⓬ Western aid for breaking with the Soviets; however, the aid did not go toward alleviating the misery of the ⓭ starving population. His regime was primarily supported by the Securitate, the secret police. With its help, minorities were brutally resettled. Ceausescu was overthrown in 1989 and executed. In 1991 opposition demonstrations were crushed by progovernment coal miners and the security forces. Although governments have alternated rapidly, the pace of reform has increased since 1997.

All three countries were accepted into the NATO Partnership for Peace program. Bulgaria and Romania are expected to become EU members in 2007.

The Albanian dictator Enver Hoxha, statue in Tirana, 1989

Joseph Stalin (left) with Georgi Dimitrov, 1936

General Secretary of the Bulgarian Communist party, Todor Zhivkov, 1987

Albanian refugees at a port in the Italian city of Bari, 1991

Ceausescu wasted economic aid on costly, prestigious buildings such as the "People's House" in Bucharest

A group of Roma carriages on a road near the Romanian capital of Bucharest, 2001

1976 | Charta 77 formed

25 Dec 1989 | Ceausescu executed

1990 | Václav Havel elected president

1 Jan 1993 | Czechoslovakia's "Velvet Divorce"

2004 | Czech Republic and Slovakia join EU

YUGOSLAVIA SINCE 1945

Yugoslavia, which was occupied by the German army in World War II, was liberated by a partisan army led by Tito (p. 485) and was not occupied by the Red Army. Tito was thus able to rebuff Stalin's intervention after 1945. He developed his own "path to Communism" and was a committed leader of the Nonaligned Movement. After his death, the state structure he had held together broke apart. The other parts of the republic set their own nationalist aspirations against the dominance of Serbia. A ❶ "nation-building war" followed and was characterized by appalling brutality.

1 Provisional bridge between the Croatian and Muslim parts of the city Mostar in Herzegovina, replaces the historic one which was destroyed during the civil war in the 1990s

Yugoslavia under Tito 1945–1980

Tito practiced a form of Communism independent of the Soviet Union. The country was a federation of republics and provinces, but the military was dominated by Serbia.

The Communist partisan army under its leader Josip Broz, widely known as ❸ Tito, was the victor in the war against the Italian and German troops that had occupied Yugoslavia during World War II. With Tito heading the National Liberation Council and then the government after 1945, Yugoslavia was given a Communist structure within a federal system, which achieved a large degree of unity. All nationalities living within Yugoslavia were promised equal rights. The king was deprived of his nationality.

Tito's government at first leaned toward the Soviet Union.

2 Head of the Yugolslav government Tito and his wife (right) as guests of the Iranian monarch, 1971

However, Stalin's attempts to assert control and ideological leadership over the Yugoslavian Communist Party were resisted by Tito, and a split resulted in 1948. Yugoslavia withstood an economic embargo imposed by Stalin with the help of Western aid, but 1955 brought a measure of ❺ rapprochement between the two governments. In 1961, Yugoslavia was a founding member of the ❹ Nonaligned Movement, an organization of states that belong to no military bloc and remained neutral in the Cold War conflict; thus the "Titoism" practiced in Yugoslavia stood for an independent form of Communism with self-governing workers and federal elements while at the same time building up good relations with ❷ non-socialist states.

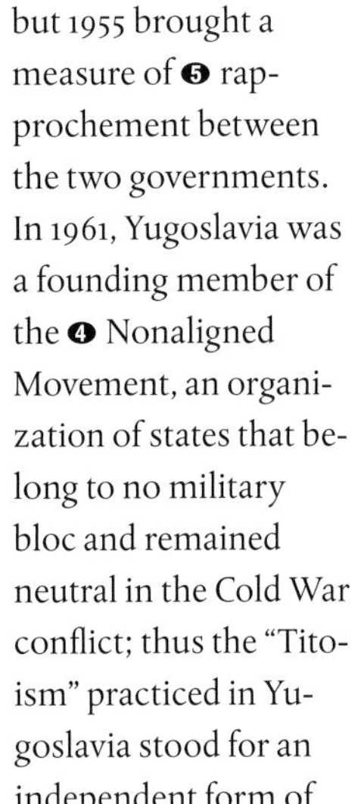

3 Tito after the end of the war in Belgrade, 1945

4 Conference of the Nonaligned Movement in Bandung, Indonesia, 1955

To accommodate the separate nationalities, Yugoslavia was divided into six republics, plus the two autonomous provinces of Vojvodina and Kosovo-Metohiya. The Communist party was restructured in 1952 to become the Federation of Communist Yugoslavia, and the police were given a federal organization in 1966. Only the army remained under the central state, which was dominated by Serbia. Despite the federal structure of the country, nationalist demonstrations, such as the "Croatian Spring" between 1969 and 1971, sometimes occurred and were violently suppressed by Tito's regime.

The autonomy of the republics increased with the constitution of 1974. After Tito's death in 1980, the chairmanship of the state committee and the party was annually rotated among the nationalities—though this was not the case within the individual republics. The dissolution of the federal state became increasingly apparent, highlighting that Tito had held Yugoslavia together.

5 Tito (right) toasts Nikita Khrushchev, 1963

1945 | Tito's government takes power in Yugoslavia
1948 | Split with the Soviet Union
1961 | Yugoslavia joins nonaligned nations
1969–71 | Croatian Spring
1974 | New constitution

The Breakup of Yugoslavia, 1980 to the Present

Almost all of the Yugoslav republics declared their independence after the collapse of the Communist central state, which was accompanied by the bloody expulsion of minorities.

After 1945, the Albanian minority in Kosovo increased to a majority of 90 percent. Disturbances began in the region in 1981. ❻ Slobodan Milosevic, later to become president, made himself the spokesman for the Serbian minority. In 1986, he rose to become first secretary of the Yugoslav Communist party, later renamed the Serbian Socialist party. Milosevic annulled Kosovo's autonomy in 1989 and replaced the Albanian elite with Serbs.

At the end of the 1980s, nationalists took over power in all of the republics. Croatia and Slovenia declared their independence on June 26, 1991. The Yugoslav army marched into both countries but soon withdrew from Slovenia. A third of Croatia, however, remained occupied; the Serbian minority living there proclaimed the Republic of Krajina.

The elections in November 1990 in Bosnia showed a majority for the Muslim Party of Democratic Action under ❽ Alija Izetbegovic, who declared the country's independence in 1991. The reaction by the Bosnian Serb minority was the proclamation of a Serbian republic under Radovan Karadzic. The Serbs were able to occupy two-thirds of Bosnia with the help of the Yugoslav army. Brutal "ethnic cleansing" through expulsion and genocide took place. The violence only ended when NATO finally intervened in 1995. By that time, 2.2 million people had ❼ fled and 200,000 had been cruelly ⓫ murdered. The country was divided under UN supervision into a Bosnian-Croatian federation and a Serbian republic which together constituted a common state.

In 1995 Croatian forces retook Krajina. The Serbian population fled or was expelled, some into Kosovo. There, in 1992, the Albanians had proclaimed the Republic of Kosovo under Ibrahim Rugova. Escalating violence between the ❾ Kosovo Liberation Army and Serbian police led to the launch of a major ❿ Serbian offensive. NATO then intervened with air strikes against Serbia and the occupation of Kosovo.

Macedonia also declared its independence in 1991. The Albanian minority in Macedonia proclaimed the Republic of Illyria and created a liberation army in 2000. About 250,000 refugees from Kosovo further increased the tension. The presence of NATO and UN troops prevented the outbreak of another war.

7 Many thousands of Muslim Bosnians, also known as Bosniaks, flee from areas held by the Bosnian Serbs, 1995

9 Kosovo Liberation Army soldiers with an Albanian flag, 1999

6 Slobodan Milosevic (center) and his wife, 1997

8 Alija Izetbegovic presents a map of the regions in Bosnia where genocide took place, 1993

10 Albanian Kosovars killed and brutally mutilated by Serbs, 1999

11 Examination of a mass grave in Bosnia, 2002

The War Crimes Tribunal in The Hague

The International Criminal Tribunal for the Former Yugoslavia (ICTY) was set up in 1993 as an auxiliary body of the UN Security Council. It deals with the prosecution of war crimes in former Yugoslavia. The Serbian leader Milosevic's trial began in February 2002 and continues today. Others such as Bosnian Serb leader Karadzic and Croat general Gotovina have not been apprehended. As of 2000, 14 prison sentences had been handed down.

Radovan Karadzic, the Bosnian Serb leader, who has been indicted for war crimes, 1993

Greece and Turkey since 1945

Before the two neighboring states Greece and Turkey became democracies, both countries suffered under dictatorial regimes. After World War II, both countries became industrial and trading nations. Conflict-laden contentious issues between them have included the mineral resources of the Aegean Sea in the territory that lies between them, which is claimed by both countries, and claims to the island of ❶ Cyprus. While Greece had been part of the European Union since the 1980s, Turkey remains a candidate for membership.

A wall separates the Greek and the Turkish parts of the Cypriot capital Nicosia, 1999

Greece: Kingdom and Dictatorship 1945–1974

After World War II and a civil war, Greece stabilized under conservative governments. The military carried out a coup against the first center-left government.

The Nazi army occupied Greece in 1943 after Greek forces had defeated Hitler's Italian allies. Various partisan movements, though also fighting among themselves, opposed the German occupation. After the war, the radical left boycotted the ❷ elections of 1946, allowing the conservative Alliance to win.This led to three years of civil war. In the 1947 peace treaty with Italy, Greece gained the ❹ Dodecanese Islands. Greece became a NATO member in 1952.

By 1952, 20 right-wing governments had ruled in succession. They were all rigidly anticommunist. The first stable government was formed by Field Marshal Alexandros Papagos with his Greek Rally party. In 1956, it became the National Radical Union, led by ❺ Konstantinos G. Karamanlis. After 20 years of a police state, the Greeks in 1963 voted into office the leftist Center Union Party led by Georgios Papandreou, who promised welfare reform in the country. However, in April 1967 conservative officers led by Colonel ❸ Georgios Papadopoulos organized a military coup and set up a dictatorial regime. A countercoup by King Constantine II in December 1967 failed. On June 1, 1973, a republic was proclaimed in Greece. Arrests, deportation, torture, and enforcement of the party line followed.

King Konstantinos II (center) with members of the government; to the far left: Georgios Papadopoulos, 1967

Konstantinos Karamanlis (right) with US President Jimmy Carter, 1978

Phaidon Gisikis became the new president in 1973 after a bloodless coup led by General Demetrios Ioannides. However, he soon came into conflict with the Turkish government over deposits in the Aegean Sea. A failed overthrow attempt against President Makarios of Cyprus, directed from Athens in 1974, eventually led to the downfall of the unpopular Greek military regime.

Greek soldiers marching to a polling station in Athens, 1946

The monastery of St. John on the Dodecanese island Patmos, one of the holiest places in Greece

The Independence of Cyprus

In order to bring about the annexation of the British colony of Cyprus to Greece, the underground movement EOKA led by General Georgios Grivas began a war against the colonial power in 1955. This was accompanied by fighting against the Turkish minority. However, the island was granted independence on August 16, 1960, which was guaranteed by Great Britain, Greece, and Turkey. The first president, Archbishop Makarios III, altered the system of government to favor the Greeks. After a bloody conflict, the Turks withdrew from the government and set up a provisional administration. In 1964, the United Nations sent in peacekeeping troops.

right: Archbishop Makarios III, bronze monument

1943 | German army occupies Greece

from 1952 | Greece member of NATO

16 Aug 1960 | Cyprus becomes independent

1967 | Military putsch led by Georgios Papadopoulos

1 Jun 1973 | Republic proclaimed

The Greek Republic since 1974

Democracy was reestablished in Greece after the end of the dictatorship. The relationship with Turkey continued to dominate foreign affairs.

In 1974, (7) General Gisikis was forced to turn over power to Karamanlis, who became prime minister. Greece returned to a parliamentary democratic form of government. Karamanlis and his New Democracy Party applied for membership in the European Community, and Greece's application was approved in 1981. In the same year, New Democracy lost its majority to the social-democratic PASOK, which appointed Andreas Papandreou as prime minister. His economic policies ignited severe social unrest in 1985, and an accusation of corruption forced him to resign in 1989.

Protected border crossing in Cyprus

After a close election victory in 1990, New Democracy under Konstantinos Mitsotakis carried out a reform program, and Karamanlis was elected president. The trade unions called a general strike in 1992 in protest over social problems. In 1993, PASOK won again with Papandreou, who had been found not guilty of the corruption charges. For health reasons, however, he stepped down in 1996 in favor of (8) Konstantinos Simitis, serving until 2004.

The postwar political history of Greece has been varied and eventful, but the country's economic growth has been consistent. Marshall Plan funds (p. 536) played a large part in this, as did membership in the European Community. Moreover, a cultural shift was running through Greece. Guest workers returning home from abroad brought not only technical know-how with them but also other concepts of living. A prolonged migration to the cities resulted in a third of all Greeks living today in the (9) (11) Athens area. Through mass (10) tourism, the Western lifestyle has come to have a permanent presence.

Animosity toward Turkey has remained the dominating foreign policy issue in the democratic republic. Disputes have arisen over rights to mineral reserves in the Aegean, issues of maritime traffic, and the rights to oil extraction. Even the NATO partnership of both states could not prevent military conflict within the context of the (6) Cyprus issue.

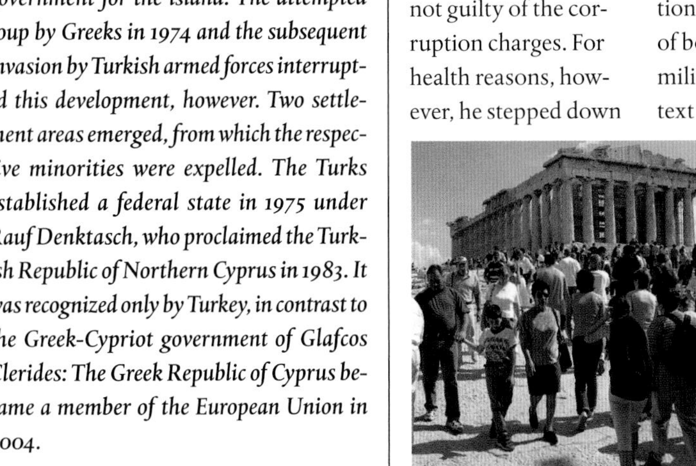

The Two States of Cyprus

A provisional administration founded by Turkish Cypriots in 1961 was meant to facilitate the realization of a federal form of government for the island. The attempted coup by Greeks in 1974 and the subsequent invasion by Turkish armed forces interrupted this development, however. Two settlement areas emerged, from which the respective minorities were expelled. The Turks established a federal state in 1975 under Rauf Denktasch, who proclaimed the Turkish Republic of Northern Cyprus in 1983. It was recognized only by Turkey, in contrast to the Greek-Cypriot government of Glafcos Clerides: The Greek Republic of Cyprus became a member of the European Union in 2004.

above: Glafcos Clerides (right) and Rauf Denktasch shake hands, 2001

Phaedon Gisikis (at the head of the table) with political leaders prior to the military rebellion, 1967

Konstantinos Simitis, 2002

Opening of the 28th Olympic Games in Athens, 2004

Tourists visit the Acropolis, 2001

Main road through central Athens, 2004

1974 | Konstantinos Karamanlis made prime minister
1981 | Joins EC
1983 | Turkish Republic of Northern Cyprus proclaimed
1992 | General strike
2004 | Greek Republic of Cyprus becomes member of EU

Turkey: On the Path to Democracy 1945–1970

Turkey became an industrialized state after World War II, but the path to democracy was not without numerous setbacks.

Anglo-French military guarantees to Turkey given just before the Second World War succeeded in keeping her neutral during the war, despite strong German pressure. Following the death of Kemal Atatürk in 1938, Ismet Inönüt became head of state. After 1945, as president, he sought support from the West, and Turkey was accepted into the Marshall Plan program (p. 536). Membership in NATO followed in 1952. The allocation of Western aid was tied to the pursuit of democratic reform. Turkey therefore adopted a multi-party system, and in the elections of 1950 the newly founded opposition, the Democratic party led by Adnan Menderes gained a majority.

2 Execution of Adnan Menderes, 1961

The economic boom at the beginning of the 1950s was followed by an economic crisis that put the Democrats under pressure. In addition, the secularist elite criticized the pro-religious policies of the party. President Menderes reacted to the criticism with suppressive measures. In May 1960, a "Committee of National Unity" led by ❶ General Cemal Gürsel organized a coup against the Menderes government. Gürsel banned the Democratic party and arrested its leadership; ❷ Menderes was executed. Although the new constitution established in 1961 had liberal characteristics, governments were henceforth subject to the scrutiny of a National Security Council dominated by the commanders of the armed forces.

The Justice party, the successor party to the Democrats, won the elections of 1965. The new head of government, ❸ Süleyman Demirel, was confronted by growing social and economic problems and rising radicalism. Demirel oriented his economic policies toward the West and followed the advice of the World Bank. Consequently, industry outstripped the ❹ agrarian sector, though only a minority profited from this development. Numerous Turks ❺ emigrated. The workers organized into unions, and the extremist factions that emerged, some of them Islamist, were further to the right and left of the two major parties. Over the decades, terrorist acts by these groups contributed to Turkey's political destabilization.

1 Cemal Gürsel, center, after 1961

3 Leader of the Justice Party Süleyman Demirel, 2000

4 Turkish women and girls in a field harvesting cotton, a main product of the Turkish economy, 1989

5 Turkish immigrant workers waiting at a German airport, 1970

The Kurdish Minority

The Kurdish people live where Turkey, Iran, and Iraq meet. The Kurds feel oppressed by the Turkish government. A separatist organization, the Kurdistan Workers' party (PKK), has made itself the mouthpiece for Kurdish autonomy. These were expressed with increasing violence after 1984. By 1999, 37,000 people had died in fighting between the PKK and Turkish forces. It was not until 1991 that the Kurds were officially recognized as a minority. The violence has decreased since the arrest of the PKK leader, Abdullah Öcalan, in 1999. Since 2002 Turkey has eased restrictions on using the Kurdish language in education and broadcasting.

Turkish soldier with the corpse of a PKK member, 1996

1938 Atatürk dies
1952 Entry into NATO
1960 Military coup under Cemal Gürsel
1961 New constitution
1965 Government of Süleyman Demirel

The Major Role of the Military since 1970

Turkey experienced two further military coups. Yet simultaneously Turkey made the transition from a developing country to a country on the threshold of economic takeoff.

In 1971 President Demirel was ousted when the army took power. By suspending civil rights, the junta brutally but effectively fought radical and terrorist factions for two years. The political system remained untouched.

7 Prime minister Tansu Çiller, photo, 1997

In 1973, the social-democratic Republican People's party under ❻ Bülent Ecevit took over government. Ecevit formed a coalition with Necmettin Erbakan's Islamist National Salvation party. Ecevit was credited with the invasion of Cyprus (p. 582) that followed the attempted Greek coup of 1974, but this did not translate into support at the polls. In the following years, he and Demirel took turns in the leading offices of state but were unable to solve the continuing problems facing the country: ❾ economic crises, ❿ Islamism, and separatist terrorism. In 1975 there were 34 victims of violence, 1500 by 1980.

On September 12, 1980, there was a third coup. General Kenan Evren dissolved parliament and disbanded political parties and unions. Thousands were jailed, tortured and executions were rife. He nonetheless succeeded in reducing the number of terrorist acts. After a new constitution was accepted by referendum in 1982, the military withdrew from power. The centralized government still allowed little autonomy to the country's provinces.

The centrist Motherland party won in the elections of 1983. Prime Minister ❽ Turgut Özal promoted democratization and market reforms, while reducing the influence of the military. In 1991, he gave the Kurds some cultural autonomy. Özal oriented himself politically and economically toward the West and in 1987 applied for membership in the European Community. In 1989 Özal was elected president, and Demirel became prime minister in the elections of 1991 as head of the True Path party. Demirel then became president after Özal's death in 1993, and his position as prime minister was filled for the first time ever by a woman, ❼ Tansu Çiller.

Since the 1980s, Islamic tendencies in Turkey have been increasing. The Islamic Welfare party first won a majority in the elections of 1995 but was banned in 1998. The electoral success of the newly founded conservative-Islamic AK party in 2002 was also a response of the populace to the economic crisis that was gripping the country.

Prime Minister ⓫ Recep Tayyip Erdogan has managed to secure the opening of membership negotiations with the European Union, which are due to begin in late 2005. However, membership remains conditional upon the continuation of political and economic reform, together with full-fledged respect of human rights. Links between the European Community and Turkey began in 1963 through an association agreement, and since 1995 the country has shared a customs union with the EU.

6 Bülent Ecevit in front of a picture of Kemal Atatürk, 1998

8 Prime Minister Turgut Özal (right) with his Greek counterpart Andreas Papandreou, 1988

9 Occupants of wooden houses, who have little hope of improvement in living conditions, slum area in Istanbul

10 Four Turkish Muslim women wearing chadors and a headscarf (right), in contemporary Istanbul

11 Recep Tayyip Erdogan after a visit to the mosque, 2003

1987 | Application for EC membership
1991 | Recognition of the Kurds as minority
1999 | PKK leader Öcalan arrested
Oct 2005 | Accession talks with the EU

The Soviet Union and its Successor States since 1945

After the Second World War, all of Eastern Europe came under the influence of Stalin's totalitarian system, which led the ❶ Soviet Union into the Cold War. The system was relaxed to a degree under his successors, who were increasingly bound to a "collective leadership." The party's claim to autocratic rule was not seriously questioned until Gorbachev. In the turbulent years of 1989–1991, the structure of the Eastern bloc crumbled, and then the Soviet Union itself collapsed, disintegrating into a federation of autonomous states. While the Central European countries sought bonds with Western Europe, autocratic presidential regimes established themselves in most of the former Soviet republics.

1 Military parade on the occasion of the 70th anniversary of the October Revolution on the Red Square in Moscow, November 7, 1987

The Soviet Union up to Stalin's Death

Joseph Stalin ensured Soviet domination of Eastern Europe after 1945 and oversaw industrial reconstruction. The USSR's increasing rivalry with the other victorious powers led to the Cold War.

In 1945, the Soviet Union was clearly one of the war's ❷ victors. At the conferences of Yalta in 1943 and Potsdam in 1945 (p. 522-527), Stalin, Roosevelt, and Churchill had agreed on the division of influence in postwar Europe. Over the next few years, Stalin systematically went about setting up Eastern European satellite states. By 1948, the Communists had taken over power almost everywhere, at first in alliance with non-socialist antifascists. The only exceptions were Greece and Yugoslavia (p. 580). In 1949 East Germany was founded (p. 539).

5 Stalin in uniform, painting, 1949

❸ Stalin had already developed his "two-camp" theory of the contrasts between the Communist and Capitalist worlds by 1946, which the United States answered in 1947 with the parallel concept of the "Cold War." The relationship between the two former allies worsened steadily and reached its nadir in the Soviet blockade of Berlin lasting from 1948–1949 (p. 539).

3 Portrait of the Russian leader Stalin, ca. 1945

4 Lavrenti Beria, the much-feared head of the Soviet secret police who enforced Stalin's reign of terror, 1953

Domestically, the terror of the Great Purges (p. 483) had passed, but the political pressure exerted by Stalin and ❹ Lavrenti Beria, the all-powerful head of the Soviet People's Commissariat for Internal Affairs (NKVD), was relentless. All soldiers and officers who had had contact with the enemy—the West—during the war were eliminated or relegated to obscure positions, including war hero Marshal Zhukov. Stalin intensified the pace of the reconstruction of ❻ industry within the framework of his fourth Five-Year Plan, which proceeded rapidly, while the development of agriculture lagged behind. By 1948, the Soviet Union's industry had reached the prewar production level of 1940, and it had doubled by 1952, but there was no rise in the population's standard of living.

The *Zhdanovshchina* carried out by cultural official Andrei Zhdanov in 1947–1948 established Stalin's ❺ personality cult and the nationalistic glorification of the Soviet Union. Writers and artists who did not adhere to this direction were vulnerable to repression and accusations of "formalism" and "cosmopolitanism." In 1952, the Stalin Note proposed to western leaders the reunification of Germany as a demilitarized and nonaligned neutral state. The Western powers quickly dismissed the offer, suspecting Stalin's motives.

2 Victory celebrations on the Red Square in Moscow: Soviet soldiers carrying flags captured from the Waffen SS, June 24, 1945

6 Workers in a locomotive factory, 1967

1943 | Yalta Conference
1945 | Potsdam Conference
1946 | Stalin's outlines his "two-camp" theory
1947-48 | *Zhdanovshchina*
1948-49 | Blockade of Berlin
Mar 1953 | Death of Stalin

Life After Stalin: Power Struggle and Khrushchev's victory

After Stalin's death, the regime relaxed his hardline policies. At first Malenkov seemed to be prevailing in the struggle to replace him, but in 1955, he was brushed aside by Khrushchev.

In January 1953, Stalin denounced a plot against his life by the Kremlin's doctors, but before a wave of further purges could be initiated, ⑩ Stalin died on March 5, 1953.

9 Georg Malenkov, leader of the Soviet Union (1953–1955), shortly after Stalin's death in 1953

11 Party Secretary Nikita Sergeyevich Khrushchev, 1960

The power struggle for the succession as leaderbegan immediately. At first Georg Malenkov, who had the government apparatus behind him, and Nikita Khrushchev, who had the support of the party, joined forces against Minister of the Interior Beria, who was deposed in June 1953 and shot in December.

⑨ Malenkov, who dominated at first, announced on August 8, 1953, a "new course" that would provide for the strengthening of the underperforming agricultural sector and the consumer industry, cultivation of new lands in the east, and "socialistic justice." A "thawing period" began in 1954 in which writers, creative artists, and intellectuals regained some freedom of expression. The first moves towards détente with the western alliance also took place. However, in May 1955, the Eastern bloc's Warsaw Pact was founded as a counterpart to NATO, and tensions returned.

In February 1956 Nikita ⑪ Khrushchev was able to win out over Malenkov at the 20th congress of the Soviet Communist party. He became party secretary and, by 1958, premier. During the 1956 congress Khrushchev famously denounced Stalin's crimes and the direction of the party under his leadership. During the wave of "de-Stalinization" that followed, revolts took place in Poland and Hungary, but both were militarily suppressed. Khrushchev relaxed ⑫ cultural policy, released many from the prison camps (*gulags*), and increasingly relied on agricultural production to improve the standard of living. He also promoted technology: The launching of ⑦ *Sputnik*, the first manmade Earth satellite, in October 1957 was a shock for the West. In 1961, ⑧ Yuri Gagarin, in his capsule Vostok I, became the first human in space.

In foreign affairs, Khrushchev fluctuated between competition with the US and the idea of "peaceful coexistence." He constantly tried to expand the Soviet Union's sphere of influence in the world. Khrushchev took advantage of the desire for independence of Asian and African countries. Following the 1956 Suez Crisis (p. 600), he also gave military and financial support to Arab countries engaged in the Middle East conflict.

10 Stalin lying in state alongside Lenin in Moscow, March 7, 1953. Eight years later his body was removed

12 Nikita S. Khrushchev and his government at a reception for Soviet artists and writers, painting, 1957

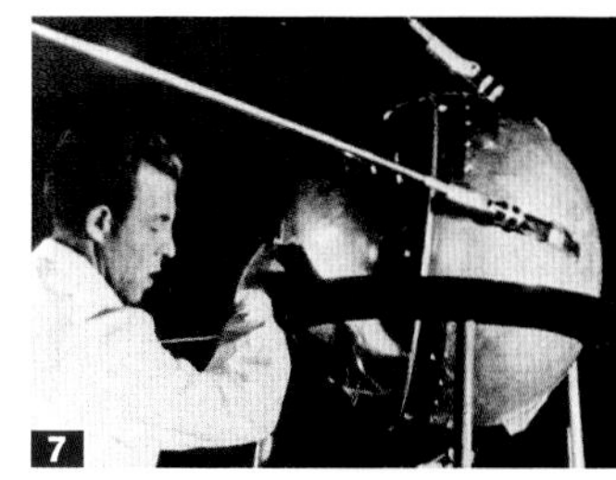

7 Technicians with *Sputnik 1*, the first man-made satellite to orbit Earth

8 Russian Cosmonaut Yuri Gagarin became the first human to orbit the Earth on April 12, 1961

Dmitry Dmitriyevich Shostakovich

The changing directions of Khrushchev's cultural policy are illustrated by the case of composer Dmitry Shostakovich. He composed many hymns glorifying Stalin and the Soviet Union in order to gain the freedom to do his own work. For a time he was a star of Soviet culture. In 1936, he was publicly denounced for the first time as being "decadent" and for "formalistic excesses." Later in 1948, he was forced to exercise "self-criticism" and ostracized. As first secretary of the Soviet Composers' Association, between 1960 and 1968, Shostakovich turned against "Western avant-gardism," again in line with party policies.

above: Dmitry Shostakovich

8 Aug 1953 | "New Course" under Malenkov
Mai 1955 | Warsaw Pact founded
1957 | "Sputnik" launched
1958 | Khrushchev becomes party secretary
14 Oct 1964 | Khrushchev deposed

Khrushchev's Downfall and the Brezhnev Era

After Khrushchev's demise in 1964, Brezhnev became the new Soviet leader; his power, however, was kept in check by other party members more than that of previous leaders. Gradually, a détente with the Western world took place in foreign policy.

In 1959 Khrushchev's foreign policy course began to lead to a growing ideological alienation from China. The stationing of nuclear missiles in Cuba brought the world to the verge of a third world war in October 1962, though escalation was avoided when the Soviet Union backed down. Khrushchev had increasingly been showing a tendency to sudden and often (for the party) unpredictable decisions and changes in course since 1961. This led to his overthrow on October 14, 1964, by the members of the Soviet presidium (Politburo).

The new strongman as general secretary of the Communist party was ❷ Leonid Brezhnev, in tandem with Premier Aleksey Kosygin as chairman of the Council of Ministers and President Nikolay Podgorny as chairman of the presidium. A one-man rule in the style of Khrushchev would not be tolerated in the future. The Brezhnev era is considered a time of "normalization" and "bureaucratization" of socialist everyday life. From the mid-1970s onward, the Soviet leadership increasingly became a ❶ political gerontocracy.

6 Worker in a factory producing locomotives in Tblisi, Georgia, 1967

1 The elderly Soviet leadership wave to the crowds during celebrations in Moscow on May 1, 1982; from left to right: Chernenko, N. Tichonow, Brezhnev, Grischin, and A. Kirilenko

The 23rd Communist party congress in 1966 cemented the dominance of ❻ heavy industry in the economy and the goal of ❺ arms parity with the United States. The immense expenditure for nuclear missiles and submarines in the 1970s resulted in, among other things, massive supply shortages for the population. The increasingly strong suppression of artists, intellectuals, and dissidents (Alexandr Solzhenitsyn and ❼ Andrey Sakharov, among others) was countered mostly with repressive measures by the state—deportation to work camps and the use of "political psychiatry."

5 Military procession taking part in celebrations marking the 50th anniversary of the Russian Revolution, Red Square, Moscow, November 7, 1967

After the Soviet leadership forcefully suppressed the "Prague Spring" (p. 578) in 1968, it greeted the ❸ policy of détente begun in 1970 by West German Chancellor Willy Brandt. From 1970 on, a series of agreements were negotiated between the Soviet Union and Western countries. These culminated in the ❹ Strategic Arms Limitation Talks (SALT I and II) in 1974 and 1979 with the United States and the 1975 Helsinki Accords on international security policy and arms control. The process of détente suffered repeated setbacks, however, including the NATO decision to counterarm in 1977, the Soviet invasion of Afghanistan in 1979, and the West's boycott of the ❽ Olympic Games in the city of-Moscow in 1980.

Some domestic reforms were successful, such as the improvement of public education and the establishment of greater political and cultural autonomy for the various nationalities that made up the Soviet republics. On the other hand, the burden of the arms race with the US increasingly undermined the performance of the economy, with resources concentrated on the military and heavy industry sectors at the expense of consumer goods. Corruption inevitably followed these supply shortages.

7 Soviet dissident and physicist Andrey Sakharov during an interview given in March 1973

2 Soviet Premier Leonid Brezhnev, who presided over détente, 1980

3 The policy of détente: The West German Chancellor Willy Brandt (right) and Brezhnev on a speedboat during a diplomatic visit to the Soviet Union, September 17, 1971

4 US President Jimmy Carter (left) and Leonid Brezhnev (right) sign the Strategic Arms Limitation Treaty II, 1979

8 Poster for the 22nd Olympic Summer Games held in Moscow between July 19 and August 2, 1980

1968 | "Prague Spring"
1974 | SALT I Agreement
1975 | Helsinki Accords
1977 | NATO decides to upgrade missile systems
1979 | SALT II Agreement and Soviet invasion of Afghanistan
1980 | Olympic Games in Moscow

Gorbachev and the End of the Soviet Union

In 1985, a radical change in direction took place with the election of Gorbachev as general secretary. His reforms led to the collapse of Soviet Communism between 1989 and 1991.

Following ❾ Brezhnev's death, first ⓫ Yuri Andropov in 1982 and then ⓭ Konstantin Chernenko in 1984 took turns to hold power. When Chernenko died on March 10, 1985, ❿ Mikhail Gorbachev was elected general secretary of the Soviet Communist party the next day. Step by step, together with Foreign Minister Eduard Shevardnadze and his younger leadership cadre, Gorbachev carried out comprehensive reforms. He renewed the disarmament talks with the United States in Geneva right away and withdrew the Soviet army from Afghanistan in 1987–1989.

11 Yuri Andropov holding an end-of-year speech, December 21, 1982

13 Interim leader: Konstantin Chernenko ruled the USSR for just over a year before his premature death

Domestically, the Soviet leadership began privatizing the economy in 1987 and legally established companies' independence in 1988. However, rapid inflation often impeded the economic reforms. Cultural and educational policies were liberalized with the slogans *glasnost* (openness) and *perestroika* (reconstruction), and Western cultural influences flooded the country. Gorbachev's reforms immediately radiated to the allied socialist states, where the people in the countries of Central and Eastern Europe forced the fall of the Berlin Wall (p. 544) in 1989 and the dissolution of the entire Eastern bloc. For his rejection of any form of violent course of action in this process, Gorbachev was awarded the Nobel Peace Prize in 1990.

10 Revolution from the top: Mikhail Gorbachev outlines his reform plans, involving *perestroika* (reconstruction) and *glasnost* (openness), to a Communist party conference, 1988

15 Meeting between Mikhail Gorbachev and US President Ronald Reagan, December 9, 1987

Gorbachev, however, came under increasing internal pressure. The traditional party cadre sabotaged his reform course, while his efforts did not go far enough to satisfy Western-oriented reformers. The catastrophic economic situation led to strikes, and the Soviet Union became increasingly dependent on extensive financial assistance from Western countries. To make matters worse, in April 1986 the worst nuclear power plant disaster to date occurred in Ukraine when the Chernobyl plant's ⓬ No. 4 reactor exploded.

In addition to these problems, separatist conflicts broke out. As early as 1986, unrest began in Kazakhstan. National reform movements and representatives of the people, particularly in the Baltic republics, sought to leave the Soviet Union in 1990. The same year, the first Russian ⓮ demonstrations against communist rule took place. On August 19, 1991, conservative hardliners attempted to execute a coup and isolated ⓯ Gorbachev, who was absent from Moscow.

14 Demanding freedom: more than 20,000 citizens demonstrate in Moscow on September 16, 1990

9 Brezhnev's funeral: leading representatives of the Soviet party and government carry his open coffin, November 15, 1982

12 Damaged reactor at the nuclear power plant in Chernobyl, 1986

Andrey Gromyko

For almost 30 years, from 1957 to 1985, Andrey Gromyko, an economist and long-standing ambassador to Washington and the United Nations, represented the interests of the Soviet Union on the world stage. The grim-mannered foreign minister became known as "Mr. Nyet" in the West. He was central to negotiations with the US over disarmament and nonaggression agreements, becoming a member of the ruling Politburo in 1973. In July 1985, Gorbachev sidelined him by making him chairman of the state council.

above: Soviet foreign minister Andrey Gromyko in 1985

Mar. 11, 1985 | Gorbachev becomes general secretary of the USSR
1986 | Nuclear disaster in Chernobyl
1987–89 | Soviet army withdraws from Afghanistan
1989 | Fall of the Berlin Wall
1990 | Gorbachev awarded Nobel Peace Prize

Russia under Yeltsin

In 1991, the Soviet empire broke down into a federation of former Soviet Socialist Republics. Sweeping reforms were carried out under Yeltsin, but the war in Chechnya also began.

Boris Yeltsin (right) humiliates Gorbachev in the Russian Duma, August 23, 1991

The Moscow coup on August 19, 1991, failed due to the resistance of the people and uncertainty in the army. When Mikhail Gorbachev returned, he found he had been ❶ deprived of virtually all power. The new leader as president of ❹ Russia was Gorbachev's former rival, Moscow mayor ❷ Boris Yeltsin. In September,

The most powerful man in Russia from 1991 on: Boris Yeltsin, 1990

Soldiers of a Russian honor guard, June 12, 1999, during a parade for the Independence Day

Yeltsin recognized the independence of the Baltic States, and in November he disbanded the Communist party of the Soviet Union. The USSR was officially dissolved on December 21, 1991, when eleven former Soviet republics—Armenia, Azerbaijan, Belarus, Georgia, Kazakhstan, Kyrgyzstan, Moldova, Tajikistan, Turkmenistan, Ukraine, and Uzbekistan—withdrew and, together with Russia, formed the Commonwealth of Independent States (CIS).

In the next few years, President Yeltsin leaned heavily on the support of the West, particularly for economic assistance. He also advanced the disarmament process. Yeltsin imposed a new constitution on the parliament in 1993, strengthening the presidency and thwarting an attempted coup by conservatives. Russia joined NATO's Partnership for Peace program in June 1994 and signed a security agreement with NATO in May 1997.

❺ Russian troops invaded Chechnya in 1994 following separatist moves, and the heavy handed military campaign proved unpopular with the Russian people. A second Chechen war began in 1999 in the wake of assassinations and bomb attacks by Chechen rebels. The Russian military offensive soon became bogged down in a brutal occupation which attracted criticism from the international community.

Following a rapid devaluation of the ruble, the Russian government was forced to default on its foreign debts in 1998. Many Russians lost their savings as inflation

Russian soldiers patrolling the region around the Chechen capital of Grozny, where Chechen rebels continued their attacks, July 1986

soared and Yeltsin became increasingly unpopular. Beset by health problems, he stepped down in favor of the former chairman of the security services, Vladimir Putin, at the end of 1999.

❸ Putin soon established himself as a popular and strong

Vladimir Putin, June 7, 2000

leader, announcing his intention to reduce corruption. However, critics inside and outside Russia have been alarmed by his curtailment of press and media freedom and his increasingly authoritarian leadership style. Putin has sought to restore Russia's international standing. After September 11, 2001, he offered support to the United States, particularly in the global fight against terrorism, and in 2002, Russia signed the Kyoto protocol on climate change. During the invasion of Iraq in 2003 he aligned himself with France and Germany to oppose the attack. After the head of Yukos, oligarch Mikhail Khodorkovsky, was arrested on tax evasion charges in 2003, Putin was reelected president with 71 percent of the vote in March 2004.

The Chechnya Conflict

The violent conflict began in December 1994 with the occupation of Chechnya by Russian troops in response to the kidnapping of a Russian soldier by separatist a militia. After seizing the capital, Grozny, President Yeltsin declared the war officially over in May 1997. The elected president of Chechnya, Aslan Maskhadov, was not recognized by Russia and went underground. A Second Chechnya War began in 1999 after a series of terrorist attacks against Russian targets by separatists. He was shot dead by Russian troops in Chechnya in 2005.

Chechen woman in front of destroyed houses in the capital Grozny, December 30, 1994

Chechen sniper watching the area in front of the presidential palace in Grozny, January 10, 1995

21 Dec 1991 | Formation of CIS
1994 | Kuchma's presidency in Ukraine
Dec 1994 | Russian occupation of Chechnya
19 Aug 1991 | Moscow coup, Yeltsin's Presidency
1993 | New constitution
Jun 1994 | Russia joins NATO's "Partnership for Peace"

Ukraine, Belarus, and Moldova

While Ukraine and Moldova have developed functioning democratic systems, the political regime in Belarus (formerly Byelorussia) remains authoritarian.

Since the middle of World War II, Ukraine had been making efforts toward autonomy. The Ukrainian Insurgent Army waged bloody battles against Soviet authorities until 1954. With the breakup of the USSR in December 1991, Ukraine became a member of the CIS, and a majority of the Ukrainians voted for continued close cooperation with Russia. ❻ Leonid Kuchma, who ruled with a firm hand as president from 1994 to 2004, began to open up the country to a market economy. Politically he leaned decidedly toward Russia. Irregularities in the elections for Kuchma's successor in 2004 led to peaceful, long-running popular ❿ protests—the "Orange Revolution," resulting in a runoff election in January 2005. The election was won by reformist politician and former prime minister ❼ Viktor Yushchenko, who declared his intention to bring Ukraine closer to the West.

6 President Leonid Kuchma (left) at a meeting with prominent regional political figures, November 29, 2004

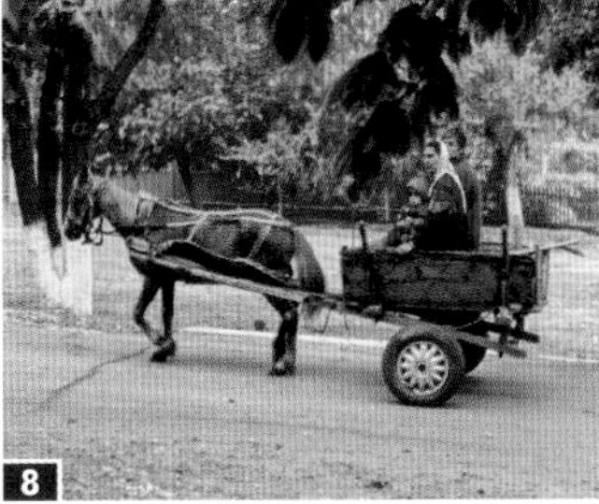

8 Moldovans on a horse-drawn buggy

Byelorussia, which declared its sovereignty as the Republic of Belarus in July 1990 and has been a member of the ⓫ CIS since 1991, has also been politically close to Russia. ❾ Alexander Lukashenko has been president since 1994. Originally seen as a market economy reformer, he increased his authority through a referendum in 1996 and since then has ruled as "Europe's last dictator." The press and opposition have been massively intimidated and political opposition suppressed. At the end of his term of office in 1999, Lukashenko simply refused to step down. Through widespread political manipulation, he was reelected in 2001, supposedly with 76 percent of the vote.

In Moldova, a member of the CIS since 1991, former Communist party members have been governing since 1994 in various alliances. There are tensions between the ethnic Moldovans, Russians, and Gagauz over the Dnestr region (Transnistria), which claims autonomy. The country is also struggling with economic problems, and approximately 80 percent of the population lives below the ❽ poverty line.

7 Viktor Yushchenko, November 22, 2004, elected president after a revote in Ukraine's 2004 election

9 Aleksandr Lukashenko, "Europe's last dictator," March 28, 1997

10 Supporters of Viktor Yushchenko demonstrating on the streets of Kiev during the "Orange Revolution," October 23, 2004

11 Lukashenko (Belarus), Nasarbajew (Kazakhstan), Putin (Russia), and Kuchma (Ukraine) during a CIS debate about a common free trade area

1996 | Lukashenko's dictatorship in Belarus

May 1997 | Security agreement with NATO

1999 | Second Chechen Conflict begins

2000 | Yeltsin resigns, Vladimir Putin takes office

March 2004 | Putin re-elected President of Russia

The Baltic States and the Caucasus

Since gaining independence the Baltic States turned toward the West, establishing democratic structures and joining the European Union. Since 2003 Georgia has moved toward democracy.

Strong independence movements emerged in the Baltic States as early as 1987, recalling the countries' traditions of independence after 1918. In 1990, Lithuania and Latvia were the first Soviet republics to declare their ❷, ❸ independence; violent coup attempts in both states by Moscow loyalists were averted. In all three Baltic Soviet republics, the people voted for independence in referendums, and independence became a reality for them in the wake of the coup attempt against Gorbachev in August 1991 (p. 589).

The Baltic nations' transition to stable democratic conditions after the Western model was made easier through membership in the United Nations (1991) and the Council of Europe (1993–1995), as well as economic assistance and cooperation treaties with the West. The ❶ withdrawal of Soviet troops and border treaties with neighboring countries were completed by 1994. Latvia was the first Baltic country to apply for ❹ membership in the European Union, on October 27, 1995, and ❽ Estonia and Lithuania soon followed. After strengthening their economies and parliamentary systems, the three were among the ten new EU members on May 1, 2004.

1 Soviet troops withdrawing from Lithuania, March 3, 1992

4 Young Lithuanians celebrating their country's accession to the European Union at a concert on the Cathedral Square in Vilnius, April 30, 2004

5 Soviet forces on the border between Armenia and Azerbaijan, January 22, 1990

2 Demonstrators wave the Lithuanian flag in front of the parliament building in Vilnius, January 9, 1991

3 A young man waving the Latvian flag during a demonstration demanding independence from the Soviet Union, Riga, January 14, 1991

In the Caucasus, bloody fighting began as early as 1989 over the ❺ Nagorno-Karabakh region, whose predominantly Armenian population declared its independence from Azerbaijan in 1991. In 1993 Armenia invaded Azerbaijan in support of the enclave; the two CIS members finally agreed to a cease-fire the next year. In Azerbaijan, the former Communists, led by Heydar Aliyev, returned to power in 1993. Nagorno-Karabakh elected its own president in 1997, although he is not recognized by the Azerbaijani government and the situation remains tense. Armenia and Azerbaijan both became members of the Council of Europe in January 2001.

Ethnic tensions also rose to the surface in Georgia during 1989, when Georgians and South Ossetians clashed; the same year, Soviet troops crushed pro-independence demonstrations in Tblisi. The national opposition, led by ❼ Zviad Gamsakhurdia, won the first multiparty elections in 1990 and declared Georgia independent in 1991. President Gamsakhurdia was deposed in January 1992 after heavy fighting and the former Soviet foreign minister, ❻ Eduard Shevardnadze, was elected as his successor. Shevardnadze stabilized the economy with the earnings from oil exports and contracts with the West, but he also consolidated his own personal power through a presidential constitution. His regime was characterized by repression and corruption. The peaceful demonstrations of the people following manipulated parliamentary elections on November 22, 2003, forced Shevardnadze to resign. New elections held in January 2004 were won by the main opposition candidate and leader of the United National Movement, Mikhail Saakashvili, who then became president.

6 Eduard Shevardnadze, president of Georgia, addressing the national parliament, April 30, 2000

7 Zviad Gamsakhurdia, the first post-Soviet Georgian president

8 Tourists in the old town of Tallinn, capital of Estonia, 2001

1989 | War over Nagorno-Karabakh between Armenia and Azerbaijan
1990 | Presidency of Niyasov in Turkmenistan
1991 | Tajikistan becomes independent
1991 | Independence of Lithuania and Latvia / Both countries join the UN
1992 | Presidency of Shevardnadze in Georgia

The Central Asian States

The former Soviet republics of Central Asia formed authoritarian presidential regimes that combined modest economic reform with old political elites.

Like their Caucasus counterparts, the former Soviet republics of Central Asia experienced political turbulence after independence. They all share a resurgent and often politicized Islamic base, whose radical adherents gained access to weapons and propaganda material through the uncontrolled borders of Afghanistan. The regimes of these states exercised a virtual monopoly over political life in the state .

9 Saparmurad Niyasov, president of the Central Asian Republic of Turkmenistan, 1997

10 Islam Karimov, the authoritarian president of Uzbekistan since 1990

12 Emomali Rahmonov, the Tajik president, 1993

In Turkmenistan, Communist party head ❾ Saparmurat Niyasov was elected president and head of government in 1990 by the Communist Assembly, and he increased his authority with a new constitution in 1992. That year, he was re-elected to the presidency unopposed. In 1999, Niyasov appointed himself president for life.

Tajikistan became independent in 1991, and ⓬ Emomali Rahmonov assumed power as head of state a year later. He declared war on Islamists and called on CIS troops to help against armed rebels in 1993–1994. After Afghan-supported rebels gained control of a part of the country in 1996, Rahmonov concluded peace talks with them and even allowed them to participate in the government in 1998. A strong personality cult supports the power of the president of Kazakhstan, an ⓫ independent state since 1990, and observers were unsurprised by his manipulated re-election in 1999 with 97 percent of the vote.

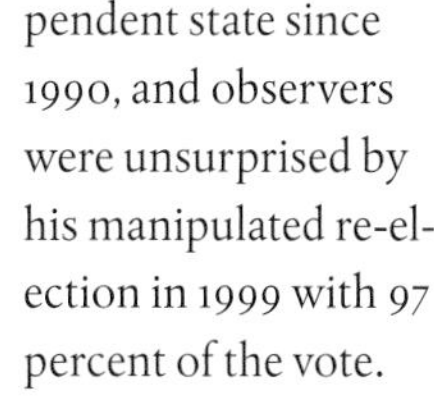

Similarly improbable election victories and autocratic tendencies have characterized the regimes of the other Central Asian states. Nursultan Nazarbayev, Kazakhstan's president since 1990, keeps his country relatively stable through economic ties with the West, cordial political relations with Russia and China, and the exploitation of the country's ⓯ oil and mineral reserves. In 2000, he assumed some lifelong powers. President ❿ Islam Karimov has held power in Uzbekistan since 1990, ruling over the ⓮ predominantly Muslim population with an iron hand. Uzbekistan provided bases for the American-led coalition during the invasion of Afghanistan in 2001. Kyrgyzstan, the smallest of the republics with perhaps 5 million citizens, was run by President ⓭ Askar Akayev from 1990 to 2005 and encouraged the development of a market economy. In 1998 Kyrgyzstan became the first former Soviet republic to join the World Trade Organization (WTO). After heavy fighting between government troops and Islamist rebels in 1999, Akayev began a severe crackdown against dissidents. In March 2005 he was forced to flee the country amid violent anti-government protests. Opposition leader Kurmanbek Bakiyev then became acting president ahead of fresh elections due in July.

11 Memorial erected to mark the country's independence from the USSR in the Kazakh capital Astana, 2004

13 Askar Akayev, president of the Central Asian Republic of Kyrgyzstan

14 Uzbek Muslims praying in a mosque in the capital city Tashkent, 2001

15 Oil production in Kazakhstan: drilling platform in the Caspian Sea, 2005

27 Oct 1995 | Latvia applies for membership in EU
22 Nov 2003 | Shevardnadze resigns
1993 | Lithuania and Latvia join European Council
2001 | Azerbaijan and Armenia become members of the European Council
1 May 2004 | Baltic States join EU

NORTHWEST AFRICA SINCE 1945

Between 1956 and 1962, the Maghreb freed itself of its political ties to France, but not always peacefully; the war of liberation in Algeria was prolonged and bloody. Although Morocco, Tunisia, and Algeria all have somewhat authoritarian regimes today, they have frequently assumed a mediating role between Europe and Africa or the Islamic world and have made progress in economic modernization. Attempts to modernize along the lines of Western industrial society have often been accompanied by efforts to keep ❶ Islamist groups out of political power.

Fighting against Islamic fundamentalists: An Algerian soldier guards the village Ben Achour, July 23, 1997

Morocco and Tunisia

After winning independence in 1956–1957, both countries achieved political stability only at the cost of entrenching authoritarian regimes.

Morocco's fight for ❸ independence was fought by the Istiqlal (Independence) party. When Sultan ❹ Muhammad V endorsed its demands in 1953, the French exiled him. Subsequent protests accelerated decolonization, which was completed on March 2, 1956. Muhammad V became king and reigned with the support of the nationalists. In 1956, Morocco regained Tangier, which had been internationalized, and raised claims to the Western Sahara.

Women in Tangiers, Morocco, September 16, 2004

In 1961 Muhammad died and was succeeded by his son, Hassan II, who faced criticism from the left-wing opposition and the Istiqlal party. He took repressive action against his opponents and in 1965 imposed martial law. An attempted coup by military units in August 1972 resulted in a fresh crackdown. In 1976, the king annexed a section of the Spanish Sahara with the civilian "Green March," later occupying the area militarily. King Hassan eased domestic restrictions after 1977 and carried out cautious modernization. He was highly regarded in Africa and the Arab world as a mediator. His son, ❺ Muhammad VI, has introduced reforms since taking the throne in 1999, pardoning thousands of political prisoners. Efforts have also been made to improve the ❷ legal position of women, while respecting the sentiments of Moroccan Islam.

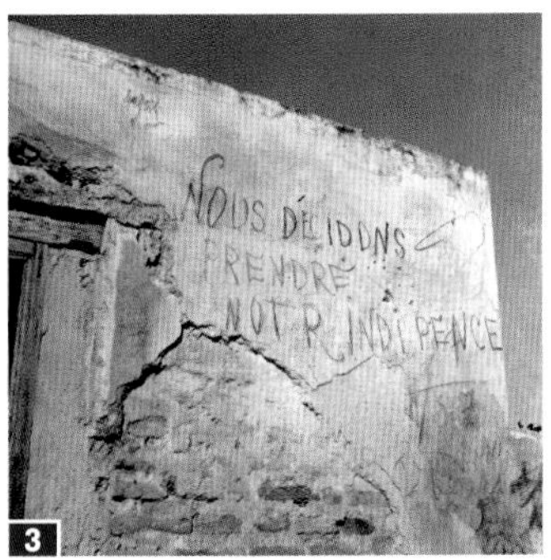

Grafitti demanding independence for the French protectorate, ca. 1944

In Tunisia, the Neo Destour Party under ❻ Habib Bourguiba led the nationalists in the fight for independence. Following the granting of autonomy from France in 1954, Tunisia became an independent republic on July 25, 1957. President Bourguiba pursued his own "path to socialism," introduced improvements in social and medical care, and sought to bring about the secularization of society. He worked for closer ties to the West and opened up Tunisia to ❼ tourism, although he took tough measures against dissidents. He was forced into retirement in November 1987 by his successor, Zine el Abidine Ben Ali, who remains in office today. After initially lifting restrictions on press freedoms, Ben Ali's rule has been characterized by fraudulent election victories and the repression of dissenters, notably from Islamic political groups.

Muhammad V during a radio broadcast, November 14, 1955

The progressive king Muhammad VI, June 20, 2000

Habib Bourguiba at his residence in Tunis, July 1957

Tamerza, a village in one of Tunisia's oases

Nov 1954 | Formation of FLN in Algeria – Beginning of the Algerian War

2 Mar 1956 | Morocco becomes independent

25 Jul 1957 | Tunisia granted independence

from 1961 | King Hassan II rulesi n Morocco

Algeria

Following the violent war of independence that lasted until 1962, the country only briefly found peace. A new civil war between government forces and Islamic militia raged from 1991 to 1999.

The war of independence in the ❾ French colony of Algeria was waged with increasing brutality by both sides. The various armed liberation movements joined together as the National Liberation Front (FLN) headed by Ahmed Ben Bellah in November 1954, and the ❽ Algerian War began. As the violence escalated, the guerrilla warfare of the independence fighters was met by military repression from the French that further alienated the Algerian people. When the French government finally declared itself ready to make concessions to Algeria, the Fourth Republic in France was toppled by an alliance between French Algerians and the French army in May 1958. General de Gaulle used his prestige to resolve the crisis, preserving French democracy and preparing the way for the French withdrawal from Algeria.

On March 18, 1962, Algeria was granted independence. ❿ Ahmed Ben Bellah became the country's new leader and let himself be elected president in September. In October, Algeria was accepted as member of the United Nations and Bellah signalized Algeria's future neutrality concerning international affairs. His one-sided domestic politics, though, caused an ⓫ exodus of Europeans, leaving the country without an economic and technical elite. In June 1965, Ben Bellah was ousted by his defense minister, ⓭ Houari Boumedienne. He introduced a new socialist agenda, nationalizing French rural estates, industry, and oil companies, while relying on the military to prop up his rule. Extensive industrial projects were initiated, primarily with Soviet aid, and an "agrarian revolution" was carried out by distributing land to poor farmers. General Chadli Ben Dschedid became president after Boumedienne's death in 1979. The radical Islamic Salvation Front (FIS) was established at the same time.

In the December 1991 parliamentary elections, the FIS won the first round and looked certain to achieve an overall majority, but the military—with tacit international approval—intervened to prevent the FIS from taking power. Military repression and a state of emergency led to revolts and assassination attempts by Islamists. In June 1992 President Muhammad Boudiaf was the victim of such an attempt as the country plunged into a ⓬ civil war that killed ca. 95,000 people.

9 Charles de Gaulle after being elected French Prime Minister in June 1958, in Algeria

11 Deifen-Bacher, the prefect of Tlemcen, asks the population to stay

Algeria Today

Peace did not return until Abdelaziz Bouteflika, president since 1999, began to pursue "national reconciliation." Though this policy has met with some success, relations between Islamist groups and the government remain tense, and sporadic violence continues. In September 2003, the army killed 150 Islamist fighters in the mountains east of Algiers, and in June 2004 security forces murdered Nabil Sahraoui, leader of the Salafist group. His second-in-command, Amari Saifi, who was captured in 2004, is presumed to be responsible for the 2003 kidnapping of 32 European tourists in the Sahara.

above: President Abdelaziz Bouteflika with his followers during an electoral campaign, April 10, 1999

8 French soldier guards the University of Algiers during the Algerian war, February 28, 1962

10 The first Minister president of Algeria, Ahmed Ben Bellah (left), and his later adversary Houari Boumedienne (right), September 10, 1962

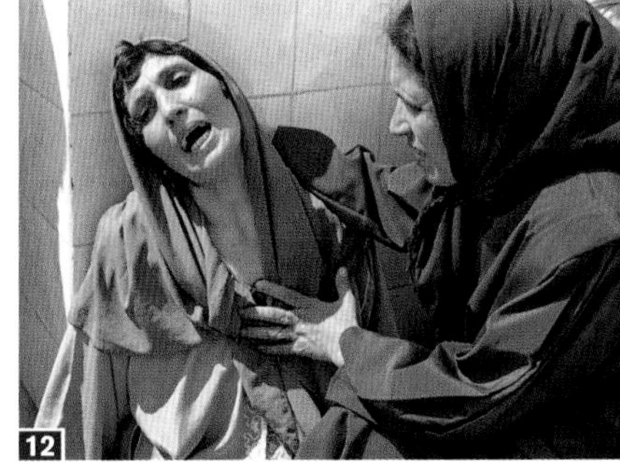

12 September 23, 1997: A woman cries for the victims of a massacre by Islamic fundamentalists, who, according to the official version, killed about 85 people in Bentalha on September 22, near Algiers

13 Houari Boumedienne (third from right), the former defense minister and eader of Algeria, gives a press conference on July 22, 1965 with members of his new government and participants in the coup against Ben Bellah

18 Mar 1962 | Algeria becomes independent

1976 | "Green March"

1987 | Ben Ali's comes to power in Tunisia

1992–99 | Civil war in Algeria

1999 | King Muhammad VI crowned in Morocco

Israel since 1948

The State of Israel's fight for ❶ existence determines its policies and identity to this day. Between the wars, and especially after 1945, many Jews settled in Palestine and cultivated and developed the country with determination and idealism. However, from the beginning, no satisfactory political solution could be found for the consequent expulsion of the Palestinians who were already living in the area. Relations with Israel's Soviet-backed Arab neighbors have long been strained to breaking point. The US-Israeli alliance has become central to both countries' foreign policies, helping to ensure Israeli supremacy in the Middle East. After a series of military defeats, most Arab countries eventually reached an accommodation with Israel, leaving the Palestinians isolated in their struggle for a state of their own.

1 Behind barbed wire: An Israeli flag flutters over a kibbutz, 1988

Israel before the Six-Day War of 1967

In 1948 Zionists fought against the British colonial authorities, Palestinian inhabitants and the neighboring Arab states to create a Jewish state. With US help it succeeded economically, militarily, and politically. Its military power brought security but not peace to the Palestinians.

The state of Israel was born in conflict. In 1939, in order to avert tensions with the Palestinians, the British mandate authorities reduced the immigration quota of Jews to Palestine to 75,000 people. Beginning in 1945, however, after the Holocaust in Europe, thousands of Jews ❷ poured into the country—most illegally, but supported by Jewish refugee organizations. They lived in communes and kibbutzim and were determined to fight for their survival. Until 1948 the British tried numerous repressive measures to stem the flow, to which the Jewish underground organizations responded with violent attacks.

❸ David Ben-Gurion, the leader of the Workers' party (Mapai), proclaimed the ❹ independent state of Israel on May 14, 1948. In 1949 the Knesset met for the first time as a single-chamber parliament and began by electing Chaim Weizmann as president and Ben-Gurion as prime minister. By 1954 the number of immigrating Jews had doubled to 576,000; they seized 750,000 acres of Arab lands, which they rapidly ❺ developed. The conflict with the Palestinians remained unresolved, and Jerusalem became a city divided between Israelis and Arabs. By 1948, 500,000 Palestinians had fled to neighboring countries, especially Jordan; a further 300,000 followed in the next few years.

With extensive financial assistance from the United States, Israel experienced rapid economic growth and established a modern and powerful military defense. Israel triumphed in the Arab-Israeli War of May–November 1948 and occupied ❼ Gaza and the Sinai Peninsula along with Britain and France in October 1956. During the Six-Day War (June 5–10, 1967), Israel crushed a coalition of Arab states led by Egypt, in the process occupying Syria's ❻ Golan Heights, East Jerusalem, and portions of the Palestinian territories.

3 First Prime Minister of Israel David Ben-Gurion, 1950

5 Tractor on a kibbutz, a collective farm community in Israeli,1962

6 The Golan Heights, occupied by Israel since 1967

2 Groups of Jewish immigrants make illegal night landings on the coast of Palestine, seeking to evade British patrols, December 1947

4 Leader of Zionist insurgency and first Israeli Prime Minister David Ben-Gurion proclaims the independence of the state of Israel in Tel Aviv, May 14, 1948

7 Mobilization for the occupation of Gaza and Sinai in Tel Aviv, October 1956

14 May 1948 | Proclamation of the state of Israel
1949 | Weizmann elected president
Oct–Nov 1956 | The Suez-Sinai War
5–10 Jun 1967 | Six-Day War
1972 | Israeli invasion of Lebanon

Israel from 1967 to the Present

The peace agreements with Egypt and Jordan were milestones in Israeli foreign policy. In the handling of the Palestinians's demands, numerous attempts at mediation have been undertaken, but the process remains contentious.

In 1972 under Prime Minister ❾ Golda Meir, Israeli troops occupied southern Lebanon, from which Palestinian guerrillas were conducting attacks into northern Israel. The Israelis were also able to repel Egypt and Syria's surprise attack in the Yom Kippur War of October 6–26, 1973. Since the Geneva Middle East Peace Conference in December 1973 and through the mediation of the United Nations, the United States, and other nations, gradual settlements have been cautiously reached with Egypt and later with Jordan, and temporarily also with Syria. The terror attacks and ⓫ militancy of the Palestine Liberation Organization (PLO) and other Palestinian groups nevertheless remained an urgent problem and led to various ⓭ diplomatic initiatives.

In 1974 Israel stood at the point of a serious financial and economic crisis. At the same time, a rift opened within the leading Israeli parties concerning understanding and agreement with the Palestinians. In 1979 peace with Egypt was reached only by strenuous effort. The office of prime minister changed hands between hard-liners and moderates who sought a permanent accord with the Palestinians. The voices of ⓬ strict Orthodox Jews and of radical settler groups grew ever louder.

Growing US pressure and secret confidence-building talks led to Israel's acceptance of the PLO as a negotiating partner in the Camp David peace talks in 1992–1993. The peace process suffered its first serious setback when Israeli prime minister Yitzhak Rabin was murdered by a Jewish fundamentalist on November 4, 1995. Despite the hard-right Benjamin Netanyahu winning the elections, Palestinian self-government began in some communities in 1997. In 2000 Ehud Barak's Labor government seemed poised to offer more concessions to the Palestinians than any previous Israeli leader—including a Palestinian state—but could not clinch a deal. After the 2001 launch of the Intifada and suicide bombings, Prime Minister ❿ Ariel Sharon answered with military retaliatory strikes and assassination attempts on militant leaders. In 2002 he began the construction of a controversial ❽ barrier, while responding to Palestinian democratization reform by announcing an Israeli pull-out from Gaza.

9 Golda Meir, Israeli Prime Minister between1969 and 1974

10 Prime Minister Ariel Sharon at a press conference, 2004

8 Israeli workers constructing the security fence unilaterally announced by Israel in 2004; Kalkilia, West Bank, November 17, 2004

11 An armed militant from the radical group Hamas guards a Palestinian refugee camp in the Israeli-occupied Gaza Strip, October 1, 2004

12 An Orthodox Jew in traditional dress praying before the Wailing Wall in Jerusalem, 1992

13 Careful advances: PLO chief Arafat talks with the Israeli Prime Minister Yitzhak Rabin during a meeting in Madrid, 1994

Yitzhak Rabin

A long-serving Israeli army chief of staff and leading strategist of the victory in 1973, Yitzhak Rabin changed his hard-line politics to a policy of understanding. As prime minister in 1992 he forbade the building of further Jewish settlements in the occupied Palestinian zones and initiated talks with the PLO. On September 13, 1993, a historic handshake took place between Rabin and PLO Chairman Yasir Arafat in the presence of US President Bill Clinton, for which the two leaders received the Nobel Peace Prize. On November 4, 1995 he was assassinated in Tel Aviv by a Jewish right-wing fanatic.

above: Yitzhak Rabin

6–26 Oct 1973 | Yom Kippur War
Dec 1973 | Geneva Middle East Peace Conference
1979 | Peace accord with Egypt
4 Nov 1995 | Murder of Yitzhak Rabin
2001 | Ariel Sharon becomes prime minister

The Arab World and the Near East

SINCE 1945

After gaining independence from European colonial rule the Arab states looked to the USSR and Pan-Arabism as alternative paths to nation-building. However, ❶ authoritarian rulers soon established themselves in the region. Since the 1970s a growing educated population lacking employment opportunities has begun to undermine many regimes, and this frustration has been exploited by politically radicalized Islamic groups. Ironically, the only freely elected Arab government in the region is that of the Palestinians, who do not have their own state.

Jordan's King Abdullah II followed by his honorary guard

Palestine and Jordan up to "Black September," 1970

In 1948 thousands of Palestinians fled the Arab-Israeli fighting that accompanied the founding of Israel. The arrival of the refugees destabilized Jordan until King Hussein II reasserted control.

The "Palestinian problem" is intimately tied to the history of Israel (p. 596-597). The UN decision on November 29, 1947, to divide Palestine into Jewish and Arab states failed. Following the founding of Israel, Palestinians fled en masse into the West Bank and Jordan, and their land was expropriated by Israel. Jordan, which was structurally weak with a small population and which had only become an independent kingdom in May 1946, struggled to cope with the waves of refugees. In 1950 it annexed part of the West Bank territory (now West Jordan). Clashes broke out between Palestinian guerrillas and Jordanian forces. While the grand mufti of Jerusalem, ❸ Amin al-Husayni, the political leader of the Palestinians, called for a war of annihilation against Israel, ❷ King Abdullah I of Jordan sought rapprochement with the Jewish state. He was assassinated by a Palestinian gunman on July 20, 1951, in al-Aqsa Mosque in East Jerusalem.

The increasingly radicalized Palestinians sought help from the rest of the Arab world and in the

Amin al-Husayni, the grand mufti of Jerusalem, 1941

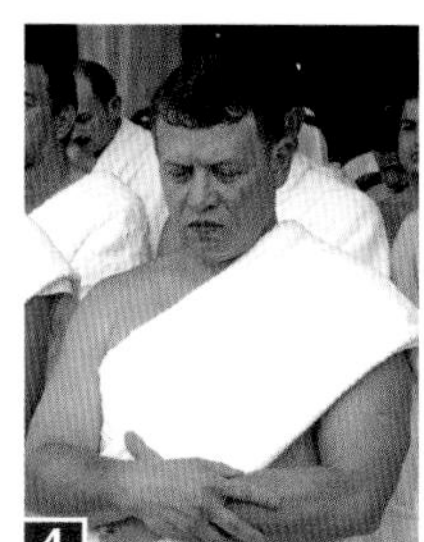

King Abdullah II of Jordan during his pilgrimage to Mecca, November 2004

King Hussein II of Jordan during his service as an air force pilot, 1955

The main street, named after King Talal, in the center of the Jordanian capital of Amman

1950s looked to Egyptian president Nasser above all. In the name of Arab solidarity, other countries in the region also became involved and armed Palestinian fighters. There were raids and skirmishes with Israel. Abdullah's grandson ❺ Hussein II had been ruling in Jordan since August 1952. In 1957, Great Britain withdrew its last soldiers from the country. Under pressure from the Palestinians, Hussein allied himself with Nasser while still maintaining contacts with the West. He survived several assassination attempts and attempted coups. His son, ❹ Abdullah II, succeeded him to the Jordanian throne in 1999.

During the 1967 Arab-Israel war, Israeli forces occupied all of Jerusalem and the West

King Abdullah I (left) of Jordan, broke with the Palestinians after 1970

Bank, leading to a new influx of Palestinians into Jordan. Following the Arab defeat, ❼ Yasir Arafat, the head of the Palestine Liberation Organization (PLO), began organizing guerrilla attacks against Israel, operating out of Jordan. The Palestinian group threatened to take control of the capital ❻ Amman until in 1970, after protracted and heavy fighting, King Hussein militarily broke the PLO's power during "Black September."

PLO leader Yasir Arafat, 1978

1947	Division of Palestine
1948	Palestine War
20 Jul 1951	Murder of King Abdullah I
1964	PLO founded
1969	Yasir Arafat becomes PLO leader
Sep 1970	"Black September"
1977	Carter initiative
1987	Start of the first Intifada

On the Path to a Palestinian State

After speaking at the United Nations, PLO leader Arafat began to gain international recognition for Palestinian claims to an independent state. Attempts at direct Palestinian–Israeli negotiations began in 1993 with the Oslo Peace Process but have yet to yield a comprehensive settlement.

In 1971 a general reconciliation took place between Jordan and the Palestinians, as well as between Jordan and its neighbors Egypt and Syria, both of which had sided with the Palestinians in 1970. From 1972 the Palestinian leadership began a series of spectacular attacks and ⓭ airplane hijackings, such as the 1977 Lufthansa seizure, with the aim of drawing international attention to their cause. After the Arab defeat in the Yom Kippur War of 1973 and Egypt's reconciliation with Israel, the Palestinians increasingly sought support from other Arab countries—especially Syria, Libya, and Iraq—while the PLO brought its goal of founding a Palestinian state before the United Nations. The United States shielded Israel from much of the pressure but also sought to mediate, notably with the 1977 "Carter Initiative." Arafat and the PLO leadership revised their thinking and increasingly sought to negotiate. However, this process suffered a major setback in 1982 when, following the occupation of West Beirut, Israel's ally, the Christian Falangist militia, carried out a massacre in the Palestinian refugee camps of Sabra and Shatila.

The Palestinian ⓾ Intifada (national uprising) began in ❽ Gaza and the West Bank in 1987. Initially peaceful, it soon deteriorated into violent street clashes between stone-throwing civilians and Israeli troops. After recognizing Israel's right to exist in 1988, Arafat stepped up his demands for an autonomous Palestinian state. The Oslo Accords, signed in 1994, set out a framework for a negotiated peace. The following year, the Palestinian Authority was set up to administer the Gaza Strip and parts of the West Bank, and in 1997 ❾ Hebron was returned to the ⓬ Palestinians. But this process was increasingly undermined by continued violence, marginalizing moderates on both sides. In 1995 Israeli prime minister Yitzhak Rabin was assassinated by a right-wing Israeli extremist. Conflict returned in 1996 when suicide bombings by the terrorist group Hamas were met with an Israeli bombardment of southern Lebanon. A second Intifada began in 2000, and after a wave of bombings, the Israeli army reoccupied the Palestinian autonomous territories in April 2001 and then besieged Arafat's headquarters. In April 2003, the United States proposed a "roadmap to peace" that envisaged a Palestinian state. President Arafat ⓫ died in November 2004, and many saw the election of his successor, the moderate Mahmoud Abbas, as an opportunity to break the deadlock.

10 Intifada: Israeli policemen fire tear gas at Palestinian youths during the first Intifada, Eastern Jerusalem, December 21, 1987

11 Palestinian mourners at Arafat's funeral in Ramallah, November 13, 2004

13 Lufthansa flight hijacked by Palestinian militants on October 13, 1977 during a forced landing in Mogadishu, Somalia

8 Israeli military checkpoint in the southern part of the Gaza Strip

9 Rooftops in the Palestinian city of Hebron, occupied by Israel until 1997

12 After signing the Hebron agreement Israeli President Benjamin Netanjahu and Yasir Arafat shake hands, 1997

Excerpt from the PLO Founding Charter of 1964

"The Palestine Liberation Organization, representative of the Palestinian revolutionary forces, is responsible for the Palestinian Arab people's movement in its struggle—to retrieve its homeland, liberate and return to it and exercise the right to self-determination in it—in all military, political, and financial fields..." (Article 26)

Arafat supporters mourn his death, November 6, 2004

1994 Oslo Accords | **1995** Autonomous authority set up | **1997** Hebron handed over to Palestinians | **2000** Start of second Intifada | **Mar–May 2002** Siege of Arafat's headquarters | **Apr 2003** US announces "Roadmap" | **Nov 2004** Arafat dies

Egypt under Nasser and Sadat, Libya under Qaddafi

Under Nasser, Egypt achieved a position of supremacy in the Arab world. His successor Sadat ended the anti-Israel course, while Libya under Qaddafi continued the path of "Nasserism."

In Egypt, the corrupt regime of King Farouk I, though supported by the British, was toppled on July 23, 1952, by a group known as the "Free Officers Movement," which proclaimed a republic on July 18, 1953. In 1954 ❸ Gamal Abdel Nasser became premier of the republic; two years later he assumed the office of president as well, being the only candidate in presidential elections. Nasser suppressed the Communists and the Muslim Brotherhood and proclaimed a path to modernize the country based on socialism and nationalism. He established himself as the voice of Pan-Arabism (p. 224) and in 1955, along with Indian prime minister Nehru and others, became a leader of the Nonaligned Movement opposing the dominance of the superpowers.

1 Anwar el-Sadat, Egyptian head of state from 1970 to 1981

2 Distributor on a pipeline on the oil field As Sarah in Libya

By nationalizing the Suez Canal in July 1956, Nasser provoked the international Suez Crisis that came to a head in October. Despite Egypt's military ❺ defeat by Israel, Great Britain, and France, Nasser generally managed to maintain his political credibility while building up great prestige in the Third World. In 1958, as an experiment in Pan-Arabism, Syria and Egypt merged as the ❻ United Arab Republic; the union lasted only until 1961, however, although it existed officially until 1971. In the 1960s Nasser initiated major construction projects such as the ❼ Aswan Dam and power plants in Egypt.

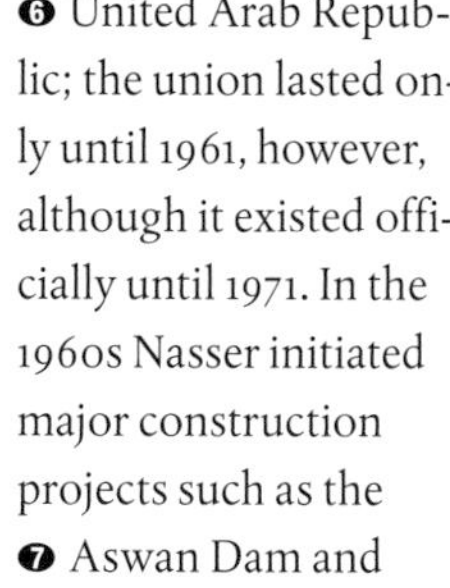

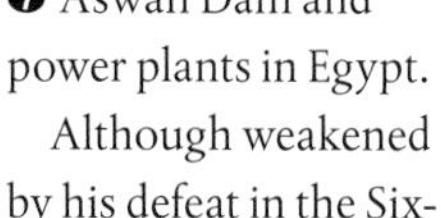

Although weakened by his defeat in the Six-Day War against Israel in 1967 (p. 596), Nasser's state doctrine ("Nasserism") became an example for neighboring countries, particularly Libya, where the Revolutionary Command Council led by Colonel ❹ Muammar al-Qaddafi seized the government on September 1, 1969. Qaddafi adopted Nasser's principle of mass mobilization and personality cult with his institutionalized revolution and radically eliminated all potential opponents. He modernized the country and achieved a rise in living standards after 1969 through nationalized ❷ oil exports. His often unpredictable policies and his support of terrorist groups led to Libya's isolation in the 1980s and 1990s, which Qaddafi has been trying to overcome since about 2000 through international compromises.

In Egypt, ❶ Anwar el-Sadat, Nasser's successor after his death in 1970, at first continued Nasser's policies, but decided in the mid-1970s to change course and moved away from socialism. He signed a peace treaty with Israel on March 26, 1979, which resulted in Egypt becoming isolated in the Arab world and Sadat's dependence on the West.

Qaddafi's Pan-Arabism

Colonel Qaddafi attempted to become the head of the Pan-Arab movement following Nasser's death. The movement seeks the unification of all Arab states. Qaddafi's ideology gave Islam a more central position. With the "Charter of Tripoli" in December 1969, he tried to bring about a merger of Libya with Egypt, Syria, and Sudan. In January 1974 he announced the impending union of his country with Tunisia, but this too failed, primarily due to Qaddafi's absolute claim to leadership.

3 Premier Gamal Abdel Nasser, 1955

4 Colonel Muammar al-Qaddafi, 1975

5 Warships on the Suez Channel during the Suez crisis, November 1956

6 Gamal Abdel Nasser and his Syrian colleague Shukri el Kuwatli after the signing of the document uniting Egypt and Syria, February 1, 1958

7 Construction of the Aswan Dam, 1963

1943	Baath Party founded in Syria
23 Jul 1952	King Farouk of Egypt deposed
18 Jun 1953	Republic of Egypt proclaimed
1956	Suez Canal nationalized
Oct 1956	Suez crisis
1956–61	Gamal Abdel Nasser's presidency
1963	Amin Hafis leads putsch in Syria

Egypt under Mubarak, Syria since Independence

Mubarak continued the presidential regime in Egypt. In Syria, the Baath party under President Assad prevailed after initial instability.

Sadat's war against Islamism, his conciliatory stance toward Israel, and his authoritarian domestic policy, expressed in the 1978 ban on all political activities, were reasons behind his ❽ assassination during a military parade on October 6, 1981. His successor, ❾ Hosni Mubarak, has continued Sadat's course, while at the same time endeavoring to reconcile with the Arab camp. He also opened up Egypt to more ❿ tourism. Egypt became a full member of the Arab League again in 1989. Mubarak's authoritarian presidential regime eased up the battle against the Muslim Brotherhood but was met with increasing criticism in the West for its lack of democracy. In February 2005, Mubarak promised to allow more presidential candidates in future elections.

8 Security staff caring for victims lying injured on the floor after the assassination of Anwar el-Sadat, October 6, 1981

9 The President of Egypt: Hosni Mubarak, March 30, 1993

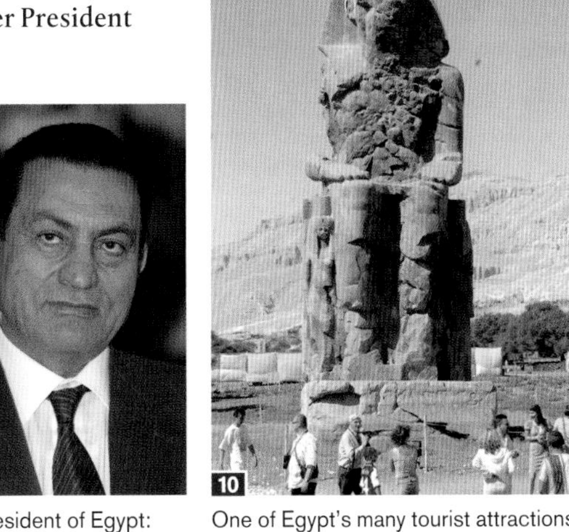
10 One of Egypt's many tourist attractions: One of the Memnon colossi, November 22, 2004

11 View over the Syrian city of Hama with a water wheel in the foreground

The conditions in ⓫ Syria, with its capital ⓮ Damascus, during the first few years after gaining independence from France in 1946 were very unstable due to the population's religious, ethnic, and political heterogeneity. After military coups in 1949 and 1951, the Baath (Rebirth) party, founded in 1943 and legalized in 1955, rose to become the leading power in the country. It propagated a Pan-Arab nationalism and socialism and cooperated with Nasser's Egypt. After the union with Egypt, driven by the Baathists, Syria withdrew again as a separate republic on September 30, 1961. In March 1963, the Baath party seized the government in a coup led by General Amin Hafis. Syria subsequently distanced itself from Nasser and turned more toward Iraq and the Palestinians. A move to the left within the Baath leadership in 1966 led to closer cooperation with the Soviet Union. In the Arab-Israeli war of 1967 (p. 596), Syria lost the Golan Heights to Israel.

Syria's support of the Palestinians in the "Black September" of 1970 (p. 598) resulted in a power struggle within the Baath party, which was won by the Alawite ⓬ minister of defense, Hafez al-Assad, in November 1970; he became president on March 11, 1971. Assad suppressed Islamic revolts, did away with possible rivals, and modernized the country on a socialist and nationalist basis. In 1976, he militarily intervened in the Lebanese civil war. The break with Iraq that had already begun in 1968 intensified through the 1970s, ultimately leading to Syria's entrance into the anti-Iraq coalition in the 1991 Gulf War. In the meantime, Assad had so consolidated the ruling position of his family in the country that after his death in 2000, the power went to his son ⓭ Bashar al-Assad. Following increasing international pressure over Syria's presence in Lebanon (p. 602), Syria was forced to withdraw its troops. After elections in 2005 in which the pro-Syrian government was voted out, and a new liberal government formed.

12 The Syrian defense minister, Colonel Hafez al-Assad, late 1960s

13 The Syrian president Bashar al-Assad, 8 April 2005

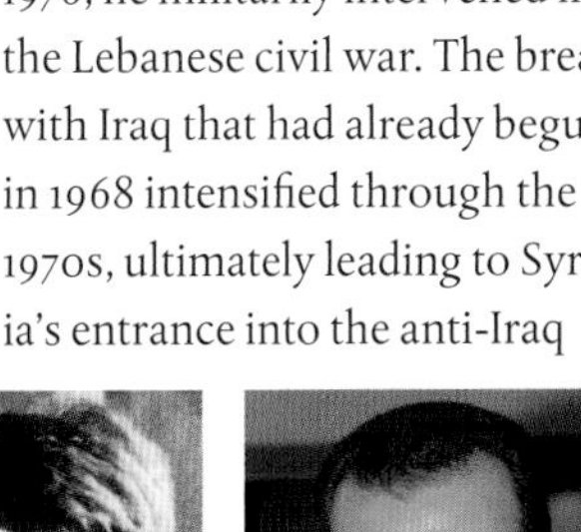

14 The old town of Damascus, in the center the Great Mosque, 1991

Lebanon

Rising tensions between Lebanon's various religious communities led to a series of political crises. These culminated in a devastating civil war between 1975 and 1990. The government was trapped between Israel's and Syria's military presences.

Since its independence from France on January 1, 1944, Lebanon has faced a number of problems. Proportional religious representation between Christians and Muslims was worked out in the National Pact of 1943, but subsequent developments polarized the population into the more prosperous and Western-oriented ❹ Christians in the north and the poorer, Arab-aligned Muslims of the south. An early civil war was waged from May to July 1958 after the reelection of the Christian president Camille Chamoun, whose government reestablished its authority with U.S. military assistance. The arrival of Palestinian refugees in southern Lebanon exacerbated sectarian tensions. A violent division of the country was prevented only by the establishment of a military administration in October 1969. Syria intervened on the side of the Muslims in the ❸ civil war that began in 1975 and in 1976 began a nearly 30-year occupation of broad areas of Lebanon.

3 Lebanese Christian Falangists at a military post in southern Lebanon, 1978

4 Church in Beirut

6 Bashir al-Jumayyil after winning the Lebanese presidential elections, August 23, 1982

7 Amin al-Jumayyil on a state visit to the Federal Republic Germany, November 25, 1987

The major fighting that destroyed Beirut and other Lebanese cities generally subsided after October 1976 through the mediation of the Arab League. In June 1982, following an assassination attempt against one of its ambassadors, Israel launched a full-scale invasion of the country, dubbed "Operation Peace for Galilee." The newly elected president, ❻ Bashir al-Jumayyil, was murdered in September 1982, which led to a ❺ massacre carried out by Christian Falangist militia in Palestinian refugee camps (p. 599). Later in the month Jumayyil's elder brother ❼ Amin was elected his successor. The following year he oversaw peace negotiations in Geneva that included all parties involved in the civil war. Israel agreed to withdraw to a security zone in the south.

1 Everyday life after the war: In front of the ruins of destroyed houses, boys play soccer in a Beirut suburb, October 2003

2 Hundreds of thousands of Lebanese demonstrators waving flags take to the streets to demand the withdrawal of Syrian forces, March 8, 2005

In 1988, combat flared again between the Christian militias of the north and the radical Shiite Hezbollah group. Maronite Christian general Michel Aoun declared a "war of liberation" against Syria in 1989. In 1991, Syria formally recognized Lebanon's independence but did not withdraw its military presence, citing the need to provide a counterbalance to the power of the militias. This left Lebanon occupied by two foreign powers. The 1975–1990 civil war took the lives of more than 144,000 people in all.

5 Aftermath of the brutal massacre carried out by the Christian Falangist militia in a Palestinian refugee camp, September 19, 1982

The situation generally ❶ stabilized after 1992 with the support of UN peacekeeping troops, but the only partially disarmed militias and the ❽ radical Palestinian movements in the country remained a problem. After the collapse of its ally, the South Lebanese Army, Israel unilaterally withdrew its forces from Lebanon in 2000. In reaction to the murder of former prime minister Rafiq Hariri in February 2005, Lebanese demonstrators demanded the ❷ withdrawal of Syrian forces as well, and in April, under heavy international pressure, Syria announced that it would comply.

8 Hezbollah guerrillas launching rockets at Israeli targets from southern Lebanon, September 1979

31 Dec 1946 | Lebanon granted independence — **Jul 1958** | Lebanese civil war — **1962–69** | Civil war in Yemen — **1964** | King Faisal in Saudi Arabia — **1975–90** | Civil war in Yemen renewed — **1976** | Syria occupies parts of Lebanon — **1979** | Islamists occupy mosque in Mecca

Saudi Arabia, the Sheikhdoms, and Yemen

Saudi Arabia and the oil-producing sheikhdoms combine monarchical forms of rule with extraordinarily wealthy elites. Following a civil war, Yemen was politically divided between 1967 and 1990.

By virtue of the country's Wahhabism, Saudi Arabia is one of the most politically and ⓬ religiously conservative of the Islamic countries. The ruling al-Saud family and its clientele have a monopoly on power and are hugely wealthy. Democratic structures are entirely lacking. This conservatism stands in strange contrast to the enormous wealth of the elite and the modern infrastructure of the country, which has been financed by the exploitation of its ⓭ oil reserves, the largest in the world.

Oil refinery near Dhahran on the East Coast of Saudi Arabia

The founder of the kingdom, ⓫ Abd al-Aziz bin Abd al-Rahman bin Faysal bin Turki bin Abdallah bin Muhammad al-Saud, or Ibn Saud, died in 1953 and was succeeded in turn by his sons Saud, Faysal, Khalid, and Fahd. In 1964 ❾ Saud was deposed by his brother, Crown Prince ❿ Faysal. Faysal carried out cautious reforms and became the leader of the conservatives of the Islamic world that stood opposed to Nasserism (p. 600). In 1975, Faysal was murdered by a member of his family and his brother Khalid succeeded him. Out of fear of the Islamic revolution in Iran (p. 607) as well as of the military dominance of Iraq, Khalid began to arm Saudi Arabia in 1980, primarily with the help of the United States. Saudi Arabia was America's most important ally in the region during the first Gulf War.

Despite growing demands for ⓮ democratic reform, the Saudi rulers have made few concessions. Similar political conditions reign in a more moderate form in Kuwait under the ruling family al-Sabah, as well as in the United Arab Emirates, Bahrain, Qatar, and Oman.

The seizure of a mosque in Mecca by Islamist extremists in November 1979, sternly dealt with by Crown Prince Fahd, was the first sign of a problem with Islamic radicalism. Today, the Saudi regime has come under pressure because many international terrorists are from Saudi Arabia.

The Saudi Arabian king Saud I, deposed by his brother in 1964

Crown Prince Faysal of Saudi Arabia, seized the crown in 1964

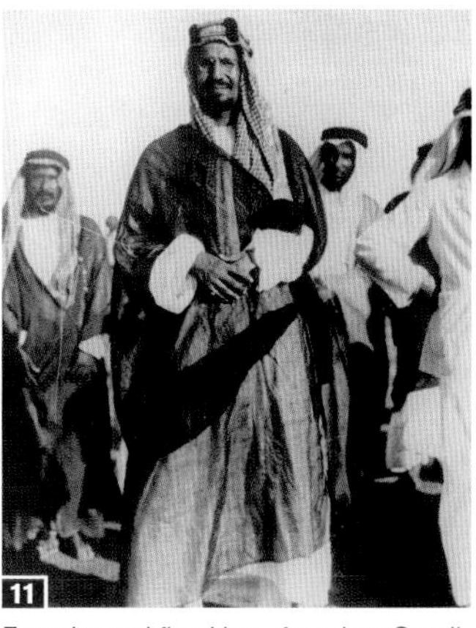
Founder and first king of modern Saudi Arabia, Abd al-Aziz ibn Saud III ruled until 1953, 1935

Thousands of Muslims circle the Kaaba in front of the Great Mosque of Haram Sharif seven times as part of their pilgrimage to Mecca, 2004

The United Arab Emirates

In 1971, seven emirates on the Persian Gulf, which had until then been British protectorates, joined together to form the United Arab Emirates (UAE). Among them, Dubai and the capital Abu Dhabi are the most important. They prosper through oil production and stand out for their modern ports, major building projects, and luxury hotels. Sheikh Khalifa of Abu Dhabi succeeded his father as UAE president in 2004; the sheikh of Dubai is also the prime minister.

The Marina Yacht Club in Dubai, a lavish oil-funded construction in the shape of a sailing ship, 2004

The special development of North Yemen's theocratic political structure ended in September 1962 with the overthrow of the absolute rule of the Zaidi imams, who had ruled the caliphate for a millennium. After the British withdrew from South Yemen in 1967, Marxist radicals seized power there, and in November 1967 the country was officially divided along lines similar to those drawn by British and Ottoman colonizers in 1849. South Yemen became a secular People's Republic on the Soviet model, supported by both the USSR and China; North Yemen remained an Arab republic. After periodic fighting, the two halves began negotiating a reconciliation in 1979. On May 22, 1990, the unified Republic of Yemen was created under President Ali Abdullah Saleh, who still holds office today.

Meeting of the Shura Council in Riyadh after the first democratic elections, February 10, 2005

1989 | Peace talks in Geneva
22 May 1990 | Reunification of Republic of Yemen
1982 | Israel occupies southern Lebanon; Hezbollah formed
1983 | Syria proclams war of liberation
Apr 2005 | Syria announces withdrawal from Lebanon

Iraq to 1979

Following the revolution of 1958, a series of nationalist presidential regimes governed Iraq. In 1968, the secular nationalist Baath party came to power in the country.

2 The Golden Mosque in Kadhimain, near Baghdad, 1958

3 The new Iraq cabinet of General Abd al-Karim Qasim, second from left, and Abd al Salam Aref (left) in Baghdad before its first meeting, July 1958

After World War II, ❷ religious (Sunni–Shia) and inter-ethnic (Kurd–Arab) tensions grew in Iraq, where ❶ King Faisal II was controlled by his cousin, the regent Abd al-Ilah, and Prime Minister Nuri as-Said, both of whom were pro-British. Great Britain controlled a large part of the country's economy (p. 488). A ❹ military coup deposed the monarchy on July 14, 1958, murdering the royal family. Brigadier ❸ Abd al-Karim Qasim, the leader of the coup, became prime minister of the new republic. He immediately undertook comprehensive administrative, social, and agrarian reforms, nationalized oil production, and in 1959 expelled the British from the country.

A revolt of the Kurds in the north began in March 1961 under Mustafa Barsani, who proclaimed a Kurdish state. All subsequent governments were compelled to negotiate with the Kurds, who were promised cultural autonomy and participation in the government in 1970.

Beginning in 1960, Qasim built up a personal dictatorship, and in 1961 he proclaimed Kuwait to be a province of Iraq. Qasim was defeated in a ❽ power struggle in February 1963 by his former second-in-command, Colonel Abd as-Salim Mohammed Arif, who seized power with the help of the Arab Socialist Baath party. Arif and the Baathists brutally persecuted Communists and other opponents, and then in November 1963, he eliminated the splintered Baathists and instead relied on traditional nationalists.

When Arif died in a helicopter accident in April 1966, his brother Abd al-Rahman Arif replaced him as ruler, but he was deposed by a military coup on July 17, 1968. Of the forces behind the coup, the revived Baath party headed by General ❼ Ahmed Hassan al-Bakr secured its supremacy over the army through numerous purges. After signing a ❺ peace deal with the ❻ Kurds in 1970, the government began to build up a socialist centralized state and initiated ambitious social projects. One major feature of this agenda was an accelerated program of land reform and irrigation projects aimed at bringing new areas into cultivation. While this process brought mixed results the nationalization of the entire oil industry, which began in June 1972, guaranteed healthy state revenues that were further boosted the following year when prices soared. The conflict with Iran over the Shatt al Arab region on the Persian Gulf was settled in March 1975. At this point Iran withdrew its financial and military support from the Iraqi Kurds who had been rebelling in the North, forcing them to accept the government's cease-fire. Fearing renewed repression, 250,000 Kurds then fled to Iran.

6 A unit of Kurdish independence fighters engaged against Iraqi national forces in the mountains of northern Iraq, posing with rifles, 196

7 General Ahmed Hassan al-Bakr, head of the Baath party, 1968

1 King Feisal II swears an oath to the constitution in front of the Iraqi national parliament after his enthronement, Baghdad, May 2, 1953

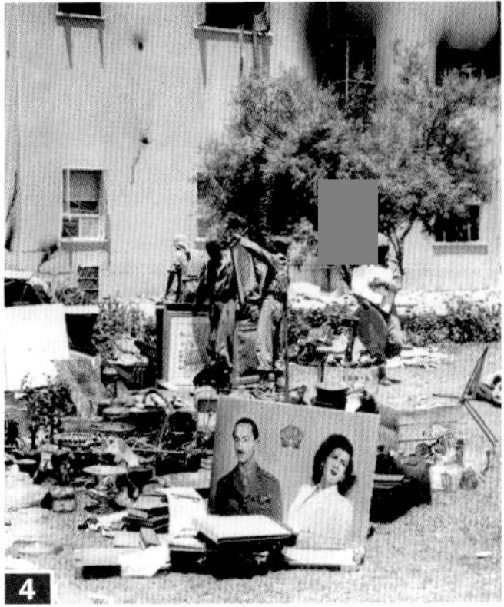

4 After the fall of the monarchy: Soldiers collect furniture and other possessions thrown out of the fire damaged royal palace following a military coup

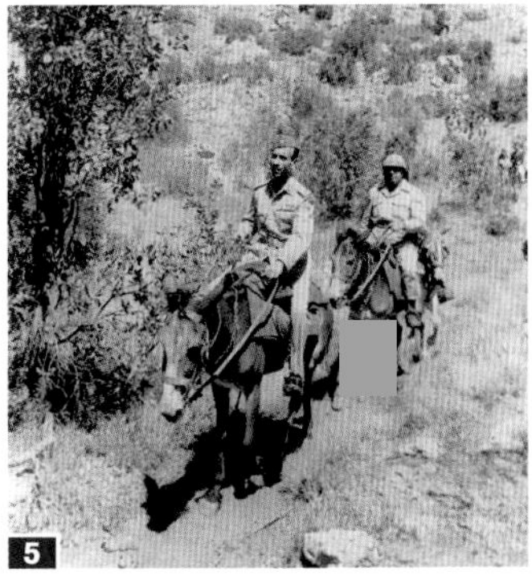

5 Iraq president in the Kurd region: Abd as-Salim Aref (front) travelling by-donkey, July 1958

8 A tank and soldiers on patrol in the streets of Baghdad two days after General Qasim was deposed in a coup, February 1963

1958 | Putsch led by Abd al-Karim Qasim
1959 | British expelled
1961 | Qasim declares Kuwait province
1961 | Kurdish revolt led by Mustafa Barsani
1963 | Putsch led by Abd as-Salim Mohammed Aref
1979 | Saddam Hussein becomes president

Iraq from Saddam Hussein to the Present

Saddam began to consolidate his personal power in 1979. After the war with Iran, he occupied Kuwait in 1990, but was defeated in 1991 and deposed in 2003.

Giant mural of the dictator Saddam Hussein, the kind of image that saturated the daily lives of the Iraqi people

General al-Bakr, the president of Iraq during the 1970s, came from Tikrit. In 1968, ❾ Saddam Hussein, who belonged to this clan, became al-Bakr's second in command, and from 1972 he dominated politics with a brutal single-mindedness. On July 16, 1979, he succeeded al-Bakr in the office of president and head of government and immediately set about eliminating possible rivals through numerous executions.

Using the general fear of an incursion by the Iranian revolution as justification, Saddam cleverly armed Iraq to become the strongest military power in the Arab world, largely with US assistance. He secured his rule through a ❿ personality cult, a skillfully devised surveillance system, and nepotism in the allocation of government offices—as was particularly evident in the roles given his sons Uday and Qusay. Saddam invaded Iran in September 1980, beginning the a war that soon stagnated into a bloody stalemate and lasted until 1988. Saddam's forces also used ⓬ poison gas to kill thousands of rebelling Kurds in February 1988.

Taking up the claims of earlier governments, Iraqi troops occupied Kuwait on August 2, 1990, declaring it to be the 19th province of Iraq. Failure to observe UN demands to withdraw led to the first Gulf War (January 16–March 3, 1991), which ended with the Iraqis being driven out of Kuwait by a UN-mandated US-led coalition. When the Shiites in the south and the Kurds in the north of Iraq took this opportunity to rebel against the defeated regime, Saddam brutally suppressed the rebellions, whereupon the Allies established protection zones for the Kurdish population. The Iraqi regime only hesitantly fulfilled the terms of commitment drawn up by a UN inspection team and the disposal of weapons of mass destruction agreed upon after the Gulf War. The trade embargo imposed by the UN affected the Iraqi people more than the leadership.

Following September 11, 2001 (p.643), Saddam Hussein's regime again came into the eye of the United States as being a part of an "axis of evil." Citing Iraq's undisclosed weapons of mass destruction as the justification, mainly US and British armed forces invaded Iraq to depose Saddam's regime on March 20, 2003. Resistance soon broke and by May Iraq was ⓫ defeated, although no evidence of the alleged weapons was subsequently found. A governing council took over the political leadership of Iraq in May 2004, followed in June by a transitional government under ⓭ Ayad Allawi. The military presence of the Coalition and the looming power struggle between the Sunnis, who had ruled until then, and the Shiite majority has led to almost daily attacks and suicide bombings since that the end of the war. The first free elections, held on January 30, 2005 (which were boycotted by the majority of the Sunnis), were won by the United Iraqi Alliance, a Shiite alliance led by Ibrahim Jaafari, who became prime minister in February 2005.

In the first few months after the election of the new government the number of insurgent attacks in Iraq seemed to increase, raising American fears of prolonged military involvement.

Saddam Hussein waving to a crowd of supporters in Kirkuk on April 2, 1988, one month after using chemical weapons against Kurdish civilians

US marines shortly after capturing Baghdad pass a statue of Saddam Hussein pulled down by an armored personnel carrier, April 10, 2003

A victim of the chemical weapons on the Iraqi-Kurd city Halabja, a father holds his dead child in his arms, between March 16 and 18 1988

The Iraq interim president Ayad Allawi, appointed after the invasion, 2005

since 1980 | Iran-Iraq war begins
Aug 1988 | Ceasefire between Iran and Iraq
2 Aug 1990 | Occupation of Kuwait
1991 | First Gulf War
20 Mar 2003 | Second US-led invasion of Iraq
Jun 2004 | Transitional government under Allawi
2005 | Ibrahim Jaafari elected president

Iran to the Overthrow of the Shah

Shah Reza Pahlavi imposed an oppressively secularist vision of society, and established an authoritarian and corrupt regime. This repression, and resentment at the perceived imperialism of western oil firms in Iran, provoked resistance in middle-class circles and among the Shiite clergy.

Mossadegh, leader of the nationalist Tudeh party, sitting in the dock at his trial in Tehran, September 9, 1953

A young Shah Muhammad Reza Pahlavi shortly after his accession in 1941

Iran was supported after 1945 by the United States and Great Britain, who had installed the young shah, ❷ Muhammad Reza Pahlavi, in 1941 (p. 490). As it was the most Western-oriented country in the Near East and, at the time, the main supplier of ❸ oil, the United States also armed Iran militarily, especially after a conflict developed with the Soviet Union over Azerbaijan in 1946. Mohammed Mossadegh, who assumed the office of prime minister in April 1951, opposed Britain's extensive involvement in the oil trade and nationalized the Anglo-Iranian Oil Company (AIOC). The shah fled the country on short notice in the subsequent power struggle, but then returned in August 1953 and toppled ❶ Mossadegh and his nationalist Tudeh party with the help of the US Central Intelligence Agency. The AIOC was restored and martial law imposed until 1957.

Beginning in 1960, the shah tried to regain control over the growing opposition within the country through a program of reforms. In January 1963, he instituted what was known as the "White Revolution" by taking land away from large landowners and initiating campaigns for literacy and ❹ women's emancipation. These initiatives primarily benefited the urban population. The ❺ Western lifestyle of the shah's family, his political ties to the West, corruption, and a disregard of Islamic traditions gradually alienated the ruler from his people. From the 1960s on, under Prime Minister Amir Abbas Hoveida, the direction became increasingly authoritarian. Regime opponents were tortured by SAVAK, the secret police, and in 1975 the de facto one-party system was institutionalized. In 1978, the shah attempted to pacify the massive opposition that had been forming since 1977 with promises of further reform. However he was undermined by regular mass demonstrations, particularly in Shiite holy cities, in support of the exiled Grand Ayatollah Ruhollah Khomeini, around whom the Islamic opposition in Iran had crystallized. In September 1978, Khomeini from exile began calling for an uncompromising war against the shah and for an "Islamic revolution," after which events took on their own momentum.

The upper class around the shah took their assets abroad and a wave of labor strikes brought oil production to a standstill. A military government installed in November could no longer control

Oil mining in Iran, in the 1970s; the largest exporter of oil in the world

The Empress Soraya and Shah Reza Pahlawi, firm allies of the West, during a state visit to the Federal Republic of Germany, 1955

the situation. In Paris, Khomeini allied with the moderate "National Front" of the opposition, and they proclaimed the common goal of an Islamic republic. On January 16, 1979, the shah fled and on February 1, the Ayatollah Khomeini returned from Paris, welcomed in Tehran ❻ by cheering crowds. The ❼ Iranian Revolution had begun.

"White Revolution:" Women gather in front of the shah's palace, to demonstrate their support for his promise to extend the electoral franchise to women, February 1963

Upon his return to Iran the Ayatollah Ruhollah Khomeini receives a triumphant welcome from the crowds in Tehran,1979

The Iranian Revolution: Angry crowds of demonstrators protest against the regime, burning pictures of the Shah and chanting anti-monarchy slogans

1951 | Muhammad Mosaddeq takes office

1953 | Mosaddeq deposed by Shah Resa Pahlavi

1963 | White Revolution begins

1963 | Khomeini exiled

1975 | One-party system institutionalized

16 Jan 1979 | Shah flees

Iran since the Islamic Revolution of 1979

Under Ayatollah Khomeini, hard-line Islamic forces dominated the revolution and the country. Only after his death did some liberalization begin to take place. Traditionalists and moderate reformers continue to struggle over the future course of the country.

9 The spiritual and political leader of the Iranian revolution, Ayatollah Ruhollah Khomeini

10 Devout women wearing full-length veils at a meeting to protest against trends toward women wearing "un-Islamic" ("provocatively revealing") clothing, Iran, 2004

Khomeini proclaimed the Islamic Republic of Iran on April 1, 1979, but did not immediately emerge as its political leader. At first, moderate opposition politicians were elected president, but the revolution was radicalized in November with the occupation of the US embassy in Tehran by students and the election victory of the strictly religious Islamic Republican party in the parliamentary elections in May 1980. A re-Islamization of public life began with the introduction of aspects of sharia Islamic law—the compulsory ➓ wearing of headscarves for women was popular among traditionalists—and a strong ideological orientation against the United States.

❾ Khomeini and the radical clergy leadership (the Mullahs) increasingly forced the splintered moderate forces out of the government or into exile. The

11 Mass public mourning at the funeral of Ayatollah Khomeini, leader of the Revolution, June 6, 1989

12 Ayatollah Ali Khamenei, President of Iran from 1981-1989

13 The Iranian president Mohammed Khatami, April 4, 2005

❽ Iran-Iraq War, launched by Iraq in September 1980, brought the final victory for the Mullahs. Even their opponents participated in the defense of the country, which Khomeini organized with the help of his fanatical "Guardians of the Faith." In 1988, Iran accepted the UN mediated cease-fire. In the meantime, the example of an Islamic revolution has inspired groups in other countries, notably the Hezbollah in Lebanon.

Only after Ayatollah Khomeini's ⓫ death on June 3, 1989, was there a relaxation of domestic pressure. His successor as spiritual leader was ⓬ Ayatollah Ali Khamenei, who also served as president from 1981–1989 and continues to represent the conservative power of the Mullahs. The office of president, however, was taken up by the pragmatic Ali Akbar Rafsanjani, who began to ease tensions and initiated a renewed economic engagement with the West. ⓭ Mohammed Khatami, who became president in 1997 and is considered a representative of moderate Islam, is seen by many reformers as their country's best hope, although he must constantly struggle against the conservative-dominated institutions in the fight for power. An anti-torture law that had already been passed by parliament was vetoed in June 2002 by the conservative Guardian Council. Since 2004, the United States has been placing heavy diplomatic pressure on Iran because of its nuclear policies; the US government is seeking guarantees that Iran will not develop nuclear weapons.

8 The bodies of two Iranian soldiers killed in border clashes with Iraqi forces during the Iran-Iraq War, March 1985

Ayatollah Ruhollah Khomeini, Describing his Program for the Establishment of an Islamic Government

"It is our duty to work toward the establishment of an Islamic government. The first activity we must undertake in this respect is the propagation of our cause; that is how we must begin. It has always been that way, all over the world. A group of people came together, deliberated, made decisions and then began to propagate their aims. Gradually the number of like-minded people would increase until finally they became powerful enough to influence a great state or even to confront and overthrow it.(...)"

Khomeini leads prayers at a mosque in Tehran,,1986

1 Feb 1979 | Khomeini returns from exile
1 Apr 1979 | Proclamation of the Islamic Republic of Iran
June 3 1989 | Death of Khomeini
1981–89 | Presidency of Ali Khamenei
1997 | Mohammed Khatami takes office

Afghanistan to the Civil War

Effective central government in ❶ Afghanistan has long been hindered by the powerful tribal culture. The monarchy was overthrown in 1973. In 1979, the Soviet Union invaded in support of an embattled left-wing regime, which led to a bloody occupation and civil war.

1 Two Afghan women carrying wood back to their village, ca. 1965

2 King Mohammad Zahir Shah of Afghanistan on a vist to the US in 1973

3 Training teachers in Afghanistan: prospective teachers taking classes, 1963

❷ Mohammad Zahir Shah ruled in Afghanistan, a country of traditional and autonomous tribal structures, from 1933, although the actual power rested with his three uncles, brothers of Nadir Shah who was murdered in 1933. Their efforts to ❸ centralize power failed due to the resistance of the tribes. From 1953, however, Prime Minister ❹ Sardar Mohammad Daud Khan, brother-in-law of the king, succeeded in introducing several social reforms with assistance from the Soviet Union. When Daud was ousted in 1963, moderate political forces introduced a constitutional monarchy in 1964 and in 1965 free parliamentary elections were held for the first time.

Daud deposed the king in a coup on July 17, 1973, and proclaimed a republic. As prime minister, he began a cautious program of land reform and the nationalization of banks. He secured the support of the Arab world and in February 1977 established an authoritarian presidential regime. Then in April 1978, the Communist-oriented People's Democratic party organized a coup with the help of the army, murdered Daud, and proclaimed the Democratic Republic of Afghanistan under Prime Minister Nur Mohammad Taraki. The new republic had close ties to the Soviet Union. The government's left-wing secularist course led to a 1979 revolt among many of the tribes and parts of the army, causing anarchy in many regions of the country. Increasingly under pressure, the new prime minister, ❺ Hafizullah Amin, called on the Soviet Union for aid. Soviet troops ❻ entered Afghanistan on December 27, 1979, and helped to install the loyal exiled politician Babrak Karmal as head of state and government. Although the new government generally respected Islam and Afghan traditions, a number of Islamic and nationalist groups were immediately formed to resist the Soviet occupation. Collectively known as the mujahideen, they began a ❼ guerrilla war against the regime in Kabul and the Soviet troops. The guerrillas were supported financially and militarily by the United States and many Arab countries.

4 The Afghan prime minister Prince Sadar Mohammad on a state visit to the Federal Republic of Germany, July 3, 1961

5 Embattled Afghan prime minister Hafizullah Amin requested Soviet aid

6 Soviet tank patrols the streets of Kabul looking for insurgents, February 1980

7 American-armed Mujahideen rebels fighting the Soviet occupation forces near the Pakistan boarder, February 14, 1980

1933 | Reign of Mohammad Zahir Shah
1953 | Mohammad Daud Khan seizes power
1965 | First free parliamentary elections
17 Jul 1973 | Proclamation of the Republic
1977 | Presidential regime under Mohammed Daud
1978 | Military putsch led by Mohammed Taraki
1979 | Soviet invasion

Afghanistan from 1979 to the Present

After the withdrawal of the Soviet troops following heavy losses, the Islamic groups fought among themselves. First the mujahideen dominated the country and then the Taliban. The latter were driven from power in 2001–2002.

Mujahideen pose before a Soviet tank abandoned during the Red Army's withdrawal, 1988

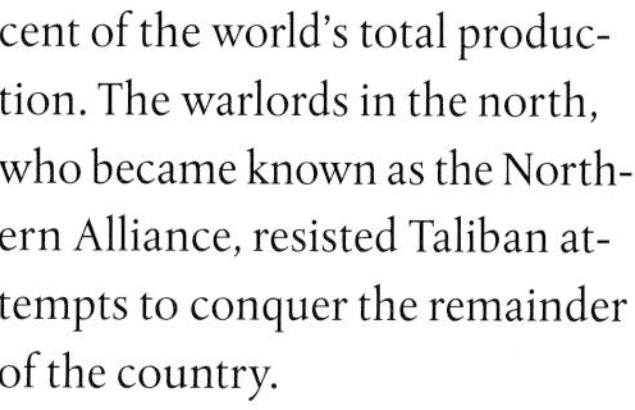

The Afghan tribal council increasingly proved to be as powerless as the government, and the mountain regions in particular became centers of a radical Islamic resistance that had extensive ties to Pakistan and to underground fundamentalist groups. By 1983, 20 percent of the population had fled to neighboring countries, particularly Pakistan; several UN peace initiatives failed to end the conflict. Atrocities committed on both sides further damaged the prospects of a peace accord. In response to Soviet pressure, Karmal was replaced by Sayid Mohammad Najibullah as secretary-general of the People's Democratic party in 1986, and in 1987 Najibullah became president. He championed a policy of national reconciliation. With the radical Islamic mujahideen increasingly winning ground, the USSR under Mikhail Gorbachev, having suffered heavy losses, ❾ withdrew its troops in 1988–1989 following a peace treaty negotiated in Geneva.

With the Soviet troops gone, Najibullah's power base collapsed. Following an attempted coup in 1990, he was finally driven out of Kabul in April 1992 by the mujahideen. The new mujahideen government, with Sebghatullah Mujaddedi as head of state and Gulbuddin Hekmatyar as prime minister, failed to gain recognition from the other resistance groups in much of the rest of the country, and the civil war thus continued. In September 1996, the Islamist Taliban militia conquered Kabul and established an oppressive regime that enforced a ❽, ⓫ fundamentalist form of Islam through coercion, while also allowing ❿ Afghan opium cultivation to reach 75 percent of the world's total production. The warlords in the north, who became known as the Northern Alliance, resisted Taliban attempts to conquer the remainder of the country.

In 1997–1998, the Taliban, led by Mullah Omar, began to expel Western aid organizations and demonstrated their open support of Islamist terrorists, particularly Osama bin Laden. In August 1998, following an attack on the US embassies in Nairobi and Dar es Salaam, the United States launched ⓬ missile strikes against terrorist training camps in Afghanistan. After September 11, 2001, when the Taliban refused to comply with the US demand for bin Laden's extradition, coordinated ⓭ offensives were launched by US and British troops and the Northern Alliance, led by the Uzbek general Abdul Rashid Dostum. Kabul was retaken on November 13 and the Taliban were soon driven toward the border with Pakistan.

NATO troops remain in the country to support the government of President Hamid Karzai.

Colossal 170 ft-high statues of the Buddha in Afghanistan, dynamited by the Taliban in 2001

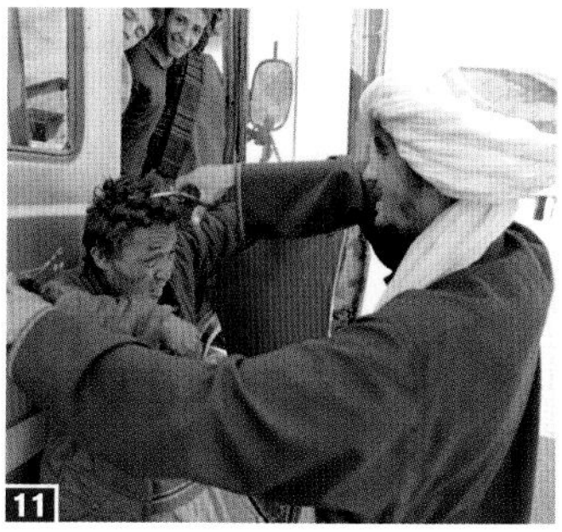

Poppy farming in Afghanistan, April 2005

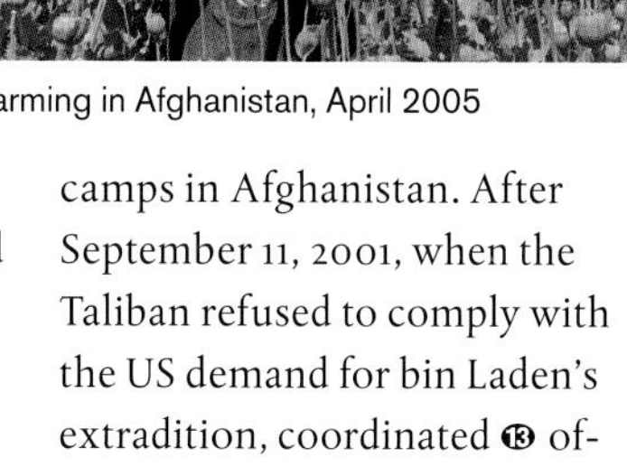

Hamid Karzai

Hamid Karzai studied international relations in India. During the 1990s he was deputy foreign minister in two mujahideen governments. As head of state, he has promised to halt opium cultivation and strengthen the rights of women. His government is still dependent on an international military presence in the main cities. His deputy, Hadji Abul Kadir, was assassinated in Kabul in July 2002, and he, too, barely escaped an attempted assassination in September of that year. Initially appointed as interim President, he won the November 2004 elections to gain a new mandate.

above: Hamid Karzai, president of Afghanistan since the US-led invasion, November 4, 2004

A Taliban militia forcibly shaves the head of a passenger in a bus

A Taliban fighter carries a wounded comrade, 1997

US special forces on patrol in Afghanistan, November 15, 2001

1988–89 | Withdrawal of Soviet troops

1992 | Najibullah ousted

1996 | Taliban conquer Kabul

1998 | US airstrikes on Bin Laden's training camps

Nov 2001 | Northern Alliance forces conquer Kabul

2002 | Hamid Karzai becomes president

Pakistan and India since 1947

From the successful war for independence against British colonial rule (p. 492), India and Pakistan emerged as two self-contained states in 1947. Both countries' claims for the Kashmir region led to a continuous political and military conflict. While India developed a democratic parliamentary democracy domestically, Pakistan was ruled by an authoritarian military government. Religious tensions led to the separation of East Pakistan as Bangladesh in 1971.

Traffic jam in Dhaka, the capital of Bangladesh, November 2004

Pakistan and Bangladesh

In 1947, Pakistan established itself as a separate Muslim state on the Indian sub-continent. In 1971, the eastern part of the country seceded as Bangladesh.

While ❻ India was struggling for independence (p. 493), Muhammad Ali Jinnah called for a separate state for the Muslim minority. Bloodshed between Hindus and Muslims led to a partition of the subcontinent and a migration of the Hindu and Muslim minorities. The primarily Muslim regions on either side of Hindu India—East Pakistan (today's Bangladesh) and West Pakistan—became the state of Pakistan, a dominion of the British Commonwealth. Jinnah became the country's first president.

Tension between secularists and political Islamists over the role of religion, exacerbated by secessionist movements within

Volunteers fight against the Pakistani army for an independent Bangladesh

the country and the conflict with India over Jammu and Kashmir, dominated politics. When the situation worsened in 1958, the secularist General Muhammad Ayub Khan seized power, stabilizing the country by imposing martial law. He followed a policy of a balance between the Cold War blocs, and in 1965 began a policy of détente with India.

The first free elections in East Pakistan were won by the Awami League with a large majority. Led by Sheikh Mujibur Rahman, the league sought autonomy for the region. When Rahman proclaimed the independent People's Republic of Bangladesh on March 26, 1971, the Pakistani government responded with force. India's ❷ military support ensured that ❶ Bangladesh became independent. Since then, democratic governments have alternated with military regimes in Bangladesh. Plagued by floods, the country is one of the poorest in the world.

After Bangladesh's secession in 1971, West Pakistan became Pakistan; it established relations with Bangladesh in 1974. Until 1977 the dictatorship of ❺ Zulfikar Ali Bhutto guaranteed a secular state, but General Zia ul-Haq seized power in a coup and planned the Islamization of society. Although the tension between secularists and Islamic forces continued to dominate politics, there was a return to free elections in 1985. ❸ Benazir Bhutto, prime minister from 1988 to 1990 and 1993 to 1996, became the first woman to lead a Muslim country. ❹ General Pervez Musharraf has led Pakistan's government after the bloodless coup in 1999. Since 2001, he has been the United States' key ally in the region, while struggling to contain internal Islamic opposition to his rule.

Pakistani prime minister Zulfikar Ali Bhutto, 1976

Pakistani prime minister Benazir Bhutto after her second victory in November 1988

General Pervez Musharraf at a press conference on February 1, 2005

Negotiating independence for India in 1947 under the leadership of the British Viceroy Lord Mountbatten and the leader of the Muslim League

14 Aug 1947 | Pakistan becomes independent
15 Aug 1947 | Indian independence
30 Jan 1948 | Mahatma Gandhi murdered
26 Nov 1949 | Foundation of the Indian Republic
26 Jan 1950 | First Indian constitution
1962 | Sino-Indian war
1966–77 | Indira Gandhi's rule

India

Since gaining independence in 1947, India has generally followed a policy of secular modernization, and political life has been dominated by the Nehru-Ghandi political dynasty. Despite numerous conflicts, the multiethnic state remains the world's largest democracy.

Shortly after independence was achieved, Muslim Pakistan broke off from India, but most of the 566 principalities of the subcontinent became a part of the new Indian state. Fighting poverty and integrating the various ethnic groups were the most pressing tasks of the country, along with the long-running conflict with Pakistan over the ❼ Kashmir region. Socially, the country fluctuated between secular modernization and traditional Hinduism.

7 Nomads in Jammu-Kashmir in the north of India

9 Jawaharlal Nehru, 1962

Mahatma Gandhi was murdered by a Hindu fanatic on January 30, 1948, and ❾ Jawaharlal Nehru, who had held the office of prime minister since 1946, became the dominant political figure in the country. Nehru pursued a socialist path, launching five-year plans to modernize the economically backward country. Constant unrest in the individual provinces and the Sino-Indian war of 1962–63 resulted in the loss of some border provinces. When Nehru died in May 1964, he was succeeded by Lal Bahadur Shastri. He too died in office in 1966, and Nehru's daughter ❿ Indira Gandhi then became prime minister. She continued the policies of her father, but shifted between delegation and centralization of authority. Gandhi presided over the Indo-Pakistani war of 1971, gaining support from the Soviets, France, and the United Kingdom in the UN Security Council. She was voted out of office in 1977, but regained power in a triumphant election victory in 1984. When in June 1984 she ordered military action against radical ❽ Sikhs who had barricaded themselves in the ⓫ Temple of Amritsar for two years, she was murdered by her own Sikh bodyguards. Her son Rajiv Gandhi then came into government, but he was killed in a 1991 bomb attack.

8 Young Sikh soldiers in Allahabad, 1993

10 Indira Gandhi, 1972

An evident radicalization of political Hinduism, separatist movements, natural catastrophes, local resistance to planned dam-building projects, and corruption scandals have led to repeated unrest in the country since the 1990s. In 2004, Sikh prime minister Manmohan Singh became the first non-Hindu to lead India's government.

The Kashmir Conflict

India and Pakistan continue to dispute ownership of the region of Kashmir, in the northern part of the Indian subcontinent. The principality, inhabited by a majority of Muslims, had been governed by Hindu rulers since 1846. Over Pakistani protests, its rulers opted to join the Indian Union in 1947. Despite UN mediation since 1951, increasingly serious and violent conflicts over the region, ignited by revolts of Pakistan-backed Muslim rebels, culminated in a war in 1965. While the two countries remain in dialogue, the conflict has sparked an arms race between them, with both announcing the acquisition of nuclear weapons in 1998.

Indian soldiers at the border to Pakistan in Kashmir open fire on guerrilla positions in the mountains, May 31, 1999

Scene from Srinagar, Kashmir, India

11 Shrine of the Sikhs: The golden Temple of Amritsar, January 9, 2003

26 Mar 1971 | Bangladesh independence proclaimed
1977 | Putsch led by Zia ul-Haq in Pakistan
1984 | Indira Gandhi murdered
1988–90 | First presidency of Benazir Bhutto
1997 | Musharraf seizes government in Pakistan
2004 | Manmohan Singh's Prime Minister in India

Southeast Asia since 1945

After 1945, most of Southeast Asia was preoccupied with the struggle for liberation from colonial rule. Many of the region's countries including ❶ Malaysia and Singapore—and in particular Indonesia, with the largest Muslim population in the world—faced the problem of maintaining cohesion among various ethnic groups. The Cold War struggle was also played out in the Pacific arena, most notably in the Vietnam War. Since 1989, the region has tended more toward stability, and democratic systems have begun to emerge in most of the states.

View over a valley with terraced vegetable-growing in central Malaysia

Sri Lanka and Indonesia

Since its independence, Sri Lanka has been preoccupied with the conflict between the Sinhalese majority and the Tamil minority. After coming to power in 1966, Sukarno ruled Indonesia for the next 32 years. The country has had a functioning democracy since 1998.

On February 4, 1948, ❾ Sri Lanka (then the British colony of Ceylon) gained independence, becoming a member of the British Commonwealth (p. 500).

Sri Lanka's President Chandrika Kumaratunga at a press conference, 1997

From the outset, the nation's difficult economic situation was further complicated by the tense relationship between the Sinhalese majority and Tamil ❸ minority. In April 1956, the Sinhalese nationalist Freedom party under Solomon Bandaranaike won the national elections. He nationalized key industries, but his attempt to make Sinhalese the official language in 1958 escalated ethnic tensions, and he was murdered by a Buddhist monk in 1959. His widow, Sirimavo Bandaranaike, then continued her husband's policies. Their daughter, ❷ Chandrika Kumaratunga, has been president since 1994. As communal relations worsened, a Tamil paramilitary force known as the "Tamil Tigers" or LTTE was formed in 1976, and Sri Lanka experienced a civil war for much of the next two decades as the Tigers in the north fought government forces. A Norwegian peace initiative in 2002 brought about a cease-fire and held out the prospect of a settlement.

A Tamil fisher woman and her child February 2005

Achmed Sukarno, June 1945

on his Political Philosophy ("Pancasila")

"The Indonesian people should not only believe in God; more than this, it should be clear that each Indonesian is allowed to pray to his own God. The Christians should serve God after the teachings of Jesus Christ. The Muslims after the teachings of the prophet Mohammed. The Buddhists should foster their religion after their books.... The Indonesian state should be a state in which everyone can pray to his God without religious jealousy! The Indonesian state should be a state to which the belief in God belongs ... on civilized way, on the path to mutual respect."

Sukarno visits the Technical University of Berlin, June 20, 1956

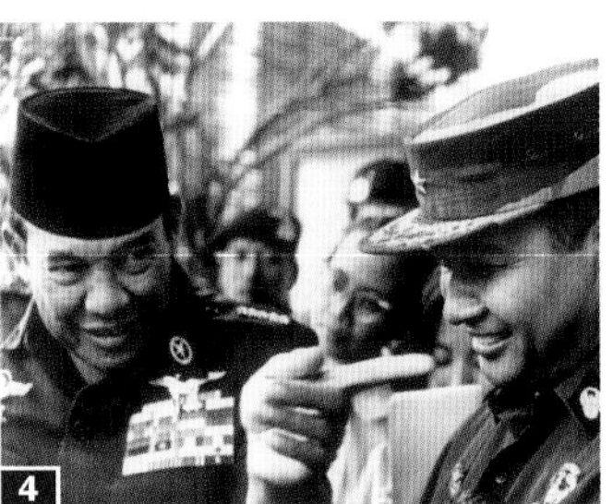

Change of government: Sukarno (left) points at Indonesia's new strong man General Suharto, September 1, 1966

Since Indonesia gained full independence in 1949, ethnic and religious conflicts have plagued the nation. While the majority of the population on the main island of Java is Muslim, Hindu or indigenous faiths tend to predominate on the other islands, such as Bali. The immediate postindependence leader was President ❹ Suharto, who looked to the USSR and domestic Communists for support and was prone to nationalistic posturing. After an attempted coup against the rule of the "Javanese" in 1960, Sukarno dissolved parliament and pursued an increasingly authoritarian

Megawati Sukarnoputri (right) president since 2001, with the former President Abdurrahman Wahid

1945 Indonesia gains independence
Feb 1948 Sri Lanka's independence
1957 Achmes Sukarno's presidency in Indonesia
1960 Parliament dissolved in Indonesia
1963 "Federation of Malaysia" founded
9 Aug 1965 Singapore leaves federation

course. In 1965 violence erupted against the pro-Communist Chinese minority, during which hundred of thousands were killed. Isolated and under pressure, Sukarno ceded power to General Suharto in March 1966.

After becoming president in 1967, Suharto cultivated ties with the West while maintaining a military-backed regime. The government took a hard line against separatist movements and in 1976 forcibly annexed the newly independent region of East Timor. The issue resurfaced two decades later when the brutal actions of the Indonesian government in crushing a Timorese revolt attracted widespread international condemnation. East Timor only became an autonomous state in 2002 after Indonesia had released it from its rule in 1999.

6 Burning houses in Dili, the capital of East Timor, December 4, 2002

❻ Popular unrest in the wake of the Asian economic crisis of 1997 forced President Suharto to step down in May 1998. After corruption allegations saw President Wahid forced out of office in 2001, ❺ Megawati Sukarnoputri, the daughter of the nation's independence leader Sukarno, held the office until 2004.

The Indonesian island of Simeulue was the epicenter of the tsunami caused by an underwater earthquake that devastated the shores of Indonesia and the surrounding countries in 2004.

Malaysia and Singapore

The Southeast Asian countries of Malaysia and Singapore achieved stability and economic growth under authoritarian governmental regimes.

7 Head of state of Singapore, Jusuf Ishak (middle), inspects a guard of honor during the celebrations for the new state Malaysia, September 15, 1963

In 1963, the Malay Peninsula, Singapore, Sarawak, and Sabah united to become the independent Federation of Malaysia, which consisted of nine sultanates and is an elective monarchy.

Political rivalries, ethnic tension, and competing economic interests caused ❼ Singapore to secede from the federation on August 9, 1965. The Sultanate of Brunei never joined the federation because of its reserves of oil; it is one of the wealthiest countries in the world. A Communist insurgency began in Sarawak in 1963 and continued until a peace was achieved in 1990.

Malaysia's head of state is the king, who is chosen every five years from the group of nine Malay sultanates, the other four states do not participate in the election of the king. The first prime minister, ❽ Abdul Rahman, sought to mediate between the Malay majority and wealthier Chinese minority following race riots in 1969 by instituting a new economic policy intended to redistribute gains and known as the New Economic Policy. Prime Minister Mahathir bin Mohammed, who governed between 1981 and 2003, oversaw a period of political stability and rapid economic growth.

Lee Kwan Yew was Singapore's first prime minister, ruling until 1990. During his time in office, the country was transformed from an economically weak former colony into a prosperous high-technology ❿ powerhouse. Public life in Singapore is staunchly conservative and subject to strict regulation by the state and its stringent legal system. Lee's successor, ⓫ Goh Chok Tong, steered the country through the Asian economic crisis of 1997–1998, signing free-trade agreements with both Japan and the United States.

8 The first prime minister of Malaysia, Tunku Abdul Rahman, signs the constitution of federation, July 1963

9 The holy city Kandy in Sri Lanka, declared a world cultural heritage site by UNESCO in 1988

10 The center of high-rise offices of banks and business of the tiny island country of Singapore

11 The prime minister of Singapore, Goh Chok Tong Commonwealth summit in Australian Coolu

1966 | Suharto takes power in Indonesia
1976 | Indonesia declares East Timor a province
1981–2003 | Mahathir bin Mohammad's premiership in Malaysia
1998 | Suharto resigns
2001 | Regency of Sukarnoputris in Indonesia

The Philippines and Myanmar

A democratic system was first introduced in the Philippines after the fall of the dictator Marcos in 1986. Myanmar (previously Burma) has been ruled by a military junta since 1962 and has garnered increasing international criticism.

The Philippines was formally granted independence from the United States on July 4, 1946, although the US continued to exert significant military and economic influence over the country. For the first two decades, a pro-Western oligarchy ruled over the relatively poor population. The nationalist ❷ Ferdinand Marcos was elected president in 1965, promising land reform, but in 1972 he declared martial law and began to build up a personal dictatorship through the imprisonment of the opposition and censorship of the press. Only after Marcos's overthrow by popular protests in 1986 did the incredible extent of the corruption under his rule come to light.

Stronger democratic structures were established under President ❹ Corazon Aquino, who held office from 1986 until 1992. Under Gloria Macapagal Arroyo, the current president, the Philippines struggles with large public debt, and corruption scandals remain frequent. Since the 1970s, there have been repeated revolts and insurgencies by Muslim separatists seeking independence for the southern islands. Between 2000 and 2003, there was a renewed government offensive against the separatist terror group Abu Sayyaf, which kidnapped Western tourists on ❶ Sipadan.

1 The extremist Muslim group Abu Sayyaf meet in their hiding place with hostages in the southern part of the Philippines

3 Aung San Suu Kyi after the end of her house arrest, 1995

Since ❺ Burma's independence in 1948, governments have struggled to contain conflicts between Buddhists and Muslims, as well as between Communists and nationalists. For the first decade, Prime Minister U Nu dominated public life. He made Burma a founding member of the Nonaligned Movement and built up a welfare state. Concerned by the rise of separatist movements, the military seized power in a coup in 1962. The coup leader, General U Ne Win, declared a "Burmese path to socialism" with an extensive nationalization program. In December 1973, the Socialist Union of Burma was proclaimed. In 1988, the military moved again, this time to install U Saw Maung, who abandoned the socialist rhetoric. Burma changed its name to Myanmar as of May 26, 1989.

Free elections in 1990 were won by the democratic opposition coalition, but the military junta refused to relinquish power. General Than Shwe, the junta's leader, continues to head the government. The international community has accused the regime of grave human rights abuses, including the use of forced labor. ❸ Aung San Suu Kyi, the leader of the prodemocracy movement and a Nobel Peace Prize winner in 1991, has spent much of the last decade under house arrest.

2 Ferdinand E. Marcos during a press conference in Manila, April 12, 1976

4 Former president of the Philippines, Corazon Aquino, 1986

5 Traffic on a busy day in the Burmese capital of Rangoon, 1997

Sithu U Thant

The third secretary-general of the United Nations was the Burmese statesman Sithu U Thant. Between 1947 and 1957, he was Burma's information minister, and represented his country in the UN from 1957 until he was elected secretary-general in 1962. In 1967, he attempted to mediate in the Arab-Israeli conflict without success. Large-scale protests erupted in 1974 when the Burmese government refused to give him a state burial because of the UN's criticism of the regime.

above: Situ U Thant, third secretary-general of the United Nations

1946 | King Rama IX in Thailand
1946 | Formal independence of the Philippines
1948 | Burma's independence
1949 | Formal independence of Laos
1962 | Ne Win in Myanmar leads coup
1965 | Ferdinand Marco's presidency

Thailand and Laos

The kingdom of Thailand has experienced frequent periods of military rule, but since 1992 civilian government has prevailed. In Laos a socialist one-party regime has been in place since 1975.

After the murder of King Rama VIII in 1946, his brother, ❻ Rama IX, ascended the throne in Thailand. He remains the head of state and is now the longest-ruling monarch in the world. Shortly after Rama IX came to the throne, Pibul Songahram established a military dictatorship with the assistance of the armed forces. He aligned the country with the West, before he himself was overthrown by a conspiracy by officers in September 1957. The new prime minister, Sarit Thanarat, and his successors continued to rule through military power; while the needs of the people were largely ignored. During the Vietnam War, the United States was permitted to station troops in Thailand (p. 617), a decision that brought some financial relief. Beginning in 1972, popular demands for democratic freedoms began to grow, and in 1973 student riots brought down the ruling Thai regime.

Too much choice: In Bangkok a passer-by looks at the election posters of the different candidates

The system of rule from then on fluctuated between unstable ❼ civilian governments and interludes of ❾ military takeover. Following the parliamentary elections of 1975, the armed forces again seized power in 1977–78. Various coalition governments were in power between 1986 and 1991 and began to open up the country's economy to international trade. Thailand's current prime minister, populist businessman Thaksin Shinawatra, won his second successive election in 2005. Despite the rapid growth of the industrial and financial sectors over the last decade, agriculture and ❿ tourism remain the most important sources of revenue.

The French colonial authority installed King Sisavang Vong in Laos in 1946 and expelled the leftist Lao Issara (Free Laos Movement) government; full independence as a constitutional monarchy came in 1954. The country was divided between right-wing royalists led by Prince ❽ Souvanna Phouma and the left-wing Pathet Lao movement led by Prince ⓫ Souphanouvong, who fought alongside the Communists in North Vietnam (p. 617) in 1950. The Pathet Lao began to conquer large stretches of the country in 1953 and in 1956 entered government. When they won the elections of 1958, a US-backed coup by royalists and the military initiated a long-running and bloody civil war. Souvanna Phouma took power in the south in 1962, while the northeast remained in communist hands and was heavily bombed by the US Air Force. Negotiations in 1973 resulted in the formation of a government of national unity. Following the communist victory in Vietnam, leftist forces deposed the king and proclaimed a socialist democratic republic. In 1991, a new constitution was imposed, and the Pathet Lao, or People's Revolutionary Party, was declared the sole political party. Khamtai Siphandon has held the office of president since 1998.

The two princes of Laos: Prince Souvanna Phouma and Prince Utthong Souphanouvong

King Rama IX with his wife Sirikit under the canopy of the throne, ca.1977

Student unrest is violently suppressed after the renewed military takeover

Western tourists walking along the street of one of the holiday resorts along the coast of Thailand

"The red prince," Prince Utthong Souphanouvong giving a speech

Cambodia

The Cambodian king Sihanouk established socialist rule in 1955. The communism propagated by the Khmer Rouge between 1976 and 1979 was accompanied by terror and genocide.

1 Guerrilla units of the Khmer Rouge in 1980

2 Cambodian dictator Pol Pot

On March 12, 1945, ❸ King Norodom Sihanouk declared Cambodia (also known as Kampuchea) independent, but the French, colonial rulers of Cambodia since 1863, fought an increasingly vicious war with Communist insurgents before finally recognizing Cambodian independence at the end of the Indochinese War in 1954. Sihanouk abdicated in 1955 in favor of his father and, after a landslide election victory, became prime minister. As a socialist, he aligned with China, causing the Western powers to support the right-wing Khmer Serai. When the US Air Force began bombing border villages in 1965, intending to stamp out Vietcong bases and supply routes, the situation deteriorated.

3 Sihanouk, king of Cambodia, during a speech in 1966

A pro-Western group led by Prime Minister ❺ Lon Nol seized power in 1970, and the leftist factions went underground and formed the Communist ❶ Khmer Rouge. Together with the followers of Sihanouk, who had fled to China, they waged a violent civil war against the government of Lon Nol. Following the withdrawal of US troops from Vietnam, the Khmer Rouge advanced rapidly, and in April 1975 took the capital Phnom Penh.

5 The pro-American prime minister Nol (left) at a champagne reception with important military leaders, 1975

The leader of the Khmer Rouge, ❷ Pol Pot, together with the nominal president, Khieu Samphan, came to power in April 1976. They subjected the country to a radical social reform process that was aimed at creating a purely agrarian-based Communist society. The city-dwellers were deported to the countryside, where they were combined with the local population and subjected to forced labor. About two million Cambodians died in ❹ waves of murder, torture, and starvation, aimed particularly at the educated and intellectual elite. Whole sections of the population were systematically wiped out. The terror gradually ended with the capture of Phnom Penh by invading Vietnamese troops in 1979, but the Khmer Rouge continued to fight on as guerrillas. Prince Sihanouk, in alliance with the Khmer Rouge, formed a government-in-exile against the Vietnamese occupation in 1982. In April 1989, a new constitution declared Cambodia to be an ideologically neutral state with Buddhism as the state religion, and a constitutional monarch where the executive power, however, is invested in the Prime Minister. In 1991 Sihanouk once again became head of state. The leader of the leftist People's party, Hun Sen, staged a coup in 1997 and became prime minister following parliamentary elections in 1998.

4 Skeletons of some 2000 victims, in the northwest of Cambodia, are reminders of the terror carried out by Pol Pot on the Cambodian population

Pol Pot

Pol Pot ("The Organizer") was born Saloth Sar. Little is known about his personal life. He studied electrical engineering in Paris, France in 1949–1953 and then worked as a teacher in Phnom Penh. There he began his steady rise through the ranks of the Communist party. Between 1975 and 1979 he gave orders for the deaths of millions of Cambodians in an extraordinarily oppressive social experiment aimed at creating a totally communist society. He was convicted of genocide and condemned to death in absentia. After his arrest in 1997, a "people's court" changed the sentence to life imprisonment. Following an escape effort into the Cambodian forest, Pol Pot died on March 15, 1998 and was cremated with only close associates in attendance.

One of the major criminals of the 20th century: Pol Pot

1946–54 | "Indochinese War"

1949 | Ho Chi Minh president in Vietnam

1954 | Ceasefire following Indochinese conference in Geneva

1957 | Begining of the second phase of the Vietnam War

Vietnam War

War for the unity and independence of Vietnam was waged from 1946 to 1976. Through the military intervention of the United States in 1964, it became one of the ❼ bloodiest conflicts of the post–World War II period.

One year after the Communists proclaimed the Democratic Republic of Vietnam in the northern Vietnamese city of Hanoi in 1945, the Indochinese War (1946–1954) broke out. Although France had granted the state under the presidency of ❾ Ho Chi Minh the status of a Vietnamese "free state" within the French Union in 1946, it tried to restore its colonial rule over the country from out of Saigon in southern Vietnam. With that, France instigated a military conflict with the Communist rulers in the north, who put up bitter resistance against the foreign troops, primarily through the guerrilla troops of the Viet Minh. Through international mediation, a cease-fire was concluded in 1954 that included a division of the country in the Geneva Accords; the Communists controlled North Vietnam, and a pro-Western Republic of Vietnam was established in the South under the Catholic leader Ngo Dinh Diem. After the withdrawal of the French from Indochina, South Vietnam received financial and military support from the United States. Corruption and oppression in the Diem regime empowered the primarily Communist opposition National Liberation Front in South Vietnam, and its military wing, the Vietcong, began a guerrilla war in 1956. With the goal of preventing the further spread of communism in Asia, direct US military intervention began in 1964.

7 The South Vietnamese head of police Nguyen Ngoc Loan shoots an officer of the Vietcong troops in Saigon on the February 1,1966

9 Ho Chi Min, Vietnamese Revolutionary

Following the claim that two US destroyers in the Gulf of Tonkin had been attacked on August 2, 1964, the Vietnam War began. North Vietnamese cities and supply channels were systematically bombed by US aircraft beginning in February 1965. In the South, continuous bombardments were intended to destroy the communist's' morale, and ❻ napalm and chemical ❽ defoliants were used to deprive the Vietcong troops of cover. Despite their military superiority, US forces were unable to defeat their opponents. The fighting that often involved civilians and incidents of excessive ❿ violence by the US troops—most infamously the My Lai massacre of hundreds of unarmed Vietnamese women and children civilians—incited international and US domestic protests against America's conduct in the war (p. 638). Following the communist's' Tet Offensive against Saigon in January 1968, the United States gradually began to withdraw from the war, shifting control of military operations to the South Vietnamese. A cease-fire was first agreed upon in January 1973, but North Vietnamese troops marched into Saigon in April 1975; on July 2, 1976, Vietnam was reunited as a socialist republic.

After Vietnam's involvement in Cambodia in 1978, violent border disputes with China followed until 1984. In 1986 the Communist regime began introducing economic reforms aimed at creating a capitalist-orientated market economy, without loosening the power monopoly of the communists. Vietnam and the US resumed diplomatic relations in 1995.

6 Soldiers and terrified children flee a village following a Napalm attack by US military planes

8 American bombers spray defoliants over the countryside

10 US soldiers destroy a Vietcong camp

2 Aug 1964 | US involvement escelates
Feb 1965 | Bombing of North Vietnam cities
Jan 1973 | Cease fire
Apr 1975 | FNL troops in Saigon
2 Jul 1976 | "Socialist Republic" of Vietnam reunited

China, Japan, and Korea since 1945

Following ❶ victory in the civil war, the communists under Mao Zedong took power in China in 1949. In the years that followed, the most populous country on Earth underwent a dramatic transformation. After World War II, Japan transformed itself to become the world's second largest economy, although it has suffered from recession since 1990. Korea broke up into a Communist dictatorship in the North and a republic in the South, which became democratic in 1987.

1 Communists marching into Beijing are welcomed by crowds, 1949

Mao Zedong Comes to Power in China

Following the proclamation of the People's Republic of China in 1949, Mao initiated a restructuring of society along communist lines that fundamentally altered China.

After the surrender of Japan in 1945, the united front between the Kuomintang under Chiang Kai-shek and the communist troops under Mao Zedong quickly fell apart (p. 494), and in 1947 civil war broke out. In 1949 the communists occupied Beijing, and within a year a defeated Chiang had fled to Taiwan, where he declared himself president and ruled until his death in 1975.

In Beijing, ❺ Mao placed himself at the head of a Central People's Government and on October 1, 1949, proclaimed the People's Republic of China (PRC). He remained state premier until 1959, with ❻ Zhou Enlai as his prime minister. The ❷ new regime occupied Tibet in 1950 and a year later annexed it to the PRC; Tibet's Dalai Lama, was exiled in 1959.

3 A tribunal accuses Huang Chin-Chi of resisting collectivization

Mao introduced a radical domestic political reorganization within the state and society and enshrined the communist monopoly on government (p. 446) in the ❹ new constitution of 1954. Sweeping aside the old elite, the government extended land reform through the ❸ collectivization of agriculture. Existing industries were nationalized and, with Soviet support, a state-led industrialization program was launched. In this period, the economy grew, while education reforms improved literacy levels. The party rapidly came to dominate all aspects of public life through a network that reached even into remote rural areas. The powerful military and security forces were ideologically loyal to the party, which rapidly became synonymous with the state. In 1956–1957 the party leadership asked intellectuals to offer criticism in the "Hundred Flowers Campaign." After a few months in which increasingly hostile critiques were published, the party put an end to the experiment and arrested the disidents.

2 Chinese troops in Tibet, 1950–1951

4 The Central People's Government enacts the new constitution on June 14, 1954

5 Mao Zedong proclaims the People's Republic of China, October 1, 1949

6 Prime Minister Zhou Enlai, Mao's right hand man, 1957

The Dalai Lama

When the Chinese occupiers brutally suppressed an uprising of the Tibetan people in 1959, Tenzin Gyatso, the 14th Dalai Lama, fled into exile in India. Since then, the important teacher of Buddhism has gained a large international audience for his pronouncements on world peace. In 1989, he received the Nobel Peace Prize as the exiled leader of a neutral Tibet, despite Chinese protests.

The Dalai Lama in Berlin, 2003

2 Sep 1945 | Japan surrenders
1 Oct 1949 | People's Republic of China proclaimed
1950 | Chinese occupation of Tibet
1951 | Tibet annexed by China
1954 | Mao's Communists come to power
1958–61 | "Great Leap Forward" program

China from the Korean War to the Cultural Revolution

To counter internal party criticism, and in opposition to the Soviet Union, Mao intensified the socialist program from the mid-1950s on. The ❼ Cultural Revolution (1966–69) he initiated proved chaotic and ruinous.

7 Members of the Red Guard with flags and banners during a mass rally in Beijing, 1960s

The PRC's unsuccessful attempts to achieve the return of Taiwan to the motherland saw tensions with the United States grow, as the United States chose to recognize Chiang Kai-shek as the sole legitimate representative of all China. Sino-American relations reached a new low when China entered the Korean War (p. 622) on the side of the North and also became involved in the conflicts in Vietnam and Cambodia (p. 616–617).

After the death of Stalin in 1953 (p. 586), China's relations with the Soviet Union deteriorated, building into an ideological and geopolitical split that remained until the collapse of the USSR. China contested the Soviet claim to leadership of the Communist world, and with the development of its own atomic weapons in 1964, clearly staked its claim to equal status with the two global superpowers, the United States and the Soviet Union.

8 Mao Zedong, left, together with his successor, Lin Biao, 1957

9 Heroic image of a young Chinese peasant working on a collective farm, propaganda poster, 1967

10 Propaganda painting of Mao Zedong,1950s

In 1958 a program of collectivization and indoctrination, or "reeducation," was launched in what was billed as the "Great Leap Forward." In contrast to the Soviet focus on heavy industry, Maoist policy concentrated on collectivizing the ❾ agricultural sector and launching local small-scale steel production. To this end, the rural population was divided into more than 25,000 "people's communes," and "production brigades" were formed. Together with mass mobilizations for the construction of roads and irrigation systems, this was expected to complete the transition to true communism.

The results of this policy were calamitous, with famines in 1960–1961 killing millions of peasants. As a result, criticism of the leadership grew within the party, particularly from Liu Shaoqi and Deng Xiaoping, who sought a more liberal, technology-focused policy. Mao Zedong stepped down in 1959 in favor of Liu, although he remained the ⓬ leading symbol of the party. With help from his "crown prince" ❽ Lin Biao, he turned the people's liberation army into the Maoist Guard and intensified the party struggle against those with "rightist" tendencies.

Toward the end of 1965, frustrated with the moderate direction of policy under his successor, Mao and his supporters proclaimed the "Great Proletarian Cultural Revolution" and publicly announced a campaign against representatives of the "capitalist way" and traditional Chinese thinking. The crusade was accompanied by a ❿ ritualized personal veneration of Mao. The ⓫ radical student Red Guards became a nationwide spy network. They terrorized and humiliated Mao's critics and harassed members of local officialdom. As their excesses increasingly grew out of control, the military and the party intervened with the approval of Mao, and by the end of 1967 order had been restored.

The Cultural Revolution led to anarchy, violence, and the displacement of much of the old party cadre. In 1969 Mao officially declared it over. Lin Biao became the designated successor of the increasingly frail Mao.

11 Young members of the Red Guard hold up copies of Mao's *Little Red Book* of quotes, Tiananmen Square, Beijing, 1965

12 "Long live our great teacher": Poster of Chairman Mao

1959 | Dalai Lama's exile begins
1959 | Mao steps down
1965 | Great Cultural Revolution
1969 | Cultural revolution ends
1989 | 14th Dalai Lama wins Nobel Peace Prize

China 1969–1989

The power struggle between Mao and the reformers around Deng, only ended with the death of the iconic leader. The group led by Deng then began to introduce reforms.

Tianjin, in the northeast of China, the second largest trading port in the world; in 1984 it became an "open city" for foreign investors, October 2001

After the Cultural Revolution, the moderate faction within the Communist party once again gained strength. Mao Zedong remained the highest authority in the state despite serious illness, although numerous party functionaries who had been expelled during the Cultural Revolution were rehabilitated. Following the unexplained death of Lin Biao in 1971, pragmatic forces within the party led by Premier Zhou Enlai and his protégé ❶ Deng Xiaoping emerged victorious for the first time. However, only after the deaths of Zhou and Mao in 1976 were the reformers around Deng finally able to have their way. The radical left-wing group called the "Gang of Four," including Mao's widow ❺ Jiang Qing, was stripped of power and condemned by a special court in 1981. Mao's successor as party chairman was Premier ❻ Hua Guofeng, while economic policies were decided by Deng. After Mao, ❹ Deng was the primary influence on the party, and he established new international economic ties. In June 1981 one of Deng's protégés, the reformer ❼ Hu Yaobang, replaced Hua as party chairman, thus clearing the path for Deng's new political direction.

Mao's widow, Jiang Qing, during her trial in Beijing, 1981

Hua Guofeng, Mao Zedong's successor as party leader

Deng then introduced economic modernization and liberalization in virtually all areas of society, and from 1979 he opened the nation to international trade with the establishment of "special economic zones." Deng also strove for a socialist but ❷ market-oriented economy, in which wage differences could exist and in which achievement had priority over other considerations. The country also liberalized politically. Everyday life became less and less dominated by ideological dogma and a Western-influenced legal system was slowly established, although freedoms of speech and assembly were forbidden and a move toward elections was not on the agenda.

Mao Zedong greeting Nixon, the first US president to visit China, 1972

In foreign policy as well, the pragmatic line held the upper hand. After serious border conflicts with the Soviet Union in 1969, a foreign political détente was evident through the admission of the People's Republic into the United Nations in 1971 and a ❸ visit from US President Nixon to China in 1972. Negotiations with the Soviets in 1982 led to a normalization of diplomatic relations and the reopening of their respective embassies in 1986. Regarding the question of Taiwan, however, the People's Republic remained adamant that only Beijing had the political right to represent China internationally and refused to recognize the government established on the island.

Deng Xiaoping

Deng Xiaoping is driven past a parade of Chinese soldiers

The reformer Hu Yaobang, June 16, 1986

1971 | Lin Biao dies
1972 | Nixon's visit to China
1979 | Special economic zones set up
1971 | People's Republic of China joins UN
9 Sep 1976 | Death of Mao
1981 | Condemnation of "Band of Four"

China since 1989

The refusal to allow political freedoms culminated in the massacre of Tiananmen Square in 1989. Despite worldwide protest, China held to the strategy of ❿ economic liberalism without a parallel political liberalization and refused to let Western demands shape its policy.

The easing of restrictions in the economy and lifestyle in China led to the growth of ❽ demands for a political voice for the people of China, particularly by students and intellectuals, and from both within and outside the party. The party's internal conflict concerning its future direction became more intense. In January 1987, following student protests, General Secretary Hu was dismissed as too liberal and was replaced by the previous premier of the State

10 The entrance to the Chinese stock exchange in Shanghai

Council, Zhao Ziyang; the new premier was Li Peng. In May 1989 in a number of cities, particularly in Beijing, students and civil rights activists demonstrated for freedom, civil rights, and democ-

12 Jiang Zemin, who continued Deng's economic reforms

8 Chinese students demonstrating for freedom and democratic reforms, June 1989

racy. Zhao was open to dialogue, but he was dismissed in June, and the hard line of Deng and Li triumphed. The months of peaceful protest in Beijing's Tiananmen Square were terminated on June 3–4, 1989, with the deployment of troops and tanks. The worldwide condemnation of this crackdown went largely unheeded and, despite economic sanctions against China from the majority of Western nations, death sentences and long prison terms were conferred on the leaders of the protests.

Li and the new party general secretary, ⓬ Jiang Zemin, guaranteed the continuation of Deng Xiaoping's economic policies in the succeeding years and even after his death in 1997. They also held onto the right of exclusive power for the party, which was expressly confirmed in 1990. The hard line taken against members of the ❾ Falun Gong religious sect in 1999–2000 showed that the party's claim to power was unbroken. The creation of a "socialist market economy" was concluded in 1993, and economic and trade relations with the Western industrial nations were intensified. A new generation appeared in the political leadership in March 2003 with Premier Wen Jiabao and President Hu Jintao, who has been general secretary of the party since November 2002. In view of the enormous ⓫, ⓭ economic potential of China, Western voices critical of the human rights situation have been muted.

In foreign affairs, China's tense relations with its neighboring states of Vietnam, Laos, and Japan were normalized between 1990 and 1993 via treaties and frontier agreements. The tone of comments relating to Taiwan became more severe after 1996; the possibility of an official Taiwanese declaration of independence has led to military threats from the People's Republic since 2004. The former British colony of Hong Kong was reintegrated into China on July 1, 1997. The fear of political pressure and the risk of a flight of capital from the financial center city prior to the handover was countered by China with the concession of special "Western" rights for Hong Kong, although there have been protests for greater democratic freedoms.

11 Chinese commuter sends a text message on his mobile phone

9 Falun Gong protest over the persecution of their Chinese members, 2001

13 Luxury apartments in the city of Shanghai, 2005

1982 | Diplomatic relations normalized with USSR
1987 | Hu Yaobang resigns
May 1989 | Demonstrations in Beijing
3–4 Jun 1989 | Tiananmen Square Massacre
1 Jul 1997 | Hong Kong reverts to China
1999–2000 | Persecution of Falun Gong Sect

Korea

The Korean Peninsula has been divided since 1948. The Communist dictatorship in the North has increasingly been isolated, while the republic in the South held its first elections in 1987.

After the 1945 defeat of Japan—which had occupied Korea (p. 419) since 1910—Korea was occupied by the Soviets in the north and by the Americans in the south. In February 1946, Kim Il Sung, formed a government along Soviet lines in the north, and on September 9, 1948, he proclaimed the People's Democratic Republic.

3 US Marines bearing the flags of Korea, the US and the UN, 1950

When the Soviet troops withdrew, Korean troops from the North invaded the South in June 1950, beginning the Korean War. Under a UN mandate, ❷, ❸ US and allied troops repelled the North Korean attack, but China intervened on the side of the North. The armistice signed on July 27, 1953, ended a conflict that cost millions of lives.

Politically, North Korea aligned with the Soviet Union and China. A ❶ state doctrine of self-sufficiency was proclaimed in 1955 by the Communist regime with a cult of personality centered on ❹ Kim. Since 1989, the dictatorship has sealed the country off from the world, although it is suspected that the populace faces massive human rights abuses and starvation. In 1997 Kim Il Sung's son, ❺ Kim Jong Il, took power. Due to the continuation of its nuclear program since 2001 despite international protests, North Korea has become a concern for East Asian security, which is now being addressed through the Six-Party Talks with both Koreas, China, Japan, the United States, and Russia.

In 1948, South Korea established an authoritarian regime aligned with the West. The president of this First Republic, ❻ Syngman Rhee, was deposed in April 1960. In August the Democratic party took over the government and established the Second Republic, which was replaced by a military government in 1961. General Park Chung Hee established the Third Republic in December 1963.

Continuing animosity between North and South Korea decreased after 1971. Various forms of military regimes followed after the assassination of General Park in October 1979. In October 1987 a new constitution introduced democratic reforms, although President Roh Tae Woo continued to counter the protests with authoritarian methods. It was only in 1997 with the election of Kim Dae Jung that democratic conditions were established and national reconciliation between North and South Korea was pursued. These policies were continued by ❼ Roh Moo Hyun, who has been president since February 2003.

6 Syngman Rhee awards a military order of merit to US General Douglas MacArthur in Seoul, October 5, 1950

7 The president of South Korea, Roh Moo Hyun, during a press conference in Seoul on June 23, 2004

1 Kim Il Sung, who developed the doctrine of self-sufficiency, raising economic autarky to national policy, 1966

2 US artillery fires on attacking North Korean troops to cover their retreat, April 27, 1951

4 The "great leader" of North Korea: Kim Il Sung, July 1976

5 The "much loved leader": Kim Il Sung's son, Kim Jong Il, in 1988 during a meeting with members of the Korean People's Army

Kim Dae Jung

Kim Dae Jung has been an activist of the Democratic party since 1956. He stood as an opposition candidate to President Park in 1971 and had to flee to Japan in 1972. The following year he was abducted and taken back to South Korea. In 1976 he demanded the reinstatement of basic rights, and for this he was sentenced to five years in prison and in 1980 sentenced to death; after international protests, the government withdrew the sentence. From 1987, Kim led the democratic opposition, and he won the presidential elections in 1997. In 2000 he was awarded the Nobel Peace Prize.

above: Kim Dae Jung, who supported the dialogue between the two Korean states, March 9, 2000

1945 Occupation of Korea | **3 Nov 1946** Japan proclaims parliamentary democracy | **9 Sep 1948** Proclamation of "Democratic People's Republic" in North Korea

1946 North Korea under Premier Kim Il Sung | **1948** First Republic under Syngman Rhee in South Korea

Japan

In Japan after 1945, the US occupation forces installed democratic structures that proved to be robust. Through rapid economic expansion, Japan became the world's second largest economy.

The emperor of Japan, Hirohito, and his wife during a walk through the Japanese countryside, 1964

After US forces secured Japan's capitulation on September 2, 1945 (p. 498), following the dropping of atomic bombs on Hiroshima and Nagasaki, the American occupation forces oversaw the rapid installation of a civilian democratic government in Japan. In January 1946, ❾ Emperor Hirohito renounced his "divine" birthright, and on November 3, Japan established a parliamentary democracy under a new constitution. Democratic political parties and worker's syndicates were established, and various coalition governments were formed. In April 1952 Japan was officially returned to full sovereignty. Administrations were often only briefly in office, but on the whole the new system proved to be stable and effective. In November 1955 the Liberal and Japan Democratic parties united as the Liberal Democratic party, which has been the ❿ majority party ever since, ruling the country in shifting coalitions. However, corruption scandals and financial dealings among its own members continue to cause difficulties. The socialists, with their various groupings, form the perennial opposition, but are nevertheless often included in the government as a result of the coalition-style government. In foreign policy, relations with neighboring states have been shaped to some extent by Japan's imperial legacy, its conduct during World War II, and the way these topics are taught in Japanese schools; these are particularly sensitive issues for China and Korea. With the end of the Cold War and the growth of economic interdependence in the 1990s, regional relations have improved somewhat. After the rapid reconstruction of the country with US financial assistance, Japan experienced a massive market-oriented ❽ modernization and industrialization drive. This led to the rejection of many ⓬ traditional society structures and therefore did not go uncriticized. The 1990s have seen the rise in the political influence of conservative religious groups.

Japanese Prime Minister Junichiro Koizumi gives a speech in Yokosuka on March 21, 2005

Business buildings in the Japanese capital Tokyo with billboards, December, 2004

Japan developed into one of the ⓫ leading Asian nations and competed successfully with the Western nations on the world market, but it has experienced a drawn-out recession since 1990 and has been affected by the vicissitudes of the global economy. It also suffers financially from earthquakes.

After the 1989 death of Hirohito, whose role prior to 1945 is not yet subject to a national consensus, his son ⓮ Akihito took office as constitutional monarch without religious legitimization. Since 1992, economic problems in Japan have shaken the postwar political consensus, resulting in rapidly changing governments. Prime Minister ⓭ Junichiro Koizumi, in office since 2001, has attempted to revive the economy by introducing financial and structural reforms.

Japanese Emperor Akihito during the inaugural meeting of the newly elected Japanese parliament on January 21, 2005

Tradition and modern technology:Three Japanese women wearing traditional kimonos and using mobile phones, 1999

Toshiki Kaifu, left, paints a lucky token on the day of the election, which he won on February 18, 1990

View over a stone bridge of the Emperor's Palace in the Japanese capital Tokyo, 1994

1955 | State doctrine of "independence" in North Korea **1997** | Kim Dae Jung's government in South Korea **2000** | Kim Dae Jung awarded Nobel Peace Prize

Jun 1950 | Korean War begins **1987** | New constitution in South Korea **1997** | Kim Jong Il takes power in North Korea

Australia, New Zealand, and Oceania since 1945

❶ Australia and New Zealand are wealthy and stable democracies based on the Anglo-Saxon parliamentary model, in which conservatives and social democrats alternate running the government. The original inhabitants in both countries—the Aborigines in Australia and the Maori in New Zealand—demand greater recognition of the centuries-long suppression of their cultural identities. As colonies of settlement in the British Empire, their transition to independence was smooth, and both voluntarily maintain strong links to Great Britain as members of the Commonwealth.

Symbol of the Australian capital: The Sydney Opera House, 1996

Australia

Since 1945, Australia has been a stable democracy, firmly aligned with the West during the Cold War. Its pluralistic society has yet to achieve a full reconciliation with the Aborigines, who remain economically and socially marginalized.

Australia, a constitutional monarchy and member of the ❹ Commonwealth, was threatened by Japan in 1942 in the Pacific War—an experience that brought the country closer to the US. This relationship was maintained after the war, and in April 1952 Australia entered into the ❺ ANZUS pact with New Zealand and the United States for security in the Pacific region. It sent troops during the Korean and Vietnam wars (p. 622, p. 617). Since 2001, Australia has been one of America's closest allies.

Elizabeth II, Australia's official head of state, March 22, 2000

Over the last two decades, Australia has looked to forge better relations with its Asian neighbors. The Australian government has worked to establish free-trade agreements with China and ASEAN (the Association of Southeast Asian Nations). It has also tried to prevent conflicts in Papua New Guinea and the Solomon Islands.

Native of Australia: An Aborigine prepares for a traditional dance

Liberals, conservatives, and social democrats compete in shifting coalitions over the formation of the government. After a long period with Labour in power (1983–1996), the Liberals won the 1996 elections and John Winston Howard became prime minister. The proposal of the constitutional assembly of 1998 to transform Australia into a republic was rejected in a referendum in November 1999, and Queen Elizabeth II remains the head of state.

Meeting of ANZUS members's representatives, August 1952

Economically, Australia is a major exporter, and since 1966 Japan has been the country's largest trading partner. Mineral resources (bauxite, nickel, oil) began to be mined more intensively in the 1950s. Liberal and competitive economic policies have attracted substantial foreign investment, especially from Europe and the United States.

Since the late 1970s there has been a growing recognition of the need to reconcile with the island's native inhabitants, the ❷, ❸ Aborigines, whose culture has long been suppressed and their living space progressively encroached upon. They have been granted wide-ranging cultural autonomy and targeted economic assistance, and in 1993 a law was passed opening the way to land restitution. Environmental issues arouse strong feelings in Australia and massive ❻ protests have taken place against nuclear tests carried out in the Pacific.

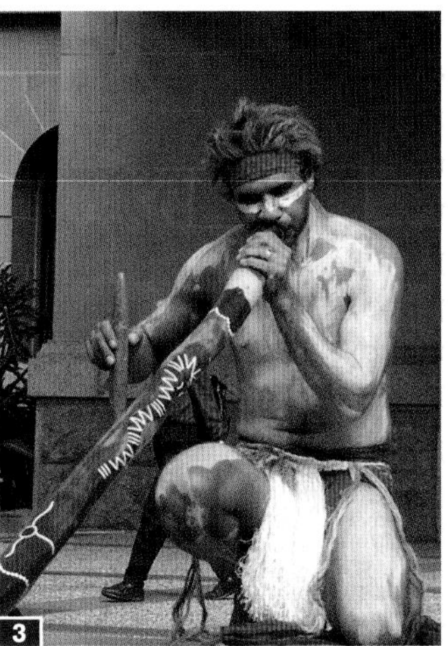

Aborigine plays in a Brisbane street, June 3, 2004

An Australian demonstrates against nuclear weapon tests, August 2001

New Zealand and the Islands of Oceania

New Zealand is a stable and prosperous democracy. The islands of the Pacific region gradually gained their independence after 1945 but for the most part maintain strong economic and political relationships with the major powers.

New Zealand became a sovereign state within the British Commonwealth on November 25, 1947. It has remained close to Australia, the United Kingdom, and the United States in its foreign policy, although there was a period of strained relations with the United States after New Zealand declared itself to be a nuclear-free zone in 1987. It joined the United States and Australia in the ANZUS defense pact. Domestically, the National Party and Labour are the two major political parties in the parliamentary system. The Labour party has led most of the governments since 1945, and since 1999 Labour's ❾ Helen Clark has been prime minister, supported by shifting coalitions. Although New Zealand has diversified significantly since the 1980s, ❿ animal husbandry, especially sheep farming, remains a key economic sector.

Men in Papua New Guinea wearing necklaces and headdresses made of plants

Helen Clark, first female prime minister of New Zealand, November 28, 1999

Most of the islands of Oceania fought for and won their independence after 1945. Relationships with former colonial powers often proved problematic. Today, most of the islands are ruled by elected governments. Conflict between ethnic groups sometimes erupts into violence, as happened on Guadalcanal in the Solomon Islands in 1998. Most of the island groups of Oceania formed the South Sea Forum with Australia and New Zealand in 1971 to promote further economic and cultural cooperation in the Pacific region.

The United States took over the administration of ⓫ Micronesia in 1947. After proclaiming the Federated States of Micronesia in 1979, the islands joined an association agreement with the United States in 1983. In 1986, the Marshall Islands also voted for a "free association" with the United States but declared independence in 1990.

In 1956–1957, the French-controlled territories of Oceania and Polynesia were given their own constitutions. Many former British territories, including Tonga and Fiji, have declared their independence; in the face of protests from Great Britain, a military regime seized power in ❼ Fiji in 1987 and declared a republic. A June 2001 peace deal put an end to a conflict between the central government of ❽ Papua New Guinea and militant separatists on the island of Bougainville that had raged since 1988–1989 and cost more than 10,000 lives.

Contrasts: Arcades from the colonial era next to a modern multi-story building on the Fiji island of Viti Levu

The Kingdom of Tonga

The Kingdom of Tonga, which is comprised of about 170 islands, has been ruled since 1965 by King Taufa'ahau Tupou IV. Although the king supports maintaining traditional lifestyles and economic structures, the government strongly promotes economic investment in the islands with tax policies designed to attract foreign companies. In 2001, a biotechnical company was granted permission to record and research the genetic makeup of the entire native population, which is considered to be one of the most homogeneous in the world.

King Taufa'ahau Tupou IV

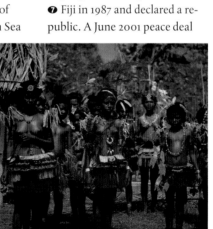

View over the green mountains of New Zealand, used for the sheep breeding that is the focus of the country's agriculture

Young women and girls wearing traditional headdresses and dancing costumes, Micronesia

1983 | Micronesia association agreement with the US

1987 | New Zealand declared nuclear-free zone

1988–89 | Civil war in Papua New Guinea

1990 | Marshall Islands's independence

from 1996 | Regency of John Winston in Australia

1 Famine: Undernourished child in a Sudanese refugee camp

Africa since the Independence of its Nations since 1945

The nations of Sub-Saharan Africa that became independent after 1957 have continued to suffer the consequences of their continent's experience of colonialism. The optimism of the early years of independence soon gave way to repeated military coups, violent conflicts, and popular disillusionment with promises to end poverty and improve living conditions. Other problems faced in parts of the region include ❸ drought and ❶ famines, limited access to drinking water, and the alarming growth of HIV/AIDS since the 1980s. These problems are compounded by authoritarian and frequently corrupt regimes.

Decolonization: Background and Problems

After World War II, weakened European colonial powers and an increased self-awareness of the native peoples led many African colonies toward self-government. Since independence, however, most have struggled to overcome serious economic, political, and social challenges.

Powerful ❺ independence movements began forming in the African colonies following World War II, leading to the creation of many new African nations since 1957. The main reason for the success of the Pan-African movement after 1945 lay in the increased self-awareness of the African nations. World War II, in which troops from many ❹ colonies fought alongside their colonial rulers, precipitated the end of European supremacy. The development of new forms of ❻ Islam, and especially of Christianity, that distinctly differed from the Western forms and were closely tied with concepts of national identity also played an important role. Most important of all, though, was a rethinking in the approach of the weakened European powers after the war.

3 Herdsman leads his emaciated cattle through a landscape marked by drought, 1985

The majority of the ❷ initiators of African independence came from the groups of native intellectuals and professional elites who had been educated in the colonial motherlands and who admired the functioning administration and material progress they encountered. They hoped that self-rule would help to create these conditions in the former colonies, too. However, on the threshold of independence, Africa was confronted by problems that were difficult to resolve and were often a legacy of colonialism (p. 422–425). The gap between the educated elite and the ❼ illiterate majority of the populace was often vast, and the economies of these nations were intricately bound to the needs of the colonial metropoles. Furthermore, many of the former colonies were not "nations" as such, but zones of European influence. Abstract borders arbitrarily divided and grouped linguistic and ethnic groups, making it difficult for the inhabitants to identify with the resultant countries. Tribal solidarity and majority-versus-minority struggles often undermined the new democratic structures. An extreme case of societal breakdown was the 1994 genocide in Rwanda (p. 629). With a colonial legacy of political instability, unclear borders, poverty, and no infrastructure, the odds were against the new states.

2 Julius Nyerere, who studied in England, became the first prime minister of Tanzania in 1964

4 Senegalese soldiers on the side of Allied forces, in German captivity, 1940

5 Members of the Senegalese population demonstrate for independence

6 A group of African Muslim men pray in Senegal, ca.1950

7 Night school for the education of illiterate adults, Cameroon

1946 | Abolition of forced labor in the colonies
1957 | Ghana's sovereignty
1960 | Independence of Nigeria and Cameroon
from 1960 | Independence of French colonies
1961 | Wars of Independence in Angola and Mozambique

The End of Colonialism

From the late 1950s, the colonial powers of Great Britain, France, and Belgium saw their rule in Africa gradually come to an end. Where possible, they sought to retain their commercial interests.

9 Sunset over the Niger River in Bamako, the capital of Mali

The three countries responded in different ways to African desires for independence. The British initially used indigenous social structures and elites in order to "indirectly" administer their

11 Kwame Nkrumah waving to the crowd after having become the first president of the Republic of Ghana

colonies cheaply and efficiently. The British slowly resigned themselves to African self-government, although African independence movements forced the pace. This was the case in

13 De Gaulle meets regional leaders fighting for independence in Brazzaville

⓫ Ghana, which became the first independent nation in Sub-Saharan Africa in 1957. One after another, colonies became sovereign members of the British Commonwealth (p. 500): Nigeria and Somalia in 1960, Uganda in 1962, Zanzibar (which joined with Tanganyika in 1964 to form Tanzania) and Kenya in 1963, and Zambia in 1964. Rhodesia and South Africa (p. 633) were exceptions, as the white populations seized power to prevent black majority rule.

France attempted at quite an early stage to grant civil rights to its Sub-Saharan African colonies and thereby to bind them to the motherland. In 1944, in order to ensure assistance in the struggle against the Vichy regime (p. 460), General de Gaulle, the leader of the French government-in-exile, assured some of the ⓭ African leaders that civil rights would be granted to all inhabitants of the French colonies. In 1946 forced labor was abolished, but as the promised benefits failed to materialize, demands for independence grew louder. De Gaulle's plan for a union of states under French leadership failed. With the exception of Algeria (p. 594), the French African colonies—including the ❿ Ivory Coast, Guinea, Cameroon, ❽ Niger, Senegal, Chad, and the Central African Republic—gained their ❾ independence peacefully after 1960; the strategically important Djibouti became politically independent only in 1977.

Of the Belgian colonies, the Congo, considered a "model colony," underwent a particularly traumatic decolonization experience via intervention by the

12 Civil war in Angola, 1976

8 Independence, Nigeria, 1965

10 The first prime minister of the sovereign Ivory Coast, Felix Hophouet-Boigny, gives a speech, ca. 1965

United States (p. 630). Rwanda and Burundi became independent in 1962.

Portugal employed mercenary troops to stifle the independence movements in its colonies, ⓬ Angola and Mozambique. Bloody fighting raged through the 1960s, and they did not win their independence until 1975 (p. 632).

Ghanaian President Kwame Nkrumah

"Our Way to Freedom," 1961

"The African independence movement, which after the Second World War gained more importance, spread far and wide across Africa like a bush fire. The clear, echoing cry for freedom... has become a powerful hurricane, that will sweep away the old colonial Africa. The year 1960 was the year of Africa. In that year alone 17 African states came into being as proud and independent, sovereign nations."

Kwame Nkrumah, the spiritual leader of Pan-Africanism and of African socialism

1962 | Rwanda und Burundi gain independence
1963 | Sovereignty of Kenya and Zanzibar
1964 | Sovereignty of Zambia
1975 | Angola gains independence
1977 | Djibouti gains independence

West Africa

Of the West African countries, Nigeria has had the most turbulent postcolonial history. Ghana, Senegal, and the Ivory Coast have slowly consolidated since their independence.

2 John Kufour at his swearing-in ceremony as the new president of Ghana, January 7, 2001

3 The name of the Biafra region became synonymous with misery, hunger, despair, and suffering

On March 6, 1957, ❶ Ghana became the first independent nation in sub-Saharan Africa. Kwame Nkrumah, one of the intellectual leaders of Africa's liberation and Ghana's prime minister since 1952, became president and installed an increasingly autocratic regime. In February 1966 he was deposed by a military coup d'état and emigrated to Guinea. After a short democratic period lasting until 1972, the military repeatedly took power in sequence of coups. At the end of 1981, Flight Lieutenant Jerry Rawlings took power in a coup, introduced democratic structures, and liberalized the economy. He then won two successive presidential elections before peacefully handing over governmental power to the victorious opposition leader ❷ John Kufuor in 2001.

After Nigeria's independence in 1960, intense clan wars took place, leading to the separation of national regions and parallel governments. From 1966 to 1999, several military coups and regimes followed one another, interrupted by short phases of democratization. A civil war broke out from 1967 to 1970 over the ❸ Biafra region, which declared itself provisionally independent. Since 1999, under the leadership of President ❻ Olusegun Obasanjo, Nigeria has begun to stabilize and seek relations with the international community. However, corruption and religious conflicts continue to afflict the country.

5 Guinea's president Lansana Conté

6 Olusegun Obasanjo

In Senegal, ❹ Leopold Sédar Senghor ruled from 1960. He was a socialist and acclaimed poet who was greatly respected as a spokesperson for the continent and as an international mediator. Senghor ruled as president until 1980 in a surprisingly liberal presidential system. His successors, Abdou Diouf (1980–2000) and Abdoulaye Wade maintained the internal political stability of the Senegalese state.

Ahmed Sékou Touré, who was president of Guinea from 1958 to 1984, established a socialist presidential government. His regime survived several coup attempts and was characterized by brutal suppression of the civilian population. His successor ❺ Lansana Conté continued this dictatorial rule. Corruption and human rights abuses have discouraged international donors and foreign investment, and in January 2005 Conté narrowly escaped an assassination attempt.

The Ivory Coast (Côte d'Ivoire) was led by President Félix Houphouet-Boigny until 1993. During this period, the country was one of the most economically prosperous and politically stable in Africa, although it fell short of a democratic system. Both his successor Henri Bédié, who ruled for seven years before being ousted in 2000, and the socialist ❼ Laurent Gbagbo used rigged elections to bolster the legitimacy of their rule. In 2002 a civil war broke out as the north and the south of the country split along political and sectarian lines. After the intervention of France, South Africa, and the United Nations, a peace deal was achieved in April 2005.

1 Shrine of an Asafo company of the Fanti at the coast of Ghana, painted cement, 1952

4 Leopold Sédar Senghor, 1986

7 Laurent Gbagbo, October 2000

1958–84 | Authoritarian government of Ahmed Sékou Touré in Guinea

from 1960 | Leopold Sédar Senghor president of Senegal

1967–70 | Civil war in Nigeria

1973 | Jean-Bedel Bokassa's regime in the Central African Republic

1981 | Jerry Rawlings's government in Ghana

Central Africa

Since 1960, authoritarian governments have predominated among Central African states.

9 Libyan tanks bomb a street in the Aouzou border area in the northern part of Chad, April 7, 1987

In Niger, President Hamani Diori established single-party rule in 1960 and tied the country firmly to France, as did his successor Seyni Kountché. Disturbances led to a military coup in 1996. In 1999 the military handed back power to President ❽ Mamadou Tandja, who introduced a multiparty system and democratized the nation.

Chad suffered from religious tensions that emerged between its Islamic north and Christian south. The conflict escalated, following revolts by the Muslim population over taxes, into a ❾ civil war in which France and Libya intervened between 1984 and 1988. In 1993 Idriss Déby was elected, and his government slowly stabilized the country and wrote a national constitution. In 1994 Libya withdrew its troops from the country after the International Court of Justice rejected its claim to a disputed strip of territory between the countries.

The Central African Republic was initially ruled by President David Dacko as an authoritarian state. In January 1966 he was toppled by army chief Jean-Bedel Bokassa, who established one of the cruelest regimes in Africa. Bokassa made himself president for life in 1973 and then in a ❿ megalomaniacal ceremony in December 1977 crowned himself Emperor Bokassa I. He was deposed in September 1979 with international approval, and Dacko returned to power, but the country remained unsettled. Even President ⓫ Ange Félix Patassé, emerging from a controversial election in 1993, was unable to ensure stability in the country. Various rebel groups launched a series of destabilizing insurrections during the 1990s.

In Cameroon between 1960 and 1982, the Francophile president Ahmadou Ahidjo presided over a one-party system. His successor, Paul Biya, initially followed the same policies but was forced to introduce a multiparty system in 1990 following popular protests. The democratic validity of following elections is disputed.

Genocide in Rwanda

After 1990, the tension between the Tutsi rebels and Hutu holders of power increased in Rwanda. When President Habyarimana was killed in an airplane crash under suspicious circumstances in April 1994, Hutu extremists began—with propagandist support from the government—systematically to massacre Tutsis and moderate Hutus throughout the country. Within only a few weeks, 800,000 people fell victim to a genocide in which virtually all layers of society took part. At the beginning of July, Tutsi troops were able to establish order and take control of the country.

A girl searches for her parents among the bodies of Rwandans who have been trampled to death, July 18, 1994

8 The democratic president of Niger, Mamadou Tandja, 1999

10 Jean-Bedel Bokassa during his coronation ceremony in Bangui, December 4, 1977

11 Ange Félix Patassé brandishes a gun at a press conference, Sept. 26,1979

Violent clashes had occurred in Rwanda since 1959 as the ethnic Hutu ⓬ majority rebelled against the Tutsi minority that had served as the ruling elite and been privileged during the colonial era. Around 150,000 Tutsis fled from Rwanda to Burundi and other neighboring states. After independence in 1962, military leaders of the Hutu ruled for the most part. However, conflicts repeatedly broke out with Tutsi rebels and led to appalling massacres in 1994.

12 A group of young soldiers of the Hutu militia at a military exercise, 1994

1990	Introduction of the multiparty system in Cameroon
1993	Idriss Deby's government in Chad
1994	Massacre of the Tutsi in Rwanda
1999	Mamadou Tandja's presidency in Niger
2001	John Kufuor elected president of Ghana
2002–2005	Civil war in the Ivory Coast

The Republic of the Congo and the Democratic Republic

Since their independence, both of these French-speaking former colonies in the ❶ Congo region have been unable to find lasting peace.

1 Traditional village huts, Belgian Congo

At the end of the 19th century, both Belgium and France claimed the Congo region (p. 424). Belgium took the territory around the capital of Léopoldville, while France claimed the area around Brazzaville.

After World War II, Fulbert Youlou established himself as the leader of the independence movement in Brazzaville. When the former French Congo became a sovereign state in 1960, Youlou became its president and quickly installed a brutal regime. He was deposed in 1963, and Alphonse Massamba-Debat, introduced a socialist state. After a power struggle, Marien Ngouabi then triumphed in 1968, setting up the Congolese Workers' Party (PCT), and in 1970 proclaimed the communist People's Republic of the Congo. Following his assassination, Denis Sassou-Nguesso was appointed president by the PCT in 1979. In 1990 he established a multiparty system and introduced democratic reform. The first election in 1992 was won by the opposition, whereupon violence erupted and a three-year civil war began. Sassou-Nguesso has held power in the Republic of the Congo since his forces seized Brazzaville in 1997, although fighting continues.

The Belgian Congo, whose ❷ mineral resources were exploited by Belgian mining companies, has been crisis-ridden since gaining ❹ independence in 1960. The leaders of the independence movement, ❸ Joseph Kasavubu and ❻ Patrice Lumumba, became president and prime minister of the new Democratic Republic of the Congo, whose capital was Léopoldville. Lumumba became an international figure in the liberation movement with his demands for a complete decolonization of Africa. In 1960, the mineral-rich province of Katanga, led by ❺ Moise Tschombé, announced its secession; a simultaneous mutiny by the army left the government helpless. The UN Security Council sent troops to oversee the disarmament of the Katangan forces. The army remained a threat and were suspected of the abduction and murder of Lumumba in January 1961.

In November 1965 General ❽ Mobutu Sese Seko led a military coup. He ruled dictatorially. Mobutu renamed the country Zaire and the capital Kinshasa, and he lavished patronage on his own clan. The corruption that enriched Mobutu and his clients was disastrous for the economy. In the early 1990s Mobutu began to share power by forming a coalition, but this imported power struggles into the government. In May 1997, while Mobutu was abroad for medical treatment, an alliance under ❼ Laurent-Désiré Kabila seized power. In 1998 the country, renamed the Democratic Republic of the Congo, became a war zone, as five neighboring states sent their own rebel fighting groups into the country. The war ended with a tentative peace in 2002 but is thought to have cost more than two million lives.

2 Industrial plant refining copper mined in the region of Jadotville, Zaire, 1959

3 Joseph Kasavubu, independence leader, 1965

4 During the ceremony marking the independence of the Democratic Republic of Congo, King Baudouin of Belgium (left) gives a speech; Joseph Kasavubu (seated) is also in attendance

5 Moise Tschombé, prime minister of the mineral-rich Congolese province of Katanga, 1961

6 Freedom fighters for the independence of Congo: Patrice Lumumba in Brussels in January 1960

7 The Zairan rebel leader Laurent Kabila, 1997

8 Mobutu Sese Seko, 1994

1960 | Fulbert Youlou's regime
1960 | Katanga cedes from "Democratic Republic of Congo"
1963–78 | Jomo Kenyatta's government in Kenya
since 1965 | Putsch led by Mobutu Sese Seko
1970 | "People's Republic of Congo" proclaimed
1971 | Belgian Congo renamed Zaire

East Africa

While Somalia and the Sudan have experienced violence and political chaos, relatively stable political systems have emerged in ⑨ Tanzania and Kenya.

Zebras grazing on a savanna in Tanzania

Premier Milton Obote during a conference in Nairobi of the Organization of African Union in the 1980s

After Tanganyika and the island of Zanzibar were granted independence from Great Britain in 1961 and 1963, they united to form Tanzania in 1964. The first president, Julius Nyerere, stayed in office until 1985 and developed a socialist one-party system. After his resignation, Ali Hassan Mwinyi oversaw the transition to multiparty politics. Despite poverty and reliance on foreign aid, the country has remained stable under his successor Benjamin William Mkapa.

Uganda became independent in 1963. Premier ⑫ Milton Obote founded a socialist one-party state in 1966. After an army coup in 1971, ⑩ General Idi Amin established one of Africa's bloodiest regimes; at least 200,000 people fell victim to his security forces. In April 1979 he was toppled, and Obote returned to power. President Yoweni Museveni, in office since 1986, has brought some stability to the country despite the rebel groups that continue to operate in the north.

Kenyan politics were dominated by the rule of Jomo Kenyatta from independence in 1963 until his death in 1978. Under growing pressure, his successor Daniel Arap Moi permitted multiparty elections after upheavals in 1991. Moi was defeated in the 2002 elections, and his successor Mwai Kbaki has pledged to fight Kenya's major corruption problem.

In 1969 military forces under General Siad Barre seized power in Somalia. Heavy fighting with rebel groups led to the flight of Barre in 1991 and to the secession of the Republic of Somaliland. In 1992–1994, US and ⑬ UN troops intervened unsuccessfully in the civil war, and since then no central government has established effective control over the country.

In Ethiopia, Emperor Haile Selassie (p. 505) was overthrown by the military in 1974. Between 1977 and 1979, thousands died under the "Red Terror" regime of Mengistu Haile Mariam, who also instigated a program of forced collectivization. He was overthrown in 1991 after the secession of the provinces of Eritrea and Tigray. The country suffered a famine in 1985 that led to a major international relief effort. Following a war with neighboring Eritrea in 1999–2000, both countries have accepted mediation.

Ever since its independence in 1956, Sudan has suffered from conflicts between Muslims, Christians, and members of African faiths. A military coup in June 1989 brought to power Islamic forces, whose attempts to introduce religion into public life caused conflict with other groups. Since 2003, a ⑪ campaign of ethnic cleansing and massacres against the population by government-backed Arab militias in Darfur has led to accusations of genocide.

In Baidoa, a Somalian child runs towards a rescue convoy; on the left, a French soldier watches closely, holding a weapon to cover the child's dash for the safety of the convoy, December 17, 1992

General Idi Amin, who later became known as the "Butcher of Africa"

Sudanese secret police intervening against rebels from the opposition, October 14, 2004

AIDS in Africa

More than 25 million Africans are infected with the human immunodeficiency virus (HIV). More than 70 percent of all HIV-infected people worldwide live in sub-Saharan Africa. Resources for prevention and treatment are lacking, although some countries, notably Uganda, have reduced new infections through educational initiatives.

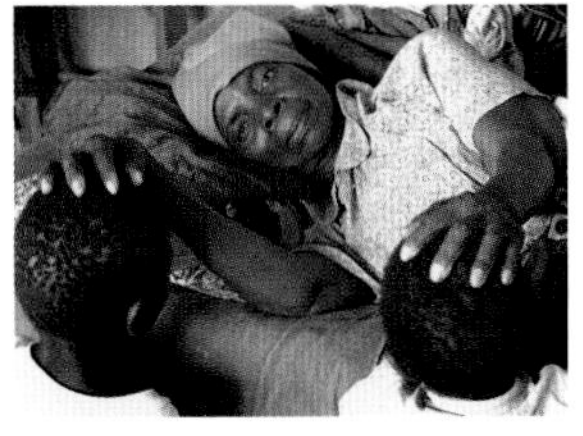

In most of Africa HIV/AIDS is the leading cause of death

1971 | Idi Amin's regime in Uganda
1974 | Emperor Haile Selassie deposed in Ethiopia
1977 | Marien Ngouabi murdered
1991 | Somaliland secedes from Somalia
1991–95 | Civil war in Somalia
1997 | Zaire renamed Democratic Republic of Congo

Southern Africa

With the exception of Zambia, the anticolonial liberation struggle in southern Africa was both protracted and bloody. An apartheid system was established in Rhodesia.

The president of Mozambique, Samora Machel, October 10, 1986

In the Portuguese colonies of Angola and Mozambique, the struggle for independence took more than a decade. In Angola, three divergent liberation movements led an armed struggle against the colonial rulers beginning in 1961. In 1975 Portugal allowed the Communists under ❻ Agostinho Neto to form an independent state.

Neto, supported by the USSR and Cuba, sought to establish a socialist people's republic but was opposed by the US-backed UNITA resistance forces under Jonas Savimbi. After 1987, Neto's successor José Eduardo dos Santos abandoned Marxism and began to negotiate with Savimbi. Since 2002 a precarious peace has held.

Mozambique became independent in 1975, and the Communists under ❶ Samora Machel attempted to set up a socialist system while fighting against rebel groups backed by the apartheid regimes of Rhodesia and South Africa. Machel's successor ❷ Joaquim Alberto Chissano, president since 1986, won free elections in 1994 and 1999.

The Zimbabwean President Robert Mugabe, April 2, 2005

Agostinho Neto, communist and poet, 1973

Prime Minister Ian Smith (middle) signs the Southern Rhodesian Declaration of Independence, November 11, 1965

The President at the ballot box: Joaquim Chissano, December 1, 2004

Zambia belonged to the British-administered Central African Federation from 1953 to 1963 as Northern Rhodesia, along with Southern Rhodesia (now Zimbabwe) and Nyasaland (now Malawi). After Zambia's independence in 1964, Premier ❽ Kenneth Kaunda became the country's president. He nationalized large parts of the economy and in 1972 established a one-party system. In 1991 multiparty elections were held and Kaunda lost to ❸ Frederick Chiluba, who survived attempted coups in 1997 and 1998. Levy Mwanawasa succeeded him in 2002.

Frederick Chiluba

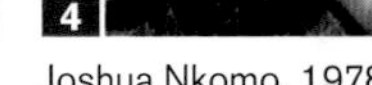
Joshua Nkomo, 1978

As a reaction to the independence of Zambia, the radical white settlers' party of Southern Rhodesia declared their nation ❼ independent despite the protests of Great Britain. In 1970 Rhodesia was declared a republic, and Ian Smith installed an apartheid regime similar to that in South Africa (p. 633). This was resisted by the African liberation forces of ZAPU under ❹ Joshua Nkomo and ZANU under ❺ Robert Mugabe. As surrounding countries were drawn in, the struggle destabilized the region. Through British mediation, negotiations took place in 1978–1979 between Smith's government and the liberation movements (who merged in 1976 to become the Patriotic Front). After guarantees for the white settlers, ZANU won elections held in February 1980. Rhodesia became the independent Republic of Zimbabwe on April 18, 1980, and since then Mugabe has been president. Subsequently competition occurred between Mugabe and Nkomo. Since 2000 he has received much international criticism due to his tacit support for the occupation of white-owned farms by black veterans of the liberation movements. All opposition is brutally suppressed and the population is thought to be close to starvation.

The first president of Zimbabwe, Kenneth David Kaunda

since 1950s | ANC begins work
1960 | Massacre of Sharpeville
1964 | Zambia's independence and Nelson Mandela condemned
1970 | Republic of Rhodesia proclaimed
1976 | Formation of the "Patriotic Front"
18 Apr 1980 | Mugabe's presidency in Zimbabwe

South Africa

In South Africa, a harsh apartheid regime ruled until 1990. In 1994, after a period of relatively peaceful political upheaval, Nelson Mandela, the formerly imprisoned leader of the opposition movement, became the first black president of South Africa.

10 Police operation using guns, tear gas, and dogs in the poverty-stricken black township of Soweto, near Johannesburg, May 12, 1986

11 Pieter Willem Botha gives a speech, February 1989

12 Hendrik Verwoerd, who was assassinated in Capetown in 1996

The white government of South Africa began implementing comprehensive apartheid laws in 1949 that segregated the black majority from the white minority and sought to reserve power for the latter. The apartheid policy of racial segregation was implemented through the creation of reservations, or "homelands," which were intended to prevent black Africans from entering the white-inhabited areas. In 1950 the African National Congress (ANC) began a campaign of civil disobedience and sought to activate mass resistance. Faced with violent repression from the security forces, the ANC fell increasingly under the influence of Nelson Mandela as the militant faction increasingly prevailed over the moderate pacifists. In 1960 there were riots and reprisals in the black townships, notably the "Sharpeville Massacre," in which scores of black demonstrators were killed by police. In the aftermath the government outlawed the ANC. From then on the ANC operated as an underground organization using guerrilla tactics. In 1964 several ANC leaders, including Mandela, were sentenced to life in prison.

In 1966 Prime Minister ⓬ Hendrik Verwoerd (1958–1966) was assassinated. His successor, Balthazar J. Vorster, enlarged the security apparatus and in 1976 several hundred blacks were killed during the uprising of the Soweto township. Such atrocities brought growing international criticism and isolation on the South African regime. After 1978, under external pressure, Vorster's successor ⓫ Pieter Botha abolished many of the apartheid laws while increasing the de facto repression of the black population. After bloody ❿, ⓭ uprisings in 1985–1986, he declared a national state of emergency. Not until Botha's successor ⓮ Willem de Klerk came to power in 1989 was the ban on the ANC lifted. Negotiations began, paving the way for apartheid's abolition. De Klerk organized a peaceful transition to democracy with Mandela, who had by then been released from imprisonment.

In 1993, a new constitution was agreed upon, and in 1994 the first elections with black participation took place. The ANC won with a clear majority and Mandela became president. He pursued a policy of reconciliation. In 1999, he was succeeded by his former comrade-in-arms and vice president, ❾ Thabo Mbeki. Mbeki was reelected with a huge majority in elections held in 2004.

13 Demonstration in Middelburg against the apartheid regime, March 9, 1986

14 Frederik Willem de Klerk, April 27, 2004

9 The third free election, ten years after the end of apartheid: President Thabo Mbeki casts his vote in Pretoria on April 14, 2004

Nelson Mandela

A onetime lawyer sentenced to life imprisonment in 1964, Nelson Mandela became the international face of black resistance to apartheid. In February 1985 he refused release from prison and demanded instead the abolition of racial segregation. He was finally released after 26 years in prison as the apartheid regime began to crumble. In negotiations with the government, Mandela secured the nonviolent handover of power, and he was subsequently elected president. He and former president de Klerk shared the Nobel Peace Prize in 1993. Mandela continues to enjoy worldwide respect as an international mediator.

Nelson Mandela, a statesman respected throughout the world, December 27, 2004

1987 | Introduction of the free market in Angola
1990 | Apartheid abolished in South Africa
1992 | Free elections in Angola
1993 | Nelson Mandela awarded Nobel Peace Prize
1994 | Free elections in Mozambique
1994 | Mandela's presidency in South Africa

CANADA SINCE 1945

Since 1931, Canada has been a sovereign nation within the framework of the British Commonwealth. It has become a ❶ modern industrial state that, as a stable democracy, has been tightly tied into the Western alliance system and the peace missions of the United Nations. The imbalance between the culturally dominate Anglophone majority and the Francophone minority has repeatedly led, particularly in the province of Quebec, to separatist aspirations. With laws and changes to the constitution, the federal government must constantly seek a cultural and linguistic balance.

1 The Toronto skyline, with the CN Tower (right)

Canada into the 1960s

Canada has constituted an integral part of the Western political world since 1945. As a result of the existence of two cultures in the country, domestic problems have sometimes arisen.

Since Canada fought on the side of the Allies in World War II (p. 525–526), the sovereign member of the Commonwealth has become politically and economically closer to the United States, although it made loans and supplied grain to Great Britain during the war. Canada has entered into several economic and defense treaties with the United States, such as agreements on the joint use of nuclear energy, and in 1963, after the Nuclear Test Ban treaty, the storage of US atomic weapons on Canadian territory. Mining of raw materials has increased, 75 percent of which is done by US firms.

As a result of the immensely rapid growth resulting from industrial mobilization during the war, Canada's growth required improved infrastructure, and in 1965 the Trans-Canada Highway, which connects all of the provinces, was completed. Through industrialization, cities experienced a rapid economic boom in the ❻, ❼ 1950s, which slowed again in the 1960s.

2 Winner of the Nobel Peace Prize Lester Bowles Pearson, June 25, 1962

3 Franco-Canadian leader of the cabinet, Pierre Elliott Trudeau, June 10, 1982

Conservative and Liberal governments have alternated. After a long period of Liberal government, Progressive Conservative John Diefenbaker became prime minister in 1957 and exiled the Liberals to the opposition benches until ❷ Lester Pearson took over government in 1963. For most of the 1968–1984 period, a Franco-Canadian, ❸ Pierre Trudeau, led the cabinet and promoted a bilingual culture. In 1969, English and French were both declared official languages.

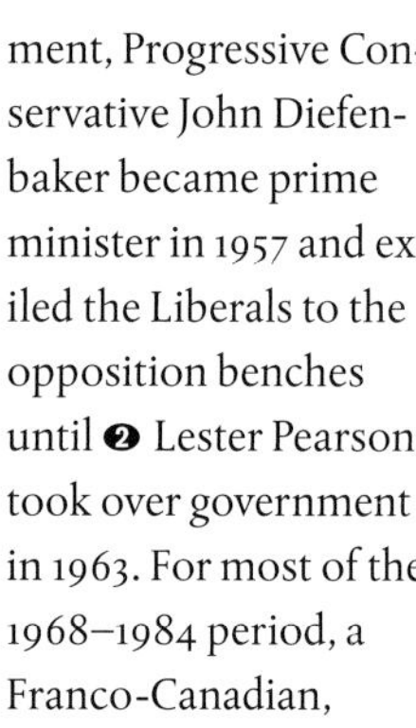

Only an uneasy balance was possible with the separatist forces in the Francophone province of Quebec. In 1967, General de Gaulle had to cut short his visit when he made a speech in which he cried, "Vive le Québec libre!"

4 Militant protester vandalizes property, Quebec, 1968

Against the background of growing social and economic dissatisfaction among French-speaking Canadians in the 1960s, especially in ❺ Quebec, strong autonomy movements formed. ❹ Militant extremist organizations made attacks on politicians. The murder of Quebec's labor minister, Pierre Laporte, in 1970 led to the declaration of a national state of emergency.

5 The old town of Quebec City

6 The skyline of Montreal

7 City of Montreal, Quebec

1957 | Pearson awarded Nobel Peace Prize
1959 | Agreement with the US on joint use of nuclear energy
1963 | Agreement with the US on basing nuclear weapons in Canada
1963–65 | Construction of the Trans-Canada Highway
1970 | Pierre Laporte murdered

Canada since the 1960s

The Canadian government has politically championed world peace. Internally the separatist tendencies of the province of Quebec are ever-present.

Since the 1960s Canada has worked, in foreign and economic politics, toward a careful disentanglement from its lopsided partnership with the United States. With its "third-opinion politics," it has sought closer relationships with Europe and Japan, and in 1970 also with the People's Republic of China, once economic agreements had been made. In the 1970s and 1980s, Canada took part in the Conference for Security and Cooperation in Europe and its successor conferences (p. 536) as well as in the (9) summits of the leading industrial nations (G7).

As a founding member of the United Nations, Canada has consistently supported UN peace efforts with (10) military troop contingents, for example, in the Congo in 1960 (p. 630) and in Cyprus in 1964 (p. 582). Diplomatically, Canada has also successfully worked to solve numerous conflicts. For his mediation efforts in the Suez Crisis (p. 600), Foreign Minister Pearson was awarded the Nobel Peace Prize in 1957.

The separatist desires of the Quebec people remain a domestic flashpoint. In 1976, the radical separatist Parti Québecois, under the leadership of Rene Lévesque, won an absolute majority in the province but failed in its 1980 referendum to secede from Canada. The 1987 Meech Lake Accord gave Quebec special rights, but the agreement was scrapped due to protests from other provinces. The "Quebec Charter of the French Language" in 1992 ultimately defined a binding language agreement for the state offices and more autonomous rights for the provinces. In 1995, the (12) vote for separation failed closely once again; with just 50,56 percent of the votes against secession, the unity of Canada was maintained for the time being.

Prime Minister Trudeau put forward the Constitution Act in 1982 requesting full political independence from the United Kingdom. The British parliament responded with the Canada Act, which severed virtually all the remaining constitutional and legislative ties between the two countries.

Under Conservative Prime Minister (13) Brian Mulroney, who governed from 1984 to 1993, tensions with the original inhabitants of Canada, the (8) Inuit and the (11) Indians, became prominent. After long unrest, in 1988 they were promised parts of the Mackenzie Valley in a preliminary treaty which was signed by representatives of the Canadian government. Under the Prime Minister Jean Chrétien, the government attempted to achieve a compromise with the native inhabitants, who in some cases were demanding all of their former lands back.

Prime Minister (14) Paul Martin, a Liberal who has been in office since 2003, is seen as a steady hand and is expected to boost the economic situation through new liberalization policies.

8 Two young Inuit girls in traditional dress, 1996

9 Paul Martin (second from left) and the ministers of finance of the leading industrial nations, Frankfurt, 1999

10 Canadian soldier of the UN peacekeeping troops in Drvar in the western part of Bosnia, April 1998

11 Canadian Indian wearing traditional clothes and headdress during a display of cultural traditions, 1990

12 People demonstrating for the unity of Canada in October 1995

13 Prime Minister Brian Mulroney, May 1989

14 Paul Martin shaking hands with US President George W. Bush, 2004

1982 | Constitution Act severs link with Great Britain

1984–93 | Brian Mulroney's government

1987 | Meech Lake Accord

1988 | Territories transferred to Canadian native inhabitants

The United States: Global Power since 1945

The ❶ United States emerged economically strengthened from World War II and, in the postwar years, became the political and cultural leader of the West as the two-state bloc system began to take shape. It stood in opposition to the Soviet Union during the Cold War, which lasted until 1991. Internally, the civil rights movement and protests against the Vietnam War ushered in a liberalization of society in the 1960s. As a global superpower, the United States has since 1991 seesawed between global cooperation and efforts toward hegemony. Since the terrorist attacks of September 11, 2001, the United States and the Western world are confronting the challenge of international terrorism.

1 Flags in the streets of Manhattan, New York, 2001

The United States under Truman

After 1945 and at the beginning of the Cold War, the United States became the leading economic and political power in the Western world.

World War II demonstrated the enormous economic and military might of the United States. The war economy created full employment and a self-sustaining economic boom that seamlessly transitioned after 1945 to a prospering peacetime economy. The development of a consumer society, which had been interrupted by the Great Depression that followed the Wall Street Crash of 1929 (p. 507), gained pace again in the 1950s and ❷ healthy economic growth continued into the 1960s. Domestically, Democratic ❸ President Harry S. Truman (1945–1953) attempted to build on the social welfare policies of the "New Deal," which had been initiated by his predecessor Franklin D. Roosevelt (p. 507).

2 The car, symbol of prosperity: poster advertising a Cadillac limousine, 1953

One of the most significant developments in US foreign policy after 1945 was that the "unnatural" war alliance with the Soviet Union (p. 522) broke apart in the face of the expansion of Communist power in Eastern Europe (p. 576-581). The new postwar order in Europe and Asia was characterized by the onset of the Cold War (p.532) between East and West. The United States definitively abandoned its isolationist stance (p. 506) and took over political and ideological leadership of the countries within its sphere of influence. After 1947, the "containment" of Soviet expansion became the central tenet of US policy. President Truman promised all free countries military and economic aid in order to preserve their independence. The reconstruction of Western Europe was generously supported and led to an economic boom there, most notably in West Germany (p. 542).

5 United States nuclear weapons test, April 22, 1952

4 American soldiers in Korea, wearing protective clothing against the rain during a cease-fire

The United States had a monopoly on ❺ nuclear weapons until the Soviets tested their atomic bomb in 1949. That same year, the states of Western Europe concluded a military alliance under the leadership of the United States, the ❻ North Atlantic Treaty Alliance (NATO), which commited its signatories to a joint military defense strategy in the event of an attack on one of the member countries. During the Korean War of 1950–1953 (p. 622), American ❹ troops fought alongside the forces of South Korea in conflict with North Korean and Chinese forces, directly engaging communist armies for the first time.

3 US Democratic President Harry S. Truman gives a speech

6 US Secretary of State Dean Acheson signs the NATO pact; Truman (center) and Vice President Barkley

since 1947 | Policy of "containment" towards USSR
1949 | Soviet atomic tests
1949 | NATO founded
1950–53 | Korean War
1953–61 | Eisenhower's presidency
1954 | American intervention in Guatemala

The United States in the 1950s

Both internally and externally, the United States of the 1950s was absorbed by the conflict with the Soviet Union. At the same time, the civil rights movement registered its first successes in the quest for equal rights for African-Americans.

Between 1953 and 1961, Republican ❽ Dwight D. Eisenhower, a popular war hero, held the US presidency. During this period, the Cold War intensified until it dominated the foreign policy agenda. With the first atomic test by the Soviets in 1949 and the circumnavigation of the Earth by the Soviet satellite *Sputnik I* in 1957, the military and technological supremacy of the United States was brought into question; the response was a large-scale rearmament program. The US government began developing space and weapons programs and increased its atomic clout. Secretary of State ❼ John Foster Dulles followed a policy of undermining Soviet influence in the Eastern bloc, known as the "rollback" strategy. In 1954, the United States intervened in Guatemala (p. 645). The Suez Crisis of 1956 (p. 600) and the Hungarian uprising of the same year (p. 576) increased tensions between East and West without bringing about a direct conflict. In 1959, the US admitted Alaska and Hawaii as the 49th and 50th states of the union. In the same year a crisis developed in "America's backyard" in the form of the communist revolution in Cuba (p. 638).

7 John Foster Dulles addresses the press, ca. 1953

9 Senator Joseph Raymond McCarthy, 1950

The Cold War was also pursued domestically during the 1950s. Senator ❾, ⓫ Joseph McCarthy and the House Committee on Un-American Activities were the driving forces behind an anti-communist wave of persecution in United States administration and public life. Unprecedented in American history, a climate of mass hysteria developed as liberals, artists, and intellectuals were defamed and fear of "treason" spread in government circles. In 1954, McCarthy was censured by his fellow senators for "bringing the Senate into dishonor and disrepute" during this period.

8 Dwight David Eisenhower, painting by Thomas E. Stephens

The continuing boom ushered in an era of affluence. A "baby boom" occurred. Cars, washing machines, and consumer goods became ❿ normal household possessions for the average family. Together with a new youth culture in ⓭ music and ⓬ film, the model of the "American way of life" spread throughout the Western world.

In the 1950s the struggle for African-American civil rights against continuing racial discrimination and segregation advanced under leaders such as Martin Luther King, Jr. In 1954, racial segregation was abolished in public schools, and in 1956 so, too, were separate seating arrangements on public transport.

Martin Luther King, Jr.

Martin Luther King, Jr. was a Baptist preacher from Atlanta who was a charismatic leader and advocate of nonviolent resistance against racial discrimination. Actions, such as the "March on Washington," made him a symbol of the protest movement at the beginning of the 1960s. As an advocate for peaceful integration, he was awarded the Nobel Peace Prize in 1964. On April 4, 1968, he was assassinated in Memphis, Tennessee, as he prepared to lead a march.

above: Martin Luther King during a speech at a rally against discrimination, ca. 1966

10 Living area with terraced houses in a suburb of Los Angeles, ca. 1958

11 McCarthy explains the spread of Communist sympathizers in the United States, ca. 1950

12 The face of the 1950s: Marilyn Monroe

13 The musical idol of the 1950s: Elvis Presley

1956 | Suez Crisis
1956 | Hungarian revolution
1959 | Alaska and Hawaii gain statehood
1964 | Martin Luther King, Jr. awarded Nobel Peace Prize
4 Apr 1968 | Martin Luther King, Jr. murdered in Memphis

Reform and Crisis: The US under Kennedy and Johnson

At the beginning of the 1960s, President Kennedy became the hope for a young and dynamic America. After his assassination, Johnson continued to implement Kennedy's domestic reforms, but also escalated involvement in Vietnam.

1 US President John Fitzgerald Kennedy, October 1961

2 A modern first lady in the White House: Jackie Kennedy, 1950s

Campaigning on a platform of promises of social reform and concessions on the race issue, ❶ John F. Kennedy won the close election of 1960. Promoting his vision of a revitalized America setting out for "new frontiers," the young and dynamic Democrat became the hope for a new generation. With his elegant wife ❷ Jackie at his side, Kennedy brought a modern style of government to the White House. His time in office, however, was not characterized by domestic change but by foreign policy crises.

The Soviet construction of the Berlin Wall (p. 540) and the unsuccessful invasion of communist Cuba attempted by US-backed Cuban exiles in 1961 (p. 644) increased tensions between ❹ East and West. After the discovery of Soviet missiles in Cuba in 1962, the world teetered for days on the brink of a nuclear war (p. 532). After this, Kennedy attempted to reduce tensions with the Soviet Union. The "hotline," a set of high-speed teleprinters linking Moscow and Washington, was set up. The United States, the Soviet Union, and Great Britain agreed in August 1963 on the Nuclear Test Ban Treaty to end atomic weapons tests, although China and France refused to sign the treaty. The ❸ assassination of Kennedy in Dallas on November 22, 1963, shocked the nation.

6 Racial unrest in Cambridge, MA, June 21, 1963

Under the slogan "Great Society," Kennedy's successor, ❺ Lyndon B. Johnson, partly implemented Kennedy's social welfare programs, including increased spending on education, Medicare, urban renewal, and a war on poverty and crime. The Civil Rights Act of 1964 guaranteed African-Americans protection when carrying out their right to vote, encouraged integration in schools, and banned racial discrimination. Economic disadvantages for blacks remained, and even President Johnson supported racist delegates from Mississippi. The black protest movement radicalized in 1964–1968, and in the inner cities ❻ unrest was not uncommon. Organizations such as the Black Panthers and the Nation of Islam, which propagated the superiority of the blacks and saw violence as legitimate, won increasing influence

Externally, Johnson decided on direct military intervention in the Vietnam conflict (p. 617) in 1964. The fighting continually escalated until the beginning of the 1970s. Military failures, and the ever stronger protest movement against the war, forced the domestic reform policy into the background and forced Johnson to renounce a run for re-election. The murders of King and popular Democrat ❼ Robert F. Kennedy in 1968 constituted a bloody end to the US reform period.

4 Kennedy and Khrushchev meet following the Cuba crisis in Vienna, 1961

3 A moment when the American nation held its breath: After President John F. Kennedy is shot, Jackie Kennedy jumps out of the car, Dallas, Texas, November 22, 1963

5 Kennedy's successor, the Democratic President Lyndon B. Johnson

7 Attorney General Robert Kennedy talks to demonstrators, June 14, 1963

1960	John F. Kennedy elected president
Oct 1962	Cuban Missle Crisis
Aug 1963	Nuclear Test-Ban Treaty
22 Nov 1963	Kennedy assassinated
1964	US involvement in Vietnam escalates
1964	Civil rights law banning racial discrimination

Division of the Nation: The United States under Nixon

The polarization between the protest movement and the Establishment destroyed the internal consensus within the United States at the end of the 1960s. Failure in Vietnam and the Watergate scandal caused a re-evaluation of the country's identity, particularly by the young.

President Richard Nixon in the White House, January 1971

Protests against the Vietnam War grew into a rebellion of the young against the "Establishment," and this spread throughout the entire Western world. Through nonconformist clothes, haircuts, and music, the young rejected the traditional order. The pacifist ❽ "hippie" movement rebelled against paternalistic government, corporate business, and traditional social mores, and taunted the representatives of middle-class values through their glorification of "free love" and drugs. The protest movement divided the mainly conservative American society. With the 1968 election of the Republican Richard Nixon, a staunch anti-Communist became president. With the slogan of "Law and Order," he proceeded aggressively against those at the heart of the protest movement.

During the ❾ Nixon Administration, a milestone was achieved in space travel: on July 20, 1969, the first human landed on the ❿ moon.

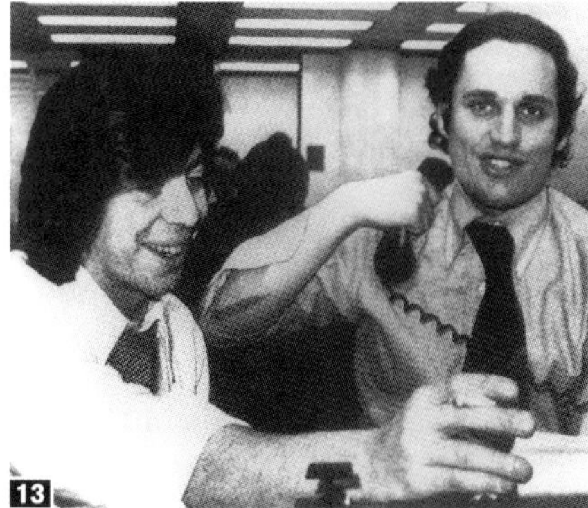

Washington Post journalists Carl Bernstein (left) and Robert Woodward who uncovered the Watergate scandal, May 7, 1973

Internationally, Nixon and his advisor ⓫ Henry Kissinger sought an improvement in relations with the leading communist states. In 1972 Nixon visited China—the first US president to do so—and in the same year the Strategic Arms Limitation Talks (SALT) with the Soviet Union, which had started three years earlier, resulted in an interim treaty. These historic visits ushered in a new phase of trade relations with both countries.

A further aim of Nixon was to achieve a peace treaty in Vietnam that was acceptable to the United States. In the face of ⓬ military disaster (p. 617), US troops began to withdraw from Vietnam gradually, starting in 1969. In 1973, after long negotiations a cease-fire was agreed upon with North Vietnam. For the first time in its history, the United States had lost a war. The Vietnam War had cost the lives of 58,226 US soldiers and caused a lasting "Vietnam syndrome" experienced by the returning veterans.

Henry Kissinger, NSA and secretary of state under Nixon, September 9, 2001

A hippie in San Francisco, 1967

In addition, the ⓭ Watergate scandal shook public confidence and trust in the presidency. In May 1973, it was revealed that Nixon had authorized a break-in at Democratic party headquarters to mount listening devices during the presidential election. Attempts by the president to hide this fact after May 1974 led to impeachment proceedings against him. On August 9, 1974, Nixon resigned the presidency.

US soldiers carrying the body of a soldier killed in action, Vietnam,1966

Woodstock

An open-air music festival in Woodstock, New York, on August 15–18, 1969, became the symbol of a hippie generation hoping for cultural and political renewal. As many as 500,000 participants peacefully celebrated the greats of rebellious pop, blues, and protest music. Joe Cocker, Jimi Hendrix, Janis Joplin, and Joan Baez gave famous performances there.

Celebrating music and the "free love" lifestyle at the Woodstock festival, film still

1968 | Robert Kennedy assassinated
1968 | Nixon elected president
1969 | US withdrawl from Vietnam
15–17 Aug 1969 | Woodstock festival
1973 | Cease-fire agreement in Vietnam
1973 | Watergate Scandal
9 Aug 1974 | Nixon resigns

Consolidation and Détente: The US under Ford and Carter

Under Ford, the tarnished office of the presidency was rehabilitated to a certain extent. His Democratic successor's term was marred by unfortunate involvement in international events.

American drivers stand in line at a gas station in Los Angeles

With Nixon's resignation in 1974, Vice President ❸ Gerald R. Ford became his successor. Ford attempted through a rigorously correct administration to improve the flawed image of the presidential office. Congress was given greater powers and from 1975, many formerly covert operations of the Central Intelligence Agency came under the scrutiny of the public and the media.

During the Ford era, many domestic problems, such as unemployment and inflation, worsened. The international ❶ oil

James Earl "Jimmy" Carter, 1983

crisis of 1973–1974 illustrated the dependence of the Western industrial nations on Arab oil exporters. In the mid-1970s, public awareness grew of environmental damage done by industrial firms which had not been properly monitored by the government. The opportunities and risks of the peaceful use of nuclear energy were discussed and generated much controversy. In foreign affairs, further SALT negotiations continued the détente policy with the Soviet Union.

In 1976, the Democratic Party candidate ❷ Jimmy Carter won the presidential election. Carter strengthened the international efforts of the United States in the areas of human and civil rights—both traditional Democratic party concerns—which was also visible in the improved relations with the regimes of Latin America (p. 644), although his approach was somewhat naive and often based on trust in corrupt and brutal regimes. His greatest foreign policy success was the ❹ mediation of a peace agreement between Israel and Egypt in 1979 (p. 597). After the signing of ❺ SALT II in 1979, the détente policy suffered a crisis in 1980 due to the invasion of Afghanistan by Soviet troops (p. 608). American wheat shipments to the Soviet Union were suspended, and the Olympic Games in Moscow were boycotted by the United States and the majority of its allies.

The Islamic Revolution in Iran in 1979 (p. 607) also caused serious difficulties for the United States, which had supported the Shah. In November 1979, more than 50 US citizens were taken hostage in the ❻ US embassy in Tehran. An unsuccessful military rescue attempt in April 1980 significantly contributed to Carter's electoral defeat in the presidential race against the conservative Ronald Reagan.

Republican President Gerald R. Ford, August 11, 1974

Signing of the peace treaty between Israel and Egypt at the White House, March 26, 1979

First encounter between Carter and Brezhnev: Signing of the SALT II treaty for the reduction of strategic weapons, Vienna, June 15, 1979

American hostages are led to the site of the US embassy in Tehran; the hostage-takers demand extradition of the deposed Shah Reza Pahlavi, Nov. 1979

The Reactor Accident at Three Mile Island in 1979

A failure in the cooling system of the Harrisburg, Pennsylvania, nuclear power station on March 28, 1979, was the worst accident in the history of the peaceful use of atomic energy up to that time. As a result of a technical mistake, radioactive gas was released. At a time when public opinion was very much divided over the issues of nuclear energy, the accident was a public relations catastrophe, as popular skepticism of atomic energy grew and awareness of the risks increased, giving impetus to the antinuclear energy lobby, particularly in the West.

View of two cooling towers at the Harrisburg. Pennsylvania, nuclear power station

Anti-communism and Disarmament: The US in the 1980s

Both internally and externally, Reagan followed a strictly anticommunist policy. With Gorbachev coming to power in 1985, the two superpowers were able to begin disarmament talks.

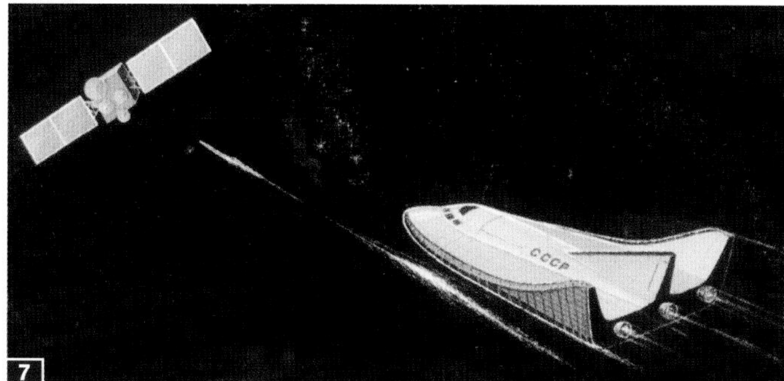

Diagram of a Soviet orbit shuttle, from a study on the military strength of the Soviet Union, April 1985

Republican President Ronald Reagan, ca. 1984

Former California governor and Republican party candidate ❽ Ronald Reagan's promise to reinstate the military and political global supremacy of the United States helped him win the presidency in 1981. With his election, a more conservative America emerged both domestically and internationally. The traditional Christian lobbies, whose power had declined in the 1960s and 1970s, gained in influence. Reagan successfully boosted the economy through cutbacks in public spending, particularly for welfare programs, while simultaneously lowering taxes. This also increased the gap between rich and poor, however. Concurrently Reagan sharply increased military spending. The planning of a ❼ space-based defense system—the Strategic Defense Initiative (SDI)—cost billions of dollars.

Reagan's rhetoric against the Soviet Union, which he described as the "Evil Empire," was backed up by his policies. He imposed economic sanctions following Soviet support of martial law in Poland in 1981 (p. 577). The United States supported anti-communist movements worldwide, particularly in Latin America and the Near East, regardless of their governance and human rights records. In Nicaragua the Contras (p. 645) who worked against the leftist Sandinistas were supported by US funds and weapons via the CIA. This led to much controversy following journalistic investigations of the administration's involvement in this proceeding.

Ronald Reagan (right) and the Soviet party leader Michail Gorbachev sign the INF treaty, 1987

US troops in 1982 intervened in the ⓬ civil war in Lebanon (p. 602) and in 1983 overthrew the left-wing government of the Caribbean island of Grenada. After failed disarmament talks with the Soviet Union in 1983, new nuclear intermediate-range ballistic missiles were stationed in West Germany as a reminder of US military power in Europe.

After his 1984 reelection, Reagan took advantage of the opportunities for adjustment offered by the Soviet reform policies (p. 586) introduced by the new general secretary, Mikhail Gorbachev. After several American-Soviet summits, in 1987 a breakthrough came on the disarmament question. Following an ❾ agreement on the worldwide reduction of land-based missiles—the Intermediate-Range Nuclear Forces (INF) Treaty—the ❿ nuclear weapons arsenal for the first time began to decrease. The sale of weapons to Iran and the diversion of the funds to the Contras in Nicaragua became public knowledge in November 1986 and became the Iran-Contra Affair, which weakened the Reagan government.

In 1988, ⓫ Vice President George H. W. Bush was elected as Reagan's successor. Under his presidency, the change in the global political situation—caused by the collapse of the Eastern bloc and the Soviet Union in 1989–1991—was completed.

Disarmament: Preparation for the destruction of the first Soviet medium-range rockets, August 10, 1988

The Republican President George H.W. Bush in October 1988

US Marines leave Beirut in armored vehicles, February 1984

Dawning of a New Age: The United States in the 1990s

In the early 1990s, the United States under President Bush was suddenly the only superpower within a "new world order." The Clinton presidency that began in 1993 was marked by increasing prosperity and a changing world role for the United States.

1 The technology stock market Nasdaq reaches a record high

2 "Operation Desert Storm": Allied troops liberate Kuwait and invade Iraq with armored tanks during the first gulf war, February 25, 1991

The mainly peaceful process of change in Eastern Europe (p. 534) was supported ideologically, politically, and economically by the Bush administration. The East–West conflict that had defined the thoughts and actions of American politics since 1945 ended with the reunification of Germany (p. 544) and the collapse of the Soviet Union in 1991 (p. 589). The United States, as the only remaining superpower, took on the undisputed leading role in the new world order, which had been taking shape since 1991. In a military intervention in Panama in December 1989, US troops overthrew the country's dictator, ❹ Manuel Noriega. Following the invasion of Kuwait by Iraq in 1990, Bush forged an ❷ international coalition that, under a UN mandate, militarily expelled Iraqi troops from ❽ Kuwait between February and March 1991. He also tightened the trade embargo on Cuba in October 1992 with the openly declared goal of bringing down Fidel Castro's communist regime (p. 647). The United States reduced its military presence in Asia and Europe and initiated further moves toward disarmament with the Soviet Union and its core successor state, the Russian Federation. Meanwhile, the American economy fell into a recession and social tension increased. Serious ❺ racial unrest shook the country in 1992 following the release of a videotape showing police brutality against an innocent African-American.

Democrat ❸ Bill Clinton moved into the White House in 1992 with promises of social reform and a revival of the economy, bringing representatives of all major ethnic minorities into his government. An ❶ economic boom set in, triggered by the development of communication and media technology, and created millions of new jobs. The legal minimum wage was raised, but Clinton's health care reforms, which provided for health insurance for all US citizens, were blocked by the conservative majority in Congress.

3 William Jefferson (Bill) Clinton and his wife Hillary at an election rally in New Hampshire, January 1992

Globally Clinton avoided asserting US dominance too strongly. In 1993, he negotiated the partial autonomy of the Palestinian territories in the Middle East (p. 599). Russia was assured of economic aid. The United States was among the initiators of the Kyoto World Climate Protocol in 1997 to reduce harmful gas emissions. Clinton was also personally involved in the difficult peace negotiations in Northern Ireland. Beginning in 1998, however, Clinton's presidency fell under the shadow of a ❻, ❼ personal scandal, leading to an impeachment process that resulted in his acquittal.

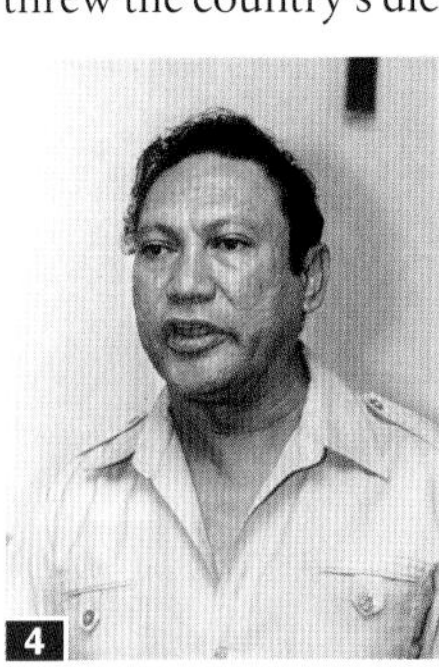

4 General Manuel Antonio Noriega, July 14, 1987

5 Race riots in Los Angeles, arson and looting of buildings and shops

6, 7 Bill Clinton and former intern Monica Lewinsky, with whom he had an affair

8 Kuwaiti people celebrate their liberation by flying US and national flags

1988 | George H.W. Bush's presidency
1992 | Trade embargo against Cuba
1992 | Bill Clinton's presidency
Jan 1999 | Impeachment proceedings against Clinton
12 Dec 2000 | George W. Bush named president

The War against Terror: The United States under Bush

Since the attacks of September 11, 2001, US foreign policy has been shaped by the international "War on Terror" and the goal of actively ensuring the spread of democracy throughout the world.

US President George W. Bush, 2005

The ⓫ presidential election of 2000, in which the Democrat candidate Al Gore ran against Republican ❾ George W. Bush, ended with an extremely narrow margin. On December 12, 2000, after weeks of legal disputes, the Supreme Court designated Bush as the 43rd president. With an agenda of conservative social and economic values, foreign policy was initially not a focus of his administration. However, the attacks carried out by the terrorist organization al-Qaida on September 11, 2001, on the New York World Trade Center and the Pentagon came as a shock to the entire country and shook ❿ society. Not since Pearl Harbor had there been a foreign attack on US soil. Bush proclaimed a "long war" against international terror and those supporting it, and since then foreign policy has dominated American politics. Domestically, immigration became more closely monitored and airport security was nationalized. In 2002, the ⓭ Department of Homeland Security was established, with a cabinet-level chief.

US Marines cover the head of a statue of Saddam Hussein with an American flag, Baghdad, April 9, 2003

Supported by a broad, worldwide anti-terror alliance, US troops ousted the Taliban regime in Afghanistan in October 2001 (p. 609). The Taliban had granted refuge to the instigator of the September 11 attacks, ⓮ Osama bin Laden, although he was able to avoid capture.

In September 2002, a controversial change was made in the national security strategy, allowing for preventive first strikes as *ultima ratio* against nations that support terrorist factions or otherwise threaten the security of the United States. In January 2002, Bush proclaimed Iraq, North Korea, and Iran to be part of an "Axis of Evil." Citing the violation of a number of UN resolutions concerning the monitoring of Iraqi nuclear materials and the possible production of weapons of mass destruction, an international coalition of primarily American and British troops invaded Iraq in March 2003. By April they had deposed the dictatorial regime of ⓬ Saddam Hussein (p. 605). Two years later, violence continues, stability remains elusive, and no date has been set for the end of US involvement.

After a polarized election campaign, Bush was elected to serve a second four-year term in November 2004.

Tom Ridge is sworn in as the first chief of homeland security, January 24, 2003

Broadcasted message from Osama bin Laden, October 18, 2003

Bush (left) and Vice President Gore following a televised presidential debate, October 11, 2000

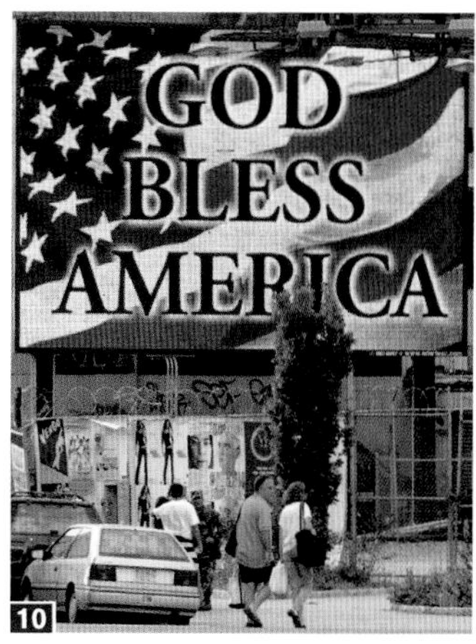

The slogan "God bless America" on a billboard, September 2001, New York

9/11

The Islamist suicide attacks on September 11, 2001, triggered a worldwide shock wave. At around 9:00 in the morning, two hijacked airliners smashed into the World Trade Center in New York City; both towers of the tallest building in the country collapsed. One and a half hours later, a third aircraft crashed into the Pentagon, the US Defense Department's headquarters near Washington, DC. A fourth plane, assumed also to be headed for Washington, crashed outside of Pittsburgh, Pennsylvania. A total of about 3000 people lost their lives in the attacks.

A second plane approaches the south tower of the World Trade Center, following the collision of the first airliner with the north tower

11 Sep 2001 | Attack on the World Trade Center and Pentagon
Oct 2001 | Military strike against the Taliban regime in Afghanistan
Mar–Apr 2003 | US-led invasion of Iraq
2004 | Bush re-elected president

Latin America since 1945

Rapidly changing authoritarian regimes, military dictatorships, and dependence on the United States were the realities of the political situation across most of Latin America until well into the 1970s. Since then, democratic regimes have emerged in most states, although they have sometimes been undermined by problems ranging from challenges to the state from the radical left and right, to poverty, corruption, and drug cartels. Enormous gaps between rich and ❶ poor continue to characterize South American societies. Attempts at political union and economic cooperation have often been undermined by the instability of the regimes in many countries.

1 Peruvians transport produce, March 2004

Problems and Development in Latin America

Stagnant economies and social conflict rooted in economic inequalities remain serious challenges to political stability and individual governments in Latin America.

Latin America has to contend with a spectrum of social and political problems. In order to promote regional economic collaboration, various unions were formed after 1945, such as the ❹ Latin American Free Trade Association in 1960 and the Latin American Integration Association in 1980. Led by Colombia, the smaller states founded the Andean Group in 1969.

The economic might of the United States has shaped the pan-American (p. 508) federations. The charter of the ❺ Organization of American States (OAS) was signed in 1948 with the intention of improving the relationship between South America and the United States. During the

3 Archbishop Oscar Arnulfo Romero (center), December 1979

Cold War, and especially after the revolution in Cuba (p. 647), the United States used the OAS for the distribution of aid but also as an instrument in the fight against Communism. The US government supported authoritarian right-wing regimes and forced the expulsion of Cuba from the OAS in 1962. Under President Carter (p. 640), the United States supported the democratization of the Latin American countries.

Internally, the ❷ gap between the rich minority and poor majority has altered little under either military or civilian rule. One of the key issues in most countries has been land reform, since the land has typically been in the hands of a small elite. The indigenous population almost always belongs to the poor and marginalized strata of society. Across the continent, ❻ urban populations have swelled with migrants from rural areas, and little provision is made for those living in shantytowns on the edge of huge cities. The wealthiest states, most notably Chile, have thriving export

2 Businessmen pass a group of street children, June 2004

sectors and well-developed infrastructure, although the wealth is unequally distributed.

The Catholic Church has played an important role in Latin America. After supporting the dictatorships, the Church in South America became influenced by "liberation theology," which championed the cause of the poor and oppressed—a dangerous stance, as shown by the case of Archbishop ❸ Oscar Romero of San Salvador, who was murdered in 1980.

4 George W. Bush welcomes the members of the Latin American Free Trade Association, 2005

5 General Secretary of the OAS, Cesar Gaviria, speaks at the annual meeting, June 3, 2001

6 Social contrasts in São Paulo: luxurious high-rise buildings next to the slums

1948 | OAS founded

1948–58 | Civil war in Colombia

1960 | Latin American Free Trade Association founded

1969 | Formation of the Andean Group

1969–75 | "Peruvian Revolution"

Central and South America: Violence and Its Reaction

Since the 1980s, fighting between rebel guerrilla groups and government forces has inhibited the emergence of democratic structures in many states of South and Central America.

Colombian paramilitary troops of the FARC, 2004

Nicaragua was ruled by dictator Anastasio Somoza from 1936 to 1947 with US support, and after his murder, his sons Luis and ⓬ Anastasio took over. After the Sandinista National Liberation Front came to power in 1979, its authority was undermined by right-wing Contra guerrillas, who were financed by the United States (p. 640). The Sandinistas were defeated in elections in 1990 by the Liberal Constitutional party, which has governed since.

The decades of civil war have cost the lives of thousands of people, Guatemala, December 1996

Government and left-wing guerrillas make peace on January 16, 1992

Armed Maoist Shining Path guerrillas in Peru, April 1991

Venezuelan President Hugo Chavez, January 17, 2003

In Guatemala after 1945, land reforms and a social welfare system were introduced. When the land reform threatened the interests of the American-based United Fruit Company in 1954, the government was overthrown by a US-sponsored military coup. Rebels resisted the military regime, and the nation descended into a ❽ civil war that finally ended with a peace deal in 1996.

The armed forces seized control of El Salvador in 1948. Power changed hands many times until the Party of National Conciliation formed an alliance with the military in 1961–1962. During the 1980s frequent guerrilla uprisings were countered with extreme violence, the government forming right-wing "death squads." Since a 1991 peace deal, ❾ democratic elections have taken place.

⓭ Colombia continues to be a turbulent country. Following the 1948 murder of a popular left-wing member of the Liberal Party, J. E. Gaitán, a civil war (known as *La Violencia*) broke out between liberals and conservatives and lasted for a decade. In 1958 a National Front coalition government was set up, staying in power until 1974. Beginning in the mid-1960s, left- and right-wing ❼ guerrilla groups formed to resist the government. The explosion of the drug trade has financed the private army and mini-state of the largest rebel group, the FARC (Revolutionary Armed Forces of Colombia). President Alvaro Uribe, who has been in office since 2002, has sought to weaken the factions with the support of the US.

Due to its large oil deposits, Venezuela is a potentially wealthy country, but revenues have been very unevenly distributed. A stable but corrupt party system was shaken by the election of left-wing populist ⓫ Hugo Chávez in 1998. He introduced some redistributive measures and has been critical of the US. Middle-class protesters failed to dislodge him in 2002, and since then he has moved to reinforce his power.

A civilian government in Peru was overthrown in 1968, and for the next six years General Juan Velasco Alvarado pursued land reform and the nationalization of sections of industry in a populist "Peruvian Revolution." After a coup by Francesco Bermúdez in 1975, a comprehensive privatization program was initiated. The Maoist ❿ Shining Path guerrilla movement started a campaign of violence in 1981. The authoritarian rule of Alberto Fujimori, which began in 1990, clamped down on the rebels. Since his fall from power in 2000, the situation in Peru has been unstable, and the current president, Alejandro Toledo Manrique, has less than 20 percent popular support.

President Anastasio Somoza with soldiers, 1979

Poverty and no prospects: children playing soccer in a street of the Colombian *barrio* El Jardin

since 1977 | Guerrilla rebellion in El Salvador

1979 | "Sandinista National Liberation Front" government in Nicaragua

1980 | Oscar Romero murdered in San Salvador

1990 | Alberto Fujimori ousted in Peru

Argentina, Brazil, and Chile

The popular postwar dictatorship of Juan Perón had a lasting effect on the political development of Argentina. In Chile the first freely elected Marxist president, Salvador Allende, was ousted from office in 1973 in a military coup.

Juan Perón became president of Argentina after elections in February 1946. With military support, he installed a dictatorship, which due to a booming economy was able to carry out social reforms benefitting the working class. All resistance to his government was suppressed. The most popular member of the regime was his wife, ❻ Eva Perón—known as Evita—who championed the interests of the poor. After her death in 1952, she attained an iconic status in the imagination of the Argentine public. As Juan Perón began to alienate employers and the Church, the military deposed him in 1955 and he was exiled. He returned after elections in 1973 to serve as president again but died one year later.

Chilean leader Salvador Allende

A repressive dictatorship under ❹ General Jorge Rafael Videla ruled from 1976. After the Argentine defeat in the Falklands (Malvinas) War against Great Britain (p. 553), ❼ military rule collapsed in 1983. President ❺ Carlos Menem was elected in 1989 and consolidated democratic structures while liberalizing the economy. His successors, from Fernando de la Rúa (1999–2001) to Néstor Carlos Kirchner (2003–), have had to face the consequences of the economic crash of 2001, when Argentina defaulted on its massive public debt.

In Brazil in 1950, the authoritarian presidential government under Getúlio Dornelles Vargas launched an industrialization program; his successor opened up the country to foreign investment. After disturbances in 1964, a military coup deposed President João Goulart and backed a series of right-wing presidents over the next two decades. The Catholic Church, especially Archbishop Dom Helder Camara, spoke out against human rights abuses. General Ernesto Geisel introduced democratic reforms in 1974, and the first free elections took place under his successor in 1982. Since then, the democratic system has been successfully consolidated, although economic inequality and a large public debt have left the country vulnerable to crises.

"Angel of the poor": The popular first lady Eva Peron next to her husband,1952

In Chile, a country with a strong democratic tradition, the independent left-wing socialist ❸ Salvador Allende was voted head of state in free elections in 1970. His revolutionary social program, "the Chilean way to socialism," aimed to nationalize industrial businesses and divide up the large rural estates. It was resisted by the conservatives in parliament. On September 11, 1973, the army overthrew the president in a ❶ coup supported by the United States in which Allende was killed. The leader of the coup, ❷ General Augusto Pinochet, then ruled in Chile as a dictator until 1990. Thousands of his opponents were murdered. After losing a referendum in 1988, Pinochet was edged out of power, and the 1990 election of Patricio Aylwin as president heralded the return to democratic government. Pinochet remained commander of the armed forces until 1998, but in 2000 the Chilean Supreme Court stripped him of his immunity from prosecution.

Units of the military in revolt shoot at the president's palace, Chile, September 11, 1973

The Chilean dictator Augusto Pinochet, 1997

Seizing of power by the military junta: Jorge Videla (middle) is sworn in, March 30, 1976

President Carlos Menem, March 4, 1997

Naked prisoners bound to posts outdoors in an Argentine prison camp during dictatorial rule under Pinochet, 1986

1910–17 | Mexican Revolution **1952** | Eva Péron dies **since 1953** | Castro's and Che Guevara's guerrilla war against the Batista regime

Feb 1946 | Jaun Péron becomes president of Argentina **1952** | Military putsch led by Fulgencio Batista in Cuba

The Special Cases of Mexico and Cuba

After World War II, both Mexico and Cuba followed independent courses vis-à-vis the United States, the political leadership of both resulting from left-wing revolutions. In 1962 Cuba was the scene of a showdown between the two Cold War superpowers.

The Mexican ⑩ revolution from 1910 to 1917 (p. 434) brought with it a social-liberal constitution that established national rights of access to mineral resources and the separation of church and state. The Institutional Revolutionary Party (PRI) held political power in a corrupt, semi-democratic system from its formation in 1946 until 2000. It pushed forward the ⑬ industrialization and nationalization of the economy, achieving high growth rates through the 1960s, and introduced social reforms. However, corruption and mismanagement of the economy led to virtual state bankruptcy in 1982, which was prevented only by US assistance. From 1988, under President Carlos Salinas de Gortari, the close connections and interlinkages between the state, the PRI, and the economy were slowly dissolved. Opposition forces gained popularity, and in the presidential election of 2000, the candidate of the right-liberal National Action party, ⑪ Vicente Fox, won to break the PRI's 54-year monopoly.

Cuba, politically and economically dependent upon the United States, was ruled by the dictator ❽ Fulgencio Batista following a military coup in 1952. Marxist revolutionary Fidel Castro, together with Che Guevara, began a ⑫ guerrilla war against Batista in 1953 and forced him to flee Havana on January 1, 1959. Castro proclaimed a socialist state and established Communist party rule. The seizure of American business assets and the close association of Cuba to the Soviet Union led to acute tensions with the United States and Cuba's expulsion from the OAS (p. 644). A US-backed attempt to invade the island in 1961 (p. 638) proved a fiasco. The Soviet move to install missiles in Cuba in 1962 brought the world to the brink of nuclear war (p. 532).

Despite its harsh repression of domestic political opposition, Castro's regime has long been an international symbol of resistance to US influence, and its social policies, such as free medical treatment, have helped keep it in power. The Cuban Communists ❾ survived the collapse of the Soviet Union in 1991, replacing Soviet subsidies with revenues from tourism, which has boomed in recent years, but the Cuban population is very poor. The island remains subject to a US trade embargo imposed shortly after the 1959 revolution.

8 Fulgencio Batista next to a statue of Abraham Lincoln, one of his favorite historical figures

9 Fidel Castro, who still holds the reins of power in Cuba, one of the last surviving communist states, May 17, 2005

10 The Mexican leader of the revolution Eufemio Zapata, December 1914

11 Mexican President Vicente Fox, February 2, 2004

12 Fidel Castro and his guerillas in the struggle against the Batista regime

13 Iron and steel factory in Mexico, ca. 1965

Ernesto "Che" Guevara

Ernesto "Che" Guevara became an icon of international Marxist revolution and one of the heroes of student protest movements in the 1960s. A doctor, born into a wealthy family in Argentina, he joined the revolutionaries of Fidel Castro in 1954 and participated in the Cuban Revolution. As president of the Cuban national bank (1959) and minister of industry (1961), he was preoccupied with social justice in the economy. He left to continue the communist revolution in other countries but was shot dead by government forces while training revolutionaries in Bolivia in 1966.

Che Guevara, who became an Communism icon after his death, 1965

1 Jan 1959 Batista flees | **1962** Cuba Crisis | **1966** Che Guevara murdered | **1970** Salvador Allende elected head of state of Chile | **11 Sep 1973** Allende deposed and murdered | **1973** Pinochet's government in Chile begins | **1976** Jorge Rafael Videla's dictatorship in Argentina

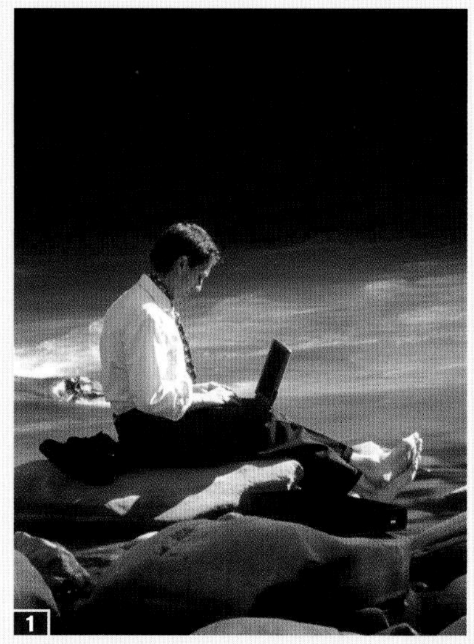

Globalization

Since the end of the East–West conflict in the early 1990s, the buzzword "globalization" has been used to refer to a various processes affecting almost all areas of life. There really is no clear definition of this contentious phrase that does justice to all the interpretations of the term, but it generally means the homogenization of standards and procedures throughout the world. Through the ❷ fast-paced progress of information technology, which makes ❶ worldwide communication possible in real time, distances and national borders are increasingly losing significance in the financial, political, and cultural decision-making processes. Networks are created among national companies, and regional events now have increased economic and political effects on faraway parts of the world. In this respect, the acquisition of knowledge and media expertise are ever more important. Particularly in industrial countries, a "knowledge society" is replacing the "industrial society."

1 Thanks to modern technology, computer work can be done outside the traditional office

Economics and the Markets of the 21st Century

With the end of the competition between ideological systems in the 1990s and the consequent opening of additional markets, the internationalization of the economic world has taken on a completely different quality. Finance, product, and service markets throughout the world are increasingly interwoven. The most progressive sector in the process of globalization is the economic globalization of international financial markets, where around the clock huge amounts of capital are transferred within seconds from one country to another, and from one continent to another. Transnational conglomerates coordinate their activities worldwide and choose the most advantageous production and delivery bases. Supply and demand are coordinated globally and ❹ price regulation is left to the market.

2 Faster and more productive: producing computer chips in Shanghai

Through this process, practically the whole world has become a ❸ market. Nations find themselves in harsh local competition for labor and the favors of mobile capital. Many states attempt to attract investors and "human capital" into the country through the lowering of taxes and the creation of advantages in the basic economic framework, by the deregulation of the labor market and the further liberalization of trade, for example. How far a state should strengthen—or balance with sociopolitical measures—the disparity between rich and poor resulting from the power of the mostly affluent businesses and investors is one of the politically contentious questions posed by the new economic world order.

4 Hustle and bustle at the stock exchange in Kuwait, March 6, 2005

3 Poster from the World Economic Forum in Davos, January 2005

Affluence and Poverty: The Consequences of a Globalized Economy

The global gross domestic product has multiplied by five since 1959. Since the mid- to late 1990s, global trade has been continually growing at a very fast pace; external investment are booming. A majority of direct investments still takes place between the industrial countries, but increasingly capital is flowing into the developing countries as well. Because ❻ labor is relatively cheap there, these nations are being integrated into the global production system of the transnational companies. Particularly in the newly industrializing nations, such as China or India, the opening of the markets has led to high growth rates and positive effects on the labor markets of the poorer countries.

On the other hand, this improvement is only relative. Sub-Saharan Africa, for example, remains cut off from the benefits of a global economy, and its popula-

5 Egyptian farmers on a donkey cart with cauliflowers, 2001

9 Nov 1989 | Fall of the Berlin Wall **3 Jun 1991** | "African Economic Community" founded **17 Dec 1992** | Founding of "North American Free Trade Zone" (NAFTA)

1990 | USSR breaks apart **1 Nov 1992** | Treaty of Maastricht comes into force

Chinese workers produce trousers for a international company

tion has ❺ little access to information technology and communication networks that are the positive consequences of globalization. Here, an increase in poverty is visible and economic output is in decline. Huge foreign debt burdens African state economies. Primary goods such as food and raw materials, which often constitute the wealth of the developing countries, are playing an ever smaller role compared to high-tech goods in the world market, and because the means for processing their own raw materials are underdeveloped in Africa, as well as in many of the countries of Latin America, these regions are increasingly reliant on imports from the developed industrial nations. Whether these developing countries will succeed in integrating themselves advantageously into the global world economy is very questionable, in view of the unstable conditions and the strong tribal and clan structures in these areas.

"One World" versus "Coca-Cola Imperialism"

Globalization is reflected in other areas of life such as culture and lifestyle. ❽ Modern mass media and increased mobility favor a sort of cultural globalization. African cooking and Indian films have become as common in Europe as Western fast food has become in Asia or Hollywood films in Arabia. Optimists see this mingling of world society as a chance to integrate ❾ "the foreign" into one's own cultural value system and in this way to increase mutual tolerance. Growing commonalities in the sense of a recognized universal value system, such as human rights, can develop in this way. This perspective presupposes free access to information and knowledge.

Two veiled Jordanian students surf the World Wide Web in an Internet cafe in 2001

In contrast, critics emphasize the economic dominance of the rich industrial nations in the media, through which they force their Western model of affluence on the weaker countries for their own economic advantage. This feeling of cultural hegemony is expressed in phrases such as "Coca-Cola imperialism" or "McDonaldization" of the world. The general commercialization and reshaping of national or regional cultures through foreign influences have in many parts of the world provoked movements seeking a return to their own traditions and values. One can trace the radical anti-Western or ❼ anti-American movements—up to and including terrorism—back to these perceived causes. The emphasis on regional, local, and new nationalist thinking can be seen as a reaction to globalization.

Global Domestic Policies

The challenges of globalization are diverse: concerns include the growing disparity between rich and poor, and the protection of the environment. The capacity of national governments to intervene directly in global economics is limited. Thus politics must essentially be globalized if mankind is to meet the worldwide problems effectively. In order to have a type of "world government" to guide the global economy, a strengthening of the system of the ❿ United Nations and a further concentration and linking-up of international relations seems unavoidable. An example of this process in action is the development of the European Union into a supranational organization; the European national states have given up a part of their sovereign state rights to the union, while still protecting national and regional identities. Even the non-governmental organizations such as Amnesty International work through worldwide networks, in which democratic cooperation and the opportunity to influence the world outside state diplomacy develop. Examples of these non-governmental organizations (NGOs) are the worldwide action network "Attac,"which is critical of globalization and fights for social control of the financial markets, and Greenpeace, which operates internationally against the negative environmental effects of a globalized of the economy.

Iranian demonstrators burn an American flag, 1997

Arabic Coca-Cola advertising in the Tunisian capital Algiers, 2004

Vote in the UN Security Council in New York on an increase of peacekeeping troops in the former Yugoslavia, November 1992

28 Feb 1994 | NATO's first military intervention in Serbia

1 Jan 1995 | WTO begins work

1 Jan 1999 | European Economic and Monetary Union takes effect

11 Jul 2000 | Founding of the African Union

18 Jun 2004 | Draft EU constitution is agreed upon

INDEX